BOOKS

CAMRA's GOOD BEER GUIDE

2012

Edited by Roger Protz

Project Co-ordinator Emma Haines

Assistant Editors Ione Brown, Katie Hunt, Simon Tuite

Head of Publishing Simon Hall

Contents

The Breweries

Special thanks to 125,000 CAMRA members who carried out research for the pubs; Rick Pickup and Steve Westby for advising on the new breweries section; John Duffy for updating the Irish breweries information; the Campaign's Regional Directors and Area Organisers, who co-ordinated the pub entries; Adrian Tierney-Jones for the feature on pp18-19; Paul Moorhouse for assembling the beer tasting notes; Michael Slaughter for checking pubs on the National Inventory; Colin Valentine for compiling the list of beer festivals; the publicans who kindly contributed their photographs; and CAMRA's National Executive for their support.

Thanks also to the following at CAMRA head office: Chief Executive Mike Benner; Marketing and Public Affairs: Lauren Anderson, Tarli Cable, John McCann, Jon Howard, Tony Jerome, Chris Lewis, Iain Loe, Jonathan Mail, Emily Ryans; What's Brewing/BEER: Claire-Michelle Pearson, Tom Stainer; Administration: Gillian Dale, Cressida Feiler, Robert Ferguson, Gary Ranson, Nicky Shipp; Membership Services: Caroline Clerembeaux, John Cottrell, Catrin Davies, Gary Fowler. Finance and Branch support: Anita Gibson, Liz McGlynn, Malcolm Harding. Warehouse: Neil Cox, Steve Powell, Barnaby Smith, Ron Stocks.

Photo credits: [Key: t = top; b = bottom; l = left; r = right] Front cover: nobleIMAGES/Alamy; p5: Terry Richards; p7: David Kilpatrick/Alamy; pp8-11 & 12(t), Cath Harries; pp18-19, Adrian Tierney-Jones; pp25-27: Cath Harries; p901: Geoff Brandwood; pp905(t x2) & 906: Apple Inc.

Production: Cover design: Dale Tomlinson; colour section design: Keith Holmes, Thames Street Studio; database, typesetting and beers index: AMA Dataset; maps David and Morag Perrot, PerroCarto; map p11, Mark Walker, MW Digital Graphics.

Printed and bound in the UK by William Clowes, Beccles, Suffolk.

Published by the Campaign for Real Ale Ltd, 230 Hatfield Road, St Albans, Herts, AL1 4LW. www.camra.org.uk

© Campaign for Real Ale 2011/2012. All rights reserved. ISBN 978-1-85249-286-1

PEFC
BMT-PEFC-0826

All of the papers used in this book are recyclable and made from wood grown in managed, sustainable forests. They are manufactured at mills certified to ISO 14001 and/or EMAS.

About the Good Beer Guide
Only the best will do

Beer quality is paramount but food and creature comforts are not ignored

For 39 years, the *Good Beer Guide* has been underlining CAMRA's work by championing real ale pubs. But it's more than a pub guide: the Breweries section makes it a unique publication, listing every brewery in the country and their regular beers, along with tasting notes.

The manner in which the Guide is compiled is made possible only by CAMRA's members. All pubs are regularly surveyed by local CAMRA branches to ensure they meet the high standards required by the Guide and every brewery has a liaison officer appointed by the Campaign, who meets his or her brewery on a regular basis to discuss the company's plans and beer range.

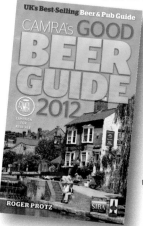

Regular inspections

Unlike most pub guides, where entries are chosen by a small editorial team or are sent in, unchecked, by members of the public, every pub in this guide is the result of regular inspection by CAMRA members, often on a weekly basis. The Guide is unique in offering only full entries, with no unchecked 'lucky dip' sections of pubs sent in at random. The Campaign comprises over 200 branches. Each branch surveys the pubs in its area

and monitors not only the quality of the cask beer in each one but also watches out for change of ownership or management that could affect the range of ales on offer.

Democracy rules when CAMRA members meet to choose their pubs for each edition of the Guide. Short lists are drawn up and votes are taken to reduce the list to the required number to meet each branch's allocation. The branches do not relax once they have chosen their entries. They continue to monitor their pubs and if one needs to be replaced – for such reasons as closure, change of ownership or poor beer quality – then it will be de-listed on both the CAMRA website and in the members' newspaper, *What's Brewing*.

Not only quality beer

Beer quality, above all, determines the choice of pubs. The *Good Beer Guide* is concerned about the history and the architecture of pubs and such important creature comforts as food, family and disabled facilities, gardens, special events and even the standard of the toilets. But it has always been our belief that if a publican looks after the real ales in the cellar – a task that requires a degree of skill and even passion – then the quality of the other facilities should be of an equally high standard.

CAMPAIGN
FOR
REAL ALE

- All CAMRA members can vote for the quality of beer in pubs by using the National Beer Scoring Scheme. The scheme uses a 0-5 scale that can be submitted online. For more information go to **www.beer-scoring.org.uk**.
- You can keep you copy of the Guide up to date by visiting the *Good Beer Guide* area of the CAMRA website: **www.camra.org.uk/gbg**. Click on 'Updates to GBG 2012' where you will find information about changes to pubs and breweries.
- The Guide is keen to hear from readers. If you wish to recommend a pub or feel that one you have visited fell below expectations, then we would like to know. Please use the Readers' Recommendations and Have Your Say forms at the back of the book or contact the editor at **camragbgeditor@camra.org.uk**.

The Guide has moved with the times: 39 years ago, entries tended to be terse; of the 'busy street-corner pub' variety. Today, the pub has to meet both the competition of high street restaurant chains and a growing tendency to stay at home and watch multi-channel television. As a result, such important matters as pub food need to be detailed. The pub entries in this edition show just how much pub food has improved. There are imaginative menus available, ranging from such staples as bangers & mash and steak & ale pie to European, Asian and Chinese specialities. And a growing number of pubs offer breakfast to help people kick start their working day. But we remain committed to the belief that the aroma and flavour of the beer in the glass is our prime consideration.

Town & country

The Guide also offers a wide cross-section of pubs in all parts of the country. In these pages you will find many delightful pubs in villages and small market towns. We are committed to helping rural pubs survive and CAMRA has argued that such pubs need special support, such as rate relief, to keep them in business. But most people live in towns and cities or visit them for a variety of reasons and we list scores of pubs in such vital hubs of communities. We happen to believe that when one so-called pub guide offers no main entries for Leeds, it's both a dereliction of duty and an insult to the people of that city.

Democracy in action:
How one CAMRA branch selects its pub entries

Choosing pubs for the *Good Beer Guide* is a labour of love. CAMRA members survey, check and – most important – drink in their local pubs all year round on a weekly and often daily basis. They get to know publicans well, understand the trials and tribulations of running licensed premises, and can help and advise with beer selections where pubs are 'free of the tie'.

Not only are all pubs entered in the Guide free of charge but the entries are up-to-date, checked and re-checked until press day. CAMRA branches attempt to involve as many of their members as possible to ensure that the choice of pubs is a truly democratic process.

The South Herts branch of the campaign is one of the most experienced in the country. It was formed in the early 1970s and has formulated and constantly improved its system of selecting GBG pubs. Its allocation of pubs for the Hertfordshire section of the guide is 27; a small number but one that is the result of painstaking work in surveying all the pubs in the branch area that serve cask beer and whittling that number

CAMRA's South Herts branch members at the Woodman, Wildhill, presenting the licensee with the 2011 Hertfordshire Pub of the Year award.

down to 27, at the same making sure there is a good geographical spread of entries.

South Hertfordshire is divided into four zones: North-east, North-west, West and South. Each zone has a co-ordinator whose role is to allocate pub inspections to branch members and to organise meetings where pubs are voted for. The zone co-ordinators report to a branch co-ordinator. Votes include proxy votes from members who can't attend meetings but vote using the branch website. For the 2012 edition of the Guide, the members chose six pubs in the North East zone, the North West zone (Amwell, Harpenden and Redbourn) had seven pubs while the South zone (Aldenham, Bricket Wood, Colney Heath, London Colney, Potters Crouch and Wildhill) had six pubs. The West zone covers just St Albans, one of the most heavily pubbed towns or cities in England, with 55 hostelries. This large number was reduced to eight for the Guide.

When selections and inspections are complete, the votes are collected by the GBG co-ordinator, who also includes proxy votes from members. The final submissions are forwarded to the regional director, a CAMRA volunteer who compiles and sorts all the entries from Hertfordshire and forwards them to the editorial team.

More than just a book...
Good Beer Guide digital editions

The *Good Beer Guide* is also available in digital formats, including an e-book, mobile app and sat-nav download. For more details see pages 905–6.

Introduction
Five-point plan to save the British pub

The real ale boom could go into reverse unless consumers stop the cull of community locals

Once again, ladies and gentlemen of the drinking public, we offer for your pleasure and delectation some 4,500 pubs throughout Britain that serve the finest pints of flavoursome real ale – beer that has matured naturally in its cask in the pub cellar, brewed with the finest malts and hops, and drawn to the bar without the unnecessary aid of applied gas.

Britain's pubs are still closing at an alarming rate and communities are suffering

The ever-growing back section of the Good Beer Guide – the brewery listings – suggests that all is well with the world of beer making. Yet again, more than 100 determined and hardy souls have invested their belief, their passion and often their redundancy money into launching small brewing ventures that add to the astonishing diversity of beer styles available in this small country. There are four times as many breweries today than when the Campaign for Real Ale was founded in 1971. As the total of British breweries edges towards 900, that's the biggest number since the 1940s.

But all is demonstrably not well at the retail end of the beer market. As many as 25 pubs close every week. The total number of pubs in Britain is down to 54,000. The pattern of closure is uneven. All too often, it's pubs in areas that have lost their industries that face the brunt of closures, robbing people of the chance to enjoy a beer once or twice a week. In some cases, the heart of a community is ripped out when the last pub closes and the chance for people from all backgrounds to meet over a pint disappears.

The growth of real ale breweries is heartening but the revival of cask beer could go into reverse unless action is taken to stop the loss of pubs. Real ale is a draught project. It can be sold only in pubs and it will go into decline, with the loss of breweries, beer and jobs, if pubs are not saved from either closure or from being turned into private homes or shops.

The *Good Beer Guide* presents a five-point plan to save the British pub as a vital outlet for real ale, a linchpin of the community and a key tourist attraction:

Beer taxes. One reason why pubs close is because the high price of a pint drives people into the cold embrace of the supermarkets. The tax on beer has risen by a staggering 35 per cent since 2008. The government piles an ever-growing burden of tax on draught beer but as a result gets back less in excise duty, VAT and other taxes as fewer people go to pubs and pub jobs disappear.

Members of CAMRA's National Executive launching a campaign in 2011 to save the British pub

The Guide calls on the government to scrap the 'duty escalator' introduced by the last Labour government and continued by its successor. The escalator automatically sparks an annual duty rise of 2 per cent above RPI inflation. By the time all the people in the beer chain – brewers, wholesalers and delivery companies, for example – have added a few more pennies to 'maintain their margins' the escalator has led to the price of a pint rising by around 10 pence every year. The government should follow the lead of the Irish government, which cut beer duty in order to boost the brewing industry and to maintain the Irish pub as a vital part of both community life and tourism.

The government should follow the lead of another EU country: France. In 2009, the French government reduced the level of VAT to 5.5 per cent on meals in bars and restaurants. This is legal under EU law and the British government should reduce VAT on pub meals and drinks here.

Tackle the power of the supermarkets. With their immense marketing power and skilful public relations departments, the high street retailers have the government in an arm-lock. The supermarkets sell beer at cost or below cost of production in a cynical misuse of marketing power. They can afford to make marginal profit or even no profit on beer as consumers will buy highly profitable goods in their stores as well. Pubs cannot compete at this level: nobody goes to the Dog & Duck for a pound of potatoes and a pair of trousers as well as a beer.

The government has suggested that supermarkets shouldn't be able to sell alcohol below the cost of duty and VAT. The fact that retailers have accepted this proposal with alacrity suggests they know it would have little impact on their sales. What is needed is a more genuine floor price based on a formula that includes duty, VAT and production costs. Duty plus VAT creates a price of 20 pence a unit of alcohol. If production costs are factored in, the price of a unit of alcohol in a supermarket would rise to 35-40 pence, dramatically decreasing the gap between high street retailers and pubs. Again, the British should learn from Europe, where the predatory pricing of alcohol is widely banned.

With their immense marketing power, supermarkets have publicans and government in an arm-lock

Tighten planning laws to stop the closure of viable pubs. At present it's legal to close a pub or change its use to other commercial uses, including pay-day loan stores or betting shops, without consulting the local community. Astonishingly, it's even possible to demolish a pub without planning permission. CAMRA is actively engaged in discussions with Bob Neill MP, who is both the Community Pubs Minister and also Planning Minister, in a bid to close this loophole.

Give the people who run pubs owned by giant pub companies more freedom to buy beer 'free of the tie' in order to give drinkers greater choice. The Guide believes that pub companies and large breweries such as Greene King and Marston's that own more than 500 tied pubs should give their tenants and lessees a 'free of tie' option in their contracts that allows them to buy beer outside their landlords' list. Where the landlord insists that the tie means a low rent, then a rent review should be carried out by a qualified and independent surveyor. Publicans who prefer to remain within the existing tie should be allowed to buy one guest cask beer.

This five-point plan is put forward to encourage a return to drinking good beer in good pubs, sold at affordable prices and with a good range on offer to consumers. We urge readers of the Guide to raise these points with both their MP and local councillors.

The pub is the heart-beat of the British way of life. Nurture it and enjoy it, and keep the real ale revival alive.

The pub is at the heart of British life and offers people from all backgrounds the chance to socialise over a pint. Pubs should be used and enjoyed or else they will continue to disappear

London Pub Marathon
Champion beer for the 2012 Olympic Games

Roger Protz goes back to his East End roots to search for the best pubs near Stratford's Olympic Park.

You don't have to talk Cockney rhyming slang if you're in striking distance of the Olympic Park but a passing knowledge won't go amiss. If, for example, a friendly local suggests visiting a rub-a-dub for a pig's ear, you'll know you're in good company, for that's an invitation to visit a pub for a beer.

The Black Lion offers East End character and fine ales

The first rub-a-dub on this tour of hostelries near Stratford is remarkable in many ways. The **Black Lion** at 59 High Street, Plaistow, E13 (see p281), dates from the 15th century and was rebuilt as a coaching inn in 1875. With heavily beamed ceilings and half-panelled walls, it's the last trace of a once rural area where Henry VIII had a hunting lodge. Today, the pub is surrounded by high-rise council flats but, in common with Mile End and Bethnal Green, is likely to be 'gentrified' in the wake of the Olympics.

The Black Lion has several claims to fame. Dick Turpin stabled Black Bess in the cobbled yard and more recently the legendary footballer Bobby Moore was a regular: West Ham United's Boleyn Ground is just 10-minutes walk away. The equally

Popular with locals, the cosy bar at the Black Lion.

legendary West Ham Boys' Boxing Club, which has produced such famous pugilists as Terry Spinks, Nigel Benn and Billy Walker, is next door.

If you believe in stereotypes then you would expect the Black Lion to be a lager-only pub. But leave your stereotypes on the pavement. The pub is a regular in the *Good Beer Guide* and on match days is packed to bursting with thirsty football fans drinking an amazing range of cask ales. The beers are chalked on boards in the main bar, with its low ceiling, beams and posts, and in a comfortable snug with wooden settles. There's a large garden to the rear, between pub and boxing club, which provides a vital overspill area on busy days.

Courage Best is a permanent beer and the guest list is ever-changing but you are likely to find the full Adnams' portfolio, including the rare Extra. There are always ales from Essex and East Anglia, including Mauldon's, while Cottage, St Austell, Sharp's, Taylor's Landlord and Young's come from further afield.

The Black Lion offers good, no-nonsense pub grub and history by the yard. The cellar was used as an air-raid shelter during World War Two and there are smugglers' tunnels running as far as Upton Park. The pub clearly has a hold on people because a barmaid called Milly Morris worked there from 1929 to 1997.

It's just a couple of minutes from Plaistow – pronounced Plarstow – Underground station while a bus to Stratford takes around 10 minutes and you can catch one outside the station.

The Palm Tree, on the edge of Mile End Park

You can also hop on a train from Plaistow to Mile End for our next pub. The **Palm Tree**, 127 Grove Road, E3 (see p280), is just over the road from the station and stands in a surprisingly sylvan area, Mile End Park, alongside the Regent's

Pictures of musicians above the bar at the Palm Tree.

Canal, where brightly-coloured canal boats are moored. The park is courtesy of the Blitz: German planes destroyed the area and the housing, apart from the pub, has never returned. It's also a part of London that had a different kind of Blitz in the 1960s and 70s: takeovers and mergers that destroyed such famous East End breweries as Charrington, Manns, Taylor Walker and Truman. The Palm has the Truman eagle logo on the cream and green facade, and inside there's a mirror advertising 'Truman's London & Burton', marking the time when London brewers rushed to Burton-on-Trent in the 19th century to brew the new style of pale ale, made possible by the salty waters of the Trent Valley.

Alf the landlord is a former dock worker and he and his family have run the Palm for 34 years. He's not sure of the precise year the pub was built but the Art Deco touches suggest it was remodelled in the 1920s. The impressive gold leaf wallpaper was chosen by Alf's wife when they took over at the pub, which has a large front room with a massive curved bar and a space for jazz and pop groups to perform live music. Above the bar there's a collection of photos of local performers and, somewhat surprisingly, one of Frank Sinatra. According to Alf, Ol' Blue Eyes dropped in with his minders one evening following a concert at the now-defunct Mile End Arena.

The smaller back bar has a fascinating collection of pre-war photos of the area along with caricatures of old sporting heroes, including boxers, golfers and footballers. This bar also has a rare example of an East End 'Fives' dartboard, with a nine-foot oche. Alf usually serves two cask beers, including Sambrook's Wandle Ale from a brewery plugging part of the gap left by Young's of Wandsworth. Guest beers come from many parts of the country. Sandwiches are served at lunchtime: see the main entry for opening hours and restrictions.

If your feet are up to a short walk you can reach the next pub via the pleasant park alongside the Palm, then pick up Grove Road again and continue along it until you reach a T-junction at Victoria Park. Turn right and after a few minutes you'll come to the **Eleanor Arms,** 460 Old Ford Road, E3 (see p279). Before you enter the pub, look further along the road and you'll see the Olympic Stadium looming over the chimney pots. The Eleanor is the closest watering hole to the games and there will eventually be a bridge from Old Ford Road to the stadium.

The pub is named after Queen Eleanor of Aquitaine, wife of Henry II: she funded a ford over the River Lea, hence the name of the road. The pub was a Fuller's house in 1879 but has been in the hands of Shepherd Neame of Kent for 30 years and is thought to be the most easterly of Shep's houses. The Eleanor is run by Frankie and Lesley Colclough and there's another Sinatra connection, as Frankie owns every track that Francis Albert recorded, though cool jazz was being played on my visit. The building stopped serving alcohol for a time when suffragettes took it over during World War One and ran it as a crèche, helping mothers improve the health of their children when infant mortality was an epidemic.

The nearest place to the Olympic stadium for a pint.

The pub has an intriguing design: the front bar is like a private living room, with wood-panelled walls, comfortable seating – including a Chesterfield donated by a local company – and a vast collection of old music hall, rock and film memorabilia. There's also a striking Watney Combe Reid brewery mirror over the brick fireplace. Small though the pub is, it has a central atrium that divided front and back bars, though a narrow passage now connects the two. The back room is bigger and has a pool table and another example of a Fives dartboard.

Frankie and Lesley serve the full range of Shep's beers and the brewery allows Frankie to add additional hops to Early Bird, which is rebadged as Early Bird Special. A fair amount of whisky is sunk in the Eleanor, as is testified by the gallon bottle of Famous Grouse with its own house label: the Famous Eleanor Arms. Filled baguettes are available at lunchtime and there are regular quizzes, jazz nights and live music. When the Olympic Park is finished it will be possible to access the Eleanor from Stratford's stations.

You can walk to the next pub, taking in the delightful greensward of Victoria Park, but it's a fair step and you can get to the **Camel**, 277 Globe Road, E2 (see p279), more easily from Bethnal Green Underground station. Save for weekends, the Camel only opens in the evening (see main entry for times). The pub, with a striking brown and cream exterior and large carriage lamp, is different in style to the previous

A little corner of Belgium in the East End.

East End 'pie and a pint' done with imagination.

ones visited and indicates the changing nature of the East End. The pavement tables and the stripped boards inside with more tables set aside for eating suggest this is the new, upwardly mobile East London.

The Camel specialises in the Cockney staple of pie and mash but it's not pie and mash as my parents would recognise it: steak and chorizo or wild mushroom and asparagus, for example, along with Thai green curry. But the pub is saved from the horror of being 'a gastro' by the excellent range of cask beers: usually Crouch Vale Brewers Gold, Harveys' Sussex Best and Sambrooks' Wandle. There are good bottled imports, too, including the divine Sierra Nevada Pale Ale from California. Owners Matt Keniston and Joe Hill saved the once derelict pub from demolition. They have revived it with a bright and airy interior dominated by a long, sweeping mahogany bar, bright floral wallpaper and a snug at one end. Once again, there's wartime history in the Camel: it was used as a refuge for children who weren't evacuated from London and were left to survive the Blitz. Fittingly, the pub is close to the Museum of Childhood.

With the **Dove**, 24-28 Broadway Market, E8 (see p280), you are well into the new, gentrified East End where some people actually pronounce

Find a quiet corner for beer and a board game in the Dove

'Ackney with an H. The bar – this is definitely not a pub – is in a revived and uplifted area that includes a street market and shops proffering organic food and designer label clothes. The Dove was once a pub called the Goring Arms but now it's a bar specialising in Belgian beer and food. There are benches and seats on the pavement and the main, spacious room at the front has ample seating, mirrors, plants and a ceiling painting based on Michaelangelo's Creation of Adam that, on closer inspection, is an advertisement for the Belgian beer Leffe. With such an introduction, Leffe Blond and Brown are naturally on tap along with such other Belgian worthies as Boon Gueuze, De Koninck, Duvel, Palm and most of the Trappist ales, including Achel, Chimay, Orval, Rochefort and Westmalle. See the bar's website for the full list.

But there is also a good range of British cask beers, including Black Hole Cosmic, Crouch Vale Brewers Gold, Grantham Gold, a rare sighting of Flowers IPA, Tim Taylor Landlord and Whitstable East India Pale Ale. If you stroll further into the Dove you'll find a warren of smaller rooms where subdued lighting, comfortable seating and wall panelling are reminiscent of bars in Bruges or Ghent. A corridor takes you to further rooms set aside for dining. One is decorated with Japanese beer prints, a second has photos of old Thailand. The food, however, offers such Belgian staples as carbonade flamande, fish soup and mussels and chips, plus vegetable cassoulet for non-flesh eaters. You can reach this imaginative addition to the drinking scene in East London from Hackney Central rail station, just three stops from Stratford.

The last pub on the crawl could hardly be more different from the Dove. The **Olde Rose & Crown**, 53-55 Hoe Street, Walthamstow, E17 (see p281), is a no-nonsense, East London boozer. No one builds pubs today like this grand three-storey, brown-brick Victorian

Pub, music venue and theatre: the Olde Rose & Crown

hostelry created in 1881 that stands on a street corner and dominates the area. It's another ex-Truman house, now owned by Enterprise Inns, and has a vigorous real ale policy. Jo, who runs the pub with Panikos, is a welcoming host and is proud of her cask beer portfolio: as well as the pumps on the bar, she points to a vast display of badges on a wall beyond the bar showing the impressive number of beers she has sold in recent years, sourced from Enterprise and the Flying Firkin wholesaler.

The bar, lit by a phalanx of hanging gas lamps, performs a dog leg and groans with handpumps and keg founts. The cask ales constantly rotate but you may find Adnams Broadside and Wood-forde's Wherry from East Anglia – 'they can go

in a day,' Jo says – along with beers from Dark Star, Fuller's, Kelham Island and Redemption. There are also several proper ciders and perries. Partitions fence off a raised area at the front of the pub where you can enjoy a quiet pint, with a sandwich or jacket potato. A second raised area to the right is used for live music while to the left and up stairs there's a small theatre: see the website for details of performances. Beyond the bar, a large back section has the ubiquitous pool table.

The Olde Rose & Crown is just a few minutes from Walthamstow Central rail, Undergrond (Victoria Line) and bus stations. The 257 bus will take you swiftly to Stratford... but you may decide to stay in the pub.

Cask ales on offer in Walthamstow

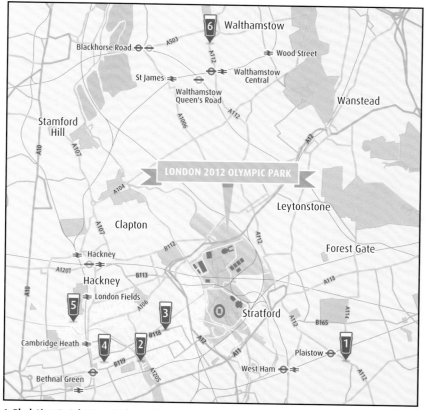

1. Black Lion, 2. Palm Tree, 3. Eleanor Arms, 4. Camel, 5. Dove, 6. Olde Rose & Crown

CAMRA's Pub of the Year

London pub takes gold

The Harp in central London was named CAMRA's 2011 National Pub of the Year – a notable award for a flag-bearer for beer from smaller breweries.

This year's Pub of the Year winner comes from London – the first time one of the capital's pubs had won the award. Despite its location in busy central London, the **Harp,** in Chandos Place, Covent Garden (see p278), retains its appeal as a true local and welcomes both regulars and first-time customers alike. The pub excelled in all the criteria for winning the award and, above all, with the quality of its beer.

Veteran publican Bridget Walsh serves eight cask beers, from such independent brewers as Dark Star, Harvey's and Sambrooks, along with real ciders and perries in a small, intimate pub festooned with mirrors, portraits and theatrical memorabilia: many of London's major theatres are close by in Charing Cross Road, Leicester Square and St Martin's Lane. The Harp has an upstairs room that is handy when the pub is packed.

Bridget Walsh is presented with National Pub of the Year award.

Described as 'a real ale pioneer', Bridget took over the Harp as a tenanted pub in 1995 but has since bought it outright. She has more than 40 years' experience in the pub trade and won CAMRA West London's Pub of the Year award in 2006, 2008 and 2010. Under her guidance, the pub has become a haven for good beer. Kimberly Martin, CAMRA's London regional director, commented: 'I never cease to be impressed or surprised by the continuing success of a pub staffed by people so passionate about real ale. The Harp's award shows how the London cask beer scene is reaching out to new drinkers.'

CAMRA's Pub of the Year competition analyses all the criteria that make a good pub, including the quality and choice of real ale, atmosphere, decor, customer service and value. The competition is judged by CAMRA's 125,000 members in regional competitions. Sixteen winners then battle it out to reach the final stages. Look out for the 🏆 symbol against pub entries in the Guide and see 'Award winning pubs' on pages 894–7.

The runners-up were:

Salutation, Ham, Gloucestershire (see p174)
Rural free house situated in the Severn Valley, popular with walkers and cyclists. The pub has two cosy bars, with a log fire and a skittle alley in front of the pub.

Beacon Hotel, Sedgley, West Midlands (see p481)
Beautifully-restored Victorian tap house and tower brewery, home of Sarah Hughes ales. There is a small island servery with hatches serving the central corridor, a small cosy snug and large main room. There is also a tap room and a family room.

Taps, Lytham St Annes, Lancashire (see p240)
Multi award-winning, one-roomed pub offering six guest ales, including a cask mild, plus a real cider. There is a plethora of memorabilia on display and the landlord has won CAMRA Branch Pub of the Year in two different pubs.

Brewing Success
Real ale is on the move...

The growing demand for real ale is forcing many brewers to move to bigger premises to increase their production.

In south-east London, **Sambrook's Brewery** is filling part of the enormous gap left by Young's of Wandsworth. Duncan Sambrook worked as an accountant in the City of London where his role included helping new businesses get investment – useful experience when you're planning a brewery in difficult economic times.

Duncan was sampling beer with a group of friends at the Great British Beer Festival and bemoaning the loss of Young's when the proverbial light bulb clicked on and he decided to launch his own small

New London Porter

brewery. He had the necessary financial skills to run a business and knew how to get investment. The next step was to go on a crash course at the Brewers' Laboratory (Brewlab) in Sunderland to learn how to make beer.

Before he started to brew, Duncan had the good fortune to meet David Welsh, the founder of Ringwood Brewery in Hampshire. David had been bought out by Marston's but he was keen to stay in brewing. He told Duncan he would invest in Sambrook's

Sambrook, Van Deventer and Welsh

but only if it produced four times as much beer as Duncan planned. David knew from experience the problems a brewery could face if demand outstripped supply.

The venture became a serious business. Further investors were found and £350,000 was raised to buy a custom-built 20-barrel brewery made in Canada. Former film studios in Battersea were found and gutted. Following trial brews, Sambrook's opened for trading in November 2008. The first draught beers were Wandle Ale and Junction Ale: the first is ·

named after the river that gives its name to Wandsworth while Junction salutes Clapham Junction railway station.

David Welsh was proved right. Sales of the beers took off and Sambrook's was soon supplying 200 pubs and producing 100 barrels a week. In November 2010 Duncan and his South African head brewer Udo Van Deventer added Powerhouse Porter, named with a deep bow in the direction of Battersea Power Station. They researched the history of London Porter but describe the 4.8% beer – available bottle conditioned and cask conditioned – as 'a modern beer brewed to an old style', using pale, brown and chocolate malts and hopped with four English varieties. It was meant as a winter seasonal beer but its success means Duncan is contemplating turning it into a regular brew.

In the summer of 2011, Duncan added Pale Ale as a new seasonal beer. All his deliveries are within the M25 but he has expanded to East and North London, including such influential areas as Islington and Stoke Newington. Sambrook's beers were also available nationwide during the summer of 2011 as part of Punch Tavern's Finest Cask scheme: quite a coup for a small brewery to be chosen by a giant pub company.

Purity Brewing is as far removed from Battersea and Wandsworth as it's possible to imagine. It's based on Upper Spernall Farm in Warwickshire, where founder and managing director Paul Halsey not only brews three cask beers – Pure Gold, Mad Goose and Pure Ubu – but also makes an important contribution to saving the environment. Purity is based in converted barns on the farm and all the used grain is re-cycled as animal feed while spent hops are spread on the land as fertiliser.

Purity take as much care of their local environment as they do brewing their beer

Paul and his staff have developed a wetlands system to process all waste water from the brewery: the wetland will turn eventually into a wild life sanctuary. Liquid waste goes through nine stages, including ponds, ditches, a reed bed and a weir before entering a water course fully purified.

'We genuinely care about our planet and we are constantly searching for new ways to help it,' Paul Halsey says. He sells beer within a 70-mile radius of the brewery and supplies a number of regular events, including CAMRA beer festivals in Birmingham and Stratford-on-Avon, Mostly Jazz Festival and Mosely Folk Festival. Beer sales are booming. When Paul launched the brewery in 2005 he sold 1,200 barrels. Today, with a staff of 12, he is brewing 9,000 barrels a year.

Hawkshead Brewery in the heart of the Lake District has been a spectacular success. It was founded in 2002 by former BBC correspondent Alex Brodie in a barn in Hawkshead where he brewed 30 barrels a week. By 2007 he was forced to find bigger premises at Staveley near Windermere. Further expansion in 2010 not only enables Alex and his large staff to brew 100 barrels a week of cask and bottled beer but also to have two bars, including the highly-praised Beer Hall where drinkers and diners can look down on the brewing plant.

The Beer Hall is open seven days a week, including evenings, and the complex includes a shop, visitor centre and conference facilities. More than 150 outlets are supplied with beers that range from Windermere Pale to the strong Brodie's Pride and include Lakeland Gold and Organic Stout.

Otley Brewery in Pontypridd, South Wales, is another brewery that could be on the move soon. It was set up in 2005 by three brothers, Nick, Charlie and Matthew Otley, and has doubled in

Hawkshead Brewery beer hall

size to 3,200 barrels a year. The brothers plan to expand to 4,000 barrels but are looking for bigger premises as demand continues to outgrow supply. They own three pubs in Pontypridd, including the acclaimed Bunch of Grapes where top-class food is matched with beer. The success of the pubs shows that top quality beer can draw the crowds even in a town such as Pontypridd that has lost both its mining industry and many traditional pubs.

Historic brews

Otley supplies beer to pubs throughout Wales and over the border into Bath and Bristol. Most of the beers have O for Otley in their titles, such as O1, the deceptively pale and strong O8 and the tongue-in-cheek O-Garden, a Belgian-style spiced wheat beer. Nick Otley also works closely with beer writers to produce historic or special brews. To date he has created beers for Pete Brown, Melissa Cole and Adrian Tierney-Jones. In 2011 he collaborated with *Good Beer Guide* editor Roger Protz to create a genuine Burton Ale called O-Roger that was based on the bottled version of the famous Burton beer Ind Coope Double Diamond Export.

Alex Brodie, Hawkshead founder

Nick Otley, looking for a new premises

It's a similar story in Scotland where **Stewart Brewing** in Loanhead on the fringes of Edinburgh is also looking for bigger premises. The company had a double celebration in 2011 – CAMRA's 40th anniversary and brewery founder Steve Stewart's 40th birthday: their 40th Ale was unveiled at the Scottish Real Ale Festival in June. Steve worked for several years for Bass at home and abroad and also had a spell with Harpoon, a craft brewery in Boston, Massachusetts. Harpoon sparked a desire to launch his own brewery back in Scotland, which he launched with his wife, Jo, in 2004.

The company quickly established itself as one of the major small breweries in Scotland. It now has nine full-time staff and several part-timers who look after and deliver five regular cask beers, a range of monthly specials and an expanding range of bottled beers. The cask beers include a traditional Scots 80 Shilling Ale, IPA, Edinburgh Gold and Cauld Reekie, a strong stout. In 2007 Edinburgh Gold was named SIBA's Supreme Champion Beer of Scotland and in 2010 Hollyroods won the title of World's Best Golden/Pale Ale in the World Beer Awards.

In June 2011 Steve said: 'After enjoying six years of solid growth, we've outgrown our current site and plans are in place to move to a bigger site. We intend to install a brand new 30-barrel brewhouse and plenty of tanks where we will have the capacity to increase our production and meet the increasing demand for our beer.'

Bill Parkinson and David Grant at Moorhouse's

Rebuilt fortunes

All these success stories almost pale into significance when you consider the remarkable case of **Moorhouse's** of Burnley. The brewery dates from 1865 and spent many of its early years producing non-alcoholic beverages to appease the rampant temperance movement. The Moorhouse family ran the company until 1978, it then changed hands four times in two years and was on the point of closure in 1985 when local businessman Bill Parkinson stepped and bought it. He hired David Grant as his managing director, a man with an impressive track record in the drinks industry and together they rebuilt the company's fortunes.

The old site could crank out just 320 barrels a week and expansion was needed when Moorhouse's won CAMRA's Champion Beer of Britain award in 2000 for Black Cat mild, a victory that created nationwide interest in all the brewery's brands, Pendle Witches Brew in particular.

Massive new brewhouse at Moorhouse's with 50,000-barrel capacity

Bill and David spent the next decade building the business, adding a small estate of six pubs, and planning a new brewery. It was unveiled in May 2011, it cost an eye-watering £4.5 million and, apart from small amounts of bottled beer, is geared solely to producing 50,000 barrels a year of cask ale. This astonishing achievement has been notched up in an area that has lost its mills and other traditional industries but, according to David Grant, still has 'fantastic pubs' in suburbs and villages.

He thinks the future is sound because real ale is not going through one of its peaks that will be followed by the inevitable trough. He says the market is changing as young people, including a growing number of women, switch to cask beer.

'The new brewery has been built to last for 30 or 40 years,' David says. His recipe for success is a simple one – sell more beer.

Cask Marque
Recognising great beer

The fact that the Cask Marque plaque is now recognised by 46% of cask ale drinkers (NOP survey) means there is a real benefit to licensees who gain the award and reflects improving beer quality in pubs.

Now, more than 7,500 licensees hold the Cask Marque award, an increase of over 15% on last year. Accredited licensees are subject to two unannounced visits each year by one of 45 Cask Marque assessors whose experience ranges from former head brewers to senior cellar service personnel. During each assessment visit they test up to six cask ales, served from the bar, checking them for temperature, appearance, aroma and taste. If any one beer fails the tests the pub will fail the whole inspection. In such cases, Cask Marque will offer to visit the cellar to try to identify the reasons why the beer was not of a high enough quality, whether an equipment fault or due to poor cellar practices.

We encourage consumers to contact us if the beer in any Cask Marque-accredited pub is not up to standard, in which cases a mystery drinker visit might be arranged.

Training

While the Cask Marque accreditation scheme is a key driver of beer quality, training is becoming a more and more important part of our activities. This year, we will deliver over 250 one-day training courses in cellar management which give pub staff an industry-recognised qualification. Most of the major pub groups are committed to this programme and we are working with the Independent Family Brewers of Britain to ensure they are supporting their licensees in cellar management training.

We also offer one-to-one cellar management training with landlords in their own pub. Although this does not provide a qualification it can give licensees valuable instruction on how to improve cellar practices.

Customers expect bar staff to provide good customer service. These training needs are taken care of through our online Cask Marque training programme, The Bar Excellence Award, which, as well as covering customer service, educates bar staff about the perfect serving of all drinks, health & safety and their legal obligations with regard to the sale of alcohol.

Our second online learning programme is 'An introduction to the cellar' for bar staff who have to enter the cellar to carry out part of their job, such as changing a cask and tapping and spiling. A clean and tidy cellar, kept at the correct temperature is vital to beer quality. All the hard work of master brewers can be ruined by poor cellar technique. More information can be found on both of these courses by visiting **www.cask-marque.co.uk**

Customer Awareness

Cask Marque is continuing to engage more with beer consumers. Previously, our regional guides listed Cask Marque pubs. However, they were expensive to produce and quickly out of date. Today we promote our Cask Marque pubs

Tapping in to beer quality at a training day

via a smart phone app, 'CaskFinder', our text messaging service and a sat nav download.

The CaskFinder smart phone app is available free of charge for iPhone or Android handsets and shows pubs in your location along with a map to help you find them and details of the beers on sale, based on our last inspection, and their Cyclops taste descriptions. It also gives information on all cask brewers and their beers. The app can also read barcodes on bottled beers to give a Cyclops description, with suggestions of other beers you could try.

For people without smart phones you can use the text message service to find your nearest Cask Marque pub.

Why not download the Cask Marque pubs file to your sat nav under 'places of interest' and you will be guided directly to the pub of your choice. You're never far from a good pub with this information to hand. More details are available on the Cask Marque website.

Find your nearest Cask Marque Pub by Sat Nav, Text or Smart Phone

www.cask-marque.co.uk

Cask Ale Week

Cask Marque are pleased to be working with CAMRA on Cask Ale Week to celebrate Britain's National Drink – cask ale. This event has now been moved in the calendar to October to coincide with the annual Cask Report, an industry report on the health of the cask ale market. It generates many good stories about cask ale and cask ale pubs. This year the main theme is 'Try Before You Buy' to encourage new drinkers to the sector as well as a chance to sample the enormous range of styles of beers available. For more information visit **www.caskaleweek.co.uk**.

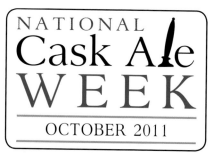

NATIONAL
Cask Ale
WEEK
OCTOBER 2011

Other Activities

Cask Marque has been busy supporting other industry initiatives:

Cyclops

Cyclops is a consumer-focused scheme, run by Cask Marque, CAMRA, SIBA and Everards which aims to de-mystify beer tasting and make real ale more accessible to drinkers. Cyclops accredited beers are described in simplified terms of their appearance, aroma and taste, providing consumers with some basic guidance on which beers among the vast range available they might like to try. Cask Marque administer the scheme and help with the marketing. For details on the scheme, visit:

CyclopsBeer.co.uk

Beer Academy

As a Director of the Beer Academy, Cask Marque supports and promotes their aim of increasing beer knowledge to the consumer. Of particular interest is the 'How to Judge Beer' course, for which more details can be found on the Academy website

BEER ACADEMY
SEMPER SITIENS
THE BEER EDUCATION TRUST

www.beeracademy.co.uk. Gift vouchers are available for the courses and are an ideal gift for the discerning beer drinker.

Cellar Equipment

Cask Marque are one of the primary instigators of encouraging the pub industry to invest in better equipment to maintain beer temperature from cellar to bar. The most important piece of equipment is known as an 'ale python' which insulates the beer lines from the cellar to the bar and maintain beer at cellar temperature 11–13°C, thus helping to deliver the perfect pint.

While the industry has invested over a £1 million in this technology there is a clear lack of knowledge and understanding on how to maintain the equipment. Frequently, the equipment breaks down resulting in warm beer. It is our objective to educate licensees about how to maintain this equipment, just as they do with other cooling equipment in the cellar, thus saving costs and improving beer quality.

When Cask Marque was formed in 1998, Simon Loftus, the then Chairman of Adnams and a keen support of Cask Marque, famously said "in five years beer quality will have improved and we will have done our job". Today, as cask beer grows in popularity, our work is far from over.

Treading the Pub Boards
The play's the thing...
plus a pint with the poets

Shakespeare enjoyed a drop at his local pub while fellow playwright Kit Marlowe met his end in one. Poet Laureate John Betjeman campaigned to save central London's Black Friar when it was in danger of demolition, while TS Eliot included a slice of pub chat in his epic The Wasteland. Meanwhile, music of all types has always been played at the pub. Sea shanties, northern soul, new wave folk, free-form jazz — if it's got a beat and a tune, chances are it'll go with a pint of real ale. The relationship that poetry, theatre and music has with beer and the pub remains as healthy today as it was when Will Shakespeare leapt on a cart outside a Southwark boozer and declaimed something about doing the show right now.

Take the **Cluny** in the Ouseburn Valley in Newcastle (see p457). At this former whisky bottling plant the ambience is light and airy, the décor bare brickwork and polished wood, and there are nine real ales on at the bar. It's all very modern in a retro sort of way. Most nights you will find a variety of folk mingling about, eager for a beer and a bite — the burgers are to die for.

Many go there for something else. Opposite the end of the bar is an entrance to a good-sized concert hall. The Cluny has an enviable reputation as a top music venue, a place where those in search of music from bands that might be big one day (or were once big) can come and be entertained.

'We took it over in 2002,' says Tony Brookes, founder of Head of Steam, the pub company that owns the Cluny, 'and invested quite heavily in a fantastic sound system and some major structural stuff. We invested far more money in the sound

than anything else and it is fantastic. Word of mouth has spread, and we have had people who are far bigger names than would normally play in this sort of venue. Last year the New York Dolls played three gigs on the trot and we also had Duffy when she was number one in the charts.'

With the hall at the back of the bar, rest assured if you want to just come in for a chat and a pint of good beer. Once the doors are shut nothing can be heard. There is a real sense of fusion in the way the Cluny operates two different styles of establishment.

Another pub that has them rocking in their pints is the **Driftwood Spars** at Trevaunance Cove, Cornwall (see p84). This is a lively, buzzy place, offering five real ales, including Lou's Brew and Red Mission, both of which are brewed onsite. Musicians have been trekking to this lovely part of south Cornwall since the 1960s, including Queen, who played there in the summer of 1971 (an occasion that was celebrated with a tribute night organised by the International Queen Fan Club).

'Music is really important to us as a pub,' says landlady Louise Treseder. 'It's part of our legacy. As well as Queen we've had Reef and Angus and Julia Stone as well as the up and coming Billy Vincent.'

Obviously not many pubs have a custom built stage with pristine sound. Does that matter? Many of my best pub musical experiences have been impromptu concerts — a couple of guys with a fiddle and guitar in the corner. Good music, superb real ale and the company of friends: an equation that cannot be beaten.

Nöel Coward suggested that Mrs Worthington (of the brewing dynasty perhaps?) shouldn't put her daughter on the stage. With that in mind, take her down the pub instead and you have pure theatre. Friends chatting and falling out and making up again; couples holding hands, then looking daggers at each other; first time dates as awkward as baby giraffes taking their first steps; old stalwarts remembering: the pub possesses a rich fabric. As the example of Shakespeare demonstrates, the play is the thing when it comes to the pub.

The **King's Head** in the Suffolk village of Laxfield (see p427) is a pub gem. Unchanged over the decades it's full of nooks and crannies and the Adnams' beers are served straight from the cask. There's a roomy garden at the back, which is where various local drama groups often congregate — and guess who's been their guiding light? 'They're

The Cluny, Ouseburn, Newcastle upon Tyne

The Driftwood Spars, Cornwall

mainly Shakespearean plays,' says the pub's landlord Bob Wilson, 'and attract quite a following.'

However, change is in the air at the King's Head, even if it isn't as dramatic as the angry young men that swept through British drama in the 1950s. 'There are also tentative plans by my daughter and a local poet-cum-scriptwriter to stage a Sweeny Todd Night in conjunction with one of our traditional Cockney pie and mash nights...'

Theatre is also a passion for Treseder at the Driftwood Spars. Like the music, this was part of the pub's legacy when she took over and she demonstrates a real fervour at the thought of performers treading the boards at the 'Drifty'.

'The St Agnes players perform about three plays here every year — one in the summer in the cliffside garden, one in the autumn and one in the spring. The latter two are in our dining room. They're all sell-outs. We allow the theatre company to use us as a venue. They charge on the door and I don't get involved in selling tickets. My benefit is the extra people in my pub and it also brings in new customers as well.'

She's echoed by Wilson, who says, 'as far as we are concerned such entertainment only appeals to a certain type of person but in its own way is good for the pub's reputation.

Morris dancing is another prime example of pleasing some and not others.' There's been an unexpected knock-on effect on the pub's thespian tendencies. Wilson: 'The plays have led to a group of poets also holding their "reading nights" here.'

Poets have long been associated with the pub and beer. Dylan Thomas is perhaps the most famous. This is the man who praised beer thus: 'I like the taste of beer. Its live, white lather, its brass bright depth. The sudden world through the wet brown walls of the glass, the tilted rush to the lips and the slow swallowing down to the lapping belly, the salt on the tongue, the foam on the corners.' Writing is obviously thirsty work.

Like the King's Head, many pubs are putting on poetry nights, such as **Baum** in Rochdale (see p324) and the **Brunswick Inn**, Derby (see p101). Recently thr Brunswick commissioned local poet (and CAMRA member) Les Baynton to deliver his words to diners on a St Valentine's Night event.

'It was a beer-themed event,' recalls Baynton, who is regularly crowned Beer King at the city's annual CAMRA beer festival. 'I wrote poems for diners' partners and read them out at the end of the evening. It proved very popular and I worked hard for my supper.'

He believes that most cities have at least one pub doing poetry nights, events that are very popular with landlords. 'They put them on not because they are poetry fans but because they will attract a slightly different crowd from the quiz/karaoke/football crowd and can fill a place on a quiet night.

'I ran a poetry night at one pub for five years that gradually increased in entertainment value. Poets cross-dressed or came in various costumes. A builder wrote a poem about his feminine side and then took off his gear to reveal a fetching set of lace underwear...'

Adrian Tierney-Jones

The Cornish Wurzels performing at the Driftwood Spars

Taking the waters

Mikron celebrates 40 years of pub pleasure

CAMRA was not alone in celebrating its 40th anniversary in 2011. For the same number of years, the Mikron Theatre group has been touring the canals of England to perform plays at waterside pubs. Canals are the lifeblood of the company, for the actors travel on a restored narrow boat, Tyseley, which they moor alongside pubs while they perform.

Mike Lucas launched Mikron after training as an actor and appearing in television, film and theatre. In common with many of the other actors, directors and writers who support the company, Mike was inspired by his love of pubs, good beer, canals and the disappearing industrial history of Britain – the early co-operative movement, the navvies who cut the canals, the brewers who make good ale and the publicans who serve it.

It's been a tempestuous 40 years. During that time, Mike has twice broken his shoulder and almost drowned on the Oxford Canal. As artistic director, he had to grapple with the loss of an Arts Council grant and launch an appeal to find new sponsors. At the age of 70, he has stopped touring but he remains the inspiration and guiding hand behind Mikron.

One of Mike's lasting legacies is Beer Street, first performed in 1994 but constantly updated to take in to account the many changes in the brewing industry and pub trade. Beer Street is a funny and rumbustious play that covers every known aspect of beer, brewing and pub-running, from the monks of Burton Abbey making ale in the 12th century to the present day problems of pubcos, excise duty and binge drinking. If all that sounds like heavy going, be assured that Beer Street offers an evening of memorable performances, hearty singing and knockabout humour, as well as food for thought. If you never thought the brewing process – from malting to tapping casks – could be explained in song, then the play will disabuse you.

Beer Street is not the company's only play. Hell and High Water, which marks the 250th anniversary of the birth of the canals, is part of the repertoire, and is a drama about the cutting of the Bridgewater Canal. In total, there have been 15 different productions over the past 40 years and new plays in 2012 will deal with the Luddites – the opponents of machinery at the birth of the industrial revolution – and the allotments movement.

If allotments sound worthy but dull, they won't be portrayed that way by Mikron. Beer Street is fast moving and brilliantly moves around in time,

with a modern pub intertwining with an ancient ale house. Brewing monks turn into modern beer-makers while customers range from bawdy boozers to respectable women in search of a port-and-lemon.

The pace is dazzling and is all the more remarkable when you consider the play is performed by just four actors – Adrian Palmer, Nicola Redman, Sally Ann Staunton and Dan Wilder – who change their costumes at lightning speed and also play guitars, banjos, fiddles and flutes. All the actors have impressive backgrounds in theatre, TV and film. Adrian Palmer is a vastly experienced actor and he uses his well-honed skills to perfection in the hilarious, show-stopping song that details the 1,001 euphemisms for the state of drunkenness.

Mikron, in common with many small, dedicated theatre groups, exists on a shoe-string. In place of the Arts Council grant, the company gets support from individual supporters and companies ranging from printers, solicitors and, naturally, brewers: Castle Rock in Nottingham, 2010 winner of the Champion Beer of Britain award, brewed a special ale to commemorate Mikron's 40th anniversary called Rock the Boat.

The company tours every spring and summer, while in the autumn it leaves the canals to perform in museums, community centres and village halls. For details of the autumn 2011 and full 2012 touring programmes go to: www.mikron.org.uk. With luck, they could be performing at a venue near you.

The Mikron four: left to right, Dan Wilder, Nicola Redman, Sally Ann Staunton and Adrian Palmer

Beer Festivals & Key Events

THE CAMPAIGN FOR REAL ALE'S BEER FESTIVALS are magnificent shop windows for cask ale and they give drinkers the opportunity to sample beers from independent brewers rare to particular localities. Beer festivals are enormous fun: many offer good food and live entertainment, and – where possible – facilities for families. Some seasonal festivals specialise in spring, summer, autumn and winter ales. Festivals range in size from small local events to large regional ones. CAMRA holds two national festivals, the National Winter Ales Festival in January, and the Great British Beer Festival in August; the latter features around 500 beers.

The festivals listed are those planned for 2010. For up-to-date information, visit the CAMRA website **www.camra.org.uk** and click on 'CAMRA Near You'. By joining CAMRA – there's a form on page 888 – you will receive the Campaign's monthly newspaper *What's Brewing*, which lists every festival on a month-by-month basis. Dates listed are liable to change: check with the website or *What's Brewing*.

JANUARY
NATIONAL WINTER ALES (MANCHESTER)
Atherton – Bent & Bongs Beer Bash
Cambridge – Winter
Colchester – Winter
Exeter – Winter
Newark – Winter
Salisbury – Winter

FEBRUARY
Battersea
Chappel – Winter
Chelmsford – Winter
Chesterfield
Derby – Winter
Dorchester
Dover – White Cliffs Winter
Fleetwood
Gosport – Winter
Liverpool
Luton
Pendle
Redditch
Stockton – Ale & Arty
Tewkesbury – Winter

MARCH
Bradford
Bristol
Burton – Spring
Coventry
Darlington – Spring
Hitchin
Hove – Sussex
Leeds
Leicester
London Drinker
Loughborough
Overton (Hampshire)
St Neots – Booze on the Ouse
Walsall
Whitehaven
Wigan
Winchester

APRIL
Barnsley
Bexley
Bury St Edmunds – East Anglian
Chippenham
Doncaster
Farnham
Glenrothes – Kingdom of Fife
Larbert – Falkirk
Maldon
Mansfield
Newcastle-upon-Tyne
Paisley
Thanet

MAY
Banbury
Cambridge
Colchester
Halifax
Kingston
Lincoln
Macclesfield
Newark
Newport (Gwent)

Northampton – Delapre Abbey
Reading
Stourbridge
Stratford-upon-Avon
Thurrock
Wolverhampton
Yapton

JUNE
Aberdeen
Braintree
Cardiff – Great Welsh
Chappel Cider Festival
Edinburgh – Scottish
Gibberd Garden – Harlow
Harpenden
Lewes – South Downs
Rugby
Salisbury
Southampton
St Ives (Cornwall)
Skipton
Stockport
Tenterden – Kent & East Sussex Railway
Woodchurch - Rare Breeds

JULY
Ardingly
Bishops Stortford
Bromsgrove
Canterbury – Kent
Chelmsford
Ealing
Derby

Devizes
Hereford – Beer on the Wye
Plymouth
Rochford – South East Essex
   Cider Festival
Stafford
Stowmarket
Winchcombe – Cotswold
Windsor
Woodcote – Steam Fair

AUGUST
GREAT BRITISH, LONDON
Barnstaple
Clacton
Grantham
Harbury
Ipswich
Peterborough
Swansea
Watnall – Moorgreen
Worcester

SEPTEMBER
Ascot
Bridgnorth – Severn Valley
Burton
Carmarthen
Chappel
Darlington – Rhythm 'N' Brews
Durham
East Malling (Kent)
Faversham – Hop
Hinckley
Jersey
Keighley
Letchworth
Lytham
Melton Mowbray
Minehead
Nantwich

Newton Abbot
North Cotswolds –
   Moreton-in-Marsh
Northwich
Ripley – Derbyshire
St. Albans
Scunthorpe
Shrewsbury
Southport
St Ives (Cambs) – Booze on the
   Ouse
Tamworth
Ulverston
York

OCTOBER
Alloa
Ayrshire Real Ale Festival -
   Troon
Barnsley
Basingstoke
Bath
Bedford
Birkenhead
Birmingham
Cambridge – Octoberfest
Carlisle
Chester
Chesterfield – Market
Eastbourne
Egremont, Cumbria
Falmouth

Gainsborough
Huddersfield – Oktoberfest
Kendal
Long Eaton
Louth
Milton Keynes
Norwich
Nottingham
Oxford
Poole
Quorn Octoberfest
Redhill
Richmond (N Yorks.)
St Helens
Sawbridgeworth
Sheffield
Solihull
Stoke-on-Trent – Potteries
Sunderland
Swindon
Thanet – Cider
Twickenham
Wallington
Weymouth
Woolston – Southampton
Worthing

NOVEMBER
Dudley
Heathrow
Rochford
Saltburn
Wakefield
Wantage
Watford
Whitchurch (Hampshire)
Woking

DECEMBER
Harwich
London – Pig's Ear

Beer Trends
Brewers are marrying old and new styles

'Innovate or die' – the famous advice to industries in danger of running out of steam – has been embraced with enthusiasm by brewers. Good beer has moved on from the era of mild, bitter and a drop of strong stuff for the winter. Today, even golden ales look a tad recherché as brewers search, with zeal and a degree of passion, for new styles to interest and even entrance drinkers.

'New styles' is something of a misnomer. Many brewers are marrying old and new in their quest for exciting additions to their portfolios. Until the arrival of the metal cask, all beer – even European lager – was stored in wood. Today, starting in Scotland, with Innis & Gunn's oak-aged beer, several British brewers are ageing strong ales in casks acquired from several sources: the Scottish malt whisky industry, bourbon barrels from Kentucky, sherry casks from Spain, and wine and Cognac barriques from France. Oak-aged beer has sparked an intense debate over which types of casks produce the best-tasting beer, as residues of the original alcohol remain locked in the wood. The jury is out but experience suggests whisky and bourbon will win as they are malt-based drinks, rather than fruit.

New expressions

The depths of flavour created by wood ageing and the different characteristics derived from the age of the cask can be seen in the work carried out at the Harviestoun brewery in Scotland. Head brewer Stuart Cail produces Ola Dubh, a strong, 8% version of the brewery's Old Engine Oil, a dark, porter-style beer: Ola Dubh is Gaelic for Black Oil. The beer is matured in casks bought from Highland Park on Orkney, recognised as

Stuart Cail of Harviestoun brewery (right) discussing whisky production with a blender at Highland Park.

one of the finest producers of single malt whisky in Scotland. Highland Park distillery produces 'expressions' of its whiskies that are aged from between 12 to 40 years. Casks sent to Harviestoun enable the brewery to produce five expressions of Ola Dubh and it's fascinating to note how the sherry/fruit, vanilla/oak character of the wood and residual whisky vapour blend with the roasted grain, burnt fruit, chocolate and bitter hop notes of the beer.

Wood-aged beer has crossed the Scottish border. Thornbridge brewery in Bakewell, Derbyshire, has experimented with ageing its St Petersburg Imperial Russian Stout in casks obtained from different whisky producers, while Fuller's in London has produced two versions of Brewer's Reserve oak-aged ale. The first was aged in single malt whisky casks obtained from the giant drinks company Diageo, the second from Cognac barriques supplied by Courvoisier. The beer used was Golden Pride and as it matured the alcoholic strength was measured at between 11.25 and 11.75%. The beer was then blended with Extra Special Bitter and the strength reduced to 8.2%: Fuller's had to satisfy the excise officers that it was not guilty of 'grogging', an 18th-century device used by brewers to increase the strength of beer by adding spirit.

The second Brewer's Reserve was launched on draught at the 2010 Great British Beer Festival but is generally available only in bottle. Innis & Gunn has also occasionally produced a cask version of its Oak Aged Beer for CAMRA beer festivals in Scotland and it's to be hoped this trend will develop.

Meantime brewery is south London has also entered the wood-aged beer scene thanks to its new micro plant in the Old Royal Naval College

Stuart Cail of Harviestoun brewery with casks obtained from Highland park distillery.

in Greenwich next to the Cutty Sark. Meantime is run by Alastair Hook who in 2010 moved his original plant to a new, custom-built site near the O2 where he is currently brewing 25,000 barrels a year but has room to grow to 100,000. As well as a proper lager, he brews cask London Pale Ale, and bottle-conditioned IPA and Porter. His most fascinating beers come from the tiny six-barrel plant in Greenwich in the baroque splendour of Sir Christopher Wren's buildings that are now a Unesco world heritage site.

In 1694 the monarchy founded a royal hospital for seamen within the naval college. Porter was brewed there to bring comfort to sick and dying sailors and Alastair has restored the tradition with his 8% Hospital Porter. This stunning beer is brewed with nine malts and English hops and, in the true fashion of early 18th-century porters, is a blend of old and young beers. Prior to blending, the old beer is matured in peated whisky casks for two years and the finished beer has a complex character of peat, roasted grain, chocolate, coffee and liquorice. There's also a hint of seaweed or phenol, which comes from whisky casks obtained from the Bruichladdich distillery on Islay. Casks from the same source are used to mature Imperial Russian Stout, also 8%, which is an unblended strong porter with a more pronounced phenolic/seaweed character. The beers can be enjoyed in the spacious restaurant alongside the brewery.

The Bowland brewery near Clitheroe, in Lancashire, has taken bottle-conditioned beer on to a new level with Artisan Gold (5.7%), produced by the méthode champenoise. The beer comes in an attractive 750ml champagne-style bottle, complete with cork and cradle. Richard Baker, the owner and brewer at Bowland, explains: 'Artisan Gold is brewed in the same way as all our ales for cask or bottle, then we transfer it to conditioning tanks with a lot of dry hops for two weeks before transferring it to a lager [storage] tank at zero degrees, where it's held for three weeks. Then it's bottled with priming glucose and a champagne yeast: secondary fermentation takes place for three to four weeks at 10-11°C.

'After two weeks of secondary fermentation, we transfer the bottles to the pupitres [racks or "pulpits"] where they're "riddled" each day – a quarter turn – allowing yeast and proteins to sediment down to the necks. We then freeze the necks in glycol at -30° C before removing the crown to allow the carbon dioxide to push the ice plug out, leaving clear, sediment-free, bottle-conditioned ale.'

Bowland are bottling beer like champagne

Richard tried ale yeast for the champagne stage but says 'it didn't work. It was too sticky and left deposits inside the bottle. We got a special champagne yeast embedded in alginate beads.' He describes Artisan Gold – brewed with Maris Otter pale malt, crystal malt and wheat, and hopped with Brewers Gold from Germany and Nelson Sauvin from New Zealand – as 'a journey rather than a product and it's changed the way we brew all our beers.'

History books

Back at Fuller's, brew master John Keeling and brewery manager Derek Prentice have delved into the brewery's history books to launch a series of bottle-conditioned beers based on recipes from the late 19th century. Wherever possible, they use ingredients that were available at the time, such as Plumage Archer barley for malting. The first beer, launched in 2010, was XX Strong Ale (7.5%), and it was followed by a strong Stout. Future beers will include Fuller's interpretation of Burton Ale, a style that emerged from the shadows in 2011. Burton-on-Trent is rightly famous as the home of pale ale and India Pale Ale but in the 18th century such major Burton brewers as Allsopp and Bass concentrated on stronger, darker and sweeter beers that became known generically as Burton Ale.

Interest in Burton Ale was prompted by Carlsberg's closure of the Tetley brewery in June 2011. Carlsberg owns Draught Burton Ale, the only beer brewed by a national brewer to win the title of Champion Beer of Britain. It started life as Ind Coope Draught Burton Ale but the beer moved to Tetley and is currently brewed in tiny batches by J W Lees.

But other Burtons remain, albeit under different names. Bass's No 1, still occasionally brewed, is labelled a barley wine but is in fact the last surviving example of a Bass Burton Ale. Burton Ale was so successful in the 18th and 19th centuries that brewers throughout the country had to have 'a Burton' in their portfolios. The style survives as Young's Winter Warmer, originally called Burton. Greene King in Suffolk was highly praised in Victorian times for its Burton and it's possible that Abbot Ale is a descendant of the brewery's Burton. It's also possible that the equally renowned Fuller's ESB developed out of its Burton.

The revival of India Pale Ale continues unabated. A style that seemed destined to be no more than a footnote to brewing history has been rekindled with enormous enthusiasm by scores of brewers. Acorn brewery in Barnsley alone produces several different versions of its IPA every year. In total there are close to 100 IPAs listed in the Guide as regular beers.

As the Guide went to press, Little Valley brewery in Yorkshire re-launched its Python IPA using organic malts and hops. The beer has a superb grassy hop, juicy malt and tangy fruit character.

All About Ale
The best beer comes naturally

Brewers call real ale 'cask-conditioned beer', a term that neatly sums up why this style is different to all other forms of beer. Cask beer has deep roots in Britain. In the 19th century, as the lager revolution spread from central Europe to most other parts of the world, Britain remained loyal to beer made in a time-honoured fashion that requires skill, commitment and even passion.

Most beer – lager as well as ale – is filtered, often pasteurised, and run into sealed containers called kegs in the brewery. When it reaches the pub or bar, it's served by applied gas pressure, either carbon dioxide or nitrogen or a mix of both.

Real ale on the other hand is a natural, living product. It's neither filtered nor pasteurised and reaches the peak of perfection in its cask in the pub cellar. It's possible – and legal – to produce something called 'beer' made with rice, maize and corn syrup, and flavoured with green juice squeezed from pulverised hops. But cask beer brewers turn their backs on such practices and prefer instead to use the finest malting barley and hops in their natural state. They may blend in darker malts and other grains, such as wheat or oats, but they avoid the cheap adjuncts used by the producers of global brands.

This insistence on quality chimes with the requirements of consumers who are concerned about how and where food and drink are made. Thanks to the work of malting companies and farmers, it's possible to trace where barley and hops are grown, even to the precise field where they are harvested. CAMRA's LocAle scheme, which encourages publicans to source some of their beers from breweries within a 30-mile radius, reduces carbon footprints. It's this insistence on locally-grown ingredients and beer brewed close to pubs that gives real ale a special appeal to the 'green generation'.

The critical difference between real ale and other types of beer is found at the brewery gate. While keg beer is finished and ready to be served, cask beer has yet to end its journey.

Before it leaves the brewery, additional hops and special brewing sugar may be added to casks to encourage a further fermentation and to increase hop aroma and flavour. In the pub cellar, each cask is 'stillaged' on its belly on a cradle.

A tap is knocked through the bung at the flat end of the cask while a peg, called a spile, is driven into a hole called the shive on top. The peg, made of porous wood, allows excess carbon dioxide to escape as the beer undergoes a secondary fermentation. As the beer has not been filtered, it retains yeast that attacks the remaining sugars in the beer. After a day, the porous peg is replaced by a hard one that keeps the remaining CO_2 inside the cask to give the finished beer a natural sparkle in the glass: the beer is said to have 'good condition'.

Meanwhile, isinglass finings added in the brewery start a natural chemical reaction that draws yeast cells and protein to the foot of the cask. When the publican or cellar manager is satisfied – by drawing a sample from the cask – that the beer has 'dropped bright', plastic tubes called lines are attached to a tap in the bung and the beer is ready to be served. The familiar handpump on the bar operates a beer engine or suction pump that draws beer from cellar to bar. In some pubs, the beer is served 'by gravity' – direct from the cask.

Real ale should be served cool: 'warm British beer' is a myth. Cask beer should be delivered to the bar at a cellar temperature of 11-13°C. Some summer beers and golden ales are served cooler at 9-10°C. The beer in your glass should be rich in malt aromas and flavours, naturally made and naturally served.

On the next two pages you can follow the brewing process in a traditional cask beer brewery, Harvey's of Lewes in East Sussex.

OLD. MILD &
WINE & SPIRIT

In the beginning is the wort...

The real-ale brewing process from mash tun to bar

Before you can raise a pint in the pub, enormous skill and the finest natural ingredients come together in the brewery to turn barley malt, hops, yeast and water into beer. Here, the *Good Beer Guide* follows the brewing skills at Harveys.

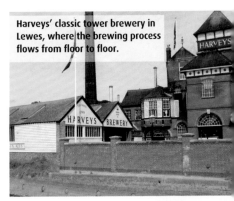

Harveys' classic tower brewery in Lewes, where the brewing process flows from floor to floor.

3.
Pure water, known as 'liquor', has percolated through the chalk downs of Sussex before reaching the brewery. Hot liquor is mixed in the mash tun with the malt grist.

▷

4.
Head brewer Miles Jenner checks the temperature of the mash as brewing gets under way. Temperature is crucial to allow malt starch to turn into fermentable sugar.

▷

7.
The hop store: Harveys uses traditional hop varieties from farmers in Sussex and surrounding counties.

▷

8.
The copper, where wort is vigorously boiled with hops: the boil extracts acids and tannins from the hops that add aroma and bitterness to the beer.

▷

11.
To keep the yeast working busily, turning malt sugar into alcohol, the fermenting beer is roused or oxygenated from time to time.

▷

12.
Beer is racked into casks in preparation for the final destination: the pub cellar where it enjoys a vigorous second fermentation.

▷

1.
Malt – partially germinated barley – is stored at the top of the brewery. Harveys uses the classic Maris Otter variety.

◁

2.
Malt is added to a hopper ready to be ground into grist. The grist is then dropped into the mash tun to start the brewing process.

◁

5.
At the end of the mash, the grain is 'sparged' or sprinkled with hot liquor to wash out remaining malt sugars.

◁

6.
The wort or sugary extract runs out of the mash tun into a receiving vessel where it is checked en route to the copper.

◁

9.
Some of the hops are added late in the boil for additional aroma and flavour. 'Late hopping' restores any aroma lost earlier during the boil.

◁

10.
After the boil the hopped wort is cooled and transfered to a fermenting vessel. Yeast is 'pitched' or blended into the wort to start fermentation.

◁

13.
In the racking hall, finings are added that will clear the beer of yeast and protein in the pub cellar.

◁

14.
And finally... checking the quality of the finished beer in the pub. Another perfect pint is poured!

◁

Britain's Classic Beer Styles

IN THE WORLD OF BEER, Britain's is best known for the style known as bitter, which in the 20th century developed from the pale ales first brewed in Victorian times. But there is far more to British beer than bitter. Older styles have reappeared while the likes of golden ale, fruit beer and wheat beer have been fashioned in recent years to give further choice to drinkers. In this briefing, **Roger Protz** gives an indication of some of the great beers available in British pubs and recommends some of his favourite versions of each style.

PORTER & STOUT

Porter was a London beer that created the first commercial brewing industry in the world in the early 18th century. Porter started life as a brown beer and became darker when new technology made it possible to roast grain at higher temperatures to obtain greater colour and flavour. The strongest version of porter was dubbed stout porter or stout for short. The name porter was the result of the beer's popularity with the large number of porters working the streets, markets and docks of 18th-century London.

Porter and stout were exported to the rest of the British Isles and, as a result, Arthur Guinness built his own porter brewery in Dublin. During World War One, when the British government prevented brewers from using heavily-roasted malts in order to divert energy to the arms industry, Guinness and other Irish brewers came to dominate the market. In recent years, porter and stout have made a spirited comeback in both Britain and the United States, with brewers digging deep in to old recipe books to create genuine versions of the style from the 18th and 19th centuries.

Look for a jet-black colour with a hint of ruby around the edge of the glass. Expect a dark and roasted malt character, with raisin and sultana fruit, espresso or cappuccino coffee, liquorice and molasses. The beer should have deep hop bitterness to balance the richness of malt and fruit.

ROGER'S ROUND:

MEANTIME LONDON PORTER

NETHERGATE OLD GROWLER

THORNBRIDGE SAINT PETERSBURG IMPERIAL RUSSIAN STOUT

MILD

Mild was once the most popular style of beer in Britain but it was overtaken by bitter in the 1950s. It was developed in the 18th and 19th centuries as a less aggressively bitter style of beer than porter and stout, and was primarily drunk by industrial and agricultural workers to refresh them after long hours of arduous labour. Early milds were much stronger that modern interpretations, which tend to fall in the 3% to 3.5% category, though Rudgate's Dark Ruby Mild at 4.4% is more in keeping with earlier strengths. Mild is usually dark brown in colour, due to the use of well-roasted malts or roasted barley, but there are paler versions such as Banks's Mild, Timothy Taylor's Golden Best and McMullen's AK. Look for rich malty aromas and flavours, with hints of dark fruit, chocolate, coffee and caramel, with a gentle underpinning of hop bitterness.

ROGER'S ROUND:

BANKS'S MILD

HOLT'S MILD

RUDGATE DARK RUBY MILD

SARAH HUGHES DARK RUBY

OLD ALE

Old ale is another style from the 18th century, stored for months or even years in wooden vessels where the beer picked up some lactic sourness from wild yeasts and tannins in the wood. As a result of the sour taste, it was dubbed 'stale' by drinkers and the beer was one of the components of the early blended porters. In recent years, old ale has made a return to popularity, primarily due to the popularity of Theakston's Old Peculier and Gale's Prize Old Ale. Contrary to expectation, old ales do not have to be especially strong and can be no more than 4% alcohol. Neither do they have to be dark: old ale can be pale and bursting with lush malt, tart fruit and spicy hops. Darker versions will have a more profound malt character, with powerful hints of roasted grain, dark fruit, polished leather and fresh tobacco. The hallmark of the style is a lengthy period of maturation, often in bottle rather than cask.

ROGER'S ROUND:

GALE'S PRIZE OLD ALE (BREWED BY FULLER'S)

THEAKSTON'S OLD PECULIER

ROBINSON'S OLD TOM

BARLEY WINE

Barley wine dates from the 18th and 19th centuries when England was often at war with France and it was the duty of patriots, usually from the upper classes, to drink ale rather that French claret. Barley wine had to be strong – often between 10% and 12% – and was stored for as long as 18 months or two years. The biggest-selling barley wine for many years was Whitbread's 10.9% Gold Label, now available only in cans. Fuller's Vintage Ale (8.5%) is a bottle-conditioned version of its Golden Pride and is brewed with different varieties of malts and hops every year. Expect massive sweet malt and ripe fruit of the pear drop, orange and lemon type, with darker fruits, chocolate and coffee if darker malts are used. Hop rates are generous and produce bitterness and peppery, grassy and floral notes.

ROGER'S ROUND:

CHILTERN BODGER'S BARLEY WINE

FULLER'S VINTAGE ALE

HOGS BACK A OVER T

IPA

India Pale Ale changed the face of brewing in the 19th century. The new technologies of the industrial revolution enabled brewers to use pale malts to fashion beers that were pale bronze in colour. First brewed in London and Burton-on-Trent for the colonial trade, IPAs were strong in alcohol and high in hops to keep them in good condition during long sea journeys. IPA's life span was brief, driven out of the colonies by German lager. But the style has made a spirited recovery in recent years, brewed with great passion in both Britain and the U.S. In Chicago, Goose Island's IPA is arguably the finest American interpretation of the style while in Britain Marston's Old Empire and Meantime's IPA are just two modern versions of the style arousing new interest. Look for a big peppery hop aroma and palate balanced by juicy malt and tart citrus fruit.

ROGER'S ROUND:

MARSTON'S OLD EMPIRE

THORNBRIDGE JAIPUR IPA

WESTERHAM INDIA PALE ALE

BURTON ALE

As the name suggests, the origins of Burton Ale lie in Burton-on-Trent, but the style became so popular in the 18th and 19th centuries that most brewers had 'a Burton' in their portfolio and the expression 'gone for a Burton' entered the English language. Bass at one time had six different versions of the beer, ranging from 6% to 11.5%: the stronger versions were exported to Russia and the Baltic States.

In the 20th century, Burton was overtaken in popularity by pale ale and bitter but it was revived with great success in the late 1970s with the launch of Ind Coope Draught Burton Ale. But when Allied Breweries broke up, the beer moved first to Tetley's in Leeds and then J W Lees in Manchester, where it's brewed in small batches but is worth seeking out: it's based on the recipe for a once-famous bottled beer, Double Diamond Export. Other Burton Ales exist under different names today: Young's Winter Warmer was originally called Burton. Bass No 1, brewed occasionally, is called a barley wine but is in fact the last remaining version of a Bass Burton Ale. Look for a bright amber colour, a rich malty and fruity character underscored by a solid resinous and piny hop note.

ROGER'S ROUND:

BURTON BRIDGE BRIDGE BITTER

MARSTON'S OWD RODGER

YOUNG'S WINTER WARMER

PALE ALE

The success of IPA in the colonial trade led to a demand for beer of a similar colour and character in Britain. IPA, with its heavy hopping, was considered too bitter for the domestic market, and brewers responded with a beer dubbed pale ale that was lower in both alcohol and hops. Pale ale was known as 'the beer of the railway age', transported round the country from Burton-on-Trent by the new railway system. Brewers from London, Liverpool and Manchester built breweries in Burton to make use of the local, mineral-rich water to make their own versions of pale ale. From the early years of the 20th century, bitter began to overtake pale ale in popularity and as a result pale ale became mainly a bottled product. A true pale ale should be different to bitter, identical to IPA in colour and brewed without the addition of coloured malts. It should have a spicy, resinous aroma and palate, with biscuity malt and tart citrus fruit. Many beers are called bitter today but are in fact pale ale, Marston's Pedigree being a case in point.

ROGER'S ROUND:

MARSTON'S PEDIGREE

REDEMPTION PALE ALE

TOWER PALE ALE

BITTER

Towards the end of the 19th century, brewers built large estates of tied pubs and they moved away from beers stored for months or years and developed 'running beers' that could be served after a few days of conditioning in the pub cellar. Bitter was a new type of running beer: it was a member of the pale ale family but was generally deep bronze or copper in colour due to the use of slightly darker malts, such as crystal, that gave the beer fullness of palate. Best is a stronger version of bitter but there is considerable crossover. Bitter falls into the 3.4% to 3.9% band, while best bitter is 4% upwards, though a number of brewers dub their ordinary bitters 'best'. A further development of bitter comes in the shape of extra or special strong bitter of 5% or more: Fuller's ESB and Greene King Abbot being well-known examples. With ordinary bitter, look for spicy, peppery and grassy hop character, a powerful bitterness, tangy fruit and juicy/nutty malt. With best and strong bitters, malt and fruit character will tend to dominate but hop aroma and bitterness are still crucial to the style, often achieved by 'late hopping' in the brewery or adding hops to casks as they leave for pubs.

ROGER'S ROUND:

HARVEY'S BEST BITTER

TIMOTHY TAYLOR LANDLORD

WOODFORDE'S WHERRY

GOLDEN ALE

Golden ales have become so popular, with brewers of all sizes producing them, that they now have their own category in the Champion Beer of Britain competition. Exmoor Gold and Hop Back Summer Lightning launched the trend in the early 1980s and other brewers

quickly followed suit in a rush to win younger drinkers away from mass-produced lagers to the pleasures of cask beer. The style is different to pale ale in two crucial ways: golden ale is paler, often brewed with lager malt or specially produced low temperature ale malt and, as a result, hops are allowed to give full expression, balancing sappy malt with luscious fruity, floral, herbal, spicy and resinous characteristics. While brewers of pale ale tend to use such traditional English hops as Fuggles and Goldings, imported hops from North America, the Czech Republic, Germany, Slovenia and New Zealand give radically different hop notes to golden ale. As a result, golden ales offer a new and exciting drinking experience. They are often served colder than draught bitter and some brewers, such as Fuller's, have installed special cooling devices attached to beer engines to ensure the beer reaches the glass at an acceptably refreshing temperature.

ROGER'S ROUND:

CASTLE ROCK HARVEST PALE

HAWKSHEAD LAKELAND GOLD

VALE GRAVITAS

WHEAT BEER

Wheat beer is a style closely associated with Bavaria and Belgium and the popularity of the style in Britain has encouraged many brewers to add wheat beer to the portfolios. The title is something of a misnomer as all 'wheat beers' are a blend of malted barley as well as wheat, as the latter grain is difficult to brew with and needs the addition of barley, which acts as a natural filter during the mashing stage. But wheat, if used with special strains of yeast developed for brewing the style, gives distinctive aromas and flavours, such as clove, banana and bubblegum that make it a complex and refreshing beer. The Belgian version of wheat beer often has the addition of herbs and spices, such as milled coriander seeds and orange peel – a habit that dates back to medieval times.

ROGER'S ROUND:

LITTLE VALLEY HEBDEN'S WHEAT

OTLEY O-GARDEN

THORNBRIDGE VERSA

FRUIT/SPECIALITY BEERS

Brewers have become restless in recent years in their quest for new flavours that will help them reach a wider and more appreciative audience for their beers. The popularity in Britain of Belgian fruit beers has not gone unnoticed and now many home-grown brewers are using fruit in their beer. Others have gone the extra mile and add honey, herbs, heather, spices, and even spirit – brandy and rum feature in a number of speciality beers.

It's important to dispel the belief that fruit and honey beers are sweet: both fruit and honey add new dimensions to the brewing process and are highly fermentable, with the result that beers that use the likes of cherries or raspberry are dry and quenching rather than cloying.

ROGER'S ROUND:

FAT CAT
HONEY CAT

ST PETER'S
GRAPEFRUIT BEER

WILLIAMS
BROTHER FRAOCH
HEATHER ALE

SCOTTISH BEERS

Historically, Scottish beers tend to be darker, sweeter and less heavily hopped that beers south of the border: a reflection of a colder climate where hops don't grow and beer needs to be nourishing. The classic traditional styles are Light, Heavy and Export, which are not dissimilar to mild, bitter and IPA. They are also often known as 60, 70 and 80 Shilling Ales from a 19th-century method of invoicing beers according to their strength. A Wee Heavy or 90 Shilling Ale, now rare, is the Scottish equivalent of barley wine. Many of the newer brewers in Scotland produce beers that are lighter in colour and with more generous hop rates.

ROGER'S ROUND:

BELHAVEN
80 SHILLING ALE

HARVIESTOUN
BITTER + TWISTED

STEWART
EDINBURGH
NO 3

Only accept perfect pints

Remember, you're the consumer, forking out a high price for beer, so don't be afraid to take your pint back to the bar if:

- It's either too cold or too warm. Cask beer should be cool, not cold – but bear in mind that some golden ales are meant to be served at a lower temperature than Milds and Bitters. At the other end of the spectrum, it's a myth that real ale should be served at room temperature. Warm beer tastes bad, as the temperature creates unpleasant off flavours. If your beer smells of acetone, vinegar or stale bread, take it back.
- The pint has no head, is totally flat and out of condition.
- It's not only flat but hazy and has yeast particles or protein floating in the liquid.

If you get the response 'Real ale is meant to be warm and cloudy', invite the publican to join the 21st century. If the offending pub has a Cask Marque plaque, get in touch with Cask Marque. Otherwise, let us know at the *Good Beer Guide* **camragbgeditor@camra.org.uk**.

And please go back to the bar if you are served a short measure – less than a pint of liquid in the glass. Drinkers lose millions of pounds a year as a result of short measure.

It's an outrageous rip-off. CAMRA beer festivals serve beer in over-size glasses that ensure drinkers always get a full pint. Most pub owners refuse to use over-size glasses, preferring brim-measure glasses that allow them consistently to serve short measure. It's a scandal. Don't put up with it.

CAMRA's Beers of the Year

THE BEERS LISTED BELOW are CAMRA'S Beers of the Year. They were short-listed for the Champion Beer of Britain competition in August 2011 and the Champion Winter Beer of Britain competition in January that year. The August competition judged Dark & Light Milds; Bitters; Best Bitters; Strong Bitters; Golden Ales; Speciality Beers; and Real Ale in a Bottle. The winter competition judged Old Ales & Strong Milds; Porters; Stouts; and Barley Wines & Strong Old Ales. Each beer was found by a panel of trained CAMRA judges to be consistently outstanding in its category and they all receive a 'full tankard' [🍺] in the Breweries section.

DARK & LIGHT MILDS
Bank Top, Dark Mild
Batemans, Dark Mild
Coastal, Merry Maidens
Goachers, Real Mild
Highland, Dark Munro
Hobsons, Mild
Mighty Oak, Oscar Wilde
Rudgate, Ruby Mild
Swansea, Deep Slade Dark

BITTERS
Arran, Arran Ale
Bryncelyn, Holly Hop
Church End, Goats Milk
Elgoods, Cambridge
Elland, Bargee
Hawkshead, Bitter
Hopdaemon, Golden Braid
Nottingham, Rock Ale Bitter
Orkney, Raven Ale
Phoenix, Navvy
Potton, Shannon IPA
Purple Moose, Snowdonia
RCH, PG Steam
Salopian, Shropshire Gold
Teignworthy, Reel Ale
Triple fff, Alton's Pride
Whim, Hartington Bitter
York, Guzzler

BEST BITTERS
Blythe, Staffie
Bollington, Best Bitter
Castle Rock, Preservation
Castle Rock, Elsie Mo
Country Life, Golden Pig
Facers, Daves Hoppy Brew
George Wright, Pipe Dream
Hall & Woodhouse, Badger
    First Gold
Houston, Peter's Well
Jarrow, Joblings Swinging Gibbet
Kelburn, Red Smiddy
Kinver, Edge
McMullen, Country Bitter
Milton, Pegasus
Otter, Amber
Purple Moose, Glaslyn Ale
Surrey Hills, Shere Drop
Timothy Taylor, Landlord

STRONG BITTERS
Adnam's, Broadside

Black Sheep, Riggwelter
Fullers, Gales HSB
Hesket Newmarket, Cat Bells
Kinver, Half Centurion
Moles, Mole Catcher
Rhymney, Export
Thornbridge, Jaipur
Tryst, Raj IPA

GOLDEN ALES
Castle Rock, Harvest Pale
Cheddar Ales, Potholer
Cumbrian Legendary Ales,
    Loweswater Gold
Dark Star, Hophead
Great Orme, Celtica
Holdens, Golden Glow
Inveralmond, Ossian
Oakham, Inferno
Salamander, Golden Salamander

OLD ALES & STRONG MILDS
B & T, Shefford Old Dark
Beowulf, Dark Raven
Box Steam, Dark & Handsome
Bragdy'r Nant, Mwnci Nell
Brunswick, Father Mike's
    Dark Ruby
Fyne, Highlander
King, Old Ale
Leeds, Midnight Belle
Marble, Chocolate

PORTERS
Acorn, Old Moor Porter
Beowulf, Finns Hall Porter
Conwy, Telford Porter
Dow Bridge, Praetorian Porter
Hammerpot, Bottle Wreck Porter
Red Squirrel, London Porter
Sulwath, Black Galloway
Wapping, Smoked Porter
Wickwar, Station Porter

STOUTS
Bull Lane, Sauce of the Niall
Cairngorm, Black Gold
Heart of Wales, Welsh Black
Hop Back, Entire Stout
Hopstar, Smokey Joes Black Beer
Milk Street, Zig Zag Stout
Milton, Nero
Thornbridge, Saint Petersburg
Titanic, Stout

BARLEY WINES & STRONG OLD ALES
Adnams, Tally Ho!
Black Isle, Hibernator
Darwin, Extinction Ale
Exmoor, Beast
Goachers, Old 1066 Ale
Heart of Wales, High as a Kite
Holdens, Old Ale
Robinsons, Old Tom

SPECIALITY BEERS
Amber, Chocolate Orange Stout
Little Valley, Hebden's Wheat
Oakleaf, I Can't Believe
    It's Not Bitter
Okells, Alt
Orkney, Atlas Wayfarer
Otley, O Garden
Salopian, Lemon Dream
Skinners, Heligan Honey
St Peter's, Grapefruit

REAL ALE IN A BOTTLE
Beowulf, Dragon Smoke Stout
Black Isle, Goldeneye
Brown Cow, Captain Oates Dark
    Oat Mild
Cropton, Two Pints Bitter
Dark Star, Imperial Stout
Fullers, Vintage (2009)
Hesket Newmarket, Doris's 90th
    Birthday Ale
Islay, Single Malt Ale
Molson Coors, Worthington
    White Shield
O'Hanlon's, Original Port Stout
Pitfield, 1850 London Porter
Prospect, Silver Tally
St Austell, Proper Job
Spire, Sgt Peppers Stout
Thornbridge, St Petersburg
Red Squirrel, Conservation Ale

CHAMPION WINTER BEER OF BRITAIN 2011
Hop Back,
Entire Stout

CHAMPION BEER OF BRITAIN 2011
Mighty Oak,
Oscar Wilde

SHETLAND

NORTHERN
ISLES

HIGHLANDS
&
WESTERN ISLES

ABERDEEN
& GRAMPIAN

TAYSIDE

LOCH LOMOND
STIRLING
& THE
TROSSACHS

FIFE

ARGYLL &
THE ISLES

EDINBURGH & LOTHIANS

GREATER
GLASGOW &
CLYDE VALLEY

BORDERS

AYRSHIRE
& ARRAN

NORTHERN
IRELAND

DUMFRIES &
GALLOWAY

NORTHUMBER-
LAND

TYNE &
WEAR

CUMBRIA

DURHAM

ISLE OF
MAN

NORTH
YORKSHIRE

LANCASHIRE

EAST
YORKS

MERSEYSIDE

WEST
YORKS

GREATER
MANCHESTER

SOUTH
YORKS

LINCOLN-
SHIRE

NW
WALES

NE
WALES

CHESHIRE

DERBYSHIRE

NOTTINGHAM-
SHIRE

SHROPSHIRE

STAFFORD-
SHIRE

LEICESTERSHIRE
& RUTLAND

NORFOLK

MID
WALES

WEST
MIDLANDS

WORCESTER-
SHIRE

WARWICK-
SHIRE

NORTHAMPTON-
SHIRE

CAMBRIDGE-
SHIRE

SUFFOLK

HEREFORD-
SHIRE

BEDFORD-
SHIRE

WEST
WALES

GLOUCS &
BRISTOL

OXFORD-
SHIRE

BUCKINGHAM-
SHIRE

HERTFORD-
SHIRE

ESSEX

GLAMORGAN

GWENT

BERKSHIRE

GREATER
LONDON

WILTSHIRE

SURREY

KENT

SOMERSET

HAMPSHIRE

WEST
SUSSEX

EAST
SUSSEX

CHANNEL
ISLANDS

DEVON

DORSET

ISLE OF
WIGHT

CORNWALL

England

BEDFORDSHIRE

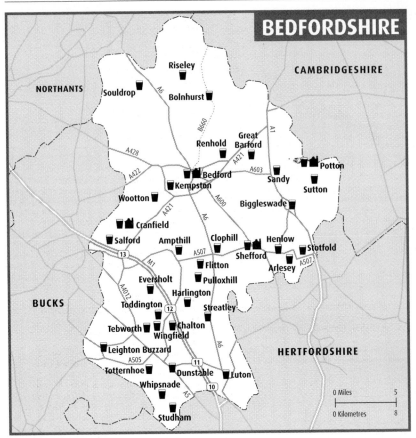

Ampthill

Albion 🄻
36 Dunstable Street, MK45 2JT TL033378
☼ 11.30-11 (midnight Fri & Sat) ☎ (01525) 634857
**B&T Shefford Bitter, Golden Fox, Dragonslayer;
Everards Tiger; guest beers** 🄷
A proper ale house with 12 handpumps dispensing
B&T and Everards beers plus a range of ever-
changing guest beers. Real cider and perry from
Westons is served and the bar is devoid of the
usual mainstream lagers. It was bought by Everards
in 2009, thoroughly refurbished and leased to the
local B&T brewery under the Project William
initiative. A good mix of clientele takes advantage
of the deceptively spacious interior and the
compact courtyard adorned with old pub signs.
🚗⊛🚪♣☝

Old Sun 🄻
87 Dunstable Street, MK45 2NQ TL034379
☼ 12-midnight (12.30am Fri & Sat); 12-11.30 Sun
☎ (01525) 405466 ⊕ theoldsunampthill.co.uk
**Adnams Bitter; Courage Directors; Fuller's London
Pride; St Austell Tribute; Young's London Gold** 🄷
Picturesque and popular two-bar pub with five ales
usually available. Real fires add to the cosy feel in
winter. A large rear garden with covered decking,
and seating in front of the pub, make this a very
pleasant outdoor venue in the summer months.
There is a games room for pool and darts with its
own serving hatch. Various local interest groups

and charity events are held throughout the year. A
newly converted function room is available.
🚗⊛🚪♣P☝

Arlesey

Vicars Inn 🄻
68 Church Lane, SG15 6UX
☼ 12-3.30 (not Mon-Thu), 5-midnight; 12-4, 7-midnight Sat &
Sun ☎ (01462) 731215
Wells Eagle IPA; guest beer 🄷
This inn is located in the north end of the village, a
short stroll from the railway station. The traditional
two-bar layout, popular with an older clientele,
makes you feel at home in a comfortable and
relaxed atmosphere. The guest beer is usually a
lower gravity session ale and excellent value.
Families make good use of the enclosed garden,
and occasional events are held in a separate
function room. Dominoes evenings are well
attended. Q⊛🚪👶⇆🚪(M2,E7)♣P

Bedford

Bedford Arms ✅
2 Bromham Road, MK40 2QA (opp HM Prison)
☼ 12-11 (midnight Thu-Sat) ☎ (01234) 214656
**Courage Best Bitter; Wells Bombardier; Young's
Bitter, Special; guest beers** 🄷
Following an extensive rebuild, this is now a
Charles Wells Speciality Ale House. Wood panelling
dominates and the wooden floor makes for

interesting acoustics. A changing range of guest beers adds choice to the four regular Wells & Young's ales. Bar meals are available daily, with a roast on Sunday. There is a quiz on Monday, a poetry club on Thursday and live music on Tuesday, Friday and all day Sunday from 1pm. ⊛◑≷⊟⌐

Castle

17 Newnham Street, MK40 3JR (½ mile E of town centre)
⊛ 12-3 (not Mon), 4.30-11; 8.30-midnight Fri & Sat; 12-10.30 Sun ☎ (01234) 353295 ⊕ thecastlepubbedford.co.uk
Courage Directors; Wells Eagle IPA; guest beers Ⓗ
Recently refurbished two-bar hostelry with a pleasant walled patio garden. A guest house at the rear provides five en-suite letting bedrooms. The pub is open to non-residents for breakfast on Friday and Saturday, and lunches and evening meals (not Sun or Mon) are also provided, though advance booking is required for Saturday evening. There is a small library of books for customers' use in the bar. The Castle is conveniently situated for Bedford Rugby Club. ⇆⊛⇄◑⊞&⊟(4,5,7)P⌐

Cricketers Arms Ⓛ

35 Goldington Road, MK40 3LH (on A4280 near rugby ground)
⊛ 5 (7 Sun)-11 ☎ (01234) 303958 ⊕ cricketersarms.co.uk
Adnams Bitter; guest beers Ⓗ
Small, friendly, one-bar pub near Bedford Blues rugby ground, popular with fans of the game and very busy on match days. It opens at noon on Saturdays for Blues home games. Live rugby is shown and the pub also opens early for live Six Nations games. Guest beers include brews from local micro-breweries. There is a covered, heated courtyard for smokers and drinkers. ⊛⊟(5)⌐

Devonshire Arms ✓

32 Dudley Street, MK40 3TB (1 mile E of town centre S of A4280)
⊛ 5 (12 Fri & Sat)-11; 12-10.30 Sun ☎ (01234) 359329
Courage Directors; Wells Eagle IPA; Young's London Gold; guest beers Ⓗ
Pleasant Victorian two-bar local in a quiet residential area east of the town centre near Russell Park and the Embankment. An annual beer festival is hosted in May. The front bar, with bare floorboards, has recently been refurbished. The carpeted rear bar is a more traditional saloon. Outside, the small, private garden has a gazebo with heating and lighting for smokers and a no-smoking lawn area. A good range of wines is sold by the glass, jug or bottle. ⋈Q⊛⊞⊟(4)⌐

Flower Pot

25 Tavistock Street, MK40 2RB (on A6 just N of town centre)
⊛ 12-11 (midnight Sat); 12-10.30 Sun ☎ (01234) 294174
Fuller's London Pride; guest beers Ⓗ
One of the oldest pubs in Bedford, with low ceilings, small windows, dark wood and subdued lighting creating a cosy, traditional atmosphere. The walls are festooned with numerous photos of old Bedford. Live music features on Friday evening and a quiz night is hosted on Wednesday. There is a patio to the side and rear with seating and a covered smoking area. ⊛◑⊟⌐

Three Cups

45 Newnham Street, MK40 3JR (200m S of A4280 near rugby ground)
⊛ 11-11; 12-10.30 Sun ☎ (01234) 352153

Greene King XX Mild, IPA, Abbot; guest beers Ⓗ
Five minutes from the town centre and close to the rugby ground, this 1770s pub with old-style wood panelling feels like a welcoming village inn. A popular lunchtime menu is available with a wide range of food served in generous portions and a roast on Sunday. The pleasant garden has a heated smoking shelter. Dogs are welcome in the public bar and garden. Quiz night is Tuesday. Q⊛◑⊞&⊟(4,5,7)♣P⌐

Wellington Arms ✓

40-42 Wellington Street, MK40 2JX (off A6 N of town centre)
⊛ 12-11 (10.30 Sun) ☎ (01234) 308033
Adnams Bitter; B&T Two Brewers; guest beers Ⓗ
Award-winning, street-corner local operated by B&T Brewery, offering a wide range of regional and micro-brewery beers, plus real cider and perry (summer only) from 14 handpumps. A good selection of draught and bottled Belgian and other imported beers is also available. The courtyard is partly covered for drinkers and smokers. A friendly pub with a mixed clientele. Local CAMRA Pub of the Year 2010. ⊛●⌐

White Horse Ⓛ ✓

84 Newnham Avenue, MK41 9PX (on A5140 just S of A4280)
⊛ 10 (12 Sun)-11 ☎ (01234) 409306
⊕ whitehorsebedford.co.uk
Wells Eagle IPA, Bombardier; guest beers Ⓗ
Large single-bar suburban pub a mile east of the town centre. Good value food is available, with a Sunday roast and occasional themed evenings. Breakfast is served Monday to Saturday. Quiz nights are Sunday and Tuesday, while Monday is 'open-mike' night. The pub has won several brewery and local business awards. A May Day weekend local beer, food and talent festival, and a November beer and banger festival are held each year. Check the website for monthly events. ⊛◑&⊟(4)P⌐

Biggleswade

Golden Pheasant Ⓛ ✓

71 High Street, SG18 0JH
⊛ 11-11 (1am Fri & Sat) ☎ (01767) 313653
⊕ goldenpheasantpub.co.uk
Wells Eagle IPA; guest beers Ⓗ
Lovely little market town pub, just five minutes' walk from the bus and train station. The low ceilings and oak beams contribute to a cosy environment where conversation takes centre stage, aided by the absence of TVs or gaming machines. Alongside the regular Eagle IPA, five guest ales rotate continuously, with small breweries from far and wide often showcased. The real cider is usually from Thatchers. Quiz and chess evenings are very popular. ⊛≷⊟♣●⌐

Stratton House Hotel Ⓛ

London Road, SG18 8ED
⊛ 11-11 (midnight Fri & Sat) ☎ (01767) 312442
⊕ strattonhouse-hotel.com

INDEPENDENT BREWERIES

B&T Shefford
Potton Potton
Wells & Young's Bedford
White Park Cranfield

Beer range varies 🄷
The front area of this hotel offers lovely armchairs and settees, popular with a mixed clientele who come to relax and enjoy a fine ale or bar meal. In addition, there is a large restaurant open every day and a function room for events. Now free of tie, the beer range is wider and the four handpumps often feature a stout or porter. A summer beer festival provides customers with a further chance to sample new ales. 🛏◖◗♿≹🚌P⅃

Wheatsheaf ✔

5 Lawrence Road, SG18 0LS
⊕ 11-4, 7-11.30; 11-midnight Fri & Sat; 12-11 Sun
☎ (01767) 222220
Greene King XX Mild, IPA 🄷
This traditional back-street beer house is very popular with the local community. A warm welcome draws you into the conversation at the bar, and the atmosphere is enhanced by a lively game of dominoes or cribbage, and live football on TV. The landlord for the last 22 years takes pride in good cellarmanship, offering high-quality conditioned ales at affordable prices. The small garden at the rear provides a quiet haven on a summer's day. ❀≹♣⅃

Bolnhurst

Plough 🄻

Kimbolton Road, MK44 2EX (on B660 S of village)
TL088587
⊕ closed Mon; 12-3, 6.30-11 (not Sun eve)
☎ (01234) 376274 🌐 bolnhurst.com
Beer range varies 🄷
Award-winning pub restaurant with roots going back to Tudor times, offering excellent food and beer, and good service. The main bar features a wood-burning stove and was recently extended to provide more space for diners. A second room is also set aside for diners. Outside is a large drinking area alongside the car park. Real ales are often from local micro-breweries. The pub is closed each year from Christmas until the second week of January. ♨Q❀◖◗♿P

Chalton

Star 🄻 ✔

33 Luton Road, LU4 9UJ (1½ miles from jct 12 M1)
TL032265
⊕ 11-11; 12-10.30 Sun ☎ (01582) 872248
Adnams Bitter; Courage Directors; Fuller's London Pride; guest beers 🄷
Good-looking, olde-worlde-style pub with a log fire in winter, usually serving an interesting guest ale alongside the regulars. Beware of the genuine, original and low ceiling beams. An extensive range of pub food is available with daily specials. On a summer's day this is a pleasant spot to sit outside on the patio or in the large garden watching the world go by. The car park is large.
♨❀◖◗♿🚌(20)P⅃

Clophill

Stone Jug

10 Back Street, MK45 4BY (off A6 at N end of village)
TL083381
⊕ 12-3, 6-11; 12-11 Fri & Sat; 12-10.30 Sun
☎ (01525) 860526
B&T Shefford Bitter; guest beers 🄷
Originally three 16th-century cottages, this popular village local has an L-shaped bar that serves two drinking areas and a family/function room. Excellent home-made lunches are available Tuesday to Saturday. The four guest beers are often from local breweries. Picnic benches at the front and a rear patio garden offer space for outdoor drinking in fine weather. Parking can be difficult at busy times. CAMRA Bedfordshire Pub of the Year 2006. Q👶❀◖🚌(S1,X44)♣🍎P⅃

Cranfield

Carpenters Arms 🄻

93 High Street, MK43 0DP (opp war memorial)
⊕ 12-2.30, 7 (6 Wed-Fri)-11; 12-11.30 Sat; 12-11 Sun
☎ (01234) 750232 🌐 carpentersarms-cranfield.co.uk
Wells Eagle IPA; guest beers 🄷
A real community pub in the middle of the village, with traditional pub games played in the public bar. Home-cooked meals are served in the lounge-cum-restaurant (no food Sun eve). There is a large car park and patio garden at the rear. Mini beer festivals are held throughout the year – check the website for details. Q❀◖◗🀄♿🚌(1,17A,V1)♣P⅃

Dunstable

Gary Cooper ✔

Grove Park, LU5 4GP
⊕ 8am-midnight (2am Fri & Sat) ☎ (01582) 471087
Fuller's London Pride; Greene King Ruddles Best Bitter, Abbot; guest beers 🄷
Large, modern Lloyds No.1/Wetherspoon venue serving a selection of up to six guest ales. Situated near the town centre in the Grove Theatre complex, it is named after the famous Hollywood actor who attended the local grammar school before the 1914-18 war. The bar tends to be busy on Friday and Saturday evenings. Be prepared for a long hike to the upstairs loos. Good value Club meals are served on Tuesday, Thursday and Sunday. Outside is a pleasant seating area overlooking the park. ❀◖◗♿🚌🍎⅃

Globe 🄻

43 Winfield Street, LU6 1LS
⊕ 12-11 (midnight Fri & Sat); 12-10.30 Sun
☎ (01582) 512300 🌐 globe-pub.co.uk
B&T Two Brewers, Shefford Bitter, Shefford Dark Mild, Dunstable Giant, Edwin Taylor's Extra Stout; guest beers 🄷
A popular beer destination and community local where 13 handpumps dispense a good range of regular B&T beers and Everards Tiger plus five ever-changing micro-brewery beers. There is also real cider and perry from Westons and 20-plus Belgian beers. Bare boards, bar stools and breweriana create a traditional town-pub atmosphere that buzzes with conversation. Tuesday night's Globe Acoustic Session features live music. Dogs are welcome. CAMRA Bedfordshire Pub of the Year 2009/10, and South Bedfordshire Pub of the Year 07/08/09/10. Q❀♿♣🍎⅃

Victoria 🄻

69 West Street, LU6 1ST
⊕ 11-12.30am (1am Fri & Sat); 12-midnight Sun
☎ (01582) 662682
Beer range varies 🄷
Popular town-centre pub that usually offers four ales including a house beer, Victoria Bitter, from

Tring Brewery. The varying guest ales are from micro and regional breweries, with one sold at a reduced rate on weekdays. Good value food is available until early evening Monday-Friday, and Saturday and Sunday lunchtimes. Darts, dominoes and crib are popular and televised sport features in the bar. Beer festivals are held several times a year. There is a separate function room available. ✿◑➡(61)♣ͱ

Eversholt

Green Man
Church End, MK17 9DU SP984325
✿ 12-2.30 (not Mon), 6-11; 5-11 Fri; 12-11 Sat; 12-7 Sun
☎ (01525) 288111 ⊕ greenmaneversholt.com
Sharp's Doom Bar; guest beers Ⓗ
This genuine free house is conveniently located near the tourist attractions of Woburn. It is an early-Victorian building with a recently refurbished interior featuring a modern flagstone floor and exposed fireplaces in the main bar area. It also has a large patio and garden and a separate restaurant serving good quality food. There are usually two guest ales, possibly including one from a local brewery. An annual beer festival is held over the May bank holiday weekend. ⋈Q✿◑➇♣Pͱ

Flitton

Jolly Coopers Ⓛ
Wardhedges, MK45 5ED
✿ 12-3 (not Mon), 5.30-11.30; 12-midnight Sat; 12-10.30 Sun
☎ (01525) 860626
Wells Eagle IPA; guest beers Ⓗ
Two ever-changing and varied guest ales are served alongside the regular Eagle. Situated in the quiet hamlet of Wardhedges at the east end of Flitton, the pub is ideally placed for some very pleasant walks in the countryside. Traditional British food is served in the bar and separate restaurant, with a choice of menus. There is a large garden to the rear and a patio with spectacular floral displays in the summer months. Dogs are welcome in the bar. ⋈✿◑➇♣Pͱ

Great Barford

Anchor Inn ✓
High Street, MK44 3LF (by river bridge 1 mile S of village centre) TL134517
✿ 12-3, 6.30 (6 Fri)-11; 12-11 Sat; 12-4, 6.30-10.30 Sun
☎ (01234) 870364
Young's Bitter, Special; guest beers Ⓗ
Busy local inn next to the church, overlooking the River Great Ouse. At least two guest beers are usually available from an extensive range offered by the pub company. Good home-cooked food is served in the bar and restaurant, as well as a fine selection of wines. The pub is popular with river users in the summer. Occasional themed nights are hosted, mainly during the winter months. ⋈Q✿◑➇Pͱ

Harlington

Old Sun Ⓛ
34 Sundon Road, LU5 6LS TL037303
✿ 12-11 ☎ (01525) 877330 ⊕ theoldsunharlington.com
B&T Shefford Bitter; Butcombe Bitter; St Austell Tribute; Thwaites Wainwright; guest beers Ⓗ

The range of ales available here has been steadily increasing – now you can sample at least five real beers including a local and two guests. This traditional, half-timbered pub dates back to 1785 and the building to the 1740s. There are two separate bars with a side room and outdoor seating plus a children's play area. Regular beer festivals are held and bar meals are served from a simple menu. It's situated in a popular commuter village and a short walk from the rail station. ⋈✿◑❶➡(X42)♣Pͱ

Henlow

Engineers Arms 🍷 Ⓛ ✓
68 High Street, SG16 6AA
✿ 12-midnight (1am Fri & Sat) ☎ (01462) 812284
⊕ engineersarms.co.uk
Beer range varies Ⓗ
This lively two-bar pub in the centre of the village is a must for real ale fans, with 10 handpumps featuring a wide range and style of beers. There are also five ciders and a perry on offer, typically from Westons. The bar room walls are covered in pictures dedicated to local history, sports stars and brewery memorabilia. Occasional live music and disco evenings are hosted, plus a regular poker session. CAMRA Branch Pub of the Year 2011. ⋈✿➇➡(82,M1)♣●ͱ

Kempston

Half Moon ✓
108 High Street, MK42 7BN
✿ 12-3, 6 (5 Fri)-11.30; 12-4, 7-11 Sat; 12-3, 7-11 Sun
☎ (01234) 852464
Courage Best Bitter; Wells Eagle IPA Ⓗ
Well-supported community pub with a comfortable lounge bar and a public bar with games, now including Wii bowling. The pub hosts a number of sports teams playing in local leagues. The large garden, which includes a children's play area, is well used in good weather. The Great Ouse a short distance away offers popular riverside walks. No food is available on Sunday. ⋈✿◑➇➡(1,V1)♣Pͱ

Leighton Buzzard

Golden Bell
4-6 Church Square, LU7 1AE
✿ 10-11 (midnight Fri & Sat); 11-11 Sun ☎ (01525) 373330
Adnams Broadside; St Austell Tribute; guest beers Ⓗ
Welcoming, lively pub with four handpumps dispensing two regular and two constantly changing guest beers. Beer can be drawn on gravity directly from the barrel if requested. The building was originally home to stonemasons erecting the nearby 13th-century church. The single bar has a low-beamed ceiling and a comfy area with sofas. Live sporting events are shown on large TVs. Traditional pub food includes home-made pies and on Tuesday market day full roast dinners are available. ✿◑➡ͱ

Luton

Bricklayers Arms ✓
16-18 High Town Road, LU2 0DD
✿ 12-11 Mon; 12-2.30, 5-11 Tue-Thu; 12-midnight Fri & Sat; 12-10.30 Sun ☎ (01582) 611017
Batemans GHA Pale Ale, XXXB; guest beers Ⓗ

Five busy handpumps serve three ever-changing guest beers, on average 10 a week, displayed on a notice-board by the bar. This officially 'quirky' town-centre pub has been run by the same landlady for the past 25 years. It is popular with Hatters fans on match days and has two TV screens showing Sky football in both bars. Quiz night is Monday and three draught Belgian beers are served. Lunchtime bar meals are served. 爵◁≒♣P'⌐

English Rose ♈
46 Old Bedford Road, LU2 7PA
☼ 12-11 ☎ (01582) 723889 ⊕ englishroseluton.co.uk
Brakspear Bitter; guest beers Ⓗ
With three frequently changing beers selected from nationwide breweries, there is always something interesting to try here. Situated in the town, this popular, family-run local has a friendly village pub atmosphere. It hosts an annual rolling beer festival during December and another in-pub festival with all ales on handpump from the large cooled cellar. Real cider or perry is from Westons. The Tuesday quiz night has been running for 12 years. Outside is a tidy paved garden with smokers' lodges. Local CAMRA Pub of the Year 2011. 爵&≒₽♠'⌐

Gardeners Call
151 High Town Road, LU2 0BX TL095221
☼ 1-11; 12-midnight Fri & Sat; 12-11 Sun ☎ (01582) 729038
Greene King XX Mild, IPA, Abbot; guest beer Ⓗ
A rare, regular outlet for dark mild. Ten minutes walk from Luton station, this is a popular community pub with a friendly and welcoming atmosphere. Several games teams play in local leagues and televised sport is shown on a large screen most nights. There is a large garden and smoking area. Chinese meals and takeaways are available whenever the pub is open, plus roasts on Sunday. The landlord has been awarded the Greene King Head Brewers Club Certificate of Excellence. 爵◁≒₽♣P'⌐

Potton

Rising Sun Ⓛ ✓
11 Everton Road, SG19 2PA
☼ 12-3, 6-midnight; 12-midnight Sat & Sun
☎ (01767) 260231
Wells Eagle IPA; guest beers Ⓗ
The main bar area of this local community pub is divided by low walls and wooden beams, and features a covered well. There is a games area and upstairs function room, plus a patio and roof-top terrace. The six handpumps offer a wide range of well-kept ales, usually including one from Oakham. Beer festivals are held on the early May and late August bank holiday weekends. Good value food is served daily until 9.30pm. CAMRA Branch Pub of the Year 2010. 爵◁▶₽(E1,E2)♣P'⌐

Pulloxhill

Cross Keys ✓
13 High Street, MK45 5HB
☼ 12-3, 5-11; 12-3, 6-10.30 Sun ☎ (01525) 712442
Adnams Broadside; Wells Eagle IPA, Bombardier Ⓗ
A rare gem of a proper village community pub that has been run by the same family for over 40 years. The attractive, half-timbered building dates back to 1640. The back bar doubles as a large function

room, which is used by various local interest groups. Busy at meal times, the pub serves a traditional English menu, and basic groceries are available. Regular events include quiz nights and live music, with jazz every Sunday evening. The large garden caters for all sorts including archers and campers. Q爵◀◁&▲₽♣P'⌐

Renhold

Polhill Arms
25 Wilden Road, MK41 0JP (at Salph End) TL083527
☼ 12-3, 5-11; 12-11 Fri & Sat; 12-10.30 Sun
☎ (01234) 771398 ⊕ polhillarms.co.uk
Greene King IPA, Old Speckled Hen; guest beers Ⓗ
One-bar, family-friendly village local with a welcoming atmosphere and large garden, play area and restaurant. An interesting collection of pub and brewery artefacts is on view. Traditional pub food is served as well as fish and chips and a choice of pizzas (no food Sun eve). Live entertainment and quiz nights feature regularly, and darts and skittles are played. At least one guest beer is usually available, with Olde Trip a popular choice. ⇔爵◁▶₽(151)♣P'⌐

Riseley

Fox & Hounds ✓
High Street, MK44 1DT
☼ 11.30-2.30, 6.30-11 (11.30 Fri & Sat); 12-3, 7-10.30 Sun
☎ (01234) 708240 ⊕ foxandhoundsriseley.co.uk
Wells Eagle IPA, Bombardier; guest beers Ⓗ
Large village inn created from two 16th-century cottages, complete with a priest's hiding hole and resident ghosts. It has a reputation for good food, with charcoal-grilled steak a speciality. Roast lunch is available on Sunday. The dining room can be reserved for parties, but there is no need to book for bar meals - relax over a pint while your food is cooked. The large lawned garden includes a covered patio with heaters. Q爵◁▶₽(152)P'⌐

Salford

Red Lion Hotel Ⓛ
Wavendon Road, MK17 8AZ (2 miles N of M1 jct 13)
SP934389
☼ 11-2.30, 6.30-11; 12-2.30, 6.30-10.30 Sun
☎ (01908) 583117 ⊕ redlionhotel.eu
Wells Eagle IPA, Bombardier Ⓗ
Friendly, traditional country hotel serving a fine choice of home-cooked food in the bar and restaurant. The cosy bar is heated by an open fire in winter and offers a selection of interesting board games. The large garden includes a covered area and a secure children's playground. Six rooms are available for overnight accommodation. ⇔Q⊠爵◀◁▶⊟&P'⌐

Sandy

Sir William Peel Ⓛ ✓
39 High Street, SG19 1AG (opp church)
☼ 12 (11 Sat)-midnight; 12-10.30 Sun ☎ (01767) 680607
Beer range varies Ⓗ
This popular free house has a spacious open-plan layout and comfortable seating. The pool table can be removed, making way for a live music event, disco or an area to host the successful spring beer festival. At the bar Batemans XB is ever-present, plus three rotating guest ales. Several real ciders

appear on a regular basis, usually from Westons and Millwhites. Although no food is served, you are welcome to bring in a take-away meal. ✿⑄⇌🖳(178)🌣P⌐

Shefford

Brewery Tap
14 North Bridge Street, SG17 5DH
✪ 11.30-11; 12-10.30 Sun ☎ (01462) 628448
B&T Shefford Bitter, Dunstable Giant, Dragonslayer; Everards Tiger; guest beers Ⓗ
The Tap was rescued and renamed by the nearby B&T Brewery in 1996. Primarily a drinkers' pub, it offers four regular beers and one guest. The open-plan interior, featuring a display of breweriana, is divided into two distinct areas, plus a family room at the rear, all served from the same bar. Pies and filled rolls are available at lunchtime. The rear patio garden is heated on cool evenings. Car park access is through an archway next to the pub.
❺✿🖳(M1,M2)♣P⌐

Souldrop

Bedford Arms ♀
High Street, MK44 1EY (½ mile W of A6) SP987617
✪ closed Mon; 12-3, 6-11; 12-midnight Fri & Sat; 12-11 Sun
☎ (01234) 781384
Black Sheep Best Bitter; Greene King IPA; Phipps NBC Red Star; guest beers Ⓗ
Large village pub created partly from a 17th-century hop and ale house. Guest beers are often from local micro-breweries. The welcoming restaurant has a central, open fireplace and serves traditional pub favourites prepared to order, with daily specials and a roast lunch on Sunday (no food Sun eve). A large games room with skittles runs off the main bar. The spacious garden and play area are popular with families in summer. CAMRA Branch Pub of the Year 2011. 🏚✿◑🖳(125)♣P⌐

Stotfold

Stag Ⓛ
35 Brook Street, SG5 4LA
✪ 12-midnight ☎ (01462) 730261 ⊕ thestag-stotfold.co.uk
Adnams Bitter; Fuller's London Pride; guest beers Ⓗ
This charming locals' pub with an open-plan layout is leased from Punch Taverns. The regular beers are supported by two guest ales, often from micro-breweries. Another handpump is dedicated to a real cider or perry, often from Welsh producer Gwynt y Ddraig. An elegant dining room is open every day, except Monday evening, with special offers on weekday meals and a Sunday afternoon carvery. There are two small patios with awnings and a large car park. ✿◑⑄🖳(97)♣🌣P⌐

Streatley

Chequers
171 Sharpenhoe Road, LU3 3PS (next to church)
✪ 12-midnight (1am Fri-Sat); 12-11 Sun ☎ (01582) 882072
⊕ thechequers-streatley.co.nr
Greene King IPA, Morland Original, Old Speckled Hen, Abbot; guest beer Ⓗ
Village pub of Georgian origin on the green next to the church. It usually has five real ales on handpump and is one of the few hostelries in the region to use oversized, lined pint glasses. Attracting locals and visitors alike, the pub is

especially popular in good weather due to its large patio area. Quiz night is Tuesday and traditional jazz plays on selected Sunday afternoons. Home-made, hearty food is served and the steak & ale pie is locally famous. Dogs are welcome.
🏚✿🍴◑⑄♣P⌐🛏

Studham

Red Lion
Church Road, LU6 2QA TL022158
✪ 12-3, 5-11; 12-11 Fri-Sun ☎ (01582) 872530
⊕ theredlion-studham.co.uk
Adnams Bitter; Fuller's London Pride; Greene King IPA; guest beers Ⓗ
Situated in a perfect location in the centre of the village adjacent to a wildlife common and in the middle of a network of countryside footpaths, this pub is the focal point of the local community. Whipsnade Zoo is only a couple of miles away, making it an ideal location to rest by the log fire after a long day at the zoo. See the blackboard for the latest guest ales. 🏚Q✿◑⑄🖳(X31)P⌐

Sutton

John O' Gaunt Inn
30 High Street, SG19 2NE
✪ 12-2.30, 7 (6 Fri)-11; 12-11 Sun ☎ (01767) 260377
⊕ johnogauntinnsutton.co.uk
Black Sheep Best Bitter; Fuller's London Pride; Woodforde's Wherry; guest beer Ⓗ
This pub is one of East Anglia's Real Heritage Pubs for its little altered early 1960s interior. A fine example of a wooden-beamed two-bar pub, the John o' Gaunt is a veteran of the Guide, featuring for more than 25 years. The petanque court and Northamptonshire skittles tables are well used by local teams. Live folk music is always popular. High quality bar meals and snacks are home-cooked. The guest ale is often Potton Porter and the real cider is Westons Traditional Scrumpy.
🏚Q✿◑⑄🖳(E1)♣🌣P

Tebworth

Queen's Head Ⓛ
The Lane, LU7 9QB
✪ 12-3 (not Sun-Wed), 6 (7 Sat)-11 ☎ (01525) 874101
Adnams Broadside; Courage Directors Ⓖ; Wells Eagle IPA Ⓗ; Young's Special Ⓖ
Marvellously traditional two-room village local with a public bar, popular for darts and dominoes, and a lounge with live music on Fridays. Apart from the Eagle, the beers are served straight from the cask. The pub has featured in this Guide for 36 continuous years, with more than 25 years under the present landlord. Just how a small village pub should be. 🏚✿🖳♣P⌐

Toddington

Oddfellows Arms
2 Conger Lane, LU5 6BP
✪ 5-11 (midnight Fri); 12-midnight Sat; 12-11 Sun
☎ (01525) 872021
Adnams Broadside; Fuller's London Pride; guest beers Ⓗ
Attractive 15th-century pub facing the village green with a heavily beamed and brassed bar featuring a vast collection of pump clips, and a games room with a pool table. Westons Old Rosie,

and often a guest cider or perry, are available, as well as a good range of bottled ciders. Beer festivals are held in the spring and autumn. The patio garden is popular in summer and has shelter for smokers. ▲❀🚲🚫♣🐕🚬

Sow & Pigs 🄻
19 Church Street, LU5 6AA
⏱ 4.30-11; 12-midnight Sat; 12-11 Sun ☎ (01525) 873089 ⊕ sowandpigs.co.uk
Greene King IPA, Abbot; guest beers Ⓗ
A 19th-century inn with a long, narrow and dog-friendly bar heated by open fires. Darts and dominoes are much played, and there is a pool room to the rear. The guest beer is usually from the local White Park Brewery. Good food is served in the upstairs restaurant, open Thursday to Saturday evenings and Sunday lunchtime. Live music alternates with a pub quiz on Saturday evening. There is a pleasant garden to the rear.
▲Q❀🚲🚫♣🐕🚬

Totternhoe

Cross Keys
201 Castle Hill Road, LU6 2DA SP979218
⏱ 11.30-3, 5.30-11; 11.30-11 Fri-Sun ☎ (01525) 220424
Adnams Broadside; Greene King IPA; guest beer Ⓗ
Attractive thatched Grade II-listed building dating from 1433 and set in a glorious damson orchard, with extensive views over Ivinghoe Beacon and the Vale of Aylesbury. In the warmer months barbecues are hosted and basket meals are served in the garden. Children are most welcome, as are dogs in the public bar. Food is served daily (except Sunday and Monday evenings).
Q❀🚲🚫🚲(61)♣🚬

Whipsnade

Old Hunters Lodge
The Crossroads, LU6 2LN
⏱ 11.30-2.30 (3 Sat), 5.30-11; 12-11 Sun ☎ (01582) 872228 ⊕ old-hunters.com
Greene King IPA, Abbot; guest beer Ⓗ

The closest inn to the world famous Zoo, this 15th-century house, thatched in Norfolk style, is one of the oldest houses in the village. There is a very comfortable bar where you can sit and enjoy a pint and a natter or good bar food, plus a separate restaurant with an à la carte menu (no food after 7pm Sun). Guest ales are from smaller breweries. The five guest rooms make this an ideal location to explore the great scenery around south Bedfordshire. ▲Q❀🛏🚲🚫(X31)P

Wingfield

Plough ✅
Tebworth Road, LU7 9QH
⏱ 12-3, 5-midnight; 12-midnight Sat; 12-11 Sun
☎ (01525) 873077 ⊕ theploughinn.com
Fuller's London Pride, ESB; Gale's HSB; guest beers Ⓗ
Charming thatched village inn dating from the 17th century, decorated with paintings of rural scenes and ploughs. Beware the low beams! Good home-cooked food is served daily except on Sunday evening when a fortnightly quiz is held. There are tables outside at the front and to the rear is a conservatory and prize-winning garden, illuminated at night in the summer. Heated umbrellas are provided for smokers. ▲❀🚫P🚬

Wootton

Chequers 🄻
Hall End, MK43 9HP (hamlet on NW edge of village) SP001457
⏱ 12-3, 6-11; 12-11 Sat & Sun ☎ (01234) 765005 ⊕ chequersinnwootton.co.uk
Wells Eagle IPA; guest beers Ⓗ
Originally a farmhouse, this handsome old inn retains a wealth of heavy wooden beams and period features. Sold by Charles Wells in 2009, it was extensively refurbished and re-opened as a free house in 2010. The range of guest beers is from local small breweries. An interesting, quality menu is served in the pleasant restaurant, and good value bar food is available throughout the pub (no food Sun eve). ▲Q❀🚫♿🚲(68)♣P🚬

Green Man, Eversholt

Great British Pubs

Adrian Tierney-Jones

Great British Pubs is a celebration of the British pub. This fully illustrated and practical book presents the pub as an ultimate destination – featuring pubs everyone should seek out and make a visit to. It recommends a selection of the very best pubs in various different categories, as chosen by leading beer writer Adrian Tierney-Jones. Every kind of pub is represented, with full-colour photography helping to show-case a host of excellent pubs from the seaside to the city and from the historic to the ultra-modern. Articles on beer brewing, cider making, classic pub food recipes, traditional pub games and various other aspects of pub life are included to help the reader truly appreciate what makes a pub 'great'.

Publishes November 2011

£14.99   ISBN 978-1-85249-265-6   CAMRA members' price £12.99   296 pages

For this and other books on beer and pubs visit the CAMRA bookshop at **www.camra.org.uk/books**

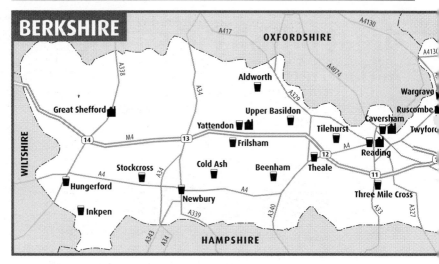

BERKSHIRE

Aldworth

Bell Inn ☆ ⃝L

Bell Lane, RG8 9SE (off B4009) SU555796
✪ closed Mon; 11-3, 6-11; 12-3, 7-10.30 Sun
☎ (01635) 578272
Arkell's 3B, Kingsdown; West Berkshire Maggs Mild, Good Old Boy, seasonal beers ⒣
One of the great classic rural pubs, it has been in the same family since the 18th century and was voted CAMRA Regional Pub of the Year in 2010. Sadly, last year saw the death of much-loved landlord 'Jack' (Iain). His son Hugh continues at this pub. In fine weather, use the beautifully kept garden, but do not miss the unusual interior features and the one-handed clock in the tap room. Home-made food is served. ⚑Q☕☺◑♣♠P

Beenham

Six Bells ⃝L

The Green, RG7 5NX SU585688
✪ 12-2.30 (not Mon & Tue), 6-11; 12-3, 6.30-10.30 Sun ☎ (0118) 971 3368 ⊕ thesixbells.co.uk
Fuller's London Pride ⒢; guest beers ⒣
This popular village pub was voted local CAMRA Pub of the Year in 2008. In addition to London Pride it offers two guest beers, usually from small local breweries, to be enjoyed in either of the two comfortable bars. High quality home-cooked food is served in the bars, conservatory and separate restaurant, which also acts as a function room.
⚑☕⌂◑ ⌐&⌑(104)♣P

Binfield

Jack o' Newbury ⛾ ⃝L

Terrace Road North, RG42 5PH SU845718
✪ 11-3, 5.30-11; 12-3, 5.30-10.30 Sun ☎ (01344) 454881
⊕ jackofnewbury.co.uk
Loddon Hoppit; West Berkshire Good Old Boy; guest beers ⒣
Friendly, family-run, Victorian free house of considerable character and tradition, situated on the outskirts of the village and featuring a separate skittle alley. Four beers mostly come from local micro-breweries. The house beer is Binfield's Best (3.9% ABV). A house cider is expected soon, and

real cider is occasionally available. Local CAMRA Pub of the Year 2011. No food is served on Sunday and Monday evening. ⚑Q☕☺◑⌑(151)♣P⅄

Victoria Arms ✅

Terrace Road North, RG42 5JA SU842713
✪ 11.30-11 (midnight Fri & Sat); 12-11 Sun
☎ (01344) 483856
Fuller's Discovery, London Pride, ESB, seasonal beers; Gale's HSB ⒣
The longest standing Guide entry in the area, this pub offers a warm welcome to a wide mix of customers and has won many awards over the years. The interior features a double-sided open fire; outside the garden has a large heated deck, and hosts hog roasts during the summer. A good range of food is available lunchtimes and evenings. Sunday is quiz night. Two TVs show selected sporting events. ⚑☕◑&⌑(53,153)P⅄

Bracknell

Old Manor ⃝L ✅

Grenville Place, RG12 1BP (on inner ring road)
✪ 8am-midnight ☎ (01344) 304490
Greene King Ruddles Best Bitter, Abbot; guest beers ⒣
Originally a 17th-century manor house, this Wetherspoon pub has plenty of character. A private residence until the 1930s, it has several rooms to drink in. The main bar usually has four guest beers and the bottom bar two more. LocAle accredited, local breweries feature prominently. Families are welcome until 9pm. Handy for Bracknell & Wokingham College. Q☕◑&⇌⌑♣P⅄

Caversham

Baron Cadogan ⃝L ✅

22-24 Prospect Street, RG4 8JG
✪ 8-11 (midnight Fri & Sat); 8-10.30 Sun ☎ (0118) 947 0626
Greene King Ruddles Best Bitter, Abbot; Loddon Cadogan's Gold ⒣; guest beers ⒢
In the centre of Caversham, this pub is open-plan in the typical Wetherspoon style, but not large or impersonal. Local history panels adorn the walls, board games are available, and there is a book swap table. The house beer is Cadogan's Gold (4.4%)

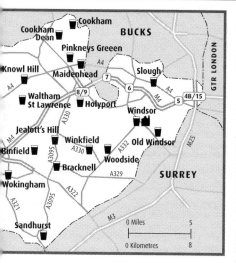

comes from the local Loddon Brewery, and three interesting guest ales are on offer.
Q◑&🚌(2,22,24)●🍴

Cold Ash

Castle Inn 🅛 ✓
Cold Ash Hill, RG18 9PS SU511697
🕕 11.30-3, 5.30-11.30; 11.30-midnight Fri & Sat; 12-11 Sun
☎ (01635) 863232 🌐 thecastleatcoldash.co.uk
Courage Best Bitter; Fuller's London Pride; guest beers Ⓗ
CAMRA Branch Community Pub in 2010, it holds a regular quiz on Monday night (the only evening no food is served), a meat raffle on Friday, and a pensioners' menu is available lunchtimes. The inside features a large single bar with many references to Courage Brewery around the walls. One of the guest beers is a LocAle from the nearby West Berkshire Brewery. The bar is dog and family friendly, as is the south-facing patio.
🏚🏵◑🚌(101)♣P🍴

Cookham

Bounty 🅛
Riverside, SL8 5RG SU907880
🕕 12-11 (winter 12-dusk Sat & Sun only; closed Mon-Fri)
☎ (01628) 520056
Rebellion IPA, Mutiny; guest beer Ⓗ
Located on Cockmarsh between Cookham and Bourne End, this quirky, characterful pub is only accessible on foot or by boat. Dogs, walkers and children are made very welcome. Summer weekends can be busy. The boat-shaped bar is packed with nautical knick-knacks and daft jokes. Bar billiards can be played while listening to the '60s music. The kitchen closes at 8pm. Note the winter opening times.
🏚🔆🏵◑▲≠(Bourne End)♣

Old Swan Uppers
The Pound, SL6 9QE
🕕 11-midnight (11 Sun) ☎ (01628) 521324
🌐 theoldswanuppers.co.uk
Brakspear Bitter; Fuller's London Pride; guest beers Ⓗ
This pub gets its name from the ancient ritual of counting and tagging swans on the river. Popular with locals, walkers and boaters, the pub offers at least five ales and traditional pub fare. In the centre of historic Cookham, it is a short walk from the station and close to local amenities. The landlord holds a number of mini beer festivals.
🏚🏵◑≠🔁P🍴

Cookham Dean

Jolly Farmer
Church Road, SL6 9PD
🕕 11.30-11 (11.45 Fri); 12-10.30 Sun ☎ (01628) 482905
🌐 jollyfarmercookhamdean.co.uk
Brakspear Bitter; Courage Best Bitter; guest beers Ⓗ
Dating from the 18th century, this village pub is situated in the heart of Cookham Dean, opposite the church. It has been owned by the village since 1987. The adults-only bar is cosy with a tiled floor and low beams. The larger Dean bar accommodates families, diners and drinkers, and features a real log fire in winter. The pub is dog-friendly and has a large beer garden with a children's play area. 🏚Q🏵◑P

Frilsham

Pot Kiln 🅛
Bucklebury Road, RG18 0XX SU552732
🕕 12-3, 6-11; closed Tue; 12-11 Sat; 12-11 (6 winter) Sun
☎ (01635) 201366 🌐 potkiln.org
West Berkshire Mr Chubb's Lunchtime Bitter, Brick Kiln Bitter; guest beers Ⓗ
Originally an ale house for the kiln workers, this rural gem now attracts a clientele that comes for the excellent and extensive restaurant, specialising in game. However, the inn still retains a small, traditional bar with a good range of classic country bar food and beers from West Berkshire Brewery, who first started up near the pub. The pub is situated in the heart of good walking country. Dogs are welcome. 🏚Q🏵◑🔁P

Holyport

White Hart
Moneyrow Green, SL6 2ND SU769889
🕕 12-11 (10 Sun) ☎ (01628) 621460
🌐 thewhitehartholyport.co.uk
Greene King IPA, Ruddles Best Bitter; guest beers Ⓗ
Welcoming, traditional two-bar pub half a mile south of the village. The public bar has wooden flooring, TV and traditional pub games including bar billiards. The wood-panelled lounge bar has leather sofas and log fires in winter. Food is available every day except Monday. Outside is a large, fenced beer garden with a children's play area and petanque pitch. Regular quiz and music nights are hosted.
🏚🏵◑🚌(6a)♣P

Hungerford

Downgate 🄻

13 Down View, Park Street, RG17 0ED SU341683
⏲ 11-11 ☎ (01488) 682708 🌐 the-downgate.co.uk
Arkell's 2B, 3B, seasonal beers Ⓗ
An Arkell's pub on the outskirts of Hungerford next to the common. The landlord is passionate about memorabilia – the walls and ceilings of the bar are adorned with model planes, automobiles and mementos from his beloved Southampton FC. Home-cooked meals include traditional Sunday roasts, with special deals for the over-60s. Look out for the tropical fish and the goals in the Gents. A good friendly welcome and atmosphere.
♨❀◖◗⇌♣P⚐

Inkpen

Crown & Garter 🄻

Inkpen Common, RG17 9QR SU378639
⏲ 12-3 (not Mon & Tue), 5.30-11; 12-5, 7-10.30 Sun
☎ (01488) 668325 🌐 crownandgarter.co.uk
Fuller's London Pride; West Berkshire Mr Chubb's Lunchtime Bitter, Good Old Boy Ⓗ
This 17th-century country inn is set in an area of outstanding natural beauty and is ideally situated for walkers and cyclists. The main bar area has a wood burner. Delicious home-cooked meals are served in the comfortable dining area. A fourth ale is usually available during the summer months. The garden includes a patio dining area and covered, heated space for smokers. Accommodation is available. ♨❀🛏◖◗🚌(13)♣P⚐▯

Swan Inn 🍷 🄻

Craven Road, Lower Green, RG17 9DX SU359644
⏲ 12-2.30, 7-11; 12-11 Sat; 12-10.30 Sun ☎ (01488) 668326
🌐 theswaninn-organics.co.uk
Butts Jester, Traditional, seasonal beers Ⓗ
Organic produce features prominently on the menu and there is an organic food shop alongside. The pub divides into several drinking spaces on different levels, including a darts and games area. Quiz night alternates with darts night on Thursdays. Outside, enjoy the country air on the terraced patio. There are 10 quality en-suite bedrooms and good wheelchair facilities. Opening hours vary in winter – ring to check. ♨Q❀🛏◖◗♿🚌(13)♣P

Jealott's Hill

New Leathern Bottle

RG42 6ET (A3095) SU868732
⏲ 12-2.30, 5-11 (10 Mon & Tue, 10.30 Wed); 12-11 Sat; 12-6 Sun ☎ (01344) 421282 🌐 newleathernbottle.co.uk
Vale Black Swan Dark Mild; Young's Bitter; guest beer Ⓗ
A friendly free house with three real ales and two real ciders usually on handpump, its two oak-beamed rooms are decorated in a traditional style with a real fire accentuating the warm ambience. Food is served lunchtimes and Wednesday to Saturday evenings, with a popular fish and chips special on Friday. There are regular Saturday themed nights, with live music on the first Saturday of the month. ♨❀◖◗🚌(53)♣●P

Knowl Hill

Bird in Hand 🄻

Bath Road, RG10 9UP SU820792
⏲ 11-11; 12-10.30 Sun ☎ (01628) 826622
🌐 birdinhand.co.uk
Beer range varies Ⓗ
A multiple CAMRA-award-winning pub, owned by the same family for over 50 years. The historic core dating from 1400 has been much extended and now includes a comfortable lounge bar with beamed ceiling. A restaurant, hotel and conference facilities are attached. Five ales in this genuine free house usually include one from the local Binghams Brewery and another from Scotland's BrewDog. Frequent beer festivals and themed nights are held. Joint local CAMRA Pub of the Year in 2010.
♨Q❀🛏◖◗🚌(127,239)●P⚐

Maidenhead

Greyhound 🄻 ✔

92-96 Queen Street, SL6 1HZ
⏲ 8am-midnight (1am Fri & Sat) ☎ (01628) 779410
Fuller's London Pride; Greene King Abbot; guest beers Ⓗ
Large Wetherspoon bar located a short walk from Maidenhead Station. It is named after the original Greyhound in the High Street where King Charles I met his children the night before his execution. Guest ales always include something from a local micro, and Westons Old Rosie and Vintage ciders are stocked. A quiet pub except for Friday and Saturday nights when music is played.
🐎◖◗⇌🚌●⚐

Maidenhead Conservative Club ✔

32 York Road, SL6 1SF
⏲ 11-11 (11.45 Fri & Sat); 12-11 Sun ☎ (01628) 620579
🌐 maidenheadconclub.co.uk
Fuller's London Pride, seasonal beers; guest beers Ⓗ
Friendly real ale outlet close to the station. Two guests from independent breweries are available, along with a selection of bottle-conditioned beers. Monday is crib night, Tuesday and Wednesday darts. Hot meals are served weekday lunchtimes. A public car park is 100 metres away. This Guide or a CAMRA membership card allows entry for a minimal fee. 🐎◖♿⇌🚌♣P⚐

Rose 🄻

16 King Street, SL6 1EF
⏲ 11-3am ☎ (01628) 621673
Binghams Brickworks Bitter; Fuller's London Pride; Rebellion Mutiny Ⓗ
A large, friendly pub convenient for the station, located on the edge of the town centre. The main bar is L-shaped and leads to a separate dining area. At the rear of the pub is a heated and partially covered courtyard with space for smokers. There is live music with a DJ on Saturday night and regular quiz, darts, pool and open mike evenings are held.
❀◖⇌🚌⚐

Newbury

Gun

142 Andover Road, Wash Common, RG14 6NE
⏲ 12-11 (midnight Fri) ☎ (01635) 580032
Adnams Broadside; Courage Best Bitter; Wadworth 6X; guest beers Ⓗ
This excellent two-bar community pub has traded under its present name since 1761. The lounge bar has a partial wall containing a wood-burning stove, which separates it from a smaller dining area. The separate public bar offers darts, pool, TV and juke-

box. There is a large car park, beer garden and outdoor covered area for smokers. Good value home-cooked meals are served daily (no food Sun eve and Mon). ⚐⚑⚒⚓⚔⚕(7)♣P⚲

Lock, Stock & Barrel ✓
104 Northbrook Street, RG14 1AA SU471672
🕐 11-11 (midnight Fri & Sat); 12-10.30 Sun
☎ (01635) 580550
Fuller's Discovery, London Pride, ESB, seasonal beers Ⓗ
Smart town-centre pub by the Kennet & Avon Canal offering high levels of comfort and service. The L-shaped bar features wooden flooring, stylish decor and various seating options. Good food is served all day until 9pm (8pm Sun). The outdoor area, extending to several levels, with quality furniture and waterside views, is popular in warm weather. The pub hosts an annual beer festival and live jazz on Sunday afternoon. Teas, coffees, free WiFi and newspapers are available. ⚐⚑⚒⚓⚔⚕⚲

Old Windsor

Jolly Gardeners ✓
92-94 St Luke's Road, SL4 2QJ
🕐 2-11 (midnight Thu & Fri); 12-midnight Sat; 12-10.30 Sun
☎ (01753) 830215 ⊕ jollygardeners.com
Courage Best Bitter; Wells Bombardier Ⓗ
Homely locals' pub with a friendly welcome. The landlord is particularly fussy about the quality of his ale, so expect an excellent pint of Bombardier. A board shows historic events of the month. Darts is a popular pastime and sports are shown on TV, but this does not dominate the pub. Sunday roasts are popular. ⚐⚑⚒⚓P⚲

Pinkneys Green

Stag & Hounds Ⓛ
1 Lee Lane, SL6 6NU
🕐 11-3, 5.30-11; 11-11 Sat; 12-10.30 Sun ☎ (01628) 630268
Rebellion seasonal beer; Sharp's Doom Bar; guest beers Ⓗ
The pub is situated in an attractive rural area. The monthly offering from Rebellion and regular Sharp's ales are supplemented by three guests, and Thatchers cider is available. The lounge bar has a real fire and dining tables, and a function room houses a carvery for Sunday lunches. Regular barbecues are held in the large garden, which is popular in summer. Beer festivals are held in May and August. Well-behaved dogs are welcome. ⚐Q⚒⚓⚔♣⚕P⚲

Reading

Eldon Arms
19 Eldon Terrace, RG1 4DX
🕐 11-3, 5.30-11.30 (midnight Fri); 11-3, 7-midnight Sat; 12-3, 7-11.30 Sun ☎ (0118) 957 3857
Wadworth IPA, 6X, Bishop's Tipple, seasonal beers Ⓗ
Licensees Brian and Anne have been in residence for more than 30 years. A public bar with a warming gas fire hosts darts matches and occasional live music. Alternatively, try the quieter lounge area. Standard offerings from Wadworth are often accompanied by rarer seasonals such as Pint Size Mild. Real cider from Westons is available. Food is served 12-2pm Monday to Saturday. Quiz night is the first Wednesday of the month. ⚒⚓⚔(19,22,144)♣⚕

Foresters Arms Ⓛ
79-81 Brunswick Street, RG1 6NY
🕐 4-11; 12-midnight Fri & Sat; 12-11 Sun ☎ (0118) 376 9128
Beer range varies Ⓗ
This back-street gem makes a welcome return to the Guide under a new licensee. Both bars are accessed via a corridor that leads through to the back garden where there is a covered terrace and seating area complete with games room and chickens for company. Local beers from Two Bridges and West Berks breweries are often available. A recent addition is hearty pub food. Folk music plays every second Thursday of the month. ⚒⚓⚔≠(Reading West)⚔♣⚕

Hobgoblin Ⓛ
2 Broad Street, RG1 2BH
🕐 11-11; 12-10.30 Sun ☎ (0118) 950 8119
Beer range varies Ⓗ
The 'Goblin' is renowned for its wide variety of ales, almost always from smaller breweries – more than 6,000 different brews have been served since 1993, and there is usually something new to try every time you go in. The Georgian building contains a small, open bar area at the front with some tables and plenty of standing room, while the back room is divided into a number of small booths. Real cider is always available; often a perry too. ⚒≠⚔⚕⚲

Nag's Head ⚐ Ⓛ
5 Russell Street, RG1 7XD
🕐 12-11; 11-midnight Fri & Sat ☎ (07765) 880137
⊕ nagsheadreading.com
Beer range varies Ⓗ
The Nag's is a destination pub for those seeking good beer and variety and can get very busy. Its reputation has been built up over a few short years and continues to grow. On entering the bar you are met with an array of a dozen handpumps – strong ales and stouts to the left, bitters and milds to the right. Current and forthcoming beers are listed on slates above the bar. Local CAMRA Pub of the Year 2011. ⚐⚒⚓≠(Reading West)⚔(15,16,17)♣⚕P⚲

Retreat Ⓛ
8 St John's Street, RG1 4EH
🕐 4.30-11; 12-11.30 Fri & Sat; 12-11 Sun ☎ (0118) 957 1593
⊕ retreatpub.co.uk
Loddon Ferryman's Gold; Ringwood Best Bitter; guest beers Ⓗ
Situated off the beaten track, the Retreat is a well-run community pub that stocks a fine selection of ales, a wide range of continental beers as well as cider and perry. It hosts a cider festival and was a recent winner of CAMRA Regional Cider Pub of the Year. With live music on Thursday night, this is a popular back-street pub attracting students and visitors to Reading who want something different. ⚔♣⚕

Zerodegrees Ⓛ
9 Bridge Street, RG1 2LR
🕐 12-midnight (11 Sun) ☎ (0118) 959 7959
⊕ zerodegrees.co.uk/location-reading.html
Zerodegrees Wheat Ale, Pale Ale, Black Lager, Pilsner, seasonal beers Ⓗ
A new-build brew-pub with a modern steel-and-glass structure (albeit with a Victorian frontage on the Gun Street entrance). The exposed I-beams, ductwork and steel spiral staircases complement the shiny brewing vessels and conditioning tanks

from which the continental-style beer is served – lightly chilled. Quality food includes speciality pizzas from Reading's only wood-fired oven. The lounge area has comfy sofas and pouffes, and muted TV. ❀◗🕭🍴⚏🖂

Sandhurst

Rose & Crown ⊘
108 High Street, GU47 8HA
❀ 12-11 (midnight Fri & Sat) ☎ (01252) 878938
⊕ roseandcrownsandhurst.co.uk
Batemans XB; Hook Norton Old Hooky; guest beers Ⓗ
The oldest pub in Sandhurst, this building has been an ale house since 1742. Eight handpumps dispense the regular beers plus five changing guests. Recently tastefully refurbished, the interior features stone floors and wood panelling decked with framed breweriana. There are front and rear decking areas with two smoking areas, and a large garden at the rear. Three en-suite rooms are available for overnight stays. ❀🛏◗⚏🍴●P🖂

Slough

Moon & Spoon ⊘
86 High Street, SL1 1EL
❀ 8am-midnight ☎ (01753) 531650
Fuller's London Pride; Greene King Abbot; guest beers Ⓗ
Large Wetherspoon shop conversion popular with a wide range of customers. One long central bar connects various spacious areas and private booths. A family dining area offers a separate children's menu. Regular steak, curry and ale nights are hosted, with discounts for CAMRA members. Three guest ales are usually available, and a real cider, often from Westons or Mr Whiteheads. ◗⚏🍴●

Rose & Crown
312 High Street, SL1 1NB
❀ 11 (12 Sun)-12.30am ☎ (01753) 521114
Beer range varies Ⓗ
This attractive Grade II-listed Regency two-bar inn is the oldest pub on the High Street and makes a pleasant contrast to its more modern surroundings. Two ales are usually available, often sourced from the North East, plus a real cider. Entertainment includes regular quiz nights and three TV screens. The annual Slough conker championship is hosted here on the second Sunday in October. ❀🛏🕭⚏🍴●⚏🖂

Stockcross

Lord Lyon Ⓛ ⊘
Ermin Street, RG20 8LL
❀ 12-3, 6-11; 12-10.30 Sun ☎ (01488) 608366
⊕ lordlyon.co.uk
Arkell's JRA, Moonlight, Kingsdown; guest beer Ⓗ
A genuine community hostelry, this Arkell's pub was originally built in 1840 for the Benham estate employees. The pub was named after Lord Sutton's 1866 Derby winning racehorse. The walls display a number of pictures of country life, including racehorses. Good home-cooked food is offered from a daily-changing menu. The landlord uses local traceable, sustainable produce and rents a field to grow his own vegetables and keep chickens. 🛏❀◗⚏(4)●P🖂

Theale

Crown Ⓛ
2 Church Street, RG7 5BT
❀ 11 (12 Sun)-11 ☎ (0118) 930 2310
⊕ thecrowntheale.co.uk
West Berkshire Good Old Boy; guest beers Ⓗ
A community pub where families are welcome. Sports screens show the day's fixtures, and a popular quiz is held on alternate Thursdays. West Berks Good Old Boy is always available alongside two varying guests, often from local breweries. The Crown Dynasty Chinese takeaway is based at the pub. A live band plays on Wednesday. Outside is a large and peaceful garden area. ❀⚏⚏(1)●P🖂

Red Lion ⊘
5 Church Street, RG7 5BU
❀ 12-11 (7 Sun) ☎ (0118) 930 2394 ⊕ redliontheale.co.uk
Beer range varies Ⓗ
A traditional village local with a landlord who is passionate about his beer. The pub takes part in the Punch Taverns Finest Cask scheme and often offers beers that are unusual for the area. Good fresh home-cooked lunchtime food with something for everyone is served Monday-Friday and Sunday. The newly-added darts area is proving popular with regulars and local teams. A traditional skittle alley and function room is available to hire.
❀◗⚏⚏(1)●P🖂

Three Mile Cross

Swan Ⓛ
Basingstoke Road, RG7 1AT
❀ 11-11; 12-3, 7-11 Sat; 12-3 Sun ☎ (0118) 988 3674
⊕ theswan-3mx.co.uk
Fuller's London Pride; Loddon Hoppit, Ferrymans Gold; Taylor Landlord; Wadworth 6X Ⓗ
Traditional 17th-century inn run by the current licensees for the past 28 years. Close to the Madejski Stadium, this pub is a popular haunt for rugby and football fans alike, and the garden is home to Mr Doyle, the gigantic Irish wolfhound mascot of London Irish RFC. Hearty home-cooked food is served. ❀◗⚏(72,82,82A)P

Tilehurst

Fox & Hounds
116 City Road, RG31 5SB
❀ 11.30 (12 Sun)-11 ☎ (0118) 942 2982
⊕ foxandhounds-tilehurst.co.uk
Courage Best Bitter; Sharp's Doom Bar; guest beer Ⓗ
An old drovers' inn, the main building is about 250 years old; shepherds and cattle-men would stop here en route to Reading Market. Nowadays, the Fox is a thriving family-friendly local with a huge community spirit. Regular charity events and poker/quiz nights are held, there is a darts team and two football teams, and a selection of board games is available. The garden features a large covered deck complete with TV, kids' play area and petanque piste. ♿❀◗🕭⚏(33A)●P🖂

Royal Oak ⊘
69 Westwood Glen, RG31 5NW
❀ 2-11; 12-midnight Sat (11 Sun) ☎ (0118) 941 6056
⊕ theroyaloak-tilehurst.co.uk
Beer range varies Ⓗ
A pub revitalised under new stewardship. Perched at the summit of a steep driveway and pre-dating most of the surrounding suburban housing, this

charmingly quirky building has been frequently extended. The bar in the old part of the building has a lower-level floor so the customer has to stoop to be served. The splendid garden (only open during summer months) was runner-up in Reading in Bloom 2010. 🏵🍽(33)♣P⁴⌐

Twyford

Waggon & Horses
61 High Street, RG10 9AJ
🕒 12-midnight (5.30 Mon); 12-11 Sun ☎ (0118) 934 0376
Courage Best Bitter; Fuller's London Pride; guest beers 🅷
Friendly edge-of-town pub with the character of a country inn. The guest beers are usually from local breweries, including Binghams, less than a mile away. There is plenty of parking and a large garden, complete with aviary and Wendy house. Inside, you can relax – or try to distinguish between genuine oak beams and replicas. Darts and crib are available to play. Hearty cooked food is served lunchtimes and evenings. 🏵🍽⇌🍽(127)♣P⁴⌐

Upper Basildon

Red Lion ⅬL
Aldworth Road, RG8 8NG SU597761
🕒 11-3, 5-11; 12-10.30 Sun ☎ (01491) 671234
West Berkshire Good Old Boy; guest beers 🅷
Situated to the north of the village, this 17th-century pub features an L-shaped bar and informal dining area. Adjoining this, and visible through the double-sided fireplace, is an elegant hop-festooned formal dining room. The extensive menu consists mainly of traditional British food, home-cooked and made with local produce wherever possible – Sunday roasts a speciality. The large garden makes for pleasant alfresco drinking. 🏵🍽(133)♣P

Waltham St Lawrence

Bell ⅬL
The Street, RG10 0JJ (opp church) SU830769
🕒 12-3, 5-11; 12-11 Sat; 12-10.30 Sun ☎ (0118) 934 1788
🌐 thebellinn.biz
Beer range varies 🅷
Classic beamed 14th-century pub owned by the local parish for several hundred years. Popular with the locals, its two bars are often bustling with activity, and visitors can be sure of a friendly welcome. There is always a wide range of beers, ciders and perries on sale. Good quality home-made seasonal dishes are served lunchtimes and evenings, with a separate dining room area. 🏵Q🍽⇌🍽(4,4A)♣

Wargrave

Wargrave & District Snooker Club
Woodclyffe Hostel, Church Street, RG10 8EP
🕒 7-11; closed Sat & Sun ☎ (0118) 940 3184
Beer range varies 🅷
You will find this regular winner of local CAMRA Club of the Year near the main Wargrave crossroads. It shares the Victorian Woodclyffe Hostel with the town library and opens weekday evenings only. There is usually only one beer on offer at a time. Games include darts, cards and bar billiards. Show this Guide or a CAMRA membership card for admittance. ⇌🍽(127)♣

Windsor

Carpenters Arms ✅
4 Market Street, SL4 1PB
🕒 10-11 ☎ (01753) 863739
Beer range varies 🅷
Situated in a narrow cobbled street between Windsor Castle and the Guildhall, this split-level Nicholson's pub has an excellent reputation for the quality and range of its ales. The entrance to a series of tunnels in the lower drinking area reputedly links it to the Castle. Mosaic floors in the porches are a reminder of the long defunct Ashby's Brewery. A former CAMRA Branch Pub of the Year. 🏵🍽⇌(Windsor & Eton Central)🍽

Duke of Connaught ✅
165 Arthur Road, SL4 1RZ
🕒 11-midnight (1am Fri & Sat); 12-11.30 Sun ☎ (01753) 840748
Greene King IPA, Abbot; guest beers 🅷
Originally No 1 Connaught Cottages, this pub was the home of Charles Wilkins, a beer retailer in 1895. An L-shaped layout lends itself to distinct drinking areas. The interior has bare floorboards and the walls are decorated with old film photographs. Major sporting events are shown on two large screens and live music is hosted at weekends. 🍺🏵🍽⇌(Windsor & Eton Central)🍽⌐

Vansittart Arms ⅬL ✅
105 Vansittart Road, SL4 5DD
🕒 12-11 (11.30 Thu; midnight Fri & Sat) ☎ (01753) 865988
Fuller's Discovery, London Pride, ESB, seasonal beers 🅷
This consistently good Fuller's pub was originally cottages housing workers from Windsor Castle. The two main bar areas have recesses and real fires. Special events are held in the garden during the summer. A covered, heated area accommodates smokers. Sport is keenly followed, with rugby taking priority on the TV screens. To the rear is a pool room with comfy sofas. No food Sunday evening. 🍺🏵🍽⇌(Windsor & Eton Central)🍽⌐

Winkfield

Old Hatchet
Hatchet Lane, Cranbourne, SL4 2EE (on A330 NW of Ascot) SU923716
🕒 11.30-11.30; 12-10.30 Sun ☎ (01344) 899911
Fuller's London Pride, ESB; Gale's HSB 🅷
Originally two 16th-century woodcutters' cottages, this Fuller's pub has stone-flagged floors and three fireplaces with real wood fires. Near Windsor Great Park, the pub serves good food. There is a new television for customers who wish to watch sporting events, while outside there is a covered smoking area and a small beer garden, which can be used to enjoy both food and drinks. 🍺🏵🍽♣P⌐

Wokingham

Crispin ⅬL
45 Denmark Street, RG40 2AY
🕒 11.30-11 (midnight Sat & Sun) ☎ (0118) 978 0309
Beer range varies 🅷
This traditional single-room pub has been reinvigorated by a new landlord. The pub serves a regularly changing range of four real ales, some local (Loddon, Windsor & Eton), others from further afield. Snacks are served at lunchtime and in the

evening, and customers are welcome to bring their own takeaway food. The large, well-kept beer garden has barbecue facilities and a smoking area. ⚞Q✿≒⊟(191)♣♠'⌐

Hope & Anchor ✅

Station Road, RG40 2AD (at jct with Shute End)
☼ 12-11 (midnight Fri; 1am Sat); 12-10 Sun
☎ (0118) 978 0918 ⊕ the-hope.net
Brakspear Bitter; Wychwood Hobgoblin; guest beers Ⓗ
The interior retains authentic wooden beams and low ceilings, tastefully combined with more modern furnishings. An enclosed garden incorporates a heated smoking shelter, barbecue and Aunt Sally pitch. The good selection of ales typically includes seasonal beers. Look for the Canadian speciality Poutine on the food menu – chips, mince and onion in gravy topped with melted cheese (no food Sat and Sun eve). Regular events include poker, darts, quizzes and live music every Saturday night. ✿⊯◑≒⊟♣'⌐

Olde Leathern Bottel ✅

221 Barkham Road, RG41 4BY
☼ 11-11 (11.30 Fri & Sat); 12-10.30 Sun ☎ (0118) 978 4222
Fuller's London Pride; Greene King Old Speckled Hen; Sharp's Doom Bar Ⓗ
A recent refurbishment has added light and colour. Take a few minutes to look at the historic local photos and paintings, as well as the open fireplaces and massive posts and beams from the original 17th-century structure. Five real ales, good food served all day and friendly, helpful bar staff make this Chef & Brewer pub a worthwhile visit for all. ⚞✿◑&⊟(144)P'⌐

Ship Inn ✅

104 Peach Street, RG40 1XH (on A329)
☼ 12-11 (midnight Thu-Sat) ☎ (0118) 978 0389
Fuller's Discovery, London Pride, ESB, seasonal beers; Gale's HSB Ⓗ
This 400-year-old former coaching inn has a flagstone floor and exposed brick walls. The public

bar, with small side room, shows televised sports, while the lounge bar is a popular meeting point for local societies and starting point for pub crawls. Food is served lunchtimes and evenings until 9pm (8pm Sun), featuring traditional pub favourites and a daily specials board. Outside is a covered, heated patio area. Quiz night is Sunday and there is free WiFi. ⚞✿◑Ⴀ⊟P'⌐

Woodside

Duke of Edinburgh ✅

Woodside Road, SL4 2DP SU927709
☼ 11-11; 12-6.30 Sun ☎ (01344) 882736
⊕ thedukeofedinburgh.com
Arkell's 2B, 3B, Moonlight, Kingsdown Ⓗ
Excellent Arkell's tied house well-known locally for good food and a friendly atmosphere. Established licensees Nick and Annie have run the Duke since 1998 and have received a number of CAMRA awards. A wide variety of food from bar and à la carte menus is served lunchtimes and evenings. Outside there is a covered and heated smoking area. The landlord often holds Chelsea FC evenings as he is a big Chelsea fan. ✿◑&P'⌐

Yattendon

Royal Oak Ⓛ

The Square, RG18 0UF SU 55229
☼ 11-11 (10.30 Sun) ☎ (01635) 201325
⊕ royaloakyattendon.co.uk
West Berkshire Mr Chubb's Lunchtime Bitter, Good Old Boy, Dr Hexter's Wedding Ale; guest beer Ⓗ
The nearby West Berkshire Brewery supplies three ales and there is a fourth changing guest. Three roaring log fires warm cold winter nights and during the summer the stunning walled garden is an added attraction. Excellent locally sourced food is served in the dining room or bar. Private feasting nights are a popular addition to the menu. Accommodation is available in five charming bedrooms. ⚞Q✿⊯◑P'⊟

Bell, Aldworth (Photo: Ian Heath)

BUCKINGHAMSHIRE

NORTHAMPTONSHIRE

Olney
Stoke Goldington
Emberton
A509
Hanslope
A422
M1
Bradwell Village
Newport Pagnell
A413
A5
Stony Stratford
A422
14
Bradwell Abbey
A509
Maids Moreton
Milton Keynes
A422
Beachampton
A421
Thornborough
A421
Fenny Stratford
A5
Padbury
A4146
A413
BEDFORDSHIRE
Marsh Gibbon
Wing
A418
Quainton
A41
Ivinghoe
A4146
Aylesbury
B489
Brill
A418
A41
Chearsley
Terrick
HERTFORDSHIRE
Ickford
Haddenham
Wendover
Long Crendon
A4129
A4010
Great Kimble
A413
A416
Prestwood
Chesham
A4128
Lacey Green
Little Missenden
A4010
Naphill
Chenies
Downley Common
Tylers Green
A355
OXFORDSHIRE
5
High Wycombe
Forty Green
A413
Wycombe Marsh
4
Seer Green
Frieth
Loudwater
A412
Marlow Bottom
M40
3
Wooburn
2
Hedgerley
Hambleden
Marlow
Common
A355
Denham
A4155
Littleworth Common
16/1A
1
M25
Burnham
A412
0 Miles   5
Iver
7
0 Kilometres   8
BERKSHIRE
M4
Dorney

Aylesbury

Broad Leys

8 Wendover Road, HP21 9LB

⏰ 11-11 (midnight Fri & Sat); 12-10.30 Sun

☎ (01296) 399979 ⊕ thebroadleys.co.uk

Loddon Hoppit; guest beers Ⓗ

Large pub next to the police station, renowned for its food, especially the popular Aylesbury duck, prepared on the premises. Although food is important, drinkers are well provided for in the well-used bar area. The large garden is partly covered for use by smokers and features a variety of statues and artefacts plus a Roman fountain. Luxurious new toilets are described as 'funky, extravagant and grand'. Well worth a visit.
🏚️🏡🕭️🚐🚏🅿️⊸

King's Head

HP20 2RW

⏰ 11-11; 12-10.30 Sun ☎ (01296) 718812

⊕ farmersbar.co.uk

Chiltern Ale, Beechwood, Three Hundreds Old Ale, seasonal beers; guest beer Ⓗ

INDEPENDENT BREWERIES

Chiltern Terrick
Concrete Cow Bradwell Abbey
Hopping Mad Olney (NEW)
Old Luxters Hambleden
Oxfordshire Ales Marsh Gibbon
Rebellion Marlow Bottom
Vale Brill

Little Gransden

Chequers L
71 Main Road, SG19 3DW
☼ 12-2, 7-11; 12-11 Fri & Sat; 12-6, 7-10.30 Sun
☎ (01767) 677348
Beer range varies Ⓗ
A village inn, owned and run by the same family for over 60 years. The unspoilt middle bar, with its wooden bench seating and roaring fire, is a favourite spot to pick up on the local gossip. The pub's Son of Sid brewhouse brews for the pub and local beer festivals. Fish and chips are a highlight on Friday night (booking essential). Real cider is usually available. Winner of numerous local CAMRA awards. ▲Q❀Ⓓ🖪(18A)♣P🕇

March

Rose & Crown L
41 St Peters Road, PE15 9NA
☼ 12-11 (midnight Fri & Sat) ☎ (01354) 652077
Beer range varies Ⓗ
Dating back 150 years, this is a traditional community pub with two rooms and low beamed ceilings. Ale lovers who are prepared to make the walk from the town centre will receive a warm welcome. Up to six ales are on offer, mainly from micro-breweries, with one Oakham beer usually available and a real cider. A mini beer festival is held at Easter time. Good quality food is served. Live music features on the last Saturday of the month. ▲Q❀Ⓓ🖪(X9,33)♣P🕇

Ship Inn L
1 Nene Parade, PE15 8TD
☼ 12-midnight (late Fri & Sat) ☎ (01354) 607878
Oakham JHB; Woodforde's Wherry; guest beers Ⓗ
Grade II-listed thatched riverside pub built in 1680, with extensive boat moorings. The unusual carved beams are said to have 'fallen off a barge' during the building of Ely Cathedral. Reopened in March 2010 as a free house after a major refit, the pub has a convivial atmosphere and quaint wobbly floor and wall to the toilets, and to a small games room with a bar billiards table. Late opening at weekends can be to 2am. ❀🖪(33,35,X9)♣♠

Milton

Waggon & Horses L
39 High Street, CB24 6DF
☼ 12-2.30, 5-11 (midnight Fri); 12-3, 6-11.30 Sat; 12-3, 7-10.30 Sun ☎ (01223) 860313
Elgood's Black Dog, Cambridge Bitter, Golden Newt; guest beers Ⓗ
Imposing mock Tudor one-room pub. The Elgood's beers are dispensed via cylinderless handpumps, and there is always a guest beer from Milton Brewery. The real cider comes from local producer Cassels. Meals are good value, and baltis are a speciality on Thursday evening. There is a challenging quiz on Wednesday evening, and bar billiards is a mainstay. Dogs on leads are welcome. ▲❀Ⓓ🖪(9,C2)♣♠P🕇🈵

Newton

Queen's Head
Fowlmere Road, CB22 7PG
☼ 11.30-2.30, 6-11; 12-2.30, 7-10.30 Sun ☎ (01223) 870436
Adnams Bitter, Broadside, seasonal beers Ⓖ
This village local has appeared in every edition of the Guide. The list of landlords since 1729 has just 18 entries, their names displayed on the wall in the simply furnished public bar. That list will soon grow to 19, as the pub is being handed from father to son once again. The cosy lounge has a welcoming fire. Simple but excellent food centres on soup and sandwiches at lunchtime. All beer is served from casks behind the bar. ▲Q◖Ⓓ🖪(31,139)♣♠P

Offord D'Arcy

Horseshoe L
90 High Street, PE19 5RH (on Godmanchester-St Neots road)
☼ 12-2.30, 5-11; 12-11.30 Fri & Sat; 12-10.30 Sun
☎ (01480) 810293 ⊕ thehorseshoeinn.biz
Fuller's London Pride; Oakham JHB; Potton Shannon IPA; guest beers Ⓗ
This family-run free house, dating from 1626, focuses on a good range of food and beers. There are two bars, a separate dining area and a family garden with children's play space. The snug, or village bar, has a TV. The pub actively supports beers from local breweries, including micros, and fresh locally sourced ingredients are used to make top-quality meals, featuring venison and rabbit as well as vegetarian options. ▲⛴❀Ⓓ🖪♿P🕇

Old Weston

Swan
Main Street, PE28 5LL (on B660 N of A14)
☼ 12-2.30 (not Mon-Fri), 6.30 (7 Sat)-11; 12-3.30, 7-10.30 Sun ☎ (01832) 293400
Greene King Abbot; Taylor Landlord; guest beer Ⓗ
Dating from the 16th century, this oak-beamed building started life as two private houses that were merged later, and has evolved through the years. At the end of the 19th century the pub had its own brewery. There is a central bar with a large inglenook, a dining area and a games section offering hood skittles and pool. At weekends a varied menu of traditional pub food is available, including home-made puddings. ▲Q⛴Ⓓ♣P

Pampisford

Chequers ✅
1 Town Lane, CB22 3ER
☼ 11-11 (10.30 Sun) ☎ (01223) 833220
⊕ thechequerspampisford.co.uk
Greene King IPA; Woodforde's Wherry; guest beers Ⓗ
A warm welcome and friendly atmosphere await you at this archetypal country pub. The character of the place stems from the wealth of exposed timbers and split-level interior – tables divided into separate berths at the lower end offer privacy while the more open top end lends itself to convivial dining. Speciality food nights are a regular feature. There is an attention to detail that sets this pub apart and ensures customers always return. ❀Ⓓ♿🖪(7)♣P🕇

Peterborough

Brewery Tap L
80 Westgate, PE1 2AA
☼ 12-11 (late Fri & Sat) ☎ (01733) 358500
⊕ oakham-ales.co.uk/brewerytap/btwelcome.asp
Oakham JHB, Citra, Inferno, Bishops Farewell; guest beers Ⓗ

Converted from an employment exchange, this spacious pub opened in 1998 and is the home of a custom-made brew plant for Oakham Ales, which can be viewed through a glass wall. The pub's future is under threat from redevelopment plans. Up to 12 draught ales are on offer plus bottled Belgian beers. Good-value Thai food is served. Furnishings include a mix of leather sofas and low tables plus tables and chairs for diners. Regular weekend entertainment is hosted and a function room is available. Handy for bus and railway stations. ⓓ≠🖵

Charters 🅛

Town Bridge, PE1 1EH (down steps at Town Bridge)
✪ 12-11 (late Fri & Sat); 12-10.30 Sun ☎ (01733) 315700
⊕ oakhamales.com/charters
Oakham JHB, Citra, Inferno, Bishops Farewell; guest beers Ⓗ/Ⓖ

Large Dutch barge moored on the River Nene by Town Bridge, the upper deck houses a fine oriental restaurant and food and snacks are also available in the bar. Live music and poetry nights are hosted. Twelve real ales are usually available plus Belgian bottled beers. Outside there is a large garden with a marquee, bar and landing stage for boats. A footpath leads to the Nene Valley Railway and Railworld. The pub gets very busy on football match days. Free use of X-Box Kinect on large-screen TV. ❀ⓓ≠🖵♣♠P🔑

Cherry Tree 🅛 ✓

9 Oundle Road, PE2 9PB
✪ 11.30-midnight; 12-10.30 Sun ☎ (01733) 703495
⊕ cherrytree-inn.co.uk
Marston's Pedigree; Taylor Landlord; guest beers Ⓗ

This 200-year-old pub was converted to a one-bar layout in 1988. Outside is a beer garden, patio and children's play area. Live music plays every Friday and Saturday night, Tuesday is karaoke night and open mike night is the last Thursday of the month. Football match days are always busy. Pensioners' lunches are available Monday to Friday. The pub is renowned for its unusual fundraising events for charity and is close to the Nene Valley Railway. Winner of a CAMRA Gold Award in April 2010. ❀ⓓ🕭≠🖵(1)♣P🔑

Coalheavers Arms

5 Park Street, Woodston, PE2 9BH
✪ 12-2 Thu only, 5-11; 12-11 Fri & Sat; 12-10.30 Sun
☎ (01733) 565664 ⊕ individualpubs.co.uk/coalheavers
Beer range varies Ⓗ

Small, friendly, one-room, back-street gem of a local, dating back to the 1850s. Four Milton beers are usually available including a mild, and four guest beers. Traditional cider and Belgian bottled beers are also stocked. The only lager is an English unpasteurised one. The large garden is popular in summer and hosts beer festivals in spring and autumn. Fresh rolls are served and on Sunday doorstep sandwiches stuffed with meat. A free-to-enter quiz is held on Sunday evening. Q❀🖵(6,7,46)♣♠🔑🖻

Draper's Arms 🅛 ✓

29-31 Cowgate, PE1 1LZ
✪ 8-midnight (1am Fri & Sat) ☎ (01733) 847570
Beer range varies Ⓗ

City-centre Wetherspoon that started life in 1899 as Armstrong's drapers and opened as the Draper's Arms in 2005. The interior is split into intimate spaces by wood-panelled dividers. Good value food

is served all day. Ten handpumps serve the regular beers plus a constantly changing selection of guest ales, often from local breweries, and traditional cider is stocked. Regular beer and wine festivals are hosted. Quiz night is Wednesday. Peterborough CAMRA Pub of the Year 2007. Qⓓ🕭≠🖵♠🔑

Hand & Heart ★ 🅛

12 Highbury Street, Millfield, PE1 3BE
✪ 3 (11 Fri-Sun)-11; 12-10.30 Sun ☎ (01733) 564653
Beer range varies Ⓗ/Ⓖ

Essentially unchanged from when it was built in 1938, this back-street community local is one of Britain's Real Heritage Pubs. A drinking corridor connects the public bar with its Art Deco fittings to the rear room served by a hatch. At least five real ales are available including one from Oakham. Two beer festivals are held annually. Traditional English and Irish music plays on the third Thursday of the month and a Cheese Club meets on the fourth Thursday. Cambridgeshire CAMRA Pub of the Year 2010. ﹏Q❀🖵(1)♣🔑

Ostrich 🅛

17 North Street, PE1 2RA (off Westgate)
✪ 11-11 (1am Fri & Sat); 12-11 Sun ☎ (01733) 746370
Beer range varies Ⓗ

The Ostrich reopened under new ownership in 2009 after major refurbishment, and revived the original name. The U-shaped bar has a small room at one end with a TV and dartboard. The walls are decorated with pictures of historic facts about the pub, bygone breweries and posters of famous acts that have appeared in the city. Up to four regularly changing real ales are on offer, many from local breweries, plus cider on handpump. Live music plays on some weekends. Outside is a small, enclosed patio. ❀ⓓ🕭≠🖵♠🔑

Ploughman 🍷 🅛

1 Staniland Way, Werrington, PE4 6NA
✪ 2-11; 12-midnight Fri & Sat; 12-11 Sun ☎ (01733) 327696
Beer range varies Ⓗ

Originally a pub with no real ale, the Ploughman has been rejuvenated and is now a thriving community hostelry with five handpumps serving local beers alongside ales from far and wide. It hosts darts and pool teams, holds regular poker nights and has live music at weekends. It holds its annual beer festival in July and is a member of Oakham Ales Oakademy of Excellence. Winner of local CAMRA Branch Gold Award in 2010 and Pub of the Year in 2011. ❀🖵(1,406,413)♣♠P🔑

Ramsey

Jolly Sailor ✓

43 Great Whyte, PE26 1HH
✪ 11 (12 Sun)-midnight ☎ (01487) 813388
Adnams Bitter, Broadside; Greene King Abbot; Wells Bombardier; Woodforde's Wherry; guest beer Ⓗ

This Grade II-listed building has been a pub for 400 years. The three linked rooms feature wooden beams dating from various periods in history as the pub has been extended over the years. Pictures and paintings of old Ramsey adorn the walls. A welcoming, friendly hostelry, it attracts a mixed clientele of all ages. Charity nights are held throughout the year. A guest beer is added to the range at weekends. No music or food is available. ﹏Q❀🕭🖵(31)♣P🔑

St Ives

Oliver Cromwell L
13 Wellington Street, PE27 5AZ
✪ 12-11 (11.30 Thu; 12.30am Fri & Sat) ☎ (01480) 465601
Adnams Bitter, Broadside; Oakham JHB; Woodforde's Wherry; guest beers Ⓗ
Cosy wood-panelled bar near the old St Ives river quay. There was a brewery here for 50 years until 1919, and an old well can be viewed through the pub floor. Two or three guest beers are offered, plus real local Cromwell cider, and an imaginative lunch menu. Entertainment includes live music on Thursday evening and occasional Sunday afternoons. There is a smoking patio at the rear. TV sport is screened on special occasions. Families are welcome until 8pm. ✿⊈◖🖵♣╚

St Neots

Pig 'n' Falcon L
9 New Street, PE19 1AE
✪ 10am-midnight (2am Fri & Sat); 11am-midnight Sun
☎ (07951) 785678 ⊕ pignfalcon.co.uk
Greene King IPA; Oakham Inferno, Citra; Potbelly Best Ⓗ**; guest beers** Ⓖ
Local CAMRA's Most Improved Pub for 2010. This small one-bar town centre venue has at least 10 real ales and four real ciders, focusing on micro-breweries and rare ales including milds, porters, stouts and barley wines. Four beer festivals are held each year. Live jazz, blues and rock nights are hosted on Wednesday, Friday and Saturday. Outside is a large, imaginative, covered and heated beer garden. CAMRA members receive a discount. ✿⊈🖵╚╚

Sawston

Black Bull L
High Street, CB22 3HJ TL485490
✪ 5-11 (11.30 Fri); 11-11.30 Sat; 12-10.30 Sun
☎ (01223) 835726 ⊕ blackbullsawston.com
Milton Pegasus; guest beers Ⓗ
Another pub rescued from closure, this traditional family-run hostelry is a welcome new entry in the Guide. The Bull offers the best choice of cask ales in the village, including Milton beers from south of the city and guest beers often from Buntingford. The oldest pub in the village, the Grade II-listed building dates from 1545 and has a wealth of wooden beams, open fires and wonky walls. ♨✿◖🖵(7)P╚

Thriplow

Green Man
2 Lower Street, SG8 7RJ
✪ closed Mon; 12-3, 7-11 (not Sun eve) ☎ (01763) 208855
⊕ greenmanthriplow.co.uk
Beer range varies Ⓗ
A friendly village local which, despite the name, is entirely blue on the outside. The welcoming interior is furnished and decorated to create a light and airy feel. The beer range varies widely but usually includes ales from East Anglian breweries. Good quality food is on offer – thankfully, without the gastro pretensions of a few years back. No fruit machine, juke-box or TV. There is outside seating, both on the green in front of the pub and in the pleasant garden. ♨Q✿◖▲🖵P╚

Tilbrook

White Horse L ✔
High Street, PE28 0JP
✪ 12 (5.30 Mon)-11 ☎ (01480) 860764
⊕ whitehorsetilbrook.com
Wells Eagle IPA; Young's Bitter; guest beers Ⓗ
Two-roomed village pub, dating back in parts to 1735, surrounded by large gardens and open fields. The public bar is furnished with sofas and bar stools and provides darts and hood skittles. There is a large lounge and bright conservatory with further seating. Traditional locally-sourced food is served all day Tuesday to Saturday and lunchtime on Sunday. The garden has swings and slides plus a petting zoo featuring ducks, chickens, goats and a goose. ✇✿◖⊟🖵♣P╚🚲

Ufford

White Hart L
Main Street, PE9 3BH
✪ 12-11 (midnight Fri & Sat); 12-9 (6 winter) Sun
☎ (01780) 740250 ⊕ whitehartufford.co.uk
Adnams Bitter; Ufford Golden Drop, White Hart, seasonal beers Ⓗ
This restored 16th-century stone-built village local was a farmhouse until the middle of the last century. The interior comprises a cosy public bar with open log fire and interesting artefacts on the walls and ceilings, plus a bar/restaurant and orangery for diners. Outside is a patio area and large beer garden with tables and children's play area. Ufford Ales Brewery is located in the car park. Occasional live music plays. ♨Q✿💤◖⊟♿🖵(201,402,403)♣P

Waterbeach

Sun
7 Chapel Street, CB25 9HR
✪ 5-11; 12-midnight Fri-Sun ☎ (01223) 861254
⊕ thesunwaterbeach.co.uk
Adnams Broadside; Woodforde's Wherry; guest beer Ⓗ
With a guiding philosophy of 'good beer, good food, good music', this village local goes from strength to strength. The small, cosy lounge is dominated by a huge fireplace while the simply-appointed public, with its wood-block floor, is always lively. Behind the bar is a small meetings room and upstairs a function room that hosts regular gigs. A changing guest beer comes from Punch's Finest Cask range. Beer and music festivals feature on the May and August bank holiday weekends. No food Monday and Sunday evening. ♨✿◖⊟♿🚲🖵(9,X9)♣╚

Whittlesey

Boat L
2 Ramsey Road, PE7 1DR
✪ 11-midnight ☎ (01733) 202488 ⊕ theboatuk.com
Elgood's Black Dog, Cambridge Bitter, Golden Newt, seasonal beers; guest beers Ⓖ
This 11th-century inn is mentioned in the Domesday Book. It attracts locals, anglers and visitors, who all receive a warm welcome. The lounge has an unusual boat shaped bar. Bar billiards is played. Up to five traditional ciders and perries supplement the real ales that are all served direct from the cask, and there is a good selection

of malt whiskies. Live music plays on Saturday evening. Outside is a petanque terrain. Accommodation is good value. CAMRA Cambridgeshire Pub of the Year 2009. 🏮🏮🛏🍴🛗⟱🚆(31,32,33)♣♦P⇆

George Hotel 🕒 ✅
10 Market Street, PE7 1AB
🕒 7am-midnight (1am Fri & Sat) ☎ (001733) 359970
Greene King Ruddles Best Bitter, Abbot; guest beers ⊞
Built in the late 1700s, the building underwent significant alterations in the mid-19th century and became a Grade II-listed building in 1974. Once a popular locals' haunt with a basic bar and comfortable lounge, it was then closed and unloved for some time, until it was bought by JD Wetherspoon. It now has several rooms and areas, with wooden decor and carpets throughout. A collection of mirrors, old photographs of the area and information on local historic figures adorns the walls. Up to eight real ales are available.
🏮Q🏮🍴🛗⟱🚆(31,32,33)♦P⇆

Letter B 🕒 ✅
53-57 Church Street, PE7 1DE
🕒 5 (12 Fri-Sun)-11 ☎ (01733) 206975
Adnams Bitter; Batemans XXXB; Oakham Bishops Farewell; Tydd Steam Scoundrel; guest beers ⊞
Two-hundred-year-old local community pub near the town centre with a warm welcome for all. It is said to be named the Letter B because there were once so many pubs in Whittlesey that they ran out of names – there was also a Letter A and a Letter C. The landlord is a real ale enthusiast and holds an annual beer festival in the spring. A member of the Oakham Ales Oakademy.
Q🏮🛏🍴⟱🚆(31,32,33)♣♦⇆

Whittlesford

Bees in the Wall
36 North Road, CB22 4NZ
🕒 12-2.30, 6-11; 12-2.30, 7-10.30 Sun ☎ (01223) 834289
Taylor Landlord; guest beers ⊞
Situated on the village's northern edge, this pub really does have bees in one wall. The public bar oozes atmosphere, especially with the fire blazing, and tends to be where the locals gather. Diners favour the long split-level lounge which opens onto a patio, huge paddock-style garden and the pub's own wood. Two guest beers are always stocked. Evening meals are served Wednesday to Saturday only. The pub may stay open all day during the summer. 🏮Q🏮🍴⟱♣P

Willingham

Duke of Wellington
55 Church Street, CB24 5HS
🕒 12-3, 5-11 (11.30 Thu & Fri); 12-11.30 Sat; 12-10.30 Sun
☎ (01954) 261622 🌐 dukeofwellington-willingham.co.uk
Greene King XX Mild Ⓖ**, IPA; guest beers** ⊞

Attractive, low-ceilinged village local which makes the most of its exposed beams and three open fires to create a relaxed, rustic feel. The main bar has big scrubbed tables, bare-boarded floors and candelabras, plus an area set aside for dining. Excellent home-cooked food majors on pies and salads. An annual garden party is held over the August bank holiday. Quiz night is Sunday. A rare outlet for Greene King Mild. 🏮🏮🍴⟱🚆(5)P⇆

Wisbech

Red Lion 🕒
32 North Brink, PE13 1JR
🕒 11.30-2.30, 6-11; 11.30-2.30, 7-11.30 Sat; 12-3, 7-11 Sun
☎ (01945) 582022
Elgood's Black Dog, Cambridge Bitter, Pageant; guest beer ⊞
This is the nearest Elgood's pub to the brewery. It is very comfortable with a pleasant, relaxed atmosphere. Both drinkers and diners are well catered for, with quality ales and excellent food served seven days a week in the revamped split-level restaurant. Wheelchair access is from the rear, where the outdoor drinking area is popular on sunny days. Q🏮🍴🛗🚆(X1)P⇆

Witcham

White Horse 🏆
7 Silver Street, CB6 2LF (1 mile from A142 jct)
🕒 closed Mon; 5-11; 12-midnight Sat & Sun
☎ (01353) 775368
Beer range varies ⊞
The only pub in the village, set in an attractive area. Three ever-changing guest beers from regional and local breweries are always available, plus occasional beer festivals. There is a pleasant lounge and dining area, offering a varied home-cooked menu in the evenings plus weekend lunches. The public bar area is basic with darts and a pool table. The village is famous for hosting the annual world pea shooting championship on the second weekend in July. Q🏮🍴🚆(106)♣⇆🚬

Yaxley

Duck & Drake 🕒
34 Main Street, PE7 3LY
🕒 12-11 (midnight Fri & Sat); 12-10.30 Sun
☎ (01733) 240476
Greene King Morland Original, Abbot; Oakham JHB; guest beers ⊞
The building dates back to the late 17th century, when it was a dwelling house for the Dutchmen who came over to drain the Fens. The main bar is part of the original house, with extensions added over the years. Bought by a local man in 2009, the pub has made a good impression on the local community, and has up to five ales on offer. The separate restaurant serves good value food. Views across the Fens are eye-catching on a clear day. 🏮Q🏮🍴🛗🚆(3,7)♣P⇆

CHESHIRE

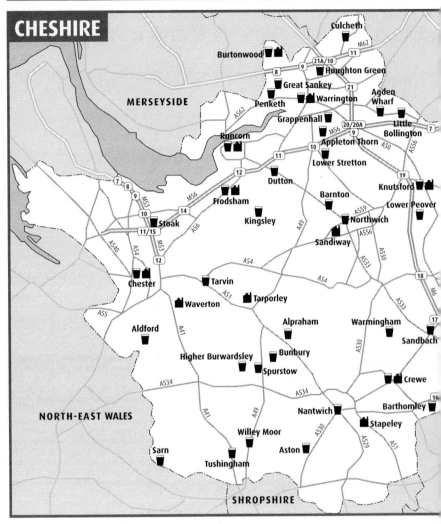

Agden Wharf

Barn Owl

Warrington Lane, WA13 0SW (off A56) SJ707872

☼ 11-11; 12-10.30 Sun ☎ (01925) 752020

⊕ thebarnowlinn.co.uk

Marston's Burton Bitter, Pedigree; guest beers ⊞

Large and friendly single-room pub set in open
countryside alongside the Bridgewater Canal with
sweeping views across farmland. Popular with a
mixed clientele of all ages, drinkers and diners
alike, it is especially busy at mealtimes, and offers
pensioners' specials. A multi-award winner for
both food and drink, five ever-changing guest ales
from micro-breweries complement the two
Marston's standards. A canalside patio offers
alfresco dining in the summer. Live music plays on
the last Saturday of the month.
✿❶♿☐(37,37A)♣P↳

Aldford

Grosvenor Arms ℒ

Chester Road, CH3 6HJ (on B5130)

☼ 11.30-11; 12-10.30 Sun ☎ (01244) 620228

⊕ grosvenorarms-aldford.co.uk

Beer range varies ⊞

Large, stylish, Victorian free house, extremely
popular with diners, with an imaginative food
menu served until 9pm. Inside there is a lively
open-plan wooden bar and attractive terracotta
floor with several quieter areas. A pleasant
conservatory leads to an outside terrace and lawn
with picnic tables. Up to five changing guest ales,
always including a Weetwood beer brewed for the
pub, are complemented by an extensive range of
wines and whiskies. Families are welcome, as are
dogs on leads. ♨Q✿❶♿☐(C56)P

Alpraham

Travellers Rest ★

Chester Road, CW6 9JA (on A51 at N end of village)
SJ578598

☼ 6.30-11; 12-4, 6-11 Sat; 12-3, 7-10.30 Sun

☎ (01829) 260523

Weetwood Eastgate; Tetley Bitter ⊞

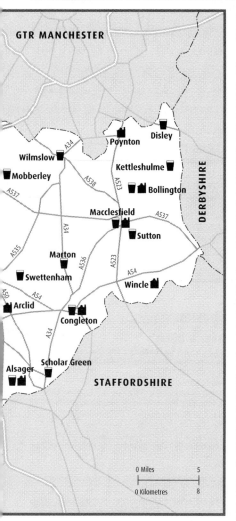

popular in summer. The pub is well served by public transport, and there is a public car park to the rear. ▲圈◐&≈₽(20)●

Appleton Thorn

Appleton Thorn Village Hall
Stretton Road, WA4 4RT SJ637838
⊕ closed Mon-Wed; 7.30-11; 1-4, 7.30-10.30 Sun
☎ (01925) 261187 ⊕ appletonthornvillagehall.co.uk
Beer range varies ⒣
CAMRA National Club of the Year 2008, the hall has a comfortable lounge and a larger bar area-cum-function room where regular events are held, including live music, quizzes and an annual beer festival in October. It offers a choice of up to seven changing beers from regional and micro-breweries, and up to eight ciders and a perry. The village hall is the hub of the local community, with popular Sunday lunches a highlight (served 1-3pm). Buses run Friday and Saturday evenings only.
Q圈&₽(8,8X)♣●P冊

Aston

Bhurtpore Inn ⓛ
Wrenbury Road, CW5 8DQ (¼ mile NW from A530 Nantwich-Whitchurch road) SJ610469
⊕ 12-2.30, 6.30-11.30; 12-midnight Fri & Sat; 12-11 Sun
☎ (01270) 780917 ⊕ bhurtpore.co.uk
Beer range varies ⒣
Friendly, welcoming, family-run hostelry in a quiet village. The pub's name refers to the successful siege of Bhurtpore Fort, in Northern India, in 1828, led by Sir Stapleton Cotton, whose portrait appears on the pub sign. Eleven handpumps serve a wide variety of real ales, mainly from small and frequently LocAle brewers, guaranteed to suit all tastes. The inn is renowned for its high quality, locally sourced food, with curries a speciality. The beer festival in July is not to be missed.
▲Q圈◐&Å≈(Wrenbury)₽(72)♣●P

Barnton

Barnton Cricket Club ⓛ
Broomsedge, Townfield Lane, CW8 4QL (200m from A533 via Stoneheyes Lane) SJ631757
⊕ 6.30 (12 Sat summer, 4 Sat winter)-11 (midnight Tue, Fri & Sat; 12.30am Thu); 12-11 Sun ☎ (01606) 77702
⊕ barntoncc.co.uk
Hydes Dark Mild, 1863; Theakston Best Bitter; guest beers ⒣
A multiple winner of CAMRA Branch and Regional Club of the Year awards, this busy club is as popular as ever. As well as the attractions of multiple sports – seven cricket teams, six squash teams, 10 bowling teams, poker, darts, dominoes and pool – there are three to four guest beers sourced from micro-breweries and a popular beer festival in November each year. Meals are available Thursday to Sunday evenings and Sunday lunchtime.
圈◐&(4)♣P

Barthomley

White Lion ★ ✪
Audley Road, CW2 5PG (jct of Audley Road and Radway Green Rd) SJ767524
⊕ 11.30-11; 12-10.30 Sun ☎ (01270) 882242
Jennings Cumberland Ale, Cocker Hoop, Sneck Lifter; Mansfield Cask Ale; Marston's Burton Bitter ⒣

Close to the Shropshire Union Canal, this genuine rural free house has been owned and run by the same family for more than 100 years. A former local CAMRA Pub of the Year, the cosy inn is always a delight to visit. The four rooms and their furnishings reflect an era when people had time to sit, sup, talk and relax. Visitors, locals, walkers, cyclists, boaters and passing motorists are always made to feel at home. Limited opening times.
Q圈⊕₽(84)♣P

Alsager

Lodge ⓛ
88 Crewe Road, ST7 2LX
⊕ 4-11; 1-midnight Fri & Sat; 3-11 Sun ☎ (01270) 873669
Beer range varies ⒣
The Lodge, a large two-roomed pub, offers an ever-changing range of ales, often sourced from micro-breweries and including ales from its own on-site brewery, Goodall's. Three draught ciders and a selection of bottled beers are also stocked, and a beer festival is held at Easter. Baps and wraps are available at all times. The garden is

This classic 15th-century thatched pub stands in an idyllic village location close to the church and river. Real fires welcome you to the main bar with its wood panelling and exposed beams, and to the more rustic upper room with wooden settles and benches. There is a small third room, no less delightful, and outside there is a patio area with tables, and seating to the front where you can watch the world go by. ▲Q☺◑P⅄

A traditional inn in the centre of this pleasant village – lively conversation in both bars helps to create a friendly atmosphere. Sports memorabilia decorate the public bar. Classic pub grub is served at reasonable prices. The four guest beers generally include representations from local breweries. Situated between the A49 and A51, it is well-worth making a detour to seek out this pub. ▲Q◑☜P

Bollington

Cock & Pheasant ⏚ ✅
15 Bollington Road, SK10 5EJ
🟢 11.30-11 (midnight Fri & Sat); 12-11 Sun
☎ (01625) 573289
Copper Dragon Golden Pippin; Storm Bosley Cloud; Tetley Bitter; guest beers Ⓗ
Large, popular pub on the main road entering Bollington, dating from 1756. Low ceilings and a stone-flagged floor make for a cosy bar, with a separate secluded dining area. A conservatory, patio and children's play area cater for all tastes. A regular outlet for Storm and Wincle local breweries, the range of well-kept cask ales complements good food from a varied menu served daily until 9pm. The bus stops right outside the front door. ꝺ☺◑♿🚌(10)♣P⅄

Poachers Inn ⏚
95 Ingersley Road, SK10 5RE
🟢 12-2 (not Mon), 5.30-11; 12-11 Sun ☎ (01625) 572086
⊕ thepoachers.org
Beer range varies Ⓗ
Friendly and welcoming family-run free house near the Gritstone Way. The licensee enthusiastically supports local breweries, including the nearby Happy Valley Brewery, with a range of five ales. Belgian beers are available in bottle. The interior is divided into comfortable seating areas, and outside there is a suntrap garden for the summer. Well regarded, good value, home-prepared food is served. Events include Wednesday pie night and a monthly quiz. Local CAMRA Pub of the Year 2010. The pub has featured in the Guide for more than 10 consecutive years. ▲ꝺ☺◑🚌(10)P⅄

Vale Inn ⏚
29-31 Adlington Road, SK10 5JT
🟢 12-2.30, 5-11; 12-11 Sat; 12-10.30 Sun ☎ (01625) 575147
⊕ valeinn.co.uk
Beer range varies Ⓗ
Single-room, family-run free house dating from the 1860s. The brewery tap for the nearby Bollington Brewing Company, it features three to five of its beers plus one or two guests, often from local breweries. Seasonal mini beer festivals are also held. Known for excellent home-cooked food, the pub is popular with the local community as well as walkers and bikers using the nearby canal and Middlewood Way footpath. It sponsors the local cricket team and games can be watched from the beer garden. Local CAMRA Pub of the Year 2008. ▲ꝺ☺◑🚌(10)♥P⅄⎕

Bunbury

Nag's Head
Vicarage Lane, CW6 9PB
🟢 10am-midnight ☎ (01829) 260027
Beer range varies Ⓗ

Burtonwood

Fiddle i' th' Bag
Alder Lane, WA5 4BJ SJ584929
🟢 12-3, 4.45-11; 12-11 Sat & Sun ☎ (01925) 225442
Beer range varies Ⓗ
On a country road running parallel with the M62, this shrine to early 20th century recorded music is famous for its eccentric advertising and enthusiastic staff who wend their way through an ever increasing range of nostalgic oddities that crowd every spare inch of space. Three handpumps dispense ever-changing beers. Tasting glasses are enthusiastically offered so that drinkers can make an informed choice. ☺◑♿🚌(329)P

Chester

Bear & Billet
94 Lower Bridge Street, CH1 1RU (near Old Dee Bridge)
🟢 12-11 (11.30 Thu; 12.30am Fri & Sat) ☎ (01244) 311886
⊕ bearandbillet.com
Okells Bitter, IPA; guest beers Ⓗ
Listed, three-storey, 17th-century building that looms over the busy street and nearby Roman walls, with a welcoming, friendly feel. Alongside the Okells and local guest ales there is a full, traditional food menu and a selection of wines. Decorative features complement tables in assorted sizes, low timber beams and a log fire. Sport is often shown on TV in the bars, but you can escape to the dining and function rooms. ▲☺◑🚌♥⅄

INDEPENDENT BREWERIES
4Ts Warrington (NEW)
Beartown Congleton
Blue Ball Runcorn (NEW)
Bollington Bollington
Borough Arms Crewe
Burtonwood Burtonwood
Chester Chester (NEW)
Coach House Warrington
DB Runcorn (NEW)
Frodsham Frodsham
Goodall's Alsager
Happy Valley Bollington (NEW)
Merlin Arclid (NEW)
Northern Sandiway
Norton Runcorn (NEW)
Offbeat Crewe (NEW)
Pied Bull Chester (NEW)
Redwillow Macclesfield (NEW)
Spitting Feathers Waverton
Storm Macclesfield
Tatton Knutsford
Tipsy Angel Warrington (NEW)
Weetwood Tarporley
Wincle Wincle
Woodlands Stapeley
Worth Poynton (NEW)

Brewery Tap 🅛
52-54 Lower Bridge Street, CH1 1RU
🕑 12-11 (midnight Sat); 12-10.30 Sun ☎ (01244) 340999
🌐 the-tap.co.uk
Spitting Feathers Thirstquencher, Old Wavertonian; guest beers Ⓗ
A former Jacobean banqueting hall, the inn won CAMRA's English Heritage Conservation and Conversion to Pub Use awards in 2009. Charles I stayed in the Grade II-listed building in 1645. Reached by steps from the street, this city-centre pub's stone floors, high ceilings and tapestries create a terrific ambience. A comprehensive, changing list of real ales from micros, many local, complements the house beers. The food is inventive and freshly prepared. An unmissable gem. Q🛈🖵🌢

Carlton Tavern ✔
1 Hartington Street, Handbridge, CH4 7BN
🕑 4-11.30 (midnight Fri); 12-midnight Sat; 12-10.30 Sun
☎ (01244) 674821
Hydes Original Bitter, seasonal beers; guest beers Ⓗ
Traditional pub in a residential area, enthusiastically managed and presented by a knowledgeable licensee and staff. Recently redecorated throughout to a high standard, the lounge and separate bar are both served from a central facility. The bar has a pool table, darts and other pub games, plus a large TV for sport. The Hydes' beers are complemented by a changing ale mainly from a local micro. Regular festivals are held with a good variety of guest beers. ⋈Q🕾🖵♣-🖢

Mill Hotel 🅛
Milton Street, CH1 3NF (by canal E of inner ring road A51/A56 jct)
🕑 12-midnight (10.30 Sun) ☎ (01244) 350035
🌐 millhotel.com
Coach House Mill Premium; Copper Dragon Golden Pippin; Phoenix Corn Mill; guest beers Ⓗ
City-centre hotel housed in a former corn mill alongside the Shropshire canal and dating back to 1830. A large range of cask beers is served from over a dozen handpumps, including a guest mild, local and regional bitters and real cider. Food ranges from bar snacks to full restaurant service. Three large TV screens ensure sports fans don't miss any of the action. Outside is a small drinking area overlooking the canal. ❀🛄🛈🕾🖵≠🌢P-

Old Harkers Arms 🅛
1 Russell Street, CH3 5AL (down steps off City Road to canal towpath) SJ412666
🕑 11.30-11; 12-10.30 Sun ☎ (01244) 344525
🌐 harkersarms-chester.co.uk
Brunning & Price Original; Flowers Original; Weetwood Cheshire Cat; guest beers Ⓗ
Upmarket pub converted from the derelict lower ground floor of a Victorian canalside warehouse. Bookcases, prints, wooden flooring and traditional wooden furniture feature throughout the interior. Blackboard listings offer imaginative tasting notes to help you choose from the variety of nine or so beers on offer, many from independent micro-breweries. Stout, porter, often a mild, and cider in summer all feature. Food is available all day with booking recommended at busy periods. Pedestrianisation allows level access and an alfresco drinking area. Q🛈🕾≠🖵🌢

Pied Bull 🅛
57 Northgate Street, CH1 2HQ
🕑 10-11 (midnight Fri & Sat) ☎ (01244) 325829
🌐 piedbull.co.uk
Adnams Broadside; guest beer Ⓗ
A pub with lots of character right in the centre of the city. The interior features extensive wood panelling and a large, ornate but unused fireplace with an old tapestry above it. The large open bar area has a cosy room leading off it, home to a local walking group. A popular quiz is held on Thursday evening. The owners are enthusiastic real ale fans and have recently opened a micro-brewery on the premises. Food is served throughout the day. 🛏🛈🕾-🌢

Telford's Warehouse
Tower Wharf, CH1 4EZ (off Raymond Street)
🕑 12-11 (1am Wed; 12.30am Thu; 2am Fri & Sat); 12-1am Sun ☎ (01244) 390090 🌐 telfordswarehousechester.com
Thwaites Original; Weetwood Cheshire Cat; guest beers Ⓗ
Converted warehouse overlooking the Shropshire Union canal with a large glass frontage providing fine views of the canal basin, and an outdoor drinking area. The lower bar, usually open in the evenings, features a stage for live music events. Food is served in the main bar and an upstairs restaurant. Three guest ales are always available from local micros and independents, plus a small selection of international bottled beers and cider. There may be an admission charge on evenings when live bands are playing. ❀🛈🕾🖵P-

Congleton

Beartown Tap 🅛
18 Willow Street, CW12 1RL
🕑 4 (12 Sat & Sun)-11 ☎ (01260) 270990
🌐 beartownbrewery.co.uk/tap.htm
Beartown Bearskinful, Honey Bear, Kodiak Gold, Polar Eclipse, Ursa Major; guest beers Ⓗ
Arguably the best-known pub in Congleton, situated just feet from the brewery. Eight ales are available with at least seven from Beartown Brewery and an occasional guest, often from a smaller brewery. Real cider is available all year round. Various events including shove-ha'penny and maggot racing help give the Tap a real community feel. ⋈❀≠🖵🌢-

Congleton Leisure Centre
Worrall Street, CW12 1DT
🕑 7-10.30; closed Sat; 8-10.30 Sun ☎ (01270) 529502
Beer range varies Ⓗ
A municipal leisure centre bar open to all, not just those participating in sporting activities. Ales usually include one from Copper Dragon plus one or two from micro-breweries. Popular beer festivals are held in March and October with a range of 20 ales plus a couple of real ciders. The venue has a welcoming atmosphere, with local CAMRA newsletters by the bar and an array of pump clips on the walls. Five minutes' walk from the bus station. ♿≠🖵P🖢

Queen's Head Hotel 🅛
Park Lane, CW12 3DE
🕑 11 (12 Sat)-midnight; 12-11 Sun ☎ (01260) 272546
Beer range varies Ⓗ
Next to the Cheshire canal and railway station, this town pub is an ideal destination for the beer

tourist. The range includes three regular ales plus three guests, often from Storm, Wincle, Coach House or Titanic. Pool, darts and boules are played. Good pub grub is available lunchtimes and evenings. Accommodation has been upgraded (booking advisable). Sport on TV is an attraction and can be viewed on sensible-sized screens around the pub. ▲❧❀⟨❍⟩❧❦⟨9,99⟩❀P⌐

Waggon & Horses
West Road, CW12 4HN
☼ 12-midnight (1am Fri & Sat) ☎ (01260) 271680
⊕ thewaggonandhorsescongleton.co.uk
Beer range varies ⊞
Community local situated on a traffic island in the West Heath area of Congleton. The beer choice takes full advantage of the breadth of Marston's group of breweries, with up to six ales available, often including a mild. The pub is busy with football followers at the weekend, and during the week darts, pool and the quiz are popular. Live music plays fortnightly on Saturday.
❧❀⟨❍⟩❦❧P⌐

Crewe

Borough Arms
33 Earle Street, CW1 2BG (on Earle Street Bridge)
SJ707557
☼ 5 (12 Fri & Sat)-11; 12-10.30 Sun ☎ (01270) 254999
⊕ borougharmscrewe.co.uk
Beer range varies ⊞
Friendly, popular free house near the town centre. A split-level single bar serves three distinct drinking areas. A further large room downstairs leads to a sheltered walled beer garden. The absence of pool, music and gaming machines encourages earnest conversation. Nine handpumps serve a wide range of ales, mainly from small and micro-brewers. Pale hoppier beers are the mainstay here, but darker beers make regular appearances. Home to the Borough Arms Brewery.
Q❧❀⟨14⟩❦⌐⊟

Hops ⌶
8-10 Prince Albert Street, CW1 2DF
☼ 11 (5 Mon)-11.30; 12-11.30 Sun ☎ (01270) 211100
Townhouse Enigma; guest beers ⊞
Friendly, family-run free house, voted CAMRA Cheshire Pub of the Year for 2011, in a quiet part of the town centre. There is a comfortable bar downstairs, more seating on the first floor, and an outside space for fine weather. The Townhouse house beer is joined by four guest ales, usually from local micro-breweries. A comprehensive range of Belgian beers, bottled and on draught, is always available. Lunchtime meals are served Wednesday to Saturday. CAMRA members are offered a discount on real ale on Monday night.
Q❀⟨❍⟩❧❦❀P

Culcheth

Cherry Tree ✔
35 Common Lane, WA3 4EX (on B5207, 400m from A574) SJ653952
☼ 11-11 (midnight Fri & Sat); 12-11 Sun ☎ (01925) 762624
Greene King Abbot; Tetley Bitter; guest beers ⊞
Large open-plan pub with an emphasis on dining offering regular meal deals. Food is served all day until 9.30pm. Three changing guest beers are offered, usually at least one from a local brewery.

Sport is shown on TV, including 3-D in the bar area. Quiz night is Wednesday, and there is a disco on Friday and Saturday. Outside is a large, impressive smokers' area with a tree growing in the middle. Free WiFi is available. There is a public car park at the rear. ❀⟨❍⟩❧❦⟨19,28,28A⟩P⌐

Disley

White Lion ♔ ⌶ ✔
135 Buxton Road, SK12 2HA
☼ 11.30 (6.30 Mon)-11 (12.30am Fri & Sat); 12-11 Sun
☎ (01663) 762800 ⊕ whitelion-disley.co.uk
Thornbridge Wild Swan; Jennings Cumberland Ale; guest beers ⊞
Large white-painted pub on the A6 towards the easterly end of the village. It offers eight real ales; six are constantly changing beers from SIBA member micro-breweries. The contemporary, largely open-plan interior has a separate dog room with blankets, water bowls and canine dinners. A comprehensive and varied food menu is served all day (except Mon) until 9pm. Quiz night is Thursday and live entertainment is hosted on the last Saturday of the month. A short walk from Peak Forest Canal (bridge 26). ▲❀⟨❍⟩❦⟨199⟩P

Dutton

Tunnel Top ⌶
Northwich Road, WA4 4JY
☼ 12-midnight ☎ (01928) 718181 ⊕ tunneltop.co.uk
Beer range varies ⊞
Friendly village pub at the heart of the local community, with two seating areas and a more formal restaurant space. There is also a separate sports pavilion that houses an eight-foot screen for football and other sports. Two handpumps dispense beers from local breweries. The pub was recently under threat of being converted into flats until a joint effort from locals and CAMRA members managed to halt this. ❀⟨❍⟩P

Frodsham

Helter Skelter ⌶
31 Church Street, WA6 6PN SJ518777
☼ 11-11 (11.30 Fri & Sat); 12-10.30 Sun ☎ (01928) 733361
⊕ helterskelter-frodsham.co.uk
Weetwood Best Bitter; guest beers ⊞
Drinkers enjoy a cosy, friendly atmosphere at the bar in this popular single-room pub situated in a busy shopping area. Seating is at ground level and also on a raised area towards the rear. There are eight handpumps – the local Weetwood beer is always available alongside ales from Cheshire and Northern micros and a changing real cider or perry. The proprietors work hard to source beers from new breweries. ⟨❍⟩❦⟨48,X30⟩❀⊟

Grappenhall

Bellhouse Club
Bellhouse Farm, Bellhouse Lane, WA4 2SG (200m off A50) SJ642862
☼ 5-11 (midnight Fri); 12-midnight Sat; 12-11.30 Sun
☎ (01925) 268633 ⊕ grappenhall.com
Beer range varies ⊞
Part of the Community Centre, this thriving club is near the cobbled Grappenhall village. Regularly changing beers, mainly from micros and regionals, are served from the main bar, which services a

large, quiet lounge area and games room. The club is home to 40 groups and offers traditional games like darts and dominoes, a quiz on Wednesday and live football fixtures on large-screen HD TV. A beer festival is held in May in the Old Barne. CAMRA members are welcome. Q✿&🍴⌂♣P⏚🖫

Great Sankey

Chapel House
380 Liverpool Road, WA5 1RU
✪ 4 (3 Fri; 12 Sat)-midnight; 12-midnight Sun
☎ (01925) 488860
Beer range varies Ⓗ
Traditional two-roomed pub with a large lounge split into two areas and a smaller, separate bar. A friendly local with a strong community focus, it caters for all age groups. Two cask beers are usually on sale with one from a family brewer such as Timothy Taylor or Black Sheep and the second from a micro-brewery. Wednesday is pie night when football is shown in the smaller of the two lounge areas. ⬚≹(Sankey)🚍(14,15)♣P⏚

Higher Burwardsley

Pheasant Inn Ⓛ
Barracks Lane, CH3 9PF (access from A534 of A41) SJ523566
✪ 11-11; 12-10.30 Sun ☎ (01829) 770434
⊕ thepheasantinn.co.uk
Weetwood Best Bitter, Eastgate, Oasthouse Gold; guest beers Ⓗ
Delightful country inn high in the Peckforton Hills with glorious views across the Cheshire Plain to the Clwydian mountains and handy for ramblers walking the nearby Sandstone Trail. The Pheasant is popular for its wholesome meals prepared from fresh, locally-sourced produce (no food Mon afternoon). The guest beer is usually from a local micro. Accommodation is in 12 en-suite rooms housed in old Cheshire sandstone buildings. ⌂Q✿🏠◑&P

Houghton Green

Millhouse Ⓛ
Ballater Drive, WA2 0LX SJ623915
✪ 12-11 (11.30 Tue & Thu; midnight Fri & Sat)
☎ (01925) 831189
Holt Mild, Bitter; guest beers Ⓗ
Built in the 1980s to cater for the expanding new estates of North Warrington, this large two-roomed open-plan pub is a popular community local. It has a spacious bar/games room with darts and pool, and a large lounge where quizzes take place on Tuesday and Thursday nights, and live music on Saturday. Food is served until 9pm (6pm Sun). ✿◑▶&🚍(23,26)♣P⏚

Plough Ⓛ ✅
Mill Lane, WA2 0SU (off Delph Lane) SJ622918
✪ 11.30-11 (11.30 Thu & Sat; midnight Fri); 12-11 Sun
☎ (01925) 815409
Wells Bombardier; guest beers Ⓗ
Set between the M62 and the estates of north Warrington, this pub is popular for both beer and food. It now offers up to seven changing cask beers alongside the regular Bombardier, with a focus on local brewers. The modern, open-plan interior complements the pub's 1774 origins. A new outdoor drinking/dining area is a further attraction

in the summer months. Food is served until 9pm seven days a week. Quiz night is Thursday. ✿◑▶&🚍(23,26)P

Kettleshulme

Swan ✅
Macclesfield Road, SK23 7QU (on B5470)
✪ 12 (5.30 Mon)-11; 12-10.30 Sun ☎ (01663) 732943
⊕ verynicepubs.co.uk/swankettleshulme
Marston's Burton Bitter; guest beers Ⓗ
Small, idyllic, 15th-century stone building with a quaint interior featuring timber beams, stone fireplaces and a real fire. Two or three changing guest beers, usually from quality micros, are always available, and a small beer festival takes place in early September. Food is of high quality from an interesting, ever-changing menu (booking advisable). Situated in the Peak District National Park, surrounded by good walking country, families and walkers are welcome. Outside there are two patios for warmer weather. ⌂✿🏠◑🚍(60,64)P

Kingsley

Red Bull
The Brow, WA6 8AN (100m from B5153) SJ522748
✪ 12-2.30, 5.30-11 (midnight Fri & Sat); 12-3, 7-11 Sun
☎ (01928) 788097 ⊕ redbullpub.co.uk
Beer range varies Ⓗ
There has been a pub on this site since 1771, first recorded as the Board in 1822. After a brief spell as the Dog & Bull, it was renamed the Red Bull in 1834. Local CAMRA Pub of the Year in 2008 and 2010, it offers a changing selection of six real ales, usually including a dark beer. Food is served daily until 9pm (not Mon eve), with fresh fish specials on Thursday, Friday and Saturday. ⌂Q✿▶🚍(48)P

Knutsford

Cross Keys Hotel Ⓛ
52 King Street, WA16 6DT
✪ 11.30-2.30, 5.30-11; 11.30-midnight Fri & Sat; 11.30-11 Sun ☎ (01565) 750404 ⊕ crosskeysknutsford.com
Beer range varies Ⓗ
This former 18th-century coaching inn is now a friendly and lively town-centre pub with modern accommodation. The lounge and vault are separated by an unusual wood and glass partition, while the dining area, reached via stairs from the lounge, has been converted from the cellar. Food is available Tuesday to Sunday with a wide choice of bar meals at lunchtime. Two or three guest beers are usually available, including at least one from a Cheshire brewery. ⌕✿🏠◑⬚≹🚍(300)♣P

Lord Eldon Ⓛ
27 Tatton Street, WA16 6AD
✪ 11-11 (midnight Thu-Sat); 12-10.30 Sun
☎ (01565) 652261
Beer range varies Ⓗ
This 300-year-old pub with sundial and hanging baskets has a surprisingly spacious interior, with a large bar area with a real fire and three separate rooms leading from it. It is generously decorated with horse brasses and pictures, many of old Knutsford. At the rear is a pleasant beer garden. Live music features twice a week, open mike on Thursday and live bands on Saturday. One of the guest ales is usually from a local brewery. ⌂Q✿◑≹🚍(300)♣⏚

Little Bollington

Swan with Two Nicks 🅛
Park Lane, WA14 4TJ (off A56)
✪ 12-11 (10.30 Sun) ☎ (0161) 928 2914
Greene King Abbot; Taylor Landlord; guest beers 🅗
Classic country pub at the rear of National Trust
Dunham Park, 10 minutes' walk from Bollin
Gate and handy for boaters on the Bridgewater
Canal. Food is served all day until 9pm (8pm Sun)
with vegetarian and gluten-free options available
in the spacious restaurant to the rear. Seven
handpumps usually include four beers from
Dunham Massey. The house beer, Swan With Two
Nicks, is brewed by Coach House. Children are
welcome and dogs too. 🏚🏵🐾◐🍴🚃P🚄

Lower Peover

Crown 🅛
Crown Lane, WA16 9QB (on B5081 off A50 S of
Knutsford) SJ737735
✪ 11.30-3, 5.30-11; 12-10.30 Sun ☎ (01565) 722074
Caledonian Deuchars IPA; Flowers IPA; Tatton Gold;
Taylor Landlord; Tetley Bitter; guest beers 🅗
A genuine country pub with attentive staff and a
warm welcome. It offers an excellent range of
beers – the always available Crown Mild is a
rebadged Woodlands Mild. The front bar with its
stone floor and low ceilings welcomes dogs and
their well-behaved owners. With a homely menu
of quality produce and tip-top beer, the Crown is
well-worth a visit. 🏚Q◐&≠(Plumley)🐾P🚄

Lower Stretton

Ring o' Bells
Northwich Road, WA4 4NZ (on A559 just off jct 10 M56)
SJ622818
✪ 12-2.30 (not Mon; 2 Tue), 5.30-11; 12-3, 5.30-midnight Fri;
12-3, 6-11 Sat; 12-4, 7-10.30 Sun ☎ (01925) 730556
Fuller's London Pride; Tetley Bitter; guest beer 🅗
A previous local CAMRA Pub of the Year, this is one
of the few traditional village locals left south of
Warrington. Conversation and banter predominate
in the main room, served by a single bar, but
refuge can be sought in one of two side rooms for
a quiet drink. There is a twice-monthly Monday
night quiz when the pub can get very busy. Boules
is played outside on a pitch next to the car park.
🏚Q🏵🚃(45,46)P🚄

Macclesfield

Baths Hotel 🅛
40 Green Street, SK10 1JH
✪ 12-11 (midnight Fri & Sat); 12-10.30 Sun
☎ (01625) 262884 🌐 bathshotel.com
Beer range varies 🅗
Friendly corner-terrace pub situated just out of the
town centre but within easy walk of the bus and
rail stations. Recently in new hands, it is now one
of a growing number of free houses in the town.
Three handpumps supply two regular beers and
one guest, giving the Baths a very individual feel.
Evening meals are served every day including
must-try home-made pizza plus popular Sunday
lunch roast. 🏚🐾🏵◐≠🚃🐾🚄

Dolphin 🅛
76 Windmill Street, SK11 7HS
✪ 12-2.30, 5-11; 12-11 Sat; 12-10.30 Sun ☎ (01625) 616179

Robinson's Hatters Mild, Dizzy Blonde, Unicorn,
seasonal 🅗
This family-run local has separate public and
lounge bars and an open fire in winter adding to
the warm and friendly feel. The regulars participate
in a number of traditional pub sports. Four
handpumps offer a range of beers throughout the
year, with Old Tom in winter. A good range of malt
whiskies is available. Home-cooked food is served
on Friday and Saturday lunchtimes. CAMRA Branch
Pub of the Year. 🏚Q🐾◐&🚃🚄🐾

Railway View 🅛
1 Byrons Lane, SK11 7JW
✪ 5 (12 Sat)-11; 12-10.30 Sun ☎ (01625) 423657
Beer range varies 🅗
An attractive local free house with stone-flagged
floors serving a constantly changing selection of
four real ales, with reduced prices on Monday
night. Real fires add warmth during the winter
months. Seasonal mini beer festivals, live music on
Friday night and a Sunday quiz are regular events.
The pub is home to local dominoes, crib, darts, bar
skittles and pool teams, and has a football side in
the local league. Very busy with fans when
Macclesfield FC play at home. 🏚🐾🏵🚃(9,14)🐾🚄

Society Rooms ✪
Park Green, SK11 7NA
✪ 9-midnight (11 Jan); 9-1am (midnight Jan) Fri & Sat
☎ (01625) 507320
Beer range varies 🅗
Large, stone-built Wetherspoon conversion of an
18th-century vicarage and college – hence the
name. Divided internally into two large areas, the
central location means the pub is busy with
shoppers and families during the day, enjoying
good value food and drinks. The bar gets more
lively and bustling on weekend evenings although
it is possible to find quieter corners. It offers six
constantly-changing guest beers and hosts mini-
beer festivals showcasing regional breweries.
🐾🏵◐&🚃🐾P🚄

Waters Green Tavern 🅛
96 Waters Green, SK11 6LH
✪ 12-3, 5.30 (7 Sat)-11; 12-3, 7-10.30 Sun
☎ (01625) 422653
Beer range varies 🅗
Award-winning hostelry close to both rail and bus
stations, making it an ideal waiting room. Now a
free house, the pub continues to trade on its core
strengths of beer quality and a welcoming
atmosphere. Recently renovated externally to its
former glory, improvements have been made to
the interior as well. Great value home-cooked food
is served every lunchtime Monday to Saturday. A
choice of up to seven beers is offered from the
north-west and beyond. 🏚🏵◐≠🚃🐾🌀🚄

Marton

Davenport 🅛
Congleton Road, SK11 9HF
✪ 12-3 (not Mon), 6-11; 12-midnight Fri-Sun
☎ (01260) 224269 🌐 thedavenportarms.co.uk
Courage Directors; Theakston Black Bull; guest
beers 🅗
Gastro-pub with a large garden and patio area with
an established reputation for good fresh food –
Tuesday curry night is a highlight. Locals as well as
diners appreciate the conscientious management
of beer quality, with two regular beers

supplemented by one or two guests, often from local brewery Storm. The bar staff are very attentive and knowledgeable and the licensees are always happy to field comments and suggestions for ale changes. ⚏🚲🏵🌒❶🅿📶

Mobberley

Bull's Head ✅
Mill Lane, WA16 7HX
🕛 12-11 (midnight Fri & Sat); 12-10.30 Sun
☎ (01565) 873395 ⊕ thebullsheadpub.co.uk
Beer range varies Ⓗ
'Local and proud' is the billing for this excellent country inn. The cobbled frontage is a promise of the delights within: three open fires, stone floors, candle-lit tables and low beams. Exposed Cheshire brick and the old back-to-back fireplace remain. Five Cheshire beers are part of the ethos of the pub along with good freshly cooked food. Each pump has tasting notes and tasters are offered to help you decide. ⚏🚲🏵🌒❶🚋♣🅿📶

Railway Ⓛ
Station Road, WA16 6LA
🕛 12-11 (1am Fri & Sat); 12-10.30 Sun ☎ (01565) 873155
⊕ railwayinnpub.co.uk
Black Sheep Best Bitter; Dunham Massey Big Tree Bitter; guest beer Ⓗ
Comfortable and welcoming country pub with a real fire and separate dining room. The railway theme includes framed buttons and badges, pictures and photographs, plus a full-sized semaphore signal in the car park. Very much a community venue, it is home to many pub teams, supports charities and hosts a music quiz using vinyl records. Cheshire ales from Dunham Massey, Tatton and Storm feature regularly. Meals are served daily. ⚏🚲🏵🌒❶🚋🚄♣🅿

Nantwich

Black Lion Ⓛ
29 Welsh Row, CW5 5ED
🕛 12-3 (not Mon), 5-11; 12-11 Thu-Sat; 12-10.30 Sun
☎ (01270) 628711
Weetwood Best Bitter, Cheshire Cat Ⓗ
Three-hundred-and-fifty-year-old black and white timbered pub on the fringe of the main shopping area, with a tranquil, relaxed atmosphere. The interior comprises a front room with roaring fire, a back room and a cosy quaint snug, all with original wooden floors, plus a conservatory to the side and an upstairs lounge. Guest beers tend to come from north-west breweries. Home-cooked food is available daily (not Mon). ⚏Q🏵🌒❶🚄🚋(45,84)📶

Crown Hotel Ⓛ
24 High Street, CW5 5AS
🕛 10-midnight ☎ (01270) 625283
⊕ crownhotelnantwich.com
Woodlands Crown Ale; guest beers Ⓗ
This Grade II-listed building burnt down in the Great Fire of Nantwich in 1583, but was quickly rebuilt. The traditional bar offers a range of guest beers, often LocAle, and a house ale brewed by Woodlands. An Italian restaurant leads off the bar. A pianist makes regular appearances throughout the week and occasional entertainment upstairs includes a monthly film night and live music. The pub hosts an annual Easter jazz and blues festival. Sky Sports is screened. ⚏🛏🌒❶👦🚋(84)🅿📶

Globe Ⓛ
100 Audlem Road, CW5 7EA
🕛 12-11 ☎ (01270) 623374 ⊕ theglobenantwich.co.uk
Woodlands Drummer Bitter, Light Oak, Oak Beauty, Best Bitter, Globe Bitter, General's Tipple; guest beers Ⓗ
Nantwich brewery Woodlands acquired and totally refurbished its only tied house in 2007 to serve as the brewery tap. Nine handpumps offer the full range with seasonal specials and an additional guest beer sourced elsewhere. There is a comfortable bar and a large restaurant area where excellent home-cooked meals are served until 9pm (8pm Sun). This is a friendly local with occasional live music and other community activities. ⚏🏵🌒❶🚄🚋(73)👦🅿📶🍴

Northwich

Penny Black Ⓛ ✅
110 Witton Street, CW9 5AB SJ661740
🕛 8am-11 (midnight Thu; 1am Fri & Sat) ☎ (01606) 42029
Greene King Ruddles Best Bitter, Abbot; Tetley Bitter; guest beers Ⓗ
Eight guest beers are available in this Wetherspoon conversion of the Grade II-listed former town post office dating back to 1914. Large and mainly open plan, quiet TVs screen news channels with subtitles. Free WiFi is available. Cheshire brewed beers are often to be found on the bar and at least one darker beer (mild, stout or porter). The car park is behind the pub off Meadow Street immediately after the new Royal Mail sorting office. Q🚲🏵🌒❶🚄(Northwich)🚋(1,45,289)👦🅿📶

Penketh

Ferry Tavern
Station Road, WA5 2UJ SJ563866
🕛 12-3.30 (not Mon), 5.30-11 (11.30 Fri); 12-11.30 Sat; 12-10.30 Sun ☎ (01925) 791117 ⊕ theferrytavern.com
Boddingtons Bitter; Greene King Ruddles County, Abbot; guest beers Ⓗ
Opened in 1762, the Ferry Tavern is accessed by crossing the railway to Fiddlers Ferry Power Station and the St Helens Canal. The pub itself looks out onto the River Mersey. Six real ales are offered, three regularly changing, and a good selection of malt whiskies is stocked. The pub is renowned for hosting events including the music festival Glastonferry and an annual vintage car rally. ⚏🏵🅿

Runcorn

Ferry Boat ✅
10 Church Street, WA7 1LR
🕛 8-midnight (1am Fri & Sat) ☎ (01928) 583380
Greene King Ruddles Best Bitter, Abbot; Marston's Pedigree; guest beers Ⓗ
Located in the centre of the old town, one minute from the main bus station, this Wetherspoon shop conversion takes its name from the ferry service that once linked Runcorn with Widnes on the opposite bank of the River Mersey. An attractive, spacious, open-plan pub, the interior is divided into several distinct seating areas and food is served all day. The pub has an enclosed, heated, decked patio to the rear. 🚲🏵🌒❶🚄🚋🅿📶

Sandbach

Lower Chequer ⓛ
Crown Bank, CW11 1FW
✪ 12 (6 Mon-Wed; 5 Thu)-11 summer; 1 (6 Mon-Wed, 5 Thu)-11 winter; 12 (1 winter)-10.30 Sun ☎ 07932 943977
Beer range varies Ⓗ
A warm welcome is assured from the award-winning licensees who have rejuvenated this black and white timbered pub set back to the rear of the cobbled square. Dating from 1570, the interior has two rooms, and outside there is seating to the front and a marquee and patio to the rear. Six real ales are on offer, all from small breweries, with Beartown Kodiak Gold and Wood Shropshire Lad the regulars. There is always a porter, mild or stout available. Q✿✿🖵(38)👄ᵗᵘ

Sarn

Queen's Head ⓛ
Sarn Road, SY14 7LN (off B5069 Threapwood Road) SJ440447
✪ closed Mon; 6 (12 Sun)-midnight ☎ (01948) 770244
🌐 queensheadsarn.co.uk
Marston's Burton Bitter; Taylor Golden Best; guest beer Ⓗ
Small, friendly village pub, known locally as The Sarn and renowned for its home-made, locally-sourced food. A twin-roomed pub with adjoining dining area, the homely lounge has a real fire and pool can be played in the games room. Outside, the covered patio is next to a converted water mill on Wych Brook. The guest beer is usually from a local micro-brewery and the pub provides a rare outlet for Taylor's light mild. ⚒Q✿✿◑&Ⓐ♣Pᵗᵘ

Scholar Green

Rising Sun ✪
Station Road, ST7 3JT (off A34)
✪ 12-3, 5-11.30; 9.30-midnight Fri; 12-midnight Sat & Sun ☎ (01782) 776235 🌐 risingsuncheshire.co.uk
Jennings Cocker Hoop; Marston's Burton Bitter, Pedigree Ⓗ
A lovely village inn comprising a main bar and adjoining restaurant with beamed ceilings and real fires. Set in an area that is ideal for walking and close to the local canal, it is popular with locals and visitors alike. The pub serves five real ales including two rotating guests from Jennings, Wychwood and Marston's. ⚒✿◑♣Pᵗᵘ

Spurstow

Yew Tree
Long Lane, CW6 9RD (E of A49, near Bunbury)
✪ 12-11 (10.30 Sun) ☎ (01829) 260274
🌐 theyewtreebunbury.com
Stonehouse Station Bitter; guest beers Ⓗ
This superb village pub, built in the 19th century, reopened after a full internal refurbishment, and it is well-worth a visit. At least six real ales are offered, including the house ale Stonehouse Station Bitter and rotating guests. The menu is first rate, featuring local produce and suppliers wherever possible. Numerous special events are hosted throughout the year. ⚒Q✿◑P

Stoak

Bunbury Arms ✪
Little Stanney Lane, CH2 4HW (signed from A5117 near M53/M56 interchange)
✪ 12-11 (10.30 Sun) ☎ (01244) 301665
Beer range varies Ⓗ
Extended 17th century red-brick building with moorings on the Shropshire Union Canal a few hundred yards away. Both the small snug and open-plan, wood-beamed lounge feature real fires. Beers, often from local breweries, are served from four handpumps. The pub is busy with diners all year and is a popular stop-off for cyclists and walkers in summer. Outside, there is a patio with heaters. Cheshire Oaks Retail Park, Blue Planet Aquarium and Ellesmere Port Boat Museum are close by. Dogs are welcome in the public bar. ⚒Q✿◑⊟&🖵(DB2)♣Pᵗᵘ

Sutton

Church House ✪
Church Lane, SK11 0DS
✪ 12-midnight ☎ (01260) 252436
Beer range varies Ⓗ
Friendly brick-built pub, popular with locals. In a good position on the main road to Langley village, it is also a favourite venue for walkers and cyclists exploring the nearby Macclesfield Forest. Three regular ales are supplemented by two from the Punch list. Dogs and children are welcome. It is near to the Jarman Farm Caravan Club campsite. ⚒▷✿◑&Ⓐ🖵(14)♣Pᵗᵘ

Sutton Hall ⓛ
Bullocks Lane, SK11 0HE
✪ 11.30-11; 12-10.30 Sun ☎ (01260) 253211
🌐 suttonhall.co.uk
Beer range varies Ⓗ
Splendid 480-year-old manor house set in its own grounds, close to the Macclesfield Canal. Tastefully refurbished by Brunning & Price, it won the 2010 CAMRA National Pub Design Refurbishment Award. The interior is notable for its many secluded areas, snug, library and seven dining areas. While there is a strong focus on food, with an excellent menu, drinkers are more than welcome to enjoy the five real ales on offer, often from local breweries. Complemented by lovely gardens, this is a real gem. ⚒Q▷✿◑&🖵Pᵗᵘ

Swettenham

Swettenham Arms ⓛ ✪
Swettenham Village, Nr Congleton, CW12 2LF
✪ 12-11 ☎ (01477) 571284 🌐 swettenhamarms.co.uk
Beer range varies Ⓗ
Established country restaurant and pub with a small bar area and separate function room. Set in beautiful countryside, it is popular with walkers. The beer is well-tended by a committed and enthusiastic real ale fan. The frequently changing range of at least three ales is regularly supplemented with beers from local breweries including Tatton in Knutsford and Storm in Macclesfield. There is fresh coffee for the driver. ⚒Q▷✿◑&👄Pᵗᵘ

Tarvin

Stamford Bridge

Tarvin Road, Stamford Bridge, CH3 7HN (on B5132, close to jct with A51)

🕒 12-11 (10.30 Sun) ☎ (01829) 740229

🌐 stamfordbridgeinn.co.uk

Brimstage Piffle; Theakston Best Bitter; Weetwood Best Bitter, Old Dog; guest beers Ⓗ

Large refurbished former coaching inn on Watling Street old Roman road. The interior features a two-level, open-plan dining area and bar and lounge areas with two real fires. The pub specialises in food – Sunday roasts are popular and booking is recommended. There is a large lawn with a children's play area, and children are welcome inside until 7pm. Camping and caravan facilities are available nearby. ⚏Q⌖🕮❶Ⓓ🖧Å🚃♣P⌕

Tushingham

Blue Bell Inn Ⓛ

SY13 4QS (signed Bell o' t' Hill from A41)

🕒 closed Mon; 12-2, 6-11; 12-3, 7-11 Sun ☎ (01948) 662172

🌐 bluebellinn.net

Oakham JHB; Salopian Shropshire Gold; guest beers Ⓗ

Magnificent timber-framed 17th-century pub with plenty of atmosphere. A cobbled front leads to an ancient front door. One wall in the dining room reveals part of the original wattle and daub. Well-behaved dogs are welcome. Four caravan pitches are available in the paddock.
⚏Q⏚⌖❶Ⓓ🖧Å♣●P⌕

Warmingham

Bear's Paw Ⓛ

School Lane, CW11 3QN

🕒 12-11 (10.30 Sun) ☎ (01270) 526 317

🌐 thebearspaw.co.uk

Beartown Kodiak Gold; Weetwood Best Bitter, Eastgate, seasonal beers Ⓗ

A welcome return to the Guide for this pub which has been much refurbished after extensive fire damage. The Bear's Paw is now part of the same chain as the Grosvenor at Pulford and Pheasant at Higher Burwardsley – and it shows. Wood panels and bare floorboards dominate, creating a comfortable and homely feel. An extensive food menu is available with most food sourced locally. The cider is usually Westons 1st Quality.
⌖🖾❶Ⓓ♣●P⌕

Warrington

Albion Ⓛ

94 Battersby Lane, WA2 7EG (200m N of A57/A49 jct)

🕒 12 (10 Sat)-midnight; 12-1am Fri & Sat; 12-11 Sun

☎ (01925) 231820

Beer range varies Ⓗ

A previous winner of CAMRA Champion Pub of Cheshire, this large, multi-roomed community pub is on the edge of the town centre. The rooms all have character, including the reading room, and the pub supports both sports teams and community activities. Regular live music plays on Saturday night. Beer festivals are held in May, August, October and over the Christmas period. Snacks and light meals are available lunchtimes daily and 5-8pm Tuesday-Friday evenings (no food Mon). Sunday roasts are a highlight.
🖾❶Ⓓ🖧≠(Central)🚃♣●⌕🍴

Lower Angel

27 Buttermarket Street, WA1 2LY

🕒 11-11 (midnight Sat); 12-4 Sun ☎ (01925) 653326

Tetley Bitter; Theakston Mild; guest beers Ⓗ

The Lower Angel has now returned to its former glory. This two-roomed, friendly, town-centre hostelry offers up to six guest beers at any one time. It is also home to the Tipsy Angel Brewery – a one-barrel plant set up in 2010. Much Walker's Brewery memorabilia is a reminder of the pub's former ownership. 🖾❶🖧≠(Central)🚃♣●⌕

Tavern

25 Church Street, WA1 2SS

🕒 2-11; 12-11.30 Fri & Sat; 12-11 Sun ☎ 07789 151610

Beer range varies Ⓗ

Warrington town centre's oldest true free house, now the main outlet for the 4T's Brewery, and offering a wide range of up to eight beers. The single main room has a wood floor and furnishings, with an emphasis on sport on TV, especially football and Rugby League. Smokers also have a TV in the rear covered courtyard. A range of Scotch and Irish whiskies is available. At weekends extra cask beers are pulled into the Tavern Music Bar next door. 🖾≠(Central)🚃♣●⌕

Willey Moor

Willey Moor Lock Tavern

Tarporley Road, SY13 4HF (300m from A49) SJ534452

🕒 12-2.30, 6-11; 12-2.30, 7-10.30 Sun ☎ (01948) 663274

🌐 WilleyMoorLock.co.uk

Greene King Abbot, Old Speckled Hen; guest beers Ⓗ

Reached by a footbridge over the Llangollen Canal, the Willey Moor is a former lock-keeper's cottage and is popular with canal boaters and walkers. There is a range of at least three beers, rising to six in summer. The interior is decorated with local watercolour paintings and a collection of teapots. It has an outside terrace and an enclosed beer garden. ⚏🖾❶ⒹP

Wilmslow

Bollin Fee Ⓛ ✅

6-12 Swan Street, SK9 1HE

🕒 9-midnight (1am Thu; 2am Fri & Sat) ☎ (01625) 441850

Beer range varies Ⓗ

Recently refurbished Lloyds No.1 bar in the town centre and handy for the railway station. Furnishings range from cosy sofas to raised bar tables, and dining is available throughout. The beer range varies, with frequent guests from local breweries. Weekend nights are very busy. The pub runs a popular beer festival during the first week of every month. Outside, two beer gardens include areas for smoking. Free WiFi access is available.
Q⏚🖾❶Ⓓ🖧≠(Wilmslow)🚃(88,130,378)●⌕

King's Arms Ⓛ

Alderley Road, SK9 1PZ

🕒 12-1am ☎ (01625) 522187

Robinson's Unicorn, seasonal beers Ⓗ

Spacious, traditional, multi-roomed pub with a large central bar, brick-built with a wood-panelled interior, there is an interesting currency collection above the bar. Sky TV attracts football fans. Next door is the Chilli Banana Thai restaurant where you can order food to eat in the pub. B&B accommodation is available, with five en-suite rooms. ⏚🖾❶Ⓓ🖧🚃♣P⌕

Camelford

Masons Arms

11 Market Place, PL32 9PB (on A39) SX106837
🟢 11–midnight ☎ (01840) 213309
St Austell Trelawny, Tribute, Proper Job Ⓗ
Unpretentious two-room town pub with open stone walls and low beamed ceilings, more than 300 years old and popular with locals and visitors alike – children are welcome. The public bar is part tiled, part wooden, the separate lounge is carpeted, and the pub is decorated with many interesting knick-knacks including long-vanished domestic products, old toys, and an ancient pen and drum flow recorder. Home-cooked meals include a selection of fresh fish. The beer garden overlooks an early stage of the River Camel.
🏚Q🏵🍴◑♿🛏🚌(510,584,594)🕯

Charlestown

Harbourside Inn Ⓛ ✅

Charlestown Road, PL25 3NJ (on harbour front) SX029516
🟢 11–11 (midnight Fri & Sat); 12–11 Sun ☎ (01726) 76955
🌐 pierhousehotel.com/harbourside_inn_in_cornwall.htm
Draught Bass; St Austell Tribute; Sharp's Doom Bar, Special; Skinner's Betty Stogs, Cornish Knocker Ⓗ
The expansive glass frontage of this lively sports-oriented modern pub affords views of the tall ships moored in Charlestown's historic harbour, which has featured in numerous film and TV productions. A former harbourside warehouse, the charming single-bar interior features exposed stonework, slate and wooden flooring, with wood furnishings throughout. Up to seven ales are available from the bar menu. Good value food is served throughout the day. Popular sporting events are screened and live music features on Saturday evening.
🏵🍴◑♿🛏🚌(25B,525)🍴🕯

Crowlas

Star Inn Ⓛ

TR20 8DX (on A30 just E of Penzance)
🟢 11.30–11; 12–10.30 Sun ☎ (01736) 740375
Penzance Crowlas Bitter, Potion No 9; guest beers Ⓗ
Cornwall CAMRA Pub of the Year for two years running, this red-bricked roadside village free house is an ale-drinkers' paradise. The single long bar is festooned with handpumps, usually dispensing some beers from the pub's micro-brewery. There is a raised seating area to the right, and a pool table. A real locals' pub where beer quality reigns supreme and conversation abounds – no music, TV or noisy machines. Best to come by bus (stop nearby), as you will stay a while.
Q🏵🚌(17,18)🍴P🕯

Edmonton

Quarryman Inn Ⓛ

PL27 7JA (off A39 near Royal Cornwall Showground) SW965727
🟢 12–11 (10.30 Sun) ☎ (01208) 816444
Beer range varies Ⓗ
Conversation and banter thrive at this characterful and convivial free house, where mobile phone usage is prohibited. The quiet, comfortable interior divides into public bar and lounge, with separate dining area; the somewhat eclectic decor features local art. An ever-changing beer menu offers up to

four quality ales, and excellent meals feature locally-sourced produce. Situated near the county showground, a diversion to this ever-popular gem of a pub, frequented by locals and tourists alike, is well worth the effort.
🏚Q🏵🍴◑♿🛏🚌(510,555,594)♣🍴P🕯

Falmouth

Front Ⓛ

Custom House Quay, TR11 3JT (behind Trago Mills) SW811325
🟢 10 (12 winter)–midnight; 11–11 Sun ☎ (01326) 212168
🌐 thefrontfalmouth.co.uk
Skinner's Betty Stogs, Heligan Honey, Cornish Knocker; guest beers Ⓗ/Ⓖ
Tucked away in a corner of the picturesque Custom House Quay, this small cellar-style pub with a low-vaulted ceiling lies below Trago Mills store. A popular student haunt, a whole range of live entertainment is on offer during the evenings – folk, shanty singers, open mike and more. Guest beers constantly vary to provide a year-round beer festival. There's no food, but you may bring your own from various nearby outlets. A selection of ciders, foreign bottled beers and alcoholic ginger beer is also available. 🏵🚃(Town)🚌🍴

Oddfellows Arms

Quay Hill, TR11 3HG (off Arwenack Street) SW810324
🟢 12–11 (10.30 Sun) ☎ (01326) 218611
🌐 theoddfellowsarms.uk.com
Sharp's Own, Special Ⓗ**; guest beer** Ⓗ/Ⓖ
Reached via steep steps, this small, unpretentious and basic pub is a real community-focused local, although visitors are quickly made welcome. No food is available, but free tastings are often on offer, including cheese, home-made pickles or (in June) baking competition entries. An interesting, ever-changing guest ale is dispensed from a spare handpump or a cask racked on the bar. As well as pub games – darts, euchre, a pool room at the rear – the local gig-rowing activities are centred here.
🚃(Town)🚌♣

Seven Stars ★

The Moor, TR11 3QA
🟢 11–3, 6–11; 12–3, 7–10.30 Sun ☎ (01326) 312111
🌐 sevenstarsfalmouth.co.uk

Draught Bass; Sharp's Special; Skinner's Cornish Knocker; guest beer G
This old town-centre drinkers' pub with listed interior is presided over by a priest, one of the same family that has run it for seven generations. Little has changed in all that time, with a narrow tap room at the front and quieter snug to the rear; the corridor retains its 'bottle and jug' hatch. The front bar is festooned with donated key fobs, while mobile phones nailed to the wall indicate their use is banned. Wheal Maiden alcoholic ginger beer is available. Q❀☀️🍴≈(Town)🚍

Fowey

Galleon Inn
12 Fore Street, PL23 1AQ
☸ 10 (12 Sun)-11 (midnight summer) ☎ (01726) 833014
⊕ galleon-inn.co.uk
Sharp's Cornish Coaster, Doom Bar; guest beers H
Riverside pub in the town centre dating back 400 years, reached off Fore Street through a glass-covered corridor with a colourful marine life mural. The only free house in Fowey, it features mainly Cornish real ales and boasts delightful harbour views from the modernised main bar and conservatory dining area. Tables outside overlook the water and there is a heated, sheltered courtyard. A wide range of meals is available daily. Accommodation is en-suite, some rooms offering river views. ⋈Q❀🛏🍴◐Ġ🚍(25,524)⧖

Gwithian

Red River Inn L
1 Prosper Hill, TR27 5BW SW586411
☸ closed Tue; 12-2.30, 5.30-10.30 (11 Wed & Thu);
12-midnight Fri & Sat; 12-10.30 Sun ☎ (01736) 753223
⊕ red-river-inn.co.uk
Sharp's Doom Bar; Skinner's Betty Stogs; guest beers H
Thriving and convivial, this family-run free house is worth seeking out. The pleasant single bar interior features wood flooring and furnishings throughout. Family-friendly, it has separate dining areas and a quiet, relaxing atmosphere where conversation thrives; wood-burning stoves add warmth. The Skinner's and Sharp's beers may change, with up to three varying guest ales. Freshly cooked meals use quality local produce, and a hog roast is held on Friday evenings in summer; occasional beer festivals also feature.
⋈Q❀☀️◐Ġ🅿🚍(515,547)♣P⧖

Helston

Blue Anchor
50 Coinagehall Street, TR13 8EL SW658274
☸ 10.30-midnight; 10.30-11 Sun ☎ (01326) 562821
⊕ spingoales.com
Blue Anchor Spingo Jubilee IPA, Middle, Special, seasonal beer H
This rambling, unspoilt 15th-century pub and former monks' retreat has its own brewery at the back producing the famous Spingo beers with their unique flavour. Inside there are two small bars with stone floors plus a snug. Outside, a beer garden with bar and barbecue, and a skittle alley are available to hire. There are no bandits or piped music, though regular live entertainment is hosted in the bars and main areas. One of the few thatched buildings in town. Q☀️❀🍴🚍(2,34,82)⧖

Kingsand

Rising Sun Inn
The Green, PL10 1NH (off B3247) SX435505
☸ 12-11 (closed Mon winter); 12-10.30 Sun
☎ (01752) 822840
Courage Best Bitter; Sharp's Doom Bar; Skinner's Heligan Honey H
This welcoming 18th-century inn, popular yet peaceful, was once the customs and excise house in this coastal village of narrow streets. The pub has a single, spacious bar room carpeted throughout, wood-panelled walls decorated with nautical prints and photos of old Kingsand, and an interesting collection of large toby jug characters gazing down from a shelf. Access by car is difficult, especially in summer, with parking limited – the village public car park is advised. Live entertainment is hosted some Thursday and Saturday evenings. ⋈❀☀️◐P

Lelant Downs

Watermill Inn L
Old Coach Road, TR27 6LQ (off A3074, on secondary St Ives road) SW541364
☸ 12-11 ☎ (01736) 757912
Sharp's Doom Bar; Skinner's Betty Stogs; guest beer H
Near Lelant Saltings station, this former 18th-century mill house is now a family-friendly two-storey free house. Standing in beautiful surroundings, downstairs is a comfortable, traditionally styled single bar, separated into drinking and dining areas and hosting the original working watermill complete with millstones, where bar meals are served. Upstairs, the former mill loft functions as a stylish evenings-only restaurant specialising in seafood. An extensive beer garden straddles the mill stream. Two beer festivals are held annually. Live music plays on Friday night. ⋈Q❀◐≈(Saltings)🚍(14,17)P⧖

Lizard

Witchball
TR12 7NJ SW704125
☸ 12-11.30 (midnight Fri & Sat) ☎ (01326) 290662
⊕ witchball.co.uk
Choughs Witch Ball; St Austell Tribute; Skinner's Betty Stogs H
Originally a farm, this 15th-century cottage was a restaurant until 2007, when the owner created a cosy pub with bar, snug and separate dining room. Situated in the picturesque but remote Lizard village, it is the most southerly pub in mainland Britain, handy for the South West Coast Path. This true free house always offers one beer from each of three Cornish breweries, and an annual beer festival is held in August. Good and varied food is available every day. ⋈Q☸❀◐Ġ🅿🚍(537)♣⧖

Lostwithiel

Globe Inn L
3 North Street, PL22 0EG (close to railway station, over bridge) SX105598
☸ 12-2.30, 6-11 (midnight Fri & Sat) winter; 12-11 (midnight Fri & Sat) summer ☎ (01208) 872501 ⊕ globeinn.com
Sharp's Doom Bar; Skinner's Betty Stogs; guest beers H
Named after a 19th-century ship on which a former owner's relative died, this cosy 13th-century pub

CUMBRIA

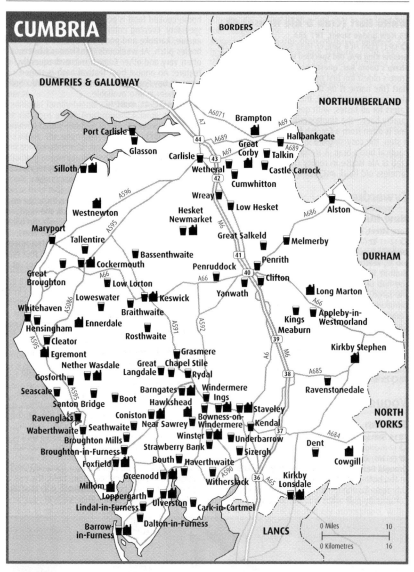

BORDERS

DUMFRIES & GALLOWAY

NORTHUMBERLAND

Brampton

Port Carlisle
Hallbankgate
Glasson
Great Corby
Talkin
Carlisle
Silloth
Wetheral
Castle Carrock
Cumwhitton
Wreay
Low Hesket
Alston
Westnewton
Hesket Newmarket
Maryport
Great Salkeld
Melmerby
Tallentire
DURHAM
Bassenthwaite
Penrith
Cockermouth
Penruddock
Great Broughton
Low Lorton
Clifton
Loweswater
Keswick
Yanwath
Long Marton
Whitehaven
Braithwaite
Appleby-in-Westmorland
Hensingham
Ennerdale
Kings Meaburn
Cleator
Rosthwaite
Egremont
Grasmere
Kirkby Stephen
Nether Wasdale
Great Langdale
Chapel Stile
Gosforth
Rydal
Seascale
Barngates
Windermere
Ravenstonedale
Santon Bridge
Boot
Hawkshead
Ings
Ravenglass
Coniston
Staveley
NORTH YORKS
Waberthwaite
Seathwaite
Near Sawrey
Bowness-on-Windermere
Kendal
Broughton Mills
Winster
Underbarrow
Dent
Broughton-in-Furness
Strawberry Bank
Sizergh
Cowgill
Foxfield
Bouth
Haverthwaite
Greenodd
Witherslack
Millom
Kirkby Lonsdale
Loppergarth
Ulverston
Lindal-in-Furness
Cark-in-Cartmel
Barrow-in-Furness
Dalton-in-Furness
LANCS

0 Miles   10
0 Kilometres   16

Alston

Cumberland Inn ♈ ⌑

Townfoot, CA9 3HX
✪ 12-11 ☎ (01434) 381875 ⊕ alstoncumberlandhotel.co.uk
Yates Bitter; guest beers ⊞
This is a family-run 19th-century inn overlooking
the South Tyne River. Close to the Coast-to-Coast
cycle route and Pennine Way, it is an ideal base to
explore the highest market town in England, with
its steep cobbled main street, South Tynedale
Railway, and the North Pennines. Two Cumbrian
beers are on handpump alongside a selection of
Northumbrian ales and beers from further
afield. Old Rosie and occasional Cumbrian ciders
and perry are stocked. Food is served all day until
9pm. Local CAMRA Pub of the Year 2009, 2010 and
2011. ⌂☎☼☞⍉⌘♿☒⊞(680)☉P⌐

Appleby-in-Westmorland

Golden Ball

4 High Wiend, CA16 6RD (off Boroughgate)
✪ 11 (12 Sun)-midnight ☎ (01768) 351493
Marston's Burton Bitter; guest beers, Pedigree ⊞
A traditional side-street pub which has changed
little over recent decades. The lounge is on the left
of the entrance and the bar is on the right, with a
TV and an excellent rock and blues juke-box. Both
bars are served from a central back-to-back bar
counter with up to six real ales. As well as a strong
local following, the pub attracts visitors, including
railway enthusiasts using the Settle to Carlisle line.
The patio has a large covered area and leads to the
garden with a children's play area.
⍟⌸⇄⊟(563)♣⌐

Barngates

Drunken Duck Inn 🅛 ✅
LA22 0NG (signed off the B5286 Hawkshead to Ambleside road) NY351013
🕒 11.30-11; 12-10.30 Sun ☎ (01539) 436347
🌐 drunkenduckinn.co.uk
Barngates Cat Nap; guest beers ⊞
Home of Barngates Brewery, the Duck always serves four of the 10 beers brewed here and brewery tours can be arranged. The bar has been extensively renovated to create a pleasing mix of local and modern styles. Lunchtime bar meals and the a la carte menu available in the dining-room in the evening are of an exceptionally high standard. The outside seating area at the front offers magnificent views of the fells to the north-east.
🏡Q❀🚌🅰🚊 ♠P⅃

Barrow-in-Furness

Duke of Edinburgh Hotel 🅛
Abbey Road, LA14 5QR
🕒 11-11.30 (midnight Fri & Sat); 11-11 Sun
☎ (01229) 821039 🌐 dukeofedinburghhotel.co.uk/thedukesbarbarrow
Lancaster Amber, Gold, Red, Black; Thwaites Original; guest beers ⊞
Situated on the edge of the town centre near the station, the Duke does not get as noisy as similar large bars in the town. The bar has an airy feel with modern, comfortable furniture and a fine open fire. Paintings by local artists are displayed around the walls. Good quality, reasonably priced bar meals are available, including pizzas. There is a separate restaurant and large function room. Beers are mainly from Lancaster (owned by the same company) and Thwaites, with guest ales too.
🏡🚌🅰👌🚊🖵

Kings Arms 🅛
Quarry Brow, Hawcoat, LA14 4HY
🕒 5.30 (4 Fri; 3 Sat)-11; 1-11 Sun ☎ (01229) 828137
Barngates Tag Lag; Copper Dragon Golden Pippin; Hawkshead Bitter ⊞
Now reopened as a free house, with a landlord who has previous CAMRA-award-winning experience and is committed to providing good quality real ale sourced mainly from local micro-breweries. There has been a pub on these premises since the 1860s and its reopening has been welcomed by people from near and far. The pub – which has very friendly staff – is small, with only two rooms, putting the emphasis on conversation. But mind your language – there is a swear box! Q🚌🖵(1)

Bassenthwaite

Sun Inn 🅛
CA12 4QP NY 230322
🕒 12-11 (10.30 Sun) ☎ (01768) 776439
🌐 thesunatbassenthwaite.co.uk
Jennings Bitter, Cumberland Ale ⊞
A traditional pub with a good selection of beers and excellent food. Exposed beams, open fires and friendly staff make this a pub with character and a welcoming atmosphere. There is seating both inside and out, often in secluded crannies that add to the atmosphere, befitting its history as a 17th-century inn. 🏡❀🅰 ♠P⅃

Boot

Brook House Inn
CA19 1TG
🕒 11-midnight ☎ (01946) 723288 🌐 brookhouseinn.co.uk
Cumbrian Legendary Langdale; Hawkshead Bitter; guest beers ⊞
Here in the heart of the Western Fells, with picturesque scenery, majestic high peaks, and waterfalls tumbling to the River Esk, this haven of top quality food and ale offers up to eight beers and ciders in summer. It is run by a dedicated family who, with two other local CAMRA award pubs, instigate the June Boot Beer Festival, when the valley throngs with real ale lovers and morris dancers, enjoying up to 100 beers. Local CAMRA Pub of the Year 2010.
🏡Q🛏❀🚌🅰🚊(Dalegarth)♠P⅃

Bouth

White Hart 🅛 ✅
LA12 8JB (off A590, 6 miles NE of Ulverston)
🕒 12-11 (10.30 Sun) ☎ (01229) 861229
🌐 whitehart-lakedistrict.co.uk
Black Sheep Best Bitter; Coniston Bluebird; Jennings Cumberland Ale ⊞
A 17th-century inn with everything you would expect from an ancient hostelry. Old farming and hunting implements adorn the walls, with horse brasses and hops on exposed beams. Slate-flagged floors and a wood-burning stove add to a welcoming atmosphere. The food is of a high standard, using locally sourced ingredients, and can be served in the bar, upstairs dining area, or on the terrace. In addition to a regular beer from Ulverston Brewery, guest ales usually come from local breweries. Magnificent views of the Rusland Valley and Coniston Old Man are a 20-minute walk away.
🏡🛏❀🚌🅰👌🅰♠P⅃

INDEPENDENT BREWERIES
Abraham Thompson Barrow-in-Furness
Barngates Barngates
Beckstones Millom
Bitter End Cockermouth
Blackbeck Egremont
Coniston Coniston
Croglin Kirkby Stephen
Cumberland Great Corby
Cumbrian Legendary Hawkshead
Dent Cowgill
Derwent Silloth
Ennerdale Ennerdale
Foxfield Foxfield
Geltsdale Brampton
Great Gable Egremont
Greenodd Greenodd
Hardknott Millom
Hawkshead Staveley
Hesket Newmarket Hesket Newmarket
Jennings (Marston's) Cockermouth
Keswick Keswick
Kirkby Lonsdale Kirkby Lonsdale
Strands Nether Wasdale
Stringers Ulverston
Tirril Long Marton
Ulverston Ulverston
Watermill Ings
Winster Valley Winster
Yates Westnewton

Bowness-on-Windermere
Royal Oak
Brantfell Road, LA23 3EG
🌐 11-11 (midnight Fri & Sat) ☎ (01539) 443970
🌐 royaloak-windermere.co.uk
**Coniston Bluebird; Jennings Cumberland Ale;
Marston's Pedigree; Taylor Landlord; Tetley Bitter;
guest beers** Ⓗ
This locals' pub offers a warm welcome to all – it is also a popular watering hole for walkers on the Dales Way route. Several old photos and adverts adorn the walls and a raised level to the rear has a pool table, electronic games and a juke-box. Many local sporting clubs use the pub as a base. Good value meals are served lunchtimes and evenings. The guest beer is often from a local micro-brewery.
🌣🛏◖❶🖥(599,618)♣P⅃⌐

Braithwaite
Middle Ruddings Country Inn Ⓛ
CA12 5RY (just off A66 at Braithwaite)
🌐 10.30-11 ☎ (01768) 778436 🌐 middle-ruddings.co.uk
Beer range varies Ⓗ
Country inn situated close to the A66 with great views of Skiddaw. It has three handpumps and only sells Cumbrian beers – the landlord visits the breweries before taking the beers. He has twice hosted a beer lover's dinner on behalf of CAMRA and is now to make it an annual event. The place is family-run and family-friendly, with children and dogs welcome. The restaurant also promotes local produce. ⚏Q❦🌣🛏◖❶🅰🖥(X5,74,74A)♣P⅃⌐🍴

Broughton Mills
Blacksmiths Arms ☆
LA20 6AX (1 mile off A593 Broughton-in-Furness to Coniston road, 2 miles N of Broughton) SD222905
🌐 12-2.30 (not Mon), 5-11; 12-11 Sat & Sun
☎ (01229) 716824 🌐 theblacksmithsarms.com
Beer range varies Ⓗ
Set in great walking country and listed in CAMRA's National Inventory of Historic Pub Interiors, this inn is well worth seeking out. It is unspoilt, featuring original beams, slate floors, oak panelling and a range, all dating back over 300 years. It comprises four public rooms of which three are available to diners; the home-cooked food enjoys considerable acclaim (no food Mon). The bar itself is reserved for drinkers, with an outside patio area making the most of the rural surroundings. Cider makes an appearance in summer. ⚏Q🌣❶🏠❹♣P

Broughton-in-Furness
Manor Arms Ⓛ
The Square, LA20 6HY
🌐 12-11.30 (midnight Fri & Sat); 12-11 Sun
☎ (01229) 716286 🌐 manorarmsthesquare.co.uk
Copper Dragon Golden Pippin; Yates Bitter; guest beers Ⓗ
This outstanding venue, where the Varty family has celebrated over 20 years of ownership, flies the flag for real ale in this popular Cumbrian village. Winner of numerous CAMRA awards, it has made it to the latter stages of the National Pub of the Year three times. The beer range promotes independent breweries and the eight handpumps are in themselves a mini beer festival. If you want to try real ale, this is the place. ⚏Q🛏🖥(7,511)♣♠🍴

Cark-in-Cartmel
Engine Inn Ⓛ
LA11 7NZ (3 miles W of Grange-over-Sands)
🌐 11.30 (12 Sun)-1am ☎ (01539) 558341
🌐 engineinn.co.uk
Beer range varies Ⓗ
Family-run traditional 17th-century inn, which took its name from the steam engines that used to service the local mills in Cark. It was tastefully refurbished during 2010, retaining the games room and restaurant area. Five en-suite letting rooms (refurbished at the same time) get booked very early for Cartmel Races and events at nearby Holker Hall. Beers from the Punch list are supplemented by ales from Ulverston and other local breweries. This venue will close earlier if quiet. Handy for the railway station.
⚏🌣🛏◖❶🅰🚃🖥(532)♣♠P⅃⌐

Carlisle
Howard Arms
107 Lowther Street, CA3 8ED
🌐 11-11; 12-10.30 Sun ☎ (01228) 532926
Caledonian Deuchars IPA; Theakston Best Bitter; guest beers Ⓗ
A beautiful original tiled exterior from pre-state management time welcomes visitors to this stalwart of the Guide. The landlord was awarded a certificate in recognition of 25 years of devotion to real ale by the local CAMRA branch (no keg here). A collection of divided rooms surrounds the horseshoe-shaped bar. Pictures of the acts that performed at the now sadly demolished theatre opposite are a reminder of bygone years.
Q🌣◖❶🚃🖥⅃⌐

King's Head Ⓛ
Fisher Street, CA3 8RF (behind old town hall)
🌐 10-11 (midnight Fri); 11-midnight Sat; 12-11 Sun
☎ (01228) 533797 🌐 kingsheadcarlisle.co.uk
Yates Bitter; guest beers Ⓗ
This CAMRA multi-award-winning pub is one of the oldest in Carlisle. Pictures of old Carlisle adorn the walls inside, and outside is an explanation of why Carlisle is not in the Domesday Book. Three guest beers include local brews, and takeaway beer cartons are available. The Lanes shopping centre and the castle and cathedral are nearby. Good-value meals are served at lunchtime. The covered smoking area to the back has a large TV and barbecue for parties. No children allowed.
🌣◖❶🖥♣⅃⌐

Linton Holme Ⓛ
82 Lindisfarne Street, CA1 2NB (E off London Road beside old tram sheds)
🌐 5 (4 Fri)-11; 12-11 Sat; 12-10.30 Sun ☎ (01228) 532637
Yates Bitter; guest beer Ⓗ
Former hotel retaining many original features including tiled mosaic floors, etched windows and a wonderful marble pillar outside. It is situated in a quiet residential area and is well worth making the effort to seek out. Inside, a variety of rooms all open out to a bar area where there is a large pool table suitable for use by wheelchair users. The guest ale is frequently from a micro-brewery. TVs show sporting events, and regular darts, pool and quiz nights are held. Local CAMRA award winner.
⚏🌣🖥(76)♣⅃⌐

Spinners Arms L
Cummersdale Road, Cummersdale, CA2 6BD (1 mile W of Carlisle off B5299)
🍺 6 (12 Sat & Sun)-midnight ☎ (01228) 532928
Beer range varies Ⓗ
Cosy family-friendly refurbished hostelry with unique animal-decorated gutters and a welcoming real fire. It is situated less than half a mile from Carlisle's south-western boundary, close to the Cumbrian Way and National Cycle Route 7, which run alongside the River Caldew. A good variety of guest ales from local, Cumbrian and northern micro-breweries is served. Live Cumbrian musicians perform on the first Saturday night of the month. Lunches are served Saturday and Sunday only, and evening bar meals 6-9pm (not Tue). Children (until 9pm) and well-behaved dogs are welcome. 🚶🕳️♿🚐(75)♣⬤

Woodrow Wilson L ✔
48 Botchergate, CA1 1QS
🍺 7am-midnight (12.30am Fri & Sat) ☎ (01228) 819942
Greene King Abbot; Marston's Pedigree; guest beers Ⓗ
Wetherspoon pub in a former Co-op building named after the former US president, who was born in Carlisle, offering the largest range of real ales in Carlisle, including a big proportion of local beers. Food is available all day till 10pm. At the rear there is a spacious heated patio for smokers. Children are welcome in some areas until 8pm. Five minutes' walk from the railway station and city centre. Q🕳️🅳♿🚋🚐⬤P⬤

Castle Carrock

Duke of Cumberland L
CA8 9LU
🍺 12-11.30; 12-midnight Sat & Sun ☎ (01228) 670341
Geltsdale Cold Fell; guest beers Ⓗ
Situated on the edge of a small village green at the foot of the northern Pennines, the Duke reopened in December 2009 after being closed for over 11 years. The open-plan L-shape format has the darts and TV area on the short leg and therefore not encroaching on the bar and dining area. The reopening coincided with the centenary of the local reservoir serving Carlisle, and some prints from the exhibition decorate the walls, creating interest for visitors. 🚶🕳️🅳♿♣P

Chapel Stile

Wainwrights Inn L ✔
LA22 9JH (on B5343 from Skelwith Bridge)
🍺 11.30 (12 Sun)-11 ☎ (01539) 438088 ⊕ langdale.co.uk/dine/wainwrights
Banks's Bitter; Jennings Cumberland Ale, Sneck Lifter; guest beers Ⓗ
Originally a farmhouse near the former Elterwater gunpowder works, the pub is now well known for its location in one of the most popular Lakeland valleys, for its quality of service and for the variety of its real ales. The stone-flagged bar area, where dogs are welcome, has four guest beers, usually from Cumbrian or small northern breweries, in addition to its regular ones. 🚶🕳️🅳♿🅰🚐(516)P⬤

Cleator

Brook 🍸 L
Trumpet Terrace, CA23 3DX (on A5086 between Cleator Moor and Egremont) NY021140
🍺 11-midnight (1am Fri & Sat) ☎ (01946) 811635
Taylor Landlord; Yates Golden Ale; guest beers Ⓗ
Candles and fairy lights, unstained beams, nooks and crannies, quirky ornaments, old photos and artworks, a chalkboard of forthcoming events (including birthdays) and a roaring fire, give this tiny, traditional Cumberland village pub a cosy and intimate community feel, where all are welcome. Food is exceptional and popular, the beers cherished by a young licensee who produces tasting notes to hand out. Runner-up CAMRA Pub of the Year three times, it deservedly gained both the local branch and Cumbria Pub of the Year Awards in 2011. 🚶🅳🚐(22,31,31A)♣⬤⬤

Clifton

George & Dragon
CA10 2ER
🍺 11-midnight ☎ (01768) 865381
⊕ georgeanddragonclifton.co.uk
Hawkshead Bitter; Lancaster Blonde; guest beer Ⓗ
Sitting on the A6, Clifton's only public house has a reputation for delicious home-cooked food, all sourced from the nearby Lowther estate. This welcoming 18th-century coaching inn has two rooms served from the bar, with comfy sofas, wooden tables, alcoves and open fires. The village is of historic interest, being the site of the last battle fought on English soil, in 1745, and there are also prehistoric burial sites close to the pub. 🚶Q🕳️�🅳🍴♿🅰🚐(106)P⬤

Cockermouth

1761
Market Place, CA13 9NH
🍺 4-11.30 (11 Mon & Tue); 2-11.30 Sat; 2-11 Sun
☎ (01900) 829282 ⊕ bar1761.co.uk
Yates Bitter Ⓗ
Named after the date from when records of the pub are available, 1761 is a traditional building with a tiled entrance, stove and fireplace, but with a modern feel. Beer is mainly from Cumbrian breweries, dispensed from four handpumps. It also offers a range of tapas and fairtrade coffee. There is a selection of board games available.
🕳️🚐(X4,X5,600)♣⬤

Swan
55 Kirkgate, CA13 9PH
🍺 6 (12 Sun)-midnight ☎ (01900) 822425
Jennings Dark Mild, Bitter, Cumberland Ale, Cocker Hoop Ⓗ
A friendly welcome from the landlady is guaranteed at this popular locals' pub. An easy five-minute walk from the Market Place, it has stone-flagged floors and low beams, helping to give a traditional feel. Regular quizzes and other community events are hosted. Well worth a visit for the Jennings Dark Mild alone, which is found in very few Jennings pubs, even in the town where it is brewed. 🚶Q♿🚐(X4,X5,600)♣

Tithe Barn
Station Street, CA13 9QW (opp Sainsbury's)
🍺 closed Mon; 4-11; 11-midnight Fri & Sat; 12-11 Sun
☎ (01900) 822179 ⊕ tithebarncockermouth.co.uk

Melmerby

Shepherds Inn Ⓛ
CA10 1HF
✪ 12 (5 Mon-Thu Oct-Feb)-11; 12-11 (10.30 winter) Sun
☎ (01768) 881741 ⊕ shepherdsinnmelmerby.co.uk
Tirril Old Faithful; guest beers Ⓗ
The original red sandstone pub dates back to 1789 but later incorporated an adjacent barn resulting in differing floor levels. The main bar is on the lower level but this too has a raised area usually used for food but also darts. Up to four guest beers are available depending on season, many of them local. Melmerby is an attractive village ideally situated to catch travellers on the scenic route from the North East to the Lakes. ⚑✿◑Ⓓ⊟Å♣P⅃

Near Sawrey

Tower Bank Arms Ⓛ
LA22 0LF (on B5285 6 miles S of Ambleside) SD370956
✪ closed 2.30-5.30 Mon-Fri winter; 11-11; 12-10.30 Sun
☎ (01539) 436334 ⊕ towerbankarms.co.uk
Hawkshead Bitter, Brodie's Prime; Cumbrian Legendary Loweswater Gold Ⓗ
All the features of a traditional 17th-century Lakeland inn are to be found here: slate floor, oak beams and a cooking range housing an open fire. Set in a beautiful rural location next to Hill Top, the former home of Beatrix Potter (which is open to the public), it can be very busy at holiday times. Food is served in the bar and restaurant. All beers are sourced locally. Children are welcome, as are dogs, but not in the restaurant. ⚑Q✿🛏◑Ⓓ♣♠P

Nether Wasdale

Strands Ⓛ
CA20 1ET NY125039
✪ 11-11; 12-10.30 Sun ☎ (01946) 726237
⊕ strandshotel.co.uk
Strands Brown Bitter, Errmmm..., Dafydd Ale, Angry Bee, T'Errmmm-inator Ⓗ
The home of an inventive brewer, up to six of his beers are on the bar. The May Festival of Beers features all 20 at once. Part of a comfortable hotel with reasonable rates and free WiFi, the bar is definitely a village pub. Interesting food is prepared from fresh, locally-sourced produce. Features include music nights, visiting morris dancers and a handy campsite – in the depths of the most beautiful scenery imaginable – making it a place not to be missed when visiting the Lake District. ⚑Q🛏✿🛏◑Ⓓ ÅP⅃

Penrith

Agricultural Hotel
Castlegate, CA11 7JE
✪ 11-11; 12-10.30 Sun ☎ (01768) 862622
⊕ the-agricultural-hotel.co.uk
Jennings Bitter, Cumberland Ale, Sneck Lifter; guest beers Ⓗ
The hotel is built from local sandstone and the bar and dining room are open plan, with steps from one to the other. There is also a small reception area. It has a Victorian shuttered bar of sash screens with four handpumps selling Jennings beers. Food is served in the large dining area as well as in the bar at quiet times. Very convenient for the railway station and nearby bus stops. ⚑Q🛏◑Ⓓ&🚲♣P⅃

Cross Keys Ⓛ
Carleton, CA11 8TP (E off A66 on A686 towards Alston)
✪ 12-2, 6-midnight; 12-midnight Sat; 12-11 Sun
☎ (01768) 865588
Theakston Black Bull Bitter; Tirril 1823; guest beer Ⓗ
Formerly a pub then closed and used as a house for many years, the Cross Keys was converted back to a pub and reopened in late 2008. With a very modern feel, the bar, pool room, darts, dining area and upstairs restaurant are spread over several levels. Food is served lunchtimes and evenings until 9pm. The LocAle is from the nearby Tirril Brewery. The owners also run Kyloes restaurant at the nearby Highland Drove pub in Great Salkeld. ⚑✿◑Ⓓ⊟&🚲(888)♣P⅃

Penruddock

Herdwick Inn Ⓛ
CA11 0QU
✪ 12-2.30, 5.30-11; 12-midnight Sat; 12-10.30 Sun
☎ (01768) 483007 ⊕ herdwickinn.com
Jennings Bitter, Cumberland Ale; guest beer Ⓗ
This charming 18th-century pub is named after the hardy breed of Cumbrian sheep. Situated north of the A66 between Penrith and Keswick, it is all that a traditional village pub should be and more. Original oak beams, open fireplaces and local stone walls add to the character of this local CAMRA award winner. The Herdwick includes a bar, games room, large garden and restaurant with excellent food. Close to the Coast-to-Coast cycle route, the inn has secure cycle storage. Accommodation is recommended. ⚑✿🛏◑Ⓓ Å♣P⅃

Port Carlisle

Hope & Anchor Ⓛ
CA7 5BU
✪ 12-11 summer; 12-2, 5-11 winter ☎ (01697) 351460
⊕ hopeandanchorinn.com
Cumberland Corby Ale; guest beer Ⓗ
A popular village pub well placed for walkers and cyclists on the Hadrian's Wall route. B&B accommodation is available in a double or family room. Car parking is shared with the bowling green across the road. A LocAle is stocked all year round, with two guest beers in summer. Meals are available all year, lunchtimes and evenings. ⚑✿🛏◑Ⓓ🚲(93)⅃

Ravenglass

Ratty Arms
The Ratty Arms, CA18 1SN (through mainline station or village car park)
✪ 11 (12 Sat & Sun)-midnight ☎ (01229) 717676
Greene King Ruddles Best Bitter; Jennings Cumberland Ale; Theakston Best Bitter; Whitehaven Ennerdale Blonde; Yates Bitter Ⓗ
A railway-themed pub deservedly popular with locals and tourists. It occupies the former station building at the junction of the main line and the 'La'al Ratty'; this narrow-gauge steam train runs deep into Upper Eskdale, with more good pubs, high fells and Roman remains to explore. Local attractions are Muncaster Castle, a Roman bathhouse, and an impressive estuary, rich in wildlife. Guest beers are often from Keswick and Whitehaven breweries. Excellent good-value food is served all day. ⚑Q✿◑Ⓓ&Å🚲🚲(6)P⅃

Ravenstonedale

Black Swan Inn L ✓

CA17 4NG (village signed off A685)
🕓 8.30am-11 (1am Fri & Sat); 11-midnight Sun
☎ (01539) 623204 ⊕ blackswanhotel.com
Black Sheep Best Bitter; John Smith's Bitter; guest beers H
An excellent example of a pub as the hub of a community, combining a Cask Marque accredited real ale outlet with the village shop, offering local produce. The bar serves up to five real ales, including two locals. It has a TV, and the lounge has adjoining dining-rooms where locally sourced food is served. Across the road is a well-maintained garden complete with stream. An annual beer and music event is held.
🏚Q❀❦❤⊕&♿🚃(564,569)♣P

Rosthwaite

Scafell Hotel (Riverside Bar)

CA12 5XB
🕓 11-11; 12-10.30 Sun ☎ (01768) 777208 ⊕ scafell.co.uk
Copper Dragon Golden Pippin; Jennings Bitter, Cumberland Ale; Theakston Old Peculier; guest beers H
The entrance to the Riverside Bar is tucked away down the side of the hotel, which may be the reason it has the feel of a real pub. Slate-flagged floors and coal fires make it welcoming on a wet day, while good weather can be enjoyed in the riverside garden. This is one of the few places in the area where Copper Dragon beers can be found regularly. Good quality food is reasonably priced.
🏚❀❤⊕♿A🚃(78)♣👤P

Rydal

Glen Rothay Hotel (Badger Bar) L

LA22 9LR
🕓 11-11 (10.30 Sun) ☎ (01539) 434500
⊕ theglenrothay.co.uk
Beer range varies H
This roadside inn dates from 1624 and is especially popular with walkers. There is a warming log fire in the main bar, where owners with dogs are welcome. The five beers on offer are all Cumbrian, reflecting the importance placed here on the environment. The separate Oak Room has a fireplace with a superb overmantel. A well-appointed dining-room looks out over Rydal Water. CAMRA members receive a discount.
🏚Q❀❦⊕❤🚃(555,599)♣P👤

Santon Bridge

Bridge Inn ✓

CA19 1UX (3 miles E of A595 at Holmrook) NY110016
🕓 11-midnight ☎ (01946) 726221 ⊕ santonbridgeinn.com
Jennings Bitter, Cumberland Ale, Cocker Hoop, Sneck Lifter; guest beers H
Once a modest mail coach halt, this venue is now an award-winning country inn with creaking floors, low beams and warming fires. A comprehensive range of Jenning's beers and home-cooked food make this a pub not to be missed. Guest beers are from the Marston range. In summer relax outside by the river and take part in the lovely mountain views. The inn hosts the immensely popular World's Biggest Liar competition in November.
🏚Q❧❀❦⊕♿A♣P👤

Seascale

Calder House Hotel

The Banks, CA20 1QP
🕓 12-2, 5.30-11 ☎ (019467) 28538 ⊕ calderhouse.co.uk
Jennings Bitter H
An imposing Victorian building which for 50 years was Calder Girls' School, in its heyday patronised by well-to-do society who sent their offspring to board in the flourishing seaside resort of Seascale. The interior retains many attractive Victorian features in good condition, as well as memorabilia echoing its past. Only 50 yards from the 18-hole golf club, it looks out across extensive sandy beaches and the Irish Sea to the Isle of Man. Local CAMRA Pub of the Season Autumn 2010.
🏚Q❧❀❦⊕♿&A⇌🚃(6,X6)♣P

Seathwaite

Newfield Inn L

LA20 6ED (6 miles N of Broughton) SD228960
🕓 11-11 ☎ (01229) 716208 ⊕ newfieldinn.co.uk
Jennings Cumberland Ale; Cumberland Legendary Dickie Doodle H
This 17th-century free house in the Duddon Valley, Wordsworth's favourite area, is an oasis for fell walkers and travellers passing through. Note the unique banded slate floor in the bar. Good food is served all day and steaks are a speciality. The spacious beer garden has excellent views towards the Coniston Fells. The pub is a venue for the Broughton Festival of Beer held each autumn.
🏚Q❀❦⊕♿&A♣P👤

Silloth

Albion

Eden Street, CA7 4AS
🕓 3 (7 Mon)-11; 4.30-11 winter; 2-midnight Fri; 12-midnight Sat & Sun ☎ (01697) 331321
Derwent Parsons Pledge; Tetley Mild H
Traditional one-bar pub with a separate family room containing a pool table and TV, well supported by friendly locals and summer visitors. Pictures of old Silloth decorate the walls along with two models of whaling trawlers. There are numerous photos celebrating the Isle of Man TT races; the local motorcycle club meets here on the first Sunday of each month and welcomes visitors. The nearby Derwent Brewery often tries out new beers at this hostelry. A holiday cottage is available next door. 🏚❧❀❦A🚃(38,60,71)♣👤

Sizergh

Strickland Arms L

LA8 8DZ (follow signs to Sizergh Castle off A590)
🕓 11.30-3.30, 5.30-midnight; 11.30-midnight Sat & summer; 12-10.30 Sun ☎ (01539) 561010 ⊕ thestricklandarms.com
Thwaites Wainwright, Lancaster Bomber; guest beers H
A fine-looking building set in a quiet location on the approach to Sizergh Castle. There are wooden and flagstoned floors in the large bar and dining area, with a further dining area upstairs. Three guest beers are all from the ever-increasing number of Cumbrian micro-breweries. Eclectic furniture and decorations abound in this warm and welcoming pub, which provides both locals and tourists with fine ales and food without compromise. 🏚Q❀⊕♿A🚃(X35,555)♣P👤

Staveley

Eagle & Child
Kendal Road, LA8 9LP
✪ 11-11; 12-10.30 Sun ☎ (01539) 821320
🌐 eaglechildinn.co.uk
Hawkshead Bitter; guest beers 🅷
A popular village local with a warm and friendly atmosphere and a welcoming fire in winter. The walls and ceiling are adorned with old prints, a collection of hats, and other memorabilia. Good value food, especially the lunchtime menu, is very popular. Local Cumbrian beers predominate in the guest beer range. The garden across the road overlooks the River Kent and holds a tented beer festival for both May and August bank holidays.
🏮☸🚪◑🖝🚉(555)🍴P⅃

Strawberry Bank

Masons Arms 🅛
Cartmel Fell, LA11 6NW SD413895
✪ 11.30-11; 12-10.30 Sun ☎ (01539) 568486
🌐 masonsarmsstrawberrybank.co.uk
Hawkshead Bitter, Lakeland Gold; Thwaites Wainwright; guest beers 🅷
Owned by the Individual Inns group, this picturesque pub is set on a hillside, with spectacular views across the Winster Valley. Two solid fuel ranges and three seating areas provide a cosy atmosphere in winter, while the outdoor seating and dining area is an idyllic location on a warm sunny day. Dogs are welcome in the garden only. The pub is very popular with walkers and the local community alike. 🏮Q🐾☸🚪◑🍴P⅃

Talkin

Blacksmiths Arms 🅛
CA8 1LE
✪ 12-3, 6-11 ☎ (01697) 73452 🌐 blacksmithstalkin.co.uk
Geltsdale Cold Fell, Brampton Bitter; Jennings Cumberland Ale; Yates Bitter 🅷
One of the most popular pubs in the area, the Blackies has been a regular Guide entry for the past 11 years. Immaculately maintained, its reputation is fully warranted – there is no TV, only subdued music, friendly staff and good food. With four real ales, it is also the best stocked bar in the vicinity. Local attractions include a nearby golf course and a country park. Now a family business, its future popularity and success appear assured.
🏮Q☸🚪◑🚉♿▲🍴P⅃

Tallentire

Bush Inn
CA13 0PT
✪ closed Mon; 5.30 (6 Tue & Wed)-midnight; 12-2, 7-11 Sun
☎ (01900) 823707
Beer range varies 🅷
Traditional Cumbrian village pub with simple decor, stone-flagged floors and low ceilings. The pub is at the centre of many village events and hosts monthly folk music evenings. Two guest beers are usually from northern and Scottish breweries; the house beer, Old Tallentire, is Robinson's Old Stockport. Meals are served in the restaurant Thursday-Saturday evenings and Sunday lunchtime. A previous CAMRA Pub of the Season and Pub of the Year runner-up. 🏮Q☸◑🚉(58)🍴P

Ulverston

Devonshire Arms 🅛
Braddyll Terrace, Victoria Road, LA12 0DH
✪ 4 (3 Thu & Fri)-11; 12-midnight Sat; 12-11 Sun
☎ (01229) 582537
Beer range varies 🅷
Situated between bus and train stations (adjacent to the railway bridge), The Dev is a large single-room pub. Distinct areas are formed by the use of comfortable bench seating. Two TVs show major sporting events, and there is a juke-box, pool, darts and dominoes. This is a real locals' pub, where all are welcome. Six handpumps serve superb ales from near and far. A beer festival is held on the May Day weekend. ☸▲🚉🚉🍴P⅃

Mill 🅛 ✪
Mill Street, LA12 7EB
✪ 11-11 (1am Fri & Sat); 11-10.30 Sun ☎ (01229) 581384
🌐 mill-at-ulverston.co.uk
Lancaster Amber, Blonde, Black, Red; guest beers 🅷
Tasteful conversion of the old town mill into a pub and restaurant by the Lancaster Brewery. The original waterwheel can be seen in the centre of the building and the mill race still runs through the elevated beer garden. Set over two floors, seating areas include a mix of sofas and armchairs. The Lancaster beer range is supplemented by four guests. Quality food is served in the bar and dining-room. ☸◑♿▲🚉🚉🍴⅃

Stan Laurel Inn 🅛
The Ellers, LA12 0AB
✪ 7-midnight Mon; 12-2.30, 6-midnight; 12-midnight Sun
☎ (01229) 582814 🌐 thestanlaurel.co.uk
Thwaites Original; guest beers 🅷
Close to the town centre and named after the town's most famous son, this welcoming pub focuses on locally produced beers – six handpulls are available in the main bar. Also popular for good value quality meals, booking is recommended (no food Mon). In summer, drinks can be enjoyed outside at picnic tables. There is a separate darts/pool room and a smaller room for diners.
☸🚪◑▲🚉🚉🍴P⅃

Swan Inn 🅛
Swan Street, LA12 7JX
✪ 3.30-11; 12-midnight Fri & Sat; 12-11 Sun
☎ (01229) 582519
Hawkshead Lakeland Gold, Brodie's Prime; Yates Bitter; guest beers 🅷
Easily accessed, just off the town centre, the Swan offers up to 10 real ales, many rare for the area, sourced from near and far, encompassing all styles and strengths. A single bar serves three drinking areas, one with a real fire. Tuesday is quiz night, and there is regular live music including an open mike session on Wednesday. The popular Oktoberfest and Easter beer festivals take place in a large marquee in the garden, with all beers on handpull. 🏮☸♿▲🚉🚉(6,6A,X35)🍴🍴⅃🚬

Underbarrow

Punchbowl Inn 🅛
LA8 8HQ
✪ closed Tue; 12-3, 6-11; 12-11 Sun ☎ (01539) 568234
Beer range varies 🅷
Traditional village inn on a scenic route between Kendal and Windermere Lake. The flagstone-floored main bar includes big leather sofas around

—an inglenook fireplace, and welcomes owners with dogs. It is popular with locals, walkers and those who love good beer with food. One beer from the Beckstones range is usually available, plus two other Cumbrian beers. There is a separate dining/ function room available. ♨Q❀◑▲♣P

Waberthwaite

Brown Cow
LA19 5YJ (on A595) SD106932
✪ 11.30-1am; 12-midnight Sun ☎ (01229) 717243
⊕ thebrowncowinn.com
Hawkshead Bitter; Stringers Dark Country; guest beers Ⓗ
Popular 100-year-old Cumbrian village pub offering up to seven interesting and varying real ales, always including a mild, often from Cumbrian and north Lancashire breweries. Meals use locally sourced food, particularly from the village butcher – by royal command. There is occasional live music, regular quiz nights and an annual beer festival. The Western Fells and Eskmeals nature reserve are close by. A winner of recent local CAMRA Branch awards. ♨⑤❀◑◑⑤▲◫(6X)♣♠P'—

Wetheral

Wheatsheaf Ⓛ ✓
CA4 8HD
✪ 12-11 (10.30 Sun) ☎ (01228) 560686
Cumberland Corby Bitter; Geltsdale Cold Fell; guest beers Ⓗ
Originally three separate rooms, now knocked into one, with a central bar, this venue is very much a local and well supported by those living nearby. It is situated a short walk up the hill from the village green in this picturesque village on the banks of the River Eden, only six miles east of Carlisle. The landlord has worked hard to increase sales of real ale and the bar now sports four handpumps, two dispensing locally brewed beers. ♨❀◑➡◫♣P'—

Whitehaven

Tavern Ⓛ
18 Tangier Street, CA28 7UX
✪ 12-midnight (2am Fri & Sat) ☎ (01946) 728283
Beer range varies Ⓗ
Popular pub with friendly staff in a building dated about 1700, close to the harbour and marina and only a short walk from the railway station, bus stop and public car park. It was closed for three years following a fire, but reopened in December 2009 completely refurbished while keeping many of its original features such as the stone-flagged floor, spiral staircase and well. It has a wood-burning stove, games room and upstairs bar. ♨⑤➡◫(6,8,30)♣'—

Windermere

Elleray Hotel ✓
2-6 Cross Street, LA23 1AE (200m from railway station)
✪ 12-11 (midnight Fri & Sat) ☎ (01539) 488464
⊕ ellerraywindermere.co.uk
Coniston Bluebird; Copper Dragon Golden Pippin; Jennings Cumberland Ale; guest beers Ⓗ
A friendly pub close to the town centre, with a large main bar and a separate restaurant. Four real ales are available throughout the year, with a stronger guest beer usually on offer during the winter months. Live music is performed most weekends, while the large beer garden is a sun-trap during the summer. CAMRA members receive a discount. ♨❀⑤◑⑤➡◫'—

Winster

Brown Horse Inn Ⓛ
LA23 3NR (on A5074)
✪ 12-11 ☎ (01359) 443443 ⊕ thebrownhorseinn.co.uk
Winster Valley Best Bitter, Old School; guest beers Ⓗ
Traditional rural pub with its own micro-brewery. It comprises a main bar with open beams and a log fire, and a separate restaurant area, but meals are served throughout. The bar has several large tables, and four real ales are always on handpump. Beware: the brewery's Lakes lager is keg. The outside seating area offers fine views of the surrounding countryside. Q❀☒◑⑤♣P'—

Witherslack

Derby Arms Hotel Ⓛ
LA11 6RN (just off A590)
✪ 12-3, 5.30-midnight; 12-midnight Sat & Sun
☎ (01539) 552207 ⊕ thederbyarms.co.uk
Cumberland Corby Ale; Hawkshead Bitter; Kirkby Lonsdale Ruskin's Bitter; Thwaites Wainwright, Lancaster Bomber Ⓗ
Part of the same group as the Strickland Arms at Sizergh, this pub was reopened, after several years of closure, by the Witherslack Community Land Trust, and remains very much a community hub. A large room with open fires is straight inside the front door, and there is more dining space in the adjoining rooms, with a snug and games room at the rear. The house beer, Jolly Boys Outing, is brewed by the Cumbrian Legendary Ales brewery. ♨Q☒◑⑤☒◫(X35)♣P'—

Wreay

Plough Inn Ⓛ
Wreay, CA4 0RL (5 miles S of Carlisle, W of A6)
✪ closed Mon; 12-2.30 (not Tue), 6-11 ☎ (01697) 475770
⊕ wreayplough.co.uk
Cumberland Corby Ale; guest beers Ⓗ
Five miles from the centre of Carlisle in a small, peaceful village, this pub is a real gem. It was bought some years ago with a view to redevelopment, but change of use was refused and it was tastefully extended by another purchaser. With a reputation for excellent food – locally sourced where possible – it is on two levels, with the main entrance and bar on the ground floor and dining tables down a few steps. ❀◑⑤▲P

Yanwath

Gate Inn ✓
CA10 2LF
✪ 12-11 (10.30 Sun) ☎ (01768) 862386
⊕ yanwathgate.com
Beer range varies Ⓗ
Cosy, convivial and welcoming 17th-century pub with a single bar area. It has an open fire, a wealth of beams, and scattered tables with candles. The restaurant is committed to quality Cumbrian ale and food, but this local dining pub of the year affords an equally warm welcome to drinkers wishing to try the three varying beers. A truly unmissable pub. ♨Q❀◑◫(108)♣P'—

DERBYSHIRE

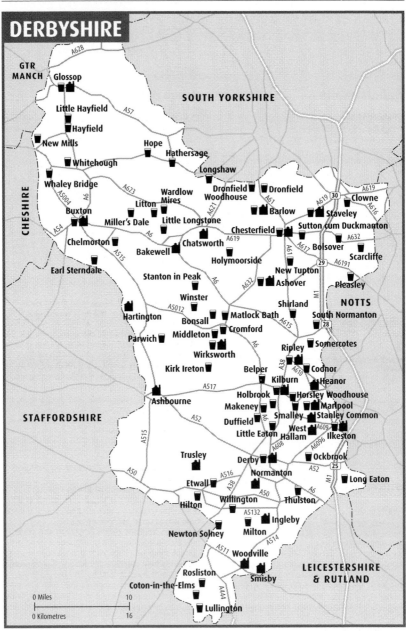

Ashover

Old Poets' Corner 🅛

Butts Road, S45 0EW (downhill from church)
☼ 12-11 ☎ (01246) 590888 ⊕ oldpoets.co.uk
Ashover Light Rale, Poets Tipple; guest beers Ⓗ
The home of Ashover Brewery, this mock-Tudor building has a warm, welcoming atmosphere, with open fires, candle-lit tables and hop-strewn beams. Choose from 10 handpumps, including regular Ashover beers, along with a range of guest ales, six traditional ciders, draught and bottled Belgian beers, and country wines. Winner of CAMRA National Cider Pub of the Year 2006 and local

CAMRA Pub of the Year 2009. Entertainment includes live music, weekly quiz, folk evenings and three beer festivals a year. Dogs are welcome.
🏚Q✿🛏◖◗&▲🚪(63,64)♣🐾P🔌

Barlow

Hare & Hounds 🅛

Commonside Road, S17 7SJ
☼ 12 (11 Sat)-11 ☎ (0114) 289 0464
Beer range varies Ⓗ
Friendly, traditional village local. The three rooms, configured around a central bar, comprise a public bar with wooden settles, a front room with

a coal fire, and a comfortable back room with panoramic views of the countryside. There is a separate games room. Beer from the Barlow Brewery, based in the village, is served via two handpumps. Fresh local produce is also for sale. ⚌Q⊟⊠(89,89A)♣P

Belper

Cross Keys
35 Market Place, DE56 1FZ
⊙ 5 (12 Sat)-midnight; 5-11 Sun ☎ (01773) 599191
Batemans Nailers Gold, XXXB; Draught Bass; guest beer Ⓗ
This early 19th-century pub was formerly used as accommodation for visiting theatre troupes, and as a meeting place for Druids and Oddfellows; it has also witnessed at least one murder in its time. The two rooms are divided by a central bar, and Nailers Gold is a bespoke house beer whose name reflects a long-gone industry in the town. Bar billiards and shove-ha'penny are played. World heritage status has rejuvenated this former mill town.
⊛⊟&⇌⊠(62,63)♣⌐

Bolsover

Blue Bell
57 High Street, S44 6HF
⊙ 12-3.30, 5-midnight; 12-3, 7-midnight Sun
☎ (01246) 823508 ⊕ bolsover.uk.com
Marston's Burton Bitter; Wychwood Hobgoblin; guest beers Ⓗ
Situated 200 metres from Bolsover Castle, and built in 1749, this historic pub still retains many of its original features. Speak nicely to the landlord and he will show you the old stable and coachman's quarters. This venue is a traditional two-roomed pub where you can rediscover the art of conversation. The panoramic view from the beer garden is spectacular, and excellent food is served lunchtimes and evenings. Q⊱⊛⊙⊟⊠♣P⌐

Bonsall

Barley Mow ⅋ Ⅼ
The Dale, DE4 2AY
⊙ closed Mon; 6-11; 12-midnight Sat; 12-10.30 Sun
☎ (01629) 825685 ⊕ barleymowbonsall.co.uk
Beer range varies Ⓗ
Tucked away in the south west of the village in an area popular with walkers – Limestone Way passes close by – this quirky one-roomed pub offers a varied range of ales from near and far, as well as real ciders. The world hen racing championship is held here in August and the enthusiastic owners also offer regular music nights, which vary from folk to rock. Limited bus service from Cromford to Bonsall. ⚌Q⊛⊙ Å⊠(M2)♣⬤P⎕

Buxton

Ramsay's Bar ⦿
Buckingham Hotel, 1 Burlington Road, SK17 9AS
⊙ 5-midnight ☎ (01298) 70481 ⊕ buckinghamhotel.co.uk
Howard Town Longdendale Light; Thornbridge Kipling; guest beers Ⓗ
This large public bar and adjoining lounge are part of the Buckingham Hotel, and offer one of the best ranges of micro-brewery beers in the area (six in summer, four in winter). Some ales are discounted during the happy hour – up to 8pm (10pm Sun &

Mon). The TV plays silently except for the occasional football match. The outdoor smoking area is heated. ⊛⊨⊙&Å⇌⊠P

Swan
40 High Street, SK17 6HB
⊙ 11-1am ☎ (01298) 23278
Greene King Old Speckled Hen; Storm seasonal beer; Tetley Bitter; guest beers Ⓗ
This is a hostelry that prides itself on being a drinkers' pub, with a friendly, welcoming atmosphere. Three rooms surround a central bar, and major sports matches are shown on TV, otherwise background music plays. There is always a Storm beer from nearby Macclesfield on handpump, and the pub has thriving darts and dominoes teams. Quiz night is Thursday, and there is a small patio outside. ⊛⊟⇌⊠♣P

Wye Bridge House ⦿
Fairfield Road, SK17 7DJ
⊙ 8-midnight (1am Fri & Sat) ☎ (01298) 70932
Greene King Ruddles Best Bitter, Abbot; Marston's Pedigree; guest beers Ⓗ
This Wetherspoon pub has a deserved reputation for serving an excellent selection of beers from local micros (usually three to five) in addition to two real ciders. The decor is modern, with a low ceiling, and a quieter area away from the bar. The substantial front patio is the best outdoor drinking area in Buxton. The place can be busy early evening. TVs play silently, and there are no sports channels. Parking nearby is limited.
Q⊛⊙&⇌⊠⬤

Chelmorton

Church Inn ⦿
Main Street, SK17 9SL
⊙ 12-3.30, 6.30-11; 12-11 Fri-Sun ☎ (01298) 85319
Adnams Bitter; Marston's Burton Bitter, Pedigree; guest beers Ⓗ
Set in beautiful surroundings opposite the local church, this traditional village pub caters for both locals and walkers. The main room is laid out for dining and good home-cooked food is on offer; however, a cosy pub atmosphere is maintained, with a low ceiling and real fire. Guest beers are usually from local micros. Parking is available at the end of the road in front of the pub and there is a patio area outside. Monday is quiz night.
⚌Q⊛⊨⊙Å♣

Chesterfield

Chesterfield Arms Ⅼ
Newbold Road, S41 7PH
⊙ 12-11 ☎ (01246) 236634
Everards Sunchaser; Fuller's London Pride; Leatherbritches CAD, Bounder; guest beers Ⓗ
Welcoming, family-run pub that is a real ale emporium, offering a selection of 10 beers – often from micros – augmented by six ciders and country wines. Oak-clad walls, open fires and hop-strewn beams create a relaxing ambience. A log-burning stove heats the barn area, open weekends, serving an extra six real ales. Tuesday is grill night, quiz night is Wednesday and curry night Thursday. Lunch is served on Sunday. Live music plays on the last Thursday of the month. Chesterfield CAMRA Pub of the Year 2010. ⚌⊛⊠(10)⬤P⌐

Wednesday and there are live events through the week. Light bar snacks are available daily.
🏨🎣⚲(Central/St David's)♣♠♨

Old Fire House
50 New North Road, EX4 4EP
✪ 12-2am (3am Fri & Sat; 1am Sun) ☎ (01392) 277279
Otter Amber; Wychwood Hobgoblin; guest beers Ⓖ
Close to the railway and bus stations, this popular city-centre pub serves good value food lunchtimes and evenings, including late-night pizzas and Sunday roasts. Up to eight (generally local) ales are available on gravity, and four real ciders adorn the bar. Regular ciders include Sam's, Autumn Mix, Sunnybrook and Sandford. The upper floor serves only bottled ales due to the distance from the cellar. There is live music Friday and Saturday evenings, and beer festivals during bank holidays.
🏨🍴&⚲(Central)🚗♠♨

Royal Oak Ⓛ ✅
79-81 Fore Street, Heavitree, EX1 2RN SX940924
✪ 11.30-11 (midnight Fri & Sat); 12-4, 7-11 Sun
☎ (01392) 254121
Adnams Broadside; Otter Amber, Ale; guest beers Ⓗ
Recently refurbished, this thatched, multi-room pub is on the B3183 into Exeter, and is close to two public car parks. Meals are served every lunchtime, while pies and pasties are available in the evenings. Outside, there is a rear courtyard with benches. A popular quiz night is held every Wednesday, and the team hope to make their summer beer festival an annual event.
🐕🍴🚗♣♨

Exmouth

First & Last Inn Ⓛ
10 Church Street, EX8 1PE
✪ 11-11 (11.30 Sat); 12-10.30 Sun ☎ (01395) 263275
Courage Directors; Otter Ale Ⓗ**; guest beer** Ⓖ
A genuine free house, this Victorian pub is near the town centre with a public car park opposite. Much enlarged by the present owners, it provides three distinct drinking areas, and an outside patio area with heated awnings. Games include pool and darts, and there is a skittle alley. Televised sport is prominent in the pub. Well-behaved dogs are welcome. The guest beer is usually from the West Country, and the cider is Thatchers Dry. The pub has air conditioning. 🐕&🎣🚗♣♠♨

Grove ✅
Esplanade, EX8 1BJ
✪ 11-11 ☎ (01395) 272101 🌐 groveexmouth.com
Wells Bombardier; Young's Bitter, Special; guest beers Ⓗ
A large Wells & Young's house at the western end of the esplanade, a 10- to 15-minute walk from the town centre, which is served by good bus and train links. Food is served 12-10pm daily. There is an upstairs bar that has good views across the bay and Exe estuary. Families are welcome, and the large beer garden is popular during the summer months. A quiz is held every Thursday evening. 🏨🐕🍴&

Holly Tree ✅
161 Withycombe Village Road, EX8 3AN (leave A376 at Gipsy Lane lights, then turn right)
✪ 11 (12 Sun)-midnight ☎ (01395) 273440
Greene King Abbot; Draught Bass; St Austell Proper Job, HSD; guest beers Ⓗ

A popular, traditional pub that concentrates on serving good beer. There are four darts, three pool and two euchre teams, and Sunday is quiz night. It is a pub much-supported by the local community, where beer and conversation predominate. Dogs are welcome at all times, and families until 7pm. There is a covered smoking area, plus two separate areas to sit outside. This is a warm, comfortable and friendly local. 🐕&🚗(97)♣P♨

Great Torrington

Royal Exchange Ⓛ
86 New Street, EX38 8BT
✪ 12-2.30 (not Mon & Tue), 5-midnight; 12-midnight Fri-Sun
☎ (01805) 623395
Forge IPA, Forged Porter Ⓗ**; guest beers** Ⓖ
Friendly, welcoming 17th-century main street local. The main bar has low beams, two handpumps, guest ales on gravity and Westons scrumpy available. The lower level side bar contains darts, pool and TV along with the rear restaurant/function/family room. Good quality food is available every day until 9pm, and Wednesday's curry night is exceptional. Children and dogs are welcome. An extremely popular, well-attended three day music and beer festival is held every year in late May/early June.
🏨🐕🐕🍴🚗(70,71,315)♣♠♨

Hartland

Anchor Inn Ⓛ
Fore Street, EX39 6BD
✪ closed Tue; 12-3, 6-11 Mon & Wed; 12-11 Thu-Sat; 12-4, 6-10.30 Sun ☎ (01237) 441414
🌐 theanchorinnhartland.co.uk
Forge Litehouse; guest beers Ⓗ
Brewery tap for the Forge Brewery situated nearby, this 16th-century coaching inn apparently has a few ghosts, but do not let that put you off. The main bar has a pool table and serves up to four real ales. The other is a cosy lounge bar. The restaurant, which can also be used for functions and entertainment, serves excellent home-cooked food using local produce. The patio area is covered and heated, with views of the local countryside. Well-behaved dogs welcome.
🏨🐕🍴🚗🌳🚗(319,519)♣P♨

Heddon Valley

Hunters Inn Ⓛ
EX31 4PY (signed from A399) SS655483
✪ 10-11 ☎ (01598) 763230 🌐 thehuntersinn.net
Exmoor Ale, Hart, Gold, Stag, Beast; guest beers Ⓗ
Popular large, renovated inn situated in a picturesque valley, where peacocks are allowed to wander freely. Several real ales are available, along with Sam's Medium cider from Winkleigh. The spacious front open area is the place to be in summer, when you might catch a visit from the North Devon Mummers. A three-day beer and music festival is held in early September. Food is served daily lunchtimes and evenings. The inn attracts walkers, hikers, cyclists, families with children, and dog owners. 🏨Q🐕🍴🍴&🌳♣♠P

Hexworthy

Forest Inn L

PL20 6SD (on unclassified road linking Holne and B3357) SX656726

☼ 11.30-3, 6-11 ☎ (01364) 631211 ⊕ theforestinn.co.uk

Teignworthy Reel Ale; guest beers H

Country inn situated in the Dartmoor Forest welcoming walkers, riders, anglers, canoeists, dogs and children. A regular Teignworthy beer is often supplemented by a guest from its range, and in summer another guest from further afield, plus local Countryman cider. Good home-made food is served using local produce wherever possible, and accommodation, including en-suite guest rooms and a bunkhouse, are offered. There are comfortable chesterfields in the bar, a cosy lounge and two dining-rooms. Horses can be stabled by prior arrangement. ♨Q☺⌂♿◑▲●P⏊

Hockworthy

Staple Cross Inn

Staple Cross, TA21 0NH

☼ closed Mon; 4 (12 Sat)-11; 12-10.30 Sun ☎ (01398) 361374 ⊕ staplecrossinn.co.uk

Otter Bitter; St Austell Tribute; guest beer H

On the border with Somerset, this attractive building (circa 1600) has been a pub since the early 1700s. There are rooms on either side of the bar, and a dining room. Wood-burning stoves are the main source of heating and provide a warm, friendly atmosphere in the winter months. The pub is frequented mainly by locals and used to be on an old trading route (wool and whisky). Good home-made food is available during opening hours. ♨Q☺◑🚗♣P

Holcombe

Smugglers Inn

27 Teignmouth Road, EX7 0LA (on A379 between Dawlish and Teignmouth)

☼ 11-11; 12-10.30 Sun ☎ (01626) 862301 ⊕ thesmugglersinn.net

Draught Bass; Teignworthy Reel Ale; guest beers H

With splendid coastal views, this roadside free house has an excellent reputation for food, served lunchtimes and evenings, the carvery being a particular attraction. The bar area has a wood-burning stove. There are two regular ales and one variable guest. The outside area is popular at all seasons, with its separate smokers' canopy. A mini beer festival is held towards the end of January, usually featuring about 14 ales, and regular entertainment is hosted. There is a car park, and buses pass the door. ♨☺◑♿▲🚗(2)P⏊

Holsworthy

Old Market Inn ♈ L ✅

Chapel Street, EX22 6AY (on A388 S of town square)

☼ 11-midnight (1am Fri & Sat); 12-11 Sun ☎ (01409) 253941 ⊕ oldmarketinn.com

Bays Gold G**; Clearwater Proper Ansome** H**; Forge Litehouse** G**, Porter** H**; Tintagel Castle Gold, Cornwall's Pride** G

Situated in an historic market town, this family-run inn is known for the quality of its beer and food. The free house has stillage for six casks at the end of the single bar, plus three handpumps and scrumpy cider from Winkleigh. Locally-sourced food is served in the spacious rear restaurant. Local comedy club acts appear regularly and during St Peter's Fair week in July a mini beer festival is held. Wednesdays are very busy thanks to a thriving livestock and food market. Local CAMRA Pub of the Year 2011. ♣🚗◑♿🚗(X9,X90)♣●P⏊

Rydon Inn

Rydon Road, EX22 7HU (½ mile W of Holsworthy on A3072 Bude road)

☼ closed Mon winter; 11.30-3, 6-11; 12-3, 6-10.30 (not winter) Sun ☎ (01409) 259444 ⊕ rydon-inn.com

Beer range varies H

This free house and licensed wedding venue is ideally situated near the market town of Holsworthy and the Cornish border. A modern extension to an original Devon longhouse, the thatched bar has a high vaulted ceiling serving West Country ales and Sam's Medium cider in winter. There is a large conservatory restaurant serving high quality locally sourced food, and a spacious garden area that leads down to a small lake with picturesque views of Holsworthy. Families with well-behaved children are welcome. ♨Q☺⌂◑♿▲🚗(X9,71,85)♣●P⏊

Honiton

Holt L

178 High Street, EX14 1LA

☼ closed Sun & Mon; 11-3, 5.30-11 (midnight Sat) ☎ (01404) 47707 ⊕ theholt-honiton.com

Otter Bitter, Amber, Bright, Ale, Head H

The Otter Brewery tap, formerly a wine bar, has been converted to a pub with a cosy bar at street level; there is a dining area upstairs. Both are smartly decorated, with plenty of exposed wood. The kitchen is in full view of the clientele. In addition to the restaurant there is a lunchtime menu, tapas, specials and smoked food available in the bar. Seasonal music festivals are held. Gastropub of the Year and winner of Taste of the West. ◑🚆🚗(20,52b,367)

Horsebridge

Royal Inn

PL19 8PJ (off the A384 Tavistock-Launceston road) SX401748

☼ 12-3, 7-11 (10.30 Sun) ☎ (01822) 870214 ⊕ royalinn.co.uk

Draught Bass; Skinner's Betty Stogs; St Austell Proper Job H**; guest beers** G

Originally built as a nunnery in 1437 by French Benedictine monks, the pub overlooks an old bridge on the River Tamar, connecting Devon to Cornwall. It now features half-panelling and stone floors in the bar and lounge, both traditional in style, with a further larger room off the lounge. The terraced gardens are suitable for children, who are welcome until 9pm. The guest beers are usually served on gravity, and the food is highly recommended. ♨Q☺◑♣P

Iddesleigh

Duke of York

EX19 8BG (off B3217 next to church) SS570083

☼ 11-11 (midnight Fri & Sat); 12-10.30 Sun ☎ (01837) 810253

Cotleigh Tawny Owl; Adnams Broadside; guest beers G

(left column partial entries, cut off at page edge)

Dartmoo[r] ...
Ⓗ/Ⓖ, Ne...
Grade II-...
back to...
farm. Th...
primarily...
lounge a...
Views of...
riverside...
by. Excell...
prepared...
♨Q☺☼...

Lee

Gramp...
Ilfracomb[e]...
office) SS4...
☼ 11-midn...
Beer rang...
Parts of t...
and, until...
there is a...
exposed s...
are from...
Winkleigh...
sourced. T...
between...
with touri...
and dogs...
every Frid[a]...

Lutton

Mounta...
Old Chapel...
☼ 12 (4.30...
Dartmoor J[a]...
A tradition[a]...
walls and...
Jail Ale, is...
guest ales,...
eight bottle...
is served d...
the foothill...
actually a c...
old local lar...

Manato[n]

Kestor I[n]...
TQ13 9UF (o[n]...
☼ 11-11 ((...
Dartmoor Le...
Spacious loc...
after a six-m...
shaped bar...
alcoves. The...
long dining...
functions. It...
selection of...
area of the...
selling basic...
in operation.

Meavy

Royal Oa[k]...
The Village, P...
☼ 11-11; 12-10...
⊕ royaloakinn.c...
Dartmoor IPA,...

✪ 12-midnight ☎ (01803) 200755
Bays Best; Butcombe Bitter; Otter Bitter; Sharp's Doom Bar; Shepherd Neame Spitfire; Wadworth 6X Ⓗ
Tucked away in the town centre and a few yards from the harbour, this is Torquay's oldest inn (circa 1540). A real ale haven with a listed cobbled floor and low-beamed ceilings, the pub has a truly nautical feel with a welcoming atmosphere, and is popular with locals and holidaymakers alike. It has a busy, roomy 70-seater restaurant serving highly-rated food. A narrow passageway outside, adorned with floral displays, makes a pleasant alfresco drinking area. Dogs on leads are welcome. Q❀◑🚋(12,32)⚊

Totnes

Bay Horse Inn
8 Cistern Street, TQ9 5SP
✪ 11 (12 Sun)-midnight ☎ (01803) 862088
🌐 bayhorsetotnes.com
Dartmoor Jail Ale; Otter Amber; guest beers Ⓗ
A 15th-century coaching inn, this quaint pub at the top of the picturesque town of Totnes serves a minimum of three real ales throughout the year. A bar menu is offered all day, with specials on a blackboard in the evening. Live jazz features on Sunday night, with folk and acoustic sessions on Monday and Thursday. Beer festivals are held at Easter, during the Totnes festival in September, and during the winter months. At the rear is a large, attractive garden with a heated patio and disabled access. ♨Q❀🛏◑🖶🚋⚊

Walkhampton

Walkhampton Inn Ⓛ
The Village, PL20 6JY SX533697
✪ 12-3, 6-11 (closed Mon); 12-3 Sun ☎ (01822) 855556
🌐 walkhamptoninn.co.uk
Dartmoor IPA, Jail Ale; guest beer Ⓗ
This pleasant 17th-century inn is tucked away in one of west Devon's many picturesque villages. It has a laid-back atmosphere and attracts locals as well as drinkers and diners from further afield. There is a good-sized beer garden to complement the wonderful interior. The husband and wife managers are very friendly, making everyone welcome. The food and drink are excellent, with Sunday lunchtime roasts a highlight, and beer and cider festivals are becoming annual fixtures. Morris dancers meet here every Wednesday evening. ♨Q❀🛏◑🚋(56)P

Whimple

New Fountain Inn Ⓛ
Church Road, EX5 2TA
✪ 12-2 (3 Sat), 6.30-11; 12-3, 7-10.30 Sun
☎ (01404) 822350
Teignworthy Reel Ale; guest beer Ⓖ
Small, friendly two-bar local in a lovely village, converted from cottages around 1890. A genuine free house, this pub has been owned by the

current licensee for 21 years. The handpumps are not in use; ale is fetched from the cellar. Extremely good value home-cooked food is served (no food Mon lunchtime, booking advisable for Sun lunch). The village heritage centre in the car park is well worth a visit. Opening hours may change; it is advisable to phone. ♨Q◑🖶🚆🚋♣P

Widecombe in the Moor

Rugglestone Inn
TQ13 7TF (¼ mile from village centre) SX721760
✪ 11.30-3, 6-midnight; 11.30-midnight Sat; 12-11 Sun
☎ (01364) 621327 🌐 rugglestoneinn.co.uk
Butcombe Bitter; St Austell Dartmoor Best; guest beer Ⓖ
Unspoilt pub in a splendid Dartmoor setting. Originally a cottage, the Grade II-listed building was converted to an inn back in 1832 and named after a local logan stone. The stone-flagged bar area has seating, with beer also served through a hatch in the passageway. An open fire warms the lounge. A wide selection of home-cooked food is available. Across the stream is a large grassed seating area with a shelter for bad weather (and smokers). Local farm cider is sold. The pub's car park is just down the road. ♨Q🐾❀◑🖶🔺♣P⚊

Yarcombe

Yarcombe Inn Ⓛ
EX14 9BD (on A30)
✪ 6 (12 Sat)-11; 11-3 Sun ☎ (01404) 861142
🌐 yarcombeinn.com
Branscombe Vale Branoc; Otter Amber; guest beers Ⓗ
Community pub run by local volunteers since 2010. Formerly a coaching inn and dating back to 1881, it was originally purchased by a member of Sir Francis Drake's family. The large traditional drinking area leads to a separate restaurant, with a skittle alley/function room upstairs. It also has a garden with wonderful views. One guest ale is served in winter, two in summer, sourced from outside the south-west. Live bands play on the last Saturday of the month; quiz night is the second Tuesday. Check the website or telephone first, as opening hours can change. ♨Q❀◑♣🍴P

Yarde Down

Poltimore Arms Ⓛ
Brayford, EX36 3HA (2 miles E of Brayford jct on A399) SS725356
✪ closed Mon; 12-2.30, 6-11; 12-3 Sun ☎ (01598) 710381
Beer range varies
Traditional Exmoor pub that has no mains electricity and is powered by generator, but offers a warm welcome with its roaring log fire and cosy atmosphere. It's now run by local landlords who have freshened up the bar and offer well-kept real ales. These are mainly from north Devon breweries and are served on gravity from behind the bar. An extensive lunchtime and evening menu is available, with excellent Sunday roasts. Well-behaved dogs are welcome. Shut-the-box and cribbage are played. ♨Q🐾❀◑♣P⚊

Yealmpton

Volunteer Inn Ⓛ
Fore Street, PL8 2JN SX578518

Good ale is the true and proper drink of Englishmen. He is not deserving of the name of Englishman who speaketh against ale, that is good ale.
George Borrow, Lavengro

✪ closed Mon; 12-3, 5-11; 12-11.30 Fri & Sat; 12-11 Sun
☎ (01752) 880463
Courage Best Bitter; Summerskills Hopscotch; guest beer Ⓗ
The popular Hopscotch may be rotated with seasonal brews from local brewer Summerskills in this cheerful two-bar village pub. The lively public bar has TV, while the welcoming lounge is more relaxed, featuring a wood-burning stove and comfortable seats and tables for dining. There is a beer garden at the rear. Food is served on Thursday, Friday and Saturday evenings, with roast dinners on Sunday lunchtime. Regular daytime buses pass the front door (not Sun).
🏰❀⬤◑⊟🚍(93,94)♣⌐

Yelverton

Rock Inn Ⓛ
PL20 6DS SX522679
✪ 11-11 (midnight Fri & Sat); 12-10.30 Sun
☎ (01822) 852022 ⊕ rockinndartmoor.co.uk
Dartmoor Legend, Jail Ale; Sharp's Doom Bar; St Austell Tribute Ⓗ
Ideally located on the Plymouth-Princetown road, this is a pub with something for everyone. The popular Lounge caters for tourists and diners, the Farmer's Bar offers a lovely fire and convivial chat, and the Back Bar caters for the younger element and those interested in sport and music. Quality ale is always in good condition. In recent times, live music and the occasional beer festival have come to the fore. 🏰Q❀◑⬤⊟🚍P⌐

Dolphin Hotel, Plymouth (Photo: Adrian Tierney-Jones)

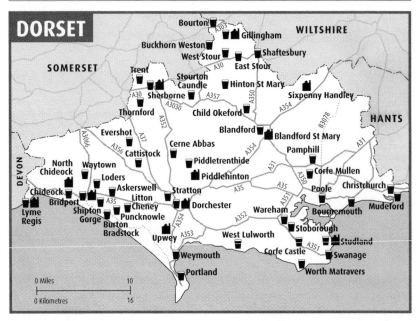

Askerswell

Spyway Inn ▼
DT2 9EP SY528933
✪ 12-3, 6-11 ☎ (01308) 485250 ⊕ spyway-inn.co.uk
Otter Bitter, Ale; guest beer G
This family-friendly 16th-century smugglers' inn is perched on a hill outside Askerswell on the road to the ancient Eggardon hill fort. In summer there is usually a guest beer and a cask of cider. The small lounge bar has beams and a woodburner; a further bar has tables for dining. The food menu features dishes made with locally-produced ingredients. Popular with locals and walkers, the sunny garden attracts families with a lovely view and a play area. Dogs are allowed in the garden. Local CAMRA Pub of the Year 2011. ▲Q✿❀♿◐ ♠P⏚—

Blandford

Dolphin ⏳ ✪
42 East Street, DT11 7DR
✪ 11.30-11 (midnight Thu-Sat) ☎ (01258) 456813
⊕ thedolphinblandford.co.uk
Dorset Piddle Jimmy Riddle, Piddle, Cocky Hop, Silent Slasher; guest beers H
Comfortable and friendly pub in the centre of town. The building dates back to the mid-1700s (becoming an inn in the mid-1800s) and retains many original features including wooden benches and oak panelling. A Dorset Piddle brewery tap, it offers the full range plus two guest ales, one from an independent micro-brewery. Excellent food is available daily lunchtimes and evenings until 9pm. Monday is quiz night and music sessions take place on Wednesday night. ▲◐➡♣

Railway Hotel ⏳ ✪
Oakfield Street, DT11 7EX (100m from B3082)
✪ 10-1am (2am Fri; 2.30am Sat) ☎ (01258) 456374
⊕ railwayblandford.com
Ringwood Best Bitter; Sixpenny Puffing Billy; guest beers H

Originally built in 1864 as a hotel serving Blandford Forum station, it lost its function when the line was axed in 1966. Now a free house, the Victorian pillared doorway leads to a central bar with sofas to the front and a dining area to the rear. This popular venue shows all major sporting events on numerous TVs, hosts live music on Saturday night and serves food until late. The outdoor heated area leads to a function room with a skittle alley. Home to the Blandford beer festival on the May bank holiday weekend. ✿◐➡(X8)♣♠⏚—

Bournemouth

Brunswick
199 Malmesbury Park Road, Charminster, BH8 8PX
✪ 11-11 (midnight Fri); 10-midnight Sat ☎ (01202) 290197
Greene King Abbot; Ringwood Best Bitter; guest beers H
This large community pub provides something for everyone. Separate public and lounge bars open on to a heated part-covered courtyard and atrium where children are welcome until 7pm. Several screens cater for sports fans. A Greene King pub, it offers a range of eight beers including guests from micro-breweries across Britain. Good value meals are available with Sunday roasts a highlight. Four minutes' walk from the bus stop with frequent services from the town centre and train station. Q❀◐⊟♿➡♣P⏚—

Cricketers Arms
41 Windham Road, Springbourne, BH1 4RN
✪ 11-11; 12-10.30 Sun ☎ (01202) 551589
Fuller's London Pride; guest beers H
A splendid Victorian gem dating back to 1847, making it Bournemouth's oldest pub. Just a short stroll from Bournemouth Travel Interchange, the public bar hosts pool, darts and shove-ha'penny. Mahogany and brass give the lounge a traditional feel. A vaulted ceiling dominates the converted stable room, once a boxing ring made famous by Freddie Mills, former world champion. Posters

advertise forthcoming guest ales. Sunday lunchtime roasts are legendary locally. Local CAMRA Pub of the Year 2009. ✿⊕&≈⊟♣P⊾

Goat & Tricycle ✓
27-29 West Hill Road, BH2 5PF
✪ 12-11 (11.30 Fri & Sat) ☎ (01202) 314220
⊕ goatandtricycle.co.uk
Wadworth Henry's IPA, 6X, JCB, seasonal beers; guest beers Ⓗ
Formerly two adjoining pubs, the buildings have been combined to form a popular and award-winning split-level venue. The cosy interior offers space for diners and drinkers alike. Eleven handpumps dispense Wadworth beers, Westons Original draught cider, and constantly changing guest beers mainly from small breweries. Good value food is served daily, with roasts on Sunday. A partly covered courtyard caters for smokers and alfresco drinking, and there is a separate meeting room available to hire. 🏠✿⊕&⊟(M1,M2)♣●⊾

Porterhouse ✓
113 Poole Road, Westbourne, BH4 9BG
✪ 11-11 (midnight Fri & Sat); 12-11 Sun ☎ (01202) 768586
Ringwood Best, Fortyniner, Old Thumper, seasonal beers; guest beer Ⓗ
Marked by a sign depicting the honest worker raising a flagon of porter, the cosy oak-panelled pub is popular with locals and visitors who come to enjoy a drink, chat and card or board games. Ringwood tied, it offers the full range, plus guests from the Marston's stable. There is also a good range of bottled beers, some notable foreign lagers, an extensive wine selection and some interesting whiskies. Lunches are served 12-2pm and dogs are welcome outside these hours.
Q⊲≈(Branksome)⊟(M1,M2)♣●

Royal Oak ♥
Wimborne Road, Kinson, BH10 7BB
✪ 10.30-11; 12-6 Sun ☎ (01202) 572305
⊕ royaloak-kinson.co.uk
Flack Manor Double Drop; Isle of Purbeck Studland Bay Wrecked; Sixpenny Best Bitter; guest beers Ⓗ
You can still play shove-ha'penny and darts in this popular two-bar community local, while enjoying a diverse range of background music from the landlord's collection. The lounge bar displays various prints of racing cars, has a real log fire and plays host to a disco on most Friday and Saturday evenings. Local CAMRA Pub of the Year 2010, but the pub is under threat of closure due to redevelopment of the area – the local branch is campaigning to keep it open. 🏠⊕⊟♣P

Bourton

White Lion Inn ✓
High Street, SP8 5AT
✪ 12-3, 5-11; 12-11 Sun ☎ (01747) 840866
⊕ whitelionbourton.co.uk
St Austell Tribute; Sharp's Doom Bar; guest beer Ⓗ
The White Lion is a traditional inn dating from 1763. Originally separate rooms, the cosy flagstoned bar has been opened out but there is always a quiet corner to be found. Taller customers are advised to 'duck or grouse'. The guest ales are often from the West Country and real cider is available. There is a cosy, intimate restaurant and, to the rear, a large beer garden. The pub is set back from the B3081 with parking opposite as well as in the car park. 🏠Q✿⊯⊲⊕⊟(158)●P

Bridport

Crown Inn ✓
59 West Bay Road, DT6 4AX (on roundabout on A35 between Bridport/West Bay)
✪ 11.30-11 (1am Fri & Sat); 11.30-10.30 Sun
☎ (01308) 422037
Palmers IPA, Copper, 200, Tally Ho! Ⓗ
A welcoming single-bar pub, much frequented by locals as well as beer and live music lovers from further afield. The full range of Palmer's beers is usually available and food is served throughout the day until 9pm. At weekends there is a great live music scene here, and a large TV screen, which can be viewed from around the bar, shows sports events. There is a beer garden and dogs are welcome. ✿⊕⊲⊟(X53)P

Tiger Inn ✓
14-16 Barrack Street, DT6 3LY
✪ 12-11 (midnight Fri); 11-midnight Sat ☎ (01308) 427543
⊕ tigerinnbridport.co.uk
Otter Bitter; Sharp's Doom Bar; guest beers Ⓗ
This bright and cheerful Victorian ale house offers a frequently changing beer list with two guests mainly from West Country breweries, plus Thatchers cider. The single split-level bar has TV for major sports events, plus pub games including a skittle alley. There is a small, attractive restaurant, a pretty garden and a heated courtyard. Close to the town centre and shops, the Tiger is a well-hidden secret worth seeking out. Separate beer and cider festivals are held annually. A CAMRA discount scheme is offered.
🏠✿⊯⊲&⊟(31)♣●⊾

Buckhorn Weston

Stapleton Arms ✓
Church Hill, SP8 5HS (between A303 and A30) ST757240
✪ 11-3, 6-11; 11-11 Sat & Sun ☎ (01963) 370396
⊕ thestapletonarms.com
Butcombe Bitter; Moor Revival; guest beers Ⓗ
Imposing village pub with a large car park and secluded garden. Inside is a relaxed and friendly spacious bar and adjacent dining area. The two guest beers often reflect the seasons, including milds in May, winter and summer ales – frequently from Moor Beer Company. Real ciders and a wide selection of draught and bottled foreign beers are always available. Excellent food is served throughout including hand-made pork pies, Scotch eggs and chutney. Children, dogs and muddy boots are welcome. Modern en-suite accommodation completes the Drink, Eat, Sleep motto.
🏠Q✿⊯⊲⊕●P

INDEPENDENT BREWERIES

Art Brew North Chideock
Dorset (DBC) Dorchester
Dorset Piddle Piddlehinton
DT Upwey (NEW)
Hall & Woodhouse/Badger Blandford St Mary
Isle of Purbeck Studland
Mighty Hop Lyme Regis (NEW)
Palmers Bridport
Sherborne Sherborne
Small Paul's Gillingham
Town Mill Lyme Regis
Wayland's Sixpenny Sixpenny Handley

Burton Bradstock

Three Horseshoes ✪
Mill Street, DT6 4QZ
☼ 11 (12 Sun)-11 ☎ (01308) 897259
⊕ three-horseshoes.com
Palmers Copper Ale, IPA, Dorset Gold Ⓗ
Old thatched cottage-style stone pub in attractive
village one mile from the sea. The L-shaped
beamed bar has a large inglenook with a log fire in
winter; furniture includes a table with bench seats
that was originally a double bed. Good value pub
food is served in the bar with a more extensive
menu specialising in local meat and fish available
in the attractive restaurant. Palmers Tally Ho! is
available when brewed. Outside is a small rear
garden and dogs and children are welcome. Very
busy in summer. ᴹ✿◑Ⓡ(X53)P

Cattistock

Fox & Hounds Inn ✪
Duck Street, DT2 0JH
☼ 12-3 (not Mon), 7-11; 12-3, 6-11.30 Thu-Sat; 12-3, 6-10.30
Sun ☎ (01300) 320444 ⊕ foxandhoundsinn.com
Palmers Copper Ale, IPA, seasonal beer Ⓗ
A warm welcome is assured at this delightful
village pub set in picturesque countryside. It offers
three well-kept Palmers ales and Thatchers cider
on handpump. Excellent home-cooked food is
served from a daily-changing menu (booking
advised). Steak night is Thursday, folk music night
is the second Monday of the month, and poetry
group is every other Tuesday. The pub is home to
several teams and clubs from crib to cricket, and a
function room is available. Dogs are welcome –
they can even enjoy their own bar snack. Taste of
Dorset Pub of the Year 2009 and 2010.
ᴹQ✿✍◑&Ⓡ(D11,212)♣♠P⁑

Cerne Abbas

Royal Oak
23 Long Street, DT2 7JG
☼ 11-3, 6-11 ☎ (01300) 341797
⊕ royaloakcerneabbas.co.uk
Badger First Gold, seasonal beer Ⓗ
A quaint thatched inn with lots of character,
atmosphere and good service. Dating from 1540,
the Royal Oak is the oldest pub in the village. The
present landlord has been welcomed back after an
absence of 15 years and offers good lunchtime and
evening menus as well as daily specials. The ales
are from Hall & Woodhouse. ᴹ✿◑⁑

Chideock

Clock House
Main Street, DT6 6JN
☼ 12-3, 6-11; 12-11 summer ☎ (01297) 489423
Otter Bitter, Ale; guest beer Ⓗ
Thatched family-owned free house a mile from the
sea. The comfortable bar has an adjoining spacious
dining room. In addition to the two Otter beers,
there is a guest beer (usually Bass) and Westons
cider on handpump. During the summer, meals are
served all day, plus takeaways. A dedicated games
annexe is home to many local teams. Dogs and
children are welcome. Community and national
charities are well supported, assisted by a large
charity library. Caravans are permitted at the
campsite. ᴹ✿◑▲Ⓡ(31,X53)♣♠P⁑

Child Okeford

Saxon Inn
Gold Hill, DT11 8HD (along narrow lane N of village)
ST829135
☼ 12-3, 6-11 ☎ (01258) 860310 ⊕ saxoninn.co.uk
Butcombe Bitter; Ringwood Best Bitter; guest beer Ⓗ
Situated at the north end of the village, close to the
iron age hill forts of Hambledon and Hod Hill near
the Stour Valley Way, this comfortable inn was
converted from three farm cottages in the 1950s.
Served by a corner bar, the main room has an open
fire and low beams, and there is an adjoining
panelled lounge with a wood-burning stove. A
delicious range of meals is offered including daily
specials. The large, quiet garden is at the rear.
ᴹQ✿✍◑&♣P

Christchurch

Olde George Inn ✪
2A Castle Street, BH23 1DT
☼ 10.30-11 (midnight Fri & Sat) ☎ (01202) 479383
Dorset Piddle Jimmy Riddle, Piddle, Silent Slasher;
guest beers Ⓗ
Lovely old coaching inn, a short walk from the
historic priory church. In earlier times the journey
could be made by secret underground passage. The
pub was the original tap for the Dorset Piddle
brewery, and the full range is usually available plus
two guests, often sourced locally. The heated
courtyard provides a pleasant seating area and
seasonal beer festivals are held in a marquee.
Excellent food is available all day. Dog friendly.
✿◑&⇌Ⓡ(1b,1c)♣⁑

Corfe Castle

Royal British Legion Club
East Street, BH20 5EQ (on A351)
☼ 12-3, 6-11; 12-midnight Sat; 12-10.30 Sun
☎ (01929) 430591
Ringwood Best Bitter; Taylor Landlord; guest beer Ⓗ
Built in Purbeck stone, this club has a small bar
area with upholstered bench seating, wooden
tables and chairs, and a lovely garden with access
to the car park and clubhouse. Traditional sports
include darts and shove-ha'penny, plus a boules
court outside. Filled rolls are available at the bar.
Major sporting events are screened on TV.
Occasionally there is live entertainment on
Saturday evening. Entry is with a CAMRA
membership card or a copy of this Guide.
✿⇌(Swanage Railway)Ⓡ(40)♣P⁑

Corfe Mullen

Lambs Green Inn ✪
Lambs Green lane, BH21 3DN (500m S of A31)
☼ 11-11 (10.30 Sun) ☎ (01202) 881974
Brains The Rev James; Ringwood Best Bitter; Sharp's
Doom Bar; guest beers Ⓗ
Part of the Mitchells & Butler Vintage Inns group,
this former farmhouse retains the original low
ceilings and small rooms, giving it a rustic feel. Six
handpumps offer up to three guest ales – a range
of beer styles is usually available. There is an
extensive dining area serving a full menu all day
every day. The large rear garden is a real sun-trap,
has extensive views over Wimborne Minster, and
hosts a beer festival in the summer.
ᴹ✿◑&▲Ⓡ(3)P⁑

Dorchester

Blue Raddle
9 Church Street, DT1 1JN
☼ 11.30-3 (not Mon), 6.30-11; 12-3, 7-10.30 Sun
☎ (01305) 267762 ⊕ theblueraddle.co.uk
Otter Bitter; Plain Ales Sheep Dip; Sharp's Doom Bar; guest beers ℍ
Popular, genuine, town-centre free house with friendly staff and an enthusiastic landlord. In addition to the three regular beers, two interesting guest ales and local ciders are also on offer. The house beer is brewed by Plain Ales. Good locally-sourced food is served lunchtimes and Thursday, Friday and Saturday evenings. The pub takes part in local events and hosts monthly folk music nights. Piped comedy and Private Eye are available in the conveniences. No children, but dogs allowed. Local CAMRA Pub of the Year 2009.
Q⑪&≠(South)🚋♣🖐

Colliton Club
Colliton House, Colliton Park, DT1 1XJ (opp county hall and crown court)
☼ 9-3, 6-11.30; 10-3.30, 7-midnight Sat; closed Sun & bank hols ☎ (01305) 224503
Greene King Abbot; Hop Back Odyssey; St Austell Tribute, Cousin Jack; guest beers ℍ
Thriving club opposite County Council HQ with six real ales always available. The club is housed in the mainly 17th-century Grade II-listed Colliton House and welcomes CAMRA members – just show your membership card. Busy in and out of office hours, this is a popular meeting place for a number of local associations. Evening snacks are served. Dogs and children are allowed. CAMRA Wessex Region Club of the Year 2007, 2008, 2010 and 2011.
Q❀⑪≠(South/West)🚋♣ᴸ

Royal Oak ✓
21-22 High West Street, DT1 1UW
☼ 7am-midnight (1am Fri & Sat) ☎ (01305) 755910
Greene King Ruddles Best Bitter, Abbot; guest beers ℍ
This former Eldridge Pope town-centre pub has been converted to a Wetherspoon, with multiple rooms on split levels. Very busy, particularly at weekends, it is popular with drinkers and diners of all ages. In addition to the two regular beers there are usually at least five varying guests, often including ales from the Cottage Brewery. Outside is a covered decked patio area. ❀⑪&≠🚋🖐ᴸ

East Stour

King's Arms
East Stour Common, SP8 5NB (on A30, W of Shaftesbury)
☼ 12-3, 5.30-11; 12-midnight Sat; 12-10.30 Sun
☎ (01747) 838325 ⊕ thekingsarmsdorset.co.uk
Palmers Copper Ale; St Austell Tribute; guest beer ℍ
This imposing roadside pub is a multi-roomed establishment served by a single bar with many areas for diners. The bar is popular with locals, who have a say in the selection of the guest beers. The Scottish-influenced food is excellent, made with locally-sourced ingredients where possible, and the all-day Sunday carvery can be very busy. The patio and large enclosed garden are a welcome addition in summer, and there is comfortable accommodation all year round. Dogs and muddy boots are welcome in the bar. ⋈❀🛏⑪&Pᴸ

Evershot

Acorn Inn ✓
28 Fore Street, DT2 0JW
☼ 11-11 (10.30 Sun) ☎ (01935) 83228 ⊕ acorn-inn.co.uk
Otter Ale; guest beers ℍ
This small, attractive 16th-century hotel has a fine pillared porch on the village main street. A large flagstoned room at the back is known as the village bar, adorned with local photographs and a wood-burning stove – a smaller bar and restaurant are at the front. There are always two ales available, and often a third, plus Somerset cider. Look out for the annual beer and cider festivals. This is the coaching inn that was mentioned in Thomas Hardy's Tess of the d'Urbervilles as 'The Sow & Acorn'.
⋈Q🐕❀🛏⑪♣🖐Pᴸ

Gillingham

Wine Bar
Queen Street, SP8 4DZ
☼ closed Mon; 12-2.30, 6.30-11 (midnight Fri & Sat); 12-midnight Sun ☎ (01747) 825825 ⊕ wineandgrill.co.uk
Fuller's London Pride; St Austell Tribute; guest beer ℍ
Once a confectionery shop, this stone-built town pub has been extensively modernised and is now a contemporary bar and grill. The regular beers are complemented by a guest ale, often from a Dorset micro. An annual beer festival is held in early August. The food is good value and there is a Sunday carvery. Music nights are held on the first and third Tuesdays, and the bar is extremely busy on Friday and Saturday nights. Outside is a large, secluded garden and decking area. ❀⑪&▲≠ᴸ

Hinton St Mary

White Horse
DT10 1NA (off B3092)
☼ closed Mon; 12-3, 6-11; 12-3, 7-11 Sun ☎ (01258) 472723
Beer range varies ℍ
This 16th-century Grade II-listed stone building is a genuine old-fashioned public house at the heart of the community. With wooden beams throughout, the public bar features stone flooring and an open fire, while the lounge is cosy and home to resident ghost. A friendly welcome is extended to all including families and pets. No music, machines or TV spoil the atmosphere. Two beers are usually available. Excellent home-prepared food is served throughout and there is a small but pretty garden.
⋈Q❀⑪&🚋(309)♣Pᴸ

Litton Cheney

White Horse ✓
DT2 9AT SY549900
☼ 12-3 (not Mon), 5-11; 12-midnight Sat; 12-10 Sun
☎ (01308) 482539
Palmers IPA, Gold, 200 ℍ
True country pub south-west of the village, beside a stream and a YHA, with friendly and helpful staff. At least two ales from the Palmer's range are offered at all times. The open-plan bar has a stone-flagged floor and wood-burning stove. Darts and dominoes are played and there is a boules pitch outside for the summer. A well-thought-out menu offers local freshly-cooked food (no food Sun eve or Mon). Disabled access is reasonable but the WC doors are narrow. Dog-friendly.
⋈Q🐕❀⑪♣🖐Pᴸ

Loders

Loders Arms
DT6 3SA
☼ 11.30-3, 6.30-11; 12-3 Sun ☎ (01308) 422431
⊕ lodersarmsbridport.com
Palmers Copper Ale, IPA, 200, Tally Ho! Ⓗ
Seventeenth-century hamstone pub in an attractive village with a long pine-panelled bar with log fire, rustic furniture, brasses and old prints. A pretty dining room offers traditional pub food with friendly service. Outside, the patio and garden have lovely views over the hillside. A skittle alley is available to hire. Popular with locals, walkers and tourists alike, children and dogs are welcome.
🏨🏠🍴◑ ▲♣ ♠P

Lyme Regis

Royal Standard ✔
25 Marine Parade, DT7 3QF
☼ 10-11 ☎ (01297) 442637
⊕ theroyalstandardlymeregis.co.uk
Palmers Copper Ale, IPA, 200 Ⓗ
Popular 400-year-old pub with a restaurant and beach-side terrace. Interior stained glass, originally from the Three Cups Hotel, depicts the the Duke of Monmouth landing on the nearby beach in the 1685 rebellion. Other Palmer's beers are available in rotation. Home-cooked meals feature local produce and freshly caught fish, with several vegetarian dishes on the menu. Ideal for families, the pub can be busy in the summer, and usually stays open late at weekends.
🏨🐾🏠🍴◑ ♿▲🚌(31,X53)♣♠

Volunteer Ⓛ
31 Broad Street, DT7 3QE
☼ 11-11; 12-10.30 Sun ☎ (01297) 442214
Branscombe Vale Donegal Ⓖ**; St Austell Tribute; guest beers** Ⓗ
Old two-room pub in the heart of this historic seaside town, a few steps from the seafront, with a lovely olde-worlde atmosphere. Popular with locals, the main bar buzzes with jolly banter and conversation. The house beer, Donegal, is Branscombe Vale Best and is stillaged behind the bar. A rotating choice of West Country ales is on offer. Dogs and well-behaved owners are allowed, and families are welcome in the dining room.
🏨🐾🍴▲🚌(31, X53)♣

Mudeford

Nelson Tavern ✔
75 Mudeford, BH23 3NJ
☼ 10-11.30 (11 Sun) ☎ (01202) 485105
⊕ nelsontavern.com
Ringwood Best Bitter, Fortyniner; guest beers Ⓗ
Situated a short walk from Avon Beach and Mudeford Quay, you are assured of a warm welcome at this traditional single-bar village pub. Ales from Yeovil and Bowman breweries regularly feature on the guest list, with a third guest and real ciders available direct from the cellar. This popular pub hosts three beer festivals a year in the garden over the bank holiday weekends. It also features regular live music, excellent Thai cuisine and Sky Sports. Dogs are welcome.
🏨🏠◑ ♿🚌(X12,1c)♣P♠

Ship in Distress ✔
66 Stanpit, BH23 3NA (off B3059 at Purewell Cross)
SZ172926
☼ 11-midnight (11 Sun) ☎ (01202) 485123
⊕ theshipindistress.com
Adnams Broadside; Ringwood Best Bitter; guest beers Ⓗ
Formerly a snuff factory, boys' school and home to the Avon Brewery before conversion to a pub in 1899, this attractive roadside establishment is steeped in history and is said to have been the home of smuggler John Streete. With a large open lounge-style main bar, a small comfortable snug and an award-winning restaurant, this pub has something for everyone. The walls are adorned with a mix of local photographs and maritime memorabilia – the original beams can still be viewed behind the bar. Q🏠🍴◑ 🍺♿🚌(1a,1c)♣P♠

Pamphill

Vine Inn ★
Vine Hill, BH21 4EE (off B3082) ST994003
☼ 11 (12 Sun)-3, 7-10.30 ☎ (01202) 882259
Fuller's London Pride Ⓗ**; guest beer** Ⓖ
Featured in CAMRA's National Inventory of Historic Pub Interiors, this old bakehouse was converted by the landlady's grandfather. It comprises a tiny public bar, lounge and upstairs family/games room. The resplendent garden has heating and a climbing frame. Ciders include Westons plus local Cider by Rosie. Sandwiches and a hearty ploughman's lunch are served (lunchtime only) – a knock on the window indicates it is ready to collect. A conker and pumpkin festival is held in September. Q🐾🏠🍴♣ ♠P♠🍴

Piddletrenthide

Piddle Inn ✔
DT2 7QF
☼ 11.30 (12 Sun)-midnight ☎ (01300) 348468
⊕ piddleinn.co.uk
Dorset Piddle Piddle; St Austell Tribute; guest beer Ⓖ
Named after the river on whose banks it stands, this is the closest pub to the Dorset Piddle Brewery serving its ales. It has a spacious single bar, and is brightly decorated throughout. A large restaurant seats 50, with dining also available in the bar. Popular locally, it hosts regular events including live music. There is a sunny garden and riverside patio. AA 4-star rooms are available. Children and dogs are welcome. 🏨🏠🍴◑ ♿🚌(D13,323)♣P♠

Poole

Bermuda Triangle
10 Parr Street, Lower Parkstone, BH14 0JY
☼ 12-2.30, 5-11 (midnight Fri); 12-midnight Sat; 12-11 Sun
☎ (01202) 748087
Beer range varies Ⓗ
As the name suggests, this bustling, multi-award-winning pub explores the mystery of the Triangle and carries a nautical theme. The single-room bar has a split-level interior and is bedecked with an intriguing range of curios, maps, newspaper cuttings and even part of an aircraft wing. Run by the same owner for 20 years, the bar has four handpumps offering an ever-changing range of ales sourced from far and wide alongside speciality German lagers and foreign beers.
🏠🚃(Parkstone)🚌(M1)

Blue Boar
29 Market Close, BH15 1NE
🕑 12-11 (midnight Fri & Sat) ☎ (01202) 682247
Fuller's London Pride, seasonal beer; Gale's Seafarers Ale, HSB Ⓗ
A former merchant's house dating back to 1750, Poole's only Fuller's house is situated a two-minute walk from the High Street. The large main bar is comfortable, while the atmospheric cellar bar hosts sports events and a quiz every Sunday. Both bars are bedecked with nautical artefacts including photographs and a brief history. Pub food is served from a reasonably priced bar menu. There are two TV screens and a large function room. A former local CAMRA Pub of the Year. ᴀₘQ🏵️🕙🌙⟰⟵

Branksome Railway Hotel
429 Poole Road, Branksome, BH12 1DQ (opp train station)
🕑 11-11 (midnight Fri & Sat); 12-10.30 Sun
☎ (01202) 769555 ⊕ branksomerailwayhotel.co.uk
Hop Back Summer Lightning; Otter Ale; guest beer Ⓗ
This Victorian station hotel dating from 1894 still serves the main Weymouth to Waterloo rail link. The large open-plan interior is divided into two areas, both served by one bar. The front area has a pool table and games machines with some seating. The rear space has more comfortable seats with views of passing trains. A DJ and occasional live music play at weekends. En-suite accommodation is offered and a function room is available for hire. ⟼◀◗🔁⟵(Branksome)🚌(M1,M2)♣P

Brewhouse
68 High Street, BH15 1DA
🕑 11-11; 12-10.30 Sun ☎ (01202) 685288
⊕ milkstreetbrewery.co.uk
Milk Street Mermaid, Beer, seasonal beers; guest beers Ⓗ
This popular local is owned by the Milk Street Brewery of Frome, Somerset. The split-level interior has a bar at street level with two pool tables at the rear. Beers include Mermaid, which is almost exclusively brewed for the people of Poole, along with two other Milk Street beers and one well-chosen guest ale. You can sit outside and watch the world go by, or there is a patio at the back. 🏵️⟵🚌♣⟵

Bricklayers Arms
41 Parr Street, Ashley Cross, BH14 0JX
🕑 12-2.30, 5-11 (midnight Fri); 12-midnight Sat; 12-11 Sun
☎ (01202) 740304
Greene King Abbot; Hop Back Summer Lightning; Ringwood Best Bitter; guest beers Ⓗ
This popular free house located in the heart of Lower Parkstone has recently been refurbished. The single L-shaped bar serves a main area with an open fireplace. There is a large beer garden at the back with a raised, decked space offering pleasant views towards the local church. Food is not served here and no children under 14 are allowed in the bar. Free WiFi is available. ᴀₘQ🏵️⟵(Parkstone)🚌(M1)

Portland

Corner House
49 Straits, DT5 1HG
🕑 10 (12 Sun)-11 ☎ (01305) 822526
Adnams Bitter; Greene King Old Speckled Hen; St Austell Tribute Ⓗ
Local street-corner community public house situated on a through route (A354) to Portland's famous lighthouse at the Bill. A shrine to the 'naval tot', this single bar pub has attractive stained glass windows and a side room with comfortable chairs. Bar snacks are available. Disabled access is good and the pub is dog and child friendly. Q⟵🏵️⟵♣

Royal Portland Arms
40 Fortuneswell, DT5 1LZ
🕑 11-11.50 (12.50am Fri & Sat); 12-11.30 Sun
☎ (01305) 862255
Beer range varies Ⓖ
Full of character, this Portland-stone pub stands alongside the main road, with public car parks nearby. More than 200 years old, George III is reputed to have stopped here for a drink and some Portland mutton on a visit to the island. Inside you will find basic, homely furnishings and a friendly welcome for all. Regular live music and other locally attended events are hosted. Bar snacks are offered and a changing range of mainly West Country ales and ciders is served on gravity dispense. Q🚌(1)♣●🗓️

Puncknowle

Crown Inn ✅
DT2 9BN
🕑 12-3, 6-11; 12-11 (not winter eve) Sun ☎ (01308) 897711
Palmers Copper Ale, IPA, 200 Ⓗ
Lovely 16th-century thatched pub in the village – pronounced 'Punnel'. The bar has an open fire and books to read if you don't want to join in the conversation with the friendly staff and locals. Tally Ho! is added to the beer range when brewed. Locally sourced home-cooked food is available in the bar and restaurant (no food winter Mon eve). There is a large garden at the back, and children and dogs are welcome. ᴀₘQ⟵🏵️⟼◀◗⟵🚌(210)●

Shaftesbury

Mitre
23 High Street, SP7 8JE
🕑 10.30-11 (midnight Fri & Sat); 12-10.30 Sun
☎ (01747) 853002
Wells Bombardier; Young's Bitter, Special, seasonal beers Ⓗ
Historic pub close to the town hall at the top of Gold Hill, with grand views overlooking the beautiful Blackmore Vale. Popular with younger drinkers but catering for all, an extensive food menu ranges from morning coffee to cream teas to good pub food. The Mitre runs crib and darts teams and hosts charity quizzes as well as occasional live music nights. Seasonal beers from the Wells & Young's range change regularly. ᴀₘ⟵🏵️◗⟵🚌♣⟵

Sherborne

Digby Tap ✅
Cooks Lane, DT9 3NS
🕑 11 (12 Sun)-11 ☎ (01935) 813148 ⊕ digbytap.co.uk
Beer range varies Ⓗ
Hidden away between the railway station and the abbey, Sherborne's only free house is worth seeking out for the building alone, which dates back to the 16th century. It was once the parish workhouse and many features of the original building remain. The interior feels like stepping back in time a generation, yet the pub remains

popular with all ages. A supporter of West Country ales, beers come from small breweries all over the region. There are benches on a paved area outside for summer drinking. Excellent value food is served at lunchtime. ᴍQ✿◑ᵹ♿⇌🚃♨

Shipton Gorge

New Inn ✪
Shipton Road, DT6 4LT SY498927
✪ 11 (12 Sun)-3, 6-11 ☎ (01308) 897302
Palmers Copper, IPA Ⓗ
Well-off the beaten track, this pub was saved from permanent closure in 2006 by a group of local people. In the past few years it has become the focal point for a range of village activities. Two Palmer's ales are available in the bar. Good food is served in the adjoining dining room lunchtimes and evenings, including vegetarian options (by arrangement only, Sun to Tue eves). The pub is closed on Sunday nights and Mondays for a few weeks each side of Christmas, but open every day from March. Q✿◑ᵹ🚃(210)P

Stoborough

King's Arms
1-3 Corfe Road, BH20 5AB (adjacent to B3075)
✪ 11-3, 5-midnight ☎ (01929) 552705
⊕ thekingsarms-stoborough.co.uk
Black Sheep Best Bitter; Isle of Purbeck Fossil Fuel; Ringwood Best Bitter; guest beer Ⓗ
This 17th-century village inn hosted Cromwell's troops in 1642 and was historically a butchers' – the old meat hooks are still evident in the canopy of the thatched roof. Featuring a wide variety of guest ales and one real cider, the pub has a pleasant, cosy atmosphere. The outdoor drinking area is a must in summer and the perfect place to enjoy the annual beer festival. A spacious restaurant-style area offers excellent pub food including light snacks, vegetarian options and locally-sourced meat. Closing time is usually later at weekends. ᴍQ✿◑ᵹ🚃(40)♨P♨

Stourton Caundle

Trooper Inn
Golden Hill, DT10 2JW (1½ miles E of A357) ST715149
✪ 12-2.30 (not Mon), 7 (6 Wed & Thu)-midnight; 12-3.30, 7-midnight Sun ☎ (01963) 362405
Beer range varies Ⓗ
Stone-built, single-room community pub with a separate function room/skittle alley. There is an attached camping and caravan site and a children's play area next to the beer garden. Good food is available lunchtimes and early evenings including a popular Friday fish and chips night. There are two changing ales and farmhouse cider, and an annual beer festival is hosted. Dogs and walkers are welcome. There are plans for a micro-brewery. Q✿◑ᵹ⚘♨P

Stratton

Saxon Arms
20 The Square, DT2 9WG
✪ 11-3, 5.15-11; 11-11 Sat & Sun ☎ (01305) 260020
⊕ thesaxon-stratton.co.uk
Ringwood Best Bitter; Taylor Landlord; guest beers Ⓗ
Celebrating its 10th anniversary in 2011, this flint and thatch pub has the feel of a country inn.

Outside, a patio area overlooks the village green. Inside, the bar divides into three areas – one a dining space serving quality food featuring locally-sourced ingredients. Already an integral part of the local community, this attractive pub is popular in the summer months. The two guest beers are often from local breweries. ᴍ✿◑ᵹ🚃P

Studland

Bankes Arms
Watery Lane, BH19 3AU
✪ 11-11 ☎ (01929) 450225 ⊕ bankesarms.com
Isle of Purbeck Best Bitter, Fossil Fuel, Solar Power, Studland Bay Wrecked, IPA; guest beers Ⓗ
This National-Trust-owned country inn, well-over 200 years old and smothered in Virginia creeper, is home to the Isle of Purbeck Brewery. Among the nine handpumps you will find most of the range, along with guest beers from other micro-breweries and home-made 'real' lager Purbex. Superb food can be enjoyed in the pub or the huge garden overlooking Poole Bay and Old Harry Rocks. There is a four-day beer festival in August.
ᴍQ✿🚪◑⚓🚃(50)♨P

Swanage

Red Lion
63 High Street, BH19 2LY
✪ 11-11.30; 12-11 Sun ☎ (01929) 423533
⊕ redlionswanage.co.uk
Palmers Copper Ale; Ringwood Best Bitter; Sharp's Doom Bar; Taylor Landlord Ⓗ; **guest beers** Ⓖ
This 17th-century hostelry retains many traditional features. It serves up to six real ales in the summer, often from local breweries, but what makes the pub special are the ciders – Westons full range, plus a variety of bottled ciders and perry. The refurbished restaurant offers an extensive selection of food. Live music occasionally features. The garden is busy in warm weather. Popular with locals and tourists, the pub is handy for the beach, Swanage steam railway and the South West Coast Path.
✿🚪◑⎕⇌(Swanage Railway)🚃(40,50)⚘♨P♨

White Swan Ⓛ
31 High Street, The Square, BH19 2LJ
✪ 11-11 ☎ (01929) 423804 ⊕ whiteswanswanage.co.uk
Dorset Piddle Piddle; Palmers Copper Ale; guest beer Ⓗ
Close to the sea in the heart of Swanage, this Dorset Piddle pub caters for all. Across four levels are a pool table, TV, sofas and dining areas; upstairs are five luxury en-suite rooms. To the rear is a walled patio and street seating at the front. The bar serves at least two ales from the Piddle range and guests from local breweries. A well-priced menu includes vegetarian and children's options, and for entertainment there is occasional live music.
⊱✿🚪◑⇌(Swanage Railway)🚃(50)⚘P♨

Thornford

King's Arms
Pound Road, DT9 6QD
✪ 12-2.30 (not Mon or Wed), 6-11; 12-2.30, 6-10.30 (closed winter eves) Sun ☎ (01935) 872294
⊕ kingsarmsthornford.co.uk
Beer range varies Ⓗ

Traditional free house in the centre of the village owned by the local Digby Estates, with three pumps normally offering beers from Otter, Butcombe and another brewery. The bar area is simple in decor, and offers a warm welcome to drinkers and diners alike. Food is also available as part of a take-away service for villagers (but no food Mon). There is also a coffee morning on Tuesday 10am-noon. ⚶⚙①⋈♣P⌐

Trent

Rose & Crown ✪
DT9 4SL 589185
✪ closed Mon; 12-3, 6-11; 12-11 Sat; 12-10 Sun
☎ (01935) 850776 ⊕ roseandcrowntrent.co.uk
Wadworth Henry's IPA, 6X, seasonal beers; guest beer Ⓗ
Large 14th-century pub in the west end of the village near the church – Charles II hid here en route to France. The bar has flagstones and beams, and the cosy snug has an open fire. Wadworth Horizon and The Bishop's Tipple alternate with seasonal and guest beers. The conservatory dining area has lovely views over the extensive garden and surrounding countryside. Excellent locally-sourced food is always popular (booking advised). Families, walkers and cyclists are all welcome here. ⚶Q⚙①&P⌐

Wareham

Black Bear Hotel
14 South Street, BH20 4LT
✪ 7.30am-midnight ☎ (01929) 553339
Ringwood Best Bitter, Fortyniner; Wychwood Hobgoblin Ⓗ
Dating from the 18th century, this coaching inn has a stone-floor corridor running through the centre, leading to a restaurant and beer garden at the back. The two front rooms feature fine wood panelling – the bar is in the room to the right. Further down the corridor is a cosy room with comfortable sofas. A large black bear above the entrance makes the hotel easily recognisable and a distinguishing feature on the town's high street. ⚶Q⚙⊨①⊟&⋈⊟(40,X53)⌐

Duke of Wellington ✪
7 East Street, BH20 4NN
✪ 11-11 (11.30 Fri & Sat); 12-11 Sun ☎ (01929) 553015
Hop Back Summer Lightning; Isle of Purbeck Fossil Fuel; Ringwood Best Bitter; guest beers Ⓗ
Bustling town-centre pub where six handpumps dispense a selection of regular and guest ales. One beer changes on a monthly basis, with local breweries well represented. Photographs of Wareham adorn the wood-panelled walls, and the restauraunt area has a distinctly maritime theme. Visitors can relax in front of the cosy fireplace in winter, and for warmer weather there is an enclosed beer garden that provides a secluded spot to enjoy a cool beer. ⚶Q⚙⊨①⋈⊟(40)♣⌐

King's Arms ✪
41 North Street, BH20 4AD
✪ 11-11; 12-10.30 Sun ☎ (01929) 552503
Ringwood Best Bitter; guest beers Ⓗ
A fine example of a traditional 16th-century public house. The frontage is unspoilt with a thatched roof and hanging baskets. The original flagstone floor and warming open fire add character to the cosy

oak-beamed interior. Fine food is available at affordable prices, with a separate dining area where a frame in one of the walls reveals a section of the original clay walls behind. Traditional ciders and perries are always available. Dogs are welcome and their owners' too. ⚶Q⚙①⊨⋈⊟(40,X53)♣⊛P⌐

Waytown

Hare & Hounds ✪
DT6 5LQ SY470978
✪ 11.30-3, 6.30 (6 summer)-11; 12-3, 6.30-11
☎ (01308) 488203
Palmers Copper Ale, IPA Ⓗ
Hidden down winding lanes, this rural gem of an unspoilt village local is well-worth seeking out. The garden, with stunning views across the Brit Valley, is a major attraction in summer with a play area and grassy expanse for children to let off steam. Bridge Farm cider is a regular and the attractive food menu features home-cooked meals and fresh local produce. A quiz replaces food on Sunday evenings in winter. Palmers 200 or Tally Ho! are available in winter months. The pub may close earlier on quiet nights or stay open later if busy. ⚶Q⚙①♣⊛P

West Lulworth

Castle Inn Ⓛ
Main Road, BH20 5RN
✪ 12-2 (3 Sat), 6-11; 12-3, 6-10.30 Sun ☎ (01929) 400311
⊕ lulworthinn.com
Palmers Best Bitter Ⓖ**; guest beers** Ⓗ**/**Ⓖ
Enchanting 16th-century thatched inn close to Lulworth Cove. It has two comfortable bars, one with a low ceiling, both beamed. Six ales (mostly local) and 13 traditional ciders are served, and the extensive food menu offers good value, home-made food in generous portions. At the rear is a tiered garden with a giant chess set. Board games are available inside. The inn has 15 bedrooms, 14 en-suite, and is dog friendly – your well-behaved dog can stay with you in your room. Q⚙⊨①⊟▲♣⊛P⌐

West Stour

Ship Inn
SP8 5RP (on A30)
✪ 12-3, 6-11; 12-11 (7 Nov-Feb) Sun ☎ (01747) 838640
⊕ shipinn-dorset.com
Beer range varies Ⓗ
Once a coaching inn, this popular roadside pub has fine views across the Blackmore Vale. The public bar features a flagstone floor and low ceiling; the separate restaurant area is light and airy with stripped oak floorboards and farmhouse furniture. There is a pretty patio and large garden to the rear. This friendly pub is renowned for superb home-cooked food (no meals Sun eve) and comfortable accommodation. Three changing beers are always available and a beer festival is held in July. Dogs are welcome in the bar. ⚶Q⚙⊨①♣⊛P⌐

Weymouth

Boot Inn ✪
High Street, DT4 8JH
✪ 11-11; 12-10.30 Sun ☎ (01305) 770327

Rookhope

Rookhope Inn
Rear Hogarth Terrace, DL13 2BG
✪ 12-midnight ☎ (01388) 517215
Beer range varies 🅗
Off the beaten track in the North Pennines, this Grade II-listed building dating from 1680 retains the original open fires and wood beams. A welcome rest stop on the coast-to-coast cycle route, this friendly community inn also offers accommodation and a function room. The big fire in the bar is welcome in the winter. Spectacular views of Upper Weardale can be enjoyed from the garden. Situated in a pretty former lead-mining village, the surrounding area provides ample opportunity for exploration. ♨Q🕮🛏🍴◑🕮♣P

St John's Chapel

Blue Bell ✪
12 Hood Street, DL13 1QJ
✪ 5 (12 Sat & Sun)-1am ☎ (01388) 537256
Beer range varies 🅗
This small, homely village local is situated in beautiful Upper Weardale, very much at the heart of the community. The pub hosts ladies' and gents' darts and pool teams and runs a quiz on Sunday night. It also has a leek club which holds an annual show, and there is a small library for customers' use. The local angling club is based here and fishing licences are on sale at the bar. The guest beers are usually from small local breweries. There is a covered and heated area outside.
♨🕮🖼(101)♣●P⅃—

Sedgefield

Ceddesfeld Hall
Sedgefield Community Association, Rectory Row, TS21 2AE
✪ 7.30-10.30 ☎ (01740) 620341
Beer range varies 🅗
Built in 1791 as the local parsonage, the hall comes complete with resident ghost, 'the Pickled Parson'. Set in extensive grounds, ideal for a summer evening, this is a private club but CAMRA members are most welcome. There is a bar, comfortable lounge and large function room. Run by volunteers from the Sedgefield Community Association, it is used by a wide variety of groups. An annual beer festival is held on the first weekend in July with reasonably priced ale. Q🕮🛏占🖼P⅃—🗗

Nag's Head
8 West End, TS21 2BS
✪ 6 (5 Fri-Sat)-midnight; 12-3, 7-11 Sun ☎ (01740) 620234
Taylor Landlord; guest beers 🅗
Situated at the centre of the village, close to Sedgefield Racecourse, this free house is a classic local attracting all age groups – families with well-behaved children are welcome. There is a comfortable bar, a smaller lounge and a restaurant serving traditional Sunday lunch prepared with fresh local produce. Meals are also served in the bar (no food Sun and Mon eve). The landlord and landlady both come from the village.
♨🕮◑占🖼♣

Shincliffe

Seven Stars Inn
High Street North, DH1 2NU (on A177, S of Durham)
✪ 11-11 (10.30 Sun) ☎ (0191) 384 8454
⊕ sevenstarsinn.co.uk
Black Sheep Best Bitter; Taylor Landlord; guest beers 🅗
Dating from 1724, this small, cosy, beamed pub is situated on the edge of a pleasant village. Local country walks and the long Weardale Way pass nearby. Walkers are welcome in the bar – just make sure your boots are clean. Well-behaved dogs are also permitted. Meals are served in the bar and traditional restaurant. Comfortable accommodation makes the pub a great base for visiting the city and other attractions in the area.
🛏🍴◑🕮🖼

Spennymoor

Frog & Ferret
Coulson Street, DL16 7RS
✪ 3 (12 Fri & Sat)-11; 12-10.30 Sun ☎ (01388) 818312
Beer range varies 🅗
This friendly, family-run free house offers four constantly-changing real ales sourced from far and wide, with local and northern micro-breweries well represented. A welcoming atmosphere greets you on arrival at the three-sided bar in the comfortably furnished lounge, with brick, stone and wood cladding. Darts and dominoes are played and bar snacks are available. Well-behaved children are permitted until 4pm. The pub hosts a quiz on Sunday evening, and a music quiz on the first Wednesday evening of the month. ♨🕮占♣P⅃—

Stockton-on-Tees

Sun Inn ✪
Knowles Street, TS18 1SU
✪ 11-11; 12-10.30 Sun ☎ (01642) 611461
Draught Bass 🅗
Popular town-centre drinkers' pub reputed to sell more Draught Bass than any other pub in the country. It was rescued from an uncertain future eight years ago by a regular at the pub who became the licensee, and who quickly increased sales of Bass to 12 18-gallon casks a week – his son-in-law is the current licensee. The pub supports darts and football teams and charitable causes. On Monday evening the function room is home to the famous Stockton Folk Club.
⇌(Stockton/Thornaby)🖼♣—

Thomas Sheraton ✪
4 Bridge Road, TS18 1BH (at S end of High St)
✪ 9-midnight (11 Sun) ☎ (01642) 606134
Greene King Ruddles Best Bitter, Abbot; guest beers 🅗
This previous local CAMRA Pub of the Year winner is a fine Wetherspoon conversion of the Victorian law courts, and named after one of the country's great Georgian cabinet makers born in the town in 1751. It comprises several distinct dining and drinking areas downstairs, with a balcony and patio upstairs. Eight guest beers are available, several sourced locally. Regular beer festivals and occasional brewery trips are arranged. CAMRA members receive a 20 per cent discount on the food menu.
🕭🕮◑占⇌(Stockton/Thornaby)🖼●—

Tudhoe

Black Horse Inn 🄻

4 Attwood Terrace, DL16 6TD (on B6288, 4 miles S of Durham)

🌼 11.30-11 ☎ (01388) 420662

Caledonian Deuchars IPA; Courage Directors; guest beers ⒣

Once closed down by a pubco as unviable, this is now a busy, atmospheric and friendly free house, reopened by the current owners in 2008 after a period of closure. Two permanent and two regularly changing guest ales are always available. Excellent food is served lunchtimes and evenings in the restaurant and bar. Buses from Durham City pass the door. This family-friendly pub is well worth a visit. 🕸🌀🔥🚆♣P'⸺

Westgate

Hare & Hounds 🅥

24 Front Street, DL13 1RX (on A689)

🌼 12-2.30 (Sat only), 6.30-11; 12-3, 6.30-9.30 Sun
☎ (01388) 517212

Black Sheep Best Bitter; Hare & Hounds Hare of the Dog ⒣

On the main road through the dale, and on the banks of the Wear, this popular village pub has a large bar with two distinct areas and a separate dining room, as well as a brewery. Bench seats along one wall, three fires and stone floors add real character. There are tables to the front, and seats to the rear overlooking the river. Three pumps dispense the popular house beer and Black Sheep, while the Sunday carvery is justifiably renowned. 🏚Q🕸🌀🔥🛆🚆(101)♣P

Willington

Burn Inn 🅥

14 West End Terrace, DL15 0HW (B6286/A690 jct at W end of village)

🌼 11-11 (midnight Sat); 12-11 Sun ☎ (01388) 746291

Beer range varies ⒣

This cosy establishment has become a first-class community pub, serving three ales from the Punch Taverns Finest Cask range. Various pub games are played here throughout the week and a quiz is held on Wednesday. It also has its own golf society, provides a meeting point for village junior football teams and acts as a venue for local Labour Party meetings. There is a heated outdoor area for smokers. 🕸🚆♣P'⸺

Witton Gilbert

Glendenning Arms 🅥

Front Street, DH7 6SY (off A691 bypass, 3 miles from city centre)

🌼 4-11; 3-midnight Fri; 12-midnight Sat; 12-11 Sun
☎ (0191) 371 0316

Black Sheep Best Bitter, Ale ⒣

Typical village community local and Guide regular with a small, comfortable lounge and a lively and welcoming bar with the original Vaux 1970s red and white handpulls. The bar is attractively decorated in a contemporary style while the lounge remains more traditional. The pub runs darts, dominoes and football teams. Situated on the village's main road, there is ample car parking. 🏚🕸🔥🚆(15)♣P'⸺

Travellers Rest

Front Street, DH7 6TQ (off A691 bypass 3 miles from city centre)

🌼 11-11; 12-10.30 Sun ☎ (0191) 371 0458

Beer range varies ⒣

Open-plan country-style pub, popular with diners. The bar area is split into three sections with a conservatory off to the side where families are welcome. There is also a more private dining room. Now owned by TR Leisure Partnership, an extensive food menu suits all tastes, with dining throughout the pub. The restaurant was redesigned two years ago and the kitchen upgraded to modern standards. Quiz nights are Tuesday and Sunday. Q🕭🕸🌀🔥🛆🚆(15)P'⸺

Witton le Wear

Dun Cow

19 High Street, DL14 0AY

🌼 6 (1 Sat; 12 Sun)-11 ☎ (01388) 448294

Black Sheep Best Bitter; Jennings Cumberland Ale; Wells Bombardier ⒣

Genuine unspoilt stone pub, dating from 1799, set back from the road in a quiet, pretty village, with a traditional single bar and seats outside the front of building. A large fireplace at one end of the room is topped by a set of impressive horns, another at the other end is guarded by a sleeping fox. Comfortable bench seats run along two walls to the left of the bar, and football memorabilia complete the decor. The view east over the Wear to Witton Castle is impressive. 🏚Q🕸🚆(88)♣P'⸺

Wolsingham

Black Bull

27 Market Place, DL13 3AB

🌼 12-11 (11.30 Sun) ☎ (01388) 527332

Caledonian Deuchars IPA; guest beer ⒣

Proper Weardale hotel in the centre of the village, providing excellent food and accommodation. It has a bar, lounge, dining room and surprise sun-trap garden, plus tables to the front. The pub runs various games nights and local Weight Watchers members enjoy the facilities after their meetings in the town hall opposite. It also serves as headquarters for the village cricket team in the summer and hosts social events. A good base for walkers and cyclists, and convenient for the Weardale Railway. 🏚Q🕸🕭🌀🕭🛆🗲⇌(Weardale Railway)🚆(101) ♣'⸺

Black Lion

21 Meadhope Street, DL13 3EN (50m N of market place)

🌼 6.30 (6 Fri; 12 Sat)-11; 12-10.30 Sun ☎ (01388) 527772

Beer range varies ⒣

On a pleasant residential street, just a few minutes walk from the village centre, this establishment is well worth a visit. Comfortable surroundings and an open fire help to create a warm, friendly atmosphere. Sport is shown on TV and opening hours may be extended for big matches, particularly cricket. Local charities are supported in various events throughout the year, including a quiz on Sunday evening. Beer festivals are held two to three times a year. 🏚Q🕸🚆(101)♣

Increasingly popular one-bar pub, situated off the High Street, with a cosy, welcoming ambience. Good quality food is served all day Monday to Saturday, and Sunday until 7pm, from an extensive menu featuring home-made pies and food made with locally-sourced ingredients. The bar and food service is quick, efficient and friendly, enhancing the feel-good factor. The walls are adorned with prints and decorative plates, and there is a fine collection of ceramic and gleaming copper jugs. ♨Q✿◗➥☷(100)P

Blackmore

Leather Bottle
Horsefayre Green, CM4 0RL
✪ 11-11 (midnight Fri & Sat); 12-11 Sun ☎ (01277) 821891
⊕ theleatherbottle.net
Adnams Bitter; Sharp's Doom Bar Ⅲ; guest beers Ⅲ/Ⅰ
Large village pub with a small flagstone-floored bar area. Most of the interior is taken up by a good quality restaurant. Two guest beers are generally available on handpump, with maybe a third on gravity at weekends in the summer, usually including a beer of around 5% or higher. Westons Old Rosie cider is also sold. An annexe to the bar has a silent fruit machine. ♨✿◗☷☷(32)●P

Braintree

King William IV Ⓛ
114 London Road, CM77 7PU (on B1053 approx 1 mile from town centre nr A120) TL749492
✪ 3-midnight; 12-1am Fri & Sat; 12-11 Sun
☎ (01376) 567755 ⊕ kingwilliamiv.co.uk
Beer range varies Ⅰ
Cosy 19th-century traditional free house with a main bar and a walk-through leading to a small back bar with a dartboard. The pub reopened in 2009, having been closed for two years. A range of three or four ales is served by gravity from a side cellar, usually featuring a Sharp's beer and Essex micro-breweries. Cider from Westons and Cornish Orchards is sold. Beer festivals are held twice a year in a marquee in the large garden. Friendly dogs are welcome. ✿☷(70,352)♣●P

Brentwood

Rising Sun Ⓛ
144 Ongar Road, CM15 9DJ (on A128, at Western Rd jct)
✪ 3-11.30 (midnight Fri); 12-midnight Sat; 12-10.30 Sun
☎ (01277) 213749
Brentwood Maple Mild; Fuller's London Pride; Hook Norton Hooky Bitter; Taylor Landlord; guest beers Ⅲ
Comfortable and friendly local with a good selection of real ales, in an area where beer choice can be fairly limited. This is very much a community pub, with a charity quiz on Monday evening, cribbage on Sunday evening and frequent darts matches. Framed prints of the local area decorate the walls. Outside is a covered, heated smokers' area and patio. ♨Q✿☷♣P⌐

Brightlingsea

Railway Tavern Ⓛ
58 Station Road, CO7 0DT
✪ 5-10; 3-11 Fri; 12-11 Sat; 12-3, 7-10.30 Sun
Crouch Vale Best; guest beers Ⅲ

Home of the Famous Railway Tavern Brewery, this friendly, traditional local sells beers that have either been brewed on site or sourced locally. At least one changing real cider is available and there is an annual cider festival on the first bank holiday weekend in May. The pub has its own football and cricket teams who are always on the lookout for opponents! The 10 Question Quiz takes place every Tuesday at around 7pm. There is no music or TV, and a real fire in winter. All own ales are vegan-friendly. ♨Q✿☷(78)●

Broads Green

Walnut Tree ✪
CM3 1DT (¾ mile S of Great Waltham village) TL694125
✪ 12-midnight ☎ (01245) 360222
Greene King IPA, Morland Bitter, Ruddles Best Bitter; guest beer Ⅰ
Handsome Victorian brick-built pub overlooking a large green. The front door opens directly into a small snug favoured by locals for conversation. To the left is the wood-panelled public bar, little changed since it was built; to the right is the more modern lounge. Outside is a garden and seating in front of the pub. There is no food – the landlord prefers to concentrate on his beers and to maintain a traditional atmosphere. An outside gents' is still in use. ♨Q✿☷(33,52)♣P

Bures

Eight Bells
Colchester Road, CO8 5AE
✪ 12-2.45, 5-midnight; 12-midnight Sat & Sun
☎ (01787) 227354
Greene King IPA; Young's Bitter; guest beers Ⅲ
Single bar pub in the heart of the village and not far from the station. The bar consists of comfortable tables and chairs in separate areas, with a large wood-burning fire enhancing the atmosphere. Sunday roasts are popular along with a daily specials board. The beer range varies, with up to five or six ales available, including regulars Greene King IPA and Young's Bitter. The landlord and landlady have been here for more than 40 years. ♨Q✿◗➥☷(753)♣P⌐

Burnham-on-Crouch

Queen's Head Ⓛ
26 Providence, CM0 8JU (in narrow lane opp clock tower)
✪ 2 (5 Mon, 12 Thu & Fri)-11; 2-midnight Sat; 12-10.30 Sun
☎ (01621) 784825 ⊕ queensheadburnham.com
Dark Star Hophead; Mighty Oak Maldon Gold; Red Fox IPA; guest beers Ⅲ
Tucked away from the high street in a popular yachting town, this award-winning and friendly pub is known for real ales and cider. The staff will always make you feel welcome here. The landlord has been a member of CAMRA for many years and has ideals well-suited for the campaign. As well as winning the National Joe Goodwin award for pub design it was runner-up in the local CAMRA Pub of the Year competition 2011. Traditional Essex huffers, special curries and home-cooked meals are available. ♨✿◗➥☷(31X)♣●⌐⊟

ENGLAND

Castle Hedingham

Bell 🏆 L

10 St James Street, CO9 3EJ (off A1017 signed Castle Hedingham)
⏲ 12-3, 5.30-11; 12-midnight Fri & Sat; 12-11 Sun
☎ (01787) 460350 🌐 hedinghambell.co.uk
Adnams Bitter; Mighty Oak IPA, Maldon Gold; guest beers G
A 15th-century coaching inn owned by Gray & Sons that is well worth a visit. There are small rooms for drinking and dining alongside the two main bars. Beers come direct from the cask, and summer and winter beer festivals are held. Live jazz plays at lunchtime on the last Sunday of the month, the pub champions local musicians on Friday evening and there is a regular quiz on Sunday night. Local Delvin End cider is usually available. Food includes Turkish specials prepared in a wood-fired stone oven. Essex CAMRA Pub of the Year 2010, and local Pub of the Year 2011. ♨Q⛺❀◐◑⊟🚌♣●P⚋

Chelmsford

Angel

160 Broomfield Road, Broomfield, CM1 7AH
⏲ 12-11 (10.30 Sun) ☎ (01245) 444917
Adnams Bitter, Broadside; guest beer H
An attractive Grade II-listed inn, recently refurbished, with open fires in the winter, in the village of Broomfield just north of Chelmsford. It has a large beer garden and car park. The guest ale is generally from a regional brewery. A wide selection of traditional pub food, including Sunday roasts, is served all day, with meat, fish and vegetarian specials daily. Frequent buses stop outside. ♨❀◐◑♿🚌P

Barista L

44-45 Duke Street, CM1 1JA
⏲ 12-11 (2am Fri & Sat); closed Sun ☎ (01245) 493333
Beer range varies G
This is a new, modern bar with comfortable leather furniture and subdued lighting. It is slightly surprising, then, to find three well-kept real ales served by gravity from the first floor cellar, and an owner who is keen to promote them. Two local beers and one from further afield are usually on offer, sometimes including a dark beer. Over-21s welcomed. ❀◐♿⇌🚌⚋

Oddfellows Arms L

195 Springfield Road, CM2 6JP
⏲ 12-11 (midnight Fri & Sat) ☎ (01245) 490514
🌐 theoddfellowsarms.com
Adnams Bitter; Greene King H&H Olde Trip; Mighty Oak Maldon Gold; Sharp's Doom Bar H**; guest beer** G
A traditional local that features a large U-shaped bar area. On one side is a pool table and on the other a back room leading out to the newly refurbished garden/smoking area. The guest beer comes from the large Gray's range, and beer festivals are held in mid-February and late July. There is monthly live music, and poker nights are held Tuesday and Thursday. Food is served lunchtimes and evenings weekdays, all day at weekends. ❀◐◑🚌♣P⚋

Orange Tree L

6 Lower Anchor Street, CM2 0AS
⏲ 12-11 (11.30 Fri & Sat) ☎ (01245) 262664 🌐 the-ot.com
Mighty Oak Oscar Wilde, Maldon Gold; Wibblers Apprentice H**; guest beers** H/G
The Orange Tree has established its place as one of the top real ale pubs in Chelmsford. There are usually six or seven beers available (often including a stout or porter), with two or three on gravity from casks behind the bar. The cider is from the Westons range. There is a charity quiz on Tuesday evening and Sunday lunch is popular. Rock/blues bands play regularly on Saturday. Q❀◐⊟♿🚌♣●P⚋

Queen's Head L

30 Lower Anchor Street, CM2 0AS
⏲ 12-11 (11.30 Fri & Sat) ☎ (01245) 265181
🌐 queensheadchelmsford.co.uk
Crouch Vale Essex Boys Bitter, Brewers Gold, Crouch Best, Amarillo; guest beers H
Crouch Vale Brewery's only pub, the Queen's Head sells four of its beers, occasionally supplemented or replaced by a beer from its seasonal list. The four guest ales from far and wide always vary, and often include a dark beer. The cider, not always available in the winter, is from the Westons range. This popular local can be busy when there is a cricket match nearby, or when clubs and societies, such as the Essex Beard Club, meet.
♨Q❀◐♿🚌♣●P

Railway Tavern L

63 Duke Street, CM1 1LW
⏲ 11-11.30; 11.30-4.30 Sun ☎ (01245) 356995
Greene King IPA; guest beers H
A new landlord has rejuvenated this pub opposite the railway station. It now offers seven real ales from the large Gray's list, with six of them constantly changing. It is a Tardis-like corner pub with a central bar, seating towards the rear laid out like a railway carriage, and a garden where you can listen to the station announcements. ❀◐⇌♣⚋

Woolpack ✔

23 Mildmay Road, CM2 0DN (S of main road into town)
⏲ 12-11 (midnight Fri & Sat) ☎ (01245) 259295
🌐 woolpack.net
Greene King H&H Bitter, St Edmunds H**, Abbot** G**; guest beers** H
Local CAMRA Pub of the Year 2010 and 2011, the Woolpack has free-of-tie beers from all over the country on one pump, as well as seven Greene King guest ales. There are darts and pool in a small public bar, while the large main lounge leads to an annexe with a large-screen TV. There is a Tuesday quiz, monthly folk music, and beer festivals at Easter and in September. An ever-changing range of speciality sausages complements the food menu, which is available Monday to Friday and Sunday lunchtime. ❀◐◑⊟🚌♣P⚋

Chrishall

Red Cow

11 High Street, SG8 8RN (2 miles N of B1039) TL445394
⏲ 12-3 (not Mon), 6-11; 12-10.30 Sun ☎ (01763) 838792
🌐 theredcow.com
Adnams Bitter; guest beers H
Thatched 14th-century pub close to an old barn in a small village near the Cambridge and Hertfordshire borders. Guest beers are usually from East Anglia. The owners welcome visitors and many local groups, including the cricket club (who run regular quizzes), the village book group, stall holders from the farmers' market, and the WI. Special occasions can be celebrated with meals from the extensive menu, either in the tiled bar or in the restaurant

the back bar and a wealth of paintings and antiques can also be found. Traditional home-cooked food is served daily. A large upstairs function room is widely used by local groups and musicians alike. Two beer festivals are held here each year. CAMRA Branch Pub of the Year for two years running in 2010 and 2011. ⋈Q❀✿◑①〜🖵(31X)P↙🖢

Queen Victoria 🄻
Spital Road, CM9 6ED
✪ 11 (12 Sun)-11 ☎ (01621) 852923
Farmer's Ales Pucks Folly; Greene King IPA, Abbot; Mighty Oak Maldon Gold ⓗ
A welcoming Victorian Gray's local with a well-kept beer range, including two local micro-brews. The single bar has a separate area for the usual pub games. The dining area offers excellent home-cooked food, with a comprehensive menu including a lighter option and an ever-changing specials board. A popular meeting place for local groups, it has five darts teams. Note the wonderful hanging baskets. On the bus route from Chelmsford. ✿◑①〜占🖵(31X)♣P↙

Queen's Head
The Hythe, CM9 5HN
✪ 11-11 (midnight Fri & Sat; 10.30 Sun) ☎ (01621) 854112
⊕ thequeensheadmaldon.co.uk
Adnams Bitter, Broadside; Farmer's Ales Pucks Folly; Taylor Landlord; guest beers ⓗ
Quayside pub, some 600 years old, on the River Blackwater. Old Thames sailing barges are moored nearby. It has a spacious outdoor seating area with sun umbrellas and an outside bar for summer use. The public bar, warmed by a log fire, is a local meeting place. Food is served in the restaurant or bar, with an extensive menu supplemented by daily specials. Well-behaved children are allowed in the restaurant. Good disabled access and WC facilities. ⋈Q✿◑①〜占♣↙

Margaretting Tye

White Hart Inn 🄻
Swan Lane, CM4 9JX TL684011
✪ 11.30-3, 6-midnight; 11.30-midnight Sat; 12-11 Sun
☎ (01277) 840478 ⊕ thewhitehart.uk.com
Adnams Bitter, Broadside; Mighty Oak IPA, Oscar Wilde; Red Fox Hunter's Gold; guest beers ⓖ
Slightly off the beaten track but still accessible, this fine pub has origins in the 17th century. Known for good food and ale, it generally has two or three guest beers on gravity. Regular club meetings are held here for cyclists, car owners, ramblers and young farmers. Very much community-focused, a book stall raises money for charities, and beer festivals are held in July and November. Local CAMRA Pub of the Year 2007 and 2008. Two rooms for accommodation are available. ⋈Q⇆✿✉◑①占♣P↙

Mill Green

Viper ☆ 🄻
Mill Green Road, CM4 0PT TL641018
✪ 12-3, 6-11; 12-11 Sat; 12-10.30 Sun ☎ (01277) 352010
Mighty Oak Oscar Wilde; Viper Ales Jake the Snake, VIPA; guest beers ⓗ
The only pub in the country with this name, the Viper is an isolated, unspoilt country pub with a lounge, public bar and wood-panelled snug. Jake

the Snake is occasionally replaced by another Viper ale. Viper Ales are commissioned from Mighty Oak and Nethergate, who also sometimes supply the two guest beers, although these may come from anywhere. Good home-cooked food is served at lunchtime, and Westons cider is sold. Beer festivals are held at Easter and over the August bank holiday. ⋈Q✿◑①〜♣♠P↙

Monk Street

Farmhouse Inn 🄻
CM6 2NR (off B184, 2 miles S of Thaxted) TL612287
✪ 11-midnight (11 Sun) ☎ (01371) 830864
⊕ farmhouseinn.org
Greene King IPA; Mighty Oak Maldon Gold, seasonal beers ⓗ
Built in the 16th century, this former Dunmow Brewery pub has been enlarged to incorporate a restaurant and accommodation; the bar is in the original part of the building. The quiet hamlet of Monk Street overlooks the Chelmer Valley, two miles from historic Thaxted. A disused well in the garden supplied the hamlet with water during World War II. The pub has a rear patio, front garden and a top field. Draught cider from Westons is usually sold in the summer. Q✿✉◑①占🖵(313)♣P↙

Mount Bures

Thatchers Arms 🄻 ✅
Hall Road, CO8 5AT (1½ miles S of Bures, 2½ miles N of Chappel) TL905319
✪ closed Mon; 12-3, 6-11; 12-11 Sat & Sun
☎ (01787) 227460 ⊕ thatchersarms.co.uk
Adnams Bitter; Crouch Vale Brewers Gold; guest beers ⓗ
This friendly pub on the Essex-Suffolk border offers stunning views over the Stour Valley and is the 2011 local CAMRA Pub of the Year. Up to five ales are available, mainly from national and local micro-breweries, plus an extensive range of British, Belgian and American bottled beers. Twice-yearly beer festivals are held in spring and winter, and the pub is also renowned for its quality home-made meals, sourced primarily from local produce. Camping is available in the garden. ✿◑①Å♣P

Old Harlow

Queen's Head 🄻
26 Churchgate Street, CM17 0JT TL483114
✪ 11.45-3, 5 (6 Sat)-11; 12-4, 7-10.30 (not winter eve) Sun
☎ (01279) 427266
Adnams Bitter; Crouch Vale Brewers Gold; Nethergate IPA ⓗ
The new town of Harlow seems a long way from this traditional village pub. It was originally built as two cottages in 1530, then joined together and converted into a pub in 1750. Wooden beams feature throughout and there is a welcoming open fire during the winter months. Guest beers are usually from East Anglian breweries. A full range of food is served. ⋈Q✿◑①〜🖵(7,59)P↙

Paglesham

Punch Bowl
Church End, SS4 2DP (signed from Rochford)
✪ 11.30-2.30, 6.30-10 Mon; 11.30-3, 6.30-11 Tue-Sat; 12-10.30 Sun ☎ (01702) 258376

Adnams Bitter; guest beers Ⓗ
Facing south in a quiet single-street village, this 16th-century building clad in white Essex boards has been an ale house since the mid-1800s, when it was supposedly frequented by smugglers. It has a single low-beamed bar displaying a large collection of mugs, brassware and old local pictures. A small restaurant to one side offers a good menu at reasonable prices. There are picnic tables at the front and in the rear garden, and ample parking all around. Q❀◑P

Pentlow

Pinkuah Arms
Pinkuah Lane, CO10 7JW (off B1064 in small lane, opp red phone box) TL816448
✪ 12-midnight (7 Mon & Sun) ☎ (01787) 280857
⊕ pinkuaharms.co.uk
Nethergate seasonal beers; Woodforde's Wherry; guest beers Ⓗ
Quite hard to find, this country pub is 350 years old, named after two spinsters who lived here. It has been tastefully refurbished, with beams, wooden floorboards, a low ceiling in part and a log fire. It has an interesting and varied menu with a good choice of Sunday roasts, and the credit crunch lunch is popular. There is outdoor seating. The pub offers many specials (quiz nights, steak nights) and themed menus. Westons Old Rosie is on handpump. Child and dog friendly. ᴹQ❀◑P

Purleigh

Bell
The Street, CM3 6QJ
✪ 11.30 (12 Sat)-3, 6-11; 12-4 Sun ☎ (01621) 828348
⊕ purleighbell.co.uk
Adnams Bitter; guest beers Ⓗ
A 14th-century traditional village pub, extensively refurbished in the 16th-century, which stands on a rare hill with fine long views over the Blackwater Estuary. The pub benefits from two open fires, one a large inglenook, and three separate heavily beamed and hop-decorated seating areas. Up to three ales are offered, with guests often from local micro-breweries. A reputation for good food is being built, from bar snacks to themed set meals, and a warm welcome is assured. ᴹQ❀◑♣P

Rayleigh

Roebuck ✪
138 High Street, SS6 7BU (close to library)
✪ 8am-midnight (1am Fri & Sat) ☎ (01268) 748430
Greene King Ruddles Best Bitter, Abbot; guest beers Ⓗ
A busy high street pub, better than the average Wetherspoon, located on the site of the Reverend James Pilkington's Baptist School. It has friendly and pleasant staff, serving a range of up to six guest ales. There is comfortable seating, with a separate family area away from the main bar. Sky Sports and News are shown on TVs. Outside is a smoking and drinking area. Well served by many buses and a railway station. ❀◑⬥≕⊟(1,7,8)♠≛

Ridgewell

White Horse Inn Ⓛ
Mill Road, CO9 4SG (on A1017 between Halstead and Haverhill) TL736407

✪ 12 (6 Mon & Tue)-11 ☎ (01440) 785532
⊕ ridgewellwhitehorse.com
Beer range varies Ⓖ
This CAMRA award-winning pub has a changing choice of beers, always including a dark mild, all gravity-dispensed, as are the two or three real ciders. The first week in March is the dark winter ale festival, and the first weekend in August the summer beer festival. This venue is famed locally for an excellent wine selection as well as for its home-made steak and ale pies and puddings, local ingredients being used wherever possible. Luxury four-star accommodation is available at reasonable prices and there are seasonal afternoon teas. ᴹ❀➡◑&♣♠P≛

Rochford

Golden Lion ♈ Ⓛ
35 North Street, SS4 1AB (200m N of town square)
✪ 11-midnight (11 Sun) ☎ (01702) 545487
⊕ goldenlionrochford.co.uk
Adnams Bitter; Crouch Vale Brewers Gold; Greene King Abbot; guest beers Ⓗ
Traditional Essex weatherboards cover this venue. Small and frequently busy, it is a 16th-century free house complete with stained glass windows. The decor includes hops above the bar and a fireplace with a traditional log-burner. It always serves six ales, including three changing guests – one a dark beer – plus a real cider. Bar snacks are available. A large-screen TV shows major sporting events, and it has its own cricket team. The patio garden at the rear is suitable for smokers. Local CAMRA Pub of the Year 2011. ᴹ❀◑≕⊟(7,8,60)♣♠≛

Horse & Groom Ⓛ
1 Southend Road, SS4 1HA
✪ 11.30 (12 Sun)-1am ☎ (01702) 544015
Mighty Oak Maldon Gold; guest beers Ⓗ
A fine locals' pub a few minutes' walk from the town centre or station, and winner of local CAMRA Pub of the Year 2009. The guest ales include a selection from Essex breweries as well as from further afield, and real cider is also always available. Occasional beer festivals are held in the function room. A separate restaurant provides good value food, especially on Friday, when a varied fish menu is on offer. ᴹ❀◑≕⊟(7,8)♠P≛

Rowhedge

Olde Albion
High Street, CO5 7ES (3 miles SE of Colchester)
✪ 12-3 (not Mon), 5-11; 12-11 Thu-Sat; 12-10.30 Sun
☎ (01206) 728972 ⊕ yeoldealbion.co.uk
Beer range varies Ⓗ/Ⓖ
Popular riverside village pub at the heart of the community. A range of ales is served, sourced mainly from micro-breweries, with 420 different ales served in the last year. The function room hosts regular beer festivals, including on St George's Day and during the village summer regatta. A greensward quay in front of the pub overlooks the River Colne, with seating for alfresco drinking. There are regular buses from Colchester and a summer weekend ferry service from Wivenhoe. ᴹ❀⊟(66)♣≛

most rooms. There is a covered courtyard with tables and a grass area on the river bank for relaxing. Rolls are available at lunchtime. The pub has its own moorings and is popular in the summer. Q✿♣●P⚲

Avening

Bell Inn ⓛ
29 High Street, GL8 8NF (on B4014 at bottom of village)
✿ 12-2.30, 5.30-11 (midnight Sat) ☎ (01453) 836422
⊕ thebellinnavening.co.uk
Box Steam Cog; Butcombe Gold; Wickwar BOB; guest beer Ⓗ
A friendly, confidently-run old inn with exposed stone walls, two bay window seats and a roaring wood-burner all combining to make this a pleasant village local, where the jovial, amicable regulars are always chatty. The pleasant open bar offers up to four different ales, all from local micros. The comfortable dining area serves a competitively priced and regularly changing menu. Catch this pleasant pub on the right evening and it can be very difficult to leave. ⚞Q◖◗♣⚲

Bledington

King's Head ⓛ ✔
The Green, OX7 6XQ (on village green) SP243228
✿ 11.30-3, 6-11; 12-10.30 Sun ☎ (01608) 658365
⊕ kingsheadinn.net
Hook Norton Hooky Bitter; guest beers Ⓗ
Local CAMRA Pub of the Year 2008, this delightful 16th-century, honey-coloured stone inn overlooks the village green, with its brook and ducks. The original old beams, inglenook with kettle plus military brasses, open wood fire, flagstone floors and high-back settles and pews create a heart-warming atmosphere. Quality food is served in a separate dining area while 12 rooms offer charming accommodation. Guest ales are varied, well-kept and carefully selected, often from Gloucestershire. Good local walks to nearby villages start close by.
⚞Q❧✿🛏◖◗🖵≠(Kingham)♣P⚲

Bourton-on-the-Hill

Horse & Groom ⓛ ✔
GL56 9AQ
✿ 11-2.30 (3 Sat), 6-11; 12-3.30 Sun ☎ (01386) 700413
⊕ horseandgroom.info
Goff's Jouster; guest beers Ⓗ
Grade II-listed Georgian stone inn serving three local real ales. This is a family-run free house in private ownership since 2005, winning awards for excellent contemporary food served in an attractive dining area. The light, airy separate bar has been tastefully refurbished with an open fire. Two miles from Moreton in Marsh and close to Batsford Arboretum, it offers five refurbished en-suite rooms for guests. The delightful sheltered garden has plenty of seating, with views over the Cotswold countryside. ⚞Q✿🛏◖◗🖵P

Bourton-on-the-Water

Mousetrap Inn
Lansdowne, GL54 2AR (300m W of village centre)
✿ 11.30-3, 6-11; 12-3, 6-10.30 Sun ☎ (01451) 820579
⊕ mousetrap-inn.co.uk
Halfpenny Anniversary; guest beers Ⓗ

This attractive, traditional and friendly Cotswold-stone pub is a family-run free house, situated in the quieter Lansdowne part of Bourton. It is popular with the local community as well as offering 10 refurbished en-suite letting rooms for visitors. Three real ales and excellent good value home-cooked meals are served. A welcoming, cosy atmosphere is created with a feature fireplace and coal-effect fire. The patio area in front with tables and hanging baskets provides a sheltered sun-trap in summer. Q✿🛏◖◗🖵(801,855)♣P

Bridgeyate

White Harte
111 London Road, BS30 5NA (on A420 jct wth A4175 E of Bristol)
✿ 11-11; 12-10.30 Sun ☎ (0117) 967 3830
Bath Ales Gem; Butcombe Bitter; Courage Best Bitter; Marston's Pedigree Ⓗ
The White Harte is a traditional pub dating from 1860, extended in 1987. It is often called the Inn on the Green because of the large village green at the front. An unusual bar counter incorporates old wooden spice drawers. Reasonably priced food attracts lunchtime diners, and the pub also gets busy in the evening with people enjoying a drink. Pub games and sporting activities are likely conversation topics, and a quiz features on Monday evening. Black Rat cider is served. There is extra parking to the rear. ⚞✿◖◗🖵(634,635)♣●P⚲

Bristol: Central

Bank
8 John Street, BS1 2HR (take lane by arcade in All Saints Lane)
✿ 12-midnight (1am Thu-Sat) ☎ (0117) 930 4691
⊕ banktavern.com
Beer range varies Ⓗ
Now well-established as one of the better real ale venues in Bristol, this compact one-bar pub is right in the centre yet well-hidden. A strong supporter of south-west micro-brewers, the Bank offers three or four constantly varying beers, and is not afraid to sell dark or very strong beers; there are also guest ciders. Food is served 12-4pm daily, including popular Sunday roasts. Many live events take place. Expect much quirky humour, and ask about CAMRA discounts. Dogs allowed.
✿◖◗≠(Temple Meads)🖵●⚲

Barley Mow
39 Barton Road, The Dings, BS2 0LP (400m from rear exit of Temple Meads Station over footbridge)
✿ 12-3 (not Mon), 5-11; 12-11 Fri & Sat; 12-10 Sun
☎ (0117) 930 4709
Bristol Beer Factory No. 7, seasonal beers; guest beer Ⓗ
A short walk from Temple Meads station brings you to this excellent pub, saved from closure by the Bristol Beer Factory in 2008. Located in the Dings renovation area, it is open plan, with a pleasant courtyard area outside. Pictures of the area and local art feature strongly, and there is occasional live music. Good food is served lunchtimes and evenings Tuesday to Saturday, with roasts 12-3pm on Sunday. Seasonal ales include the award-winning Milk Stout, and a guest beer often appears. ⚞✿◖◗≠(Temple Meads)🖵⚲

Bell ✅

Hillgrove Street, Stokes Croft, BS2 8JT (off Jamaica St)

☼ 12-midnight (1am Fri); 4.30-1am Sat; 12-10.30 Sun

☎ (0117) 909 6612 ⊕ bell-butcombe.com

Bath Ales Gem; Butcombe Bitter, Gold, seasonal beer Ⓗ

Pleasant, eclectic, two-roomed pub where DJs spin their discs from 10pm nightly in the back room. Friday evenings attract drinkers on their way to nearby clubs. Local workers are regular customers for the lunchtime and early evening food. Sunday lunches are popular, too. A surprising feature is the pleasant rear garden with a patio, which is heated in colder weather. Local art on the wood-panelled walls adds a Bohemian feel. ⊛◖◗❒¹⌐

Bridge Inn

16 Passage Street, BS2 0JF

☼ 12-11.30 (11 Sun) ☎ (0117) 929 0942

Bath Ales SPA, Gem; guest beers Ⓗ

Tiny pub close to the station and surrounding hotels, yet only a short walk from the city centre. Music industry memorabilia features and a collection of vinyl records is available to play on a deck. Regular quizzes and other events are held, and there is free WiFi. The pub is quite adventurous in its choice of real ales, with two from Bath Ales usually available plus two from high-quality micro-breweries. Breakfast is served 8-11am Friday only, and lunch 12-3pm weekdays. All beer prices reduced on Monday. ⊛◖≠(Temple Meads)❒

Cornubia

142 Temple Street, BS1 6EN (opp fire station by former Courage Brewery)

☼ 12-11; closed Sun ☎ (0117) 925 4415

Quantock Sunraker; guest beers Ⓗ

Welcome back to this multi-award-winning CAMRA favourite, superbly revitalised by former winners of the National Pub of the Year award. A great selection of four or five guest beers is on offer, plus a house beer brewed by Arbor and a changing real cider. The atmosphere is convivial with subtle lighting, award-winning pictures, patriotic flags and numerous pump clips on the walls, and a turtle tank too. Food is served at lunchtime, and there is seating outside. Once again, a must-visit pub in Bristol. Q⊛◖≠(Temple Meads)❒♣

Eldon House

6 Lower Clifton Hill, BS8 1BT (off top of Jacobs Wells Rd)

☼ 12-3, 5-midnight; 12-1am Fri & Sat; 12-11 Sun

☎ (0117) 922 1271 ⊕ bathales.com/pubs/eldon-house.html

Bath Ales Spa, Gem; guest beers Ⓗ

Pleasant listed pub greatly extended during 2009, giving it a much more spacious feel. Good quality pub food is served daily plus popular Sunday roasts. There is free WiFi, and many regular events. It is close to the city museum and the QEH theatre, and buses run nearby – get off at the top of Park Street and head down Jacobs Wells Road. Although run by a director of Bath Ales, three of the five guest beers are from well-chosen independent brewers. Bath Ales seasonals may also appear. Q◖≠(Clifton Down)❒

Grain Barge

Mardyke Wharf, Hotwells Road, Hotwells, BS8 4RU (moored on opp bank to SS Great Britain)

☼ closed Mon; 12-11 (11.30 Fri & Sat) ☎ (0117) 929 9347

⊕ grainbarge.com

Bristol Beer Factory Acer, No. 7, Sunrise, seasonal beers Ⓗ

This moored boat was built in 1936 and converted into a floating pub by Bristol Beer Factory in 2007, with great views of the SS Great Britain, the floating harbour and passing boats from the two top decks. Popular themed food nights are held some weekdays. The kitchen is open lunchtimes and evenings. Thatchers cider is served. A downstairs bar and function room are available. Voted among the top 50 nation's bars by the Independent newspaper. ⊛◖❒♣¹⌐

Green Man

21 Alfred Place, Kingsdown, BS2 8HD

☼ 4 (12 Fri & Sat)-11; 12-10.30 Sun ☎ (0117) 930 4824

⊕ thegreenmanbristol.org

Dawkins Green Barrel; guest beers Ⓗ

This small, dimly-lit Dawkins pub, formerly known as The Bell, offers a selection of four or five independent real ales. Home-cooked food comes from a small but interesting changing menu; mainly organic or ethically produced (served all day Monday to Saturday, 12-4pm Sunday). Organic ciders are offered too. The pub hosts two beer festivals per year and a quiz on the last Sunday of the month. Morris men appear sometimes. Q◖❒(20)♣

Highbury Vaults

164 St Michaels Hill, Kingsdown, BS2 8DE (top of steep hill next to Bristol Royal Infirmary)

☼ 12-midnight (11 Sun) ☎ (0117) 973 3203

Bath Ales Gem; Brains SA; Bristol Beer Factory Exhibition; St Austell Tribute; Young's Special; guest beers Ⓗ

In the same hands, and in this Guide, for many years, the pub is popular with university students and hospital staff. Dating from the mid-19th century, its interior is dark and dimly lit, with a small front snug bar, a main drinking area and a bar billiards table. Outside is a large heated patio and garden. Good-quality food is served every lunchtime and weekday evenings. Owned by Young's, the establishment is allowed a lot of freedom with the beer range. Toilets are down steep stairs. Q⊛◖≠(Clifton Down)❒(8,9)♣¹⌐

Hillgrove Porter Stores

53 Hillgrove Street North, Kingsdown, BS2 8LT

☼ 4-midnight (1am Fri); 2-1am Sat; 2-midnight Sun

☎ (0117) 924 9818

Dawkins Brassknocker, Bob Wall, seasonal beers; guest beers Ⓗ

This was the first of the Dawkins Taverns, the brainchild of a local entrepreneur who also bought Matthews Brewery in 2009. An excellent community pub, it usually dispenses eight guest ales, including two more from Dawkins, dark beers and rare styles, plus Westons cider. The interior is horseshoe-shaped, with a wonderfully comfortable lounge area hidden behind the bar. Outside is a pleasant patio. Sunday is quiz night. Frequent themed mini beer festivals are held in conjunction with the other Dawkins pubs. Food is served 6-9pm. Q⊛◖≠(Montpelier)❒♣♣¹⌐

Hope & Anchor

38 Jacobs Wells Road, BS8 1DR (between Anchor Rd and top of Park St)

☼ 12-11 (10.30 Sun) ☎ (0117) 929 2987

Beer range varies Ⓗ

Popular and friendly city local offering up to six changing real ales, mostly from West Country micro-breweries. The pub has achieved a happy balance between those who come to eat the high-quality food, served all day, and those who just want a pint. Subdued lighting, candles on the tables and hanging hop bines over the bar create atmosphere. On summer days the terraced garden at the rear is pleasant, with a recently re-opened well. Street parking is limited. ⊛◑▶🚃-

Old Fishmarket ✅

59-63 Baldwin Street, BS1 1QZ (200m from city centre)
☼ 12-11 (midnight Fri & Sat); 12-10 Sun ☎ (0117) 921 1515
Butcombe Bitter; Fuller's Discovery, London Pride, ESB, seasonal beers Ⓗ
This spacious Fuller's pub, once a fish market, has become the main venue for those who enjoy a great pint with their TV sport – all big events are screened. It has a large front bar and an indoor patio to the side, as well as several discrete seating booths behind the bar for those wishing to avoid the sport. Thai and English meals are served lunchtimes and evenings (until 5pm only on Sun). ◑▶&⇌(Temple Meads)🚃

Orchard Inn

12 Hanover Place, Spike Island, BS1 6XT (off Cumberland Rd near SS Great Britain)
☼ 12 (11 Sat & Sun)-11 ☎ (0117) 926 2678
Bath Ales Gem; Fuller's London Pride Ⓗ**; guest beers** Ⓖ
CAMRA National Cider Pub of the Year 2009, this is a popular one-bar, street-corner local, 10-minutes' walk from the centre along the harbourside. The ferry service stops nearby. It serves up to seven guest beers on gravity, and up to 24 different ciders at once. Good hearty food is served at lunchtimes, with snacks at most other times. Folk music features on Sunday. ⊛◑🚃(500)♣🌢-

Robin Hood

56 St Michaels Hill, BS2 8DX
☼ 12-midnight (1am Fri & Sat) ☎ (0117) 929 4433
Beer range varies Ⓗ
Former Wadworth's pub refurbished and reopened as a free house in early 2010, on a steep hill next to the maternity hospital. A large plain front window looks in on light oak floors and pastel walls. Toilets and a function room are upstairs and there is a small rear outside patio. Four or five changing beers often include one from Moor brewery, plus Thatchers cider and continental beers. Two TVs show sport and good food is served all day until 9pm. Dogs welcome. ⊛◑▶🚃(8,9,20)

Seven Stars 🍺

1 Thomas Lane, Redcliffe, BS1 6JG (just off Victoria St)
☼ 12-11 (10.30 Sun) ☎ (0117) 927 2845
Beer range varies Ⓗ
This small free house was local CAMRA Pub of the Year 2010 and 2011. Generous discounts are offered to CAMRA members at all times and to all customers on Wednesdays and weekday afternoons. The pub has a pool table, rock-oriented juke-box and silent TVs set to sport channels, with outdoor seating in fine weather. Eight changing pumps dispense a full range of styles and strengths, plus ciders and perries. Live acoustic music plays on Thursday evening and weekend afternoons. 'Beeriodical' beerfests are held on the first Monday to Wednesday of every month. ⊛⇌(Temple Meads)🚃(1,54,X39)♣🌢-

Shakespeare ✅

68 Prince Street, BS1 4QD
☼ 11-11 (midnight Fri & Sat); 12-11 Sun ☎ (0117) 929 7695
Greene King IPA, Old Speckled Hen, Abbot; guest beers Ⓗ
Traditional Grade II-listed two-bar pub near the waterside and handy for the SS Great Britain, harbourside and the centre. Two interesting guest beers come from the extended Greene King list from the likes of Hydes, Batemans and Holden's, changing monthly or so. Good value food, including Sunday roasts, is served all day. Families (until 6pm) and dogs are welcome. The small patio at the front is a sun-trap at times. Tuesday is quiz night. There is a public car park nearby. ⊛◑▶🚃-

Three Tuns

78 Georges Road, Hotwells, BS1 5UR (300m from cathedral towards Hotwells)
☼ 12-11 ☎ 07590 519659
Beer range varies Ⓗ
The pub is five minutes' walk from the city centre past the cathedral. Now run by Arbor Ales, this is independent beer nirvana. Seven pumps dispense the full range of beer styles, with two from Arbor and the rest mainly from top-rated British brewers. Bottled beers feature BrewDog and rarities from the US. The L-shaped interior has scrubbed wooden tables and mixed seating. Quality food is served daily, and there is free WiFi. Live folk music is on Monday, and numerous other events include unmissable beer festivals. Outside is a covered, heated patio. ♨⊛◑🚃🌢-

Zerodegrees

53 Colston Street, BS1 5BA (opp Bristol Royal Infirmary)
☼ 12-midnight (11 Sun) ☎ (0117) 925 2706
⊕ zerodegrees.co.uk
Zerodegrees Pale Ale, Wheat Beer, Mango Beer, Black Lager, Pilsner, seasonal beers Ⓗ
This brew-pub won the 2005 CAMRA National New Build Pub award and has proved hugely popular with a good mixed local clientele. The high-tech brewery is on full view. All beers are served at continental-style temperatures, much lower than the norm for pubs in this Guide. A large restaurant serving all day is spread over two floors and features an open kitchen (booking advisable at peak times). Two balconies and a terraced patio provide an escape from the ever-present music. ⊛◑▶&🚃(20)-

Bristol: East

Chelsea Inn

60-62 Chelsea Road, Easton, BS5 6AU
☼ 1-midnight ☎ (0117) 902 9186 ⊕ thechelseabs5.co.uk
Beer range varies Ⓗ
Street-corner community local with one large room and a collection of vintage sofas, armchairs and other furniture. Pictures from local artists are for sale or commission. In a cosmopolitan area, it attracts a varied crowd, many relatively young. Free WiFi and a small exchange library are available. Up to five beers are served, some from the Marston's range, plus varied guest beers and two ciders. Live music plays on Tuesday (jazz), Wednesday and Saturday. Look for the interesting graffiti in the garden. ⊛⇌(Stapleton Rd)🚃(6,7)♣🌢-

Old Stillage ⓛ

145-147 Church Road, Redfield, BS5 9LA (on A420)
☉ 4-11; 12-midnight Fri & Sat; 12-10.30 Sun
☎ (0117) 939 4079
Arbor Ales Hunny Beer, Single Hop, seasonal beers; guest beers Ⓗ
Arbor's first pub acts as the brewery tap and testing ground for its many one-off brews. Low lighting and simple decor feature in this traditional town venue. A pool table, dartboard and juke-box are all available. Food was introduced in 2010, served Friday-Sunday only, and the rear patio area opened up for the first time. There is live music or a DJ at weekends, and Irish night on the last Thursday of the month. CAMRA members receive a discount on real ales. ⊛⧄≠(Lawrence Hill)⊟♣≒

Bristol: North

Annexe

Seymour Road, Bishopston, BS7 9EQ
☉ 11.30-3, 5-11.30; 11.30-11.30 Sat; 12-11 Sun
☎ (0117) 949 3931
Courage Best Bitter; St Austell Tribute; Sharp's Doom Bar; Skinner's Cornish Knocker; Wye Valley HPA; guest beer Ⓗ
Community pub close to the county cricket ground behind the larger Sportsman pub and not far from the Memorial Stadium. Inside is a converted skittle alley and a large conservatory/family room to one side. Several TVs show live sport, including one out on the partially covered patio outside. Good simple food, including quality pizzas, is served, and a pool table is available. Monday is quiz night in this continuously improving pub, which is getting more adventurous with guest beers, too.
Q⧄⊛⧄⬥♿⊟♣≒

Duke of York

2 Jubilee Road, St Werburghs, BS2 9RS
☉ 5-11; 4-midnight Fri; 3-midnight Sat; 3-11 Sun
☎ (0117) 941 3677
Beer range varies Ⓗ
This well-hidden free house serves an eclectic clientele. Visit in daylight for the enchanted forest mural exterior, then at night experience the warm glow of the grotto-like interior. The decor comprises fairy lights, odd memorabilia, wooden floors, a rare skittle alley and much more. There are two rooms, and an extra bar upstairs offering a very different feel. Four handpumps offer unusual beers, real ciders from polypins and a good range of bottled ales. Local CAMRA Pub of the Year 2008.
⊛⧄≠(Montpelier)⊟(5,25)♣●≒

Miners Arms

136 Mina Road, St Werburghs, BS2 9YQ (400m from M32 jct 3)
☉ 4-midnight (1am Fri); 2-1am Sat; 12-midnight Sun
☎ (0117) 907 9874
Brains SA Gold; St Austell Tribute; guest beers Ⓗ
Located close to St Werburghs city farm and Bristol Climbing Centre, this is an excellent three-roomed street-corner local, part of the local Dawkins chain and now free of previous beer ties. The split-level interior houses a hop-adorned bar where two guest beers and two from Dawkins join the regulars and Westons cider. Another small, quiet bar lies to the side, and a larger pool room to the rear. Children and dogs are welcome. The function room can be booked. Thursday is quiz night.
⋈⊛⧄≠(Montpelier)⊟(5,25)♣●≒

Bristol: South

Windmill

14 Windmill Hill, Bedminster, BS3 4LU (next to Bedminster station)
☉ 11-11 (midnight Fri); 12-midnight Sat; 12-10.30 Sun
☎ (0117) 963 5440 ⊕ thewindmillbristol.com
Bath Ales Gem; Bristol Beer Factory No. 7, Sunrise Ⓗ
With pastel colours and wooden flooring throughout, the pub is on two levels, with a family room on the lower area where children are welcome until 8pm. Two beers from the nearby Bristol Beer Factory are always on offer, plus real cider and foreign bottled beers. Good food is served all day. Board games are available, there is free WiFi and an old 1970s juke-box. Outside is a small patio area to the front.
⋈⧄⊛⧄≠(Bedminster)⊟(75,76,77)●≒

Bristol: West

Cambridge Arms

Coldharbour Road, Redland, BS6 7JS
☉ 12-11 (11.30 Fri & Sat) ☎ (0117) 973 9786
Butcombe Bitter; Fuller's Discovery, London Pride, ESB; seasonal beers Ⓗ
Large, red-brick Edwardian Fuller's house, not far from the Downs, with an L-shaped bar, wooden floors and pastel walls. The pub can get busy with diners and those seeking refreshment after sporting exertions. There is a large south-facing garden at low level behind the pub. Fuller's seasonal beers and those from the former Gale's brewery are often available. Sunday roast is popular but no booking is allowed. Dogs are welcome. ⋈⊛⧄⊟(583)P≒

Lansdown

8 Clifton Road, Clifton, BS8 1AF
☉ 4-11; 12-11 Fri & Sat; 12-10.30 Sun ☎ (0117) 973 4949
⊕ thelansdown.com
Bath Ales Barnstormer; St Austell Tribute; guest beers Ⓗ
Traditional pub that now specialises in a great real ale offering. Four of the five beers come from within 20 miles and the range always features an excellent mix of styles, including a dark beer and a golden ale. Arbor ales alternate with Tribute. All beers are sold at similar upper-end prices irrespective of strength. There is an upstairs lounge/dining room available for functions. Food is available evenings (except Sun) and lunchtimes when open. The courtyard garden is heated and covered. ⊛⧄⊟(8,9)≒

Merchants Arms

5 Merchants Road, Hotwells, BS8 4PZ
☉ 4 (12 Fri-Sun)-11 ☎ (0117) 904 0037
Bath Ales SPA, Gem, Barnstormer, seasonal beer Ⓗ
Traditional local located just before the Cumberland Basin, on all the main Bristol to north Somerset bus routes. It won a national CAMRA award for its refurbishment when Bath Ales first took it on. Conversation dominates in the two drinking areas, although live music is held occasionally and a quiz night on Thursday. The concealed TV is brought out now and again for football. Food is limited to bar snacks. Well-behaved dogs are welcome, and there is free WiFi access. ⋈Q⊟

Portcullis

3 Wellington Terrace, Clifton, BS8 4LE (close to Clifton side of Suspension Bridge)

Pig Inn the City ⓁL
121 Westgate Street, GL1 2PG
✪ 11-midnight (1.30am Fri & Sat) ☎ (01452) 421960
⊕ piginnthecity.co.uk
St George's Dragons Blood; Uley Pig's Ear; guest beers Ⓗ
An imposing, listed, 19th-century facade belies the vibrant atmosphere inside this welcoming family-run pub. Humorous piggy bric-a-brac is displayed, and pig portraits adorn the walls. Up to four craft ales are sourced nationwide, and ciders from Gwatkin and Broadoak feature in summer. Excellent home-made food is available every lunchtime (and evenings except Tue, Fri and Sun, when there is entertainment). An upstairs function room is available for hire. Local CAMRA City Pub of the Year 2009-2011. ✿❍⬥⬥≈♣●ᵇ—

Ham

Salutation Ⓛ
Ham Green, Berkeley, GL13 9QH (from Berkeley take road signed Jenner Museum) ST681984
✪ 12-2.30 (not Mon), 5-11; 11-11 Sat; 12-10.30 Sun
☎ (01453) 810284 ⊕ salutationinn.biz
Cotswold Spring Old English Rose; Severn Vale Dursley Steam Bitter; guest beers Ⓗ
Finalist for CAMRA National Pub of the Year 2011, this rural free house is situated in the Severn Valley within walking distance of the Jenner Museum, Berkeley Castle and Deer Park. This friendly local sources its beers from nearby breweries and is popular with walkers and cyclists. The pub has two cosy bars with a log fire and a skittle alley/function room. Food is served lunchtimes and early evening. There is a child-friendly garden at the front.
⋈Q✿❍⬥⬥♣●P

Hartpury

Royal Exchange Ⓛ ✅
Gloucester Road, GL19 3BW (on A417)
✪ 11.30 (12 Sun)-11.30 ☎ (01452) 700714
Beer range varies Ⓗ
A traditional, rural pub that started as a beer house in the mid-1800s, situated on an old turnpike road. With a large garden, it has good open views towards the Malverns and May Hill. Inside there are three adjoining drinking/dining areas, plus a pool/darts room, all with either a real fire or log-burner. The local Mummers meet for a session every second Tuesday of the month, to enjoy the five local ales offered. ⋈⭲✿❍⬥▲▦(132,351)●P—

Hawkesbury Upton

Beaufort Arms Ⓛ
High Street, GL9 1AU (off A46, 6 miles N of M4 jct 18)
✪ 12-11 (10.30 Sun) ☎ (01454) 238217
⊕ beaufortarms.com
Wickwar BOB; guest beers Ⓗ
This 17th-century Grade II-listed, Cotswold stone free house is close to the historic Somerset Monument. It has separate public and lounge bars, dining room and skittle alley/function room. The interior is adorned with an ever-increasing plethora of ancient brewery and local memorabilia. It serves four ales and Wickwar Screech cider. With an attractive garden, this fine village inn is the hub of local community activities. A local CAMRA award winner where a warm welcome is assured.
⋈Q✿❍⬥⬥▦♣●P

Lechlade

Crown Inn Ⓛ ✅
High Street, GL7 3AE (opp traffic lights at A417/A361 jct)
✪ 12-midnight (11 Sun) ☎ (01367) 252198
⊕ crownlechlade.co.uk
Halfpenny Ha'penny Ale, Thames Tickler, Four Seasons, Old Lech, seasonal beer Ⓗ
Local CAMRA Pub of the Year 2010, this twin-roomed, wooden-floored brew-pub has flourished, with up to six Halfpenny ales available, to the obvious delight of its regular clientele. Renowned locally for its parties and unusual choice of games, this enthusiastic establishment makes for a memorable drinking experience. Two fireplaces flank the front room, whose walls feature an eclectic array of paraphernalia, while smokers can watch the brewing from a covered patio at the rear. ⋈✿⬥▲▦♣—

Marshfield

Catherine Wheel
High Street, SN14 8LR (off A420 between Chippenham and Bristol)
✪ 12-11 ☎ (01225) 892220 ⊕ thecatherinewheel.co.uk
Courage Best Bitter; guest beers Ⓗ
Beautifully restored Georgian-fronted pub on the village high street, with a pretty dining room. An extensive main bar leads down from the original wood-panelled area, via stone-walled rooms, to the patio area at the rear. A superb open fire warms in winter. There are up to two local guest ales available, and imaginative and well-presented food is served in the bar or garden (no meals Sun eve). Children are allowed and free WiFi is available. ⋈Q✿⬥❍⬥▦(635)P—

May Hill

Glasshouse
GL17 0NN (off A40 W of Huntley) SO710213
✪ 11.30-3, 6.30-11; 12-3 Sun ☎ (01452) 830529
Butcombe Bitter; Sharp's Doom Bar Ⓖ
Recently extended old pub, sympathetically refurbished using reclaimed bricks and timber. A safe and enclosed garden makes this popular with families on warm, sunny days. There is an interesting seat and canopy in the car park made out of an old yew hedge. Flagstone floors, an old cooking range and various nooks and crannies make this a venue worth looking out for. Good home-cooked food and two ales are available. ⋈Q✿❍P—

Mayshill

New Inn ✅
Badminton Road, BS36 2NT (on A432 between Coalpit Heath and Nibley)
✪ 11.45-3, 5.30-11; 11.45-11 Fri & Sat; 12-10 Sun
☎ (01454) 773161
Beer range varies Ⓗ
A 17th-century inn hugely popular for its food, so book ahead. Expect three changing guest beers from far and wide, one of them likely to be dark, plus a changing cider. The main bar is warmed by a real fire in winter, and the rear area is more of a restaurant. Children are welcome until 8.45pm. The garden is pleasant in summer. Generous beer discounts are available to CAMRA

members on Monday and Tuesday evenings. Local CAMRA Pub of the Year 2009. Free WiFi. ⚌Q✿◗⌷(X42,342)●P⌂⌐

Minchinhampton

Weighbridge Inn �🍺
Longfords, GL6 9AL (on road from Nailsworth to Avening near Longford Mill)
✪ 12-11 (10.30 Sun) ☎ (01453) 832520 ⊕ 2in1pub.co.uk
Uley Old Spot; Wadworth 6X; guest beer ⊞
The Weighbridge Inn is on the original packhorse trail to Bristol, which is now a footpath and bridleway. The road at the front of the inn became a turnpike in 1822, when the weighbridge served the local mills. Today the pub is known for its 2-in-1 pies. Inside there are many exposed beams and open logs fires to provide winter warmth. The guest beer is often from a local micro-brewery. Children and dogs are welcome. ⚌Q✿◗⌷⌐⚁▲P⌂⌐

Moreton in Marsh

Inn on the Marsh
Stow Road, GL56 0DW (on A429 at S end of town)
✪ 12-2.30, 7-11; 11-3, 6-11 Thu-Sat and summer; 12-3, 7-11 Sun ☎ (01608) 650709
Banks's Mild; Marston's Burton Bitter, Pedigree; guest beer ⊞
A charming Marston's pub that usually has an interesting house guest ale, often from Ringwood. Next to a duck pond, this former bakery has woven hanging baskets on display. The bar area has a dedicated popular locals' section, and a welcoming lounge area with open fire and comfortable seating. The large conservatory serves food with a Dutch East Indies influence, and is ideal for parties. If you are lucky, the enthusiastic landlord may even play his guitar. Close to Moreton, and it has a car park. ⚌Q✿◗⌷⚁▲⇌⌷⚁●P⌂⌐

Nettleton Bottom

Golden Heart �🍺
GL4 8LA (on A417)
✪ 11-3, 5.30-11; 11-11 Fri & Sat; 12-10.30 Sun
☎ (01242) 870261 ⊕ thegoldenheart.co.uk
Brakspear Bitter; Festival Gold; guest beers ⊞
This 300-year-old Cotswold free house stands beside the short single-carriageway section of the Swindon to Gloucester road. Little has changed here in a century and the large log fire, bare stone walls, mixed furniture and assorted mementos ooze rustic charm. The best locally-sourced produce contributes to the national award-winning food, and children are catered for. To the rear, a large stone-paved patio and lawn abut a cow pasture. Two en-suite bedrooms are available. ⚌Q✿▲◗P⌂⌐

Newent

George Hotel �🍺 ✅
Church Street, GL18 1PU (off B4215 and B4216 opp church)
✪ 11-11 (midnight Fri & Sat); 12-10 Sun ☎ (01531) 820203 ⊕ georgehotel.uk.com
Butcombe Bitter; Sharp's Doom Bar; guest beers ⊞
This attractive town-centre coach house and post inn dates back to the mid-17th century - records state 1649. Despite it being a three-star hotel, a dartboard, fruit machines and TV screens are

located in the rear area of the open bar, with the coach house now a restaurant. It plays host to the Newent Onion Fayre Beer and Cider Festival in September. Several function rooms, nine en-suite bedrooms and three flats are available. ⚌✿▲◗⚁⌷♣●P⌂⌐

Oldbury on Severn

Anchor Inn
Church Road, BS35 1QA
✪ 11.30-2.30, 6-11; 11.30-12 Sat; 12-10.30 Sun
☎ (01454) 413331 ⊕ anchor-inn-oldbury.co.uk
Butcombe Bitter; Draught Bass; Otter Bitter; guest beer ⊞
Converted riverside mill with two bars and a restaurant. People come from afar for the food, which is served in all areas when busy. The lounge has an L-shaped bar, wooden beams and an open fire. The more spartan public bar is popular with locals. One guest beer is added on Thursday until it runs out. The large enclosed garden to the rear has a boules piste and access to the river footpath. Children are welcome in the restaurant. ⚌Q✿◗⌷⚁♣●P⌂⌐

Quenington

Keepers Arms
Church Road, GL7 5BL (from Fairford turn right at village green)
✪ 12-3 (not Mon & Tue); 7-11 ☎ (01285) 750349
⊕ thekeepersarms.co.uk
Butcombe Bitter; guest beer ⊞
Given a fresh breath of life under its young, enthusiastic landlord, this once-basic village local has been slowly transformed into a modern pub. The new wood of the counter and floor make an attractive combination in the refurbished bar, with the other two rooms now set aside for dining (except for quiz nights), with regular themed dining evenings. Two fireplaces give a pleasant glow in winter. The tiny front garden is popular with cyclists, ramblers and smokers alike. ⚌✿◗⚁♣P

Rodborough

Prince Albert 🍷 🍺 ✅
Rodborough Hill, GL5 3SS
✪ 4.30 (5 Sat)-11.30; 4.30-12.30am Fri & Sat; 12-10.30 Sun
☎ (01453) 755600 ⊕ theprincealbertstroud.co.uk
Fuller's London Pride; Stroud Budding; Taylor Landlord; guest beers ⊞
This lively, cosmopolitan pub near Rodborough Common is bohemian, homely and welcoming, with an eclectic mix of furniture and fittings, the walls covered with myriad film and music photos/posters. It hosts three beer festivals a year, plus art exhibitions and themed nights – quizzes, backgammon, live music and comedy. Some Tuesday events are ticketed, so please check first. Children, dogs and walkers all welcome. No food is served Monday-Wednesday. Local CAMRA Pub of the Year 2011. ⚌✿⇌♣⌐

Sheepscombe

Butchers Arms ✅
GL6 7RH (off A46 N of Painswick, or off B4070 N of Slad)
SO893105

in a secluded paved garden. Look out for Phil's famous secret beer festival, following the August bank holiday. ♨Q❀☷✿▣☖

George
Butts Road, GU34 1LH
🕒 10-11 (midnight Thu-Sat) ☎ (01420) 82331
Black Sheep Best Bitter; St Austell Tribute; Sharp's Doom Bar; guest beer ⊞
Refurbished in a contemporary style in 2008 and renamed the George, there is live music every Friday, three or four real ales are on offer at all times, and 30 different wines by the glass. Meals are available at all sessions with a seasonal menu changing monthly. Breakfast is served from 10am to noon. Small gardens can be found at the side and rear of the pub. ♨❀◑&▣P☖

Railway Arms ⎣
26 Anstey Road, GU34 2RB
🕒 12-11; 11-midnight Fri & Sat ☎ (01420) 82218
Triple fff Alton's Pride, Moondance, Stairway, seasonal beers; guest beers ⊞
Friendly pub close to the Watercress Line and mainline station, owned by Triple fff Brewery, whose own beers are supplemented by ales from a host of micros. The cider is from Mr Whitehead's. A rear function room, with its own bar, is available for hire. The patio area, designed with a traditional railway theme, incorporates a covered, heated smoking area. There are tables outside at the front, under a striking sculpture of a steam locomotive. Well-behaved dogs are welcome. ❀☷▣♣●☖

Bank

Oak Inn
Pinkney Lane, SO43 7FE (just S of A35 W of Lyndhurst) SU286072
🕒 11.30-3, 6-11; 11.30-11 Sat; 12-10.30 Sun
☎ (023) 8028 2350
Fuller's London Pride, seasonal beers; Gale's Seafarers Ale, HSB; guest beer ⊞
The Oak is a white-painted brick-and-slate house, in a quiet hamlet, yet overlooking a wild part of the New Forest. Inside is a small, cosy, wood-panelled bar, often busy. Fortunately, there is more space in the side garden with many tables, plenty under cover. The same friendly and efficient staff have been running the pub for seven years. The food, featuring fish and local forest products, is popular with locals and tourists alike. ♨❀◑&P☖

Basingstoke

Basingstoke Rugby Club ✔
Pack Lane, RG22 5HH
🕒 6-11; 12-2am Sat (6 Sun) ☎ (01256) 323308
⊕ basingstokerfc.com
Butcombe Bitter; Fuller's London Pride; guest beer ⊞
Founded in 1948 but moving to its current location in 1971, the club is home to several adult, youth and veteran rugby teams. A full programme of social activities is held throughout the year, and the clubhouse and grounds are available for hire. CAMRA members are welcome. Opening hours are flexible when sporting fixtures are held. ❀◑▣(1,5)P☖

Basingstoke Sports & Social Club ✔
May's Bounty, Fairfields Road, RG21 3DR (10 minutes' walk S of Top of Town area)

🕒 12-3, 5-11; 12-11 Fri & Sat; 12-10.30 Sun
☎ (01256) 331646 ⊕ basingstoke-sports-club.co.uk
Adnams Bitter; Fuller's London Pride; Gale's Seafarers Ale, HSB; guest beers ⊞
Founded in 1865 by local brewery owner and entrepreneur, Col. John May, the club is home to cricket, rugby, football and hockey clubs as well as providing squash courts. County cricket week attracts large crowds in the summer. The wide-screen TV in the bar is dedicated to sports events. A full programme of social activities is held throughout the year, and the clubhouse and grounds are available for hire. CAMRA members are welcome. Opening hours are flexible when sporting fixtures are held. ❀◑▶▣P

Maidenhead Inn ✔
17 Winchester Street, RG21 7ED (at top of town)
🕒 9-midnight (1am Fri & Sat); 7-midnight Sun
☎ (01256) 316030
Greene King Ruddles Best Bitter, Abbot; guest beers ⊞
This attractive Wetherspoon pub is situated in the historic Top of Town area, with five pumps to dispense local and guest ales. Local beers from Andwell, Loddon and Triple fff breweries regularly feature. A large dining area leads to the compact bar, with further seating to the rear over two levels, complemented by an outdoor heated beer garden. Q❀◑&☷▣☖

New Inn
57 Sarum Hill, RG21 8SS
🕒 9-11 (midnight Thu-Sat); 12-10.30 Sun ☎ (01256) 323292
Triple fff Alton's Pride ⊞
Local to the town centre, the pub offers frequent social and live music opportunities, including bands on Saturdays and pool, darts and karaoke at other times during the week. There is just one real ale pump at the moment, but it has been a permanent fixture for some time now. Limited bar food is available, including breakfasts. ❀◑☷▣(4,5)☖

Way Inn
Chapel Hill, RG21 5TB (opp Holy Ghost church)
🕒 12-11 (10.30 Sun) ☎ (01256) 321520
Caledonian Deuchars IPA; Greene King Abbot; Taylor Landlord; guest beers ⊞
This extensively refurbished pub provides a comfortable environment for all age groups. It has a spacious bar area at the front and rear (the rear bar area is available for group reservations) with access to the large car park, outside patio and south-facing sun-drenched garden. There are no

TVs or bar games but there is an online juke-box. The menus offer a wide range of home-cooked traditional food, available lunchtimes and evenings (no food Sun eve), with a good vegetarian range. The two guest beers are sourced via SIBA. ⏚✿◑↧⇄⊟P⅃

Binsted

Cedars
The Street, GU34 4PB (follow London Rd from Holybourne) SU772411
✿ 12-3, 6 (4.30 Fri)-11.30; 12-11.30 Sat; 12-11 Sun
☎ (01420) 22112 ⊕ thecedarspub.co.uk
Courage Best Bitter; guest beers Ⓗ
Country pub with a quiet and cosy bar area where customers can enjoy pub games, with many teams in local leagues. There is an extensive garden that children will love. Occasional musical events are held as well as an annual beer festival. A warm welcome is extended to walkers, cyclists and campers at this convivial, friendly community pub. Caravans are also permitted. ⏚Q✿◑⚶♣P⅃

Bishop's Sutton

Ship Inn ✓
Main Road, SO24 0AQ (on B3047)
✿ 12-2.30 (not Mon), 6-11; 12-3, 7-10.30 Sun
☎ (01962) 732863
Palmers Copper Ale; guest beers Ⓗ
This comfortable, genuine family-run free house has a split-level bar and a log fire providing a cosy, relaxing atmosphere. There are separate areas for pub games, families and dining, plus a restaurant. The food is home-cooked, with many daily specials on the board. Popular with walkers from the nearby St Swithun's Way, this pub is the hub of the village. The regular bus between Winchester and Alton stops outside, and the Watercress Line preserved steam railway is nearby.
⏚Q➤✿◑⊟(64)♣P⅃

Bishop's Waltham

Bunch of Grapes
St Peter's Street, SO32 1AD (follow signs to church)
✿ 12-1.45, 6-10.30 (not Sun eve) ☎ (01489) 892935
Courage Best Bitter; Goddards Ale of Wight Ⓖ
A gem on the lane that leads to St Peter's Church, this small pub has a homely atmosphere, possibly because the landlord has lived here for more than 30 years, 25 as licensee. There is a waiting list to join the pub's golfing society, so expect to hear discussion of the noble game. The pub serves wine from the local Webbsland vineyard, which the landlord partly owns – opening can be slightly delayed if the landlord is making deliveries. Prices are at the top end but a price list is posted outside.
Q✿⊟(8,69)♣

Boldre

Red Lion ✓
Rope Hill, SO41 8NE (on Rope Hill/Boldre Lane crossroads)
✿ 11-3, 5.30-11; 11-11 Sat summer; 12-4, 6-10.30 (12-10.30 Jul & Aug) Sun ☎ (01590) 673177 ⊕ theredlionboldre.co.uk
Marston's Pedigree; Ringwood Best Bitter, Fortyniner; guest beer Ⓗ
Traditional 15th-century pub now incorporating old cottages and original stables decorated with tack. It

has a cosy, multi-roomed interior with three log fires, low beams and authentic decor. The locally-sourced and home-cooked traditional menu often includes game and seafood. An outside table area incorporates barbecue fittings. Accommodation in season is on a weekly let basis, and for weekends out of season. The bus service stops outside but only Monday-Friday daytime. Guest beers are from the Marston's list. ⏚Q✿↧◑⊟(112)P⅃

Braishfield

Newport Inn
Newport Lane, SO51 0PL (lane opp red phone box) SU373249
✿ 12-2.30 (not Mon), 6-11; 7-10.30 Sun ☎ (01794) 368225
Fuller's London Pride, seasonal beers; Gale's Seafarers Ale, HSB Ⓗ
Run by the same family for nearly 70 years, this two-bar pub, hidden away down a country lane, attracts a loyal clientele from miles around. Visitors would be forgiven for thinking they had strayed into an earlier age. There is often a folk session on Thursday evening, and on Saturday night the landlady leads a singalong around the piano. The simple bar menu offers sandwiches or ploughman's (choose ham or cheese) and their quality is legendary. ⏚Q✿⊟♣P

Catisfield

Limes at Catisfield
34 Catisfield Lane, PO15 5NN
✿ 12-2.30 (not Tue & Wed), 5-11; 12-3, 7-11 Sat; 12-10.30 Sun ☎ (01329) 842926
Fuller's London Pride; Gale's HSB; Hop Back Summer Lightning; Ringwood Best Bitter, Fortyniner; Sharp's Doom Bar Ⓗ
This large free house, formerly a farmhouse and country club, is a traditional drinker's pub where the emphasis is on quality beer. Various clubs use its facilities, including the floodlit petanque arena. A long public bar has darts and pool, and there is a small lounge bar and function room. Friendly conversation is the norm most evenings, but the bars can become busy when petanque or darts teams are playing at home. Seasonal beers may be available, including Ringwood XXXX Porter in winter. ✿⊟(26,28)♣P⅃

Charter Alley

White Hart
White Hart Lane, RG26 5QA (1 mile W of A340, opp turning for Little London) SU593577
✿ 12-2.30 (3 Sat), 7-11; 12-10.30 Sun ☎ (01256) 850048
⊕ whitehartcharteralley.com
Palmers Best Bitter; guest beers Ⓗ
This cosy coaching inn, built in 1819, is the epicentre of this rural village, and all comers are assured of a friendly greeting. Welcoming features include log fires, oak beams and a capacious restaurant, serving a variety of quality food and home-made gourmet pies. The breweriana-decorated main bar has six pumps dispensing an array of ales that changes so frequently that an email notification service is available by subscription. It's been a stalwart Guide entry for the past 22 years. ⏚Q✿↧◑⊟(56)♣P⊟

Greywell

Fox & Goose Ⓛ

The Street, RG29 1BY (E end of village) SU721518
✪ 11-11; 12-10.30 Sun ☎ (01256) 702062
⊕ foxandgoosegreywell.co.uk
Courage Best Bitter; Ringwood Fortyniner; guest beers Ⓗ
Sixteenth-century inn set in a picturesque village and well-frequented by locals, a short distance from the Basingstoke Canal and King John's Castle, from where he rode to Runnymede to seal the Magna Carta in 1215. It is an ideal stop-off for local walkers and cyclists. There is a large field behind the pub used for various events. The two regular beers are accompanied by up to two guests. No food is served Sunday or Monday evenings.
🏚Q❀◑♿Pﹺ

Havant

Old House At Home ✓

2 South Street, PO9 1DA
✪ 11-11 (11.30 Fri & Sat); 12-10.30 Sun ☎ (023) 9248 3464
Fuller's Chiswick Bitter, London Pride, ESB, seasonal beers; Gale's HSB Ⓗ
One of the oldest buildings in town and one of only two survivors of the 1760 fire. Originally five cottages, it then became a bakery and, finally, a pub. The public bar has a bare floor (part tiled and part wood). The decoration includes an old Gale's price list with HSB at 15p a pint. The larger lounge is carpeted and comfortably furnished. To the rear is the pub's garden – probably one of the best secrets in town. No evening meals Friday to Sunday. 🏚❀◑♿➡➡♣ﹺ

Hawkley

Hawkley Inn

Pococks Lane, GU33 6NE SU747291
✪ 12-3, 5.30-11; 12-11 Sat; 12-10.30 Sun ☎ (01730) 827205
⊕ hawkleyinn.co.uk
Beer range varies Ⓗ
A long-standing Guide entry, where six beers are usually on offer, but it can be up to nine. Two real ciders and a perry are also stocked, two of which hail from local producer Mr Whitehead's. Two small bars serve three rooms, the largest of which has a moose head above the fireplace. Outside there is a large front veranda, and the big secure rear garden hosts events including beer festivals. Well-behaved dogs welcome. 🏚Q❀➡◑♣

Hill Head

Crofton Ⓛ ✓

48 Crofton Lane, PO14 3QF
✪ 11-11; 12-10.30 Sun ☎ (01329) 314222
⊕ thecroftonpub.co.uk
Oakleaf Hole Hearted; Sharp's Doom Bar; guest beers Ⓗ
This 1960s estate pub is situated in a housing area not far from the sea, and over the years has undergone many facelifts. Four guest beers are usually available, with beers from SIBA breweries in addition to those from the Punch Taverns portfolio. As well as the two bars, the function room has a skittle alley where special events are held, including a beer festival in November. Home-cooked food is served all day at weekends.
🏚Q❀◑♿➡(33,35)♣Pﹺ

Holybourne

Queen's Head

20 London Road, GU34 4EG
✪ 12-11 (11.30 Thu; 12.30am Fri & Sat; 10.30 Sun)
☎ (01420) 86331
Greene King IPA; guest beers Ⓗ
This traditional, friendly pub highlights the best of Greene King, featuring a flexible and interesting guest beer list. The Queen's comprises two rooms plus an extension and a covered smoking area. Hearty food, served lunchtimes Monday to Sunday and evenings Thursday to Saturday, features local produce. Regular live music events take place throughout the year. The extensive garden has a children's play area. Alton Station is a 15-minute walk. Q❀◑➡➡(Alton)➡(X65)♣Pﹺ

Hook

Crooked Billet ✓

London Road, RG27 9EH (on A30 approx 1 mile E of Hook) SU737548
✪ 11.30-3, 6-11; 11.30-11 Sat; 12-10.30 Sun
☎ (01256) 762118 ⊕ thecrookedbilletpub.co.uk
Courage Best Bitter; Sharp's Doom Bar; guest beer Ⓗ
Recently extended, air-conditioned, spacious pub beside the River Whitewater, run by the same landlord for the past 20 years. The hostelry is renowned for its good food as well as its beer. There are two guest ales. An open log fire is welcoming in winter and there is plenty of space for both drinkers and diners, especially in summer when the riverside garden is at its best. Thatchers is stocked for cider drinkers and a covered area is available for smokers. Families are welcome.
🏚Q❀◑♿➡(10)Pﹺ

Hursley

King's Head Ⓛ ✓

Main Road, SO21 2JW
✪ 11-11 ☎ (01962) 775208
Ringwood Best Bitter; Sharp's Doom Bar; guest beers Ⓗ
The King's Head is an imposing four-square building, originally a coaching inn, built in 1810. Bought in 2009 by a group of local farmers, they upgraded it to a gastro-pub with accommodation. Inside are three linked areas: a rustic lower room, the main bar with fire, and the dining area. In the cellar is a skittle alley. Free of tie and with up to three guests, the inn is a good place to try local ales – Andwell, Botley, Bowman, Itchen Valley and Triple fff often feature. 🏚❀➡◑➡(46,66)P

Hythe

Ebenezer's Ⓛ

Pylewell Rd, SO45 6AR
✪ 11-2.30, 5-11 (11.30 Fri & Sat); 12-11 Sun
☎ (023) 8020 7799
Beer range varies Ⓗ
This delightful little pub started life in 1845 as a chapel; it still serves bread and wine, but not in the same context. A single storey, low-ceilinged bar offers three real ales that change on a regular basis, but at least two are always local beers: Bowman, Flowerpots, Goddards and Hop Back often feature. Outside is a large covered smoking area. Q❀◑♿➡(8,9)ﹺ

Kingsclere

Swan Hotel ⓛ
Swan Street, RG20 5PP
✪ 11-3, 5.30-11 (11.30 Fri); 11-3, 6-11.30 Sat; 12-3.30,
7-10.30 Sun ☎ (01635) 298314 ⊕ swankingsclere.co.uk
Theakston XB; Young's Bitter; guest beers Ⓗ
Traditional inn frequented by an eclectic mix of
customers, serving four beers including two
frequently-changing local guests. The 400-year-old
pub is one of the county's oldest coaching inns,
dating from 1449 and associated with the Bishop
of Winchester for 300 years. The Grade II-listed
building, close to the Watership Down beauty spot,
retains original oak beams and fireplaces, and
offers nine en-suite bedrooms. Good food is served
in both the dining room and the bar (no food Sun).
🏨Q🛏🕽🍴🚃♣P⅄

Langley

Langley Tavern
Lepe Road, SO45 1XR
✪ 11-11 (midnight Fri & Sat) ☎ (023) 8089 1402
Ringwood Best Bitter; guest beers Ⓗ
Large roadhouse built by the Brickwood Brewery in
the 1930s, this pub has a separate public bar with
pool table, dartboard and sports TV. Next door, the
lounge serves four real ales, with the guest beers
usually from local brewers. Food is offered from a
varied menu and there is accommodation in three
en-suite bedrooms. A large beer garden with
children's play area aids the family welcome. Quiz
night is Sunday and there are music nights
monthly. 🏨Q🕽🛏🍴🚃(9)♣

Lasham

Lasham Gliding Society Bar
Lasham Airfield, The Avenue, GU34 5SS SU677438
✪ 12-2, 5-11; 12-11 Sat & Sun ☎ (01256) 384906
Sharp's Doom Bar; guest beer Ⓗ
This club has a friendly, comfortable lounge bar and
an excellent restaurant with a resident chef. Check
in advance for availability of evening meals. It is
open to the public at all times and children are
welcome. An extensive patio area is a good place
to enjoy your pint while watching the aircraft. The
club holds a mini beer festival every Easter. Voted
local CAMRA Club of the Year 2007-2009 and
Wessex Regional Club of the Year 2009.
Q🕽🍴P⅄

Lee on the Solent

Bun Penny ⓛ ✓
36 Manor Way, PO13 9JH
✪ 11-11 (midnight Fri & Sat); 12-10.30 Sun
☎ (02392) 550214 ⊕ bunpenny.co.uk
Otter Bitter Ⓖ; guest beers Ⓗ
You are always assured of a warm welcome at this
excellent free house noted both for its good food
and guest ales drawn from many Hampshire and
West Sussex breweries. It also stocks two real
ciders. It has a large safe garden and caters for
families, situated just three minutes' walk from the
beach. A regular live music venue, it is also dog-
friendly. 🏨Q🕽🍴🚃♣P

Linwood

Red Shoot Inn ✓
Tom's Lane, BH24 3QT SU187094
✪ 11-11 (01425) 475792 ⊕ redshoot.co.uk
**Red Shoot New Forest Gold, Muddy Boot, Tom's
Tipple; Wadworth Henry's IPA, 6X, seasonal beers** Ⓗ
Named after a nearby wood, this Wadworth-
owned brew-pub and its camping and caravan site
provides an excellent base for exploring the
western New Forest area. The large L-shaped bar is
simply furnished, offering a good view of the pub's
brewery. Food is available every session and all
day on summer weekends. Evening entertainment
includes a Thursday quiz and live music on Sunday.
There are beer festivals in April and October and a
cider festival in June. 🏨🕽🍴🚃♣P

Little London

Plough Inn ▾ ⓛ
Silchester Road, RG26 5EP SU621596
✪ 12-3, 5.30 (6 Sat)-11; 12-3, 7-10.30 Sun
☎ (01256) 850628
Palmers Dorset Gold; Ringwood Best Ⓗ**; guest
beers** Ⓖ
Wonderful village pub and recent CAMRA Regional
Pub of the Year, where in winter you can enjoy a
glass of beer in front of one of the log fires or play
a game of bar billiards. A good range of baguettes
is available (no food Sun eve). There is a secluded
garden at the side of the pub. It is ideal for
ramblers and cyclists visiting the extensive Roman
ruins at nearby Silchester or Pamber wood. CAMRA
Branch Pub of the Year 2011. 🏨Q🕽🍴(44)♣P⅄

Long Sutton

Four Horseshoes
RG29 1TA SU748471
✪ 12-2.30 (not Mon & Tue), 6.30-11 (not Sun eve)
☎ (01256) 862488 ⊕ fourhorseshoes.com
Beer range varies Ⓗ
This friendly local has a single bar divided by a
fireplace. A small enclosed veranda offers fine
views. Home-cooked meals are tasty and
reasonably priced. Up to three beers may be
available, usually one under 4%. The second and
fourth Tuesdays of the month are jazz nights, and
the fourth Thursday is quiz night. Take-home real
ale is only £1.50 a pint. Accommodation is
available as well as camping (enquire in advance).
🏨Q🕽🍴🚃(201,C43)P

Lower Froyle

Anchor Inn
Lower Froyle, GU34 4NA (off A31 Alton-Farnham Rd)
✪ 11 (12 Sun)-11 ☎ (01420) 23261
Triple fff Alton's Pride; guest beers Ⓗ
Dating from about the 17th century, this
refurbished and historic country inn retains many
original features. Adjacent to the bar, a
comfortable snug has been created, with oak-
panelled walls and photographs of a bygone era.
While the emphasis is on locally-produced
wholesome food, beers from local micros feature
strongly. Alongside the Alton's Pride from Triple fff
are two guest ales, and Andwell and Bowman
breweries frequently represented. Seasonal events
are held throughout the year.
🏨Q🕽🍴🚃(44)♣P⅄

Lower Upham

Woodman
Winchester Road, SO32 1HA (on B2177, opp B3037 jct)
✿ 12-2.30, 7.15-11; 12-6.30, 7.30-11.30 Sat & Sun
☎ (01489) 860270
Beer range varies Ⓗ
Seventeenth-century pub, recently changed to a free house. The landlord has lived here for more than five decades. A cosy lounge and a friendly public bar serve two or three different real ales (usually one local); Otter, Sharp's and Palmers often feature. There are also more than 150 whiskies. Sandwiches and ploughman's are normally available at lunchtimes. A blues band plays on the first Wednesday of each month and a mini beer festival is held on the weekend of St George's Day. ₳Q❀➌➡(69)♣P⎯🛏

Lower Wield

Yew Tree Ⓛ
SO24 9RX SU636398
✿ closed Mon; 12-3, 6-11; 12-10.30 Sun ☎ (01256) 389224
⊕ the-yewtree.org.uk
Triple fff Alton's Pride; guest beer Ⓗ
Out-of-the-way rural local set in picturesque rolling Hampshire countryside, with an old yew tree growing outside (hence the name), situated on a quiet country lane opposite the local cricket pitch. The house beer is Alton's Pride and the guest comes from a local brewery. The pub has a separate dining area and is a winner of a Good Food Award for 2010. The nearest bus stop is Medstead on route 28, Basingstoke-Alton, 1½ miles away. ₳Q❀➌P

Lymington

Wheel Inn Ⓛ
Sway Road, Pennington, SO41 8LJ (Ramiley Rd/ Pitmore Lane jct, 2 miles W of Lymington)
✿ 11 (12 winter)-midnight (1am Fri & Sat); 12-11 Sun
☎ (01590) 676122 ⊕ thewheelinnpub.co.uk
Ringwood Best Bitter; guest beers Ⓗ
Large family-friendly public bar specialising in sourcing local guest ales for originality and differing styles. The separate Krua Thai 88 restaurant with takeaway service occupies the lounge bar (no food Mon). A stand-up comedy club takes place on the second Tuesday of the month, there is acoustic music every Monday, and a pool table is available. There is background music and karaoke, but this is mainly a fine pub for enlightened conversation. Camping is for caravans only. No weekend or evening bus service. ₳❀➌&🏕➡(X2)P⎯

Milford on Sea

Red Lion
32 High Street, SO41 0QD (on B3058)
✿ 11.30-2.30, 6-11; 12-3 Sun ☎ (01590) 642236
⊕ redlionpubmilfordonsea.co.uk
Fuller's London Pride; Ringwood Best Bitter; guest beers Ⓗ
Imposing 18th-century inn with a notable fireplace. Run by Paul and June for 13 years, it has featured in the Guide for 11 years. Friendly, comfortable and relaxing, the single bar area is split up and arranged on several levels. One area is reserved for pool and darts, with an unobtrusive gaming

machine. Good value quality food is served (no food Sun eve) and occasional musical events are staged. The cider is from Lilley's Cider Barn. No evening buses. ₳Q❀➌&🏕➡(X2)♣🖤P⎯🛏

North Waltham

Fox Ⓛ ✅
Popham Lane, RG25 2BE (off Frog Lane, between village and A30) SU563458
✿ 11-11 (midnight Fri & Sat); 12-10.30 Sun
☎ (01256) 397288 ⊕ thefox.org
Brakspear Bitter; Ringwood Best Bitter; West Berkshire Good Old Boy; guest beer Ⓗ
This is a lovely free house country pub, overlooking farmland and close to the M3/A30. The pub is divided into two – a popular restaurant and a public bar where food is also served (you need to book in advance). Outside there is an extensive beer garden and a children's adventure play area. Once a year the pub holds an oyster festival, with a beer tent and many other stalls and attractions. ₳Q❀➌&➡P⎯

North Warnborough

Lord Derby
Bartley Heath, RG29 1HD SU730526
✿ 11.30-3, 5.30-11; 11.30-11 Wed-Sat; 12-10.30 Sun
☎ (01256) 702283
Fuller's London Pride; Gale's HSB; guest beers Ⓗ
A well-presented country roadside pub in what is now a no-through road. Its central servery supplies the bar and restaurant. The bar has a flagstone floor with bar stools and tables and chairs. Two regular ales are on offer, plus up to two guests, usually one from the local Andwell Brewery. The restaurant area is open plan but cosy, with an open fireplace and hop-covered oak beams. Quality meals, including local game dishes, are served. ₳Q❀➌➌P⎯

Oakhanger

Red Lion
GU35 9JQ SU770360
✿ 12-3, 6-11 (not Sun) ☎ (01420) 472232
Courage Best Bitter; Ringwood Fortyniner; guest beer Ⓗ
Traditional unspoilt village pub catering for locals and visitors. There are views across the countryside from the front window seats. The restaurant has a good range of meals and in winter the pub is warmed by log fires – there is an inglenook fireplace. Dating from 1550, the pub was called the Rising Sun from 1700 until 1824. Acquired by Farnham United Breweries in 1927 and latterly Courage in 1951, the Red Lion is now an Enterprise Inn. ₳Q❀➌➌♣P⎯

Odiham

Odiham & Greywell Cricket Club Ⓛ
King Street, RG29 1NF
✿ 5 (2 Sat)-9; 12-10 summer; 1-7 (12-10 summer) Sun
☎ (01256) 703302 ⊕ odihamandgreywell.play-cricket.com
Andwell seasonal beers; guest beer Ⓗ
The first recorded match at this club was in 1764, making it one of the oldest cricket clubs in the country. It is set in countryside just south of the village, so you can enjoy a quiet beer while watching cricket in summer. A guest ale is

available alongside one of the beers from Andwell Brewery. Although a private members' club, CAMRA members are welcome. ▲✿♣P♿

Overton

Greyhound
46 Winchester Street, RG25 3HS SU516495
🕓 5-11 (11.30 Fri); 12-3, 6-11.30 Sat; 12-3, 7-10.30 Sun
☎ (01256) 770241
Caledonian Deuchars IPA, seasonal beer; Greene King IPA, Abbot; Ringwood Fortyniner Ⓗ
Near the village centre and bus stops, this is a typical village pub, with a welcoming bar between a comfortable TV lounge and the games area with a pool table and dartboard. This local is an integral part of village life, supporting the cricket club and most pub games and activities including cribbage and quizzes. At the rear is a well-lit courtyard area with seating and floral displays, and access to the external toilets. ▲Q✿🖳(74,76,86)♣♿

Red Lion Ⓛ
37 High Street, RG25 3HQ SU513497
🕓 12-3, 6-11; 12-4 Sun ☎ (01256) 773363
Cheriton Flowerpots Bitter; Triple fff Moondance Ⓗ
Close to the village centre, this pub has a good reputation for high quality, freshly-cooked food at reasonable prices. The main menu includes a vegetarian dish and there are daily specials. Three smartly decorated areas include a restaurant, main bar and snug with upholstered bench settees. There is a car park at the rear and a partially covered patio area. No food Sunday evening. ▲Q✿❶🖳(74,76,86)P♿

Park Gate

Sir Joseph Paxton ✅
272 Hunts Pond Road, PO14 4PF
🕓 12-11.30 (midnight Fri & Sat); 12-11 Sun
☎ (01489) 571111 🌐 sirjosephpaxton.co.uk
Otter Bitter; Ringwood Fortyniner; St Austell Tribute Ⓗ
A friendly pub in a residential part of Park Gate, named after the famous English gardener and architect who designed the Crystal Palace. The pub changed ownership at the end of 2009 and the new landlord is committed to serving consistently good real ale. Three handpumps are offered, with brands popular with the regulars. The pub has ample parking, a beer garden and offers occasional live music. A selection of traditional pub food is served all day, together with various seasonal special offers. ▲Q✿❶🖳(80)P♿

Petersfield

Good Intent ✅
40 College Street, GU31 4AF
🕓 11-3, 5.30-11; 12-3, 7-11 Sun ☎ (01730) 263838
🌐 goodintentpetersfield.co.uk
Fuller's London Pride, seasonal beer; Gale's Seafarers Ale, HSB; guest beers Ⓗ
A 16th-century pub just a few minutes' walk north from the town centre, on the old main road to London. It has a single bar to serve two rooms. One doubles as a restaurant, while the main room has low wood beams and a split-level floor. There is a small garden/patio at the front, live music on Sunday evening, and a quiz on Monday. Food is served at all sessions. ▲✿🚲❶≠P

Portsmouth

Artillery Arms Ⓛ ✅
Hester Road, PO4 8HB
🕓 12-3, 6-11.30; 12-midnight Fri; 11-midnight Sat; 11-11.30 Sun ☎ (023) 9273 3611
Bowman Swift One; Fuller's ESB; guest beers Ⓗ
Traditional local back-street free house selling a wide selection of up to six ales from many southern breweries. Located just minutes from Fratton Park football ground, it can get lively on match days. The pub has a large walled garden with equipment for children. It is famous for its good value Sunday lunches, and rolls are available on match days. The pub also supports darts and pool teams. Q✿🚲🖳(1c,6,17)♣P♿

Barley Mow Ⓛ ✅
39 Castle Road, Southsea, PO5 3DE
🕓 12 (11 Sat)-midnight; 12-11 Sun ☎ (023) 9282 3492
🌐 barleymowsouthsea.com
Fuller's London Pride; Gale's HSB; guest beers Ⓗ
Good-sized Victorian street-corner pub with pool and darts in the public bar, and a wood-panelled lounge bar. There are usually five guest beers on offer, one a mild, stout or porter. This lively community pub hosts a wide range of events from theme nights to quizzes and music and is home to darts, bridge, billiards, chess, pool, golf and cricket teams. The award-winning garden has a covered area so can be appreciated all year round. ✿🚲♿≠(Portsmouth & Southsea)🖳(1,23,40)♣👜

Duke of Devonshire Ⓛ
119 Albert Road, PO5 2SR
🕓 11-midnight (1am Fri & Sat); 12-11.45 Sun
☎ (023) 9282 3682
Fuller's London Pride; guest beers Ⓗ
A busy traditional street-corner local in the Albert Road area of Southsea. The single bar has comfortable seating throughout and a real old-world feel; it is a step back in time. Known as Mollie's, it has a thriving ladies' darts team. On milder days drinkers can enjoy the walled patio garden to the rear. You are certain of a warm welcome and fine ale no matter what the weather. ✿🖳(17,18)♣♿

Eldon Arms Ⓛ
15 Eldon Street, Southsea, PO5 4BS
🕓 12-11 (11.30 Fri & Sat; 10.30 Sun) ☎ (023) 9229 7963
Fuller's London Pride; guest beers Ⓗ
A traditional tiled exterior belies an expansive interior, as the building encompasses the neighbouring cottage. This extension houses the games area with pool, darts and billiards; the other end of the bar has board games piled on a piano. Guest beers are both light and dark. There is a good community spirit, with a mixed clientele; although popular with students, this is not a student pub. Food is served lunchtimes with a carvery on Sunday. The smoking shelter is heated. ✿❶≠(Portsmouth & Southsea)🖳(15)♣👜♿

Fifth Hants Volunteer Arms ✅
74 Albert Road, Southsea, PO5 2SL
🕓 3-midnight; 12-1am Fri-Sun ☎ (023) 9282 7161
Fuller's London Pride; Gale's Seafarers Ale, HSB Ⓗ
A traditional two-bar, street-corner local popular with all ages, run by the same landlord for more than 25 years. The public bar has bare boards, a dartboard and probably the best rock juke-box in town. The smaller lounge is comfortably furnished,

featuring military memorabilia and pictures of the pub's dogs past and present. One wall displays certificates commemorating the pub's many years in this Guide. ⏰🍽(17,18)♣

Florence Arms
18-20 Florence Road, Southsea, PO5 2NE
✪ 12-midnight (11 Sun) ☎ (023) 9287 5700
Adnams Bitter, Broadside; Shepherd Neame Spitfire; guest beers Ⓗ
One of Southsea's hidden gems, the Flo has a genuine public bar, a more select lounge, and a dining room serving excellent home-cooked meals (no food weekends except Sun lunch). Live entertainment includes jazz, folk and poetry. Guest beers come from local independent breweries. The excellent range of cider and perry, including at least 25 real ciders and perries on draught and 40-plus in bottles, earned it CAMRA's Regional Cider Pub of the Year title in 2010. Q◐⏰🍽(1,5,6)♣●

Fountain Inn Ⓛ
163 London Road, North End, PO2 9AA
✪ 12 (11 Sat)-11.30; 12-11 Sun ☎ (023) 9266 1636
Gale's HSB; Irving Frigate Ⓗ
This is a large Grade II-listed pub handy for North End shops. Previously a Brickwoods house, the present building dates from around 1898 and was designed by renowned Portsmouth architect AE Cogswell, although there has been a coaching inn on the site since the 1700s. The U-shaped single bar displays an assortment of historic pub photographs on the walls. There is a separate family/games room to the rear which may be hired. A quiz is held on Thursday. Well-served by buses. ⛟🌳♿🍽(1,1a,3)♣⌐

Hole in the Wall Ⓛ
36 Great Southsea Street, Southsea, PO5 3BY
✪ 4-11; 12-midnight Fri; 4-midnight Sat; 2 (4 summer)-11 Sun ☎ (023) 9229 8085 ⊕ theholeinthewallpub.co.uk
Oakleaf Hole Hearted Ⓖ; **guest beers** Ⓗ/Ⓖ
The Hole is one of the smallest pubs in Portsmouth, but has one of the best beer ranges from local breweries and agencies. The current selection of five or six beers is displayed on the website. Hole Hearted, originally brewed for and named after the pub, is on gravity. Real cider and 'weapons grade' ginger beer are also served. Food is available most evenings – quality sausages and suet puddings are the speciality. No admittance after 11pm. Local CAMRA Pub of the Year 2007 and 2009. Q◐⇌(Portsmouth & Southsea)🍽(1,3,23)●⌐

Leopold Tavern 🍷 Ⓛ ✅
154 Albert Road, Southsea, PO4 0JT
✪ 11 (10 Fri & Sat)-midnight; 12-11 Sun ☎ (023) 9282 9748
Bowman Swift One; Hop Back Summer Lightning; Oakleaf Hole Hearted; guest beers Ⓗ
A spacious pub with a single bar divided into three drinking areas, the outside retains the original decor advertising the Portsmouth & Brighton United Breweries, while the interior has been given a modern but subtle makeover. Three guest beers are served, at least one from a local brewery. Local real cider is often available and sometimes a perry too. A small patio garden completes this excellent watering hole. Local CAMRA Pub of the Year 2010 and 2011. ♿🍽(17,18,19)♣●⌐

Northcote Hotel
35 Francis Avenue, Southsea, PO4 0HL
✪ 11-midnight (1am Fri & Sat) ☎ (023) 9278 9888

Hop Back Summer Lightning; Taylor Landlord; Wadworth 6X Ⓗ
An imposing two-bar pub in the Albert Road area of Southsea. The spacious public bar has a dartboard and pool table, while the smaller comfortable lounge is decorated with memorabilia from the early days of the cinema, including Charlie Chaplin and the Marx Brothers, and the famous fictional detective, Sherlock Holmes. The bar back is unusually fitted with plain glass rather than mirrors, allowing customers in the lounge to watch a darts match in the public bar. To the rear is a large heated patio area. ♿🌳🍽(17,18,19)♣

Old Canal Inn Ⓛ
2 Shirley Avenue, Milton, PO4 8HF
✪ 3-midnight (1am Fri & Sat) ☎ (023) 928 25750
Oakleaf Pompey Royal; Ringwood Old Thumper Ⓗ
This street-corner pub retains the traditional green tiles and etched windows of the old Portsmouth United Breweries. Inside, wooden tables and chairs surround the L-shaped bar. Although the cask range is limited there are also a few bottled beers. In a residential area, this is very much a friendly community pub, with men's and ladies' darts and pool teams and popular Saturday night live music. The landlord is proud to uphold traditional pub values and this place is being sympathetically redecorated. ⛟♿♣⌐

Old Customs House
Gunwharf Quay, PO1 3TY
✪ 9-midnight (10.30 winter; 2am Fri & Sat); 9-11 Sun ☎ (023) 9283 2333 ⊕ theoldcustomshouse.com
Fuller's London Pride, ESB, seasonal beers; Gale's Seafarers Ale, HSB Ⓗ
Award-winning conversion of the former Naval Pay Office in HMS Vernon, the layout of this Grade II-listed building comprises several rooms spread over the ground and first floors, many with period fittings. Some of the history of the building, particularly while in Royal Navy service, can be found on display boards. Set within the modern Gunwharf Quays retail and leisure complex, this pub is popular with locals and visitor alike. Q♿◐♿⇌(Portsmouth Harbour)🍽⌐

Pembroke
20 Pembroke Road, Southsea, PO1 2NR
✪ 10-midnight (11 Mon); 12-4, 7-11 Sun ☎ (023) 9282 3961
Draught Bass; Fuller's London Pride; Greene King Abbot Ⓗ
Purpose built as a street-corner hostelry in 1711, this now single-room bar has a horseshoe-shaped interior and an L-shaped servery decorated with naval memorabilia. It is mentioned in the Captain Marryat novels under its original name of the Little Blue Line. It changed its name to the Pembroke in 1900. This pub is a rare haven for the discerning drinker, which explains its varied clientele, and it still serves probably the best pint of London Pride in Portsmouth. 🍽(6,6a)

Phoenix
13 Duncan Road, Southsea, PO5 2QU
✪ 10-midnight (1am Fri & Sat); 12-midnight Sun ☎ (023) 9278 1055
Beer range varies Ⓗ
Hidden in the back streets off Albert Road, this solidly traditional pub is well worth seeking out. The public bar is decorated with memorabilia of the local football team and has a large-screen TV for major matches. The lounge is adorned with many

photographs of actors, actresses, comedians and others who have performed at the nearby Kings Theatre. There is a games room with a pool table, separated from the rest of the pub by a small walled garden. ✿🍴🖂(17,18)♣🚭

Rose In June ✪
102 Milton Road, PO3 6AR
🕐 12-11.30 ☎ (023) 928 24191 🌐 theroseinjune.co.uk
Fuller's London Pride; Gale's HSB; Hop Back Summer Lightning; Ringwood Best Bitter; Sharp's Doom Bar; guest beer Ⓗ
Imposing, two-bar pub near Kingston Prison and 20 minutes' walk from Fratton Park, originally owned by Allen's Buckland Brewery. It has an extensive garden with adventure playground, barbecue and marquee. The publican keeps birds of prey. The guest beer changes every weekend; annual beer festivals are hosted in February and June. There is a regular quiz on Tuesday, and darts and pool teams. Monthly fish and chips night is on the first Wednesday. The cider is Thatchers Cheddar Valley. ✿🍴🖂(1c,6,6a)♣🚭

Royal Marines Artillery Tavern
58 Cromwell Road, Eastney, PO4 9NL
🕐 6-midnight (1am Fri-Sun) ☎ (02392) 820896
Fuller's London Pride; Gale's Seafarers Ale, HSB Ⓗ
A back-street drinkers' local opposite what used to be the old main gate of the Royal Marine barracks from which the pub takes its name. The beer range is from Fuller's and the old Gale's beer list. The pub provides free entertainment most weekends; it is also home to the last remaining skittle alley in Portsmouth. It's within walking distance of the seafront at Eastney and the Royal Marines museum. ✿🄰🖂(1c,6,6a)♣🚭

Sir Loin of Beef
152 Highland Road, PO4 9NH
🕐 11-11.30 (midnight Fri & Sat); 12-11.30 Sun
☎ (02392) 820115
Beer range varies Ⓗ
A true free house with around eight beers sourced mainly from southern independent breweries. A good range of bottle-conditioned beers is also stocked to complement the range of draught ale. The pub has a nautical theme – submarine paraphernalia adorns the walls and a klaxon is used to signal time. A warm welcome with a continental feel awaits. 🄰🖂(1c,6,6a)♣🍴

Winchester Arms Ⓛ
99 Winchester Road, Buckland, PO2 7PS
🕐 3 (4 Mon)-11; 12-11 Sat & Sun ☎ (023) 9266 2443
🌐 thewinchpub.co.uk
Oakleaf Hole Hearted; Shepherd Neame Spitfire; guest beer Ⓗ
Friendly two-bar local pub with two beers and one varying guest. An open fire is set in the winter. The pub has a dartboard and runs its own teams. A beer festival takes place on the spring bank holiday each year, and on Sunday evening there is live music. There is a covered area in the garden for smokers. The pub may stay open beyond 11pm on Friday and Saturday evenings if busy. ✿Q✿🍴♣🍴🚭

Preston Candover

Purefoy Arms
Alresford Road, RG25 2EJ SU606416
🕐 closed Mon; 12-3, 6-11; 12-6 Sun ☎ (01256) 389777
🌐 thepurefoyarms.co.uk

Beer range varies Ⓗ
Recently remodelled into a modern, rustic-style dining pub, opposite the church in the charming village of Preston Candover. An extensive and imaginative menu changes daily and has a Michelin Bib Gourmand Award. The interior provides informal, well-spaced dining, with a small bar area serving two real ales and cider. There is a large rear garden. Q✿🍴♿🖂(41,42)🍴P

Ringwood

Inn on the Furlong ✪
12 Meeting House Lane, BH24 1EY
🕐 10 (11 Sun)-11 ☎ (01425) 475139
Jennings Cocker Hoop; Ringwood Best Bitter, Fortyniner, Old Thumper; guest beers Ⓗ
Former Ringwood Brewery tap, this substantial Victorian house is a popular meeting place for mature customers. A raised bar serves a series of interlinked rooms including a family area and a sunny conservatory used mainly by diners. Outside are two small patio gardens, one heated and covered. All Ringwood beers are served plus guest beers from Marston's; the real cider is from Cheddar Valley. An Indian buffet is available on Wednesday night. 🄰Q✿✿🍴♿🄰🖂♣🍴🚭

Rockbourne

Rose & Thistle ✪
SP6 3NL
🕐 11-3, 6-11; 11-11 Sat; 12-10.30 (8 winter) Sun
☎ (01725) 518236 🌐 roseandthistle.co.uk
Fuller's London Pride; Palmers Copper Ale; Taylor Landlord; guest beer Ⓗ
Delightful 16th-century thatched chalk cob local with a beamed ceiling, two log fires and cottage garden frontage close to the Roman villa. A locally-sourced guest ale is available in summer when the pub is also frequented by local cricket teams. The cider is Westons First Quality. Local game, fish and home-made sorbets and ice cream feature on the imaginative menu (no food Sun eve), and the restaurant area has a collection of Simon Drew animal caricatures. Surrounded by good walking and cycling country. 🄰Q✿🍴♣🍴P🚭

Romsey

Abbey Hotel Ⓛ
11 Church Street, SO51 8BT
🕐 11-3, 6-11; 11-11 Sat; 12-3, 7-10.30 Sun
☎ (01794) 513360 🌐 abbeyhotelromsey.co.uk
Courage Best Bitter, Directors; Young's Bitter Ⓗ
Lovely old hotel opposite the world-famous Romsey Abbey. Stepping through the door, to your left is a small secluded dining area with a varied menu available, to the right a curved, well-stocked bar that serves three real ales. A popular pub near the town centre, it is also close to the tourist information office and the medieval King John's House. There is a tranquil garden beyond the car park. 🄰Q🍴🍴➰🖂(4)P🚭

Bishop Blaize ✪
4 Winchester Road, SO51 8AA
🕐 12-11 (midnight Fri & Sat); 12-10.30 Sun
☎ (01794) 511777
Ringwood Best Bitter; guest beer Ⓗ
The Bishop Blaize gets its name from the patron saint of woolcombers; built in the 1700s, this

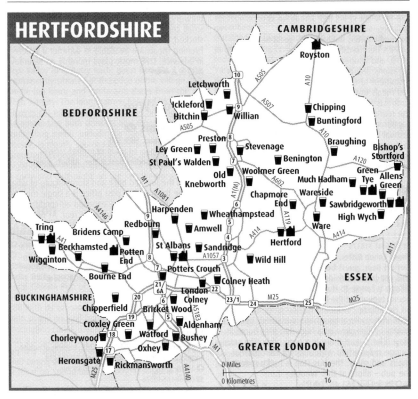

HERTFORDSHIRE

Aldenham

Roundbush
Roundbush Lane, WD25 8BG TQ144984
🕐 12-11 (10.30 Sun) ☎ (01923) 855532
⊕ theroundbush.com
Courage Directors; Wells Eagle IPA, Bombardier; guest beers ⊞
A genuine country pub it caters for all, with two adjoining bars, darts and flagstones at one end, carpet and an open fire at the other. The traditional interior features exposed timbers and a display of bygone items mostly found within the pub itself. A separate restaurant area at the back offers a brasserie menu. There are gardens front and rear – one for adults and one for children. No children after 9pm. ❀◗☺🖳(302,602,632)♣P

Allens Green

Queen's Head 🍷 🅻
CM21 0LS TL455170
🕐 12-2 (not Mon & Tue), 5-11; 12-2.30, 5-11 Thu-Sat; 12-10.30 Sun ☎ (01279) 723393 ⊕ shirevillageinns.co.uk
Fuller's London Pride Ⓖ; **Mighty Oak Maldon Gold; guest beer** ⊞
Small, traditional village inn with a large garden, popular with locals, cyclists and walkers. Although the location is rural, it is well-worth seeking out. Hot snacks are available unless the pub is busy. Every third weekend of the month is for beer lovers, with up to seven local and unusual ales on offer. Beer festivals take place most bank holidays. Some expansion work is now underway – when complete all beers will be served by gravity. Q❀&♣P

Amwell

Elephant & Castle ✅
Amwell Lane, AL4 8EA TL167131
🕐 12-2.30, 5.30-11; 12-11 Sat; 12-10.30 Sun
☎ (01582) 832175
Greene King IPA, H&H Bitter, Abbot; guest beer ⊞
Hidden away in a beautiful and peaceful setting, this welcoming and deservedly popular pub dates from 1714. Two real fires warm the interior and there is a 200-feet deep well in the back bar. With two large gardens (one for adults only), this is an excellent example of a successful rural pub. Lunches are served daily and evening meals Tuesday to Saturday. The pub hosts Amwell Day, a local charity fund-raising event, in June. ᄊ❀◗☺🖳(304,320,366)P⅃

Benington

Lordship Arms
42 Whempstead Road, SG2 7BX TL307228
🕐 12-3, 6 (7 Sun)-11 ☎ (01438) 869665
⊕ lordshiparms.co.uk
Black Sheep Best Bitter; Crouch Vale Brewers Gold; Taylor Landlord; guest beers ⊞
A repeat winner of local and county CAMRA Pub of the Year. The single bar is decorated with telephone memorabilia – even some of the handpumps are modelled on telephones. Wednesday evening curries and Sunday roasts are popular. Bar snacks are served 12-2pm. The large garden is an attraction, with superb floral displays in summer. There are classic car gatherings on the second Tuesday of the month from May to September. ᄊQ❀☺🖳(384)♣P🖵

Berkhamsted

Crown
145 High Street, HP4 3HH SP992077
❂ 8am-midnight (1am Fri & Sat) ☎ (01442) 863993
Greene King Ruddles Best Bitter, Abbot; guest beers Ⓗ
Historically always a pub, this Wetherspoon hostelry with low ceilings and interesting alcoves has more character than many conversions within the pub chain. Guest beers often come from Tring and Rebellion, and beer festivals are hosted throughout the year. There is a large tree-lined patio area to the rear. It opens at 8am for breakfast. ❀◖⑃⇌⌧⌐

Rising Sun ⑃
1 Canal Side, George Street, HP4 2EG SP997078
❂ 12-11 (midnight Thu) summer; 3-11 (midnight Thu) winter; 12-midnight Fri & Sat; 12-10.30 Sun
☎ (01442) 864913 ⊕ theriser.co.uk
Tring Riser; guest beers Ⓗ
Cider and perry drinkers are well catered for at the Riser, voted Local and Regional CAMRA Cider Pub of the Year in 2010. However, ale drinkers are not neglected, with three guests on the bar and three beer festivals a year held on the outside patio. Outside there is lock-side seating alongside the Grand Union Canal. CAMRA card-carrying members are offered a discount on drinks. Dogs are welcome. ❀◖⇌⌧♣P⌐

Bishop's Stortford

Bricklayers Arms
61 Hadham Road, CM23 2QY TL482214
❂ 12 (5 Mon)-midnight; 12-1.30am Fri & Sat; 12-11.30 Sun
☎ (01279) 657803
Beer range varies Ⓗ
Local beers are showcased here, usually including at least one each from Buntingford Brewery and Saffron Brewery. Built on the site of a former brickworks, this popular pub has served the local community for 150 years. Once a Benskins house, it is now free of tie. There is a quiet, comfortable lounge and a lively sports-oriented public bar and pool room with several Sky HD screens. Outside there is a covered, heated smokers' patio and a large, secluded deck. Dogs are welcome throughout the pub. ♨Q❀⌸⇌P⌐

Red Cow ⑃
58 Dunmow Road, CM23 5HL TL494211
❂ 12-11 (10.30 Sun) ☎ (01279) 755784
Greene King IPA, Abbot; guest beer Ⓗ
The third handpump serves a Buntingford Brewery guest beer, varying according to season. This cosy neighbourhood pub in a Georgian detached house with leaded windows has been serving beer since 1840. There are two generally quiet drinking areas and a pool room, but the main feature is the three-sided central bar – if you sit here on one of the traditional high stools you will inevitably be drawn into a wide-ranging conversation with the welcoming landlord and his regulars. ❀⇌⌧P

Bourne End

White Horse ⑃
London Road, HP1 2RH (½ mile from A41 jct) TL023062
❂ 11-11; 12.30-10.30 Sun ☎ (01442) 863888
McMullen AK, Country Ⓗ

Roadside country pub just a short stroll from the Grand Union Canal. Cosy log fires warm the pub in winter and outside there is a large garden and patio for summer sun. The older dining area, with beamed ceilings, is to the front, and there is a large open-plan space adjacent to the bar area at the rear. Efficient service and good food make it popular with diners, and the quality McMullen beers delight drinkers. Children are welcome, but not dogs. ♨Q❀◖⑃⌧(500,501)P⌐

Braughing

Golden Fleece ⑃ ✅
20 Green End, SG11 2PG
❂ 11.30-3, 5.30-11; 11.30-11 Sat; 12-10.30 Sun
☎ (01920) 823555 ⊕ goldenfleecebraughing.co.uk
Adnams Bitter; guest beers Ⓗ
Large rural pub built in the early 1700s, with wooden floors, beams and the original fireplace. It closed as a pub in 2003 but reopened in 2010 after extensive remodelling of the interior layout. Guest ales come from local breweries such as Buntingford, Tring and Red Squirrel. The food menu is mainly gluten free and includes a changing range of daily specials. ♨Q⟳❀◖⌧(331,386)P

Bricket Wood

Old Fox ⑃
School Lane, AL2 3XU (follow School Lane out of the village) TL126004
❂ 2-11 Mon, Wed & Thu; closed Tue; 12-11.30 Fri & Sat; 12-10.30 Sun ☎ (01923) 675354
Tring Side Pocket for a Toad, Ridgeway; guest beer Ⓗ
This rural pub, located in natural woodland, is reached via School Lane, formerly a through road but now cut off by the M1. It is situated a short walk from Garston railway station or a far longer but interesting walk from Bricket Wood station. A popular local, it features open fires in winter and plenty of green space outside for a sunny summer's day with friends. ♨Q❀⌸A⇌(Garston)⌧P⌐

Bridens Camp

Crown & Sceptre ⑃
Red Lion Lane, HP2 6EY (from A4146 at Water End take Red Lion Lane up hill for 1km) TL043111
❂ 12-3, 5.30-11; 12-11 Sat & Sun ☎ (01442) 234660
⊕ crownandsceptrepub.co.uk
Greene King IPA, Abbot; St Austell Tribute; guest beers Ⓗ
Genuine country free house with three interconnecting rooms around a U-shaped bar, with some low beams (tall people beware!). Guest ales often come from LocAle breweries, eg Tring and Vale, and vary in number depending on the season. Outside is a large patio and beer garden, plus an outside bar used for beer festivals and functions.

INDEPENDENT BREWERIES

Buntingford Royston
Green Tye Green Tye
McMullen Hertford
Old Cross Hertford
Red Squirrel Potten End
Sawbridgeworth Sawbridgeworth
Tring Tring
Verulam St Albans

The pub is home to a number of leisure activities and is popular with walkers. There is a cricket pitch in an adjacent field. No food Sunday evening.
ᴹᴬQ✿◑🞿🍴(X31)P♿⭆

Buntingford

Brambles ⃝L
117 High Street, SG9 9AF TL360298
✪ 12-11 (10.30 Sun) ☎ (01763) 273158
Fuller's London Pride; Gale's HSB; guest beers Ⓗ
Brambles has two bars, both warmed by real fires, and eight handpumps dispensing the ales. Beers from local breweries including Buntingford and Red Squirrel are usually available, and guests are often from Nethergate and Church End. The clientele is varied and can get exuberant at weekends. One of the few pubs in the area to use oversized glasses.
ᴹᴬ✿🞿🍴(331,700)♣P⚲

Bushey

Swan
25 Park Road, WD23 3EE TQ132954
✪ 11-11; 12-10.30 Sun ☎ (020) 8950 2256
Greene King Abbot; Jennings Cumberland Ale; Young's Bitter, Special Ⓗ
Making its 33rd appearance in the Guide, the Swan is set in a residential street off Bushey High Street, its single bar offering a constant range of ales. The walls are adorned with various local photos and breweriana. Two real fires add to the homely and welcoming feel. Bar snacks are available all day including toasties and pies. There is also a Wednesday night home-made meal. The Ladies is in the back garden. Free WiFi is available.
ᴹᴬ✿🞿🍴♣⭆

Chapmore End

Woodman ✪
30 Chapmore End, SG12 0HF (off B158 between Bengeo and A602 roundabout) TL328164
✪ 12-2.30 (not Mon), 5.30 (5 Fri)-11; 12-11 Sat & Sun
☎ (01920) 463143 🌐 woodmanware.co.uk
Greene King IPA, Abbot; guest beer Ⓖ
Classic two-bar country pub in a quiet hamlet, popular with walkers. At this unspoilt gem the beer is served straight from cooled casks in the cellar behind the public bar. A local favourite is 'mix': half IPA and half Abbot. Home-made food is available Tuesday to Sunday (no food Sun eve). The Wednesday Supper Special features seasonal meals. The large rear garden has a safe children's play area and petanque. Look out for beer and music festivals. ᴹᴬQ✿◑▲♣P⭆

Chipperfield

Royal Oak
1 The Street, WD4 9BH (at village crossroads) TL042017
✪ 12-3, 6-11; 12-3, 7-10.30 Sun ☎ (01923) 266537
Adnams Broadside; Fuller's London Pride; Young's Bitter Ⓗ
This traditional pub has featured in the Guide for 30 years. Interesting collections of book matches cover the wall and foreign bank notes hang from the ceiling. Unusual wooden cask stools in the public bar, copper-topped tables and decorative brasses make for a proper pub atmosphere. Classic car club meetings are held here and old car photos decorate the walls. Good lunchtime food is served,

with evening meals and a separate function room available by arrangement. Well-behaved children and dogs are welcome. ᴹᴬQ◑🞿🍴(352,R9)P⭆

Chipping

Countryman
Ermine Street, SG9 0PG TL356319
✪ closed Mon-Thu; 12-11 Fri & Sat; 12-10.30 Sun
☎ (01763) 272721
Beer range varies Ⓗ
Built in 1663 and an inn since 1760, the Countryman is a single-bar, split-level pub. The interior boasts some well-executed carvings on the bar front, an impressive fireplace and some obscure agricultural implements. Two real ales are usually available from a varying range and tend to be around 4-4.5%. Note the restricted opening hours. ᴹᴬQ✿🞿(331)P⭆

Chorleywood

Rose & Crown ⃝L
Common Road, WD3 5LW TQ026963
✪ 11.30-2.30, 5.30-11 (midnight Fri); 11.30-11 Sat; 12-10
Sun ☎ (01923) 283841 🌐 roseandcrownchorleywood.co.uk
Fuller's London Pride; Young's Bitter; guest beers Ⓗ
Small, dog-friendly free house on the western border of Chorleywood Common, dating back to the mid-19th century. The back bar is now a popular restaurant (no food Sun or Mon eves). The drinking area can get crowded, particularly when the restaurant overspills. There are two guest beers, one always from a LocAle brewery, typically Buntingford, Rebellion or Vale, and the other occasionally from further afield.
ᴹᴬ✿◑⇌⊖🞿(336)♣P

Colney Heath

Crooked Billet ⃝L
88 High Street, AL4 0NP TL202060
✪ 11-2.30, 4.30-11; 11.30-11 Sat; 12-10.30 Sun
☎ (01727) 822128
Tring Side Pocket for a Toad; guest beers Ⓗ
Popular and friendly cottage-style village pub dating back more than 200 years. A genuine free house, it stocks three to five guest beers from national, regional and micro-breweries. A wide selection of good-value home-made food is served lunchtimes and Friday and Saturday evenings. Summer barbecues and Saturday events are held occasionally. This is a favourite stop-off for walkers on the many local footpaths. Families are welcome in the large garden, where there is play equipment, and in the bar until 9pm.
ᴹᴬ✿◑🞿(304)♣♣P⭆

Croxley Green

Sportsman ⃝L
2 Scots Hill, WD3 3AD (at A412 jct with the Green)
TQ069953
✪ 12-11 (10.30 Sun) ☎ (01923) 443360
🌐 croxleygreen.com/sportsman
Red Squirrel Conservation Bitter; Tring Side Pocket for a Toad; guest beers Ⓗ
Comfortable family-run pub with a warm welcome for all. Up to four guest beers, which tend to come from craft brewers such as Red Squirrel, Dark Star or Downton, and a changing real cider are available. An external function room hosts

community groups such as a jazz workshop on Monday evening. Entertainment includes a popular quiz night on Wednesday, regular live music on Saturday evening (can be noisy), a monthly book club, and twice-yearly beer festivals. ⏛(320,321)♣♠P╘─⚘

Green Tye

Prince of Wales ⅃

SG10 6JP (Green Tye signed from Much Hadham) TL444184
🕘 12-3 (3.15 Wed), 5.30-11 (1am Fri & Sat); 11.15-10.30 Sun
☎ (01279) 842517 ⏺ thepow.co.uk
Green Tye Union Jack; Wadworth Henry's Original IPA; guest beers Ⓗ
You can be sure of a warm welcome from Gary and Jenny at this traditional and friendly village local, whether you are a walker, cyclist, dog owner or just plain thirsty. Smaller East Anglian breweries are showcased throughout the year, as well as Green Tye, situated at the rear of the pub. Beer festivals are held on the May Day weekend and in September. Hearty sandwiches are available at lunchtime. Regular live folk and other musical events are held. ₳Q☮◑♿♠P

Harpenden

Carpenters Arms

14 Cravells Road, AL5 1BD
🕘 11-3, 5.30-11; 12-3, 7-10.30 Sun ☎ (01582) 460311
Adnams Bitter; Courage Best Bitter; Greene King Abbot; Harveys Sussex Best Bitter; guest beer Ⓗ
Harpenden's smallest pub is cosy, comfortable and welcoming. Five real ales are available including one guest. The pub is beautifully furnished with an open fire warming the bar in colder weather. Occasional themed food nights are held throughout the year (booking essential). In summer there are barbecues on the stylish, secluded patio. ₳Q◑⏛(321)P╘─

Cross Keys ⅃ ✅

39 High Street, AL5 2SD (opp war memorial)
🕘 11-11 (late Fri & Sat); 12-10.30 Sun ☎ (01582) 763989
⏺ cross-keys-harpenden.co.uk
Rebellion IPA; Taylor Landlord; Tring Jack O'Legs; guest beer Ⓗ
This two-bar pub with a fine pewter bar top and flagstoned floors has retained its traditional charm. The original oak-beamed ceiling has tankards used by past and present customers hanging from it. In spring and summer enjoy your pint in the secluded, attractive rear garden where Necessity the bear resides. Traditional home-cooked lunches are served Monday to Saturday lunchtimes. The pub may stay open until 1am on Friday/Saturday, with latest entry 11pm. Q♿◑⇌♣♠

Heronsgate

Land of Liberty, Peace & Plenty ♈ ⅃

Long Lane, WD3 5BS (about ¾ mile from jct 17 M25) TQ023949
🕘 12-11 (midnight Fri & Sat) ☎ (01923) 282216
⏺ landoflibertypub.com
Tring Liberty Ale; guest beers Ⓗ
Welcoming country community pub named after a nearby 19th-century Chartist settlement. Six beers from smaller breweries are usually available, as well as a good selection of ciders, perries and malt whiskies. Although no children are allowed in the bar, there is a covered pavilion outside and a large garden where petanque and Aunt Sally are played. Regular beer festivals and other events are held. CAMRA Pub of the Year National Finalist in 2007. About 15/20-minutes' walk from Chorleywood station. ₳☮☀⏛(R4)♣♠P╘─⚘

Hertford

Old Barge ✅

2 The Folly, SG14 1QD (ask for Folly Island and you will find the Old Barge) TL326128
🕘 11-11 (midnight Fri & Sat); 12-11 Sun ☎ (01992) 581871
⏺ theoldbarge.co.uk
Black Sheep Best Bitter; St Austell Tribute; Sharp's Doom Bar; guest beers Ⓗ
The Old Barge is now a free house and hosts three beer festivals a year (one during St George's Day week). It is also rightly proud of its home-cooked food, often made with locally-sourced produce. Here you can enjoy great beer watching passing narrowboats. A film night is held on the first Thursday of the month, jazz nights on the second and last Thursdays. Watch out for the Folly at the Folly Sunday festival in August and the Crayfish Festival on August bank holiday for children under 12. ₳◑⇌(East)⏛♣♠P╘

Old Cross Tavern ⅃

8 St Andrew Street, SG14 1JA TL323126
🕘 12 (4 Mon)-11; 12-10.30 Sun ☎ (01992) 583133
Fuller's London Pride; Old Cross Tavern Laugh 'n' Titter; Taylor Landlord; guest beers Ⓗ
Superb town free house offering a friendly welcome. Up to eight real ales, usually including a dark beer of some distinction, come from brewers large and small, including the pub's own micro-brewery, and there is a fine choice of Belgian bottle-conditioned beers. A popular beer festival is held over the spring bank holiday. No TV or music here, just good old-fashioned conversation. Filled rolls and pork pies are available well into the evening Monday to Saturday. ₳Q⇌(East/North)⏛♣

White Horse

33 Castle Street, SG14 1HH TL326124
🕘 12-11 (midnight Fri & Sat); 12-10.30 Sun
☎ (01992) 503911
Fuller's Discovery, London Pride, ESB; Gale's Seafarers Ale, HSB; guest beers Ⓗ
A 'must see' for visitors to Hertford, this charming old timber-framed building has two downstairs bars and additional rooms upstairs, one featuring bar billiards, others where children are welcome. The Fuller's beers are typically suplemented by Adnams and Butcombe bitters and a monthly guest. The landlord prides himself on the quality of the home-made food. Regular events include music nights and gourmet-themed evenings. There are no gaming machines or TVs to distract from conversation. Dog-friendly. ₳Q◑♿⇌(East/North)⏛♣

High Wych

Rising Sun ⅃

High Wych Road, CM21 0HZ TL463141
🕘 12-2.30 (not Tue, 2 Wed), 5.30-11; 12-3, 7-10.30 Sun
☎ (01279) 724099

This free house [...] 1728. The pub [...] and open log fi [...] it is dog- and fa [...] during the Aug [...] facilities availa [...] music plays on [...] cooked food is [...] Saturday and S [...] Ashford and Fa [...] Friday and ever [...] evenings or Sur [...]

Benender [...]

Bull ⅃

The Street, TN17 [...]
🕘 12-midnight ☎ [...]
⏺ thebullatbenen [...]
**Dark Star Hophe [...]
Larkins Tradition [...]**
Imposing free h [...] century, located [...] The comfortable [...] exposed oak be [...] fireplace. A sep [...] serves locally-g [...] also served in t [...] for the Friday fi [...] steak night and [...]

☼ 10-11; 12-10.30 Sun ⊕ castleinn-kent.co.uk
Harveys Sussex Best Bitter; Larkins Traditional Ale, seasonal beer Ⓗ
Sitting at the centre of this picturesque National Trust village, the Castle dates back to 1420. Tasteful recent refurbishment has not spoilt its charm, including a traditional public bar popular with walkers and dogs, and a more plush saloon bar and separate restaurant. There is also a function room for hire. As you might expect from a pub situated just up the road from an established local micro-brewery, its beers are always available here, including the stunning winter warmer, Larkins Porter. ㅿQ❀◑♣

Chiddingstone Hoath

Rock
TN8 7BS (1½ miles S of Chiddingstone via Wellers Town) TQ497431
☼ 12-4 Mon; 12-3, 6-11; 12-11 Fri & Sat; 12-5 Sun
☎ (01892) 870296
Larkins Traditional Ale, seasonal beers; Sharp's Doom Bar Ⓗ
Unspoilt country inn on high ground to the west of Penshurst. The pub is named after one of the nearby rocky outcrops and is now a free house after many years tied to the nearby Larkins brewery, though its beers still dominate. The main bar has a brick floor that has seen years of use, and there is a smaller, cosy saloon on the right. Try your luck at Ring the Bull near the well-used, inviting wood stove, and enjoy this timeless and friendly place with a well-deserved pint. ㅿQ❀◑♣P

Chipstead

Bricklayers Arms ✅
39 Chevening Road, TN13 2RZ (by entrance to sailing club)
☼ 11.30-3.30, 5.30-11; 11.30-11 Fri & Sat; 11.30-10.30 Sun
☎ (01732) 743424 ⊕ the-bricklayers-arms.co.uk
Harveys Sussex Best Bitter Ⓖ, **seasonal beers** Ⓗ
A friendly village inn in an old row of cottages with a lakeside view. The varied clientele of locals, sailors, fishermen and walkers rub shoulders in a pub with an ever-growing reputation. A stone-flagged front room leads to a bar dominated by beer casks, which see plenty of action, and a regularly roaring fire. The pub serves a popular range of food (no food Sun eve), with regular steak and curry nights. Quiz night is Tuesday, complemented by monthly live music events. ㅿ❀◑♿🚌(402)♣🛏

Cobham

Darnley Arms
40 The Street, DA12 3BZ
☼ 12-11 (10.30 Sun) ☎ (01474) 812218
Dark Star Hophead; Greene King IPA; guest beers Ⓗ
Cosy village local with a variety of interesting artefacts including a time recording clock and apprentice indenture papers. The single bar has several distinct drinking areas. The decor features a wide range of local memorabilia including the coat of arms of the Darnley family, who lived at nearby Cobham Hall. The extensive food menu features fish as a speciality. ㅿQ❀🍴◑♿🚌(416)P

Coldred

Carpenter's Arms
The Green, CT15 5AJ
☼ 6 (7 Sun)-11 ☎ (01304) 830190
Beer range varies Ⓗ/Ⓖ
One of CAMRA's Real Heritage Pubs, this 18th-century two-roomed pub, situated on the village green, is a village local and community hub. Remaining largely unchanged for 50 years, the simple furniture and decor includes a display of the village's multiple awards and silhouettes of locals from times past. Two or three real ales are normally available, usually from local breweries Hopdaemon and Ramsgate, but no keg beer or lager are sold. Darts, dominoes and skittles are played. Dog-friendly. ㅿQ❀🍴🚌(88A)♣

Cooling

Horseshoe & Castle Ⓛ
Main Road, ME3 8DJ TQ759761
☼ 11.30 (5.45 Mon)-11 (midnight Fri & Sat); 12-11.30 Sun
☎ (01634) 221691 ⊕ horseshoeandcastle.co.uk
Shepherd Neame Master Brew; guest beer Ⓗ
Nestling in the quiet village of Cooling, this pub is near a ruined castle once owned by Sir John Oldcastle, on whom Shakespeare modelled his Falstaff character. The local graveyard was used in the film version of Great Expectations, where young Pip met the convict Magwitch. Snacks and bar food is available as well as an a la carte menu served in a separate dining area (no food Mon). Draught Addlestones cider is available. Accommodation is high quality. ㅿQ❀🛏◑♿🖤P🛏

Crockham Hill

Royal Oak
Main Road, TN8 6RD (on B2026)
☼ 12-3, 6-11 (midnight Fri); 12-11 Sun ☎ (01732) 866335
Westerham Finchcocks Original, British Bulldog, seasonal beers Ⓗ
A smartly refurbished ex-Shepherd Neame pub, now the first run by the successful local Westerham Brewery, restoring brewing links with the nearby town. It serves both its regular real ales, and often more than one seasonal beer, in a friendly community atmosphere, with nice decor such as comfortable leather sofas. Popular home-cooked traditional pub food is on offer (no food Sun or Mon eve), especially lunchtime roasts on Sunday, for which booking is advisable. Families, walking groups and societies are welcome. ㅿQ❀◑🍴♿🚌♣🛏

Dartford

Malt Shovel
3 Darenth Road, DA1 1LP
☼ 12 (3 Mon)-11; 12-midnight Fri ☎ (01322) 224381
St Austell Tribute; Young's Bitter, Special, London Gold; guest beer Ⓗ
Attractive country cottage-style pub just outside the town centre. The low-ceilinged tap room, which now features an original Dartford Brewery mirror, dates from 1673 and still exudes a rustic charm. The main bar has recently been extensively

Ash

Cheque
4 Chequer
☼ 11 (5 Mo
⊕ thechequ
Greene Ki
Communi
featuring
comfortal
pub neve
music, fo
cider is o
is served
Tue), roas
cooked pi
festival, f
club, and
ㅿ❀◑🚌

Ashfo

County
10 High S
☼ 8 (9 Sun
Greene Ki
beers Ⓗ
A welcon
this pub

refurbished but retains the large wooden malt shovel on display. A large modern conservatory leads to the garden that overlooks the parish church. Good food is available lunchtimes and evenings (no food Mon lunch and Sun-Tue eves), with fish night on Friday. Quiz night is Monday. ✿◑◖⊟≠⊟♣P'—

Wat Tyler

80 High Street, DA1 1DE (next to parish church)
✿ 9-11 (midnight Fri & Sat); 10.30-10.30 Sun
☎ (01322) 272546
Courage Best Bitter; John Smith's Bitter; guest beers Ⓗ

A small friendly corner pub, this town-centre local is a short bus ride from Ebbsfleet International Station and Bluewater shopping centre. Two regular beers, plus three different guests ranging from mid-red to stouts and porters, reflect the preferences of the regulars. A raised area is situated at the rear of the bar. Frequent trains to London and Medway towns are just a few minutes' walk away. ⊟&≠⊟♣♠

Deal

Magnet Inn

267 London Road, CT14 9PW
✿ 11-midnight (1am Fri & Sat) ☎ (01304) 360842
Shepherd Neame Master Brew, Late Red; guest beers Ⓗ

Large, welcoming, down-to-earth pub situated on the edge of Deal, easily accessible by bus. The large room is divided by the bar, from which the range of Shepherd Neame real ales is served, including beers from Shep's micro-brewery, and occasional guest beers from across the country. The local motorcycle club meets every Thursday and occasional live music is hosted. Bar billiards, pool and darts are played. There is a large patio garden, which can be covered in inclement weather. ✿&⊟(13,82)♣P'—

Ship

141 Middle Street, CT14 6JZ
✿ 11 (12 Sun)-midnight ☎ (01304) 372222
Caledonian Deuchars IPA; Dark Star Hophead; Fuller's London Pride; Ramsgate Gadds' No 7, Gadds' Seasider; guest beers Ⓗ

Traditional, unspoilt pub in the middle of Deal's conservation area, just 10 minutes from the town centre. The wood-floored bar features beers from south-east breweries, such as Ramsgate and Dark Star. The inviting lounge is an ideal place for conversation or reading. The back bar overlooks a large patio-style garden, reached by a staircase, with a covered area for smokers. Nautical memorabilia adorn the walls. Daily discount sessions are popular (not Sun), as are occasional music events. ⊞✿≠⊟(15,15A)'—

Dover

Blakes of Dover

52 Castle Street, CT16 1PJ
✿ closed Sun; 12-11 ☎ (01304) 202194
⊕ blakesofdover.com
Beer range varies Ⓗ /Ⓖ

A short walk from the town centre and bus station, this pleasant cellar bar can be easily missed. The stone-flagged room is a quiet haven from the bustle of the town, where a good selection of real ales from handpumps and stillage is on offer. This is complemented by ciders from local cidermakers such as East Stour and Broomfield, and a good range of whiskies. A small courtyard garden provides a pleasant place to relax in summer. Lunches are available, including excellent sandwiches. Q✿✿◑◖≠⊟♠'—

Eight Bells ✓

19 Cannon Street, CT16 1BZ
✿ 8-11 (midnight Fri & Sat) ☎ (01304) 205030
Greene King Ruddles Best Bitter, Abbot; Shepherd Neame Spitfire; guest beers Ⓗ

Situated on the main shopping street, this family-friendly Wetherspoon is part of the former Metropole Hotel. Entrance to the large, single-room, traditional-style bar is through an outdoor seating area overlooking the pedestrian precinct. This, as well as the sofas at the front of the pub, are popular with locals. The long bar serves a wide variety of real ales, featuring occasional beers from Kent micro-breweries, such as Wantsum. As usual, an excellent range of good value food is available. ◑&≠⊟♠'—

Louis Armstrong

58 Maison Dieu Road, CT16 1RA
✿ 2 (7 Sun)-late ☎ (01304) 204759
Hopdaemon Skrimshander IPA; guest beers Ⓗ

Local music venue, playing blues, jazz and rock at the weekend. The L-shaped bar, with seating and a stage, is adorned with music-related pictures and posters. Up to four real ales, many from Kent, are served, and an occasional local cider, such as Stour Valley. With a fine rear garden, beer festivals are normally held in August and at Christmas. Good value food is served on Wednesday. On Dover's one-way system, it is on most local bus routes and has a public car park opposite. ⊞✿◑⊟'—

East Malling

Rising Sun Ⓛ

125 Mill Street, ME19 6BX
✿ 12-11 (10.30 Sun) ☎ (01732) 843284
Goacher's Fine Light; guest beers Ⓗ

A long-established, family-run free house offering good value food and drink to local residents at weekday lunchtimes and on Thursday evening. Sport is popular here and all major football matches and other sports events are shown. The pub is home to several teams including darts, football and cricket. The two guest beers come from far and wide. A collection of malt whiskies sits above the bar. A lunchtime meat raffle is held on Sunday. The large patio garden to the rear is popular for summer drinking. ✿◑≠⊟(58)♣'—

Edenbridge

Old Eden Ⓛ

121 High Street, TN8 5AX (by roundabout just S of bridge over River Eden)
✿ 12-11 (midnight Fri & Sat); 11-11 Sun ☎ (01732) 862398
Harveys Sussex Best Bitter; Westerham British Bulldog, 1965; guest beers Ⓗ

A traditional pub with origins as a late 15th-century Kentish hall house. With its three open fires the atmosphere is certainly homely, comfortable and relaxed. A plaque in the bar shows the water level in the 1968 floods from the nearby River Eden. Local Westerham beers are ever-present among the five handpumps, along with two seasonal brews such as Hepworth Old or Whitstable Native in winter or Westerham Summer Perle. Westons Old Rosie cider also appears in the warmer months. Popular with diners (but no food Sun and Mon eves). ᴍ☺◑&≠₩(231,233)●Pᶜ

Farningham

Chequers
87 High Street, DA4 0DT (250m from A20 jct 3 M25)
☼ 12-11.30 (10.30 Sun) ☎ (01322) 865222
Fuller's London Pride, ESB; Harveys Sussex Best Bitter; Taylor Landlord; guest beers ⊞
Popular, cosy, one-bar corner local in an attractive riverside village. The unusual decor includes murals depicting local scenes, two large decorative candelabra and a life-size model waiter. Ten handpumps dispense four regular beers and up to six guests. Food is served Monday to Saturday lunchtimes. Parking is difficult as the pub is situated in the village on a dangerous corner. ◑₩(421,427)♣

Faversham

Anchor
52 Abbey Street, ME13 7BP
☼ 12-11 (midnight Fri & Sat); 12-10 Sun ☎ (01795) 536471
Shepherd Neame Master Brew, Kent's Best, Spitfire, Late Red, Bishops Finger, seasonal beers ⊞
At the end of Abbey Street, a fine medieval road, this superb example of a traditional British pub dates back more than 300 years. The interior has a wealth of nautical memorabilia and original features such as oak beams and an open fireplace. The pub proudly stocks a large range of Shepherd Neame ales, and has an impressive bar menu, as well as two restaurant areas and a large garden. It is popular with locals, walkers and tourists. Live music plays most Sunday evenings.
ᴍ☺◑◁≠₩ᶜ

Chimney Boy
59 Preston Street, ME13 8PG
☼ 11-11 (midnight Fri & Sat); 11.30-10 Sun
☎ (01795) 532007 ⊕ chimneyboy.co.uk
Shepherd Neame Master Brew, Spitfire, Late Red, seasonal beers ⊞
A short walk from the railway station, this historic pub is one of many handsome old buildings in the market town. It is large and spacious, with character to boast of, and no fewer than three inglenook fireplaces. The pub takes its name from the largest of these fireplaces – inside are the steps the sweep's boy used to climb. Outside is a planted courtyard with seating. Traditional lunchtime fare is served along with an a la carte option in the evening. ☺◑≠₩Pᶜ

Elephant ♥ ⌂ ✔
31 The Mall, ME13 8JN
☼ closed Mon; 3 (12 Sat)-11; 12-7 Sun ☎ (01795) 590157
Beer range varies ⊞
Local CAMRA Pub of the Year 2011 for the fifth consecutive year and East Kent Pub of the Year 2010. A charming, traditional ale house, with five beers, usually including a mild, presenting the best ale selection in town. The beers are mainly sourced

from the south-east, including Kent micro-breweries, and there is real cider, an open log fire in winter, and a walled garden for the summer. Live music from local bands/artists regularly features. Beer festivals are held in July and November. ᴍ☺≠₩♣●

Leading Light
20-22 Preston Street, ME13 8NZ
☼ 8am-11 ☎ (01795) 535075
Greene King Ruddles Best Bitter, Abbot; guest beers ⊞
Located in the street leading from the station, this former Co-op is a typical Wetherspoon conversion. The pub offers the usual fare that you would expect, with a variety of food, ales and themed events. East Kent micro-breweries are well represented. The cider, usually Westons, is kept in a fridge. There is a covered outside patio and children are welcome until 6pm in the area at the rear of the pub. Popular with locals and visitors to this historic town. ☎☺◑&≠₩●ᶜ

Old Wine Vaults ⌂ ✔
75 Preston Street, ME13 8PA
☼ 11-11 (10.30 Sun) ☎ (01795) 591817
⊕ theoldwinevaults.com
Beer range varies ⊞
Situated in the centre of town, this popular local dates back to the 17th century. The small street frontage opens to a deceptively large interior with ample seating throughout. The traditional bar is set in the middle, with a mix of tables and chairs and many cosy corners. One ale from Hopdaemon is always available plus two rotating guests. A Kentish cider is offered, normally Biddenden. There is an extensive menu using locally-sourced ingredients, and a pleasant beer garden. ☎☺◑≠₩●ᶜ

Phoenix Tavern
98-99 Abbey Street, ME13 7BH
☼ 12-11 ☎ (01795) 591462
⊕ thephoenixtavernfaversham.co.uk
Harveys Sussex Best Bitter; guest beers ⊞
Traditional English public house situated in the heart of medieval Abbey Street, offering something for everyone. It boasts two open fires, a large refurbished and comfortable restaurant, plus a variety of quality ales including two or three guests, often from local micro-breweries. The food is good quality and competitively priced. The pub also offers an impressive and varied events calendar, including poetry and quizzes, with something for everyone. Outside is a secluded walled garden. ᴍQ☺◑≠₩♣ᶜ

Shipwright's Arms ⌂
Ham Road, Hollowshore, ME13 7TU (1½ miles N of Faversham) TR017636
☼ closed Mon eve winter; 11-3, 6-10; 12-4, 6-11 Sat & summer; 12-4, 6-10.30 Sun ☎ (01795) 590088
⊕ theshipwrightsarmspub.co.uk
Goacher's Real Mild Ale, Shipwrecked; Hopdaemon Golden Braid; Whitstable East India Pale Ale; guest beers Ⓖ
Historic wood-clad pub behind the sea wall at the confluence of Faversham and Oare creeks. Beers are sourced mainly from Kentish micro-breweries. Many nooks and crannies are to be found, together with artefacts that reflect its maritime history. The place is dog-friendly and popular with walkers, ramblers and boat owners from the adjacent

moorings. Numerous welcoming log fires blaze in winter and its large garden is well-used in summer. In severe winter weather telephone to confirm opening hours. No food Sunday or Monday evenings. ♨Q❀◑P┗

Finglesham

Crown Inn
The Street, CT14 0NA
✪ 12-11.30 ☎ (01304) 612555
⊕ thecrownatfinglesham.co.uk
Beer range varies ℍ
Welcoming rural pub and 16th-century restaurant that has recently been sympathetically refurbished. Three to four real ales and Biddenden cider provide refreshment. Good home-made food is available all day in summer – the pub has a passion for fresh fish. 'Beer o'clock' on Friday is popular with locals and visitors, along with quiz nights and occasional live music. May and August feature beer festivals, and bat and trap is played in summer. The large garden has a children's play area. ♨❀◑●P┗

Folkestone

British Lion ✪
10 The Bayle, CT20 1SQ (close to church off the pedestrian part of Sandgate Road)
✪ 12-4, 7-11 (10.30 Sun) ☎ (01303) 251478
Greene King IPA, Abbot; guest beers ℍ
This former Hanbury, Mackeson and Whitbread house dates from 1460 and is now the oldest pub in Folkestone, visited by Charles Dickens when writing Little Dorrit. Situated close to the town centre, near to the church, a comfortable and relaxed atmosphere prevails. Two guest ales are normally stocked from the Punch Taverns Finest Cask selection, together with two real ciders. Good pub food is served in generous portions lunchtimes and evenings (no food Tue eve). ♨Q🕭◑🖫♣●┗

Chambers ⌐
Radnor Chambers, Cheriton Place, CT20 2BB (off the Hythe end of Sandgate Road)
✪ 12-11 (1am Fri & Sat); 7-10.30 1st Sun of month only ☎ (01303) 223333 ⊕ pubfolkestone.co.uk
Adnams Lighthouse; Hopdaemon Skrimshander IPA; Whitstable Kentish Reserve; guest beers ℍ
Chambers is a spacious cellar bar beneath a licensed coffee shop. Two guest beers, often from local micro-breweries, and two real ciders are usually available. A beer festival is held over the Easter weekend. Food includes Mexican and European dishes, and daily specials are served (no food Mon and Fri eves and Sun). Live music features on Thursday, disco on Friday and a quiz on the first Sunday of the month. No under-18s unless dining. ◑≢🖫♣●

East Cliff Tavern
13-15 East Cliff, CT19 6BU (from harbour, up hill straight on past lifeboat and second right)
✪ 5-11; 12-11 Sat & Sun ☎ (01303) 251132
Beer range varies ℍ
Friendly little back-street pub, a short walk from the harbour. A warm welcome to visitors may include a local history lesson from the landlord. Two beers are usually available – one from a Kent or Sussex micro-brewery – plus cider from

Biddenden. Little Switzerland camp/caravan site is about a mile north-east. Old photographs of Folkestone harbour and pubs decorate the walls, and community events include weekly raffles. Q🕭▲♣●┗

Guildhall
42 The Bayle, CT20 1SQ (off pedestrian part of Sandgate Road nearest to the Old High Street)
✪ 12-11 (midnight Fri & Sat); 12-10.30 Sun
☎ (01303) 251393
Greene King IPA, Ruddles County; guest beers ℍ
A welcoming, traditional single-bar pub, close to the town centre. Large windows give the interior a light, airy feel. This is an ideal place to take a break from the hustle and bustle of the town centre and enjoy good ale. Two guest ales are normally stocked from the Punch Tavern's Finest Cask selection. A real cider may be stocked in the summer. Good-value food is served at lunchtimes and occasionally evenings if pre-booked. ❀◑🖫♣●P┗

Pullman
7-9 Church Street, CT20 1SE (off Rendezous St in pedestrian zone)
✪ 12-11 (9 Thu; 6 Sun winter) ☎ (01303) 240538
Harveys Sussex Best Bitter; guest beers ℍ
Re-opened in 2009 after major refurbishment, the interior features wood panelling, mainly dark stained but with one area painted white to good effect. There are three distinct drinking areas on two levels. Up to three guest beers are stocked from regional and micro-breweries from around the country. Food is served throughout the week. The smoking area is covered and heated. There are plans for en-suite accommodation. ♨Q🕭❀◑🖫♣┗

Fordwich

Fordwich Arms ⌐
King Street, CT2 0DB
✪ 11-midnight (1am Fri & Sat); 12-11 Sun
☎ (01227) 710444 ⊕ fordwicharms.co.uk
Flowers Original; Shepherd Neame Master Brew; Wadworth Henry's IPA, 6X ℍ
Classic 1930s building opposite the ancient town hall in England's smallest town. The large bar has a superb fireplace and there is a separate dining room with wood panelling. Excellent meals are served in both areas (no food Sun eve). The garden and terrace overlook the River Stour and church. Run by the same landlord and landlady for 17 years, the pub hosts regular themed evenings including a popular pudding night on the second Wednesday of the month, plus a folk club every second and fourth Sunday night. There is jazz in the garden on summer Sunday afternoons. ♨Q❀◑&≢(Sturry)🖫(4,6,7)P┗

Frittenden

Bell & Jorrocks ✪
Biddenden Road, TN17 2EJ TQ815412
✪ 12 (11 Sat)-11; 12-10 Sun ☎ (01580) 852415
⊕ thebellandjorrocks.co.uk
Adnams Bitter; Harveys Sussex Best Bitter; Woodforde's Wherry; guest beer ℍ
A coaching inn from the early-18th century, in the centre of the village, both geographically and

socially. There is more history in its name and the Heinkel propeller over the main fireplace. Originally multi-bar, the interior has now been knocked through but retains cosiness in all parts, helped by a log fire in cold weather and the absence of gaming machines. Live music is held periodically and a main beer festival in mid-April with occasional mini festivals. Lunches are served Wednesday to Sunday and evening meals Friday and Saturday. ﷯

Gillingham

Frog & Toad ✅
38 Burnt Oak Terrace, ME7 1DR TQ774688
☗ 1 (4 Mon)-11; 12-10.30 Sun ☎ (01634) 852231
⊕ thefrogandtoad.com
Fuller's London Pride; guest beers Ⓗ
This is a typical local pub, hidden in the back streets among housing. A previous three-times winner of the local CAMRA Pub of the Year title, the pub is a 15-20 minute walk from Gillingham train station. It carries a range of guest beers plus Magic Bus cider and a selection of Belgian beers. A large patio garden area to the rear of the pub has bench tables and seats, and an outside bar hosts several beer festivals a year. Sandwiches are served throughout the week. Q﷯(176)﷯

Will Adams ♆
73 Saxton Street, ME7 5EG TQ770683
☗ 7-11; 12.30-4 Sat; 12-3, 8-11 Sun ☎ (01634) 575902
⊕ thewilladams.co.uk
Beer range varies Ⓗ
A friendly single-bar local that was local CAMRA Pub of the Year in 2006 and 2011, the pub has a well-deserved reputation for well-kept beer. Three ales are usually on offer from breweries and micros across the country, plus draught ciders and perry – Old Rosie is the usual regular. The pub is named after a local navigator adventurer, whose exploits are depicted on a mural. Opening times vary for Gillingham FC home games. Away fans are always welcome. ﷯

Gravesend

Jolly Drayman
1 Love Lane, Wellington Street, DA12 1JA
☗ 12-11.30 (midnight Fri & Sat); 12-11 Sun
☎ (01474) 352355 ⊕ jollydrayman.com
Dark Star Hophead; St Austell Tribute; guest beers Ⓗ
Comfortable pub with original low ceilings just outside the town centre. The entrance is via what used to be the back of the pub, which looks out onto the alleyway opposite. It was once part of the Walkers Brewery. It hosts men's and women's darts teams, and daddlums (Kentish skittles) is played on alternate Sundays. Four ales are available, with guest beers often from Dark Star. Lunches are served Monday to Saturday, with evening barbecues some summer evenings. Beer festivals are held twice yearly. ﷯(490,499)﷯

Rum Puncheon
87 West Street, DA11 0BL (on one-way system, next to Tilbury Ferry)
☗ 11 (12 Sat)-11; 12-9 Sun ☎ (01474) 353434
Beer range varies Ⓗ

Large riverside building between the ferry and town pier. The L-shaped bar has a log fire and chandeliers. Upstairs, a function room opens onto a balcony with river views. A rear terrace also provides these views. Six ales rotate regularly though beers from Adnams and Kent micros often appear. Music is usually Classic FM or Jazz, and live jazz or folk evenings are planned. Meals are available lunchtimes and Friday and Saturday evenings. ﷯(480,499)﷯

Ship & Lobster
Mark Lane, Denton, DA12 2QB (end of Mark Lane)
☗ 11-11; 12-4 Sun ☎ (01474) 324571
⊕ shipandlobster.co.uk
Beer range varies Ⓗ
Mentioned by Dickens as the Ship in Great Expectations, this welcoming historic pub can be found at the eastern end of the town, past the canal basin at the end of Mark Lane. It has a nautical theme and is used by walkers on the Saxon Shore Way and by locals fishing the River Thames. The outside drinking area is on the sea wall overlooking the river. ﷯

Great Mongeham

Leather Bottle
103 Mongeham Road, CT14 9PE
☗ 5 (12 Sat & Sun)-11 ☎ (01304) 375931
Beer range varies Ⓗ
This street-corner free house looks out over the village of Great Mongeham. Recent renovations give the large bar room a relaxed, smart, modern feel. A range of beers is featured on its two handpumps, including occasional beers from smaller micro-breweries. Sports feature heavily; large-screen TVs broadcast regular events and there are five darts and pool teams. Occasional live music, karaoke and quiz nights take place. Outside there is a small covered patio for smokers and a large garden. Dog-friendly. ﷯(14,82)﷯

Halstead

Rose & Crown ⓛ
Otford Lane, TN14 7EA (just off main Knockholt road)
☗ 12-11 ☎ (01959) 533120
Larkins Traditional Ale; Whitstable East India Pale Ale; guest beers Ⓗ
An attractive and welcoming two-bar flint-faced free house, built in the 1860s. The public bar contains a cluster of small tables and a dartboard, well-used by the pub team. The saloon bar is also used by casual drinkers and diners' and acts a tea room in the afternoon. Despite changing hands recently, the Rose & Crown continues to be renowned for its ale quality and range, with a leaning towards local breweries. The menu offers home-cooked food. The garden has a child's play area and shaded seating. Local CAMRA Pub of the Year in 2008 and 2009. ﷯(R5,R10,402)﷯

Hastingleigh

Bowl Inn ⓛ
The Street, TN25 5HU TR095449
☗ closed Mon; 5-11.30 (midnight Sat); 12-10.30 Sun
☎ (01233) 750354 ⊕ thebowlonline.co.uk

Harveys Sussex Best Bitter; Hopdaemon Incubus; guest beers Ⓗ
Lovingly restored village pub, this listed building retains many period features including a tap room (now used for playing pool) and is free from juke-box and games machines. Quiz night is Tuesday. The lovely garden has a tame European eagle owl and a cricket pitch to the rear where matches are played most Sundays in the summer. A beer festival is held over the August bank holiday. Excellent sandwiches and baguettes are available weekends. ⚫Q♿🐕🅰️◑♣♠P🚭🚲

Herne

Butcher's Arms Ⓛ

29A Herne Street, CT6 7HL (opp church)
✪ closed Mon; 12-1.30, 6-9 (or later); 12-2 Sun
☎ (01227) 371000 ⊕ micropub.co.uk
Dark Star Hophead; Fuller's ESB; guest beers Ⓖ
The smallest pub in Kent, a real ale gem, and the inspiration for other micro-pubs. Once a butcher's shop, it still has the original chopping tables, with hooks and other implements. There is seating for 12 customers and standing room for about 20 – the compact drinking area ensuring lively banter. A variety of guest beers is offered, and customers can also buy beer to drink at home. The pub has won five CAMRA awards and has been Kent Pub of the Year. Q🚲(4,6)

Smugglers Inn Ⓛ

1 School Lane, CT6 7AN (opp church)
✪ 11-11 (1am Fri & Sat); 12-11 Sun ☎ (01227) 741395
Shepherd Neame Master Brew, seasonal beers Ⓗ
Friendly village local with a smuggling history, situated just inland from Herne Bay. A regular in this Guide, it has been run by the same landlord for 17 years. Dating back to 1840, it was previously called the Prince Albert. The comfortable saloon bar is reputed to be haunted and has a low ceiling with birch thatching, hanging hops and wood panelling. The public bar is in a more recent extension and has a pool table and dartboard. The garden has a bat and trap pitch and hanging flower baskets. Beers from Shepherd Neame's micro-brewery are occasionally available. Q🅰️🗓️♿🚲(4,6)♣🚭

Herne Bay

Prince of Wales Ⓛ

173 Mortimer Street, CT6 5DS (at E end of town, between seafront and High St)
✪ 10am (12 Sun)-midnight ☎ (01227) 374205
Beer range varies Ⓗ
Victorian pub full of memorabilia, winner of the 2006 CAMRA Design Award for the best pub refurbishment. The stylish woodwork and glass are not overwhelmed by discreet TV screens for sporting events, and it has a unique collection of water jugs. Only a few yards from the seafront, the four bars include a large games room with pool and darts, and a small, beautifully-decorated back bar. There is a patio with seating. The range of Shepherd Neame beers varies, but usually includes Master Brew Bitter. ⚫🐕♿🗓️🚲(4,6)♣🚭

Higham

Stone Horse

Dillywood Lane, ME3 8EN (off B2000 Cliffe Road)
TQ732713
✪ 12-3, 6-11; 12-11 Fri & Sat; 12-3.30, 7-10.30 Sun
☎ (01634) 722046
Courage Best Bitter, guest beers Ⓗ
Country pub with a large garden situated on the edge of Strood, surrounded by fields and handy for walkers. The unspoilt public bar sports a wood-burning range. Good value food is served and locals can participate in the cookery club. The pub is dog-friendly but no children are allowed in the bar. Up to three guest beers are usually available. Roasts are on offer Tuesday and Wednesday, no food Sunday. ⚫Q🅰️◑♿🗓️🚲(133)♣P🚭

Hildenborough

Cock Horse

London Road, TN11 8NH (on B245 between Sevenoaks and Tonbridge) TQ553499
✪ 12-11 ☎ (01732) 833232
Shepherd Neame Master Brew, Spitfire Ⓗ
Originally named The Old Cock, this family-run 16th-century pub was a coaching inn on the busy road between Tunbridge Wells and Sevenoaks. The homely interior contains a cosy bar with an inglenook fireplace. Home-cooked food is available all week and is especially popular at weekends, with busy lunchtimes (booking recommended). Check the chalkboard for the daily menu. Popular with walkers, who enjoy a well-earned rest on the split-level rear decked area overlooking the garden and stream. The two cask beers are always in top condition. ⚫Q🅰️◑♿🗓️🚲(402)P

Hythe

Three Mariners Ⓛ

37 Windmill Street, CT21 6BH
✪ 4-10 Mon; 12-11 (midnight Fri & Sat) ☎ (01303) 260406
Young's Bitter; guest beers Ⓗ
This traditional two-bar back-street local is the jewel in the crown and a cask ale mecca in a town with several potential Guide candidates. Refurbished in 2009 from a run-down Shepherd Neame establishment, the friendly and relaxed atmosphere makes this worthwhile finding for its range of guest ales, usually including two from local micro-brewers. Beer festivals are held on the spring and August bank holidays. ⚫🐕🅰️◑♣♠🚭

Iden Green

Peacock

Goudhurst Road, TN17 2PB (1½ miles E of Goudhurst at A262/B2085 jct) TQ747374
✪ 12-11 (6 Sun) ☎ (01580) 211233
Shepherd Neame Master Brew, Late Red, Bishops Finger, seasonal beer Ⓗ
Attractive timber-framed building with white weatherboarding, set back from the road with a large car park to the front. The two welcoming bars are simply furnished and decorated with lots of local memorabilia and photos. The original bar has an inglenook fireplace and old beams and provides a pleasant ambience as a dining area. The newer

rear bar opens onto the large garden and has a friendly atmosphere enhanced by the local patrons enjoying a traditional English public house.
♨Q✿◑⊞♿🚌(297)♣P⌐

Ightham Common

Old House ★

Redwell, Redwell Lane, TN15 9EE (½ mile SW of Ightham village, between A25 and A227) TQ590588
⏲ 7-11; 12-3, 7-10.30 Sat & Sun ☎ (01732) 886077
Lodden Shrimpers; guest beers 🄶
Kentish red-brick and tile-hung cottage hidden away down a steep, narrow lane. Enter through a small lobby to find a public bar to the left with a Victorian wood-panelled counter, parquet flooring and a large inglenook fireplace. The parlour to the right houses a chaise longue in the bay window. Up to six beers are served by gravity from a stillage in a back room. The pub often closes at 9pm on Monday and Tuesday if not busy. A rural gem not to be missed. ♨Q✿⊞⛺♣P⌐

Ivychurch

Bell Inn 🏆 ✔

TN29 0AL (signed from A2070 between Brenzett and Hamstreet) TR028275
⏲ 12-11 (10.30 Sun) ☎ (01797) 344355
🌐 thebellinnromneymarsh.co.uk
Black Sheep Best Bitter; Sharp's Doom Bar; Wadworth Henry's IPA; guest beers 🄷
Like many marsh pubs, this house is adjacent to the church; in fact, it was carved off from the churchyard. Popular for its excellent ales and ciders as well as the selection of food, a warm welcome awaits. The current licensees have achieved an enviable reputation for the establishment, gaining the honour of CAMRA Branch Pub of the Year in 2010 and 2011. Well worth finding, it was once the centre of the Owlers (smugglers).
♨♞✿◑⊞♿♣●P⌐

Knockholt

Three Horseshoes ✔

The Pound, TN14 7LD
⏲ 11.30-3, 6-11; 12-4, 7-10.30 Sun ☎ (01959) 532102
Harveys Sussex Best Bitter; Westerham SPA; guest beers 🄷
Attracting drinkers and diners alike, this pub is also dog-friendly, making it especially popular with numerous walkers. It always has three real ales, with the emphasis on local micro-breweries. It features a large, separate dining room where reasonably priced, home-cooked food is served. There is also a garden for enjoying alfresco beer and food. Regular events include a monthly quiz in aid of Kent Air Ambulance, cribbage league matches, and a monthly classic vehicles rally.
Q✿◑⊞♿🚌(402,R5)♣P⌐

Lower Halstow

Three Tuns

The Street, ME9 7DY
⏲ 12-11 (midnight Fri & Sat); 12-10.30 Sun
☎ (01795) 842840 🌐 the-tuns.co.uk
Shepherd Neame Kent's Best; guest beer 🄷
A Grade II-listed building said to date from 1468, which was issued an ale licence in 1764. The spacious pub is the only one remaining in this small, quiet village. There is a log fire in winter and a large garden with decking for the summer, plus a games room with a pool table. You will always find one guest beer, two at busy times. The restaurant is open lunchtimes and evenings, with a varied bar menu all day Monday to Saturday, and Sunday lunches 12-6pm. ♨✿◑♿🚌(327)♣P⌐

Luddesdown

Cock Inn 🏆 Ⓛ ✔

Henley Street, DA13 0XB (1 mile SE of Sole Street station) TQ664672
⏲ 12-11 (10.30 Sun) ☎ (01474) 814208
🌐 cockluddesdowne.com
Adnams Bitter, Lighthouse, Broadside; Goacher's Real Mild Ale; Shepherd Neame Master Brew; guest beers 🄷
Independent free house under the same ownership since 1984. The building dates from 1713, with two distinct bars and a conservatory creating a homely atmosphere. It is also home to many clubs and societies. The landlord hosts a challenging quiz every Tuesday. Bar billiards can be played in the public bar, dominoes and other games are set out in the conservatory, and petanque is played in the garden. The purpose-built covered and heated smoking area has a dartboard. ♨Q✿◑⊞♣●P⌐▯

Lynsted

Black Lion

Lynsted Lane, ME9 0RJ (close to church) TQ943609
⏲ 11-3, 6-11; 12-3, 7-10.30 Sun ☎ (01795) 521229
Goacher's Real Mild Ale, Light, Dark, seasonal beers 🄷
With three or four beers from Goacher's on offer, this friendly village pub is sought out by drinkers. The main bar room has real fires in winter, and a further bar is home to a bar billiards table. Wooden floors throughout add to the character. Food is available daily and there is a large garden. The 345 bus runs every two hours or so from Sittingbourne via Teynham (not eves or Sun). There are three letting rooms separate from the pub.
♨Q✿🛏◑⊞🚌(345)♣P⌐

Maidstone

First & Last

40 Bower Place, ME16 8BH
⏲ 4-11.30; 2-midnight Sat & Sun ☎ (01622) 683151
Adnams Bitter; Ringwood Best; Taylor Landlord; guest beer 🄷
Cosy town pub situated on an acute-angled corner, approximately 10 minutes' walk from the centre of Maidstone. Built in 1835 by William Cleaver on what was originally the main road, it was known as the Cradle & Coffin. Three real ales are always available, with a fourth often added as a guest. Live music, from unusual local bands, features monthly on a Saturday evening. A charity cricket match is held annually to support the Kent Air Ambulance. ♨Q⇌(West)🚌(8)♣

Flower Pot ☺ ⓛ ✅

96 Sandling Road, ME14 2RJ (off A229 N of town centre)
🕒 12 (11 Sat)-11; 12-10.30 Sun ☎ (01622) 757705
🌐 flowerpotpub.com
Goacher's Gold Star; Kent Brewery Pale; guest beers Ⓗ

This split-level, street-corner free house is a real ale lovers' paradise. Nine handpumps adorn the bar, dispensing ales from Kent micros and the rest of Britain. Dark Star and BrewDog often feature. A TV screen displays not only the beers on offer, including the strength and price, but also forthcoming events such as music and jam nights. Occasional beers festivals are held, and several ciders are sold. A must when visiting the county town. CAMRA Kent Regional Pub of the Year 2011.
🏚Q🅿⌑≠(East)🚲(101,155)♣♠⁵⌐

Pilot ✅

23-25 Upper Stone Street, ME15 6EU (on A229 southbound)
🕒 12-3 (not Mon), 6-11; 12-midnight Fri & Sat; 12-11 Sun
☎ (01622) 691162
Harveys Mild, Sussex Best Bitter, Armada Ale, seasonal beers Ⓗ

A welcome return to this Guide for Maidstone's country pub in the town. The Grade II-listed pub has a beamed interior with an inglenook fireplace. On Sunday roasts are served at lunchtime, followed by live music in the afternoon and a fun quiz in the evening. There are folk nights on alternate Mondays, and a monthly jam night. Food is not available on Monday, Tuesday or Sunday evening. Petanque is played in the garden.
🏚🅿⌑≠(West)🚲♣♠⁵⌐

Rifle Volunteers ⓛ

28 Wyatt Street, ME14 1EU
🕒 11-3, 6 (7 Sat)-11; 12-3, 7-10.30 Sun ☎ (01622) 758891
Goacher's Real Mild Ale, Fine Light, Crown Imperial Stout Ⓗ

Quiet street-corner, single-bar pub owned by the local Goacher's Brewery. It retains most of its original features and has been a regular in this Guide for several years. The pub fields two quiz teams in the local league. Note the display of interesting old bottled beers and the unusual toy soldiers used to indicate a beer in the wood. A good old-fashioned pub free from music and fruit machines. Q🅿≠(East)♣⁵⌐

Swan ⓛ ✅

2 County Road, ME14 1UY (opp prison, near County Hall)
🕒 12-11 ☎ (01622) 751264 🌐 theswaninnmaidstone.co.uk
Shepherd Neame Master Brew, Kent's Best; guest beers Ⓗ

Originally called The County Arms, this friendly locals' pub dates back to 1840 and is situated two minutes' walk from Maidstone East station and close to County Hall and Maidstone Prison. Shepherd Neame beers include seasonals and brews from the brewery's pilot micro-brewery, and the pub hosts regular mini festivals. The interior is adorned with swans in all shapes and sizes, and historic brewery and pub pictures. Occasional live music plays at weekends, plus folk nights and fun quiz nights on alternate Wednesdays.
🏚🅿≠(East)♣⁵⌐

Marden

Stile Bridge ⓛ ✅

Staplehurst Road, TN12 9BH (S of Maidstone on A229 at foot of Linton Hill by jct with B2079)
🕒 11-11 ☎ (01622) 831236 🌐 stile.co.uk
Adnams Lighthouse, Broadside; guest beers Ⓗ

Imposing, blue-painted, roadside pub and seafood restaurant with a welcoming atmosphere offering a mixture of pub and separate dining. There is even a snug bar. Every wall is adorned with pub- and drink-related memorabilia. Five real ales and three ciders are always available, supported by genuine continental beers and lagers. Popular Bridgestock beer and music festivals are held on the spring and summer bank holidays. There are regular theme nights, quizzes and live music events. Traditional home-cooked meals are also served.
🏚🅿⌑🚲(5)♠P⁵⌐☗

Margate

Lifeboat Ale & Cider House

1 Market Street, CT9 1EU
🕒 12-2, 5-10 (11 Fri & Sat); 12-6 Sun ☎ (07837) 024259
🌐 thelifeboat-margate.com
Beer range varies Ⓗ

Opening in 2010, this former wine bar in Margate old town has been transformed into a welcome addition to the town's meagre real ale scene. Wooden stillaging divides the pleasant space into a front and back room, and the pub offers a changing selection of around six gravity-dispensed, mainly Kentish, beers, and a similar number of real ciders. It is well placed to cater to visitors expected at the brand-new Turner Contemporary Gallery a short distance away. 🏚⌑≠🚲♠

Northern Belle

4 Mansion Street, CT9 1HE
🕒 11 (12 Sun)-11 ☎ (07810) 088347
Shepherd Neame Master Brew, Kent's Best; guest beers Ⓗ

Margate's oldest standing pub is down a tiny alleyway opposite the stone pier. In the year 1680 two fishermen's cottages were combined and a new pub, Aurora Borealis, was created. The pub owes its present name to a merchant ship that ran aground in 1857. Low ceilings and quirky little nooks make this a cosy establishment. Live music sometimes plays. ⌑≠🚲(8,34)♣

Sheldon's

127-129 High Street, CT9 1JT
🕒 11-11 (midnight Fri & Sat) ☎ (01843) 223578
Fuller's London Pride; Ramsgate Gadds' No. 5 Ⓗ

A popular free house at the top of Margate's pedestrianised high street, and part of the Thorley Taverns chain. It has a large seating area and offers home-cooked food as well as locally-sourced ale. The building dates from 1935. Formerly the Saracen's Head, this is a well-run pub in the heart of Margate. 🅿⌑≠🚲

Mersham

Farriers Arms

The Forstal, TN25 6NU (from village turn right into Church Rd. Pub is on left-hand side approx 1km)

Sandwich

Red Cow
12 Moat Sole, CT13 9AU
🕛 11-11 ☎ (01304) 613243
St Austell Tribute; Sharp's Doom Bar; guest beers H
Timber-framed, town-centre pub 10 minutes from the railway station. The bar, lounge and dining area have a traditional feel, with wooden floors and exposed beams. Real ales from Ramsgate and Wantsum feature alongside ciders from Biddenden and Westons. The family-friendly pub has a large enclosed garden, with children's games, ideal in summer. Mini beer festivals are held. A good range of pub food is offered, with occasional special deals. Major football matches are shown on TV in the bar. 🏠🕙≠🖪(13,14,87)●P⁵⁻

Seal Chart

Crown Point Inn
Sevenoaks Road, TN15 0HB
🕛 11.30-11; 12-10.30 Sun ☎ (01732) 810669
Beer range varies H
Large road house on the A25 between Ightham and Sevenoaks, with three separate drinking areas plus a dining area and carvery, and an Italianate garden for summer drinking and dining. The pub is happy to support local breweries and always features at least one ale from one of them – tasters are willingly supplied. There is an extensive, excellent-value menu available all day, every day. 🏠🏵🕙🅰🖪(308)P⁵⁻

Sevenoaks

Anchor
32 London Road, TN13 1AS
🕛 11-3, 6-midnight; 10.30-midnight Fri; 10.30-4.30, 7-midnight Sat; 12-midnight Sun ☎ (01732) 454898
Harveys Sussex Best Bitter; Sharp's Doom Bar; guest beer H
Over the past 30 years the landlord has moved from young upstart to elder statesman of the local pub scene. His enthusiasm for his work is undiminished and shows in the welcome extended to locals and strangers alike. The pub is entered through an unusual circular lobby and has a single-bar room with a games area for pool and darts and an unobtrusive TV at one end. The recent addition of a third handpump for the changing guest beer, often from a local source, has been a success. Live music, often blues, and open mike sessions are hosted. 🕙🖪(402)●⁵⁻

White Hart
Tonbridge Road, TN13 1SG (S of town centre on A225)
🕛 11-11; 12-10.30 Sun ☎ (01732) 452022
🌐 whitehart-sevenoaks.co.uk
Fuller's London Pride; Harveys Sussex Best Bitter; Shepherd Neame Spitfire H
A whitewashed 17th-century coaching inn, once next to the Sevenoaks turnpike, now refreshing modern travellers. Recently taken over by Brunning & Price, a small pub chain from north-west England, the pub has a rapidly growing reputation for high-quality food and drink. It usually serves at least half a dozen cask beers, including a house beer from Phoenix in Manchester, plus real cider, and holds twice yearly beer festivals. Although it is

a large multi-level building, the pub still manages to be cosy, with several real fires, low lighting and intriguing wall prints. A welcome new entry. 🏠Q🏵🕙🛆🖪(402)♣●P⁵⁻

Shatterling

Frog & Orange
CT3 1JR
🕛 12-11 (10.30 Sun) ☎ (01304) 812525
🌐 thefrogandorangepub.co.uk
Beer range varies H
Family-run pub, on the Canterbury to Sandwich road, built in the modern style with a red-brick interior comprising the bar area, with comfortable seating and wooden floors, and a restaurant. Real ales often include beers from the Ramsgate Brewery. The daily grumpy time is popular with locals, as are the blacksmith's puzzles held behind the bar. A varied menu of home-made food is offered. Regular classic car club meetings, an annual steam rally and tug o' war take place. Dogs are welcome outside mealtimes, and there is an excellent children's playground. 🏵🏠🕙🖪(13,13A)♣P⁵⁻

Sheerness

Red Lion
61 High Street, Blue Town, ME12 1RW TQ911750
🕛 11-midnight (1am Thu-Sat); 12-midnight Sun
☎ (01795) 664354
Beer range varies H
An oasis of choice in Sheppey. Facing the former naval dockyard wall, this is the only real ale outlet remaining in the old Blue Town district of Sheerness, with its cobbled High Street. Three beers from regional and micro-breweries are served, with customers having a say in the choice. No meals are served, but there is a free buffet on Sunday. Outside are tables and a heated, covered smoking area. 🏠🏵≠🖪♣⁵⁻

Snargate

Red Lion ★ L
TN29 9UQ (on B2080, 1 mile NW of Brenzett) TQ990285
🕛 12-3, 7-11 (10.30 Sun) ☎ (01797) 344648
Beer range varies G
A 16th-century building owned by the same family for 100 years, universally known as Doris's, located on the road that separates Walland Marsh from Romney Marsh. The interior of this superb, unspoilt, three-room pub is decorated with posters from World War II and the Women's Land Army and features in CAMRA's National Inventory of Historic Pub Interiors. It serves beer from small breweries, usually including Goacher's, and hosts a beer festival in June and a mini festival in October. 🏠Q🏵♣●P⁵⁻

Stalisfield Green

Plough Inn L
ME13 0HY TQ955529
🕛 closed Mon; 12-3 (not Tue), 6-11; 12-11.30 Sat; 12-6 Sun
☎ (01795) 890256 🌐 stalisfieldgreen.com
Beer range varies H

Built some time between 1350 and 1450, this historic multi-roomed pub is in an attractive setting on the North Downs. Beers are almost always from Kent's micro-breweries and feature on a rotating basis. The extensive menu offers locally-sourced produce and has won many awards. The pub has a large family-friendly garden. Live music plays on some Fridays (see website for details). There is a beer festival over the August bank holiday weekend. The 660 bus from Faversham is infrequent, but may be of use.
△△⊛⊘▶ 本田(660)♣P

Stansted

Black Horse 🄻

Tumblefield Road, TN15 7PR (1 mile N of A20 jct 2) TQ606620
☼ 11.30-11; 12-10.30 Sun ☎ (01732) 822355
Larkins Traditional; guest beers Ⓗ
Situated in the heart of the North Downs, this welcoming village free house is surrounded by rolling hills and woodlands, attracting ramblers and cyclists. The large garden includes a children's play area. Thai meals are served Tuesday to Saturday evenings until 9.30pm and good bar meals at lunchtime, with popular Sunday roasts. Irish folk music sessions are held on the second Sunday of each month. △△Q☲⊛⊛⊘▶本♣♦P⅃

Staple

Black Pig

Barnsole Road, CT3 1LE (signed off Staple-Woodnesborough road)
☼ closed Mon; 12-midnight (10.30 Sun) ☎ (01304) 813000
⊕ theblackpig.co.uk
Beer range varies Ⓗ
On the outskirts of Staple, this charming 16th-century rambling building, said to be constructed from the timbers of local shipwrecks, hosts a traditional country pub. A varied menu of home-made food is complemented by a range of up to three real ales, regularly featuring Sharp's beers. Occasionally cider is on offer. Families are welcome and a function room is available for special occasions. Benches outside the front of the pub and a large enclosed garden are popular in summer. Regular live music is hosted and there is a beer festival in August. △△⊛☲⊘▶P

Staplehurst

Lord Raglan 🄻

Chart Hill Road, TN12 0DE (½ mile N of A229) TQ786472
☼ 12-3, 6.30-11.30; closed Sun ☎ (01622) 843747
Goacher's Fine Light; Harveys Sussex Best Bitter; guest beers Ⓗ
Pleasant rural pub with an orchard aspect. The hop-decorated bar runs across the front room of the pub and has a log fire at either end. A side room gives access to the large garden, lovely on a sunny summer evening, and there is a further room tucked away behind the bar. Hot meals and snacks can be taken in any of the rooms. The friendly staff ensure that diners and drinkers are made equally welcome. △△Q⊛⊘▶田(5)♦P

Tenterden

White Lion Hotel

57 High Street, TN30 6BD (in centre of High Street on A28)
☼ 10-11 (midnight Fri & Sat); 10-10.30 Sun
☎ (01580) 765077
Jennings Cumberland Ale; Marston's Pedigree; guest beers Ⓗ
A 16th-century coaching inn with an elegant frontage, pillared porch, bowed and dormer windows, and the original coaching entrance. It was built facing the wide tree-lined High Street that includes many historic buildings and is convenient for the Kent & East Sussex Railway. Inside there are aged ship timbers, inglenook fireplaces and local memorabilia. The pub has the full range of Marston's beers to choose from and encourages customers to request the beers they want. △△Q☲☲⊘▶田占田(293,295,400)P

Tilmanstone

Plough & Harrow

Dover Road, CT14 0HX (signed off A256 between Dover and Sandwich)
☼ 12-11 (10.30 Sun); winter hours vary ☎ (01304) 617582
⊕ ploughandharrowtilmanstone.co.uk
Shepherd Neame Master Brew, Spitfire; guest beers Ⓗ
Wooden floors, sofas and an interesting collection of Kent coalfield memorabilia give this rural pub a traditional feel. Real ale includes beers from Shepherd Neame's micro-brewery and occasional guests. Traditional home-cooked food is served all day, every day (12-6pm Sun) in the conservatory restaurant, with a senior citizen's menu on Tuesday. Entertainment includes bar billiards, charity quizzes and an annual pumpkin competition. A large garden has a heated, covered area for smokers and a barbecue for customers' use. △△⊛☲⊘▶田(87,88,88A)♣P⅃

Tonbridge

Humphrey Bean 🅥

94 High Street, TN9 1AP (near castle and river)
☼ 7am-midnight (1am Fri & Sat) ☎ (01732) 773850
Greene King Ruddles Best Bitter, Abbot; guest beers Ⓗ
The Bean has moved on from its rather chequered past to become a stalwart of the Tonbridge drinking scene. The large Wetherspoon venue was previously a post office and is named after the landlord of a pub that once occupied the site. It has a bright and airy feel, thanks to large roof windows, with quieter corners. The rear garden has views across the River Medway to the castle. Guests beers from south-eastern breweries are regularly served. National Wetherspoon beer festivals are promoted with enthusiasm. Real cider (often Thatchers) is also available. ⊛⊘▶占⇌田(77,402)♦P⅃

Punch & Judy

11 St Stephens Street, TN9 2AB (behind police station)
☼ 12-midnight (11 Sun & Mon) ☎ (01732) 352368
Harveys Sussex Best Bitter; Sharp's Doom Bar Ⓗ
A thriving community local tucked away on a road behind the police station. It is built on two levels,

⊕ 12-2 (not Mon-Wed), 5-11; 12-midnight Fri & Sat; 12-11 Sun ☎ (01282) 612173

Moorhouse's Black Cat, Premier Bitter, Pride of Pendle, Blond Witch; guest beers Ⓗ

One of just six Moorhouse's tied houses and the only one in Pendle. The famous old hill, with its witchcraft connections, can be viewed from the front patio area. Dog-friendly and still retaining its traditional tap room, it has a collection of breweriana in the parlour. Bar snacks and meals are served daily (all day until 7pm at weekends). The Rising Sun is thought to be the last pub still serving the Pendleside delicacy of 'Stew an' Hard'. The licensee is a CAMRA member.
▲Q❀❶🕀🖫(P70,P71)♣P

Blackpool

Blackpool Cricket Club Ⓛ ✓

Barlow Crescent, West Park Drive, FY3 9EQ

⊕ 7-11; 12-11 Sat & Sun ☎ (01253) 393347

Thwaites Wainwright; guest beers Ⓗ

The club is adjacent to Stanley Park and has a number of teams playing in local cricket leagues; occasional Lancashire county cricket matches are also played here. The premier suite is available for social functions and meetings. The club is a supporter of Blackpool football club and all premier league matches are shown on large-screen TV. There are three handpumps and a LocAle is usually available. Food is served all day at weekends.
❀❶ᴴ&Pᴸ

Gillespies

87-89 Topping Street, FY1 3AA (off Church St and close to Winter Gardens)

⊕ 10-11 (midnight Fri & Sat) ☎ (01253) 627882

Greene King St Edmunds; guest beers Ⓗ

There is always a warm and friendly welcome in this popular locals' pub, situated on the fringe of Blackpool's bustling bar, restaurant and night club scene. It is round the corner from the famous Winter Gardens and approximately 500m from the promenade. Gillespies won the CAMRA Pub of the Season award for summer 2010, and has four cask ales always available. The pub is sport-oriented and houses a pool table, two big screens and four TVs. Food is served until 6pm every day. Families are welcome. ❶≢(North)🖫

No 4 & Freemasons Ⓛ ✓

Layton Road, FY3 8ER (at jct with Newton Drive, B5266)

⊕ 12-11 (midnight Tue; Fri-Sun) ☎ (01253) 302877

Thwaites Original, Wainwright, Lancaster Bomber; guest beers Ⓗ

This smart suburban pub fronts on to Newton Drive and is located one mile inland from the seafront, with bus stops directly outside. The main lounge has both dining and drinking areas with TV screens and pictures of Blackpool's heyday. The rear games room has pool and darts. Beers are served in top condition, including two guest beers, and meals are served lunchtimes and evenings Monday-Friday, and all day Saturday and Sunday.
❀❶🕀&🖫(2,15)♣Pᴸ

Pump & Truncheon Ⓛ

13 Bonny Street, FY1 5AR (opp Bonny St police station)

⊕ 11-11; 10-midnight Fri-Sun summer ☎ (01253) 624099

⊕ thepumpandtruncheon.co.uk

Beer range varies Ⓗ

This bare brick and wood former Hogshead pub makes the most of its location. Police badges and painted friezes are a wry and amusing reflection of the pub's connections. Hearty and generous home-cooked meals are served. A good selection of malt whiskies is stocked, together with foreign bottled beers. There is a 10 per cent discount for CAMRA members on food and real ale. Three changing guests in winter, six in summer, and local Fuzzy Duck beers feature regularly. Families are welcome in this genuine free house.
▲❶🕀&🕀(Central Pier)🖫♣

Ramsden Arms Ⓛ

204 Talbot Road, FY1 3AZ (on A586 nr North railway station)

⊕ 10.30-midnight (1am Sat); 12-midnight Sun ☎ (01253) 291713

Beer range varies Ⓗ

A new management team has brought back quality real ale to this pub on the edge of the town centre, distinct thanks to its black and white appearance, close to North railway station. The Rammy is a superb addition to Blackpool's real ale scene – real ale, real fires, real people. Three changing guest beers are served. An array of beer tankards and sporting trophies adorns the walls, along with TV screens. Bar snacks are available until 6pm every day. ▲❀🕀≢(North)🖫Pᴸ

Shovels Ⓛ ✓

260 Common Edge Road, FY4 5DH (on B5261, ½ mile from A5230 jct)

⊕ 12-11 (midnight Thu-Sat) ☎ (01253) 762702

Lytham Shovels Best; guest beers Ⓗ

A large open-plan roadside venue that has won CAMRA Local Pub of the Year more than once. Six handpumps offer a range of guest beers, mainly from micros; the house beer is brewed exclusively for the pub by Lytham Brewery. A beer festival is held every October, attracting people from all over. The pub is home to many sports clubs and has a large screen for sporting events. Good food is popular with diners and is served all day.
▲❀❶&🜨🖫(17)♣Pᴸ

Blackpool: Bispham

Bispham

Red Bank Road, FY2 9HY (300m from promenade)

⊕ 12 (11 Sat)-11; 12-10.30 Sun ☎ (01253) 351752

Samuel Smith OBB Ⓗ

Well-maintained mid-1930s Art Deco main road pub, a popular local, well-known for its low-priced ale drawn from oak casks. There's no food, music or children – a haven for a pint and a chat. It is four minutes' walk from the sea front and the Blackpool-Fleetwood tramway. The pub sign features one of the older trams, a reminder that there used to be a tram depot behind the pub. A quiz is held Thursday and Sunday. Upstairs meeting room available. Q❀🕀&🕀🖫ᴸ

Brindle

Cavendish Arms ✓

Sandy Lane, PR6 8NG

⊕ 12-11 (midnight Fri-Sun) ☎ (01254) 852912

⊕ cavendisharms.co.uk

Banks's Bitter; guest beers Ⓗ

At the heart of this attractive village and opposite the 13th-century church, the Cavendish was sadly boarded up for most of 2008. Now under new management, the pub and village have been revitalised. With a small room on the left as you enter and the large main bar area with rooms off, the pub has been tastefully restored and expanded inside. Three guest beers are from the Marston's list. A beer festival is held in a marquee annually in June. ♨Q❀◑◐▯➾(118)P

Burnley

Boot Inn L ✓
18 St James St, BB11 1NG
❀9am-11 (midnight Fri & Sat) ☎ (01282) 463720
Greene King Ruddles Best Bitter, Abbot; guest beers ⑭
This Grade II-listed building was completed in 1911 and has been a Wetherspoon pub since the summer of 2009. Previously owned by Thwaites and latterly a Yates Wine Lodge, the pub had been shut for more than 12 months, but is now a smart, welcoming and comfortable hostelry in typical Wetherspoon style, with a good choice of ales from many excellent East Lancs local brewers. An extensive outdoor drinking area is well used in the summer months. ◑占≠╚

Bridge Bier Huis L
2 Bank Parade, BB11 1UH (behind shopping centre)
❀closed Mon & Tue; 12-midnight (1am Fri & Sat); 12-11 Sun ☎ (01282) 411304 ∰ thebridgebierhuis.co.uk
Hydes Bitter; guest beers ⑭
This free house has a large open-plan bar area with a small snug to one side. It supports the LocAle scheme and serves up to four guest beers, mainly from micro-breweries, as well as a real cider or perry. Five Belgian or foreign beers are on tap, with an extensive and changing range of foreign bottled beers. Quiz night is Wednesday and occasional live music is hosted at weekends. A regular CAMRA award-winner. ❀◑≠(Central)➾♣♠

Gannow Wharf L
168 Gannow Lane, BB12 6QH (next to Leeds-Liverpool canal on Gannow bridge)
❀7 (5 Fri)-11; 3-11 Sat & Sun ☎ (07855) 315498
Beer range varies ⑭
This ever-popular local offers a friendly welcome to bikers and all lovers of real ale. A varying range of six beers is sold, mostly sourced from local breweries as part of the LocAle scheme. Try the gallon challenge if you dare. Activities include quiz nights, live music, karaoke, pool and satellite TV. At the rear, overlooking the canal, is a heated, covered area for smoking. ❀≠(Rose Grove)➾(4,65)╚

Ministry of Ale L
9 Trafalgar Street, BB11 1TQ (100m from Burnley Manchester Road station)
❀closed Mon; 7.30-11 Tue; 6-11 Wed & Thu; 3.30-midnight Fri; 12-midnight Sat; 1-11 Sun ☎ (01282) 830909 ∰ ministryofale.co.uk
Beer range varies ⑭
Home of the Moonstone Brewery, which opened in 2000, and the 2.5 barrel brew-plant can be seen in the front room of this small local. Two Moonstone beers are always available, alongside two changing guests from other micro-breweries. The pub always provides a warm, friendly welcome, good beer and good conversation. Art exhibitions are regularly held, with works displayed on the walls. Quiz night is every Thursday. Accredited LocAle member. ❀≠(Manchester Rd)➾(X43,X44)╚

Talbot Hotel L ✓
65 Church Street, BB11 2RS (on A56 close to town centre)
❀4-midnight (late Fri); 12-late Sat; 12-midnight Sun ☎ (01282) 412074
Copper Dragon Golden Pippin; Holt Bitter; Moorhouse's Premier; Taylor Landlord, Ram Tam; Thwaites Wainwright ⑭
There is always a warm welcome at this recently refurbished free house, which dates back to the 1800s. The licensee is a cask ale enthusiast and offers two guest beers in addition to the six regular ales. Guests might be from any of the following: Coniston, Ossett, Cairngorm or Camerons. Live bands feature regularly at weekends. There are two pool tables, and a large-screen TV for major sporting events. A private car park is available for residents. The Talbot has its own Facebook page. ▭❀◪≠➾(X43, X44)╚

Burscough

Farmers Arms ✓
36 New Lane, L40 8JA (turn into Higgins Lane off A59 and continue into New Lane) SD428126
❀11-midnight; 11.30-11.30 Sun ☎ (01704) 896021
Black Sheep Best Bitter; Jennings Cumberland Ale; Tetley Dark Mild, Bitter ⑭; **guest beers** ⑭/℗
Situated on the Leeds-Liverpool canal, the pub is handy for passing barges, which can moor alongside, and also close to the busy Burscough industrial estate. The Farmers has a reputation for good food, with (late) breakfasts available too. There is a real coal fire in winter, and in summer there are tables outside. The Wildfowl and Wetlands Trust centre at Martin Mere is also nearby. Food is served lunchtimes and evenings weekdays, all day on Sunday. ♨Q▭❀◑占▵≠(New Lane)P╚

Hop Vine ♈ L
Liverpool Road North, L40 4BY (on A59, almost opp Burscough Bridge station)
❀10.30-midnight (12.30am Fri & Sat) ☎ (01704) 893799 ∰ thehopvine.co.uk
Burscough Priory Gold, Ringtail Bitter; Moorhouse's Pendle Witches Brew; Prospect Hop Vine; guest beers ⑭
Situated in the attractive village of Burscough, the Hop Vine brew-pub dates from 1874 and was originally a coaching stop. Recently refurbished, the pub sports a classic country pub interior, with wood panelling, mixed wood/tile flooring, and is decorated throughout with historic local maps, photographs and rare vintage bottled ales. The pub commenced brewing (as the Burscough Brewing Co.) in 2010 in the charming cobbled flower garden at the rear. Excellent home-cooked food is served throughout the day. Close to Manchester-Southport railway. ♨❀◑▯≠(Burscough Bridge)➾(2A,2B)P╚

Catforth

Running Pump
Catforth Road, PR4 0HH (½ mile off B5269)
❀12-midnight (11 Sun) ☎ (01772) 690265
Robinson's Unicorn ⑭
This historic country pub with stunning fell views, named after the spring-fed water pump at the front, remains largely unchanged. Local history decorates the walls of its three rooms, all with

Eccleston

Original Farmers Arms
Towngate, PR7 5QS (on B5250)
✿ 12-midnight (11.30 Sun) ☎ (01257) 451594
Black Sheep Best Bitter; Fuller's London Pride; Tetley Bitter; Wells Bombardier; guest beers Ⓗ
This white-painted village pub has expanded over the years into the cottage next door, adding a substantial dining area. However, the original part of the pub is still used mainly for drinking. The two rotating guest beers are predominantly sourced from local micros – Bowland, Three B's and Southport breweries are favourites. Meals are available throughout the day seven days a week, and there is accommodation in four good-value guest rooms. ✿⊯◑🖥(113,347)P⌐

Edgworth

White Horse Ⓛ
2-4 Bury Road, BL7 0AY SD742168
✿ 5-11 Mon & Tue; 12-3, 5-midnight Wed & Thu; 12-midnight Fri & Sat; 12-11 Sun ☎ (01204) 852929
Bank Top Flat Cap; Greene King Ruddles Best Bitter; Marston's Pedigree; Taylor Landlord; guest beers Ⓗ
Situated prominently at the Bolton-Bury road crossroads in Edgworth, this local is a large, decorative corner building. The impressively decorated interior has tables set for diners who come to enjoy exquisite cuisine. The range of real ales on five handpumps includes some from LocAle breweries; a good selection of wine is also available. The pub name has heraldic origins, dating back to 1714-1800 – white being the colour of peace and the horse representing stead: readiness for all events in the name of the king. A wall plaque outside explains more. ♨✿◑♿P⌐

Euxton

Euxton Mills ✪
Wigan Road, PR7 6JD (at A49/A581 jct)
✿ 11.30-10.30 (11 Wed & Thu; 11.30 Fri); 12-11.30 Sat; 12-10.30 Sun ☎ (01257) 264002
Jennings Bitter, Cumberland Ale, Cocker Hoop; guest beers Ⓗ
A village inn that has won several Best Kept Pub awards, as well as local CAMRA Pub of the Season. Outside, a large collection of hanging baskets and flowerpots are particularly attractive during the summer months. The pub is renowned for the quality of its food and serves up to three guest beers from the extensive Marston's range. Two beer festivals are held each year, with eight ales available at any one time. Quiz night is Wednesday. ✿◑≢(Balshaw Lane)🖥(16,109)P⌐

Fence

White Swan Ⓛ ✪
300 Wheatley Lane Road, BB12 9QA (off A6068)
✿ 12-2.30 (not Mon), 5-11; 12-11.30 Fri & Sat; 12-10.30 Sun ☎ (01282) 611773 ⊕ whiteswanatfence.co.uk
Taylor Best Bitter, Golden Best, Landlord Ⓗ
Known locally as t'Mucky Duck, this is currently one of only two Timothy Taylor tied houses in Lancashire. A fourth handpump regularly dispenses one of Taylor's other beers. Good, wholesome food made with fresh local ingredients is served lunchtimes and evenings. Situated at the heart of the village community, a warm welcome awaits,

especially in winter, when two open fires heat the small pub. Satellite TV is screened in the bar area. ♨Q◑🖥(65)P⌐

Feniscowles

Feildens Arms Ⓛ
673 Preston Old Road, BB2 5ER (at jct of A674/A6062, 3 miles W of Blackburn)
✿ 12-midnight (1am Fri & Sat); 12-10.30 Sun
☎ (01254) 200988
Black Sheep Best Bitter; Flowers IPA; guest beers Ⓗ
Stone-built pub on the outskirts of Blackburn, three miles west of the town centre. The bar has six handpulls, one featuring a beer from a local brewery such as Moorhouse's or Three B's. There is a coal fire in the lounge. Football is regularly shown on Sky TV. Customers can play darts, cards, pool and dominoes. ♨✿♿≢(Pleasington)🖥(124,152)♣P⌐

Fleetwood

Thomas Drummond ✪
London Street, FY7 6JY (between Lord St and Dock St)
✿ 9am-11; 11-midnight Fri & Sat ☎ (01253) 775020
Greene King Ruddles Best Bitter, Abbot; guest beers Ⓗ
The pub, which celebrated its 10th anniversary in 2011, is situated in former congregational church rooms, and is named after the builder who helped construct Fleetwood. Displays honour the founders of the town, which celebrated its 175th anniversary in 2011 – Sir Peter Hesketh Fleetwood and his architect Decimus Burton. Food is served until 10pm daily. A regularly changing list of guest ales includes local beers when possible. Marcle Hill and Old Rosie ciders are available. A covered, heated area for smokers is provided. 🛏✿◑♿⊖(London St)🖥(1,14)●⌐

Freckleton

Coach & Horses
Preston Old Road, PR4 1PD
✿ 11-midnight (11 Sun) ☎ (01772) 632284
⊕ coachandhorsesfreckleton.co.uk
Boddingtons Bitter; guest beers Ⓗ
This community village local has retained its cosy atmosphere. It is home to Freckleton's award-winning brass band; a cabinet displays an impressive collection of trophies. A special place is reserved for mementos of the 8th Air Force, who served locally during World War II. The pub also has a golfing society and holds charity events on bank holiday weekends in the car park. Good value pub food is served and a large-screen TV shows Sky Sports. ✿◑♿🖥(68,78)P⌐

Garstang

Wheatsheaf
Park Hill Road, PR3 1EL
✿ 10-midnight (1am Fri & Sat); 11.30-11.30 Sun
☎ (01995) 603398
Courage Directors; Theakston Best Bitter; guest beers Ⓗ
Built as a farmhouse in the late 18th century, this is now a Grade II-listed building and was greatly extended in 2002. The pub serves breakfast, lunch and supper, and there is a covered outdoor smoking area. A disco is held every Friday. It's a

welcoming establishment that attracts a varied clientele from all age groups.
❀◑♿⛺🚌(40,42)♣P⚟

Goosnargh

Stag's Head
990 Whittingham Lane, PR3 2AU
⏲ 12-11 (11.30 Fri; midnight Sat) ☎ (01772) 864071
Theakston Best Bitter; Thwaites Wainwright; guest beers Ⓗ
Large public house with two restaurants, close to the haunted Chingle Hall. Four seating areas are served by a central bar, and outside there is a huge garden with a marquee and a heated area for smokers. Up to four guest beers come from the Cellarman's Reserve list, with Caledonian ales often featuring, and a mild or dark usually offered. Live music is hosted and there is an annual beer festival. All food is from local producers and home-made pickles and chutneys are available to take away. ♨❀◑♿⛺🚌♣P⚟

Great Eccleston

White Bull
The Square, PR3 0ZB (in village square)
⏲ 11 (4 Tue; 12 Sun)-midnight ☎ (01995) 670203
Black Sheep Best Bitter; Everards Tiger; St Austell Tribute; guest beers Ⓗ
Historic coaching inn in the heart of the village. A family-friendly, welcoming pub with flagged floors and an unspoilt atmosphere, it has a games room with pool, darts and the usual pub games. Three quieter rooms are for talking, drinking and eating. Locally sourced home-cooked food is good quality and excellent value. Interesting guest ales come from breweries on the SIBA list. CAMRA Branch Pub of the Season summer 2010.
♨Q❀◑⛺🚌(82,42)⚟

Great Harwood

Royal Hotel Ⓛ
2 Station Road, BB6 7BE (jct of Princess St and Park Rd)
⏲ 4 (12 Sun)-11; 12-midnight Fri & Sat ☎ (01254) 883541
Beer range varies Ⓗ
Genuine local, attracting both young and old to sample the eclectic atmosphere. It has a large games room and a more sedate lounge for conversation; a classic juke-box provides excellent background music. Up to eight ales are available at the L-shaped bar, with at least one dark beer. Most ales are from local independents such as Hopstar, Bank Top and Three B's. Several draught wheat and fruit beers are on offer, also continental bottled beers. A separate concert room hosts bands weekly, and there is a beer festival each May Day weekend. Served by buses from Blackburn, Accrington and Clitheroe. ❀🛏⛺🚌(6,7)♣🗑

Victoria ★ Ⓛ ✔
St John's Street, BB6 7EP
⏲ 4 (3 Fri; 12 Sat)-midnight; 12-10.30 Sun
☎ (01254) 885210
Bowland Gold; Caledonian Deuchars IPA; Taylor Landlord; guest beers Ⓗ
Cosy, welcoming pub built in 1905 by Alfred Nuttall, with much fine woodwork, cream and green Art Nouveau tiling, and etched internal windows. It sits alongside a disused railway line, now a well-used cycle path; the local name of 'Butcher Brig' refers to the railway bridge which once stood nearby. The central horseshoe-shaped bar serves a main room and a corridor. There are five other rooms including a small snug, a darts room with original wooden lathe bench seating, and a comfortable lounge with fine views.
Q❀⛺♣●⚟

Haslingden

Holden Arms
Grane Road, BB4 4PD (jct of A6177 and B6235) SD775225
⏲ 12-midnight (2am Fri & Sat) ☎ (01706) 231461
Banks's Bitter; Jennings Cocker Hoop; guest beers Ⓗ
Set in the West Pennine hills, the Holden is an award-winning pub with a large function room for parties and receptions. There is always a quiet corner available in the main pub and good food is served at all times. The landlord is passionate about keeping a good atmosphere and is always friendly. Local bands and charity groups often hold events in the pub. ◑♿🚌(11,244)P⚟

Heapey

Top Lock
Copthurst Lane, PR6 8LS (alongside canal at Johnson's Hillock)
⏲ 12-11 (10.30 Sun) ☎ (01257) 263376
Beer range varies Ⓗ
Excellent canalside pub with an upstairs dining room where nine real ales are served, mostly from micros, including a mild and either a porter or stout, together with a Timothy Taylor and a Coniston beer, and up to three real ciders. An annual beer festival is held in October with around 100 ales available in the pub and a marquee. There is a covered smoking area. Genuine Indian cuisine prepared by Indian chefs is a speciality. Winner of local CAMRA Pub of the Year. Q❀◑●P⚟🗑

Helmshore

Robin Hood Ⓛ
288 Holcombe Road, BB4 4NP (on B6235)
⏲ 4-11; 12-midnight Sat & Sun ☎ (01706) 213180
Hydes Original, Jekyll's Gold; guest beers Ⓗ
Near Helmshore Textile Museum, the Robin Hood is a small heritage pub and a vital part of the community. It has a good atmosphere, added to by the friendly locals. The pub now has a range of Hydes beers and two local guests. The interior retains some original features and is divided into three rooms, so it is easy to find a corner near the open fires in the winter. A warm, welcoming pub with much character and a wide selection of spirits.
♨🚌♣

Heysham

Royal 🍷
7 Main Street, LA3 2RN (70m towards St Patrick's Chapel from Heysham Village bus terminus)
⏲ 12-11 (midnight Fri & Sat); 12-10.30 Sun
☎ (01524) 859298 🌐 heyshamonline.co.uk/royal/royal.html
Thwaites Lancaster Bomber; guest beers Ⓗ
A 15th-century inn in the heart of the village. As you enter, a tiny locals' bar is on the right, a restaurant is on the left, while the main bar is accessed via a winding passage and opens onto a

LEICESTERSHIRE & RUTLAND

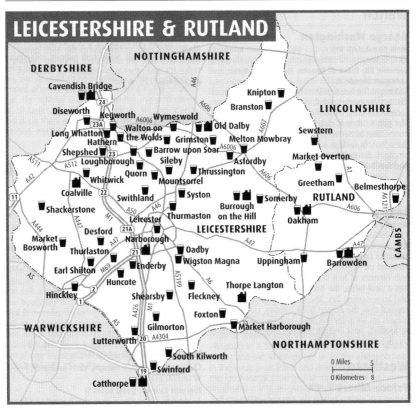

Asfordby

Horseshoes

128 Main Street, LE14 3SA

☼ 12-4, 7-11; 12-midnight Fri; 12-4, 7-11.30 Sat (10.30 Sun)

☎ (01664) 813392

Batemans XB, seasonal beers Ⓗ

Friendly single-room locals' pub in the centre of the village. The Batemans house offers at least two of the brewery's beers, and often another from the seasonal range. A proper drinkers' pub, the ale is always of a high standard. The No. 5 bus between Melton Mowbray and Leicester stops almost outside the front door. ᐅ☷(5,5A)⁵⁻

Barrow upon Soar

Hunting Lodge

38 South Street, LE12 8LZ

☼ 11-midnight ☎ (01509 412337) 412337

⊕ probablythebestpubsintheworld.co.uk

Adnams Broadside; Fuller's London Pride; guest beers Ⓗ

A comfortable bar, restaurant and inn with open fires and leather furniture. Good food from snacks to an à la carte menu can be enjoyed in the restaurant or alfresco in the large garden to the rear, with views towards Charnwood Forest. Accommodation is in six individually-styled bedrooms. ᐅ☷⛺⑴&♿⮑(2)P⁵⁻

Soar Bridge Inn

29 Bridge Street, LE12 8PN

☼ 12-11; 12-10.30 Sun ☎ (01509) 412686

Everards Sunchaser, Tiger, Original; guest beer Ⓗ

Situated next to the bridge that gave it its name, this pub is popular with walkers, boaters and drinkers. The large single-room interior divides into distinct areas, with a separate restaurant, function room and skittle alley. Outside there is a floodlit petanque court, beer terrace and garden. Well-behaved dogs and children are welcome. Home-made food is available Tuesday to Sunday. The first Monday of the month is Grand Union Folk Club night and a weekly quiz is held on Thursday. The annual beer festival is a highlight.
ᐅ☷⑴♿⮑(K2,CB27)♣P⁵⁻

Barrowden

Exeter Arms Ⓛ

28 Main Street, LE15 8EQ (1 mile S of A47)

☼ 12-2.30 (not Mon), 6-11; 12-3.30, 6-11 Sat; 12-5 Sun

☎ (01572) 747247

Barrowden Beech, Pilot, Hop Gear, Own Gear, seasonal ales; Greene King IPA Ⓗ

INDEPENDENT BREWERIES

Barrowden Barrowden
Belvoir Old Dalby
Dow Bridge Catthorpe
Everards Narborough
Grainstore Oakham
Langton Thorpe Langton
Long Lane Coalville (NEW)
Parish Burrough on the Hill
Shardlow Cavendish Bridge

Collyweston stone-built pub with a fantastic view overlooking the village green, duck pond and Welland Valley. It offers a warm welcome and serves highly-regarded food. The patio drinking area outside is a wonderful place to spend a summer's day. Petanque is played in the summer, dominoes in the winter and darts all year round. Folk music and quiz nights alternate on Mondays. Barrowden Brewery is situated in a barn building behind the pub. ▲Q☺❄🐕◑&🖵(12)♣P💲

Belmesthorpe

Blue Bell ℒ

Shepherds Walk, PE9 4JG TF042102

❂ 12-2 (not Mon), 6-11 (5-11.30 Fri); 12-11.30 Sat; 12-10.30 Sun ☎ (01780) 753081

Draught Bass; guest beers ℍ

Historic village pub three miles from Stamford. Low ceilings, a roaring fire and stone walls give the Bell its charm. There are five handpulls carrying a wide range of well-kept guest beers, including at least one LocAle and a real cider. Good honest home-made pub food is available Tuesday evening until Sunday lunchtime (booking advisable). Dogs on leads are welcome in the bar area. ▲Q☺♣●P💲

Branston

Wheel

Main Street, NG32 1RU

❂ closed Mon; 11-11; 12-10.30 Sun ☎ (01476) 870376

Batemans XB; guest beers ℍ

Like most of the buildings in the village, this attractive 18th-century pub is built using local stone. There is a small bar with some seating and a larger restaurant area that was originally two small rooms, now sympathetically renovated. The deceptively large outdoor area is quiet and relaxing in the summer months. An extensive lunch and evening food menu uses locally-sourced ingredients where possible, including produce from the nearby Belvoir Estate. ▲Q☺◑&&●P💲

Burrough on the Hill

Grant's Free House ℒ

Main Street, LE14 2JQ

❂ closed Mon; 6-11 Tue; 12-2, 5-11 (midnight Sat); 12-11 Sun ☎ (01664) 452141 or 454801

Parish PSB, Farm Gold, Burrough Bitter ℍ**, Baz's Bonce Blower** ⒢

Formerly a 16th-century inn known as the Stag & Hounds, Grant's Free House is a refurbished three-room, split-level pub, firmly established as the home of the Parish Brewery. A full range of Parish beers is always available from the adjacent brewhouse. A beer festival is held annually over the late-May bank holiday weekend. ▲Q☺◑🖵P💲

Catthorpe

Cherry Tree

Main Street, LE17 6DB

❂ 12-2.30, 5-11.30 (12.30am Fri); 12-12.30am Sat; 12-11.30 Sun ☎ (01788) 860430 ⊕ cherrytree-pub.co.uk

Adnams Bitter; guest beers ℍ

Excellent village free house, welcoming to all. Locally-sourced food is available, plus changing guest ales, including beers from Catthorpe's own micro-brewery, Dow Bridge. Railway and aviation

memorabilia adorn the walls while in the corner is a jet fighter ejection seat. Outside is a south-facing decked area and small garden overlooking the River Avon. Beer festivals are held each year. ▲Q☺◑▲🖵♣P💲

Cavendish Bridge

Old Crown ✅

Shardlow, DE72 2HL (off A6)

❂ 11-11.30 (12.30am Fri & Sat); 11-11 Sun ☎ (01332) 792392 ⊕ brilliantpubs.co.uk/oldcrownshardlow

Jennings Dark Mild, Cumberland Ale, Cocker Hoop; Marston's Pedigree, Old Empire; guest beers ℍ

Coaching inn dating from the 17th century with the original oak-beamed ceiling displaying an extensive collection of old jugs. The walls are covered with pub mirrors, brewery signs and railway memorabilia, which even extend into the toilets. The cosy open-plan interior is divided into two areas with a large inglenook on the right. Good value food includes curry night on Wednesday. Quiz night is Monday and live music features on Tuesday. Local CAMRA Branch Pub of the Year 2009. ▲☺🍴◑🖵P💲

Desford

Blue Bell Inn

39 High Street, LE9 9JF

❂ 11-11 (11.30 Tue & Thu; midnight Fri); 12-midnight Sat; 12-11 Sun ☎ (01455) 822901

Everards Beacon, Tiger, Original, seasonal beer; guest beers ℍ

Welcoming pub in the centre of the village with two rooms and a restaurant area with a central servery. A general knowledge quiz is held on Tuesday night. Food is available lunchtimes and evenings throughout the week including the traditional Sunday lunch. Dominoes and darts are played. Outside, the garden has a children's play area and there is a heated and covered space for smokers. Close to Mallory Park, B&B accommodation is provided. ☺🍴◑&🖵(152,153)♣P💲

Diseworth

Plough Inn ✅

33 Hall Gate, DE74 2QJ

❂ 11.30-3, 5-11; 11.30-11 Fri & Sat; 12-10.30 Sun ☎ (01332) 810333 ⊕ theploughdiseworth.co.uk

Draught Bass; Greene King Abbot; Marston's Pedigree; guest beers ℍ

Situated in a village with many half-timbered buildings, this is a cosy, multi-roomed pub with parts dating back to the 13th century. Low-beamed ceilings and exposed brickwork are just some of the original features discovered during renovation work in the 1990s. There is an interesting display of old photographs of the area. Tasty home-made food is served. The spacious, well-presented beer garden is popular in summer. Local CAMRA Village Pub of the Year 2009. ▲☺◑&🖵♣●P💲

Earl Shilton

Red Lion ✅

168 High Street, LE9 7LQ

❂ 12-11 (2.30am Fri & Sat); 12-midnight Sun ☎ (01455) 843356

Draught Bass; Greene King Abbot; guest beers ℍ

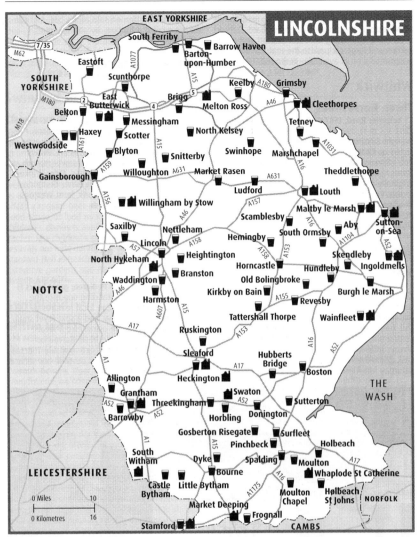

LINCOLNSHIRE

Aby

Railway Tavern ▼
Main Road, LN13 0DR (off A16 via S Thoresby)
☼ 12-midnight (closed Tue winter) ☎ (01507) 480676
Beer range varies Ⓗ
Cosy village pub worth searching out for its varied beer list and excellent food. A real community pub (regional winner of the best community pub in the 2010 Great British Pub awards) with a warm welcome for all, it has an open fire and a Wednesday quiz night. Dogs are permitted and there are plenty of good walks close by. Food is home-made with locally-sourced ingredients to the Taste of Lincolnshire standard, and is usually available until 8.30pm. ᴍQ❀◑♠️P⅃

Allington

Welby Arms ✅
The Green, NG32 2EA (1 mile from A1 Gonerby Moor jct or A52)
☼ 12-2.30, 6-11; 12-10.30 Sun ☎ (01400) 281361

Jennings Cumberland Ale; John Smith's Bitter; Taylor Landlord; guest beers Ⓗ
This a cosy, welcoming, traditional village inn overlooking the village green. The pub holds a regular quiz (third Monday of the month). The bar is split into three areas, with a separate restaurant. Look out for the blackboard listing the available beers. It's a good base for exploring local attractions such as Belton House and the Vale of Belvoir. ᴍQ❀🚪◑♿P⅃

Barrow Haven

Haven Inn
Ferry Road, DN19 7EX (approx 1½ miles E of Barrow-upon-Humber) TA063230
☼ 11.30-11 ☎ (01469) 530247 ⊕ thehaveninn.co.uk
Black Sheep Best Bitter; Taylor Landlord; Tom Wood Best Bitter Ⓗ
The Haven Inn was built in 1730 as a coaching inn for travellers using the nearby ferry, and has remained a place renowned for hospitality, good food and comfortable lodgings ever since. Full of

character, the bars have traditional, beamed ceilings, and a warm welcome awaits the weary traveller by the open fire in the lounge. Themed food events such as pie night and stew/curry night make this a great pub for both good food and good beer. ♨✿🏠🕪🍽🟈🟈🍴🟈P🛏

Barrowby

White Swan 🍷 ✅
High Road, NG32 1BH
✪ 12-midnight (1am Fri-Sat) ☎ (01476) 562375
Adnams Bitter, Broadside; guest beers ⊞
Voted Grantham CAMRA Country Pub of the Year for the third year running, this is a traditional village local with a warm welcome, close to the A1 and A52. The busy public bar has a pool table, and plays host to darts and crib teams. The lounge is a quiet room, with comfortable seating and an open fire. There is a regular quiz on the first Sunday of the month and occasional live music.
♨Q✿🕪🟈🚂(6)🍴P🛏

Barton-upon-Humber

Sloop Inn
81 Waterside Road, DN18 5BA (follow Humber Bridge viewing signs)
✪ 11-11; 12-10.30 Sun ☎ (01652) 637287
Wold Top Bitter, Mars Magic; guest beers ⊞
Welcoming pub with nautical-themed decoration and areas named after parts of a ship. The central bar serves a games area, a drinking/dining area and two further rooms, one with an original Delft tiled fireplace. Real ales are from the local Tom Wood Brewery plus guests. A wide range of home-cooked food, popular with locals and walkers, is on offer, with many specials, including the pub's own sausages and an onion ring mast. Far Ings Nature Reserve, Waters Edge Visitor Centre, Ropewalk and Humber Bridge are nearby.
Q✿🕪🟈🚂(250,350)🍴P

Wheatsheaf ✅
3 Holydyke, DN18 5PS
✪ 12-11.30 (12.30am Fri & Sat); 12-11 Sun ☎ (01652) 633292
Batemans XB; Black Sheep Best Bitter; Theakston Best Bitter; Wells Bombardier; guest beers ⊞
Occupying a prominent position on the main road through Barton, this pub dates back to the 18th century, with a list of former licensees going back to 1791. It has an unspoilt, traditional atmosphere, with regulars enjoying classic bar games of dominoes and crib. The pub has a bar, snug and large drinking/dining area, plus a summer beer garden and a private car park. A range of excellent food is served at lunchtime and in the evening.
♨Q✿🕪🚂(250,350)🍴P🛏

Belton

Crown
Church Lane, Churchtown, DN9 1PA (off A161, behind church)
✪ 10.30-midnight (1.30am Fri & Sat) ☎ (01427) 872834
Bradfield Farmers Blonde; Jennings Cumberland Ale, Cocker Hoop; guest beers ⊞
Difficult to find but well worth the effort, this hidden gem always offers six cask ales. Rotating guest beers from Glentworth and Tom Wood breweries are featured alongside the three

regulars. Quizzes, live music and pub games are enjoyed at this friendly local, which also holds occasional beer festivals. Winner of Doncaster CAMRA's District Pub of the Season award for Autumn 2010. ♨✿▲🚂(399)🍴P🛏

Blyton

Black Horse
93 High Street, DN21 3JX
✪ closed Mon; 11.45-midnight ☎ (01427) 628277
⊕ blackhorseblyton.co.uk
Caledonian Deuchars IPA; guest beers ⊞
A 250-year-old establishment selling 'real ale, real food from a real pub', it's a very well-appointed and comfortable local but with a clean, fresh twist, serving good, home-made food made with fresh local meat, fish and vegetables prepared in a five-star-hygiene-rated kitchen. Guest beers often come from Lincolnshire's micro-breweries plus a Westons cider. Pool is played and darts and quiz nights are regular events. The pub has a real community feel while remaining welcoming to visitors. ♨✿🕪🟈🚂🍴🟈P🛏

Boston

Carpenters Arms
20 Witham Street, PE21 6PU (near market place)
✪ 12-midnight (1am Fri); 11-1am Sat ☎ (01205) 362840
Batemans XB, XXXB; Draught Bass; guest beer ⊞
This is a multi-roomed, low-ceilinged traditional local hidden in the maze of side streets off the medieval Wormgate and overlooked by the magnificent Boston Stump. Although a Bateman's house, the Carpenters always has a guest beer available. There is a patio area outside for sunny days. The pub is close to the town centre but you may need to ask for directions more than once to find it. ♨✿🟈🚂

Cowbridge
Horncastle Road, PE22 7AX (on B1183, N of Boston)
✪ 11 (7 Mon; 12 Sun)-11 ☎ (01205) 362597
Brains SA; Greene King Old Speckled Hen; guest beer ⊞
Just out of town, this pub attracts drinkers and diners. It divides into three main areas. The public

INDEPENDENT BREWERIES

8 Sail Heckington
Bacchus Sutton-on-Sea
Batemans Wainfleet
Blue Bell Whaplode St Catherines
Blue Cow South Witham
Brewsters Grantham
DarkTribe East Butterwick
Fulstow Louth
Grafters Willingham by Stow
Hopshackle Market Deeping
Leila Cottage Ingoldmells
Malt B Maltby le Marsh
Melbourn Stamford
Newby Wyke Grantham
Oldershaw Grantham
Poachers North Hykeham
Riverside Wainfleet
Sleaford (Hop Me Up) Sleaford (NEW)
Swaton Swaton
Tom Wood Melton Ross
Willy's Cleethorpes

bar is a no-nonsense drinking room with darts, dominoes and a large collection of local street signs adorning the walls. The smaller lounge is cosy, with a welcoming open fire, and beyond that a restaurant serving excellent home-cooked food. The pub is popular with fishermen and handy for Boston Golf Club. ♨Q⚲☺❄❍ ⊟Ġ♣P﹏

Moon Under Water ⊘
6 High Street, PE21 8SH
☼ 9-midnight (1am Fri & Sat) ☎ (01205) 311911
Greene King Ruddles Best Bitter, Abbot; guest beers ⊞
A large, lively, town-centre Wetherspoon pub near the tidal section of the River Witham. Formerly a Government building, an imposing staircase leads from the lounge up to the toilets. A spacious conservatory-style dining area is supplemented by a second child-friendly dining room adjacent to the lounge. The pub offers a good number of guest ales and a large range of continental bottled beers. Local history photographs and information boards highlight important people associated with Boston. ❄❍Ġ⇌❏﹏

Bourne

Smith's of Bourne ⑤
25 North Street, PE10 9AE
☼ 8am-11 (midnight Fri & Sat); 9am-11 Sun
☎ (01778) 426819 ⊕ smithsofbourne.co.uk
Fuller's London Pride; Ufford White Hart; guest beers ⊞
Winner of a CAMRA/English Heritage award for the successful and imaginative conversion of this three-storey building and family grocer's shop to produce a multi-roomed public house. With a large, well-equipped patio, it hosts an annual beer festival in July. Breakfast is served until 11am and evening meals are available Monday to Saturday. The large beer garden has a grassed area for children. Wednesday is wine night, Thursday is real ale jug night, there is live music on Saturday evening and a quiz on alternate Sundays. ♨Q❄❍ ⊟Ġ❏(101,102)♠﹏

Branston

Waggon & Horses
High Street, LN4 1NB
☼ 12-2 (not Mon, or Tue winter), 5-midnight; 12-1am Fri & Sat; 12-midnight (6 winter) Sun ☎ (01522) 791356
⊕ branstonwaggon.co.uk
Batemans XB; Sharp's Doom Bar; John Smith's Bitter; guest beers ⊞
A welcoming community pub in the heart of the village, two guest beers feature on the five handpumps. The bar is lively and recently decorated, and regular fundraising events are held. The comfortable lounge hosts the Monday quiz night, Tuesday jam session and live entertainment on Saturday. Excellent-value home-cooked food is available until 9pm, and roasts until 6pm on Sunday. ❄⇌❍ ⊟❏(2)♣P﹏

Brigg

Black Bull ⊘
3 Wrawby Street, DN20 8JH
☼ 11-3, 7-11.30 Mon; 11-11 ☎ (01652) 652153
John Smith's Bitter; guest beer ⊞

A popular, friendly, town-centre public house with a large bar area and a large-screen TV at one end. The guest beers change frequently. Home-cooked meals are available in the bar area and restaurant every lunchtime and Thursday to Sunday evenings until 7pm. The pub operates a no-swearing policy. A smoking area is provided at the rear of the building. ❄❍⇌❏(909)P﹏

Dying Gladiator
Bigby Street, DN20 8EF
☼ 11-11 (midnight Fri & Sat) ☎ (01652) 652110
Batemans XXXB; Black Sheep Bitter; Tom Wood Bomber County, Dying Gladiator ⊞
Traditionally styled town-centre local, with an open-plan layout and four discrete drinking areas, simply but tastefully decorated and furnished, with sofas in one alcove. Four real ales are served including Dying Gladiator, the house beer brewed by Tom Wood. This uniquely-named pub has a statue of the stricken gladiator over the entrance, drawing in passing tourists for a photo opportunity. Meals are not served, but sandwiches are available. Poker night is Wednesday, and a pool/snooker hall is being added at the rear of the pub. ♨❄Ġ⇌❏♣﹏

Burgh le Marsh

Red Lion
East End, PE24 5LW
☼ 11-midnight; 12-11 Sun ☎ (01754) 810582
Beer range varies ⊞
Located off the main road, this low-ceilinged pub, with its large open fire and interesting artefacts, has a cosy feel. It offers a varied beer range, usually from independent brewers. For a small pub it has quite a high weekly turnover of beer, and the landlord is enthusiastic about his ales. It is one of the rare pubs nowadays not to provide food, concentrating on beer quality instead. ♨⚲❄⊟Ġ⇌♣P

Castle Bytham

Castle Inn ⑤
High Street, NG33 4RZ
☼ 10-2 (Sun only), 6-11 ☎ (01780) 410504
Newby Wyke Bear Island; Woodforde's Wherry; guest beers ⊞
A 17th-century pub with a splendid selection of real ales, farmhouse ciders and perry, all kept in peak condition in a traditional cellar. Guest ales are sourced both locally and nationally, and change regularly. There is regular folk music, and an excellent range of good food is available every evening and Sunday lunchtime. ♨Q❄❍❏♠﹏

Cleethorpes

No. 2 Refreshment Room ♟
Station Approach, DN35 8AX (on station)
☼ 7.30am-midnight ☎ (07905) 375587
Greene King H&H Olde Trip; Hancock's HB; M&B Mild; Worthington Bitter; guest beers ⊞
Located under one of the last wooden railway clock towers, this small, friendly pub is just a short walk from the town centre. In addition to the regular beers, there are two different guests. Thursday is quiz night, and a free buffet is provided on Sunday evening. Smokers may use a covered and heated area on the station concourse. ❄⇌❏﹏

Willy's
17 High Cliff Road, DN35 8RQ
☼ 11-11 (2am Fri & Sat); 12-10.30 Sun ☎ (01472) 602145
Willy's Original; guest beers H
With panoramic views across the Humber estuary, and an excellent range of beer and cider, this pub is a perennial Guide favourite. Good-value, home-cooked food is served daily at lunchtime as well as Monday to Thursday evenings. Award-winning beers are brewed in the in-house brewery, which can be viewed from the bar. The upstairs bar is available for hire. The pub is served by several bus routes and about half a mile from Cleethorpes railway station. ⬢⬤⬛(9)⬤⬤⬤

Donington

Black Bull
Marketplace, PE11 4ST
☼ 11 (12 Sun)-midnight ☎ (01775) 822228
⬢ blackbulldonington.co.uk
John Smith's Bitter; guest beers H
Busy local just off the A52. Four handpumps feature a varying selection of guest beers from small brewers as well as larger regionals; Westons cider is on handpump. The comfortable bar has low, beamed ceilings, wooden settles and a cosy fire in winter. The restaurant offers a good choice of reasonably-priced evening meals; lunches are served in the bar. Tables in the car park are used for outdoor drinking. Buses run from Boston and Spalding (not Sun). ⬢⬤⬛(59)⬤⬤⬤

Dyke

Wishing Well Inn ✪
Main Street, PE10 0SA
☼ 11-3, 5-11; 11-11 Fri-Sun ☎ (01778) 422970
Greene King Abbot; guest beers H
A comfortable pub with a changing range of guest beers, generally including one from Oakham Brewery. Despite its popularity for meals there is still a pub atmosphere in the bar. The pub is housed in what was once a row of three shops. The well that gives the pub its name can be seen in the restaurant. The village takes its name from the nearby Roman Car Dyke. ⬤⬛⬤⬤⬤

East Butterwick

Dog & Gun 🄻
High Street, DN17 3AJ (off A18 at Keadby Bridge E bank)
SE837058
☼ 5 (12 Sat & Sun)-11 ☎ (01724) 782324
DarkTribe Spruce Goose, Sternwheeler; John Smith's Bitter H
Traditional village local nestling alongside the River Trent. It has three drinking areas, all simply decorated and furnished, with a roaring real fire in the bar. Home to the on-site DarkTribe micro-brewery, two beers from its extensive range are always available. Darts is popular here, and the pub hosts monthly Wheels nights in summer featuring vintage vehicles, kit cars and motorbikes. Tables are set out on the riverbank in spring and summer overlooking the river. Assisted wheelchair access is available on request. ⬢⬤⬛⬛⬤(12)⬤⬤⬤

Eastoft

River Don Tavern 🄻
Sampson Street, DN17 4PQ (on A161 Goole-Gainsborough road)
☼ closed Tue; 5-12.30am; 12-1am Sat; 12-12.30am Sun
☎ (01724) 798040
Beer range varies H
Traditionally-styled, village-centre pub, popular with local clientele and visitors alike. The bar serves a single large room, divided into a bar area and lounge, the latter used for dining. The pub offers evening meals Wednesday to Saturday, plus an all-day carvery on Sunday. Two rotating guest ales are available (three in summer), generally from Yorkshire, Nottinghamshire and Lincolnshire micros. A large orchard is set out with tables for outdoor drinking in summer. ⬢⬤⬤⬛(356)⬤⬤⬤

Frognall

Goat 🄻
155 Spalding Road, PE6 8SA
☼ 11-3, 6-11; 12-10.30 Sun ☎ (01778) 347629
⬢ thegoatfrognall.com
Beer range varies G
Friendly pub with a low-ceilinged bar, dining area and separate restaurant. The range of six cask ales, mostly from micros and independents, includes a low gravity beer and normally a strong dark ale. A large range of single malt whiskies is also on offer, as well as good quality food. The large garden has a play area for children and one for toddlers. A beer festival is held in June. ⬢Q⬤⬤⬤⬛(22,102)⬤P⬤

Gainsborough

Blues Club
Northolme, North Street, DN21 2QW (adjacent to Gainsborough Trinity football ground)
☼ 7am-12, 5-1am Fri; 12-1am Sat; 12-midnight Sun
☎ (01427) 613688
Beer range varies H
CAMRA members are always welcome at this club on production of a membership card or copy of the Guide. The club has a bar area with several TVs showing sport, a quieter lounge and a large function room that hosts regular live entertainment (admission charges may apply). Two changing real ales are always available, kept in good condition, and details of forthcoming beers can be sent to customers by email on request. ⬤⬤⬤

Canute 🄻
14-18 Silver Street, DN21 2DP (50m S of market place)
☼ 9am-midnight ☎ (01427) 678715
Wells Bombardier; guest beers H
A typical, lively, town-centre pub that has been chosen as the local CAMRA Pub of the Season for Winter 2009 and 2010. Wells Bombardier is a permanent feature and landlord Neil is keen to provide a varying range of other beers – there are usually four real ales available. Good quality and value food is served until 9pm and live sport is shown on many screens. The pub can be busy on Friday and Saturday nights. ⬤⬤⬤⬤⬛⬤⬤

Eight Jolly Brewers 🄻
Ship Court, Silver Street, DN21 2DW (behind the Canute)
☼ 11 (12 Sun)-midnight ☎ (07767) 638806

Greene King Ruddles Best Bitter, Abbot; guest beers Ⓗ

Family-friendly Wetherspoon pub housed in the old Ritz Cinema, a building that has been a key feature of the High Street since it opened as a cinema in 1937. In 1998 it reopened as a pub with Art Deco-style furnishings complemented by signed photographs of stars who performed at the Ritz in its glory days. Guest beers always include at least one from a local brewery. Westons Marcle Hill and Scrumpy ciders are regular favourites. ⏃Ⓓ🚗🚃🌼🔔

Strugglers Ⓛ
83 Westgate, LN1 3BG
✪ 12-11 (midnight Tue & Wed; 1am Thu); 11-1am Fri & Sat
☎ (01522) 535023

Black Sheep Best Bitter; Draught Bass; Greene King Abbot; Rudgate Ruby Mild; Taylor Landlord; guest beers Ⓗ

Compact community pub under the castle walls in the historic cathedral quarter. The cosy snug with open fire adjoins the main long public bar, which dispenses ales from seven handpumps, at least two of which are guests, sometimes more, from SIBA and LocAle suppliers. Frequent live music features at Sunday teatime, while the surprisingly large garden has a TV for sports events. Simple bar snacks are always available. Well-behaved dogs are welcome. ▲Q🌼🍺🔔(7,8)🔔

Tap & Spile ●
21 Hungate, LN1 1ES
✪ 4-midnight; 12-1am Fri & Sat ☎ (01522) 534015
⊕ tapandspilelincoln.co.uk

Greene King Abbot; Fuller's London Pride; guest beers Ⓗ

Formerly the White Horse and situated off the High Street, the pub's friendly atmosphere welcomes all ages. A centre bar has eight handpumps hosting two regular beers plus guests and Old Rosie cider. The rugged walls have pictures of musicians, and there is live music on Friday and Saturday nights, theme night on Wednesday, plus a Sunday teatime jam session followed by a general knowledge quiz. The unusual circular chess is played on Thursday. 🌼🚃♣🌼🔔

Victoria
6 Union Road, LN1 3BJ
✪ 11-midnight (1am Fri & Sat); 12-midnight Sun
☎ (01522) 541000

Batemans XB; Castle Rock Harvest Pale; Taylor Landlord; guest beers Ⓗ

A small traditional Victorian pub located next to the castle's West Gate, now in its 27th consecutive year in the Guide and a place where old and young alike feel welcome. It features a long, narrow bar with four alternating guest ales and three regulars, plus a cider or perry brought from the cellar. Pictures of Victoria herself decorate the walls of the lounge bar. Outside there is a large heated seating area plus a children's play area facing the castle wall. Q🌼Ⓓ🍺🔔(7,8)🌼🔔

Wig & Mitre
30-32 Steep Hill, LN2 1LU
✪ 3.30-11.30; 8.30-10.30 Sun ☎ (01522) 535190
⊕ wigandmitre.com

Batemans XB; Black Sheep Ale Ⓗ**; guest beer** Ⓐ

The Wig is located in the historic uphill area of the city at the top of the aptly named Steep Hill, equidistant from the castle and cathedral.

Occupying an interesting mix of 14th, 16th, and 20th-century buildings, this multi-roomed, multi-levelled pub is renowned for its high-quality food that is served all day. Child-friendly throughout and dog-friendly downstairs, it welcomes drinkers as well as diners. Q Ⓓ 🚃

Little Bytham

Willoughby Arms Ⓛ ●
Station Road, NG33 4RA
✪ 12-11 (10.30 Sun) ☎ (01780) 410276
⊕ willoughbyarms.co.uk

Batemans XB; Ufford White Hart; guest beers Ⓗ

There is always one dark ale among the guest beers supplementing the Batemans XB and the LocAle Ufford White Hart at this former railway station building on the outskirts of the village. It holds two beer festivals annually in May and October and serves home-cooked food daily. There is occasional live music at weekends. ▲🌼🚗Ⓓ🍺▲🌼Ⓟ🔔

Louth

Cobbles Bar
2 New Street, LN11 9PU (off Cornmarket)
✪ 10-midnight (2am Fri & Sat); 12-10 Sun ☎ (07736) 275262

Black Sheep Best Bitter; guest beers Ⓗ

Traditional pub-style bar based in the centre of town, with friendly staff at all times. This small but accommodating venue has multiple personalities, from bustling coffee shop serving light lunches to a busy pre-club local with DJs and live music at the weekend. It has a good beer trade, with two contrasting cask ales, as well as a huge selection of exotic spirits. Disabled access is right through the front doors. 🌼Ⓓ🍺🔔(9,10,51)

Greyhound Inn
40 Upgate, LN11 9EX (near St James's Church)
✪ 11-midnight; 12-11 Sun ☎ (01507) 604685

Black Sheep Best Bitter; Brains Flowers Original; Taylor Landlord; guest beers Ⓗ

A modern town pub with multiple rooms and a separate restaurant that opens Wednesday to Sunday from 5.30pm until late. There are large comfortable chairs in all rooms and a quiet room with a big open fire in the winter months, with plenty of whisky containers all around. The back room has Sky TV and opens onto a spacious outdoor courtyard, with tables for dining and drinking, plus a smoking area. ▲Q🌼Ⓓ🍺🌼Ⓟ🔔

Newmarket Inn
133 Newmarket, LN11 9EG
✪ 12-3 (not Mon & Tue), 5-midnight; 12-midnight Sat & Sun
☎ (01507) 605146

Adnams Bitter; guest beers Ⓗ

Friendly, family-run, classically decorated free house, set only five minutes' walk from the town centre. Two guest ales are always available, plus the regular Adnams. A free quiz is held every Sunday night, and the local folk club meets here on a Tuesday evening. The popular bistro serves traditional home-cooked food using locally-sourced produce; booking is advisable. Food is available Wednesday to Saturday lunchtimes and evenings; food on Sunday is served 12-3pm. Q🌼Ⓓ🌼

ENGLAND

Ludford

White Hart Inn
Magna Mile, LN8 6AD
🌣 12-2 (not Mon-Thu; 2.30 Sat), 6-11; 12-3.30, 7-10.30 Sun
☎ (01507) 313489
Beer range varies Ⓗ
This 18th-century coaching house was local CAMRA Pub of the Year 2009. A two-roomed rural village pub close to the Viking Way, it is popular with hikers and ramblers. It offers four different guest beers; the licensees pride themselves on serving real ale from micro-breweries. All food is home made, using ingredients from local suppliers, and meals are available lunchtimes and evenings. There is guest accommodation separate from the pub. ⋈Q✿🛏🍴◖◗♣P

Maltby le Marsh

Crown Inn 𝕃
Beesby Road, LN13 0JJ (jct of A157 and A1104)
🌣 12-11.30 (11 Sun) ☎ (01507) 450100
Batemans XB; Malt B Old Reliable, PEA, Smarty's Night Porter; guest beers Ⓗ
Up to six beers are on offer as well as ciders, including Westons Old Rosie. A small micro-brewery has been installed mainly to supply the Crown. The inn and its outdoor tables are in a good position for the nearby coastal strip with its many visitors, especially in summer. Bar skittles and shove-ha'penny are played. Meals are available both in the bar and restaurant.
✿🛏◖◗🍴&🅰🚃(10)♣♠P⅃

Market Rasen

Aston Arms
18 Market Place, LN8 3HL
🌣 11-11 (11.30 Fri & Sat); 12-11 Sun ☎ (01673) 842313
John Smith's Bitter; Wells Bombardier; guest beer Ⓗ
This large, popular pub holds a commanding position on the market square. In 2010 the pub's association with local lad Bernie Taupin, a long-time lyricist for Elton John, was awarded recognition in a national list of 100 famous pubs. A central bar serves three open-plan drinking areas. The games area features pool, darts and shove-ha'penny. Good-value food is served daily until 8pm, making it popular with families, walking groups and racegoers. There is a covered, heated patio area with ramp access.
⋈✿◖◗&🚲🚃(3,23)♣⅃

Marshchapel

White Horse
Sea Dyke Way, DN36 5SX
🌣 4 (12 Sun)-midnight; 12-1am Fri & Sat ☎ (01472) 388280
Beer range varies Ⓗ
Two-roomed coaching inn formerly part of Grimsby's Hewitts Brewery estate, it is now an Enterprise Inns pub. Saint Mary's Church, known as the Cathedral of the Marsh, dates from the 15th century. The two beers come from a changing range including Greene King, Theakston, Black Sheep and Caledonian. Food is locally sourced, with Thursday and Friday fish and chips especially popular. Meals are served Friday-Sunday lunchtimes, Wednesday-Saturday evenings. There is bingo and the quiz is free to join.
⋈✿◖◗🍴🚃(50)♣P⅃

Messingham

Bird in the Barley
Northfield Road, DN17 3SQ (½ mile from Messingham on A159)
🌣 closed Mon; 11.30-3, 5-11; 11.30-3.30, 5.30-10.30 Sun
☎ (01724) 764744
Jennings Snecklifter; Marston's Pedigree; guest beers Ⓗ
A country pub with a mix of traditional and modern design. The interior features oak beams, wooden flooring and a dining conservatory. A seated drinkers' area includes leather sofas and armchairs. There are two beer gardens; one includes a large canopy and heater. Good home-cooked food is made from locally-sourced ingredients. Two regular real ales from the Jennings and Marston's ranges are stocked, plus one or two guest beers. Cyclops tasting notes are displayed on the handpumps. ⋈✿◖◗&🚃(100,353)P⅃

Horn Inn
61 High Street, DN17 3NU
🌣 11-11 (midnight Sat) ☎ (01724) 762426
Black Sheep Best Bitter, Ale; guest beers Ⓗ
In the village centre on the A159, this venue is popular with locals and visitors both for its regular and changing real ales and its excellent food. Quality home-made meals are available lunchtimes and evenings (not Wed and Sat). Quiz night is Monday and local bands entertain on Wednesday and Saturday. There are several distinct drinking areas, plus a sheltered garden for use in the warmer months. ⋈Q✿◖◗&🚃♣P⅃

Moulton

Swan ✪
13 High Street, PE12 6QB
🌣 11 (11.30 Sun)-2am ☎ (01406) 370349
Wells Bombardier; guest ales Ⓗ
Family-run pub in the centre of an attractive village which enjoys a good daytime bus service. Three changing guest ales are available. The pub has an excellent reputation for food, with an interesting and varied menu, and credit crunch specials Monday-Wednesday. It is family and dog friendly, with a pleasant and popular garden. Enter before 11pm if you wish to take advantage of late hours.
⋈🍴✿◖◗🚃(505)♠P⅃

Moulton Chapel

Wheatsheaf
4 Fengate, PE12 0XL
🌣 12-2.30 (not Mon), 5.30-11; 12-2, 6.30-11 Sat; 12-2, 7-10.30 Sun ☎ (01406) 380525
Beer range varies Ⓗ
The small quarry-tiled bar is at the heart of this village pub, with its splendid old black range that positively glows on winter evenings, and no noisy machines or TV to sully the atmosphere. The beer could be from far or near but is as consistently good as the home-cooked food. Fish and chips night and other good value specials feature during the week. Two pleasant dining-rooms showcase paintings by local artists. A games room is due to open soon. ⋈Q✿◖◗🚃♣P

TV for sports. The smaller bar opposite has a dartboard and Crows Nest upstairs room.
◖⇌⊖(Charing Cross/Embankment)🚃

WC2: Covent Garden

Cambridge ✪
93 Charing Cross Road, WC2H 0DP
✪ 10-11 (11.30 Fri & Sat); 12-11 Sun ☎ (020) 7494 0338
Fuller's London Pride; Sharp's Doom Bar; Taylor Landlord; guest beers Ⓗ
On the eastern edge of W1 Soho but with a WC2 postcode, there has been a pub on this site since 1744 when it was called the King's Arms. The present building dates from 1887. The current name comes from Prince George, Duke of Cambridge. There is a comfortable downstairs bar plus another bar and further seating on the first floor. ◖▶⊖(Leicester Sq/Tottenham Ct Rd)🚃

Cross Keys Ⓛ
31 Endell Street, WC2H 9BA
✪ 11-11; 12-10.30 Sun ☎ (020) 7836 5185
⊕ crosskeyscoventgarden.com
Brodie's English Best, IPA, seasonal beers Ⓗ
The striking exterior, with its elaborate decoration obscured by extensive foliage, forms an immediate impression upon approaching this pub. Inside is a fascinating collection of bric-a-brac, ranging from copper kettles to musical instruments, and even including a diving helmet. There are also brewery mirrors, a large collection of pictures and portraits adorning the walls, and two notable clocks. Leased by East London brewers Brodie's, this pub showcases a good range of its beers. ◖⊖🚃♣🍴

Freemasons Arms ✪
81-82 Long Acre, WC2E 9NG
✪ 12-11 (11.30 Fri & Sat; 10.30 Sun) ☎ (020) 7836 3115
⊕ freemasonsarmscoventgarden.co.uk
Shepherd Neame Master Brew, Spitfire, Bishops Finger, seasonal beers Ⓗ
Located near Freemasons Hall and convenient for theatreland, this pub was first licensed in 1704 and known as the Bull's Head until 1778. The Football Association was founded here in 1863. The interior is comfortably furnished with leather banquettes and wood panelling. Staff are welcoming and sport is popular: there are several screens where matches can be viewed. ◖▶⊖🚃

Harp Ⓛ ✪
47 Chandos Place, WC2N 4HS
✪ 10.30-11.30 (11 Mon); 12-10.30 Sun ☎ (020) 7836 0291
⊕ harpcoventgarden.com
Dark Star Hophead; Harveys Sussex Best Bitter; Sambrook's Wandle, Junction; guest beers Ⓗ
This small, friendly, independent free house has become a haven for beer choice, generally including a mild or porter, plus Dark Star and London micro-brewery seasonals. The narrow bar is adorned with mirrors, theatrical memorabilia and portraits. There is no intrusive music or TV and a cosy upstairs room provides a refuge from the busy throng. Numerous past awards culminate in the ultimate accolade, CAMRA National Pub of the Year 2010. A brief description cannot do justice to this outstanding pub.
Q⇌(Charing Cross)⊖(Charing Cross/Leicester Sq)🚃🍴

WC2: Holborn

Ship Tavern ✪
12 Gate Street, WC2A 3HP
✪ 11-11 (midnight Thu-Sat); 12-10.30 Sun
☎ (020) 7405 1992 ⊕ theshiptavern.co.uk
Caledonian Deuchars IPA; Greene King Old Speckled Hen; Theakston Best Bitter; Wells Bombardier; guest beers Ⓗ
A pub has been on this site since 1549. This former Younger's house, with six handpumps, runs frequent regional beer festivals. Stripped oak flooring, booths and maritime prints add to the atmosphere, which is far removed from the bustle of High Holborn. Look out for the pie night promotions. The upstairs restaurant can be booked for private functions. ◖▶⊖🚃

WC2: Temple

Devereux ✪
20 Devereux Court, WC2R 3JJ
✪ 11-11; closed Sat & Sun ☎ (020) 7583 4562
Fuller's London Pride; Young's London Gold; guest beers Ⓗ
This attractive, listed pub was built in 1844; part of the site used to be the Grecian Coffee House. The comfortable lounge has a wood-panelled bar with five handpumps dispensing beers from the Punch list. There are prints on the walls showing local places of interest and historical figures; judges' wigs reflect proximity to the Law Courts. Upstairs is a restaurant available to hire. Q◖▶⊖🚃

Edgar Wallace ✪
40 Essex Street, WC2R 3JF
✪ 11-11; closed Sat & Sun ☎ (020) 7353 3120
Crouch Vale Brewers Gold; Nethergate Edgar's Pale Ale; guest beers Ⓗ
There has been a pub on this site since 1777. Now leased from Enterprise, this one has so far collected about 140 of the 170 or so books written by Edgar Wallace. The comfortable downstairs room has a fine wooden bar with seven handpumps. Many of the prints and photos on the walls celebrate rugby and football. There is more seating available upstairs. Look out for beer festivals. Q◖▶⊖🚃

EAST LONDON
E1: Aldgate

Dispensary
19A Leman Street, E1 8EN
✪ 12-11; closed Sat & Sun ☎ (020) 7977 0486
⊕ thedispensarylondon.co.uk
Beer range varies Ⓗ
A former local CAMRA Pub of the Year, the Dispensary is an imposing building with a high-ceilinged interior. There is a large main bar with other small rooms. The landlady describes the beer range as a lucky dip, as the five real ales change frequently, although Dark Star and Harveys feature often. Florence NightingAle from the Nethergate brewery is the house beer. The owners are considering introducing Saturday opening; phone to check. CAMRA members enjoy a discount on real ales. ◖▶⊖(Aldgate East)🚃🍴⤆

Goodman's Field ✪
87/91 Mansell Street, E1 8AN
✪ 10 (12 Sat & Sun)-11 ☎ (020) 7680 2850

Fuller's London Pride; Greene King IPA, Abbot; guest beers Ⓗ
The cobalt blue tiles behind the bar of this modern, fresh-looking Wetherspoon's gives a striking impression against the grey granite bar top. An impeccably clean, family-friendly, City-edge pub favoured by office workers and builders from nearby construction sites, it is handy for out-of-towners and close to a Travelodge and a Premier Inn. Once a farm area, Goodman's field was the scene of one of highwayman Dick Turpin's shootouts in 1737. Food includes breakfasts.
Q✿☐☻♿≹(Fenchurch St)⊖(Tower Hill/Tower Gateway DLR)🚋

Still & Star ✪
1 Little Somerset Street, E1 8AH
✪ 11-11; closed Sat & Sun ☎ (020) 7488 3761
⊕ stillandstar.co.uk
Adnams Lighthouse; Fuller's London Pride; Young's Bitter; guest beer Ⓗ
Having been under threat of demolition, the Still & Star is now safe, although the surrounding area is to be redeveloped. Situated just off Aldgate, almost next door to the bus station, the single bar is larger than the outside would suggest. The guest beer is from the Coors list. Food is served all day and there is a large outdoor drinking area. Inside is a dartboard. Saturday opening may be introduced.
✿☐≹(Fenchurch St)⊖🚋♣'–

White Swan
21-23 Alie Street, E1 8DA
✪ 11-11; closed Sat & Sun ☎ (020) 7702 0448
Shepherd Neame Master Brew, Spitfire, seasonal beer Ⓗ
Just a short walk from the City, the White Swan has a City feel when busy at lunchtimes and early evening, but later has the local friendly atmosphere of the East End. Wooden floors, wood panelling and big leather sofas enhance the relaxed drinking ambience. Upstairs is used for diners or by small groups for meetings.
Q☐≹(Fenchurch St)⊖(Aldgate/Aldgate East)🚋'–

E1: Spitalfields
Pride of Spitalfields
3 Heneage Street, E1 5LJ
✪ 11-midnight (2am Fri & Sat); 11-11 Sun
☎ (020) 7247 8933
Crouch Vale Brewers Gold; Fuller's London Pride, ESB; Sharp's Doom Bar Ⓗ
Just off Brick Lane, down a small street, there is always a warm welcome in this small one-bar, two-roomed pub, a traditional and unspoilt local. It is especially cosy on cold winter days when the real fire is roaring away. The walls have plenty of old photographs of the old Truman Brewery and the local area. Ideally positioned for the curry houses nearby, it serves home-cooked food weekday lunchtimes and Sunday roasts.
🚌✿☐≹(Liverpool St/Shoreditch High St)
⊖(Aldgate East)🚋'–

E1: Wapping
Town of Ramsgate
62 Wapping High Street, E1 2PN
✪ 12-midnight (11 Sun) ☎ (020) 7481 8000
Fuller's London Pride; Sharp's Doom Bar; Young's Bitter Ⓗ

Dog and children-friendly riverside local, with an inviting historic atmosphere. It took its name from the fishermen of Ramsgate who would land their catch at nearby Wapping Old Stairs to avoid river taxes at Billingsgate. A long, narrow bar leads to a delightful patio overlooking the River Thames, which can be very popular in the summer. Home-cooked food is served until 9pm, Tuesday is steak night and Wednesday curry night.
✿☐≹🚋(100,D3)♣

E2: Bethnal Green
Camel 🅛
277 Globe Road, E2 0JD
✪ 4 (12 Fri & Sat)-11; 12-10.30 Sun ☎ (020) 8983 9888
Crouch Vale Brewers Gold; Sambrook's Junction, Wandle; guest beers Ⓗ
Small street-corner hostelry with a noteworthy tiled exterior, which now seems in safe hands after being closed a few years ago. A LocAle pub with six handpumps, it also sells Millwhites cider and a menu of speciality pies and mash. The interior is dimly lit, with candles on the tables creating an intimate atmosphere. There are tables outside on the pavement for warmer weather and busy times.
✿☐≹(Bethnal Green/Cambridge Heath)⊖🚋♠

Carpenters Arms
73 Cheshire Street, E2 6EG
✪ 12 (4 Mon)-11.30 (12.30am Fri & Sat) ☎ (020) 7739 6342
⊕ carpentersarmsfreehouse.com
Adnams Bitter, seasonal beer; Taylor Landlord Ⓗ
A friendly street-corner free house handy for Brick Lane curry houses. There is a cosy single bar and an unusual separate room along with a heated enclosed patio. It is well worth a visit for the wide selection of bottled beers from the UK and worldwide, and also ciders. Home-cooked food is served 1-10pm.
✿☐≹(Bethnal Green/Shoreditch High St)🚋'–

E2: Haggerston
Albion in Goldsmith's Row 🅛
94 Goldsmith's Row, E2 8QY
✪ 12-11 (1am Fri & Sat) ☎ (020) 7739 0185
Sharp's Doom Bar; Taylor Landlord; guest beers Ⓗ
Excellent one-bar community pub, handy for Columbia Road and Broadway markets, with a strong sporting emphasis (the landlord is a West Brom fan). Spot your club among all the sporting memorabilia. Darts and shove-ha'penny are played and occasional live bands supplement regular Friday open mike nights. The guest beers hail from local micro-breweries, often including Brodie's from Leyton, and a range of bottled American craft beers is stocked. ✿≹(Cambridge Heath)🚋♣'–

E3: Bow
Eleanor Arms
460 Old Ford Road, E3 5JP
✪ 12 (4 Mon)-11; 12-10.30 Sun ☎ (020) 8980 6992
⊕ eleanorarms.co.uk
Shepherd Neame Kent's Best, Spitfire, seasonal beers Ⓗ
Run by a real ale enthusiast, this pub serves some of the best Shepherd Neame beers found anywhere. The single bar room has two distinct areas – at the back is a pool table and a TV for rugby and major sporting events. The front section is for

socialising. On Friday and Saturday the guv'nor plays DJ from his eclectic CD collection, and live jazz features twice a month. Filled baguettes are available. ❀⊞⊖(Bow Rd/Bow Church DLR)🚌(8)⌐

Palm Tree

127 Grove Road, E3 5RP (in Mile End Park, road access via Haverfield Rd)
✿ 12.30-midnight (2am Sat); 12-midnight Sun
☎ (020) 8980 2918
Beer range varies Ⓗ
A great standalone pub in Mile End Park on the banks of the Regent's Canal, run by the same landlord for 34 years. The beers come mainly from micro-breweries. With its unique 1930s Truman's interior, this is one of London's Real Heritage Pubs. There is no TV but music groups play at weekends, when the doors close at 10.30pm on Saturday, 10.45pm on Sunday. ❀⊞&⊖(Mile End)🚌♦P⌐

E4: Chingford

Station House

134-138 Station Road, E4 6AN
✿ 12-11 (1am Fri & Sat) ☎ (020) 8529 8576
Banks's Bitter; Marston's Pedigree, seasonal beer; guest beer Ⓗ
Situated opposite Chingford bus and railway stations, this Guide debutante was originally a shop. Two regular beers are accompanied by two others from the Marston's stable and/or guests. The open-plan interior includes a pool table and dartboard. TVs are usually muted and background music is kept at a reasonable volume. For Friday and Saturday discos, under 25s are not admitted without a residents' ID card. The pub is fully wheelchair accessible (entrance via side door). ❀①&▲⇌🚌♣P⌐

E4: Chingford Mount

Obelisk

30-32 Old Church Road, E4 8DD
✿ 10-11 (midnight Thu; 1am Fri & Sat); 12-11 Sun
☎ (020) 8523 9706
Draught Bass; Wells Bombardier; Young's Bitter Ⓗ
Previously converted from a shop and taken over by the Barracuda chain four years ago, this community pub has three large TV screens in use at any one time showing big football games. Customers range from OAPs in for breakfast to young people on Friday and Saturday nights, when door monitors are employed. Trips to beer festivals and breweries are organised throughout the year; check in pub for details. ①&🚌⌐

E5: Clapton

Anchor & Hope ✔

15 High Hill Ferry, E5 9HG (800m N of Lea Bridge Rd, along river path)
✿ 1-11 (midnight Fri & Sat); 12-11 Sun ☎ (020) 8806 1730
Fuller's London Pride, ESB; guest beer Ⓗ
This Fuller's tenancy and regular Guide entry is right next to the bank of the Lee Navigation, with outside tables overlooking the water and Walthamstow Marshes. The pub itself is small and has not been modernised, giving it a traditional charm. It has a strong local following and is also popular with passing walkers and cyclists. Barbecues are held on Saturdays and Sundays during the summer. ❀⇌🚌(393)♣⌐

E8: Hackney

Pembury Tavern

90 Amhurst Road, E8 1JH
✿ 12-11 ☎ (020) 8986 8597 ⊕ individualpubs.co.uk/pembury
Milton Minotaur, Sparta, Nero; guest beers Ⓗ
Sixteen handpumps serving five beers from Milton Brewery, rotating guests and a real cider make the Pembury a beer island in the hustle and bustle of Hackney. This large one-room free house, subdivided with wooden settles to create a more intimate atmosphere, offers bar billiards, pool and board games in peaceful surroundings without gaming machines or TV. Beer festivals are held twice a year, with extra stillage for more beers. Q①▶&⇌(Hackney Central/Downs)🚌♣♦⌐⊟

E8: South Hackney

Dove

24-28 Broadway Market, E8 4QJ
✿ 12-11 (midnight Fri & Sat) ☎ (020) 7275 7617
⊕ dovepubs.co.uk
Crouch Vale Brewers Gold; Taylor Landlord; guest beers Ⓗ
There are six handpumps and four changing guest beers here, alongside a wide choice of Belgian beers on draught and in bottles. Tastings take place at regular intervals throughout the year; ring for details. The food menu is good and the pub gets busy in the evening. The Belgium fanatic should make every effort to find this gem. No music but WiFi access is available.
Q①▶&⇌(London Fields)🚌(236,394)

E9: Homerton

Kenton Arms

38 Kenton Road, E9 7AB
✿ 4-11 (midnight Fri); 12-midnight Sat; 12-11 Sun
☎ (020) 8533 5041
Hop Back GFB; Taylor Landlord Ⓗ
This dog-friendly neighbourhood pub, with its mixture of oddly-matched furniture and bare wooden floors, gives a feeling of 'come in and enjoy'. The food is good basic pie and mash, and Sunday roasts. Entertainment is an eclectic mix: live music, world cinema screenings, DJs, quizzes, ladies night (cocktails, cupcakes and jumble sale), rock-paper-scissors game, and the infamous Rock 'n' Roll Bingo. There are also monthly arts exhibitions, comedy nights, free WiFi and plenty of board games. ❀①▶⇌🚌

E10: Leyton

Drum Ⓛ ✔

557-559 Lea Bridge Road, E10 7EQ
✿ 9-midnight (1am Fri & Sat) ☎ (020) 8539 9845
Greene King Ruddles Best Bitter, Abbot; guest beers Ⓗ
An early example of a Wetherspoon pub, now offering a choice of up to 10 different beers and ciders, usually including at least one local ale. Two Wetherspoon festivals are held each year alongside the pub's own mini beer festivals, beer tastings, Meet the Brewer events and brewery trips. This split-level establishment is a friendly place with a conservatory seating area and small patio garden. ❀①▶⇌(Leyton Midland Rd)🚌♦⌐

Leyton Orient Supporters Club 🗽

Matchroom Stadium, Oliver Road, E10 5NF
🟢 from 12.30 Sat match days; 5.30 weekdays, not during game. Closing time varies ☎ (020) 8988 8288
🌐 orientsupporters.org
Mighty Oak Oscar Wilde; guest beers Ⓗ
Leyton Orient fans are lucky to have what is widely considered to be the best real ale supporters' club bar in the country. The clubhouse is in Orient's modern West Stand, where you will find eight changing handpumps, usually serving local ales, and a real cider and perry. It opens on match days and on other ad hoc occasions; check the website for details. Beer festivals are held twice a year. CAMRA members showing their membership cards are welcome. ♿🌳🚃♣🚃

E11: Leytonstone

Birkbeck Tavern

45 Langthorne Road, E11 4HL
🟢 11-11 (midnight Fri & Sat); 12-11 Sun ☎ (020) 8539 2584
Rita's Special; guest beers Ⓗ
This basic and friendly Victorian corner pub in a back street behind Leyton Underground Station is split into two parts: one with a pool table and smaller bar, the other with a larger bar, screens to watch football, three dartboards and more seating. Alongside house beer Rita's Special are three changing guests, many from micro-breweries and normally up to 4.5%. Outside is a pleasant garden. ♿🚭♿🚃(Leyton)🚃♣🚃

North Star

24 Browning Road, E11 3AR
🟢 4 (12 Sat)-11; 12-10.30 Sun ☎ (07961) 226197
Wells Bombardier; guest beers Ⓗ
Built in 1851 for Charrington and now owned by Enterprise Inns, this pub is situated in a conservation area of Leytonstone. The back bar, served by a hatch, has now had the chimney demolished to give a roomier feel. Three guest beers from the SIBA list change quickly. In the summer, music groups play in the rear garden and barbecues are held. To check on regular Thursday music performances, visit Whatscookin.co.uk. ♿🚭🚃♣

E11: Wanstead

Nightingale ✅

51 Nightingale Lane, E11 2EY
🟢 12-midnight (1am Fri); 10.30-1am Sat ☎ (020) 8530 4540
Courage Best Bitter; guest beers Ⓗ
Tucked away in the back streets of Wanstead, this Enterprise establishment is a popular community pub, with two main rooms round the bar plus an alcove and a separate room that can be used for meetings. The current leaseholder has been here for 22 years. Four guest beers change regularly and an excellent all-round menu is available during the day. Thursday is quiz night and Wednesday Irish music night. ☕🍴🚃(Snaresbrook)🚃(W12)

E13: Plaistow

Black Lion ✅

59-61 High Street, E13 0AD
🟢 11-11; 12-10.30 Sun ☎ (020) 8472 2351
Courage Best Bitter; guest beers Ⓗ
An early 16th-century coaching inn rebuilt about 280 years ago, retaining some original features

including low ceilings, oak beams and a cobbled courtyard. East Anglian breweries regularly appear on the guest list in this top-quality free house in what is otherwise a real ale desert. Excellent home-cooked food is served lunchtimes and early evenings. A function room is available for hire and there is a local boxing club alongside. ♿🍴🚃🚃🚃♣🚃

E17: Walthamstow

Coppermill

205 Coppermill Lane, Walthamstow, E17 7HF
🟢 11-11 (midnight Fri & Sat) ☎ (020) 8520 3709
Greene King IPA; Fuller's London Pride; Marston's Pedigree; guest beer Ⓗ
Making a welcome return to the Guide after a number of years, this is a small back-street pub that is popular with locals. A genuine free house, it offers three regular ales and a guest (usually over 4%) that changes twice a week. Sunday is quiz night and the pub also holds occasional live entertainment. Football is shown on a TV screen. There are tables outside the pub, which is on the way to the delightful Walthamstow Marshes. ♿🚊(St James St)🚃(158,230,W12)

Nag's Head 🗽

9 Orford Road, E17 9LP
🟢 4 (2 Fri; 12 Sat)-11; 12-10.30 Sun ☎ (020) 8520 9709
🌐 thenagshead17.com
Mighty Oak Oscar Wilde; Maldon Gold; Nethergate The Itinerant, Augustinian; Taylor Landlord Ⓗ
A perennial Guide favourite, this one-room Enterprise tenancy in the Walthamstow Village conservation area always has a nice relaxed atmosphere. It has a small courtyard garden and is cat friendly, with a couple of resident and four visiting felines. Beer festivals are held occasionally, with the ale names having a cat theme. Regular events, including a monthly book club, are held either in an upstairs room or in the bar itself. ♿🚊🚃(Walthamstow Central)🚃(W12)🚃

Olde Rose & Crown 🗽 ✅

53-55 Hoe Street, E17 4SA
🟢 10-11 (midnight Fri & Sat); 12-11 Sun ☎ (020) 8509 3880
🌐 yeolderoseandcrowntheatrepub.co.uk
Beer range varies Ⓗ
Large, friendly, community corner pub, with six handpumps serving changing beers from the SIBA range and two boxed real ciders on the back bar. With two function rooms, it hosts theatre productions, shellac night, comedy night, film club, quiz night, folk and other live music, poetry and art or craft exhibitions; check with the pub. Home-cooked food is available during the week (1-3pm) and Sunday roasts (1-3.30pm). ♿🚊🚃(Walthamstow Central)🚃🚃

Waltham Forest Corporation Sports & Social Club

Waltham Forest Town Hall, Forest Road, E17 4JF
🟢 12-11 (midnight Fri; 10.30 Sun); closed Sat
☎ (020) 8527 3944
Crouch Vale Essex Boys Bitter; guest beers Ⓗ
Private members club, located to the side of the Town Hall, which welcomes CAMRA members and visitors with a copy of the Guide. Two changing guest ales are available and beer festivals are held in April and November. Food is served lunchtimes and Friday evening. There is a main bar and the

smaller Hatters bar. The club offers big-screen sport, darts, crib, pool and a traditional full-sized snooker table. A charge of £1 on Friday covers live entertainment. ⊛◖⊟⛱

Chadwell Heath

Eva Hart ✪

1128 High Road, RM6 4AH (on A118)
✪ 9am-midnight ☎ (020) 8597 1069
Courage Best Bitter, Directors; Greene King Ruddles Best Bitter, Abbot; guest beers ⊞
This large, comfortable Wetherspoon pub, previously the local police station, is named after a local singer and music teacher who was one of the longest-living survivors of the Titanic disaster; photographs and memorabilia are on display. A splendid choice of four or more guest ales is normally available on handpump, usually including at least one stout or porter. Real Thatchers Old Rascal cider is available. Good value food is served 8am-10pm. Q⊛◖&≠⊟●P⅃

Collier Row

Colley Rowe Inn ✪

54-56 Collier Row Road, RM5 3PA (on B174)
✪ 9-11.30 ☎ (01708) 760633
Courage Directors; Greene King Ruddles Best Bitter, Abbot; guest beers ⊞
Pleasant Wetherspoon pub with some cosy alcoves, which provides some of the best real ale in the Romford area. Three or four guest beers are normally available, plus three real ciders from Westons, or sometimes a perry. Food is served all day, every day, 9am-10pm. The Colley is a 10-minute bus ride from Romford railway station (five routes). The manager is a CAMRA member. Q◖&⊟●

Dagenham

Eastbrook ★ ✪

Dagenham Road, RM10 7UP (by A1112, at jct with Rainham Road South)
✪ 11-11 (midnight Fri & Sat) ☎ (020) 8592 1873
Brakspear Oxford Gold; Fuller's London Pride; guest beer ⊞
One of Britain's Real Heritage Pubs, with wood panelling in abundance, this is a friendly, Grade II*-listed inn dating from 1938 in an area with little real ale. Popular with sports fans, and close to Dagenham & Redbridge FC, it has numerous TV screens showing live sports. The separate public bar features darts and pool. Lunchtime food is available from 11.30-2.30pm, Sunday roasts from 12-3pm. Families are welcome.
⊛⌂◖⊟&⊟(103,174)♣P⅃

Gants Hill

Bar ♈

19 Sevenways Parade, Woodford Avenue, IG2 6JX (by A1400 at jct with A12 and A123)
✪ 12-11 (1am Fri & Sat); 12-10.30 Sun ☎ (020) 8551 7441
Beer range varies ⊞
Small, friendly free house by Gants Hill tube station, with a front patio. It has a good mixed clientele and a great range and variety of beers (mainly from East London and Essex micro-breweries), bringing much-needed choice to an area served by just a few mainstream real ales. It

has seasonal beer festivals, light bar snacks are available, and shuffleboard is played. Karaoke/live music, jam'n & blues take place every Sunday afternoon, and sport is screened on TV. Parking is at the rear (eves only). Local CAMRA Pub of the Year 2011. ⊛⊖⊟♣P⅃

Hornchurch

JJ Moons ✪

Unit 3, 46-62 High Street, RM12 4UN (on A124)
✪ 9am-midnight (12.30am Fri & Sat; 11.30 Sun)
☎ (01708) 478410
Greene King Abbot; guest beers ⊞
An impressive range of guest beers greets you at this busy Wetherspoon's pub, near the end of the High Street. The usual collection of local historic photographs and information includes a feature on John Cornwall, the boy hero of the Battle of Jutland. Breakfast is served until midday and food up to 11pm. A family area is available until 6pm. At the back is a covered smoking area.
Q◖&≠(Emerson Park)⊟⅃

Rainham

Phoenix

Broadway, RM13 9YW (on B1335, near clock tower)
✪ 11-11; 12-3, 7-10.30 Sun ☎ (01708) 553700
Courage Directors; Fuller's London Pride; Greene King Abbot; John Smith's Bitter ⊞
Busy, spacious town pub close to Rainham station and convenient for the RSPB Rainham Marshes nature reserve. It has two bars: a public bar with dartboard, and a saloon for dining. Poker is played on Wednesday; quizzes and live entertainment/music alternate on Thursday; more entertainment features on Saturday. The large garden has five aviaries and a barbecue area. A family fun day is held every bank holiday Monday. Accommodation comprises seven twin and one single room.
⊛⌂◖⊟&⊟♣P⅃

Romford

Moon & Stars ✪

99-103 South Street, RM1 1NX
✪ 9-midnight (1am Fri & Sat) ☎ (01708) 730117
Courage Directors; Greene King Ruddles Best Bitter, Abbot; guest beers ⊞
Popular Wetherspoon pub, handy for Romford railway station and buses. Five rotating guest beers range in strength from session bitters to strong ales, catering for all tastes. Friday and Saturday evenings are busy, which makes for an exciting atmosphere, although finding a table may be difficult. Breakfast is available from 7am to noon (beer from 9am), and good value coffees are served. The full menu is available until 10pm. Real ciders are from the Westons range. Q◖&≠⊟●⅃

Woodford Green

Cricketers ⎍

299-301 High Road, IG8 9HQ (on A1099)
✪ 11.30 (12 Sun)-11 ☎ (020) 8504 2734
McMullen AK, Country Bitter, seasonal beers ⊞
A pleasant, cosy local with a dartboard in the public bar and plaques in the saloon for all 18 first-class cricket counties, together with photographs of former local MP Sir Winston Churchill, whose statue stands on the green almost opposite. Good value

food (including pensioners' specials) is served Monday to Saturday lunchtimes. There is patio seating at the front, and a covered smoking area with seating. Boules is played on a pitch behind the pub. Q✿◑⬚⬚🖵(179,W13)♣P⬚⬚

Travellers Friend
496-498 High Road, IG8 0PN (on slip road off A104)
✿ 12-11; 12-4, 7-11 Sun ☎ (020) 8504 2435
Adnams Broadside; Courage Best Bitter; Wells Bombardier; guest beer Ⓗ
An absolute gem, and one of London's Real Heritage Pubs, this friendly, comfortable local features oak-panelled walls and rare original snob screens. There are normally two guest beers. Small beer festivals are held in April and September. As far as is known, the pub has never sold keg bitter. There is a covered, heated patio/smoking area at the rear, picnic tables at the front and a small car park. Local CAMRA Pub of the Year 2008 and 2010. Q✿&🖵(20,179,W13)P⬚⬚

NORTH LONDON
N1: Canonbury
Lord Clyde
340-342 Essex Road, N1 3PB
✿ 12-11 (midnight Sat; 10.30 Sun) ☎ (020) 7288 9850
⊕ thelordclyde.com
Harveys Sussex Best Bitter; guest beer Ⓗ
A welcoming locals' pub with original Charrington woodwork carefully blended to feel traditional yet comfortable. The ethos of real ale and great service marries well with good fresh pub food at pub prices. It has a separate public bar, a tranquil sunny decked area at the back for enjoying a Sunday roast, and seating in front. Chill out with friends, join the popular quiz every other Monday or just relax with a quiet pint and your newspaper.
⛬✿◑⬚≒(Essex Rd)🖵♣⬚⬚

N1: Hoxton
Baring
55 Baring Street, N1 3DS
✿ 12-11 (10.30 Sun) ☎ (020) 7359 5785
⊕ thebaringpub.co.uk
Shepherd Neame Spitfire; Taylor Landlord; guest beers Ⓗ
Local authority listed, imposing back-street corner pub close to the Regent's Canal and former Gainsborough film studios. It was fully refurbished a few years ago, including repairs to damage inflicted by the Luftwaffe. The modern decor does not detract from a warm feeling on entry. Artwork for sale around the bar is by a local artist. The pub is proud to have its own cricket team. When it is open, a sign on New North Road gives directions.
✿◑≒(Essex Rd)🖵♣♦

Prince Arthur
49 Brunswick Place, N1 6EB
✿ 11.30-midnight (may close earlier); 12-6 Sat & Sun
☎ (020) 7253 3187
Shepherd Neame Master Brew, Kent's Best, Spitfire, seasonal beers Ⓗ
A friendly back-street locals' pub conveniently located for Old Street station and run by the same landlord for more than 30 years. The split-level bar features a regularly used dartboard in the lower section at the rear. The walls are adorned with pictures from the landlord's previous boxing career

and there is also a strong horse racing theme. There is an outdoor drinking area at the front, and light snacks are available. ✿≒⊖(Old St)🖵♣⬚⬚

N1: Islington
Charles Lamb
16 Elia Street, N1 8DE
✿ 12 (4 Mon & Tue)-11; 12-10.30 Sun ☎ (020) 7837 5040
⊕ thecharleslambpub.com
Dark Star Hophead; Triple fff Alton's Pride; guest beers Ⓗ
This small, popular, two-room free house is situated in a residential area close to the Regent's Canal just east of Angel. One of the regularly rotating guest beers is usually locally sourced and cider is now often available. Interesting food is served, mainly in the rear room, but it does not overwhelm the pub. Board games and shove-ha'penny are available and boules is played outside on Bastille Day. Covered outside seating is provided. ✿◑⊖(Angel)🖵♣♦⬚⬚

N1: King's Cross
King Charles I Ⓛ
55-57 Northdown Street, N1 9BL
✿ 12-11 (1am Fri); 5-11 Sat; closed Sun ☎ (020) 7837 7758
Beer range varies Ⓗ
Cosy and popular pub tucked away off Caledonian Road, just a short distance from the busier area around King's Cross. Besides a Brodie's beer, on handpump or gravity, is a rotating selection of up to three guests. Snacks are available at the bar. The decor is interesting (African masks on the wall) and there is a bar billiards machine along with various games. Outside is a partly covered seating area.
✿≒⊖(King's Cross/St Pancras)🖵♣⬚⬚

N1: Kingsland
Duke of Wellington Ⓛ ✔
119 Balls Pond Road, N1 4BL
✿ 3-midnight (1am Thu & Fri); 12-1am Sat; 12-11 Sun
☎ (020) 7275 7640 ⊕ thedukeofwellingtonN1.com
Sambrook's Wandle; guest beers Ⓗ
This pleasant two-room inn alongside a busy main road won local CAMRA Pub of the Season not long ago. The front room has an island bar with many original features. The back room is more relaxed but can get busy when major sports events are shown on the large screen. Guest ales are usually from small independents. Bar snacks are popular and beer festivals are held twice a year.
⛬◑≒(Dalston Jct/Dalston Kingsland)🖵♣♦⬚⬚

N1: Newington Green
Nobody Inn ✔
92 Mildmay Park, N1 4PR
✿ 12-11 (midnight Thu-Sat) ☎ (020) 7249 6430
Dark Star Hophead; Sharp's Doom Bar; guest beers Ⓗ
Spacious pub facing Newington Green, with up to four rotating guests. The pub is divided into three areas, including one with a pool table and TV sports, and another featuring a traditional telephone box. All areas have modern North London decor and are furnished with a mix of scrubbed tables, chairs and sofas. The cider is Westons Traditional Scrumpy. Thai food is served lunchtimes and evenings, all day at the weekend.
⛬◑≒(Canonbury)🖵♣♦

Black Sheep Best Bitter; Sambrook's Wandle; guest beers H
This large Victorian pub's front room is now a restaurant, serving gastro-style food. The rear wood-panelled room with bar leads to another room that has been extended into a conservatory in a large, attractive garden area. Keen to promote LocAles, it usually offers at least one more besides the house beer. The pub is dog friendly in the bar area, which also hosts two major beer festivals annually, with a discount for CAMRA members. Local CAMRA 2008 Pub of the Year.
Q❄️🍴➪⊖(Tufnell Pk)🚆(134)⟵

Pineapple
51 Leverton Street, NW5 2NX
🕐 12-11 (10.30 Sun) ☎ (020) 7284 4631
Draught Bass; guest beers H
Grade II-listed, this is one of London's Real Heritage Pubs, original features in the front bar including a splendid bar-back and traditional mirrors. Alcoves and corridors behind lead to a spacious conservatory, where Thai food can be enjoyed, and finally to a heated garden. Four varying guest beers are served, with festivals twice yearly. A true community pub, it was saved from closure by its many regulars some years ago. Local CAMRA Pub of the Year 2010. Q❄️🍴&➪⊖🚆⟵

Southampton Arms 🍷
139 Highgate Road, NW5 1LE
🕐 12-11 (11.30 Fri & Sat) ☎ (020) 7485 1511
⊕ thesouthamptonarms.co.uk
Beer range varies H
Local CAMRA Pub of the Year, this pub has established itself in a short time as a must-visit for London's ale lovers. Twelve pumps adorn the long thin bar, 10 for beer and two for cider, with six more ciders behind. All-day snacks include the most wonderful pork baps. Music is played on vinyl, mostly jazz, blues and soul, except on Sunday and Wednesday when there is a pianist. Outside is an attractive seating area.
🚶➪(Gospel Oak/Kentish Town)
⊖🚆(214,C2,C11)♣🍴⟵

NW8: St John's Wood

Clifton ✓
96 Clifton Hill, NW8 0JT
🕐 12-11 (10.30 Sun) ☎ (020) 7372 3427
⊕ cliftonstjohnswood.com
Greene King IPA, Abbot; guest beers H
A hunting lodge 200 years ago, before gaining a licence, this pub was given hotel status by King Edward VII so that he could visit Lily Langtry here. Royalty could not visit pubs. The front has a decorative wooden island bar, with bronze inserts. To the rear are two rooms, one a restaurant. Many board games are available. The beer range varies, with rotating guests and seasonals.
❄️🍴➪(Kilburn High Rd)⊖(Kilburn Pk)🚆

Eastcote

Case is Altered ✓
Eastcote High Road, HA5 2EW
🕐 11-11 ☎ (020) 8866 0476 ⊕ caseisalteredpinner.co.uk
Greene King IPA, Morland Bitter; Sharp's Doom Bar; guest beers H
Old English pub from the 17th century and one of London's Real Heritage Pubs. Set in the attractive village of Old Eastcote, next to the cricket pitch, at the front is a large beer garden. Inside, there is one bar with three seating areas. The barn to the back is a recent refurbishment and provides extra seating. There is a real fire in the main bar during the winter months. 🚶❄️🍴&🚆(282,H13)P⟵

Harefield

Harefield
41 High Street, UB9 6BY
🕐 12-11 (10.30 Sun) ☎ (01895) 820003
Ringwood Best; Taylor Landlord; guest beers H
An Admiral pub that has had several name changes before settling on the current one in 2007 after a complete refurbishment. It is well known for its good food, made with fresh local produce, and for the quality and variety of its beers. There is a full Sunday roast. A beer club on Wednesday offers discounted real ales. Outside there is a patio, and limited parking. It hosts two popular beer festivals every year. 🚶❄️🍴➪🚆(331,U9)P⟵

Old Orchard
Park Lane, UB9 6HJ
🕐 11.30-11; 12-10.30 Sun ☎ (01895) 822631
⊕ oldorchard-harefield.co.uk
Brunning & Price Original; Fuller's London Pride; Tring Side Pocket For A Toad; guest beers H
Little is known of the history of this pub but it did start out as a country house. It reopened in 2010 following a major refurbishment as a Brunning & Price establishment, having previously been a restaurant. There are commanding views of the Colne Valley from the terrace and extensive beer garden. Three guest beers are usually available, mostly from local breweries. The Original is brewed by Phoenix. 🚶Q❄️🍴&(U9)♣P⟵

Harrow

Moon on the Hill ✓
373-375 Station Road, HA1 2AW
🕐 7am-midnight (12.30am Fri & Sat) ☎ (020) 8863 3670
Greene King Ruddles Best Bitter, Abbot; guest beers H
Small, busy Wetherspoon pub located close to Harrow-on-the-Hill station and served by numerous bus routes. Serving food all day, it is popular with price-conscious regulars, office workers and students from the nearby University of Westminster. The pub gets extremely busy when there are sporting events on at nearby Wembley Stadium and plastic glasses may be used on these occasions. Q🍴➪⊖🚆

Harrow-on-the-Hill

Castle ★ ✓
30 West Street, HA1 3EF
🕐 12-11 (midnight Fri & Sat) ☎ (020) 8422 3155
Fuller's Discovery, London Pride, ESB, seasonal beers; Gale's HSB H
Situated in the heart of historic Harrow-on-the-Hill, this is a popular and friendly Fuller's house. Built in 1901 and Grade II-listed, it is one of Britain's Real Heritage Pubs. Food is served until 9pm every day; reservations are recommended for Sunday lunchtime. Three real coal fires help to keep the pub warm and cosy in the colder months and a secluded beer garden is popular during the summer. 🚶Q❄️🍴➪🚆(258,H17)⟵

Pinner

Queen's Head
31 High Street, HA5 5PJ
🕓 11-11 ☎ (020) 8868 4607 🌐 thequeensheadpinner.com
Adnams Bitter; Greene King Abbot; Wells Bombardier; Young's Special; guest beers Ⓗ
Historic pub in a conservation area, a Grade II-listed building dating back to 1540. Despite its suburban location, it has the appearance and feel of a traditional country inn, with its Tudor frontage, low ceiling and exposed beams. It is closely involved in local activities and celebrates St George's Day with a hog roast. There is no music or TV but a quiz is held on Monday. Q❀🕽&❤🖼P▙

Ruislip Common

Woodman ✔
Breakspear Road, HA4 7SE
🕓 11 (12 Sun)-midnight ☎ (01895) 635763
Courage Best Bitter; Draught Bass; guest beer Ⓗ
A cheerful and welcoming two-bar local in the northern area of Ruislip close to Ruislip Lido and woods, opposite Hillingdon Borough Football Club. The cosy lounge bar is traditional in atmosphere with no intrusive electronic machines, although the TV may be on for sports matches. Note the collection of bottled beers on display. There is also a good selection of single malt whiskies. The public bar is friendly and comfortable, with a dartboard and other pub games. Q❀🕽🖳&🖼(331)♣▙

Ruislip Manor

JJ Moons ✔
12 Victoria Road, HA4 0AA
🕓 9-midnight (1am Fri & Sat) ☎ (01895) 622373
Courage Directors; Fuller's London Pride; Greene King Ruddles Best Bitter, Abbot; guest beers Ⓗ
Large, busy Wetherspoon's opened in 1990 in a former Woolworths, frequented mainly by locals and busy on Friday and Saturday evenings. There is a large raised area to the rear for diners. Accredited for LocAle in 2009, it offers guest ales from nearby breweries such as Twickenham, Rebellion and Tring. A real ale club every Wednesday helps the enthusiastic manager to decide which beers to order. Two Westons ciders are also regularly available on handpump.
🏃❀🕽&❤🖼(114,398,H13)♣▙

SOUTH-EAST LONDON
SE1: Borough

Brew Wharf
Brew Wharf Yard, Stoney Street, SE1 9AD
🕓 12-11 (5 Sun) ☎ (020) 7378 6601 🌐 brewwharf.com
Beer range varies Ⓗ
Near the busy Borough Market, this is a modern brew-pub with adjoining restaurant and outside courtyard seating area next to Wine Wharf, both sharing the same owners as the Vinopolis wine museum. The bar and restaurant areas are contemporary, and behind them through a large window can be seen the brewing kit. Two of its own beers are always available (the resident brewer prides himself on never brewing to the same recipe twice) and a good range of bottled beers. ❀🕽⇌❤(London Bridge)🖼▙

Market Porter
9 Stoney Street, SE1 9AA
🕓 6-8.30am, 11-11; 12-11 Sat; 12-10.30 Sun
☎ (020) 7407 2495
Harveys Sussex Best Bitter; guest beers Ⓗ
Busy pub next to Borough Market that has been in the Guide for years. The walls and ceiling display pump clips from the vast range of ales that have been served. The pub was featured in Harry Potter and the Prisoner of Azkaban as the Third Hand Book Emporium. The upstairs restaurant is open for lunch and available to hire for functions in the evening. 🕽⇌❤(London Bridge)🖼♣

Rake
14 Winchester Walk, SE1 9AG
🕓 12 (10 Sat)-11; 12-8 Sun ☎ (020) 7407 0557
Beer range varies Ⓗ
One of the smallest pubs, but with a big selection for the beer connoisseur: three draught beers, several rare foreign beers on tap, and a large range of bottled beers across the back wall. Run by Utobeer and set on one side of Borough Market, it has an outside covered deck area to give drinkers more space, and the Gents is one of the market's toilets. Simple, good-quality bar snacks are served. ❀🕽&⇌❤(London Bridge)🖼

Royal Oak ✔
44 Tabard Street, SE1 4JU
🕓 11 (12 Sat)-11; 12-6 Sun ☎ (020) 7357 7173
Harveys Sussex XX Mild, Pale, Sussex Best Bitter, seasonal beers; guest beer Ⓗ
Traditional local, with two Victorian-style bars featuring decorative glass, carved woodwork and subdued corner lighting, creating a cosy atmosphere thankfully not marred by noisy music or fruit machines. A rarity in London, this pub is owned by Harveys, and many interesting photos of the brewery hang on the walls. Draught cider is available, excellent food is offered and there is a handy meeting room upstairs. The guest beer is from the Fuller's range.
Q🕽⇌(London Bridge)❤🖼♣

Wheatsheaf
24 Southwark Street, SE1 1TY
🕓 11 (12 Sat)-11; 12-10 Sun ☎ (020) 7407 9934
Nethergate Redcar Best Bitter; Young's Bitter, Special; guest beers Ⓗ
Located in atmospheric brick cellars beneath the old Hop Exchange building, this bustling Red Car pub replaced the original Young's house round the corner, which had to close for rail developments. Low arched ceilings and long tables evoke a tavern culture long associated with Southwark, while leather sofas and stylish photos of old Wheatsheaf regulars bring it up to date. A great selection of ales from breweries across the country is complemented by a range of foreign beers and good food. 🕽⇌❤(London Bridge)🖼♣

SE1: Southwark

Charles Dickens ✔
160 Union Street, SE1 0LH
🕓 12 (2 Sat)-11 ☎ (020) 7401 3744
🌐 thecharlesdickens.co.uk
Beer range varies Ⓗ
A wooden-floored free house with a rear patio, this tranquil pub is minutes away from major railway stations and makes a pleasant escape from the

usual busy London atmosphere. There is always a choice of six guest beers from small British brewers. The lower walls are wood-panelled; upper walls carry framed illustrations from Dickens' stories. Quiz night with the Fat Controller is Wednesday. Closing time may be later on Saturday, earlier on Sunday.
Q❄️⏹️🍴🚇(Waterloo East)⊖(Borough/Southwark) 🚌🚹

SE1: Waterloo

Hole in the Wall
5 Mepham Street, SE1 8SQ
🕐 11-11 (11.30 Fri & Sat; 10.30 Sun) ☎ (020) 7928 6196
Adnams Bitter; Greene King IPA; Hogs Back TEA; Sharp's Doom Bar; Young's Bitter; guest beer Ⓗ
Appropriately named for its unusual location, this pub is in a railway arch just across from the main entrance to Waterloo Station. A two-bar free house, it is something of an institution, popular with locals and commuters alike, having served an impressive range of real ales for longer than most people can remember. It gets busy most nights, and screens sporting events. Outside is a patio beer garden with heaters. ❄️⏹️🍴🚇⊖🚌🚹

SE3: Blackheath

Princess of Wales ✅
1a Montpelier Row, SE3 0RL
🕐 12-11 (10.30 Sun) ☎ (020) 8852 5784
🌐 princessofwalespub.co.uk
Fuller's London Pride; Sharp's Doom Bar Ⓗ
Long associated with Blackheath Rugby Club, the pub sits on the edge of the heath. Summer drinkers spill out both onto the vast green space and into the spacious walled garden. The L-shaped bar allows for large tables for groups as well as cosy sofas. The pub's food is popular and its Sunday roasts are renowned. Guest beers come from micros and national breweries, with Purity and White Horse ales frequently featuring. Real cider is often available in boxes. ❄️⏹️🍴👦🚇🚌🚹P

SE4: Brockley

Talbot
2 Tyrwhitt Road, SE4 1QG
🕐 11-11 (midnight Sat) ☎ (020) 8692 2665
Harveys Sussex Best Bitter; Sambrook's Junction; guest beers Ⓗ
The sister pub of the Prince Regent in Herne Hill is building quite a reputation in the short space of time since it re-opened in 2009. Serving a selection of ales and locally-sourced quality food, it strikes a nice balance between the old and the new, with modern decor and wooden furniture to give it a retro touch. Outside is a large seating area, perfect for enjoying the sunshine when the warmer weather is here. ❄️⏹️👦🚇(St Johns)🚌🚹

SE5: Camberwell

Bear
296a Camberwell New Road, SE5 0RP
🕐 1-10.30 Mon; 12-11 (midnight Fri & Sat); 12-10.30 Sun
☎ (020) 7274 7037 🌐 thebear-freehouse.co.uk
Beer range varies Ⓗ
A free house, this family-owned Victorian corner pub clearly once had separate saloon and public bars. Original external tiling is matched by a

sensitive interior decor combining both the modern and the classic. Two real ales are available, with more for beer festivals. The menu is traditional English, including Sunday roast, and French country, with snails on toast at times. The pub attracts a mixed, discerning clientele. Tuesday is quiz night. Upstairs is an artists' exhibition space. ⏹️🍴🚌♣️🚹

Hermit's Cave
28 Camberwell Church Street, SE5 8QU
🕐 12-midnight (2am Fri & Sat) ☎ (020) 7703 3188
Brodie's Mild, Red, IPA; Loddon Gravesend Shrimpers Bitter Ⓗ
Close to a busy junction, yet you can escape from it all in this corner pub with an eye-catching curved frontage. Watch the world go by through the etched glass Victorian windows that illuminate the grand marble fireplace beautifully. The bar has a homely atmosphere, bare floorboards, a variety of seating – banquette, small café tables and chairs, and bar stools. This is a family-run pub, serving bar snacks, and is ideal for a break from shopping or an evening out. Q🚇(Denmark Hill)🚌👦

Tiger ✅
18 Camberwell Green, SE5 7AA
🕐 4-11 (midnight Thu; 1am Fri); 12-1am Sat; 12-11 Sun
☎ (020) 7703 5246 🌐 thetigerpub.com
Beer range varies Ⓗ
This traditional Victorian-themed pub, near Denmark Hill Station and facing the green, reverted to its original name on reopening in 2010 after many years as the Silver Buckle. One of the Antic pub chain, it attracts a trendy clientele but provides an oasis where drinkers and diners can relax and watch the hustle and bustle of Camberwell outside. Good hearty food is served.
❄️⏹️👦🚇(Denmark Hill)🚌♣️P🚹

SE5: Denmark Hill

Fox on the Hill ✅
149 Denmark Hill, SE5 8EH
🕐 8am-midnight (12.30am Fri & Sat) ☎ (020) 7738 4756
Fuller's London Pride; Greene King Ruddles Best Bitter, Abbot; guest beers Ⓗ
Large welcoming Wetherspoon's on a steep hill, with friendly staff and customers. Its layout includes numerous cosy, low-screened booths. Outside is a spacious garden. Unusually for the company, this not a new build or a conversion from shop premises but occupies what was formerly a Charrington's pub. John Ruskin and other local notables are remembered in well-researched wall displays. Between four and six guest beers are served and, as well as national festivals, mini beer festivals featuring locally-brewed beers are sometimes held. 🐕⏹️👦🚇🚌♣️P🚹

SE5: East Dulwich

Hoopers ✅
28 Ivanhoe Road, SE5 8DH
🕐 5.30 (5 Fri)-11 (11.30 Wed; midnight Thu & Fri); 12.30-midnight Sat; 12.30-11 Sun ☎ (020) 7733 4797
🌐 hoopersbar.co.uk
Redemption Ivanhoe Ale; guest beers Ⓗ
A community pub with a wedge-shaped footprint, the area at the point of the building providing space for performers during monthly comedy nights or for live music. The main bar area is of

good size and is contrasted by a more sombre snug to the rear. Most of the time there are three real ales, and beer festivals are held in April, October and December. A quiz is held on Thursday.
🏚🛏🍴�Mᐅᚹ(P13)♣♠P🚭🍴

SE6: Catford

London & Rye ✓
109 Rushey Green, SE6 4AF
🕐 9-midnight ☎ (020) 8697 5028
Adnams Bitter; Fuller's London Pride; Greene King Ruddles Best Bitter, Abbot; guest beers Ⓗ
To judge from its first-floor appearance, this Edwardian building may have originally been a house. However, it was converted to a shop long ago, eventually becoming a Wetherspoon's in the 1990s. Forecourt seating overlooks Rushey Green, the quaint local name for the A21, also the inspiration for the pub name. The internal decor features some fascinating displays on local history. This pleasant pub has 10 handpumps, always a good selection of micro-brewery beers and often real cider. 🏞ᐅᚹ≠(Catford/Catford Bridge)🚍♦

SE8: Deptford

Dog & Bell 🗟 ✓
116 Prince Street, SE8 3JD
🕐 12-11.30 ☎ (020) 8692 5664
Fuller's London Pride, ESB; guest beers Ⓗ
From the 1860s this pub was the Royal Marine – its current name dates back to an earlier pub that existed here. A calm and relaxed place, it offers three guest ales, a wide selection of bottled Belgian beers and also a considerable choice of single malt whiskies. The modern kitchen is reassuringly open to view from its walled yard behind the pub. Cuisine is uncomplicated and matches the traditional pub atmosphere.
🏚Q🏞ᐅᚹ≠🚍(47,188,199)♣🍴

SE9: Eltham

Park Tavern
45 Passey Place, SE9 5DA
🕐 12-11 (midnight Fri & Sat); 12-10.30 Sun
☎ (020) 8850 8919
Fuller's London Pride; Harveys Sussex Best Bitter; St Austell Tribute; Taylor Landlord; guest beers Ⓗ
Attractive traditional Victorian pub with a tiled frontage and historic Truman's signage. The beautifully and warmly refurbished interior has elegant drapes, bar lamps and chandeliers, an impressive wood bar and a real log fire. Decorative plates and pictures line the walls. Vases of fresh flowers add to the relaxed atmosphere, with jazz and light classical background music, and an impressive selection of ales, whiskies and wines. A rear garden is available plus seating to the front and side. 🏚Q🏞ᐅ≠🚍♣🍴

SE10: Greenwich

Gate Clock
210 Creek Road, SE10 9RB
🕐 7am-midnight (1am Fri & Sat) ☎ (020) 8269 2000
Fuller's London Pride; Greene King Ruddles Best Bitter, Abbot; guest beers Ⓗ
Wetherspoon pub situated in a new building next to Cutty Sark DLR station in Greenwich town centre. There is a large bar area with plenty of seating,

with a smaller bar upstairs and some outdoor seating at the front. The pub is popular with locals, visitors and students alike, and is about five minutes from Greenwich Park, the Old Royal Naval College and the National Maritime Museum.
🏞ᐅ&≠Ө(Cutty Sark DLR)🚍

Greenwich Union 🗟
56 Royal Hill, SE10 8RT
🕐 11-11; 11.30-10.30 Sun ☎ (020) 8692 6258
Dark Star Hophead; Sambrook's Junction; guest beers Ⓗ
This Meantime pub is always bustling in the evenings with a mix of students, tourists and local beer connoisseurs. Meantime's international reputation is growing as fast as its range of beers; from chocolate to raspberry, there is something for everyone. Cask beers from other local breweries are also showcased here, or you could be adventurous and sample a bottle of the smoky heaven that is Aecht Schlenkerla Marzen (5.1%).
🏞ᐅ≠Ө(DLR)🚍🍴🚭

Old Brewery
Pepys Building, Old Royal Naval College, SE10 9LW
🕐 11-11; 12-10.30 Sun ☎ (020) 3327 1280
🌐 oldbrewerygreenwich.com
Meantime Pale Ale; guest beers Ⓗ
The original brewery on this site was commissioned in 1717 to make beers for the pensioners of the Royal Hospital; we can safely say that the beers have improved quite considerably since then. The brand new brewery with its Meantime flagship pub is impressive, with a small bar area leading to the large dining space. Daily brewery tours are available but should be booked in advance. 🏞ᐅ&≠Ө(Cutty Sark DLR)🍴🚭

SE10: North Greenwich

Pilot Inn ✓
68 River Way, West Parkside, SE10 0BE
🕐 11-11 ☎ (020) 8858 5910
Fuller's Discovery, London Pride, ESB, seasonal or guest beer Ⓗ
The pub dates from 1801 and offers an isolated gem of historic architecture on the Greenwich Peninsula in striking contrast to the modern O2 Arena within whose shadow it lies. It is deceptively large but, being spread over three different levels, retains a cosy and welcoming feel. There is a pleasant garden area to the rear. Quiz night is Tuesday. 🏞🛏ᐅ&Ө🚍♣P🚭

SE13: Lee

Dacre Arms
11 Kingswood Place, SE13 5BU
🕐 12-11 (10.30 Sun) ☎ (020) 8852 6779
Black Sheep Best Bitter; Courage Best Bitter; Greene King IPA; Sharp's Doom Bar; Wells Bombardier; guest beer Ⓗ
Charmingly traditional, this single-roomed back-street pub whisks you back to ale houses of yesteryear with its pub dog, wood panelling, curios hanging from every surface and patterned, upholstered banquette seating throughout. Original glazed partitions add to the cosy, warm and friendly feel, as do the dried hops hanging above the bar, and the courtyard garden behind the pub is a perfect summer retreat.
Q🏞≠(Blackheath)🚍(54,89,108)🍴

Traditional informal pub with one bar running the length of the interior. There are usually three changing guest ales from smaller breweries, often unusual ones for the area. Live music is performed on a Friday and Sunday and karaoke on Tuesday, and there is a poker league on Thursday evening. The railway memorabilia is in keeping with the name and location of the pub. ⚿⚫🍽♣⌐

Bexleyheath

Furze Wren ✓
Broadway Square, 6 Market Place, DA6 7DY
✪ 9-11.30 ☎ (020) 8298 2590
Greene King Ruddles Best Bitter, Abbot; Shepherd Neame Spitfire; guest beers Ⓗ
Located in the heart of Bexleyheath shopping centre, this modern pub is named after a once-local bird, the Dartford Warbler. The large open-plan space and big windows afford great opportunities for people-watching, and an unrestricted view of the clock tower from which a bust of William Morris surveys all below. Unusually for a Wetherspoon pub, it is all on one level, including the toilets. ⬢⬤👪⌐♣

Robin Hood & Little John ♈ ⅃
78 Lion Road, DA6 8PF
✪ 11-3, 5.30 (7 Sat)-11; 12-4, 7-10.30 Sun
☎ (020) 8303 1128
Adnams Bitter, Broadside; Brakspear Bitter; Fuller's London Pride; Harveys Sussex Best Bitter; guest beer Ⓗ
Well-worth a visit, this little back-street pub dating from the 1830s has been run by the Johnson family since 1980 and offers eight ales, including two guests. Its popular home-cooked food is available at lunchtime (no food Sun) with themed specials and regular Italian dishes, which can be eaten at tables made from old Singer sewing machines. London Regional CAMRA Pub of the Year three times and the current local CAMRA Pub of the Year. Over 21s only. Q⚿⬤

Bromley

Bitter End Off Licence
139 Masons Hill, BR2 9HW
✪ 12 (11 Sat)-9; 12-2, 7-9 Sun ☎ (020) 8466 6083
⊕ thebitterend.biz
Beer range varies Ⓖ
A unique off-licence offering a changing choice of gravity-dispensed ale to take away in containers, minipins and firkins, also selling an impressive selection of real ciders and now more than 160 different bottled beers. The owners are only too happy to advise and chat about beer and cider, and the constant custom certainly does make it feel like a beer festival in a shop. ⚫(Bromley South)⌐♣

Bromley Labour Club
HG Wells Centre, St Marks Road, BR2 9HG
✪ 12-11 (10.30 Sun) ☎ (020) 8460 7409
⊕ blcbromley.co.uk
Shepherd Neame Master Brew, Kent's Best Ⓗ
A former CAMRA Club of the Year, this comfortable, friendly club is a good place to escape the hubbub of the many shops in the area. Situated in a quiet side street off the main road, it has a pool table and shows football and other sports on a large-screen TV. The club is open to CAMRA members. ⚿👪⚫(Bromley South)⌐P⌐

Partridge ✓
194 High Street, BR1 1HE
✪ 12-11.30 (12.30am Fri & Sat); 12-11 Sun
☎ (020) 8464 7656
Fuller's Discovery, London Pride, ESB, seasonal beers; Gale's HSB Ⓗ
Formerly a National Provincial Bank, the 1927 listed building was converted to a pub by Fuller's in 1996. Original features include a black-and-white marble floor and bank counters, and two beautiful chandeliers illuminate the high ceilings in the main bar. An impressive mirrored display area behind the bar showcases a selection of beers and wines. There is a quiet snug with half-timbered walls, a separate dining area, and outside seating. The pub is popular with town workers and shoppers. ⚿⬤👪⚫(Bromley North)⌐⌐

Red Lion
10 North Road, BR1 3LG
✪ 11 (12 Sun)-11.30 ☎ (020) 8460 2691
Greene King IPA, Abbot; Harveys Sussex Best Bitter; guest beers Ⓗ
A true gem of a pub nestling in the back streets of Bromley, with a wonderful flower display in the outdoor seating area at the front. The husband and wife team never lose their enthusiasm and passion for running this beautifully-kept establishment, with many traditional features such as Victorian tiling and flagstone and timber flooring. A blackboard describes the guest ales of the month, with notes on the three regulars. Historic photographs display the art of beer making and hop growing. ⌂Q⚿⬤⚫(Bromley North)⌐(314)♣⌐

Bromley Common

Two Doves
37 Oakley Road, BR2 8HD
✪ 12-3, 5-11; 12-11 Fri & Sat; 12-10.30 Sun
☎ (020) 8462 1627
Courage Best Bitter; St Austell Tribute; Young's Bitter, Special Ⓗ
Beautiful leaded windows and a warm welcome await in this immaculately kept pub with old plates, jugs and saucy postcards in the Gents. Set in a semi-rural conservation area, it is home to the Ravensbourne Morris Men and a perfect stop for walkers, with a large garden at the rear. You will not find any big-screen TVs but you will get real conversation with locals and everything you could hope for in a traditional pub. ⌂⚿⬤👪⌐(320)♣⌐

Chelsfield

Five Bells ✓
Church Road, BR6 7RE
✪ 11-11 (midnight Fri & Sat); 12-10.30 Sun
☎ (01689) 821044 ⊕ thefivebells-chelsfieldvillage.co.uk
Courage Best Bitter; Harveys Sussex Best Bitter; Sharp's Doom Bar; guest beers Ⓗ
Far off the beaten track, a warm welcome awaits at this rural gem, built around 1680 to celebrate the installation of five new bells in the nearby village church. Original beams, photographs and plates on the walls contribute to a cosy atmosphere. With two bars and a popular restaurant, regular theme nights and open mike nights are held here, and walkers, families and dogs can enjoy the large, pleasant garden. The bus stops right outside. Q⚿⬤⬢⌐(R3)♣⌐

Chislehurst

Ramblers Rest ✅
Mill Place, BR7 5ND (off Old Hill)
🕛 11.30-11; 12-10.30 Sun ☎ (020) 8467 1734
Courage Best Bitter; Fuller's London Pride; Sharp's Doom Bar; Wells Bombardier; Young's Bitter; guest beers Ⓗ
Fair-weather drinkers at this weatherboarded building in a scenic location on the edge of Chislehurst Common have a choice of the rear patio or the open green at the front. Internally, this two-bar pub is laid out on two levels: a lower roomy bar and a cosy upper bar, favoured by locals. Hot or cold food is available at lunchtimes only.
🏚Q✿♿⌖≠➲(162,269)♣P⌐

Crayford

Crayford Arms Ⓛ
37 Crayford High Street, DA1 4HH
🕛 2-11; 12-midnight Thu-Sat; 12-11 Sun ☎ 07505 141433
🌐 thecrayfordarms.com
Shepherd Neame Master Brew, Kent's Best, Spitfire, Bishops Finger, seasonal beer Ⓗ
A pub boasting five handpumps and a traditional atmosphere with many original features. To the right is a cosy public bar and to the left a wood-panelled saloon bar from which an attractive oak staircase leads up to a function room. Occasional live music is performed. The pub sells the full range of Shepherd Neame beers but only five are available at the bar at any one time.
✿➲≠➲(96,428,492)♣P⌐

Croydon

Builders Arms ✅
65 Leslie Park Road, CR0 6TP
🕛 12-11 (midnight Fri & Sat); 12-10.30 Sun
☎ (020) 8654 1803
Fuller's Chiswick Bitter, London Pride; Gale's HSB; guest beers Ⓗ
An attractive, detached pub in a back street, one bar has comfortable seating, with more tables to the extended rear, which leads to a pleasant sheltered garden. The other bar has a more public bar feel. There are sports TVs in both bars. Children are welcome until 8pm. Substantial food is served lunchtimes and evenings until 9pm (8pm weekends). There is live music once a month, and occasional guest beers.
🏚✿♿◑➲♿≠(E Croydon)⊖(Lebanon Rd Tramlink)➲♣⌐

Dog & Bull
24 Surrey Street, CR0 1RG
🕛 11-11 (11.30 Fri-Sat); 12-10.30 Sun ☎ (020) 8667 9718
Wells Bombardier; Young's Bitter, Special, seasonal beers Ⓗ
Historic pub on the town's famous street market; its origins date back to the 16th century. The comfortable interior features a main room with an island bar, and two adjoining rooms. The pub has a pleasant walled garden (one of Croydon's best kept secrets) where summer barbecues are held. Other events include a monthly comedy night (first Tuesday) and quizzes (alternate Tuesdays). There is a small upstairs function room available for hire.
✿◑➲≠(E/W Croydon)⊖(Church St/George St Tramlink)➲⌐

George 🏆 ✅
17-21 George Street, CR0 1LA
🕛 8-midnight (1am Fri & Sat) ☎ (020) 8649 9077
Dark Star Hophead; Fuller's London Pride; Thornbridge Jaipur IPA; guest beers Ⓗ
The current local CAMRA Pub of the Year, this Wetherspoon pub occupies a prime location in central Croydon and is almost always busy. There are two serving bars in the long single room, with some tables in booths towards the rear, and access to the large patio garden. The more than usual number of guest beers are mostly from small breweries and there are normally two draught ciders. A range of Dark Star beers is on the rear bar.
✿◑♿≠(E/W Croydon)⊖(George St Tramlink)➲●⌐

Glamorgan
81 Cherry Orchard Road, CR0 6BE
🕛 12 (4 Sat)-midnight; closed Sun ☎ (020) 8688 6333
Harveys Sussex Best Bitter; guest beers Ⓗ
A welcoming corner pub, often busy with trade from local offices. Its three rooms provide areas for drinking, dining and games, with a dartboard, pool table and TV (not used for live football). The pub specialises in good quality food, and the menu has a distinct South African flavour. A pleasant patio garden also serves as a smoking area. Bookings are taken for private functions, especially on Sunday when the pub is usually closed.
✿◑≠(E Croydon)⊖(E Croydon Tramlink)➲⌐

Green Dragon Ⓛ ✅
58-60 High Street, CR0 1NA
🕛 10-midnight (1am Fri & Sat); 12-10.30 Sun
☎ (020) 8667 0684 🌐 greendragoncroydon.co.uk
Dark Star Hophead; Harveys Sussex Best Bitter Ⓗ; Hogs Back TEA Ⓖ; Taylor Landlord; Wells Bombardier Ⓗ; guest beers Ⓗ/Ⓖ
Buzzing Town & City pub near Croydon's historic market, enthusiastically run by young staff with a keen interest in ale. Six handpumps and two gravity casks dispense a variety of beers including some locally brewed. Real draught cider is usually available. Lunchtimes are quieter than evenings; a wide variety of music is performed upstairs including live jazz on Sunday afternoon. Popular with both young and not-so-young, this was the 2008 local CAMRA Pub of the Year.
◑♿≠(E/W Croydon)⊖(George St Tramlink)➲●

Half & Half Ⓛ
282 High Street, CR0 1NG
🕛 12 (3 Sat)-midnight; 3-11 Sun ☎ (020) 8726 0080
🌐 halfandhalf.uk.com
Dark Star Hophead; guest beer Ⓗ
A smart, friendly lounge bar on two floors, conveniently located for the south Croydon restaurants and well away from Croydon nightlife. Sofas, comfortable bar stools and soft background music create the atmosphere. The rotating guest beer is from Sambrook's, complemented by a small but interesting range of Belgian beers and one Czech beer on the tall fonts. There is free WiFi and the basement room is available for private functions. ⊖(George St Tramlink)➲🍴

Royal Standard ✅
1 Sheldon Street, CR0 1SS
🕛 12-midnight (1am Fri & Sat); 12-11 Sun
☎ (020) 8688 9749
Fuller's Chiswick Bitter, London Pride, ESB, seasonal beers; Gale's HSB; guest beers Ⓗ

High Lane

Royal Oak
Buxton Road, SK6 8AY
✪ 12-3, 5-11; 12-10.30 Sun ☎ (01663) 762380
Marston's Burton Bitter; Jennings Cocker Hoop; guest beers Ⓗ
A well-appointed pub with a pleasing exterior. Although it has an open-plan layout, there are three distinct drinking areas, one used for games. Live entertainment is hosted most Fridays and an innovative food menu is served at all sessions. The garden and outdoor play area make this a good summer and family pub. Up to six handpulled beers are sourced from the Marston's range.
Q✿✪◗🛈🖳(199,394)P🕭

Hindley

Hare & Hounds Ⓛ
31 Ladies Lane, WN2 2QA
✪ 3 (6 Tue)-midnight; 12-midnight Sat & Sun ☎ 07900 990 681
Beer range varies Ⓗ
A classic community boozer with a warm and friendly atmosphere. There are two rooms – a bar area with darts and dominoes and a TV area showing sport, and a lounge with pleasant surroundings to sit and chat with a drink. Children are welcome until 7pm. There is a small beer garden with an ample covered smoking area. The pub is home to men's and women's darts and dominoes teams. Thursday is quiz night. 🏛🕭🖳≠🕭

Holcombe Brook

Hare & Hounds ✔
400 Bolton Road West, BL0 9RY (on A676 at jct with Longsight Road)
✪ 12-11 (midnight Thu-Sat) ☎ (01706) 822107
🌐 hareandhoundsbury.com
Beer range varies Ⓗ
Winner of the Publican Awards Cask Ale Pub 2008 and highly commended in 2010, this large rural community pub has a bright, friendly atmosphere where young, old and their dogs are all welcome. Ten cask ales from across the country are on handpump – the list can be viewed on the pub's webcam. There is also a range of continental lagers on tap and two beer festivals are held annually. A small function room is available plus free WiFi.
🏛✿✪◗🖳(472,474)♣P🕭

Horwich

Crown
1 Chorley New Road, BL6 7QJ (jct A673/B6226)
SD634118
✪ 11-11 (midnight Fri & Sat); 12-11.30 Sun
☎ (01204) 693109
Holt Mild, Bitter, seasonal beers Ⓗ
A grand local landmark, handy for the Reebok Stadium, Rivington Pike and the West Pennine Moors. Lever Park across the road was a gift from Lord Leverhulme, the soap magnate and great benefactor to his home town. Darts and dominoes teams play on Tuesday and Thursday evenings and there is a vault and games room at the rear. Various artists provide entertainment on Sunday evening. Children are welcome at lunchtime when dining. ✿✪◗🛈🖳(125,575)♣P🕭

Original Bay Horse
206 Lee Lane, BL6 7JF (on B6226, 200m from A673)
✪ 1-midnight; 12-12.30am Fri & Sat; 12-midnight Sun
☎ (01204) 696231
Bank Top Flat Cap; Coach House Gunpowder Mild; Lees Bitter; Moorhouse's Pride of Pendle; guest beers Ⓗ
Dating from 1777, this stone-built pub with small windows and low ceilings has been run by the same family for many years and is locally known as the 'Long Pull'. In the lounge, pool and darts are played and live sports coverage on TV is popular, while on the left a cosy, traditional vault has some interesting football memorabilia. A Moorhouse's beer is usually available. Nearby Lever Park is ideal for lovely woodland walks. ✿🕭🖳(125,575)♣♣🕭

Victoria & Albert
114 Lee Lane, BL6 7AF (opp Horwich public hall on B6226)
✪ 12-11 (midnight Fri & Sat) ☎ (01204) 770837
Holt Bitter, IPA Ⓗ
Formally the Albert Arms, the pub is situated on the B6226 opposite Horwich public hall. Recently refurbished, this is now a modern and comfortable lounge-style pub with three separate seating areas. It is handy for the West Pennine Moors and walkers are always welcome. Two guest beers are offered, one usually from Moorhouse's. The toilets have disabled access. Outside is a beer garden. Over-21s only. 🖳(125)🕭

Hyde

Cheshire Ring
72 Manchester Road, SK14 2BJ
✪ 2 (1 Thu & Fri)-11; 12-11 Sat; 12-10.30 Sun
☎ (07917) 055629
Beartown Kodiak Gold, Bearskinful, seasonal beers; guest beers Ⓗ
A warm welcome is assured at this friendly pub, one of the oldest in Hyde and comprehensively overhauled by Beartown. Seven handpumps offer a range of Beartown ales and guests from micros in addition to ciders, perries and continental beers. A range of bottled beers is also stocked and occasional beer festivals offer additional drinking choice. Gentle background music plays and live bands perform. The opening hours vary with the season. ♻✿🕭🖳≠(Central)🖳♣🕭

Cotton Bale ✔
21-25 Market Place, Market Place, SK14 2LX
✪ 9am-midnight (1am Fri & Sat) ☎ (0161) 351 0380
Beer range varies Ⓗ
A reminder of when cotton was king in Hyde, this popular, vibrant town-centre pub offers up to 12 handpumped real ales at Wetherspoon's value-for-money prices. A number of indoor drinking areas and another outside provide flexible space for drinking and dining, and TV screens are provided. Families are welcome and food is available all day. Hyde market and good public transport links are nearby. ✿◗🛈≠(Central)🖳🕭

Queen's Inn
23 Clarendon Place, SK14 2ND
✪ 11-11 ☎ (0161) 368 2230
Holt Mild, Bitter, seasonal beers Ⓗ
A town-centre community pub with a warm welcome. Home to several sports teams, the interior is divided into four distinct areas to cater for all needs, including a large function room that is

a favourite for wedding receptions. Situated close to Hyde bus station and the market, the Queen's is popular with shoppers during the day. A late licence is available for special events throughout the year.

ᐳ❀❁ᐸ≅(Central/Newton for Hyde)�♣🚬

Sportsman 🅛

57 Mottram Road, SK14 2NN
✪ 11-11; 12-10.30 Sun ☎ (0161) 368 5000
Moorhouse's Black Cat; Rossendale Floral Dance, Halo, 1047, Pitch Porter, Sunshine Ⓗ
This Rossendale Brewery tied house offers the full range of its Pennine Ales beers plus three guests from micros. Bar snacks are served and there is a restaurant upstairs specialising in genuine home-cooked Cuban food and tapas. This former CAMRA Pub of the Region retains its character. The rear patio includes a covered and heated smoking area.

ᐍQ❀◑≅(Central/Newton for Hyde)🚃♦P🚬

Leigh

Boar's Head 🍸 🅛

2 Market Place, WN7 1EG
✪ 11-11 (1am Thu-Sat) ☎ (01942) 673036
Beer range varies Ⓗ
Opposite Leigh's parish church, the imposing red-brick exterior contains clues to the pub's history, from the Bedford Brewing Company to Walker's Warrington Ales, plus the odd Firkin brew-pub memento inside. A real free house, there are four pumps, two dispensing Moorhouse's beers and two ever-changing guests. The large pool room houses a collection of Rugby League team photographs from various eras, the dining area displays Lancashire colliery plates. A carvery is available on Sunday. Live music sessions are held most Saturdays, a quiz with hotpot on Sunday.

❀◑🚃♣🚬

Leigh Rugby Union Club

Round Ash Park, Hand Lane, WN7 3NA (off Beech Walk)
✪ 7-11; 12-11 Sat & Sun ☎ (01942) 673526
Beer range varies Ⓗ
A true community pub with not only men's and women's rugby teams but also crown green bowls, darts and dominoes. Put that together with an enthusiastic, hard-working bar team and a friendly crowd of locals and you cannot go wrong. Well-worth the 10-minute walk from Leigh bus station. It has an annual Scrumdown beer festival in May, with more than 30 real ales and ciders. Greater Manchester Club of the Year 2008, 2009 and 2010.

❀P🚬

Thomas Burke 🅛 ✓

20A Leigh Road, WN7 1QR
✪ 9am-midnight (1am Fri & Sat) ☎ (01942) 685640
Beer range varies Ⓗ
Popular with all ages, this Wetherspoon pub is named after a renowned Leigh tenor, known as the Lancashire Caruso. The building was the Hippodrome Theatre that was later converted into a cinema. The pub divides into three areas: the main long bar, a raised dining area and, in what was once the cinema foyer, lounge-style seating. Ten handpumps offer a changing range of beers from local to distant breweries. ◑ᐸ🚬

Littleborough

Moorcock

Halifax Road, OL15 0LD (on A58, 1 mile NE of town centre)
✪ 11.30-midnight (11.30 Sun) ☎ (01706) 378156
⊕ themoorcockinn.com
Taylor Landlord; guest beers Ⓗ
Situated at the foot of the Pennines with spectacular views of the surrounding hills and moors, this traditional country inn was originally a farmhouse built in 1681 and first licensed in 1840. It has a warm, convivial ambience with guest beers from local micro-breweries including Pictish. Bar food is always available, with a full à la carte menu in the restaurant lunchtimes and evenings. Seven en-suite bedrooms make this an ideal base to explore the attractive local area.

ᐍ❀🛏◑ᐸᐂ🚃(528)P🚬

White House

Halifax Road, OL15 0LG (on A58 towards Halifax)
✪ 12-3, 6.30-midnight; 12.30-10.30 Sun ☎ (01706) 378456
Theakston Best Bitter; guest beers Ⓗ
The Pennine Way passes this 17th-century coaching house, a landmark at 1300 feet that benefits from outstanding views. A family-run inn for the past 27 years, it extends a warm and friendly welcome to all. There are two bars, both with log fires. Four handpumps serve one regular and three guest beers, usually from local breweries. World bottled beers, cider and a good selection of wine complement the excellent food menu and daily specials board. Meals are served all day on Sunday. ᐍQ❀◑ᐂ🚃(528)♦P🚬

Lydgate

White Hart

51 Stockport Road, OL4 4JJ (on A6050 nr jct with A669)
✪ 12-midnight (11 Sun) ☎ (01467) 872566
⊕ thewhitehart.co.uk
Lees Bitter; Taylor Golden Best, Best Bitter, Landlord; guest beers Ⓗ
True free house in a classic weathered Yorkshire stone building dating from 1788, atop a hill with impressive views over Greater Manchester and beyond. The multi-room layout has log-burning stoves in two rooms. Guest beers are from far and wide, usually including a light and a dark beer. Quality food is served daily from an award-winning kitchen in both the pub and separate restaurant. A good range of foreign bottled beer is also stocked.

ᐍQ❀🛏◑ᐸ🚃(180,184)P

Manchester: City Centre

57 Thomas Street

57 Thomas Street, M4 1NA (off Shudehill)
✪ 11.30-midnight ☎ (0161) 832 0501
Beer range varies Ⓖ
This one-roomed bar was converted from a deli in 2010 by Marble Brewery, and sells the full range of Marble ales, but not all at the same time. Beers are served straight from the casks that are situated on the bar – up to four at a time. Bottled Belgian and German beers and an interesting variety of meals and snacks are available at all times.

❀◑ᐸ≅(Victoria)⊖(Shudehill)

Angel

6 Angel Street, M4 4BQ (off Rochdale Rd)
✪ 11-midnight; closed Sun ☎ (0161) 833 4786

Bob's White Lion; guest beers Ⓗ
A thriving free house just north of the city centre – upstairs there is a well-established restaurant and downstairs drinkers are catered for in an L-shaped room with bare floorboards and a warming fire in winter. The bar is adorned with 10 handpumps – two reserved for real cider and perry. A wide range of beers is available from all over the country, with small breweries to the fore. Quiz night is Monday. CAMRA Branch Pub of the Year 2010.
🏬🍴🍶🍽≈(Victoria)⊖(Shudehill)🚌🚶P🚭

Bar Fringe
8 Swan Street, M4 5JN (30m from A62/A665 jct)
🕐 12-midnight (12.30am Fri & Sat) ☎ (0161) 835 3815
Beer range varies Ⓗ
Popular continental-style bar with five handpumps dispensing ales from all over the country, plus an extensive range of draught and Belgian bottled beers. Thatchers Cheddar Valley cider is also available, and sometimes another guest. Enjoy the eccentric decor while supping – how many ornamental rats can you count? – and do not miss the 'secret' beer garden at the rear. Hot snacks are available until 4pm.
🍶🍽≈(Victoria)⊖(Shudehill)🚌🚶🚭

Bull's Head
84 London Road, M1 2PN (jct Fairfield St)
🕐 11.30-11; 12-10.30 Sun ☎ (0161) 236 1724
Banks's Mild; Jennings Cumberland Ale; Marston's Pedigree; guest beers Ⓗ
Situated across the road from the back entrance to Piccadilly Station, the Bull's Head attracts both travellers and locals. While the interior is basically open plan, it nevertheless has the kind of cosy intimacy you might expect from a more suburban location. Run with superb professionalism across the board, the Bull's Head never disappoints and is a beacon for quality. Guest beers are usually from the Marston's stable, but beer festivals and promotions support other breweries. Evening food is 5.30-8.30pm Monday-Thursday.
Q🍴♿≈(Piccadilly)⊖(Piccadilly)🚌(192,201)

Cask
Liverpool Road, Castlefield, M3 4NQ
🕐 12-11 ☎ (0161) 819 2527 ⊕ caskmanc.co.uk
Beer range varies Ⓗ
Corner location near the historic Castlefield district. In addition to the three constantly-changing guest ales this establishment specialises in continental and world beers in bottled and draught form. The layout is open plan, tables and chairs at the front, an open area by the bar and at the rear a spacious lounge with sofas and booths. No food is served on the premises apart from the usual nuts and crisps; however you may bring your own food in.
≈(Deansgate)⊖(Deansgate/Castlefield)🚌🚭

Castle Hotel
66 Oldham Street, M4 1LE (near Warwick St)
🕐 11-1am; 12-10.30 Sun ☎ (0161) 237 9485
⊕ thecastlehotel.info
Beer range varies Ⓗ
Part of Robinson's Brewery estate since 1946, the pub is a Northern Quarter must-see. Renovation was completed in 2010, restoring many of the Grade II-listed building's features. The newly re-opened performance space is gathering attention from local promoters for week-night shows, including a spoken word night. Most of the Robinson's range is available on its seven

handpumps, the rest is in bottles including the popular Chocolate Tom. The latest seasonal ales also feature.
🍶🍴≈(Victoria/Piccadilly)⊖(Market St)🚌🚶🚭

City Arms ✓
46-48 Kennedy Street, M2 4BQ
🕐 11.30-11 (midnight Fri); 12-midnight Sat; 12-8 Sun
☎ (0161) 236 4610
Beer range varies Ⓗ
There is always a friendly welcome at this traditional, compact, two-room, city-centre pub with seven ever-changing guest beers plus real cider. At least seven malt whiskies are also available. To eat there are pies. A regular entry in the Guide for the past 15 years, the pub is always busy and has a lot of regular clients – like a local in the city centre. Expect a crowd on Friday and Saturday. 🍶🍴≈(Oxford Rd)⊖♣

Common
37-41 Edge Street, M4 2HW (corner of Hare St)
🕐 11-midnight (2am Thu-Sat) ☎ (0161) 832 9245
⊕ aplacecalledcommon.co.uk
Flowers IPA; guest beer Ⓗ
The most striking feature of this building is that it is an ever-changing art gallery – inside and out. Opened in 2005, the bar started selling real ale in early 2010. The guest beer changes often and is chosen from a wide variety of breweries. Food is good, served until 10pm every day. The bar generally attracts a younger clientele, but the staff offer a warm welcome to all.
🍴≈(Victoria)⊖(Shudehill)🚌(Shudehill)

Crown & Kettle
2 Oldham Road, Ancoats, M4 5FE (corner of Oldham St and Great Ancoats St)
🕐 12-11; 12-midnight Fri & Sat; 12-10.30 Sun
☎ (0161) 236 2923 ⊕ crownandkettle.com
Greenfield Crown & Kettle Ale; guest beers Ⓗ
In co-operation with English Heritage, the developers re-opened this Grade II-listed pub in 2005 after a closure of 16 years. The building has a drinking hall, modern snug and separate vault with the original ornate ceiling. The pub has quickly gained a good reputation for offering up to four quality beers from near and far, including ales from Ossett, Weetwood and Howard Town. Occasional beer festivals also feature. Live folk plays on a Friday night once a month. Food is served up to 4pm daily.
🍶🍴♿≈(Victoria)⊖(Piccadilly Gardens)🚌🚶🚭

Grey Horse
80 Portland Street, M1 4QX (jct Princess St)
🕐 11-11; 12-10.30 Sun ☎ (0161) 236 1874
Hydes Mild, Original Bitter, seasonal beers Ⓗ
Certainly one of the smallest pubs in the city, if not the country, this is a cosy, one-roomed refuge from the hectic world outside. Football matches are screened, and the pub can get busy on match days when space is at a premium. However there is little else in the way of distraction – the beer quality speaks for itself. A rarity these days – the Gents toilet is out the back.
≈(Oxford Rd)⊖(St Peter's Sq)🚌(1,3)🚭

Knott Bar Ⓛ
374 Deansgate, M3 4LY
🕐 12-11.30 (midnight Thu; 12.30 am Fri & Sat)
☎ (0161) 839 9229
Beer range varies Ⓗ

A converted railway arch adjacent to Deansgate station, the bar serves an ever-changing mix of beers from leading micro-breweries such as Pictish, Acorn, Hornbeam and Dark Star, and at least one from Marble Brewery is usually available. Real cider is also served alongside an extensive selection of bottled and draught foreign beers. Quality meals served until 8pm seven days a week have an excellent reputation – check the blackboard for details of monthly themed Epicurean Nights. CAMRA Greater Manchester Regional Pub of the Year 2010.
🛏🕯🍺🕭🚆⊖🖾🕯🗝

Marble Arch 🍺 ☆

73 Rochdale Road, M4 4HY (on A664, 200m from A665 jct)
🕛 12-11.30 (12.30am Sat); 12-midnight Sun
☎ (0161) 832 5914
Marble Pint, Manchester, Best, Ginger, seasonal beers; guest beers ⓗ
Superb Victorian street-corner pub with a grand marble exterior and glazed-brick interior, featuring a sloping floor and an ornately worded frieze displaying various drinks. Above this, the arched ceiling adds further interest. The back room, which is used for dining, is a lot plainer, but part of the in-house brewery can be observed from here. Excellent, highly-regarded food is served until 9pm (8pm Sun).
🍴🛏🕯🍺🚆(Victoria) ⊖(Shudehill)🖾🕯🗝

Micro Bar

Unit FC16, Manchester Arndale, 49 High Street, M4 3AH (inside Arndale Market, High St entrance)
🕛 11-6; 12-5 Sun ☎ (0161) 277 9666
Boggart Hole Clough Rum Porter; guest beers ⓗ
Boggart Hole Clough Brewery's only outlet, this innovative market bar doubled in size in 2010, but is still one of the smallest around. Friendly bar staff dispense the Newton Heath brewery's many ales, plus guests from all over the country and real cider, on five handpumps. An impressive selection of domestic and international bottles also attracts regular custom. Although the hours are limited due to the bar's location, it is well worth a visit.
🚆(Victoria) ⊖(Shudehill)🖾🕯🗓

Old Wellington Inn 📛

4 Cathedral Gates, M3 1SW (next to Cathedral)
🕛 10-11 (midnight Fri & Sat); 10-10.30 Sun
☎ (0161) 839 5179
Jennings Cumberland Ale; Thwaites Lancaster Bomber; guest beers ⓗ
Impressive remodelled 16th-century inn – part of the Nicholson's of London estate. Over the past 40 years, this tourist attraction pub has been moved due to various developments. It now serves up to eight real ales, with favourites from Kelham Island, Thornbridge and BrewDog breweries among others. The pub is on three levels, with an extended bar downstairs for drinkers and informal dining, and more formal dining upstairs. This Tudor pub is noted for its pies. Food is served up to 10pm.
Q🛏🕯🍺🕭🚆(Victoria) ⊖(Victoria)🖾

Paramount 📛

33-35 Oxford Street, M1 4BH (jct Portland St)
🕛 9-midnight (1am Fri & Sat) ☎ (0161) 233 1820
Elland Paramount; Greene King Abbot; Phoenix Lancashire Pale Ale; Thwaites Wainwright; guest beers ⓗ

Named because of its location in Manchester's old theatreland, this large and extremely popular Wetherspoon pub has a lively, yet always controlled atmosphere. What really sets it apart is the enthusiasm of the team for its wide and interesting range of cask beers. Old photographs of now closed theatres and cinemas adorn the walls, and it is handy for many modern-day venues including Manchester Central Conference Centre, Palace Theatre and Bridgewater Hall.
🍺🕭🚆(Oxford Rd) ⊖(St Peter's Sq)🖾(1,3)🕯🗝

Peveril of the Peak ★

127 Great Bridgewater Street, M1 5JQ
🕛 12-3 (not Sat), 5-11; 5-10.30 Sun ☎ (0161) 236 6364
Caledonian Deuchars IPA; Copper Dragon Golden Pippin; Everards Tiger; Jennings Cumberland Ale ⓗ
Dating from around 1829, this classic pub boasts an array of original details – and features in CAMRA's National Inventory of Historic Pub Interiors. Named after the stagecoach that ran from London to Manchester, the pub was saved from demolition in the 1970s after a campaign by the locals and CAMRA. The landlady celebrated 40 years as licensee in January 2011. The pub opens at noon on Saturday if Manchester United are playing at home.
🛏Q🕯🍺🕭🚆(Oxford Rd) ⊖🖾🍀🗝

Rising Sun 📛

22 Queen Street, M2 5HX
🕛 11-8 Mon; 12-10.40 Tue-Thu; 12-11 Fri & Sat; 1-7 Sun
☎ (0161) 834 1193
Beer range varies ⓗ
Traditional, historic, city-centre pub, off Deansgate, with entrances on Queen Street and Lloyd Street (one of only three pubs in Manchester with two entrances). Six handpumps dispense beers from Punch Tavern's Finest Cask list and regular real cider. Food is served lunchtimes Monday to Friday, including Mr Smith's world famous home-made chilli. Local CAMRA Pub of the Season Autumn 2010, it hosts regular Meet the Brewer events and beer festivals. An improving pub, worth tracking down. 🍺🚆(Deansgate) ⊖🖾

Sandbar

120-122 Grosvenor Street, All Saints, M1 7HL (off Oxford Rd A34/B5117 jct)
🕛 12-midnight (1am Thu; 2am Fri); 4-2am Sat; 4-11 Sun
☎ (0161) 273 1552 🌐 sandbaronline.net
Moorhouse's Black Cat; Phoenix All Saints; Taylor Landlord; guest beers ⓗ
This gem, in the heart of the university area, attracts custom from both students and lecturers alike, who come for the bohemian atmosphere and excellent range of British and foreign (notably, German) beers, both draught and in bottle. The craft cider is a changing guest from a small producer. Occasional exhibitions of photographs or paintings usually line the walls, while DJs or live music often feature in the evening. Food is available until 7pm weekdays. Free WiFi available.
🍺🚆(Oxford Rd)🖾(42,43)🕯🗝

Smithfield Hotel & Bar

37 Swan Street, M4 5JZ (on A665 between Rochdale Rd and Oldham Rd)
🕛 12-midnight ☎ (0161) 839 4424
🌐 the-smithfield-hotel.co.uk
Robinson's Dark Hatters; Facers Smithfield Bitter; guest beers ⓗ
Situated in the Northern Quarter, this small and intimate city-centre bar has the atmosphere of a

local. The front room is dominated by a pool table, but a recently created snug opposite the bar offers more seating. The house bitter is from Facers and the guests come from micros and family brewers, with rarities during the numerous beer festivals held throughout the year. Reasonably priced accommodation is available in nine bedrooms. ⇔≠(Victoria)⊖(Shudehill)🖵♣

Waterhouse L ⊘
67-71 Princess Street, M2 4EG (opp town hall)
❂ 8am-midnight ☎ (0161) 200 5380
Elland Waterhouse IPA; Greene King Ruddles Best Bitter, Abbot; Phoenix Wobbly Bob; guest beers Ⓗ
This multi-roomed Wetherspoon pub is very different in character to the chain's more usual large open-plan establishments. It provides a constantly changing range of cask ales as well as real ciders. Food is well-presented from Wetherspoon's typical menu. Regular Meet The Brewer evenings are held. The Sunday evening CAMRA Club offers a discount on real ale to card-carrying CAMRA members. Q☎🏠❶&≠(Oxford Rd)⊖🖵♠♪

Marple

Hare & Hounds ⊘
Dooley Lane, Otterspool, SK6 7EJ
❂ 11.30-11; 12-10.30 Sun ☎ (0161) 427 0293
Hydes Bitter, Jekyll's Gold, seasonal beers Ⓗ
Attractive pub by the River Goyt on the Marple-Romiley road. It is difficult to imagine that when this pub was built it was at the end of a row of terraced cottages, demolished long ago when the road was realigned. The pub's Hydes beers now provide some welcome variety in the area. The interior is open plan with a separate dining area and conservatory plus an improved and pleasant outdoor space. The pub offers something for everyone including good-value food. Q☎❶●P♪

Hatters Arms
81 Church Lane, SK6 7AW
❂ 12-midnight ☎ (0161) 427 1529 ⊕ hattersmarple.co.uk
Robinson's Hatters, Unicorn, seasonal beers Ⓗ
At the end of a row of stone-built hatters' cottages, this tiny pub was enlarged only a few years ago and retains an intimate atmosphere. There are three small rooms and an attractive panelled bar area. Numerous photographs on the walls reflect the pub's brass band connections. Much is done to attract regular custom, including games evenings and a quiz on Thursday. ☎❶&≠(Rose Hill)

Railway
223 Stockport Road, SK6 6EN
❂ 12-11 (11.30 Fri & Sat) ☎ (0161) 427 2146
Robinson's Hatters, Unicorn, seasonal beers Ⓗ
This impressive pub first opened in 1878 alongside Rose Hill Station and many rail commuters still number among its customers. The pub has changed little externally, and is handy for walkers and cyclists on the nearby Middlewood Way. Two open-plan airy and relaxing rooms are complemented by an outside veranda and drinking area. A deservedly popular pub. ☎❶&≠(Rose Hill)🖵P♪

Marple Bridge

Hare & Hounds
19 Mill Brow, SK6 5LW (from A626 Lane Ends along Ley Lane for ¾ mile) SJ980896
❂ 12-3 (Fri only), 5-1am; 12-1am Sat; 12-midnight Sun
☎ (0161) 427 4042
Robinson's Hatters, Dizzy Blonde, Unicorn Ⓗ
Winner of the 2010 Robinson's Unicorn Shield for best-kept cellar, this is a hidden gem in the beautiful hamlet of Mill Brow. Extensively refurbished in 2008 to a high standard, this excellent country pub with great atmosphere and a roaring fire in winter is the perfect place for both discerning drinkers and diners. Meals are freshly prepared and food is locally sourced. A genuine local that caters for everyone, including walkers, with some of the best views in the area. ⇔☎❶&🖵(394)♣●P♪

Middleton

Olde Boar's Head L ⊘
111 Long Street, M24 6UE
❂ 12-11 (10.30 Sun) ☎ (0161) 643 3520
Lees Bitter, seasonal beers Ⓗ
Venerable half-timbered pub that dates back to at least 1632. Inside, old and new mix easily, with stone-flagged floors and carpeted lounge areas. The pub has a variety of rooms and there is a nook or cranny to suit all. The large Sessions Room at the side was once a court, but now hosts a slimming club and other more modern activities. Note the viewing panel for the original wattle-and-daub walls near the bar. ☎❶&🖵(17)P♪

Ring o' Bells
St Leonard's Square, M24 6DJ (up New Lane from Long St, Middleton)
❂ 5-midnight (1am Fri); 12-1am Sat; 12-midnight Sun
☎ (0161) 654 9245 ⊕ ringobellsmiddleton.co.uk
Lees Bitter, seasonal beers Ⓗ
Old village pub at the rear of Jubilee Park opposite the historic parish church, this popular JW Lees house has a regular local clientele and hosts an annual May bank holiday maypole event and the Pace Egg play on Easter Monday. Regular entertainment includes live music, a quiz, poetry and speciality nights. The upstairs function room is for hire and contains unique memorial collages created from hundreds of butterflies. Outside is a covered and lit smoking area. ☎♣♪

Tandle Hill Tavern L
14 Thornham Lane, M24 5SD (1 mile up unmetalled lane from either A664 or A627)
❂ 5 (12 Sat & Sun)-midnight ☎ (07826) 853890
⊕ tandlehilltavern.co.uk
Lees Brewers Dark, Bitter; guest beers Ⓗ
Set on the top of a hill in the Tandle Country Park, this neat little pub nestles among a number of farms. It comprises a main bar and lounge area with a separate side room. In summer, the walled rear beer garden is a suntrap and benches to the front and side provide plenty of outdoor seating. The pub is popular with walkers, farmers and locals, and dogs are welcome. Hearty home-cooked meals are available at weekends – ring first at other times. ⇔☎❶

Monton

Park Hotel

142 Monton Road, M30 9QD (corner of Hawthorne Avenue)
🕐 11-11 (11.30 Thu; midnight Fri & Sat); 12-10.30 Sun
☎ (0161) 787 8608
Holt Mild, IPA, Bitter, seasonal beers; guest beers 🅷
Rebuilt in 1971, this is a thriving community local. The interior comprises a vault, large lounge and the smaller Bridgewater Room – a separate quiet room, with an interesting map of the nearby canal – all served by a central bar. A regular quiz is hosted on Sunday evening, and live entertainment on Saturday. Sport is shown on 3-D TV and the pub is home to darts teams. The locals are keen anglers. Q🕮♿🚃(33,68)♣P⌐

Mossley

Britannia Inn

217 Manchester Road, OL5 9AJ
🕐 2.45 (11.45 Sat)-11 (midnight Fri & Sat); 11.45-midnight Sun ☎ (01457) 832799
Marston's Burton Bitter; guest beers 🅷
The 'Brit' is a fine gritstone building next to the erstwhile Britannia Mills and close to the station. Five guest ales on offer are frequently from local breweries, often including a beer from Millstone. The pub is semi-open plan, with a secluded dining area. Meals are served daily until 7.30pm (5pm Sun). A partially covered patio at the front provides for outdoor drinking and smoking. Thursday is poker evening. ♿◑≠(Mossley)🚃(343,350)♣⌐

Dysarts Arms

Huddersfield Road, OL5 9BT (on B6175 ½ mile S of A635)
🕐 12-midnight (1am Fri & Sat) ☎ (01457) 832103
🌐 dysartsarms.com
Robinson's Hatters, Unicorn, seasonal beers 🅷
Robinson's acquired this pub when it took over Schofield's of Ashton-under-Lyne in 1926. The present steeply-pitched, Swiss-style roof dates from 1928; prior to this the pub had another storey. The interior comprises a spacious, comfortable bar area and a cosy lounge with a real fire in winter. A partially covered patio to the side allows for outdoor drinking and smoking. The licensees organise the pub's walking and cycling clubs. No food is available on Monday. 🛏♿◑▲🚃(350)♣P⌐

Rising Sun

235 Stockport Road, OL5 0RQ
🕐 12-midnight ☎ (01457) 238236 🌐 risingsunmossley.co.uk
Black Sheep Best Bitter; Millstone Tiger Rut; Taylor Landlord 🅷
From its bracing location nearly a mile from the station but a good deal higher, this pub offers good views eastwards over the Tame Valley towards Saddleworth Moor. The ever-changing range of up to seven guest ales is complemented by a splendid variety of bottled beers from around the world. A pavement patio and covered area are available for smokers. The Blue Grass Boys meet here on Tuesday evening and a band performs on Monday. 🛏♿🚃(353)♣♠P⌐

New Springs

Crown Hotel 🅻

106 Wigan Road, WN2 1DP (on B5238 by canal bridge)
🕐 7-midnight (1am Fri); 2-1am Sat; 2-11 Sun

Beer range varies 🅷
This is a community pub well worth a visit. A free house, it has three handpumps offering a selection of Prospect beers. Two real fires welcome visitors on winter evenings, and there is a pool table, dartboard and large-screen TV. Outside is a beer garden and smoking area. Cabaret entertainment is hosted on Friday evening and karaoke on Saturday. Opening times may vary in winter. Close to the canal bridge and Haigh Country Park. 🛏♿P⌐

Oldham

Ashton Arms 🅻

28-30 Clegg Street, OL1 1PL (rear of Town Square shopping centre)
🕐 11.30-11 (11.30 Fri & Sat); 11.30-7 Sun
☎ (0161) 630 9709
Beer range varies 🅷
Once owned by Gartside Brewery, this free house is a permanent beer festival offering seven changing real ales from new and established brewers. Third-of-a-pint measures are always available. The Ashton was local CAMRA Pub of the Year 2010 and a finalist in a regional newspaper contest. Continental beers, traditional ciders and perries (Gwynt y Ddraig and guests) are stocked. Good value food is served lunchtimes (no food eves). Note the stone fireplace that is more than 200 years old. 🛏◑🚃♣♠⌐🎖

Three Crowns ⊘

1 Manchester Street, OL1 1LE (by bus station)
🕐 12-8 (10 Sat); 12-4 Sun ☎ (0161) 628 6123
Beer range varies 🅷
This tidy, well-appointed town-centre pub has a smartly painted black-and-white exterior and attracts a varied mix of customers of all ages. Lunchtimes are often busy here, with shoppers and office workers taking a well-earned break. Beers, including seasonals, are from the Marston's stable. The pub has three distinct drinking areas, one often used for small functions, and offers full disabled access and facilities. Quality food is served seven days a week. ♿◑♿🚃♣⌐

Orrell

Running Horses

146 James Road, WN5 7AA
🕐 4 (12 Sat)-midnight; 1-11.30 Sun ☎ (01942) 512604
Beer range varies 🅷
Dating back to the 1800s, with a large extension added in 1920 and further modernisation in 2004, the pub offers a warm, cosy interior, with sofas arranged around a fireplace. There is a separate pool and darts room. Sports events are shown on large-screen TVs. Quality guest ales cover all tastes. Lunches are served on Sunday only (booking advisable). The pub hosts a regular Sunday night quiz and charity events. Outside is a small covered smoking area. ♿≠P⌐

Patricroft

Queen's Arms

Green Lane, M30 0SH (next to rail station)
🕐 7 (5 Fri)-11; 12-11 Sat & Sun ☎ (0161) 789 2019
Boddingtons Bitter; guest beer 🅷
Wonderful classic pub, listed at the instigation of the local CAMRA branch. Built in 1828, in readiness for the opening of the Liverpool & Manchester

Railway, it claims to be the world's first railway pub. Three unspoilt rooms are served from a central bar. A recent innovation is the addition of a weekend guest beer. The pub received a local CAMRA branch award as a fine example of a traditional unspoilt pub. Q❀❀⊞≢⊟♣P⅃

Stanley Arms ★

895 Liverpool Road, M30 0QN (on A57, opp fire station)
✪ 12-11 (10.30 Sun) ☎ (0161) 788 8801
Holt Mild, Bitter Ⓗ
Visit the Stanley and you go back in time to the mid-19th century. This pub is totally unspoiled, with a separate vault, an attractive tiled corridor, and two comfortable rooms, one with a cast-iron range. Note the old bell push switches built into the seating, once used to summon a waiter, and the interesting photographs of early local scenes. The pub has featured in the Guide for more than 10 years and is well worth a visit.
Q❀❀⊞≢⊟(10,22,67)♣⅃

Pendlebury

Lord Nelson

653 Bolton Road, M27 4EJ (A666 near B5231 jct)
✪ 11-11 (11.30 Fri); 12-11 Sun ☎ (07827) 850254
Holt Mild, Bitter Ⓗ
Large two-room venue with a dividing central bar, typical of many built in the late 1960s. The capacious vault has a pool table and large screen. The even bigger lounge, with a stage, resembles a club room, though one corner is tucked away to provide a sort of snug. The Nelson is notable for regularly selling Holt's Mild, which has been ousted from much of the brewery's estate by the keg Holt's Black. The pub can get busy.
⊞≢(Swinton)⊟(8,484)♣P⅃

Ramsbottom

First Chop

43 Bolton Street, BL0 9HU
✪ closed Mon; 4-midnight Tue; 12-midnight Wed & Sun; 12-1am Thu-Sat ☎ (01706) 827722 ⊕ thefirstchop.co.uk
Beer range varies Ⓗ
A passion for beer, food and music is evident at this friendly bar set over two floors. Four local cask ales, plus more than 40 world-wide bottled beers, are available alongside good home-cooked, locally-sourced food. The background music is eclectic, unobtrusive and of high merit – expect folk, blues, reggae, soul, hip-hop, punk rock, plus live acoustic sessions on Thursday. A loyalty card scheme offers a free pint when you buy five pints of cask ale in a week. ◑≢⊟♠

Major Hotel

158-160 Bolton Street, BL0 9JA
✪ 4-11 Mon; 12-midnight Tue-Sat; 12-11 Sun
☎ (01706) 826777
Taylor Landlord; guest beers Ⓗ
This traditional stone-built pub comprising a lounge and a bar was originally three terraced houses. The excellent home-cooked food is a mix of old favourites and contemporary dishes (no eve meals Sat and Sun). The pub is the unofficial tap for the nearby Irwell Works Brewery and its beers often feature among the four ales on offer. The pub is dog-friendly and there is outdoor seating with a heated smoking area. ❀◑⊞⊟(472,474)♣P⅃

Rochdale

Baum

33-37 Toad Lane, OL12 0NU (follow signs for Co-op Museum)
✪ 11.30-11 (midnight Fri & Sat); 11.30-10.30 Sun
☎ (01706) 352186 ⊕ thebaum.co.uk
Beer range varies Ⓗ
A hidden gem within a local conservation area and part of the same building as the original Pioneer Museum. A split-level hostelry with old world charm and wooden floors, at the rear is a large beer garden with two full-sized petanque pistes, overlooked by a conservatory. The wide range of beers is served by friendly staff from six handpumps (one dedicated to cider), and there is also a good choice of foreign beers. Good food is served daily. CAMRA Branch Pub of the Year 2009. ❀◑≢⊟♣P⅃

Cask & Feather

1 Oldham Road, OL16 1UA
✪ 11-midnight (1am Fri & Sat); 12-midnight Sun
☎ (01706) 711476
Greenmill Gold; Phoenix Navvy; guest beers Ⓗ
Free house situated a few minutes' walk from the railway station. The interior is open plan with a long bar and pool area. Cask beer is keenly priced with the guests sourced from local micros. The rear of the pub is home to the Greenmill Brewery. Good value lunches are served daily. Outside is a beer garden and covered smoking area. Pool and poker are played on Monday and Tuesday, there is a heavy rock disco on Friday and live music on Sunday. ❀◑≢⊟♣⅃

Flying Horse Hotel

37 Packer Street, OL16 1NJ (next to town hall)
✪ 11-midnight (1am Fri & Sat); 12-midnight Sun
☎ (01706) 646412 ⊕ theflyinghorsehotel.co.uk
Lees Bitter; Taylor Best Bitter, Landlord; guest beers Ⓗ
Striking stone-built Edwardian free house owned by the same family for more than a decade. Guest beers always include an offering from the local Phoenix Brewery, with up to 10 beers available. Live sport is shown on TV and regular live music plays on Thursday, Friday and Saturday. The menu features meat from the local butcher's and pies made on the premises. There is a function room for hire and a heated smokers' area outside. The main bus station is three minutes' walk away. ◑⊟♣⅃

Healey Hotel

172 Shawclough Road, OL12 6LW
✪ 11.30-11.30; 12-midnight Fri-Sat ☎ (01706) 645453
Robinson's Hatters, Unicorn, seasonal beers Ⓗ
A three-roomed stone-built terraced property, this busy, friendly pub has been recently refurbished but retains many original features including a heritage bar. The pub is renowned for home-cooked food served seven days a week, with rag pudding a speciality. The large garden has well-kept flower beds and features a petanque piste. Healy Dell Nature Reserve is nearby and there is a bridleway to the rear. Approximately two miles from Rochdale centre, the 476 bus stops outside. Q❀◑Å⊟(446,466)P⅃

Regal Moon Ⓛ ✔

The Butts, OL16 1HB (next to bus station)
✪ 9am-midnight (1am Fri & Sat) ☎ (01706) 657434
Greene King IPA; Thwaites Wainwright; guest beers Ⓗ

Large, imposing former cinema in the centre of town adjacent to the bus station. Traces of its former existence include period fittings. Note the mannequin above the bar. The Regal Moon is the 2011 Wetherspoon Cask Pub of the Year and boasts 18 handpumps serving a varied mix of beers from near and far, all of the highest quality. Standard JDW food menus are offered all day until late. The pub opens at 8am for breakfast. Real cider is from Westons. ⊛⊄▷🜸🖵●⌐

Rusholme

Ford Madox Brown ✅
Unit 3 Wilmslow Park, Oxford Road, M13 9NG (opp Whitworth Park)
🕑 9-midnight ☎ (0161) 256 6660 ⊕ jdwetherspoon.co.uk
Greene King IPA, Abbot; guest beers Ⓗ
Built on the site of the old Rusholme Hall, this Wetherspoon pub is handy for the University, Curry Mile, MRI Hospital and Whitworth Art Gallery. It is named after the eminent Victorian Pre-Raphaelite painter whose works hang in Manchester Town Hall and the City Art Gallery (he lived nearby in Victoria Park). Although a modern open-plan establishment, it has a warmer feeling than you might expect and goes out of its way to build on this with charity and community events.
Q⊛⊄▷&🖵(42,43)●⌐

Sale

J P Joule Ⓛ ✅
2A Northenden Road, M33 3BR
🕑 8am-midnight (1am Fri & Sat) ☎ (0161) 928 9889
Beer range varies Ⓗ
Popular Wetherspoon venue run by a young, enthusiastic manager and his team who are continually trying to attract new customers to real ale, with brewery and tasting evenings held occasionally. The pub has two floors connected by a stunning staircase that cannot be missed as you enter the building. Two extensive bars host a total of 14 handpumps. Real cider from Westons is available. J P Joule, the physicist famous for heat experiments, lived locally. ⊛⊄▷&⊖🖵●⌐

Volunteer Hotel
81 Cross Street, M33 7HJ
🕑 12-midnight (11 Sun)
Holt Mild, Bitter, seasonal beers Ⓗ
Dating back to the late-19th century, this once multi-roomed pub has been opened up into one large room served by a single bar. The interior is warm and welcoming, with friendly, helpful staff. Three darts teams are based here, which makes for some lively evenings, while quiz night takes place most Thursdays. There is a fine oak-panelled room upstairs available for meetings. ⊛&⊖🖵P⌐

Salford

Crescent
18-21 The Crescent, M5 4PF (opp Salford University)
🕑 12-midnight (last entry 11pm); 12-10.30 Sun
☎ (0161) 736 5600 ⊕ thecrescentsalford.co.uk
Beer range varies Ⓗ
Said to be a meeting place for Karl Marx and Friedrich Engels, this Grade II-listed Salford pub – a circuit favourite and local institution – is now under new management. The new landlord has big plans, but continues to offer a wide variety of beers, with

12 handpumps dispensing a fast-changing selection from brewers such as Three B's, Hydes and AllGates. The pub hosts a regular quiz night on Monday, 'open mike' on Sunday and curry night on Wednesday. Up to four ciders are available. ⚞⊛⊄▷⇌🜸♣●P⌐

King's Arms
11 Bloom Street, M3 6AN (off Chapel Street)
🕑 12-11 (midnight Fri & Sat); closed Sun ☎ (0161) 839 8726
Beer range varies Ⓗ
Built in 1879, this imposing Grade II-listed building is in the Gothic style and retains exterior architectural features such as the royal coat of arms, mosaics and leaded lantern in the roof. The public areas include a large oval room with a bar and a separate lounge. Upstairs is reserved for theatrical and musical events and the outside smoking area is decorated with interesting artefacts. With half a dozen quality ales on handpump, this pub is a must-visit.
Q⊛⊄▷⇌(Central)🖵(3)P⌐

New Oxford
11 Bexley Square, M3 6DB (by magistrates court)
🕑 12-midnight ☎ (0161) 832 7082 ⊕ thenewoxford.co.uk
Beer range varies Ⓗ
A famous Salford premier pub situated in the corner of historic Bexley Square. This once-tied Vaux house has been transformed by a committed management team into the rising star of the Greater Manchester pub scene. The light and airy well-appointed two-roomed pub is dedicated to the worship of beer, with up to 18 handpumps dispensing quality ales, with two for cider. House beers come from Phoenix and Empire. Belgian beers are a speciality. Food is served until 4pm (3pm Sat). ⊛⊄&⇌(Central)🖵●⌐

Racecourse Hotel
Littleton Road, Lower Kersal, M7 3SE (next to River Irwell)
🕑 12-11 (midnight Fri & Sat); 12-10.30 Sun
☎ (0161) 792 1420
Oakwell Dark Mild, Barnsley Bitter Ⓗ
This riverside mock-Tudor pub, built in 1930, served the Manchester racecourse until the 1960s. Entering through revolving doors, visitors are greeted by a massive central bar. Inside, there are separate lounges and an alcove with an Art Deco fireplace, plus a separate vault. A gargantuan community pub, it is used frequently by local groups – ladies' football, student hockey and darts teams meet here – and serves the locals well. The pub won a CAMRA Best Refurbishment award in 2005. Q♿⊛⊄🖵(93,95)♣P⌐

Star Inn
2 Back Hope Street, Higher Broughton, M7 2PR (off Great Clowes St)
🕑 1.30-11 (midnight Fri & Sat) ☎ (0161) 792 4184
⊕ staronthecliff.co.uk
Star Starry Night; guests Ⓗ
Britain's first urban pub co-operative to be owned and run by its customers, this is now a brew-pub. The local brewery, Bazens, moved to the pub in 2010 and changed its name to Star Brewery. Outside, the pub looks like a Devon country inn. Inside, the pub is no less welcoming – the tiny bar vault leading to a lounge with attractive bay windows. A back room is mainly used as an overspill, in demand more often since the takeover by locals in 2009. ⊛⊄🖵(98)♣⌐

Stalybridge

Old Hunter's Tavern

51-53 Acres Lane, SK15 2JR
⏲ 12-midnight ☎ (0161) 303 9477
Robinson's Hatters, Unicorn, seasonal beers Ⓗ
A true local, this splendid street-corner pub, full of character, appeals to all. The brass poles with their circular shelves for standing drinkers are an unusual feature and complement the eye-catching brass-work in the pub. The decorative bar is also impressive. Outside, there is a pavement patio and a covered area for smokers. The licensees often organise activities and events for their locals. Food is not served at weekends. ❀◖⇌🚌♣P⁓

Stalybridge Labour Club ✔

Acres Lane, SK15 2JR
⏲ 12-4 (4.30 Sat & Sun), 7.30-11 ☎ (0161) 338 4796
Beer range varies Ⓗ
Here is a club that is truly enthusiastic about beer. Two cask ales are available, often three at weekends, generally chosen from members' recommendations. A classic car club meets fortnightly; other regular events include line dancing and jiving sessions. The large function room is available to hire (and catering can be arranged). The games room has a full-sized billiard table. A copy of this Guide or a CAMRA membership card will secure entry. ♿⇌🚌♣P

Stalybridge Station Refreshment Rooms (Buffet Bar) ☆

Rassbottom Street, SK15 1RF (Platform 1)
⏲ 10-11; 12-10.30 Sun ☎ (0161) 303 0007 🌐 buffetbar.org
Boddingtons Bitter; Flowers IPA; guest beers Ⓗ
Nobody minds delayed or missed trains at Stalybridge. This institution for educated drinkers serves an ever-changing range of up to nine cask beers, usually from micros, plus often rare brews. Foreign bottled beers are also available. These can be enjoyed in convivial Victorian splendour by the roaring fire, or outside watching the world and the trains go by. The conservatory adds to the charm and character of this gem. A folk club plays on Saturday, quiz night is Monday.
⛰Q❀◖◗⊟♿⇌🚌●P⁓

Stockport

Arden Arms ★

23 Millgate, SK1 2LX (jct Corporation St)
⏲ 12-11 ☎ (0161) 480 2185 🌐 arden-arms.co.uk
Robinson's Hatters, Unicorn, Double Hop Ⓗ**, Old Tom** Ⓖ**, seasonal beers** Ⓗ
Grade II-listed and on CAMRA's National Inventory of Historic Pub Interiors, the Arden's distinctive curved, glazed bar, its hidden snug, chandeliers and grandfather clock conjure up a Victorian ambience. Conveniently close to Stockport's historic market, the place is abuzz at lunchtimes, but more intimate in the evenings. The cellars, a former mortuary, retain body niches in their walls. A beautiful courtyard shows off the old stables and outbuildings. Voted CAMRA Branch Pub of the Year in 2009, this is an unmissable gem.
⛰🛏❀◖⊟🚌(300,384)♣⁓

Armoury

31 Shaw Heath, SK3 8BD (on B5465, jct Greek St)
⏲ 10.30-midnight (2am Fri & Sat); 11-midnight Sun
☎ (0161) 477 3711
Robinson's Hatters, Unicorn, Old Tom, seasonal beers Ⓗ
Comfortable, recently refurbished multi-roomed local with a strong community involvement. It caters for a varied clientele from sports watchers to darts teams (with two leagues often playing on the same night) to quiet bookworms alike. Excellent well-priced food from a varied menu is now available (served 12-4pm), with efficient, friendly service. Handy for the train station and football ground to boot, outside is a pleasant suntrap of a beer garden. CAMRA Branch Pub of the Year 2007 runner-up. Q❀◖⊟⇌🚌(310,369)♣⁓

Crown

154 Heaton Lane, SK4 1AR (jct King Street West under viaduct)
⏲ 12-11 (10.30 Sun) ☎ (0161) 480 5850
🌐 thecrowninn.uk.com
Beer range varies Ⓗ
CAMRA National Pub of the Year 2009 runner-up, the Crown is a busy pub, especially in the evenings. It offers around 16 ever-changing beers – with helpful and knowledgable staff to advise those confused by the choice. Pictish and Copper Dragon are regulars, and there is usually a mild, stout/porter and a craft cider. Four rooms radiate from the busy bar: two compact snugs, a large lounge and a stand-up bar. Food is served until 3pm weekdays. Live music is a feature, with the rear yard often showcasing local bands at the weekend. A real gem. ⛰❀◖⊟⇌🚌(192)♣●⁓

Magnet 🏆

51 Wellington Road North, SK4 1HJ (A6 jct Duke St)
⏲ 4 (12 Thu-Sun)-11 ☎ (0161) 429 6287
🌐 themagnetfreehouse.com
Beer range varies Ⓗ
Once a failing keg pub, the Magnet was rescued then renovated to become CAMRA Branch Pub of the Year 2011. It boasts 14 handpumps for beer and a draught cider. A large foreign bottled range completes the now rosy picture. It has a bustling vault to the left, leading to a lower pool room, and a series of rooms separated by arched doorways on the right. Monday cheese nights are always popular. The pub is home to the Cellar Rat Brewery.
⛰Q❀⊟🚌(22,192)♣●P⁓

Olde Vic

1 Chatham Street, SK3 9ED (jct of Shaw Heath)
⏲ closed Mon; 5 (7 Sat)-late (last entry 10.15); 1-10.30 Sun
☎ (0161) 480 2410 🌐 yeoldevic.com
Beer range varies Ⓗ
This quirky but extremely well-run free house was the first Stockport pub to offer changing guest beers, and continues to do the business to this day. The beers come from micros near and far, and the guest cider often comes from a smaller maker. Larger-than-life landlord Steve runs a tight ship (strictly no swearing) where conversation and banter are the order of the day. Immerse yourself in the atmosphere during Steve's famous quiz.
⛰❀⇌🚌(310,369)●⁓

Pineapple

159 Heaton Lane, SK4 1AQ (off A6, near viaduct)
⏲ 12-11 (10.30 Sun) ☎ (0161) 480 3221
Robinson's Hatters, Cumbria Way, Unicorn, seasonal beer Ⓗ
While this three-roomed pub in sight of Stockport's famous viaduct can be justly described as a community local in the town centre, it is

nevertheless welcoming to shoppers, office workers and visitors to the nearby Hat Works and Plaza Theatre alike. The walls of the comfortable lounges are adorned with numerous plates brought back from foreign parts by the regulars. At the rear is a more basic pool and darts room displaying an array of trophies. ✪◖≥⊟(192)♣⌐

Railway
1 Avenue Street, SK1 2BZ (jct Great Portwood St/A560)
✪ 12-11 (10.30 Sun) ☎ (0161) 429 6062
Pennine Floral Dance, Hameldon Bitter, Porter, seasonal beers; guest beers Ⓗ
Bustling, street-corner house with 11 handpumps showcasing the ranges of Pennine and Outstanding breweries, plus other guests. A changing mild and a real cider are also stocked, and a wide selection of Belgian, German and other bottled beers. CAMRA Branch Pub of the Year 2007. Note the model railway atop the bar canopy, and the amusing loco mural at the back. A bar billiards table is well-used. Q✪◖⊟(325,330)♣♦⌐

Swan with Two Necks ★
36 Princes Street, SK1 1RY
✪ 11-7 (11 Fri & Sat); 12-6 Sun ☎ (0161) 480 2341
Robinson's Hatters, Dark Hatters, Unicorn, Old Tom, seasonal beers Ⓗ
Narrow-fronted with a mock-Tudor facade, the building was bought by Robinson's in 1924. Rejuvenated by a young couple with ideas and vigour, it is impressively panelled in light oak throughout in familiar Robinson's style, with labelled doors to match. The front door leads to a vault, then the bustling bar-corridor, then a cosy snug with an attractive skylight, and at the rear a small lounge and diner. Outside is a compact, walled drinking area. Quality lunchtime meals are served weekdays. Cider is Westons Scrumpy. ✪◖⊟(300,330)♦

Strines

Sportsman
105 Strines Road, SK6 7GE (on B6101)
✪ 12-3, 5-11; 12-11 Sat & Sun ☎ (0161) 427 2888
⊕ the-sportsman-pub.co.uk
Beer range varies Ⓗ
Standing on the edge of the Goyt Valley with a great picture window giving views over the wooded countryside, a monumental fireplace accommodates log fires in winter and there is a small separate tap room. Five ever-changing guest beers, mainly from micros, are available and the landlord welcomes beer suggestions. Outside, a terrace and balcony are popular in summer and the pub is close to the Peak Forest Canal. ᴹQ✪◖≥⊟(358)♣P⌐

Summerseat

Footballers Inn Ⓛ ✪
28 Higher Summerseat, BL0 9UG
✪ 2-midnight (1am Fri & Sat); 12-midnight Sun
☎ (01204) 883363 ⊕ footballersinn.co.uk
Acorn Barnsley Bitter; Moorhouse's Black Cat, Pride of Pendle, Blond Witch; Taylor Landlord Ⓗ
Extremely welcoming, with a great ambience and friendly staff, this popular village pub has been run by the same couple for nine years. Live music is hosted on Saturday evening and quiz nights on the first and third Wednesdays of the month. WiFi

access is available, most major sporting events are screened, and dogs are welcome. A guest beer is sometimes added to the range. The East Lancashire Steam Railway is within easy walking distance. ✪≈♣P⌐

Swinton

Park Inn
135 Worsley Road, M27 5SP (A572, between A6 & A580)
✪ 11-11 ☎ (0161) 793 1568
Holt Bitter Ⓗ
A Holt's pub since 1878, the mock-Tudor facade is a more recent inter-war addition. The front and back rooms to the right of the entrance have been opened out into one large lounge, but the front vault and tiny snug are largely unaltered. The vault is popular and the serving hatch near the entrance is often populated by drinkers who prefer to stand. After recent trials of Mild and seasonal beers, this tenancy has reverted to the in-demand Bitter. ⊟⊟(12,73)♣⌐

White Horse ✪
384 Worsley Road, M27 0FH (on A572, near Moorside Rd)
✪ 12-11 (midnight Fri & Sat) ☎ (0161) 794 2404
Boddingtons Bitter; Marston's Pedigree; Wells Bombardier; guest beers Ⓗ
Swinton's oldest pub, dating back to the mid-1700s. It has been opened out inside but retains many nooks and crannies, making it a talking pub, popular with locals and families. Six different real ales are offered, the ever-changing list including beers from Everards, Thwaites and Adnams breweries. The pub hosts a Tuesday night quiz, grill club also on Tuesday, and curry on Wednesday. Food is served until 8.45pm daily. Annual themed days feature, especially for petrol heads. ✪◖♿⊟(12,26)P⌐

Tyldesley

Half Moon
115-117 Elliot Street, M29 8FL
✪ 11-4, 7-midnight; 12-midnight Sat; 12-11 Sun
☎ (01942) 883481
Holt Bitter; guest beers Ⓗ
Well-kept town-centre, two-room local popular with a clientele of all ages. The comfortable main lounge has various seating and standing areas, while the second lounge is cosy and ideal for get-togethers. In summer the outside patio area is a good place to take in the views of Winter Hill. ✪♣⌐

Mort Arms
235-237 Elliot Street, M29 8DG
✪ 12-midnight (1am Fri & Sat); 12-11 Sun ☎ (01942) 883481
Holt Mild, Bitter Ⓗ
From the facade to the interior, this popular 1930s pub is recognisable as a Holt's hostelry. The entrance has two etched doors directing you into the tap room or lounge, with a central bar serving both rooms. The tap room is a bright contrast and just how a tap room should be. A meeting place for the Tyldesley Brass Band, at the rear is a secluded patio area. ⊟♣

Uppermill

Cross Keys

Off Running Hill Gate, OL3 6LW (off A670, up Church Rd)
🌣 12-11.30 (midnight Fri & Sat) ☎ (01457) 874626
Lees Brewer's Dark, Bitter, Coronation Street, seasonal beers Ⓗ
This attractive 18th-century stone building overlooks Saddleworth Church. It has exposed beams throughout and the public bar features a stone-flagged floor and Yorkshire range. Home-cooked food, served all day, includes puddings, pies and real chips. The pub is especially busy during annual events such as the Rushcart Festival and the Road & Fell Race in August. A folk night is hosted on Wednesday. Dogs are welcome and the smoking area is heated and covered.
🏛Q🌣🌓🖢♣Pɬ

Hare & Hounds

68 High Street, OL3 6AW
🌣 11-midnight (1am Sat); 12-11 Sun ☎ (01457) 873115
Lees Bitter Ⓗ
A traditional stone inn in the centre of the village. The spacious interior has two distinct areas comprising a comfortable lounge to one side and a more open area with pool table to the other. Run by enthusiastic licensees, the friendly pub has a strong local following and welcomes dogs and well-behaved children. Two guest beers supplement the popular Lees Bitter. Monday is quiz night and the pub is home to crib and darts teams.
🚇(Greenfield)🚌(184,350)

Waggon Inn

34 High Street, OL3 6HR
🌣 11.30-11 (12.30am Fri & Sat); 12-10.30 Sun
☎ (01457) 872376 🌐 thewaggoninn.co.uk
Robinson's Unicorn, Dizzy Blond, Old Tom, seasonal beers Ⓗ
This mid-19th-century stone inn is set in a picturesque village opposite Saddleworth Museum and the Huddersfield Narrow Canal. It has a central bar, three rooms and a restaurant, plus high quality en-suite B&B. The pub is the venue for many annual events including the Whit Friday Brass Band contest, July Folk Festival and in August the Wartime Weekend and Rushcart Festival. Good home-cooked food includes senior specials and themed events (no eve meals Sun or Mon). Old Tom is available in the winter only.
Q🌣🛏🌓🅰🚇🚌(184,350)♣Pɬ

Wardley

Morning Star

520 Manchester Road, M27 9QW (opp Bagot St)
🌣 12-midnight ☎ (0161) 794 4927
Holt Mild, Bitter, seasonal beers Ⓗ
Built in 1890, this fine red-brick building is an excellent, smart and tidy community local. As you enter, the vault is to the left, with darts and TV. To the right is a small front room leading to the much larger main lounge. The three rooms are served by a central bar. For the locals there is regular live entertainment, quiz nights, darts and dominoes teams. Live sport is screened on TV.
🌣🅶🚇(Moorside)🚌(36,37)♣Pɬ

Westhoughton

Robert Shaw ✅

34-40 Market Street, BL5 3AN (200m from town hall)

🌣 8-midnight (1am Fri & Sat) ☎ (01942) 844110
Greene King Ruddles Best Bitter, Abbot Ⓗ
This large open-plan public house was formerly the Co-op. It is named after the actor who was born in Westhoughton. Wood panelling and bare brick dominate the decor in this modern Wetherspoon pub. Old photographs of the local Pretoria Pit Mine disaster that happened 100 years ago feature on the walls. The pub hosts four beer festivals a year.
Q🛏🌓🅳🚌(540)♣Pɬ

Whitefield

Eagle & Child

Higher Lane, M45 7EY (on A665, 300m from A56)
🌣 12-11 (midnight Fri & Sat)
Holt Mild, Bitter, seasonal beers Ⓗ
Detached, inspiring double-fronted pub with a floodlit bowling green and patio at the rear. Set back from the road, the existing pub dates from 1936 although the site has been used since the 1800s. This large building has a spacious lounge and public bar, both served by a central bar. A smaller room is ideal for meetings or private parties. The bowling green is superbly maintained and well-used by the pub's 11 teams. There is a covered patio for smokers.
🏛🌣🅶⊖(Besses o' th' Barn)🚌(98,135)♣Pɬ

Wigan

Anvil Ⓛ ✅

Dorning Street, WN1 1ND (next to bus station)
🌣 11-11 (10.30 Sun) ☎ (01942) 239444
🌐 allgatesbrewery.com/our_pubs/the_anvil/#
Beer range varies Ⓗ
A popular town-centre pub and winner of many local CAMRA awards – note the array of certificates. Six handpumps offer beers from the nearby AllGates Brewery plus guests. A mild is always available. Draught continental and bottled beers are also stocked. There is a beer garden to the rear and a heated, covered smoking area. Two large-screen TVs show sport.
🌣🚇(Wallgate/N.Western)🚌♣ɬ

Boulevard Ⓛ

Wallgate, WN1 1LD
🌣 2-2am (2.30am Fri & Sat); 2-midnight Sun
☎ (01942) 497165
Beer range varies Ⓗ
It is easy to miss the entrance to this surprisingly spacious basement pub. A long flight of stairs leads you down to the bar room which has a TV for sporting events, gaming machines and a juke-box. From the bar you enter a large back room where regular live music is played. Local beers and a cider are available. 🚇(Wallgate/North Western)🚌♣

Bowling Green

106 Wigan Lane, WN1 2LS
🌣 4-11; 2-1am Fri; 12-1am Sat; 12-11 Sun
☎ (01942) 519871
Beer range varies Ⓗ
This red-brick pub, built in 1904, was once used as a soup kitchen. It has an unspoilt interior with gantried bar, real fires, lots of panelling and an intact vault and lounge, plus a pool room out of the way at the back. Outside is a beer garden with a covered area for smokers. Upstairs, a function room is available to hire. The beer range includes four ever-changing guests. 🏛🌣🅶🚇🚌♣ɬ

Brocket Arms 🅛 ✅

Mesnes Road, Swinley, WN1 2DD

☻ 7am-midnight (1am Fri & Sat) ☎ (01942) 403500

Greene King Ruddles County, Abbot; Marston's Pedigree; guest beers Ⓗ

The Brocket Arms was built by brewer Peter Walker and opened by Lord Brocket in 1957. Now a Wetherlodge, the open-plan interior is spacious, light and airy, with intimate booths and flexible seating to accommodate groups of all sizes. Two conference rooms are available for hire and a patio area to the front caters for smokers. There is a Sunday carvery in addition to the usual menu. Guest beers from local micro-breweries feature. Regular charity events are held.
🏃🏵🏚🌙🍴🕭♿P⁵⁻

Millstone 🅛

67-69 Wigan Lane, WN1 2LF

☻ 12-midnight (1am Fri & Sat) ☎ (01942) 245999

Thwaites Original, seasonal beers; guest beers Ⓗ

The Millstone is a modern pub with a conservatory extension but has a traditional feel. There is a beer garden to the rear and a sheltered smoking area. Five TVs throughout the premises show sporting events. Two beers from the Thwaites range are served and usually one local ale, plus a range of bottled continental beers. The pub gets busy at weekends and when Wigan rugby and football teams are playing. 🏵⁵⁻

Royal Oak 🅛

Standishgate, WN1 1XL (on A49 N of town centre)

☻ 4-midnight; 12-1am Fri & Sat; 12-midnight Sun

☎ (01942) 323137

Beer range varies Ⓗ

The Royal Oak was built in the early-17th century and is now a listed building. It has always been a landmark pub on the town circuit due to its location on the A49 and close to Wigan centre. The multi-room interior is served by a long bar stocking a range of beers including some locals, plus foreign draught and bottled beers. Live music and food festivals are hosted. The pleasant beer garden is ideal for summer. 🏵♿⁵⁻

Tudor House

New Market Street, WN1 1SE

☻ 11-11 (1am Fri & Sat) ☎ (01942) 242190

Beer range varies Ⓗ

A former nunnery, the pub has two rooms, one with a stage and dance floor. The decor includes a mixture of haphazardly arranged furniture. There are two beer gardens with smoking areas. The pub is a favourite with students, although it is away from the main areas in Wigan usually frequented by younger people. Live acts and poetry evenings are hosted and there are two TVs and a juke-box. Local beers are served. 🏵🚆🕭⁵⁻

Woodford

Davenport Arms (Thief's Neck)

550 Chester Road, SK7 1PS (on A5102, jct Church Lane)

☻ 11-11; 12-10.30 Sun ☎ (0161) 439 2435

Robinson's Hatters, Unicorn Ⓗ**, Old Tom** Ⓟ**, seasonal beers** Ⓗ

This is the 25th consecutive year in the Guide for this unspoilt farmhouse-style pub – the licence has belonged to the same family for more than 75 years. The cosy rooms are warmed by real fires, and children are welcome at lunchtimes in the right-hand snug. Excellent food is mostly home made, with some adventurous specials. Outside, the spacious forecourt and attractive garden, set well-away from the road, are popular in summer, when impressive floral displays are on show.
🏚Q🏃🏵🌙🍴🕭🚌(157,X57)♣P⁵⁻

Worsley

Barton Arms ✅

2 Stablefold, M28 2ED (at side of Bridgewater Canal on Barton Rd)

☻ 11.30 (12 Sun)-11 ☎ (0161) 728 6157

Black Sheep Best Bitter; Taylor Landlord; Thwaites Bitter; guest beers Ⓗ

This is a 1990s new-build pub with, on the outside, a modern take on mock-Tudor, in keeping with rest of the scenic Worsley village. The pub's new ethos is for more of an accent on real ales, with around five available from the Mitchells & Butlers beer list. There is also the Ember Cask Ale Club, where customers can state a preference on whether a guest beer returns. The modern lounge serves good food until 10pm daily. Children are permitted if dining. 🏚Q🏃🏵🌙🍴🕭🚌(33,68)P⁵⁻

Bridgewater Hotel ✅

23 Barton Road, M28 2PD (on B5211 200m S of M60 jct 13)

☻ 10-11 ☎ (0161) 794 6206

Boddingtons Bitter; Greene King IPA; guest beers Ⓗ

A large, family-friendly hostelry near the Bridgewater Canal. The exterior is quite impressive and the equally smart interior radiates from the large bar out to a series of rooms and alcoves, some on a raised level. There are usually four guest beers that change regularly and come from the Punch Taverns list. Wheelchair access is via the rear car park. The emphasis here is on food, with a range of meals served until 9pm.
🏚🏵🌙♿🚌(33,68)P⁵⁻

Worthington

Crown Hotel 🅛

Platt Lane, WN1 2XF

☻ 12-11 (10.30 Sun) ☎ (08000) 686678

🌐 thecrownatworthington.co.uk

Beer range varies Ⓗ

CAMRA Greater Manchester Regional Pub of the Year and National Pub of the Year runner-up in 2009, this country inn offers seven cask beers and at least one cider dispensed from eight handpumps. High-quality, home-cooked food is served in the bar and conservatory restaurant, while a decked sun terrace at the rear has patio heaters. Regular themed evenings and mini-beer festivals are hosted, plus a yearly cider festival. There are 10 en-suite bedrooms and function rooms. Q🏵🏚🌙🕭♿P⁵⁻

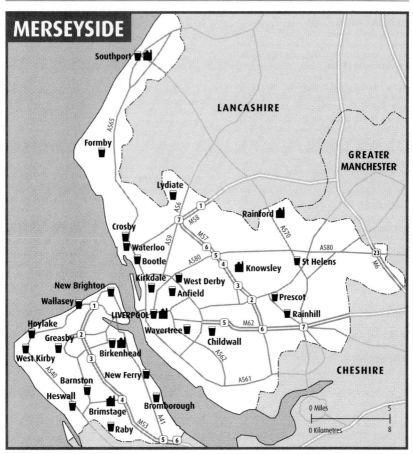

MERSEYSIDE

Barnston

Fox & Hounds ✓
107 Barnston Road, CH61 1BW (on A551)
☼ 11-11; 12-10.30 Sun ☎ (0151) 648 7685
⊕ the-fox-hounds.co.uk
Brimstage Trappers Hat; Theakston Best Bitter, Old Peculier; guest beers ℍ
Village pub with bar, lounge and snug full of bric-a-brac, clocks, flying ducks, horse brasses, local photos and other memorabilia. The lounge, converted from tea rooms, is quiet with no music or games machines. The pub retains its original character including real fires in the bar and snug. The stone courtyard is a profusion of colour in the summer. Popular for its cask ales and real lunchtime food, it offers a fish dish of the day, daily specials and traditional Sunday roasts. Local CAMRA Pub of the Year 2008. ₳Q❄⊛◑◱⬚≠⊟♣℗ᴸ

Birkenhead

Gallaghers Pub & Barbers Shop ❢ ⃞
20 Chester Street, CH41 5DQ
☼ 11-11 (midnight Fri & Sat) ☎ (0151) 649 9095
Brimstage Trappers Hat; guest beers ℍ
Genuine free house close to the famous Mersey ferries, resurrected after closure and refurbished in 2010 by a former Irish Guardsman as a unique pub with barber's shop. One long bar sports six

handpumps mainly serving beers from local breweries plus a real cider and perry. A fascinating range of memorabilia includes military hats and photographs as well as a collection of Mersey shipping images. TV sport adds to a lively atmosphere. CAMRA Wirral Pub of the Year 2011. ⊛◑⊟☐♣

Bromborough

Knockaloe Bar & Restaurant ⃞
28 Bridle Road, CH62 6AR
☼ 12-11 (midnight Fri & Sat) ☎ (0151) 328 5690
Brimstage Trappers Hat; Tetley Bitter; guest beer ℍ
Formerly the Associated Octel Social Club, the 'OC' is now a pub open to all. The club has undergone a tasteful refurbishment attracting a wide variety of

drinkers. There are extensive sports facilities, function and meeting rooms, plus a patio area. A well-attended quiz night is hosted. Local beers from Brimstage are popular – the brewery usually supplies the guest ale. Children are welcome until 9.30pm. Food is available throughout the day until 9pm (7pm Sun). ✿◑🕭≉🖵P

Crosby

Stamps Bar 🅛
4 Crown Buildings, L23 5SR
✪ 12-11 (midnight Fri & Sat) ☎ (0151) 286 2662
🌐 stampsbar.co.uk
Beer range varies 🖽
Once the local post office, this two-level bar provides a comprehensive and imaginative menu of real ales. There are usually five beers available with local breweries well represented, and one real cider, which changes regularly. Excellent food is served during the day and with live music at weekends Stamps has something for everyone. A number of local artistic and music festivals are supported throughout the year. Free internet access and WiFi is also available.
◑🕭≉(Blundellsands & Crosby)🖵●

Formby

Freshfield Hotel ✪
1a Massams Lane, Freshfield, L37 7BD (from Freshfield station turn inland into Victoria Rd and then left into Gores Lane)
✪ 12-11 (midnight Fri & Sat) ☎ (01704) 874871
Greene King IPA, Ruddles County, Abbot; Morland Original 🖽
Up to 12 beers and a cider are usually available at this popular community local. A Greene King pub, it offers a varied and interesting beer choice, with micros always well represented. A successful comedy club takes place on the first Wednesday of the month, along with regular jazz nights and charity fundraisers. This award-winning pub focuses on the quality of its product along with service. The red squirrel reserve and beach are nearby.
🚶✿◑🕭≉(Freshfield)🖵(162,165)♣●P⁵

Greasby

Irby Mill ✪
Mill Lane, CH49 3NT (on roundabout between Greasby and Irby)
✪ 12-11 (midnight Fri & Sat) ☎ (0151) 694 0194
🌐 irbymill.co.uk
Adnams Bitter; Brains The Rev James; Greene King Abbot; Wells Bombardier; guest beers 🖽
Formerly Lumsdens Café and once frequented by touring motorcyclists, the pub sits on the site of a former mill. It comprises a small, L-shaped, stone-floored bar and a lounge used mainly by diners. The pub has an excellent reputation for its home-made food. The nearby Royden Park and Thurstaston Common provide the pub with many passing hikers to supplement the strong local following. 🚶Q✿◑🕭🖵P

Heswall

Dee View Inn 🅛
Dee View Road, CH60 0DH
✪ 12-midnight (11 Sun) ☎ (0151) 342 2320

Black Sheep Best Bitter; Taylor Landlord; guest beers 🖽
Homely, traditional local built in the late 1800s offering a warm welcome. Redecorated in 2008, it has retained its character and friendly atmosphere. It sits on a hairpin bend by the war memorial and famous mirror, with views over the Dee Estuary and close to the Wirral Way path. A popular and entertaining quiz night is held on Tuesday and live music is a frequent attraction. Traditional home-cooked food is served and children are welcome if dining. ✿◑🖵♣P⁵

Johnny Pye
Pye Road, CH60 0DB (next to bus station)
✪ 11-11 (11.30 Thu; midnight Fri & Sat); 12-11 Sun
☎ (0151) 342 8215
Banks's Bitter; Marston's Burton Bitter; guest beers 🖽
Situated on the site of an old bus depot, this lively, modern pub is named after a local entrepreneur. Johnny Pye is associated with some other buildings nearby, and was responsible for starting the local bus service. A signed caricature of England's 1966 World Cup-winning goalie, Gordon Banks, adorns the bar. The pub has wide-screen TVs, a strong football following and ladies' and gents' darts teams. Children are welcome on the patio area.
✿◑🕭🖵♣P⁵

Hoylake

Ship Inn
Market Street, CH47 3BB
✪ 12-11 ☎ (0151) 632 4319
Brimstage Trappers Hat; Caledonian Deuchars IPA; Greene King Abbot; Wells Bombardier 🖽
Popular town-centre pub, first licensed in 1754 (recent testing has dated the building to 1730). Although modernised in recent years, with a single L-shaped bar area, old beams have been retained in the back lounge. Beers can include guests from local micro-breweries. Good value bar meals are served every lunchtime and in the evening (not Sat/Sun). The large, secluded garden at the rear has a pond. ✿◑≉(Hoylake/Manor Road)P

Liverpool: Anfield

Strawberry Tavern
Breckfield Road South, L6 5DR
✪ 2 (3 Wed; 1 Fri)-11; 12-10 Sat; 1-10.30 Sun
☎ (0151) 261 9364
Oakwell Bitter, Dark Mild 🖽
The Strawberry continues to supply an excellent drop of the two Oakwell standard beers. The interior is divided to give a separate games area with pool table and dartboard. Lying between Breck Road and West Derby Road, the pub provides a welcome oasis for thirsty fans visiting Liverpool football club, as well as shoppers from the nearby supermarket. ✿🕭🖵♣P⁵

Liverpool: Bootle

Merton Inn ✪
42 Merton Road, L20 3BW
✪ 8am-11 (11.30 Thu; midnight Fri & Sat)
☎ (0151) 934 7790
Greene King Ruddles Best Bitter, Abbot; guest beers 🖽
The Merton Inn was once a hotel created when two villas were combined in the 1930s. Used as a

hospital during World War II, it was converted to a pub in the 1970s. This spacious multi-level venue, with wood panelling complemented by subdued lighting, retains some of the character of its villa origins. Several abstract paintings have been commissioned depicting the local landscape. Up to 10 handpumps are available, often featuring ales from local and micro-breweries.
⊛◑♿≉(Oriel Road/New Strand)⊟P

Wild Rose ✓
2a & 1b The Triad Centre, L20 3ET
✪ 7am (8am Sat & Sun)-midnight ☎ (0151) 922 0828
Greene King Ruddles Best Bitter, Abbot; guest beers Ⓗ
An open-plan Wetherspoon situated at the base of the Triad tower block, which at 240ft dominates the skyline. With wooden panelling throughout, the bar area boasts eight handpumps and an ever-changing range of ales. The name recalls William Gladstone, MP for Liverpool, who served four terms as Prime Minister. After spending part of his childhood at nearby Seaforth, he wrote: 'I have seen wild roses growing upon the very ground that is now the centre of Bootle.'
◑♿≉(New Strand)⊟

Liverpool: Childwall

Childwall Fiveways Hotel ✓
179 Queens Drive, L15 6XS
✪ 8am-11.30 ☎ (0151) 738 2100
Greene King Ruddles Best Bitter, Abbot; guest beers Ⓗ
This large single-roomed pub opened as a Wetherspoon outlet in 2010. A former Higson's tied house, the pub is located in a leafy suburb, has good motorway links and a spacious car park. The refurbished interior is tastefully decorated with wood panelling and there is a beer garden to the rear. A popular establishment with locals, it can get very busy, especially at weekends. ⊛◑♿⊟P

Liverpool: City Centre

Augustus John Ⓛ
Peach Street, L3 5TX (off Brownlow Hill next to Blackwell's bookshop)
✪ 11.30 (12 Sat)-11; closed Sun ☎ (0151) 794 5507
⊕ liv.ac.uk/educatering/augustus_john.htm
Tetley Bitter; guest beers Ⓗ
Artist Augustus John was a lecturer at the University of Liverpool in 1901 – this pub was opened by his son and continues to be run by the university. An open-plan venue popular with students, lecturers and locals alike, up to four guest beers are available. Handpulled cider is also stocked, usually from Gwynt Y Ddraig. Pizzas are served at all times. Sport is shown on a multitude of TV screens and there is a juke-box. Closed over Christmas and New Year.
⊛♿≉(Lime St)⊖(Central)⊟(79)♠←

Baltic Fleet Ⓛ
33 Wapping, L1 8DQ
✪ 12-11 (midnight Sat); 10-10.30 Sun ☎ (0151) 709 3116
⊕ wappingbeers.co.uk
Wapping Bitter, Stout, Summer, seasonal beers; guest beers Ⓗ
Located near the Albert Dock, the building is Grade II-listed and based on a flat-iron shape, with interior decoration on a nautical theme. Five

handpumps serve beer from the Wapping brewery located in the cellar plus occasional guests from Liverpool One brewery. Good value lunches and evening meals are available, all using locally-sourced ingredients. Tunnels in the cellar have led some to speculate on a dark period in the pub's history involving smuggling and press gangs.
⚒Q◑⊞⊖(James St)⊟(500)

Belvedere Ⓛ ✓
8 Sugnall Street, L7 7EB (off Falkner Street)
✪ 12-11 (10.30 Sun) ☎ (0151) 709 0303
Beer range varies Ⓗ
A few years ago after closure, permission was granted to convert this 1830s listed building into a house. Fortunately it has now reopened as a pub and many of its original fixtures and fittings feature in the two small rooms, including some interesting glasswork. Only a mile from the city centre, it is very much a community pub and its proximity to the Philharmonic Hall makes it a popular watering hole for members of the orchestra, even mid-performance. ⚒Q⊛◑⊞≉(Lime St)⊖⊟⊡

Caledonia Ⓛ
22 Caledonia Street, L7 7DX (on corner of Catherine St behind Philharmonic Hall)
✪ 12-11 (midnight Fri & Sat) ☎ (0151) 708 0235
Taylor Golden Best; guest beers Ⓗ
Situated at the back of the Philharmonic Hall in the Georgian Quarter of the city, this pub has been tastefully refurbished with traditional wooden floorboards and a wooden bar. A one-room pub on two levels, there is a total of four handpumps offering a wide selection of ever-changing guest ales. Music is a focal point, with open mike nights every Thursday evening, jazz on Friday (the house band performs fortnightly) and blues every other Sunday. ⊖(Central)⊟

Cracke Ⓛ
13 Rice Street, L1 9BB (off Hope St near Philharmonic Hall)
✪ 12-11.30 (midnight Fri & Sat) ☎ (0151) 709 4171
Thwaites Original; guest beers Ⓗ
A multi-roomed back-street pub with two bars, the Cracke is full of character and steeped in history – it is claimed that John Lennon used to drink here in his days as an art student. One room bears the name 'The War Office' – a plaque on the wall stating that between 1899 and 1902 this was the place where the locals discussed the Boer War. Ales on offer include a wide range from micro-breweries and up to three LocAles.
⊛◑≉(Lime St)⊖(Central)⊟(86)♠

Dispensary Ⓛ
87 Renshaw Street, L1 2SP
✪ 12-11 (midnight Fri & Sat) ☎ (0151) 709 2180
Cains Bitter; George Wright Mild; guest beers Ⓗ
An excellent city-centre hostelry previously called The Grapes. The large bar features prominently in this single room pub, with seven handpumps dispensing guest beers from local and other interesting micro-breweries. The licensee prides himself on his cellar work, which is reflected in the beer quality on offer. Real ales increase to 10 during mini beer festivals, which are always very popular. Local CAMRA Pub of the Year 2010.
≉(Lime St)⊖(Central)⊟

Doctor Duncan's 🅛

St John's House, St John's Lane, L1 1HF (opp St George's Gardens)

🕭 11.30 (11 Sun)-11 ☎ (0151) 709 5100

Cains IPA, Bitter, FA, seasonal beers Ⓗ

A flagship Cains pub, Doctor Duncan's is named after the first chief medical officer of health to be appointed in Britain, who was also a campaigner against poor living conditions in Liverpool during the Victorian era. The interior is split into four distinct rooms, including a magnificent tiled room with mosaic floor and fireplace that is used during the winter months. The full range of Cains beers is on offer as well as up to two guests.

🏨🏵🗗🕭⇌(Lime St)⊖(Lime St)🚃⬩—

Fall Well ✅

St Johns Way, L1 1LS

🕭 7am-11.30 (midnight Fri); 8am-midnight Sat; 8am-11.30 Sun ☎ (0151) 705 2050

Greene King Ruddles County, Abbot; guest beers Ⓗ

Previously a pet shop but now a Wetherspoon's, the pub is situated in a pedestrianised shopping area handy for the Playhouse, Royal Court and bus stops. The Fall Well was once an important source of water for the area and fed the fountain and garden of William Roe, a merchant who gave his name to Roe Street. The well stood on the site of the neighbouring Royal Court. Seasonal beer festivals are hosted.

🏵🕭🗗🕭⇌(Lime St)⊖(Lime St)🚃⬩—

Fly in the Loaf ✅

13 Hardman Street, L1 9AS

🕭 11-11 (midnight Fri & Sat) ☎ (0151) 708 0817

Okells Bitter; guest beers Ⓗ

Housed in what was once Kirkland's bakery, the pub gets its name from the old slogan 'no flies in the loaf'. Owned by the Isle of Man brewer Okells, handpumps dispense the brewery's own beers, as well as up to seven guests often from micros. There is also a good range of imported bottled beers on offer. Upstairs, a function room has its own handpumps. Large TV screens broadcast Sky Sports. Food is served until 7pm (5pm Sun).

🕭🗗🕭⇌(Lime St)⊖(Central)🚃⬩—

Globe ✅

17 Cases Street, L1 1HW (opp Liverpool Central Station)

🕭 11 (10 Sat)-11; 12-10.30 Sun ☎ (0151) 707 0067

Black Sheep Best Bitter; Cains Bitter; guest beers Ⓗ

Small, traditional two-roomed local in the city centre, close to railway stations and the main shopping area. A lively pub, it is popular with locals and visitors to the city. Drinkers need to be aware of the unique sloping floor that leads through to a quiet back room, which has a brass plaque commemorating the inaugural meeting of the Merseyside branch of CAMRA, held here in 1974.

⇌(Lime St)⊖(Central)🚃

Grapes 🅛

60 Roscoe Street, L1 9DW

🕭 3.30-1am (2am Thu-Sat) ☎ (0151) 709 3977

⊕ thegrapesliverpool.co.uk

Beer range varies Ⓗ

Traditional single-room, street-corner hostelry. Built around 1804 on Roscoe Street, the pub has been expanded over the years and now incorporates two adjoining houses on Knight Street. The focal point is the wooden bar, boasting six handpumps. Erotic artwork in wood adorns the walls. At the rear is a cosy beer garden decorated

with planters. The exterior of the pub bears the sign 'Mellors noted wines and spirits'. Live music is a regular feature, with jazz every Sunday night.

🏵⇌(Lime St)⊖(Lime St)🚃

Lady of Mann

19 Dale Street, L2 2EZ

🕭 12-11 ☎ (0151) 236 5556

Okells Bitter; guest beers Ⓗ

The Lady of Mann, named after the eponymous Manx ferry, is owned, like Thomas Rigby's, by Okells Isle of Man brewery and both premises share a large outside drinking area. Essentially open plan, with a single bar located in a separate smaller drinking area, it is approached from the courtyard via a flight of steps. Cold food is available at all times. The large rear room can be booked for events. Q🏵🕭▶⊖(Moorfields)🚃

Lion Tavern ☆ 🅛 ✅

67 Moorfields, L2 2BP

🕭 11-11; 12-11 Sun ☎ (0151) 236 1734 ⊕ liontavern.com

Caledonian Deuchars IPA; Copper Dragon Golden Pippin; Moorhouse's Pride of Pendle; Young's Bitter; guest beers Ⓗ

The Lion is named after the locomotive that worked the Liverpool to Manchester railway and features exquisite artwork, etched and stained glass and most notably a recently restored cupola in the rear lounge, which is why it is Grade II-listed and one of Britain's Real Heritage Pubs. The pub attracts a varied clientele and hosts regular society meetings and events including occasional Meet the Brewer evenings. Food is excellent value, with pork pies a speciality. 🕭🗗🕭⊖(Moorfields)🚃(26)

Monro

92 Duke Street, L1 5AG

🕭 12-11.30 (1am Fri & Sat); 12-9.30 Sun ☎ (0151) 707 9933

⊕ themonro.com

Jennings Cumberland Ale; guest beers Ⓗ

A Grade II-listed building, the Monro takes its name from the 19th-century three-masted sailing ship James Monro and the fifth President of the United States James Monroe (1817-1825). The interior has two main dining areas and a small bar with a large fireplace that is used in the winter months. Renowned for excellent food, there are four cask ales on offer from the Marston's range. Food attractions are numerous and include a monthly pudding club. 🕭▶⊖(Central)🚃(82)⬩—

Peter Kavanagh's ★

2-6 Egerton Street, L8 7LY (off Catharine St)

🕭 12-midnight (1am Fri & Sat) ☎ (0151) 709 3443

Greene King Abbot; guest beers Ⓗ

Situated in the Georgian area of Liverpool, this splendid back-street local is a gem and features in CAMRA's National Inventory of Historic Pub Interiors. It boasts stained glass windows with wooden shutters, and two snugs with wooden benches – note the carved armrests, allegedly caricatures of the politically incorrect Peter Kavanagh. There are also murals by Eric Robinson, which are thought to have been commissioned to cover a debt. Up to four rotating guest beers are offered. Q🚃(86)

Philharmonic ★ ✅

36 Hope Street, L1 9BX

🕭 10-11 (midnight Fri & Sat) ☎ (0151) 707 2837

Cains Bitter; guest beers Ⓗ

popular with hikers and bikers. An extensive menu is available for traditional meals as well as Thai food. Other services include a takeaway, car wash and breakfasts (8-11am). ❀❍▶ᵴ♠🖃(48)P↻

Binham

Chequers Inn 🟦

Front Street, NR21 0AL (in centre of village 2 miles S of Stiffkey) TF983396

❀ 11.30-2.30, 6-11; 12-2.30, 7-11 Sun ☎ (01328) 830297
⊕ binhamchequers.co.uk

Front Street Binham Cheer; guest beers 🅗

The Chequers is a short walk from English Heritage's historic and picturesque Binham Priory. The single-room bar has welcoming roaring fires in winter. The pub is the home of the Front Street micro-brewery, with a large range of ales, three of which are always available. There is also an extensive range of Belgian beers, bottled as well as on draught. Excellent meals are served at all sessions. ▲❀❍▶ᵴ🖃(46)P↻

Blakeney

King's Arms

Westgate Street, NR25 7NQ (nr Blakeney harbour) TG026440

❀ 11-11; 12-10.30 Sun ☎ (01263) 740341

Adnams Bitter 🅖; **Greene King Old Speckled Hen; Marston's Pedigree; guest beers** 🅗

Situated close to the harbour in one of Norfolk's most picturesque coastal villages, this old building was originally three fishermen's cottages, with an interior comprising a series of interconnecting rooms. Note the plaque half-way up the wall denoting the 1953 flood level. Real ales here are dispensed by handpump and gravity. There is a patio and large garden to the side of the pub. Children and dogs are welcome and food is served all day. En-suite accommodation is available. ▲Q❀🛏❍▶♠🖃(Coasthopper)P

Brancaster Staithe

Jolly Sailors

Main Road, PE31 8BJ

❀ 11-11; 12-10.30 Sun ☎ (01485) 210314
⊕ jollysailorsbrancaster.co.uk

Adnams Bitter; Woodforde's Wherry; guest beer 🅗

A cosy inn with several small drinking areas and two dining-rooms. Beers are available from the pub's own brewery (not on site) which produces a varying range of ales. There is regular live music in the winter and a beer festival in June. Food offerings include stone-baked pizza, with the oven visible from the bar. Only a short walk to Brancaster harbour and the Norfolk coast path. ▲Q❀❍▶(Coasthopper)P↻

Broome

Artichoke

162 Yarmouth Road, NR35 2NZ (just off A143) TM352915

❀ closed Mon; 12-11 (midnight Fri & Sat) ☎ (01986) 893325
⊕ theartichokeatbroome.co.uk

Adnams Bitter 🅗, **Broadside** 🅖; **Elgood's Black Dog** 🅗; **guest beers** 🅗/🅖

Just off the A143, this early 19th-century inn was the home of the long-defunct Crowfoot Brewery. Flagstones, wooden floors and a large fireplace

with a real fire give a rural ambience to this friendly establishment. Home-cooked food is available, served in the bar, dining room or garden. A range of up to eight beers is offered, with an emphasis on local breweries, with some served by gravity from a tap room. The pub also boasts a range of around 70 malt whiskies. Local CAMRA Pub of the Year 2009. ▲Q❀❍▶♠🖃(580,588)P↻

Burnham Thorpe

Lord Nelson

Walsingham Road, PE31 8HN (off B1355)

❀ 12-11 (12-3, 6-11 winter); 12-10.30 Sun
☎ (01328) 738241 ⊕ nelsonslocal.co.uk

Greene King Abbot; Woodforde's Wherry 🅖

A 17th-century pub in the village of Nelson's birth, frequented by the local hero when he had no ship from 1786 to 1793. You can even sit on the same high-backed settle where he spent many hours. The dispense is all by gravity from a traditional tap room. The modern world is catered for by an extensive menu and occasional live bands. Guided tours of the village are available at weekends in summer. There is a Nelson memorabilia shop. ▲Q❀❍▶♠♣P↻

Burston

Crown Inn 🟦

Crown Green, IP22 5TW (2 miles W of A140) TM138834

❀ 12-11 (10.30 Sun) ☎ (01379) 741257
⊕ burstoncrown.com

Adnams Bitter; Greene King Abbot 🅖; **guest beer** 🅗

Lovely 16th-century Grade II-listed pub with exposed beams, deep sofas and a blazing fire in the huge inglenook fireplace in the right-hand bar. The two regular ales are served straight from the cask. The guest beers on handpump come from East Anglian breweries including Elmtree. A small restaurant serves locally-sourced, freshly-cooked food (no food Sun eve). Live music takes place on alternate Sunday evenings. Families are welcome. ▲❀❍▶ᵴ🖃P↻

Catfield

Crown Inn

The Street, NR29 5AA TG387218

❀ closed Mon; 12-2.30, 7-11; 12-3, 7-midnight Sat; 12-3, 7-10.30 Sun ☎ (01692) 580128 ⊕ thecatfieldcrown.co.uk

Greene King IPA; guest beer 🅗

Cosy, tastefully furnished, 300-year-old traditional village inn with a real fire in winter. The guest beer range changes regularly and often includes St Austell Tribute. The landlord is also the chef and excellent food, including Italian dishes, is a speciality. Fresh local ingredients are used where possible. There is a separate function/dining-room and a secluded garden in summer. En-suite accommodation is in a detached converted hall that was once the doctor's surgery. Close to the Broads and north Norfolk coast. ▲Q❀🛏❍▶🖃(12)P

Chedgrave

White Horse ✔

5 Norwich Road, NR14 6ND (just off A146) TM360993

❀ 12-11 ☎ (01508) 520250 ⊕ whitehorsechedgrave.co.uk

Taylor Landlord; guest beers 🅗

A genuinely welcoming family-friendly pub with an open-plan interior that includes a log fire in winter. A changing list of up to four guest beers is available. The separate restaurant serves meals every lunchtime and evening, with roasts all day Sunday. Beer festivals are staged in April and October each year and and there is occasional live music plus other themed events. The building is wheelchair-friendly. Pub games including backgammon and chess are played and in summer the bowls green is busy. Outside, there is a covered smoking area with tables. ⋈❀◐⌂&⊟(X2)♣P⅃

Colton

Ugly Bug Inn ⌷

High House Farm Lane, NR9 5DG (2 miles S of A47. Turn off on roundabout on Honingham Road) TG104908
⏱ 12-2.30 (not Tue), 5-10.30; 12-3, 6-10 Sun
☎ (01603) 880794 ⊕ uglybuginn.co.uk
Beeston Worth the Wait; Humpty Dumpty Cheltenham Flyer Ⓗ
Large remote rural pub with extensive gardens, six en-suite bedrooms and a spacious dining room. The single bar has exposed beams and comfortable seating. The two regular ales are from the local Humpty Dumpty and Beeston micro-breweries, and a guest beer, usually from East Anglia, is added in summer. The pub is closed Tuesday lunchtime. Live jazz takes place monthly. ❀⇐◐&P

Cromer

Red Lion

Brook Street, NR27 9HD (on top of cliffs above pier and lifeboat station near parish church)
⏱ 10-11 (10.30 Sun) ☎ (01263) 514964
⊕ redlion-cromer.co.uk
Adnams Bitter; Woodforde's Wherry; guest beers Ⓗ
A Victorian pub situated at the top of the cliff, with commanding views of the promenade, sea and Cromer pier. The interior comprises two bars: one, a traditional Edwardian bar with mahogany panels, the other with flint and brick walls adorned with photographs of Cromer's maritime past. The guest beers usually come from local micro-breweries. There is also the Galleons Restaurant offering an extensive menu. ⇐◐&▲⇌⊟(Coasthopper)♣P

Dersingham

Coach & Horses

77 Manor Road, PE31 6LN
⏱ 12-midnight (11 Sun) ☎ (01485) 540391
⊕ norfolkinns.co.uk/coachhorse
Woodforde's Wherry; guest beers Ⓗ
Busy 19th-century carrstone pub close to Sandringham House. Entertainment includes quiz nights, bingo, poker games and live music on Friday night and some Sundays. It is a popular pub for food, enjoyed by locals as well as tourists. There is a large beer garden including a children's play area, music stand, old red phone box and heated smoking shelter. Three en-suite rooms are available to let. A beer festival takes place in September, with around 20 real ales and some cider. ⋈Q❀⇐◐⊞▲⊟(41A)P⅃

Docking

Railway Inn

Station Road, PE31 8LY

⏱ 12-11 ☎ (01485) 518620
Buffy's Bitter; guest beers Ⓗ
Lovely cosy pub situated at one end of the village near the old railway house and adjacent to the disused railway line. A railway theme is continued inside including railway pictures and a high-level working model train. The main bar boasts three handpumps, two dispensing different guest beers. Another bar has lounge settees and a small dining area. The main restaurant is a large conservatory built on the side, serving locally-produced food. ⋈⌛❀◐⊞&♣P⅃

Downham Market

Crown Hotel

12 Bridge Street, PE38 9DH
⏱ 9.30 (11 Sun)-11 ☎ (01366) 382322
Adnams Bitter; Greene King IPA, Abbot; Woodforde's Wherry; guest beers Ⓗ
A 17th-century coaching inn found at the heart of the old town near the famous town clock. You enter through a room with a lovely staircase. The bar has a beamed ceiling, a large fireplace and five handpumps with four regular beers and one guest. It features a restaurant and a separate function room that caters for parties and weddings. Always busy, there is plenty of outside seating starting at the old coaching arch. ⋈Q⌛❀⇐◐⇌⊟P⅃

Railway Arms ⌷

Downham Market Railway Station, PE38 9EN
⏱ 10am-5.30 (10.30 Thu & Fri); 10-12.10, 4-10.30 Sat; 12-2.30 Sun ☎ (01366) 386636
Beer range varies Ⓗ
A unique experience, the Railway is shoehorned into the waiting rooms at Downham rail station. All beers are on gravity; the range often features Elgood's ales but a good variety is sourced from further afield. Traditional cider comes from Cambridgeshire's Pickled Pig. The pub still acts as a waiting room and has a small model railway running around at ceiling height. Light snacks made from locally-sourced ingredients are available. Make sure you check out the library and record collection. ⋈⇌♣●

White Hart ⌷

58 Bridge Street, PE38 9DH
⏱ 11-midnight (1am Fri & Sat); 12-midnight Sun ☎ (01366) 387720
Elgood's Black Dog; guest beers Ⓗ
A typical basic pub in an 18th-century building, the White Hart has two large bars, one featuring a pool table. The excellent Elgood's Black Dog is always on, plus a range of guests. The pub also provides a good stop-off between the two other Guide pubs in Downham and is a short walk from the railway station. ⋈❀⇐⇌⊟♣P⅃

Earsham

Queen's Head ⌷

Station Road, NR35 2TS (turn left off A143 signed to Earsham) TM321891
⏱ 12-11 (10.30 Sun) ☎ (01986) 892623
Waveney East Coast Mild, Lightweight; guest beer Ⓗ
Seventeenth-century pub with a large front garden overlooking the village green. The main bar has a flagstone floor, wooden beams and a large fireplace with a roaring fire in winter. Home to the

Waveney Brewing Co, two Waveney beers are usually on offer along with a seasonal, plus a guest from another brewer. Food is served at lunchtime (not Mon and Tue). Two of the Waveney seasonals feature unusual fruit flavourings, medlar and bullace, and are highly recommended.
🏚️❀◑➡(580)♣P⤶

East Dereham

George Hotel
Swaffham Road, NR19 2AZ (in centre of town near war memorial)
🕽 11-11 (11.30 Fri & Sat); 12-10.30 Sun ☎ (01362) 696801
🌐 lottiesrestaurant.co.uk
Adnams Bitter, Broadside; Fuller's London Pride; Woodforde's Wherry; guest beer Ⓗ
Well-appointed 18th-century coaching inn just to the north end of the market place of this busy mid-Norfolk town. The comfortable bar has wood panelling, leather chairs and pictures of local historic interest. There is an air-conditioned conservatory with disabled access, a heated outdoor patio lined with bamboo for drinkers, and a separate smokers' corner. The guest beer varies but mainly comes from a local brewery. Food is available lunchtimes and evenings, all day on Sunday. 🏚️🍴❀◑➡🖂⤶(X1)P⤶

Edgefield

Pigs
Norwich Road, NR24 2RL (on B1149) TG098343
🕽 11-3, 6-11; 12-10 ☎ (01263) 587634
🌐 thepigs.org.uk
Adnams Bitter, Broadside; Greene King Abbot; Woodforde's Wherry; Wolf Old Spot; guest beer Ⓖ
Multi-award-winning pub with its own local news sheet, The Grunter, and famed for its barter system where fresh produce can be exchanged for beer. Enter through the foyer displaying fresh local produce for sale. Beer is served by gravity from casks behind the bar. There is a room to the left, a restaurant area to the right and outdoor seating areas to the front and rear. The pub can become busy during peak times. Accommodation is available. 🏚️🍴❀◑➡🖂♣P⤶

Elsing

Mermaid Inn
Church Street, NR20 3EA (opp church) TG053165
🕽 12-3, 7 (6 Sat)-11; 12-3, 6.30-10.30 Sun
☎ (01362) 637640
Adnams Broadside; Wolf Golden Jackal; Woodforde's Wherry; guest beers Ⓖ
A 17th-century pub opposite the village church. The large single room has a log-burning fire at one end and a pool table at the other. There is also a restaurant. Cask ales sold here are mainly from local brewers and are dispensed by gravity. Food is served every lunchtime except Monday, and every evening. The pub features an interesting range of pies, with the current specials listed on the Pie Chart on the bar wall. 🏚️❀◑⟶AP⤶

Geldeston

Locks Inn
Locks Lane, NR34 0HW (through village centre, turn left into Station Rd, after 300m turn left onto track across marshes) TM390908

🕽 12-midnight Fri & Sat and summer; 5-midnight (closed Mon & Tue) winter; 12-midnight (7 winter) Sun
☎ (01508) 518414 🌐 geldeston.locks.co.uk
Green Jack Canary Pale Ale, Orange Wheat Beer, Grasshopper, Gone Fishing, seasonal beers; guest beers Ⓗ
Originally a mill-keeper's cottage, there has been a pub on this site since the 17th century. It is located on the banks of the River Waveney and accessed by a long, meandering track between dykes and marshes. The small main bar, with low ceiling beams and clay pamment floor, retains an authentic, welcoming feel, with the candlelight adding to the atmosphere. Modern extensions allow it to maintain an active live music scene. Owned by the Green Jack Brewery, its range of beers is supplemented by guests and a selection of real ciders and perries. 🏚️Q🍴❀◑➡♣⤶P

Gorleston-on-Sea

Mariners Compass
21 Middleton Road, NR31 7AJ
🕽 9.30am-1am (2.30am Fri & Sat); 10-midnight Sun
☎ (01493) 659494
Greene King IPA; guest beers Ⓗ
On the town route to Lowestoft, this large two-bar pub was opened in the 1930s and fitted out in Brewers Tudor style. It was saved from demolition in 2008 and since then has become one of the major real ale venues for the area. It retains many of its original fittings inside. The pub has two defined drinking areas, the real ale bar occupying the old saloon area. Beers are always changing and invariably interesting. Good value bar snacks are always available. ❀◑➡🖂♣⤶P⤶🍺

New Entertainer
80 Pier Plain, NR31 6PG (off Englands Lane)
🕽 12-11 ☎ (01493) 441643
Greene King IPA; guest beers Ⓗ
Traditional street-corner local with an interesting design and layout including a triangular-shaped corner. There is always a fine choice of beers on offer, including at least six guests, many coming from local brewers. This dedicated free house is only a short walk from the seafront, and is well worth seeking out, though the signposting is not always obvious. Some Belgian beers are also available. A pool table and dartboard are available. Q🖂♣⤶

Great Cressingham

Windmill Inn
Water End, IP25 6NN (off A1065 S of Swaffham) TF846019
🕽 9-11 ☎ (01760) 756232 🌐 oldewindmillinn.co.uk
Adnams Bitter, Broadside; Greene King IPA; Hancock's Windy Miller Ⓗ**; guest beers** Ⓗ/Ⓖ
A maze-like pub with every type of environment you could wish for, where you can sit next to the fire in or the sunshine in a conservatory. A good choice of real ales includes the house beer, Windy Miller by Hancock's, while guest beers are rotated weekly. A new feature is real cider on the bar. Thirty different malt whiskies are stocked. The pub offers live music and a talent night. Good home-cooked food is available. A perfect stop-off on the Peddars Way. 🏚️Q🍴❀◑➡🖂A♣⤶P⤶

Great Massingham

Dabbling Duck ▼
11 Abbey Road, PE32 2HN
☼ 12-11 (10.30 Sun) ☎ (01485) 520827
⊕ thedabblingduck.co.uk
Adnams Broadside; Beeston Worth the Wait; Greene King IPA; Woodforde's Wherry; guest beers Ⓗ
Situated between two duck ponds in an attractive village, the pub features a large bar area as well as a separate restaurant for the many customers attracted by the food. However, there is ample room for those who just wish to try one of the five or six beers on offer. The extensive garden is used for the occasional beer festival, and in winter there is a roaring fire. See the wall map for details of local walks. Norfolk CAMRA Branch Pub of the Year for 2011. ▨✿✦◐⏦⊟(48)♣P⅃

Great Yarmouth

Mariners Tavern Ⓛ
69 Howard Street South, NR30 1LN (between harbour and market place, 20m from police station)
☼ 11-11 (1am Fri-Sat); 12-11 Sun ☎ (01493) 332299
Elgood's Mariners Ale; Greene King IPA, Abbot; guest beers Ⓗ
Voted local CAMRA Branch Pub of the Year 2010, this former Lacons pub is a family-run, friendly community local. With a pleasant red brick-and-flint exterior, the pub comprises a main bar and a smaller cider bar. Most of the seven guest ales come from local micros, and there is a selection of foreign beers available. It hosts a number of themed beer festivals during the year, including one to coincide with the Yarmouth maritime weekend in September.
▨⏦✿◐A⇌⊟(X1)♣♠⅃☐

Oliver Twist Ⓛ
62-63 North Market Road, NR30 2DX (to NE of Market Gates complex)
☼ 12-11 (1am Sat) ☎ (07768) 120714
Blackfriars Bitter, Old Habit; guest beer Ⓗ
This is a cosy street-corner pub that has been extended over the years. Beers from Blackfriars Brewery are always available. The landlord is a music fan and scooter aficionado, as is evident from the large original juke-box with more than 2,000 tunes to choose from and the interesting display cabinet of memorabilia. Live music features rock 'n' roll and skiffle. A range of local ciders is available alongside the real ales.
⏦✿◐&⇌(Yarmouth Vauxhall)⊟♣♠⅃☐

St John's Head Ⓛ
58 North Quay, NR30 1JB
☼ 12-midnight (10.30 Sun) ☎ (01493) 843443
Elgood's Cambridge Bitter; guest beers Ⓗ
Now a free house, this former Lacons Brewery pub is reputed to be built on land confiscated from monks of the Carmelite Order. It has a traditional flintstone facade and oval windows at the front. Four real ales include the Elgood's regular plus three changing guests. A single bar houses a large TV screen for live sport, which is popular here. There is a pool table in one area, plus a smoking shelter, which is minimalist but heated.
✿&⇌(Yarmouth Vauxhall)⊟♣P⅃

Heacham

Fox & Hounds Ⓛ
22 Station Road, PE31 7EX
☼ 12-11 (10.30 Sun) ☎ (01485) 570345
Adnams Broadside; guest beers Ⓗ
Popular with locals and visitors, this is the home of the Fox Brewery and was CAMRA's West Norfolk Branch Pub of the Year 2008. There are eight beers on offer including a selection from Fox whose bottled beers are also available plus a range of imported beers. The restaurant offers beer recommendations to match the cuisine. There is live music on Tuesday evening (mainly blues) and a quiz on Thursday. Beer festivals are hosted throughout the year. Nice posh loos.
▨✿◐&⊟(40,41)♣P⅃

Hempton

Bell
The Green, NR21 7LG (turn by the Fakenham Garden Centre off the A1065) TF913293
☼ 11-2.30 (not Tue), 5-midnight; 11-midnight Sat; 12-4, 7-midnight Sun ☎ (01328) 864579 ⊕ hemptonbell.co.uk
John Smith's Bitter; Woodforde's Wherry; guest beer Ⓗ
In a small village on the outskirts of Fakenham, this pub has been at the centre of the village community for around 400 years. A rare example of a rural pub that does not serve food, the Bell is friendly, very traditional, and retains a two-bar layout little altered since the early 1970s. Pub games including dominoes, crib and darts are popular – you'll be welcome to get involved. The guest beer is always changing and usually comes from a micro or independent brewery. ◐P⅃

Hethersett

King's Head Ⓛ
36 Norwich Road, NR9 3DD (just off the B1172) TG154045
☼ 11-11 (midnight Fri & Sat) ☎ (01603) 810206
⊕ kingsheadhethersett.co.uk
Adnams Bitter; Fuller's London Pride; Taylor Golden Best; guest beer Ⓗ
In this 18th-century, two-roomed country pub the comfortable saloon bar boasts a large inglenook fireplace with a roaring fire in winter and a suit of armour. The public bar is a gem, unchanged for the past 50 years. The guest beer comes from the Woodforde's range and changes on a regular basis. There is a separate dining-room. Food is served lunchtimes and evenings Monday to Wednesday, all day Thursday to Saturday, and Sunday lunchtime. ▨✿◐⏦⅃

Heydon

Earle Arms Ⓛ
The Green, NR11 6AD (W of B1149, opp village green) TG113273
☼ closed Mon; 12-3, 6-11; 12-10.30 Sun ☎ (01263) 587376
⊕ earlearms.vpweb.co.uk
Adnams Bitter; Panther Red; Woodforde's Wherry Ⓗ
Lovely old coaching inn in the centre of this picture-postcard village opposite the green. The village, which is privately owned, has often been used as a film location. The bar is mainly candlelit, with a welcoming atmosphere and a log fire in winter; it also has an interesting collection of

horse-racing memorabilia. The food is locally sourced, cooked to order and of the highest quality. The restaurant is separate, and booking is advisable. Superb pub, not to be missed.
♨❀◐◑●P

Hockering

Victoria

The Street, NR20 3HL (just off A47) TF863355
⏲ 1 (12 Sat)-3, 6-11; 12-6 Sun ☎ (01603) 880507
Mighty Oak Oscar Wilde; Sharp's Doom Bar; guest beer Ⓗ
Just north of the A47 and opposite the X1 bus stop, this friendly pub offers a warm welcome and a real fire in winter. The guest beer varies but is normally a golden ale. The large single bar has a dartboard and also offers shut-the-box and cribbage. Beer festivals are held in summer and at Christmas.
♨❀♿🚌(X1)♣P⁄–

Horsey

Nelson Head

The Street, NR29 4AD (300m E of B1159 coast road)
⏲ 11-11; 12-10.30 Sun ☎ (01493) 393378
🌐 nelsonheadhorsey.co.uk
Woodforde's Wherry, Nelson's Revenge Ⓗ
Rural pub close to the coast, Horsey Mere Nature Reserve, the Broads and a famous mill. It is quiet, with a timeless atmosphere enhanced by a log fire in winter. The bar has a large collection of marshman's implements. A good selection of home-cooked meals made with locally-sourced produce is available lunchtimes and evenings. Families are welcome, and there is a large garden area for children. This venue is popular with artists, walkers, boaters and locals alike. Well worth seeking out. ♨Q🐴❀◐◑♿P⁄–

Kenninghall

White Horse

Market Place, NR16 2AH
⏲ 12-3 Thu & Fri, 5.30-11; 12-11 Sat; 12-10.30 Sun
☎ (01953) 888857
Adnams Bitter; guest beer Ⓗ
This establishment has a main bar that features a large inglenook fireplace and beams, as well as a games room and restaurant. The guest beer is chosen from a variety of local micro-breweries, including Elmtree, Wolf, Buffy's and Humpty Dumpty. Food is served every lunchtime and Wednesday to Saturday evenings. The pub also offers accommodation with five letting rooms.
♨❀🛏◐◑♿♣P⁄–

King's Lynn

Crown & Mitre

Ferry Street, PE30 1LJ
⏲ 12-2.30, 6-11 ☎ (01553) 774669
Beer range varies Ⓗ
This is not an average pub. Off Tuesday Market Place, overlooking the river, it is stuffed full of interesting memorabilia, much of it with a railway or maritime connection. There are usually five or six guest beers on offer, mostly from small breweries, and it has a good reputation for food. However the opening hours are variable and it may well be closed during the Mart in the last two weeks of February. ♨Q❀◐◑●

Lattice House ✔

Chapel Street, PE30 1EG
⏲ 9-11 (1am Fri & Sat) ☎ (01553) 769585
Greene King Ruddles Best Bitter, Abbot; guest beers Ⓗ
Just off the Tuesday Market Place, this historic pub is now owned by Wetherspoon. It is smaller and more intimate than many of its houses, with the interior divided into a number of separate areas, including an upstairs bar. The lack of TV screens is more than compensated for by the gallery, ancient wall paintings and other interesting features. The usual food options are available and the keen management ensures a fine selection of around 10 beers is on offer. There is a public car park by the pub. ♨Q🐴❀◐◑●

Stuart House Hotel

35 Goodwins Road, PE30 5QX
⏲ 6-11; 7-10.30 Sun ☎ (01553) 772169
🌐 stuart-house-hotel.co.uk
Beer range varies Ⓗ
This may be an independent hotel bar, but it is well used by locals as well as guests. The two or three beers are often from East Anglia and food is served in the bar or separate dining-room. Special events such as murder mystery nights, themed meals, live music (some Fridays) and the annual beer festival (last week in July) are popular. There is a beer garden for summer and a real fire for winter. Ask about special accommodation deals for CAMRA members. ♨Q❀🛏◑P

Langham

Bluebell ✔

22-24 Holt Road, NR25 7BX (take B1156 S from Blakeney, then turn right into village) TG012411
⏲ 11-3 (4 Sat), 7-11; 11-11 Fri; 12-4, 7-11 Sun
☎ (01328) 830502
Adnams Bitter; guest beer Ⓗ
Situated two miles inland from the Norfolk coast road at Blakeney, this village local is small from the outside but visitors, including families and dogs, can be sure of a big welcome inside. The main bar area is at the front, with a split-level dining-room to the side. To the rear is a games room, leading to the large rear garden. Home-cooked food, using locally-sourced products where possible, is available every day lunchtime and evening (no food Tue). ♨❀◐◑♿🚌(46)♣P⁄–

Larling

Angel Inn

NR16 2QU (off A11 between Thetford and Norwich, signed by B1111 East Harling) TL983890
⏲ 10-midnight; 11-11 Sun ☎ (01953) 717963
🌐 angel-larling.co.uk
Adnams Bitter; guest beers Ⓗ
A brilliant all-around pub run by the same family since 1913, recognised as CAMRA's Norfolk Pub of the Year for 2010. Five real ales are always on handpump, including a mild. There is superb food, over 100 whiskies, and both the lounge and bar have open fires. The bar is frequented by friendly locals, passers-by and campers who enjoy the Angel's caravan park. A summer beer festival features more than 70 ales and the pub also hosts a whisky week.
♨Q❀🛏◐◑🅿♿⛺⇌(Harling Road)P⁄–

Lessingham

Star Inn
School Road, NR12 0DN (300m off B1159 coast road) TG388283
✪ 12-3 (not Mon), 6-11 ☎ (01692) 580510
⊕ thestarlessingham.co.uk
Adnams Bitter; Buffy's Bitter; Greene King IPA; guest beer Ⓗ
This excellent village local offers well-kept beers to regulars from near and far, and a warm welcome is extended to all. Situated near the north-east Norfolk coast, it has an easy-going feel, and is convenient for those visiting nearby East Ruston Old Vicarage Garden. The large beer garden is perfect for summer drinking. The cider is Westons Old Rosie. Dogs are welcome in the bar. Bar snacks and freshly prepared high-quality lunches and dinners are available daily (no food Mon, and Sun eve). ▲Q❄✿☞◑▲⚑(34,36)♣♠P

Newton by Castle Acre

George & Dragon Ⓛ ✅
Swaffham Road, PE32 2BX (on main road between Fakenham and Swaffham)
✪ 12-2.30, 6-11; 12-3 Sun ☎ (01760) 755046
Beer range varies Ⓗ
Situated by a busy road, the large car park and entrance are at the rear. On arrival you pass a cosy meeting room into the main bar, where the interior is split into three rooms featuring wooden beams, a restaurant and a welcoming open fire. The pub supports LocAle and two local beers are available at all times. A varying food menu is offered and entertainment includes regular music evenings and quiz nights. ▲Q♿✿◑⊟⚑P

North Creake

Jolly Farmers
1 Burnham Road, NR21 9JW
✪ closed Mon & Tue; 12-2.30, 7-11 (10.30 Sun)
☎ (01328) 738185 ⊕ jollyfarmers-northcreake.co.uk
Greene King IPA Ⓗ; Woodforde's Wherry; guest beers Ⓖ
Run by Heather and Adrian for 10 years, this traditional, cosy inn has small rooms with pine furniture, beams and tiled floors, which are enhanced by a roaring log fire in the winter. The Jolly Farmers is both a local pub and a place for visitors to eat. The menu features local produce, including game in winter and seafood in summer. Classical music plays in the background at lunchtime and jazz in the evening. ▲♿✿◑⚑&P⅃

North Elmham

Railway
Station Road, NR20 5HH TF995202
✪ 11 (12 Sun)-11 ☎ (01362) 668300
Beer range varies Ⓗ/Ⓖ
This rural gem, situated close to an ancient Anglo-Saxon cathedral, is a fine example of a community local. There is an adjacent function room with a first-floor balcony that hosts many local events, plus a patio at the rear of the pub. Most of the beers on sale here are from local and microbreweries such as Grain, Elgood's and Cottage. Home-cooked meals using mainly locally-sourced ingredients are available at lunchtimes and in the evenings. ▲❄☞◑▲P

North Lopham

King's Head
The Street, IP22 2NE (2 miles N of A1066) TM037834
✪ 11.30-3 (not Mon), 5-11; 11.30-midnight Sat; 12-10.30 Sun
☎ (01379) 688007 ⊕ lophamkingshead.co.uk
Adnams Bitter; Woodforde's Wherry; guest beer Ⓗ
Two-bar timber-framed pub dating from the 16th century and set back from the main road through the village. The public bar has an inglenook fireplace and a pool table, while the comfortable saloon and dining area have a wood-burner. The guest beer varies but is normally over 4%. Food is served lunchtimes and evenings Wednesday to Saturday and Sunday lunchtimes. The pub has its own crazy golf course; clubs and balls can be borrowed free of charge. ▲❄◑&♣P

North Wootton

Red Cat Hotel
Station Road, PE30 3QH (300m from North Wootton church)
✪ 4.30-11; 12-2, 7-11 Sun ☎ (01553) 631244
⊕ redcathotel.com
Adnams Bitter; Greene King Ruddles County; Woodforde's Wherry Ⓗ
Informal yet friendly family-run country inn, built of local 'gingerbread' carrstone. Set in the picturesque village of North Wootton, it dates back to 1898. Recently refurbished to a high standard, it provides comfortable seating and a warm welcome from the staff. The three regular ales are of superb quality. The restaurant is available every evening and offers home-cooked food in a relaxing environment. A WiFi hotspot zone is offered for those who wish to surf the net. Q☞◑⊟⚑(43)P⅃

Norwich

Beehive
30 Leopold Road, NR4 7PJ (between Newmarket and Unthank roads)
✪ 12 (5 Mon)-11; 12-midnight Fri & Sat ☎ (01603) 451628
⊕ beehivepubnorwich.co.uk
Fuller's London Pride; Wolf Golden Jackal; guest beers Ⓗ
Situated between the Unthank and Newmarket roads, this popular community pub serves a good range of guest ales from East Anglia as well as the two regulars. The pub is home to three darts teams, and pool and korfball teams. A weekly quiz is held on Wednesday, and free WiFi and pub games round out the entertainment. It also hosts a popular beer festival in the first week of July along with regular charity barbecues during the summer months. Food is served lunchtimes only. ❄◑⚑(12,24)♣⅃

Cottage Ⓛ
9 Silver Road, NR3 4TB (5 mins from Anglia Square shopping area)
✪ 12-11 ☎ (01603) 665535 ⊕ thecottagenorwich.co.uk
Crouch Vale Brewers Gold; Mauldons Bitter, Blackadder; guest beers Ⓗ
Mauldons' second public house opened late in 2009 to an enthusiastic welcome from local drinkers. The pub was completely refurbished and a range of Mauldons ales installed, along with up to six guests from around East Anglia. The pub holds an annual St George's beer festival, and bar snacks are available daily. Weekly quiz nights, live music on Friday night and Sunday afternoon, along

Rothwell

Rowell Charter L ✅

Sun Hill, NN14 6AB (on old A6)
☼ 12-11 ☎ (01536) 710453
Fuller's London Pride; Gale's Seafarers Ale; guest beers Ⓗ
A new entry to the Guide, this pub was built from Northamptonshire ironstone in 1642, with new rooms added to provide three split levels, with low door lintels and ceilings. Originally the Sun, the name was changed 25 years ago to commemorate the signing of the Charter by King John in 1204 when the town was officially permitted to hold the annual fair and market. A proclamation is held every year on the first Monday after Trinity Sunday when the pub opens at 6am. Five guest ales are offered, two from local micros.
🛏️❀🛌◗🖩(19)🖐️P🕭

Rushden

Rushden Historical Transport Society

Station Approach, NN10 0AW (on ring road)
☼ 7.30 (6 Fri)-11, 12-11 Sat; 12-10.30 Sun
☎ (01933) 318988 ⊕ rhts.co.uk
Grainstore Phipps IPA; Oakham Bishops Farewell; guest beers Ⓗ
This former run-down railway station has been turned into CAMRA's National Club of the Year 2010. A real gem, the bar occupies the former ladies' waiting room, with gas lighting and a roaring fire. The walls are adorned with enamel advertising panels and railway photos plus many CAMRA awards. The former parcels office is now a museum with many artefacts, and a former postal railway coach is now a skittles alley and small lounge. Open weekends are held during the summer with steam- and diesel-hauled train rides. In May a traction engine and vintage vehicles cavalcade is held. 🛏️Q❀🛌🖩(X46,M50)🖐️🖐️🕭🖵

Slipton

Samuel Pepys L

Slipton Lane, NN14 3AR (off A6116)
☼ 12-3, 5-11; 12-11 Sat & Sun ☎ (01832) 731739
⊕ samuel-pepys.com
Digfield Fools Nook Ⓗ**; guest beers** Ⓗ/Ⓖ
A splendid 16th-century ironstone village pub with a lovely low-beamed and brick-floored traditional bar where locals and visitors can chat or relax in cosy armchairs in front of a real fire. The stone-built main dining lounge bar and the conservatory restaurant are decorated and furnished in smart modern style. Five guest beers may come from local micros and in summer Hop Back Summer Lightning and real cider are available on gravity. A recent CAMRA Pub of the Season.
🛏️Q❀◗🖩🖐️(16)P🕭

Stoke Bruerne

Boat Inn

Bridge Road, NN12 7SB (opp canal museum)
☼ 11-11; 12-10.30 Sun ☎ (01604) 862428 ⊕ boatinn.co.uk
Banks's Bitter; Frog Island Best Bitter; Jennings Cumberland Ale; Marston's EPA, Pedigree, Old Empire Ⓗ
Situated on the banks of the Grand Union Canal, at the southern end of the Blisworth tunnel, the Boat Inn has been run by the same family since 1877. The delightful Tap Bar's inter-connecting rooms have canal views, open fires and window seats. A large extension houses a lounge, restaurant and cocktail bar. A small shop sells basic groceries, refreshments and souvenirs for this popular spot on the canal. Northants skittles is played here.
🛏️Q🍴❀◗🖩🖩🛌🖩(86)🖐️🖐️P🕭

Sutton Bassett

Queen's Head L

Main Street, LE16 8HP (on B664)
☼ 12-2.30, 6-11; 12-10.30 Sun ☎ (01858) 463530
Adnams Bitter; Greene King IPA; guest beers Ⓗ
An 18th-century two-roomed pub with a rear terrace overlooking the Welland Valley, with low-beamed ceilings and walls adorned with pictures. In the rear bar is an open fire and a piano covered in silverware won by the pub's darts teams. Three guest beers are available, including one from a local micro. Locally sourced home-cooked food is served, with Sunday roasts especially popular (booking recommended). The pub takes part in the unique Welland Valley Beer Festival in June, served by vintage buses from Market Harborough.
🛏️Q❀◗🖩(167)🖐️🖐️P🕭

Thornby

Red Lion

Welford Road, NN6 8SJ (on A5199)
☼ 12-2.30 (not Mon), 5-11; 12-11 Sat & Sun
☎ (01604) 740238 ⊕ redlionthornby.co.uk
Greene King IPA; Wadworth Henry's IPA; guest beers Ⓗ
Situated on the old A50, this traditional village pub dates back more than 400 years. The compact bar has two drinking areas with a wood-burning open fire in the lounge. A motley collection of beer tankards, steins and paintings is displayed throughout. To the rear is the restaurant, which occupies two linked rooms, one heavily beamed. Regular guest beers are from Church End, Elgood's and Grainstore, with five to choose from. During the summer, classic car meetings are held along with pig roasts. No food Monday. 🛏️❀◗🖢P🕭

Tiffield

George Inn L ✅

21 High Street, NN12 8AD (off A43)
☼ 12-3 (not Tue), 6-midnight; 12-3, 5.30-1am Fri; 12-1am Sat; 12-7 Sun ☎ (01327) 350587 ⊕ thegeorgeattiffield.co.uk
Vale Best Bitter, VPA; guest beers Ⓗ
A popular and welcoming village pub near Towcester dating from the 16th century with Victorian and more recent additions. It has three rooms – a cosy bar, games room featuring Northants skittles and a back room with an eclectic range of furniture and artwork. Two ever-changing guest beers and Old Rosie cider are on offer, with current and forthcoming beers detailed on the website. The George provides a hub for local groups, and hosts an occasional Saturday quiz and other events including two beer festivals.
🛏️🍴❀◗🖐️🖐️P🕭

Walgrave

Royal Oak

Zion Hill, NN6 9PN (2 miles N of A43)

🕐 11.30-2.30, 5.30 (5 Fri & Sat)-11; 12-10.30 Sun
☎ (01604) 781248
Adnams Bitter; Greene King Abbot; guest beers Ⓗ
A comfortable ironstone village inn dating from the 1840s, set back from the main road. The front bar is partitioned into a main central area with two dining spaces either side. The traditional interior boasts beams with hanging jugs and a stone inglenook fireplace. A small back bar serves a cosy lounge and a separate function area. Outside, there is a room for Northants skittles and children's play equipment in the garden. Three changing guest beers often come from local breweries.
🏚️⊛◑🚌(39)♣P⅃

Weldon

Shoulder of Mutton Ⓛ
12 Chapel Road, NN17 3HP
🕐 11-11 ☎ (01536) 266453 ⊕ myspace.com/
theshoulderofmutton
Beer range varies Ⓗ
This large, friendly pub has recently been refurbished providing two large bars. The front room was originally three rooms that have been made into one, with an open fire at one end. The rear bar has a pool table, dartboard, plasma TV and games machine, and leads to an enclosed outside area with space for smokers and non-smokers. Four local real ales are always on offer, including Great Oakley brews. A beer festival is held annually.
🏚️⊛◑🚌(X4)♣P⅃

Welford

Wharf Inn
NN6 6JQ (on A5199 N of village)
🕐 12-11 (10.30 Sun) ☎ (01858) 575075 ⊕ wharfinn.co.uk
Marston's EPA, Pedigree; guest beers Ⓗ
Situated on the Leicestershire border, this brick-built inn lies at the end of the Welford Arm of the Grand Union Canal and is popular with narrow boat travellers, locals and tourists alike. Inside, the main bar and dining area are separated by a large open fire. A smaller bar is on a lower level to the front. A beer festival is hosted in the summer and themed events are held regularly. Four guest beers always include an Oakham ale. Well-behaved children and dogs are welcome. 🏚️Q⊛🚅◑❶🚌♿♣▲♣P⅃

Wellingborough

Coach & Horses 🍷 Ⓛ
17 Oxford Street, NN8 4HY
🕐 12-11 ☎ (01933) 441848
Adnams Bitter; guest beers Ⓗ
Town-centre local with an enthusiastic landlord who is fully committed to offering a good choice of real ales. Up to 10 are available, with beers from local micro-breweries Great Oakley and Potbelly regularly featuring. Traditional home-cooked food is served lunchtimes and evenings. Lots of breweriana adorn the front bar area, which has a real fire. The large garden has a heated smoking shelter. CAMRA East Midlands Regional Pub of the Year runner-up in 2009. The cider is Westons scrumpy. 🏚️⊛◑♿♣♣⅃

Weston by Welland

Wheel & Compass
Valley Road, LE16 8HZ (off B664)

🕐 12-11 (10.30 Sun) ☎ (01858) 565864
⊕ thewheelandcompass.co.uk
Greene King Abbot; Marston's EPA, Burton Bitter, Pedigree; guest beers Ⓗ
The pub stands on the edge of the village surrounded by open countryside. Inside it has two open drinking areas and a large dining room to the side serving good quality food at reasonable prices. A large family-friendly garden contains swings and slides – a big attraction in the summer. Two guest beers come from all over the country. A regularly changing real cider has now been added to the range. 🏚️Q⊛◑♿🚌(167)♣P⅃

Woodford

Duke's Arms
83 High Street, NN14 4HE (off A14/A510)
🕐 12-11 ☎ (01832) 732224
Elgood's Bitter; Greene King IPA; guest beers Ⓗ
This popular village pub overlooking the village green was once called the Lord's Arms, named after the Duke of Wellington, who was a frequent visitor to Woodford. A games-oriented hostelry, it features Northants skittles, darts and pool. Home-cooked food is served daily (no food Sun eve). A beer festival is held on the Whit Sunday bank holiday weekend. Guest beers include one from Oakham. 🏚️🚅⊛◑♿♿🚌(16)♣♣P

Wootton

Wootton Working Men's Club
High Street, NN4 6LW (off A508 near jct 15 M1)
🕐 12-2 (3 Fri, not Wed & Thu), 7-11 (11.30 Fri); 12-11 Sat; 12-10.30 Sun ☎ (01604) 761863
Great Oakley Wagtail; guest beers Ⓗ
This ironstone building was previously the Red Lion pub and is a multi-award-winning club. It was rescued from closure by the regulars, and is now home to local sports groups. There are many intimate areas in which to enjoy a pint, including the bar, cosy lounge, function room and games room with Northants skittles. Up to five guest beers are available. Show this Guide or a CAMRA membership card for admittance. Local CAMRA Club of the Year 2008. Q🚌(15,36)♣P

Yardley Hastings

Rose & Crown Ⓛ
4 Northampton Road, NN7 1EX
🕐 5-11; 12-midnight Fri & Sat; 12-6 Sun ☎ (01604) 696276
⊕ roseandcrownbistro.co.uk
Grainstore Phipps IPA; Greene King IPA, Abbot; guest beers Ⓗ
Big ironstone pub dating from 1740 that was extensively refurbished in the 1980s and is now a single large-roomed establishment in olde-worlde style. It retains stone-flagged floors and beamed ceilings throughout, and has a small drinking area in the bay window. The emphasis is on traditional home-cooking with the menu varying daily, good service and some tempting dishes. Regular live music events from jazz to rock to blues feature, along with a new boules court. The landscaped gardens are wonderful in the summer.
⊛◑🚌(P1)P⅃

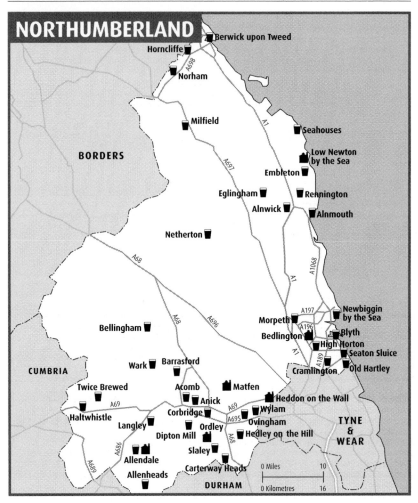

NORTHUMBERLAND

Berwick upon Tweed
Horncliffe
Norham
Milfield
BORDERS
Seahouses
Low Newton by the Sea
Embleton
Eglingham
Rennington
Alnwick
Alnmouth
Netherton
Newbiggin by the Sea
Morpeth
Bedlington
Blyth
High Horton
Seaton Sluice
Old Hartley
Cramlington
Bellingham
Wark
Barrasford
CUMBRIA
Acomb
Anick
Matfen
Heddon on the Wall
Twice Brewed
Corbridge
Wylam
Haltwhistle
Langley
Ordley
Ovingham
Hedley on the Hill
TYNE & WEAR
Dipton Mill
Slaley
Allendale
Carterway Heads
Allenheads
DURHAM

0 Miles 10
0 Kilometres 16

Acomb

Miners Arms
Main Street, NE46 4PW
☼ 5 (12 Sun)-midnight ☎ (01434) 603909
⊕ theminersacomb.com
Wylam Bitter, Gold Tankard; Yates Bitter; guest beers Ⓗ
Superb, traditional, family-run 1746 inn with an emphasis on real ale, which is served in oversized lined glasses. The pub hosts regular music and folk nights. The bar has a genuine, cosy feel and is divided by a central staircase – energetic dogs often greet the visitor here. The miners have long gone but this pub is a superb legacy that lives on in this popular hamlet. ⋈⛟☸◑🍴♿🚌(880,882)♣♪🖨

Allendale

Allendale Inn
Market Place, NE47 9BJ
☼ 12-midnight ☎ (01434) 683246
Greene King Old Speckled Hen; Taylor Landlord; guest beer Ⓗ
Pleasant pub with a friendly landlord nestling in the corner of Market Square. Popular with visitors

and locals, the pub is well supported and has darts, dominoes and pool teams. The nearby Allen Banks and superb countryside attract large numbers of ramblers who gladly quench their thirst here. Food is served lunchtimes and early evenings. Outside is a superb refurbished beer garden. Handy for the PlusBus via Hexham rail station.
⋈⛟☸◑🍴♿🚌(688)♣♦

King's Head
Market Place, NE47 9BD (opp Co-Op)
☼ 12-11 ☎ (01434) 683681
Banks's Mild; Jennings Cumberland Ale; guest beer Ⓗ
A welcoming, upmarket inn situated in the town square, next door to the Golden Lion. The refurbished bar retains original features such as an open log fire. Traditional pub food is served all day.

INDEPENDENT BREWERIES

Allendale Allendale
Hexhamshire Ordley
High House Farm Matfen
Northumberland Bedlington
Ship Inn Low Newton by the Sea
Wylam Heddon on the Wall

The pub is popular with ramblers, cyclists and day trippers taking advantage of nearby countryside walks. Rail links to Allendale are good, and it is handy for the PlusBus via Hexham rail station. Well worth seeking out in this small market town. ᴍQ🐕🍴◖◗🍽�¬(688)

Allenheads

Allenheads Inn ⓛ
NE47 9HJ
☼ 12-4, 7-11; 12-11 Fri & Sat; 12-10.30 Sun
☎ (01434) 685200 ⊕ allenheadsinn.co.uk
Black Sheep Best Bitter; guest beers Ⓗ
Superb rural pub, popular with local ramblers and tourists. Originally the home of Sir Thomas Wentworth, the 18th-century multi-room building has a public bar with log fire, games room and dining room. The premises are bedecked with memorabilia and knick-knacks from a bygone age. Good bar meals are available at a decent price. Take care (and skis) in the winter.
ᴍ🐕❀🍴◖◗🍽(688)♣P

Alnmouth

Red Lion Inn ✪
22 Northumberland Street, NE66 2RJ
☼ 11-midnight ☎ (01665) 830584 ⊕ redlionalnmouth.com
Black Sheep Best Bitter; High House Farm Nel's Best; Wylam Bitter; guest beer Ⓗ
Charming, family-run, 18th-century coaching inn with a cosy lounge bar. Three guest beers often come from northern English or Scottish micro-breweries, and a small range of continental bottled beers is available. Panoramic views across the Aln estuary can be enjoyed from the decked area at the bottom of the garden. Occasional live music plays – outside in summer. Well patronised by tourists and locals, dogs are also welcome. An annual beer festival is held in October. Excellent B&B facilities. ᴍQ🐕❀🍴◖◗🍽(518)●P

Alnwick

John Bull Inn
12 Howick Street, NE66 1UY
☼ 7-11; 12-3, 7-10.30 Sun ☎ (01665) 602055
⊕ john-bull-inn.co.uk
Beer range varies Ⓗ
Current local CAMRA Pub of the Year, this 180-year-old inn thrives on its reputation as a back-street boozer. The passionate landlord offers four cask-conditioned ales at varying strengths, real cider, the widest range of bottled Belgian beers in the county and 120 single malt whiskies. There is a newly inaugurated darts team in the local league and the pub upholds the north-east tradition of an annual leek show. Q❀♣●¬

Anick

Rat Inn
NE46 4LN (follow the sign at Hexham A69 roundabout)
☼ 12-11 (3 Mon); 12-10.30 Sun ☎ (01434) 602814
⊕ theratinn.com
Beer range varies Ⓗ
Superb 1750 country inn with spectacular views across the Tyne Valley. The pub has a welcoming and friendly feel to it, with an open log fire surrounded by chamber pots hanging from the ceiling. Good food prepared with locally-sourced ingredients has earned the pub an excellent local reputation, enhanced by inclusion in the prestigious Michelin Red Guide. Half portions are available for children. Well worth the short taxi ride from Hexham rail station. ᴍQ🐕❀◖◗●P¬

Barrasford

Barrasford Arms
NE48 4AA
☼ 12-2 (not Mon), 6.30-11 (midnight Fri); 12-midnight Sat; 12-11 Sun ☎ (01434) 681237 ⊕ barrasfordarms.co.uk
Beer range varies Ⓗ
Splendid, unspoilt 1870s country pub located in the heart of Barrasford village in the North Tyne Valley. The friendly bar is complemented by good ale and customer banter. It regularly hosts quoits tournaments, hunt meets, darts finals and vegetable competitions. Top chef Tony Binks has won several culinary awards. The nearby former railway station is now used by Scouts but the bar has several railway pictures from yesteryear that add to the ambience. ᴍQ🐕❀🍴◖◗♣P

Bellingham

Riverdale Hall Hotel
NE48 2JT (W of Bellingham on road to Kielder)
☼ 11-11 (10.30 Sun) ☎ (01434) 220254
⊕ riverdalehallhotel.co.uk
Beer range varies Ⓗ
Originally built as a Victorian mansion for a leading railway developer in 1866, the present owners, the Cocker family, purchased the hotel from Lord Stafford in the 1970s. The bar is a popular rendezvous for residents, locals and visitors. The superb patio enjoys excellent views over the rear garden with full-size cricket pitch. A folk night is held on the last Thursday of the month, and an annual music and beer festival over the May bank holiday. ᴍQ🐕❀🍴◖◗🍽♿▲🍽(880)P

Berwick upon Tweed

Barrels Ale House
59-61 Bridge Street, TD15 1ES (in old part of town)
☼ 12-midnight (11.30 Sun) ☎ (01289) 308013
⊕ thebarrels.com
Stewart Pentland IPA; guest beers Ⓗ
There is an original Olde Curiosity Shop ambience to this pub, located in the old part of Berwick next to the original road bridge over the Tweed. The excellent real ale no doubt helps customers brave the dentist's chair at the side of the bar. The downstairs bar is used by DJs and bands at weekends. Outside is a unique open drinking area surrounded by high walls. Winner of CAMRA Pub of the Year awards. ❀🍽¬

Pilot
31 Low Greens, TD15 1LZ
☼ 12-midnight ☎ (01289) 304214
Caledonian Deuchars IPA; guest beers Ⓗ
Well patronised by locals and sought out by train trippers who have heard about this gem. The stone-built end of terrace pub dates from the 19th century and is noted in CAMRA's Regional Inventory of Historic Pub Interiors. It retains the original small room layout and boasts several nautical artefacts over 100 years old. The pub runs darts and quoits teams and hosts music nights. The bar staff are welcoming and friendly. ᴍ🍴◖◗🍽♣

Blyth

Olivers
60 Bridge Street, NE24 2AP
✪ 12-11; 12-10.30 Sun ☎ (01670) 368346
Caledonian Deuchars IPA; guest beers Ⓗ
This warm and friendly one-roomed hostelry was converted from a former newsagent's and is a welcome real ale outlet within a beer desert. It is located close to the regenerated quayside of a port better known for the FA Cup exploits of its famous Spartans Football Club. Three real ales are available, one usually locally sourced. Bus 308 passes outside and the bus station for services to Blyth is a short walk. ◖�🚲♣

Carterway Heads

Manor House Inn Ⓛ
DH8 9LX (on A68 S of Corbridge)
✪ 11-11; 12-10.30 Sun ☎ (01207) 255268
⊕ themanorhouseinn.com
Beer range varies Ⓗ
Excellent country inn run by a licensee keen on supporting local micros. The multi-room interior with three open fires has a comfortable and welcoming feel. Just off the A68, it is popular with tourists. A double-glazed window in a wall allows customers to view the cellar. Proper home-cooked food is served including unusual and exotic meat dishes. Excellent accommodation is available.
🛏🚫🕸🛌◖🍴🅑♣♠Ⓟ⌐

Corbridge

Angel Inn
Main Street, NE45 5LA
✪ 11 (12 Sun)-11 ☎ (01434) 632119
⊕ angelofcorbridge.co.uk
Hadrian & Border Tyneside Blonde; Taylor Landlord; guest beers Ⓗ
Superb former 1726 coaching inn located on the main road with good transport links. Family friendly, the pub has a reputation for good food. Seven handpulls offer a range of ales, and a wonderful selection of malt whiskies is also stocked. A separate lounge area has comfortable leather seating and outside is a relaxed seating area. The town has strong links with the Romans and Hadrian's Wall is nearby. Popular with tourists, ramblers and locals. 🛏Q🚫🛌◖🍴🅑➡🚌(10,685)Ⓟ

Dyvel's Inn ✅
Station Road, NE45 5AY (adjacent to Tynedale Rugby Club)
✪ 12-11 ☎ (01434) 633633 ⊕ dyvelsinn.co.uk
Caledonian Deuchars IPA; guest beers Ⓗ
Family-friendly country inn easily accessible by train along the beautiful Tyne Valley. Cosy in winter and open and sunny in summer, the two-room pub has a secluded garden and private car park, making it an ideal place to visit in a historic Tyne Valley town. Food is served throughout (ring first on Mondays, January-March). There are beautiful town and country walks on the doorstep. Tynedale Rotary, chess club and canoe club meet here monthly. 🛏🚫🕸◖🍴🅑♣▲🚌(10,685)Ⓟ

Cramlington

Plough
Middle Farm Buildings, NE23 1DN

✪ 11-3 (3.15 Wed), 6-11; 11-11 Fri & Sat; 12-10.30 Sun
☎ (01670) 737633
Ruddles County; guest beers Ⓗ
Owned by the Fitzgerald pub chain and located within the old village centre of Cramlington, now surrounded by new town development, this is a sympathetic conversion of what used to be farm buildings into a traditional pub, including the time-honoured division between bar and lounge. Among the interesting architectural features is the former gin gan – a circular building in which a horse would be harnessed to a wheel to grind corn – incorporated within the lounge. The bar is smaller and busy with doors leading to an outdoor seating area. Children are welcome during the day.
🕸◖🅑Ⓟ⌐

Dipton Mill

Dipton Mill Inn Ⓛ
Dipton Mill Road, NE46 1YA
✪ 12-2.30 (2 Wed), 6-11; 12-3 Sun ☎ (01434) 606577
⊕ diptonmill.co.uk
Hexhamshire Devil's Elbow, Shire Bitter, Devil's Water, Whapweasel, Old Humbug, Blackhall English Stout Ⓗ
The tap for Hexhamshire Brewery, this small inn is run by a keen landlord who brews his own excellent beers. Lineside won local brewery best bitter in the Battle of the Beers at the Newcastle Beer Festival 2010. To complement the ales there is great home-cooked food. A cosy atmosphere and warm welcome make the pub well worth seeking out. The large garden has a stream running through it and there is plenty of countryside to explore.
🛏Q🕸◖♠Ⓟ

Eglingham

Tankerville Arms
15 The Village, NE66 2TX
✪ 12-11 (12.30am Fri & Sat); 12-10.30 Sun
☎ (01665) 578444 ⊕ tankervillearms.com
Hadrian & Border Tyneside Blonde; guest beers Ⓗ
Well-appointed traditional country pub dating from 1851, serving three locally-sourced beers. The bar has several framed pictures that enhance the surroundings. Popular with tourists and ramblers, families are always welcome and dogs too. Local golf and cricket clubs meet here. An excellent open beamed restaurant complements this establishment. The comfortable bedrooms are en-suite. Well worth a visit. 🛏Q🚫🕸🛌◖🍴Ⓟ

Embleton

Greys Inn ✅
Stanley Terrace, NE66 3UY
✪ 12-11 (10.30 Sun) ☎ (01665) 576983
Black Sheep Best Bitter; Hadrian & Border Tyneside Blonde, Farne Island; guest beer Ⓗ
Pleasant traditional pub located at the rear of a lovely seaside hamlet, just a short walk from a wonderful beach. The bar is warmed by three open fires and a framed 1904 grocery list hangs on the wall. This is an excellent venue to enjoy a bite to eat washed down with a locally sourced real ale – hopefully while enjoying the sunshine on the superb outdoor patio. Home to a ladies' darts team, clay pigeon club and golf club.
🛏🚫◖🚲🚌(501,518)♣⌐

Haltwhistle

Black Bull

Black Bull Lane, Market Square, NE49 0BL

☼ 12-11 (midnight Fri & Sat); 12-10.30 Sun

☎ (01434) 320463

Caledonian Deuchars IPA; guest beers Ⓗ

Warm, friendly two-room pub close to Hadrian's Wall, situated just off Market Place down a cobbled lane. Popular with locals and ramblers, the pub has a traditional ambience with a low beamed timber ceiling, open fire, horse brasses and six handpulls on the bar. Regular themed nights are held. Ring to check meal times and winter hours as they can vary. ⚲Q❧◑▣(685)

Hedley on the Hill

Feathers ✔

NE43 7SW (take Lead Road out of Greenside and follow road signs)

☼ 12 (6 Mon)-11 ☎ (01661) 843607 ● thefeathers.net

Hadrian & Border Gladiator; Mordue Workie Ticket; guest beers Ⓗ

Much acclaimed country pub set in a pleasant hamlet with superb views of three counties. The interior has a genuine comfortable feel with exposed stone walls and beams. Young and welcoming staff serve high quality home-cooked food that complements the real ales. A beer festival is held every Easter and an uphill barrel race on Easter Monday. The pub has won awards for food – Sunday lunch is a highlight (booking recommended). ⚲Q❧✿◑P⌐

High Horton

Three Horse Shoes

Hathery Lane, NE24 4HF (off A189 N of Cramlington, follow A192) N7276793

☼ 11-11 (midnight Fri & Sat); 12-11 Sun ☎ (01670) 822410

● 3horseshoes.co.uk

Greene King Abbot; Tetley Bitter; guest beers Ⓗ

Extended former coaching inn at the highest point in the Blyth Valley, with views of the Northumberland coast. The pub is open plan with distinct bar and dining areas plus a conservatory. Dedicated to real ale, it hosts regular beer festivals. A house beer is brewed by Carlsberg. Guest ales are sourced from all over the country but regularly come from local micro-breweries, also available in two pint carry-outs. An extensive range of meals and snacks is served lunchtimes and evenings, all day Friday to Sunday. Q✿◑▣(X5)●P⌐

Horncliffe

Fishers Arms

Main Street, TD15 2XW

☼ 12-3 (3.15 Wed), 6-10.30; closed Tue; 12-3, 6-11 Fri & Sat; 12-2, 6-10.30 Sun ☎ (01289) 386866

Beer range varies Ⓗ

Traditional pub at the heart of community life, offering a once-a-month buskers' session, food-themed nights, quiz nights, OAP lunch every Thursday, and the Hooky Mats club on Wednesday lunchtime. Part of a terrace in the village centre, the pub has separate dining and drinking areas. Reasonably priced home-cooked food is popular. The Tweed Cycle Way is nearby. B&B includes en-suite facilities. ⌂◑▣▣(67)♣

Langley

Carts Bog Inn Ⓛ

NE47 0NS (3 miles off A69 on A686 to Alston)

☼ 12-2.30 (not Mon; 2 Wed), 5-11; 12-10.30 Sun

☎ (01434) 684338 ● cartsbog.co.uk

Mordue Bog Bitter; guest beers Ⓗ

Recently refreshed and re-opened, this excellent rural pub serves the local community at Langley and visitors to the area. The building dates from 1730 and was built on the site of an ancient brewery (circa 1521). Carts really did get bogged down here. A large open fire divides the two-room interior. The walls proudly display pictures of bygone days including the old railway station nearby, which closed in 1930 and is now a tourist attraction called the Garden Station. Home to three quoits teams and a darts team. ⚲Q❧✿◑▣♿▣(688)♣P⌐

Milfield

Red Lion

Main Road, NE71 6JD

☼ 11-2, 5-11 ☎ (01668) 216224 ● redlioninn-milfield.co.uk

Black Sheep Best Bitter; guest beers Ⓗ

A true local pub at the heart of the village, just eight miles inside the border, dating back to the mid-1700s. Rescued by the current licensee from the tight grip of Heineken, the Red Lion is a proper free house, with many varied guest beers served through the third handpump. Freshly-prepared food is available, with blackboards proudly displaying where local produce is sourced. Home to the leek-growing club. ⚲✿◢◑▣P⌐

Morpeth

Old Red Bull Ⓛ ✔

Dark Lane, NE61 1ST (opp Morrisons)

☼ 12-11 (11.30 Wed); 12-midnight Fri & Sat; 12-10.30 Sun

☎ (01670) 513306

Beer range varies Ⓗ

The walls of this pub proudly display the level of the recent floods in Morpeth at the latter end of 2008 – the pub has since been renovated and has a modern yet comfortable feel. There is a main bar area, and a smaller second room with a pool table and dartboard. Three real ales are available, with guest beers sourced both locally and from further afield. ⚲♣P⌐

Tap & Spile Ⓛ

23 Manchester Street, NE61 1BH

☼ 12-2.30, 4.30-11; 12-11 Fri & Sat; 12-10.30 Sun

☎ (01670) 513894

Everards Tiger; Greene King Abbot; Hadrian & Border Tyneside Blonde; Mordue Geordie Pride; Taylor Landlord; guest beers Ⓗ

Cosy, popular local, welcoming to all and handy for the nearby bus station. It has a busy narrow bar to the front and quieter lounge to the rear. A good choice of ales is offered, with beers from Northumbrian breweries often available. Westons Old Rosie real cider is also stocked as well as a selection of fruit wines from Lindisfarne Winery. A traditional folk group plays on Sunday lunchtimes. Winner of local CAMRA awards. ⚲Q◑▣♣●⌐

Castle Rock Harvest Pale; Draught Bass; guest beer Ⓗ
This 200-year-old listed pub in the far north of the
Vale of Belvoir has been carefully restored to retain
its original character. The large bar offers
comfortable seating for drinkers and diners, with a
further separate raised restaurant area. The pub
serves freshly-prepared meals lunchtimes and
evenings, and three cask beers, one always a
LocAle. Mini-festivals are held occasionally
throughout the year, with upcoming events well
publicised on the website. ⚉Q⚉✍◑♿P

Sutton-in-Ashfield

Masons Arms Ⓛ
Eastfield, NG17 4JZ
✪ 12-11 ☎ (01623) 472704 ⊕ themasonsarmspub.co.uk
Beer range varies Ⓗ
Hard to miss – look for the solar panels on the roof
– this pub has a warm and friendly atmosphere.
The public bar and separate lounge with
comfortable seating are served from a central bar.
Two handpumps dispense ever-changing beers
sourced from local micros including Blue Monkey
and Springhead – see the blackboard for details of
what is available. Darts is popular in the public bar
with three dartboards. ⚉❹♿🚃♣P℄

Picture House ✪
Fox Street, NG17 1DA
✪ 8am-midnight (1am Fri & Sat) ☎ (01623) 554627
Greene King Ruddles Best, Abbot; guest beers Ⓗ
Open-plan Wetherspoon pub housed in a former
1920s cinema, situated close to the bus station.
The interior is in Art Deco style with a high ceiling
and wood panels, with ample seating available
throughout. Good value food is served every day
until 10pm. Live sports events are shown on a large
screen above the front entrance. ◑♿🚃🌸

Tollerton

Air Hostess
Stanstead Avenue, NG12 4EA
✪ 12-11.30 (midnight Fri & Sat) ☎ (0115) 937 7388
⊕ airhostesspub.co.uk
Everards Beacon, Tiger, Original; guest beers Ⓗ
Excellent community pub named due to its
proximity to Nottingham Airport, reflected in its
iconic large carved 'trolley dolly' sign. The
traditional public bar with darts, dominoes and
pool is complemented by a spacious, comfortable
lounge. Outside, there is a drinking area alongside
the petanque piste. Wednesday is quiz night and
live music plays every Sunday. An ever-changing
menu of good-value food is offered lunchtimes and
evenings. The Tollerton Plough Play is performed
here annually. ⚉◑❹♿🚃♣🌸P℄

Upper Broughton

Golden Fleece Ⓛ
Main Street, LE14 3BG
✪ 12-11 (10.30 Sun) ☎ (01664) 822262
Beer range varies Ⓗ
Large, attractive inn situated just off the main A606
Nottingham to Melton road. A dining pub, the
spacious interior has a large bar and seated area for
drinkers and a separate restaurant and
conservatory. There is also an attractive beer
garden for warmer months. The wide and varied
food menu receives good reports locally. Guest ales

often come from micro-breweries, with one pump
dedicated to LocAle. Occasional beer festivals are
hosted. ⚉❥⚉◑♿🚃(19)♣P℄

Watnall

Queens Head
40 Main Road, NG16 1HT
✪ 12-11.30 ☎ (0115) 938 6774
Adnams Broadside; Everards Tiger, Original; Greene
King Old Speckled Hen; Wells Bombardier; guest
beers Ⓗ
A 17th-century rural gem with a lounge/dining
space, a small snug hidden behind the bar and an
unusual locals' area with a grandfather clock. The
extensive garden has children's play equipment
and a marquee, making the pub popular all year.
The internal fittings around the bar are original,
and old photos adorn the walls adding to the pub's
ambience. Home-cooked English food is served
lunchtimes and weekday evenings. The pub is
reputedly haunted. Occasional beer festivals and
live music feature. ⚉Q⚉◑❹Ⓐ🚃(331)P℄

Wellow

Olde Red Lion
Eakring Road, NG22 0EG (opp maypole)
✪ 12-11 ☎ (01623) 861000
Beer range varies Ⓗ
This 400-year-old village pub is situated opposite
the village green with its maypole and participates
in a large event on May Day. The traditional wood-
beamed interior includes a restaurant, lounge and
bar areas with photographs and maps depicting the
history of the village. Three real ales are available
including a house beer from the local Maypole
Brewery. Situated close to both Sherwood Forest
and Clumber Park. Q⚉◑❹P🚃

West Bridgford

Southbank Ⓛ
1 Bridgford House, Trent Bridge, NG2 5GJ
✪ 11-midnight (2am Fri); 10-2am Sat; 10-midnight Sat
☎ (0115) 945 5541 ⊕ southbankbar.co.uk
Fuller's London Pride; Mallard Duck 'n' Dive; guest
beer Ⓗ
Sports bar situated on Trent Bridge, close to
Nottingham Forest's football ground and other
sporting venues. A large island bar dominates the
centre of the room, with plenty of seating and a
number of different-sized screens showing a range
of sports. Outside, the large, partly-covered patio
overlooks the River Trent. Live music plays on most
nights. An extensive varied food menu is served
including an early breakfast on Saturday and
Sunday. CAMRA members receive a discount.
⚉◑♿🚃(1-11)℄

Stratford Haven Ⓛ
2 Stratford Road, NG2 6BA
✪ 10.30-11 (midnight Thu-Sat); 12-11 Sun
☎ (0115) 982 5951
Batemans XB, XXXB; Castle Rock Harvest Pale, Elsie
Mo; Everards Tiger; Hop Back Summer Lightning;
guest beers Ⓗ
A former retail premises, this is now one of the
Castle Rock estate's flagship outlets. It has a single
narrow bar with a larger seating area at the back
and a secluded snug to one side. Up to 10 cask ales
are available at any one time, including LocAles

from the Castle Rock portfolio. A wide range of food includes curry night on Monday and pie night on Tuesday. Sunday is quiz night and a brewery evening is held on the second Tuesday of the month. Q❀◑🌐♿🖵(6-9)🏃

West Stockwith

White Hart
Main Street, DN10 4ET
⏱ 12-11 ☎ (01427) 890176
Beer range varies Ⓗ
Small country pub with a little garden overlooking the River Trent, Chesterfield Canal and West Stockwith Marina. One bar serves the through bar, lounge and dining area. Idle Brewery is situated in outbuildings at the side of the pub and the range of five real ales usually includes three from Idle. The area is especially busy during the summer, due to the river traffic. Q◑♿🅰🖵🐾P

Westwood

Corner Pin 🅛
75 Palmerston Street, NG16 5HY (off B6016)
⏱ 1-11 (midnight Fri); 12-midnight Sat & Sun
☎ (07908) 531901
Naked Brewer Blush, Hopsession, Oracle, Palindrome; guest beer Ⓗ
A genuine free house and winner of a number of CAMRA branch awards, this corner pub has a lounge and separate public bar with an open fire. There is a pool table and a function room. Six handpumps dispense beers from local micros and the on-site Naked Brewer located in the skittles alley. The landlady is also the head brewster. An annual St George's beer festival is hosted. Dogs are welcome. ᛗ❀🍴🅰🖵(1,90)🐾●P🏃

Woodthorpe

Vale 🅛 ✅
Mansfield Road, NG5 3GG
⏱ 12-11 (midnight Fri & Sat) ☎ (0115) 926 8864
Adnams Broadside; Castle Rock Harvest Pale; guest beers Ⓗ
This imposing late-1930s building sits on a prominent corner position, the main entrance leading to the original timber and glass porch. Inside there is much wood panelling – the HB circular plaques refer to the original owners, Home Brewery. The beer range includes two regulars and four guests. To the rear of the lounge is a dining area where good value food is available all day. Outside is a covered and heated area for cooler evenings. ♿❀◑🖵P🏃

Worksop

Mallard
Station Approach, S81 7AG (on railway platform)

⏱ 11-11; 12-10.30 Sun ☎ 07973 521824
Beer range varies Ⓗ
Formerly the Worksop station buffet, the Mallard is situated within the railway station buildings, with access from the car park. The pub offers a warm welcome as well as three real ales including a porter, a selection of foreign bottled beers and country fruit wines. A further room is available downstairs for special occasions such as the three beer festivals the pub holds each year. Q🅰🚲🖵P

Shireoaks Inn
Westgate, S80 1LT
⏱ 11.30-4, 6-11; 11.30-11 Sat; 12-10.30 Sun
☎ (01909) 472118
Beer range varies Ⓗ
Warm, friendly pub converted from cottages. The public bar houses a pool table and large-screen TV, and the comfortable lounge bar has a separate dining area. Tasty home-cooked food represents good value for money. The two handpulls dispense regularly changing guest ales. A small outside area with tables is available in the summer.
Q❀◑🍴🅰🚲🖵🐾🏃

Station Hotel
Carlton Road, S81 7AG (opp railway station)
⏱ 11-11 (10.30 Sun) ☎ (01909) 474108
Acorn Barnsley Bitter; guest beers Ⓗ
Formerly the Regency, the Station Hotel has now reverted to its original name, situated opposite Worksop railway station, on the edge of the town centre. Four real ales are available, always including Barnsley Bitter. One bar serves a large bar area with a separate dining room, and a further small room suitable for meetings. Food is available lunchtimes and evenings. ❀◑🅰🚲🖵P

Wysall

Plough Inn 🅛
Main Street, Keyworth Road, NG12 5QQ (jct of Widmerpool Rd and Main St)
⏱ 12-midnight (1am Fri & Sat) ☎ (01509) 880339
🌐 ploughatwysall.co.uk
Draught Bass; Greene King Abbot; Taylor Landlord; guest beers Ⓗ
A pub for more than 150 years, and owned by the same family for the past 12 years, this pleasantly updated village free house retains many period features and much original character. A sensibly priced menu of traditional home-cooked pub favourites is available at lunchtime. Three regular and three guest beers include popular LocAles from breweries such as Castle Rock – with a generous discount for CAMRA members. Though a little off the main routes, this south Nottinghamshire gem is well worth a visit. Quiz night is Tuesday.
ᛗQ❀◑🖵(51)🐾P🏃

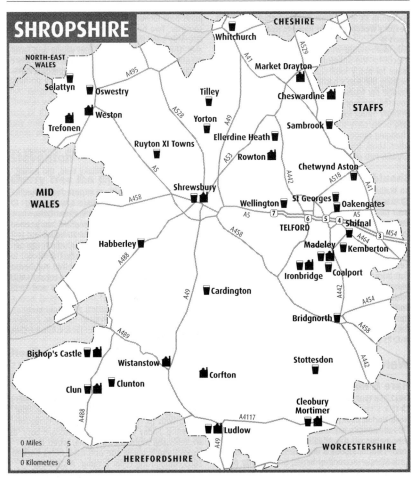

SHROPSHIRE

CHESHIRE
Whitchurch

NORTH-EAST WALES

Selattyn
Oswestry
Tilley
Market Drayton
Cheswardine
STAFFS

Weston
Yorton
Sambrook

Trefonen
Ellerdine Heath

Ruyton XI Towns
Rowton
Chetwynd Aston

MID WALES
Shrewsbury
Wellington
St Georges
Oakengates
Shifnal

Habberley
TELFORD
Madeley
Kemberton

Ironbridge
Coalport

Cardington

Bridgnorth

Bishop's Castle
Stottesdon

Wistanstow
Corfton

Clun
Clunton

Cleobury Mortimer

Ludlow

0 Miles 5
0 Kilometres 8
HEREFORDSHIRE
WORCESTERSHIRE

Bishop's Castle

Crown & Anchor Vaults

High Street, SY9 5BQ
☼ 4 (2 Sun)-11 ☎ (01588) 638966
Ludlow Gold; Monty's Sunshine; Wye Valley HPA; guest beer ⊞
Known locally as The Vaults, this no-frills pub has recently been purchased by the current landlady. Extensive alterations to the interior have created an open space around the central bar so customers can appreciate the pub's regular music sessions. It relies entirely on beer sales to survive so that while customers bringing in their own food are not frowned upon, it's always best to ask first. Dogs are most welcome. ✿▲➡♣⊷

Six Bells

Church Street, SY9 5AA
☼ 12-2.30 (not Mon), 5-11; 12-11 Sat; 12-3.30, 7-10.30 Sun
☎ (01588) 638930 ⊕ sixbellsbrewery.co.uk
Six Bells Big Nevs, Ow Do!, Cloud Nine; guest beers ⊞
This is the Six Bells brewery tap – the adjoining Six Bells Brewery was re-established on the site of the original one, which closed in the early 1900s. You can be sure of a friendly greeting in the wooden beamed bar where three ales are on handpump, plus monthly specials and real cider in summer.

Excellent fresh food is served in the dining/lounge bar (no food Sun, Mon – except bank hols – or Tue eve). The local beer festival in July offers around 90 ales and real ciders plus live music in the courtyard.
🍴Q✿➀◗⊟▲➡(553)♣♦⊷

Three Tuns

Salop Street, SY9 5BW
☼ 12-11 (10.30 Sun) ☎ (01588) 638797
⊕ thethreetunsinn.co.uk
Three Tuns 1642, XXX, Cleric's Cure; guest beer ⊞
One of the truly historic pubs in the country, this is one of the Famous Four who were still brewing in the early 1970s. Together with the adjoining, but separately owned, Three Tuns Brewery, from where it gets all its beers, it has been on this site since 1640. On one side is the dining lounge, on the other the ever-popular front bar leading to the central snug and timber-framed, glass-sided dining room. As well as good food, the pub offers music sessions, including jazz, in the top room. Dogs are welcome. 🍴Q✿➀◗⊟⅙▲➡(443,745)♣⊷

Bridgnorth

Bell & Talbot ⌶

2 Salop Street, High Town, WV16 4QU

◑ 5-11.30 (midnight Fri & Sat); 5.30-11 Sun
☎ (01746) 763233 ⊕ odleyinns.co.uk
Bathams Best Bitter; Hobsons Twisted Spire, Town Crier; guest beers Ⓗ
A community pub used by many groups for informal meetings, popular with musicians, bikers, walkers, cyclists and bridge players. Guest beers are always LocAle bitters; cider is occasionally served in summer. The pub supports three quiz teams, and the larger bar is the venue for live music on Friday and Sunday evenings. A ukulele band meets in the conservatory on occasional Wednesday evenings. Outside in the small courtyard is an umbrella-covered smoking area. An old inn with limited accommodation.
爲☷✍➘⊞♣℄

Black Boy Ⓛ

58 Cartway, WV16 4BG
◑ 12 (5 Mon-Thu, 3 Fri winter)-midnight; 12-midnight Sun
☎ (01746) 761432
Hook Norton Hooky Bitter; Kinver Black Boy Bitter; Wye Valley HPA; guest beer Ⓗ
This Grade II-listed 17th-century ale house is the last remaining inn on Bridgnorth's Cartway. Both the bar and separate lounge have open fires and exposed beams. From the garden terrace there are views over the River Severn. The pub is a popular music venue on Friday and Saturday nights showcasing local talent. It also supports darts, dominoes and quiz teams, and holds a beer festival in summer. Outside is a covered smoking area.
爲Q☷✍Ⓖ☷➘⊞♣℄

Golden Lion Ⓛ ✅

83 High Street, High Town, WV16 4DS
◑ 11.30-2.30, 5-11; 11-11 Fri & Sat; 12-10.30 Sun
☎ (01746) 762016 ⊕ goldenlionbridgnorth.co.uk
Greene King IPA; Hobsons Town Crier; Wye Valley HPA; guest beers Ⓗ
This 17th-century coaching inn is a traditional town-centre inn with separate public and lounge bars. Pictures on the walls of the two comfortable lounge bars record the history of the pub. The public bar is the venue for sports teams. A fine collection of pump clips adorns the beams throughout. At the rear there is an outdoor patio drinking area near the car park, and a covered smoking area. All accommodation is en-suite with freeview TV. Q☷✍Ⓖ➘⊞♣P℄

Hare & Hounds Ⓛ

8 Bernards Hill, Low Town, WV15 5AX (just off Hospital St A442)
◑ 5-midnight; 3-1am Sat & Sun ☎ (01746) 768819
⊕ hareandhounds.biz/index.php
Hobsons Mild, Town Crier; guest beers Ⓗ
This traditional English pub is made up of two drinking areas. The L-shaped bar has a large open fire and quiet background music. The lounge is smaller and well-furnished with a TV and smaller open fire. There are four handpulls and real cider. The food speciality is pie, chips and peas. Outside is a covered and heated smoking area, and a beer garden with stunning views of the Severn Valley and steam railway. 爲☷✍Ⓐ➘⊞♣℄

King's Head Ⓛ

3 Whitburn Street, High Town, WV16 4QN
◑ 11-11 (midnight Fri & Sat); 12-10.30 Sun
☎ (01746) 762141 ⊕ kingsheadbridgnorth.co.uk
Hobsons Best Bitter, Town Crier; Holden's Golden Glow; Wye Valley HPA, Butty Bach; guest beers Ⓗ

Sympathetically renovated Grade II-listed, 16th-century coaching inn complete with timber beams, flagstone floor, leaded windows and roaring log fires in winter. The King's Head bar has two regular and two guest beers. The extensive menu includes a pub grub section and daily blackboard specials that use locally-sourced produce. The Stable Bar to the rear has seven handpulls and an impressive display of wine bins. The courtyard has a pleasant seated area. 爲Q☷✍➘⊞℄

Railwayman's Arms Ⓛ

Hollybush Road, WV16 5DT (follow signs for SVR)
◑ 11.30-4, 6-11; 11.30-11 Fri; 11-11 Sat; 12-10.30 Sun
☎ (01746) 764361 ⊕ svr.co.uk
Bathams Best Bitter; Hobsons Best Bitter; guest beers Ⓗ
A licensed refreshment room since 1861, this SVR-owned drinking spot filled with railway memorabilia is always busy at weekends and on summer days. The platform drinking area is perfect for attracting beer drinkers and heritage railway enthusiasts. The bar has five guest beers – usually three bitters, a mild, a stout and one Belgian beer. A selection of local and European bottled beers is also available. A CAMRA beer festival is hosted in the car park in September. Dog-friendly except Friday and Saturday evenings. 爲Q☷➘⊞♣P℄

White Lion Ⓛ

3 West Castle Street, WV16 4AB
◑ 10.30-11 (midnight Fri & Sat; 10.30 Sun)
☎ (01746) 763962 ⊕ whitelionbridgnorth.co.uk
Banks's Bitter; Ludlow Gold; St Austell Tribute; Titanic Mild; guest beers Ⓗ
This 18th-century inn with two bars offers a warm welcome to regulars and visitors. Murals by a local artist adorn the bars and outside walls. Good, traditional food is served daily, with home-made bar snacks available. Six handpulls offer LocAles and national beers. Outside is a terrace, lawned beer garden and children's play area. The pub hosts live music and quizzes and is a regular venue for the local storytelling group and folk club. Beer festivals are held in summer and winter. Dog-friendly. 爲Q☷✍➘⊞♣●℄

Cardington

Royal Oak

SY6 7JZ

Luxborough

Royal Oak Inn

TA23 0SH (about 2½ miles from B3224 between Wheddon Cross and Raleghs Cross)
✪ 12-2.30, 6-11; 12-11 Sat & Sun ☎ (01984) 640319
⊕ theroyaloakinnluxborough.co.uk
Cotleigh Tawny; Exmoor Ale; St Austell Tribute; guest beers Ⓗ

Ancient village pub known locally as the Blazing Stump, with an original stone-flagged public bar, serving hatches, large inglenook fireplace and a further bar/children's room to the rear. Alongside is a hotel and dining complex. The pub is popular in season with shooting parties and walkers as well as locals. Quiz evenings are held. Rich's Farmhouse and Thatchers Cheddar Valley real ciders are sold. In an Exmoor valley, it is an ideal base for walking. ⚄Q☀✆❀◑ ⌸♣♠P⌐

Middlezoy

George Inn Ⓛ

42 Main Street, TA7 0NN (off A372, 1 mile NW of Othery)
✪ closed Monday; 12-3, 7 (6 Fri & Sat)-midnight; 12-3, 7-11 Sun ☎ (01823) 698215 ⊕ thegeorgeinnmiddlezoy.co.uk
Butcombe Bitter; guest beers Ⓗ

Friendly 17th-century free house with stone flag floors and exposed beams. Beers are mainly from south-west England. Excellent locally-sourced food is available Wednesday to Saturday. The South African landlord keeps his beers in top condition and runs a beer festival each year at Easter. This pub may be a little remote but is well-worth finding. Closed on Monday. ⚄Q☀☀◑▲⌸(16)♣♠P⌐

Minehead

Queen's Head Ⓛ

Holloway Street, TA24 5NR (off the Parade)
✪ 11-11 (midnight Wed-Sat) ☎ (01643) 702940
Exmoor Gold; Sharp's Doom Bar; St Austell Tribute; guest beers Ⓗ

Situated in a side street just off the Parade, this popular town pub sells up to eight ales. The spacious single bar has a raised seating area for dining and families. There is a games room at the rear and a skittle alley. Good-value food is served daily lunchtimes and evenings – try the home-made pies. A carvery is offered every Tuesday, Thursday and Sunday lunchtime. Twice-yearly beer festivals are held. ◑&▲⇄⌸(18,28,39)♣⌐

Moorlinch

Ring o' Bells Ⓛ

Pit Hill Lane, TA7 9BT (between A39 and A361 near Street)
✪ 5-8 Mon; 12-2, 5-11 Tue-Fri; 12-midnight Sat; 12-10.30 Sun ☎ (01458) 210358 ⊕ ringobellsmoorlinch.co.uk
Beer range varies Ⓗ

Traditional village inn offering at least two West Country beers, all served by handpump. Locally sourced home-cooked food is available in the public bar, big lounge bar or in the separate dining-room. Darts, skittles and pool are played and there is a juke-box. Families are welcome and dogs too. Although a little off the beaten track, this pub is well worth seeking out. ⚄Q☀◑⌸&⌸(19)♣P⌐

Mudford

Half Moon

Main Street, BA21 5TF (on A359 between Yeovil and Sparkford)
✪ 12-11 (10.30 Sun) ☎ (01935) 850289
⊕ thehalfmooninn.co.uk
Beer range varies Ⓖ

Welcoming 17th-century village free house that is popular with diners. There is a huge, varied menu on well-appointed blackboards. The ales are on stillage behind the bar and takeaway purchases are offered at reduced prices. A selection of ciders and perries from Westons is also stocked. Only guide dogs are allowed. This is a pub where you can relax with a great choice of food, drinks and newspapers. For those warmer days there is an outside courtyard, and overnight accommodation is available. Q☀✆◑&⌸(1)♠P⌐

Norton Fitzwarren

Cross Keys Ⓛ ✅

TA2 6NR (at A358/B3227 jct W of Taunton)
✪ 11-11; 12-10.30 Sun ☎ (01823) 333062
Beer range varies Ⓗ

Large roadside pub divided into several areas, with plenty of exposed beams in contemporary style. The wide-ranging menu offers good food at reasonable prices. Up to four different beers are available, often from local breweries, as well as from other parts of the UK, including regional brewers as well as micros. There is a large garden bordered by a stream where you can relax on a sunny summer's day. ⚄☀◑⌸(25,28)P⌐

Pitney

Halfway House Ⓛ

Pitney Hill, TA10 9AB (on B3153)
✪ 11.30-3, 5.30-11; 12-3.30, 7-11 Sun ☎ (01458) 252513
⊕ thehalfwayhouse.co.uk
Butcombe Bitter; Hop Back Summer Lightning; Otter Bright; Teignworthy Reel Ale; guest beers Ⓖ

Thriving traditional village pub serving a variety of local ales on gravity alongside many international bottled beers. Superb home-cooked food is served based on local produce (ploughman's only Sun lunch, no food Sun eve). No music or fruit machines disturb the buzz of conversation here. It was CAMRA National Pub of the Year 1996, Telegraph Pub of the Year 2007, and local CAMRA Pub of the Year on several occasions. Local ciders, including Wilkins and Hecks, are served. A real gem, definitely not to be missed. ⚄Q☀◑⌸(54)♠P⌐

Porlock

Ship Inn Ⓛ ✅

High Street, TA24 8QD
✪ 11-midnight ☎ (01643) 862507 ⊕ shipinnporlock.co.uk
Cotleigh Tawny Owl; Exmoor Ale; Otter Bitter; St Austell Tribute, Proper Job; guest beers Ⓗ

Known locally as the Top Ship, this 13th-century inn was recorded in RD Blackmore's Lorna Doone. The bar appears not to have changed much since then, with flagstoned floors, inglenook fireplaces and a good selection of real ales and Cheddar Valley cider. Located at the bottom of the notorious Porlock Hill, this gem offers good home-cooked food, a three-tiered patio garden, skittle alley and

four en-suite bedrooms. The dog-friendly hostelry also welcomes well-behaved children.
🏨Q🕑🌁☺🍴◑🔌🍽�(39,300)♣🐾P⅃

Porlock Weir

Ship Inn 🔲
TA24 8PB (take B3225 from Porlock)
🔶 11-11 (10.30 Sun) ☎ (01643) 863288
⏏ thebottomship.co.uk
Exmoor Ale, Stag, Beast; St Austell Tribute, Proper Job 🔲
The Ship has possibly the best view from any pub in Somerset, overlooking the small harbour and Bristol Channel towards the South Wales coast. Located in the Exmoor National Park, it is more than 400 years old. Good-value food is served by friendly staff. Friday night in winter is 'fish, chips and a pint' night. Ideal for walkers, the pub is close to Porlock village and the famous hill. The large nearby Pay & Display car park can be busy during holiday periods. 🏨Q🕑🌁◑🚿🚭(39)♣🐾P⅃

Portishead

Windmill Inn
58 Nore Road, BS20 6JZ (next to municipal golf course above coastal path)
🔶 11-12.10.30 Sun ☎ (01275) 843677
Butcombe Gold; Courage Best Bitter; Draught Bass; RCH Pitchfork; guest beers 🔲
Large split-level free house with a spacious patio to the rear, with a recent extension enjoying panoramic views. Above the coastal path on the edge of town, the Severn Estuary and both Severn bridges can be seen on clear days. A varied menu is served all day and is enormously popular. One large area is set aside for families. The two guest ales are often locally sourced and there is an Easter beer festival. Thatchers cider is stocked.
Q🕑🌁◑🚿🚭(359)🐾P⅃

Priddy

Hunters Lodge
BA5 3AR (isolated crossroads 1 mile from A39) ST549500
🔶 11.30-2.30, 6.30-11; 12-2, 7-11 Sun ☎ (01749) 672275
Blindmans Mine Beer; Butcombe Bitter; Cheddar Potholer 🇬; **guest beers** 🔲
Timeless, classic roadside inn near Priddy, the highest village in Somerset, popular with cavers and walkers. The landlord has been in charge for well over 40 years. Three rooms include one with a flagged floor; the beer casks are behind the bar. Wilkins cider is served. Simple home-cooked food is excellent and exceptional value. A folk musicians' drop-in session is held on Tuesday evening in the back room. The garden is pleasant and secluded. Mobile phones are not welcome but dogs are. 🏨Q🕑🌁◑🚿🚭♣🐾P

Queen Victoria Inn ✅
Pelting Drove, BA5 3BA (on minor road to Wookey Hole)
🔶 12-3, 6-11; 12-11.30 Sat; 12-11 Sun ☎ (01749) 676385
Butcombe Bitter, Gold; guest beer 🔲
Creeper-clad inn, a pub since 1851, with four rooms that feature low ceilings, flagged floors and three log fires. This is a wonderfully warm and relaxing haven on cold winter nights, and is popular during the Priddy Folk Festival in July and the annual fair in August. Reasonably priced,

home-cooked food is a speciality. Children and dogs are allowed and there is a play area by the car park. Cheddar Valley cider is sold. Beers are now via handpump, not gravity as before.
🏨Q🌁◑🍴🚿♣🐾P⅃

Priston

Ring o' Bells
High Street, BA2 9EE
🔶 12-3, 6-midnight ☎ (01761) 471467
Blindmans Ring of Bells; Milk Street Beer; Moles Tap; Wickwar Bob 🔲
In the centre of a pretty village in good walking country. The pub is a traditional old English inn with a stone floor, serving substantial bar and restaurant meals using locally-sourced ingredients. Morris men feature regularly, including on New Year's day, along with a duck race on the river. Three luxury rooms are available for B&B accommodation. 🏨Q🌁🚿◑🔌🚭♣🐾P

Radstock

Fromeway
Frome Road, BA3 3LG (¾ mile from Radstock centre on A362 Frome Road) ST697547
🔶 closed Mon; 12-3, 6-11; 12-11 Sun ☎ (01761) 432116
⏏ fromeway.co.uk
Butcombe Bitter; Wadworth 6X; Plain Indulgence 🔲
This friendly free house has been in the same family for five generations. The present landlord has been in charge for more than 35 years and produces his own sausages, faggots and home-cured hams for the excellent bar and restaurant meals. Well used by locals, the Fromeway has a warm and relaxing atmosphere. A single bar serves a number of adjoining areas, and there are regular guest beers. The pub organises many functions, quizzes and walks for charity. Q🕑🌁🚿◑🔌🚭P⅃

Rickford

Plume of Feathers ✅
Leg Lane, BS40 7AH (off A368 2 miles from A38 jct)
🔶 12-11 ☎ (01761) 462682 ⏏ theplumeoffeathers.com
Butcombe Bitter; Cheddar Ales Potholer; guest beers 🔲
This 15th-century, Grade II-listed building has been a pub since the 1800s. If approaching from Churchill, the left turn towards the pub is tricky. The interior is part divided into bar, restaurant and family room. The changing menu is chalked up on a crowded blackboard. Enthusiastic owners have made this into a pleasant and convenient base from which to walk, fish or explore the Mendips. The garden at the rear has a stream running the length of the pub, leading to a ford. Parking is limited. 🏨Q🕑🌁🚿◑🐾P

Rowberrow

Swan Inn ✅
Rowberrow Lane, BS25 1QL (signed off A38)
🔶 11.30-3, 6-11; 11.30-11 Sat; 12-10.30 Sun
☎ (01934) 852371
Butcombe Bitter, Gold, seasonal beer; guest beer 🔲
Believed to date from around the late 17th century, this Butcombe Brewery-owned country pub enjoys an attractive setting, nestling beneath the Dolebury Iron Age hill fort. A convenient stop for walkers on the Mendip Hills, the emphasis is on

ales are available from the Marston's portfolio and snacks are on offer. The large rear garden is popular during the summer and provides an excellent view of the cathedral. Darts, dominoes and board games are played and a charity quiz is held on Thursday night. The pub is dog-friendly. ▲⊛⊛▲≈(City)🖵♣P¦﹘

Horse & Jockey
8-10 Sandford Street, WS13 6QA
✪ 11.30-11 (11.30 Fri & Sat) ☎ (01543) 410033
Fuller's London Pride; Holden's Golden Glow; Marston's Pedigree; guest beers Ⓗ
Just one year on from becoming a free house, the Horse & Jockey is now one of the most popular real ale pubs in the city. At least three guest ales, mainly from local micros, flank the regular beers on the large U-shaped bar. The pub is host to darts and dominoes teams. Good-value food is served at lunchtimes (not Sun), and pork pies are available at all times. The pub is dog-friendly. Note that there is an over-21 entry policy. ▲⊛⊕≈🖵♣P¦﹘

Longdon

Swan With Two Necks
40 Brook End, WS15 4PN (250m off A51)
✪ 12-3, 5-11 (11.30 Fri & Sat); 12-10.30 Sun
☎ (01543) 490251
Marston's Pedigree; Taylor Landlord; guest beers Ⓗ
A meeting place for locals from the village and surrounding countryside, this fine pub has been in the Guide for more than 30 years. Up to three guests, mainly from local micro-breweries, are offered, with Bathams Best Bitter a Friday regular. Bar meals are of a high quality, and the restaurant area opens on Friday and Saturday evenings. Takeaway fish and chips is also available. With three open coal fires, this is a cosy pub for the winter. ▲Q⊛⊕&P¦﹘

Lower Penn

Greyhound Ⓛ
Market Lane, WV4 4UN (at Market Lane/Greyhound Lane jct)
✪ 12-3.30, 5.30-11; 12-11.30 Thu; 12-midnight Fri & Sat; 12-11 Sun ☎ (01902) 620666
⊕ thegreyhoundlowerpenn.co.uk
Enville Ale; Wye Valley Hare of the Dog; guest beers Ⓗ
Dating from 1830, this village pub is situated approximately three miles from Wolverhampton city centre. It is popular with walkers and cyclists using the South Staffordshire Railway Walk, and canal moorings are available at nearby Dimmingsdale. The bar area contains photographs of Wolves teams from the last 120 years, and the gents' toilet has pictures of boxing and horse racing. Local beers from Kinver, Wye Valley and Slater's are regularly available. The restaurant sells good food. ▲⊛⊕🖵&P¦﹘

Marchington

Bulls Head
Bag Lane, ST14 8LB
✪ 5 (12 Sat)-11; 12-3, 6-10.30 Sun ☎ (01283) 820358
⊕ bullsheadmarchington.co.uk
Marston's Pedigree; guest beer Ⓗ
Not far from the town of Uttoxeter in the small village of Marchington, the Bulls Head is a genuine

community pub. Log fires in both the bar and lounge are welcoming in winter, and in the summer the large patio is popular for alfresco drinking. Home to various clubs, regular quizzes and music nights are also hosted at the pub. An ideal place to take a break when out walking or cycling in the local countryside. ▲Q⪢⊛⊕♣P¦﹘

Milwich

Green Man Ⓛ
ST18 0EG (on B5027)
✪ 5 (12 Fri & Sat)-11; 12-10.30 Sun ☎ (01889) 505310
⊕ greenmanmilwich.com
Backyard The Hoard; Draught Bass; Greene King Abbot; guest beers Ⓗ
A pub since 1775, this free house offers guest beers from regional and micro-breweries nationwide – see the website for forthcoming guests. It also hosts regular beer festivals and stocks real cider from Westons or Thatchers. Run by the same licensee for more than 20 years, a list displays his predecessors dating back to 1792. A popular pub with walkers and cyclists, there is a small restaurant area off the bar. Stafford Branch CAMRA Pub of the Year 2007.
▲Q⪢⊛⊕&♣P¦﹘

Newcastle-under-Lyme

Castle Mona ✪
4 Victoria Street, ST5 1NT
✪ 4 (12 Sat)-midnight; 12-11.30 Sun ☎ (01782) 257764
Marston's Pedigree; Wells Bombardier; Wychwood Hobgoblin; guest beer Ⓗ
Classic terraced pub, well worth a visit, with a comfortable lounge and a traditional bar area with the bar as the focal point in the centre. Outside is a large and pleasant beer garden. A beer festival is held annually and the licensee is proud to display a local CAMRA Branch Pub of the Month award. The pub has a genuine community spirit and a warm welcome is guaranteed. Major sports fixtures are screened. ⊛🖵♣¦﹘

Old Brown Jug ✪
Bridge Street, ST5 2RY
✪ 3-midnight (1am Wed & Thu); 12-2am Fri & Sat; 12-1am Sun ☎ (01782) 711393 ⊕ oldbrownjug.com
Marston's Pedigree; guest beers Ⓗ
This large, one-roomed Marston's pub at the edge of town is popular with both locals and students, and renowned for its beer and cider as well as for its varied live music. A popular jazz venue, it also hosts a salsa night and a rock and blues evening – check the website for forthcoming gigs. Winner of local CAMRA Cider Pub of the Year, it has a large beer garden to the rear and is well worth a visit. ⊛🖵♣♦P¦﹘

Newtown

Ivy House
62 Stafford Road, WS6 6AZ (on A34)
✪ 12-11.30 (10.30 Sun) ☎ (01922) 476607
⊕ ivyhousepub.co.uk
Banks's Mild, Bitter; Marston's Pedigree; guest beers Ⓗ
Winner of local CAMRA Pub of the Year five times in recent years, the Ivy House was first listed as an ale house in 1824. This traditional pub has three rooms on split levels, and a separate restaurant serving

food all day. The beer garden retains a country feel, backing onto open farm land. A visit is highly recommended and a warm welcome assured. Q❀◑&🖂(1,2,351)♣P⅃

Norton Bridge

Railway Inn
Station Road, ST15 0NT
✪ 4.30 (12 Sat)-11; 12-10.30 Sun ☎ (01785) 760289
Thwaites Original, Lancaster Bomber; guest beer ⓗ
Saved from closure, this local is now a thriving and popular community village inn. A good range of home-cooked evening meals is served (not Sun) and highly recommended. The food can be savoured with a traditional pint in a cosy atmosphere. Traditional pub games are popular and the North Staffordshire BSA Motorcycle Owners Club meets here regularly. Draught cider appears during the summer and soon all year round.
🏚Q🏕❀◑🕹&🛆🖂(490)♣🐾P⅃

Onecote

Jervis Arms Ⓛ
ST13 7RU (on B5053 N of A53 Leek-Ashbourne road)
✪ 12-midnight summer; 12-3, 7 (6 Sat)-midnight winter; 12-midnight Sun ☎ (01538) 304206
Joule's Pale Ale; Titanic Iceberg; Wadworth 6X; guest beers ⓗ
A regular in this Guide, the pub has shown a long-term commitment to the real ale scene. Situated in the Peak District National Park, it is close to Alton Towers. Family friendly, the beer garden has a river running through it and a good children's playground; there is a large car park just beyond. The landlord is fanatical about real ale, sourcing his guest beers from breweries both near and far.
🏚🏕❀◑&🛆🐾P⅃

Oulton

Brushmakers Arms ✅
8 Kibblestone Road, ST15 8UW (500m W of A520, 1 mile NE of Stone)
✪ 12-3, 6-midnight; 12-1am Fri & Sat; 12-midnight Sun ☎ (01785) 812062
Thwaites Original, Lancaster Bomber; guest beer ⓗ
Named after a local cottage industry, the 'Brush' is a pub where time stands still. It has a traditional quarry-tiled bar and a small ornate lounge, and pictures and postcards adorn the walls, reflecting a bygone era. The small rear patio garden is a real sun-trap and doubles as a smoking area. With no games machines or juke-box, conversation flows in this excellent village local. Well-behaved dogs are welcome. The guest ale may come from a local micro. 🏚Q❀🕹&🖂(250)♣P⅃

Penkridge

Littleton Arms Ⓛ ✅
St Michaels Square, ST19 5AL
✪ 12-11 (midnight Fri & Sat); 12-10.30 Sun ☎ (01785) 716300 ⊕ thelittletonarms.com
Purity Pure Gold; Slater's Premium; guest beer ⓗ
Dating as far back as 1793, the Littleton Arms has recently benefitted from extensive refurbishment to provide a modern, comfortable interior and outside patio area. A regularly updated food menu is served throughout the day using locally-sourced and freshly prepared food. The independently

managed pub hosts popular themed nights on the last Friday of the month. Fantastic service and a CAMRA Pub of the Month award make this a very popular pub. 🏚Q❀🛏◑🕹&🚃🖂P⅃

Penn Common

Barley Mow ✅
Pennwood Lane, WV4 5JN (follow signs to Penn Golf Club from A449) SO901949
✪ 12-2.30, 6-11; 12-11 Sat; 12-10.30 Sun ☎ (01902) 333510
Greene King Abbot; Taylor Landlord; guest beers ⓗ
On the edge of Penn Common and sharing an access driveway with Penn Golf Club, this charming pub is worth seeking out. Built around 1630, it has low-beamed ceilings and steps leading down to the drinking and dining areas. The compact single bar has a display of beer mats, foreign banknotes and a selection of five quality real ales. The licensee is also the local butcher, so take the opportunity to sample the excellent fare.
Q❀◑P⅃

Rugeley

Plaza ✅
Horsefair, WS15 2EJ
✪ 9-11.30 (12.30am Fri & Sat) ☎ (01889) 586831
Greene King Abbot; Ruddles Best Bitter; guest beers ⓗ
A typical Wetherspoon pub with lots of character, converted from a cinema in 1988 and the heartbeat of the town ever since. Take a step inside and you will see that much of the old cinema still remains. This fine pub offers mostly local ales, including an ever-present beer from Blythe Brewery. It also hosts regular Meet the Brewer evenings. Outside is a large beer garden for warmer days. Q❀◑&🚃🖂(825)🐾P⅃

Yorkshireman
Colton Road, WS15 3HB
✪ 12-3, 6-11; 12-8 Sun ☎ (01889) 583977
⊕ wine-dine.co.uk
Blythe Bagots Bitter, Palmers Poison; guest beer ⓗ
Situated next to the Trent Valley rail station, this classic pub reopened in 2007 after a short period of closure, and has flourished ever since. Known as much for quality cuisine as fine ale, the restaurant hosts occasional themed nights such as Asian or Mexican. Casual drinkers are welcome in the elegant bar where the well-regarded local Blythe ales have featured for some years. Q❀◑&🚃P⅃

Salt

Holly Bush Inn ✅
ST18 0BX (turn left off A518 opp Weston Hall) SJ959277
✪ 12-11 (10.30 Sun) ☎ (01889) 508234
⊕ hollybushinn.co.uk
Adnams Bitter; Marston's Pedigree; guest beer ⓗ
The Holly Bush claims to have origins going back as far as 1190 and it is believed to be the second oldest inn to be granted a licence. With extensions and alterations over the centuries, it has three distinct areas: a bar, dining room and snug. Many awards have been won for the superb quality meals. The oldest part of the building retains a thatched roof. There are plans to host summer beer festivals in the garden. 🏚Q❀◑&🛆🖂P⅃

Icklingham

Red Lion
The Street, IP28 6PS
✪ closed Mon; 12-2.30, 6-11; 12-2.30 Sun
☎ (01638) 711698 ⊕ lockwoodrestaurants.co.uk
Cliff Quay Tolly Roger; Earl Soham Gannet Mild;
Humpty Dumpty Norfolk Nectar ⊞
A timber-framed, thatched 16th-century free house
set well back from the road with ample parking
and up to five usually local beers on offer. In the
back bar customers can play darts, cribbage or even
I Spy, while home-cooked food is served in the
front bar/restaurant. In colder months log fires
greet customers in both bars; for warmer weather
there is a patio area overlooking the surrounding
fields and the River Lark. ▲Q❀❄❍♣P⌐

Ipswich

Brewery Tap
Cliff Quay, IP3 0BS
✪ 11-3, 6-11; 11-11 Sat; 11-10.30 Sun ☎ (01473) 225501
⊕ thebrewerytap.org
Cliff Quay Bitter, Tolly Roger, seasonal beers; guest
beer ⊞
Historic brewer's house adjacent to the former Tolly
Cobbold Brewery with an extensive food menu
based on quality, home-produced fare alongside
excellent beers, mainly brewed by a nearby micro.
Themed food nights, home-made pickled eggs and
various bar snacks are offered. There are stunning
views of the River Orwell through a bay window in
the bar, despite new sea defences being added.
Live music plays regularly. Two private function
rooms are available and there is a secluded garden
to the rear. ▲☎❀❍♿⊞(1,6)♣P⌐

Dove Street Inn ♈
76 St Helens Street, IP4 2LA TM170445
✪ 12-midnight (10.30 Sun) ☎ (01473) 211270
⊕ dovestreetinn.co.uk
Adnams Broadside; Crouch Vale Brewers Gold; Fuller's
London Pride ⊞**; Elgoods Black Dog Mild** �servG**; guest**
beers ⊞/⒢
This busy ale house regularly serves more than 20
real ales in oversized glasses – including milds and
traditional ciders – plus an array of continental
beers. Three beer festivals are held annually with
more than 60 cask ales available. Good home-
cooked food and bar snacks are on offer at all
times. Well-behaved dogs and children are
welcome during the day. Last entry is 10.45pm.
New accommodation is available.
Q☎❀⚏❍♿⊞♣♠⌐☷

Fat Cat
288 Spring Road, IP4 5NL TM181448
✪ 12-11 (midnight Fri & Sat) ☎ (01473) 726524
⊕ fatcatipswich.co.uk
Crouch Vale Brewers Gold; Fuller's London Pride;
Woodforde's Wherry; guest beers ⒢
Popular beer house with up to 16 beers dispensed
from a tap room behind the bar. This cosy drinking
pub is a joy to visit, with no background music or
games machines. Original enamel signs, posters
and other artefacts are scattered around the walls.
The garden and patio provide extra space for
occasional barbecues on summer afternoons.
Snacks are available and plates provided for
customers to order in takeaways (not Fri or Sat
eve). Children and dogs are not permitted.
Q❀≈(Derby Rd)⊞(2,75)♣⌐

Greyhound
9 Henley Road, IP1 3SE
✪ 11-2.30, 5-11; 11-midnight Fri & Sat; 10-10.30 Sun
☎ (01473) 252862 ⊕ greyhound-ipswich.com/
Adnams Bitter, Explorer, Broadside, seasonal beers;
guest beers ⊞
This popular pub offers a cosy, small public bar at
the front and a larger drinking and dining area to
the rear. An outside drinking space is also busy in
the summer months. Fresh home-made food from
a blackboard menu is served daily. Occasional live
music and arts events are hosted. TVs screen
sporting events. The new landlord has been a chef
for many years and is gradually refurbishing the
pub – cooked breakfasts are now available on
Sunday, 10-11.30am. ❀❍⚏♿≈⊞♣P⌐

Mannings ✪
8 Cornhill, IP1 1DD (next to town hall)
✪ 11-8 (11 Thu-Sat); 12-5 Sun ☎ (01473) 254170
Adnams Bitter, Broadside; Fuller's London Pride;
Greene King Old Speckled Hen ⊞
This narrow-fronted 16th-century town pub
provides an oasis of calm in the town centre,
especially on Friday and Saturday evenings. The
ales are of excellent quality and outdoor tables and
chairs in the summer provide the perfect place to
sit and watch the world go by. There is also a small
enclosed patio to the rear. A popular provisions
market is held on the Cornhill four days a week.
Q❀⚏♿≈⊞⌐

Plough ✪
2 Dog's Head Street, IP4 1AD
✪ 11-11 (midnight Fri & Sat); 12-7 Sun ☎ (01473) 288005
Adnams Bitter; Marston's EPA; guest beers ⊞
This popular large bar in the town centre gets busy
with local football fans on match days. All major
sport events are screened on TVs around the bar
and live bands perform regularly on Saturday
evenings. A function room is available for private
parties or dining, and there is a separate pool table
area. Outside, the enclosed patio has two smoking
shelters with heaters. The bus station is next door.
Over-18s only. ❀❍≈⊞♣⌐

Robert Ransome ✪
Trafalgar House, Tower Street, IP1 3BE
✪ 9am-midnight (2am Fri & Sat); 11-11 Sun
☎ (01473) 341920
Beer range varies ⊞
This spacious two-storey pub next to the Tower
Ramparts bus station is a Lloyds No.1 branded
venture. It opened in 2009 to replace the Yates
nightclub that was formerly in the same building.
Two bar serveries usually offer up to seven draught
beers alongside Wetherspoon's standard value-for-
money fare. The ground floor bar is popular all day.
Occasional live music or discos feature in the
evening and at weekends. ❍♿≈⊞♦

Ixworth

Greyhound
High Street, IP31 2HJ
✪ 11-2.30, 6-11; 12-3, 7-11 Sun ☎ (01359) 230887
Greene King XX Mild, Ruddles Best Bitter; Yorkshire
Terrier ⊞
Situated on the town's pretty High Street, this
traditional inn has three bars including a lovely
central snug. The heart of the building dates back
to Tudor times. The pub is a rare outlet for XX Mild.

Good value lunches and early evening meals are served in the restaurant. A beer festival is held in November. Dominoes, crib, darts and pool are played in leagues and for charities. ⊛◑⊟⊠♣P

Kettleburgh

Chequers ✓
The Street, IP13 7JT TM263600
❀ 12-2.30, 6-11; 12-2.30, 7-10.30 Sun ☎ (01728) 724369
⊕ thechequers.net
Elgood's Black Dog Mild; Greene King IPA; guest beers Ⓗ
Substantial single-bar pub built in 1913 to replace an earlier building destroyed by fire. The massive rear garden eventually leads to the River Deben and provides an excellent location for a relaxing afternoon on sunny days. An unusual arrangement of branches, lights and other ornaments adorns the pub ceiling and gives the bar much character. Food includes various a la carte options and specials that change regularly. ⋈⍅⊛◑P

Laxfield

King's Head (Low House) ★
Gorams Mill Lane, IP13 8DW (behind churchyard)
TM296724
❀ 12-3, 6-midnight; 11-midnight Fri & Sat summer; 12-4, 7-11 Sun ☎ (01986) 798395 ⊕ laxfieldkingshead.co.uk
Adnams Bitter, Broadside, seasonal beers; guest beer Ⓖ
This gem dates from the 16th century and has changed little over the years, with a warren of rooms, low ceilings and high-back settles. Beers are served straight from casks in the tap room with no bar counter. Home-cooked food is available in a separate dining room. Outside, there is a large seating area and garden where croquet is played. Beer festivals are held in May and September. En-suite accommodation is available. Adnams Pub of the Year 2010. ⋈Q⊛⇦◑⊟⊠♣P'⍹

Long Melford

Crown
Hall Street, CO10 1JL
❀ 11.30-11; 12-10.30 Sun ☎ (01787) 377666
⊕ thecrownhotelmelford.co.uk
Adnams Bitter; Greene King IPA; Taylor Landlord; guest beers Ⓗ
In the antiques centre of Long Melford, the Crown is a family-run free house dating back to the 17th century. The last reading of the Riot Act in West Suffolk took place here in 1885. The bar area is set round a central servery, with a choice of seating for diners and drinkers inside or on the patio. Excellent food ranges from traditional favourites to modern cuisine. The 12 en-suite guest rooms vary in style. ⋈⊛⇦◑⛔⊟P'⍹

Lower Ufford

White Lion
Lower Street, IP13 6DW
❀ 11.30-2 (not Mon), 6-11; 12-3 Sun ☎ (01394) 460770
⊕ uffordwhitelion.co.uk
Adnams Bitter, Broadside; guest beers Ⓖ
Cosy, small, single-bar pub with a quarry-tiled bar close to the historic church on the edge of a tiny settlement. Many special events are held in the evening including highly popular bingo sessions

and themed food events such as hog roasts. Food is available lunchtimes and evenings (not Mon). The large garden leading to the River Deben is the perfect place to relax and enjoy the gravity beers. A large marquee hosts parties and entertainment on summer days. ⋈Q⍅⊛◑♣P

Lowestoft

Mariner's Rest
60-62 Rotterdam Road, NR32 2HA
❀ 11-midnight (2am Fri & Sat); 12-11.30 Sun
☎ (01502) 218077
Beer range varies Ⓗ/Ⓖ
This welcoming local is called the Rest due to the closeness of the nearby cemetery. It has a comfortable open-plan bar with TV screen and unique darts alley. A large array of real ales is served on both handpump and gravity feed, plus a good selection of ciders – it was local CAMRA's Cider Pub of the Year in 2011. Live music plays on some weekends. Outside is a covered and heated smoking area and garden. A discount is available for CAMRA members. ⊛⇌⊟🐾'⍹

Norman Warrior ✓
Fir Lane, NR32 2RB
❀ 11-midnight (12.30am Fri & Sat); 12-10.30 Sun
☎ (01502) 561982 ⊕ thenormanwarrior.co.uk
Greene King IPA; Marston's Pedigree; Sharp's Doom Bar; guest beers Ⓗ
Large estate pub on the northern side of town with ample parking. The public bar has a pool table and dartboard, and the comfortable lounge area leads to a spacious restaurant serving reasonably priced home-cooked food daily (booking advisable). Outside, the terraced garden hosts an annual beer and cider festival over the August bank holiday weekend with live music. Local CAMRA Branch Pub of the Year in 2010. CAMRA members receive a discount. ⊛◑⊟⇌(Oulton Broad North)⊠♣🐾P'⍹

Oak Tavern
Crown Street West, NR32 1SQ
❀ 10.30-11; 12-10.30 Sun ☎ (01502) 537246
Adnams Bitter; Greene King Abbot; guest beers Ⓗ
Popular with all ages, this lively drinkers' back-street local has an open-plan interior – one end with a pool table and Sky TV (for sporting events), the other festooned with Belgian memorabilia. Four handpumps serve local real ales, usually including a dark beer in the winter months. A large range of mainly Belgian continental beers is also available. Outside there is a patio. ⊛⇌⊠♣P'⍹

Triangle Tavern ♈
29 St Peters Street, NR32 1QA
❀ 11-11 (midnight Thu; 1am Fri & Sat); 12-10.30 Sun
☎ (01502) 582711 ⊕ thetriangletavern.co.uk
Green Jack Excelsior, Orange Wheat, Trawler Boys, Lurcher Stout, seasonal beers; guest beers Ⓗ/Ⓖ
This lively town tavern is the flagship for the Green Jack Brewery. The characterful front bar is decorated with many brewery and pub awards, and is home to live music every Friday evening. The contrasting back bar with pool table and juke-box is adorned with memorabilia. Alongside Green Jack's beers are guest ales, real ciders and an ever-changing selection of continental draught and bottled beers (mainly Belgian). Quarterly beer festivals are held. Customers are welcome to bring in their own food. ⋈⊛⊟⇌⊠🐾

Market Weston

Mill Inn
Bury Road, IP22 2PD TL979776
🌣 11-3, 5-11; 12-3, 7-11 Sun ☎ (01359) 221018
Old Chimneys Military Mild, Scarlet Tiger Ⓗ
This striking white brick-and-flint faced inn stands at a crossroads and is the closest outlet to the Old Chimney's Brewery, located on the other side of the village. Run by the same landlady for more than 12 years, it offers an excellent choice of beers complemented by a good menu of home-cooked meals (no food Mon eve). ⚖Q◑➍P

Mellis

Railway
Yaxley Road, IP23 8DU TM100746
🌣 6 (12 Sat)-11; 12-10.30 Sun ☎ (01379) 783416
🌐 railwaytavernmellis.co.uk
Adnams Bitter; guest beers Ⓗ
A two-bar pub close to the mainline railway crossing point (the station is no longer used). Guest beers come from local breweries. Themed food evenings include a self-service Indian buffet every Wednesday evening (booking advisable). The huge green was the scene of the county's only fatality during the English Civil War when on 11th April 1644 Edward Gibes of Thrandeston was 'slain at muster, shot through the bowels'. ⚖➌◑➍P

Naughton

Wheelhouse
Whatfield Road, IP7 7BS (450m off B1078)
🌣 5-11 (9 Mon; 8 Tue); 6-11 Sat; 12-10.30 Sun
☎ (01449) 740496
Beer range varies Ⓗ
A thatched, timber-framed building, with a low ceiling in the main bar that remains a hazard, despite the tiled floor now being much lower than it once was. The more spacious public bar is brighter and leads to a games room with pool table and darts. This splendid rural pub is well worth seeking out, with an interesting selection of beers always available. Opening times may vary to suit local demand. Dog-friendly. ⚖Q✿&➍P

Newbourne

Fox ✪
The Street, IP12 4NY TM273431
🌣 11-11; 12-10.30 Sun ☎ (01473) 736307
🌐 debeninns.co.uk
Adnams Bitter, seasonal ales; guest beers Ⓗ
Olde-worlde charm can be found in abundance at this cosy pub with a quarry-tiled floor and low-beamed ceiling. A full a la carte menu is offered daily, with gluten free options, daily specials and occasional themed food evenings. During the winter there is live music and in summer regular visits from local morris dancers. Popular with families, ramblers and locals alike, the garden has a pond with fish and ducks. ⚖Q➌✿◑&➍P

Orford

Jolly Sailor
Quay Street, IP12 2NU TM424496
🌣 11.30-3, 5.30-11; 12-11 Sat; 12-10.30 Sun
☎ (01394) 450243 🌐 thejollysailor.net
Adnams Bitter, Broadside, seasonal beers Ⓗ

Situated close to the modern quay this late 16th-century building is constructed from old ship timbers and was formerly six fishermen's cottages. Sympathetically refurbished, it retains much character. A tiny snug and three other rooms are used as restaurants, offering fresh fish dishes and plenty of local produce. Shove ha'penny, dominoes and boules are played. A highlight is sea shanty singing once a month. ⚖Q✿✿◑&▲➍P⌐

Pakefield

Oddfellows
6 Nightingale Road, NR33 7AU
🌣 11-11; 12-10.30 Sun ☎ (01502) 538415
Adnams Bitter; guest beers Ⓗ
This popular pub is situated near Pakefield cliffs and a stone's throw from the sea. The interior comprises three open-plan spaces with wooden flooring and panelling throughout. The main drinking area has a central fireplace and two TV screens showing sports. Substantial meals are served in the dining area (booking advisable). Up to four beers are available, usually including one from Green Jack Brewery. Outside seating. ✿◑➍

Rattlesden

Five Bells
High Street, IP30 0RA
🌣 12-12.30am (11.30 Sun) ☎ (01449) 737373
Beer range varies Ⓗ
Set beside the church on the high road through a picturesque village, this is a good old Suffolk drinking house – few of its kind still survive. Three well chosen ales on the bar are usually sourced direct from the breweries. The cosy single-room interior has a games room on a lower level. Occasional live music plays. Pub games include shut the box and shove ha'penny, and petanque and croquet in summer. ⚖Q✿

Rickinghall

Bell Inn ✪
The Street, IP22 1BN (adjacent to Botesdale)
🌣 11-11 (midnight Fri & Sat); 9-11 Sun ☎ (01379) 898445
Adnams Bitter, Broadside Ⓗ
The Bell Inn dates back to the 17th century when it was used by travellers going to and from Great Yarmouth, Bury St Edmunds and London. It was a popular stop-off because of its extensive stabling, accommodation and lively bar. More recently, it has become the focal point of the village. The lounge has a log fire and beamed ceilings. Children and dogs are welcome. ⚖✿✿◑➍P⌐⊟

Rumburgh

Buck
Mill Road, IP19 0NS
🌣 11.45-3, 6.30-11; 12-3, 7-10.30 Sun ☎ (01986) 785257
Adnams Bitter, seasonal beers; guest beers Ⓗ
Originally this pub and the parish church were part of a Benedictine priory. Extensions have added two dining areas, with a public bar and games room retained around the historic core. The bar is timber framed with a flagstone floor. Full of character and at the heart of village life, folk music evenings, quiz nights and darts matches are hosted. Guest beers are mainly local and the food is renowned (booking advisable). ✿◑⊟▲➍P

Shadingfield

Fox

London Road, NR34 8DD (on A145)
✪ 12-3, 6-11.30; 12-5 Sun ☎ (01502) 575100
⊕ shadingfieldfox.co.uk
Fuller's London Pride Ⓗ; **guest beers** Ⓗ/Ⓖ
Dating back to 16th-century, the original arched doors and carved fox heads on beams have been retained. The interior comprises a bar with comfortable seating, conservatory plus a dining area. Outside, a sun terrace has umbrellas and chimera heaters, and there is a small garden. Two beer festivals are held each year – one over the Father's Day weekend and the other close to Guy Fawkes Night. Live music every Friday evening features local artists. In the summer months extra beers are served on gravity. ﹛Q☎❀✪➊P⊱

Southwold

Lord Nelson ✪

42 East Street, IP18 6EJ
✪ 10.30-11; 12-10.30 Sun ☎ (01502) 722079
Adnams Bitter, Explorer, Broadside, seasonal beers Ⓗ
A regular entry in the Guide, this busy and lively hostelry is popular with locals and visitors enjoying the coastal views from the nearby cliff top. The pub has a flagstone floor and open fire in winter months, and the large central bar offers the full range of Adnams beers. Children are welcome in the side room and the partly covered and heated garden to the rear. The walls are adorned with naval memorabilia and photographs of old Southwold. ﹛❀☎✪➊▲➟⊱

Stanningfield

Red House

Bury Road, IP29 4RR
✪ 12-3, 5-11.30; closed Wed; 12-11 Sat & Sun
☎ (01284) 828330
Greene King IPA; guest beers Ⓗ
Built in 1866 in Victorian red brick, the building was originally a cobbler's workshop, but licensed in 1900 and now a free house. Neat and clean inside and out, the single-bar local has a relaxed and comfortable atmosphere. Live music plays monthly and pub games and sport are well supported. Food is served lunchtimes Monday to Saturday and evenings Monday to Thursday. Accommodation is in an en-suite family room. ﹛❀➟✪➊➤➟♣P⊱

Stansfield

Compasses

High Street, CO10 8LN
✪ closed Mon; 12-2 (not Tue), 5-11; 12-11 Sat & Sun
☎ (01284) 789486 ⊕ compasses.uk.com
Adnams Bitter; Woodforde's Wherry; guest beers Ⓗ
A pleasant, friendly 200-year-old village pub, the age of the building limits development and thus it retains much of its original charm. The wooden-floored bar area is bright and welcoming. Behind the brick chimney breast is a smaller tiled dining area, and another room is home to a bar billiards table. The friendly Dutch landlord will set up the shuffleboard on request. A selection of locally-sourced food is available. Well-behaved dogs are welcome. ﹛Q❀✪➊▲➟(343)♣P⊱〒

Stowmarket

King's Arms

Station Road, IP14 1RQ
✪ 11-11 ☎ (07590) 033202
Woodforde's Wherry Ⓗ; **guest beers** Ⓗ/Ⓖ
Built in about 1850, closed in 1958, this excellent and much-needed addition to the town re-opened again in 2009. A back-to-basics three-roomed establishment, it is deceptive in size and can get busy in the evenings. An ideal stop-off for train travellers, it is just a short walk from the town centre. A beer festival and barbecue are hosted in July. Dogs are welcome during non-busy periods. ➟❀✪➊➤➟(Stowmarket)➟(87B,88)♣P⊱

Royal William

53 Union Street, IP14 1HP (off Stowupland St)
✪ 11-11; 12-10.30 Sun ☎ (01449) 674553
Beer range varies Ⓖ
Tucked away down a side street and just a short walk from the station and town centre, this is a gem of a pub. An end of terrace back-street boozer, it is well supported by locals and visitors alike. Regular darts and crib matches are played and sports shown on TV. Ales are served from a cellar behind the bar by gravity dispense. ❀➟➤➟♣⊱

Stradbroke

Ivy House

Wilby Road, IP21 5JN TM230738
✪ 12-3, 6-11 (10.30 Sun) ☎ (01379) 384634
⊕ ivyhousestradbroke.co.uk
Adnams Bitter; guest beers Ⓗ
Recently refurbished to a high standard, this comfortable split-level cottage-style bar and restaurant is located close to the village centre and nearby sports fields and swimming pool. The menu is described by the landlord as 'modern British with a twist', and includes various curry dishes. Modern board games are available. Q❀✪➊➤➟♣P

Sudbury

Brewery Tap

21 East Street, CO10 2TP (200m from Market Place)
✪ 11-11 (midnight Fri & Sat); 12-10 Sun ☎ (01787) 370876
⊕ blackaddertap.co.uk
Mauldons Mole Trap, Silver Adder, Suffolk Pride; guest beers Ⓗ
Mauldons Brewery's first pub, after many years of searching. Formerly the Black Horse, this street corner local has been transformed. All Mauldons beers are available here, as well as guests. Snacks are served and takeaway meals can be ordered in. Live music plays including jazz on the first Sunday of the month. On the last Sunday breakfast is served 10-11.15am (booking essential). Dog-friendly. Q❀✪➊➤➟➤➟♣⊱〒

Tattingstone

White Horse

White Horse Hill, IP9 2NU TM136382
✪ 12-3, 6-11; 12-11 Fri & Sat; 12-10.30 Sun
☎ (01473) 328060 ⊕ whitehorsetattingstone.co.uk
Adnams Bitter; Crouch Vale Brewers Gold; guest beers Ⓗ
This 17th-century, Grade II-listed inn retains much character. The beamed main bar with log-burning stove hosts folk nights and other events. The guest

beer is from a local brewery. Excellent home-cooked food available lunchtimes and evenings (not Sun eve) includes gluten-free options, and curry night on the last Thursday of the month is always popular. Beers include a changing mild. Dog- and biker-friendly, there is a caravan and campsite at the rear. Excellent outside toilets. ♨Q☆❀◐▲➡♣P

Thurston

Fox & Hounds ▼ ✔

Barton Road, IP31 3QT
☼ 12-2.30, 5-11; 12-midnight Fri & Sat; 12-10.30 Sun
☎ (01359) 232228 ⊕ thurstonfoxandhounds.co.uk
Adnams Bitter; Greene King IPA; guest beers Ⓗ
Dating from 1800, this listed building is now a regular entry in the Guide. A busy village local, it offers a good selection of ever-changing real ales on handpump, served by the cheerful landlord and staff. Good home-cooked food is available. The public bar has a pool table, darts and Sky TV while the lounge is quieter and more comfortable. Local CAMRA Pub of Year. ☆❀◐⊟▲➡➡♣P⅃

Walberswick

Anchor ✔

Main Street, IP18 6UA
☼ 11-4, 6-11; 11-11 Sat; 12-11 Sun ☎ (01502) 722112
⊕ anchoratwalberswick.com
Adnams Bitter, Broadside, seasonal beers Ⓗ
Situated in an idyllic coastal village, this hotel caters for holiday makers and locals alike. It has two cosy alcove areas heated by a real fire on both sides, a side room for families, and a spacious restaurant serving local produce. The large garden and patio are located to the rear, and a converted barn is used for beer festivals. Voted Wine Pub of the Year by Harpers in 2011, it also stocks an extensive range of world-wide bottled beers. ♨Q☆❀◐⊟▲P⅃

Walsham-le-Willows

Six Bells ✔

Summer Road, IP31 3AA (opp church)
☼ 11.30-2.30, 5.30 (6.30 Sat)-11; 12-2.30, 7-11 Sun
☎ (01359) 259726
Greene King XX Mild, IPA, Morland Original Bitter, Abbot Ⓗ
A former wool merchant's house in the centre of a pretty village, this thatched building partly dates from the 16th century. A huge fireplace and dark timbers create a cosy atmosphere, together with exposed, heavily-carved timbers in the main bar. This traditional community pub, home to darts and crib teams, is run by a local couple who were regulars before taking it on 15 years ago. The emphasis here is firmly on beer. ♨Q❀⊟➡♣P⅃

Wissett

Plough

The Street, IP19 0JE
☼ 10.30-12.30am; 11.30-11.30 Sun ☎ (01986) 872201
Adnams Bitter; guest beers Ⓗ
This 17th-century inn has a large garden where visitors can pitch their tents during the summer months. An annual beer festival is held during July with live music and barbecue. Inside there is a central bar area, wooden floors and original

wooden beams adorned with agricultural artefacts. The centre of community life, the pub holds regular quiz evenings, charity events and themed food nights. There is a village shop in a converted outbuilding. ♨❀◐▲P

Woodbridge

Angel

2 Theatre Street, IP12 2NE TM270491
☼ 12-3, 5-11 (midnight Fri & Sat); 12-10.30 Sun
☎ (01394) 383808 ⊕ theangelwoodbridge.co.uk
Adnams Bitter; Sharp's Doom Bar; Woodforde's Wherry; guest beers Ⓗ
A 16th-century inn just off the market square with a quarry-tiled entrance and wooden floors in three separate bar areas. One bar is used for dining, with a good menu of home-made food on offer (with meal deals Mon-Wed). The remaining bar areas are furnished in a homely style with settles, armchairs and tables, warmed by two open fires. Background music includes jazz and blues. Families welcome. ♨❀◐⊟➡P⅃

Cherry Tree Inn

73 Cumberland Street, IP12 4AG
☼ 7.30am-11; 9am-11 Sat & Sun ☎ (01394) 384627
⊕ thecherrytreepub.co.uk
Adnams Bitter, Explorer, Broadside, seasonal beers; Elgood's Black Dog Mild; guest beers Ⓗ
Spacious open-plan bar with a large central counter that helps to create several distinct seating areas. The long-standing landlord has a good reputation for keeping quality real ale. Eight beers are usually on offer and two beer festivals are held. Traditional food is served all day. Family games are available to play. Accommodation is offered in a converted barn beside the garden and car park. Weelchair, child and dog friendly. Q☆❀◐⊟➡♣P

Old Mariner

26 New Street, IP12 1DX
☼ 11-3.30, 5 (6 Sat)-11; 12-10.30 Sun ☎ (01394) 382679
Adnams Bitter; Fuller's London Pride; Shepherd Neame Spitfire; Young's Bitter Ⓗ
Cosy, intimate, two-bar pub with a small restaurant area to the rear. The decor is simple and traditional throughout, with quarry-tiled floors and scrubbed wooden tables. The large TV is well used on rugby days, when the locals gather in the lively front bar. Food is popular, with casseroles, stews and roasts all freshly prepared on the premises (booking recommended for Sun lunch). Outside is a smoking area and garden. ♨Q❀◐➡⊟P⅃

Yaxley

Cherry Tree

Old Norwich Road, IP23 8BH TM121743
☼ 12-3, 7-11; 12-3, 5-midnight Fri; 12-3, 6-midnight Sat; 12-6 Sun ☎ (01379) 788050
Earl Soham Victoria; guest beers Ⓗ
Pleasant village local with a separate games area and a popular local stores. There is an enclosed garden to one side of the building and seating to the front. The landlord's policy is to sell only beers from East Anglian breweries – with more than 250 different ales offered in seven years. Beer festivals are regular features and barbecues are held on summer days. ♨☆❀◐♿♣P

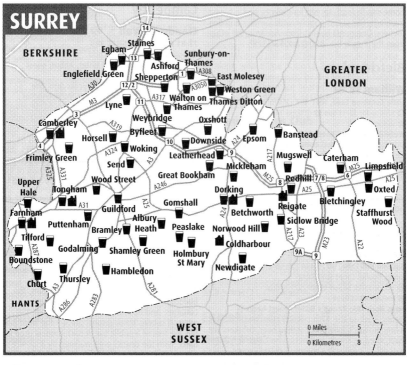

SURREY

BERKSHIRE
Staines
Egham
Englefield Green
Ashford
Shepperton
Sunbury-on-Thames
East Molesey
Weston Green
Lyne
Walton on Thames
Thames Ditton
GREATER LONDON
Camberley
Weybridge
Oxshott
Horsell
Byfleet
Downside
Epsom
Banstead
Frimley Green
Woking
Leatherhead
Mugswell
Caterham
Limpsfield
Send
Mickleham
Redhill
Upper Hale
Tongham
Wood Street
Great Bookham
Dorking
Reigate
Bletchingley
Oxted
Farnham
Guildford
Gomshall
Betchworth
Sidlow Bridge
Staffhurst Wood
Tilford
Puttenham
Bramley
Albury Heath
Peaslake
Norwood Hill
Coldharbour
Godalming
Shamley Green
Holmbury St Mary
Newdigate
Boundstone
Thursley
Hambledon
Chert
HANTS

WEST SUSSEX

0 Miles 5
0 Kilometres 8

Albury Heath

William IV 🅻
Little London, GU5 9DG TQ066467
🍺 11-3, 5.30-11; 12-3, 7-10.30 Sun ☎ (01483) 202685
🌐 williamivalbury.com
Hogs Back TEA; Surrey Hills Ranmore Ale, Shere Drop; Young's Bitter Ⓗ
This secluded and unspoilt 16th-century inn is situated on a small country lane south of Shere, in an area popular with walkers. Features include a flagstone floor, wood beams and a magnificent wood-burning fireplace that warms the cosy main bar. Meals served in the restaurant include Gloucestershire Old Spot pork from the pigs kept in the field behind the pub (no food Sun eve). In summer the tables in the front garden are in demand. ▲Q🕮🐕♣P🚭

Ashford

King's Fairway ✪
91 Fordbridge Road, TW15 2SS (on B377)
🍺 11.30-11 (midnight Fri & Sat) ☎ (01784) 423575
Adnams Broadside; Courage Directors; Sharp's Doom Bar; guest beers Ⓗ
Well-run Ember Inn opposite Ashford Manor Golf Course with extensive parking. Six handpumps dispense three regular real ales and three frequently changing guests. A quiet, largely food-oriented family friendly pub (children over 14 allowed if dining), with no live music or large-screen sports. Two gas fires provide a comfortable ambience in the winter months. Quiz night is Wednesday and curry night Thursday. There is a heated and covered smokers' refuge in the garden. 🕮🐕&🚌(290)P🚭

Banstead

Woolpack ✪
186 High Street, SM7 2NZ (on B2217)
🍺 11-11; 12-10 Sun ☎ (01737) 354560
🌐 thewoolpackbanstead.co.uk
Shepherd Neame Master Brew Bitter, Spitfire, Bishops Finger; guest beers Ⓗ
Bright and friendly pub at one end of the High Street, the Woolpack offers excellent beer with two ever-changing guests, usually from local breweries. Food is all home-made and of high quality. The single bar is divided into a number of areas, with plenty of room for all. A beer festival is held over the August bank holiday. Live jazz plays on the first Tuesday afternoon of the month. ▲🕮🐕&🚌P🚭

Betchworth

Red Lion ✪
Old Road, RH3 7DS (off A25) TQ214504
🍺 11-11 (midnight Fri & Sat); 11-10 Sun ☎ (01737) 843336
🌐 redlionbetchworth.co.uk
Sharp's Doom Bar; guest beers Ⓗ
Parts of the building date back to the early 16th century – the oldest part is the rounded barn beneath the pub – and the wisteria is believed to be more than 230 years old. Well known for its

commemorate Queen Victoria's review of her troops nearby. Marine bric-a-brac and various drinking jugs are on display along with awards for previous entries in this Guide. The generous food is home cooked. The pub closes on some winter Saturday evenings – ring to check. ▲Q✿◑♣P⧛

Mickleham

King William IV 🅛
Byttom Hill, RH5 6EL (off A24 southbound) TQ174538
✪ 11-3, 6.30-11; 12-4.30 Sun ☎ (01372) 372590
⊕ king-williamiv.com
Hogs Back TEA; Surrey Hills Shere Drop; Triple fff Alton's Pride; guest beer Ⓗ
Friendly 18th-century free house clinging to a hillside overlooking the Mole Valley and Norbury Park. It has two separate rooms, both with real fires. An extensive home-cooked menu offers traditional pub food plus more exotic dishes and vegetarian options. The patio and terraced garden are popular on sunny days, and barbecues are hosted. Opening hours are extended in the summer. Steep steps can make access difficult. The shared car park is on the A24. ▲Q✿◑🚊(465)P⧛

Mugswell

Well House Inn 🅛 ✅
Chipstead Lane, CR5 3SQ (off A217) TQ259552
✪ 12-11.30 (10.30 Sun) ☎ (01737) 830640
⊕ wellhouseinn.co.uk
Adnams Bitter; Fuller's London Pride; Surrey Hills Shere Drop; guest beers Ⓗ
The ghost of Harry the Monk is said to be a regular visitor at this Grade II-listed, 16th-century pub. The interior comprises two drinking areas plus a conservatory, the main bar featuring an impressive collection of pewter and ceramic tankards. The restaurant serves generous portions of good food made with local ingredients (not Sun or Mon eves). The Domesday Book mentions the well outside – known as Mag's Well, hence the area's name. ▲Q✿◑🚊♣P⧛

Newdigate

Surrey Oaks 🏆
Parkgate Road, Parkgate, RH5 5DZ TQ205436
✪ 11.30-2.30 (3 Sat), 5.30 (6 Sat)-11; 12-10.30 (8 Nov-Feb) Sun ☎ (01306) 631200 ⊕ surreyoaks.co.uk
Harveys Sussex Best Bitter; Surrey Hills Ranmore Ale; guest beers Ⓗ
This award-winning 16th-century pub continues to excel. It offers an interesting selection of ales from micro-breweries, with hoppy beers and dark ales always popular. Very good home-made food is served in the bar and restaurant (not Sun or Mon eves). Low beams, flagstones and an inglenook feature in the bar, outside are two boules pitches and there is now a skittle alley. Third of a pint glasses are available. Beer festivals are held on the late spring and August bank holidays. Local CAMRA Pub of the Year 2011. ▲Q✿◑♣●P

Norwood Hill

Fox Revived 🅛
RH6 0ET TQ240435
✪ 11 (9.15 Sat)-11.30; 9.15-11 Sun ☎ (01293) 862312
⊕ thefoxrevived.co.uk
Dark Star Hophead; guest beers Ⓗ

Smart country inn situated on a rural crossroads within easy reach of Gatwick Airport. The front bar, complete with book collection and real fire, has a warm and comfortable feel to it. Further in, the interior is more modern and spacious, leading to two conservatories and a large garden with orchard and good views. All meals are home-made and of a high standard, served lunchtimes and evenings during the week and all day at the weekend, including breakfast. Guest beers are mostly LocAles. ▲✿◑P⧛

Oxshott

Bear
Leatherhead Road, KT22 0JE (on A244)
✪ 12-11 (10.30 Sun) ☎ (01372) 842747
⊕ thebearoxshott.co.uk
Young's Bitter, Special, seasonal beers Ⓗ
This Young's pub dates from before 1816, but is decorated in a contemporary style. The central bar is surrounded by several distinct areas and there is a restaurant to the rear. Two spare handpumps may feature either Wells beers or Young's seasonals. There is a decked area at the front, part covered and heated for smokers, and a garden at the rear with a barbecue. Food is served lunchtimes and evenings and all day on Sunday. ▲✿◑♿🚊(408)P⧛

Oxted

Crown 🅛
53 High Street, Old Oxted, RH8 9LN (off A25)
✪ 12-3, 5.30-11; 12-11 Sat; 12-10.30 Sun ☎ (01883) 717853
Adnams Bitter; Fuller's London Pride; guest beers Ⓗ
Dating from the 17th century, the pub was extended in the 1880s when it also incorporated a brewery. This interesting building has many nooks and crannies and is of sufficient age to house a resident ghost. The ground floor is effectively the public bar and has a log fire, while upstairs is used more for dining. Board games are popular and there is a large beer garden with a children's play area. One guest beer will be supplied by Westerham. ▲✿◑🚊(410)♣⧛

Peaslake

Hurtwood Inn 🅛
Walking Bottom, GU5 9RR TQ086446
✪ 12-11 (midnight Fri); 12-10.30 Sun ☎ (01306) 730851
⊕ hurtwoodinnhotel.com
Hogs Back TEA; Surrey Hills Shere Drop; guest beers Ⓗ
Peaslake is in the heart of Surrey Hills walking country, making it a popular lunch stop for ramblers and cyclists. The bar at this three star hotel, which dates from 1920, has a bright contemporary design with a new inglenook fireplace. The beers, mostly LocAle, complement the wide range of main meals and bar snacks served. There are 21 en-suite rooms available. ▲✿⌀◑🚊(25)P

Puttenham

Good Intent ✅
60-62 The Street, GU3 1AR (off B3000) SU931478
✪ 12-3, 6-11.30 (11 Mon); 12-11.30 Sun; 12-10.30 Sun
☎ (01483) 810387 ⊕ thegoodintentpub.co.uk
Otter Bitter; Sharp's Doom Bar; Taylor Landlord; guest beers Ⓗ

Sitting under the North Downs, this welcoming 16th-century inn is popular with villagers, cyclists, walkers and their dogs alike. The inglenook fireplace is especially welcoming during the winter months. Three guest beers join the regulars and an annual beer festival is held over the late May bank holiday weekend. Fish and chip night is every Wednesday, but no food is served Sunday or Monday evenings. The village boasts the last field still growing hops in Surrey. ⚌Q❀❍◗▲♣P⌐

Redhill

Garland ✓
5 Brighton Road, RH1 6PP (on A23)
❂ 11.30-11.30 (12.30am Fri; midnight Sat); 12-11.30 Sun
☎ (01737) 760377
Harveys Sussex XX Mild, Hadlow Bitter, Sussex Best Bitter, Armada Ale, seasonal beers Ⓗ
This classic Victorian street-corner local is one of the older buildings in Redhill. Although close to the town centre, it has the atmosphere of a country pub, and is home to a number of darts, bar billiards and quiz teams. Eight handpumps supply the full range of Harveys beers, including all seasonal and one-off brews. A side room is available for private use and well-behaved children are welcome until 7.30pm. Lunchtime meals during the week offer good value. ❀❍≢⊟♣P⌐

Jolly Brickmakers ✓
58-60 Frenches Road, RH1 2HP
❂ 12-11 ☎ (01737) 789388 ⊕ jollybrickmakers.co.uk
Brakspear Bitter; Ringwood Best Bitter; guest beer Ⓗ
This basic, friendly pub is very much part of the local community. The wood-panelled interior is effectively two bars with a public section containing some unusual moulded heraldic wall badges. The saloon area is distinguished by a Bass mirror, bar billiard table and a library of paperback books. Occasional beer festivals are held in the small garden. The guest beer comes from the Marston's list. No meals, but cutlery and plates are provided for takeaways. ❀⊟(430,435)♣⌐

Send

New Inn
Send Road, GU23 7EN
❂ 11-11; 12-10.30 Sun ☎ (01483) 762736
Adnams Bitter; Fuller's London Pride; Greene King Abbot; Ringwood Best Bitter; guest beer Ⓗ
The New Inn is located on the bank of the Wey Navigation, which opened in 1653 to join Guildford to the Thames and was used for commercial transportation for 300 years. Today's traffic is all for pleasure and many crews find time to stop at the New Inn for a pint or a bite to eat. The pub is well presented and the long single room is divided into a number of areas by exposed brick partitions. ⚌❀❍⊟(462,463)P⌐

Shamley Green

Bricklayers Arms Ⓛ
The Green, GU5 0UA
❂ 11-11 ☎ (01483) 898377 ⊕ bricklayersarmspub.co.uk
Fuller's London Pride; guest beers Ⓗ
Despite its age, this traditional 200-year-old village pub has a bright new feel and offers a warm welcome. Comfortable leather sofas are arranged by the open fire, there is a pool table in the back

area and a restaurant to the side of the horseshoe-shaped bar. Up to five guest ales frequently include beers from LocAle breweries. Events, including a spring beer festival, appeal to all members of the local community. ⚌Q❀❍◗⊟(53,63)♣P⌐

Shepperton

Barley Mow ♥ Ⓛ
67 Watersplash Road, TW17 0EE
❂ 12-11 (10.30 Sun) ☎ (01932) 225326
Hogs Back TEA; Hop Back Summer Lightning; guest beers Ⓗ
Friendly side-street local situated in Shepperton Green a 10-minute walk from the town. Local CAMRA Pub of the Year 2011 and highly commended. The landlord likes to deal direct with local breweries such as Ascot, Twickenham and Windsor & Eton. Live rock 'n' roll or rhythm 'n' blues bands play on Saturday night, with jazz on Wednesday and a quiz on Thursday. Well behaved dogs are welcome. A charity meat raffle is held on Sunday afternoons. ❀≢⊟(438,458)♣♦P⌐

Sidlow Bridge

Three Horseshoes Ⓛ
Ironsbottom, RH2 8PT (off A217) TQ252461
❂ 12-11 (7.30 Sun) ☎ (01293) 862315 ⊕ sidlow.com
Fuller's London Pride, ESB; Harveys Sussex Best Bitter; Young's Bitter; guest beers Ⓗ
The Shoes is a fine old-fashioned country pub, with parts of the building dating back 300 years. It was once home to a forge, hence the name, and was once a coaching inn on the London to Brighton route. Three guest beers are available, often including local ales, and a beer festival is held on the first May bank holiday. Good food, with daily specials, is available lunchtimes and evenings, with barbecues held in the large garden. Q❀❍◗P⌐

Staffhurst Wood

Royal Oak Ⓛ ✓
Caterfield Lane, RH8 0RR TQ407485
❂ 11-11 (closed 3-5 Mon & Tue winter); 12-10.30 Sun
☎ (01883) 722207
Adnams Bitter; Harveys Sussex Best Bitter; Larkins Traditional; Westerham Staffhurst Ale Ⓗ**; guest beers** Ⓗ/Ⓖ
This splendid rural free house is well worth seeking out for both food and drink. Guest ales usually come from local micro-brewers and a range of interesting bottled beers is stocked along with real ciders and perry. Excellent quality meals made from locally-sourced ingredients are available in the bar and restaurant (not Sun eve). This dog-friendly pub enjoys superb views across the countryside. CAMRA members receive a discount on real ales and bar meals. ⚌Q❀❍◗♣♦P⌐

Staines

Bells
124 Church Street, TW18 4ZB
❂ 12-3, 5-11; 12-midnight Fri & Sat; 12-11 Sun
☎ (01784) 454240
Courage Best Bitter; Young's Bitter, Special, seasonal beers; guest beer Ⓗ
This 18th-century pub opposite St Mary's Church and close to the Thames but within easy walking distance of the town centre serves regular and

seasonal Wells and Young's beers plus a guest from its seven handpumps. Good quality food is served – the Honours Club, a discount scheme on food and drink, is available for regular customers lunchtimes and early evenings. The pleasant rear patio garden, with a large heated smokers' canopy, is especially popular in summer, attracting local workers and shoppers. Q❀◐▸&🖳(305)'←

George ✓
2-8 High Street, TW18 4EE
❂ 8-midnight (1am Fri & Sat) ☎ (01784) 462181
Courage Best Bitter; Greene King Ruddles Best Bitter, Abbot; guest beers 🅗
Ever-popular large, two-storey town-centre Wetherspoon pub built in the 1990s. The spacious downstairs bar with its mixture of tables and intimate booths is always busy but a quieter bar can be reached via a spiral staircase. Up to six guest ales are dispensed from one bank of handpumps, with the national brands and two real ciders from Westons on the rear bank. A good selection of foreign bottled beers is also stocked. Value-for-money pub food is served all day. ◐▸&🖳♣'←

Swan Hotel ✓
The Hythe, TW18 3JB (overlooking Thames by Staines Bridge)
❂ 11-11 (midnight Fri & Sat) ☎ (01784) 452494
Fuller's London Pride, ESB, seasonal beers; Gale's Seafarers Ale 🅗
Expect to see all Fuller's draught beers over the course of a year, plus the occasional guest, in this rambling 18th-century hotel. Much enlarged and refurbished over the years, the warren of rooms includes two separate bars and a restaurant. On the walls evocative pictures of Thames life include swans, swan upping and eel catching, and racks of newspapers are available. The long riverside terrace above the hotel's moorings is ideally placed to view the multitude of swans that congregate here. ➳🚲❀🛏◐▸&🖳(51,446)'←

Wheatsheaf & Pigeon 🅛 ✓
Penton Road, TW18 2LL (off B376, corner of Wheatsheaf Lane and Penton Road) TQ 038701
❂ 11-11; 12-10.30 Sun ☎ (01784) 452922
⊕ thewheatsheafandpigeon.co.uk
Courage Best Bitter; Fuller's London Pride; Sharp's Doom Bar; guest beer 🅗
This welcoming and friendly community local is situated between Staines and Laleham, a short walking distance from the Thames Path and Staines Town FC. The cosy bar's wide selection of ales includes guests from the Windsor & Eton range and good food is served every day except Sunday evening; there is also a small dining area. Outside there is plenty of seating for the summer months plus a covered smoking area. Quiz night is Sunday. The pub is particularly busy on football match days. ❀◐▸'←

Sunbury-on-Thames

Grey Horse 🅛
63 Staines Road East, TW16 5AA
❂ 11-11; 12-10.30 Sun ☎ (01932) 782981
Fuller's London Pride; Shepherd Neame Spitfire; Twickenham Original 🅗
This small but welcoming local with an almost rural feel situated between Sunbury Cross and Kempton Park is popular with racegoers. The large garden to the rear is pleasant in the summer despite its close

proximity to the M3. All food is home cooked using locally-sourced produce. Darts matches are played on Monday. Meals are served weekday lunchtimes and Monday to Thursday evenings. Well-behaved dogs are welcome. Mary the ghost is said to reside here. ➳❀◐▸🍴🖳♣'←

Thames Ditton

George & Dragon
High Street, KT7 0RY (on B364)
❂ 11 (12 Sun)-11 ☎ (020) 8398 2206
Shepherd Neame Master Brew Bitter, Spitfire, Late Red, seasonal beers 🅗
Friendly, traditional local often busy with sports fans. Its open-plan interior is divided into several separate drinking areas. The pub welcomes families and has a local jazz band playing on Tuesday evenings. Home-cooked traditional food is served lunchtimes, with a roast on Sunday, and evenings Wednesday to Saturday. Smokers have a heated, covered area with a TV. Shepherd Neame Community Pub of the Year 2010.
Q❀◐▸🍴🖳(514,515)P'←

Thursley

Three Horseshoes
Dye House Road, GU8 6QD (off A3) SU903397
❂ 12-3, 5.30-11; 12-11 Sat; 12-10.30 Sun ☎ (01252) 703268
⊕ 3hs.co.uk
Hogs Back TEA; Surrey Hills Shere Drop; guest beers 🅗
Saved from closure and bought by local supporters in 2004, this pub is now a thriving concern. The hospitable and welcoming inn boasts a traditional bar and separate restaurant areas, roaring log fires, a friendly cat and a two-acre garden popular with families. The excellent guest ale range includes beers from local breweries, and quality home-cooked food is served. The Devil's Punch Bowl and Thursley Nature Reserve are within walking distance. Well worth a detour off the A3.
➳Q❀◐▸&♣P'←

Tilford

Donkey
Charles Hill, GU10 2AU (on B3001) SU893443
❂ 11.30 (12 Sun)-11 ☎ (01252) 702124
⊕ donkeytilford.co.uk
Beer range varies 🅗
A lovely country pub, offering a range of beers usually from Otter and local breweries such as Hogs Back, Surrey Hills and Triple fff. The bar area is small and cosy with a real fire and there is a larger restaurant serving excellent seasonal food. The decor is traditional with wooden beams, and the staff are friendly. Outside, the garden has plenty of seating and space for children to play. Adults and children alike will love the resident donkeys.
➳❀◐▸&♣(46)P'←🚲

Tongham

White Hart 🅛 ✓
76 The Street, GU10 1DH (off A31)
❂ 12-11 (midnight Fri & Sat); 12-10.30 Sun
☎ (01252) 782419 ⊕ whitehartongham.co.uk
Beer range varies 🅗
Three-room pub in the centre of the village, offering a warm welcome to drinkers, with at least four real ales and one cider on offer – check the

blackboard before ordering. Beer festivals are held in March and September. Snacks are served all day, and basket meals in the evening until 9pm (not Sun). Newspapers, books and games are available. Live bands play and there is a quiz every other Tuesday. Children are welcome until 9.30pm, and dogs on leads are allowed.
🏰🕸️🐕🍽️🚂(3,20)♣️👜P🍺

Upper Hale

Alfred Free House
9 Bishops Road, GU9 0JA SU837490
🕒 5 (12 Sat & Sun)-11 ☎ (01252) 820385
🌐 thealfredfreehouse.co.uk
Brakspear Bitter; Ringwood Best Bitter; guest beers Ⓗ
This establishment was previously known as the King Alfred. A classic family-run pub, it serves traditional ale and home-cooked food (weekends only). The cosy main bar is truly welcoming, as is the smart restaurant area next to it. The Alfred aims to be a community pub where conversation reigns. Look out for beer festivals in the spring and October. 🏰Q🕸️🐕🍽️P🍺

Walton on Thames

Regent ✓
19 Church Street, KT12 2QP (on A3050)
🕒 9-midnight (1.30am Fri & Sat) ☎ (01932) 243980
Fuller's London Pride; Greene King Ruddles Best Bitter, Abbot; guest beers Ⓗ
A pleasantly furbished Wetherspoon pub in what was previously a cinema dating from the 1920s. Art Deco in style, it has reflecting lights hanging from the long curved ceiling and high wood panels around the walls. A long bar runs along the right-hand side. Steps at the far end lead to a raised seating area, which is also used by families. Westons cider is sold. Q🕸️🐕👵🍽️👜🍺

Weston Green

Marney's Village Inn
Alma Road, KT10 8JN (off A309)
🕒 11-11; 12-10.30 Sun ☎ (020) 8398 4444
Fuller's London Pride; Young's Bitter; guest beer Ⓗ
This 18th-century hunting lodge became an inn known as the Alma Arms in the mid-1800s. The current name comes from the family that once ran a wood yard next door. The pub is hidden from the main road next to a church and village pond. There is a small bar area with only two tables and a low ceiling, plus a raised area with more seating usually given over to dining, which leads out to the garden. 🕸️🐕🚂(Esher)🍽️(515)P

Weybridge

Jolly Farmer
41 Princes Road, KT13 9BN (off A317)
🕒 11-3, 5.30-midnight; 11-midnight Fri & Sat; 12-midnight Sun ☎ (01932) 856873
Ringwood Best Bitter; Sharp's Doom Bar; guest beers Ⓗ
Traditional old English pub down a back street near the cricket green. Popular with locals, it has a low beamed ceiling and L-shaped bar. Large mirrors and pictures of old Weybridge decorate the walls. Live music features most Saturdays and darts teams play during the week. There is no regular TV although Six Nations rugby is shown. The spacious

garden is popular in the summer and smokers are catered for with heated canopies. Three guest pumps may feature local beers. 🕸️🐕🍽️(459)♣️🍺

Old Crown
83 Thames Street, KT13 8LP (off A317)
🕒 10-11; 12-10.30 Sun ☎ (01932) 842844
🌐 theoldcrownweybridge.co.uk
Courage Best Bitter, Directors; Young's Bitter; guest beer Ⓗ
Weatherboarded, Grade II-listed building dating from the 16th-century. This second generation, family-run pub is alongside the River Thames where it meets the Wey. The garden runs to the waterside where there is access for small boats. Wood-panelled drinking areas include a snug, public bar and dining room, with a conservatory to the rear. Food is available lunchtimes all week and evenings Thursday to Sunday. A meeting place for groups including divers and sailors. Q🕸️🐕🍽️♣️P

Woking

Herbert George Wells 🍺 ✓
51-57 Chertsey Road, GU21 5AJ
🕒 8-midnight (1am Fri & Sat) ☎ (01483) 722818
Courage Best Bitter, Directors; Greene King Abbot; Hogs Back TEA; guest beers Ⓗ
Long-established Wetherspoon pub serving an ever-changing range of up to four guest beers plus four ciders (including two from Mr Whiteheads). There is something for everyone here – office workers and shoppers during the day and a wide range of drinkers young and old in the evening. Named after HG Wells, who lived locally, artefacts include a magnificent invisible man bandaged in tin. Close to both bus and rail stations, this a comfortable alternative to a waiting room. Local CAMRA Pub of the Year 2011. Q🕸️🐕👵🚂🍽️🍺

Woking Railway & Athletic Club
Goldsworth Road, GU21 6JT
🕒 10.30-11; 12-10.30 Sun ☎ (01483) 598499
Beer range varies Ⓗ
Friendly and lively social club tucked away near Victoria Arch serving two constantly changing real ales at reasonable prices, often from local breweries such as Ascot and Bowman. One side of the bar shows various sports events on TV and the other is quieter where conversation rules. Children are welcome and there is wheelchair access to the side. For entry show a CAMRA membership card or copy of this Guide. Local CAMRA Club of the Year 2011. 🚂🍽️♣️🍺

Wood Street

Royal Oak Ⓛ
89 Oak Hill, GU3 3DA
🕒 11-3, 5-11; 12-3, 7-10 Sun ☎ (01483) 235137
Courage Best Bitter; Surrey Hills Shere Drop; guest beers Ⓗ
This free house features regularly in the Guide and has won CAMRA awards for many years. It offers four regularly changing guest beers from micro-breweries, always including a mild, and two real ciders on gravity. Above the bar are 'coming next' pump clips and a cherished Hodgson's Brewery rights-of-way sign. Traditional wholesome food is served every lunchtime and on evenings, Thursday to Saturday. Outside is a large quiet rear garden. Q🕸️🐕🍽️(17)♣️👜P

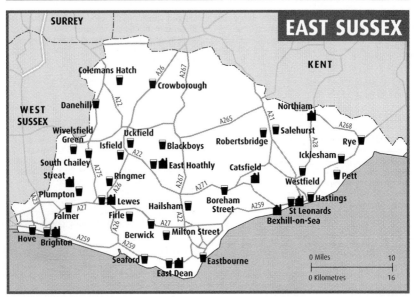

SURREY

EAST SUSSEX

KENT

Colemans Hatch
Crowborough
Danehill
Northiam
WEST SUSSEX
Wivelsfield Green
Uckfield
Salehurst
Rye
Isfield
Blackboys
Robertsbridge
Icklesham
South Chailey
East Hoatly
Catsfield
Streat
Ringmer
Westfield
Pett
Plumpton
Falmer
Lewes
Hailsham
Boreham Street
St Leonards
Hastings
Bexhill-on-Sea
Firle
Hove
Brighton
Berwick
Milton Street
Seaford
Eastbourne
East Dean

0 Miles 10
0 Kilometres 16

SUSSEX (EAST)

Berwick

Cricketers' Arms 🛢 ✅
Berwick Village, BN26 6SP (S of A27)
🕐 11-3, 6-11; 11-11 Sat & summer; 12-10.30 Sun
☎ (01323) 870469 ⊕ cricketersberwick.co.uk
Harveys Sussex Best Bitter, Armada Ale, seasonal beers Ⓖ
Close to the South Downs Way and popular with walkers, this tied house serves ales on gravity from the 'cellar' room behind the bar. Rustic in appearance, it was originally two cottages that were converted into a pub during the 18th century. Peaceful cottage gardens make this an ideal place to idle away the hours on a hot summer's day. Good quality food is served all day. ᴍQ✿◖♣P

Blackboys

Blackboys Inn ✅
Lewes Road, TN22 5LG (on B2192 S of village)
🕐 12-11.30 (midnight Sat & Sun) ☎ (01825) 890283
⊕ theblackboysinn.co.uk
Harveys Hadlow Bitter, Sussex Best Bitter, seasonal beers Ⓗ
This cosy 14th-century pub is decorated with old prints, hop bines and interesting Moroccan artefacts, and has a number of intimate, quiet drinking areas. Outside is a large terraced area overlooking a duck pond, with a covered smoking area, spacious gardens and a large green. Food is served lunchtimes and evenings, all day at weekends. New this year are a children's play area, Wi-Fi, B&B accommodation and a function room. ᴍQ✿✿◖⊟♣P⸻

Boreham Street

Bull's Head 🛢 ✅
BN27 4SG
🕐 12-3, 6-11; 12-11 Fri & Sat; 12-10.30 (6 winter) Sun
☎ (01323) 831981 ⊕ bullsheadborehamstreet.co.uk

Harveys Hadlow Bitter, Sussex Best Bitter, seasonal beers Ⓗ
Harveys' first tied house continues to gain popularity since it re-opened after closure a few years ago. A traditional village pub with wooden floors and panelling, it has a main bar area with a real fire plus two smaller rooms. Harveys seasonal beers are served, with Old Ale throughout the winter and Olympia during the summer. Quiz night is Monday. Good quality, locally-sourced food is served every lunchtime and Tuesday to Saturday evenings. ᴍQ✿◖Ⓐ⊟(98)♣P⸻

Brighton

Basketmakers Arms
12 Gloucester Road, BN1 4AD
🕐 11-11 (midnight Fri & Sat); 12-11 Sun ☎ (01273) 689006
⊕ thebasketmakersarms.co.uk
Fuller's Discovery, London Pride, ESB, seasonal beers; Gale's Seafarers Ale; guest beers Ⓗ
Two-room Victorian street-corner pub on the outer edge of the North Laine area of the city. Eight handpumps serve beers from the Fuller's range plus guests. Reasonably priced home-made pub food is served, including a traditional roast on Sunday. An array of metal boxes and signs covers the walls. Real ale in a bottle is available to take away. ◖⇌⊟⸻

Evening Star 🏆
55-56 Surrey Street, BN1 3PB (150m S of station)
🕐 12-11; 11.30-midnight Fri & Sat; 12-11 Sun
☎ (01273) 328931 ⊕ eveningstarbrighton.co.uk
Dark Star Hophead, seasonal beers; guest beers Ⓗ
A Guide regular and firm favourite with discerning drinkers of all ages. Ignore the somewhat spartan furnishings – you are here to enjoy the great beer. As a flagship Dark Star house, four of its beers are available plus three from other micros, as well as real cider and sometimes perry, together with a varied selection of bottled beers and European beers on draught. All this and occasional beer festivals and live music nights too. ✿⇌⊟♣⸻

Greys
105 Southover Street, BN2 9UA (500m E of A270 opp The Level)
🕒 4-11 (11.30 Thu; 12.30am Fri); 12-12.30am Sat; 12-11 Sun
☎ (01273) 680734 🌐 greyspub.com
Harveys Sussex Best Bitter; Taylor Landlord Ⓗ
A welcoming establishment in the Hanover district of the city offering a wide selection of Belgian beers. Excellent food is served from an a la carte menu in the evening as well as a popular Sunday lunchtime roast. The pub hosts regular live music events often featuring international artists and an annual Belgian beer festival. A quiz night is held every Sunday and a music quiz on the third Monday of the month. Look for the list of local pubs past and present displayed on the wall. ⊛◑🖴(37,37B)🏃

Hampton Arms
57 Upper North Street, BN1 3FH (behind Argos)
🕒 12-midnight (1am Fri & Sat) ☎ (01273) 731347
Arundel Trident; WJ King Brighton Best; guest beers Ⓗ
Lively single bar pub close to the main shopping area with plenty of tables inside and a south-facing patio outside. A popular choice for the younger (or young at heart) beer lovers, there are generally four or five well kept ales, mostly from Sussex breweries. Music is played at a reasonable volume, with occasional live music or a DJ. Quiz night is Monday. Food is served lunchtimes and evenings, all day at the weekend. ⊛◑🖴🏃

Lord Nelson Inn ✔
36 Trafalgar Street, BN1 4ED
🕒 11.30-11; 12-10.30 Sun ☎ (01273) 695872
🌐 thelordnelsoninn.co.uk
Harveys XX Mild, Hadlow Bitter, Sussex Best Bitter, Armada Ale, seasonal beers Ⓗ
A Guide and Ale Trail regular, popular with locals as well as visitors to the city. It is conveniently located for the station and many bus routes. The entire range of Harveys regular and seasonal beers is stocked. There is a folk club on the first Monday of the month, occasional live music and a quiz night on Tuesday. The conservatory can be booked for meetings and functions. Outside is a covered patio with a smoking area. Real cider is available on handpump. ⊛◑🖴♣🏃

Mitre Tavern ✔
13 Baker Street, BN1 4JN
🕒 10.30-11; 10.30-midnight Fri & Sat; 12-10.30 Sun
☎ (01273) 683173 🌐 mitretavern.co.uk
Harveys XX Mild, Sussex Best Bitter, Armada Ale, seasonal beers Ⓗ
Welcoming, traditional, street-corner local situated close to the busy London Road shopping area. A former Charrington pub, it is now owned by Harveys of Lewes. Five or more well-kept Harveys beers are always available, including two seasonal beers. Lunchtime food can be ordered by the bar staff from a local café (11.30-2.30 Mon-Sat). There is a small, secluded courtyard with a smoking area. ⊛◑&🖴♣🏃

Prestonville Arms ✔
64 Hamilton Road, BN1 5DN (between Preston Circus and Seven Dials)
🕒 5-11; 12-midnight Fri & Sat; 12-11 Sun ☎ (01273) 701007
🌐 theprestonvillearms.co.uk
Fuller's London Pride, seasonal ales; Gale's Seafarers Ale, HSB; guest beers Ⓗ

This Fuller's tied house is a vibrant, popular local in a residential area. The half-panelled interior has a variety of seating round a horseshoe-shaped bar. Entertainment includes live music on some weekends, a music quiz on Tuesday, a quiz on Sunday and a Wednesday curry night. There is usually a guest beer to complement the Fuller's/ Gale's range. ⊛◑🖴🏃

Pump House ✔
46 Market Street, BN1 1HH (near town hall)
🕒 10-11; 10-midnight Fri & Sat ☎ (01273) 827421
Harveys Sussex Best Bitter; Sharp's Doom Bar; guest beers Ⓗ
One of the oldest buildings in Brighton and originally a tea house serving sea water bathers, this pub in the famous Brighton Lanes is now a Nicholson's house. Four to five real ales are usually available including changing guest beers; prices are reasonable for the area. The interior is well lit with plenty of seating. A good range of pub food is served until 9pm, with sausages a speciality. The fireplace is said to bear the initials of a Miss Elliott who purchased the building in 1766. 🏚⊛◑🖴🏃

Sir Charles Napier ✔
50 Southover Street, BN2 9UE
🕒 4-11.30; 3-12.30am Fri; 12-12.30am Sat; 12-11 Sun
☎ (01273) 601413
Fuller's London Pride, seasonal beers; Gale's Seafarers Ale, HSB; guest beers Ⓗ
A splendid Victorian corner local where little has changed over past decades. Although a single bar pub it naturally divides into two areas where all can feel at home. A good mixed clientele comes here for food (pizza, sausage and mash), beer, a game of cribbage or just a chat. The regular Sunday night quiz is well supported, along with other events such as Beaujolais Nouveau Night. The landlord is a winner of Fuller's Master Cellarmanship Award. 🏚Q⊛◑🖴(37,81)♣🏃

Station Hotel
1 Hampstead Road, Preston Park, BN1 5NG (opp Preston Park station)
🕒 11-11 (midnight Thu-Sat); 12-11 Sun ☎ (01273) 501318
🌐 stationhotelbrighton.co.uk
Harveys Sussex Best Bitter; guest beers Ⓗ
Traditional back-street local overlooking Preston Park railway station with panoramic views across Brighton, offering a good range of regularly changing beers. Reasonably priced home-made pizzas are available throughout the day with complementary bar snacks on Friday evening. The large L-shaped bar has a TV screen showing live sport. Quiz night is Thursday and live music plays on Saturday evening, with various other events throughout the year.
🏚⊛◑⇌(Preston Park)🖴(5,27)♣🏃

INDEPENDENT BREWERIES
1648 East Hoathly
Beachy Head East Dean
Fallen Angel East Hoathly
FILO Hastings
Franklin's Bexhill-on-Sea (NEW)
Full Moon Catsfield
Harveys Lewes
Hastings St Leonards (NEW)
Kemptown Brighton
Rectory Streat
Rother Valley Northiam

Falmer

Swan Inn ✔
Middle Street, BN1 9PD (just off A27 in N of village)
🕒 12-11 (10.30 Sun) ☎ (01273) 681842
Palmers Best, Tally Ho; guest beers Ⓗ
This three bar pub, enjoyed by locals and visitors alike, has a central snug and two larger bars either side. The snug, with 'Public Bar' and a swan etched on the windows, is where you will find the three handpumps. Two German lagers, Erdinger and Hacker-Pschorr, are available on draught. A German model railway sits above the bar and the landlord will run it if you ask. Other German railway and more general transport memorabilia abound. ＭＱ❀◑⬗ᵫ≉ₘ(28,29)♣Ｐ⅃

Firle

Ram Inn
The Street, BN8 6NS TQ 469074
🕒 11.30 (9 Sat & Sun)-11 ☎ (01273) 858222 ⊕ raminn.co.uk
Harveys Sussex Best Bitter, seasonal beers; guest beers Ⓗ
This village local acted as a court house until the 19th century and retains many early features including the tiled floor around the bar area, bench seating and bay windows from the 1930s. Toad in the hole is still played on a very old board in the low-ceilinged games room. The focus is now on food (booking for meals recommended), but there is still a good pub vibe at the bar, attracting visitors, locals and walkers on the South Downs Way. Westons perry is usually available. ＭＱ▷❀⬗◑⬗(25,125)♣●Ｐ⅃

Hailsham

King's Head ♜ ✔
146 South Road, BN27 3NJ
🕒 5-11; 12.30-3, 4.30-11 Fri; 12-3, 6-11 Sat; 12-3, 7-10.30 Sun ☎ (01323) 440447
Harveys Sussex Best Bitter, seasonal beers Ⓗ
This popular local dates from 1700 and has been a Harveys tied house since 1841. The interior comprises two main bars and a quiet snug, with exposed beams and open fireplaces. Outside is a large beer garden. A friendly hostelry that supports the local community, it even has a knitting club and hosts traditional pub games including toad in the hole. A beer festival is an annual feature. Local CAMRA Pub of the Year 2011. ＭＱ❀ᵫₘ♣Ｐ⅃ᵫ

Hastings

Dolphin ✔
11-12 Rock-a-Nore Road, TN34 3DW
🕒 11-11 (midnight Sat) ☎ (01424) 431197
Courage Directors; Dark Star Hophead; Harveys Sussex Best Bitter; guest beers Ⓗ
Overlooking the unique Hastings fishermen's huts at Rock-a-Nore, this old town pub is at the heart of the fishing community. It is decorated with fishing memorabilia and is busy at weekends and holidays. Good food includes the speciality fish platter (no evening meals are available at the weekend). Live music and quiz nights take place during the week. ＭＱ❀◑⬗ₘ⅃ᵫ

First In Last Out Ⓛ
14-15 High Street, TN34 3EY (in old town, near Stables Theatre)

🕒 12-11 (midnight Fri); 11-midnight Sat ☎ (01424) 425079
⊕ thefilo.co.uk
FILO Mike's Mild, Crofters, Ginger Tom, Cardinal, Gold; guest beers Ⓗ
Dating from the 1500s, this building has been an inn since at least 1896. Formerly home to the FILO Brewery (now 300m up the road), the popular old town pub has a large bar warmed by a central open fire. Four beers are usually available, sometimes including guests. Fresh home-cooked food is served Monday to Saturday, with tapas on Monday evening. Beer festivals are held in the rear function room/restaurant on most bank holiday weekends, with real cider also available. ＭＱ◑⬗ₘ♣ᵫ

Stag Inn
14 All Saints Street, TN34 3BJ
🕒 12-midnight (11 Sun) ☎ (01424) 425734
Shepherd Neame Kent's Best, Spitfire, Bishops Finger, seasonal beers Ⓗ
Probably the oldest surviving pub in Hastings, in its present form it dates from 1547 and has many interesting and quirky features (including mummified cats on display). As a tied house, it is one of a few pubs to take beers from Shepherd Neame's micro-brewery and these are often available to complement the regular ales. Food is usually on offer (check first in winter months). Monday is quiz night, Tuesday folk night, Wednesday bluegrass and Thursday singers. ＭＱ❀◑⬗ₘ♣⅃

White Rock Hotel Ⓛ
1-10 White Rock, TN34 1JU (opp pier)
🕒 10 (12 Sun)-11 ☎ (01424) 422240
⊕ thewhiterockhotel.com
Beer range varies Ⓗ
This large hotel has a stylish, contemporary bar with ample seating and an extensive outside terrace overlooking the seafront. A good range of freshly prepared food is available from 7am until 10pm; the four beers on offer are always from independent Sussex breweries. Many of the guest rooms have fantastic sea views; all are en-suite and decorated and furnished to a high standard. Local CAMRA Pub of the Year 2008. Ｑ❀ᵫ◑⬗ᵫ≉ₘ●

Hove

Downsman
189 Hangleton Way, BN3 8ES (N of Hangleton)
🕒 11.30-4, 6-11; 12-4, 7-11 Sun ☎ (01273) 711301
Harveys Sussex Best Bitter; guest beers Ⓗ
A comfortable 1956 family-run estate pub with a lovely garden overlooking the start of the Old Dyke Railway Trail. The central mock Tudor bar serves three distinct areas – a dining area, lounge and public bar. Two guest beers are offered if the turnover is adequate to keep them in good condition. Reasonably priced pub meals include a hugely popular Sunday roast (no food Sat or Sun eve). ＭＱ❀◑⬗ᵫₘ(5B)Ｐ⅃

Icklesham

Queen's Head
Parsonage Lane, TN36 4BL (signed off A259, opp village hall)
🕒 11-11; 12-10.30 Sun ☎ (01424) 814552
⊕ queenshead.com

Harveys Sussex Best Bitter; guest beers Ⓗ
Local CAMRA Pub of the Year 2009 and a Guide regular, there are always five beers on offer here and up to eight at weekends, with local beers and cider prominent. The interior has five areas warmed by three log fires in winter, adorned with an eclectic mix of decorations and memorabilia. There is an interesting, affordable menu, live music most Sunday afternoons and an annual autumn mini beer festival. A spacious garden offers great views towards Rye. ▲♣☺◐� (100)♣♠P⁵-ⓉⓊ

Robin Hood Ⓛ
Main Road, TN36 4BD
☺ 11-3, 7-11; 11-11 Fri & Sat; 12-5, 7-10.30 Sun
☎ (01424) 814277
Beer range varies Ⓗ
A family-run roadside pub dating from 1607 with parts rebuilt in 1812 following fire damage. Up to five beers are available, often from local breweries. There are two bars, one with a pool table and open fire, the other leading to a dining area where good home-cooked food is served (no food Tue eve). There is a large garden to the rear and a spacious car park. In July the pub hosts the popular Icklesham village beer festival.
▲♣☺◐♧♿▲old (100)♣♠P⁵-

Isfield

Laughing Fish ◐
Station Road, TN22 5XB (off A26 between Lewes and Uckfield) TQ452172
☺ 11.30-11 ☎ (01825) 750349 ⊕ laughingfishonline.co.uk
Greene King IPA, H&H Olde Trip, seasonal beers; guest beers Ⓗ
Built in the 1860s as the Station Hotel, the pub was renamed in the 1960s by local request. The railway line was closed in 1969 but the preserved Lavender Line now uses the station. Tenants since 2001, Andy and Linda have made many improvements including disabled access, a heated outdoor smoking area and a large children's play area. Annual events include the Easter beer race and the village fete. The pub is home to successful pool, darts and toad in the hole teams.
▲♣☺◐♧♿▲🅰old (29,29B)♣P⁵-

Lewes

Brewers Arms
91 High Street, BN7 1XN (near Lewes Castle)
☺ 10-11; 12-10.30 Sun ☎ (01273) 475524
⊕ brewersarmslewes.co.uk
Harveys Sussex Best Bitter; guest beers Ⓗ
This pub is a favourite with CAMRA members, boasting a frequently changing range of ales including three or four guests alongside the Harveys Best. It also attracts football fans, with Sky Ultimate showing on two screens in the back bar, and other major sports events including cricket and rugby also screened. Food is served until 6.30pm; traditional breakfasts daily. There has been a public house on this site since the 17th century.
Q♣☺◐♧old (28,29)♣♠-

Elephant & Castle
White Hill, BN7 2DJ (off Fisher St, near old police station)
☺ 11.30-11 (midnight Fri & Sat); 12-11 Sun
☎ (01273) 473797 ⊕ elephantandcastlelewes.co.uk
Harveys Sussex Best Bitter; Taylor Landlord; guest beers Ⓗ

This community pub attracts young and old alike. Commercial Square Bonfire Society has its headquarters here and it is also a meeting place for groups including a folk club on Saturday evening and a discussion group, Lewes Skeptics in the Pub, once a month. Toad in the hole, table football and darts are played and the pub runs a Sunday football team. In winter the guest beer is often WJ King's Old; the real cider is Westons Old Rosie.
▲♣☺◐≈old (127)♣♠-

Gardener's Arms
46 Cliffe High Street, BN7 2AN
☺ 11-11; 12-10.30 Sun ☎ (01273) 474808
Harveys Sussex Best Bitter; guest beers Ⓗ
Compact, two-bar, genuine free house decorated with pictures of bygone days. Harveys Best is a regular and the ever-changing guests come from small independent breweries; at least one real cider is always available. The pub is home to cricket, stoolball and toad in the hole teams. Many community groups are also supported including the Cliffe Bonfire Society. Locally-sourced pies, sausage rolls and pasties are on offer. A former landlord's football allegiances can be viewed in the Gents.
≈old (28,29)♣♠

John Harvey Tavern ◐
Bear Yard, Cliffe High Street, BN7 2AN (opp Harveys Brewery)
☺ 11-11; 12-10.30 Sun ☎ (01273) 479880
⊕ johnharveytavern.co.uk
Harveys Hadlow Bitter Ⓗ, Sussex Best Bitter Ⓖ, Armada Ale, seasonal beers Ⓗ
Situated in the lane opposite Harveys brewery shop, the pub occupies what was once the stables of the Bear Hotel, where John Harvey first brewed. Despite its modernity the main bar has character – some of the seats are made from wooden fermenting vessels. There is a second quiet room and another room upstairs which can also be used for functions. In winter Old Ale is available on gravity. Live music is performed at the weekend.
▲Q♣☺◐≈old (28,29)⁵-

Lewes Arms ◐
1 Mount Place, BN7 1YH
☺ 11-11 (midnight Fri & Sat); 12-11 Sun ☎ (01273) 473152
⊕ thelewesarms.co.uk
Fuller's London Pride, ESB; Gale's Seafarers Ale, HSB; Harveys Sussex Best Bitter; guest beer Ⓗ
Historic pub with three rooms, offering five regular Fuller's beers plus Harveys Best and one guest. It is the home of the world pea-throwing championships, dwyle flunking and other unusual events, and in 2009 it hosted its first August bank holiday festival – a three-day event of music, poetry and a toad in the hole competition – and now a regular event. It also puts on a pantomime in the upstairs function room and is a venue for writing and bonfire groups.
▲Q☺♣☺◐♧≈old (28,29)♣⁵-

Lewes Constitutional Club
139 High Street, BN7 1XZS
☺ 4.30-10; 12-midnight Fri & Sat; 12-8 Sun
☎ (01273) 473076 ⊕ lewesconclub.co.uk
Harveys Sussex Best Bitter, seasonal ales; guest beers Ⓗ
The Con Club, as it is known locally, was CAMRA Sussex Club of the Year in 2010. Harveys Old is available in winter, usually outselling all others. For entry, show your CAMRA membership card or a

Oakleaf Hole Hearted; Ringwood Best Bitter; guest beers Ⓗ
This early 19th-century pub was built on the site of the village market and subsequently extended into a neighbouring shop. The newer area is mainly used for dining (no food Sun eve or Mon), leaving the remainder of the L-shaped bar with its real fire for drinkers. There is an outside bar in the yard that comes into its own during beer festivals, when the usual diet of local micros is supplemented by beers from far and wide.
🛏Q🏠🌳🕦&🚆(Emsworth)🚌(11,36)🍴🐾💷

Worthing

Cricketers Ⓛ ✔
66 Broadwater Street West, Broadwater, BN14 9DE (on A24 opp Broadwater Green)
☼ 11-11 (11.30 Fri & Sat); 12-10.30 Sun ☎ (01903) 233369
⊕ cricketersworthing.co.uk
Fuller's London Pride; Harveys Sussex Best Bitter; Sharp's Doom Bar; Shepherd Neame Bishops Finger; guest beers Ⓗ
This traditional English pub stands opposite the south east corner of Broadwater green and has a mature rear garden where three beer festivals are held each year – the largest one in July. Dogs are welcome, as are well-behaved children until 9pm, with a play area in the garden. Live music plays on Saturday; Tuesday is quiz night. Well served by buses from Worthing, with roadside parking nearby. 🛏🏠🕦🍴🐾💷

George & Dragon Ⓛ ✔
1 High Street, Tarring, BN14 7NN (S end of High Street)
☼ 11-11 (midnight Fri & Sat); 12-10.30 Sun
☎ (01903) 202497 ⊕ ganddtarring.co.uk
Courage Directors; Greene King Abbot; Harveys Sussex Best Bitter; Hop Back Summer Lightning; Young's Bitter; guest beers Ⓗ
Situated in a well-preserved village street, the 17th-century G&D is a thriving traditional locals' pub with wide appeal. The welcoming bar with low exposed oak beams has several distinct drinking areas, a cosy snug and a tranquil patio garden. Locally-sourced home-cooked food is served lunchtimes and early evenings (Tue-Thu). Entertainment includes pub games, a Wednesday night quiz, jazz on the first Tuesday of the month and occasional live music. The pub is home to a golf society and holds a meat raffle on Sunday.
🏠🕦🚆(West)🚌(6,16)🍴💷

Richard Cobden Ⓛ ✔
2 Cobden Road, BN11 4BD
☼ 11-11 (11.30 Fri & Sat); 12-10.30 Sun ☎ (01903) 236856
⊕ therichardcobden.co.uk
Hop Back Summer Lightning; Ringwood FortyNiner; guest beers Ⓗ
Traditional street corner pub with an L-shaped bar with a real fire at one end and a dartboard at the other, and an attractive enclosed courtyard outside.

Pub food is served alongside changing guest beers often including a mild. Shuffleboard is played on Sunday evening and a slate shove-ha'penny and cribbage board are among the pub games available. Jazz on Thursday and regular live entertainment add to the enjoyment of this classic establishment. Morris men help to dance in the new year. 🛏🏠🕦&🚆🚌(1,5,7)🍴💷

Selden Arms Ⓛ
41 Lyndhurst Road, BN11 2DB (nr Worthing Hospital)
☼ 11-11 (11.30 Fri); 12-11.30 Sat; 12-10.30 Sun
⊕ seldenarms@ntlworld.com
Dark Star Hophead; guest beers Ⓗ
A frequent winner of CAMRA Local Pub of the Year, this one-bar free house provides a continuously changing range of interesting ales on the five guest handpumps. The enthusiastic owners always stock a dark beer plus a selection of bottled Belgian beers. A January beer festival, generous pub lunches, occasional acoustic music and quiet TV sport are other attractions. Situated between the town centre and the hospital, several buses run close by. No lunches on Sunday. 🛏🕦🚆🚌(106)🍴

Swan Inn Ⓛ
79 High Street, BN11 1DN
☼ 11-11 (midnight Fri & Sat); 12-11 Sun ☎ (01903) 232923
Greene King Abbot; Harveys Sussex Best Bitter; Shepherd Neame Spitfire; guest beers Ⓗ
The Swan is a traditional hostelry with a dedicated publican whose cellarmanship is second to none. The pub has an open plan U-shaped interior with a drinking area on one side and a games area with a bar billiards table on the other. The brass and copper artefacts adorning the ceiling are always gleaming. Children are allowed until 7.30pm.
🛏🏠🕦🚆🚌(9,106)🍴💷

Yapton

Maypole Inn ♉
Maypole Lane, BN18 0DP (off B2132 1km N of village; pedestrian access across railway from Lake Lane)
SU978042
☼ 11.30-11 (midnight Fri & Sat); 12-11 Sun
☎ (01243) 551417 ⊕ themaypoleinn.co.uk
Dark Star Hophead; Skinner's Betty Stogs; guest beers Ⓗ
This small, flint-built inn is hidden away from the village centre, down a narrow lane ending in a pedestrian crossing over the railway. The cosy lounge boasts two open fires and a row of eight handpumps, dispensing a variety of up to four guest beers including a mild, often from Arundel. The public bar has a juke-box, darts, pool and a TV for sports events. A skittle alley/function room with bar billiards table can be booked and there is a covered veranda for smokers. Local CAMRA Pub of the Year 2011.
🛏Q🏠🕦🍴&🅰🚆(Barnham)🚌(66,66A,700)🍴💷

A quart a day keeps the doctor away

A judicious labourer would probably always have some ale in his house, and have small beer for the general drink. There is no reason why he should not keep Christmas as well as the farmer; and when he is mowing, reaping, or is at any other hard work, a quart, or three pints, of really good fat ale a-day is by no means too much.
William Cobbett, Cottage Economy, 1822

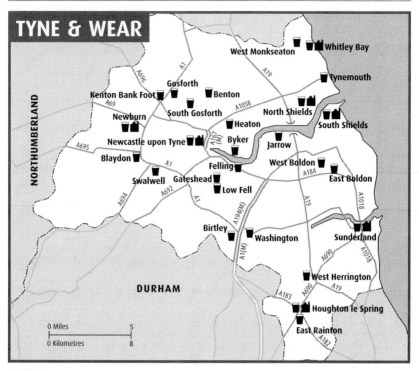

Benton

Benton Ale House

Front Street, NE7 7XE

✪ 11-11 (midnight Fri & Sat); 12-11 Sun ☎ (01912) 661512
⊕ bentonalehouse.com

Banks's Bitter; Jennings Cumberland Ale; Marston's Pedigree; Ringwood Boondoggle; guest beers Ⓗ

Well-appointed traditional pub with a horseshoe bar and large bay windows giving a light and airy feel. Run by a friendly manager and staff, the beer lines are cleaned in front of customers. Reasonably priced, good quality food is served from a menu that proudly boasts 'fresh meat in home-made dishes and Sunday lunches supplied by Lemington butchers'. Families are welcome and a quiz night is hosted on Wednesday. ⛺❍❻♣Pↄ

Birtley

Barley Mow Inn ✪

Durham Road, Barley Mow, DH3 2AG (jct of Durham Road and Vigo Lane)

✪ 11-midnight; 10-11.30 ☎ (01914) 104504
⊕ thebarleymowinn.co.uk

Harviestoun Bitter & Twisted; Rudgate Viking; guest beers Ⓗ

With nine handpulls and seven guest beers (often from northern England), this 1930s roadhouse on the edge of Tyne & Wear offers the widest variety of real ales for some distance. There is a dog-friendly public bar and split-level lounge leading to the dining area. Run by experienced tenants, the pub hosts a weekly quiz and has darts (the landlord is a keen player) and dominoes teams. Regular, varied live music plays and two music and beer festivals feature in February and August.
✿❍❻♿♣Pↄ

Blaydon

Black Bull ✪

Bridge Street, NE21 4JJ

✪ 2-11; 12-midnight Fri & Sat; 12-11 Sun ☎ (01914) 142846

Adnams Broadside; Black Sheep Best Bitter; Caledonian Deuchars IPA; guest beer Ⓗ

Two roomed pub with traditional values – 'No pool table, no juke-box, no bandit' boasts the proud landlord. There has been a pub on this site since the 1800s, and the bar displays over 40 framed photographs of old Blaydon. Two folk nights feature weekly, plus a buskers' night, quiz night and live bands once a month. Barbecues are held in the superb rear beer garden during the summer months. There are excellent views of the River Tyne and Tyne Valley. The premises are patronised by the local blind club. ♨Q⛺❻♿➹(10,602)♣♠P

Byker

Cluny

36 Lime Street, Ouseburn, NE1 2PQ

✪ 11.30-11; 12-10.30 Sun ☎ (01912) 304474
⊕ theheadofsteam.co.uk/newcastle-outlets-the-cluny/

Beer range varies Ⓗ

An imaginative and sympathetic conversion of a stone and brick building standing in the heart of a former heavily industrialised area now regenerated as a leisure venue. As well as the main bar that showcases many works by 'Stuckist' and other artists, there is a family-friendly seating area featuring local artists, and a well established live music venue. The pub has an excellent reputation for its home-made food. Beers from small independent brewers are enthusiastically supported. ✿❍❻♠

Cumberland Arms 🖹

James Place Street (off Byker Bank), Ouseburn,
NE6 1LD

⊕ 4.30-11; 12.30-10.30 Sun ☎ (01912) 656151
⊕ thecumberlandarms.co.uk/
Wylam Rapper; guest beers Ⓗ

Three-storey pub rebuilt more than 100 years ago
and relatively little changed since. It stands in a
prominent position looking down and across the
lower Ouseburn Valley. Home to traditional dance
and music groups, the house beer Rapper from
Wylam Brewery is named after a traditional dance.
A multiple winner of CAMRA's regional Cider Pub of
the Year award, it usually offers up to six ciders or
perries. Winter and summer beer festivals are held
each year. ᏯQ☻✍❤❋♦P

Free Trade Inn 🖹

St Lawrence Road, Ouseburn, NE6 1AP

⊕ 11-11 (midnight Fri & Sat); 12-10.30 Sun
☎ (01912) 655764
Mordue IPA; guest beers Ⓗ

Renowned for its splendid views up river to the
Tyne Bridges and the Newcastle city skyline, this
pub offers a changing selection of beers with local
independent breweries well represented. The pub
is reassuringly basic and homely with friendly,
knowledgeable staff and a high standard of graffiti
in the gentlemen's toilets. Well-behaved dogs are
made welcome. Ꮿ❀☻(Q2,106)♦

East Boldon

Grey Horse

Front Street, NE36 0SJ

⊕ 12-11; 11-midnight Fri & Sat ☎ (0191) 519 1796
Beer range varies Ⓗ

Large mock-Tudor pub on the main road through
the village, next to Boldon Auction Rooms.
Downstairs, it has a single open-plan room with a
number of separate seating areas, and upstairs is a
function room. The guest beers are mainly from
larger independent brewers. Sunday is quiz night.
ᏯQ❀❶♿☻☻(9,30)P⸚

East Rainton

Olde Ships Inn 🖹

Durham Road, DH5 9QT (off A690, behind Highfield
Hotel)

⊕ 12-11 Fri-Sun & summer; 4-11 (closed Mon) winter
☎ (0191) 5840944
Maxim Lambton's; Theakston XB; guest beer Ⓗ

Traditional, family-friendly pub with a welcoming
atmosphere, popular with locals and visitors alike.
The large open-plan L-shaped room has a nautical
theme with walls covered in marine charts and
many framed photographs of Sunderland
shipbuilding. There are no gaming machines or
juke-box, just unintrusive background music. The
pub hosts a local cricket team and book club and is
a regular stop for local walkers. Quiz night is
Tuesday. Freshly cooked, traditional pub food is
served until 9pm (4pm Sun). ❶☻(20,22)♣P⸚

Felling

Old Fox

10-14 Carlisle Street, NE10 0HQ

⊕ 2-11; 1-midnight Fri & Sat; 12-11 Sun ☎ (01914) 404815
Fuller's London Pride; Castle Rock Harvest Pale; guest
beers Ⓗ

Pleasant real ale pub a short walk from Felling
Metro. The open fire gives the bar a homely feel. A
live band plays on the first Saturday of the month
and Monday is local buskers' night. The present
landlord has returned after several years away and
is busy restoring the pub to its former glory.
Ꮿ❀☻✍❶☻☻(27,93,94)♣P⸚

Wheatsheaf 🖹

26 Carlisle Road, NE10 0HQ

⊕ 5 (12 Fri & Sat)-11; 12-10.30 Sun ☎ (01914) 200659
Big Lamp Bitter, Prince Bishop Ale, Sunny Daze,
seasonal beers; guest beer Ⓗ

One of two pubs belonging to Big Lamp Brewery,
this street corner local has a loyal band of regulars
who travel quite a distance to drink here, but offers
a warm welcome to all. The pub features some
original details, mismatched furniture and, when
needed, real coal fires. There's a fortnightly
Monday quiz, traditional folk music night featuring
keen local musicians on Tuesday, and Wednesday
is dominoes night. Ꮿ❀❶☻☻(27,93,94)♣♦

Gateshead

Central ☆

Half Moon Lane, NE8 2AN

⊕ 12-midnight (1am Fri & Sat) ☎ (01914) 782543
⊕ theheadofsteam.co.uk/gateshead
Beer range varies Ⓗ

A mid-19th century Grade II-listed four-storey,
wedge-shaped building recently revived by the
Head of Steam group. It now has a revamped
public bar, two function rooms, a rooftop terrace
and is a live music venue. The Buffet has been
retained as fitted-out circa 1900 with a carved U-
shaped counter and bar back, plasterwork frieze
and panelling and features in CAMRA's National
Inventory of Historic Pub Interiors. The 14 handpulls
dispense many local micro-breweries' beers.
❶♿☻☻♣♦⸚

Gosforth

County ✔

High Street, NE3 1HB

⊕ 12-11 (10.30 Sun) ☎ (01912) 856919
Black Sheep Best Bitter; Caledonian Deuchars IPA;
Daleside Blonde; Fuller's London Pride; Wells
Bombardier; guest beers Ⓗ

Standing at the southern edge of Gosforth High
Street, the County is one of the best known real ale
outlets in Newcastle. The large L-shaped bar
attracts a variety of visitors, from office workers to
students, and can get busy, especially at
weekends. Up to four regular beers are available. A
separate room at the back offers respite from the
hustle and bustle of the main bar, and also doubles
as a small function room. ❀❶P

Job Bulman 🅛 ⊘
St Nicholas Avenue, NE3 1AA
☻ 9am-11.30 ☎ (01912) 236230
Greene King Ruddles Best Bitter, Abbot; guest beers Ⓗ
Impressive Wetherspoon conversion of the old post office building just off the busy High Street. The unusual horseshoe-shaped interior houses a large bar area in the centre, complemented by more discrete dining areas to each side. There is an outside courtyard for smokers. Two regular beers are complemented by a constantly rotating guest list, with up to eight ales at any one time. At least two guests are usually from local micro-breweries. A church group and war widows group meet here monthly. ⍩⊙♣ᵔ

Queen Victoria 🅛
206 High Street, NE3 1HD
☻ 11-11; 12-10.30 Sun ☎ (01912) 856917
Mordue Workie Ticket; guest beers Ⓗ
Big establishment on the corner of the High Street with a large upper storey bay window. Closed for a long period, it has recently been acquired by Leopard Leisure and refurbished to a high standard. Previously called Northern Lights and Ye Olde Jockey, the pub has now reverted to its original name. Six handpumps serve beers from the Punch list. ♿

Heaton

Chillingham 🅛
Chillingham Road, NE6 5XN
☻ 11-11 (midnight Fri & Sat); 12-11 ☎ (01912) 655915
Black Sheep Best Bitter; Jarrow Rivet Catcher; Mordue Workie Ticket; guest beers Ⓗ
A large two-roomed pub with contrasting styles – the public bar in traditional dark wood with panelling and a historic mirror recalling the past glories of nearby Wallsend, and the lounge with a contemporary feel, flat screen sports TVs and excellent artwork depicting the sights of Newcastle. Popular with the widest possible customer base, the upstairs function room holds live music and comedy nights. An excellent choice of local micro-brewery beers is always on offer, and look out for bottled beer, whisky and wine of the month. ⊙🖵🚆(62,63)♣♣P

Houghton le Spring

Copt Hill 🅛
Seaham Road, DH5 8LU (on B1404)
☻ 11-midnight; 11.30-11.30 Sun ☎ (0191) 584 4485
Beer range varies Ⓗ
With a spectacular vista over the Houghton countryside, this former Vaux pub has a close connection with the local Maxim Brewery and acts as its unofficial tap, so at least one of its beers is always available, complemented by four guest ales, usually sourced locally. Excellent food is served all day from an extensive menu – booking for the recently refurbished restaurant is advisable as it can get busy at evenings and weekends. Live music plays every Sunday night. ⊛⊙♿🖵(20)P

Jarrow

Robin Hood 🅛
Primrose Hill, NE32 5UB
☻ 11-11 (midnight Fri & Sat) ☎ (0191) 4285454
⊕ jarrowbrewery.co.uk
Jarrow Bitter, Rivet Catcher, Westoe IPA Ⓗ
Originally a coaching inn dating back to 1824, the Robin Hood is tastefully decorated and retains its old charm. A previous CAMRA local Pub of the Year, and the original home of the Jarrow Brewery, it is adorned with awards for both the brewery and the pub. It has three function rooms, live entertainment every Friday and Sunday, and a good range of award-winning Jarrow ales constantly on offer plus one guest. ⍩Q⍩⊛🖵♿⊖(Fellgate)Pᵔ🖵

Kenton Bank Foot

Twin Farms
22 Main Road, NE13 8AB
☻ 11-11 (11.30 Fri & Sat); 12-10.30 Sun ☎ (01912) 861263
Black Sheep Best Bitter; Taylor Landlord; guest beers Ⓗ
Large stone-built building, a former farmhouse, standing in its own grounds. Comfortably furnished, it has various areas inside and out to sit and enjoy the extensive selection of beers on offer. The management runs events for regulars, including brewery visits and Meet the Brewer sessions. The pub aims to reduce food miles and the ingredients used in meals are locally-sourced from named suppliers. ⍩Q⍩⊛⊙♿⊖(X77,X78)P

Low Fell

Aletaster 🅛
706 Durham Road, NE9 6JA
☻ 12-11 (midnight Fri); 12-midnight Sat ☎ (01914) 870770
Black Sheep Best Bitter; Everards Tiger; Jennings Cumberland Ale; Taylor Landlord; Theakston Old Peculier; Wylam Gold Tankard; guest beers Ⓗ
In the Guide under the same stewardship for nearly 20 years and with 11 handpulls, this suburban ale house offers the greatest number of real ales (and a real cider) for miles around. There is an L-shaped public bar with bare boards and TVs, plus a cosy, smaller lounge with its own bar counter. The pub hosts a lively weekly quiz and occasional live music. The four guest beers often come from micro-breweries in the north of Britain. ⊙🖵♣♣P

Newburn

Keelman
Grange Road, NE15 8NL
☻ 11-11; 12-10.30 Sun ☎ (01912) 671928
Big Lamp Sunny Daze, Bitter, Summerhill Stout, Prince Bishop, seasonal beers Ⓗ
This tastefully converted Grade II-listed former pumping station is now home and brewery tap to the Big Lamp Brewery. A conservatory has been added to accommodate the growing band of diners and drinkers who come to enjoy the full range of Big Lamp beers. Quality accommodation is provided in the adjacent Keelman's Lodge and Salmon Cottage. Attractively situated by the Tyne Riverside Country Park, Coast to Coast cycleway and Hadrian's Wall National Trail. ⍩⊛🛏⊙♿🖵(22)Pᵔ

Newcastle upon Tyne

Bacchus 🄻
42-48 High Bridge, NE1 6BX
✪ 11.30-midnight; 12-10.30 Sun ☎ (01912) 611008
Jarrow Rivet Catcher; guest beers 🄷
Local CAMRA Pub of the Year three years running, this smart, comfortable, city-centre pub boasts nine handpumps offering a wide range of rapidly changing guest ales, with one pump dedicated to beer from Orkney's Highland Brewing Company and another to cider. A seasonal house beer is brewed by Yorkshire Dales, and a large range of draught and bottled foreign beers is available. Regular beer and food matching events are held. Photographs and posters showing the industries in which this region used to lead the world cover the walls. ◑♿⊖(Monument)♣

Bodega 🄻
12 Westgate Road, NE1 6BX
✪ 11-11 (midnight Fri & Sat); 12-10.30 Sun
☎ (01912) 211552
Big Lamp Prince Bishop; Durham Magus; guest beers 🄷
Two fine stained-glass domes are the architectural highlights of the pub, which stands next to the Tyne Theatre and is popular with football and music fans. TVs show sporting events and the pub can be busy on match days. The interior offers a number of standing and seating areas, with separate booths for more intimate drinking. A number of old brewery mirrors adorn the walls. A good selection of foreign bottled and draught beers is available. ◑≠(Central)⊖(Central)♣

Bridge Hotel 🄻
Castle Garth, NE1 1RQ
✪ 11.30-11 (midnight Fri & Sat); 11.30-10.30 Sun
☎ (01912) 326400
Black Sheep Best Bitter; Caledonian Deuchars IPA; guest beers 🄷
This large Fitzgerald pub is situated next to Stephenson's spectacular High Level Bridge, the rear windows and the patio have views of the city walls, River Tyne and Gateshead Quays. The main bar area, adorned with many stained glass windows, is divided into a number of seating areas with a raised section to the rear. Several guest beers come from far and wide. Among the live music events held in the upstairs function room is what is claimed to be the oldest folk club in the country. ❀◑≠(Central)⊖(Central)♣⊱

Centurion 🄻 ✔
Central Station, NE1 5DG
✪ 10-11 (midnight Fri & Sat) ☎ (01912) 616611
⊕ centurion-newcastle.co.uk/bar.asp
Black Sheep Best Bitter; Caledonian Deuchars IPA; Jarrow Rivet Catcher; guest beers 🄷
This beautiful bar, recently enhanced with improved lighting, was built in 1893 as a sumptuous waiting lounge for first class passengers – note the exquisite tiling which is today worth £3.8 million. It was closed in the 1960s, when the Transport Police used it as cells. Since its restoration, the grandeur of the John Dobson-designed interior is now enjoyed by thousands of customers, both locals and visitors to Newcastle. A popular starting point for Whistle Stops II real ale outings. ⊱◑◑♿≠(Central)⊖(Central)🚌♣♣

Crown Posada ★ 🄻
33 Side, NE1 3JE
✪ 12-11 (1am Fri & Sat); 7-10.30 Sun ☎ (01912) 321269
Hadrian Gladiator; Jarrow Bitter; Mordue Workie Ticket; guest beers 🄷
An architecturally fine pub, listed in CAMRA's National Inventory of Historic Pub Interiors. Behind the narrow street frontage with two impressive stained glass windows lies a small snug, the bar counter and a longer seating area. There is an interesting coffered ceiling, locally relevant photographs and cartoons of long-gone customers and staff on the walls. Local small brewers are enthusiastically supported. The building has been sympathetically refurbished over the years by the owners and is an oasis of calm and peace near the busy Quayside drinking, dining and clubbing circuit. Q🚌(Q1,Q2)⊱

Duke of Wellington
High Bridge, NE1 1EN
✪ 12-11 (10.30 Sun) ☎ (01912) 618852
⊕ thedukeofwellington.info
Taylor Landlord; guest beers 🄷
A small, single-roomed pub run by an enthusiastic real ale supporter. Situated in an area full of vintage clothing and record shops, The Duke has retained its independent identity with a mixed clientele drawn by the selection of beers from near and far. The pub is near the infamous Bigg Market area but just far enough away to ensure that it's off the young revellers' circuit. Home-made lunchtime/afternoon food is simple and good value. Busy on match days. ◑⊖(Monument)♣

LYH
10 Northumberland Road, NE1 8JF
✪ 11-2am; 12-10.30 Sun ☎ (01912) 325231
Caledonian Deuchars IPA; guest beers 🄷
Just off the main city centre shopping street, this pub has had a number of owners and names over the years but has now settled down as part of the well-respected Head of Steam chain, offering a good selection of beers and ciders. The frontage is small, but once inside the building opens out into a large bar with separate sitting area and a mezzanine floor. The pub is popular with football fans before the match or when live games are televised, and also stages live rock music nights. ◑⊖(Haymarket)♣

Mile Castle ✔
Westgate Road, NE1 5XU (corner of Grainger St and Westgate Rd)
✪ 7-midnight (1am Thu-Sat) ☎ (01912) 111160
Greene King Ruddles Best Bitter, Abbot; guest beers 🄷
Opened in 2009, this Lloyds No.1 bar boasts 20 handpulls over three floors. Impressively redecorated, there is a boothed area for diners on the second floor, although meals are served throughout the day to all areas. The name refers to the Roman forts that were built a mile apart and one is reputed to have been situated nearby. Transport links are excellent, with rail and Metro stations nearby and a main bus stop outside the front door. ⊱◑◑♿≠(Central)⊖(Central/Monument)🚌♣

New Bridge 🄻
2 Argyle Street, NE1 6PF
✪ 11-11 (11.30 Thu-Sat); 12-10.30 Sun ☎ (01912) 321020
Jarrow Rivet Catcher; guest beers 🄷

Slightly out of the city centre, this pub attracts a wide range of customers, with weekday lunchtimes always busy with office workers and students enjoying the good quality home-made food. As part of the independent, locally based SJF real ale chain, the pub has access to an excellent selection of rapidly changing beers from all parts of the country. The Thursday night quiz is popular. ◑⊖(Manors)🖳

Newcastle Arms

57 St Andrew's Street, NE1 5SE (by Chinese Arch at Gallowgate end of Stowell St)
✪ 11-11; 12-10.30 Sun ☎ (01912) 602490
Caledonian Deuchars IPA; guest beers Ⓗ
Popular single roomed pub near St James' Park and China Town, the 'Top Arms' is a multiple winner of CAMRA Local Pub of the Year competitions, demonstrating the staff's commitment to giving customers what they want. An impressive range of beer sourced from far and wide is available, including a seasonal house ale from Big Lamp Brewery. Beer festivals are held regularly, when a portable bar brings the number of beers available up to 13. Q🍴🚳🛒⊖(Monument/St James)🖳🏮

North Shields

Magnesia Bank

1 Camden Street, NE30 1NH
✪ 12-11 (midnight Fri & Sat) ☎ (01912) 574831
⊕ magnesiabank.com
Durham Magus; guest beers Ⓗ
The Maggie Bank is so called due to its former days as a bank; it then became a social club before conversion to a pub. Now a popular music venue, free live music plays every Wednesday, Friday and Saturday, and Monday is buskers' night. As well as the pub, the Café Black Door, open Wednesday to Saturday evenings, provides an extensive food menu. A much improved outlet and previous local CAMRA Pub of the Year. ◑

Oddfellows

7 Albion Road, NE30 2RJ
✪ 11 (12 Sun)-11 ☎ (01912) 574288
⊕ oddfellowspub.co.uk
Greene King Abbot; Jarrow Bitter; guest beer Ⓗ
The walls of this small, friendly, single-room lounge bar are covered with historic maps and photographs of pre-war North Shields, which are also shown on the large flat-screen TV and relayed to the outside smoking area. The pub has strong sporting links with past boxing champions and current national darts players. Home to football and darts teams, it fundraises for charity and hosts a beer festival annually in May. 🚳🛒🖳(306)🏮🏮

Prince of Wales

2 Liddell Street, NE30 1HE
✪ 3 (12 Wed-Sat)-11; 12-10.30 Sun ☎ (01912) 962816
Samuel Smith OBB Ⓗ
Records for this pub date back to 1627 but the current building, faced with green glazed brick, dates from 1927. The premises lay empty for some years, before restoration in traditional style by Samuel Smith, and re-opened in 1992. A rare outlet for Sam Smith's this far north, it is well worth a visit. Close to the fish quay where the fish and chips are renowned, there is a replica 'wooden dolly' outside, which gives the pub its nickname. 🏚Q🚳🛒🖳(333)

South Gosforth

Brandling Villa ✔

Haddricks Mill Road, NE3 1QL
✪ 12-midnight ☎ (01912) 840490 ⊕ brandlingvilla.co.uk
Jarrow Rivet Catcher; Wylam Gold Tankard; guest beers Ⓗ
Large double-fronted pub with keen, enthusiastic staff. The bar offers a constantly changing selection of beers from far and near along with two ciders. A tiny, locally based brewery uses the pub to showcase its beers which are always well received by customers. The imaginative manager organises various well-attended events, such as the Sausage Fest when local butchers present artisan sausages and pies alongside a vast selection of British and imported beers and ciders. 🏚🚳◑🛒⊖🏮

South Shields

Alum Ale House ✔

Ferry Street, NE33 1JR (next to South Shields Ferry Landing)
✪ 11-11 (midnight Fri & Sat); 12-11.30 Sun
Banks's Mild, Bitter; Jennings Cumberland Ale; Cocker Hoop; Marston's Pedigree; Wychwood Hobgoblin Ⓗ
The Alum Ale House is situated on the south bank of the River Tyne, adjacent to the Ferry Landing and close to the Market Place. The open plan bar, with its six handpumps, is the venue for a fortnightly buskers' night on alternate Thursdays and a lively Irish music session on the first Sunday of the month. In addition to traditional bar games such as dominoes, the pub also hosts a chess club and organises quiz nights. 🏚Q🚳🛒⊖🖳🏮P🏮

Maltings Ⓛ

Claypath Lane, NE3 4PG (off Westoe Road)
✪ 12-11.30 (10.30 Sun) ☎ (0191) 427 7147
⊕ jarrowbrewery.co.uk
Beer range varies Ⓗ
Located on the first floor of the building, above the Jarrow Brewery, this former dairy has been transformed into real gem of a pub. The staircase or lift leads you to a partitioned room with a large central bar and lots of seating. At least two Jarrow beers are always available on handpull complemented by a selection of guests, bottled Jarrow ales, and a range of imported European draught and bottled beers. Food is available daily with authentic Thai food a speciality. Q🚳◑🛒⊖🖳🏮🏮

Stag's Head ☆ Ⓛ

45 Fowler Street, NE33 1NS
✪ 12-11 (midnight Fri-Sun) ☎ (0191) 427 2911
Draught Bass; guest beer Ⓗ
Traditional single-room town-centre pub dominated by an attractive alcove back bar. Listed on CAMRA's National Inventory of Historic Pub Interiors, it has retained many original design features including colourful entrance tilework and a wide acid-etched bay window at the front. Three beers are usually available, always including Bass. This popular local can get busy at times. Upstairs is an extra room complete with its own small bar – also available to hire for private functions. Karaoke features on Sunday. ⊖🖳🏮

Steamboat 🏆 ✔

Coronation Street, Mill Dam, NE33 1EQ (follow signs for Customs House)

12-11 (midnight Thu-Sat); 12-11.30 Sun
☎ (0191) 454 0134
Beer range varies Ⓗ
Bursting with character and atmosphere, close to the South Shields ferry and Custom House theatre, the Steamboat has been awarded CAMRA Local Pub of the Year for the past two years and boasts eight handpumps offering an impressive range of beers from independent and micro-brewers all over the country. It has a large bar with a raised seating area and a small lounge. The friendly staff host regular beer festivals, cheese and ale and Meet the Brewer nights. ⊖🖵♣🐾

Trimmers Arms Ⓛ
34 Commercial Road, NE33 1RW
12-midnight (1am Fri-Sun) ☎ (0191) 597 9023
Marston's EPA; Yard Of Ale Yardarm Ⓗ
This was originally two pubs – the Trimmers Arms and the West End Vaults – which burned down. In 2004 the present Trimmers Arms emerged, comprising a large bar area with raised seating and a spacious lounge leading off. As well as the regular ales there are four guests and Old Rosie cider. A carvery is held every Sunday, live music plays at the weekend and a quiz night is hosted on Tuesday. ⊖(Chichester)🖵🐾

Sunderland

Avenue Ⓛ
26 Zetland Street, Roker, SR6 0EQ (just off Roker Avenue)
12-11; 11-midnight Fri & Sat; 11-11 Sun
☎ (0191) 5677412
Beer range varies Ⓗ
A lively local pub with a bar and function room on the ground floor plus a games room upstairs containing a full size snooker table and two dartboards. The bar room is rectangular with an area at one end used for music/busker nights. The function room is opened for live football matches on TV, bingo nights and other regular functions. Close to the Stadium of Light, it can get busy on match days. ❀⊖(Saint Peters)🖵(E1,E6)♣🐾

Clarendon Ⓛ
143 High Street East, SR1 2BL
12-midnight (11 Sun) ☎ (0191) 510 3200
⊕ bull-lane-brewing.co.uk
Bull Lane Nowtsa Matta Ⓗ
This brew pub is located just outside the city centre, with six handpumps offering Bull Lane beers. The single-room public bar has a large rear window with panoramic views across the River Wear. The pub is a lively community local, where the focus is clearly on beer. It hosts a buskers' night on Wednesday and live music on Sunday afternoon. A warm welcome is assured and the pub is well worth the walk from Sunderland centre. ♿🖵(5,5A)

Cliff
Mere Knolls Road, Roker, SR6 9LG
12-11.30 (12.30am Fri-Sun) ☎ (0191) 548 6200
Caledonian Deuchars IPA Ⓗ
This friendly and welcoming bar in a largely residential area has a spacious open-plan lounge featuring an L-shaped bar with a raised pool and board games area at one end. The pub offers three cask ales including two guests and has a spacious smoking area. Popular on Sunderland AFC match days, a shuttle bus is laid on to take fans to the

Stadium of Light. Large-screen TVs have their volume muted to be unobtrusive. Quiz nights are Tuesday and Wednesday. Home to an active golf society. ❀♿🖵(18,19,E1)♣🐾

Fitzgerald's Ⓛ
10-12 Green Terrace, SR1 3PZ
11-11 (midnight Fri & Sat); 12-10.30 Sun
☎ (0191) 567 0852 ⊕ sjf.co.uk
Taylor Landlord; guest beers Ⓗ
Sunderland's largest range of cask beers can be found at this busy town-centre pub run by the real-ale-friendly Sir John Fitzgerald group. There are two separate rooms, with the smaller Chart Room quieter than the main bar. The pub is an enthusiastic supporter of north-east micro-breweries and nine guest beers are usually on offer. Quizzes are held Tuesday and Thursday. CAMRA members receive a discount on ale. ❀◧⇌⊖(University)🖵🐾

Harbour View Ⓛ
Benedict Road, Roker, SR6 0NU
10.30-11.30 (midnight Fri & Sat) ☎ (0191) 567 1402
Beer range varies Ⓗ
A modern, open plan bar with good views of the River Wear and the sea. It offers two regular ales – Caledonian Deuchars IPA and Taylor Landlord – as well as a good choice of four guests. Quiet during the week, the pub is livelier at weekends – match days are best avoided if you like a peaceful pint as it can get hectic. Buses stop directly outside. ♿🖵(E1,19)🐾

King's Arms Ⓛ
Beach Street, Deptford, SR4 6BU
12-11 (midnight Fri & Sat) ☎ (0191) 567 9804
⊕ threehorseshoesleamside.co.uk/kings_arms.aspx
Taylor Landlord; guest beers Ⓗ
Dating back to 1834 and situated in the old industrial heartland of Deptford, the pub has views over the River Wear. A walled beer garden with marquee hosts live music, barbecues and small beer festivals. Seven guest beers from north-east micro-breweries are regularly available. CAMRA Local Pub of the Year from 2005 to 2007 and North East winner 2006 to 2008. ⋈❀⊖(Millfield)🖵(10,11)🐾🍴🍺

Museum Vaults Ⓛ
33 Silksworth Row, Millfield, SR1 3QT
12-11 (3 Tue; midnight Thu-Sat); 12-10.30 Sun
☎ (0191) 5659443
Beer range varies Ⓗ
A blazing open fire welcomes you to this small, friendly hostelry, managed by the same family for more than 30 years. The former Vaux pub has a long connection to both the brewery and the local football team, with numerous pieces of memorabilia adorning the walls. Three handpulled beers are available, one always from Maxim Brewery, the others alternating between local and national micro brews. A selection of bottle-conditioned beers is also stocked, often from Durham Brewery. ⋈❀⊖(University)🖵(10,11)P🐾

TJ Doyles Ⓛ
Hanover Place, Deptford, SR4 6BY
4-11; 12-midnight Sat & Sun ☎ (0191) 510 1554
⊕ tjdoyles.com
Bull Lane Neck Oil; guest beers Ⓗ
This former Vaux pub is now a stylish Irish bar providing a range of beers from local micro-

breweries – ales from Bull Lane, Maxim and Jarrow are regularly available as well as guest beers from further afield. The bar is large with comfortable Chesterfield leather sofas for relaxed drinking. Live music plays at weekends. ❀🚲♿ (Millfield) 🚆 (11,36A/C) ♣P⁵⌐

Wolsey
40 Millum Terrace, Roker, SR6 0ES
☼ 11-11 (midnight Fri & Sat) ☎ (0191) 567 2798
Theakston Best Bitter; guest beer Ⓗ
This family-friendly pub overlooks Roker Marina and is only a short walk from the beach. A blazing wood fire welcomes you to the cosy open-plan lounge/bar. Two handpumps dispense the regular beer and a guest. Live music plays every Saturday evening and a popular free quiz takes place on Thursday night. Good reasonably priced food is available every day – specials such as curry night on Wednesday and steak night on Thursday are popular. 🏚Q❀◖♿🚆(E1)P

Swalwell

Sun Inn ❷
Market Lane, NE16 3AL (just off roundabout at end of Front St)
☼ 11-midnight; 12-11 Sun
Beer range varies Ⓗ
Situated in the modern village of Swalwell just a stone's throw from the Metrocentre shopping complex, this pub has been in existence for more than 100 years. A genuine community pub, entertainment ranges from sword dancers to a monthly pie competition to buskers' night on Saturday. The enthusiastic landlord has increased the handpulls from one to four and also has real cider on draught. Bar food and snacks are available, free on Sunday. 🍴❀🚆♣♦⌐

Tynemouth

Cumberland Arms ❷
17 Front Street, NE30 4DX
☼ 12-11 (10.30 Sun) ☎ (01912) 571820
⊕ cumberlandarms.co.uk
Courage Directors; Jennings Cumberland Ale; Tetley Bitter; guest beers Ⓗ
Cosy split-level pub with friendly bar staff. A side alley gives access to the upper bar. Attractive stained glass windows and historic artefacts feature throughout and beer is dispensed in both rooms from a cabinet with six handpulls. Families are welcome in the dining area at the rear, which

Beer changes

As the Guide went to press, we learned that Theakston Traditional Mild had become a seasonal beer, rather than a regular member of the brewery's portfolio. It will be brewed every May to coincide with CAMRA's Make May a Mild Month promotion but other periods have not been decided.

Adnams Bitter has been renamed Adnams Southwold Bitter.

serves good-value food – themed events include grill night on Wednesday and curry night on Thursday. 🍴◖♿♿🚆(306)♣

Turk's Head ❷
41 Front Street, NE30 4DZ
☼ 11-11; 12-10 Sun ☎ (01912) 576547
Caledonian Deuchars IPA; Courage Directors; Wells Bombardier; guest beers Ⓗ
Popular main street pub with two linked rooms – the front bar tends to be more lively with the rear room much quieter, welcoming families up to 7pm. Food is available all day and TVs throughout screen live sport. Of architectural note, the exterior is white tiled with stained glass windows; the interior is home to the famous stuffed dog. A wide range of seating and wooden floors add character. 🏚🍴◖♿🚆(306)♣

Tynemouth Lodge Hotel
Tynemouth Road, NE30 4AA
☼ 11-11; 12-10.30 Sun ☎ (01912) 577565
⊕ tynemouthlodgehotel.co.uk
Belhaven 80/-; Caledonian Deuchars IPA; Draught Bass; guest beer Ⓗ
This attractive externally tiled free house was built in 1799 and has featured in every issue of the Guide since 1983 when the current owner took over – the 25th anniversary celebrations were duly held in 2009. The comfortable U-shaped lounge has the bar on one side and a hatch on the other. It is noted in the area for its Scottish ales and for selling reputedly the highest volume of Draught Bass on Tyneside. The pub is next to Northumberland Park and near the Coast to Coast cycle route. 🏚Q❀◗P

Washington

Courtyard Ⓛ
Arts Centre, Biddick Lane, Fatfield, NE38 8AB
☼ 11-11 (midnight Fri & Sat); 12-11 Sun ☎ (0191) 417 0445
Taylor Landlord; guest beers Ⓗ
Located within the arts centre just outside Washington town, this light and airy cafe/bar offers a warm welcome to drinkers and food lovers alike. Seven handpumped beers and one real cider are available, with a mix of local micro-brews and national ales. The pub offers an extensive range of food served throughout the day, with three separate food menus. Outside seating is available within the spacious courtyard. Two popular beer festivals are held twice a year on the Easter and August bank holidays. Q❀◖♿🚆(M1)♣♦P⁵⌐❒

William de Wessyngton ❷
2-3 Victoria Road, Concord, NE37 2SY (opp bus station)
☼ 8am-11.30 (10.30 Tue) ☎ (0191) 418 0100
Greene King Ruddles Best Bitter; Marston's Pedigree; guest beers Ⓗ
Large open-plan Wetherspoon pub housed in a former snooker hall and ice cream parlour. It is named after a Norman knight and lord of the manor whose descendants later emigrated to the United States. A real ale oasis, it is the only cask beer outlet in Concord and offers value-for-money beer and food. The regular ales are complemented by up to four guests and occasional beer festivals are held. Q🍴◖♿🚆♦⌐

Church End Goat's Milk; Tunnel Late OTT, seasonal beers; Wychwood Hobgoblin; guest beer Ⓗ
A deserved regular Guide entry, this delightful family-friendly village pub has a decor themed around Lord Nelson. The bar overlooks the public playing fields and children's playground across the road. Two restaurants on either side are always popular. There are five handpulls on the bar. Beer festivals are held in the garden where the Tunnel Brewery was founded in 2005 in buildings at the rear. The bus stop is right outside. 🅰️🏵️◑ ⊟🖥️P!~

Ashorne

Cottage Tavern
CV35 9DR (1½ miles from B4100 at Fosse Way Island) SP304577
✪ 5 (12 Fri & Sat)-11; 12-2.30, 5-11 Wed & Thu; 12-10.30 Sun
☎ (01926) 651410
John Smith's Bitter; guest beers Ⓗ
A small village local with a pleasant atmosphere and a friendly welcome. Both the split-level bar and the dining area have a log fire in winter months. Four changing guest ales are mainly from micro-brewers and complement the weekly food promotions. Seasonal dishes on the menu are home cooked using local produce. A popular quiz night is held on the last Sunday of the month and traditional pub games like shut the box are enjoyed by locals and visitors alike. 🅰️🏵️◑🖥️(77)♣!~

Atherstone

New Dolphin Inn
162 Long Street, CV9 1AE
✪ 12-3, 6-11; 12-11 Fri-Sun ☎ (01827) 713167
Beer range varies Ⓗ
Friendly, open-plan pub with a mix of comfortable seating, wood panelling and widescreen TVs. Note the large stained glass panel featuring a dolphin. Keenly priced, interesting ales are sourced from micro-breweries near and far, with two usually available. The pub is home to darts and dominoes teams. Dog-friendly. 🏵️⇌🖥️(48,765)♣!~

Baddesley Ensor

Red Lion
The Common, CV9 2BT (from Grendon roundabout on A5 go S up Boot Hill)
✪ 7 (4 Fri)-11; 12-3, 7-11 Sat; 12-3, 7-10.30 Sun
☎ (01827) 718186
Everards Tiger; Greene King IPA; Marston's Pedigree; guest beers Ⓗ
Popular community local where ale is king and food does not feature. Enjoy instead the open fire and the buzz of conversation in a music-free environment. Two or three guest ales are featured, and the landlord willingly removes the sparkler. Off-road parking is available directly opposite the pub. 🅰️Q🖥️(765,777)♣🍴

Baxterley

Rose Inn ✅
Main Road, CV9 2LE (off B4116, W of Atherstone) SP277970
✪ 12-3, 7-11; 12-11 Sat; 12-10.30 Sun ☎ (01827) 713939
🌐 roseinnbaxterley.com
St Austell Tribute; Draught Bass; Wells Eagle IPA, Bombardier; guest beer Ⓗ

Picturesque country pub complete with duck pond. Though at heart an ale drinker's pub, the Rose is also well regarded for food. As befits a former mining village, the bar has an open coal fire, and welcomes dogs. There are three further intimate areas, a restaurant with a scenic view, and a skittle alley where you can work up a thirst. 🅰️🏵️◑⊟🖥️(777)♣P

Bodymoor Heath

Dog & Doublet
Dog Lane, B76 9JD (take Bodymoor Heath Road off A4091, turn right after canal bridge)
✪ 11-11 ☎ (01827) 872374 🌐 doganddoubletinn.co.uk
Greene King Old Speckled Hen, Abbot; Wells Bombardier; guest beer Ⓗ
Traditional pub beside the Birmingham & Fazeley Canal. Built in 1786, it became a pub around 1835. Grade II-listed, it features wood-panelled walls and oak beams. The single bar is TV-free and popular with diners. Plenty of brasses and old photographs of the local area adorn the walls. Outside there is a children's play area, and seating alongside the canal. Look out for the sign above the exit saying 'T'rar a bit!' 🏵️🛏️◑ 🅖♣P

Bubbenhall

Malt Shovel Ⓛ
Lower End, CV8 3BW SP362725
✪ 12-11 ☎ (024) 7630 1141
🌐 themaltshovelbubbenhall.co.uk
Hook Norton Hooky Bitter; Wells Bombardier; guest beers Ⓗ
Friendly village free house situated in Bubbenhall conservation area. The 17th-century Grade II-listed building comprises a large L-shaped lounge bar at the front and a small public bar to the rear. Behind the spacious car park lies the large walled garden and adjacent bowling green, with woods available in the summer. Traditional home-cooked food featuring locally-sourced produce is available including daily specials. At least one guest beer is usually local. Convenient for Ryton Pools Country Park. Q🏵️◑⊟🅐🖥️(539)♣P!~

Corley Moor

Bull & Butcher
Common Lane, CV7 8AQ SP279850
✪ 10-midnight (1am Fri & Sat); 10-11 Sun ☎ (01676) 540241
Draught Bass; Greene King Abbot; M&B Brew XI; guest beer Ⓗ
A deserved regular in the Guide, you can be sure of a warm welcome at this popular village pub. The wood-beamed flagstone bar leads to the cosiest of

snugs, both with open fires. The restaurant at the back is busy with diners but food service doesn't detract from the traditional pub atmosphere. Festooned with hanging baskets for most of the year, the pub has a large garden with plentiful play equipment for family fun. ⚫Q🌑◑ 😀⑂ ⚫P⏚

Five Ways

Case is Altered

Case Lane, CV35 7JD (off Five Ways Road near A4141/A4177 jct) SP225701

⚫ 12-2.30, 6-11; 12-2, 7-10.30 Sun ☎ (01926) 484206

Greene King IPA; Wye Valley Butty Bach; guest beers Ⓗ

A traditional unspoilt country pub with a bar and separate snug. The current landlady has been there 32 years, taking over from her grandmother. The traditional bar billiards table still takes the old sixpences, which have to be bought from the bar. Monday night is cribbage night. Don't miss the Victorian print in the bar of a former Leamington brewery plus a clock from another old local brewery. There is even a propeller from a World War I fighter on the ceiling. ⚫Q🌑♣P⏚

Hampton Lucy

Boar's Head

Church Street, CV35 8BE

⚫ 11-3, 5-11; 11-11 Fri & Sat; 12-10 Sun ☎ (01789) 840533

⊕ theboarsheadhamptonlucy4food.co.uk

Beer range varies Ⓗ

This friendly, comfortable village pub dates back to the 17th century. Situated on a Sustrans route and close to the river Avon, it is popular with cyclists, walkers and visitors to nearby Charlecote Park (NT), as well as the local Young Farmers. The walled garden has fire pit tables and the food menu includes locally-sourced rare meats including pheasant and squirrel. Up to six frequently changing beers are available. Local CAMRA's Pub of the Year 2009/10 plus Warwickshire County Pub of the Year 2010. ⚫Q🌑◑P⏚

Harbury

Old New Inn

Farm Street, CV33 9LS (SW of village)

⚫ 3 (12 Sat & Sun)-midnight ☎ (01926) 614023

Beer range varies Ⓗ

This fine stone-built pub on the edge of the village has a splendid garden at the rear that is a blaze of colour in summer. Inside, the two rooms have low ceilings reflecting the age of the building. Sport is popular here, with TVs screening major fixtures – there can be rugby in one room and football in the other. Pub teams are also well supported – darts, dominoes and pool all feature. The beer range changes regularly. There is plenty of space in the car park. ⚫Q🌑😀⑂Å⊒(64A,65,66)♣P⏚

Hartshill

Malt Shovel

39 Grange Road, CV10 0SS

⚫ 12-11.30 ☎ (024) 7639 2501

Banks's Bitter; Marston's Pedigree; guest beer Ⓗ

Handy for the Coventry Canal and Hartshill Hayes Country Park, the pub is well known for Sunday roasts but has good value meals available all day every day to accompany the range of Marston's

beers on offer in either the restaurant or separate bar. Football matches are normally screened in the bar. Seating is available outside, together with a children's play area. ⚫🌑◑ 😀⊒(48,765)P⏚

Kenilworth

Clarendon Arms Ⓛ

44 Castle Hill, CV8 1NB

⚫ 11.30-3, 5.30-11.30; 11.30-12.30am Fri & Sat; 12-11.30 Sun ☎ (01926) 852017 ⊕ clarendonarmspub.co.uk

Beer range varies Ⓗ

Multi-roomed pub opposite Kenilworth Castle warmed by a log-burning stove in winter. The house beer, Clarendon Ale, a pale ale brewed by Slaughterhouse, is supplemented by three frequently changing guest ales, mostly from Purity, Slaughterhouse and Church End breweries in Warwickshire, and Hook Norton. An excellent range of food is available all day. There is a function room upstairs and a paved patio outside with tables and umbrellas. The TV screens Six Nations and World Cup sport only. ⚫🌑◑⊒(540)⏚

Old Bakery

12 High Street, CV8 1LZ (near A429/A452 jct)

⚫ 5.30 (5 Fri & Sat)-11; 5-10.30 Sun ☎ (01926) 864111

⊕ theoldbakery.eu

St Austell Tribute; Wye Valley Bitter; guest beers Ⓗ

Open evenings only, this pleasant two-roomed bar is in an old town hotel near Abbey Fields with a convivial atmosphere and mainly mature clientele. The Wye Valley Bitter is sold as Old Bakery Bitter. Two guest pumps often feature midlands independents such as Hobsons and Church End. Monday is fish and chips night, served from 5.30-7.30pm. Disabled access is via the rear car park and small outside patio area. Four en-suite bedrooms are available. Q🌑🛏⑂⊒(12)P

Virgins & Castle

7 High Street, CV8 1LY (A429/A452 jct)

⚫ 11-11.30 (12.30am Fri); 10-midnight Sat; 10-11.30 Sun ☎ (01926) 853737 ⊕ virginsandcastle.co.uk

Everards Beacon Bitter, Sunchaser Blonde, Tiger Best Bitter, Original; guest beer Ⓗ

Kenilworth's only Everards pub, this is a welcoming, historic inn dating from 1563 with a multi-roomed interior and L-shaped bar. Oak panelling, assorted furniture and pictures of old Kenilworth fill the pub with character. English and Filipino food is available lunchtimes and evenings. Monday is quiz night. There is limited parking at the front but a public car park close by. Dogs are welcome. ⚫Q🌑◑⊒(12)⏚

Wyandotte Inn

Park Road, CV8 2GF (jct of Park Rd and Stoneleigh Rd)

⚫ 11.30-midnight ☎ (07827 017470)

⊕ thewyandotteinn.com

Jennings Cocker Hoop; guest beers Ⓗ

Originally a brew-pub built in 1868, it is named after the Native American tribe – the landlord and son are honorary chiefs. The pub has been tied to Marston's for much of its recent history and the two guest beers are from the Banks's range. Thatcher's Heritage cider is also available. Many sporting events are shown on big screens and live music and a DJ often feature; however, this is still very much a community pub. A well-known landmark for buses around the country – just ask for 'The Wyandotte'. ⚫🌑⊒(X17,16)♣🍺P⏚

Leamington Spa

Benjamin Satchwell ✪

112-114 The Parade, CV32 4AQ SP318658
✪ 7-midnight (1am Fri & Sat) ☎ (01926) 883733
Greene King Ruddles Best Bitter, Abbot; guest beers Ⓗ

The Benjamin Satchwell, named after a former Leamington benefactor, bears all the hallmarks of typical Wetherspoon style. (The real Benjamin Satchwell discovered Leamington's second spring in 1784.) Converted from two shops, the pub is large, stretching back to Bedford Street. The split level interior has been used well to create comfortable seating areas, and the upper level hosts an impressively long bar. On the walls are panels depicting the history of Leamington and its people. A rare real cider outlet for the town.
⬗⭋⚞⇄⛶⚓

Somerville Arms ☖ ✪

4 Campion Terrace, CV32 4SX
✪ 12-2, 5.30-11; 12-11 Sat & Sun ☎ (01926) 426746
⊕ somervillearms.co.uk
Adnams Bitter, Broadside; Everards Beacon, Sunchaser, Tiger, Original; guest beer Ⓗ

An excellent Victorian local situated on a street corner in a pleasant suburb of north-east Leamington. The pub has recently been acquired by Everards and undergone a subtle and sympathetic refurbishment. The 'Ville' retains a simple bar room and a small, comfortable snug. The wooden bar sports a fine new set of seven matching handpumps. A popular community venue, regular open music nights are well supported. The courtyard has won awards for its flowers. Local CAMRA Pub of the Year 2011.
⌂Q☸⚞⛶(67)♣⚓⅃

Talbot Inn

34 Rushmore Street, CV31 1JA
✪ 12-11 (midnight Fri & Sat) ☎ (01926) 428883
Wye Valley HPA, Butty Bach; guest beers Ⓗ

This pub – although easily accessible and clearly visible from the canal thanks to its large mural – is described by the regulars as their 'secret' due to its location in a maze of residential terraces. The extended part of this Victorian house contains the public bar and the adjoining lounge area is in the original part of the building. Impromptu barbecues are hosted in the south-facing garden during the summer, often on bank holidays. One changing draught cider is always available. Q☸⛶♣⚓⅃

Long Itchington

Green Man ✪

Church Road, CV47 9PW
✪ 5 (12 Sat & Sun)-midnight ☎ (01926) 812208
⊕ greenmanlongitchington.co.uk
Black Sheep Best Bitter; Fuller's London Pride; Tetley Bitter; guest beer Ⓗ

Parts of this fine country inn date back to the early 1700s and it has retained the original beams and low ceilings in the bar areas. The building has a number of linked drinking areas and a function room at the rear. It is home to several pub teams and an annual beer festival in May, which the landlord helps organise. The front courtyard has benches that are also used by punters of the visiting fish and chips van on a Friday evening with a pint to wash them down. ⌂Q☸⚞⛶⚐(64)♣⚓P

Harvester Inn Ⓛ

6 Church Road, CV47 9PG (off A423 at village pond, then first left)
✪ 12-2.30, 6-11; 12-3, 7-10.30 Sun ☎ (01926) 812698
⊕ theharvesterinn.co.uk
Hook Norton Best Bitter; guest beers Ⓗ

This friendly village local is situated on the corner of a small village square. The unassuming building is split into two drinking areas and a separate restaurant serving good value and popular food. An annual highlight is the May bank holiday beer festival – the number of beers appearing over the weekend grows each time, with 50 at the last count! Look out for local pickles on sale and the rare Budvar Dark. Q⬗⭋⚞⛶(64)P

Two Boats Inn ✪

Southam Road, CV47 9QZ
✪ 12-11 ☎ (01926) 812640
Adnams Broadside; Greene King Abbot; Wells Eagle IPA; guest beer Ⓗ

This fine canal-side pub is three storeys tall looking from the canal but four tall from the car park where access is via steps at the side. The property was originally three mid-18th century cottages. Access from the towpath leads either to the bar or separate lounge where a good range of meals is served. The pub participates in the village May Day weekend beer festival. An extra guest beer is added during the summer to be enjoyed by the many boaters. ⌂☸⬗⚞⛶(64)♣P

Moreton Morrell

Black Horse

CV35 9AR
✪ 11.30-3, 7-11; 12-3, 7-10.30 Sun ☎ (01926) 651231
Hook Norton Hooky Best; guest beer Ⓗ

A rural pub in the heart of the village, where beer and banter come first. Nothing seems to have changed since the 1960s, including the music on the juke-box. Wooden settles are arranged around the walls of the cosy, compact bar. It's a popular destination for walkers, but also handy for travellers on the Fosse Way and just off the M40 at junction 12. The landlord takes great pride in the quality of his ales, and the guest beer is of highish gravity (4.5% plus) and usually from a small independent brewery. Q⭋⚞⛶(77)

Nether Whitacre

Gate Inn

Gate Lane, B46 2DS
✪ 12-11 (10.30 Sun) ☎ (01675) 481292 ⊕ thegateinn.com
Banks's Mild, Bitter; Jennings Cumberland Ale; Marston's Pedigree; Ringwood Fortyniner; guest beer Ⓗ

Welcoming community local dating from the 19th century, where diners tend to favour the conservatory and large lounge, while drinkers gravitate to the quarry-tiled bar. The guest ale is from the Marston's portfolio. A large, child-friendly garden is to the rear. Do not miss the yearly beer festival. Local eggs are sold at the bar.
☸⬗⚞⛶♣P⅃

Nuneaton

Bilberries

Bond Gate, CV11 4AE
✪ 10-10 (7.30 Mon & Tue); 10-1am Sun ☎ (024) 7632 6614

Beer range varies Ⓗ
Formerly known as the Granby Head, this is a large open-plan pub in a town centre location. Handy for a drink after doing your shopping, it is also close to the bus and railway stations. Three regularly changing guest ales are served at reasonable prices, often including one from the local Tunnel Brewery. The pub usually has music playing and gets busy on Friday and Saturday nights. Outside is a small drinking area with tables. No food is served. ≉🚃

Crown
10 Bond Street, CV11 4BX
🕓 12-11 (midnight Fri & Sat) ☎ (024) 7637 3343
🌐 thecrownnuneaton.com
Oakham JHB; guest beers Ⓗ
The Crown is situated between Nuneaton railway and bus stations. The board listing beers and ciders available on the 10 handpulls faces you as you walk through the door. A selection of foreign beers and malt whiskies is also available. Live rock bands feature on Saturday night. A function room is available to hire and the pub has an outdoor space for drinkers. Beer festivals are held in June and December. 🏰✿≉🚃💗P🏆⌐

Royal Oak ✅
The Square, Attleborough, CV11 4JY
🕓 12-midnight (4.30-midnight Mon-Thu winter); 12-11 Sun
☎ (024) 7638 2977
Draught Bass; Greene King Old Speckled Hen; guest beers Ⓗ
Historic and atmospheric, this pub has retained a village local feel due to the main road bypassing the old village and keeping it in a time warp. The basic red-tile-floored public bar at the front of the pub is usually lively with conversation. The lounge, approached by a passage and steps, is the venue for socials, quiz nights and karaoke. Lounge service is via a hatch to the bar where there are six handpulls. Beer festivals are held in the garden. 🏰✿🚃⌐

Royal Oak
Arbury Road, Stockingford, CV10 7NQ
🕓 11-11 (10.30 Sun) ☎ (024) 7637 1480
Fuller's London Pride; Greene King Abbot; guest beer Ⓗ
Large, detached split-level local pub. Enter by the door on the side as the main door has been blocked off. The games room on the right holds table football competitions every Friday. The long lounge to the left has a games area at the end with a pool table, which is moved to stage monthly gigs by local bands. Karaoke also figures. Six handpulls on the bar frequently include a guest from a local brewery such as Tunnel. ✿🚃♣P

Ratley

Rose & Crown
OX15 6DS SP38304741
🕓 12-2.30, 6-11; 12-4, 7-11 Sun ☎ (01295) 678148
Greene King Abbot; St Austell Tribute; Wells Bombardier; Wye Valley HPA; guest beer Ⓗ
One of many golden stone buildings in this secluded village, the 11th-century pub has exposed beams and a carpeted bar with wood-burning stoves for winter warmth. Alongside the four regular beers a fifth handpump dispenses a guest ale that changes each week. A cosy snug serves as a children's room and can also be used for

functions. Delicious food is available every day and Aunt Sally is played in the garden during the summer months. Sunday newspapers are available. 🏰Q☜✿🕪❶🚃(269)♣⌐

Ridge Lane

Church End Brewery Tap
109 Ridge Lane, CV10 0RD (2 miles SW of Atherstone) SP295947
🕓 closed Mon-Wed; 12 (6 Thu)-11; 12-10.30 Sun
☎ (01827) 713080 🌐 churchendbrewery.co.uk
Beer range varies Ⓗ/Ⓖ
At least eight beers are available from the adjoining brewery at this friendly tap, with a mild always on. Why not try a 'coffin' of third-of-a-pint tasters? A range of Belgian bottled beers is joined by at least one real cider. Dogs are allowed inside, but children and smokers are relegated to the beer garden. Customers are welcome to bring their own food. Q✿🕭Å♣💗P⌐

Rowington

Rowington Club
Rowington Green, CV35 7DB (just E of B4439, opp village hall) SP1998070150
🕓 2 (12 Sat & Sun)-11 ☎ (01564) 782087 🌐 rowington.org/Rowington/rowington_club.html
Flowers IPA; Wye Valley HPA; guest beers Ⓗ
A popular community club with a garden overlooking the village cricket ground. Annual membership is encouraged, but day membership is available for a small fee and is free to card-carrying CAMRA members. The bar features guest ales and real ciders. An annual beer festival is held, along with regular music, bingo and other interesting and seasonal social events including barbecues in summer and an autumn game fair. Pleasant cycling and walking country is nearby. Well worth a visit. 🏰☜✿👤≉(Lapworth)♣💗P⌐

Rugby

Alexandra Arms
72 James Street, CV21 2SL (next to John Barford multi-storey car park)
🕓 11-11 (11.30 Fri & Sat); 12-11 Sun ☎ (01788) 578660
🌐 alexandraarms.co.uk
Alexandra Petit Blonde; Fuller's London Pride; Greene King Abbot; guest beers Ⓗ
Conveniently situated close to the town centre, the pub has a comfortable lounge where lively debate flourishes among the friendly locals. The back bar/games room features a fabulous rock juke-box. Good value pub food is served at lunchtimes. The large, comfortable garden serves as a venue for summer beer festivals complete with live jazz. At the rear of the pub is a micro-brewery that is home to the Alexandra Ales and Atomic ranges. Seven times winner of local CAMRA Pub of the Year. Q✿❶🕭≉♣⌐

Bell ✅
High Street, Hilmorton, CV21 4HD
🕓 12-midnight (11 Fri & Sat) ☎ (01788) 544465
M&B Brew XI; Sharp's Doom Bar; Wadworth 6X; guest beer Ⓗ
Popular family-friendly pub with a restaurant and spacious bar, offering three excellent real ales. Locals recommend the food – particularly the home-made steak and ale pie. Activities include

live music on Saturday night, a regular quiz night and summer barbecues. The large garden with fish pond also has ducks, rabbits and chickens.
🏚Q🕸🕪🍴🍽🚭♿P♪

Lawrence Sheriff ✓

28-29 High Street, CV21 3BW
☼ 7-midnight (1am Thu-Sat) ☎ (01788) 517640
Greene King Ruddles Best Bitter, Abbot; Shepherd Neame Spitfire; guest beers Ⓗ
Opened in 2009 on the site of Boots the Chemist, this Wetherspoon Lloyds No.1 bar is named after Lawrence Sheriff, an Elizabethan gentleman and grocer to Elizabeth I who founded Rugby School. The pub caters for all ages but late on weekends becomes the heart of the local 'real ale' disco scene. 🕪♿🍽🚭♪

Merchants Inn ✓

5-6 Little Church Street, CV21 3AW (behind Marks & Spencer)
☼ 12-midnight (1am Fri & Sat); 12-11 Sun
☎ (01788) 571119 ⊕ merchantsinn.co.uk
B&T Shefford Bitter; Batemans XB; Oakham Bishops Farewell; Purity Mad Goose; guest beers Ⓗ
Ten regularly changing real ales, two ciders by gravity dispense and a large range of Belgian beers make this a 'must visit' pub. The owner continues to add to the large collection of breweriana that adorns the warm, cosy interior, with comfortable sofas, flagstone floors and an open fire. Home-cooked food is served every lunchtime. Live rugby is shown on big screens at weekends. Beer festivals are held in April and October, plus an annual Belgian night in February. Warwickshire County CAMRA Pub of the Year in 2003 and 2007.
🏚🕪♿🍽♣♪⌐

Raglan Arms 🏆

50 Dunchurch Road, CV22 6AD
☼ 4-midnight; 3-1am Fri; 12-1am Sat & Sun
☎ (01788) 544441 ⊕ raglanarmsinn.co.uk
Fuller's London Pride, ESB; Greene King Abbot; Raglan Original Bitter; guest beers Ⓗ
Opposite Rugby School playing fields, the Raglan Arms was awarded local CAMRA Pub of the Year in 2010, for the third consecutive year. The interior has a comfortable feel and a friendly atmosphere. A large choice of real ales is kept in the pub's two cellars. A cosy snug bar with a coal effect fire is available for general use and meetings. Snacks are sold all day. Major sporting events are screened on Sky TV. Q🕸🕪🍴🍽🚭♣P♪⌐

Squirrel Inn Ⓛ

33 Church Street, CV21 3PU
☼ 12 (4 Sun)-11 ☎ (01788) 544154
Dow Bridge Pretorian Porter; Marston's Pedigree; guest beers Ⓗ
The bright pink exterior makes the Squirrel an easy find. This true town local offers a warm greeting to all, with visitors always welcome to join in the ever-changing topical discussions at the bar. A supporter of LocAle – Dow Bridge is the brewer of choice – and a mild is usually among the range. Excellent live music plays until late on Wednesday and Saturday evenings (yes bands do fit in!). A large range of indoor games is available.
🏚Q♿🍽🚭♣♥

Three Horseshoes Hotel ✓

22 & 23 Sheep Street, CV21 3BX (town centre pedestrian precinct)

☼ 11-11 ☎ (01788) 544585 ⊕ threehorseshoesrugby.co.uk
Wells Bombardier; Greene King IPA, Abbot; guest beer Ⓗ
Welcoming former coaching inn dating from the 17th century in a town centre location near Rugby School. Three cask ales are available in the cosy traditional bar. Excellent home-cooked meals are served at all times (no food Sun eve). It's a meeting place for many local community groups, with function rooms and catering if required.
🏚Q🕸🛏🕪🍴♿🚆🚭⌐

Victoria Inn

1 Lower Hillmorton Road, CV21 3ST
☼ 4 (12 Thu)-midnight; 12-1am Fri & Sat; 12-midnight Sun
☎ (01788) 544374 ⊕ downthevic.com
Atomic Strike, Fission, Half Life, Bomb, Winter; guest beers Ⓗ
The Atomic Brewery tap also offers guest beers from other micros on its 14 handpumps plus bottled Belgian beers. Regular beer festivals are held during the year. This Victorian hostelry has a traditional bar with a comfortable lounge and two small snug rooms. Regular quiz nights are held and Sky Sports and ESPN are screened. Dogs are welcome. Q🕸🍴🚆🚍⊖🚭♣👟⌐

Shustoke

Griffin Inn

Church Road, B46 2LB (on B4116)
☼ 12-2.30, 7-11; 12-3, 7-10.30 Sun ☎ (01675) 481205
Hook Norton Old Hooky; Jennings Dark Mild; Marston's Pedigree; RCH Pitchfork; Theakston Old Peculier; guest beers Ⓗ
Thriving family-run Guide regular with its own brewery next door. A Griffin beer is usually one of the five guests. Occasional beer festivals are massively popular. Children are welcome in the conservatory and outside on the patio and meadow play area. Food is served Monday to Saturday lunchtimes; local eggs and cheeses are on sale at the bar. 🏚Q🍴🕸🕪AP♪⌐

Stratford-upon-Avon

Bear at the Swan's Nest Hotel ✓

Swan's Nest Lane, CV37 7LT (S end of Clopton Bridge)
SP20545480
☼ 12-11 ☎ (01789) 265540 ⊕ thebearfreehouse.co.uk
Everards Tiger; Hook Norton Old Hooky; guest beers Ⓗ
A traditional English pub with a waterside location, five minutes' walk from the town centre, serving seven real ales. The focus tends to be on local and regional brewers such as Wye Valley, Hook Norton, Hobsons and Warwickshire Brewing Co, with seasonal beers available. The Bear is decked out with wood panelling, a pewter bar and picnic tables for riverside drinking. Excellent, home-made bar meals are served in a warm, friendly, welcoming atmosphere. Board games and newspapers are always available.
🍴🛏🕪🚆(23)♣P

West End

9 Bull Street, CV37 6DT (from town hall, 400m SW, cross road junction into Bull St)
☼ 11.30 (12 Mon & Sun)-11 ☎ (01789) 268832
⊕ thewestendstratford.co.uk
Hook Norton Bitter; Taylor Landlord; Uley Pig's Ear; guest beer Ⓗ

Stratford's hidden gem. Although situated just a short walk from the town centre, the pub has the feel of a village local with themed food nights (eg Pig Roast) and Meet the Brewer. Live music and a monthly quiz are hosted. Freshly-prepared food using local produce, a range of daily specials and Sunday roast are served in a separate dining area. The large patio is a sun-trap in summer. A family and dog-friendly pub. Q⊛⏏❍❞╲≈♣⌐

Stretton-on-Fosse

Plough Inn
GL56 9QX
✪ 11.30-2.30, 6-11; 11.30-3, 6-11 (closed eve Oct-Apr) Sun
☎ (01608) 661053 ⊕ strettononfosse.co.uk/plough_inn.htm
Hook Norton Hooky Bitter; guest beers Ⓗ
A welcoming 17th-century stone-built inn boasting flagstone floors and oak beams. The inglenook fireplace is used to cook Sunday lunchtime roasts in winter. A friendly, cosy pub, it offers a range of home-made dishes prepared using locally-sourced produce. Sunday nights are dedicated to quizzes and folk music in the summer but closed in winter. Pub games are played, including Aunt Sally. Traditional cider is available. Winner of local CAMRA Pub of the Year 2008 and Morning Advertiser Best Freehouse East and West Midlands 2010.
Q⊛❍♣●P⌐

Studley

Little Lark
108 Alcester Road, B80 7NP (Tom's Town Lane jct with A435) SP075632
✪ 12-3, 6-11; 12-midnight Fri & Sat; 12-10.30 Sun
☎ (01527) 853105
Adnams Bitter; Taylor Landlord; guest beer Ⓗ
This popular village local serves a great selection of traditional fruit wines and single malt whiskies as well as real ale. The Lark used to publish its own newspaper and the walls are decorated with

framed front pages. Food is served lunchtimes and evenings – the Desperate Dan Cow Pie is a speciality. The pub runs themed food evenings, an annual cheese festival and regular beer festivals.
⚐Q❍◗❞╲❰❭(67,246,247)●⌐

Warings Green

Blue Bell Cider House
Warings Green Road, Hockley Heath, B94 6BP (S of Cheswick Green, off Ilshaw Heath Road) SP1286074275
✪ 11.30-11; 12-10.30 Sun ☎ (01564) 702328
⊕ thebluebellciderhouse.co.uk
Wye Valley HPA, Butty Bach; guest beer Ⓗ
Friendly canal-side free house offering three real ales and three draught ciders. The large lounge and cosy bar have real fires in winter, and families are welcome in the spacious conservatory and garden. Reasonably priced food and a Sunday carvery are popular. Wednesday is quiz night and occasional live music is hosted. Eight temporary moorings make it a popular stop for boaters and the area is pleasant for fishing, cycling and walking around the local lakes. ⚐Q❍⊛❞❰❭╲♣●P⌐

Warwick

Old Fourpenny Shop
27/29 Crompton Street, CV34 6HJ (near racecourse, between A429 and A4189)
✪ 12-11 ☎ (01926) 491360 ⊕ 4pennyhotel.com
RCH Pitchfork; guest beers Ⓗ
This Georgian building dating from around 1800 lies a short distance from the town centre, close to both the racecourse and the castle. The single, split-level room has a contemporary feel and the relaxed atmosphere is enhanced by the absence of machines and loud music. Ask the staff the origin of the pub's name while ordering one of five real ales available at all times. The old stable block has been converted into accommodation. CAMRA Branch Pub of the Year 2010. Q⊷❞Å❭P⌐

Boar's Head, Hampton Lucy

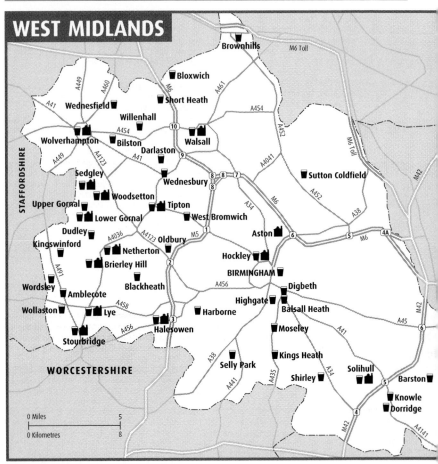

WEST MIDLANDS

Amblecote

Maverick ✓
Brettell Lane, DY8 4BA (on jct of A491 and A461)
🕐 12-midnight (1am Wed, Fri & Sat); 12-11 Sun
☎ (01384) 824099
Jennings Cumberland Ale; guest beers 🅷
A former CAMRA Branch Pub of the Year, the Maverick is a large street-corner hostelry. A Wild West room doubles as a live music venue, featuring blues, folk, rock and much more. There is also a Mexican-themed room. There are always four beers on handpump, usually including two from micros. Several screens show Sky Sports when no live music is playing. A corridor leads past a second bar servery to a covered, heated smoking area outside and a small garden.
Q❀⊞🖼(256,257)♣ᴸ

Starving Rascal ✓
1 Brettell Lane, DY8 4BN
🕐 4 (12 Sat & Sun)-11 ☎ 07843 670163
Holden's Golden Glow; guest beers 🅷
Guest beers from local breweries, sourced through the SIBA direct delivery scheme, are generally served at this establishment, which was voted most improved pub 2010 by the local CAMRA branch. A central bar, located between three linked rooms, provides the hub of this friendly hostelry where there is always a welcoming atmosphere.

Pub games, including table skittles, are available and the wide selection of single malt whiskies is worth investigating. 🏛🖼(246)♣P

Swan
10 Brettell Lane, DY8 4BN (on A461, ⅓ mile after A491)
🕐 12-2.30 (not Tue-Thu), 7-11; 12-3, 7-11 Sun
☎ (01384) 76932
Beer range varies 🅷
The Swan is a free house that boasts a comfortable lounge, a separate public bar and a delightful garden. There is a TV in the bar for watching sporting events. This friendly neighbourhood pub supports several local charities including the Air Ambulance. Drinkers can choose from three varied real ales on offer, and there is also an interesting selection of whiskies. A heated smoking area is provided at the side of the pub. Cobs are on sale at lunchtime. ❀⊞🖼(246)♣ᴸ

Barston

Bull's Head ✓
Barston Lane, B92 0JU (in village, on main road)
SP2073378090
🕐 11-2.30, 5-11; 11-11 Fri & Sat; 12-10.30 Sun
☎ (01675) 442830 ⊕ thebullsheadbarston.co.uk
Adnams Bitter; Hook Norton Hooky Bitter; Purity Mad Goose; guest beer 🅷

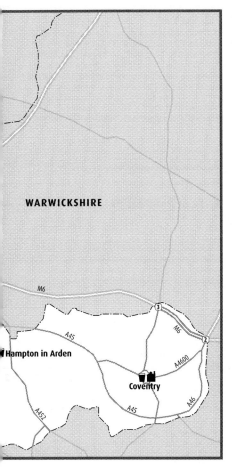

WARWICKSHIRE

M6

3

A45

M6

Hampton in Arden

A4600

2

Coventry

A45

A46

A452

A45

A lovely, genuine village pub, a former coaching inn and four-times winner of the local CAMRA Pub of the Year award. Inside are two friendly and comfortable bars, plus a 20-cover restaurant; food is seasonal and available in all three rooms. Four handpumps offer regularly changing guest ales. With a pleasant beer garden outside, the pub is popular with locals, cyclists and ramblers alike, and you are always assured of a warm welcome. ⚍Q♿❀◑🍴⏣P↳

Bilston

Olde White Rose
20 Lichfield Street, WV14 0AG
✪ 11-11 Sun & Mon; 11 (10 Fri & Sat)-11.30
☎ (01902) 498339
Beer range varies Ⓗ
Grade II-listed pub that has undergone a major refurbishment to coincide with the opening of its new hotel. It offers a choice of 12 changing real ales and Westons cider, together with a varied food menu. Situated close to both the metro and bus station, it is easily accessible by public transport. The hotel caters for all visitors including people attending the Robin 2 music venue nearby. Quiz nights are hosted on Tuesday and Wednesday evenings. ⚍◑♿❀(Central)🚋♦

Trumpet Ⓛ
58 High Street, WV14 0EP
✪ 12-4, 7.30-11.30 ☎ (01902) 493723 ⊕ trumpetjazz.org.uk
Holden's Mild, Bitter, Golden Glow, Special; guest beers Ⓗ
Busy and compact, this one-room local serves Holden's award-winning ales at reasonable prices. Plenty of musical memorabilia are on display, including posters from Louis Armstrong to Charlie Parker and musical instruments on the walls and ceiling. There is live jazz and blues seven nights a week plus Sunday lunchtime, which relies on a collection bucket passed around for the bands (all present are expected to contribute). Outside at the back is a drinking and smoking area. The bus and metro stations are a five-minute walk away. ❀⊖(Central)🚋↳

Birmingham: Balsall Heath

Old Moseley Arms Ⓛ
53 Tindal Street, B12 9QU
✪ 12-11 (10.30 Sun) ☎ (0121) 440 1954
Black Sheep Best Bitter; Enville Ale; Wye Valley HPA; guest beers Ⓗ
All are welcome at this popular back-street local. The two-doored entrance leads to separate bar areas, one with a large-screen TV, the other with a more relaxed feel, leading to an even quieter seated area. The large outdoor area is pleasant on clement days and hosts festivals twice a year. Two more festivals are held in an upstairs meeting room in winter. A good food menu is offered, with home-made curry nights on Tuesday and Thursday. Quiz night is Tuesday. Chaos acoustic club performs on Sunday evening. ❀◑⏣🚋(50)↳

Birmingham: City Centre

Brasshouse ✪
44 Broad Street, B1 2HP
✪ 10-midnight (1am Thu; 2am Fri & Sat) ☎ (0121) 633 3383
Banks's Bitter; Marston's EPA, Pedigree; Taylor Landlord; guest beers Ⓗ
Large multi-roomed pub at the city-centre end of Broad Street. Renowned for its good value food, the pub is also developing a reputation for its quality beers and is planning to increase the range available. Handy for the Brindley Place area, National Indoor Arena and Symphony Hall, its excellent canalside location makes this pub popular with families and local workers alike, although children are only allowed if eating and must leave by 6pm. ◑≢(New Street)🚋(9,22)

Bull
1 Price Street, B4 6JU (off St Chads Queensway)
✪ 12-midnight; closed Sun ☎ (0121) 333 6757
⊕ thebull-pricestreet.com
Adnams Broadside; Marston's Pedigree; guest beer Ⓗ
Country pub in the city centre located near Aston University. This popular back-street local with friendly staff is one of Birmingham's oldest pubs, and feels as if you are visiting someone's home. Two distinct drinking areas surround a U-shaped bar; there is a smaller back room with settees for more privacy. A large collection of water jugs abound, alongside a number of old paintings, pictures and memorabilia. Good value food is served and guest beer changes regularly. A small garden area is at the rear.
Q❀⚍◑♿≢(Snow Hill)⊖(Snow Hill)🚋P↳

Old Contemptibles ✪

176 Edmund Street, B3 2HB (100m from Snow Hill Station)

✪ 10-11; 12-6 Sun ☎ (0121) 200 3310

Beer range varies Ⓗ

Popular with the business community, this Nicholson's pub has a long wood-panelled bar leading to a comfortable snug at the rear. Seven handpulls dispense a range of ales from micros and regionals from far and wide, and cover all styles. Pump clips have tasting notes attached that invite you to 'sip before you sup'. Two real ciders are also available and good quality food is served until 10pm. Can get busy with after-work crowds. ◖Ⅱ◗&≷(Snow Hill, New St)⊖(Snow Hill)➡●

Old Fox Ⓛ ✪

54 Hurst Street, B5 4TD (opp Hippodrome Theatre)

✪ 12-midnight (2am Fri & Sat); 12-10 Sun

☎ (0121) 622 5080

Greene King Old Speckled Hen; St Austell Tribute; guest beers Ⓗ

Victorian two-roomed pub nestling between the Chinese and Gay quarters, attracting a clientele from nearby theatres as well as regular drinkers. The wooden-floored front room has plenty of brass, partly-stained glass windows and bar screens, and a large TV. The lounge/dining area features mirrored columns etched with fox designs. Old theatrical posters decorate the walls. Traditional food is served until 7.30pm. The reasonably priced guest beers are usually from micros, often local, with Slater's and Backyard particularly favoured. ◖Ⅱ◗&≷(New St)➡(45,47)

Old Joint Stock Ⓛ ✪

4 Temple Row, B2 5NY (opp St Philip's Cathedral)

✪ 11-11; 12-5 Sun ☎ (0121) 200 1892

⊕ oldjointstocktheatre.co.uk

Fuller's Chiswick, Discovery, London Pride, ESB; Gale's HSB; guest beers Ⓗ

Imposing Victorian, Grade II-listed building, formerly the Old Joint Stock Bank. It boasts elaborate decorative features externally and internally, with a large island bar, columns and pictures, and features a club room at the rear and a balcony drinking area. Upstairs is a theatre that also showcases local comedians. Good-quality food is served, and it gets busy with the after-work crowd. Poker night is Monday. Guest beers are from local breweries. The paved patio smoking and drinking area has a stairlift. ➣✿◖Ⅱ◗≷(New St/Snow Hill)⊖(Snow Hill)➡●⌐

Prince Of Wales Ⓛ

84 Cambridge Street, B1 2NP (behind ICC/NIA and Rep Theatre)

✪ 12-11 (2am Sat); 3-10.30 Sun ☎ (0121) 643 9460

Caledonian Deuchars IPA; Purity Mad Goose; St Austell Tribute; Taylor Landlord; Wells Bombardier; guest beers Ⓗ

Back-street pub with a local feel that is welcome to all and attracts a number of people from nearby Broad Street, canal boaters and those attending events at the NIA and Symphony Hall. It has an open-plan L-shaped layout with a wooden-floored main bar and a narrower carpeted seating area. Good value meals are served 12-2pm and 5-7pm (no food Sun). There is piped music and a pull-down TV screen for terrestrial sporting events, and live music on Sunday afternoon. Guest beers are from the Punch list. ◖Ⅱ◗&≷(New St)➡(9,23)

Pub Du Vin Ⓛ

25 Church Street, B3 2NR

✪ 12 (1 Sat)-11; closed Sun ☎ (0121) 200 0600

Kinver Light Railway; Purity Mad Goose; guest beer Ⓗ

Downstairs bar of the Hotel Du Vin, with a square central bar with lounge-style seating and a large-screen TV and piped music, and a separate Snuggles lounge for hire and more secluded moments. It is popular with all types but specifically office workers. Beer festivals feature smaller brewers, and the guest ale is also locally sourced. A vast range of wines and whiskies is stocked, with bookable tastings. Board games are available and children are welcome. The pub can close on Saturday for functions – check ahead. ⊨◖Ⅱ◗&≷(Snow Hill/New St)⊖(Snow Hill)➡

Sacks of Potatoes ✪

10 Gosta Green, B4 7ER

✪ 11-11.30 (midnight Thu & Fri; 1am Sat); 12-midnight Sun

☎ (0121) 503 5811

Caledonian Deuchars IPA; Harviestoun Bitter and Twisted; Marston's EPA; guest beers Ⓗ

Standing alone on the edge of the Aston University campus, this wooden-floored pub is popular with students and office workers alike. The U-shaped bar has several distinct seating areas. Outside there are tables overlooking the campus. Good value food is available and beer prices are low for the area. Plenty of TV screens give sports coverage but the sound is normally off. Three new handpumps have been installed for the guest ales. ✿◖Ⅱ◗≷(Snow Hill)⊖(Snow Hill)➡(14,66)●⌐

Shakespeare ✪

31 Summer Row, B3 1JJ

✪ 11-11 (midnight Fri & Sat; 10.30 Sun) ☎ (0121) 236 8702

Black Sheep Best Bitter; Marston's EPA, Pedigree; Taylor Landlord; guest beer Ⓗ

A newly refurbished, cosy, two-roomed pub located next to M&B's headquarters and part of the Nicholson's brand. The pub boasts many original features that add to its character. An outdoor patio area with a covered smoking shelter can be found at the rear. A quality traditional food menu is available throughout the day. Situated within easy walking distance of the National Indoor Arena and International Convention Centre. ✿◖Ⅱ◗&≷(New St/Snow Hill)⊖(Snow Hill)➡●⌐

Wellington Ⓛ

37 Bennetts Hill, B2 5SN (5 minutes from New Street station)

INDEPENDENT BREWERIES

ABC Birmingham: Aston
Angel Halesowen (NEW)
Backyard Walsall
Bank's & Hanson's (Marston's) Wolverhampton
Batham Brierley Hill
Black Country Lower Gornal
Byatt's Coventry (NEW)
Craddock's Stourbridge (NEW)
Highgate Walsall
Holden's Woodsetton
Olde Swan Netherton
Sadler's Lye
Sarah Hughes Sedgley
Silhill Solihull (NEW)
Toll End Tipton
Two Towers Birmingham: Hockley

⏰ 10-midnight ☎ (0121) 200 3115
🌐 thewellingtonrealale.co.uk
Black Country Ales BFG, Pig On The Wall; Oakham Citra; Purity Mad Goose; Wye Valley HPA; guest beers Ⓗ

A frequent local CAMRA Pub of the Year award recipient, this busy pub has 17 handpumps serving a wide range of ales, including many from new and local micros advertised on large-screen TVs. Two changing ciders complement the range, making every day a mini-festival. No food is served but customers are welcome to bring their own – plates and cutlery are provided. Regular cheese and quiz evenings are held, plus quarterly beer festivals from January. Foreign bottled beers are also stocked.
Q≉(New St/Snow Hill)⊖(Snow Hill)🚇🍴

Birmingham: Digbeth

Anchor ★ Ⓛ
308 Bradford Street, B5 6ET
⏰ 11-11.30 (midnight Fri & Sat); 12-11 Sun
☎ (0121) 622 4516 🌐 anchorinndigbeth.co.uk
Hobsons Mild; guest beers Ⓗ

Currently CAMRA Branch Pub of the Year bronze winner, the Anchor is a must-visit for any real ale enthusiast. It is situated behind the coach station in the centre of Birmingham's Irish quarter and easily walkable from the city centre. The Keane family have been running the pub for 38 years and always ensure a changing range of ales is available, often from small micros, as well as real cider. Regular themed beer festival weekends are held. Live sporting events are shown on large screens.
Q❀◑♨♿≉(New St/Moor St)🚇(37,50)🍴

White Swan ★ Ⓛ
276 Bradford Street, B12 0QY
⏰ 12-11 (1am Fri & Sat) ☎ (0121) 622 2586
Banks's Mild, Bitter; Jennings Cumberland Ale, Cocker Hoop; guest beer Ⓗ

Two-roomed unspoilt Victorian red-brick pub with the same wonderful landlady since 1969 – a fact acknowledged by the local CAMRA branch. The main drinking area has a wooden bar with a large bar-back and etched mirrors, plus stools and bench seating around the walls. An impressive, ornately tiled hallway leads to a small lounge and smoking area. It gets busy when sporting events are shown on large pull-down TV screens. Sandwiches, pies and pasties are available. Guests are from the Marston's/Jennings portfolio. Digbeth coach station is close by.
♨♿≉(New St/Moor St)🚇(2,12,31,50)🍴

Birmingham: Harborne

Green Man ✅
2 High Street, B17 9NE
⏰ 12-11 (1am Fri & Sat) ☎ (0121) 427 0961
M&B Brew XI; Purity UBU; guest beer Ⓗ

An imposing, busy M&B community pub furnished like others in the Ember Inns chain (including a real fire). It offers reasonably priced food until 10pm. Beer is also priced competitively. There is outside seating at the front and a covered area to the rear. Frequent discos, quizzes and other community charity fundraising activities are organised with the regulars. Because of its location, the pub is considered by some to be ideally placed for the start of a pub crawl. 🚍❀◑♿🚇(21,23,29)P🍴

Harborne Club Ⓛ
39 Albany Road, B17 9JX (200m down road, last house on left)
⏰ 5.30-10; 1-3 Sun ☎ (0121) 427 1638
🌐 theharborneclub.co.uk
Holden's Black Country Bitter; guest beer Ⓗ

Private members club that offers a warm welcome to CAMRA members and guests (a signing-in book is available). Sited at the top of Albany Road, there is no discernible sign of the club as it blends in with the rest of the houses. The one-roomed lounge-style layout has seating around tables. The guest beer is usually from a local micro-brewery and can be a Two Towers ale. The club has been in existence for 112 years, formed as a drinking establishment for businessmen returning from work in Birmingham. Q🚇(21,22,29)

Junction ✅
212 High Street, B17 9PT
⏰ 12-midnight; 10-10.30 Sun
☎ (0121) 428 2635 🌐 thejunctionharborne.co.uk
Purity Pure UBU; Sharp's Doom Bar; guest beers Ⓗ

Imposing Edwardian pub, narrow at the front and wider at the rear. It has a wood-floored and tiled bar area, leading to a further drinking area and then to the main dining area serving bar snacks and main meals in the evening, and a family space where children are welcome until 7pm. There is a TV in the bar for sporting events. Guest beers can be unusual and local; three ciders and continental lagers are also stocked. There is a large covered tiled garden and a smoking area with benches. Board games are available. 🚍❀◑♿🚇♣🍴

Plough Ⓛ ✅
21 High Street, B17 9NT
⏰ 11-11 (midnight Thu & Fri); 10-midnight Sat; 10-10.30 Sun
☎ (0121) 427 3678 🌐 theploughharborne.co.uk
Purity Mad Goose; Wye Valley Butty Bach; guest beer Ⓗ

An attractive, popular pub that appeals on many levels. It has a good selection of ales; presently two regular beers, one local and another a changing guest. The food menu features home-cooked dishes, with special 2-for-1 deals Monday-Wednesday and a breakfast for shoppers on Saturday. Live music plays on Thursday and a quiz is held on Tuesday. The large, quirkily designed pub garden has an under-cover area for smokers. Cakes and traditional sweets, along with more usual bar snacks, are also available. ❀◑♿🚇(21,23,29)🍴

Birmingham: Highgate

Lamp
157 Barford Street, B5 6AH (500m from Pershore Rd nr bottom of Hurst St)
⏰ 12-11 ☎ (0121) 688 1220
Everards Tiger; Stanway Stanney Bitter; guest beers Ⓗ

One-room tavern that has been run by Eddie, the ever-present landlord, for 19 years. The pub is a hidden gem located just off the Hurst Street entertainment area. There is a changing range of four or five guest beers, often from micros, as well as the regular beers, sourced from around the country, and a local mild is always available. The function room at the rear is available for live acts and meetings. The pub sometimes has a late licence. ♿≉(New St)🚇(35,45,47)

and a couple of vending machines. Baguettes are available in the evenings, hot sandwiches and chips at weekends. The enclosed rear garden is ideal for smokers and sun worshippers. A Guide regular for 14 years. Q✿❀🖼(9)♣♨—🍺

Waggon & Horses 🅛

21 Stourbridge Road, B63 3TU (on A458, ½ mile from bus station)
✿ 12-11.30 (12.30am Fri & Sat) ☎ (0121) 550 4989
Bathams Best Bitter; Bob's White Lion; Holden's Golden Glow; Oakham Inferno; guest beers 🄷
A splendid traditional hostelry with an impressive battery of pumps. Fourteen ales are on at any one time, complemented by up to nine Belgian beers on draught and three real ciders. Mild or stout is also usually available. The traditional bar has sloping floors and church pews, with a quieter room at either end where snacks using the best-quality ingredients are served. A true community pub with a national reputation. Awards include CAMRA County Pub of the Year. Q◖🖼(9)♣♨🍺

Hampton in Arden

White Lion ✅

High Street, B92 0AA (opp church) SP2035080820
✿ 12-11 (11.30 Thu-Sat); 12-10.30 Sun ☎ (01675) 442833
🌐 thewhitelioninn.com
Black Sheep Best Bitter; M&B Brew XI; Purity Mad Goose; Sharp's Doom Bar; St Austell Tribute; guest beer 🄷
Charming 17th-century timber-framed building with Grade II status. The White Lion has been licensed since 1838, and is a popular local with a cosy lounge and public bar, both with lovely real fires. The separate restaurant is ideal for intimate dining. Traditional bar meals are available, served lunchtimes and evenings. Local CAMRA Most Improved Pub 2007. ⋈Q✦◖◗⦾♿⇌🖼♨

Kingswinford

Park Tavern ✅

182 Cot Lane, DY6 9QG (corner of Cot Lane and Broad Street) SO884884
✿ 11-11 (1am Fri & Sat) ☎ (01384) 287178
Bathams Best Bitter; Enville Ale; Purity Mad Goose; guest beers 🄷
This popular, lively old pub in the back streets of Kingswinford has finally returned to the standard of five years ago. The separate bar and lounge each has its own feel, but TV does dominate when there are sporting events on. The landlord has worked hard to raise the quality and quantity of real ales, currently serving six. For the peckish, try the Tiger cobs, which are popular. There is also a large marquee attached to the rear for smokers and sports enthusiasts alike. ◖🖼(256,257)♣P♨

Knowle

Vaults

St John's Close, B93 0JU (off High Street, A4141) SP181767
✿ 12-2.30, 5-11; 12-11.30 Fri & Sat; 12-11 Sun
☎ (01564) 773656
St Austell Tribute; Tetley Bitter; Wadworth 6X; guest beers 🄷
A popular drinkers' pub, this was local CAMRA Branch Pub of the Year from 2005 to 2008. Diners often call here for a pint of real ale before visiting

one of Knowle's many restaurants. The range of guest beers varies, and includes ales from small breweries and old favourites. Real cider from the Westons range is also available. Lunchtime meals are served Monday-Saturday. The pub holds regular beer festivals. Major sports events can be seen on ESPN. ◖🖼(S2,S3)♨—

Lower Gornal

Black Bear

86 Deepdale Lane, DY3 2AE
✿ 5 (4 Fri; 12 Sat)-11; 12-10.30 Sun ☎ (01384) 253333
Kinver Black Bear IPA; guest beers 🄷
Embedded in the landscape for several centuries, this stone building has withstood the ravages of time. It was once a farmhouse and is now a traditional Black Country pub. Subsidence has taken its toll and there is a distinct slope to the split-level interior, and large buttresses support the downhill exterior walls. The views are stunning, the natives friendly, the ambience warm, dogs are welcome, and the bus stops are close. ⋈✿🖼(257,297)♣

Five Ways

375 Himley Road, DY3 2PZ (jct of B4176/4175, 3 minutes from Gornal Wood bus station)
✿ 8-midnight (1am Fri & Sat); 7-midnight Sun
☎ (01384) 252968
Bathams Best Bitter; guest beer 🄷
Warm and welcoming wayside watering hole on the western edge of the West Midlands conurbation. Its one crook-shaped room divides the bar into two distinct areas. There is a raised decking area overlooking the car park at the back of the pub that also incorporates a covered smoking shelter. Buses 257 and 297 pass close by, and Gornal Wood bus station is just a short walk away. Opens early at 8am (7am Sun) for home-cooked breakfast seven days a week.
⋈♿🖼(257,297)♣P♨

Fountain

8 Temple Street, DY3 2PE (on B4157 5 minutes from Gornal Wood bus station)
✿ 12-11 (10.30 Sun) ☎ (01384) 242777
Greene King Abbot; Hobsons Town Crier; Hook Norton Old Hooky; RCH Pitchfork; guest beers 🄷
Regular finalist and twice winner of Dudley CAMRA Pub of the Year, this excellent free house serves nine real ales accompanied by draught and bottled Belgian beers, real cider and 12 fruit wines. The busy, vibrant bar is complemented by an elevated dining area serving excellent food Monday-Friday lunchtimes and evenings, all day Saturday, and Sunday lunches until 5pm. During the summer months the rear garden is a sun-trap and a pleasant area to while away an hour or two. You may need to ask about cider. 🛌✿◖♿🖼(527)♣♨

Lye

Windsor Castle Inn

7 Stourbridge Road, DY9 7DG (at Lye Cross)
✿ 12-11 ☎ (01384) 897809
Sadler's Stumbling Badger, JPA, Worcester Sorcerer, Red House, Thin Ice, Mud City Stout; guest beer 🄷
The Sadler's Ales Brewery tap house featured on the TV series Oz and James Drink to Britain. The brewery was rehoused in Lye in 2004 by descendants of the original brewer. The interior is split into several seated areas, with an open space

in front of the bar with brewers' barrels as tables. This venue won 2007 local CAMRA Pub of the Year. Most of the Sadler's ranges of beers are available plus seasonal specials. Brewery tours are Monday evening or by arrangement.
Q❀🕙◗🕭♿🚲🚃(9,276)P↳

Netherton

Olde Swan ☆ 🅛
89 Halesowen Road, DY2 9PY (on A459 Dudley-Old Hill road)
🕙 11-11; 12-4, 7-11 Sun ☎ (01384) 253075
Olde Swan Original, Dark Swan, Entire, Bumble Hole; guest beer Ⓗ
One of the last four remaining English home-brew pubs from 1974. Deservedly on CAMRA's National Inventory of Historic Pub Interiors, it is also home to the Olde Swan Brewery, resurrected in 2000. The front bar is an unspoilt treasure and there is a cosy rear snug. Food is available in the lounge Monday-Friday lunchtimes and Monday evening. The upstairs restaurant is highly regarded for its a la carte menu, open Tuesday-Saturday. Sunday lunches are also served (booking essential).
🏛Q❀🕙◗🕭♿🚃(243,244)P

Oldbury

Jolly Collier 🅛
43 Junction Street, B69 3HD (off A457)
🕙 12-3, 5-11; 12-11 Fri & Sat; 12-10.30 Sun
Beer range varies Ⓗ
At the end of a side street, this friendly locals' pub is popular with a broad clientele. Traditional pub games and comprehensive TV coverage of live sporting events are available here. There is a heated, covered smoking patio and a large elevated decked area overlooking the garden with its grassed children's games area. The beers, which change regularly, are nearly always LocAles. Three beer festivals are held each year, usually one coinciding with Cask Ale Week. Sandwiches are available at the bar.
🚲♿🕭🚃(Sandwell & Dudley)🚃(87,120)♣↳

Waggon & Horses ★ 🅛 ✓
17A Church Street, B69 3AD (opp Sandwell council house)
🕙 12-11 (midnight Fri & Sat); 12-10.30 (7 Nov-Apr) Sun
☎ (0121) 552 5467
Enville White; Salopian Shropshire Gold; guest beers Ⓗ
Deservedly popular community pub and a peaceful haven from the bustle of Oldbury town centre a short distance away. Up to five guest beers are served, usually including one from owners SA Brains and another from the Salopian stable. In CAMRA's National Inventory of Historic Pub Interiors, the pub has some wonderful noteworthy architectural features such as the copper ceiling, ornately tiled walls and Holt Brewery etched windows. A tasty selection of freshly cooked good-value food includes a vegetarian option (served every lunchtime, Tue-Fri eves).
🏛Q🚲🕙◗🕭♿🚃(Sandwell & Dudley) 🚃(87,120,404)

Sedgley

Beacon Hotel ★ 🅛
129 Bilston Street, DY3 1JE (on A463)

🕙 12-2.30 (3 Fri), 5.30-11; 12-3, 6-11 Sat; 12-3, 7-10.30 Sun
☎ (01902) 883380
Sarah Hughes Pale Amber, Surprise, Dark Ruby; guest beers Ⓗ
Classic, beautifully restored Victorian tap house and tower brewery, the home of Sarah Hughes ales. The heart of this atmospheric, popular pub is the small island servery with hatches serving the central corridor and a small cosy snug, and the large panelled main room. Off the corridor is a traditional benched tap room and a family room with access to a well-equipped garden and play area. Cobs are available. CAMRA Branch Pub of the year 2008-2011, and National Pub of the Year runner-up 2010. The strong barley wine Snowflake is on sale during the Christmas period.
Q🚲❀🕭🚃(229,545)P↳

Bull's Head
27 Bilston Street, DY3 1JA (A463)
🕙 9-11 ☎ (01902) 661676
Holden's Mild Ⓗ**, Bitter** Ⓗ/Ⓟ**, Golden Glow; guest beer** Ⓗ
Not far from the centre of Sedgley village, on a street corner, sits this listed double-fronted building. It is a locals' pub with a bar at the front and, following the modern trend for diversification, now has a Thai restaurant occupying what used to be the lounge at the rear. Opening at 9am, breakfast and lunch are served with a choice of English or Thai dishes available. A free car park (height restriction applies) is available at the rear of the pub. 🏛🚲❀🕙◗🚃(541,558)♣↳🖵

Mount Pleasant (Stump)
144 High Street, DY3 1RH (on A459)
🕙 6.30 (7 Mon & Tue)-11; 12-3, 7-10.30 Sun
Beer range varies Ⓗ
Known locally as The Stump by its many regulars, this friendly, popular free house serves an interesting selection of eight beers. It possesses a Tardis-like interior and a mock-Tudor frontage. The front bar has a convivial, warm atmosphere while the lounge has an intimate feel with two rooms on different levels housing various nooks and crannies and two real coal stoves. Food is limited to ham or cheese cobs. Dog-friendly, it is on the 558 Dudley/Wolverhampton bus route, or five minutes' walk from Sedgley centre. 🏛Q❀🕭🚃(558)♣P↳

Shirley

Bernie's Real Ale Off-Licence
266 Cranmore Boulevard, B90 4PX (off A34, opp TRW research site) SP1287077635
🕙 11.30-2, 4-10; 11.30-10 Sat; 6-9 Sun ☎ (0121) 744 2827
Taylor Landlord; guest beers Ⓗ
This long-standing Guide entry had quite a makeover in 2010, and is now totally refurbished inside with smart new fittings. Happily the regularly changing guest beers are still available, served from a completely new cellar. Most are from small or micro-breweries, with plenty of pale hoppy beers from the north of England. Various takeaway containers are supplied and a vast array of bottled beers complements the draught ales. Traditional Rich's cider is permanently on sale too.
♿🚃(5,6,76)♣

Mug House L

12 Severnside North, DY12 2EE (150m from river bridge)

✪ 12-11 (midnight Fri; 11.30 Sat; 11 Sun) ☎ (01299) 402543
🌐 mughousebewdley.co.uk

Taylor Landlord; Wye Valley HPA; guest beers Ⓗ

Situated alongside the River Severn, this attractive little pub has a beamed bar serving up to five real ales including beers from local independents such as Bewdley Brewery. There is a real fire in winter, a pleasant garden and a restaurant serving fine food. The dog-friendly pub offers accommodation and hosts a popular beer festival over the May Day weekend. The name originates from when trow haulers and carriers struck a deal over a mug of ale.
🏨Q🕮🍴◑♿≋(SVR)🚌🐾¹⌐

Waggon & Horses

91 Kidderminster Road, DY12 1DG (on Bewdley-Kidderminster road, Wribbenhall side of river)

✪ 12-11; 11.30-1am Fri & Sat ☎ (01299) 403170

Banks's Mild, Bitter; Bathams Best Bitter; guest beer Ⓗ

Popular locals' pub with a single bar serving three distinct areas. The small wooden floored snug has settles, tables and a dartboard; the larger room has bench seating, a TV and a large roll-down screen for major sporting events. An old kitchen range in the dining area adds to the cottagey feel. Food is available lunchtimes and evenings, with a carvery on Sunday. A terraced garden is to the side. Guest ales come from local independents.
Q🕮◑♿≋(SVR)🚌♣🐾P⌐

Woodcolliers Arms L ✓

76 Welch Gate, DY12 2AU

✪ 5-midnight; 12-12.30am Fri & Sat; 12.30-11 Sun
☎ (01299) 400589 🌐 woodcolliers.co.uk

Hobsons Twisted Spire; Kinver Edge; Ludlow Gold; St Georges Friar Tuck; Three Tuns 1642; guest beers Ⓗ

A short walk from Bewdley centre, this friendly pub keeps a constantly changing range of local guest beers as well as a bottled beer menu. The Cordon Bleu chef offers a speciality Russian menu as well as traditional food – no microwave used. The old style, dog-friendly pub has open fires and beams, and stores bikes and fishing tackle for visitors. A special service is run for Severn Way walkers: ring for details. Quiz night is Tuesday.
🏨Q🕮🍴◑♿🚌♣🐾P⌐

Birlingham

Swan L

Church Street, WR10 3AQ

✪ 12-3, 6.30-11 (10.30 Sun) ☎ (01386) 750485
🌐 theswaninn.co.uk

Wye Valley Bitter; guest beers Ⓗ

Black-and-white thatched free house dating back over 500 years in a quiet village. The open bar/lounge boasts exposed beams and a wood-burning stove. As well as the Wye Valley Bitter and two real ciders (Thatchers and Moles Black Rat), more than 300 guest ales are served over a year. There are two beer festivals in May and September. Traditional home-cooked food is available in the conservatory (not Sun eve). Crib, darts and dominoes are played in the bar. There is a large car park opposite and a pleasant south-facing garden.
🏨🕮◑♣🐾P⌐

Bretforton

Fleece Inn ★

The Cross, WR11 7JE

✪ 11-11.30 (closed 3-6 Mon & Tue Oct-Mar); 11-10.30 Sun (12-10.30 Oct-Mar) ☎ (01386) 831173 🌐 thefleeceinn.co.uk

Hook Norton Hooky Bitter; Uley Pig's Ear; guest beers Ⓗ

Famous old National-Trust-owned village pub, sympathetically restored after a fire in 2005 and voted Worcestershire CAMRA Pub of the Year 2006. It houses a renowned collection of 17th-century pewter. Up to five ciders are available, including one produced at The Fleece itself using apples from various NT premises. The pub has its own orchard garden with play equipment, plus a medieval barn for functions and weddings. Pebworth Morris meet here and there is dancing and music all year including a folk session every Thursday.
🏨Q🕮🍴◑🍴♿🏕(554)♣🐾¹⌐

Broadway

Crown & Trumpet L ✓

14 Church Street, WR12 7AE (on road to Snowshill)

✪ 11-11 (closed 2.30-5 Mon-Thu winter) ☎ (01386) 853202
🌐 cotswoldholidays.co.uk

Beer range varies Ⓗ

Unpretentious 17th-century Cotswold stone inn, popular with locals and tourists. Oak beams, log fires and Flowers Brewery memorabilia create a warm ambience. The pub offers an unusual range of games plus live jazz and blues on alternate Thursdays. Locally-sourced, traditional home-cooked food is served daily. Guest beers are from Cotswold Spring and Stroud breweries, plus Gwatkin cider. 🏨🕮🍴◑♿🚌(559)♣🐾¹⌐

Bromsgrove

Golden Cross Hotel ✓

20 High Street, B61 8HH (S end of High Street)

✪ 8-midnight (1am Fri & Sat) ☎ (01527) 870005

Greene King Ruddles Best Bitter, Abbot; Purity Gold; guest beers Ⓗ

Originally a coaching inn, the venue was re-opened by Wetherspoon in 1994 and is its oldest establishment outside the M25. It has a long room with a raised area at one end and cosy seating compartments on the side, and interesting facts about Bromsgrove's local history are displayed on panels around the walls. Ten or more ales are offered, specialising in local breweries, and monthly events featuring different beers are held. Good value food includes special meal deals. CAMRA members receive a discount.
🏨🕮◑♿🚌🐾P⌐

INDEPENDENT BREWERIES

Bewdley Bewdley
Birds Bromsgrove
Brandy Cask Pershore
Cannon Royall Uphampton
Joseph Herbert Smith Hanley Broadheath
Malvern Hills Malvern
St George's Callow End
Teme Valley Knightwick
Weatheroak Hill Weatheroak
Wyre Piddle Peopleton

Greyhound L ✔

Rock Hill, B61 7LR SO952697

🕐 12-midnight; 11-1am Sat; 11-10.30 Sun

☎ (01527) 835391

Wye Valley HPA; guest beers H

A tastefully decorated, comfortable pub to the south of town, it serves four real ales. A single bar serves an open plan L-shaped room which has distinct areas for drinking, dining and darts. Traditional pub fare is of an exceptionally high standard, with weekly changing specials.
🏚Q🕮🐕🍴◑🚍(144)♣P

Ladybird L

2 Finstall Road, Aston Fields, B60 2DZ (on B4184) SO969695

🕐 11-11; 12-10.30 Sun ☎ (01527) 878014

🌐 theladybirdinn.co.uk

Bathams Best Bitter; Wye Valley HPA; guest beers H

This popular local has grown in recent years and now boasts a bar, lounge, Italian restaurant, beer garden and attached 45-room Travelodge. A beer from local Bromsgrove brewer Birds is always served. The lounge has a light, airy feel with polished wooden floors to contrast with the busy drinkers' bar. Various pictures and local memorabilia adorn the walls. Its location next to the railway station makes it popular with those wishing to explore the West Midlands.
🕮🐕🍴◑🚲♿🚉🚍(140,141,143)P♿

Caunsall

Anchor Inn L

DY11 5YL (off A449 Kiddie-Wolverhampton road)

🕐 11-4, 7-11; 11-3, 7-10.30 Sun ☎ (01562) 850254

🌐 theanchorinncaunsall.co.uk

Enville Ale; Hobsons Best Bitter, Town Crier; Ludlow Gold; Wye Valley Butty Bach, HPA; guest beer H

Popular, friendly, traditional local run by the same family since 1927, renowned for its six real ales, ciders and well-filled cobs. A central doorway leads to the little changed bar with its original 1920s furniture and horse racing memorabilia. The friendly staff welcome an impressive mix of customers, and the bar gets especially busy at lunchtime. Easily reached from the nearby canal, this gem is well worth visiting. Dog-friendly.
Q🐕♿♣●P♿

Chaddesley Corbett

Swan

The Village, DY10 4SD SO892737

🕐 11-11 ☎ (01562) 777302

Bathams Mild Ale, Best Bitter, XXX (winter); guest beer H

Lovely village pub dating from 1606 with a large lounge, snug and comfortable public bar. Lunch is available daily, but no hot food Monday to Wednesday. Evening meals are served Thursday to Saturday in the restaurant. Filled rolls and pork pies are recommended. A jazz night is held every Thursday evening. Popular with walkers, dogs are welcome in the public bar and garden. There is a large garden and play area at the rear.
🏚Q🕮🐕🍴◑♿🚍(X3,333)♣●P♿

Talbot

The Village, DY10 4SA SO892736

🕐 11-3, 5-11; 11-11 Sat summer; 12-3, 6-11 Sun

☎ (01562) 777388 🌐 talbotinn.net

Banks's Mild, Bitter; guest beers H

This half-timbered historic building occupies a site that has been an inn since 1600. Inside there is a public bar with pool table, two cosy wood-panelled lounges with hidden alcoves and an upstairs restaurant. Food is served daily lunchtimes and evenings. Guest beers are from the Marston's portfolio. Outside there is a large rear veranda shaded by a grape vine, car park and garden with children's play area. Live music features occasionally. 🏚Q🕮🐕🍴◑♿🚲🚍(X3,333)♣P♿

Clifton upon Teme

New Inn L

Old Road, WR6 6DR (signed 200m off B4204) SO724609

🕐 5 (12 Sat & Sun)-midnight ☎ (01886) 842226

🌐 newinnclifton.com

Greene King Abbot; Wye Valley HPA; guest beer H

The New Inn dates back several centuries, as does the imposing yew tree in the garden that doubles as a smoking shelter. The pub's elevated position provides magnificent views over the Teme and Severn valleys, arguably the best in the county. Where better to enjoy fine ales and home-produced meals from locally-sourced produce? Meals are served daily until 9pm and the Sunday roast until 4pm or until it's finished – no waste here. The char-grilled steaks are a speciality. There is lawn mower racing in the summer.
🏚Q🕮🐕🍴◑♿🚲🚍(308,310)♣●P♿

Clows Top

Colliers Arms

Tenbury Road, DY14 9HA (on main A456 Kidderminster-Tenbury road)

🕐 11-3, 6-11; 11-11 Sat; 11-6 Sun ☎ (01299) 832242

🌐 colliersarms.com

Hobsons Best Bitter, Town Crier; guest beer H

A family-owned and run free house set in the Worcestershire countryside with fine views from the restaurant and beer garden. The lounge area has comfortable seating and a pool table. Friendly staff provide excellent service and advice on the range of beers and food served. Beers come from local independent breweries and excellent quality, home-cooked food is made from seasonal, locally-sourced ingredients. The pub features regularly in Michelin and AA food guides. 🏚Q🕮◑♿🚲P

Dodford

Dodford Inn

Whinfield Road, B61 9BG SO939729

🕐 12 (5 Mon)-11 ☎ (01527) 575815 🌐 dodfordinn.com

Beer range varies H

Set in four acres of rolling countryside, this single roomed pub is known as 'the pub in the field'. The real ale haven attracts walkers, ramblers, bikers and horse riders. It features up to four real ales, often from local breweries, and regular beer festivals. One real cider is served. Themed food events and occasional music evenings are hosted. Home-cooked food includes hot lava rock grills. Family-friendly and dogs are welcome.
🏚🕮🐕◑♿🅰●P♿

Droitwich

Hop Pole 🍺 L

40 Friar Street, WR9 8ED SO898634

evenings and every weekend. A quality food menu is offered. There is a large covered, heated outdoor area to the front and a garden to the rear. The car park is small but there is ample parking in the environs. A no-swearing rule is enforced.
⛫❀◐◑⥃(Malvern Link)🚌(44,44A,362)♣●P⚟

Star 🄻

59 Cowleigh Road, WR14 1QE
✪ closed Mon; 4.30-10.30; 12-11.30 Fri & Sat; 12-10.30 Sun
☎ (01684) 891918 🌐 star-malvern.co.uk
Beer range varies 🄷
A fusion of Chinese cooking and English pub cultures, drinks and simple meals are served in the bar and there is a separate restaurant for more formal dining (booking recommended Fri and Sat). Evening food is from 5pm, Sunday lunches 12-3pm. There is also a takeway service available – have a pint while you wait. An outside patio includes a sheltered smoking area. Wye Valley HPA and Wood's Shropshire Lad make regular appearances on the bar (note the ornate bar back).
◑⊟⥃(Malvern Link)🚌(44,362,675)P⚟

Wyche Inn 🄻

Wyche Road, WR14 4EQ (Upper Wyche) SO769437
✪ 12 (11 Sat)-11; 11-10.30 Sun ☎ (01684) 575396
🌐 thewycheinn.co.uk
Hobsons Bitter; Wye Valley Brewery HPA; guest beers 🄷
Set on the side of the Malvern Hills adjacent to the Wyche Cutting, this free house has panoramic views towards the Cotswolds. Ideally situated for hill walkers, it offers two bars, one with traditional games, a dining area and a patio. Tony and Stephanie, formerly of the Rose & Crown, Brierley Hill, serve an ever-changing ale list, even converting lager drinkers (check the website for current and upcoming beers). Good home-cooked food includes popular themed nights.
❀🛏◐◑⊟🚌(362,363,675)♣

Pensax

Bell 🄻

Clows Top Road, WR6 6AE (on B4202 Clows Top-Great Whitley road)
✪ closed Mon; 12-2.30, 5-11; 12-10.30 Sun
☎ (01299) 896677
Bewdley Worcestershire Way; Exmoor Gold; Hobsons Best; Wye Valley HPA; guest beers 🄷
A consistent Guide entry and local CAMRA Pub of the Year winner, this pub is not to be missed. The friendly hostelry offers at least five superbly kept, constantly changing ales plus local ciders and perry. The wooden floors, hanging hops, open fires and pew seating give a true country feel. It has a separate dining room with superb views and a snug where families are welcome. Good pub food features local seasonal ingredients. A beer festival is held at the end of June. Dog-friendly.
⛫Q🐎❀◐◑⊟⛺●P⚟

Pershore

Brandy Cask

25 Bridge Street, WR10 1AJ
✪ 11.30-2.30, 7-10.30 (11.30 Thu); 11.30-3, 7-11.30 Fri & Sat; 12-3, 7-11 Sun ☎ (01386) 552602
Brandy Cask Whistling Joe, Brandysnapper, John Bakers Original; guest beers 🄷
At least three house ales are always available as well as a wide range of guest beers from around the country. Cheddar Valley cider is also normally stocked. Food is good and reasonably priced (not Tue in winter). The beautifully kept rear garden runs down to the River Avon where mooring for boats is available. This is a classic brew pub, well worth a visit. ⛫Q❀◐◑🚌(382,550,551)●

Redditch

Gate Hangs Well ✔

98 Evesham Road, B97 5ES (on Evesham-Redditch road) SP037659
✪ 11-2.30, 6-11; 11-2.30, 5.30-11.30 Fri; closed Sat; 11-11 Sun ☎ (01527) 401293 🌐 gatehangswell.com
Greene King Abbot; Hobsons Bitter; Hook Norton Hooky Bitter; St Austell Tribute; Wadworth 6X; guest beer 🄷
Traditional cosy local with up to six beers usually available. Future guest beers are advertised in advance. The single room has a dartboard at one end and is home to sports and games teams. Small TVs screen mainly sporting events and there is no loud music. A quiz is held on Sunday and Monday nights from 9pm. Good value bar snacks are offered weekday lunchtimes. Children are not permitted. There is a free public car park at the top of nearby Birchfield Road. ⛫Q❀◐♿🚌(70)♣⚟

Woodland Cottage

102 Mount Pleasant, Southcrest, B97 4JH SP038668
✪ 12 (5 Tue)-midnight ☎ (01527) 402299
Sharp's Doom Bar; Taylor Landlord; guest beers 🄷
Friendly locals' pub with a single room open-plan interior. Sport is shown on TV and darts is played in the bar area. A balcony with a sheltered smoking area overlooks the garden outside. Local bands play live most Saturday evenings and occasionally on other nights. Four real ales are served.
⛫❀⥃🚌P⚟

Shenstone

Plough

Shenstone Village, DY10 4DL (Off A450/A448) SO865735
✪ 12-3, 6 (7 Sun)-11 ☎ (01562) 777340
Bathams Mild Ale, Best Bitter, XXX (winter); guest beer 🄷
Dating from 1840, the Plough is a traditional rural community pub at the heart of the village. A long single bar serves the lounge and public room areas, with real fires in both areas. A large enclosed courtyard serves as an overflow area where children are permitted. The pub runs regular trips to other Bathams houses and is a host to local morris dancing teams in the summer. Pork pies are worthy of mention. ⛫Q🐎❀⊟♿♣P⚟

Stanford Bridge

Bridge Hotel 🄻

WR6 6RU (signed 100m off B4203) SO716658
✪ 12-midnight (1am Thu-Sat) ☎ (01886) 812771
🌐 stanfordbridgepub.co.uk
Hobsons Twisted Spire; Wye Valley HPA; guest beers 🄷
A former hotel in a pleasant riverside location, this community pub is popular with locals and has a lively, friendly atmosphere. Four real ales are offered, two from local breweries, and Thatchers

Heritage real cider, plus Westons perry in summer. Traditional pub games include pool and darts in the separate games room. Food is served Friday to Sunday lunchtimes and Tuesday to Saturday evenings. A summer beer festival is hosted with live bands and lawn mower racing. Outside, there is a heated seating area. ⌖✿⊕◐↹♣♠P↩

Stourport-on-Severn

Angel ✪
14 Riverside, DY13 9EW
✿ 11-11 ☎ (01299) 822661
Banks's Mild, Bitter; guest beer Ⓗ
Overlooking the River Severn downstream of the barge lock into the canal basins, there are public moorings nearby. An old-fashioned single-bar pub, it is home to crib, darts and dominoes teams. A separate room has a pool table. Up to four guest beers are offered from April to September, plus holiday periods. Home-made food is a speciality in the summer. ⌖✿↹◐▲➡♣♠P↩

Hollybush
Mitton Street, DY13 9AA
✿ 12-11.30 (midnight Fri & Sat); 12-10.30 Sun)
☎ (01299) 827435
Black Country BFG, Pig On The Wall, Fireside; guest beers Ⓗ
A traditional pub specialising in real ales – the three regulars from Black Country are served alongside three ever-changing guests from independent breweries. A single bar serves three distinct areas – the main bar, a small lower room with a dartboard, and a side room where the pub quiz is held. An upper function room leading to the beer garden is used for beer festivals and jam nights. ⌖Q⌖✿◐➡♣♠↩

Uphampton

Fruiterer's Arms Ⓛ
Uphampton Lane, WR9 0JW (off A449 at Reindeer pub)
SO838648
✿ 12.30-3.30, 5-11.30; 12.30-midnight Fri; 12-midnight Sat; 12-11.30 Sun ☎ (01905) 620305
Cannon Royall Fruiterer's Mild, Kings Shilling, Arrowhead, IPA; guest beer Ⓗ
The Fruiterer's Arms is situated in a lovely rural location down a lane off the A449 Worcester to Kidderminster road, served by a regular bus during the day. Reasonably priced ales are provided by the Cannon Royall Brewery at the rear of the pub, which is a separate business. The cosy oak-beamed lounge is decorated with working horse memorabilia and pictures. Filled rolls are available Friday to Sunday and a range of home-made pickles is sold at the bar. Children under 14 are permitted until 9pm. ⌖Q✿➡♣P↩

Weatheroak

Coach & Horses
Weatheroak Hill, B48 7EA (Alvechurch-Wythall road)
SP057741
✿ 11.30-11; 12-10.30 Sun ☎ (01564) 823386
Hobsons Mild, Bitter; Holden's Special; Weatheroak Hill Icknield Pale Ale, WHB Bitter; Wood Shropshire Lad; guest beers Ⓗ
This attractive rural pub on the corner of Icknield Street and Weatheroak Hill is the home of the Weatheroak Hill Brewery. It has a quarry-tiled

public bar with real fire, a split level lounge/bar and a modern restaurant with disabled access and toilets. Meals are served lunchtimes and evenings, on Sunday until 4.30pm. Outside is a large, family-friendly garden and patio, and beer festivals, barbecues and morris dancing are frequent attractions. A recipient of numerous local CAMRA awards. No under-14s in the bar. ⌖Q⌖✿◐➡↹♣♠P↩

West Malvern

Brewers Arms Ⓛ
Lower Dingle, WR14 4BQ (down track by pub sign on B4232) SO76404565
✿ 12-3, 6-midnight; 12-midnight Fri-Sun ☎ (01684) 568147
⊕ brewersarmswithaview.co.uk
Marston's Burton Bitter; Malvern Hills Black Pear; Wye Valley HPA; guest beers Ⓗ
This comfortable, traditional pub is both the centre of the village community and an ideal refreshment stop for visitors to the Malvern Hills. Up to eight real ales are available and a beer festival is held in October. Home-cooked food is served lunchtimes and evenings. The cosy bar can get busy at times, but extra dining space is available in the function room or the garden with its award-winning view to the Black Mountains. ⌖Q✿◐➡(675)↩

Wildmoor

Wildmoor Oak Ⓛ
Top Road, B61 0RB SO953757
✿ 5-10.30 Mon; 12-11 (midnight Fri); 11-midnight Sat; 12-10.30 Sun ☎ (0121) 453 2696 ⊕ wildmooroak.com
Wells Bombardier; guest beers Ⓗ
This rural country inn by a stream is a local pub as well as a destination restaurant, serving both traditional British food and international cuisine cooked by an award-winning chef. Monthly themed nights ranging from comedy to quizzes, Chinese buffet to cheese and wine, attract a varied clientele. An interesting real ale range is offered, with two guest beers. One or two local real ciders and perries also feature. ⌖✿⌖◐➡♣♠P↩

Worcester

Bell
35 St Johns, WR2 5AG (W side of Severn off A44)
✿ 10 (11 Sun)-11.30 ☎ (01905) 424570
Fuller's London Pride; Sharp's Doom Bar; guest beers Ⓗ
A community pub with two rooms on one side of a central corridor and the main bar on the other. At the rear is a second bar used only at busy times, and available for functions. There is also a highly popular skittles alley. Three guest beers are served alongside the regulars, one from Hobsons and two usually from local independent brewers. Live music often features at the weekend. ⌖✿➡♣↩

Berkeley Arms
School Road, WR2 4HF
✿ 12-2, 5-midnight; 12-12.30am Fri & Sat; 12-2, 8-11.30 Sun ☎ (01905) 421427
Banks's Mild, Original ℗; Jennings Dark Mild; guest beers Ⓗ
Family-run local with a single bar serving two drinking areas, popular for pub games. A room at the rear is used for meetings or as a children's

room, and outside is a partially enclosed patio. Two guest beers are supplied by Marston's, usually from their smaller breweries or seasonal brews. Draught Thatchers Heritage cider is available.
❀🖃(44,44A)♣♦P⁵⊷

Bridges

Hindlip Lane, WR3 8SB (off A3456/B4550)
❀ closed Mon; 12-3, 6-11.30; 12-3 Sun ☎ (01905) 757117
⊕ bridgesworcester.co.uk
Beer range varies 🅷
Lively and vibrant bar, carvery and entertainment venue – if you're looking for a quieter moment go Sunday lunchtime or early doors. The landlord is fanatical about the quality of his ales – mainly local with one from Teme Valley – which can be enjoyed with the show, in the small bar or outside in a seating area with a large heated gazebo. Guide dogs are welcome and there is good wheelchair access. ⬙❀🝙🖫🖢♦P⁵⊷

Dragon Inn

51 The Tything, WR1 1JT (on A449, 300m N of Foregate St station)
❀ 4.30 (12 Fri & Sat)-11; 12-3, 4.30-11 Wed & Thu; 1-4.30, 7-10.30 Sun ☎ (01905) 25845 ⊕ thedragoninn.com
Beer range varies 🅷
The owner of this real-ale-centric pub is passionate about beer quality, offering six ever-changing ales from smaller independent brewers, with one or more usually from the co-owned Little Ale Cart Brewery in Sheffield. Bottle-conditioned Belgian beers are also stocked. The walls feature mementos of life in the pub, but beware the list of banned conversation topics. There is a partially-covered rear patio for warmer weather. Good-value lunchtime meals are offered on Friday and Saturday. Well-behaved dogs are welcome.
❀🝙⇌(Foregate Street)🖃♦⁵⊷

Firefly

54 Lowesmoor, WR1 2SE
❀ 4-midnight (1am Thu); 3-1am Fri; 1-2am Sat; 1-11 Sun
☎ (01905) 616996
Beer range varies 🅷

Offering period comfort in a regenerated part of the industrial city, the old vinegar works manager's Georgian residence is now a delightful bar with soft furnishings, subtle lighting and a cosy fire. Downstairs is a candlelit snug with bench sofas. The upstairs bar opens at weekends and occasionally during the week for live music. There is a sun terrace overlooking the city and a paved beer garden. Pie and mash are served Wednesday to Sunday. Member of the Oakademy Of Excellence.
🏔❀🝙⇌(Shrub Hill/Foregate St)🖃♦⁵⊷

Plough

23 Fish Street, WR1 2HN (next to fire station)
❀ 12 (4.30 Thu)-11 (11.30 Fri & Sat); 12-10.30 Sun
☎ (01905) 21381
Hobsons Best Bitter; Malvern Hills Black Pear; guest beers 🅷
This friendly Grade II-listed pub is a must for any visitor to Worcester. Four changing guest ales come from nearby breweries and the surrounding counties, and draught cider and perry are also from local producers. A flight of stairs leads to a bar flanked by two rooms, both with many original features. A small outside patio area provides views towards the cathedral. ⬙❀⇌(Foregate St)♣♦⁵⊷

Postal Order ✓

18 Foregate Street, WR1 1DN
❀ 8-midnight (1am Fri & Sat) ☎ (01905) 22373
Greene King Ruddles Best Bitter, Abbot; Marston's Pedigree; guest beers 🅷
This classic Wetherspoon pub was once the Worcester telephone exchange. The Postal Order has one of the largest real ale sales in the chain's West Midlands region and offers a wide range of beers. It holds regular mini festivals featuring beers from local breweries. Traditional cider is also available. Good-value food is served daily until 10pm. Foregate Street railway station is close by.
Q⬙🝙🖫⇌(Foregate St)🖃♦⁵⊷

Beers on the edge

Four famous cask beers – Draught Bass, Boddingtons Bitter and Flowers Original and IPA – are in danger of disappearing, unloved and unwanted by the world's biggest brewer, AB InBev. The beers have been owned by the global giant following the departure from brewing by Bass and Whitbread early in the 21st century. AB InBev is interested only in big volume brands such as American Budweiser and Stella Artois and has put the cask brands on the market for £15 million.

Draught Bass was once, by far, the biggest-selling premium cask ale in Britain, worth close to one million barrels a year. It's a classic Burton beer, with its roots in the pale ales and IPAs brewed in the town in the 19th century. Under-promoted first by Bass and then InBev, sales have fallen to around 37,000 barrels a year, still a respectable amount. It has a legion of admirers and its passing would be mourned by beer lovers everywhere. It's brewed today for AB InBev by Marston's, ironically once the major competitor to Draught Bass with Pedigree.

Boddingtons is now brewed under licence by Hydes in Manchester while the Flowers beers are brewed by Brains in Cardiff. There's been no rush to buy the beers, mainly because AB InBev would retain the rights to the iconic Bass trademark, the Red Triangle, the first registered trademark in Britain. Without the trademark, any new owner of Draught Bass would be unable to use the Red Triangle in promotions and exports.

ENGLAND

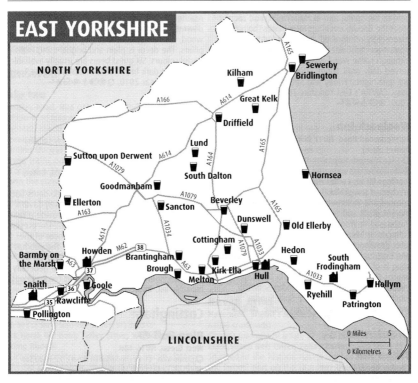

EAST YORKSHIRE

NORTH YORKSHIRE

Kilham
Sewerby
Bridlington

A166
A614
Great Kelk

Driffield

Lund
A165

Sutton upon Derwent A614
A164
A1079
South Dalton
Hornsea

Goodmanham

Ellerton
A1079
A163
Sancton
Beverley
A165

Dunswell
Old Ellerby

Cottingham
A1079
A1033

Barmby on
the Marsh
A63
Howden M62 38
Brantingham
Brough A63
Hedon
South
Frodingham
A1033

Snaith
37
36
Goole
Kirk Ella
Melton
Hull
Hollym

Rawcliffe
Ryehill
Patrington

35
Pollington

LINCOLNSHIRE

0 Miles 5
0 Kilometres 8

YORKSHIRE (EAST)

Barmby on the Marsh

King's Head Ⓛ ✅
High Street, DN14 7HT (3 miles from Knedlington crossroads on B1228 near Howden on no through road) SE688286
☼ 12-2 (not Mon & Tue), 5-11; 12-midnight Sat & Sun
☎ (01757) 630705 ⊕ thekingsheadbarmby.co.uk
Black Sheep Best Bitter; guest beers Ⓗ
Busy village pub that is well worth the three-mile trip from the nearest main road. Refurbished and extended in 2008, the pub is now a spacious and welcoming watering place and eatery. Four handpumps are in constant use, with three guest beers regularly from local breweries. The pub is renowned for its food quality and has a separate restaurant – weekends can get busy.
🏨⚜◖&♣P⁵⁻

Beverley

Cornerhouse
2-4 Norwood, HU17 9EY
☼ closed Mon; 5-midnight (1am Fri); 10-1am Sat; 10-11 Sun
☎ (01482) 882652
Abbeydale Deception; Black Sheep Best Bitter; Roosters Yankee; Tetley Bitter; Taylor Landlord; guest beers Ⓗ
The Cornerhouse looks like a gastro-pub, but the customers are mainly here for the real ale on 12 handpumps, and the real cider on two handpumps. Yorkshire brewers feature prominently and there is usually a mild available. A coal fire warms the far end of the bar and there is unusual gallery seating off the bar. Curry night is Tuesday and quiz night

Wednesday. Food is served 5-9pm weekdays, 1.30-9pm weekends, plus breakfasts 10am-1pm. Guest accommodation is planned. 🏨⚜◖🚌●⁵⁻

Dog & Duck
33 Ladygate, HU17 8BH
☼ 11-4, 7-midnight; 11-midnight Fri & Sat; 11.30-3, 7-11 Sun
☎ (01482) 862419
Black Sheep Best Bitter; Copper Dragon Best Bitter; John Smith's Bitter; guest beers Ⓗ
Just off the main Saturday Market, next to the historic Picture Playhouse building (now Browns), the Dog & Duck was built in the 1930s and has been run by the same family for more than 35 years. It comprises three areas: a bar with a period brick fireplace and bentwood seating, a front lounge, and a rear snug. The good value, home-cooked lunches are popular. Guest accommodation is in six purpose-built, self-contained rooms to the rear. Local CAMRA Town Pub of the Year 2008.
🏨🍴◖🚌♣

Green Dragon ✅
51 Saturday Market, HU17 8AA
☼ 11-11 (midnight Thu-Sat); 12-11 Sun ☎ (01482) 889801
Beer range varies Ⓗ
Historic Tudor-fronted inn renamed the Green Dragon in 1765. Up to seven beers from breweries throughout the UK are featured. Beer festivals are

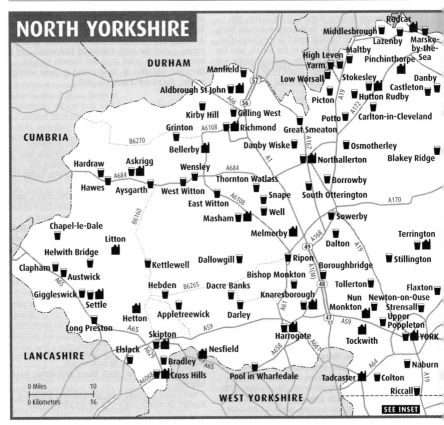

award winner, including Pub of the Year 2010, it comprises two bars that, uniquely, sandwich a sweet shop. The house ale, Beckwatter, is organically brewed by North Yorkshire, while guests are sourced locally. A painting of the Murk Esk by Algernon Newton has been hanging outside the pub since 1944 – donated as a thank you during his seven-year residency. Sandwiches, pies and beer cake are always available. ▲▲Q❀✿⏩⏪◑⊟❧P

Bishop Monkton

Lamb & Flag
Boroughbridge Road, HG3 3QN (off A61)
🕒 12-2 (not Mon & Tue), 5.30-11; 12-3, 7-10.30 Sun
☎ (01765) 677322
Tetley Bitter; guest beers Ⓗ
Warm and cosy inside, this immaculately kept traditional village pub supports local charities and fundraising events. Two comfortable rooms adorned with knick-knacks and brasses are served from one central bar, but each has its own open coal/log fire. Good home-cooked food is offered and AA 4-star accommodation is available. A garden and large car park are at the rear, with tables at the front. ▲▲Q❀✿⏩⏪◑▲⊟(56)❧P

Blakey Ridge

Lion Inn
YO62 7LQ (from south, join A170, turn off at Hutton le Hole sign, follow this road 6 miles past village) SE 679997
🕒 9am-11 ☎ (01751) 417320 ⊕ lionblakey.co.uk

Black Sheep Best Bitter; Copper Dragon Golden Pippin; Greene King Old Speckled Hen; Theakston Best Bitter, XB, Old Peculier Ⓗ
In an isolated position above Rosedale and Farndale, this is the highest pub in the North Yorkshire Moors. The area is steeped in history, from ancient crosses to 19th-century iron workings. This historic inn has offered food, drink and shelter for well over 400 years. The heavily beamed and bare-stone-walled interior has several interconnected seating areas and a separate restaurant with several roaring fires in winter. Westons Old Rosie scrumpy is also available. There is camping for walkers only.
▲▲❀✿⏩◑⊟▲⊟(Moorsbus)❧P⸺

Boroughbridge

Black Bull Inn
6 St James Square, YO51 9AR
🕒 11-midnight; 12-11 Sun ☎ (01423) 322413
John Smith's Bitter; Taylor Best Bitter; guest beer Ⓗ
In the main square, this 13th-century, Grade II-listed inn is popular with locals and visitors. There are several discrete dining and drinking areas as well as a separate restaurant that boasts an international menu. A traditional snug has wall settles, a larger distinctive bar serves good value beers, and there is a wide choice of bar meals. This classic pub, complete with friendly locals, is well worth a visit. Free town parking is nearby, plus limited pub parking. ▲▲Q⏩◑⊟▲⊟❧P

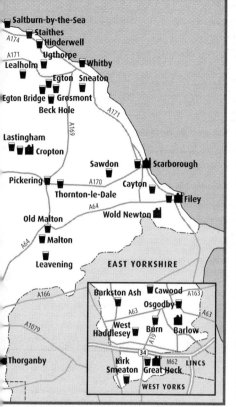

Burn

Wheatsheaf L

Main Road, YO8 8LJ (on A19 3 miles S of Selby)
SE594286

⌚ 12-11 ☎ (01757) 270614 ⊕ wheatsheafburn.co.uk

John Smith's Bitter; Taylor Best Bitter; guest beers Ⓗ
Renowned roadside free house stocking four reasonably priced guest beers, often from local breweries including Brown Cow and Great Heck. A narrow entrance leads to the bar and spacious lounge with its huge open fire. A collection of bottled beers, artefacts from bygone days, and memorabilia of 578 Squadron stationed at Burn in World War II adorn the walls. Food is served every lunchtime and Thursday to Saturday evenings. Frequent beer festivals and monthly jazz nights are held. ▲Q❀◑◧➡♣Pᐟ

Carlton-in-Cleveland

Blackwell Ox Inn

Main Street, TS9 7DJ (400m off A172)

⌚ 11.30-11 ☎ (01642) 712287 ⊕ theblackwellox.co.uk

Black Sheep Best Bitter; Tetley Bitter; guest beers Ⓗ
Located in a beautiful area on the edge of the National Park, this impressive, multi-roomed village inn is renowned for its good-value cuisine. Winter Monday evening Thai buffets, washed down with a pint or three, can easily become habit-forming. Look out also for early-evening year-round specials. But you don't have to eat! Drinkers are made most welcome. Four handpumps provide an eclectic range of varying beer styles including two interesting guests. The garden has an extensive children's play area. ▲Q❀◪◑▲➡(80,89)P

Castleton

Eskdale Inn

Station Road, YO21 2EU (next to railway station, 400m N of village centre)

⌚ 12-midnight (11 Sun) ☎ (01287) 660333 ⊕ eskdaleinn.co.uk

Black Sheep Best Bitter; Tetley Bitter; guest beer Ⓗ
Situated between the railway station and the Esk, this former station hotel offers a friendly welcome to all. The casks of beer sit in a cool cellar directly beneath the handpumps and well away from the warming fire. The guest beer is often chosen by the locals themselves and is usually something interesting. A good-value range of food includes a specials board and an extensive children's menu. The pub supports two darts and one pool team. Two letting bedrooms are available. ▲Q❀◪◑⧖⇌➡♣Pᐟ⛊

Borrowby

Wheatsheaf

Main Street, YO7 4QP (1 mile from A19 in village centre)
⌚ 5.30-11; 12-4, 7-10.30 Sun ☎ (01845) 537274
⊕ borrowbypub.co.uk

Daleside Bitter; guest beers Ⓗ
Attractive 17th-century free house in an attractive village close to the North York Moors. The thriving, welcoming and friendly community pub has a cosy low-beamed public bar dominated by a huge stone fireplace, with another drinking area to the rear and also a small dining-room. Home-cooked food is available Wednesday-Saturday evenings and Sunday lunchtimes, when roast dinners are popular. ▲☎❀◑⧖▲♣Pᐟ

Bradley

Slaters Arms L

Crag Lane, BD20 9DE 003481
⌚ 12-3, 5-11; 12-10.30 Sun ☎ (01535) 632179
⊕ theslatersarms.co.uk

Taylor Golden Best; Tetley Bitter; guest beers Ⓗ
Two-roomed rural situated at the eastern end of the village. It is half a mile from the Leeds-Liverpool canal and enjoys extensive views of the Aire Valley from the patio. The main lounge has an open fireplace and a real fire. Dogs are permitted in the back room only, and well-behaved children are welcome if dining. There is an extensive outdoor area, and the venue is popular with diners. ▲❀◑◧➡(78a)♣Pᐟ

Cawood

Ferry Inn L

2 King Street, YO8 3TL
⌚ 3 (12 Tue)-11; 12-midnight Wed & Thu; 12-1am Fri & Sat; 10-11 Sun ☎ (01757) 268515

Caledonian Deuchars IPA; Copper Dragon Best Bitter; Taylor Landlord; Wychwood Hobgoblin Ⓗ
On the banks of the River Ouse, tucked away just off the main street, with three open fires providing a warm welcome in winter. In summer the riverside terrace, with views of the adjacent Cawood swing bridge and open country on the opposite bank, is a pleasant place to take in the air

and enjoy a pint. One of two pubs in the village, it holds regular quizzes and live music nights. ⋈Q✿◑⊟℗⊞(42)♣P⌐

Cayton

Blacksmiths Arms

89 Main Street, YO13 3RP
✿ 12 (5 Mon)-midnight (1am Fri & Sat) ☎ (01723) 584886
Wold Top Bitter; guest beers Ⓗ
Friendly real ale pub in the centre of the village and also close to numerous holiday parks and campsites, with regular bus services passing the door. It has a separate lounge/restaurant and a large public bar with three distinct areas, as well as a covered outside smoking area and patio. Food is available, and there is live music twice a month. The guest ales all come from Yorkshire breweries and occasionally a cider is offered. A warm welcome awaits all who enter, making it well worth seeking out. ⋈✿◑⊟℗▲⊞♣P⌐

Chapel-le-Dale

Hill Inn

LA6 3AR (on B6255) SD374477
✿ closed Mon; 12-11 ☎ (01524) 241256 ⊕ oldhillinn.co.uk
Black Sheep Best Bitter; Dent Aviator; Theakston Best Bitter Ⓗ
The inn dates from 1615 and is beloved of generations of hikers and potholers. Well-worn paths run from here to both Whernside (Yorkshire's highest peak) and Ingleborough (its best known). Lots of exposed wood and some stonework feature in the bar. Run by a family of chefs, the pub is popular with diners – puddings are a speciality, and there is a sugar sculpture exhibition in an adjoining room (booking advisable for meals). ⋈Q✿⊟◑▲P⌐⊟

Clapham

New Inn

LA2 8HH
✿ 11-midnight ☎ (01524) 251203 ⊕ newinn-clapham.co.uk
Black Sheep Best Bitter; Copper Dragon Best Bitter, Golden Pippin; guest beers Ⓗ
Situated in a major tourist village, this spacious 18th-century coaching inn features two lounge bars. One includes oak panelling, the other has walls with photos and cartoons depicting caving, and is home to pub games. Children are welcome in the restaurant. The railway station is a mile away. ⋈✿⊟◑⅙≷⊟(581)♣P

Colton

Old Sun Inn Ⓛ ✓

Main Street, LS24 8EP (left into village, along Colton Lane, 1 mile S of Bilbrough Services on A64) SE542448
✿ 12-2.30, 6-11; 12-11 Sun ☎ (01904) 744261
⊕ yeoldsuninn.co.uk
Black Sheep Best Bitter; Moorhouse's Bitter; Rudgate Bitter; Taylor Landlord; guest beers Ⓗ
A 17th-century village pub with an award-winning restaurant and deli. It has four cosy dining areas, together with a newly developed drinkers-only bar with six handpumps. The interior features traditional low-beamed ceilings and in winter there are two real fires. For the summer there is a patio and a large picnic area. Next door is a B&B owned by the publican. ⋈Q✿⊟◑⅙P⊟

Cropton

New Inn Ⓛ

Woolcroft, YO18 8HH (5 miles off the A170 Pickering-Kirkbymoorside road) SE755888
✿ 11-11; 11.30-10.30 Sun ☎ (01751) 417330
⊕ newinncropton.co.uk
Cropton seasonal beers; guest beers Ⓗ
Set on the edge of North Yorkshire Moors National Park, this is a perfect base for walking and cycling. It is the brewery tap for Cropton Brewery, with a fantastic beer range, good food and accommodation. A beer festival is held every November, plus a music festival in summer. The New Inn sets the standard for how a rural pub should be run. For those not wanting to drive, the Moors bus service runs regularly from both Pickering and Kirkbymoorside. Q⅍✿⊟◑▲⊟♣P⊟

Cross Hills

Old White Bear Ⓛ

6 Keighley Road, BD20 7RN (on A6068, close to jct with A629)
✿ 11.30-11; 12-10.30 Sun ☎ (01535) 632115
⊕ oldwhitebear.co.uk
Naylor's Pinnacle Mild, Bitter, Blonde, seasonal beer Ⓗ
Four-room village pub, built in 1735 with timbers said to have come from a ship of the same name. The top room, with stone-flagged floor, is used mainly for dining; there are three other rooms, two with open fires. The back room has darts and Ring the Bull. Quiz night is Thursday. A regular outlet for the local Naylor's Brewery, it was local CAMRA Pub of the Year 2009. ⋈✿◑⊟(66,66A)♣P⌐

Dacre Banks

Royal Oak Inn

Oak Lane, HG3 4EN
✿ 11.30-11; 12-10.30 Sun ☎ (01423) 780200
⊕ the-royaloak-dacre.co.uk
Rudgate Jorvik Blonde, Viking, Ruby Mild Ⓗ
A family-run, Grade II-listed pub built in 1752, close to Brimham Rocks and Upper Nidderdale. Rudgate ales are served in the bar with views over Nidderdale. There is further seating at the front of the pub with a real fire. Boules is played alongside the car park. Food focuses on local produce and is served in the bar and separate restaurant. ⋈Q✿⊟◑⊟(24)♣P

Dallowgill

Drovers Inn

HG4 3RH (2 miles W of Laverton on road to Pateley Bridge) SE210720
✿ closed Mon; 6.30-11.30 (7-11 winter); 12-3, 6.30-11 Sat & Sun ☎ (01765) 658510
Black Sheep Best Bitter; Hambleton Bitter; Old Mill seasonal beer Ⓗ
Close by large areas of moorland, this traditional stone-built inn is used by walkers, shooting parties and the local farming community. All are made welcome at the small one-roomed pub. In winter there is a blazing coal fire adjacent to the tiny bar. Excellent value home-cooked meals are available daily until 8.30pm. ⋈Q✿◑▲♣P

Dalton

Jolly Farmer

Brookside, YO7 3HY (off A19 or A168)
✪ 7-11 Mon-Wed; 12-3, 6 (7 Sun)-11 ☎ (01845) 577359
Theakston Traditional Mild, Best Bitter Ⓗ
Popular with locals, this family-run pub dating from the mid-1800s is at the heart of the village. Its six handpumps feature beer from local micros chosen by the regulars, as well as a real cider and perry. Freshly prepared home-made dishes using local produce are served from the kitchen (booking advisable for Sunday lunch). Three en-suite rooms provide an ideal base for exploring the Dales and North Yorkshire Moors. ⅏Q⊛🚃🕛🌡🅿🏠

Danby

Duke of Wellington

2 West Lane, YO21 2LY (200m N of railway station)
✪ 12-3 (not Mon), 7-11; 12-11 Fri & Sat; 12-3, 7-10.30 Sun
☎ (01287) 660351 ⊕ dukeofwellingtondanby.co.uk
Copper Dragon Scotts 1816; Daleside Bitter; guest beer Ⓗ
An 18th-century inn and 2010 local CAMRA Pub of the Season winner, set in idyllic National Park countryside, close to the Moors Visitor Centre. It was used as a recruiting post during the Napoleonic Wars, and a cast-iron plaque of the first Duke of Wellington, unearthed during restorations, hangs above the fireplace. All the ales come from local breweries, while the menu offers traditional British home-cooked meals, using locally-sourced meat, fish and game. Cider and perry are served Easter-October. ⅏Q⊛🚃🕛🚃🚆🌡🍴

Danby Wiske

White Swan Ⓛ

DL7 0NQ (approx 3 miles N of Northallerton off A167) 336986
✪ 11-11 Easter-October; closed Tue, 12-3, 6-11 winter
☎ (01609) 775131
Beer range varies Ⓗ
On the route of Wainwright's 190-mile coast-to-coast walk, this attractive pub has changed greatly but still retains much character and ambience. It re-opened in 2010 following two years' closure and extensive refurbishment, serving up to four cask beers including two from the Wall's Brewery in Northallerton. Facilities for coast-to-coasters include en-suite B&B plus camping. Food is available during the summer months – phone to check in winter. ⅏Q⊛🚃🌡🍴🅿

Darley

Wellington Inn

HG3 2QQ (on B6451 to W of village)
✪ 11.30-11; 12-10.30 Sun ☎ (01423) 780362
⊕ wellington-inn.co.uk
Black Sheep Best Bitter; Copper Dragon Golden Pippin; Taylor Landlord; Tetley Bitter Ⓗ
Spacious stone roadside inn much extended in the 1980s. The beer garden gives excellent views over Nidderdale, an area of outstanding natural beauty. The original bar operates as a tap room. The extension has an impressive inglenook fireplace and is used more as a dining area. There is a separate restaurant and the pub makes an ideal starting point for exploring the Dales. ⅏⊛🕛🚃🖥🍴🅿

East Witton

Cover Bridge Inn ☗ Ⓛ

DL8 4SQ (½ mile N of village on A6108) SE144871
✪ 11-midnight; 12-11.30 Sun ☎ (01969) 623250
⊕ thecoverbridgeinn.co.uk
Black Sheep Best Bitter; John Smith's Bitter; Taylor Landlord; Theakston Best Bitter, Old Peculier; guest beers Ⓗ
On a sharp bend on the Middleham to Masham road, this ancient inn has won countless CAMRA awards, which are on display in the bar. You will need to fathom out the door latch before you enter the ancient public bar, but its splendid hearth and open fire make it worthwhile. A tiny lounge leads to an attractive garden with a play area backing on to the River Cover. The pub has an enviable reputation for food, with lunchtime and evening meals served daily. ⅏Q⏰⊛🚃🕛🖥(159)🍴🅿☗

Egton

Wheatsheaf Inn

High Street, YO21 1TZ
✪ closed Mon; 11.30-2.30, 5.30-11; 11.30-11 Sat & Sun
☎ (01947) 895271 ⊕ wheatsheafegton.com
Caledonian Deuchars IPA; Taylor Landlord; guest beer Ⓗ
A CAMRA multi-award-winner, this Grade I-listed 19th-century pub is now in its 12th year in the Guide, and remains under the stewardship of a licensee who has had 25 years of continuous Guide recognition. Church pews, collectables from auctions and a roaring range add to the character. The upmarket menu features local meats, fish and game. The grassy area to the front and boules to the rear are ideal for summer. Six bedrooms and a holiday cottage are available. ⅏⊛🚃🕛🚃🖥🚆(99)🍴🅿🏠

Egton Bridge

Horseshoe Hotel

YO21 1XE (down hill from Egton station)
✪ 11.30-3, 6.30-11; 11.30-11 Sat; 12-11 Sun
☎ (01947) 895245
Black Sheep Best Bitter; John Smith's Bitter; guest beers Ⓗ
Secluded gem in a hollow accessed from the station or across the stepping stones of the Esk. Old-fashioned settles and a large fire adorn the bar, while a raised grassy area makes outdoor drinking a pleasure. Five handpumps provide a wide selection, with one of the three guests usually sourced from Durham. A weekend beer festival is held close to Yorkshire Day, 1 August. The regular menu and specials are locally sourced and good value. Accommodation is in six bedrooms. ⅏Q⏰⊛🚃🕛🌡🚆🖥(99)🅿🏠

Elslack

Tempest Arms ✪

BD23 3AY (off A56 Skipton-Colne road)
✪ 11-11; 12-10.30 Sun ☎ (01282) 842450
⊕ tempestarms.co.uk
Dark Horse Hetton Pale Ale; Theakston Best Bitter Ⓗ
Award-winning establishment in a pleasant rural setting, this large country inn offers a wide choice of excellent food in the restaurant area and bar. The decor reflects the historic association with the

local Tempest family. During the winter months there is a welcoming log fire that greets you as you enter. Conference facilities, a function room and accommodation are all available. A member of the small Individual Inns group, the house beer is by Cuerden Brewing. ▲⛺🛏️◑♿🚆(215)P

Filey

Bonhommes Bar ☻
Royal Crescent Court, The Crescent, YO14 9JH
🕙 11 (12 winter)-midnight; 11-1am Fri & Sat; 12-midnight Sun ☎ (01723) 515325
East Coast Bonhomme Richard; Tetley Bitter; guest beers ⓗ
Situated just off the fine Victorian Royal Crescent Hotel complex, the bar's name celebrates John Paul Jones, father of the American Navy. His ship, the Bonhomme Richard, was involved in a battle off nearby Flamborough Head during the War of Independence. Six handpumps serve one East Coast beer plus five rotating guests. A fun quiz is held on Saturday, and the main quiz on Sunday. Voted local CAMRA Rural Pub of the Year 2008 and 2009. ⇌🚆●

Flaxton

Blacksmith's Arms ⎣
YO60 7RJ (1 mile from A64, opp York Lane jct) SE678 624
🕙 closed Mon; 6-11 Tue-Sat; 12-3 Sun ☎ (01904) 468210
⊕ blacksmithsarmsflaxton.co.uk
Black Sheep Best Bitter; Taylor Landlord; Theakston Best Bitter; York seasonal beer; guest beers ⓗ
Built in the 1700s as a coaching inn, the Blacksmiths Arms has retained plenty of charm and character. Owned and run by one family, this village pub has an L-shaped main bar with a dining room and snug off to one side, and a real fire for the winter months. Four regular ales are served, all Yorkshire-brewed, with an occasional guest also available. The snug houses a Yorkshire board for darts matches. Good food is served evenings and Sunday lunchtime. ▲⛺🛏️◑♿🚆(180,181)♣P

Giggleswick

Hart's Head Hotel ⎣
Belle Hill, BD24 0BA (on B6480 ½ mile N of Settle)
🕙 12-2.30 (not Tue & Thu), 5.30-11; 12-11.30 Fri & Sat; 12-11 Sun ☎ (01729) 822086 ⊕ hartsheadinn.co.uk
Copper Dragon Golden Pippin; Tetley Bitter; guest beers ⓗ
Open-plan 18th-century coaching inn, the bar area has pub games and sport on TV, while the comfortable lounge area has sofa seating. Freshly prepared meals from a varied menu are served in the adjacent dining-room. The pub is ideally situated as a base for touring the Dales, and is a member of the Walkers and Cyclists Welcome scheme. Four changing guest beers are available, often from Dent, Barngates, Black Sheep and Bowland breweries. Local CAMRA Pub of the Season Summer 2010.
▲⛺🛏️◑♿🅰️🚆(580,581)♣P⅃

Gilling West

White Swan Inn ⎣
51 High Street, DL10 5JG (2 miles W of Scotch Corner, off A66)
🕙 12-11 (3am Mon); 10.30-11 Sun ☎ (01748) 821123

Jennings Cumberland Ale; guest beers ⓗ
Friendly 17th-century country inn with an open-plan bar with a real fire and a dining-room offering an extensive menu. This free house sources its three guest beers from local and national micro-breweries, and is the brewery tap for the local Mithril Ales. The bar's beams are covered in banknotes, old and new. The beer garden has tables, chairs, sunshades and features an unusual collection of objects. Live acoustic music plays on alternate Wednesdays. Avoid the Grumpy Seat. CAMRA Pub of the Season 2011.
▲Q⛺◑🅰️🚆(29)♣⅃

Great Heck

Bay Horse
Main Street, DN14 0BQ (follow signs to village from A19) SE594210
🕙 closed Mon; 5-11 (midnight Fri & Sat); 12-10.30 Sun ☎ (01977) 661125
Old Mill Bitter; guest beers ⓗ
Part of the Old Mill Brewery group, there are two distinct areas: an open space around the bar with two fireplaces and exposed beams, and a raised area for dining. There are usually three beers on handpump including two guests from Old Mill. Old Rosie cider is available in summer. Outside is ample car parking across the front of the converted cottages that make up the pub. To the rear is a patio and covered area for smokers. Food is served Friday only. ⛺◑●P⅃

Great Smeaton

Black Bull
DL6 2EH (on A167)
🕙 5 (12 Sat & Sun)-late ☎ (01609) 881219
Daleside Blonde; John Smith's Bitter; guest beer ⓗ
Popular 17th-century coaching inn situated at the end of a row of roadside cottages on the Darlington to Northallerton road, with a linked bar, lounge and games room, with low-beamed ceilings. Underneath the games room were once cells that detained the legendary highwayman Dick Turpin on the way to his execution in York. The guest beer is from a local micro. The pub is handy for exploring the North Yorkshire Moors and Yorkshire Dales, with the Croft Circuit nearby. Dogs are welcome and accommodation is available in four rooms.
▲🛏️⛺🛏️◑♿🅰️🚆(72)♣P⅃

Grinton

Bridge Inn
DL11 6HH (on B6270, 1 mile E of Reeth) SE046984
🕙 12-midnight (1am Fri & Sat; 11 Sun) ☎ (01748) 884224
⊕ bridgeinngrinton.co.uk
Jennings Bitter; guest beer ⓗ
The wood-panelled bar, lounge and two restaurant rooms at this old coaching inn are often busy with a throng of tourists and locals alike, all enjoying a friendly and welcoming atmosphere. Close to the River Swale and the towering hills of Fremington Edge and Harkerside, the premises have the added quirk of Grinton Beck running through them, as well as clear warnings about the use of mobile phones. A wide range of seasonal produce is served throughout the day.
▲Q🛏️⛺🛏️◑🖴🅰️🚆(30,36,831)♣P

Grosmont

Crossing Club
Co-operative Building, Front Street, YO22 5QE (opp NYMR car park)
🌣 closed Mon winter; 8-11 ☎ (01947) 895040
Beer range varies Ⓗ
Opposite the NYMR and Esk Valley railway stations, this railway-themed private members' club was converted from the Co-operative store's delivery bay. Five handpumps, one usually dedicated to Wold Top, have served more than 700 different beers during the club's 11-year existence. A warm welcome is always extended to CAMRA members. Access is gained by ringing the door bell. Beer is supplied for the Music Train that runs up and down the Esk Valley on Friday evenings during the summer. Q☰🖵(99)♣

Hardraw

Green Dragon Ⓛ
DL8 3LZ 868913
🌣 10-1am (2am Fri & Sat) ☎ (01969) 667392
⊕ greendragonhardraw.com
Taylor Landlord; Theakston Best Bitter Ⓗ, **Old Peculier** Ⓖ; **guest beers** Ⓗ
Old pub of character at the entrance to England's highest single-drop waterfall, Hardraw Force, a noted beauty spot (for admission pay at the bar), which hosts a folk weekend in July and brass band competition in September. The bar has flagged floors, low beams and two impressive ranges. Meals are served all day. Wordsworth and Turner both stayed here and two, in suites named after them or even in a bunkhouse. A new visitor centre details the history of the waterfall and serves teas and other refreshments.
🏔☀🛏🕭🍴Ⓛ♣P

Harrogate

Blues Bar
4 Montpelier Parade, HG1 2JJ (by Betty's Tea Room)
🌣 10 (12 Sun)-1am ☎ (01423) 566881 ⊕ bluesbar.org.uk
Beer range varies Ⓗ
Small single-room bar in the town centre overlooking the lovely Montpelier gardens. Noted for live music seven days a week, with two sessions on a Sunday, it is popular with music lovers and can get busy. Modelled on an Amsterdam café bar, it has been going for more than 20 years. Food is served lunchtimes (except Sun) and upstairs there is an Egyptian restaurant open from Tuesday to Saturday. 🍴☰🖵

Coach & Horses Ⓛ
16 West Park, HG1 1BJ (opp The Stray)
🌣 11-11; 12-10.30 Sun ☎ (01423) 561802
⊕ thecoachandhorses.net
Copper Dragon Golden Pippin; Daleside Bitter; Taylor Landlord; Tetley Bitter; guest beers Ⓗ
A central bar is surrounded by snugs and alcoves, creating a cosy atmosphere. Excellent meals are served at lunchtime and there are frequent themed food evenings. Many of these, together with a Sunday night quiz, raise money for a local children's hospice. Five real ales are usually sourced from local breweries, including one from Rooster's always available. A few tables and chairs are placed outside for smokers in summer. Window boxes provide year-round colour, with a quite spectacular display in summer. Q🍴☰🖵(36)

Hales Bar ✪
1-3 Crescent Road, HG1 2RS
🌣 12-midnight (1am Thu-Sat; 11.30 Sun) ☎ (01423) 725570
⊕ halesbar.co.uk
Copper Dragon Golden Pippin; Daleside Old Legover; Draught Bass; Taylor Golden Best, Landlord Ⓗ
Harrogate's oldest pub, on CAMRA's Regional Inventory of Historic Pub Interiors, and used in the filming of Chariots of Fire, the lounge has a Victorian-style interior with gas lighting over the bar, and there is a separate snug. There are six handpumps, one serving a changing range of guest beers. Karaoke features on a Thursday night, also poker and quiz nights, and occasional party nights are hosted (see the website for details). The pub prides itself on its floral displays in season. Food is available lunchtimes and evenings. 🍴🛏🍴☰🖵🍴

Old Bell Tavern ✪
6 Royal Parade, HG1 2SZ (500m W of A61)
🌣 12-11 (10.30 Sun) ☎ (01423) 507930
Black Sheep Best Bitter; Theakston Best Bitter; guest beers Ⓗ
Originally the site of the Blue Bell Inn, which closed in 1815 and was later demolished, the Old Bell opened in 1999. In 2001 it expanded into the former Farrah's toffee shop – plenty of Farrah memorabilia is still on show. Eight real ales are always available; many are local and the guest ales always include a Rooster's, Timothy Taylor and a mild, plus a good range of bottled beers. Excellent quality bar food is served every day and a separate upstairs restaurant opens evenings (not Sun). Q🍴☰🖵

Swan on the Stray ✪
17 Devonshire Place, HG1 4AA (just off Skipton Rd)
🌣 12-11; 12-10.30 Sun ☎ (01423) 524587
Black Sheep Best Bitter; Daleside Blonde; Ilkley Mary Jane; Taylor Landlord Ⓗ
Extensively and tastefully refurbished in a modern style, the pub opened in late 2009. Eight real ales are available, four changing regularly, with many from Yorkshire micros, though not exclusively so. A range of foreign beer is available on draught, plus an added selection in bottles. Allied to a good wine choice, the pub appeals to all age groups. Well-behaved children are welcome. Q🍴🖵P

Tap & Spile Ⓛ
Tower Street, HG1 1HS (100m E of A61)
🌣 11.30-11; 12-10.30 Sun ☎ (01423) 526785
Rooster's Yankee; Theakston Old Peculier; guest beers Ⓗ
A central bar links the three drinking areas in this quality ale house. Visitors are spoilt for choice with a range of guest beers, many sourced from local micros. The number of real ales sold is fast approaching 2,000. The venue is well established and popular with all age groups. A quiz is held on Monday evening, folk music on Tuesday, and rock music on Thursday. Darts is played on alternate Tuesdays and Wednesdays. Some outdoor seating is provided. ☀☰🖵(36)♣🍴

Hawes

Crown Ⓛ ✪
Market Place, DL8 3RD
🌣 11-11 ☎ (01969) 667212 ⊕ thecrownhotelhawes.co.uk
John Smith's Bitter; Theakston Best Bitter, Black Bull Bitter, XB, Old Peculier Ⓗ

Large pub on the main street of this tiny but bustling Dales town, run by the same family for 30 years. The interior has been opened out to form two main rooms, and a recent refurbishment has given much of the bar area a more contemporary feel, with wood beams lining the ceilings, bare floorboards and real fires. A separate bar is partitioned off to the side. The beer garden has extensive views over Wensleydale.
🏚🏵🍴🌔🕭❺👌▲🖵(156,157)🐾-

Fountain Hotel 🅛
Market Place, DL8 3RD
🟢 11.30-midnight ☎ (01969) 667206
🌐 fountainhawes.co.uk
Black Sheep Best Bitter, Ale, Golden Sheep, Riggwelter; Copper Dragon 1816; guest beer Ⓗ
Hawes is home to the Creamery of Wensleydale cheese fame, along with a ropeworks and Countryside Museum. It also lies on the Pennine Way and is a centre for many other walks and events, keeping the local inns busy, particularly on Tuesday market days. Under the same management for more than 20 years, the Fountain's comfortable front bar serves bar meals, and there is a large dining-room to the rear. In good weather the pavement-side patio is a great place to watch the world go by.
🏚🛏🏵🍴🌔▲🖵(156,157)🐾P

Hebden

Clarendon Hotel 🅛 🅞
BD23 5DE
🟢 10.30-3, 5.30-11; 10.30-11 Sat & Sun ☎ (01756) 752446
🌐 theclarendonhotel.co.uk
Black Sheep Ale; Taylor Best Bitter; Tetley Bitter; guest beers Ⓗ
Small family-owned hotel not far from Grassington, close to the riverside path along the River Wharfe and ideally situated for exploring the surrounding fells and dales (walkers with clean boots welcome). There is a comfortable lounge bar and separate dining-room with a reputation for fine steaks. Morning coffees and afternoon teas are also served. Pride of the Dales bus 72 operates Monday-Saturday. 🏵🍴🌔🖵(72)🐾P

Helwith Bridge

Helwith Bridge 🅛 🅞
BD24 0EH (turn off B6479 at Helwith Bridge and cross river) SD810695
🟢 2.30 (12 Fri-Sun)-11 ☎ (01729) 860220
🌐 helwithbridge.com
Caledonian 80; John Smith's Bitter; Three Peaks Pen-y-Ghent Bitter; Wells Bombardier; guest beers Ⓗ
Despite its relative isolation in the tiny hamlet of Helwith Bridge, this is a welcoming, thriving, no-frills community local, run with warmth and a sense of humour. Three separate rooms are stone-flagged and adorned with railway artefacts, paintings and photos. Pie and peas are available when full meals are not. The four guest ales are usually sourced from the Heineken list and the house beer is from Three Peaks Brewery. The beer list is fastened to the ceiling.
🏚🏵🌔👌▲🖵(B1)🐾P-

High Leven

Fox Covert
Low Lane, TS15 9JW (on A1044, 3km E of Yarm)
🟢 11.30-11 (midnight Fri & Sat); 12-11 Sun
☎ (01642) 760033 🌐 thefoxcovert.com
Caledonian Deuchars IPA; Theakston Old Peculier Ⓗ
A previous local CAMRA Pub of the Season award winner, this popular, long-established and uniquely-named inn has been in the same family for more than 25 years. Originally a farmhouse, it was built in the traditional longhouse style, with whitewashed walls and a pantiled roof. Inside it is warm and cosy, with two open fires and two drinking areas offering superbly kept beers. The pub is noted for its food, served all day every day. Conference facilities are available.
🏚🏵🌔👌🖵(507)P

Hinderwell

Brown Cow
55 High Street, TS13 5ET (on A174)
🟢 11 (12 Sun)-1am ☎ (01947) 840694
Beer range varies Ⓗ
Between the moors and the coast, this family-run pub has a strong local following as well as attracting holiday visitors. Two busy handpumps serve weaker beers mid-week and stronger beers at weekends. The pub supports darts teams, charity nights, dominoes and whist drives, and has a separate pool room. Children and dogs are welcome. Smokers are also well provided for. There are snacks in addition to lunchtime and evening meals. Accommodation is in three bedrooms. A previous local CAMRA Pub of the Season award winner. 🏚🛏🏵🍴🌔🕭❺👌🖵(5)🐾P-

Hutton Rudby

King's Head
36 North Side, TS15 0DA (W end of village)
🟢 12-11 (10.30 Sun) ☎ (01642) 700342
Camerons Strongarm; Jennings Cocker Hoop, Cumberland Ale; guest beer Ⓗ
Set in a beautiful village, this previous local CAMRA Pub of the Season award winner is a traditional locals' pub where a friendly welcome is assured. It comprises a main bar and a snug where children are welcome. Four busy handpumps include a guest from the Marston's range. Real fires, a popular quiz night on Tuesday, steak nights on Wednesday and Friday and live music on Saturday all add to the experience. Outside is a smokers' paradise, complete with TV. 🏚🛏🏵🖵(82)-

Kettlewell

King's Head 🅛
The Green, BD23 5RD (top of village near church)
🟢 11-midnight (12.30am Fri & Sat); 12-midnight Sun
☎ (01756) 760242 🌐 kingsheadkettlewell.co.uk
Black Sheep Best Bitter; Taylor Landlord; Tetley Bitter; Yorkshire Dales Butter Tubs; guest beer Ⓗ
Situated in a village mentioned in the Domesday Book, this 17th-century hostelry boasts an impressive inglenook fireplace and flagstone floors. The simple single-bar interior welcomes visitors to the Yorkshire Dales as well as providing a haven for locals. Accommodation is available, and the place welcomes walkers and dogs. It is a regular outlet for the local Yorkshire Dales Brewery,

with additional guest beers in summer. Westons Original cider is on offer occasionally. ▨❀☛◖ ▲▨(72,72R,874)♣P

Kirby Hill

Shoulder of Mutton ⓛ

DL11 7JH (2½ miles from A66, 4 miles NW of Richmond)
🕑 12-3 (Sat & Sun only), 6-11.30 (11 Sun)
☎ (01748) 822772 ⊕ shoulderofmutton.net
Daleside Bitter; guest beers Ⓗ
Ivy-fronted country inn in a beautiful hillside setting overlooking Lower Teesdale and the ruins of Ravensworth Castle. The pub has an open front bar that links the lounge with a cosy restaurant to the rear. Three guest beers (four in summer) are chosen by the pub's regulars. On the edge of the Yorkshire Dales, this is a popular venue for walkers. There are five en-suite guest bedrooms. Highly recommended, excellent food is available Wednesday to Sunday, although the bar area remains for drinkers. ▨Q❀☛◖ ▣♣P½━

Kirk Smeaton

Shoulder of Mutton

Main Street, WF8 3JW (follow signs from A1)
🕑 5 (11.30 Sun)-midnight; 12-1am Fri & Sat
☎ (01977) 620348
Black Sheep Best Bitter; guest beer Ⓗ
In the centre of the village, this is a cosy pub with three open fires and two rooms, including a lounge and a snug with dark panelling. Outside there is a beer garden with a covered, heated area for smokers. The beer range usually includes an ale from Dark Horse, often the house beer, and real cider is available too. ▨❀▣▨(409)P½━

Knaresborough

Blind Jack's

18a Market Place, HG5 8AL
🕑 4 (5.30 Mon; 3 Fri)-11; 12-11 Sat; 12-10.30 Sun
☎ (01423) 869148 ⊕ blindjacks.co.uk
Black Sheep Best Bitter; Harviestoun Bitter & Twisted; Marble Blind Jack's Bitter; Taylor Landlord Ⓗ
Cosy, multi-roomed pub with bare brick walls, wooden floorboards and dark wood panelling. A vibrant, award-winning ale house, it provides a focal point for both locals and the many visitors who appreciate the excellent selection of ales, cosy ambience and lively banter. The changing guest beers usually include a mild. Cheese and pâté platters complement the beers. Of particular interest is the trompe-l'oeil painting to the exterior, which features the pub's namesake, Blind Jack Metcalfe. Q⇌▨(100,101,102)🏳

Cross Keys ❷

Cheapside, HG5 8AX (near town centre)
🕑 12-11 (midnight Fri & Sat) ☎ (01423) 863562
Fuller's London Pride; Ossett Yorkshire Blonde, Big Red Bitter; Silver King Ⓗ
Recently fully-refurbished pub just off the town centre, with a stone-flagged floor in front of the single bar and wood floors to the sides. Eight handpumps dispense four regular beers and four changing guests, often from other local micros though not exclusively so. Monday is pie night and Thursday quiz night. Good food is available daily with a special menu on Sunday. ◖⇌▨(1,1A,1B)

Mitre Hotel ❷

4 Station Road, HG5 9AA (opp railway station)
🕑 12-11 (midnight Fri & Sat) ☎ (01423) 868948
Black Sheep Ale; Copper Dragon Golden Pippin; Thwaites Wainwright; guest beers Ⓗ
The Mitre offers a split-level lounge, side function room, brasserie/restaurant and an outside drinking area. There are five guest ales including a dark beer, rotating ales from the Rooster's/Outlaw label, Timothy Taylor and often local beers. Look out for the speciality bottled beer menu; some foreign beers are also available on draught. There is live acoustic music on Sunday evening, and dogs are welcome. Q☾❀☛◖ &⇌▨(1,1A,1B)

Union ❷

Calcutt, HG5 8JL (½ mile from Knaresborough centre in Calcutt village)
🕑 12-2 (not Mon & Tue), 5-11; 12-11 Fri & Sat; 12-10.30 Sun
☎ (01423) 862084 ⊕ theunionknaresborough.co.uk
Jennings Cumberland Ale; Marston's EPA Ⓗ
Warm, welcoming, traditional two-roomed pub. Each room has its own bar selling between three and five ales from the Marston's stable, with an occasional Harviestoun product. A good menu of pub food is available. Summer visitors will enjoy the outside drinking area looking down over the local cricket ground. Situated half a mile from Knaresborough town centre, the pub is well worth a visit. ▨Q❀◖ ▣▨(56,56A,57)♣P

Lastingham

Blacksmith's Arms

Front Street, YO62 6TL (4 miles N of A170 between Helmsley and Pickering) SE728904
🕑 12-11.30 ☎ (01751) 417247
⊕ blacksmithslastingham.co.uk
Theakston Best Bitter; guest beers Ⓗ
Pretty stone inn in a conservation village opposite St Mary's Church, famous for its 11th-century crypt. The interior comprises a cosy bar with a York range lit in winter, a snug and two dining-rooms. Excellent quality food, including local game, is served alongside interesting guest beers. A secluded beer garden is to the rear. This remote pub is popular with locals, walkers and shooting parties. Twice winner of York CAMRA Country Pub of the Season. ▨Q❀☛◖

Lazenby

Lazenby Social Club

High Street, TS6 8DX (in centre of village, off A174)
🕑 11.30-11; 12-10.30 Sun ☎ (01642) 453905
Brains The Rev James; guest beer Ⓗ
Wedged between the remnants of Teesside's heavy industries and the Cleveland Hills, this private members club welcomes CAMRA members. A free house, it comprises a lounge, a large bar/ games room, a concert room and a conservatory that houses a full-size snooker table. Sadly it was dry for years during Teesside's industrial heyday, but the club has now gained a deserved reputation for selling fine real ales. The guest beer is usually sourced locally. ❀▣&♣P½━

Lealholm

Board Inn

Village Green, YO21 2AJ (by River Esk)
🕑 9am-midnight (2am Fri & Sat) ☎ (01947) 897279

Black Sheep Best Bitter; Camerons Strongarm; guest beers Ⓗ
Family-run, picturesque 17th-century free house serving four ales, four real ciders and a huge selection of whiskies. The menu, which reflects the seasons, is virtually all sourced within 500 metres of the pub. Breakfasts are served from 9am, with the restaurant staying open all day. And how many licensees air-cure their hams, keep 45 laying hens, own a herd of prime beef, and also have local fishing rights? A beer festival is held at Easter on the covered riverside patio. There are five letting bedrooms. ⚲Q⛄⚙☕❶Ⓗ⚑Å⇌🚆(99)♣🚶P⌐

Leavening

Jolly Farmers
Main Street, YO17 9SA SE785631
✪ 7 (6 Fri; 12 Sat & Sun)-midnight ☎ (01653) 658276
Taylor Landlord; Tetley Bitter; guest beers Ⓗ
Seventeenth-century pub on the edge of the Yorkshire Wolds between York and Malton. The multi-room interior has been extended but still retains a cosiness in two small bars, a family room and dining rooms. Former local CAMRA Pub of the Year, varied guest beers from independent breweries and two beer festivals a year make this an essential visit. The extensive menu includes locally caught game dishes in season.
⚲⛄⚙❶&♣P⌐🍴

Long Preston

Maypole Inn Ⓛ ✔
Main Street, BD23 4PH
✪ 11 (12 Sun)-11 ☎ (01729) 840219 ⊕ maypole.co.uk
Moorhouse's Premier Bitter; Taylor Landlord; guest beers Ⓗ
On the village green complete with maypole, this friendly, welcoming pub has been in the same capable hands for 27 years. Dogs are welcome in the tap room, which has carved Victorian bench seating. Good quality home-cooked food is available all day in the dining-room and in either bar. Two guest beers are usually available, often from Bowland, Moorhouse's or other local breweries, and two Westons ciders are served. Local CAMRA Branch Pub of the Year 2010.
⚲Q⚙❶⚑Å⇌🚆(580)♣🚶P⌐

Low Worsall

Ship
TS15 9PH (on B1264)
✪ 12-11 (10.30 Sun) ☎ (01642) 780314
Greene King Old Speckled Hen; guest beers Ⓗ
The Ship sits beside the old Richmond to Yarm turnpike and close to a disused quay that marks the centuries-old limit of navigation for boats on the River Tees. Guest beers are usually premium bitters. The pub is well known for the quality of its good value food, served all day every day. Smaller portions are available for those unable to tackle the usual impressively large helpings. The pub is child-friendly, with a small play area in the garden.
Q⚙❶&P⌐

Maltby

Manor House
High Lane, TS8 0BN (at jct of A1044 and A1045, 4 km east of Yarm and just W of A19)

✪ 11-11; 12-10.30 Sun ☎ (01642) 764153
Black Sheep Best Bitter; guest beers Ⓗ
Situated on the western outskirts of this pretty village, at the junction of High Lane and Low Lane, the pub is adjacent to one of Europe's largest private housing estates. This large, busy establishment, now in its third year of operation following major renovations, has a welcoming cosiness and warmth to it. Food is served all day every day, and enthusiastic staff ensure that two, usually three, guest beers provide an interesting mix of different styles. Quiz night is Monday. ⚙❶&P⌐

Malton

Crown Hotel (Suddaby's)
12 Wheelgate, YO17 7HP
✪ 11-11 (11.30 Fri & Sat); 12-11 Sun ☎ (01653) 692038
⊕ suddabys.co.uk
Suddaby's Double Chance, seasonal beers; Thwaites Original; guest beers Ⓗ
This Grade II-listed market-town pub has been in the same family for 139 years and the Guide for 25. Double Chance is brewed by Leeds Brewery, other Suddaby's beers by Brown Cow. Beer festivals are held at Easter, summer and Christmas. The on-site shop stocks more than 200 different beers, specialising in Belgian and local British micro-breweries, plus wine and breweriana. A covered smoking patio is at the rear. Accommodation is available, with a discount for CAMRA members staying two nights or more. ⚲Q⚙⚑⇌🚆♣P⌐

Manfield

Crown Inn Ⓛ
Vicars Lane, DL2 2RF (500m from B6275)
✪ 5 (12 Sat)-11.30; 12-11 Sun ☎ (01325) 374243
Village White Boar; guest beers Ⓗ
Yorkshire CAMRA Pub of the Year 2005 and a regular local award winner, this attractive 18th-century inn sits in a quiet village. Recently refurbished, it has two bars, a games room, a large beer garden and a trellised heated smoking area. A mix of locals and visitors creates a friendly atmosphere. Seven guest beers come from micro-breweries countrywide, along with up to two ciders or perries. Two beer festivals and a cider festival are held, and there is a monthly quiz on a Tuesday night. ⚲Q⚙❶🚆(29)♣🚶P⌐🍴

Marske-by-the-Sea

Frigate
49 Hummershill Lane, TS11 7DH (300m E of A1085, next to cricket club)
✪ 3-11 (11.30 Wed & Thu); 12-12.30am Fri (1am Sat; midnight Sun) ☎ (01642) 483270
Camerons Strongarm; guest beers Ⓗ
What still remains a locals' pub for the regulars has been transformed by an enthusiastic licensee into a venue providing an eclectic mix of both beer and blues/R&B music. Up to five guests are served at this large one-roomed free house. The pub supports both pool and darts teams. The atmosphere heats up at 9pm on Thursday, Saturday and Sunday evenings when live bands perform, and when a quiet drink is not really on the cards. An ideal party venue. ⚙⇌🚆♣🚶P⌐🍴

Masham

Bay Horse
Silver Street, HG4 4DX
✪ 11-midnight (1am Fri & Sat; midnight Sun)
☎ (01765) 689236 ⊕ bayhorsemasham.co.uk
Black Sheep Best Bitter; Greene King H&H Olde Trip; Theakston Best Bitter Ⓗ
Welcoming pub with two bars separated by a low partition, with traditional wooden floors and furniture of character, including several settles. Each bar has a roaring real fire in winter with an invitation to stoke up as needed. Many old artefacts adorn the walls and mantelpieces. A wide variety of home-cooked food is available, with ingredients coming mainly from local suppliers. There are six letting rooms and a holiday cottage sleeping six close by. Dogs are welcome throughout. ▲Q❀⇌⬧ ÅⱤ♣⸌

Black Sheep Brewery Visitor Centre ✔
Wellgarth, HG4 4EN (follow the brown tourist signs)
✪ 10.30-4.30 (11 Thu-Sat) ☎ (01765) 680101
⊕ blacksheepbrewery.com
Black Sheep Best Bitter, Ale, Riggwelter, Golden Sheep Ⓗ
Popular tourist attraction that is housed in the spacious former maltings. As well as offering the opportunity to sample the brewery's products at the 'baaar', there is a high quality café/bistro serving snacks and full meals, with an emphasis on local ingredients. A 'sheepy' shop stocks the bottled product and Black Sheep souvenirs. Visitors can book a 'shepherded' tour of the brewery. A small garden overlooks scenic lower Wensleydale and the River Ure. Q❀⬧ ÅⱤ(159)Pⓗ

White Bear ✔
12 Crosshills, HG4 4EN (follow brown tourist signs on A6108)
✪ 11-midnight ☎ (01765) 689319
⊕ thewhitebearhotel.co.uk
Caledonian Deuchars IPA; Theakston Best Bitter, Black Bull Bitter, XB, Old Peculier Ⓗ
A recently extended and refurbished brewery tap – the extension making extra room for diners as well as adding 14 bedrooms and conference facilities. The pub has not lost any of its charm as an award-winning hostelry and is a great favourite with the locals, as well as directors and staff from the Theakston Brewery. The full range of the brewery's products is usually available. Outside is a pleasant drinking and dining area. ▲❀⇌⬧ ⬧Å ⱤⱤ♣P⸌

Middlesbrough

Star
14 Southfield Road, TS1 3BX (opp university)
✪ 11-11 (1am Fri & Sat); 12-11 Sun ☎ (01642) 245307
Beer range varies Ⓗ
A large and popular pub situated opposite the university campus, recently sympathetically modernised. With a licensee dedicated to promoting a wide variety of real ales, four beers are usually available, together with Westons Old Rosie cider. A contemporary, relaxed atmosphere prevails, with sofas and easy chairs adding to the ambience. The pub attracts a wide-ranging clientele and can get extremely busy at weekends. Good value pub food is on offer. The outdoor areas are heated and covered. ❀⬧⬧≈Ⱡ♣⸌

Naburn

Blacksmiths Arms
Main Street, YO19 4PN (W of A19 on S side of York)
SE598455
✪ 12-11 ☎ (01904) 623464 ⊕ blacksmithsarmsnaburn.co.uk
Marston's Burton Bitter, Pedigree; guest beer Ⓗ
Village pub that is a true centre of the community, catering for all tastes and ages. It has a unique library in the corner of the bar where people can swap books on an honesty basis. Situated close to the York-to-Selby cycle path and the River Ouse, it is popular with cyclists and boaters. It has a bar area and lounge, both with TVs (on mute unless requested), and a dedicated games room. Well worth seeking out. ▲♿❀⇌⬧ ⬧Å ⱤⱤ(42)♣P⸌

Newton-on-Ouse

Dawnay Arms Ⓛ
YO30 2BR (on main street of village) SE510601
✪ closed Mon; 12-2.30, 6-11; 12-11 Sat; 12-10 Sun
☎ (01347) 848345 ⊕ thedawnayatnewton.co.uk
Taylor Golden Best; guest beers Ⓗ
The landlady is committed to developing a country pub with locally-sourced food and beer, and the modern British menu often includes local game. It is on the Top Gastro Pubs list and booking is advisable. The interior is a mix of rustic wooden tables and comfortable upholstered chairs. There are two open fires in the winter, and a pleasant garden that leads down to the River Ouse. The pub is handily placed for the bus to/from York. ▲Q❀⬧ ⬧Å Ⱡ(29)P⸌

Northallerton

Standard
24 High Street, DL7 8EE (on A167, 400m N of town centre opp Sainsbury's)
✪ 12-2.30, 5-11.30; 12-11.30 Fri-Sun ☎ (01609) 772719
⊕ thestandard-pub.co.uk
Caledonian Deuchars IPA; Copper Dragon Golden Pippin; Hambleton Stallion; Taylor Landlord; guest beer Ⓗ
Named after the nearby Battle of the Standard, an English defeat of the Scots in 1138, the Standard is now home to a more modern piece of military history, with its own Jet Provost aircraft in the beer garden. Just north of the town centre, near Sainsbury's, this is a real community local, offering good value, wholesome meals (no food Sun-Tue eves) in the stone-flagged bar, and is home to Northallerton Stallions, the local Rugby League club. Spring bank holiday sees an annual beer festival. Q❀⬧Ⱡ♣⸌

Tithe Bar & Brasserie Ⓛ ✔
2 Friarage Street, DL6 1DP (just off High Street near hospital)
✪ 12-11 (midnight Fri & Sat) ☎ (01609) 778482
Beer range varies Ⓗ
Just off the town's busy High Street, the bar has the feel of a continental beer café, and offers six different ales from smaller brewers, supplemented by an array of foreign beers. Part of the small Market Town Taverns chain, renowned for its strong commitment to cask beer, it offers good-value meals, and there is a brasserie upstairs open Tuesday-Saturday evenings. Q⬧⬧≈Ⱡ♣

Old Malton

Royal Oak

47 Town Street, YO17 7HB (400m off A64 Malton bypass)

✪ closed Mon; 5-midnight; 12-1am Fri & Sat; 12-midnight Sun
☎ (01653) 699334

Tetley Bitter; York Guzzler; guest beers Ⓗ
Popular hostelry set in a picturesque village close to the Eden Camp military museum. At the front of the pub is a cosy snug, to the rear is a larger room leading to an extensive beer garden with a large covered smoking area. Guest beers are usually from York or Moorhouse's. Traditional meals featuring locally-sourced produce are served weekend lunchtimes, Friday and Saturday night – Thursday is pie night. The bus stops outside. Finalist for local CAMRA Pub of the Year 2009.
🏨Q🕽◖▲≠⊟♣P╚

Osgodby

Wadkin Arms Ⓛ ✪

Cliffe Road, YO8 5HU (just off A63 in village) SE641335
✪ 12-11 (midnight Fri & Sat) ☎ (01757) 702391
⊕ wadkinarms.co.uk

Copper Dragon Golden Pippin; John Smith's Bitter; guest beers Ⓗ
Cosy old pub in the centre of the village, featuring real fires and wholesome food served at limited times – tea times can be busy. Guest beers regularly come from nearby breweries such as Great Heck and Brown Cow, and a dark mild and a pale beer are usually available. An annual beer festival is now established. The pub has a good local atmosphere and is frequented both by Osgodby residents and nearby villagers alike.
🏨🗗🕽♣P╚

Osmotherley

Golden Lion

6 West End, DL6 3AA (in village centre, 1 mile E of A19)
✪ 12-2.30 (not Mon & Tue), 6-11; 12-midnight Sat; 12-10.30 Sun ☎ (01609) 883526 ⊕ goldenlionosmotherley.co.uk

Beer range varies Ⓗ
A hugely popular centre for walking on the North York Moors, Osmotherley is also at the end of the Lyke Wake walk, and the tables outside the pub are at a premium in good weather. Inside, while much of the accent is on dining, for which there is a fine reputation, the recently reconfigured bar area caters much more for drinkers and there is a strong local trade. Guest ales are generally from local Yorkshire micro-breweries and a beer festival is hosted in November. 🏨Q🗗◖▲⊟(80,89)

Pickering

Sun Inn

136 Westgate, YO18 8BB (on A170 400m W of traffic lights in town centre)
✪ 4-11; 2.30-midnight Fri; 12-midnight Sat; 12-11 Sun
☎ (01751) 467080

Leeds Best Bitter; Tetley Bitter; guest beers Ⓗ
Small, friendly, CAMRA-award-winning pub a short walk from the busy town centre and NYMR steam railway, with all guest beers from Yorkshire. Well-behaved children, walkers and dogs (on leads) are welcome. There is just one room, cosy in winter with real fires, with pub games and newspapers provided. The large garden is popular in summer

and sometimes hosts music events. An acoustic open session features in the bar on the third Sunday afternoon of the month. Menus for local takeaways are available. 🏨🕽≠⊟(128)♣●╚

Picton

Station

TS15 0AE (at level crossing on Kirklevington-Picton Rd, 300m E of village)
✪ 11-2.30 (Sat only), 6-11; 11-11.30 Sun ☎ (01642) 700067
Black Sheep Best Bitter; Tetley Bitter Ⓗ
Situated beside the Middlesbrough to York railway, this remote pub is well worth the journey, though sadly not by train, as the adjacent station was closed in the 1960s. The one-roomed bar is warmed by an open fire, where railway memorabilia adorn the walls. The two ales sit alongside an impressive and varied food menu, featuring local produce where possible. Meals, renowned for their generosity, are served in an equally impressive conservatory. 🏨Q🕽◖P

Pool in Wharfedale

Hunters Inn

Harrogate Road, LS21 2PS (on A658 between Otley and Harrogate)
✪ 11-11; 12-10.30 Sun ☎ (0113) 2841090
Tetley Bitter; Theakston Best Bitter; guest beers Ⓗ
When you enter this welcoming roadside pub, do not forget to check out the impressive range of up to nine cask ales shown on the board on the right. A separate board gives tasting notes. The large single-room interior incorporates a raised area with a warming real fire during the colder months. Well-behaved children are allowed in the pub until 9pm accompanied by an adult.
🏨🕽⊟(767,X52,X53)♣●╚

Potto

Dog & Gun ✪

2 Cooper Lane, DL6 3HQ
✪ 3-midnight; 12-midnight Fri & Sat; 12-11 Sun
☎ (01642) 700232 ⊕ thedogandgunpotto.com
Beer range varies Ⓗ
Country ale house under the stewardship of an enthusiastic licensee who now also runs the Captain Cook Brewery. Friendly staff ensure that a laid-back ambience prevails in this contemporary setting, which comprises a comfortable main bar, classy restaurant, private dining areas, five luxury bedrooms and conference facilities. Alongside the selection of beers from Captain Cook, a guest sourced from a local micro-brewery is also served. Outside, open terraces are ideal for summer drinking. Live acoustic music plays on Friday.
🏨🗗◖⑁&P

Riccall

Greyhound Inn Ⓛ ✪

Main Street, YO19 6TE (on A19 10 miles S of York) SE620380
✪ 12 (3 Mon-Wed Nov-Feb)-midnight; 12-11.30 Sun
☎ (01757) 249101 ⊕ thegreyhoundriccall.co.uk
Copper Dragon Golden Pippin; Tetley Mild, Bitter; guest beer Ⓗ
Situated in a quiet village between Selby and York, this pub offers a friendly welcome and an enthusiastic guest beer policy. Home-made food is

available daily except Monday (Sat and Sun lunchtime only), plus takeaway fish and chips. Home to keen darts and dominoes teams, the pub is also popular with cyclists and walkers using the York-Selby cycle path (note the old Cyclists Touring Club emblem). There is a large garden to the rear for summer meals and drinks. ⚶Q❀⇦❶◗🖥(415)♣P⅃

Richmond

Ralph Fitz Randal 🄻 ✅
6 Queens Road, DL10 4AE (edge of town centre on main Scotch Corner road)
☼ 9am-midnight (1am Fri & Sat) ☎ (01748) 828080
Greene King Ruddles Best Bitter, Abbot; guest beers Ⓗ
Converted from a former post office, the large single bar is on three levels, with an informal seating area near the main entrance leading down to the main bar area and a large family dining area beyond. The simple and contemporary Wetherspoon interior is modern, and low-volume flat-screen TVs cater for sports fans. Up to eight guest beers and themed monthly beer festivals – often focusing on a particular brewery or beer style – have helped the pub build up a good following from real ale fans in recent years. Opens at 8am for breakfast. ❀◗&🖥♠⅃

Ripon

Magdalens ✅
26 Princess Road, HG4 1HW (5-minute walk from city centre past fire station)
☼ 12 (4 Mon; 1 Tue-Wed)-midnight ☎ (01765) 604276
Caledonian Deuchars IPA; John Smith's Bitter; Taylor Landlord; Theakston Best Bitter Ⓗ
A real community pub with darts, dominoes, pool and football teams. The landlord, who is a keen gardener, has created an award-winning beer garden, which is a mass of flowers in summer. A grassed play area for children is provided at the rear of the pub car park. Inside, the walls are covered with old photographs, and a large cabinet filled with trophies is witness to the prowess of customers over the years. ❀🖥(36)P⅃

One-Eyed Rat ✅
51 Allhallowgate, HG4 1LQ (near bus station)
☼ 5 (12 Fri & Sat)-11; 12-10.30 Sun ☎ (01765) 607704
⊕ oneeyedrat.com
Black Sheep Best Bitter; guest beers Ⓗ
Set in a terrace of 200-year-old houses, the small frontage gives no clue to the award-winning beer garden at the rear. This independent family-run pub is everything a good cask ale house should be, with a warm and welcoming atmosphere complete with coal fire, plus one regular and seven changing guest beers. There is always a pump dedicated to a stout/mild or porter, and another for a stronger beer at around 5%. A must-visit when in Ripon. ⚶Q❀🖥(36)♣👝⅃

Royal Oak ✅
36 Kirkgate, HG4 1PB (just off Market Square)
☼ 11-11 (midnight Fri & Sat); 12-10.30 Sun
☎ (01765) 602284 ⊕ royaloakripon.co.uk
Taylor Golden Best, Best Bitter, Landlord, Dark Mild Ⓗ
Adjacent to the cathedral and Market Square, this old coaching inn retains its original facade but has an airy feel to its interior. While stocking the full

range of Taylor's beers, there is also an emphasis on locally-sourced food. Nearby attractions are Fountains Abbey and Ripon racecourse. At the obelisk in nearby Market Square at 9pm every night the Ripon hornblower sets the night watch – which has happened for 1,000 years. The pub has six en-suite bedrooms. ⚶❀⇦❶◗🖥(36)⅃

Saltburn-by-the-Sea

Saltburn Cricket, Bowls & Tennis Club
Marske Mill Lane, TS12 1HJ (next to leisure centre)
☼ 8-midnight (1am Fri & Sat); 2-midnight Sat match days; 11.30-3, 8-midnight Sun ☎ (01287) 622761
Beer range varies Ⓗ
Casual visitors are made welcome at this 2011 local CAMRA award-winner. A private sports club supported by the local community, it fields cricket, tennis and bowls teams, and is also the watering hole for the local diving club. The bar sits in a spacious, comfortable lounge, which can be divided for different functions and social events. The balcony, ideal for those lazy summer afternoons, overlooks the cricket field. Two changing beers are served. ❀&⇋🖥(X4,48)♣P⅃

Sawdon

Anvil Inn
Main Street, YO13 9DY (2 miles off A170)
☼ closed Mon & Tue; 12-2.30, 6-11; 12-3, 6-10.30 Sun
☎ (01723) 859896 ⊕ theanvilinnsawdon.co.uk
Daleside Bitter; guest beers Ⓗ
A heart-of-the-village pub, on the edge of the North York Moors National Park, Dalby Forest and close to the coast, in excellent walking, cycling and mountain biking country. Formerly the village blacksmith's, it still retains the forge and, of course, the anvil. A cosy bar, with a separate lounge and dining area, serves two guest beers from local independents, and food of the highest standard; booking is recommended. There are two well-appointed letting cottages. ⚶❀◗♣P

Scarborough

Angel ✅
46 North Street, YO11 1DF
☼ 11 (12 Sun)-midnight ☎ (01723) 365504
Copper Dragon Golden Pippin; Cropton Two Pints; Tetley Bitter; Wells Bombardier Ⓗ
Friendly town-centre local close to the main shopping area, with a single-room horseshoe bar displaying an excellent collection of saucy seaside postcards. An interest in sport and games is reflected in the impressive array of trophies won by various pub teams and the large-screen TVs for viewing sporting events. Occasional guest beers are added in summer. Note the Tardis-like quality of the surprisingly spacious and well-appointed patio garden at the rear. ❀⇋🖥♣⅃

Cellars
35-37 Valley Road, YO11 2LX
☼ 4-11; 12-midnight Sat; 12-10.30 Sun ☎ (01723) 367158
Camerons Strongarm; Jennings Sneck Lifter; guest beers Ⓗ
A family-run pub converted from the cellars of a Victorian house. Six handpumps dispense four, mainly northern, guest beers. Excellent locally-sourced, home-cooked food is available lunchtimes

Thornbridge Wild Swan, Lord Marples, Kipling, Jaipur IPA; guest beers ⊞

Opened in 2009, this was originally the first-class refreshment room for Sheffield Midland station, built in 1904. After years of neglect the main bar area has been carefully restored and retains many original features, including the ornamental bar fittings and tiled walls. Further seating has been provided in the corridor leading from the Sheaf Street entrance, and two more rooms have been opened up to the right of the bar. A CAMRA Conversion to Pub Use design award winner. A small range of bar snacks is available. Q✿&≠⊖⊟

Sheffield: East

Carlton

563 Attercliffe Road, S9 3RA
🕐 11-11; 12-9 Sun ☎ (0114) 244 3287
Beer range varies ⊞

Built in 1862, this former Gilmour's house lies behind a deceptively small frontage, but offers the most impressive range of real ales in the area. The main room around the bar is comfortably furnished in traditional style. To the rear is the refurbished games room leading on to a newly established snug and a recently created garden. A strict no-swearing policy enhances the friendly atmosphere. Beers are mainly from small breweries, with some local but mostly from further afield.
✿⊖(Woodbourn Rd)⊟(52,69)♣'-

Sheffield: North

Gardeners Rest ℓ

105 Neepsend Lane, S3 8AT
🕐 3-11; 12-midnight Fri & Sat; 12-11 Sun ☎ (0114) 272 4978
⊕ gardenersrest.com
Sheffield Crucible Best, Five Rivers, seasonal beers; guest beers ⊞

The tap of the Sheffield brewery re-opened in 2009 after refurbishment following severe flooding in 2007. The clean, bright interior has retained the cosy lounge. The main bar features art exhibitions, live music Friday and Saturday, and the restored bar billiards table. To the rear is a conservatory leading to the beer garden overlooking the River Don. There are usually four Sheffield beers, together with up to eight guests from other local and regional breweries. The popular quiz night occurs on a Sunday.
Q✿&⊖(Infirmary Rd)⊟(53)♣●'-⊟

Hillsborough Hotel ℓ

54-58 Langsett Road, S6 2UB
🕐 12-11 (midnight Fri & Sat) ☎ (0114) 232 2100
⊕ hillsborough-hotel.com
Crown HPA, Traditional Bitter, Stannington Stout, seasonal beers; guest beers ⊞

Family-run hotel serving home-cooked food. The guest ales are supplemented by beers from the house brewery in the cellar, which brews under the Crown name, with at least four of its range always available. Brewery tours can be booked. The conservatory and raised terrace at the rear feature panoramic views along the upper Don Valley. Attractions include seasonal beer festivals, regular themed events, folk music on Sunday and a popular quiz night on Tuesday.
Q✿🛏◑&⊖(Langsett Primrose View)⊟♣'-

New Barrack Tavern ℓ

601 Penistone Road, S6 2GA
🕐 11-11 (midnight Fri & Sat); 12-11 Sun ☎ (0114) 234 9148
Acorn Barnsley Bitter; Bradfield Farmers Bitter; Castle Rock Harvest Pale, Screech Owl; guest beers ⊞

Multi-roomed pub offering up to seven guest beers including seasonal ales from Castle Rock. The home-cooked food is available daily, with a late night takeaway service, and a carvery on Sunday. The front bar has darts, the main room features live music Friday and Saturday, there is a comedy club on the first Sunday of the month, plus folk on Monday. A wide choice of continental beers, single malts and a real cider are served. Outside is an award-winning heated, covered patio garden.
🛏Q✿◑▶⊖(Bamforth St)⊟(53,77,78)♣●'-

Rawson Spring ℓ ✅

Langsett Road, Hillsborough, S6 2LN
🕐 7am-11.30 (midnight Fri & Sat) ☎ (0114) 285 6200
Greene King Ruddles Best Bitter, Abbot; guest beers ⊞

Large Wetherspoon converted from the former Hillsborough swimming baths, popular on match days and featuring past Wednesday team photos, along with other historic prints. The pub takes its name from the local spring that supplied fresh water to the nearby barracks. The eponymous house beer is provided by Bradfield, and six other handpumps supply a range of guest ales. Food is available every day until 10pm. Family-friendly throughout, it has a beer garden and a covered, heated patio area. ✿◑&⊖(Hillsborough)⊟●'-

Wellington ℓ

1 Henry Street, S3 7EQ
🕐 12-11; 12-3.30, 7-10.30 Sun ☎ (0114) 249 2295
Millstone Baby Git; guest beers ⊞

Popular street-corner pub, also known as the Bottom Wellie, that champions a varying range of beers from small independent brewers, with 10 handpumps always offering a stout or porter and a real cider, plus a range of continental bottled beers. The house brewery, which adjoins the secluded garden at the rear, recommenced brewing late in 2009. It now produces a wide range of brews, usually pale and hoppy, under the Little Ale Cart name, normally with three on sale.
🛏Q✿⊖(Shalesmoor)⊟●'-⊟

Sheffield: South

Archer Road Beer Stop ℓ

57 Archer Road, S8 0JT
🕐 11 (10.30 Sat; 5 Sun)-10 ☎ (0114) 255 1356
⊕ archerroadbeerstop.com
Beer range varies ⊞

Small corner shop off-licence featuring four hand-pulled ales, mainly from local micro-breweries. It also stocks a large number of bottle-conditioned beers and an equally impressive range of Belgian, continental and world favourites. The shop has been a long-standing entrant in this Guide and also winner of local CAMRA awards. Well worth a visit for those seeking a bottle or three for a quiet night in. ⊟(97,98)

Sheaf View

25 Gleadless Road, Heeley, S2 3AA
🕐 11.30-11.30 ☎ (0114) 249 6455
Bradfield Farmers Blonde; Kelham Island Easy Rider; guest beers ⊞

Welcoming free house offering at least six rotating guest ales sourced largely from independent micro-breweries throughout the UK, and featuring an impressive range of Belgian and continental bottled beers and a splendid selection of malt whiskies. The Sheaf has developed a fine reputation for high quality and exceptional value, and this consumer focus has made it a beacon of excellence in the local area.
Q❀&♿🚌(20,20A,53)♣♠P⌐

Sheffield: West

Ball Inn ✓
171-173 Crookes, S10 1UD
🕐 11-11.30 (12.30am Fri & Sat); 12-11.30 Sun
☎ (0114) 266 1211
Greene King IPA, Ruddles County, Old Speckled Hen, Abbot; guest beers Ⓗ
Situated at the heart of Crookes, this is a traditional pub dating back to around 1901, replacing an earlier inn that started life as a farmhouse. The old-fashioned wooden decor incorporates the oak panelling of the former tap room. The Ball has become a popular cask ale house thanks to the policy of rotating guest beers mainly from local brewers. A good selection is usually available, ranging from pale to dark, to complement the core range from Greene King. ❀&🚌(52)♣⌐

Champs Sports Bar
315 Ecclesall Road, S11 8NX
🕐 10-midnight (1am Fri & Sat) ☎ (0114) 266 6333
🌐 champssportsbar.co.uk
Kelham Island Champs Special, Pale Rider; Thornbridge Wild Swan, Lord Marples, Jaipur IPA; guest beers Ⓗ
At the heart of the Ecclesall Road drinking circuit, the pub comprises a large open-plan bar area and a raised restaurant space. A refurbishment in 2009 saw the introduction of 10 additional handpumps, which dispense up to four beers each from Kelham Island and Thornbridge, in addition to guests from local and regional breweries. Meals are served throughout the day, starting with breakfast at 10am, and last orders in the restaurant is 9.30pm (10pm Sat and Sun). ❀◑&🚌

Cobden View
40 Cobden View Road, Crookes, S10 1HQ
🕐 1-midnight (1am Fri); 12-1am Sat; 12-midnight Sun
☎ (0114) 266 1273
Black Sheep Best Bitter; Bradfield Farmers Blonde; Caledonian Deuchars IPA; Greene King Old Speckled Hen; Wychwood Hobgoblin Ⓗ
Off the main Crookes thoroughfare, this busy community pub caters for a varied clientele, ranging from students to retired folk. The original room layout is still apparent, with the bar serving a snug at the front, a games area with pool table to the rear, and a lounge to the right of the front entrance. A quiz is held on Sunday evening and there is live music most Thursdays and Saturdays. The well-kept rear garden hosts summer barbecues. ❀&🚌♣♠⌐

Francis Newton ✓
7 Clarkehouse Road, S10 2LA
🕐 7am-midnight (1am Thu-Sat) ☎ (0114) 267 3660
Greene King Ruddles Best Bitter, Abbot; guest beers Ⓗ
Broombank House, the former home of Victorian steel magnate Francis Newton, was converted to pub use in the 1990s and re-opened as a Wetherspoon in 2010. The open-plan interior is divided into several separate areas and the extensive grounds adjoin Lynwood Gardens, a community nature reserve. The pub is family-friendly and food is available all day until 10pm.
♨Q❀◑&🚌(30,40,120)♠P⌐

Ranmoor Inn Ⓛ ✓
330 Fulwood Road, S10 3GD
🕐 11.30-11; 12-10.30 Sun ☎ (0114) 230 1325
Abbeydale Moonshine; Bradfield Farmers Bitter, Farmers Blonde; Taylor Landlord; guest beers Ⓗ
Renovated Victorian local with original etched windows lying in the shadow of Ranmoor Church. Now open plan, the seating areas reflect the old room layout. A friendly, old-fashioned pub, it has a diverse clientele that includes choirs and rugby and cricket teams. The piano by the bar is often played by regulars. Outside, there is a small front garden plus the former stable yard, which has been opened as a partly covered and heated drinking area. Lunches are available Tuesday to Saturday. Q❀◑🚌(40,120)♣⌐

Rising Sun Ⓛ ✓
471 Fulwood Road, S10 3QA
🕐 12-11 ☎ (0114) 230 3855 🌐 risingsunsheffield.co.uk
Abbeydale Daily Bread, Brimstone, Moonshine, Absolution, seasonal beers; guest beers Ⓗ
Operated by local brewer Abbeydale, this is a large suburban roadhouse in the leafy western side of the city. The two rooms are comfortably furnished, with a main bar and raised area to the rear. A range of Abbeydale beers is always available, with up to six guests, mainly from micros, dispensed from the impressive bank of handpumps. Entertainment includes live music on Monday and quizzes on Sunday and Wednesday. An annual beer festival, Sunfest, is held in July. Q❀◑&🚌(40,120)♣P⌐

University Arms Ⓛ
197 Brook Hill, S3 7HG
🕐 12-11 (midnight Fri & Sat); closed Sun ☎ (0114) 222 8969
Thornbridge Jaipur IPA; guest beers Ⓗ
Owned by the University of Sheffield, this former staff club became a pub in 2007. There is a bar with a small alcove seating area adjoining, and a main lounge area. A conservatory at the rear leads to the extensive beer garden. Up to six guest beers usually include one from Thornbridge, with the others mostly sourced locally. There is no food on Saturday evening. Entertainment includes a quiz on Tuesday night and regular live jazz and blues at weekends.
Q❀◑⊖(Sheffield University)🚌(51,52)♣⌐

York
243-247 Fulwood Road, S10 3BA
🕐 10-11 (midnight Fri & Sat) ☎ (0114) 266 4624
🌐 theyorksheffield.co.uk
Brew Company Anvil Porter; guest beers Ⓗ
Occupying a prominent site in the centre of Broomhill, after a period of closure following its disposal by a pubco, the York re-opened as a free house in 2010. Extensively refurbished, with parquet flooring and wood-panelled walls, it now offers high quality dining complemented by a range of up to five mainly local guest ales and two real ciders. Q❀◑&🚌(40,52)♠⌐

South Anston

Loyal Trooper 🅛 ✅
34 Sheffield Road, S25 5DT (off A57, 3 miles off M1 jct 31 heading for Worksop)
☼ 12-11 (midnight Fri & Sat) ☎ (01909) 562203
Adnams Bitter; Taylor Landlord; Tetley Bitter; guest beers 🅗
Friendly oak-beamed village local selling a range of real ales and good wholesome food at reasonable prices. Guest beers often come from local breweries. Largely unchanged since the 1960s, parts of the building date back to 1690. The interior comprises a public bar, snug, lounge and a function room upstairs used by many local groups, including a thriving folk club. Close to St James's Church, it is on the Five Churches walk and handy for Anston Stones Wood and the nearby Butterfly Farm.
Q❀🕸🅘🖥🖾(19,19B,29)P⅃

Sprotbrough

Boat Inn ✅
Nursery Lane, DN5 7NB (down hill from village; walk along canalside)
☼ 12-11 (10.30 Sun) ☎ (01302) 858500
Beer range varies 🅗
Situated near the Transpennine Trail, this attractive riverside pub is popular with walkers, diners and drinkers. Good food from an extensive menu is served throughout the day. Beer is sourced from independent breweries, with a new batch of specials from the Vintage Inns list becoming available each quarter. The pub is multi-roomed and has a large courtyard drinking area outside with ample parking. 🏰❀🕸🅘&P⅃

Sunnyside

Woodman
Woodlaithes Road, Woodlaithes Village, S66 3ZL (off A631, 1½ miles from M18 jct 2, nr roundabout on Woodlaithes Road)
☼ 11-11 (midnight Fri & Sat); 12-11 Sun ☎ (01709) 533854
Marston's Pedigree, seasonal beers; guest beers 🅗
A new pub situated on the Woodlaithes village estate, opened around four years ago by Marston's, with the guest beers sourced from its portfolio. This family-friendly pub offers an extensive menu of locally-sourced food, with popular curry nights. Poker and quiz nights are held regularly, and there is occasional live music. The beer garden contains a children's play area. Winner of local CAMRA Pub of the Season awards in 2008 and 2011.
❀🕸🅘&🖾(3,3A)P⅃

Sykehouse

Old George ✅
Broad Lane, DN14 9AD
☼ 12-midnight ☎ (01405) 785635
Tetley Bitter; guest beers 🅗
A 200-year-old building in this linear village, the Old George is well worth seeking out. Featuring an open fire in winter and a warm welcome from staff, it is a free house, the guest ales sourced from countrywide breweries, usually two in summer. Excellent meals are served, including OAP specials and a Sunday carvery. Outside is a patio area where barbecues are held in summer, and a large playground including a children's bathing pool.
🏰❀🕸🅘&🅐🖾(89)♣P⅃

Thorne

Victoria Inn 🅛
Southend, DN8 5QN (adjacent to Thorne South railway station)
☼ 4 (2 Sat & Sun)-11 ☎ (01405) 813163
Beer range varies 🅗
A delightful, traditional pub where conversation and good fellowship take precedence over jukebox and gambling machines. Four handpumps all serve local beers. Old photographs and curios add to a pleasant old-fashioned atmosphere in the bar. There is a separate lounge and conservatory, and even a bric-a-brac shop to browse. Quiz night is Thursday, and sing-along with knees-up on Saturday night. Outside is a paved drinking and smoking area. Q❀🛏🅘&🖾♣P⅃

Windmill Inn 🅛
19 Queen Street, DN8 5AA (mid-way between Thorne North station and centre of town)
☼ 2-11 (midnight Fri & Sat); 12-midnight Sun
☎ (01405) 812866
Thorne Pale Ale; guest beers 🅗
Well-kept, popular community pub, appealing to young and old alike. Although sports fans are catered for, conversation among the friendly clientele is never intruded upon by TV sound levels. The pub comprises a lounge and public bar divided into two distinct areas. Outside there is a large beer garden with a covered, heated area for smokers. A local beer is always available, plus guest beers from independent breweries. Sunday is quiz night. ❀&🖾P⅃

Thorpe Salvin

Parish Oven
Worksop Road, S80 3JU (from M1 jct 31 take A57, then B6059)
☼ 12-2.30 (not Mon), 5.30-11 (11.30 Fri); 12-midnight Sat; 12-10.30 Sun ☎ (01909) 770685 ⊕ theparishoven.co.uk
Black Sheep Best Bitter; guest beers 🅗
Built on the site of a former farmhouse and communal bakery in 1972, this award-winning pub is a popular venue for Sunday lunch and evening meals, offering a variety of home-cooked dishes (booking advisable). There is a large children's play area outside, and well-behaved dogs are welcome in the bar area. It is situated on the Five Churches and Round Rotherham walks, and close to the Chesterfield Canal Cuckoo walk and the ruins of medieval Thorpe Salvin Hall. Live music plays most Saturdays. ❀🅘&P⅃

Thurlstone

Huntsman 🅛
136 Manchester Road, S36 9QW (on A628)
☼ 6-11; 12-10.30 Sun ☎ (01226) 764892
⊕ thehuntsmanthurlstone.co.uk
Black Sheep Best Bitter; Taylor Landlord; Tetley Bitter; guest beers 🅗
This friendly roadside pub sitting on a major east-west route is an ideal stopping place for travellers. It is, however, also a locals' pub hosting varied activities, quizzes, old-fashioned pub games and a road-running club. Good cheer and fellowship abound; it must, for instance, be the most dog-friendly pub anywhere. While not regularly serving food, an eclectic Sunday lunch is offered. The guest ale pumps sport an ever-rotating supply of mainly LocAle beers. 🏰Q🖾(20,20A)♣

Tickhill

Scarbrough Arms

Sunderland Street, DN11 9QJ (on A631 between motorway bridge and the Buttercross)
✪ 12-11 (10.30 Sun) ☎ (01302) 742977
Greene King Abbot; Shepherd Neame Spitfire; John Smith's Bitter; guest beers Ⓗ
A deserving entry since 1990, this three-roomed stone-built pub has won several local CAMRA awards over the years. Originally a farmhouse, the building dates back to the 16th century. Although structural changes have taken place, the snug is a delight, with its barrel-shaped furniture and real fire, while bar billiards can be played in the bar. An outbuilding doubles as a covered smoking area and beer festival extension in the summer.
🏚Q✤✿⌑◖⊟🚆(22,205)♣P⌐

Wath upon Dearne

Church House Ⓛ ✔

Montgomery Square, S63 7RZ
✪ 9am-midnight ☎ (01709) 879518
Greene King Ruddles Best Bitter; Marston's Pedigree; guest beers Ⓗ
Large pub with an impressive frontage set in a pedestrian square in the town centre, with excellent access to local bus services. It was built in 1810, consecrated by the nearby church in 1912, became a pub in the 1980s, and then a Wetherspoon in 2000. Handy for exploring the RSPB Old Moor Wetlands Centre and for Manvers, it serves a wide variety of beers from both national and local brewers, including the nearby Acorn and Wentworth breweries. Westons ciders are on handpull. 🏚✿◖⑊⊟🚆(22,220,229)●P⌐

Wentworth

George & Dragon Ⓛ

85 Main Street, S62 7TN (stands back from road on B6090)
✪ 10-11 (10.30 Sun) ☎ (01226) 742440
🌐 georgeanddragonwentworth.co.uk
Taylor Landlord; Wentworth WPA, seasonal beers; guest beers Ⓗ
In a picturesque village, just 500 metres from Rotherham's only brewery, this free house offers up to four ales from the brewery along with beers from local and national brewers. The pub has a car park and patio, and a grassed area at the rear with a children's adventure playground and a craft shop. Home-cooked food is popular here. This local is handy for historic Wentworth Woodhouse and Hoober Stand, and has been licensed since 1804.
🏚Q✿◖⊟🚆(44,227)P⌐

West Melton

Plough Inn ✔

144 Melton High Street, S63 6RG
✪ 12-12.30am (2am Fri & Sat) ☎ (01709) 872995
John Smith's Bitter; guest beers Ⓗ
Popular pub standing back from the road – the front bar serves as both a lounge and tap area. There is a separate function room, family room and sizeable outside area. Food is served every lunchtime (except Mon), Tuesday to Friday evenings, and all afternoon on Sunday. Poker matches are played here. Handy for the RSPB Old Moor Wetlands Centre and Manvers. 🛏✿◖⑊⊟🚆(220,229)♣P⌐

Whiston

Hind ✔

285 East Bawtry Road, S60 4ET (on A631 link road between M1 and M18)
✪ 12-11 (midnight Thu-Sat) ☎ (01709) 704351
Taylor Landlord; Tetley Bitter; guest beers Ⓗ
Large pub, built for Mappins Brewery of Rotherham in 1936, on the border of Whiston and Rotherham and serving the extensive estates in the area. Originally known as King Edward VIII, it was renamed when the king abdicated. Since refurbishment the interior has been opened out, creating good disabled access. There are extensive gardens and a patio to the rear, with a snooker table upstairs (membership required to play). Daytime and evening food is popular, and third-of-a-pint tasting racks are available. Historic Canklow Woods are a short walk away.
🏚Q✿◖◑⑊⊟🚆(10,10A,19B)P⌐

Wombwell

Anglers Rest Ⓛ

66 Park Street, S73 0HS (on Park St 5 mins' walk from Wombwell town centre)
✪ 5 (7 Wed winter)-midnight; 12-midnight Sat & Sun ☎ (01226) 751031
Acorn Old Moor Porter; guest beers Ⓗ
Local CAMRA award-winning pub and fantastic community local. The landlady has been at the helm for three years. In that time the range of cask ales has extended, with up to four sourced from the nearby Acorn Brewery or other local micros. The pub is small and cosy, with a fantastic rear courtyard complete with a wood-burning stove. The landlady is a huge cider fan, and draught cider is always available. The pub hosts regular theme and fund-raising nights.
Q✿✤◖⑊⊟🚆(222,226)♣●P⌐

Wortley

Wortley Arms Ⓛ

Halifax Road, S35 7DB
✪ 12-11 (10.30 Sun) ☎ (01142) 885218
🌐 wortley-arms.co.uk
Acorn Barnsley Bitter; Taylor Landlord Ⓗ
Originally built as a coach house in 1753 at a cost of 188 pounds and 66 shillings. After an extensive period of renovation the revolving door re-opened in 2006, with Montagu's restaurant upstairs. The pub boasts features such as exposed stone, oak beams and wood panelling. In front of an impressive inglenook fireplace you can enjoy LocAles from three nearby breweries, and try a famous Wortley pie as featured in the pub's charity cookbook. 🏚Q◖◑⑊⊟🚆(23,29)P

YORKSHIRE (WEST)

Ackworth

Angel

Wakefield Road, WF7 7AB (on A638 ½ mile W of A628/A638 roundabout)
✪ 12-3, 5-11 (11.30 Fri & Sat); 12-11 Sun ☎ (01977) 611276
Black Sheep Best Bitter; guest beer Ⓗ
One of six real ale pubs and clubs in Ackworth, the Angel has a thoughtful and well-designed open-plan layout centred around a large arched wooden bar. High quality home-made bar meals using local

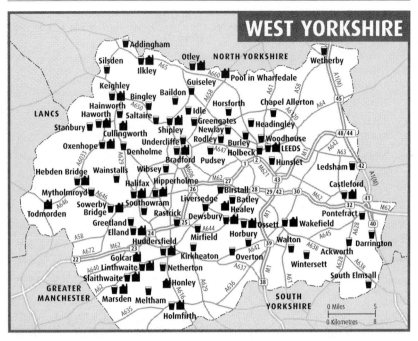

WEST YORKSHIRE

produce are served Monday to Saturday lunchtimes and evenings, plus a Sunday carvery 12-4pm. There is a popular quiz on Wednesday evening. The adjacent Dando Way provides a good start and finish point for walking/cycling in the nearby country park and surrounding area. The Ackworth Road Runners set out from here on Tuesday and Thursday evenings. ♠♣☰♦⛟(35,245,485)P≒⊟

Addingham

Swan Inn ⬡ ✪
106 Main Street, LS29 0NS
🕓 12-2 (not Mon & Tue), 5.30-11 (5.30-11 only Mon-Thu winter); 12-midnight Sat; 12-10.30 Sun ☎ (01943) 831999
🌐 swan-addingham.co.uk
Tetley Bitter; guest beers Ⓗ
The central bar serves three of the four rooms in this traditionally laid-out, friendly village local. The stone-flagged bar, snug and tap room are all warmed by real fires in winter, and bands play in the evening (Monday folk, Tuesday acoustic, and a live band most Saturdays), while Wednesday is quiz night. Local breweries' ales are featured as Brewery of the Month. Walkers and well-behaved dogs are welcome. ♠♣☰(X84,762,765)♣P

Baildon

Junction ⬡
1 Baildon Road, BD17 6AB (on Otley road)
🕓 12-midnight (1am Fri & Sat) ☎ (01274) 582009
Fuller's ESB; Oakham JHB; Saltaire Blond; Tetley Bitter; guest beers Ⓗ
A friendly community local, this CAMRA award-winning pub has three rooms: a main bar, lounge, and games room with a pool table, dartboard and pinball machine. Beers change constantly, including ales from local micros, and one pump is dedicated to those from the nearby Saltaire Brewery. Home-cooked food is served on weekday

lunchtimes. Regular Sunday evening jam sessions are held and sporting events are shown on TV. There is an annual beer festival and a separate annual cider festival.
❀◖➤(Shipley)☰(656,658,653)♣♦≒

Batley

Cellar Bar
51 Station Road, WF17 5SU (opp rail station)
🕓 4-11; 12-midnight Fri & Sat; 12-11 Sun ☎ (01924) 423419
Black Sheep Best Bitter; Copper Dragon Golden Pippin; guest beers Ⓗ
The easternmost pub on the Transpennine Rail Ale Trail, this atmospheric single-room bar in the basement of a Grade II-listed building, in a historic area that is sometimes used as a film set, always provides a friendly welcome. Comfortable seating and candles on tables add to the ambience. Quiz night and jam session alternate on Thursday nights, and live music plays every weekend on either Friday or Saturday. ➤♣≒

Bingley

Brown Cow ⬡ ✪
Ireland Bridge, BD16 2QX
🕓 12-3, 5-11 (midnight Fri); 12-midnight Sat; 12-10.30 Sun ☎ (01274) 564345
Taylor Dark Mild, Golden Best, Best Bitter, Landlord, Ram Tam Ⓗ
On the riverside next to a 13th-century bridge, a warm welcome awaits both drinkers and diners at this comfortable hostelry. Not all tables are set for dining, and settees, armchairs and bar stools are provided. An upstairs function room plays host to a variety of local groups. A small range of Belgian bottled beers is stocked. Live music features on Saturday, quiz night is Tuesday. Book ahead for meals, especially at weekends. Free WiFi provided. ♠❀◖➤(662)P≒

Myrtle Grove ⓛ ✪

141 Main Street, BD16 1AJ

☼ 8am-midnight ☎ (01274) 568637

Greene King Ruddles Best Bitter, Abbot; guest beers Ⓗ

This town-centre Wetherspoon outlet is in its 12th year. Originally a cinema, it is a large single room with a high ceiling. Cosy alcoves with comfortable high-backed settles occupy the back wall. It is popular with all age groups and has a well-established clientele of regulars. Five guest beers are always available, with local breweries represented such as Saltaire, Naylor's, Elland, Ossett, Moorhouse's and Daleside. There are regular Meet the Brewer evenings. The train station and bus stop are close by.

Q◑▶&≉➡(662)●

Birstall

Horse & Jockey

97 Low Lane, WF17 9HB (200m W of market place)

☼ 12-midnight ☎ (01924) 472559

Copper Dragon Golden Pippin; guest beers Ⓗ

A country-style pub first licensed in the 1750s, formerly called the Horse & Groom, a short walk from the village centre. The open-plan bar has half-panelled walls and a beamed ceiling and is divided into four alcoves. Darts and dominoes are played and there is a popular pool room. Outside is a paved patio drinking and smoking area. Good value pub food is served 12-3pm and 5-7pm, Sunday 12-3pm only (no food Wed). A policy of the pub is that hats must be removed. ❀◑➡♣P⅃

Bradford

Castle Hotel ⓛ

20 Grattan Road, BD1 2LU

☼ 12-midnight ☎ (07967) 144474

Jennings Cumberland Ale; guest beers Ⓗ

An established real ale pub in the city centre within easy reach of the transport network, this former Webster's house now stocks a changing range of beers, supporting local breweries, including an ale from Old Spot Brewery. A real cider is often available. The 19th-century building features a semi-circular wraparound bar, forming two almost separate areas, with a dartboard and TV at one end. Live music is on Friday. The pub may close early if quiet. &≉(Forster Square/Interchange)➡(662)●

City Vaults ⓛ ✪

33 Hustlergate, BD1 1NS

☼ 10.30-11 (midnight Fri & Sat) ☎ (01274) 739697

Black Sheep Best Bitter; Copper Dragon Golden Pippin; Salamander Golden Salamander; Saltaire Blonde; Tetley Bitter Ⓗ

Bustling city-centre pub in former bank premises opposite the famous Wool Exchange. There are now five ales on handpump, with local breweries strongly supported. Home-cooked food is served 11-9pm weekdays (7pm Friday) and until 6pm Saturday and Sunday. The pub retains a traditional feel, with fine stained glass and a wrought-iron spiral staircase to the upper drinking area. There is live music every alternate Saturday, jazz every Sunday evening, and a popular quiz on Wednesday.

❀◑&≉(Forster Square/Interchange)➡⅃

Corn Dolly

110 Bolton Road, BD1 4DE

☼ 11.30-11; 12-10.30 Sun ☎ (01274) 720219

Black Sheep Best Bitter; Draught Bass; Everards Tiger; Moorhouse's Dolly Bitter; guest beers Ⓗ

Popular award-winning local a short walk from the city centre, a Guide entry for many years. This cosy pub, which dates from 1834, was originally called the Wharfe. Four guest beers complement four regulars. The open-plan layout incorporates a separate games area. Good value food is served weekday lunchtimes. A large collection of pump clips adorns the beams and bar area, which can be admired while enjoying the beers.

🏨❀◑&≉(Forster Square/Interchange)

➡(612,640,641)♣P⅃

Fighting Cock ♈

21-23 Preston Street, BD7 1JE

☼ 11.30-11; 12-10.30 Sun ☎ (01274) 726907

Copper Dragon Golden Pippin; Greene King Abbot; Taylor Best Bitter, Landlord; Theakston Old Peculier; guest beers Ⓗ

Popular, unassuming pub, just a short walk or bus ride from the city centre. Twelve real ales are usually available, including at least one dark beer.

Additionally, ciders, foreign bottled beers and fruit wines are stocked. The pub attracts a wide variety of customers from loyal locals to well-travelled real ale enthusiasts. Lunches are served Monday to Saturday. A regular award winner and local CAMRA Pub of the Year 2011. ⚏⚏⚏⚏⚏⚏

Haigy's ⓁⒶ
31 Lumb Lane, Manningham, BD8 7QU
⚏ 5 (12 Sat)-2am; 2-11 Sun ☎ (01274) 731644
Tetley Bitter; guest beers Ⓗ
Friendly locals' pub, a former Bradford CAMRA Pub of the Year, on the edge of the city centre. It offers up to four guest ales, mainly from local micros. Tetley Dark Mild is on when available. The comfortable lounge sports a fine collection of porcelain teapots and an extensive range of pictures. It has a heated, covered smoking area and large-screen TV, and is popular with Bradford City and away real ale fans on match days.
⚏⚏(Forster Square/Interchange)⚏(620,621)P⚏

New Beehive Inn ★ Ⓛ
171 Westgate, BD1 3AA
⚏ 12-11 (1am Fri & Sat); 6-11 Sun ☎ (01274) 721784
⚏ newbeehive.co.uk
Beer range varies Ⓗ
Gas-lit pub on the fringe of the city centre. Built in 1901, this imposing building deserves its place on CAMRA's National Inventory of Historic Pub Interiors for its multi-roomed interior. Note its external features, too. Beers are almost exclusively from micros, with local ales prominent. A separate cellar bar offers occasional music, and folk and jazz can sometimes be experienced in the pub itself. See the splendid paintings in the back bar. No food is sold on Sunday. Three-star en-suite accommodation is available.
⚏⚏⚏⚏⚏⚏(Forster Square)⚏(617,618)
⚏⚏P⚏

Sir Titus Salt Ⓛ Ⓐ
Unit B, Windsor Baths, Morley Street, BD7 1AQ (behind Alhambra Theatre)
⚏ 9am-midnight (1am Fri & Sat) ☎ (01274) 732853
Greene King Ruddles Best Bitter, Abbot; guest beers Ⓗ
Excellent conversion of former public baths, this Wetherspoon site is a former local CAMRA Pub of the Season. Named in honour of a local industrialist, the interior decoration includes photographs and other artefacts relating to his life and times. Close to the National Media Museum and the city's famous curry houses. Q⚏⚏⚏(Forster Square/Interchange)⚏⚏

Brighouse

Old Ship Inn Ⓛ
34 Bethel Street, HD6 1JN
⚏ 12-11 (midnight Fri & Sat; 10.30 Sun) ☎ (01484) 719543
⚏ theoldshipinn.t83.net
Black Sheep Best Bitter; Copper Dragon Golden Pippin; Dark Horse Shipwrecked; guest beers Ⓗ
Friendly pub in the town centre with a growing reputation for real ale. The bar area has a stone-flagged floor and wood-panelled walls. In addition to the four regular beers, the pub serves four constantly changing guests. Home-cooked food is available at lunchtime, using ingredients sourced from local suppliers. Winner of local CAMRA Pub of the Year 2010. An annual beer festival (FestivALE) is held in March. ⚏⚏⚏⚏⚏⚏

Red Rooster ⓎⓁ
123 Elland Road, Brookfoot, HD6 2QR (on A6025)
⚏ 3 (12 Fri & Sat)-11; 12-10.30 Sun ☎ (01484) 713737
Abbeydale Deception; Marble Pint; Moorhouse's Blond Witch; Taylor Landlord; guest beers Ⓗ
Small stone pub that lies on the inside of a sharp bend approximately half a mile out of town. Its former four-roomed layout is still apparent, with a stone-flagged floor throughout. A charity week is held in mid-August and a beer festival in September. Part of the decking area to the front is covered to provide a smoking shelter. Live music features on the afternoon of the last Sunday of the month. Guest ales always include a dark beer.
⚏⚏(571,E8)⚏⚏

Richard Oastler Ⓛ Ⓐ
Bethell Street, HD6 1JN SE145227
⚏ 9am-11 (1am Fri & Sat) ☎ (01484) 401756
Greene King Ruddles Best Bitter, Abbot; guest beers Ⓗ
A Grade II-listed former Methodist chapel converted to a successful Wetherspoon pub. It has a magnificent but inaccessible upper floor with original chapel pews, and the impressive ceiling is retained. Eight guest beers are served, always including a dark beer. Local micro-breweries are regularly featured. Two traditional ciders from the Westons range are also available. Winner of local CAMRA 2009 winter Pub of the Season.
⚏⚏⚏⚏⚏⚏

Castleford

George V WMC Ⓛ Ⓐ
124 Front Street, Glasshoughton, WF10 4RN (on main road from Pontefract to Castleford)
⚏ 12-11; 11-midnight Fri & Sat ☎ (01977) 552775
John Smith's Bitter; Samuel Smith OBB; Tetley Bitter Ⓗ
A friendly, popular and traditional club which has LocAle and Cask Marque accreditation. The adults-only bar is well frequented by sports fans enjoying racing, Rugby League and football. A quieter round-the-corner area provides for those who simply want to sup and natter. A separate large family concert room hosts regular entertainment. There is outside table seating with a children's play area adjacent. The club runs its own football team and arranges trips and outings.
⚏⚏⚏⚏(Glasshoughton)⚏⚏P⚏

Glass Blower Ⓛ Ⓐ
15 Bank Street, WF10 1JD (just off town centre)
⚏ 8am-midnight (1am Fri & Sat) ☎ (01977) 520390
Greene King Ruddles Best Bitter, Abbot; guest beers Ⓗ
Characterful former post office converted by Wetherspoon. The name refers to the town's history of glass bottle manufacture, with some examples on display. Locally-born sculptor Henry Moore is represented via reproductions adorning the walls. A good selection of LocAles is generally available. It is a popular venue for families and rugby supporters on match days, and Meet the Brewer events and brewery visits are held. Excellent value food is served all day and children are welcome in the family area. Q⚏⚏⚏⚏⚏⚏

Junction Ⓛ
Carlton Street, WF10 1EE
⚏ 12-11 (12-midnight Fri & Sat) ☎ (01977) 278867

Beer range varies Ⓗ
After several years in the wilderness, this free house has had a renaissance, thanks to its current owner. The pub, which is undergoing an extensive refurbishment, is a large single room with a horseshoe-shaped bar; a snug is planned. Up to six guest beers, mainly from Yorkshire micros, and a good selection of Sam Smith's bottled beers are available. The pub has bar billiards and darts and is dog-friendly. Well-behaved children are welcome until 6pm. ♨️➽🚃🖵♣

Shoulder of Mutton Ⓛ
18 Methley Road, WF10 1LX (on A6032 500m from town centre)
✪ 12-3, 7-midnight; 12-4, 7-1am Sat; 12-4, 7-midnight Sun
☎ (01977) 736039
Tetley Dark Mild, Bitter; guest beers Ⓗ
A traditional free house that started life as a farmhouse in 1632 and is now packed with breweriana. The landlord, 'Tetley Dave' Parker, is a great supporter of local micro-breweries and a fount of knowledge on pub-keeping. He is justifiably proud of the many awards he has received for his cellarmanship. There is no pool table or juke-box, just lively conversation. Live music plays on the last Sunday of the month and the George Formby Society meets here on the last Wednesday of each month.
♨️Q🏵🍴👤🚃🖵(153,189)♣P⅃

Darrington

Spread Eagle
Estcourt Road, WF8 3AP (W of A1 on main road through village)
✪ 12-3 (not Mon), 5-11; 12-10.30 Sun ☎ (01977) 699698
Black Sheep Best Bitter; guest beers Ⓗ
Friendly and welcoming community pub in the heart of the village. The landlord is particularly adventurous in his choice of guest beers. Good-quality food is served both in the bar and a small dining area (no food Sun eve or all day Mon). Monday is quiz night. There is a pleasant function room for hire and a patio outside. It is said there have been sightings here of the ghost of a boy who was shot for horse rustling in 1685.
Q🏵🕪👤🚃🖵(408,409)P⅃

Denholme

New Inn Ⓛ
Keighley Road, BD13 4JT
✪ 4 (2 Sat & Sun)-11 ☎ (01274) 833871
Old Spot Light But Dark; Tetley Bitter; guest beers Ⓗ
Rescued from closure by experienced licensees, this is now a must-visit free house supporting local micros, particularly Goose Eye, Old Spot and Salamander. A warm welcome is assured. Keenly priced real ale attracts a mixed clientele, and a real cider, changed monthly, adds to the attraction. Free snacks are served from 6pm on Thursday.
♨️Q🖵(696/697)♣👤P⅃

Dewsbury

Huntsman Ⓛ
Chidswell Lane, Shaw Cross, WF12 7SW (400m from A653/B6128 jct)
✪ 12-3 (not Mon), 7 (5 Thu-Sat)-11 ☎ (01924) 275700
Taylor Landlord; guest beers Ⓗ

Ian Mann and his family have created a homely country pub on Chidswell Lane, with a warm atmosphere and a good choice of ales. With one large room and two smaller rooms, the converted farm cottages are made cosy with horse brasses, a Yorkshire range and other period features. Lunches are served Tuesday to Saturday, evening meals 5-7.30pm Thursday and Friday. The house beer, Chidswell Bitter, is brewed by Highwood. The pub has been a regular Guide entry for more than 10 years. ♨️🏵🕪👤🚃🖵(117,205)P

Leggers Inn
Calder Valley Marina, Mill Street East, WF12 9BD (off B6409; follow brown signs to Canal Basin)
✪ 10.30-11 (midnight Fri & Sat); 11-10.30 Sun
☎ (01924) 502846
Everards Tiger; guest beers Ⓗ
Once the hayloft of stables by the canal basin, this pub has been in the Guide for the 13 years it has been open. Low beams and quirky items on display make a unique atmosphere. Six beers include ales from Abbeydale and Rooster's, with one cider pump. Outside, a large decked area is excellent in summer. Light meals are served all day until 8pm and there is a function room. Bus and rail stations are within a mile. ♨️🏵🕪♣👤P⅃

Shepherds Boy Ⓛ ✔
157 Huddersfield Road, WF13 2RP (on A644 ½ mile from town centre)
✪ 3-11; 12-midnight Fri & Sat; 12-11 Sun ☎ (01924) 454116
Ossett Excelsior, Pale Gold; guest beers Ⓗ
Ten minutes' walk from the railway station, this Ossett Brewery pub, with its nicely reconstructed interior, has many retained or reinstated original features and four separate, comfortable drinking areas. A trademark brick arch separates the front and rear of the pub. The well-balanced range of beers includes several from the Ossett group; varying guest beers include one from Fuller's. Real cider or perry is always available. Tuesday is quiz night. The pub hosts two well-supported annual beer festivals. Lunches Sunday only.
🏵👤🚃🖵♣👤P⅃

West Riding Licensed Refreshment Rooms 🍷 Ⓛ ✔
Railway Station, Wellington Road, WF13 1HF (platform 2 Dewsbury Station)
✪ 12-11 Mon; 11-11 Tue, Wed & Sun; 11-midnight Thu & Fri; 10-midnight Sat ☎ (01924) 459193 🌐 imissedthetrain.com
Black Sheep Best Bitter; Taylor Dark Mild, Landlord; guest beers Ⓗ
Multi-award-winning pub in a Grade II-listed Victorian building. A Transpennine Rail Ale Trail mainstay, the pub serves a broad range of rotating beers from local independents; one of the eight pumps is reserved for the local Anglo-Dutch Brewery. The pub is famed for good value, quality food. An annual beer festival is held in June, with music Friday and Sunday in summer. A large, decked, partially-covered patio serves as a beer garden. Lunches are available daily, evening meals Tuesday to Thursday only. ♨️🏵🕪👤🚃🖵👤⅃

Elland

Drop Inn ✔
12 Elland Lane, HX5 9DU
✪ 4-11; 12-12.30 Thu-Sat; 12-10.30 Sun ☎ (01422) 387484

Ossett Pale Gold, Yorkshire Blonde, Excelsior; guest beer Ⓗ
Stone flags and floorboards, and a brick arch between rooms, exhibit the Ossett Brewery pub style. French Renaissance pictures add to the decor along with cigar containers, stone jars and tankards. A stove occupies a large cottage fireplace in the side room. A Fuller's beer is sold along with three or four guests, including Ossett-owned Fernandes and Riverhead brews. Food is served 12-2pm Thursday to Saturday. To Reach Elland Lane take the Dewsbury road, then Westbury Street from the centre. ➽❀◖▯(278,503)♣⏚

Greengates

Albion Inn ❷
25 New Line, BD10 9AS (on main Keighley-Leeds road)
✪ 12-11 (midnight Fri & Sat) ☎ (01274) 613211
Acorn Barnsley Bitter; Tetley Bitter; guest beers Ⓗ
Busy roadside local with an L-shaped lounge and a separate tap room where pub games are played. The pub is home to a thriving social club, and strangers are made most welcome. Traditional values are maintained in this friendly neighbourhood pub. Moonshine cider and Broadoak perry are usually available. Buses pass close by. ◖▯(760)♣♠P

Greetland

Greetland Community & Sporting Association
Rochdale Road, HX4 8JG (on B6113)
✪ 5-11; 4-midnight Fri; 12-midnight Sat; 12-11 Sun
☎ (01422) 370140
Coach House Cheshire Gold; guest beers Ⓗ
Award-winning sports and social club set back from the road at the top of Greetland village, with a modern but cosy bar, with seating at the front and an area for pool players beyond. The club is a past winner of both the CAMRA Yorkshire and National Club of the Year awards. It has a wooden decked area outside, which in summer affords excellent views over Halifax. A warm welcome is offered to all visitors. ❀▯(557,559)P⏚

Guiseley

Coopers Ⓛ ❷
4-6 Otley Road, LS20 8AH (opp Morrisons on A65)
✪ 12-11 (midnight Fri & Sat) ☎ (01943) 878835
Black Sheep Golden Sheep; Copper Dragon Golden Pippin; Taylor Golden Best; guest beers Ⓗ
One of the Market Town Taverns chain, this light, airy, modern bar/diner is a conversion of a former Co-operative store. Eight ales are served, generally from Yorkshire and northern micros and independents, with one pump dedicated to dark beers. It also stocks a large selection of continental bottled beers. A diverse range of meals is available until 9pm in a separate dining area. The large upstairs function room has regular events and also serves as a dining room.
Q❀◖▯&≠▯(33,33A,97)♠⏚

Guiseley Factory Workers Club Ⓛ ❷
6 Town Street, LS20 9DT
✪ 1-4 (5 Mon), 7-11; 1-midnight Fri; 11.30-midnight Sat; 11-midnight Sun ☎ (01943) 874793
Tetley Bitter; guest beers Ⓗ

Founded over 100 years ago by the Yeadon and Guiseley Factory Workers Union, this is a friendly club serving three changing guest ales; normally one of these will be a dark beer. There is a small lounge bar, a larger concert room and a snooker room with two tables. In February 2011 the club served its 1000th different real ale. Show your CAMRA membership card or a copy of this Guide for entry. National CAMRA Club of the Year 2009.
❀≠▯(33A,97,737)♣P⏚

Hainworth

Guide Ⓛ
Keighley Road, BD21 5QP (Keighley Rd/Rycroft Rd jct) SE065387
✪ 4-11 (midnight Fri); 12-midnight Sat; 12-11 Sun
☎ (01535) 272138
Beer range varies Ⓗ
Bradford CAMRA's most isolated pub and well worth a visit, not least for a taste of the very local Old Spot ale. This two-roomed pub features a log fire and pictures of motorbikes and landscapes. Everyone is welcome to sample the local award-winning ales and the excellent atmosphere provided by the locals. It's a recent local CAMRA Pub of the Season. There is no bus service on Sunday. ♨Q❀⋀▯(915)♣P⏚

Halifax

Barum Top Ⓛ ❷
17 Rawson Street, HX1 1NX
✪ 9-midnight (1am Fri & Sat) ☎ (01422) 300488
Greene King Ruddles County, Abbot; guest beers Ⓗ
Situated in the heart of the Halifax theatre quarter close to the 19th-century Victoria Theatre, this stone-built Wetherspoon establishment is popular and successful. The pub has a large open-plan layout overlooked by an upper gallery. As with most Wetherspoon's, it has regular seasonal beer festivals, curry club nights and Sunday roasts.
◖▯&▯♠

Big Six
10 Horsfall Street, Saville Park, HX1 3HG (off A646 Skircoat Moor road at King Cross)
✪ 4 (3.30 Fri)-11; 12-11 Sat & Sun ☎ (01422) 350169
Adnams Bitter; guest beers Ⓗ
An unusual pub in the middle of a terrace of houses adjacent to the Free School Lane recreation ground. Dogs are always welcome at this busy and friendly venue. A through corridor separates the bar and games room from the two lounges. Memorabilia from the Big Six mineral water company, which operated from the premises a century ago, adorn the walls. Three changing guest beers are served. There is a beer garden to the rear of the pub.
♨Q❀▯♣

Shears Inn Ⓛ
1 Paris Gates, HX3 9EZ (rear of flats by Shay Stadium, then head for the mill chimney) SE097241
✪ 11.30-midnight ☎ (01422) 352936
🌐 shearsinnparisgates.co.uk
Taylor Golden Best, Best Bitter, Landlord; guest beers Ⓗ
This family-run true free house is located between Shaw Lodge Mills (formerly Moquette) and Hebble Brook. It is now a single room but with two back-to-back fireplaces in the centre. Pictures on display show the valley bottom and local terraced housing.

The two guest beers are from regional and larger micro-breweries. Food, including the home-made pie of the day, is available at all sessions except Sunday evening. There is an unheated smoking shelter. ♨️❀◑🅿️🚪(531)P

Three Pigeons ★ 🅛 ✪
1 Sun Fold, South Parade, HX1 2LX
🕐 4 (12 Fri-Sun)-11.30 ☎ (01422) 347001
Ossett Pale Gold, Big Red, Excelsior; guest beers Ⓗ
Close to the Shay football/Rugby League ground, this welcoming and friendly inn has something rare and special: the best example of Art Deco styling in the country. The centrepiece is the octagonal drinking lobby from which the three rooms and the servery all radiate. Owned by the Ossett Brewery, it serves beers from the group as well as an ale from Fuller's and four guests. There is also a good selection of Belgian bottled beers. ♨️❀🚉🚪🚬🍺

Westgate
28 Westgate, HX1 1DJ
🕐 11-11 (10 Sun) ☎ (01422) 362232
Greene King Old Speckled Hen; Tetley Bitter; Wychwood Hobgoblin Ⓗ
Handy for restaurants, the nearby arcade and the borough market, the Westgate is a true locals' pub in the heart of the town. It is popular with racing and Rugby League enthusiasts as well as shoppers and after-work drinkers. The pub takes its name from the adjacent street leading to the west gate of the historic Piece Hall. The elaborate frontage in Union Street belonged to the former Town Hall Tavern, with which it was merged in 1962. 🚉🚪♣

William IV ✪
247 King Cross Road, HX1 3JL
🕐 11-11; 11.30-10.30 Sun ☎ (01422) 354889
Tetley Bitter Ⓗ
A busy shopping-street pub popular with a wide range of customers, with TV screens catering for sports lovers. There is a standing area, seating opposite the bar, and a raised lounge area that was once a separate shop. The one cask ale sells well, especially as 'smooth' is not sold. Buses from Halifax towards Sowerby Bridge and Hebden Bridge stop outside the door. Benches are provided to the rear of the pub for smokers and drinkers. Lunches are served Monday to Friday. ❀◑🚪♣🍺

Haworth

Fleece Inn 🅛 ✪
67 Main Street, BD22 8DA
🕐 12-11 (11.30 Fri); 10-11.30 Sat; 10-10.30 Sun
☎ (01535) 642172 ⊕ fleece-inn.co.uk
Taylor Dark Mild, Golden Best, Best Bitter, Landlord, Ram Tam Ⓗ
A three-storey former coaching inn situated half-way up the historic steep cobbled Haworth main street. The Haworth Brass Band can be heard from outside on some evenings rehearsing in their band room above the pub. Offering good beer, food and accommodation, the Fleece is popular with locals as well as visitors. The beer garden is three storeys up from the bar. A large range of foreign bottled beers is stocked.
♨️❀🏨◑🅿️🚉🚪(663,664,665)♣

Haworth Old Hall Inn ✪
8 Sun Street, BD22 8BP (bottom of cobbled main street)
🕐 12-11 (10.30 Sun) ☎ (01535) 642709
⊕ hawortholdhall.co.uk

Jennings Bitter, Cumberland Ale, Cocker Hoop, Sneck Lifter; guest beers Ⓗ
On entering this magnificent Yorkshire-stone Tudor manor house through the substantial studded oak door, you find stone floors, arches, mullioned windows, two huge fireplaces and a splendid wood-panelled bar serving the full range of Jennings beers plus guests. Good home-cooked food is served and the pub can get busy at weekends. ♨️❀🏨◑🚻🔥🚉🚪(663,664,665)P🍺

Hebden Bridge

Moyles 🅛
4-10 New Road, HX7 8AD (on A646 opp canal marina)
🕐 12-midnight ☎ (01422) 845272 ⊕ moyles.com
Pictish Brewers Gold; guest beers Ⓗ
A modern hotel bar tastefully furnished with leather seats and stylish tables. The beer engines are set back behind the wood-faced bar. The current list of beers along with tasting notes is displayed on the bar top. Bar snacks are served Monday to Saturday 12-6pm, and a fixed-price two- or three-course menu is available in the restaurant Monday to Saturday 12-2.30pm, 6-9pm and Sunday 12-8pm.
♨️Q❀🏨◑🔥🚉🚪(590,591,592)🍺

New Delight Inn 🅛 ✪
Jack Bridge, Colden, HX7 7HT SD962282
🕐 12-2.30, 5-11; 12-11 Sat; 12-10 Sun ☎ (01422) 846178
Bridestones Sandstone, Bottleneck Bride; guest beers Ⓗ
Cosy rural pub in the delightful Colden Valley, well placed for the Pennine Way and Calderdale Way footpaths, as well as the Pennine Bridleway. Cyclists and dog walkers are welcome. To one side of the bar is a comfortable lounge, on the other a stone-flagged room favoured by locals and hikers. This hostelry is family-run, as is the nearby Bridestones Brewery. Guest beers come from Moorhouse's, Thwaites and further afield. Camping is available in the grounds. No food Saturday and Sunday evenings. ♨️❀◑🔥⛺🚪(E)P

Stubbing Wharf 🅛
King Street, HX7 6LU (on A646 ½ mile W of Hebden Bridge)
🕐 12-11 (midnight Fri & Sat; 10.30 Sun) ☎ (01422) 844107
⊕ stubbingwharf.com
Black Sheep Best Bitter; Copper Dragon Golden Pippin; Taylor Landlord; guest beers Ⓗ
Sandwiched between canal and river, this popular venue for diners and drinkers has a mix of flagged, floorboarded and carpeted rooms. Hops hang above the bar and in the rooms that open towards the bar. Three guest beers from small breweries are complemented by guest ciders, two on handpump and one or two in boxes behind the bar. Apple days and cider festivals are proving increasingly popular, with family attractions including apple juices and barge trips.
♨️❀◑🔥🚪(590,592)🍺P🍺

Hipperholme

Travellers Inn 🅛 ✪
53 Tanhouse Hill, HX3 8HN
🕐 12-midnight (11 Mon; 11.30 Tue & Wed)
☎ (01422) 202494
Fuller's London Pride; Ossett Pale Gold, Yorkshire Gold, Excelsior; guest beers Ⓗ

Opposite the former railway station, this traditional 18th-century, stone-built local has taken in adjoining cottages to create a series of distinct spaces. The floor is stone-flagged in the lower area, with plain floorboards in the upper part. Children and dogs are welcome until 7pm when quiet. There is a small south-facing roadside seating area. A covered yard with heating is provided for smokers. Guest beers include two from Ossett, Riverhead or Fernandes, and a dark beer. ♨⚜🚃(255,548,549)♣⁓

Holmfirth

Rose & Crown (Nook) 🅛 ✅
7 Victoria Square, HD9 2DN (down alley off Hollowgate)
✪ 11.30 (12 Sun)-midnight ☎ (01484) 682373
⊕ thenookbrewhouse.co.uk
Nook Yorks, Best, Blond, Red, Oat Stout; guest beers Ⓗ
Right in the centre of Last of the Summer Wine tourist country, the Rose & Crown is a favourite of locals and visitors alike. The pub dates from 1754, and has appeared more than 30 times in the Guide. Known as the Nook, it not only serves home-cooked food all day, but has been serving beers from its own Nook brewery since 2009. Well known for its great live music, there is a popular folk club every Sunday evening. ♨⚜🕪♿🚃(308,312,313)♣●⁓

Horbury

Boons 🅛 ✅
6 Queen Street, WF4 6LP (off High Street)
✪ 11-3, 5-11; 11-11 Fri & Sat; 12-10.30 Sun
☎ (01924) 277267
Clark's Classic Blonde; John Smith's Bitter; Taylor Landlord; guest beers Ⓗ
Centrally situated just off the High Street, this Clark's brewery tied house caters for all age groups and is a real community pub. Four rotating guest beers are always available alongside beers from the Clark's range. At the back of the pub is a large outdoor drinking area that is used for the annual summer beer festival. ♨⚜🚃(126,127,231)♣

Cricketers Arms 🅛
22 Cluntergate, WF4 5AG (on E edge of shopping centre)
✪ 12-11; 11-midnight Fri & Sat ☎ 07788 506797
Black Sheep Best Bitter; Taylor Dark Mild, Landlord; guest beers Ⓗ
Located on the edge of the town centre, this former Tetley's house has now re-opened as a genuine free house. The pub has had a tasteful refurbishment that has extended the length of the bar. There is a bus stop close by with a frequent service to Wakefield and Dewsbury. ♨Q♿⚜🚃(126,127)♣●P⁓

Huddersfield

Cherry Tree ✅
16-18 John William Street, HD1 1BA
✪ 9am-midnight (1am Fri & Sat) ☎ (01484) 448190
⊕ undertheviaduct.com
Greene King Ruddles Best Bitter, Abbot; guest beers Ⓗ
What this town-centre pub lacks in aesthetic appeal, it more than makes up for in good beer. It has one large room on the ground floor, with a

raised family dining area at the rear and a small downstairs seating space. There are eight guest beers, tending towards the dark, with usually at least one LocAle and a real cider. Management and staff are happy to advise before you buy. Q🕪♿🚃🍴

Grove 🅛
2 Spring Grove Street, HD1 4BP
✪ 12-11 (midnight Thu-Sat) ☎ (01484) 430113
⊕ groveinn.co.uk
Taylor Golden Best, Landlord; Thornbridge Jaipur IPA; guest beers Ⓗ
The Grove has a huge choice of beer – three permanent ales, seven pumps dedicated to rotating beers from Thornbridge, Fuller's, Gadds', Dark Star, Marble, Durham and BrewDog breweries, and a further eight guest ales, many rare for the region. Mild, stout and strong ale are all available. These are complemented by 250-plus bottled beers and foreign draughts. Enjoy your beers in airy, traditional surroundings and decide which are more bizarre – the bar snacks, the artwork or the keg fonts. Q⚜🚃🍴⁓🕪

King's Head
St George's Square, HD1 1JF (in station buildings, on left when exiting station)
✪ 11.30-11; 12-10.30 Sun ☎ (01484) 511058
⊕ the-kings-head-huddersfield.co.uk
Bradfield Farmers Blonde; Taylor Landlord; guest beers Ⓗ
A regular Guide entry, this pub's quirky and distinctive character gives it an unmistakable individuality. Sound management and loyal staff ensure that the 10 beers available are all top quality at competitive prices. There are always two dark ales, and real cider is available. A mosaic-tiled floor dominates the main room, which hosts live bands on Sunday afternoons, piano singalongs on Tuesday evenings and monthly folk and blues sessions. It can get busy at weekends, but is well worth discovering. ♨♿🚃●⁓

Marsh Liberal Club
31 New Hey Road, Marsh, HD3 4AL (on A640, 1½ miles from town centre)
✪ 12-2 (Mon, Thu & Fri), 7-11; 12-11 Sat & Sun
☎ (01484) 420152 ⊕ marshlib.co.uk
Taylor Golden Best, Best Bitter, Landlord; guest beers Ⓗ
Housed in a striking Grade II-listed building, this friendly club celebrated its 150th anniversary during 2008. The main bar area has been recently reorganised and refurbished. Two guest beers are normally available, usually from independent micros. Snooker, pool, darts, dominoes and crown green bowls are all played here, and there are regular social events. The building has wheelchair access and a disabled WC. Show this Guide or a CAMRA membership card to be signed in. ⚜♿🚃(370,371,372)♣P

Rat & Ratchet 🍷 🅛 ✅
40 Chapel Hill, HD1 3EB (on A616 below ring road)
✪ 3-midnight; 12-12.30am Fri & Sat; 12-11 Sun
☎ (01484) 542400
Ossett Pale Gold, Yorkshire Blonde, Silver King, Excelsior; guest beers Ⓗ
This multi-award-winning pub has been a permanent fixture in the Guide for many years. Among the 13 handpumps, Fuller's, Mallinsons and Pictish always feature. Riverhead and Fernandes

are also often available, and the guest beers always include a mild and stout/porter. The pub was runner-up Yorkshire CAMRA Cider Pub of the Year 2010, and at least six ciders and two perries are always on offer. Beer festivals are held in May (mild and cider only) and September.
❀⇒🖫♣👜P🕾

Sportsman 🍺 🗟 ✅
1 St John's Road, HD1 5AY
🕚 12-11; 11-midnight Fri & Sat ☎ (07766) 131123
Black Sheep Golden Ale; Taylor Landlord; guest beers 🖬
A 1930s pub, sympathetically restored with a contemporary twist, while retaining notable historic features such as Hammonds Brewery etched windows and a corner vestibule door, which won it a CAMRA English Heritage Conservation Pub Design award. Eight handpumps serve LocAle beers, including a mild and a beer from Mallinsons brewery. Rotating real ciders are also available. The pub has quickly become a firm favourite on the local drinking scene, and on the Real Ale Rail Trail. Food is available all day Monday to Friday, 11-6pm Saturday, and 12-3pm Sunday. Local CAMRA Mild Pub of the Year 2010, and former Pub of the Season. 🏚❀🕽⇒🖫👜🕾

Star Inn
7 Albert Street, Folly Hall, HD1 3PJ (off A616)
🕚 closed Mon; 5 (12 Sat)-11; 12-10.30 Sun
☎ (01484) 545443 🌐 thestarinn.info
Pictish Brewers Gold; Taylor Best Bitter, Landlord; guest beers 🖬
A pub with a warm welcome for locals and visitors alike. There is always a range of changing guest ales, including milds, stouts and porters, which are sourced nationally and locally. With no juke-box, pool table or games machine, there is always a great atmosphere, with lively conversation around the bar and a real fire during winter months. Each year the pub holds three beer festivals in its marquee, which are recognised as being among the best in the country. 🏚Q❀⛆🖫🕾

White Cross Inn
2 Bradley Road, Bradley, HD2 1XD (on A62, 3 miles from town centre)
🕚 11.45-11 (midnight Sat); 12-10.30 Sun ☎ (01484) 425728
Copper Dragon Golden Pippin; John Smith's Bitter; guest beers 🖬
At the busy Leeds Road and Bradley Road crossroads, the White Cross is a cheerful pub serving a wide range of the community. The pub dates from 1806 and has a large lounge extending across both sides of the central bar, where the two regular beers are supplemented by four varied guests. Home-cooked food is served each lunchtime. The games area offers pool, darts and dominoes. A popular beer festival is held in February in the upstairs meeting room.
❀🕽⛆🖫(202,203,229)♣P🕾

Idle

Brewery Tap 🗟
51 Albion Road, BD10 9QE
🕚 3-11 (midnight Thu-Sat); 2-11 Sun ☎ (07515) 469441
Copper Dragon Golden Pippin; Harviestoun Bitter & Twisted; Tetley Bitter; Theakston Old Peculier; Wells Bombardier; guest beers 🖬
Single-roomed pub with an island bar, behind which is the cellar trap door and its vertiginous

steps. This pub was part of the Trough Brewery estate until its demise. Locally famous for its regular live rock bands, it attracts talent and customers from afar. The garden area is well sheltered. Look around you for pithy mottoes as well as evidence of the Trough era, and ask about the ashes in the niche.
🏚❀⛆🖫(640,641,760)♣P🕾

Symposium Ale & Wine Bar 🗟 ✅
7 Albion Road, BD10 9PY
🕚 12-2.30 (not Mon & Tue), 5.30-11; 12-11 Fri-Sun
☎ (01274) 616587
Copper Dragon Golden Pippin; Thwaites Wainwright; guest beers 🖬
A Market Town Taverns pub that always has six real ales available. It is a popular bar/restaurant with a rolling beer festival, predominantly featuring northern breweries. Beers from many parts of the world are on sale in draught and bottle, and the wine list is impressive. Excellent meals are available from an inventive menu. The rear snug leads to an elevated terrace, popular in summer. A warm and quiet pub in an old suburban village, remarkably easy to find. Q❀🕽🕽🖫(610,611,612)🕾

Ilkley

Bar T'at 🗟 ✅
7 Cunliffe Road, LS29 9DZ
🕚 12-11 ☎ (01943) 608888
Black Sheep Best Bitter; Copper Dragon Golden Pippin; Ilkley Mary Jane; Taylor Landlord; guest beers 🖬
Popular side-street pub from the Market Town Taverns group, renowned for the quality of its beer and food. Guest ales usually include a mild, stout or porter, plus brews from Yorkshire micros. A wide range of good foreign beers is available in bottles and on draught. Bottled gluten-free beer is also available. Home-cooked food is on the menu every day. This three-storey building has a music-free bar area. It stands next to the main town centre car park. Q❀🕽🕽⇒🖫👜🕾

Riverside Hotel
Riverside Gardens, Bridge Lane, LS29 9EU
🕚 10-midnight (11.30 Sun) ☎ (01943) 607338
🌐 ilkley-riversidehotel.com
Copper Dragon Best Bitter; Ilkley Mary Jane; Taylor Landlord; Tetley Bitter 🖬
Family-run hotel with 12 en-suite rooms, set by the River Wharfe in a popular park. The adjacent fish and chip shop and ice cream servery, The Cabin, are also run by the hotel. Meals are served 12-8pm every day. The open fire is a welcome sight in cold weather. Disabled access is available on request. The start of the Dalesway is at the old Pack Horse Bridge close to the hotel. 🏚❀🛏🕽🕽⇒🖫P🕾

Keighley

Boltmakers Arms 🗟 ✅
117 East Parade, BD21 5HX
🕚 11-midnight (11 Mon); 12-11 Sun ☎ (01535) 661936
Taylor Dark Mild, Golden Best, Best Bitter, Landlord, Ram Tam; guest beers 🖬
Classic Keighley town-centre pub – the de facto Taylor's brewery tap. It has a tiny split-level layout, but this adds to the character of the place. The licensees take pride in the pub and it is always welcoming. Brewery, whisky and music

memorabilia adorn the walls. The guest beer and handpulled cider are from various sources at the licensee's whim, and there is a fine selection of single malts. Quiz night is every Tuesday and occasional live music plays. ⋈⊛≋⊟♣♠♦'⌐

Brown Cow L ✅

5 Cross Leeds Street, BD21 2LQ (bottom of West Lane, corner of Oakworth Rd)
🕓 4-11; 12-10.30 Sun ⊕ browncowkeighley.co.uk
Taylor Golden Best, Best Bitter, Landlord, seasonal beers; guest beers ⊞
A popular, comfortably furnished pub featuring local breweriana, including the original sign from Bradford's Trough Brewery. It also has a good collection of police helmets, truncheons, and the like. The licensees are keen local historians. A Timothy Taylor tied house, it offers two regularly changing guest beers sourced mainly from micro-breweries. Bad language is banned. ⋈⊛⊟♣P

Cricketers Arms

Coney Lane, BD21 5JE
🕓 11.30-11 (midnight Fri & Sat); 12-11 Sun
☎ (01535) 669912 ⊕ cricketersarmskeighley.co.uk
Yates Bitter; guest beers ⊞
Back-street pub revitalised by frequent live music sessions, with bands from near and far. The ground-level bar is now complemented by a downstairs bar (open Fri and Sat eves). An interesting montage of photographs taken of regulars is at the top of the stairwell. The pub serves four guest beers from regional and micro-breweries nationwide, plus a range of foreign bottled beers, and hosts occasional beer festivals. The downstairs bar has real cider. ⊛≋⊟'⌐

Kirkheaton

Yeaton Cask L

4 Town Road, HD5 0HW (at crossroads in centre of village)
🕓 4-9 Mon; 4-11 Tue; 12-11 Wed & Thu; 12-11.30 Fri & Sat; 12-10.30 Sun ☎ (07796) 641003 ⊕ yeatoncask.co.uk
Hawkshead Red; Taylor Landlord; guest beers ⊞
Well-loved community local that reopened in 2010 after a full renovation, where modern sits happily alongside traditional. This genuine free house is now a comfortable real ale oasis, having sold 300-plus guests in nine months. Featuring seven handpumps, a real cider and 10 continental and bottle-conditioned beers, the pub is a former local CAMRA Pub of the Season. The Yeaton Cask house beer is brewed by changing local micro-breweries. Home-cooked food is served lunchtimes Wednesday to Saturday. Live music features occasionally. ⋈⊛◖⊟(262)♦P'⌐

Ledsham

Chequers Inn

Claypit Lane, LS25 5LP (near A1M jct 42)
🕓 11-11; closed Sun ☎ (01977) 683135
⊕ thechequersinn.f9.co.uk
Brown Cow Ledsham Sessions, seasonal beers; John Smith's Bitter; Taylor Landlord; Theakston Best Bitter ⊞
A cosy old English pub with a well-regarded restaurant and attractive garden in the picturesque village of Ledsham, across the road from All Saints, possibly Yorkshire's oldest church. It has two main rooms each side of the bar, plus two smaller rooms

complete with oak beams, wood fires, jugs, brasses, sporting memorabilia, old photographs and beer mats from previous guest beers. An extensive range of meals and sandwiches is served 12-9.15pm – outside in the summer. ⋈⊛◖⊟(175)P'⌐

Leeds: Burley

Fox & Newt L

9 Burley Street, LS3 1DS
🕓 12-11 (1am Fri; midnight Sat) ☎ (0113) 245 4527
Burley Street Laguna Sec, Monza; guest beers ⊞
Just outside the city centre, this brew-pub changed hands recently and is now the home of Burley Street Brewery. The single room is wood-floored with a raised section at one end. The centrally placed bar has eight handpumps, three dispensing the house regular and seasonal beers. Guest beers on the other pumps come mainly from the many excellent local micro-breweries. Friday usually features live music and Wednesday hosts an open mike session. ⊛◖♿⊟(49,50,50A)

Leeds: Chapel Allerton

Further North

194 Harrogate Road, LS7 4NZ (on main road 300m N of centre)
🕓 5.30-11 (midnight Thu); 5-midnight Fri; 1-midnight Sat; 1-11 Sun ☎ (0113) 237 0962 ⊕ furthernorth.co.uk
Beer range varies ⊞
A mass of pictures and 32 lights, each with a different lampshade, give an unusual look to this bare-boarded, single-room bar measuring just 21 by 14 feet. It offers a changing beer range, usually from Rooster's, Salamander, Elland, Marble and Riverhead. Draught Lindeboom, Bacchus, Framboise and foreign bottled beers are served by knowledgeable staff happy to guide and assist those unfamiliar with them. Snacks of bread and cheese are available all day. ♿⊟♣

Regent L ✅

15-17 Regent Street, off Harrogate Road, LS7 4PE
🕓 11-11 (midnight Fri & Sat); 12-10.30 Sun
☎ (0113) 262 0524
Caledonian Deuchars IPA; Leeds Pale; Taylor Landlord; Tetley Mild, Bitter; guest beers ⊞
Two-roomed stone-built local, with a warm welcome and a beer range that has increased from three to seven, including a mild by popular demand, under a landlord determined to showcase the best between micros and regionals. Guest beers from near and far vary between micros and regionals. Food is served until 9pm Monday to Thursday and until 6pm at weekends. One bar has a 3-D TV showing all sports channels, with viewing glasses provided. ⊛◖⊟♣P'⌐

Leeds: City Centre

Hop L ✅

The Dark Arches, Granary Wharfe, Neville Street, LS1 4BR
🕓 12-midnight ☎ (0113) 243 9854 ⊕ the-hop.co.uk
Ossett Pale Gold, Yorkshire Blonde, Big Red, Silver King, Excelsior; guest beer ⊞
Opened in 2010, this is Ossett Brewery's first venture into the Leeds area, gaining instant recognition by being voted local CAMRA Pub of the Season in summer 2010. In the arches directly

under platform 17 of Leeds railway station, the arrival and departure of train services is clearly distinguishable. Live music features on Friday and Saturday nights on the open gallery stage on the first floor. There is disabled access to the ground floor only. A dress code applies when Leeds United are at home. ✿≉⬤🌣

Mr Foley's Cask Ale House 🅛

159 The Headrow, LS1 5RG

✪ 11-11 (1am Fri & Sat) ☎ (0113) 242 9674

Beer range varies 🅗

A grand street-corner pub, usually dispensing four beers from York Brewery, plus six guests, often including strong and dark beers. The pub divides itself into four areas, with few seats being out of sight of sport TV. So whether you want to stand up and sup by the bar, relax in one of the two comfortable lounges, or lord it over everyone from the minstrels' gallery, you are sure to find somewhere to suit you. ◖🌣⬤≉🖼

North 🅛

24 New Briggate, LS1 6NU

✪ 12-2am (1am Mon & Tue; midnight Sun)

☎ (0113) 242 4540 ⬤ northbar.com

Outlaw Wild Mule; guest beers 🅗

The first in a mini chain of bars, North is a well-established fixture on the Leeds drinking scene. With ever-changing art on the walls and beer on the pumps, quality bar snacks and knowledgeable bar staff, North manages to be interestingly innovative and reassuringly traditional at the same time. The long bar dispenses global beers, always a dark real ale, occasional real cider, and hosts at least three festivals a year. ◖≉🖼⬤

Palace 🅛

Kirkgate, LS2 7DJ

✪ 10-11.30 (midnight Fri & Sat; 11 Sun) ☎ (0113) 244 5882

Fuller's London Pride; Rooster's Special; Taylor Landlord; Tetley Bitter; guest beers 🅗

White-painted pub just on the edge of the city centre. The one large drinking area wraps around the long bar; it is not difficult to see where three of the four former rooms used to be. There are two outdoor drinking areas; the rear one, bedecked with fairy lights, is popular all year round. The Palace has for many years been a supporter of local brewed real ales as well as guests from near and far. Sausages are a speciality. ✿◖🌣🖼⬤

Scarbrough Hotel 🅛 ✅

Bishopgate Street, LS1 5DY

✪ 11-midnight; 10-10.30 Sun ☎ (0113) 243 4590

Fuller's London Pride; Tetley Bitter; guest beers 🅗

Busy city-centre pub conveniently close to the main train station. Named after an early owner, Henry Scarbrough, although in his time the venue was known as the King's Arms; the name was changed in the 1890s. At either end of the long bar are comfortable seating areas. Alongside the regular beers a selection of guests is served, mostly from local breweries. Normally both real cider and perry are available. The menu includes an extensive range of pies. ✿◖🌣≉(City)🖼(1)⬤🌣

Templar

2 Templar Street, LS2 7NU

✪ 11-11; 12-10.30 Sun ☎ (0113) 245 9751

Tetley Mild, Bitter; guest beers 🅗

Burmantoft cream and green tiling adorns the exterior, complemented by stained glass windows

with heraldic symbols including the Bowing Courtier, and there is wood panelling throughout. This former Melbourne Brewery hostelry is split into two distinct areas. A red tiled fireplace is the centrepiece of one end, with drinking booths at the other. There are large-screen TVs throughout the pub. Guest beers vary, from local breweries such as Leeds to those further afield. ◖≉🖼⬤

Town Hall Tavern 🅛 ✅

17 Westgate, LS1 2RA

✪ 11.30-11; closed Sun ☎ (0113) 244 0765

⬤ townhalltavernleeds.co.uk

Taylor Golden Best, Best Bitter, Landlord, Ram Tam 🅗

Situated near to the Leeds courts and legal offices, this spacious open-plan pub reveals plenty of wood panelling, giving a fresh and modern feel to the interior. Many framed pictures adorn the walls and snug-like alcoves. The pub sells third-of-a-pint tasters of the Taylor range. Originally a Musgrave & Sager pub, it now caters for a wide range of drinkers, with good value meals, pies and jackets served at lunchtimes 11.30-2pm. ◖🌣≉🖼⬤

Veritas Ale & Wine Bar 🅛 ✅

43 Great George Street, LS1 3BB

✪ 11-11; 12-10.30 Sun ☎ (0113) 242 8094

Ilkley Mary Jane; Thwaites Wainwright; guest beers 🅗

A new addition to Market Town Taverns, this bar has one large L-shaped wood-floored room divided into four areas. Guest beers concentrate on local micro-breweries and a good range of beer styles is always available. Good food is served all day; a unique feature is the deli bar with cold meats and an extensive selection of local artisan cheeses. As its name suggests, a good range of wines is present, along with draught and bottled foreign beers. Q◖🌣≉🖼

Victoria Family & Commercial ✅

28 Great George Street, LS1 3DL (behind town hall)

✪ 11-11 (midnight Fri); 10-midnight Sat; 12-8 Sun

☎ (0113) 245 1386

Acorn Barnsley Bitter; Leeds Best; Tetley Bitter; guest beers 🅗

Situated behind the town hall, the pub retains the original Victorian frontage and signs, although the hotel function has now ceased. The interior displays Victorian grandeur but is, however, mostly quality reproduction. The central hallway leads to a main long bar on the right. Two smaller lounges to the left and centre can be hired for meeting rooms. Six guest beers are usually available and food, specialising in sausages, is served up to 10pm. Live modern jazz features every Thursday night. ◖≉🖼

Whitelocks First City Luncheon Bar ★ 🅛 ✅

Turks Head Yard, off Briggate, LS1 6HB (near Marks & Spencer)

✪ 11-11 (midnight Fri & Sat); 12-6 Sun ☎ (0113) 245 3950

Leeds Whitelocks Ale, Midnight Bell; Theakston Best Bitter, Old Peculier; guest beers 🅗

A long, narrow classic Leeds yard pub said to be 'the very heart of Leeds' by Sir John Betjeman. The pub goes back to 1715, with the present delightfully atmospheric Victorian interior dating from 1895. The fine ceramic bar counter and brewery mirrors are of particular note. Six changing guest beers are offered. There is a restaurant (open 12-8pm) famous for its hearty fare, plus bar snacks. The newer bar, Ma Gamps, further up the yard, is open at weekends. ▲Q✿◖≉🖼

Greene King Ruddles Best Bitter, Abbot; guest beers Ⓗ
The typical conversion by Wetherspoon from a previous use – formerly a Co-op department store, this example opened originally as a Lloyds No.1, but was converted to the standard format nearly two years ago. Real ale usually centres on local breweries, with Greene King products also on the bar. Regular Meet the Brewer nights are held.
Q◑♿⇌🚌🍎

Silsden

King's Arms 🏆 Ⓛ ✔
9 Bolton Road, BD20 0JY
⏲ 12-midnight ☎ (01535) 653216
Saltaire Blonde; Theakston Best Bitter; guest beers Ⓗ
There is always something going on at the King's of an evening: Tuesday is folk night, Thursday open mike, Wednesday quiz, with themed food nights and more wedged in when there is the time. The licensees' efforts have made it a deserved winner of local CAMRA Branch Pub of the Year 2011. Guest beers are from the Punch Finest Cask list, and Westons cider and perry are regularly sold. The bus between Keighley and Addingham stops outside. Dogs and well-behaved children are permitted.
🔥❀◑🚌(70,712,762)♣🍎P🚭

Slaithwaite

Commercial Ⓛ
1 Carr Lane, HD7 5AN (village centre, off A62)
⏲ 12-midnight (1am Fri & Sat) ☎ (01484) 846258
🌐 commercial-slaithwaite.co.uk
Empire Moonraker Mild, Commerciale; guest beers Ⓗ
Since re-opening in 2009, this family-run free house has enjoyed enviable success. Nine handpumps provide ample variety, and the house beer from nearby Empire Brewery is keenly priced. A rotating real cider is available, often from Westons. Very community-focused, it nonetheless has a varied clientele including locals, enthusiasts tackling the Transpennine Rail Ale Trail and ramblers and their dogs – the pub is dog-friendly. Light snacks and beverages are served Friday-Sunday. An upstairs function room is available free of charge. Q❀⇌🚌♣🍎🚭

South Elmsall

Barnsley Oak ✔
Mill Lane, WF9 2DT (on B6474, off A638 Wakefield-Doncaster road)
⏲ 11.30-11.30 ☎ (01977) 643427
John Smith's Bitter; guest beer Ⓗ
This former mining area is fortunate to be served by this fine community pub. It has built up a loyal following for cask ale and often features a guest ale brewed in Yorkshire. Excellent value food is served all day until 7.45pm (4.30pm Sun), and there are occasional themed food evenings. Children are welcome and meals can also be taken in the conservatory, which affords panoramic views. Quiz nights are Tuesday and Sunday.
❀◑⇌(South Elmsall/Moorthorpe)🚌(46,496)P🚭

Southowram

Shoulder of Mutton Ⓛ
14 Cain Lane, HX3 9SB
⏲ 12-midnight (11 Sun) ☎ (07707) 358697
Saltaire Blonde; guest beers Ⓗ
Busy village local whose awards include Best Community Pub in Yorkshire and the north-east, and a Pubs in Bloom award for its floral display enhancing the roadside frontage. The building is thought to be more than 300 years old. The interior has an L-shaped lounge and a busy pool room. Blonde and gold beers are favourites for the two guest beers. Quiz night is Thursday.
🚌(571,572)♣🚭

Sowerby Bridge

Firehouse Ⓛ
1 Town Hall Street, HX6 2QD
⏲ 4 (12 Fri-Sun)-11.30 ☎ (01422) 832586
🌐 firehouserestaurant.co.uk
Taylor Golden Best, Landlord; guest beers Ⓗ
Close to the bridge crossing the River Calder in the centre of Sowerby Bridge, this prominent building, dating from 1874, has been stylishly converted from offices, and is a popular venue for those who like to eat out with the option of a traditional pint. It is a family-run outlet that has built a popular reputation for food and real ale, in particular the open pizza oven that produces authentic Italian pizzas. There is always a guest beer from a local or regional brewer. ◑♿⇌🚌🚭

Jubilee Refreshment Rooms Ⓛ
Station Road, HX6 3AB (at railway station)
⏲ 12-10 ☎ (01422) 648285
🌐 jubileerefreshmentrooms.co.uk
Beer range varies Ⓗ
Historic refreshment room in a railway building adjacent to the westbound platform. Fairly basic inside, it has an increasing display of posters and memorabilia. The three to six beers are from small breweries. Breakfasts are available Monday to Saturday before opening time, and snacks lunchtimes and early evenings. A winner of several awards including Pub of the Season from the local CAMRA branch and West Riding SPBW branches, plus Olive Restaurant Award 2010 (BBC Good Food Magazine) and Railway Heritage Trust Conservation Award 2010. 🔥Q♿⇌P

White Horse Ⓛ
Burnley Road, Friendly, HX6 2UG
⏲ 12-11 (10.30 Sun) ☎ (01422) 831173
Tetley Bitter; guest beer Ⓗ
White-painted pub set back from the busy A646 Burnley Road, on the main bus route from Halifax to Todmorden and next to a bus stop. The welcoming local has a tap room and a large lounge partitioned in two. A strong community following includes members of the Friendly Brass Band and dominoes club. There is a smoking area to the rear and an outside seating area to the front.
❀♿🚌(590,591,592)♣P🚭

Works Ⓛ
12 Hollins Mill Lane, HX6 2QG (opp swimming pool)
⏲ 12-11 (10.30 Sun) ☎ (01422) 834821
🌐 theworkssowerbybridge.co.uk
Taylor Golden Best, Best Bitter, Landlord; guest beers Ⓗ
Converted from a former joinery, the pub won Best Conversion to Pub Use in 2007. This large open-plan local features exposed beams and floorboards, and is beside the Rochdale Canal on the western side of the town centre. Nine real ales are served including three from Timothy Taylor and six

rotating guests. Food, made 'with love', is served both lunchtimes and teatime. Entertainment most evenings features jazz, folk or comedy.
ﯗﯗﯗﯗ

Stanbury

Old Silent Inn L

Hob Lane, BD22 0HW SE002371
12-11 (midnight Sat; 10.30 Sun) ☎ (01535) 647437
⊕ old-silent-inn.co.uk
Taylor Landlord; Theakston Old Peculier; guest beers H
A 400-year-old roadside inn at the west edge of the village, only five minutes' walk from the bus stop. With oak beams, flagged floors and open fires, it is a building with considerable charm. The emphasis is on food, winning Morning Advertiser 2010 Food Pub of the Year, among others. Walkers will find it close to the Pennine Way, Bronte Way and Millennium Way. Drinkers are also welcome. Rotating guest beers are usually from local breweries. ﯗﯗﯗﯗ(664)P

Undercliffe

Milners Arms L

126 Undercliffe Road, BD2 3BN (300m from Eccleshill library)
4-11 (11.30 Fri); 12-11.30 Sat; 12-11 Sun
☎ (01274) 639398
Beer range varies H
Friendly two-roomed traditional community pub a short bus ride from Bradford city centre. The small bar serves a tap room and lounge. Wednesday quiz night is popular, with a regular, loyal clientele. Three handpumps offer a varied range of beers from both national and local breweries, with up to seven different ales served each week. There is a pleasant beer garden at the side of the pub and ample on-street parking. Bradford CAMRA Pub of the Season Autumn 2010. ﯗﯗﯗﯗ(670)♣♣

Wainstalls

Cat i' th' Well L

Wainstalls Lane, Lower Saltonstall, HX2 7TR SE041284
11.30-3, 5-11; 11.30-11 Fri & Sat; 12-10.30 Sun
☎ (01422) 244841
Taylor Golden Best, Best Bitter, Landlord; guest beers H
Set in a steep valley on the edge of moorland, this old and little-changed pub has a cosy atmosphere enhanced by panelling rescued from a nearby castle on its demolition. The bar lounge area has an open fire, the side lounge displays local pictures. The pub and its split-level beer garden face down the attractive Luddenden Valley. One or two guest beers are usually from nearby small breweries. No lunchtime meals Monday and Tuesday.
ﯗﯗﯗﯗ

Wakefield

Black Rock ✓

19 Cross Square, WF1 1PQ (at top of Westgate, near Bull Ring)
11-11 (midnight Sat); 12-10.30 Sun ☎ (01924) 375550
Tetley Bitter; guest beers H
An arched, tiled facade leads into this compact city-centre local, where the warm welcome and comfy interior with many photographs of old Wakefield

add to the proper pub feel. The Rock has been a bastion of comfort for the ale drinkers of Wakefield, and now offers three guest beers. Drinkers are encouraged to suggest beers they would like to try. It is an enclave from the surrounding bars and discos of the youth zone. A three-minute walk from the bus station. ﯗ(Westgate/Kirkgate)ﯗ

Bull & Fairhouse L

60 George Street, WF1 1DL (left out of Westgate station, right at the lights, left at the bottom of the hill and the pub is 200m on the left)
5-11; 12-midnight Fri & Sat; 12-11 Sun ☎ (01924) 362930
Bob's Brewing Co White Lion; Great Heck Golden Bull, seasonal beer; guest beers H
Recently taken over by the Great Heck Brewery, the pub has reverted to the original name, which reflects the fact that the local cattle market was just across the road. There are plans to relocate the toilets to the rear room and to create a lounge area in the space. Comfortable sofas, secluded corners and a real fire complement the warm welcome. A popular bingo quiz is held on Thursday and there is live music at the weekend.
ﯗﯗﯗ(Westgate/Kirkgate)ﯗ(443,444)

Fernandes Brewery Tap & Bier Keller L ✓

5 Avison Yard, Kirkgate, WF1 1UA (turn right 100m S of George St/Kirkgate jct)
Pub: 4-11 (11.30 Thu); 12-late Fri & Sat; 12-11 Sun; Bier keller: 4-midnight Fri & Sat; 12-10.30 Sun ☎ (01924) 386348
Beer range varies H
This outlet is owned by Ossett Brewery and the beer range includes Ossett, Fernandes and Fuller's beers. The pub has 10 handpulls, one dedicated to a mild, stout or porter. The Bier Keller has 12 premier foreign beers on draught plus Ossett Silver King and a cider on handpump. There is live music on Sunday afternoon, with free stew on Sunday evening. Pie and peas are served on Tuesday evening, for which there is a small charge. Pets are welcome. Qﯗ(Westgate/Kirkgate)ﯗ

Harry's Bar L

107B Westgate, WF1 1EL (out of Westgate Station, turn left and cross the road, then take 2nd alley on right)
5 (4 Sat)-1am; 12-midnight Sun ☎ (01924) 373773
Leeds Pale; Ossett Silver King; guest beer H
Winner of local CAMRA Pub of the Year for 2007, this small, one-roomed pub has an exposed brick and wood interior complemented by a sun deck and a shady yard. Hidden away down an alley off Westgate, it is secluded from the fizz and music youth zone of the city centre. Harry's is a thriving community local with many new friends to meet. Live music features on Wednesday. There is a Pay & Display car park adjacent.
ﯗﯗﯗ(Westgate/Kirkgate)ﯗ

Hop L ✓

19 Bank Street, WF1 1EH (left off Westgate down Bank Street, opp opera house)
4-midnight; 3-2am Fri; 12-2am Sat; 4-11 Sun
☎ (01924) 367111
Fuller's London Pride; Ossett Pale Gold, Silver King, Excelsior; guest beers H
This converted Victorian building has been transformed into a multi-faceted venue for drinking, socialising, music appreciation and conversation. It retains the bare brick walls, fireplaces and other original features. The draught beers are complemented by an extensive wine list

GLAMORGAN

MID

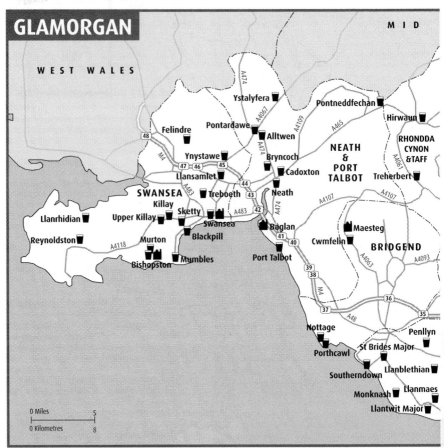

WEST WALES

Authority areas covered: Bridgend UA, Caerphilly UA, Cardiff UA, Merthyr Tydfil UA, Neath & Port Talbot UA, Rhondda, Cynon & Taff UA, Swansea UA, Vale of Glamorgan UA

Aberdare

Red Cow ♈ Ⓛ
6 Merthyr Road, Llwydcoed, CF44 0YE (on B4276)
☼ 6 (12 Wed-Sun)-11 ☎ (01685) 873924
⊕ theredcowpub.co.uk
Beer range varies Ⓗ
Excellent, friendly pub with superb well-prepared and reasonably priced food. The landlord is enthusiastic about his beer, with a range that varies on a weekly basis – see the website for this week's ales. The family-friendly house hosts sporting days and is a sponsor of local children's sport. In summer the conservatory opens out onto the enclosed garden, overlooking a conservation area. Two first-rate beer festivals are held each year with live music. ⋈☀◑ঐ☐(6)♥P≒

Aberthin

Hare & Hounds
Aberthin Road, CF71 7LG (on A4222)
☼ 12 (4 Mon)-midnight ☎ (01446) 774892
Marston's EPA Ⓖ, **Pedigree; guest beer** Ⓗ
A stone-built pub on the main road through the village. The comfortable and welcoming inn has a pleasant bar with a real fire, wooden settles and a collection of historic photographs and prints.

Outside is seating to the front and a large garden for warmer weather. There is live music on Saturday and a thriving darts team. The guest beer comes from the Marston's group of breweries. ⋈Q☀◑ঐ☐(E11)♣≒

Alltwen

Butchers at Alltwen
Alltwen Hill, SA8 3BP (off A474)
☼ 12-4, 6-11; 12-midnight Fri & Sat; 12-11 Sun
☎ (01792) 863100 ⊕ thebutchersarmsalltwen.co.uk
Beer range varies Ⓗ
This recently refurbished public house retains an easy atmosphere for a quiet drink, although the main focus is on serving quality food in the bar and restaurant. Two guest ales are available – check the blackboard on the bar for the next beers to be tapped. Live music features twice a month on Sunday afternoon. The outdoor drinking area has a panoramic view of the Swansea Valley. ⋈☀◑ঐ☐(122,222)P≒

Barry

Barry West End Club Ⓛ
54 St Nicholas Road, CF62 6QY
☼ 2 (11.30 Sat)-11.30; 12-10.30 Sun ☎ (01446) 735739

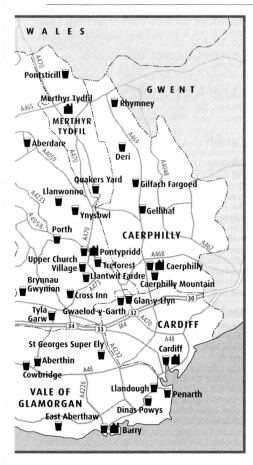

Greene King Ruddles Best Bitter, Abbot; guest beers Ⓗ

This spacious Wetherspoon pub is named after Sir Samuel Romilly, a landowner and legal reformer in the 1800s. It opened in 2009 in a building that was previously a market hall, theatre and bank. The bank vault remains and is used as a seating area. A large mural above the side entrance depicts life in old Barry, with many more pictures of the town inside. A typical range of guest ales includes regular appearances from Bullmastiff and Vale of Glamorgan breweries. Q❀🕐▷&≭🚐💷🍴⌐

Bishopston

Joiners Arms
50 Bishopston Road, SA3 3EJ
☼ 11.30 (2 Mon)-11; 12-10.30 Sun ☎ (01792) 232658
Courage Best Bitter; Marston's Pedigree; Swansea Bishopswood, Three Cliffs Gold, Original Wood; guest beers Ⓗ

Situated in the heart of the village, this 1860s pub is popular with locals and busy in both bars. Home of the Swansea Brewing Company, beer festivals and music events are held occasionally, adding to the excellent ale range. Good value-for-money food is served and social events are organised. The pub has won several local CAMRA awards. There is a small car park – if full, try 100 metres down the hill. ⌂Q❀🕐▷🚐(14,114)P🍴⌐

Blackpill

Woodman ✓
120 Mumbles Road, SA3 5AS (on A4067, near turn off for B4436)
☼ 12-11 (10.30 Sun) ☎ (01792) 402700
Adnams Explorer; Greene King IPA; Wells Bombardier; guest beers Ⓗ

Local scenes of yesteryear decorate the various rooms and nooks of this spacious, recently refurbished establishment situated between the seafront and the entrance to Clyne Gardens. Popular with both families and diners, the pub is also welcoming to those wishing to forego the ubiquitous electronic sounds and screens. A constantly changing range of guest ales is offered. There are three outside seating areas including a small beer garden. Meals are served until 10pm (9.30pm Sun). ⌂Q❀🕐▷&P🍴⌐

Bryncoch

Dyffryn Arms
Neath Road, SA10 7YF (on A474)
☼ 12-midnight ☎ (01639) 636184

Brains Dark, Bitter; guest beers Ⓗ

Set on a hill overlooking Barry Old Harbour, this club is housed in a red brick building. Many original features remain, and the walls of the bar are adorned with pump clips from guest beers. Home to traditional pub games and sports, the club has a welcoming atmosphere. An ever-changing range of guest ales and real ciders is offered, and a beer festival is held in September featuring Welsh beers. A regular award winner, the club was local CAMRA Club Of The Year 2011. Q❀🚐&≭🚐♣🍴⌐

Castle Hotel
44 Jewel Street, CF63 3NQ
☼ 12-11.30 (midnight Fri & Sat); 12-11 Sun
☎ (01446) 408916
Brains Bitter, SA; guest beers Ⓗ

This friendly multi-roomed Victorian hotel on the corner of two streets is full of character. The entrance hall and grand stairway still take centre stage in the lounge. A Brains tied house but offering up to three guest beers, this is a welcome beer oasis. A full size snooker table and skittle alley add to the pub games. The pub is well supported by local groups and societies and the bar has a large screen TV. Food is available Sunday lunchtime only. Q❀🕐🚐≭(Docks)🚐♣

Sir Samuel Romilly ✓
Romilly Buildings, Broad Street, CF62 7AU
☼ 7-midnight (1am Fri & Sat) ☎ (01446) 724900

WALES

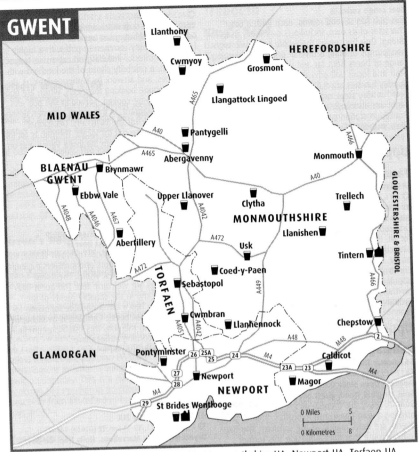

GWENT

Authority areas covered: Blaenau Gwent UA, Monmouthshire UA, Newport UA, Torfaen UA

Abergavenny

Angel Hotel
15 Cross Street, NP7 5EW
🕐 10-3, 6-11 (11.30 Fri & Sat); 12-3, 6-10.30 Sun
☎ (01873) 857121 ⊕ angelhotelabergavenny.com
Sharp's Doom Bar; Wye Valley HPA; guest beer Ⓗ
Imposing town-centre hotel with a long-established tradition for excellent draught ales. The Foxhunter Bar is wood panelled with a mix of large tables and comfortable leather settees. A separate quiet lounge features interesting artwork and artefacts, and outside the enclosed courtyard has tables for dining and drinking on warmer days. Also renowned for quality food and accommodation, the establishment is popular with locals and travellers alike. ⚲Q❀☕◑⇄🚪P

Grofield Ⓛ
Baker Street, NP7 5BB
🕐 5 (11 Tue & Wed)-11; 5-11.30 Thu-Sat; 11-11 Sun
☎ (01873) 858939
Rhymney Bitter; Sharp's Doom Bar; guest beers Ⓗ
Modern lounge bar with comfortable seating and decor, serving lunchtime meals only. Just off the main thoroughfare, you won't find the rowdy crowd here. Two regular ales and a guest are always top quality, occasionally supplemented by another guest from a micro-brewery. Q❀◑🖳♣⁺ⁱ

King's Head Hotel
60 Cross Street, NP7 5EU
🕐 10.30-11; 12-4, 7-10.30 Sun ☎ (01873) 853575
⊕ kingsheadhotelabergavenny.co.uk
Wells Bombardier; guest beer Ⓗ
Adjacent to the Victorian town hall and market place, the open-plan interior is broadly divided into two sections, each with a fireplace. The pub is a popular haunt of market folk and shoppers during the day, with a large screen for big sporting occasions and live music on Friday night. A function room and good-quality accommodation are to be found upstairs. The affiliated Venue 59 restaurant offers tasty lunches and an a la carte menu. ⚲❀🍴◑⇄🚪♿⁺ⁱ

Station
37 Brecon Road, NP7 5UH
🕐 5 (2 Wed; 1 Thu)-11; 1-11.30 Fri; 12-11.30 Sat; 11.30-11 Sun ☎ (01875) 854759
Draught Bass; Fuller's London Pride; Wye Valley HPA; guest beers Ⓗ

INDEPENDENT BREWERIES

Kingstone Tintern
Warcop Saint Brides Wentlooge

Featuring in CAMRA's Real Heritage Pubs of Wales, this is a classic town pub with a large public bar and much smaller and quieter lounge. Railway memorabilia decorates the interior of this establishment that once served the long-gone Brecon Road station. Pictures of jazz greats also adorn the walls – the landlord is a well-known jazz drummer on the south Wales music circuit. Three guest beers often include choices that are unusual for the area. ⏣🚍(X4,X43)♣P⅃

Abertillery

Pontlottyn ●
Somerset Street, NP13 1DJ
❂ 8am-midnight ☎ (01495) 322930
Greene King Ruddles Best Bitter, Abbot; guest beers Ⓗ
A recent conversion of a long-disused building, previously a supermarket and before that the much-loved department store that gave the pub its name. An attractive and well-lit interior leads to a sunken terrace, which is protected from prevailing weather conditions. In a near real ale desert, rarely can the arrival of one pub have had such an impact on the local scene, introducing some hitherto rare ales to local drinkers. Changing ciders are also available. ⏥Q❂⏃&🚍(X15,X16)●⅃

Brynmawr

Hobby Horse
30 Greenland Road, NP23 4DT
❂ 12-3, 7-11; 11.30-midnight Sat & Sun ☎ (01495) 310996
⏚ freewebs.com/hobbyhorseinn/home.htm
Beer range varies Ⓗ
With ales sourced from all parts of the country, this recently refurbished back-street local, a few minutes from the town centre, is well worth the search. Always a contender for the Blaenau Gwent in Bloom competition (runner-up in 2010), summer is a good season to witness this pub in all its glory. With a regular Thursday night quiz, darts and sports on TV, this pub is a community meeting place, and is home to clubs and societies including potholers, walkers and charities. ❂⏤⏃⏣🚍(X4,X15)♣P⅃

Caldicot

Castle
64 Church Road, NP26 4HN
❂ 12-11 (midnight Fri & Sat) ☎ (01291) 420509
Beer range varies Ⓗ
Two miniature cannons at the front remind visitors that this attractive pub lies close to Caldicot Castle and Country Park. The pleasant low-beamed interior has a lounge/dining room on one side of the servery, with a cosy bar with a large fireplace as its focal point on the other. Two changing guest ales are sourced from national, regional and family brewers. Food is popular, with plenty of choice from an extensive menu. The garden includes a large play fort for children. ⏥❂⏃⏣🚍(14,74)P⅃

Chepstow

Bell Hanger ●
St Mary's Street, NP16 5EW
❂ 8am-midnight ☎ (01291) 637360
Greene King Ruddles Best Bitter, Abbot; Marston's Pedigree; guest beers Ⓗ

This imaginative and comfortable conversion and extension of two former shops has proved deservedly popular with ale lovers and a broad range of the community, including families and senior citizens, since it opened in 2008. Two beer festivals with varying themes, including Wales, supplement Wetherspoon's national festival. Guest beers invariably include a Butcombe ale and often one or more from Newmans, with the emphasis on distinctive character and variety of style. Chilled bag-in-a-box draught ciders are from Westons. Q❂⏃&⇌🚍●⅃

Chepstow Athletic Club
Mathern Road, Bulwark, NP16 5JJ (off Bulwark Rd)
❂ 7-11 (11.30 Fri & Sat); 12-3.30, 7-11 Sun
☎ (01291) 622126
Brains SA; Flowers IPA; Rhymney Bitter; guest beers Ⓗ
A true community club where CAMRA members are always welcome and everyone gets involved, from sports people to local clubs and societies including the ever-thirsty Chepstow Male Voice Choir. The comfortable main bar is supplemented by a large function room upstairs, where real ale is also available. Guest beers often include a seasonal Cottage brew. Ale quality and value, plus a warm welcome, are enduring features of the 'Athy', where conversation rules the day – at least until the televised rugby begins! ❂⏣🚍(14,74)♣P⅃

Coach & Horses 🏆 Ⓛ
Welsh Street, NP16 5LN
❂ 12-11 (10.30 Sun) ☎ (01291) 622626
⏚ coachandhorsesinn.co.uk
Brains Bitter, SA, The Rev James; guest beers Ⓗ
Family-run pub, popular with locals and visitors, with a single split-level bar providing a range of seating. Brain's beers are complemented by guests – often rare and distinctive light-coloured brews from all around the UK. One beer gives way to a cider in summer. The pub hosts Chepstow's beer and sausage festival in October, plus a major festival in July when up to 50 beers, ciders and perries energise the town's renowned folk and morris-dance celebrations. Local CAMRA Town Pub of the Year 2011. ❂⏃⇌🚍●⅃

Clytha

Clytha Arms 🏆 Ⓛ
NP7 9BW (on B4598 old road between Abergavenny and Raglan) SO366088
❂ 12-3 (not Mon), 6-11; 12-11 Sat; 12-10.30 Sun
☎ (01873) 840206 ⏚ clytha-arms.com
Beer range varies Ⓗ
Multi-award-winning, family-run pub and restaurant with good quality accommodation. Set in large and well maintained grounds, it is an ideal venue for the annual Welsh beer and cheese festival held over the August bank holiday, and the Welsh cider and perry festival in May. A wide variety of changing beers and ciders always includes examples from Welsh independents and often beers unusual for the area, sought by the enthusiastic and knowledgeable licensee. ⏥Q❂⏤⏃⏣🚍(83)♣●⅃

Coed-y-Paen

Carpenters Arms
NP4 0TH SO986334

❂ 12-3 (not Mon), 6-11; 12-11 Sat; 12-10.30 Sun
☎ (01291) 672621 ⊕ thecarpenterscoedypaen.co.uk
Beer range varies Ⓗ
A smart and sympathetic refurbishment has
maintained the feel of this interesting village local.
Convenient for Llandegfedd Reservoir, with
facilities for boating, fishing and wind-surfing,
there are also good walks and golfing in the area.
The large beer garden has camping facilities
adjacent. The food menu emphasises the choice of
local produce, as do the beers where one guest ale
is usually from Wye Valley Brewery. The pub hosts
an open mike night on the last Wednesday of the
month. Q❂➀❿⑱♿ ÅPⁿ⌐

Cwmbran

Queen Inn
Upper Cwmbran Road, Upper Cwmbran, NP44 5AX
❂ 12-midnight (11 Sun) ☎ (01633) 484252
Beer range varies Ⓗ
With a backdrop of Mynydd Maen and to the front a
rushing mountain stream with wildfowl, this is an
attractive location in a former industrial community
on the fringe of town. This old Rhymney Brewery
house with a three-room layout has developed into
a popular drinking and dining venue. The excellent
outdoor play facilities for children add to its family
appeal. Three beers are sourced from breweries
large and small, local or from afar.
❂➀❿⑱(1,8)♣Pⁿ⌐

Cwmyoy

Queen's Head
NP7 7NY SO311221
❂ 11-2.30 Mon & Thu, 6-11; closed Wed; 11-3, 6-11 Sat; 12-3,
7-10.30 Sun ☎ (01873) 890241
Beer range varies Ⓗ
Known locally as Billy's, after the landlord who has
been here for 35 years, the stone-built pub's single
room is heated by a large log burner on cold days,
and has a low ceiling and a flagged and tiled floor.
Situated at the start of the beautiful Llanthony
Valley in the Brecon Beacons National Park, the
grounds slope down to the River Honddu. Hillside
views on all sides attract walkers and trekkers.
Food is available at lunchtimes only. ⋒Q➀P

Ebbw Vale

King's Arms Ⓛ
Newchurch Road, NP23 5BD
❂ 7 (5 Sat)-12.30am; 12-10.30 Sun ☎ (01495) 352822
Brains The Rev James; guest beer Ⓗ
Large modernised pub set high above Ebbw Vale
Rugby Club, so close to the ground you can pop out
at half time for a quick drink (it opens 1pm on
match Saturdays). The rugby connection leads to a
sporting emphasis in the public bar but the larger
lounge offers more tranquil surroundings. Very
much a family-run pub, there are plans to further
improve the facilities. A function room is available.
Check for a date for the summer beer and cider
festival. Q❂➀❿⑱(X4,22)♣Pⁿ⌐

Grosmont

Angel Inn
NP7 8EP
❂ 12-2.30 (not Mon), 6-11; 12-11 Sat; 12-3, 7-11 Sun
☎ (01981) 240646 ⊕ grosmont.org/group/the-angel-inn

Beer range varies Ⓗ
The Angel is strong on music, with live music often
playing until the early hours on Saturday night. The
pub is owned by a consortium of local residents,
which goes some way to explaining its community
spirit. It offers a range of three beers, usually
including one from the Wye Valley Brewery in
Herefordshire. There are cider and beer festivals in
the summer as a bonus. Situated just a hundred
yards away from Grosmont Castle, it is on the Three
Castles Walk. ❂➀❿⑱♣P

Llangattock Lingoed

Hunters Moon Inn
NP7 8RR SO363201
❂ 12-3 (not Mon-Fri March-October), 7-midnight; 12-2.30,
7-midnight Sun ☎ (01873) 821499
⊕ hunters-moon-inn.co.uk
Wye Valley HPA; guest beer Ⓗ
Attractive 13th-century country inn set in a tiny
hamlet near Offa's Dyke and alongside the equally
ancient St Cadoc's Church. The old stone-flagged
bar is full of character while the adjoining
restaurant with its thick stone walls forms part of
the original building. Welsh guest beers are regular
visitors poured straight from casks behind the bar.
Outside drinking is tempting with a decked patio
looking towards the church and another area
beside a waterfall and pool. Q❂➀❿⑱♣P

Llanhennock

Wheatsheaf
Caerleon, NP18 1LT SO353927
❂ 11-11; 12-3, 7-10.30 Sun ☎ (01633) 420468
⊕ thewheatsheafllanhennock.co.uk
Fuller's London Pride; guest beers Ⓗ
This 19th-century traditional country pub has fine
views from its enclosed garden area. Inside, to the
left of the entrance is a small snug, to the right a
cosy bar, both full of bric-a-brac and old
photographs. Boules has a strong competitive
following here. One of the two guest ales is usually
from a local brewery. Last year marked the 25th
consecutive year in this Guide under the same
ownership. ⋒❂➀❿⑱♣P

Llanishen

Carpenters Arms
NP16 6QH
❂ closed Mon; 12-3 (not Tue), 5.30 (6 Tue)-11; 12-3, 7-10.30
Sun ☎ (01600) 860812
Wadworth 6X; guest beer Ⓗ
This 400-year-old roadside inn maintains a fine
reputation for high-quality cask ale and good-value
home-cooked food. Two distinct areas of the main
bar, separated by a partition, provide for drinkers,
diners and pool players, while a small side room
seats more diners at busy times. Curries and
seafood are particularly popular. The guest ale is
nearly always from a local Welsh brewery, often
Kingstone. Two self-catering flats provide
accommodation for those wishing to stay awhile to
explore this beautiful corner of Wales.
❂➀❿⑱(65)♣P

Llanthony

Half Moon
NP7 7NN SO286279

❄ 12-3 (not Oct-Apr), 7-11; closed Tue; 11-11 Sat; 12-4, 7-10.30 Sun ☎ (01873) 890611
Bullmastiff Son of a Bitch; guest beers Ⓗ
Remote inn set in idyllic countryside near the ruins of Llanthony Priory on a lane that hugs the valley between high ridges before rising to cross the dramatic Gospel Pass. Local trade is increased substantially by walkers and pony trekkers at weekends and during the summer. A wood burner provides warmth for winter visitors, but note that opening is limited between October and April. Accommodation makes this a good base for a National Park based holiday. ♨Q⊛☕◐⛁P

Magor

Golden Lion Ⓛ
The Square, NP26 3HY
❄ 11-11; 12-10.30 Sun ☎ (01633) 880312
⊕ thegoldenlionmagor.co.uk
Brains The Rev James; St Austell Tribute; Wye Valley Bitter; guest beer Ⓗ
Attractive pub with a covered courtyard leading to the public bar, garden and play area. The lounge is cosy and gives access to a pleasant restaurant. An impressive fireplace at one end provides a focal point, particularly when the fire is lit on cold days. There are lamps with old coaching scenes and an old-fashioned inn sign – a reminder of when the pub temporarily changed its identity for a period costume drama. The menu is extensive and monthly gourmet evenings are popular.
♨⊛◐⛁(14,74)♣⌐

Monmouth

King's Head Hotel ✔
8 Agincourt Square, NP25 3DY
❄ 7am-midnight ☎ (01600) 713417
Greene King Ruddles Best Bitter, Abbot; guest beers Ⓗ
Successful Wetherspoon refurbishment of an old residential hotel, with several rooms and areas in which to enjoy a drink or a meal. Many of the original ornate ceiling decorations and some fireplaces have been retained – note the impressive plaster cast believed to have been salvaged from nearby Monmouth Castle. Plenty of books are on display while large pictures and pictorial histories of famous people and organisations associated with the town are displayed around the walls. Q⊛☕◐⛁♣⌐

Newport

Godfrey Morgan ✔
158 Chepstow Road, Maindee, NP19 8EG
❄ 8am-midnight (1am Fri & Sat) ☎ (01633) 221928
Brains SA; Greene King Ruddles Best Bitter, Abbot; Rhymney Export; guest beers Ⓗ
Pleasant, airy pub in a former cinema in the vibrant Maindee area of Newport, featuring photographs of early movie stars with local connections. Godfrey Morgan was a survivor of the Charge of the Light Brigade. A selection of up to 10 well-kept ales is offered, including some more unusual examples. The car park at the rear of the pub is Pay & Display, refundable at the bar when you order.
Q⊛◐⛁♣P⌐

John Wallace Linton Ⓛ ✔
10-12 Cambrian Centre, Cambrian Road, NP20 1GA (off Queensway)
❄ 7am-midnight (1am Fri & Sat) ☎ (01633) 251752
Greene King Ruddles Best Bitter, Abbot; Rhymney Export; guest beers Ⓗ
Handily placed for the railway station, local bus services, market, shops and evening entertainment venues, this is understandably a popular rendezvous for locals and visitors. The open plan interior has colourful artwork on display either side of a large mirror, and a pictorial history of Newport is dotted around the walls. TV channels silently deliver the news and sport. Note the area commemorating those who served on HMS Turbulent, whose heroic commander was John Wallace Linton VC. Q⊛◐♿⛁⌐

Olde Murenger House
53 High Street, NP20 1GA
❄ 11-11; 12-2.30, 7-10.30 Sun ☎ (01633) 263977
Samuel Smith OBB Ⓗ
This 16th-century Tudor inn stands out amid Newport's more modern architecture. Admire the facade and leaded front windows before enjoying the dark wood decor, high back settles and subdued lighting that help to create a cosy, relaxing ambience in its various linked areas. Dotted around the walls are pictures depicting mainly local scenes and personalities of bygone days. Conversation and laughter dominate here among customers sampling the impressive Sam Smith's range of drinks, especially the keenly priced Old Brewery Bitter. ◐⛁

Red Lion
47 Charles Street, NP20 1JH
❄ 12-midnight (1am Fri & Sat); 12-11.30 Sun ☎ (01633) 264398
Beer range varies Ⓗ
One of the last remaining traditional pubs in the city centre, the Red Lion retains a local feel while welcoming visitors from far and wide. There is an emphasis on sport, particularly Rugby Union, it being a haunt of followers of Newport based teams. The shove ha'penny board is well used and draws interest from those unfamiliar with this little known pub game. Well worth seeking out and just far enough away from the night club scene to retain a convivial atmosphere.
♨⊛⛁(1,151)♣⌐

St Julian Inn ✔
Caerleon Road, NP18 1QA
❄ 11.30-11.30 (midnight Fri & Sat); 12-11 Sun ☎ (01633) 243548 ⊕ stjulian.co.uk
John Smith's Bitter; Wells Bombardier; Young's Bitter; guest beer Ⓗ
Well-run riverside pub fully deserving its high popularity rating. A central bar serves adjoining but discrete areas, which include a lounge panelled with wood from the Doric, a former ocean liner. The riverside balcony gives superb views of the countryside and towards historic Caerleon. Pub games include boules, pool and skittles, while golfers might like to test their skills at the Celtic Manor Resort a short drive away. Interesting guest ales sit alongside the core range.
⊛◐⛁(28,60)♣P⌐

Pantygelli

Crown Inn ⌊

Old Hereford Road, NP7 7HR

✪ 12-2.30 (not Mon), 6-11; 12-3, 6-10.30 Sun
☎ (01873) 853314 ⊕ thecrownatpantygelli.com

Rhymney Best Bitter; Wye Valley HPA; guest beers ⊞
This superb country inn of 15th-century origin is a
recent Gwent CAMRA Country Pub of the Year
winner. The interesting interior, with much old
wood and stone in evidence, is a complex of cosy
dining areas, while drinkers settle in and around
the bar and near the fireplace. The food is highly
recommended and can be washed down with a
good selection of ales, including local brews. On
clear days enjoy the scenic views towards the
Skirrid Mountain. ㎫Q❀◑♣P⁵⌐

Pontymister

Commercial ◐

Commercial Street, NP11 6BA

✪ 11 (12 Sun)-11.30 ☎ (01633) 612608
⊕ thecommercialpontymister.com

Beer range varies ⊞
Three times local CAMRA Town Pub of the Year
winner, this is a comfortably furnished hostelry
with adjoining lounge and bar/games areas. At the
front is a spacious patio that can be covered by a
retractable awning when required. The menu
offers a good range of popular main meals plus
lighter bites. A good selection of frequently
changing ales is available and cider appears in
summer. A bus stop is a few minutes walk away,
as is Pontymister/Risca railway station.
❀◑⊟⑆≠(Risca/Pontymister)⊟♣⁵⌐

St Brides Wentlooge

Lighthouse Inn

Beach Road, NP10 8SH SO300816

✪ 12-11 ☎ (01633) 680451 ⊕ lighthouseinnstbrides.co.uk

Beer range varies ⊞
A friendly free house on the coast of the Severn
Estuary with good walks nearby, especially on the
sea wall overlooking the high tidal flow. The pub is
popular with locals as well as visitors. The upstairs
has been converted to a rustic style restaurant
specialising in steaks served on a steak-stone,
open Friday and Saturday evenings. One ever-
changing guest ale is always on, with promises to
increase this if demand warrants it. Live music
plays on Friday and Saturday. ㎫❀◑⊟(31)♣P⁵⌐

Sailors arms

Up the street, in the Sailors Arms, Sinbad
Sailors, grandson of Mary Ann Sailors,
drew a pint in the sunlit bar. The ship's
clock in the bar says half past eleven. Half
past eleven is opening time. The hands of
the clock have stayed still at half past
eleven for fifty years. It is always opening
time in the Sailors Arms.
Dylan Thomas, Under Milk Wood

Sebastopol

Open Hearth

Wern Road, NP4 5DR

✪ 11.30-12.30am (1.30am Fri & Sat); 12-11.30 Sun
☎ (01495) 763752

Wye Valley HPA; guest beers ⊞
Welcoming canalside pub with spacious outdoor
areas that are popular in fine weather. The historic
building has gradually expanded over many years –
it was once owned by the Great Western Railway –
and has several rooms for diners and drinkers. The
function room hosts Torfaen Jazz Society on Friday
evenings, and other occasional live music. Beers
are selected from popular family and regional
breweries, and tasty food can be chosen from an
appetising menu. Last admittance is 11pm.
❀◑⊟⊟(X3,X24)♣⁵⌐

Sebastopol Social Club

Wern Road, NP4 5DU

✪ 12-11 (midnight Fri & Sat); 12-10.30 Sun
☎ (01495) 763808 ⊕ sebastopolsocial.org.uk

Beer range varies ⊞
Thriving social club that has once again added
Regional CAMRA Club of the Year to its long list of
honours. It offers a range of exciting new ales as
well as returning favourites from breweries near
and far. The main room hosts live entertainment,
bingo and league darts. Major sporting events are
screened, most regularly in the comfortable rear
room. Skittles is played downstairs and pool in the
upstairs function room. Non-members are
welcome subject to visitor rules.
❀⊟(X3,X24)♣●P⁵⌐

Tintern

Anchor Inn

Chapel Hill, NP16 6TE (off A466 at Tintern Abbey)

✪ 11-11; 12-10.30 Sun ☎ (01291) 689582
⊕ theanchortintern.co.uk

Wye Valley Bitter, Butty Bach; guest beers ⊞
The massive old cider press in the main bar is a
reminder of one former function of this ancient
riverside building – a source of sustenance for
monks toiling in the great abbey next door. Today
the Anchor sustains drinkers and diners in a choice
of comfortable rooms, including a restaurant with a
delightfully tiny and secretive annexe. A
summertime café and large garden are popular
with families. Guest beers often include brews rare
in south Wales. Draught cider, often from Westons,
is also available. ㎫❀◑⊟(69)●P

Moon & Sixpence

Monmouth Road, NP16 6SG (at N end of village on
A466)

✪ 12-midnight (12.30am Sun) ☎ (01291) 689284
⊕ moonandsixpencetintern.co.uk

Wye Valley Bitter, Butty Bach; guest beer ⊞
This welcoming roadside pub is perched safely
above the highest tides of the fast-flowing River
Wye close by. Several small adjoining rooms at
different levels provide a charming and cosy
environment, enhanced by the sound and sight of
a natural spring in one corner. A 15-minute stroll
from Tintern Abbey, the pub is popular with visitors
exploring this scenic and historic valley. A split-
level terrace outside provides good views. The
guest beer is often Kingstone Gold from the nearby
brewery. Q❀◑⊟(69)♣P⁵⌐

Trellech

Lion Inn
NP25 4PA

☼ 12-3, 6 (7 Mon)-11 (midnight Thu); 12-midnight Fri & Sat; 12-4.30 Sun ☎ (01600) 860322 ⊕ lioninn.co.uk

Beer range varies ⊞

Cosy and welcoming pub on the B4293 Monmouth to Chepstow road. Entrance is to the main bar, with a larger restaurant area to the left. Once a regular in this Guide, the pub has returned to its former high standards. Annual beer festivals with live music are held in June and November, with a cider festival in August. ⚇✿🏠◑️⏰🍴🚐(65)P⇌

Upper Llanover

Goose & Cuckoo ⓛ
NP7 9ER SO292073

☼ closed Mon; 11.30-3, 7-11; 11.30-11 Fri & Sat; 12-10.30 Sun ☎ (01873) 880277 ⊕ gooseandcuckoo.com

Beer range varies ⊞

This charming, unspoilt country inn has featured on TV as one of the Great Little Pubs of Wales. A real fire adds to the cosiness of the main room, with an old piano in the corner acting as a repository for tourist information, books and magazines. The visitors' book bears testimony to the pub's popularity, especially with passing walkers. Beer and music festivals feature on the Whitsun and August bank holidays. ⚇Q✿🏠◑️P⇌

Usk

King's Head Hotel
18 Old Market Street, NP15 1AL

☼ 11 (1 Tue)-11; 12-10.30 Sun ☎ (01291) 672963

Fuller's London Pride; Taylor Landlord ⊞

Entrance is through a short corridor into a cosy bar on two levels, with much hunting and fishing

memorabilia scattered about, along with a good number of books. The pub has plenty of olde world charm with its low beamed ceilings. A good selection of food is available both in the bar and the adjoining Lionel Sweet room. A mix of en-suite and budget accommodation makes this a useful base for exploration of the area. ⚇Q🏠◑️🚐(60,63)P

Nag's Head ⓛ
Twyn Square, NP15 1BH

☼ 12-2.30, 5-11 (10.30 Sun) ☎ (01291) 672820

Brains The Rev James; Sharp's Doom Bar; guest beer ⊞

This fascinating old pub dating back to 1641 has been in the same family for more than 40 years and is a long time Guide entry. Situated in the main town square, the multi-roomed establishment is well known for a good range of food featuring locally-sourced produce. Note the unusual brass taps (not in use) on the front panel of the bar. A fine collection of plaques from businesses, numerous old photos and adverts adorn the walls. Q◑️🚐(60,63)⇌

Usk Conservative Club ⓛ
16 Maryport Street, NP15 1BH

☼ 12 (11 Tue)-3, 7-11; 12-3, 7-10.30 Sun ☎ (01291) 672820

Rhymney Bitter; guest beer ⊞

Well-appointed private members club set in its own grounds. As you enter, there is the welcoming sight of three handpulls on an elegant bar at the centre of a comfortably furnished lounge, with a games area on one side and a dining room on the other. A large function room is at the rear. An air of old-fashioned gentility prevails in this friendly club. Non-members are welcome but entry rules may be applied. Q✿◑️🚐(60,63)♣P⇌

Goose & Cuckoo, Upper Llanover (Photo: Cris Bartlett)

MID-WALES

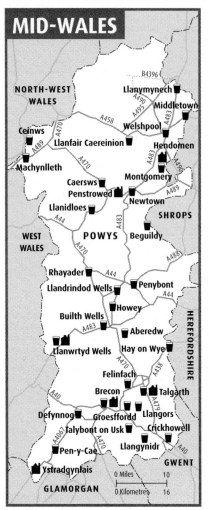

Authority area covered: Powys UA

Picturesque and somewhat isolated, this 16th-century roadside inn lies close to the English border. It has a snug low-roofed bar and comfortable adjoining dining area leading to a larger seating area. The guest beers are sourced from a range of breweries including Breconshire, Hobson's, Six Bells and Wye Valley. No meals are served on Sunday evening. The outdoor smoking area is heated. Q✿◑⬚♣P⃗

Brecon

Boar's Head
Ship Street, LD3 9AL (by bridge over River Usk)
✪ 11-midnight (2am Fri & Sat); 12-1am Sun
☎ (01874) 622856
Breconshire Welsh Pale Ale, Golden Valley, Cribyn, Ramblers Ruin, seasonal beers Ⓗ
The Breconshire Brewery tap is a popular and lively town-centre pub with two distinct bars – the wood-panelled front bar houses the majority of the handpumps and tends to be a little quieter than the larger back bar, which has a pool table and gets busy on match days when rugby internationals are shown on TV. Live music evenings and quiz nights are held throughout the year, and the pub is a favourite spot during the jazz festival. The riverside patio garden enjoys superb views over the river and up to the Brecon Beacons.
⚌✿◑⬚&⧉(X43)♣♠P⃗

George Hotel
George Street, LD3 7LD (just off the Struet)
✪ 11 (12 Sun)-midnight ☎ (01874) 623421
⊕ george-hotel.com
Evan Evans BB, Cwrw, seasonal beers Ⓗ
Smart yet friendly hotel bar in the centre of Brecon. A large conservatory addition to the main bar area provides more tables for drinkers and diners. Food is locally sourced, including venison, beef and fish. The bar features beers from Evan Evans Brewery, which owns the hotel. An enclosed courtyard is a pleasant place to relax in warmer weather, and there is also large function room. ⚌✿⛢◑⬚&⧉⬚

Aberedw

Seven Stars
LD2 3UW (off B4567)
✪ 12-3, 6.30 (6 Fri & Sat)-11; 12-3.30, 6.30-10.30 Sun
☎ (01982) 560494 ⊕ 7-stars.co.uk
Beer range varies Ⓗ
Situated a few miles outside the market town of Builth Wells in the small village of Aberedw, the Seven Stars has links back to the 13th century and the legend of the fall of Llywelyn ap Gruffydd, last Prince of Wales. The main bar is friendly but rugged with a real fire and exposed stonework, while the restaurant is comfortable and popular with locals and visitors. Real cider from Gwynt y Ddraig is available. ⚌Q◑&♠P

Beguildy

Radnorshire Arms ✪
LD7 1YE (on B4355)
✪ closed Mon; 7-midnight (1am Fri & Sat); 12-3, 7-midnight Sun ☎ (01547) 510354
Fuller's London Pride; guest beers Ⓗ

Builth Wells

Greyhound Hotel
3 Garth Road, LD2 3AR
✪ 12-midnight (1am Fri & Sat) ☎ (01982) 553255
⊕ thegreyhoundhotel.co.uk
Beer range varies Ⓗ
Pleasant modern hotel with open-plan bars, a restaurant and a large function room. Excellent food, including a Sunday carvery, is served, with the menu featuring local produce. A glass panel above the door harks back to when there was a brewery at the hotel. A beer festival is held every year. ✿⛢◑&⧉♣P⃗

Caersws

Red Lion
Main Street, SY17 5EL (on B4569)
🟢 3-11 (midnight Fri, Sat & summer) ☎ (01686) 688023
Beer range varies Ⓗ
Friendly wood-beamed village pub with two bars, attracting a varied clientele of all ages. Early evenings can be busy as many villagers call in on their way home from work. The four changing ales usually include two locally-produced beers, and a local cider is also sold. A summer beer festival is held in the large car park and there are drinking areas outside to the front and rear.
🏨❄🍴◑▣🚃🚍(X75,X85)♣🐕P

Ceinws

Tafarn Dwynant
SY20 9HA (off A487 3 miles N of Machynlleth) SH759059
🟢 closed Mon; 5.30 (3 Sat & Sun)-11 ☎ (01654) 761660
🌐 tafarndwynant.co.uk
Purple Moose Snowdonia Ale; guest beer Ⓗ
Situated in a quiet village, this friendly community free house is three miles from the nearest town. The landlord's own artwork is on display. Home-prepared food uses locally and ethically sourced ingredients (evening meals served Tue-Sun in summer, Wed-Sat in winter). Occasional mini beer festivals are held and the front patio is used for alfresco drinking. Local bus 34 stops near the pub; longer-distance buses stop on the main road, just across the river from the village.
🏨❄◑Å🚍(34)♣🍽

Crickhowell

Bear Hotel
High Street, NP8 1BW
🟢 11-3, 6-11; 11-3, 7-10.30 Sun ☎ (01873) 810408
🌐 bearhotel.co.uk
Brains The Rev James; Draught Bass; guest beer Ⓗ
Originally a 15th-century coaching inn, the Bear is now an award-winning hotel. The multi-roomed bar enjoys grand surroundings with exposed beams, wood panelling and fine settles, and an eclectic selection of furnishings and decorations. There are open fireplaces in both bar rooms and a side room. An excellent and varied food menu is offered, featuring much local produce. The hotel is an excellent base for exploring the surrounding Black Mountains and Brecon Beacons National Park. 🏨Q❄🍴◑▣🛏🚍(X43)P🍽

Defynnog

Tanners Arms
LD3 8SF
🟢 5 (12 Sat & Sun)-midnight ☎ (01874) 638032
🌐 tannersarmspub.com
Beer range varies Ⓗ
Family-run country pub famous for its warm welcome, set in the delightful village of Defynnog in the Brecon Beacons National Park. The pub has traded continuously since 1870 but the original buildings (cottages for workers at the nearby tannery) date to circa 1806. The public bar has a pool table, dartboard and bar games, and there is a separate restaurant and function room with its own bar. To the rear is a large south-facing beer garden.
🏨❄🍴◑Å🚍(X63)♣🐕P

Felinfach

Griffin
LD3 0UB (just off A470 3 miles NE of Brecon)
🟢 12-11.30 ☎ (01874) 620111 🌐 eatdrinksleep.ltd.uk
Breconshire Cribyn; Wye Valley Butty Bach; Otley 01 Ⓗ
The pub's ethos – the simple things in life done well – says it all. A welcoming country pub, restaurant and hotel, the emphasis here is on good beer and excellent food. The multi-roomed layout allows for discrete areas for drinking and dining. The huge fireplace between the bar and the main dining area dominates during the winter, while a full-sized Aga lurks in a side room, providing warmth throughout the building. The large garden, popular in summer, affords superb views of the Brecon Beacons and Black Mountains.
🏨Q❄🍴◑🛏🚍P🍽

Groesffordd

Three Horseshoes
LD3 7SN 075280
🟢 12-3 (not Mon), 5-11; 12-11 Fri-Sun ☎ (01874) 665672
🌐 threehorseshoesgroesffordd.co.uk
Beer range varies Ⓗ
Busy village centre pub in the heart of the Brecon Beacons, boasting superb views from both the front and rear outdoor seating areas. The pub is just a 10-minute walk from the Brynich Lock on the Brecon & Monmouth Canal, and is a popular stopping off point for boaters and other visitors to the area. Excellent food, sourced locally, is on offer, and quizzes and other events take place regularly.
🏨❄◑🛏Å♣🐕P🍽

Hay on Wye

Kilverts ✓
The Bull Ring, HR3 5AG
🟢 11-11 (midnight Fri & Sat) ☎ (01497) 821042
🌐 kilverts.co.uk
Breconshire Kilverts Gold, Ramblers Ruin; Wye Valley Butty Bach; guest beers Ⓗ
Popular with locals and visitors alike, the inn has a large beer garden and 12 en-suite rooms. The focus here is on quality beer, with tutored tastings, food pairings, regular Meet the Brewer events and an August bank holiday beer festival featuring 50 Welsh ales. Food is served in the bar and restaurant, with fresh fish the speciality. Tuesday is open mike night and jazz plays on the lawn throughout the summer. Hay Brewery is located in the garden. 🏨❄🍴◑🛏🚍🐕P🍽

Howey

Laughing Dog
LD1 5PT
🟢 6 (5.30 Fri)-11; 11-11 Sat; 11-10.30 Sun
☎ (01597) 822406 🌐 thelaughingdog.co.uk
Felinfoel Double Dragon; Wye Valley Bitter; guest beers Ⓗ
Located on an old drovers' road outside Llandrindod Wells, this 18th-century building has been a pub since the 19th century. The interior is rustic and friendly with solid timber furniture. There is a separate games room and restaurant, with food served on Friday and Saturday evenings and Sunday lunchtime. As the name implies, friendly dogs are always welcome. 🏨❄◑Å♣

Llandrindod Wells

Conservative Club
South Crescent, LD1 5DH
🕓 11-2, 5.30-11; 11-11.30 Fri & Sat; 11.30-10.30 Sun
☎ (01597) 822126
Hancock's HB; Marston's Pedigree; guest beer Ⓗ
Located in the centre of historic Llandrindod Wells, the Conservative Club is a smart and friendly destination for those wishing to enjoy a quiet drink. Visitors will find a large lounge, TV room, games bar, snooker and pool tables and a small front patio. Lunches are available Thursday to Saturday. Live entertainment is hosted occasionally in the evening. CAMRA members are welcome but non-members must be signed in. Q❀◖Ь⇌🖫🖴

Llanfair Caereinion

Goat Hotel
High Street, SY21 0QS (off A458)
🕓 11-11 (midnight Fri & Sat) ☎ (01938) 810428
Beer range varies Ⓗ
This excellent inn has a welcoming atmosphere and attracts both locals and tourists. The plush lounge, dominated by a large inglenook with an open fire, has comfortable leather armchairs and sofas, complemented by a dining room serving home-cooked food and a games room at the rear. The choice of three real ales always includes one from the Wood Brewery. ♨❀🖦◖♣P

Llangors

Castle Inn
LD3 7UB
🕓 5-11; 12-midnight Fri-Sun ☎ (01874) 658819
Beer range varies Ⓗ
Hospitable and traditional village local with stone walls, wood bar, large fireplace and great service. Popular with locals and visitors, the pub provides a hub for ramblers, boaters, horse riders and explorers. Excellent beers are brought in from near and far, and locally-sourced food is served in the evenings and at weekends. ♨❀Ь人⇌🖫♣P

Llangynidr

Red Lion
Duffryn Road, NP8 1NT (off B4558)
🕓 11-11; 12-10.30 Sun ☎ (01874) 730223
Rhymney Best Bitter Ⓗ
Popular village local, off the beaten track, which offers a warm welcome to walkers, boaters, families and dogs. The beer range changes regularly and good-value home-cooked food is served in the bar. A separate games area, outside seating and children's play area make this a pub for all. ♨🏖❀🖦◖🖫♣P

Llanidloes

Angel Hotel
High Street, SY18 6BY (off A470)
🕓 11.30-2.30 (not Wed), 5-1am; 12-3, 7-midnight Sun
☎ (01686) 412381
Everards Tiger; Greene King Abbot; guest beer Ⓗ
Friendly edge-of-town pub with two comfortable bars. The larger of the two rooms has a big stone fireplace and old photographs on the wall, and the smaller room has an interesting bar inlaid with old pennies. There is a restaurant at the rear that can

seat 40 people (booking recommended). The pub was built in 1748 and Chartists held meetings here between 1838 and 1839. Outside seating is available at the front of the pub.
♨❀◖🖫(X75,525)♣

Crown & Anchor Inn ★
41 Long Bridge Street, SY18 6EF (off A470)
🕓 11-11; 12-10.30 Sun ☎ (01686) 412398
Brains The Rev James; Worthington's Bitter Ⓗ
Wonderful, unspoilt town-centre gem with a relaxed and friendly atmosphere, featuring in CAMRA's National Inventory of Historic Pub Interiors. The landlady has been in charge since 1965 and throughout that time the pub has remained unchanged, retaining its public bar, lounge, snug and two further rooms, one with a pool table and games machine. Serving hatches connect the small end rooms to the bar and there is another hatch to pass drinks into the games room. 🖫(X75,525)♣

Red Lion Hotel
Long Bridge Street, SY18 6EE (off A470)
🕓 11-midnight (1am Fri & Sat) ☎ (01686) 412270
Brains The Rev James; Taylor Landlord; guest beers Ⓗ
Wood-beamed town-centre hotel with a plush lounge and red leather sofas. The public bar is divided into two areas – the front area has an interesting wood-panelled fireplace, the rear space has a pool table and games machines. Up to four real ales are usually available. There is a patio outside for alfresco drinking in warmer weather.
♨❀🖦◖🖫(X75,525)♣

Llanwrtyd Wells

Neuadd Arms Hotel
The Square, LD5 4RB
🕓 9.30-midnight (1am Fri & Sat) ☎ (01591) 610236
⊕ neuaddarmshotel.co.uk
Felinfoel Double Dragon; Heart of Wales Irfon Valley, Aur Cymru, Bitter, Welsh Black, Noble Eden, Innstable, seasonal beers Ⓗ
Large Victorian hotel serving as the tap for the Heart of Wales brewery. The Bells Bar features a large fireplace and an eclectic mix of furniture. The bells that once summoned servants remain on one wall, along with the winners' boards from some of the town's more unusual competitions, such as bog-snorkelling or man v horse. The lounge bar is a little more formal, with deep carpets, sofas and paintings on the walls. The hotel takes part in the town's annual events, including food festivals and a beer festival in November. Gwynt y Ddraig cider is served. ♨Q❀🖦◖🖫人⇌♣●P

Stonecroft Inn
Dolecoed Road, LD5 4RA
🕓 5-midnight; 12-1am Fri-Sun ☎ (01591) 610332
⊕ stonecroft.co.uk
Brains The Rev James; Rhymney Best Bitter; guest beers Ⓗ
This warm and friendly community pub participates in the town's many and varied festivities – bog-snorkelling, beer and food festivals, real ale rambles and much more. The hostelry has three main areas for drinking, dining and games, plus a large riverside garden with an aviary. Excellent food complements the fine range of beers. Lodge accommodation is popular with walkers and mountain bikers. ♨❀🖦◖人⇌♣●P🖴

Llanymynech

Bradford Arms ✓
North Road, SY22 6EJ (on A483)
☼ 11.30-3, 6-11 ☎ (01691) 830582
⊕ bradfordarmshotel.com
Black Sheep Best Bitter; guest beers Ⓗ
Small but popular hotel near Offa's Dyke with a varied clientele. The cosy bar has a real fire and the walls are adorned with pump clips and RAF photographs. Three beers are available, with guest ales coming from local breweries – third of a pint glasses are available for sampling. A real cider is added in the summer months. This AA four-star hotel has a restaurant to the rear and five guest rooms. ♨⊯◑ᴴ&♣P

Machynlleth

White Horse
42 Maengwyn Street, SY20 8DT
☼ 12-3 (Wed-Fri only), 7 (6 Fri)-11.30; 12-11.30 Sat & Sun
Beer range varies Ⓗ
Friendly locals' pub on the main street of this bustling market town, once the capital of Wales – just across the street is the site of Owain Glyndwr's Parliament House of 1404. Both bars have open log fires in winter, and there is a pool table. Two real ales are usually on offer, drawn from a wide range of family and micro-brewers. The beer garden at the rear affords access for disabled customers. ♨✿◑ᴴ&ᴰ⇌□♣P⬱

Wynnstay Arms
Maengwyn Street, SY20 8AA
☼ 12-2.30, 6-11.30 ☎ (01654) 702941
⊕ wynnstay-hotel.com
Greene King IPA; guest beers Ⓗ
This 18th-century country-town hotel lies close to the Victorian Gothic clock tower. Known for its food – award-winning chef Gareth Johns makes extensive use of local produce, especially seafood – it has a dining room and a large bar-dining area with an open log fire. The drinkers' bar is small but comfortable and busy. Up to four real ales may be available, often from Wales or the borders. At the rear a separate pizzeria serves pizzas baked in a wood-fired oven. ♨✿⊯◑ᴴ⊞⇌□♣P⬱

Middletown

Breidden Hotel
SY21 8EL (on A458)
☼ 12-2.30, 5-11; 12-midnight Sat; 11-midnight Sun
☎ (01938) 570880
Beer range varies Ⓗ
This village local has a large wood-beamed, L-shaped interior with comfortable seating, a pool table and games machines. At one end of the bar is a small, cosy restaurant area, and the pub has a good reputation for eastern cuisine. The hotel takes its name from Breidden Hill, topped by the 18th-century Admiral Rodney's Pillar, which dominates the neighbourhood. Outside is a large partly-covered drinking area. ♨✿◑ᴰ□(X75)♣P⬱

Montgomery

Crown Inn
Castle Street, SY15 6PW
☼ 11-11 (midnight Sun) ☎ (01686) 668533
Beer range varies Ⓗ

This pub attracts a mixed clientele from the local area, with a wood-burning stove and wall seating at the front and a long public bar with a pool table and games machines at the rear. The walls are covered with local photographs. There is also a small lounge bar with a comfortable sofa and sports trophies. Three beers are on offer, at least one from a local brewery. ♨⊟♣

Newtown

Elephant & Castle
Broad Stree, SY16 2BQ (off A483)
☼ 11-11 ☎ (01686) 626271 ⊕ elephantandcastlehotel.co.uk
Six Bells Big Nev's; guest beers Ⓗ
Open-plan town-centre hotel next to the River Severn with a number of drinking areas off the main bar. Old photographs and prints adorn the walls and several TVs show sporting events. Three local beers are on offer, usually from Monty's or Six Bells breweries. To the rear is a separate building used for functions. Outside, there is bench seating by the river wall. ✿⊯◑ᴰ⇌♣P

Railway Tavern
Old Kerry Road, SY16 1BH (off A483)
☼ 12-2.30, 6-midnight Mon, Wed & Thu; 11-1am Tue, Fri & Sat; 12-11 Sun ☎ (01686) 626156
Draught Bass; Worthington's Bitter; guest beer Ⓗ
Traditional pub on the edge of the town centre and handy for the railway station. The establishment owes its welcoming atmosphere and devoted following to the long-serving landlord and landlady who have been in charge for more than 25 years. It is home to a successful darts team and match nights can get busy. Guest beers come from a wide range of independent breweries. ✿⇌□(X75)♣

Sportsman Ⓛ ✓
Severn Street, SY16 2BQ (off A483)
☼ 12-11 ☎ (01686) 623978
Monty's Sunshine, Midnight; guest beers Ⓗ
This refurbished town-centre local is now Monty's Brewery's first pub. Four of its beers are always available plus a guest from an independent brewery, and a real cider. There are three areas to drink in – the main bar with a brick inglenook and wood-burning stove, a quiet area with comfortable leather seating, and the rear slate-tiled games area with a pool table and TV. A mute TV in the main bar shows silent comedies and classic cartoons. ♨✿&⇌⬤

Pen-y-Cae

Ancient Briton ♈
Brecon Road, SA9 1YY (on A4067 between Ystradgynlais and Dan-yr-Ogof caves)
☼ 12-midnight ☎ (01639) 730273 ⊕ ancientbriton.co.uk
Wye Valley Butty Bach; guest beers Ⓗ
Excellent country inn within the Fforest Fawr Geopark, close to Dan-yr-Ogof Caves and Henrhyd Waterfall, frequently used by walkers, cavers and cyclists. Thirteen handpumps regularly dispense up to six real ales and two real ciders, and an annual beer festival is held in September. The restaurant has a la carte and bar meals and there is en-suite accommodation. Winner of local CAMRA Branch Pub of the Year on three occasions and runner up for South and Mid Wales in 2010.
♨Q✿⊯◑ᴰ▲□(X63)♣⬤P⬱

cosy single bar has a roaring fire in winter. Beer and good conversation are the main features of this regular local CAMRA Pub of the Year winner. Five handpumps feature ales from local breweries and a varying and interesting range of guests. ⋈Q❄☗⊛☖⌂♣P

Carrog

Grouse Inn

LL21 9AT (on B5437) SJ113435
✪ 12-1am ☎ (01490) 430272 ∰ thegrouseinncarrog.co.uk
Lees Bitter, seasonal beers Ⓗ
Situated in a beautiful location alongside the River Dee, with spectacular views of the valley and the Berwyn Mountains, the Grouse was originally a farm and brew house. Today, the long-standing Guide entry has a single bar serving two agreeable and separate dining rooms, a games room and an outside covered patio area. The western terminus of the Llangollen Railway is a short walk away. Lees seasonal beers are available occasionally. ⋈Q⊛◑Å⇌⊡(X94)P⌂

Cefn Mawr (Trefor Isa)

Mill

Mill Lane, LL14 3NL SJ275424
✪ 12-midnight (1am Fri & Sat) ☎ (01978) 821799
Beer range varies Ⓗ
Small unspoilt locals' pub hidden down a one-way narrow lane in the lower part of an old industrial village. A games room and small snug with upholstered benches lead off the central bar. The smoking area backs on to the gurgling mill stream. Beers are usually sourced from local micros. Nearby are the famous Pontcysyllte Aqueduct on the Llangollen Canal and Cefn Druids FC. Parking can be difficult but buses pass nearby. ⊛☗⊡(2,5)♣⌂

Cefn-y-Bedd

Ffrwd

Ffrwd Road, LL12 9TS (1 mile along B5102 from A541)
✪ closed Mon; 6.30-midnight; 12.30-10 Sun
☎ (01978) 757951
Beer range varies Ⓗ
The Ffrwd (Fast Flowing Stream) is a typical roadside pub, situated on the edge of a small wood and stream. It has a bar and large dining area decorated with timber beams, both served by a single bar. Good home-cooked meals are available throughout the day, lunchtime only on Sunday. A TV shows most sporting events. The spacious car park is situated across the road from the pub. ⋈⊛◑☗&⇌⌂⌂

Cilcain

White Horse

The Square, CH7 5NN (signed from A451 Mold to Denbigh road) SJ177651
✪ 12-3, 6-11; 12-11 Sat; 12-10:30 Sun ☎ (01352) 740142
Banks's Bitter; guest beer Ⓗ
Located in the centre of a charming village, the White Horse has separate entrances for bar and lounge. The bar, where the prices are lower, is used by locals and walkers exploring the nearby Moel Famau and Offa's Dyke. The lounge has four areas, decorated with pictures of old Cilcain. The beer is from the Marston's list, looked after by a landlord of long standing. ⋈Q⊛◑☗Å♣P⌂

Clawddnewydd

Glan Llyn Ⓛ

LL15 2NA (on B5105) SJ083524
✪ 5-midnight (1am Sat); 12-11 Sun ☎ (01824) 750754
Facer's Flintshire Bitter; guest beers Ⓗ
This traditional 16th-century multi-roomed pub in the centre of the village is larger than the exterior suggests. A busy community pub, the single room is home to local football, pool, darts and dominoes teams. Beams and stonework, together with period cinema posters, are striking features, while a central fireplace gives a homely feel on colder days. The house beer is brewed by Facer's, and food is served on Friday and Saturday evenings as well as Sunday lunchtime. ⋈❄⊛◑☖&♣⌂P⌂

Denbigh

Brookhouse Mill Ⓛ

Ruthin Road, LL16 4RD SJ072658
✪ 12-3, 6-11.30; 12-11 Sun ☎ (01745) 813377
∰ brookhousemill.co.uk
Conwy Welsh Pride; guest beers Ⓗ
Situated by the River Ystrad, this former water mill has been converted into a smart restaurant, with a central bar serving a number of satellite dining areas. Upstairs is a conservatory and separate function area. The old mill cogs and wheels can still be seen in the low-beamed interior. Two cask beers are available from local north Wales microbreweries. ⊛◑&Å⊡(51,53,150)P

Railway

2 Ruthin Road, LL16 3EL SJ059664
✪ 12-midnight ☎ (01745) 812376
Beer range varies Ⓗ
Classic unspoilt local, about half a mile from Denbigh town centre and its historic castle. The pub still retains the original five small rooms, although new fittings and sports video screens are now in place to suit modern tastes. The pub's name and heritage are reflected throughout the interior decorations. Two cask ales are available, with Purple Moose a local favourite. ☗Å⊡(51,76,150)♣P⌂

Dolphin

Glan Yr Afon Inn Ⓛ

CH8 8HE SJ195739
✪ 12-11 (11.30 Fri & Sat); 12-10.30 Sun ☎ (01352) 710052
∰ glanyrafoninn.co.uk
Beer range varies Ⓗ
Set in a quiet location just off the A55, this 16th-century coaching inn was once a changing point for stage coaches on the Holyhead-Chester-London route. With spectacular views over the Mediterranean-style patio and garden over the Dee Estuary, the pub welcomes families, ramblers and their dogs. The interior includes a function area and a separate restaurant. Fresh locally-sourced food is served all day and the house beer is brewed nearby at Facer's. ⋈Q⊛☖◑⊡(126)P

Dyserth

New Inn

Waterfall Road, LL18 6ET (on B5119 close to Dyserth Waterfall) SJ055794
✪ 12-11 ☎ (01745) 570482 ∰ thenewinndyserth.co.uk

Banks's Mild; Marston's Burton Bitter, Pedigree; guest beer Ⓗ
Close to the foot of Dyserth Waterfall, this 400-year-old pub – now greatly modernised and extended – focuses on food. Nevertheless, five real ales are a good reason to call in for a drink at this TV-free zone. Pictures of days gone by reflect the age of the pub and village. There is a pleasant outdoor drinking area. ⚐☎☺◑&⊟(35,36)P᠊

Eryrys

Sun Inn
Village Road, CH7 4BX
☾ 3.30-11; 1-10.30 Sun ☎ (01824) 780402
Flowers IPA; guest beers Ⓗ
Welcoming village inn built from local stone and set in an attractive countryside location close to the Flintshire/Denbighshire border. Popular with locals, walkers and cyclists, the small bar serves a low-beamed lounge with wood-burning stove and TV. A separate quiet room at the back is mostly used for dining. One or two guest ales are available, often sourced from local micros. Good quality home-produced food is served lunchtimes and evenings (no food Mon or Sun eve).
⚐☎◑⊟P᠊

Flint

Royal Oak
6 Church Street, CH6 5AE (at intersection of A548 with A5119 traffic lights)
☾ 10-11.30 (1am Fri & Sat); 11-midnight Sun
☎ (01352) 732239
Oakwell Old Tom Mild, Barnsley Bitter, Senior Ⓗ
A basic but friendly town pub, appreciated by the locals, with two drinking areas and the widest cask ale range in Flint; it is also the only mild outlet for miles. An establishment for those who are sports-minded, this venue also hosts a weekly quiz evening and a number of pub games evenings during the week; it can be busy at weekends when there is karaoke and also occasional live music.
☺◑⊖⇌⊟(11a,X11,18)♣᠊

Graianrhyd

Rose & Crown
Llanarmon Road, CH7 4QW (on B5430, off A5104) SJ218560
☾ 4 (12 Fri & Sat)-11; 12-10.30 Sun ☎ (01824) 780727
⊕ theroseandcrownpub.co.uk
Flowers IPA; guest beers Ⓗ
Welcoming 200-year-old village pub, appealing to the local community and walkers alike. The main bar area has an open fire and traditional copper-topped tables, and the smaller side bar has a log-burning stove and satellite TV. Two ever-changing guest ales feature, mainly sourced from local micro-breweries, and real cider is also on offer from time to time. Excellent value hearty food is popular, with lunchtime bar snacks and full evening meals available (no eve meals Mon).
⚐Q◑⊖♣P᠊

Graigfechan

Three Pigeons Inn
LL15 2EU (on B5429 about 3 miles S of Ruthin) SJ145545
☾ 12-3, 5.30-11; 12-11 Sat; 12-10.30 Sun ☎ (01824) 703178
⊕ threepigeonsinn.co.uk

Hancock's HB; guest beers Ⓗ/Ⓖ
Spacious, traditional, rural pub with superb views over the Clywydian range. Two rooms are served from a central bar, one with an open fire, the other a wood-burner, and the separate dining room (closed Sun eve) serves quality, locally-sourced food. The interior is decorated with shipping artefacts including a model of Bismark. Four beers, including regularly changing guests, are available straight from the cask (see website for ales of the week). Staff support July's Route 76 inter-pub beer festival and have their own festival on St David's Day. ⚐Q☺◑⊖&A⊟(76)●P᠊

Gresford

Griffin
Church Green, LL12 8RG
☾ 4-11 ☎ (01978) 852231
Adnams Bitter; Courage Best Bitter; guest beers Ⓗ
Bright, tidy, community pub adjacent to the 15th-century All Saints Church – its bells are one of the Seven Wonders of Wales. The inn is a picturesque white building just off the road in an attractive part of the village. A variety of pictures adorns the walls. The bar area offers lively conversation, but there are also plenty of quiet corners. A lawn to the side of the building has more seating. Children are welcome in some areas until 8pm. Q☺⊟(1)♣P᠊

Pant-yr-Ochain
Old Wrexham Road, LL12 8TY (off A5156, E from A483, follow signs to The Flash) SJ347534
☾ 12-11 (10.30 Sun) ☎ (01978) 853525
⊕ pantyrochain-gresford.co.uk
Brunning & Price Original; Flowers Original; Purple Moose Snowdonia Ale; guest beers Ⓗ
Extensive converted manor house set in award-winning landscaped gardens, overlooking a small lake to the rear. Inside, a central bar serves two main areas, but a walk around will reveal numerous other large rooms plus nooks and crannies for more intimate seating. You can sit by the splendid 16th-century inglenook fireplace in the winter or relax in the modern garden room or on the lawns in summer. High-quality food is popular. ⚐Q☺◑&P᠊

Halkyn

Blue Bell Inn Ⓛ ✅
Rhosesmor Road, CH8 8DL (on B5123) SJ209703
☾ 5-11 (midnight Fri); 12-midnight Sat; 12-11 Sun
☎ (01352) 780309 ⊕ bluebell.uk.eu.org
Beer range varies Ⓗ
Winner of many awards – as can be seen from the number of CAMRA certificates on display – the pub hosts regular events including conversational Welsh classes, and is the headquarters for free guided walks around Halkyn Mountain and the surrounding countryside. Four cask beers are usually available including two house beers from Facer's, three ciders, and often a perry. A discount is available for CAMRA members.
⚐Q☺◑A⊟(126)♣●P᠊

Hendre

Y Dderwen (The Oak)
Denbigh Road, CH7 5QE (on A541) SJ191677
☾ 7-midnight ☎ (01352) 741466 ⊕ ydderwen-theoak.com
Beer range varies Ⓗ

WALES

Roadside pub with a strong community focus, hosting social activities most evenings. The central bar serves two rooms, both festooned with an impressive pottery collection and old photographs of local interest, including Hendre Spa Mines. Two cask ales are usually available, with at least one from a local micro-brewery. The pub is a popular meeting point for ramblers and visitors to the surrounding countryside. ♨Q✿❀Ⓓ&Å➡(14)♣P╚

Hendrerwydd

White Horse Ⓛ
LL16 4LL (signed from B5429, near Llandyrnog) SJ121635
✿ 12-3 (not Mon & Wed), 6-11; closed Tue; 11-11 Sat;
12-10.30 Sun ☎ (01824) 790218
⊕ whitehorserestaurant.co.uk
Facer's Splendid Ale; guest beer Ⓗ
Modernised 16th-century hostelry, rescued from closure, retaining a small locals' bar, the Snug. The restaurant has a growing reputation for quality food, with produce coming from within a five-mile radius of the establishment. Live music on Sunday evenings is 'ad hoc' with everyone welcome to join in. The family-run pub blends in with the local community and takes part in the Route 76 inter-pub beer festival each July.
♨Q➳✿Ⓓ Å➡(76)P╚

Holt

Peal o' Bells
12 Church Street, LL13 9JP (400m S of Holt-Farndon bridge)
✿ 4 (6 Mon)-11; 4-12.30am Fri; 12-12.30a. Sat; 12-10.30 Sun
☎ (01829) 270411 ⊕ pealobells.co.uk
Beer range varies Ⓗ
Family-friendly village pub situated next to St Chad's church on the road to the River Dee. The bar serves two front rooms and a back room with a dartboard and pool table. The large fully-enclosed garden with a small play area has excellent views of the Dee Valley and Peckforton Hills. Real cider or perry is available and guest ales come from the SIBA list. The pub usually stages a beer festival on one of the May bank holidays.
♨Q✿&➡(C56)♣P╚

Llanarmon Dyffryn Ceiriog

Hand at Llanarmon
LL20 7LD (end of B4500 from Chirk) SJ157328
✿ 11-11 (12.30am Fri & Sat); 12-11 Sun ☎ (01691) 600666
⊕ thehandhotel.co.uk
Beer range varies Ⓗ
Superbly situated inn at the head of the Ceiriog Valley surrounded by the Berwyn Mountains. Once you've settled into the cosy and atmospheric bar with its black beams and inglenook fireplace, it's hard to leave. There is always a cask beer on offer from an independent such as Weetwood, and two at busier times. Food and accommodation are both of a high standard. This is a popular base for walkers and cyclists, and well-behaved dogs are welcome. ♨Q➳✿❀Ⓓ &➡♣P╚

Llanarmon-yn-Ial

Raven Inn Ⓛ
Ffordd-Rhew-Ial, CH7 4QE (signed off B5430) SJ191562
✿ closed Mon; 5-10.30 (11 Fri); 12-11 Sat; 12-6 Sun
☎ (01824) 780833 ⊕ raveninn.co.uk

Beer range varies Ⓗ
Situated in a designated area of outstanding natural beauty, the Raven has been run by the local village community since 2009, with any surplus profits used to fund village community projects. The pub hosts numerous events and offers locally-sourced food and real ales, with a central bar serving separate drinking areas. Three cask ales are usually available, including a house beer from Purple Moose, as well as a locally produced cider. ♨Q✿Ⓓ&Å♣♦P╚

Llandyrnog

Golden Lion Ⓛ ✔
LL16 4HG (on B5429, opp village stores) SJ108650
✿ 4-11 (12.30 Thu); 2-1am Fri & Sat; 2-11 Sun
☎ (01824) 790373
Facer's DHB; Tetley Bitter; guest beer Ⓗ
Situated at the heart of the village, this welcoming drinkers' pub has strong links with the local football team – players and supporters like to drink here after matches. Live music and ESPN TV also feature at weekends. The pub has two main areas, a public bar and a room with wooden fixtures, wood floor and a pool table. The pub participates in July's Route 76 inter-pub beer festival, and real cider is usually available in the summer.
♨❀❀➡(76)♣♦╚

White Horse (Ceffyl Gwyn) ✔
LL16 4HG SJ108651
✿ closed Mon & Tue; 12-3, 6-11 ☎ (01824) 790582
Tetley Bitter; guest beer Ⓗ
Situated next to the village church, this pub has a good reputation for food, which is its main business. There are three seating areas – two for diners and the bar area with exposed beams and a flagstone floor. The pub participates in the Route 76 beer festival held each July. If dining, it is advisable to book, especially at weekends.
♨❀Ⓓ Å➡(76)♦P╚

Llangollen

Abbey Grange Hotel Ⓛ
Horseshoe Pass Road, Llantisylio, LL20 8DD (on A542, 1½ miles NW of Llangollen)
✿ 11-11; 12-midnight Fri & Sat; 12-11 Sun
☎ (01978) 860753 ⊕ abbey-grange-hotel.co.uk
Beer range varies Ⓗ
This former slate quarry owner's residence boasts an enviable location in eight acres of countryside at the foot of the Horseshoe Pass, a few minutes drive from the attractions of Llangollen. Close by are the evocative ruins of the Cistercian Valle Crucis Abbey that dates from the 13th century. Up to four cask ales are available, mostly from the hotel's own brewery, which began operations in 2010. Good value meals are served throughout the day.
♨➳✿🛏Ⓓ&ÅP╚

Corn Mill
Dee Lane, LL20 8PN (on town side, W of River Dee bridge) SJ214421
✿ 12-11 (10.30 Sun) ☎ (01978) 869555
⊕ brunningandprice.co.uk/cornmill
Beer range varies Ⓗ
A splendidly converted flour mill incorporating the water wheel, with a series of open plan rooms spread over three levels. The large outside decking area has great views across the River Dee to the

restored steam railway station. Frequently changing beers are from independent breweries, particularly local micros, with Brunning & Price Original a favourite. High quality food is served most of the day. The bus service is limited in the evening. Q✿❶❷&🖼🕿

Sun Inn
49 Regent Street, LL20 8HN (½ mile E of town centre on A5)
❸ 12 (5 winter)-1am; 12 (3 winter)-2am Fri & Sat; 12 (3 winter)-1am Sun ☎ (01978) 860079
Purple Moose Snowdonia, Dark Side of the Moose; Salopian Shropshire Gold; guest beers Ⓗ
A superb free house usually serving at least two changing ales from micro-breweries, together with continental beers and a wide range of whiskies. The large room at the front, with two real fires and a games area, hosts live music Wednesday to Saturday evenings, featuring folk, jazz and rock bands. A small snug at the back of the bar leads to a covered outside seating area with a large-screen TV. ♨✿❹&🖼♣🕿

Llangynhafal

Golden Lion Inn
LL16 4LN (at village crossroads) SJ131634
❸ closed Mon; 6-11; 4-midnight Fri; 12-midnight Sat; 12-11 Sun ☎ (01824) 790451 ⊕ thegoldenlioninn.com
Holt Bitter; guest beer Ⓗ
Cheerful, welcoming inn at the village crossroads. An L-shaped central counter serves a public bar with a pool table plus a lounge and dining area. The pub is an outlet for Holt's beers, which the landlord collects himself, as well as regularly-changing guests, often from Facer's. The inter-pub Route 76 beer festival is an annual highlight in July. In recent years the pub has twice been voted local CAMRA Pub of the Year and it won the regional award in 2009. ♨Q✿🚲❶ ❹Å🖼(76)♣ ♠P🖥

Mold

Glasfryn Ⓛ
Raikes Lane, CH7 6LR (just off A5119) SJ240500
❸ 11.30-11; 12-10.30 Sun ☎ (01352) 750500
⊕ glasfryn-mold.co.uk
Facer's Flintshire Bitter; Flowers Original; guest beers Ⓗ
The Glasfryn is situated in its own grounds, near Theatr Clwyd, with views of the town and the Clwydian mountains. Originally a residence for circuit judges attending the court opposite, Brunning & Price converted it into a pub and restaurant in 1999. Its spacious interior is popular with diners as well as cask ale drinkers – a wide range of beers is available, many originating from north Wales breweries. ♨✿❶&🖼(28)♠P🖥

Gold Cape ✅
6 Wrexham Road, CH7 1ES (near Market Square)
❸ 9am-midnight ☎ (01352) 705920
Greene King Ruddles Best Bitter, Abbot; guest beers Ⓗ
The pub is named after the 4,000 year old gold peytrel discovered at Mold in 1831 (a replica can be seen in Mold Heritage Centre and Museum). This Wetherspoon establishment is an enthusiastic supporter of cask beer and often has an ale from the local Plassey Brewery alongside the usual range. Handily situated in the market town centre

and offering a discount to CAMRA members, the pub is a popular venue for local real ale fans. Q✖❶🖼♦🖥

Overton-on-Dee

White Horse Inn
21 High Street, LL13 0DT (on A528)
❸ closed Mon; 12-2.30, 5.30-midnight (10.30 Tue); 12-midnight Sat; 12-11 Sun ☎ (01978) 710111
⊕ thewhitehorseoverton.co.uk
Joule's Pale Ale; guest beers Ⓗ
This attractive red-brick, mock-Tudor building is situated in the heart of the village and is part of the small but impressive Joule's estate. A CAMRA pub design winner, inside it features frosted and latticed windows, pristine wooden partitioning and restored fireplaces. A former pantry, coal shed and wash house to the rear have been converted into dining spaces, each decorated with Joule's breweriana. ♨✿❶ ❹&🖼(146)♠🖥

Prestatyn

Halcyon Quest Ⓛ
17 Gronant Road, LL19 9DT (on A547 just E of town centre) SJ069826
❸ 3-11 (midnight Fri); 12-midnight Sat; 12-11 Sun
☎ (01745) 852442 ⊕ halcyonquest-hotel.com
Facer's Flintshire Bitter; guest beers Ⓗ
The Halcyon Quest has a pleasant, one-roomed lounge full of sporting memorabilia, including cricket, golf and baseball equipment and a rowing boat suspended from the ceiling. The Flintshire Bitter, brewed locally by Facer's, is complemented by guest beers. Accommodation is in nine bedrooms. The northern end of Offa's Dyke is nearby. ✿🛏Å≈P🖥

Rhyl

Caskeys ✅
19-23 Vale Road, LL18 2BT (next to The Little Theatre)
❸ 12-11 ☎ (01745) 798285
Marston's Pedigree; guest beer Ⓗ
Situated immediately south of the railway bridge, this recently refurbished pub is close to the town centre. Tastefully furnished, with a large, open-plan layout, a brick arch leads to a separate dining room; there is also a games room with pool table off the main drinking space. Sports fans are well catered for, with several large TVs. Outside, a covered and decked area provides space for drinking and smoking. ✖✿❶≈🖼♣🖥

Sussex ✅
26 Sussex Street, LL18 1SG
❸ 9am-midnight (1am Sat); 9am-10.30 Sun
☎ (01745) 362910
Greene King Ruddles Best Bitter, Abbot; Marston's Pedigree; guest beers Ⓗ
Popular Wetherspoon outlet situated in a pedestrianised part of the town centre and convenient for the sea front. The interior is largely open plan, covering three areas. Originally a Welsh Wesleyan Chapel and later The Old Comrades Club, it was converted to a pub in 1992 before its current owners took over in 2001. The walls are decorated with a pictorial history of Rhyl's cultural and social past, together with modern art. Guest beers sometimes come from the Conwy Brewery. Q✖❶&≈🖼♦

public bar. Meals are served in a separate quieter lounge and bar snacks are also available. There is outdoor seating in the front car park, and at the rear is a larger parking area and courtyard. Three bedrooms offer good-value accommodation.
🏠Q❄️🌟🍴◀️🍺(X94)♣P🍃

Llandudno

Cottage Loaf 🅛 ✅
Market Street, LL30 2SR SH781824
🕐 11-11 (11.30 Fri & Sat) ☎ (01492) 870762
🌐 the-cottageloaf.co.uk
Conwy Welsh Pride; Courage Directors Bitter; guest beers Ⓗ
This building used to be a bakery, hence the name. The interior features stone-flagged floors, an impressive fireplace and raised timber floor area – much of the wood came from The Flying Foam, a schooner shipwrecked at Llandudno's West Shore. With great home-cooked food served daily, the Loaf is a popular meeting place for people of all ages. Live bands play on Saturday and Sunday evenings, and there is an annual beer and music festival in the summer. 🏠❄️🌟◀️🍺🍃

King's Head ✅
Old Road, LL30 2NB (next to Great Orme Tramway) SH778827
🕐 12-11 (midnight Fri & Sat) ☎ (01492) 877993
🌐 kingsheadllandudno.co.uk
Greene King IPA, Abbot; guest beers Ⓗ
The 300-year-old King's Head is the oldest inn in Llandudno. It has a traditional split-level bar dominated by a large open fire and a grill restaurant at the rear serving good quality food. The pub makes an ideal stop after walking on the Great Orme or riding on Britain's only cable-hauled tramway. Quiz night is Wednesday and folk night the first Sunday of the month. 🏠❄️🌟◀️🍴❖P🍃

Llanelian-yn-Rhos

White Lion
LL29 8YA (off B583) SH863764
🕐 closed Mon; 11.30-3, 6-midnight; 12-4, 6-11 Sun
☎ (01492) 515807 🌐 whitelioninn.co.uk
Marston's Burton Bitter, Pedigree; guest beer Ⓗ
In the Guide for 20 years, this 16th-century inn situated in the hills above Old Colwyn, next to St Elian's Church, greets you with a warm welcome. Gracing the entrance are two stone white lions, leading into the bar area with its slate-flagged flooring and large comfortable chairs around the log fires. Decorative stained glass is mounted above the bar in the tiny snug. A spacious restaurant serves delicious home-cooked food, with a wide menu choice. Jazz night is Tuesday, quiz night Thursday. 🏠Q❄️🌟◀️🍴♣P🍃

Llanrwst

Pen-y-Bryn 🅛
Ancaster Square, LL26 0LH SH798617
🕐 4.30-11; 12-midnight Sun ☎ (01492) 640678
Beer range varies Ⓗ
Traditional stone-built pub much favoured by locals, with a hospitable landlord and friendly regulars offering a warm welcome. A long bar serves a large, comfortable open-plan lounge area with an original inglenook fireplace. This is a great community pub with a games room at the rear for

pool and darts. Traditional pub games are featured and there is a TV for sporting events. Tuesday is poker night. Beers are mainly from the local Nant Brewery, with Mwnci Nell always a favourite. ❄️🌟◀️🍴◀️🍺♣🍃

Maentwrog

Grapes Hotel
LL41 4HN (on A496 near A487 jct)
🕐 12-late ☎ (01766) 590365 🌐 grapes-hotel.co.uk
Evan Evans Cwrw, Best, Warrior, seasonal beers Ⓗ
A former coaching inn, this hotel dates back to the 17th century and overlooks the Vale of Ffestiniog. The interior comprises a lounge, public bar, veranda and large dining room. All the beers are from the local Evan Evans Brewery in Llandeilo, including the full seasonal range. Good value food is popular, especially the ribs. The railway station nearby is on the Ffestiniog line. 🏠Q❄️🍴◀️🍴❖▶️◀️🍺♣P🍃

Menai Bridge

Tafarn y Bont (Bridge Inn)
Telford Road, LL59 5DT
🕐 11-midnight; 12-10.30 Sun ☎ (01248) 716888
Banks's Bitter; Marston's Pedigree; guest beers Ⓗ
Mid-19th-century former shop and tea rooms, close to the famous bridge, now a brasserie-style pub with an excellent restaurant. A beamed interior, log fires and numerous hideaway rooms give the pub an old-fashioned feel. Snowdonia is a short drive away and the Anglesey Coastal Path is close. Local CAMRA Pub of the Season winter 2009. 🏠❄️🌟◀️🍴🍃

Victoria Hotel
Telford Bridge, LL59 5DR (between bridge and town centre)
🕐 11-11; 12-10.30 Sun ☎ (01248) 712309
Draught Bass; guest beers Ⓗ
Situated 300 metres from the Menai Suspension Bridge, this 19-room hotel overlooks the Straits and affords delightful views from the garden and patio. It is licensed for weddings and has a spacious function room with wide-screen HD TV for sport. Live music is a regular added attraction. There is easy access to Snowdonia and the hotel is near the Anglesey Coastal Path. ❄️🌟🍴◀️🍴❖P🍃

Old Colwyn

Red Lion
385 Abergele Road, LL29 9PL (on main Colwyn Bay to Abergele road) SH868783
🕐 5-11; 4-midnight Fri; 12-midnight Sat; 12-11 Sun
☎ (01492) 515042
Brains Dark; Marston's Burton Bitter; guest beers Ⓗ
This free house serves up to five guest ales from independent and local brewers. A winner of many CAMRA awards, the popular local is a former Branch Pub of the Year. It has a cosy L-shaped lounge featuring a real coal fire, antique brewery mirrors and other memorabilia, and a traditional public bar with a pool table, darts and TVs. To the rear is a superb Victorian-style covered and heated smoking conservatory. The Real Ale Club every Thursday offers nine beers at reduced prices. Guest ciders. 🏠Q❄️🍺♣🍴🍃

Penrhyn Bay

Penrhyn Old Hall

LL30 3EE SH816815

✪ 12-3, 5.30-11; 12-3, 7-10.30 Sun ☎ (01492) 549888

Draught Bass; guest beer Ⓗ

The main Tudor lounge dates back to 1420 and features a wood-panelled bar and a large fireplace concealing a priest hole. Good-value meals are served daily in the restaurant at the rear – Sunday lunches are a speciality. The hall is available for hire for functions and has a skittle alley. The Penrhyn Bay Players stage occasional pub theatre here. ⊛◑ ♠🏠♣P✔

Penrhynside

Cross Keys Ⓛ ✅

Pendre Road, LL30 3DD SH814815

✪ 5-midnight (11 Mon); 3-midnight Fri; 12-midnight Sat & Sun ☎ (01492) 547070 ⊕ crosskeys-inn.co.uk

Facer's Flintshire Bitter; guest beer Ⓗ

Awarded local CAMRA Most Improved Pub of the Year 2010, this family-owned and run 19th-century free house has been tastefully refurbished. It has a cosy front room with a central bar, rear pool room with views and juke-box, and comfortable lounge with a window seat boasting unrivalled views of the surrounding area towards Penrhyn Bay and Rhos-on-Sea. Occasional karaoke and live music nights are highlights. ⊛🏠♠🏠♣

Penrhyn Arms Ⓛ

Pendre Road, LL30 3BY (off B5115) SH814816

✪ 5.30 (4.30 Thu; 4 Fri)-midnight; 12-1am Sat; 12-11 Sun ☎ (07780) 678927 ⊕ penrhynarms.com

Banks's Bitter; Marston's Pedigree; guest beers Ⓗ

This pub is a winner of many awards including local CAMRA Pub of the Year plus regional, Welsh and national cider awards. The welcoming local has up to four guest beers including local ales, Belgian beers and a winter ale on gravity at Christmas. The spacious L-shaped bar has pool, darts and a wide-screen TV. Thursday is cheese night. Accommodation is available in a self-contained flatlet for up to eight people. ⛺⊛🏠♠🏠♣🍺✔

Penysarn

Bedol

LL69 9YR

✪ 12 (2 winter)-11; 12-11 Sat & Sun ☎ (01407) 832590

Robinson's Hartleys XB, Unicorn, seasonal beers Ⓗ

Built in 1985 to serve a small village, regulars now come to The Bedol (Horseshoe) from a much wider area. This Robinson's tied house hosts regular live entertainment and offers good food all day (no food Mon). Anglesey's beautiful beaches and the coastal path are nearby. Ring to check opening times and food availability mid-week in winter. Q⊛◑♠🏠(62)♣P✔

Porthmadog

Ship Inn

14 Lombard Street, LL49 9AP

✪ 12-2.30, 5.30-11 (11.30 Thu-Sat) ☎ (01766) 512990

Beer range varies Ⓗ

Traditional pub set in a picturesque location behind the park in the centre of this harbour town. Friendly and efficient staff dispense frequently changing ales and serve quality food, including pub

favourites steak and ale pie, lasagne and barbecue ribs. The pub has a separate bar and lounge, and a room available for private events, and is popular with locals and tourists. A quiz is hosted on Thursday night. ⛺Q🏠🦴◑🏠≢🏠(1,3,X32)P

Spooner's Bar

Harbour Station, LL49 9NF

✪ 10-11; 12-10.30 Sun ☎ (01766) 516032 ⊕ festrail.co.uk

Beer range varies Ⓗ

An all-year-round mini beer festival – Spooner's has built its reputation on an ever-changing range from small breweries, including the local Purple Moose. Situated in the terminus of the world-famous Ffestiniog Railway, steam trains are outside the door most of the year. Food is served every lunchtime, but out of season only Thursday to Saturday in the evening. Local CAMRA Pub of the Year 2005 and 2007. Q🦴⊛◑♿≢🏠P

Station Inn

LL49 9HT (on mainline station platform)

✪ 11-11 (midnight Thu-Sat); 12-11 Sun ☎ (01766) 512629

Brains The Rev James; Purple Moose Snowdonia; guest beer Ⓗ

Situated on the Cambrian Coast railway platform, this pub is popular with locals and visitors alike. It has a large lounge and smaller public bar, and can get busy at the weekend and on nights when live football is shown on TV. A range of pies and sandwiches is available all day. ⊛🏠♿♠≢🏠♣P

Red Wharf Bay

Ship Inn ✅

LL75 8RJ (off A5025 between Pentraeth and Benllech)

✪ 11-11 (10.30 Sun) ☎ (01248) 852568

⊕ shipinnredwharfbay.co.uk

Adnams Bitter; Brains SA; guest beers Ⓗ

Red Wharf Bay was once a busy port exporting coal and fertilisers in the 18th and 19th centuries. Previously known as the Quay, the Ship enjoys an excellent reputation for its bar and restaurant, with meals served lunchtimes and evenings. It gets busy with locals and visitors in the summer. The garden has panoramic views across the bay to south-east Anglesey. The resort town of Benllech is two miles away and the coastal path passes the front door. Beers can be expensive. CAMRA Pub of the Season summer 2009. ⛺Q🦴⊛◑🏠P✔

Rhos-on-Sea

Colwyn Bay Cricket Club ✅

Penrhyn Avenue, LL28 4LR

✪ 11.30-2, 4.30-11 (midnight Fri); 11.30-midnight Sat; 12-3, 7-11 (12-11 summer) Sun ☎ (01492) 544103

⊕ colwynbaycricketclub.co.uk

Tetley Dark Mild, Bitter; guest beers Ⓗ

A frequent local CAMRA Club of the Year winner, this comfortably furnished venue features wide-screen TVs showing sporting events, usually cricket. The games room has two full size snooker tables. Several function rooms are for hire. Good value snacks are available. Glamorgan County Cricket Club play at least one of their home matches here. An annual beer festival is held over the spring bank holiday weekend. ◑🏠P

Toad

West Promenade, LL28 4BU SH847795

✪ 11-11.30 (10.30 Sun) ☎ (01492) 532726

Jennings Cumberland Ale; guest beers H
Attractively furnished traditional inn on the Colwyn Bay promenade with stunning sea views from the pub and front beer garden. A winner of many awards for food including local CAMRA Pub Food of the Year in 2009, it serves modern British cuisine freshly prepared with quality local produce, and excellent value Sunday lunches. The downstairs pool room is enjoyed by people of all ages. Professional, friendly and approachable staff offer a warm welcome to locals and visitors. ❀◖◗➡♣P⅃

Rhoscolyn

White Eagle

LL65 2NJ (off B4545 signed Traeth Beach) SH271755
✿ 12-3, 6-11; 12-11 Sat; 12-10.30 Sun ☎ (01407) 860267
🌐 white-eagle.co.uk

Marston's Burton Bitter, Pedigree; Weetwood Eastgate Ale; guest beers H
Saved from closure by new owners, this pub has been renovated and rebuilt with an airy, brasserie-style atmosphere. It has a fine patio enjoying superb views over Caernarfon Bay and the Lleyn Peninsula to Bardsey Island. The nearby beach offers safe swimming with a warden on duty in the summer months. The pub is also close to the coastal footpath. Excellent food is available lunchtimes and evenings, all day during the school holidays. ▲Q❀◖◗➡♿ÅP

Rhydlydan

Giler Arms

LL24 0LL SH892508
✿ 12-3 (not Mon-Thu), 6 (7 winter)-11
☎ (01690) 770612 01690 🌐 giler.co.uk/
Bathams Mild Ale, Best Bitter, XXX H
Friendly country hotel in six acres of grounds including a one acre fishing lake, camping and touring caravan site with recently refurbished facilities, and picturesque gardens beside the small River Merddwr. It offers a welcoming, comfortable lounge, a separate public bar popular with locals, and a small pool room. The restaurant has lovely views over the lake. Quiz night is the middle Wednesday of the month. B&B accommodation is in seven bedrooms and children and dogs are welcome. ▲Q➾❀❀◖◗♿Å➡♣P⅃

St George

Kinmel Arms

LL22 9BP SH974758
✿ closed Sun & Mon; 12-3, 6-11 (11.30 Fri & Sat)
☎ (01745) 832207 🌐 thekinmelarms.co.uk
Thwaites Original; guest beers H
A local CAMRA Pub of the Year winner, this former 17th-century coaching inn is set on the hillside overlooking the sea. A central bar serves a large combined dining and drinking area with a real log fire in one corner and a spacious conservatory at the rear. Two guest beers come from independent breweries, plus a Welsh cider or perry and a selection of Belgian and continental beers. The pub has a reputation for good food. Luxury accommodation is available in four comfortable suites. ▲Q❀◖◗♿➡●P⅃

Tremadog

Golden Fleece

Market Square, LL49 9RB (on A487)
✿ 11.30-3, 6-11; 12.30-3, 6-10.30 Sun ☎ (01766) 512421
🌐 goldenfleeceinn.com

Draught Bass; Purple Moose Glaslyn Ale; guest beer H
Situated in the old market square, this former coaching inn is now a friendly local. The pub has a lounge bar, snug and a covered area outside with decking and bench seats. Bar meals are good value and there is a bistro upstairs (booking advisable). Guest beers come from small breweries. Live acoustic music plays on Tuesday night.
▲Q➾❀❀◖◗♿ÅⒽ

Trofarth

Holland Arms 🅛

Llanrwst Road, LL22 8BG SH840708
✿ 12-3 (not Thu), 7 (6 Fri & Sat)-11; closed Wed; 12-10.30 Sun ☎ (01492) 650777 🌐 thehollandarms.co.uk
Beer range varies H
Family-run pub with a warm welcome for locals and visitors alike, the 18th-century coaching house is set in a country landscape within sight of Snowdonia. Recently tastefully refurbished in keeping with its origins, it has a pleasantly furnished bar, lounge and restaurant areas. Excellent good-value meals are available lunchtimes and evenings. A big supporter of LocAle, it features beers from Conwy, Great Orme, Purple Moose and Nant. Local CAMRA awards include Most Improved Pub 2009, LocAle 2010 and Food Pub 2011. ▲Q❀◖◗♣P

Tudweiliog

Lion Hotel

LL53 8ND (on B4417)
✿ 11-11 (12-2, 6-11 winter); 11.30-11 Sat; 11-10.30 (12-3 winter) Sun ☎ (01758) 770244
Beer range varies H
The origins of this free house go back more than 300 years. A village inn set on the glorious, quiet north coast of the Lleyn Peninsula, cliffs and beaches are a mile away by footpath, a little further by road. Up to three beers are served depending on the season, with Purple Moose a firm favourite. The pub is accessible by number 8 bus from Pwllheli during the day only. Closed Monday lunchtimes in winter. Q➾❀❀◖◗♿➡P

Waunfawr

Snowdonia Park 🅛

Beddgelert Road, LL55 4AQ
✿ 11-11 (10.30 Sun) ☎ (01286) 650409
🌐 snowdonia-park.co.uk
Beer range varies H
Home of the Snowdonia Brewery, this is a popular pub for walkers, climbers and families, with children's play areas inside and outside. Meals are served all day. The pub adjoins Waunfawr station on the Welsh Highland Railway – stop off here before continuing on one of the most scenic sections of narrow gauge railway in Britain (you can watch the trains while enjoying your drink in the beer garden). There is a large campsite by the pub on the riverside. Q➾❀❀◖◗♿Å⇌➡♣P

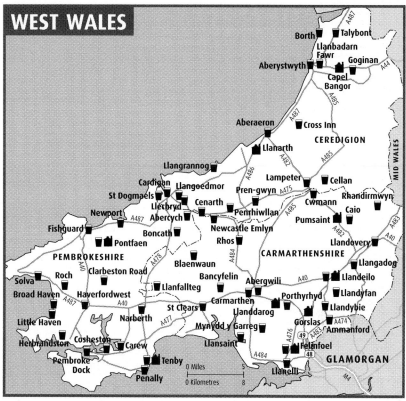

WEST WALES

Borth · Talybont
Llanbadarn Fawr
Aberystwyth · Goginan
Capel Bangor
Aberaeron · Cross Inn
CEREDIGION
Llanarth
Llangrannog · Lampeter · Cellan
Cardigan · Llangoedmor · Pren-gwyn · Rhandirmwyn
St Dogmaels · Cenarth · Cwmann · Caio
Newport · Abercych · Penrhiwllan · Pumsaint
Fishguard · Boncath · Newcastle Emlyn
Pontfaen · Rhos · Llandovery
PEMBROKESHIRE · Blaenwaun · CARMARTHENSHIRE · Llangadog
Roch · Clarbeston Road · Bancyfelin · Abergwili · Llandeilo
Solva · Llanfallteg · Llandyfan
Broad Haven · Haverfordwest · Carmarthen · Porthyrhyd · Llandybie
Little Haven · St Clears · Llanddarog
Narberth · Mynydd y Garreg · Gorslas · Ammanford
Herbrandston · Cosheston · Llansaint · Felinfoel
Pembroke Dock · Carew · Llanelli · GLAMORGAN
Tenby
Penally
0 Miles 5
0 Kilometres 8

Authority areas covered: Carmarthenshire UA, Ceredigion UA, Pembrokeshire UA

Aberaeron

Harbourmaster

2 Quay Parade, SA46 0BT (off A487, overlooking harbour)
☼ 8am-11.30 ☎ (01545) 570755 ⊕ harbour-master.com
Purple Moose HM Best, Glaslyn; guest beer Ⓗ
Light, comfortable and expertly renovated bar and restaurant overlooking Aberaeron harbour. Welsh culture is celebrated, staff are bilingual, paintings by Welsh artists adorn the walls and award-winning food is locally sourced. The guest beer, available Easter to October, comes from a Welsh brewery. While the bar is usually free of electronic entertainment, an exception is made for rugby internationals on TV. In the summer, pints can be enjoyed outside overlooking the water.
Q❀⇌❍&⚲☒(X40,X50,550)P⁓

Abercych

Nag's Head

SA37 0HJ (on B4332 between Cenarth and Eglwyswrw)
☼ 11-3 (not Mon), 6-11; 12-10.30 Sun ☎ (01239) 841200
Beer range varies Ⓗ
This well-restored old smithy boasts a beamed bar and riverside garden. The bar area is furnished with collections of old medical instruments, railway memorabilia, beer bottles and timepieces showing the time in various parts of the world. House beer Old Emrys is brewed for the pub. Abercych is a hamlet in the beautiful Cych valley, which features in the medieval Welsh tales of the Mabinogion.
⌂⅍❀❍&P⁓

Abergwili

Black Ox

High Street, SA31 2JB
☼ 12-midnight ☎ (01267) 231257
Marston's Pedigree; Ringwood Fortyniner; guest beers Ⓗ
Friendly village local a couple of miles from the county town of Carmarthen. It has an open plan bar, a separate dining room serving good value food, and a small covered beer garden to the rear. Live music plays on alternate Saturdays and occasional quiz and bingo evenings are hosted. The Carmarthenshire County Museum in the former Bishops Palace is close by. ❀❍&☒♣P⁓

Aberystwyth

Glengower Hotel ✓

3 Victoria Terrace, SY23 2DH
☼ 12-11 ☎ (01970) 626191 ⊕ glengower.co.uk

WALES
MID WALES

Purple Moose Cwrw Glaslyn; guest beer ⊞
Popular with students but welcoming to all, this seafront hotel sits towards the north end of Aberystwyth's promenade. Large windows provide plenty of natural lighting for the spacious and airy front bar, which overlooks Cardigan Bay with its famous sunsets. Outside seating on decking at the front is popular in warm weather. Pool and televised sport hold sway to the rear. The guest beer is usually from a micro-brewery in Wales or the borders. Bar meals finish at 6pm on Sunday. ⊛⇔⊄❿≠☷(2)⌐

Ship & Castle ☸
1 High Street, SY23 1JG
⊛ 2-midnight (1am Fri & Sat) ☎ (07773) 778785
⊕ shipandcastle.co.uk
Wye Valley HPA; guest beers ⊞
Following successful refurbishment in 2009, this established mecca for the area's real ale drinkers continues to improve – a recent innovation being the 'five pump platter' tasting tray. Five ever-changing guest beers are drawn largely but not exclusively from micro-breweries in Wales and the borders, while cider and perry are from Welsh award-winner Gwynt y Ddraig. There are beer festivals in spring and autumn, and occasional quiz nights, often run by the local CAMRA branch. Local CAMRA Pub of the Year in 2010 (and regional winner for South and Mid Wales) and 2011. ⚒≠☷♣♠

Ammanford

Ammanford Hotel
Wernolau House, 31 Pontamman Road, SA18 2HX
⊛ 5.30 (1 Sat)-11; 12-10.30 Sun ☎ (01269) 592598
Beer range varies ⊞
Originally a colliery manager's house, this pleasant hotel stands on the outskirts of the town, set in two acres of landscaped grounds and woodland. It is renowned not only for the choice and quality of its beer but also for the warm welcome. Log fires burn in winter and there is a large function room catering for weddings and private events. ⚒Q⊛⇔❿☷P

Bancyfelin

Fox & Hounds
SA33 5ND (just off A40)
⊛ 11-midnight summer; 11-3, 5.30-midnight winter
☎ (01267) 211341 ⊕ foxandhounds-bancyfelin.co.uk
Beer range varies ⊞
Situated in the heart of the village, this is a pub with a real Welsh welcome. Lunches and evening meals are served in the lounge/dining area and there is a separate locals' bar with a pool table, juke-box and games machines for those who prefer a more traditional bar atmosphere. Two guest beers are usually offered from a mix of small and larger breweries. Q☷⊛❿⊞☷☷♣P

Blaenwaun

Lamb Inn
SA34 0JD SN236271
⊛ 4.30-midnight ☎ (01994) 448899
Beer range varies ⊞
Friendly and comfortable pub with a welcoming landlord and a good selection of well-kept real ales. Three beers and a cider are available during

the winter months, four or more ales and two ciders during the summer. Guest beers change frequently. The pub has an olde-worlde look with drop beams and an open fire, and wonderful panoramic views. Entertainment includes TV, pool, darts and occasional quiz nights. ⚒⊛❿☷♠☷☷♠⌐

Boncath

Boncath Inn
SA37 0JN (on B4332 between Cenarth and Eglwyswrw)
⊛ 11-11; 12-8.30 Sun ☎ (01239) 841241
Worthington's Bitter; guest beers ⊞
Pembrokeshire CAMRA Pub of the Year 2006 and 2007, this pub dates back to the 18th century and is the centre of life in this attractive village, which developed as a result of the opening of the now long-closed Whitland-Cardigan railway. The interior is divided into several seating areas creating an intimate atmosphere, and the walls display items of local historic interest. The home-cooked meals are recommended. A beer festival is held each August bank holiday weekend. ⚒⊛❿☷♠☷(430)♣P⌐

Borth

Victoria Inn ✔
High Street, SY24 5HZ
⊛ 5-11; 12-midnight Sat & summer; closed Mon winter; 12-10 (midnight summer) Sun ☎ (01970) 871919
Black Sheep Best Bitter; guest beer ⊞
The only pub on the sea side of the street, the Victoria makes good use of its location with a sun terrace and patio overlooking Borth's famous strand. Inside, the refurbished split-level room retains separate drinking areas. One guest beer is served in winter, three in summer, and there are occasional beer festivals. Members of the Hard Peg Club pay £1 to charity and get 30p off a pint of real ale. Though Sky Sports is shown, this is not a sport-dominated pub. The bus from Aberystwyth stops outside, but rail is best evenings and Sundays. ⊛❿☷♠≠☷(4,512)♣⌐

Broad Haven

Galleon
35A Enfield Road, SA63 3JW (on seafront)
⊛ 10-midnight (1am Fri & Sat) ☎ (01437) 781152
Brains Bitter, SA, The Rev James; guest beer ⊞
The Galleon's hospitable and welcoming landlady helps to bring a cosy atmosphere to this friendly pub with splendid views over St Brides Bay. Converted from a tea room in the 1980s, the pub has now become a widely appreciated feature of the Havens community. With a delightful sandy beach, Broad Haven remains popular as a holiday resort for day trips and longer stays. ⚒Q☷⊛❿☷♠☷(311)♣♠⌐☷

Caio

Brunant Arms
SA19 8RD (off A482 near Pumsaint)
⊛ 11-11 (1am Fri & Sat) ☎ (01558) 650483
Beer range varies ⊞
Family-run pub in the centre of the village near the Dolaucothi Gold Mines. Good food is served until 9pm every day. Plenty of outdoor pursuits nearby include pony trekking and there is a horse tethering rail provided at the pub. A legendary

Welsh wizard is buried in the church opposite. One real ale is offered in winter, two in summer.
ⓂⓈ🌃🍴◑🅰♣🏠

Cardigan

Black Lion

High Street, SA43 1HJ (E side of main street)
🌑 10am-midnight ☎ (01239) 612532
Brains The Rev James; Fuller's London Pride; Worthington's Bitter Ⓗ
This large Victorian hotel in the centre of a popular west Wales town serves three ales and good food. Three separate rooms offer different surroundings, with real fires during colder months. There is occasional live music in an upstairs function room but generally this is a quiet pub during the week, livelier at weekends. Ⓜ🛏🌃🍴◑🔑🚃🏠

Grosvenor

Bridge Street, SA43 1HY
🌑 11 (12 Sun)-11 ☎ (01239) 613792
Worthington's Bitter; Greene King Abbot; guest beer Ⓗ
Situated on the edge of the town centre next to Cardigan Castle and the River Teifi, this large pub provides a good choice of ales, including a selection of bottled beers. The large open-plan bar/lounge provides various areas to relax, eat and drink, and there is an extra room upstairs for dining or functions. Good value food is served lunchtimes and evenings every day. 🌃◑🔥♿🚃🏠

Carew

Carew Inn

SA70 8SL (off A477 before Pembroke Dock)
🌑 11-11 (11.30 Sun) ☎ (01646) 651267 ⊕ carewinn.co.uk
Brains The Rev James; Evan Evans Cwrw Ⓗ
Situated close to Carew's historic Celtic Cross, castle and tidal mill, this former estate pub of the Trollope-Bellew family makes an ideal stop-off with its village location and many local attractions. A pine-boarded bar features photographs of the local area from the past. Outside there is a marquee and a large grassed garden with a children's play area. Ⓜ🌃◑🅰🚃(361)Ⓟ🏠

Carmarthen

Hen Dderwen ✓

47-48 King Street, SA31 1BH
🌑 9-midnight (11 Sun) ☎ (01267) 242050
Greene King Ruddles Best Bitter, Abbot; guest beers Ⓗ
This Wetherspoon pub opened in 2000 and is named after the Carmarthen legend of Merlin and the Old Oak – the story is told in pictures and plaques on the walls. The interior is divided into two distinct spaces – the principal drinking area is at the front while the area to the rear tends to be mainly used by diners. A good selection of real ales is offered. Food is served all day including the chain's standard meal deals. ◑🍴🚃♣🏠

Friends Arms 🍷

Old St Clears Road, Johnstown, SA31 3HH
🌑 12-11 (midnight Fri); 11-midnight Sat; 11-11 Sun
☎ (01267) 234073
Beer range varies Ⓗ
Excellent local hostelry within half a mile of Carmarthen town centre, with a cosy and friendly atmosphere and a warm welcome, enhanced by two open fires. Popular with sports fans, it has Sky Sports and ESPN on two screens, plus pool and darts. A quiz is held on the the first and third Tuesday of the month and bingo on the second and fourth Tuesday. Two real ales are usually offered; happy hour is 5-6pm Monday to Friday. Local CAMRA Branch Pub of the Year 2011, with its own micro-brewery underway. ⓂQ🌃🚃🏠

Queen's Hotel

Queen Street, SA31 1JR
🌑 11-11 ☎ (01267) 231800
Beer range varies Ⓗ
Town-centre pub near Carmarthenshire county hall with a bar, lounge and small function room. The public bar is used by locals and has TV for sporting events. Local beers are usually on sale. The patio nestles beneath the castle walls and is a sun-trap during the summer months. Upstairs function rooms are available, and the local CAMRA branch meets here. 🌃♿🚃🏠

Cellan

Fishers Arms

SA48 8HU (on B4343)
🌑 4.30 (12 Sat & Sun)-11 ☎ (01570) 422895
Beer range varies Ⓗ
Situated close to the River Teifi, one of Wales' premier trout and salmon rivers, the pub dates from 1580 and was first licensed in 1891. The main bar has a log-burner and flagstone floor. The guest beer changes weekly and is usually from a Welsh micro-brewery. Meals are available 6.30-8.45pm on Thursday, Friday and Saturday. Live music plays every Sunday afternoon. The pub is served by buses from Lampeter and Aberystwyth until early evening (not Sun). ⓂQ🌃◑♿🅰🚃(585)♣P

Cenarth

Three Horse Shoes

SA38 9JL
🌑 11 (12 winter)-11 ☎ (01239) 710119
Evan Evans Best Bitter Ⓗ
A gem of an inn in a popular tourist village in west Wales. The interior has been modified in recent years but retains an abundance of original features including an inglenook fireplace that is big enough to sit in and huge, exposed beams. The pub can be touristy in high season but retains a local atmosphere. Good food is available lunchtimes and evenings. Ⓜ🌃◑🅰🚃(460)Ⓟ🏠

Clarbeston Road

Cross Inn ✓

SA63 4UL SN019211
🌑 12-midnight (1am Fri & Sat) ☎ (01437) 731506
Courage Directors; Worthington's Bitter; guest beer Ⓗ
Multi-roomed village inn, well worth seeking out, with stone and wood floors and original oak beams in abundance. The large bar area housing pool, TV (for sport) and juke-box is complemented by two small snugs and a restaurant where reasonably-priced home-cooked food is served. Outside there are more spacious drinking areas. A beer festival is held in the summer. The village of Clarbeston Road grew up around the junction of the railways to Fishguard Harbour and Milford Haven (both still open). Ⓜ🌃◑♿🚃(313)♣P🏠

ABERDEEN & GRAMPIAN

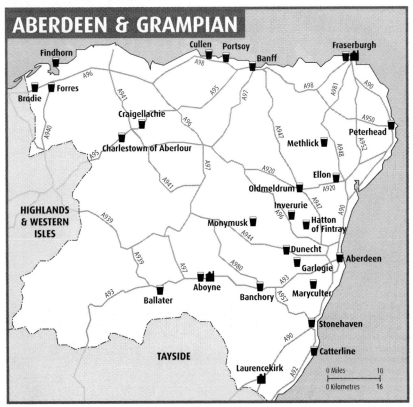

Authority areas covered: Aberdeenshire UA, City of Aberdeen UA, Moray UA

Aberdeen

Aitchies Ale House
10 Trinity Street, AB11 5LY
☼ 8am-10 (11 Fri & Sat); closed Sun ☎ (01224) 581459
Orkney Dark Island Ⓗ
This small corner bar is the closest real ale outlet to the city rail/bus stations and the Union Square shopping complex. Renovated in 1994, it retains the flavour of an old-fashioned Scottish pub. Bar food is best described as traditional Scottish pub grub, including roast beef stovies. A good selection of whiskies includes Bell's special edition decanters. The friendly service here is second to none. ♿⇌🖾♣

Archibald Simpson ✪
5 Castle Street, AB11 5BQ (corner of Union St & King St)
☼ 8am-midnight (1am Fri & Sat); 10am-11 Sun
☎ (01224) 621365
Greene King Abbot; guest beers Ⓗ
This Wetherspoon is in one of many monumental granite buildings in central Aberdeen designed by local architect Archibald Simpson. The former local headquarters of Clydesdale Bank, it retains many original architectural features. The main room is the high-ceilinged central hall, and there are additional seating areas to the side. The long bar features 12 handpumps offering a variety of beers, frequently from the local Deeside Brewery, with house ales supplied by Skye and Houston. Local CAMRA Pub of the Year 2009. Free WiFi.
🛏🌐♿⇌🖾♣

Brentwood Hotel
101 Crown Street, AB11 6HH
☼ 11-2.30 (not Sat), 4.30-midnight; 6-11 Sun
☎ (01224) 595440 ⊕ brentwood-hotel.co.uk
Beer range varies Ⓗ
This mirrored cellar bar (formerly known as Carriages) in the basement of a modernised hotel has lots of comfortable couches and seating areas. A winner of numerous local CAMRA awards, it offers 10 changing beers, usually a mix of national brands and Scottish micro-brews. Lunches are available in the bar, and the adjoining restaurant serves good food in the evening. Railway and bus stations are easily reached by descending the stairs from nearby Crown Terrace to Bridge Street. Free WiFi. 🛏🍴⇌🖾🅿♿

Grill ★
213 Union Street, AB11 6BA
☼ 10-midnight (1am Fri & Sat); 12.30-midnight Sun
☎ (01224) 573530 ⊕ thegrillaberdeen.co.uk
Caledonian 80; Deeside Talorcan; Harviestoun Bitter & Twisted; Shepherd Neame Spitfire; guest beer Ⓗ
With an exquisite interior redesigned in 1926 and remaining largely unchanged since, this is the only pub listed in CAMRA's National Inventory of Historic Pub Interiors in the area. For men only until 1975,

ladies toilets were eventually provided in 1998. Situated across from the Music Hall, musicians often visit during concert breaks. The pub has a large selection of whiskies and has won numerous awards from lovers of the malt. Bar snacks are available. &⬥≠🚃

Moorings

2 Trinity Quay, AB11 5AA (opp quayside near Market St)
✪ 12-midnight; 1-3am Fri & Sat; 1-midnight Sun
☎ (01224) 587602
Inveralmond Moorings Ale; guest beers Ⓗ
This historic harbourside bar changes character from laid-back local to raucous rock bar on weekend evenings, when there may be a cover charge. The eclectic juke-box is in regular use by the varied clientele. Sword dancers and a classical quartet have both been spotted. Local CAMRA City Pub of the Year winner 2008, 2010 and 2011. A discount is offered to CAMRA members. ≠🚃💀🍴

Old Blackfriars ●

52 Castle Street, AB11 5BB
✪ 11-midnight (1am Fri & Sat) ☎ (01224) 581922
⊕ old-blackfriars.co.uk
Caledonian Deuchars IPA; Greene King Abbot; Inveralmond Ossian Ale; guest beers Ⓗ
Located on the Castlegate in the historic centre of the city, this Belhaven pub is on two levels, with bars on both, and offers up to six guest beers, many from Scottish micros the obligatory ones from the Greene King range. Unobtrusive background music plays and there is no TV. The pub has a reputation for good pub food served daily until 9.30pm. Quiz night is every Tuesday and occasional themed beer festivals are hosted. ◗&≠🚃

Prince of Wales ●

7 St Nicholas Lane, AB10 1HF (opp Marks & Spencer)
✪ 10-midnight (1am Fri & Sat); 11-midnight Sun
☎ (01224) 640597
Caledonian 80; Inveralmond Prince of Wales; guest beers Ⓗ
One of the oldest bars in Aberdeen, the Prince of Wales has possibly the longest bar counter in the city, a friendly atmosphere and a large following of regulars. It is also blessed with the total absence of television. A regular winner of CAMRA City Pub of the Year, it is listed in Scotland's True Heritage Pubs and offers a varied selection of Scottish and English ales and a house beer. Folk music plays on Sunday evening and a quiz is hosted on Monday. Good value food is served daily. Q◗≠🚃

St Machar Bar

97 High Street, Old Aberdeen, AB24 3EN
✪ 12-11 (7 Sun) ☎ (01224) 483079 ⊕ themachar.com
Caledonian Deuchars IPA; Inveralmond Ossian Ale; guest beers Ⓗ
Located in the photogenic and historic Old Aberdeen conservation area amid the university buildings and close to Kings College, the long bar is frequented by academia and locals alike. Up to three guest beers are normally from Scottish micro-breweries – the range may be reduced out of term time. The back gantry shelves hold a comprehensive selection of whiskies. A splendid mirror from the long-gone local Thomson Marshall Aulton Brewery adorns the wall just inside the front door. CAMRA members receive a discount. Open till midnight during university term.
&🚃(20)🍴

Under the Hammer

11 North Silver Street, AB10 1RJ (off Golden Square)
✪ 5 (4 Fri)-midnight (1am Thu & Fri); 2-1am Sat; 6-11 Sun
☎ (01224) 640253
Caledonian Deuchars IPA; Inveralmond Ossians Ale; guest beer Ⓗ
Located in a quiet side street near Golden Square just off Union Street, this regular Guide entry is located in a basement next to an auction house – hence the name. Works by local artists displayed on the walls are for sale if they take your fancy. Convenient for the Music Hall and His Majesty's Theatre, the large noticeboard has posters advertising forthcoming events in town. Guest beers tend to contrast in style from the two regulars, with local Deeside beers frequent favourites. Pleasant background music plays. ≠🚃

Aboyne

Boat Inn

Charleston Road, AB34 5EL (N bank of River Dee next to Aboyne Bridge)
✪ 11-11 (midnight Fri & Sat) ☎ (01339) 886137
⊕ theboatinnaboyne.co.uk
Beer range varies Ⓗ
Popular riverside inn with a food-oriented lounge featuring a log-burning stove and spiral staircase leading to the upper dining area. Junior diners (and adults) may request to see the model train, complete with sound effects, traverse the entire pub at picture-rail height upon completion of their meal. Three ales are served, mainly from Deeside, Cairngorm and Inveralmond breweries, with an occasional Isle of Skye brew. The local Rotary Club meets here. Self-catering accommodation is available, one room with facilities for the disabled.
🛏️🏵️🍴◗🍽️&🧍♣P

Ballater

Alexandra Hotel

12 Bridge Square, AB35 5QJ (E of village on A93, adjacent to Dee bridge)
✪ 11-2.30, 5-midnight; 11-midnight Fri-Sun
☎ (013339) 755376 ⊕ alexandrahotelballater.com
Beer range varies Ⓗ
Originally built as a private home in 1800 and becoming the Alexandra Hotel in 1915, this smart and recently refurbished lounge bar is popular with locals for bar suppers. Two ales are normally from Cairngorm and Inveralmond, with Deeside a possible third in summer, alternating with an occasional English ale. Handy for a stop off on your way to Braemar for the Highland Games or for a visit with the royals at Balmoral. 🏵️🛏️◗&🧍♣⌐

Banchory

Douglas Arms Hotel

22 High Street, AB31 5SR
✪ 11-midnight (1am Fri & Sat); 11-11 Sun
☎ (01330) 822547 ⊕ douglasarms.co.uk
Caledonian Deuchars IPA; guest beers Ⓗ
The public bar of this small hotel is a classic Scottish long bar with etched windows and vintage mirrors – one of Scotland's Real Heritage Pubs. The separate lounge area is in three parts, divided by former external and internal walls and fireplace, and is primarily used for bar suppers. Outside there is a large south-facing terrace, ideal for summer drinking. All bar areas feature plasma TV systems

where different sports can be watched. Two guest ales, usually one from Deeside, supplement the regular beer. ⚏🍽🏨❄🍺◑⚅🔥🅿🚶(201,202)♣

Ravenswood Club (Royal British Legion)

25 Ramsay Road, AB31 5TS (N of main A93)
❂ 11-11 (midnight Fri & Sat) ☎ (01330) 822347
⊕ banchorylegion.com
Beer range varies Ⓗ
Large British Legion Club with a comfortable lounge adjoining a pool and TV room, and a spacious function room used by local clubs and societies as well as members. Darts and snooker are popular and played most evenings. The two handpumps offer excellent value and the beer choice is constantly changing, with ales consistently the best quality in the village. An elevated terrace has fine views of the Deeside hills. Show your CAMRA membership card or a copy of this Guide for entry.
🍽◑⚅🔥🅿

Banff

Ship Inn

8 Deveronside, AB45 1HP (at mouth of Deveron, close to harbour)
❂ 12-midnight (1am Fri & Sat) ☎ (01261) 812620
⊕ theshipbanff.co.uk
Greene King Old Speckled Hen; guest beer Ⓗ
The interior of this historic nautical-themed inn featured in the film Local Hero. It has a wood-panelled bar and lounge with sea views through the small windows. A blocked carriage arch hints at the earlier history of the building. Banff Marina, Duff House Gallery (National Gallery of Scotland) and the Macduff Aquarium are close by, as are several golf courses. The pub has a fine view across the mouth of the Deveron to Macduff. Bar snacks are served all day. Karaoke and live music feature at weekends. WiFi available. ⚏◑⚅🔥🚶(305)♣

Brodie

Old Mill Inn

IV36 2TD (on main A96 between Forres and Nairn)
❂ 11.30-11 ☎ (01309) 641605 ⊕ oldmillinnbrodie.com
Beer range varies Ⓗ
This gem is a spacious, family-friendly pub-restaurant with a cosy fireside area, smart restaurant, function room and a charming conservatory with views of the old watermill and garden. Up to five ales are on handpump, mainly from Scottish micros. Light lunches, cream teas and traditional Scottish high teas are served, plus a full restaurant menu with steak on Monday, fish on Friday and roasts on Sunday. Live Scottish/Irish instrumental music plays on Sunday evening. Brodie Castle is nearby and the popular shopping destination Brodie Country Fare is opposite.
⚏Q🍽❄🍽◑⚅🔥🚶(10,11,305)🅿

Catterline

Creel Inn

AB39 2UL (on coast off A92, 5 miles S of Stonehaven)
NO868782
❂ 12-3, 6-midnight (1am Fri); 12-1am Saturday; 12-midnight Sun ☎ (01569) 750254 ⊕ thecreelinn.co.uk
Beer range varies Ⓗ
This small pub in a scenic clifftop location has been successfully extended to incorporate a restaurant in

an adjacent row of fishermen's cottages. A walk round the back to enjoy the view from the cliff top is strongly recommended. The pub is primarily a food venue but the bar area remains dedicated to drinking and serves as the village local. Up to four beers, usually from Scottish micros, and over 100 bottled beers from around the world are on offer. Crawton Bird Sanctuary, Todhead Lighthouse and Kinneff Old Church are all nearby. ⚏Q❄◑♣🅿

Charleston of Aberlour

Mash Tun

8 Broomfield Square, AB38 9QP (follow sign for Speyside Way Visitor Centre)
❂ 12-12.30am (1am Fri & Sat); 12.30-12.30am Sun
☎ (01340) 881771 ⊕ mashtun-aberlour.com
Beer range varies Ⓗ
Built in 1896 as the Station Bar, a pledge in the title deeds allowed a name change if the railway closed – but it must revert to the Station Bar if a train ever pulls up again outside. Patrons may now drink their ale on the former station platform and enjoy the view of the old railway line running past the door, now the Speyside Way. At least one beer comes from Cairngorm, with another local Scottish ale added in summer. The bar also offers more than 100 varieties of malt whisky.
Q🍽❄🍽◑⚅🔥(336)🅿🚶

Craigellachie

Highlander Inn

10 Victoria Street, AB38 9SR (on A95)
❂ 12-11 (12.30am Fri & Sat) ☎ (01340) 881446
⊕ whiskyinn.com
Cairngorm Trade Winds; guest beers Ⓗ
Picturesque whisky and cask ale bar on Speyside's Whisky Trail, close to the Speyside Way. It offers a fine selection of malt whiskies and good value tasting sessions, alongside a selection of ales from three handpumps (two in winter). CRAC (Craigellachie Real Ale Club) meets on the first Wednesday of the month, and its members, whose etched glass tankards hang above the bar, help to choose the pub's guest ales with the support of the owners and staff. The area is good for fishing and walking. Q❄🍽◑⚅🔥(336)♣🅿🚶

Cullen

Three Kings

17-21 North Castle Street, AB56 4SA
❂ 12-2, 5-11 (12.30am Thu-Sat) ☎ (01542) 840031
Beer range varies Ⓗ
Small, family-run pub converted 40 years ago from 150-year-old railway workers' cottages. A low-beamed roof and real fire help to create a cosy atmosphere on colder days. There is a separate restaurant to the rear and a large outdoor drinking area complete with petanque courts. Beers tend to be from Scottish micros including Deeside, Cairngorm and Orkney. ⚏❄🍽◑⚅🔥(305)♣

Dunecht

Jaffs

AB32 7AW (on A944 at B977 jct)
❂ 12-2, 4.30-11 (midnight Fri & Sat); 12.30-11 Sun
☎ (01330) 860808 ⊕ jaffsbarandrestaurant.co.uk
Inveralmond Ossian Ale; Taylor Landlord; guest beer Ⓗ

Attractive multi-level bar and restaurant created from a range of former farm buildings in this picturesque village. Relaxed and informal, the pub is a popular venue for locals and extends a friendly welcome to all visitors. Quiz night is the last Sunday of the month. An occasional guest beer may replace one of the regulars, usually from Inveralmond. 🕭🍴🚲(X15,215)♣P⏴

Ellon

Station Hotel

Station Brae, AB41 9BD (½ mile W of village centre)
🕭 11-11 (1am Fri; midnight Sat) ☎ (01358) 720209
⊕ stationhotelellon.co.uk
Beer range varies Ⓗ
This imposing family-owned hotel, dating from 1891, is situated half a mile west of Ellon town centre and close to the Formartine and Buchan Way, a long-distance footpath popular with walkers and cyclists. The large public bar offers one regularly changing beer, usually from a well-known national brewery. There is a separate restaurant, function facilities and accommodation in 16 rooms. 🍴🕭🔌♿P⏴

Tolbooth

21-23 Station Road, AB41 9AE
🕭 12-11 (midnight Thu; 12.30am Fri & Sat); 12.30-11 Sun
☎ (01358) 721308
Greene King Abbot; guest beers Ⓗ
A large pub, popular with all ages, close to the centre of the town and recently refurbished. There are separate seating areas on split levels as well as an airy conservatory. The range of ales depends on availability, but tends to focus on national brands, but not exclusively, as beers from nearby BrewDog are occasionally on offer. No food is served. 🕭♿🚲⏴

Findhorn

Kimberley Inn

94 Findhorn, IV36 3YG
🕭 12-midnight ☎ (01309) 690492 ⊕ kimberleyinn.com
Beer range varies Ⓗ
Styling itself as Moray's seafood pub, it is situated right on the shore of Findhorn Bay, with superb views from the tables on the patio outside. The bar is wood-panelled with snugs at either end. Two handpumps dispense a wide variety of beers, mainly from Scottish micros. The menu of home-cooked food features local fish and even local ice cream. Findhorn is a breezy village with views over the sands to the Moray Firth, framed by distant hills. 🅰Q🕭🔌♿▲🚲(336)♣P⏴

Forres

Carisbrooke Hotel

Drumduan Road, IV36 1BS (just off A96 at E of town)
🕭 11-12.30am (1.30am Fri & Sat); 12-12.30am Sun
☎ (01309) 672585
Courage Directors; Greene King Old Speckled Hen; Houston Killellan Ⓗ
Looking much like one of the houses in the area, this hotel sports a neat, comfortable lounge bar with wood panelling, pool table, juke-box, darts and widescreen TVs. The bar is popular with locals and sports teams. Tuesday is quiz night. 🅰🚲🕭🍴🔌🚲(10,11,305)⏴

Mosset Tavern

Gordon Street, IV36 1DL (just off High Street)
🕭 11-11.30 (1.30am Fri & Sat); 12-11.30 Sun
☎ (01309) 672981 ⊕ mossettavern.com
Beer range varies Ⓗ
'The country pub in the heart of Forres', this smart, extremely popular Scottish lounge bar/restaurant is situated next to the Mosset burn and pond, with swans and ducks. The friendly, efficient staff serve ale from a single handpump in the lounge, usually selected from the Cairngorm range. The bar has pool tables and large screens showing sport, and a spacious function room is available. 🕭🚲🔌🍴♿🚲🚲(10,11,305)♣⏴

Fraserburgh

Elizabethan Lounge 🏆

36 Union Grove, AB43 9PH (jct Union Grove and Dennyduff Rd)
🕭 9.30am (11 Sun)-1am ☎ (01346) 515148
Beer range varies Ⓗ
Located in the middle of a housing estate, with a large bar and two lounges with TV sport usually showing. The pub has a formidable reputation for a regular supply of quality ales from far and wide, increasing local CAMRA membership as a direct result of the landlord's avid promotion of real ale. Beers mainly come from the local BrewDog and other Scottish micros, plus a variety of English ales. The bar also features well over 150 malts – the largest collection in the area. Local CAMRA Pub of the Year 2011, CAMRA members receive a discount. 🚲♿▲🚲(267,268,269)⏴

Garlogie

Garlogie Inn

AB32 6RX (on B9119)
🕭 11-2.30, 5-10.30 (11.30 Fri & Sat); 12.30-9 Sun
☎ (01224) 743212 ⊕ garlogieinn.co.uk
Beer range varies Ⓗ
This roadside inn dating from the early 19th century has been run by the Quinn family for 25 years. Numerous extensions have been added to the original building, forming a large restaurant area, and the pub has a reputation for excellent food (booking advised). Drinkers are welcome in the small bar area, with beers from Scottish breweries including Harviestoun, Stewart and Caledonian. Drum Castle and Cullerlie stone circle are close at hand. 🅰Q🕭🔌♿🚲(210)P

Hatton of Fintray

Northern Lights

AB21 0YG
🕭 11.30-midnight (12.30am Fri; 1am Sat); 12.30-11 Sun
☎ (01224) 791261
Beer range varies Ⓗ
Tucked away down a back lane between houses in the village centre, this small pub was converted from a pair of cottages. The wood-panelled bar room is heated by a large log fire. The lounge is predominantly used as a restaurant, with occasional live music on Friday evening, and the quiet conservatory provides more space for drinking and dining. Food is available evenings only during the week, all day at weekends. 🅰🚲🔌P

Inverurie

Edwards
2 West High Street, AB51 3SA
☼ 10-11 (2am Fri & Sat) ☎ (01467) 629788
⊕ edwardsinverurie.co.uk
Caledonian Deuchars IPA; guest beers Ⓗ
Tastefully converted from a town-centre hotel into a bar diner a few years ago, the decor is modern with just a hint of Art Deco. Situated in the heart of a thriving town and close to the railway station, the upstairs function room doubles as a disco at weekends. Three beers are always available, guests sourced mainly from Scottish breweries such as Highland, Orkney and Inveralmond.
⊛◑♿⇌🖼(10,307,737)╚

Maryculter

Old Mill Inn
South Deeside Road, AB12 5FX (jct B979/B9077)
☼ 11-11 ☎ (01224) 733212 ⊕
Caledonian Deuchars IPA; Taylor Landlord; guest beer Ⓗ
Small, privately-owned hotel, dating from 1797, in a rural location on the south bank of the River Dee. Real ale is served in the comfortable lounge bar, furnished with sofas and decorated with fishing memorabilia, as well as in the restaurant. The guest beer is normally sourced from the local Deeside Brewery. Children's attraction Storybook Glen and the Blairs Museum of Scotland's Catholic Heritage are close by. ⊛🛏◑🖼♿▲P╚

Methlick

Ythanview Hotel
Main Street, AB41 7DT
☼ 11-2.30, 5-11 (1am Fri); 11-12.30am Sat; 11-11 Sun
☎ (01651) 806235 ⊕ ythanviewhotel.co.uk
Beer range varies Ⓗ
Traditional inn in the village centre, home to the Methlick Cricket Club and numerous other local clubs. The small public bar at the rear is heavily sport-themed. Bands play on some Saturdays and quiz nights are also hosted. A log fire warms the large lounge/restaurant. The pub is renowned for Jay's special curry with whole chillies – a challenge worth taking. Beers mainly come from Scottish micros and from the Waverley guest list. Haddo House, Tolquhon Castle and Pitmedden Garden are close by. ⋈⊛🛏◑🖼🍴

Monymusk

Grant Arms Hotel
The Square, AB51 7HJ (on village green)
☼ 11-11 (11.45 Fri & Sat) ☎ (01467) 651226
⊕ monymusk.com
Taylor Landlord; guest beer Ⓗ
Former coaching inn dating from the 18th-century with later additions, now a small hotel with lounge and public bars. Food is served in the lounge and a separate restaurant area. Situated at the centre of a conservation area, this is a popular haunt for walkers as well as salmon and trout fishermen on the River Don (the hotel owns the fishing rights to more than 10 miles of the river). The Pitfichie and

Cairn William mountain bike trails are close by. A guest beer is added occasionally in summer. A premium is paid for half pint drinking.
⋈Q⊛◑🛏♿🖼(X20,220,421)♣

Oldmeldrum

Redgarth Hotel
Kirk Brae, AB51 0DJ (off A947 towards golf course)
☼ 11-3, 5-11 (11.45 Fri & Sat); 12-3, 5-11 Sun
☎ (01651) 872353
Beer range varies Ⓗ/Ⓖ
This renowned local hotel and pub has imposing views over the eastern Grampian mountains. A winner of many local CAMRA awards, it retains a strong reputation for its imaginative choice of beers, sourced from, among others, Timothy Taylor, Highland and Inveralmond breweries. A successful blend of popular family restaurant and marvellous real ale pub, it is appreciated by a dedicated core of regulars. During occasional Brewers in Residence evenings, three handpumped ales may be supplemented by many more on gravity.
🛏⊛🛏◑▲🖼(305,325)♣P╚

Peterhead

Cross Keys ✪
23-27 Chapel Street, AB42 1TH
☼ 7am-11 (midnight Fri & Sat) ☎ (01779) 483500
Caledonian Deuchars IPA; Greene King Abbot; Isle of Skye Cross Keys; guest beers Ⓗ
This welcome Wetherspoon outlet in a beer desert opened in 2008, named after the chapel dedicated to St Peter that previously stood on the site. The long single room interior has the bar towards the front and a large seating area to the rear. A sheltered and heated area outside caters for hardy souls and smokers. There are at least two guest ales, typically one Scottish and one English. Open from 7am for coffee and breakfast, children are welcome until 8pm if dining. ⊛◑♿🖼(260)●╚

Portsoy

Shore Inn
Church Street, AB42 2QR
☼ 11-11 (midnight Thu; 1am Fri & Sat) ☎ (01261) 842831
Beer range varies Ⓗ
This ancient 18th-century coastal inn situated on the oldest harbour on the Moray coast exudes an old-time atmosphere with its low ceilings and dark wooden bar fittings. Up to three ales are stocked (only one off-season), often from Deeside and Houston breweries. The village hosts an annual boat festival in early July and an outside bar is set up during this time, with additional beers on offer. Meal service times vary according to the season – phone ahead to check. ⊛◑▲🖼(305)♣

Stonehaven

Marine Hotel
9-10 Shorehead, AB39 2JY (on harbour front)
☼ 11-midnight (1am Fri & Sat); 11-midnight (11 winter) Sun
☎ (01569) 762155 ⊕ marinehotelstonehaven.co.uk
Caledonian Deuchars IPA; Inveralmond Dunnottar Ale; Taylor Landlord; guest beers Ⓗ
Small harbourside hotel featuring simple wood panelling in the bar and a rustic lounge with an open fireplace. Upstairs, the restaurant has been recently refurbished and has its own handpumps.

Outside seating is available with a splendid view of the harbour. The pub makes a point of offering beers from local and regional brewers as guest ales. There is also an unusual selection of Belgian beers on draught and a large choice of bottled beers from around the world – ask for the beer menu. Historic Dunnottar Castle is one mile south. Local CAMRA Pub of the Year 2009 and 2010. ᴍ☸♿◐▲ᕫ(107,117)ᵎ⊟

Ship Inn
5 Shorehead, AB39 2JY (on harbour front)

☸ 11-midnight (1am Fri & Sat) ☎ (01569) 762617
⊕ shipinnstonehaven.com
Beer range varies ⊞

Traditional harbour-front hotel, with a maritime themed, wood-panelled bar and an outdoor seating area overlooking the water. In the bar, a mirror from the defunct Devanha Brewery is a prominent feature. Two beers are offered, one usually from the Inveralmond Brewery, and an extensive range of malt whiskies is stocked. A modern restaurant, with panoramic harbour views, is adjacent to the bar, with food available all day at the weekend. ᴍ☸♿◐ᕫ(107,117)ᵎ

Marine Hotel, Stonehaven

SCOTLAND

ARGYLL & THE ISLES

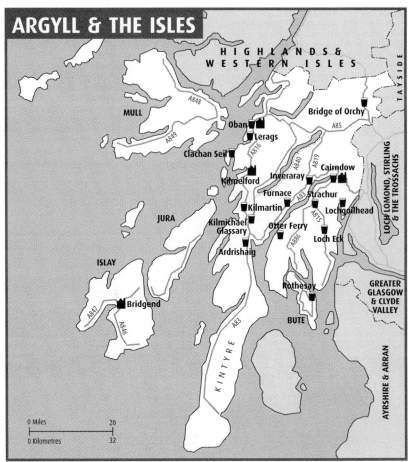

Authority area covered: Argyll & Bute UA

Ardrishaig

Argyll Arms Hotel

65 Chalmers Street, PA30 8DX (on main lochside road)
⏰ 11-1am; 12-1am Sun ☎ (01546) 602352
Beer range varies Ⓗ
Whitewashed building on the main street overlooking Loch Fyne, the compact bar room has a corner counter with a single handpump serving local and national beers. A TV shows sport and news. Near the fireplace and cushioned bench seating, a model boat is set into the wood-panelled wall. There is a dining room and an upstairs function room. Frequented by locals, hotel guests and users of the Crinan Canal. ⚶✿⇘⏰₽

Lorne Bar

Chalmers Street, PA30 8DY (on lochside)
⏰ 12-midnight (1am Thu-Sat) ☎ (01546) 605263
Fyne Highlander Ⓗ
Locals' bar on the main A83 through Ardrishaig near the loch. Recently renovated following a fire, the long bar counter, made from church pews, runs half the length of the room towards a corner with a pool table, and the wooden floor tiles come from Glasgow University. A single handpump usually serves Fyne Highlander, a favourite of the regulars. Sport is shown on TV and the walls display pictures of historic scenes. ⚶₽⅃

Bridge of Orchy

Bridge of Orchy Hotel ✓

PA36 4AD (on A82 at N end of Glen Orchy between Tyndrum & Glencoe) NN296396
⏰ 11-11 (midnight Fri & Sat); 12.30-11 Sun
☎ (01838) 400208 ⊕ bridgeoforchy.co.uk
Caledonian Deuchars IPA; guest beers Ⓗ
A good place to take a break for travellers on the A82 between Glasgow and Fort William. The cafe-style bar usually sells a mixture of Scottish and English real ales, and does a good trade in coffee and bistro-style meals for passing trade including coach parties and wedding guests at the hotel. The village has a station on the scenic West Highland Line and for walkers the West Highland Way passes close by, with bunkhouse accommodation available on-site. ⚶⇘✿⇘⏰⇌⊟(914)₽

Cairndow

Stagecoach Inn

PA26 8BN (near head of Loch Fyne just off A83) NN181109
⏰ 11-11 (1am Fri & Sat) ☎ (01499) 600286
⊕ cairndowinn.com
Beer range varies Ⓗ

One of the oldest Highland coaching inns, on a small road off the A83, offering views over Loch Fyne and a lochside garden. A large pub with several distinct areas, archways lead from the main bar to the dining room and a spacious lounge with a log-burning fireplace. The bar has comfortable seating, rustic tables and two handpumps serving a changing range from Fyne Ales – the brewery is just down the road. Glasgow CAMRA Argyll Pub of the Year 2010. ▲☎☆🏠◑🕏👤🚃(926,976)♣P⬥

Clachan Seil

Tigh an Truish

PA34 4QZ (on B844 5 miles W of A816 jct, by Clachan Bridge) NM784197

🕒 11-11; 11-2.30, 5-10 winter; 12-10 Sun
☎ (01852) 300242 🌐 tighantruish.co.uk
Beer range varies 🅗

Set beside the Atlantic Bridge joining Seil Island to the mainland, this friendly, traditional, 18th-century pub is worth seeking out. Two beers are usually from Scottish micros, notably Fyne Ales, and in summer food is available, either in the bar, the small lounge or dining area. There is a fine view of the bridge and sound through the bay windows and from the inviting, sheltered beer garden and front patio. Local CAMRA Argyll Pub of the Year 2009. ▲Q☆◑👤🚃(418)P

Furnace

Furnace Inn

PA32 8XN NN004000

🕒 12-11 (1am Fri) summer; 5-11 Oct-Easter; 12-1am Sat; 12-11 Sun ☎ (01499) 500200
Beer range varies 🅗

Tall stone building lying off the main A83 south of Inveraray, in a village famed for iron smelting. The main L-shaped room has a log-burning fireplace, TV showing sport and bare stone walls giving a rustic feel. A pool table sits at one end and an archway leads to the dining area with a wood-burning stove. Two handpumps dispense a changing range of beers from Fyne Ales, and a good selection of malt whiskies is available. ▲☆◑🚃P

Inveraray

George Hotel

Main Street East, PA32 8TT

🕒 11 (12 Sun)-12.45am ☎ (01499) 302111
🌐 thegeorgehotel.co.uk
Beer range varies 🅗

The George was formed in the middle of the 19th century from two houses built some 70 years earlier in the centre of this conservation town. The original flagstone floor and roaring log and peat fires provide a bygone ambience in the central restaurant and bar. There is a smaller, livelier public bar to one side with TVs. Both bars serve two beers, at least one from the local Fyne Ales brewery. ▲Q☆🏠◑🕏👤🚃(926,976)P⬥

Kilmartin

Kilmartin Hotel

PA31 8RQ (on A816 10 miles N of Lochgilphead) NR835989

🕒 12-midnight Apr-Oct; 5-midnight Nov-Mar; 12-midnight Fri-Sun ☎ (01546) 510250 🌐 kilmartin-hotel.com
Caledonian Deuchars IPA; guest beers 🅗

White-fronted building on a hillside commanding an impressive view over scenic Kilmartin Glen. One of the two guest ales is usually from Fyne Ales and the other from a Scottish micro. The dining rooms of this family-run hotel serve a wide range of excellent home-made meals. Kilmartin is a must for anyone interested in exploring prehistoric features including stone carvings, standing stones, burial cairns and other relics dating back some 5,000 years. Q☎☆🏠◑🕏👤🚃(423)P⬥

Kilmichael Glassary

Horseshoe Inn

Bridgend, PA31 8QA (in Bridgend village, off A816 3 miles N of Lochgilphead) NR852928

🕒 5-11; 12-midnight Sat; 12-10 Sun ☎ (01546) 606369
🌐 horseshoeinn.biz
Beer range varies 🅗

Converted farmhouse in a quiet village. The lounge and public bar both have a handpump, offering beers usually from local Fyne and Oban Ales. Note the coloured glass panels in the doors. There is a games room to the rear, and a separate dining area where good food is available. The area boasts plenty of sights to enjoy, including the scenic Kilmartin Glen, the ancient hilltop Dunadd Fort and the Crinan Canal. ▲☎☆🏠◑ 🕏🚃(423)P⬥

Lerags

Barn

Cologin, PA34 4SE (down minor road off A816) NM853260

🕒 12-midnight summer; closed Mon-Thu, 5-11, 12-midnight Sat & Sun winter ☎ (01631) 571313 🌐 myspace.com/barnbar
Fyne Highlander; guest beer 🅗

A popular local for those staying in nearby holiday accommodation and regulars from the Oban area. The guest beer is from Fyne or Oban Ales and a range of 50 single malt whiskies is offered. A centre for outdoor activities, scenic circular forest walks and various rights of way to the sea shore start here. In summer the Barn is popular for its food and for live music on a Wednesday night. Folk music plays on Sunday afternoon. ☆◑P⬥

Loch Eck

Coylet Inn

PA23 8SG (on A815 near S end of Loch Eck) NS143885

🕒 closed Mon (also closed Tue winter); 11-11; 12-10 Sun
☎ (01369) 840426 🌐 coyletinn.co.uk
Fyne Highlander; guest beers 🅗

A 17th-century coaching inn on the banks of scenic Loch Eck in the heart of the Cowal Penisula. While beers from the local Fyne Ales brewery dominate, a selection of guests from other breweries can be found throughout the summer months. The small cosy bar is frequented by locals and travellers. The hotel location has excellent views of the loch and hills opposite, plus Allt Na Gaibhre (local name Linn of Agnes), a 400m watercourse.
▲☆🏠◑🚃(484)P⬥

SCOTLAND

Whistlefield Inn

PA23 8SG (jct of A815 and unclassified road to Ardentinny) NS144933
✿ 12.30-11 ☎ (01369) 860440 ⊕ whistlefield.com
Beer range varies Ⓗ
This 15th-century inn on a former drovers' road is now popular with musicians for its monthly folk nights. Three handpumps offer ales from around the west of Scotland. Sited high on the glen side, with impressive views, the hotel is on the cycle route around Loch Eck and close to many forest walks and the Cowal Way. Fishing Loch Eck offers the rare chance to net Arctic char.
🏚Q🛏️👧🏃◑🞔Pᵔ

Lochgoilhead

Shore House Inn Ⓛ

PA24 8AD (at head of Loch Goil) NN198015
✿ 12-11 (midnight Fri-Sun) ☎ (01301) 703340
⊕ theshorehouse.net
Fyne Highlander; guest beer Ⓗ
At the head of Loch Goil, the views from the lochside gardens and restaurant of this 1850s former parish manse are magnificent. It is within Argyll Forest and Loch Lomond and the Trossachs national parks, so is an ideal base for outdoor activities. The guest beer is from Fyne Ales. The restaurant has a varied menu, with traditional wood-fired oven pizzas a speciality. The inn can be reached easily by yacht. In winter phone before you set off to confirm opening times.
👧🏃◑♿▲🞔(484)Pᵔ

Oban

Lorne Bar ◉

Stevenson Street, PA34 5NA
✿ 12-1am (midnight Mon; 2am Fri-Sun) ☎ (01631) 570020
Caledonian Deuchars IPA; guest beer Ⓗ
A short walk through the back streets is all you need to find this traditional pub near the river in the Gateway to the Isles. It is well-worth a visit for its distinctive decor. The main room is dominated by a unique island bar with elephantine brass furniture. An extended beer range is available in summer when the sheltered garden area is a treasure, and a varied selection of food is available and popular with regulars. 🏃◑🚆🞔(976)ᵔ

Otter Ferry

Oystercatcher Ⓛ

PA21 2DH (on B8000 on E coast of Loch Fyne) NR930845
✿ 11-11 ☎ (01700) 821229 ⊕ theoystercatcher.co.uk
Fyne Highlander; guest beer Ⓗ
Impressive white pub/restaurant set in an idyllic location on the eastern shore of Loch Fyne, with a spacious lawn leading directly to the beach. It is accessible from Strachur via the B8000 that hugs the shore, providing a scenic journey, or alternatively by boat as the pub has its own pontoon and moorings. Three handpumps serve mostly Fyne ales and occasionally other beers, and locally-sourced food is available in both the bar and restaurant. Telephone to check opening hours in winter. 🏚🏃◑♿♣P

Rothesay: Isle of Bute

Black Bull Inn

3 West Princess Street, PA20 9AF (opp harbour)
✿ 11-11 (midnight Fri & Sat); 12.30-11 Sun
☎ (01700) 502366
Caledonian Deuchars IPA; guest beer Ⓗ
The attractive Isle of Bute is just a ferry ride from the architectural wonder of Wemyss Bay railway station. This two-bar pub is conveniently situated opposite the harbour, making it easy to find on arrival and the perfect place to wait for your ferry to come in before returning. With good food served in a separate dining area, you can also refuel here after a walk along the seafront or over the hill on the West Island Way. The Deuchars is regularly supported by a guest ale. ◑🞔🚆

Strachur

Creggans Inn

PA27 8BX (on A815, near A886 jct) NN087022
✿ 11-1am; 12-1am Sun ☎ (01369) 860279
⊕ creggans-inn.co.uk
Beer range varies Ⓗ
An old coaching inn that dates back to the 18th century and is sited where Mary Queen of Scots caught the ferry across the loch. McPhunn's Bar, named after a half-hung local laird, features photographs of the local shinty team and is warmed by a real fire. The adjacent restaurant serves a variety of meals including a daily special. There is usually one beer in the winter and two in summer, with at least one coming from Fyne Ales.
🏚Q👧🏃◑🞔(484,486)Pᵔ

The ale diet

Boniface: Sir, I have now in my cellar ten tun of the best ale in Staffordshire; 'tis smooth as oil, sweet as milk, clear as amber, and strong as brandy; and will be just 14 years old the fifth day of next March, old style.

Aimwell: You're very exact, I find, in the age of your ale.

Boniface: As punctual, sir, as I am in the age of my children. I'll show you such ale! I have lived in Lichfield, man and boy, about eight-and-fifty years, and, I believe, have not consumed eight-and-fifty ounces of meat.

Aimwell: At a meal, you mean, if one may guess your sense by your bulk.

Boniface: Not in my life, sir, I have fed purely upon ale; I have eat my ale, drank my ale, and I always sleep upon ale.

George Farquhar, The Beaux-Stratagem, 1701

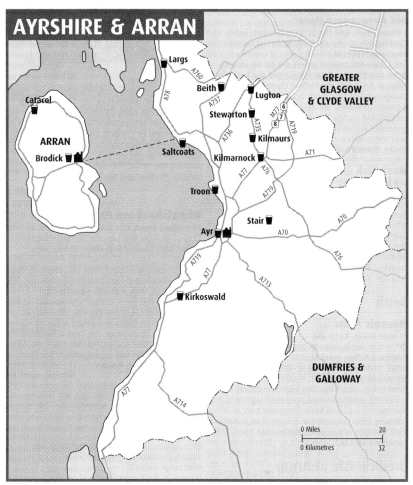

AYRSHIRE & ARRAN

Authority areas covered: East Ayrshire UA, North Ayrshire UA, South Ayrshire UA

Ayr

Abbotsford Hotel
14 Corsehill Road, KA7 2ST
⊕ 10-12.30am (midnight Sun) ☎ (01292) 261506
⊕ abbotsfordhotel.co.uk
Caledonian Deuchars IPA; guest beer Ⓗ
This family-run hotel, situated in a residential area south of the town centre, is convenient for the seafront, local golf courses, Burns-related attractions and other delights of the area. Two real ales are offered in the Copper Bar – its name accurately describes its decor. Meals are served in both the bar and a separate restaurant area. There is also a pool/TV room and a function room/ conservatory. The guest beer tends to be from a larger brewery. ⑤❀✍⬤🍴P⌐

Geordie's Byre
103 Main Street, KA8 8BU (N of centre, over river towards Prestwick)
⊕ 11-11 (midnight Thu-Sat); 12.30-11 Sun
☎ (01292) 264925
Beer range varies Ⓐ
This CAMRA award-winning gem of a pub serves up to four guest ales, sourced from far and near,

dispensed using traditional Scottish tall founts. Both the public bar and the lounge feature a wealth of memorabilia. A wide range of malt whiskies and rums is also available – ask for the list. Local CAMRA Pub of the Year 2009.
⊞⇌(Newton-on-Ayr)🚍

Glen Park Hotel
5 Racecourse Road, KA7 2DG
⊕ 10-12.30am (midnight Sun) ☎ (01292) 263891
⊕ glenparkhotel.com
Ayr Leezie Lundie, Jolly Beggars; guest beer Ⓗ
A short walk from the town centre, this attractive 1860s B-Listed Victorian building is a splendid modern hotel offering guests and non-residents alike the warmest of welcomes. Home to Ayr Brewing Company, the guest beer is its seasonal brew, and the restaurant features fresh local produce. The front patio has fine sunset views in the summer months. ⛺❀✍⬤🖕⇌🚍(A9)P⌐

INDEPENDENT BREWERIES

Arran Brodick: Isle of Arran
Ayr Ayr

SCOTLAND

BORDERS

Authority area covered: Scottish Borders UA

Allanton

Allanton Inn
TD11 3JZ
☼ 12-11 (midnight Fri & Sat); closed winter afternoons
☎ (01890) 818260 ⊕ allantoninn.co.uk
Beer range varies Ⓗ
A warm welcome is assured at this old coaching
inn dating back to the 18th century, with hitching
rings by the door for those arriving by horse.
Quality food is served in the restaurant in the front
rooms, while the bar at the back always offers an
interesting ale or two. Accommodation is available
for those looking for a base to explore Berwickshire
and Northumbria. Dogs are welcome. Free WiFi.
🏨Q🌭🛏🌗🛝♣P

Auchencrow

Craw Inn
TD14 5LS (signed from A1)
☼ 12-2.30, 6-11 (midnight Fri); 12-midnight Sat; 12.30-11
Sun ☎ (01890) 761253 ⊕ thecrawinn.co.uk
Beer range varies Ⓗ
This friendly 18th-century village inn is very much
the hub of the community. The traditional single
bar features beams festooned with pump clips and
a wood-burning stove. Excellent home-cooked
food is served every day in both the bar and the
well-appointed restaurant. Summer drinking and
dining can be enjoyed on the recently installed
decking. A beer festival is held in November.
Children welcome. Free WiFi. 🏨Q🌭🛏🌗&🛝♣P

Burnmouth

First & Last
Upper Burnmouth, TD14 5SL
☼ 11-11.45 (12.45am Fri & Sat); 12.30-11.45 Sun
☎ (01890) 781306
**Belhaven St Andrew's Ale; Houston Killellan; guest
beer** Ⓗ
Frequented by locals and travellers on the adjacent
A1, this pub, with bar, dining room and pool room,
has built a good following for real ale. The guest
beer changes regularly. The bar area is decorated
with old photographs and nautical artefacts, giving
the pub a cosy and traditional feel. Meals are
served all day Friday-Sunday. Children are
welcome until 9pm. Free WiFi. 🏨🌭🌗&🛝P

Coldingham

New Inn
1 Bridge Street, TD14 5NG
☼ 12-midnight (1am Fri & Sat) ☎ (01890) 771315
Beer range varies Ⓗ
Well-appointed village pub with two dining rooms
in addition to the main bar. The emphasis is on
food, and the pub has a growing reputation for

quality meals. Three real ales are offered (two in winter), usually from smaller breweries. Lively jam sessions are hosted on Saturday evening. Meals are served all day Sunday and families are welcome. ⚲Q🌑🌑🍴♿♣🅿️⛔

Coldstream

Besom ✅
75-77 High Street, TD12 4AE
🕛 11-midnight (1am Fri & Sat); 12.30-midnight Sun
☎ (01890) 882391
Caledonian Deuchars IPA; guest beer ⓗ
One of the first and last pubs in Scotland, this three-roomed gem has remained relatively unchanged since it was built in the 1890s and revamped circa 1910. The cosy bar retains its original counter and gantry, while the diverse range of memorabilia, bookshelves and comfortable seating creates the feel of a living room rather than a pub. Leading through from the lounge (where children are welcome) is a room dedicated entirely to the memory of the Coldstream Guards. Dogs are permitted in the bar. ⚲Q🌑🌑🍴♣🅿️⛔

Denholm

Auld Cross Keys Hotel
Main Street, TD9 8NU
🕛 12-11 (midnight Thu; 1am Fri & Sat); 12.30-midnight Sun
☎ (01450) 870305 🌐 crosskeysdenholm.co.uk
Beer range varies ⓗ
Overlooking the village green, this small hotel still retains the character of an inn. The plain and functional public bar may be favoured by drinkers, however there is also a more comfortable lounge bar. The beer is from either Hadrian & Border or the Scottish Borders breweries. Folk music sessions and concerts are regular events. Meals are served 1-7pm on Sunday. The bedrooms are of a good standard. Children are welcome until 9pm, and dogs permitted in the bar. Free WiFi. ⚲Q🌑🍴🌑♣🅿️

Fox & Hounds Inn 🛏
Main Street, TD9 8NU
🕛 11.30-3, 5-midnight Mon & Wed; 11.30-midnight (1am Fri & Sat); 12.30-midnight Sun ☎ (01450) 870247
Wylam Gold Tankard; guest beer ⓗ
Village local, built in 1728, overlooking the green. The small bar is half wood panelled, and a real fire gives a cosy feel in winter. Pictures and memorabilia decorate the walls. The rear lounge has a coffee house feel, and an upstairs dining room is used in the evening. The courtyard offers shelter for smokers as well as an alfresco drinking space in warmer weather. Beers are from Wylam and Scottish Borders breweries. Children are welcome until 8pm. ⚲🌑🍴🌑♣⛔

Galashiels

Ladhope Inn 🛏
33 High Buckholmside, TD1 2HR (A7, ⅓ mile N of centre)
🕛 4-11 (midnight Thu); 3-midnight Fri; 12.30-midnight Sat; 12.30-midnight Sun ☎ (01896) 752446
Caledonian Deuchars IPA; guest beer ⓗ
Comfortable, friendly local with a vibrant Borders atmosphere. Originating circa 1792, the building has been altered considerably inside. Now a single

room, it is decorated with whisky jugs and a large map of the Galashiels area. A wee alcove has a golfing theme. Three flat-screen TVs ensure the pub is busy during sporting events, and frequent live music is hosted. The guest beer is often from Hadrian & Border but changes regularly. Excellent home-made soup is served on Sunday. Dogs are welcome. 🌑♣⛔♣

Innerleithen

St Ronan's Hotel
High Street, EH44 6HF
🕛 11-midnight (12.45am Fri & Sat); 12-midnight Sun
☎ (01896) 831487 🌐 stronanshotel.co.uk
Beer range varies ⓗ
This village hotel takes its name from a local saint. The functional public bar is long and thin, with a brick and wooden fireplace. There are two alcoves, one with seating, the other with a dartboard and a wide-angle photograph of the village. There is also a room with a pool table. Meals are served daily until 10pm (times and menu vary in winter). A pick-up service is available for Southern Upland Way walkers. ⚲🌑🍴🌑⛔♣🅿️

Traquair Arms Hotel 🛏
Traquair Road, EH44 6PD (B709, off A72)
🕛 11-11 (midnight Fri & Sat); 12-11.30 Sun
☎ (01896) 830229 🌐 traquairarmshotel.co.uk
Caledonian Deuchars IPA; Taylor Landlord; Traquair Stuart Ale ⓗ
Elegant 18th-century hotel in the scenic Tweed Valley. The comfortable lounge bar features a welcoming real fire in winter and a relaxing tropical fish tank. An Italian bistro area and separate restaurant provide plenty of room for diners, with food served all day at weekends. This is one of the few outlets for draught ales from Traquair House. Children are welcome, as are dogs. ⚲🌑🍴🌑♿⛔♣(62)🅿️

Kelso

Cobbles Inn 🛏
7 Bowmont Street, TD5 7JH (off NE side of town square)
🕛 11-3, 5-10 (1am Fri); 11.30-late Sat & Sun summer; 12-3, 5-10 Sun ☎ (01573) 223548 🌐 thecobblesinn.co.uk
Beer range varies ⓗ
An award-winning gastro pub offering an eclectic mix of British classics, Pacific Rim and modern European cuisine, made with the finest locally-sourced and seasonal ingredients. To the right of the main dining area is a lounge bar where beers from the inn's own micro-brewery are featured. Though the focus is on food, drinkers are welcome. Private functions are catered for upstairs. Children are welcome. Free WiFi. ⚲🌑🌑♿⛔

Kirk Yetholm

Border Hotel
The Green, TD5 8PQ
🕛 11-midnight (1am Fri & Sat); 12-11 winter; 12-midnight Sun ☎ (01573) 420237 🌐 theborderhotel.com
Beer range varies ⓗ
This 260-year-old coaching inn is a mecca for walkers, situated at the official end of the Pennine Way and on the ancient St Cuthbert's Way. Those completing the Pennine Way are entitled to a free half pint – a tradition continued from Wainwright's time. The hotel is noted for its hearty food served

EDINBURGH & THE LOTHIANS

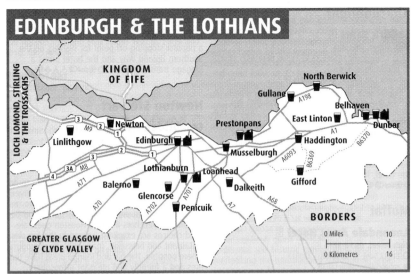

Authority areas covered: City of Edinburgh UA, East Lothian UA, Midlothian UA, West Lothian UA

Balerno

Grey Horse L
20 Main Street, EH14 7EH (off A70, in pedestrian area)
🌣 10 (12.30 Sun)-1am ☎ (0131) 449 2888
⊕ greyhorsebalerno.com
Caledonian Deuchars IPA; Greene King Old Speckled Hen; guest beers Ⓗ
Traditional stone-built village centre inn, dating back 200 years. The public bar retains some original features, with wood panelling and a fine Bernard's mirror. The pleasant lounge has green banquette seating. The restaurant next door is part of the pub so you can have a drink with your meal in the evening. Children are welcome in the lounge until 9pm, and dogs are offered water and biscuits. Free WiFi. ﷯Q☸◑呂⊞♣⌐

Belhaven

Masons Arms L
8 High Street, EH42 1NP (1 mile W of Dunbar)
🌣 12-3, 5-11; 12-midnight Fri & Sat; 12.30-11 Sun
☎ (01368) 863700
Beer range varies Ⓗ
Friendly pub close to Belhaven Brewery with fine views to the Lammermuir Hills. The bright, comfortable public bar has banquette seating around the edges and the walls are decorated with pictures of old sailing ships. There is also a pleasant dining room where food from a quality menu is served (no food Sun eve). One of the three real ales available is usually from Belhaven.
﷯☸◑呂人呂♣

Dalkeith

Blacksmith's Forge ✪
Newmills Road, EH22 1DU
🌣 8am-11 (1am Fri & Sat); 10-11 Sun ☎ (0131) 561 5100
Caledonian Deuchars IPA; Greene King Abbot; guest beers Ⓗ
A Wetherspoon establishment with a mix of seating areas. Although busy at the weekends, it has a reasonably quiet atmosphere. Dimmed

lighting helps to create a soothing ambience, despite two small TVs and a gaming machine. Meals are served all day and children and dogs are welcome. An outdoor drinking area can be used until 10pm. Free WiFi. ☸◑占呂⌐

Dunbar

Volunteer Arms
17 Victoria Street, EH42 1HP (near swimming pool)
🌣 12-11 (midnight Thu; 1am Fri & Sat); 12.30-midnight Sun
☎ (01368) 862278
Beer range varies Ⓗ
Close to Dunbar harbour, this is a friendly, traditional locals' pub. The cosy panelled bar is decorated with lots of fishing and lifeboat oriented memorabilia. It offers two real ales, usually from smaller breweries, and local real cider is occasionally available. Upstairs is a restaurant serving an excellent, good value menu with an emphasis on seafood. In summer meals are served all day until 9.30pm. Children are welcome until 8pm and dogs after 9pm. ☸◑人≑呂♣♠⌐

East Linton

Crown
25-27 Bridge Street, EH40 3AG (village square)
🌣 12-11 (1am Thu-Sat; midnight Sun) ☎ (01620) 860335
⊕ thecrowneastlinton.co.uk
Beer range varies Ⓗ
Small 18th-century stone-built hotel in the centre of a historic conservation village. The functional, cosy bar has a real log fire, lots of wood panelling and original Dudgeon windows. To the rear is a large lounge/restaurant serving pub meals (no food Mon or Tue). There is a side room leading off the bar devoid of all electronic distractions.

Children are welcome in the lounge and a small family room. Dogs are also welcome.
🏠🐕☕🍴🍲🅿️♣⌐

Edinburgh

Abbotsford Bar & Restaurant ★
3 Rose Street, EH2 2PR (city centre)
🕐 11-11 (midnight Fri & Sat); 12.30-11 Sun
☎ (0131) 225 5276 ⊕ theabbotsford.com
Beer range varies Ⓗ
A traditional Scottish bar listed on CAMRA's National Inventory of Historic Pub Interiors. The magnificent island bar and gantry in dark mahogany have been a fixture since 1902, and the ornate plasterwork and corniced ceiling, highlighted by concealed lighting, are also outstanding. Beers are usually from Scottish micro-breweries. Food is served all day in the bar from an extensive menu and there is also a restaurant upstairs, where children (over five) are welcome and you can ask for beer from downstairs.
Q🕐🍴➡(Waverley)🅿️

Athletic Arms (Diggers) Ⓛ ✅
1-3 Angle Park Terrace, EH11 2JX (1 mile SW of centre)
🕐 11 (12.30 Sun)-1am ☎ (0131) 337 3822
Caledonian Deuchars IPA; Stewart 80/- Ⓐ**; guest beers** Ⓗ
Situated between two graveyards, the name 'Diggers' became synonymous with this Edinburgh pub legend, which opened in 1897. Banquette seating lines the walls, and a compass drawing in the floor aids the geographically challenged. A smaller back room has a dartboard and further seating. Quieter now than in its heyday, though packed when Hearts are at home, it continues to extend a warm welcome to local characters and visitors alike. Dogs welcome. ➡(Haymarket)🅿️♣

Bennets of Morningside Ⓛ
1 Maxwell Street, Morningside, EH10 5HT (1½ miles S of city centre)
🕐 11-12.30am (1am Wed-Sat); 12.30-12.30am Sun
☎ (0131) 447 1903
Black Isle Yellowhammer; Caledonian Deuchars IPA; Taylor Landlord; guest beers Ⓐ
Friendly and welcoming hostelry in the upmarket Morningside area of the city. A major refurbishment has taken place since the pub was sold by the Bennet family, and it remains popular among its customers due to the excellent selection of six beers, including three guests. Simple bar snacks are available all day. There is a paved drinking area outside at the front. Dogs on leads welcome. 🍴🅿️⌐

Blue Blazer Ⓛ
2 Spittal Street, EH3 9DX (SW side of centre)
🕐 11 (12.30 Sun)-1am ☎ (0131) 229 5030
Cairngorm Trade Winds Ⓐ**; Orkney Dark Island** Ⓗ**; Stewart Pentland IPA** Ⓐ**, 80/-; guest beers** Ⓗ
Nestling in the shadows of Edinburgh castle, this two-roomed inn has a traditional feel, with wooden floors, high ceilings and old brewery window panels complemented by candles in front of the handpumps when the sun goes down. Beers from Scottish micros are the speciality here. Named after a local school uniform, there is a blue blazer inlaid on the floor. Keep up to date on Facebook page, I Love The Blue Blazer. The pub stays open later during the city festival in August. Dogs welcome. ➡(Haymarket)🅿️⌐

Bow Bar 🍷 Ⓛ
80 West Bow, EH1 2HH (Old Town, off Grassmarket)
🕐 12-11.30; 12.30-11 Sun ☎ (0131) 226 7667
Caledonian Deuchars IPA; Stewart 80/-; Taylor Landlord; guest beers Ⓐ
One of the first re-creations of a classic Scottish one-roomed ale house, dedicated to traditional Scottish air pressure dispense and perpendicular drinking. The five guest beers can be from anywhere in the UK. The walls are festooned with original brewery mirrors and the superb gantry does justice to an award-winning selection of about 200 single malt whiskies. Bar snacks are available at lunchtime (not Sun). Dogs are welcome and free WiFi is available.
Q➡(Waverley)🅿️

Café Royal ☆ Ⓛ ✅
19 West Register Street, EH2 2AA (off E end of Princes St)
🕐 11-11 (midnight Thu; 1am Fri & Sat); 12.30-11 Sun
☎ (0131) 556 1884 ⊕ caferoyal.org.uk
Caledonian Deuchars IPA; guest beers Ⓗ
One of the finest Victorian pub interiors in Scotland, listed on CAMRA's National Inventory of Historic Pub Interiors. It is dominated by an impressive oval island bar with ornate brass light fittings and magnificent ceramic tiled murals of innovators made by Doulton from pictures by John Eyre. The superb sporting windows in the Oyster Bar were made by the same firm that supplied windows for the House of Lords. Guest beers are usually from Harviestoun, Inveralmond and Kelburn. Meals are served all day and children are welcome in the restaurant. 🍴➡(Waverley)🅿️

Cask & Barrel Ⓛ
115 Broughton Street, EH1 3RZ (E edge of New Town)
🕐 11-12.30am (1am Thu-Sat); 12.30-12.30am Sun
☎ (0131) 556 3132 ⊕ caskandbarrel.co.uk
Caledonian Deuchars IPA, Draught Bass; Hadrian & Border Broughton St Domestic Ale; Harviestoun Bitter & Twisted; Highland Orkney Best; Young's Special; guest beers Ⓗ
Spacious and busy ale house drawing a varied clientele of all ages, ranging from business people to football fans. The interior features an imposing horseshoe bar, bare floorboards, a splendid cornice and a collection of brewery mirrors. Old barrels act as tables for those who wish to stand up, or cannot find a seat. The guest beers, often from smaller Scottish breweries, come in a range of strengths and styles. Sparklers can be removed on request. 🍴➡(Waverley)🅿️♦

Cask & Barrel Southside
24-26 West Preston Street, EH8 9PZ (1 mile S of centre)
🕐 12-midnight (1am Fri); 11-1am Sat; 12.30-midnight Sun
☎ (0131) 667 0856
Caledonian Deuchars IPA; Highland Orkney Best; Stewart 80/-; guest beers Ⓗ
Modern re-creation of a Scottish city or tenement boozer, which if it were true to history would have a lot less furniture. A room with windows front and back is divided by a horseshoe bar with a dark wood gantry, adorned with decorative wooden casks. The walls support a fine range of old photos, framed advertisements and historic brewery and distillery mirrors. A good place to try beers from Scottish breweries, along with a few from 'down south'. 🅿️

Cloisters Bar L

26 Brougham Street, EH3 9JH (SW edge of centre)
☼ 12-midnight (1am Fri & Sat); 12.30-midnight Sun
☎ (0131) 221 9997
Cairngorm Trade Winds; Highland Scapa Special;
Stewart Pentland IPA, Holy Grale; guest beers ⊞
A former parsonage, this bare-boarded ale house is
popular with a broad cross-section of drinkers.
Appropriately, old pews give the pub a friendly
feel. A fine selection of brewery mirrors adorns the
walls and the wide range of single malt whiskies
does justice to the outstanding gantry. A spiral
staircase makes visiting the loo an adventure. Bar
meals are served daily (not Mon or Fri & Sat eve)
and freshly prepared from local ingredients. Free
WiFi. Q◑♪⊟♣♨

Dagda Bar

93-95 Buccleuch Street, EH8 9NG (¾ mile S of centre)
☼ 12 (1 Sun)-1am ☎ (0131) 667 9773 ∰ dagda.co.uk
Beer range varies ⊞
Convivial, cosy bar in the university area attracting
a wide-ranging clientele. The single room has
banquette seating on three sides and the bar
counter on the other. The stone flagged floor is a
little uneven in places. The staff are happy to let
you sample the four real ales before you buy,
which usually come from smaller breweries. Fresh
ground coffee and quality tea are also available.
Dogs welcome. ⊟♣

Guildford Arms

1 West Register Street, EH2 2AA (off E end of Princes St)
☼ 11-11 (midnight Fri & Sat); 12.30-11 Sun
☎ (0131) 556 4312 ∰ guildfordarms.com
Caledonian Deuchars IPA; Fyne Avalanche;
Harviestoun Bitter & Twisted; Orkney Dark Island;
guest beers ⊞
This large city-centre pub was built in the golden
age of Victorian pub design. The high ceiling,
cornices and friezes are spectacular, as are the
window arches and screens. An unusual gallery
above the main bar, where the restaurant is
located, is also noteworthy. There is a large
standing area around the canopied bar plus seating
areas to the rear. The diverse beer range includes
various Scottish micro-brews, with specific
breweries regularly showcased.
◑≹(Waverley)⊟♣

Halfway House

24 Fleshmarket Close, EH1 1BX (up steps opp station's
Market St entrance)
☼ 11-midnight (1am Fri & Sat); 12.30-midnight Sun
☎ (0131) 225 7101 ∰ halfwayhouse-edinburgh.com/
realale.php
Beer range varies ⊞
Cosy, characterful pub hidden halfway down an old
town 'close'. Railway memorabilia and current
timetables adorn the interior of this small, often
busy, bar. Four interesting beers from smaller
Scottish breweries are usually offered, and good
quality, reasonably priced food is served all day.
CAMRA members receive a discount on ale. The
pub may stay open until 1am at busy times of the
year. Children over five and small dogs are
welcome. ❀◑≹(Waverley)⊟♣≞

Kay's Bar L

39 Jamaica Street West, EH3 6HF (New Town, off India
St)
☼ 11-midnight (1am Fri & Sat); 12.30-11 Sun
☎ (0131) 225 1858 ∰ kaysbar.co.uk

Caledonian Deuchars IPA; Theakston Best Bitter;
guest beers ⊞
This small, cosy and convivial pub is a popular
haunt for lawyers in the early evening. It offers an
impressive range of beers for the size of the bar.
One wall is decorated with whisky barrels, and
there is also a good whisky selection behind the
bar. If the front bar is busy, try the small room at
the back. Lunches consist mainly of traditional
Scottish fare. The building was originally used as a
wine merchants. Dogs are welcome once lunch is
finished. ▲Q◑⊟♣

Malt & Hops L

45 The Shore, Leith, EH6 6QU (1½ miles S of centre)
☼ 12-11 (midnight Wed & Thu; 1am Fri & Sat); 12.30-11 Sun
☎ (0131) 555 0083
Caledonian Deuchars IPA; guest beers ⊞
One-roomed public bar dating from 1749 and in
the heart of 'new' Leith's riverside restaurant
district. Wood panelling gives an intimate feel,
with numerous mirrors, artefacts and a large oil
painting adding interest. The superb collection of
pump clips, many from now defunct breweries,
indicates the interesting and ever-changing range
of guest beers on offer, often from Scottish
breweries. Meals are served on Friday only.
Children and dogs welcome. ▲❀◑⊟♣

McCowan's Brewhouse

Fountain Park Complex, Dundee Street, EH11 1AF (1
mile S of centre)
☼ 12-1am (midnight Mon); 12.30-1am Sun
☎ (0131) 228 8198
Caledonian Deuchars IPA; guest beers ⊞
American-style brew pub in a modern
entertainment complex. Sadly the on-site brewery
is unused. On two levels with a glass front wall and
exposed metal roof beams and ventilation ducts,
the interior has a light and airy feel with an
industrial ambience. It is furnished with a mixture
of tables, chairs and comfortable settees. Regular
entertainment features on Friday evening. Food is
served all day and children are permitted until
6pm. ❀◑≹(Haymarket)⊟P≞

Mitre ✪

131 High Street, EH1 1SG (Old Town)
☼ 10-midnight (1am Fri & Sat); 12.30-midnight Sun
☎ (0131) 652 3902
Caledonian Deuchars IPA, 80; guest beers ⊞
Lively bar on the famous Royal Mile, popular with
locals and tourists. The young, friendly bar staff are
enthusiastic about the real ales on sale. Olde
worlde in style, the interior has high ceilings,
bookshelves and pictures of old Edinburgh, with a
large dining area to the rear. Meals are served all
day and there is also an excellent choice of bar
snacks available. The pub is located close to
religious reformer John Knox's house. Children are
welcome until 8pm if eating.
❀◑≹(Waverley)⊟≞

Oxford Bar ★

8 Young Street, EH2 4JB (New Town, off Charlotte Sq)
☼ 11-midnight; 12.30-11 Sun ☎ (0131) 539 7119
∰ oxfordbar.com
Cairngorm Trade Winds; Caledonian Deuchars IPA;
guest beers ⊞
Small, basic, vibrant New Town drinking shop
unchanged since the late 19th century. It is
renowned as one of the favourite pubs of Inspector
Rebus and his creator Ian Rankin, and a haunt of

many other famous and infamous characters over the years, so you never know who you might bump into. Guest beers are normally from Scottish micro-breweries. A real taste of New Town past, and listed on CAMRA's National Inventory of Historic Pub Interiors. Bar snacks are available. Dogs welcome. 🚌♣🏠

Sheep Heid Inn ✔

43 The Causeway, Duddingston, EH15 3QA (1½ miles SE of centre)
⊛ 11-11 (midnight Fri & Sat); 12-11 Sun ☎ (0131) 661 7974
Beer range varies Ⓗ
An historic pub, dating from the 14th century, with several drinking areas. The comfortable lounge has dark wood panelling. A traditional skittle alley at the rear can be hired. Despite its location in one of the most exclusive areas of Edinburgh, it has a varied clientele of all ages including students from nearby halls of residence and residents of a large council housing scheme. Meals are served all day. Dogs are permitted in the bar and courtyard.
🚾🕮🕽&🚌♣🏠P🏠

Stable Bar Ⓛ

Mortonhall Park, 30 Frogston Road East, EH16 6TJ (SE edge of city)
⊛ 11-11 (midnight summer); 12.30-midnight Sun
☎ (0131) 664 0773 🌐 mortonhall.co.uk/home/bar/stablebar.htm
Caledonian Deuchars IPA; Stewart Edinburgh Gold, 80/- Ⓗ
Perched on the southern edge of the city, the Stable has all the qualities of a country pub with the convenience of a city one. The comfortable main bar is dominated by a large stone fireplace, which has a roaring log fire in the winter. Horse brasses and photographs of old Edinburgh adorn the walls. With the three real ales coming from within three miles, this is as LocAle a pub as you can find. Food is served all day until 9pm (10pm in summer). Children and dogs welcome. Free WiFi.
🚾🕮🕽▲🚌♣P🏠

Starbank Inn

64 Laverockbank Road, EH5 3BZ (Newhaven, 1½ miles N of centre)
⊛ 11-11 (midnight Thu; 1am Fri & Sat); 12.30-11 Sun
☎ (0131) 552 4141 🌐 starbankinn.co.uk
Belhaven 80/-; Greene King IPA; Taylor Landlord; guest beers Ⓗ
Bright, airy, bare-boarded ale house, in a prominent position overlooking the sea, with superb views across the Firth to Fife. The interior has a U-shaped layout extending into a conservatory dining area, and the walls sport several rare brewery mirrors. Up to five interesting guest ales, often from Scottish independent breweries, are usually available. Meals are served all day Friday-Sunday. Children are welcome until 9pm. Dogs allowed if on a lead. Q🕮🕽&🚌♣🏠

Stockbridge Tap Ⓛ ✔

2-4 Raeburn Place, Stockbridge, EH4 1HN (¾ mile S of centre)
⊛ 12-midnight (1am Fri & Sat); 12.30-midnight Sun
☎ (0131) 343 3000
Cairngorm Trade Winds; Stewart Pentland IPA, 80/-; guest beers Ⓗ
Very much a specialist real ale house, the pub offers unusual and interesting beers from all over the UK, and holds occasional beer festivals. The L-shaped room, with a bright bar area, boasts mirrors

from lost breweries including Murray's and Campbell's. The seating is a mixture of soft chairs and church pew style benches, with ample room for vertical drinking. The food menu is excellent, available all day until 7pm Friday to Sunday. Dogs welcome. 🕽&🚌♣

Teuchters Landing

1c Dock Place, Leith, EH6 6LU (1½ miles N of centre)
⊛ 11 (12.30 Sun)-1am ☎ (0131) 554 7427
🌐 aroomin.co.uk/teuchters-landing/index.html
Caledonian Deuchars IPA; Highland Dark Munro; Inveralmond Ossian; Taylor Landlord; guest beer Ⓗ
Converted from the former waiting room for the Leith to Aberdeen ferry, to the front is a comfortable bar where the walls are half wood-panelled, half stone, with a series of Scottish place names listed around the top. The wood-panelled ceiling is in the shape of an upturned boat. To the rear is a larger restaurant and bistro, with a conservatory extension that opens out onto a pontoon floating on the Water of Leith. Meals are served all day. Children are welcome until 10pm. Free WiFi. Q🕮🕽&🚌🏠

Thomson's Bar Ⓛ ✔

182-4 Morrison Street, EH3 8EB (W edge of centre)
⊛ 12-11.30 (midnight Thu & Sat; 1am Fri); 4-11.30 Sun
☎ (0131) 228 5700
Caledonian Deuchars IPA; Harviestoun Bitter & Twisted Ⓐ**; guest beers** Ⓗ
This award-winning pub is dedicated to the style of Glasgow architect Alexander 'Greek' Thomson and the traditional Scottish air pressure dispense system. The superb hand-made gantry is inlaid with scenes from Greek mythology and the walls contain a range of mirrors, adverts and elaborate point of sale material from long-forgotten Scottish breweries. Beers from Oakham are often guests along with a wide range of Scottish ales. No food is available on Sunday and pies only on Saturday. Dogs welcome. Q🕮🕽≠(Haymarket)🚌♣🏠

Windsor Buffet

45 Elm Row, EH7 4AH (¾ mile N of centre)
⊛ 11 (12.30 Sun)-1am ☎ (0131) 556 4558
Caledonian Deuchars IPA; guest beers Ⓗ
This late Victorian bar, on busy Leith Walk, has been significantly altered in recent years. Still very much a locals' bar, it retains a traditional look but is now brighter and more open plan. Comfortable green leather armchairs and bench seating throughout complement the extensive wood panelling. The beer range has been expanded, with the three guests coming from a range of Scottish breweries. Dogs welcome. Free WiFi. 🕮≠(Waverley)🚌

Winston's Ⓛ ✔

20 Kirk Loan, Corstorphine, EH12 7HD (3 miles W of centre off St Johns Rd)
⊛ 11-11.30 (midnight Thu-Sat); 12.30-11 Sun
☎ (0131) 539 7077
Caledonian Deuchars IPA; guest beers Ⓗ
A comfortable single-room lounge bar situated in Corstorphine, just over a mile from Murrayfield stadium and close to the zoo. The small, modern building houses a warm and welcoming community pub. Popular with old and young alike, children are welcome until 3pm. The decor is golf and rugby themed, along with historic photographs of Corstorphine. Lunchtime food includes wonderful home-made pies (not available Sun). Dogs welcome. Free WiFi. 🕮🕽🚌🏠

SCOTLAND

Gifford

Goblin Ha' Hotel
Main Street, EH41 4QH
✪ 11-11 (1am Fri & Sat) ☎ (01620) 810244 ⊕ goblinha.com
Caledonian Deuchars IPA; Hop Back Summer
Lightning; Taylor Landlord; guest beer Ⓗ
Long-established inn near the village green. The focus is on food in the smart, contemporary lounge bar and conservatories, with colourful decor and light-stained wood, though an area is available for drinking. Non-diners may prefer the more rustic public bar, with its half wood, half stone walls, leading to a games room with pool table. Occasional live music is hosted. Gluten free meals are available. The patio and garden are popular in summer. Dogs welcome. Free WiFi.
🏚️🌸🚪◑🍴🛠️🚍♣

Glencorse

Flotterstone Inn Ⓛ
Milton Bridge, EH26 0PP (off A702 by Pentlands visitor centre)
✪ 11.30 (12.30 Sun)-11 ☎ (01968) 673717
⊕ flotterstoneinn.com
Stewart Pentland IPA; guest beers Ⓗ
Family-run pub with a large rectangular lounge bar with church pew seating and numerous toby jugs and plates around the walls. A modern timber-clad extension overlooks the enclosed garden and provides additional space. Good food is served all day in two dining rooms, which have bare stone walls and wooden ceilings. A handy place to recover from a day on the nearby Pentland Hills, the pub gets busy at weekends, and children are welcome. Dogs allowed if on a lead.
🌸◑🛠️🚍(100)♣P⬩⬩

Gullane

Old Clubhouse Ⓛ
East Links Road, EH31 2AF (W end of village, off A198)
✪ 11-11 (midnight Thu-Sat); 12.30-11 Sun
☎ (01620) 842008 ⊕ oldclubhouse.com
Caledonian Deuchars IPA; Taylor Landlord Ⓟ; guest beer Ⓗ
There is a colonial touch to this pub, built in 1890 to accommodate members of the original Gullane golf club, with views over the links to the Lammermuir Hills. The half-panelled walls are adorned with historic memorabilia and stuffed animals. Caricature statuettes of the Marx Brothers and Laurel and Hardy look down from the gantry. Food features highly and is served all day – the extensive menu includes seafood, pasta, barbecue, curries, salads and burgers. Gullane's only real ale outlet, children are welcome until 8pm. Dogs are also welcome. 🏚️🌸◑🚍♣⬩⬩

Haddington

Tyneside Tavern Ⓛ ✔
10 Poldrate, EH41 4DA
✪ 11-11 (midnight Thu & Sun; 1am Fri & Sat); 12.30-11 Sun
☎ (01620) 822221 ⊕ tynesidetavern.co.uk
Caledonian Deuchars IPA; guest beers Ⓗ
Dating from the 18th century, this community pub lies next to an old water mill by the River Tyne. On the left on entering is the long narrow main bar, popular for TV sport. On the right is the more spacious lounge bar. The pub is known for its

excellent selection of guest ales. Hearty good-value pub food is freshly made with locally sourced seasonal ingredients, served in both bars and are available all day at weekends. Children and dogs are welcome and free WiFi is available.
🏚️🌸◑🍴♿🚍

Victoria Inn & Avenue Restaurant
9 Court Street, EH41 3JD
✪ 11-11 (midnight Fri & Sat); 12.30-11 Sun
☎ (01620) 823332 ⊕ theavenuerestaurant.co.uk
Beer range varies Ⓗ
Recognised by its colourful window baskets in summer, the focus is on quality food at this stylish town-centre inn. However, drinkers are made most welcome. The contemporary and comfortable bar with its horseshoe counter has bar chairs and tall tables for drinkers as well as a dining area. Upstairs is more dining space as well as five comfortable bedrooms. Food is served all day on Sunday. Children welcome until 10pm if eating. Free WiFi.
🏚️Q🌸🚪◑♿🚍

Waterside Bistro Ⓛ
1-5 Waterside, EH41 4AT (by Nungate Bridge)
✪ 12 (12.30 Sun)-11; closed Mon & weekday afternoons winter ☎ (01620) 825674 ⊕ watersidebistro.co.uk
Stewart Pentland IPA; guest beer Ⓗ
Occupying a picture-postcard setting by the old Nungate Bridge, this bistro enjoys views across the River Tyne to historic St Mary's Collegiate Church. The bar features a long light oak counter, comfortable seating, a wood-burning stove, exposed stone walls and two rather incongruous metal pillars. Upstairs are various dining rooms and a retail outlet selling bottled beers and wines. Scotland's larder is the inspiration for the quality food, with the emphasis on seasonal, locally-sourced produce. Children are welcome. Dogs welcome in the bar area and free WiFi is available.
🏚️Q🌸◑🚍P

Linlithgow

Four Marys ♈ Ⓛ ✔
65-67 High Street, EH49 7ED
✪ 12-11 (midnight Wed & Thu; 12.30am Fri & Sat); 12.30-11 Sun ☎ (01506) 842171 ⊕ thefourmarys.co.uk
Belhaven 80/-, St Andrews Ale; Caledonian Deuchars IPA; guest beers Ⓗ
Much commended pub in the main street opposite Linlithgow Palace, the birthplace of Mary Queen of Scots, and named after her ladies-in-waiting. The pub walls are decked with mementos of Mary. The building has seen many uses in its 500-year history, from dwelling-house to shop. It holds popular beer festivals in May and October when 20 or more beers from around the UK are available in two bars. Local CAMRA Pub of the Year 2011.
🌸◑🍴🚆🚍⬩⬩

Platform 3 ✔
1A High Street, EH49 7AB (next to railway station)
✪ 10.30-midnight (1am Fri & Sat); 12.30-midnight Sun
☎ (01506) 847405 ⊕ platform3.co.uk
Caledonian Deuchars IPA; guest beers Ⓗ
Small, friendly pub of great character conveniently situated next to the train station, hence the name, and only a short walk to bus connections. Look out for the model train that makes regular journeys along the suspended track. With an increasing number of handpumps, the bar offers a good range of guest ales from Cairngorm, Harviestoun or

Stewart breweries. Live music includes regular folk sessions. Dogs are most welcome, with biscuits 'on tap'.

Lothianburn

Steading

118-120 Biggar Road, EH10 7DU (on A702, just S of bypass)
11-11 (midnight Fri & Sat); 12.30-11 Sun
(0131) 445 1128
Caledonian Deuchars IPA; Taylor Landlord; guest beer H
Originally created from a row of farm cottages, the bar is divided into different areas, with comfortable chairs and settees ideal for relaxing with a drink, and higher tables for dining. The popular restaurant includes a large conservatory extension (food is served all day). Outside, there are excellent views of the Pentland Hills, and the pub is ideally placed for a relaxing pint after walking in the hills or visiting the nearby dry ski slope. May close early if quiet. Children and dogs welcome. Free WiFi. P

Musselburgh

Levenhall Arms

10 Ravensheugh Road, EH21 7PP (B1348, 1m E of centre)
12-11 (midnight Thu & Sun; 1am Fri & Sat); 12.30-11 Sun
(0131) 665 3220
Stewart Pentland IPA P**; guest beers** H
This three-roomed hostelry dates from 1830 and is popular with locals and racegoers. The lively, cheerfully decorated public bar is half timber-panelled and carpeted. A smaller area leads off, with a dartboard and pictures of old local industries. The quieter lounge area, with vinyl banquettes, is used for dining (food served all day until 8pm). Children are permitted in the lounge until 8.30pm. Opening times and the menu may vary in winter. Q(Wallyford)P

Volunteer Arms (Staggs)

81 North High Street, EH21 6JE (behind Brunton Hall)
12-11 (11.30 Thu; midnight Fri); 11-midnight Sat; 12.30-11 Sun (0131) 665 9654 staggsbar.com
Caledonian Deuchars IPA; guest beers H
Superb pub run by the same family since 1858. The bar and snug are traditional with wooden floors, wood panelling and mirrors from defunct local breweries. An attractive gantry is topped with old casks. The more modern lounge opens at the weekend. Three guest beers are available, often pale and hoppy, and changing regularly. Dogs are welcome in the bar, but don't bring the kids. Local CAMRA Pub of the Year 2010.

Newton

Duddingston Arms

13-15 Main Street, EH52 6QE (1 mile W of South Queensferry on A904 Boness/Linlithgow road)
12-2.30, 4.30-10; 12-11 Fri & Sat; 12.30-11 Sun
(0131) 331 1948 duddingstonarms.com
Beer range varies H
Decked out with hanging baskets, this establishment is easy to spot on the main road through the village – and well worth delaying your journey for. The pub has been a family-owned business since 1832, with three handpulls serving beers from Tryst, Stewart and Kelburn, and some from further afield making regular appearances. The pub acts as a gallery for local artists, with pictures available for sale. Very much a community pub, ramblers, cyclists, fishermen and dogs are all welcome. (474)

North Berwick

Nether Abbey Hotel

20 Dirleton Avenue, EH39 4BQ (on A198 ¾ mile W of city centre)
11-11 (midnight Thu; 1am Fri & Sat) (01620) 892802
netherabbey.co.uk
Caledonian Deuchars IPA; Taylor Landlord A**; guest beers** H
Originally a grand seaside villa built at the turn of the 19th century, this busy, family-run hotel has a bright, contemporary interior. The open-plan, split-level room has a bar on the lower area and a restaurant on the upper level. The marble-topped bar counter displays a row of modern chrome founts – the middle ones, with horizontally moving levers, dispense the real ales. Food is served all day at weekends. Children are welcome until 9pm. Dogs are also welcome. Free WiFi. P

Penicuik

Navaar

23 Bog Road, EH26 9BY
12-1am (midnight Sun) (01968) 672683
Stewart Pentland IPA H
A lively pub with a strong community spirit, situated in an old private house, built circa 1870. The large bar is open plan with a log/coal fire and TV screens. The restaurant, with an extensive a la carte menu, serves meals all day. Snacks are available in the bar. A large patio and decking are popular in summer. Dogs welcome. P

Prestonpans

Prestoungrange Gothenburg ☆

227 High Street, EH32 9BE
closed Mon; 12-3, 5-11; 12-midnight Fri & Sat; 12.30-11 Sun (01875) 819922 thegoth.co.uk
Beer range varies A
Superb Gothenburg pub that features in CAMRA's National Inventory of Historic Pub Interiors. The 100-year-old listed building's magnificent painted ceiling in the bar has to be seen to be appreciated. Fowler's micro-brewery can be viewed from the bar area. There is also a bistro and upstairs is a lounge and function room with superb views over the Forth. The walls throughout are covered in murals and paintings depicting past local life. Meals, including gluten-free options, are served lunchtimes and evenings, all day Friday to Sunday. Children welcome. P

Keep your Good Beer Guide up to date by visiting the CAMRA website **camra.org.uk**, then Good Beer Guide, then Updates.

SCOTLAND

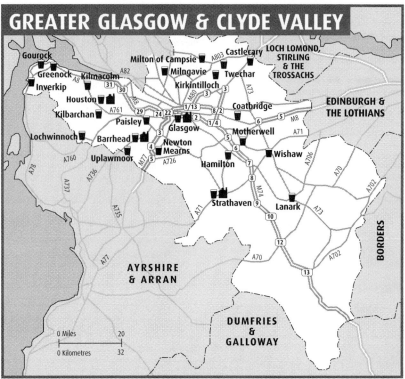

GREATER GLASGOW & CLYDE VALLEY

Authority areas covered: Argyll & Bute UA, Ayrshire UAs, City of Glasgow UA, Dunbartonshire UAs, Inverclyde UA, Lanarkshire UAs, Renfrewshire UAs

Barrhead

Cross Stobs Inn 🅛

2-6 Grahamston Road, G78 1NS (on B7712)
🕒 11-11 (midnight Thu & Sat; 1am Fri); 12.30-11 Sun
☎ (0141) 881 1581
Kelburn Misty Law; guest beer 🅗
Eighteenth-century coaching inn on the road to Paisley. The public bar has a real coal fire and retains much of its original charm with antique furniture and service bells. The lounge is spacious and leads out to an enclosed rear garden. There is also an outside drinking area at the front of the pub. The bar leads to a pool room and a function suite that can be hired privately. The guest beer is always from the nearby Kelburn Brewery.
🏛Q🕸🕐▷🔅&⚞🍴🚌(51,101)

Waterside Inn

The Hurlet, Glasgow Road, G53 7TH (A736 near Hurlet, on edge of Barrhead)
🕒 11-11 (midnight Fri & Sat); 12.30-11 Sun
☎ (0141) 881 2822 ⊕ thewatersideinn.net
Kelburn Red Smiddy; guest beer 🅗
Comfortable and friendly bar and restaurant near Levern Water. Food is the main focus here, but there is a cosy area with a real log fire for those just wanting to enjoy a relaxing drink. The decor includes old local photographs on the walls. Themed nights are held fairly regularly, often musical, such as an Abba tribute night. The guest beer is always from the local Kelburn Brewery.
🏛🕸🕐▷&🚌(103,X44B)P

Castlecary

Castlecary House Hotel

Castlecary Road, G68 0HD (just off A80 near M80 jct 4)
🕒 11-11 (11.30 Thu-Sat); 12.30-11 Sun ☎ (01324) 840233
⊕ castlecaryhotel.com
Beer range varies 🅗
Large hotel situated just off the new Glasgow to Stirling motorway and the old Glasgow to Edinburgh train viaduct. It has long been a provider of real ales, delivering an ever-changing range of beers from local Scottish micro-breweries as well as English brewers – look for the blackboard to see what's available. Its own-label Bottleneck (brewed by Tryst) is also often available. The three bars are connected to a central service area.
Q🕸🛏🕐▷&🚌(X37,X39)P🚺

Coatbridge

Vulcan ⊘

181 Main Street, ML5 3HH (jct with Dunbeth Rd)
🕒 11-1am; 12-midnight Sun ☎ (01236) 437972
Caledonian Deuchars IPA; Greene King Abbot; guest beers 🅗
Modern bar in a late 20th-century style, situated in the centre of a town once known as the Iron Burgh. Appropriately named after an old local iron works, it is conveniently close to the Summerlee Museum of Scottish Life. Now a Wetherspoon pub, it is smaller than the norm for this chain, which gives it a local feel. As well as two regular beers, the bar offers three guests, usually from Scottish micros.
🕐▷&⚞(Sunnyside)🚌(62)●

Glasgow

Babbity Bowster
16-18 Blackfriars Street, Merchant City, G1 1PE
(between High St and Walls St/Albion St)
☼ 11 (12.30 Sun)-midnight ☎ (0141) 552 5055
Caledonian Deuchars IPA; Kelburn Misty Law; guest beer Ⓐ

Tall, pale building with large windows in a small, secluded street, just off the busy High Street. This is a welcoming haven where a cosmopolitan mix of drinkers and diners provide a hubbub of lively conversation. Three traditional tall founts dispense ales to accompany the bar menu that includes superb local dishes, with more Scottish fare served in the upstairs restaurant. The sheltered beer garden with flower boxes and trees is a city-centre rarity and a pleasure in summer.
⚌Q❀❄◑≢(High Street/Argyle St/Queen St)
⊖(Buchanan St)◫P⌐

Blackfriars Ⓛ
36 Bell Street, Merchant City, G1 1LG
☼ 11 (12.30 Sun)-midnight ☎ (0141) 552 5924
⊕ blackfriarsglasgow.com
Beer range varies Ⓗ

Traditional corner local in Glasgow's modern Merchant City. A café bar area overlooks the street, the bar is in the middle and to the rear is a quiet dining section. Friendly staff serve Kelburn and other ales from Scotland and Britain from five handpumps. There is also an interesting selection of American and European bottled beers. Meals are served until 10pm. Entertainment includes quiz night on Monday, live bands Tuesday and Sunday, tango club on Wednesday and club nights on Saturday and Sunday.
❀◑≢(High St/Argyll St/Queen St)
⊖(Buchanan St)◫(18,62)♣⌐

Bon Accord ♟ Ⓛ ✪
153 North Street, G3 7DA
☼ 11-midnight; 12.30-11 Sun ☎ (0141) 248 4427
⊕ bonaccordweb.co.uk
Caledonian Deuchars IPA; Marston's Pedigree; guest beers Ⓗ

The Bon Accord opened in 1971 and in just a few years established itself as one of the foremost real ale pubs in Glasgow. The present owners took over 10 years ago and have maintained the high standards, winning several CAMRA branch Pub of the Year awards in the process. There are eight guest beers available from local and more distant breweries. In addition, there is a large range of malt whiskies and a thriving whisky club.
❀◑≢(Charing Cross/Anderston)◫(62)♣⌐

Crystal Palace ✪
36 Jamaica Street, G1 4QD
☼ 11 (12.30 Sun)-midnight ☎ (0141) 221 2624
Caledonian Deuchars IPA; Greene King Abbot; guest beers Ⓗ

Two sides of this listed, former furniture store are made almost entirely of glass. There are bars on two floors, each with a different beer range. The main bar downstairs can be busy, with occasional TV sports, but quieter areas include a back room where children are welcome during the day. It is also more peaceful upstairs. Note the original cage lift, providing access for wheelchairs. A wide choice of ales is available and the pub attracts city workers, travellers and pre-clubbers.
Q👶❀◑⛫≢(Central)⊖(St Enoch)◫

Drum & Monkey ✪
91 St Vincent Street, G2 5TF (corner with Renfield St)
☼ 12-11 (midnight Fri & Sat); 12.30-11 Sun
☎ (0141) 221 6636
Caledonian Deuchars IPA, 80; guest beers Ⓗ

Situated in the centre of Glasgow, on the junction with Renfield Street, this corner pub is a feast of wood panelling, ornate plasterwork and interesting curios from a bygone age. Formerly a bank, the main bar room is on two levels, providing separate seating areas around a peninsula bar, which serves up to five real ales. Food is available, with a rear room for dining. Expect to while away several hours in this busy but cosy bar.
◑⛫≢(Central/Queen St)⊖(Buchanan St)◫

Esquire House ✪
1487 Great Western Road, Anniesland, G12 0AU
☼ 11-11 (midnight Thu-Sat); 12.30-11 Sun
☎ (0141) 341 1130
Caledonian Deuchars IPA; Greene King Abbot; guest beers Ⓗ

A community pub in the north west of the city, established more than 10 years ago. Unusually for Wetherspoon, this was a new-build, and is one of the smaller pubs in the chain, helping to develop a good local ambience. Up to eight guest beers are on offer, many from small local breweries, served by interested and helpful staff. Open from 9am for breakfast, the pub is easily accessible by rail and bus. ❀◑⛫≢(Anniesland)◫(20,66,118)♣P⌐

Granary ✪
10 Kilmarnock Road, G41 3NH (jct with Pollokshaws Rd)
☼ 12-11 (midnight Fri & Sat); 12.30-midnight Sun
☎ (0141) 649 0594 ⊕ nicholsonpubs.co.uk/thegranaryshawlandsglasgow/
Beer range varies Ⓗ

A triangular building sandwiched between the Y-junction of two major roads, the pub is on main bus routes from the city centre. Cask ales are in the central bar, the largest of the three public rooms, and on either side are areas used for dining. With a selection of fine malt whiskies and unusual European bottled beers and wines, the Granary caters for a wide variety of discerning drinkers.
◑⛫≢(Crossmyloof)◫

Mulberry St
778 Pollokshaws Road, G41 2AE
☼ 11-11 (midnight Fri & Sat); 12.30-11 Sun
☎ (0141) 424 0858 ⊕ mulberrystbarbistro.com
Harviestoun Bitter & Twisted; guest beer Ⓗ

Welcoming cafe-bar and restaurant at the heart of the community. Moray Place, designed by local architect Alexander 'Greek' Thomson, and Queen's Park are close by. Up to two real ales are served, supplemented by a small selection of foreign bottled beers. Food is available in both bar and restaurant until late. The pub can get extremely busy at weekends, although the large windows help to create a roomy feel even when there's a crowd. A quiz is held on Monday night.
❀◑⛫≢(Queen's Park/Pollokshields West)◫⌐

INDEPENDENT BREWERIES

Clockwork Glasgow
Houston Houston
Kelburn Barrhead
Strathaven Strathaven

SCOTLAND

Cobbs at Nevisport

Airds Crossing, High Street, PH33 6EU (beneath
Nevisport shop) NN110742
🕓 11-11 (1am Fri & Sat); 12.30-11 Sun ☎ (01397) 704790
⏣ cobbs.info
Beer range varies ▣
Convenient for Glen Nevis and at the end of the
West Highland Way, this large but cosy bar is a
favourite meeting place for walkers, climbers and
skiers. A collection of mountaineering photographs
and paraphernalia adorns the walls and a large
warming open fire welcomes winter visitors.
Traditional Scottish breakfasts, bar meals and
home-baked cakes are served in the bar and the
upstairs restaurant where children are welcome.
Beers are mainly Scottish, often from the Atlas and
Isle of Skye breweries. 🏨🍽🏮🚲🕭🅰♿🚌🚃

Grog & Gruel ✪

66 High Street, PH33 6AE
🕓 12 (4 Mon-Fri winter)-11.30; 12-12.30am Thu-Sat; 12 (5
winter)-11.30 Sun ☎ (01397) 705078 ⏣ grogandgruel.co.uk
Beer range varies ▣
This recently refurbished traditional ale house
keeps up to six beers in summer, fewer in winter,
and holds regular live music and beer festivals. The
beers are predominantly Scottish, often from the
local Glenfinnan Brewery, and the bar is busy with
locals, outdoor enthusiasts and tourists. Home-
cooked food is available in the upstairs restaurant
and light meals and snacks in the bar.
🍽🍴🅰♿🚌🚃

Fortrose

Anderson

Union Street, IV10 8TD
🕓 4-11.30; 12.30-11.30 Sun ☎ (01381) 620236
⏣ theanderson.co.uk
Beer range varies ▣
Homely bar, restaurant and rooms in a quiet
seaside village. The owners are an international
beer writer and self-confessed beer geek, and his
wife, a New Orleans-trained chef. Serving ale and
cider from more than 250 breweries since 2003,
this beer drinkers' mecca also offers more than 240
malts and 100 Belgian beers, earning it several
awards. Entertainment includes winter beer
festivals, regular quizzes, music sessions and
knitting nights. Food is reasonably priced, high-
quality international cuisine. CAMRA members are
offered a discount on accommodation in winter.
🏨🍽🏮🍴🅰🚌🚃(26)♣♿🅿♿

Gairloch

Old Inn 🄻

Flowerdale, IV21 2BD (opp harbour) NG811751
🕓 11-1am (11.45 Sat); 12-11.15 Sun ☎ (0800) 542 5444
⏣ theoldinn.net
**An Teallach Ale; Isle of Skye Red Cuillin; Old Inn The
Erradale; guest beers** ▣
Family-owned traditional Highland coaching inn, in
a delightful setting at the foot of Flowerdale Glen.
The finest quality local produce, including home-
cooked game and freshly landed seafood, takes
pride of place on the menu. A range of Scottish and
English ales is served, including brews from the
inn's own in-house micro-brewery. Close to Loch
Maree, Inverewe Gardens and the Beinn Eighe
Nature Reserve, this is an ideal base for exploring
the delights of Wester Ross. 🏨🍽🏮🍴🅰♣🅿

Glencoe

Clachaig Inn 🄻

PH49 4HX (on slip road ½ mile off A83) NN128567
🕓 11-11 (midnight Fri; 11.30 Sat); 11-11 Sun
☎ (01855) 811 252 ⏣ clachaig.com
Beer range varies ▣
A legend among mountain climbers and other
outdoor enthusiasts, the Clachaig provides a
welcome refuge after a hard day on the hills or a
long drive. The Boots Bar has up to 10 handpumps
serving real ale, usually from Cairngorm and other
Scottish breweries, while the Bidean Lounge has
three pumps. A real cider is also usually available.
The pub stages beer festivals twice a year and
there is regular live music at weekends. Good pub
grub is available in both bars.
🏨🅀🍽🏮🍴🅰🚌(916)♿🅿♿

Inverie

Old Forge

PH41 4PL (100m from ferry terminal)
🕓 11 (winter 4pm; 1 Sat)-midnight; 11-1am Fri & Sat; 11 (1
winter)-midnight Sun ☎ (01678) 462267
⏣ theoldforge.co.uk
Beer range varies ▣
The most remote pub in mainland Britain can be
reached only by ferry from Mallaig or a 15-mile
hilly walk. In a spectacular setting on the shore of
Loch Nevis, it provides an ideal location for walking
the rough bounds of Knoydart. Moorings welcome
waterborne visitors. Two handpumps usually
include a beer from Isle of Skye or Glenfinnan
breweries. Excellent food is served all day featuring
locally caught seafood and game. 🏨🅀🍽🍴🅰♿

Inverness

Blackfriars 🄻 ✪

93-95 Academy Street, IV1 1LU
🕓 11-midnight (1am Fri; 12.30am Sat); 5-11 Sun
☎ (01463) 233881 ⏣ blackfriarshighlandpub.co.uk
Caledonian Deuchars IPA; guest beers ▣
This popular traditional pub has a spacious single-
room interior with a large standing area by the bar
and ample seating in comfortable alcoves. The five
handpumps are dedicated to a wide variety of
Scottish ales, often from Inveralmond, An Teallach
and Highland. A further two handpumps dispense
real cider. Good value meals feature home-cooked
Scottish fare with daily specials. A welcoming
music-oriented venue, it features ceilidh, folk,
blues and country, with local bands performing at
weekends. 🍴♿🚌🚃♿

Castle Tavern 🄻

1 View Place, IV2 4SA (top of Castle Street) NH666449
🕓 11-1am (12.30am Sat); 12.30-midnight Sun
☎ (01463) 718178 ⏣ castletavern.net
**Cairngorm Trade Winds; Highland Scapa Special;
Houston Peter's Well; Isle of Skye Flora MacDonald's;
guest beers** ▣
Listed building with fine views across the River
Ness towards Inverness Cathedral. A buzzing city-
centre pub with all the friendliness of a village
local, it has six handpumps dispensing an Isle of
Skye house beer plus changing guests, mostly from
Scottish independents. A Victorian-style canopy
covers the beer garden, where there is an extra bar
during the pub's September Real Ale Festival. Bar
meals are served all day, and there is a restaurant
on the first floor. 🍽🍴🅰🚌🚃(6,7,14)🚃

Clachnaharry Inn

17-19 High Street, Clachnaharry, IV3 8RB (on A862 Beauly Road) NH648466
☼ 11-11 (1am Thu-Fri; 12.30am Sat); 12-11.45 Sun
☎ (01463) 239806 ⊕ clachnaharryinn.co.uk
Beer range varies Ⓗ
Popular with locals and visitors, this friendly 17th-century coaching inn offers high-quality food made with locally-sourced ingredients lunchtimes and evenings, and families are made welcome. Five handpumps dispense mainly Scottish guest beers, often from Inveralmond, Orkney/Atlas and Cairngorm breweries. The large patio area affords fine views over the Caledonian Canal sea lock and Beauly Firth toward the distant Ben Wyvis. The beer garden was once the platform of the old village station on the north railway line. Dogs are welcome in the public bar.
ⓆⓆ⌂⏺♿⛲🅿(18A)♣P

Kings Highway ✅

72-74 Church Street, IV1 1EN
☼ 11-11 (midnight Thu & Sat; 1am Fri); 12.30-11 Sun
☎ (01463) 251830
Caledonian Deuchars IPA; Greene King Abbot; guest beers Ⓗ
This former hotel is now a Wetherspoon pub with a 27-room lodge attached. The vast single roomed bar is broken up by several pillars and plenty of comfortable seating in alcoves. Up to 10 handpumps serve the regular ales alongside a good mix of guests, including beers from Houston, Cairngorm and Isle of Skye breweries. Real cider is also available. Food is standard Wetherspoon, with breakfasts served from 7am. Customers are the typical eclectic mix and the pub gets busy at weekends. 🍴⏺♿🚲♣

Snowgoose ✅

Stoneyfield, IV2 7PA (on A96)
☼ 12-11 (10.30 Sun-Thu Jan-Mar) ☎ (01463) 701921
Caledonian Deuchars IPA; guest beers Ⓗ
This traditional inn supports a popular bar trade, with an area reserved for drinkers. Situated next to a Holiday Inn and a Travelodge, most of its custom comes from the local area. A converted 1788 coach house, the single large L-shaped room has alcoves and log fires to give it a more cosy and intimate feel. A wide variety of food is offered all day at reasonable prices. The two guest handpumps feature ever-changing ales from the Mitchells & Butlers Vintage Inn list. ⓆⓆ⌂⏺♿(1,10)P

Kincraig

Suie Hotel Ⓛ

PH21 1NA
☼ 5-11 (1am Fri & Sat) ☎ (01540) 651344 ⊕ suiehotel.com
Cairngorm Trade Winds, Stag Ⓗ
Cosy wooden extension to a seven-bedroomed Victorian character hotel, run by only the second owner in 105 years. The wooden floored bar features a large stove and open fire, and has an alcove with a pool table and juke-box. Close to the River Spey and Loch Insh, the bar is popular with locals, hillwalkers, skiers and cyclists. Traditional Scottish music features occasionally. Good food is served. ⓆⓆ⌂⏺🚲♣P

Nairn

Braeval Hotel ♀ ✅

Crescent Road, IV12 4NB
☼ 12-midnight (12.30am Thu-Sat); 12.30-midnight Sun Apr-Dec; 12 (12.30 Thu-Sat)-2.30, 5-midnight; 12.30-midnight Sun winter ☎ (01667) 452341 ⊕ braevalhotel.co.uk
Beer range varies Ⓗ/Ⓖ
The Bandstand Bar is part of the Braeval Hotel, close to Nairn Beach. It has up to eight handpumps offering a wide range of Scottish ales, often from Fyne Ales, Highland and other local breweries, and a range of English ales is also stocked. The restaurant in this family-run hotel enjoys spectacular sea views overlooking the Moray Firth. The bar hosts a beer festival every spring, featuring at least 50 ales. CAMRA Highlands & Western Isles Pub of the Year 2009 and 2011.
ⓆⓆ⌂⏺♿⛲🅿

Newtonmore

Glen Hotel Ⓛ ✅

Main Street, PH20 1DD
☼ 11 (12.30 Sun)-midnight ☎ (01540) 673203
⊕ theglenhotel.co.uk
Beer range varies Ⓗ
Small, welcoming, family-run hotel in Monarch of the Glen country in the Cairngorms National Park. It has a good local trade and is also popular with outdoor enthusiasts and tourists. The large bar room has separate games and dining rooms, and regular quiz and games nights are held. Up to four handpumps dispense mainly Scottish beers, usually including one from Cairngorm, plus a Westons cider or perry. An extensive menu includes a good selection of vegetarian dishes. ⓆⓆ⌂⏺♿⛲♣P

Plockton

Plockton Hotel Ⓛ ✅

41 Harbour Street, IV52 8TN NG803335
☼ 11-midnight; 12.30-11 Sun ☎ (01599) 544274
⊕ plocktonhotel.co.uk
Beer range varies Ⓗ
Sheltered by mountains and fanned by the warm air of the Gulf Stream, the hotel is at the edge of Loch Carron and boasts breathtaking views across the bay. Seafood is the speciality on an excellent menu that also features locally-reared beef and Highland venison. The village has much to offer and is a regular haunt for outdoor enthusiasts. Brews from the local Plockton Brewery are regularly on handpump. ⓆⓆ⌂⏺♿⛲♣P

Plockton Inn Ⓛ ✅

Innes Street, IV52 8TW NG803333
☼ 11-1am (12.30am Sat); 11-11 Sun ☎ (01599) 544222
⊕ plocktoninn.co.uk
Plockton Plockton Bay Ⓗ
Popular village inn owned and run by a local family for many years. Locally caught fish and shellfish take pride of place on the menu – the seafood platter includes fish smoked on the premises. Every Tuesday and Thursday there are live music sessions in the public bar and all are welcome to join in. A regularly changing selection of real ales includes locally-brewed Plockton Brewery ales. ⓆⓆ⌂⏺♿⛲♣P

bar food is served at lunchtime. The pub received a Best Bar None award in 2008, 2009 and 2010 from Fife Constabulary. ⊛(ċ&₪'⌐

Freuchie

Albert Tavern ▼
2 High Street, KY15 7EX
🕔 5 (12 Fri & Sat)-midnight; 12.30-midnight Sun ☎ 07876 178863
Beer range varies ⊞
Friendly village local, reputedly a coaching inn when nearby Falkland Palace was a royal residence. Wainscot panelling and two old brewery mirrors adorn the walls of the bar, and both bar and lounge have beamed ceilings. A TV in the lounge screens sport. Four handpumps offer weekly-changing guest beers, usually including a dark mild. There is a small patio area outside. A multi-award winner, including Scottish CAMRA Pub of the Year, National Pub of the Year runner-up, and local CAMRA Pub of the Year for the past three years. ♨Q⊛⊛₪(X54,64)P'⌐

Lomond Hills Hotel
High Street, KY15 7EY
🕔 11-2, 5-midnight; 11-midnight Fri & Sat; 12.30-midnight Sun ☎ (01337) 857329 ⊕ lomondhillshotel.com
Beer range varies ⊞
Comfortable country hotel with a marvellous view of the Lomond Hills. The small, welcoming public bar sports a carved bar top and wood panelling on the walls. A plasma screen shows sport. Two beers are always available. Meals are served in the family lounge and a separate dining room. Outside there is a smoking area and beer garden. The hotel has a leisure area with heated pool and sauna available to guests and a conservatory available for functions. ♨ゑ⊛⊛(Ď ⊞&₪(X54,64)P'⌐

Glenrothes

Golden Acorn ⦿
1 North Street, KY7 5NA (next to bus station)
🕔 11 (12.30 Sun)-midnight ☎ (01592) 751175
Greene King Abbot ⊞
Large Wetherspoon venue with its own accommodation. In the bar, scenes of the local area in days gone by decorate various pillars. Real ale on four handpumps and an occasional cider are on offer, as well as the usual Wetherspoon beer festivals and special deals. The local Fyfe Brewing Company sometimes also holds a beer festival. Breakfast is served from 7.30am. Plasma screens show sport, and there is a smoking and seating area outside. ⊛ฅ(Ď&Å▐⊛P'⌐

Kinghorn

Auld Hoose
6-8 Nethergate, KY3 9SY
🕔 12 (11 Sat; 12.30 Sun)-midnight ☎ (01592) 891074
Fuller's London Pride; guest beers ⊞
Busy village local situated on a steep side street leading off the east end of Kinghorn main street, handy for the station, Kinghorn beach and the Fife Coastal Path. Popular with locals and visitors, the main bar has a TV and pool table to keep sports fans happy and features dominoes competitions at the weekend. Bar snacks are available. The lounge is quieter and more comfortable, with a relaxed atmosphere. ⊞&₪(6,7)♣

Crown Tavern
55-57 High Street, KY3 9UW
🕔 11 (12.30 Sun)-11.45 ☎ (01592) 890340
Beer range varies ⊞
Bustling two-roomed local, also called The Middle Bar, situated to the west end of the High Street. Two ever-changing ales are dispensed by cheery bar staff. Attractive stained glass panels adorn the windows and door, and the high ceilings feature ornate plaster work. Mainly a sports bar, two TVs and a large projector screen show games. There is also a pool table in a side room. A collection of footballs autographed by Scottish Premier League players is displayed at the end of bar. ⇒₪(6,7)♣

Ship
2 Bruce Street, KY3 9TJ
🕔 12 (12.30 Sun)-midnight ☎ (01592) 890655
Caledonian Deuchars IPA; guest beer ⊞
This is one of the oldest buildings in Kinghorn, originally built as a house for Bible John, who printed the first bibles in Scotland. The unobtrusive entrance door facing the main road opens into a fine timber-panelled interior with a long bar counter, ornate gantry and a welcoming coal fire. The small jug bar is probably one of the finest surviving traditional interiors in Fife. An attractively decorated dining area has been added at the rear. A busy local, it has a good mixed clientele. ♨(Ď⊞&⇒₪(6,7)'⌐

Kirkcaldy

Harbour Bar
471-475 High Street, KY1 2SN
🕔 11-3, 5-midnight; 11-midnight Thu-Sat; 12.30-midnight Sun ☎ (01592) 264270
Beer range varies ⊞
Situated on the ground floor of a tenement building, this unspoilt local with a brewery on the premises has been described by regulars as a village local in the middle of town. It has a light and airy lounge with ornate cornices. Six handpumps sell up to 20 different beers each week from micros all over Britain, including its own Fyfe Brewery ales. Fife CAMRA Pub of the Year on numerous occasions and Scottish Pub of the Year runner-up in 2000. Q⊟P'⌐

Robert Nairn ⦿
2-6 Kirk Wynd, KY1 1EH
🕔 11 (12.30 Sun)-midnight ☎ (01592) 205049
Caledonian Deuchars IPA; Greene King Abbot ⊞
A Wetherspoon Lloyds No.1 with a split-level lounge and pictures of old Kirkcaldy on the walls. Six handpumps dispense a variety of beers including local ales from Fyfe Brewery – check the noticeboard to see which beers are on and what to look forward to. There is also a good selection of bottled ciders. Beer festivals are held throughout the year. The lively pub attracts a mixed clientele, young and old, who all enjoy the real ales. Meals are served until 10pm. (Ď&₪⊛'⌐

Leslie

Burns Tavern

184 High Street, KY6 3DB

🕐 12 (11 Fri & Sat)-midnight; 12.30-midnight Sun

☎ (01592) 741345

Taylor Landlord; guest beers Ⓗ

Typical Scottish two-room main-street local in a town once famous for paper making. The public bar is on two levels, the lower lively and friendly with an open fire, the upper with a large-screen TV, pool table and football memorabilia on the walls. The lounge bar is quieter and more spacious. Competitions and quizzes are held weekly, with karaoke on Saturday. Leslie folk club meets and plays here on a Sunday. Two beers are usually available. A real gem. ᴴQ🏠🅰🚆(X1,201)♣P⌂

Fettykil Fox ✅

Leslie Roundabout, KY6 3EP (next to Holiday Inn Express)

🕐 12-11 (10.30 Sun) ☎ (01592) 749613

Caledonian Deuchars IPA; guest beer Ⓗ

This is a traditional olde-worlde style building with coal fires at both ends. The decor is a mix of stone, wood panelling and rough plaster on the walls, with oak-beamed ceilings throughout. The bar is furnished with comfortable couches and wooden tables, and decorated with pictures of the local village of Leslie. Food is served all day in two dining areas. The soft background music is a joy. There is also a large enclosed beer garden. ᴴQ🏠🅾🅱🚆🅰🚆(X1,201)P⌂

Limekilns

Ship Inn

Halkett's Hall, KY11 3HJ (on promenade)

🕐 11-11 (midnight Fri & Sat); 12.30-11 Sun

☎ (01383) 872247

Beer range varies Ⓗ

Traditional white coastal building on the waterfront with seating outside providing superb views of the River Forth to watch the ships go by. There is always a friendly welcome here, with fresh flowers, cosy alcoves and a maritime theme throughout. Three guest ales on handpump are complemented by the occasional real cider. Meals are served lunchtimes and evenings, with fish and seafood the speciality. Bar snacks are available outside regular meal times. Q🏠🅾🚆(73,76)P⌂

Lower Largo

Railway Inn

1 Station Wynd, KY8 6BU

🕐 11 (12.30 Sun)-midnight ☎ (01333) 320239

Beer range varies Ⓗ

Small two-room pub with a cosy real fire close to the picturesque harbour. The bar has a railway theme and displays photographs of the last trains to pass on the viaduct overhead before the Beeching measures of the 1960s. TV screens in each room show sport. The four handpumps serve various beers from all over Britain. Bar snacks are available. ᴴQ🏠🚆⌂

St Andrews

Central Bar ✅

77-79 Market Street, KY16 9NU

🕐 11-11.45 (1am Fri & Sat); 12.30-11.45 Sun

☎ (01334) 478296

Courage Directors; Fuller's London Pride; Inveralmond Lia Fail; Theakston Old Peculier Ⓗ

A good mix of students, locals, business folk and tourists makes this an interesting, bustling hostelry. It has a Victorian-style island bar, large windows and ornate mirrors creating a late 19th-century feel. There are tables outside on the pavement, weather permitting. This is the only pub in town where food is available until 10pm. The bar manager is dedicated to his ales and the staff are friendly. Local CAMRA Pub of the Year runner up 2010 and 2011. CAMRA members receive a discount on real ale. 🏠🅾🚆⌂

Criterion

99 South Street, KY16 9QW

🕐 11-midnight (1am Fri & Sat); 12.30-midnight Sun

☎ (01334) 474543

Caledonian Deuchars IPA; guest beers Ⓗ

This lovely pub has a big picture window and oak-panelled walls adorned with photographs of St Andrews in days gone by. The hostelry is famous for its home-made pies including steak and ale, chicken and ham, and lamb and rosemary, served until 5pm. Background music plays and a plasma screen shows sport. Open music night on Monday is popular with local artists, and a regular quiz night is hosted during the week. 🅾🚆

Whey Pat Tavern ✅

1 Bridge Street, KY16 9EX

🕐 11-11.30 (11.45 Fri & Sat); 12.30-11.30 Sun

☎ (01334) 477740

Caledonian Deuchars IPA; Greene King IPA; guest beers Ⓗ

Town-centre pub on a busy road junction just outside the old town walls. There has been a hostelry on this site for several centuries. The front bar is L-shaped with a dartboard and TV, and there is an airy lounge and meeting room to the rear. Seven beers are served on handpump. A mixed clientele of all ages frequents this usually busy venue. ᴴ🅾🅱🚆♣⌂

Strathkinness

Tavern

4 High Road, KY16 9RS (just off A91)

🕐 5-11; 12-midnight Fri-Sun ☎ (01334) 850085

🌐 strathkinnesstavern.co.uk

Beer range varies Ⓗ

Public bar with seating and a comfortable lounge at one end, with two handpulls offering a choice of changing guest ales. There is a separate room with a dartboard, pool table and Sky TV, and brain-teaser games to test your wits. Lunches and evening meals are served in the bar or you can dine in the restaurant. There is a beer garden to the rear and the front of the pub affords lovely views over the river estuary – a good location for plane spotting. Q🏠🅾🅱🅰🚆(64,96)♣P⌂

LOCH LOMOND, STIRLING & THE TROSSACHS

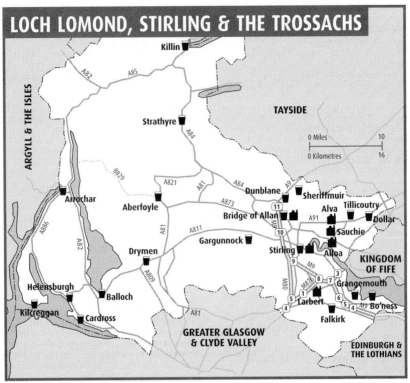

Authority areas covered: Argyll & Bute UA (part), Clackmannanshire UA, Falkirk UA, Stirling UA, West Dumbartonshire UA

Aberfoyle

Forth Inn Hotel 🗘

Main Street, FK8 3UQ

🕓 11-midnight (1am Fri & Sat) ☎ (01877) 382372
🌐 forthinn.com

Harviestoun Schiehallion; guest beers Ⓗ
This hundred-year-old, family-run inn with a wood-panelled bar and a cosy atmosphere is a magnet for tourists and locals. Entertainment is laid on most weekends and the pub hosts a three-day beer festival once a year. The restaurant uses local produce and accommodation is available. The inn is situated on a riverside within the Trossachs National Park. 🏯Q🌸🚪🕪🍴🔥🍽🏧🛢P🕾

Arrochar

Village Inn ✅

Shore Road, G83 7AX (on A814) NN293034

🕓 11-midnight (1am Fri & Sat); 12-midnight Sun
☎ (01301) 702279 🌐 villageinnarrochar.co.uk

Beer range varies Ⓗ
A regular in the Guide, impressive views over Loch Long and the Arrochar Alps are to be enjoyed from the bay window of the comfortable, rustic bar and the inviting beer garden at this traditional inn. A selection of up to three guest ales from Scottish breweries is available, plus others from all over Britain. Good food from a varied menu is served in the bar and restaurant.
🏯Q🌸🚪🕪🍴🛢🏧(926,976)P🕾

Balloch

Tullie Inn 🗘 ✅

Balloch Road, G83 8SW (next to rail station)

🕓 11-midnight (1am Fri & Sat) ☎ (01389) 752052

Caledonian Deuchars IPA; Greene King Old Speckled Hen, Abbot; guest beers Ⓗ
A lively, spacious pub, the guest ales may be something local from Fyne Ales or from the Caledonian Brewery. The pub has regular music and quiz nights and serves freshly cooked food. Well-furnished patios and grass areas surround the building, with plenty of sheltered tables and a heated smoking area. Balloch is easily accessible by train from Glasgow and offers boat trips on and easy walks by Loch Lomond. 🌸🚪🕪🍴🛢🏧🚆🛢P🕾

Bo'ness

Riverview

16 Church Wynd, EH51 0EQ

🕓 5 (12 Sat)-midnight (1am Fri & Sat); 12.30-midnight Sun
☎ (01506) 826450 🌐 riverview.bo-ness.org.uk

Beer range varies Ⓗ
From the shores of the River Forth, Bo'ness rises up a steep slope. Half-way up is the Riverview, with spectacular views over the Forth. The bar area, separate from the restaurant (open Wed-Sun), offers up to three ales from local breweries as well as from further afield. Although the TV is turned on for sporting events, conversation is key to this pub's friendly character. 🌸🕪🍴🛢🏧🍴P🕾

Bridge of Allan

Allanwater Brewhouse L

Queens Lane, FK9 4NU (behind Adamo Hotel)
🕑 12-5 (closed Mon & Tue winter) ☎ (01786) 834555
Tinpot 70/-, 80/-; guest beers Ⓗ
The brewery tap of Tinpot, this local is furnished with many historic pieces of brewing equipment, and offers free brewery tours and tastings. The staff are friendly and the pub is popular with visiting tourists, CAMRA members and locals. Tinpot's seasonal beers include the unusual and interesting Thai Pot, Marmalade Pot and Chocolate Pot, among others. Q➤❦P

Cardross

Coach House Inn

Main Road, G82 5JX (opp golf club) NS347775
🕑 12-midnight (1am Thu-Sat) ☎ (01389) 841358
⊕ coachhouseinn-cardross.com
Caledonian Deuchars IPA; guest beer Ⓗ
This inn is an ideal base for walks on the Clyde coast and to Loch Lomond. The interior of this friendly, family-run hostelry has distinct dining, seating and drinking areas, plus an area with a pool table. The Deuchars is usually supported by a guest ale towards the end of the week.
🏰❦◗&➤❦(216)♣P'➚

Dollar

King's Seat ✔

19-23 Bridge Street, FK14 7DE
🕑 12-midnight (1am Fri & Sat); 12.30-midnight Sun
☎ (01259) 742515 ⊕ kingsseat.com
Harviestoun Bitter & Twisted; guest beers Ⓗ
This old coaching inn, with low ceilings and a cosy, comfortable feel, is located in the main street of a historic and attractive village on the southern edge of the Ochil Hills. Up to five ales are on handpump with the guests usually including a Harviestoun seasonal beer. The restaurant (open Wed-Sun) offers high quality meals at reasonable prices, and there are two double bedrooms upstairs.
❦❦◗▲❦(23,65,70)❦'➚

Drymen

Clachan Inn

2 Main Street, Drymen Square, G63 0BL
🕑 11-11 (midnight Fri & Sat); 12-11 Sun ☎ (01360) 660824
⊕ clachaninndrymen.co.uk
Beer range varies Ⓗ
The oldest registered licensed premises in Scotland, dating from 1774, run by the same family since 1981. Two handpumps serve ales mainly from local Scottish breweries including Kelburn and Houston. Food is served in the separate restaurant and it is wise to book. Drymen is a popular resting place for walkers on the West Highland Way and for visitors touring Loch Lomond. 🏰❦◗❦▲❦

Dunblane

Tappit Hen ✔

Kirk Street, FK15 0AL (opp cathedral)
🕑 11-midnight (1am Fri & Sat); 12.30-midnight Sun
☎ (01786) 825226
Greene King IPA; Caledonian Deuchars IPA; guest beers Ⓗ

Local CAMRA Pub of the Year 2010, the Tappit Hen offers an ever-changing range of five real ales from local breweries and from further afield. Visitors are assured of a friendly welcome from the knowledgable staff, and beer festivals held in May and October are popular with locals and visitors alike. Entertainment includes a folk night on Tuesday every week. ➤❦♣

Falkirk

Behind the Wall ✔

14 Melville Street, FK1 1HZ
🕑 5-9 (11 summer); 5-1am Fri & Sat; 12.30-midnight Sun
☎ (01324) 633338 ⊕ behindthewall.co.uk
Caledonian Deuchars IPA; guest beers Ⓗ
This spacious venue for drinking, dining and entertainment was once a bra factory. Popular for watching live sports events, it has plenty of seating and several wide screens in a large room that doubles as a live music venue for local bands. Eglesbrech is the ale and whisky bar upstairs, divided into two rooms with timber furnishings and a large wood-burning stove, offering a choice of cask beers. 🏰❦◗❦❦➤❦

Carron Works L ✔

Bank Street, FK1 1NB (near rail and bus stations)
🕑 9.30am-11 (midnight Thu; 1am Fri & Sat); 12.30-11 Sun
☎ (01324) 673020
Caledonian Deuchars IPA; Greene King Abbot; guest beers Ⓗ
In a converted cinema, this is an excellent Wetherspoon venue with helpful staff dispensing the chain's guest beers. Centrally situated, with a spacious interior, it is popular with locals and CAMRA members. It has frequent festivals and is keen to promote real ale. The standard Wetherspoon menu is available all day. ❦◗➤❦♣

Wheatsheaf Inn ✔

16 Baxters Wynd, FK1 1PF
🕑 11-midnight (1am Fri & Sat); 12.30-midnight Sun
☎ (01324) 638282
Caledonian Deuchars IPA; guest beers Ⓗ
A public house that dates from the late-18th century and retains much of its original character. The wood-panelled bar is furnished in traditional style with plenty of interesting features from the past. Guest beers come from micro-breweries in Scotland and England, with two on offer mid-week and three at the weekend. A must-visit venue, it was a finalist Forth Valley CAMRA Pub of the Year 2011. ❦➤(Grahamston/Falkirk High)❦

Gargunnock

Gargunnock Inn

Main Street, FK8 3BW
🕑 5-11 (1am Fri); 12-1am Sat; 12-11 Sun ☎ (01786) 860333
⊕ cafealbert.co.uk
Beer range varies Ⓗ

SCOTLAND

NORTHERN IRELAND

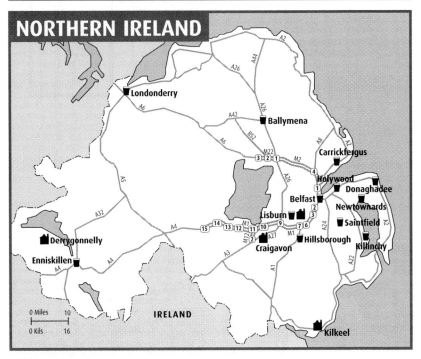

Ballymena

Spinning Mill ✓
17-21 Broughshane Street, BT43 6EB
✪ 8am-11 (midnight Fri & Sat) ☎ (028) 2563 8985
Greene King Abbot; guest beers ⊞
Town house in one of Northern Ireland's main shopping areas, it has two bars, one with a cosy fireplace area, dispensing up to eight real ales. Open for breakfast from 8am, with specialist food menus during the week, but in common with other Wetherspoon pubs in the province alcohol is not served until 11.30am. ▲☎⬢⬢⬢⬢⬢

Belfast

Botanic Inn
23-27 Malone Road, BT9 6RU
✪ 11.30-1am; 12-midnight Sun ☎ (028) 9050 9740
Whitewater Belfast Ale ⊞
Recently refurbished to extend the smoking area, the Botanic Inn remains a popular bar for students and locals. Live sport on screen is a major draw and the bar is often packed for big sporting events. The other attraction is the real ale, with Whitewater's Belfast Ale a continuous presence. Try ordering the ale from the smaller public bar where it should be a bit cheaper. Bar food is available until 7.45pm and live bands play regularly. ⬢⬢⬢⬢(8B)⬢

Bridge House ♀ ✓
37-43 Bedford Street, BT2 7EJ (near City Hall)
✪ 7am-midnight (1am Fri & Sat) ☎ (028) 9072 7890
Greene King Abbot; guest beers ⊞
This Wetherspoon venue is local CAMRA's Pub Of The Year for 2011. In addition to the ubiquitous Abbot, a range of constantly changing guest ales is served. Brews from the local Hilden stable are also available regularly. This is a large, often busy, establishment near Belfast city centre. The upstairs

dining area has its own bar and is more of a family-friendly area. Breakfast is available from 7am but no alcohol is served before 11.30am (12.30 Sun). ⬢⬢⬢(Gt Victoria St)⬢⬢⬢

Crown ★ ✓
46 Great Victoria Street, BT2 7BA (opp Europa Hotel and Great Victoria St station)
✪ 11.30-midnight; 12.30-11 Sun ☎ (028) 9024 3187
⊕ crownbar.com
Whitewater Belfast Ale, Crown Glory; guest beer ⊞
Sitting at the corner of Great Victoria Street and Amiens Street, there are few pubs in the UK as unspoilt as the Crown. Its exterior tiling and well-preserved interior are increasingly rare sights in public houses. CAMRA Northern Ireland is proud that this gem sells real ale. There are three handpumps in the middle of the granite topped bar, dispensing beers from Whitewater Brewery. The first stop on any real ale trip to Belfast. ⬢⬢⬢(Gt Victoria St)⬢

John Hewitt
51 Donegal Street, BT1 2FH (100m from St Anne's Cathedral)
✪ 11.30 (12 Sat)-1am; 7pm-midnight Sun
☎ (028) 9023 3768 ⊕ thejohnhewitt.com
Hilden Ale; guest beer ⊞
Situated in the Cathedral Quarter, the John Hewitt is one of Belfast's independents. It is run by the Belfast Unemployed Resource Centre and the profits are used to finance the organisation's work among the unemployed and others. There are two

real ale handpumps dispensing beer from Hilden. The bar hosts music most week nights and other events such as art exhibitions and charity quizzes. Popular food is served at lunchtime and the pub can be busy. Q◖⅃⅄🖃

King's Head

829 Lisburn Road, BT9 7GY (opp Kings Hall at Balmoral)
❂ 12-1am (midnight Mon); 12-midnight Sun
☎ (028) 9050 9950
Beer range varies Ⓗ
Opposite the King's Hall lies one of Belfast's classier real ale pubs. The King's Head is characterised by a mixture of drinking, dining and music. The ale, often Whitewater Belfast Ale or another of the brewery's beers, is on two handpumps in the public bar. Food is served in the bar and the restaurant upstairs. Music plays downstairs and in the attached Live Lounge. The pub is easily accessible and on bus and train routes.
Q❀◖⅃⅄≠(Balmoral)P⅃⅄

McHughs

29-31 Queens Square, BT1 3FG (near Albert Clock)
❂ 12-1am (midnight Sun) ☎ (028) 9050 9999
⊕ mchughsbar.com
Whitewater Belfast Ale; guest beer Ⓗ
Long-established, traditional hostelry that has been sympathetically upgraded and extended to incorporate the adjacent premises, formerly a renowned brothel. Accommodation comprises a basement function room, a ground floor bar of cosy interlinked drinking spaces, and a galleried restaurant on the first floor. The new arrangements are mellowing nicely and patrons include dedicated regulars, tourists and visitors to nearby music venues. Live traditional music is played on Wednesday evening. ◖⅃⅄≠(Central)🖃⅃⅄

Molly's Yard

1 College Green Mews, Botanic Avenue, BT7 1LN
❂ 12-9 (9.30 Fri & Sat); closed Sun ☎ (028) 9032 2600
⊕ mollysyard.co.uk
Beer range varies Ⓗ
The Good Food Guide's Restaurant of the Year for Northern Ireland is this charming venue, accessed through a narrow passageway and courtyard. This lends it the air of a hidden gem and helps to create a peaceful ambience. The emphasis is on good locally-produced food and drink. Two handpumps in the downstairs bar serve College Green and Hilden ales, all brewed at Hilden Brewery. Beer is only available when purchasing food.
❀◖⅃≠(Botanic)🖃(7A)⅃⅄

Carrickfergus

Central Bar ✓

13-15 High Street, BT38 7AN (opp Carrickfergus Castle)
❂ 8am-11 (1am Fri & Sat) ☎ (028) 9335 7840
Greene King Abbot; guest beers Ⓗ
This two-storey town-centre Wetherspoon pub has mellowed into a community local and haunt of dedicated regulars. It provides a lively ground-floor public bar and a quieter first floor, family-friendly sitting room/restaurant with many windows affording excellent views of Belfast Lough and the 12th-century castle. Handpumps on both levels dispense two house beers plus up to three guests, usually from Scottish and English micros or speciality ales from various breweries. Alcohol is served from 11.30am (12.30 Sun).
Q⅄◖⅃⅄≠🖃(563)❀

Donaghadee

Moat Inn

102 Moat Street, BT21 0ED
❂ 11.30-11.30; 12.30-11 Sun ☎ (028) 9188 3297
⊕ moatinn.co.uk
Beer range varies Ⓗ
On the main road into Donaghadee, the Moat has a public bar, bistro and a larger restaurant upstairs. There is also a beer garden for summer days. The real ale is on two handpumps, mainly from Whitewater Brewery. This is the bar's second year in the Guide, a testament to the enthusiasm of the owner. A friendly, welcoming place, it is perfect for a relaxing pint. ❀◖⅃⅄🖃(7)P⅃⅄

Enniskillen

Linen Hall ✓

11-13 Townhall Street, BT74 7BD
❂ 8am-midnight (1am Sat; 11 Sun-Tue) ☎ (028) 6634 0910
Greene King Abbot; guest beer Ⓗ
A very popular Wetherspoon establishment in the centre of town opposite the bus station, it has four distinct areas: the front entrance, bar, rear door area, and a family space at the back. The bar features five handpumps dispensing ale and cider. In common with other Wetherspoon's in the province, large screens show sports news, usually with the sound turned off. Alcohol is served from 11.30am (12.30 Sun). ⅄❀◖⅃⅄❀⅃⅄

Hillsborough

Hillside

21 Main Street, BT26 6AE
❂ 11.30-11.30 (1am Fri & Sat); 11.30-11 Sun
☎ (028) 9268 9233 ⊕ hillsidehillsborough.co.uk
College Green Headless Dog; Hilden Ale Ⓗ
One of CAMRA Northern Ireland's favourite bars, Hillside has recently changed its beer supplier from Whitewater to Hilden, with two ales usually available. The bar is traditionally styled with open fires and pictures of old Hillsborough and hunting scenes on the walls. Food is available in the bistro and restaurant, and there is a beer garden and smokers' area at the side. Live music features on Saturday. The annual beer festival continues to be a popular event. ⋈Q❀◖⅃⅄🖃(38,238)⅃⅄

Holywood

Dirty Duck Ale House

3 Kinnegar Road, BT18 9JN (300m from railway station)
❂ 11.30-11.30 (1am Thu-Sat); 12.30-midnight Sun
☎ (028) 9059 6666 ⊕ thedirtyduckalehouse.co.uk
Beer range varies Ⓗ
This cheerful inn on the County Down side of Belfast Lough is a previous CAMRA Northern Ireland Pub of the Year and a recent winner of Northern Ireland Gastro Pub of the Year. From the picture windows in the bar and upstairs restaurant there are superb views of shipping in the Lough and the Country Antrim coast. Home to a golf society, the pub also hosts a quiz night on Tuesday and live music on Thursday, Friday and Sunday nights. ⋈❀◖⅃≠⅃⅄

Killinchy

Daft Eddy's

Sketrick Island, BT23 6QH (2 miles N of Killinchey at Whiterock Bay)

⚙ 11.30-11.30 (1am Fri); 12-10.30 Sun ☎ (028) 9754 1615
⊕ dafteddys.com
Beer range varies Ⓗ

Set in glorious surroundings, this old favourite has recently undergone major renovation. A new log-cabin-style public bar with a large TV screen has been built inside the restaurant, and the old public bar has been replaced with a new coffee bar. The restaurant continues to serve quality local food, with oysters and lobster among the specialities. One ale is available from Whitewater.
Q❀✪⟨⟩⬅⬡P꜌

Lisburn

Tap Room

Hilden Brewery, Hilden, BT27 4TY (5 minutes' walk from Hilden railway halt)

⚙ 12-2.30, 5-9 (closed Mon); 12-3 Sun ☎ (028) 9266 3863
⊕ hildenbrewery.co.uk
Hilden Hilden Ale; guest beer Ⓗ

The Tap Room restaurant sits alongside Hilden Brewery in the grounds of the Scullion family's huge Georgian mansion. Quality food is mainly made from local produce and goes down well with the ale brewed next door – the choice of ales varies but can only be ordered with a meal. Alfresco dining can be enjoyed on a summer's day. The venue also hosts music nights and beer festivals.
🏔Q❀✪⬅⬄(Hilden)⬡(325H)P꜌

Tuesday Bell ⊘

4 Lisburn Square, BT28 1TS

⚙ 8am-11 ☎ (028) 9262 7390
Greene King Abbot; guest beers Ⓗ

Two-level Wetherspoon venue in the city centre of this former linen-making town, close to the Linen museum and not far from Hilden Brewery. The ground floor offers plenty of seating and a compact bar where drinkers queue politely to be served. The family-friendly first floor accommodates a split-level lounge. Handpumps on both levels dispense the two house ales and up to three varied guest beers from the Wetherspoon list. Alcohol is served from 11.30am (12.30 Sun). ✪⬄⬅⬡●꜌

Londonderry

Diamond ⊘

23-24 The Diamond, BT48 6HP (centre of walled city)

⚙ 8am-1am (11 Mon & Tue; midnight Wed & Thu); 8am-midnight Sun ☎ (028) 7127 2880
Greene King Abbot; guest beers Ⓗ

Located in the Diamond square, inside the walled part of the Maiden City, this is a two-storey Wetherspoon pub with good views over the city from the upper floor. There are large bars on both floors – the upstairs is more family-oriented. A varied range of guest ales is usually available alongside the regulars. As with other pubs in the chain, alcohol is served from 11.30am (12.30 Sun). ⬄✪⬄⬅●꜌

Ice Wharf ⊘

Strand Road, BT48 7AB

⚙ 7am-midnight (1am Thu-Sat) ☎ (028) 7127 6610
Greene King Abbot; guest beers Ⓗ

From the city's bus station, turn towards Guildhall Square. At the end of the Square, turn right into Strand Road to reach this hostelry. A former hotel, it was Wetherspoon's first Lloyds No.1 in Northern Ireland. Now a large single-floor pub, screens divide the bar area from the seating space. As well as the regular and guest ales, cider is available on gravity. Alcohol is served from 11.30am (12.30 Sun). ⬄✪⬄⬅⬡꜌

Newtownards

Spirit Merchant ⊘

54-56 Regent Street, BT23 4LP (next to bus station)

⚙ 9am-11 (midnight Fri & Sat) ☎ (028) 9182 4270
Greene King Abbot; guest beers Ⓗ

Formerly the Jolly Judge, the bar is situated opposite the bus station and close to the town centre. Breakfast is served daily from 9am, beer from 11.30am (12.30 Sun). Two regular ales and up to three guests make up the beer choice. The standard Wetherspoon food menu includes daily specials. There are three TV screens for sport, with the sound turned off. At the front is a smoking area and to the side a heated courtyard. A friendly establishment with welcoming, helpful and knowledgeable staff. ❀✪⬄⬅⬡(5,7,9)●P꜌

Saintfield

White Horse

49 Main Street, BT24 7AB

⚙ 11.30-11.30; 12-10.30 Sun ☎ (028) 9751 1143
Whitewater Copperhead Ale, Belfast Ale, Crown Glory; guest beers Ⓗ

Owned by Whitewater Brewery, the pub has four handpumps on the bar, mainly dispensing Whitewater ales plus occasional guests. The interior is bright and modern with several drinking areas and a bistro serving good food. Downstairs is a function room leading to the beer garden. Live music plays in the main bar. A previous local CAMRA Pub of the Year, its annual beer festival is one of the most popular among CAMRA members. 🏔❀✪⬄⬡(15,215)꜌

Perhaps the workman spends, night after night, more than he should on beer. Let us remember, if he needs excuse, that his employers have found him no better place and no better amusement than to sit in a tavern, drink beer (generally in moderation), and talk and smoke tobacco. Why not? A respectable tavern is a very harmless place; the society which meets there is the society of the workman; it's his life; without it he might as well have been a factory hand of the good old time – such as hands were 40 years ago; and then he should have but two journeys a day – one from bed to mill, and the other from mill to bed.
Walter Besant, As We Are and As We May Be, 1903

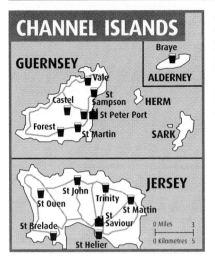

ALDERNEY
Braye

Coxswain Bar
Braye Street, GY9 3XT
✪ 9-11 ☎ (01481) 822421
Randalls Patois Ⓗ
The small Coxswain Bar and Boathouse Bistro together form The Moorings, a venue that is popular with locals as well as visitors. The bar's welcoming landlords are enthusiastic about quality real ale. Another attraction is the lovely location just 100 metres from the harbour. Good value food is served from April to October. ▲◑▸

GUERNSEY
Castel

Fleur du Jardin ✅
Kings Mills, GY5 7JT
✪ 10.30-11.45 ☎ (01481) 257996 ⊕ fleurdujardin.com
Badger Best Bitter; Greene King Old Speckled Hen Ⓗ
A building of unique charm with two bars – one traditional, small and cosy, attached to the restaurant, the other recently renovated in a more contemporary style to enjoy a comfortable, relaxing area to enjoy a beer. A door from this area leads to a large covered patio and out to the garden. Menus in both the bar and restaurant feature fresh local produce. ▲Q⊛✍◑♿P⌁

Rockmount Hotel
Cobo, GY5 7HB
✪ 10.30-midnight (12.45am Fri & Sat) ☎ (01481) 256757
Randalls Patois Ⓗ
A pub for all seasons with a choice of bars – a public to the rear, and a newly-refurbished front bar by the road. A warming fire in winter makes it a cosy retreat from the gales. A good range of tasty food is served and the pub is just across the road from a sandy beach. The perfect place to relax and enjoy one of Guernsey's legendary sunsets. ▲◑🖳P⌁

Forest

Deerhound ✅
Le Bourg, GY8 0AN

✪ 11-11 ☎ (01481) 238585
Beer range varies Ⓗ
Modern pub on the main road to the airport. The emphasis is on food, and a popular choice of meals is served (note that there is no pre-booking of tables) – the bar can get busy in the evenings. Outside, there is a large, sunny, decked patio perfect for summer dining, as well as benches dotted about on the grass. The car park fills up quickly at busy times. ⊛◑▸P

St Martin

Captain's Hotel ✅
La Fosse, GY4 6EF
✪ 11-11 (midnight Fri & Sat); 12-4 Sun ☎ (01481) 238990
Fuller's London Pride; Taylor Landlord Ⓗ
In a secluded location down a country lane, this is a popular locals' pub with a lively, friendly atmosphere. It has a small, raised area in front of the bar furnished with a sofa to make a comfy zone. Meals can be eaten in the bar or bistro area, or you can take away a pizza. A meat draw is held on Friday. The car park to the rear fills up quickly. 🛏◑▸P⌁

St Peter Port

Cock & Bull
Lower Hauteville, GY1 1LL
✪ 11-2.30, 4-12.45am; 11-12.45am Fri & Sat; 4-11 Sun
☎ (01481) 722660
Beer range varies Ⓗ
Popular pub, just up the hill from the town church, with five handpumps providing a changing range of beers. Live music takes place throughout the week, with salsa, baroque or jazz on Monday, open mike on Tuesday, jazz on Wednesday, Irish on Thursday and on Saturday a silent set – gentle music that won't hinder good conversation. Seating is on three levels. The pub only opens on Sunday when there is rugby on. CAMRA Branch Pub of the Year 2008. ⌁

Cornerstone Café Bar ♈
La Tour Beauregard, GY1 1LQ
✪ 10 (8am Thu & Fri)-midnight; 12-6 Sun ☎ (01481) 713832
⊕ cornerstoneguernsey.co.uk
Randalls Patois; guest beers Ⓗ
Situated across the road from the States Archives, this café has a small bar area to the front with bar stools, and further seating to the rear. Regular quiz evenings are held. The menu offers a wide range of good quality hot and cold meals, plus a daily specials board (no food Sun). There is a large screen for sporting events. Ales from Randalls or Liberation Brewery are usually on handpump – check the website for what's on now and what's up and coming. ◑

Drunken Duck
La Charroterie, GY1 1EL (opp Charles Frossard House)
✪ 11 (12 Sun)-12.45am ☎ (01481) 726170
Badger Hopping Hare; Fuller's London Pride; Taylor Landlord Ⓗ
Now the refurbishments are complete and the pub has returned to its distinctive name, this is once

INDEPENDENT BREWERIES
Liberation St Saviour: Jersey
Randalls St Peter Port: Guernsey

ISLANDS

again a welcoming locals' hostelry. The bar is divided into two areas. At the front the comfortable zone with a couple of sofas has been retained, alongside plenty of traditional pub seating. To the rear the original bench seats around the walls have returned and there is now a dartboard. Light bites such as baguettes and toasties are available. ⌐

Ship & Crown ✓

North Esplanade, GY1 2NB (opp Crown Pier car park)
✪ 10-12.45am; 12-10 Sun ☎ (01481) 721368
⊕ crowsnestguernsey.com
Beer range varies ⊞

Now a free house, the Ship & Crown has a nautical theme. Situated across the road from Victoria Pier, this busy pub attracts a varied clientele of all ages. Real cider is part of the range available on handpump. Excellent bar meals are served in generous portions throughout the day until 9pm, with a daily changing range of specials. The Crows Nest above the pub serves meals lunchtimes and evenings but has no handpump, only bottles. ◑♠

St Sampson

Pony Inn ✓

Les Capelles, GY2 4GX
✪ 11-10.30 ☎ (01481) 244374
Taylor Landlord ⊞

The pub was heavily modernised some years ago and the emphasis now is on good quality food, with families welcome. The handpump is on the bar in the dining area. To the side there is a public bar with its own entrance – although there is no handpump here the bar staff will happily bring you a pint from the main bar. To the front is a large car park. ⊛◑♼P

Vale

Houmet Tavern ✓

Rousse, GY6 8AR (between Vale Church and Rousse Tower)
✪ 10-12.45am; 10-6 Sun ☎ (01481) 242214
Beer range varies ⊞

The Houmet has a public bar to the rear, popular with locals, with pub games and a TV to watch sporting events. To the front there is a large lounge with an attached conservatory, giving fabulous views of the bay and local fishing boats. Bar meals are served in the lounge lunchtimes and evenings (not Sun eve). The pub may shut around 11.45pm. ◑♼🚐P⌐

JERSEY
St Brelade

Old Smugglers Inn ✓

Le Mont du Ouaisne, JE3 8AW
✪ 11-11 (winter hours vary) ☎ (01534) 741510
⊕ oldsmugglersinn.com
Draught Bass ⊞; **Greene King Abbot** ⒼG; **Wells Bombardier; guest beers** ⊞

Perched on the edge of Ouaisne Bay, the Smugglers has been the jewel in the crown of the Jersey real ale scene for many years. It is set on several levels within granite-built fishermen's cottages dating back hundreds of years. Up to four real ales are usually available including one from Skinner's, and mini beer festivals are regularly held. The pub is well known for its good food and fresh daily specials. ▲Q◑

St Helier

Forum ♈ ⌊ ✓

13 Grenville Street, JE2 4UF
✪ 11-11.30 ☎ (01534) 768105
Liberation Ale, seasonal beers; guest beers ⊞

Ideally situated just on the outskirts of the town centre, the pub is named after the cinema that once occupied the site opposite. It has a modern interior but with a classic feel and includes a number of brass plaques that were taken from the old Royal Court building. This is not a quiet pub – live sport and background music often feature. Three real ales are always available, and a large range of real ciders. Food is served in the bar from the Indian restaurant directly above. CAMRA Pub of the Year 2010. ◑&♠⌐

Lamplighter ⌊ ✓

9 Mulcaster Street, JE2 3NJ
✪ 11-11 ☎ (01534) 723119
Ringwood Best Bitter, Fortyniner; Wells Eagle IPA, Bombardier ⊞; **guest beers** ⒼG

A traditional pub with a modern feel. The gas lamps that gave the pub its name remain, as does the original antique pewter bar top. An excellent range of up to eight real ales is available including one from Skinner's – four are served direct from the cask. A real cider is sometimes also on offer. Local CAMRA Pub of the Year 2008 and 2009. ◑🚐(5)♠

Peirson ⌊ ✓

17 Royal Square, JE2 4WA
✪ 10 (11 Sun)-11 ☎ (01534) 722726
Draught Bass; Liberation Ale ⊞; **guest beer** ⒼG

The pub is nestled in the corner of the Royal Square in the centre of St Helier. Named after Major Francis Peirson, it contains historical reminders of the Battle of Jersey in 1781. Two ales are always on handpump and an occasional additional ale on gravity. Excellent food is served at lunchtime throughout the year, with evening meals also offered during the summer. The pub has a good reputation with locals and visitors alike. Outside seating is extremely popular in the summer months. Q⊛◑&⌐

Post Horn ⌊ ✓

Hue Street, JE2 3RE
✪ 10 (11 Sun)-11 ☎ (01534) 872853
Liberation Ale, seasonal beers; guest beer ⊞

Busy, friendly pub adjacent to the precinct and five minutes' walk from the Royal Square. Popular at lunchtimes with its own nucleus of regulars, it offers three draught ales plus a guest. Addlestones Cider is also on draught. The large L-shaped public bar extends into the lounge area where there is an open fire and TV showing sport. A good selection of freshly cooked food is served. There is a large function room on the first floor, a drinking area outside and a public car park nearby. ▲⊛◑&⌐

St John

L'Auberge du Nord

La Route du Nord, JE3 4AJ
✪ 11-11 ☎ (01534) 861697 ⊕ theboathousegroup.com
Ringwood Best Bitter ⊞

A 10-minute walk towards the north coast from St John village, this 16th-century farmhouse was converted to a pub in the 1950s. The restaurant was refurbished in 2009 and joins The Boat House, Tree House and Beach House in this popular chain serving locally-sourced produce. A guest ale often replaces the Ringwood on the bar. Parking and outside seating make the pub a useful meeting place for the north coast. ♠Q❀◗▣(5)P⸚

St Martin

Royal
La Grande Route de Faldouet, JE3 6UG
❀ 9.30 (11 Sun)-11 ☎ (01534) 856289
Draught Bass; Ringwood Best Bitter Ⓗ; guest beer Ⓖ
Large, traditional, country-style inn at the centre of St Martin with sizeable public and lounge bars and a restaurant area. Owned by Randalls, it has been under the same management team for 25 years. The interior features traditional furnishings, cosy corners and a real fire in the colder months. Guest ales are from the Marston's, Sharp's and Skinner's stables. Quality food is popular with locals and visitors alike, with a good menu served lunchtimes and evenings until 8.30pm (no food Sun). ♠Q❀◗▣⬥▲▣(3)P⸚

St Ouen

Farmers Inn ⓛ ✓
La Grande Route de St Ouen, JE3 2HY
❀ 10 (11 Sun)-11 ☎ (01534) 485311
Draught Bass; Liberation Ale, seasonal beers Ⓗ
Situated in the hub of St Ouen, the rustic Farmers Inn is a typical country pub offering up to three ales as well as a locally made cider when available (usually April-July). Traditional pub food is also served in generous portions. Best described as a

friendly community local, there is a good chance of hearing Jersey French (Jerriais) spoken at the bar. ♠❀◗⬥▲▣(8,9)♣P⸚

Moulin de Lecq ✓
Le Mont de la Greve de Lecq, JE3 2DT
❀ 11-11 (winter hours vary) ☎ (01534) 482818
⊕ moulindelecq.com
Greene King Old Speckled Hen Ⓗ, Abbot Ⓖ, seasonal beers; Wells Bombardier; guest beers Ⓗ
Another free house on the island offering a range of real ales, the Moulin is a converted 12th-century watermill situated in the valley above the beach at Greve de Lecq. The waterwheel is still in place and the turning mechanism can be seen behind the bar. A restaurant adjoins the mill. There is a children's play area and a barbecue area used extensively in the summer. ♠Q❀◗▣(9)♣P⸚

Trinity

Trinity Arms ⓛ ✓
La Rue es Picots, JE3 5JX
❀ 11-11 ☎ (01534) 864691
Liberation Mary Ann Best Ⓐ, Ale Ⓗ
Sporting the parish's ancient symbol of the Trinity, this 1976-built pub is modern by Jersey country pub standards but has plenty of character. Owned by the Jersey Brewery, the pub is central to and popular in village community life. It has a public bar and restaurant where food is served lunchtimes and evenings. Outside is seating, a children's play area and car parking. ❀◗⬥▣(4)♣P⸚

Peirson, St Helier, Jersey (Photo: Adam Bruderer)

Good Bottled Beer Guide

Jeff Evans

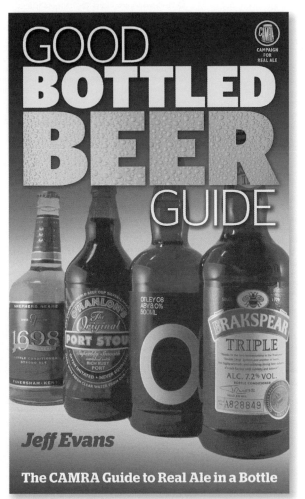

A pocket-sized guide for discerning drinkers looking to buy bottled real ales and enjoy a fresh glass of their favourite beers at home. The 7th edition of the **Good Bottled Beer Guide** is completely revised, updated and redesigned to showcase the very best bottled British real ales now being produced, and detail where they can be bought. Everything you need to know about bottled beers; tasting notes, ingredients, brewery details, and a glossary to help the reader understand more about them.

£12.99   ISBN 978-1-85249-262-5   CAMRA members' price £10.99   384 pages

For this and other books on beer and pubs visit the CAMRA bookshop at **www.camra.org.uk/books**

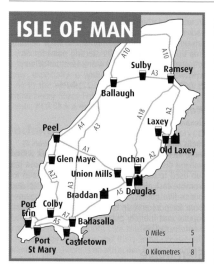

ISLE OF MAN

Sulby
Ramsey
Ballaugh
Peel
Laxey
Glen Maye
Onchan
Old Laxey
Union Mills
Braddan
Douglas
Port
Erin
Colby
Ballasalla
Port
St Mary
Castletown

0 Miles 5
0 Kilometres 8

Ballasalla

Whitestone ✪
Station Road, IM9 2DD
☼ 12-11 (midnight Fri & Sat) ☎ (01624) 822334
Okells Bitter; guest beer Ⓗ
Large multi-roomed pub in the centre of the village
with a small, separate public bar with pool and TV,
which can be lively at weekends. There is plenty of
space for diners and non-diners, with the main
area divided into a dining space and two
comfortable lounge areas. The Okells Bitter is
complemented by a changing guest. The pub hosts
entertainment most weekends.
Q✿◖🖰&≒🖾(1,2)♣P⌐

Ballaugh

Raven ✪
The Main Road, IM7 5EG
☼ 12-11 (midnight Fri & Sat) ☎ (01624) 896128
Okells Ravens Claw, Bitter; guest beers Ⓗ
Situated on the TT course adjacent to Ballaugh
Bridge, it's a family-friendly locals' establishment,
offering good pub food. The house brew is Ravens
Claw, brewed by Okells. The comfortable bar has
three areas, one mainly for dining, plus a separate
games room with pool and darts. Outside, the
paved patio adjacent to the car park is ideal for
watching the TT and Manx Grand Prix races. No
food Sunday evening. Q✿◖&🖾(5,6)♣P⌐

Castletown

Castle Arms (Glue Pot) ✪
The Quay, IM9 1LD
☼ 12-11 (midnight Fri & Sat) ☎ (01624) 824673
Okells Bitter; guest beers Ⓗ
Situated next to Castletown harbour and opposite
Castle Rushen, the Castle Arms is an attractive,
historic pub. It is popularly known as the Glue Pot
due to a less salubrious past. The two small ground
floor rooms have nautical and Manx motor racing
themes. The patio is ideal on warm days for
watching quayside vessels and waterfront wildlife.
Draught Bass is a regular guest beer, with up to
three more ales available during the summer
months. ✿◖≒(IMR)🖾(1,2)♣⌐

Sidings
Victoria Road, IM9 1EF (next to railway station)
☼ 11.30-11.30 (12.30am Fri & Sat) ☎ (01624) 823282
Bushy's Ruby Mild, Bitter, Castletown Bitter; guest
beers Ⓗ
Popular with locals and visitors, The Sidings has
two large lounges and a pool room. On entering,
turn left into the bar area and the first thing you
notice are 10 handpumps stretching the length of
the bar, with several guest and local beers among
the range. This is a welcome sight for bus and train
travellers calling in while they await their
departure. The only recent addition to mar the
view is a Heineken font slap bang in the middle.
The annual beer festival is held in July.
🖗✿◖≒(IMR)🖾(1,2)♣P⌐

Colby

Colby Glen Hotel ✪
Main Road, IM9 4LR
☼ 12-2.30, 5-11.30 (midnight Fri); 12-midnight Sat; 12-11
Sun ☎ (01624) 834853
Okells Bitter; guest beers Ⓗ
Making its first appearance in the Guide, this
refurbished, modernised and tastefully redecorated
pub is situated in the heart of the village. The
comfortable local has two separate bar rooms and
a games room at the rear. Quiz nights are a regular
feature during the week, and wholesome food
attracts local diners and visitors from further afield.
A function room is available and there is ample
parking. Q✿✿◖&Å🖾(1)♣P⌐

Douglas

Albert Hotel ✪
3 Chapel Row, IM1 2BJ (next to bus station)
☼ 10-11 (11.45 Fri & Sat); 12-11 Sun ☎ (01624) 673632
Bushy's Castletown Bitter; Okells Mild, Bitter; guest
beer Ⓗ
The nearest Guide pub to the sea terminal, the
Albert is an unspoilt local with many regulars. It has
a traditionally-laid-out central bar, dark wood
panelling, a pool table in one room and interesting
pictures of Steampacket boats in the other. Sport
on TV is a frequent feature but never loud enough
to spoil conversation. Four reasonably priced ales
are available – two from Okells, Bushy's Castletown
Bitter and a changing guest. Q✿≒(IMR)🖾♣

Cat With No Tail ✪
Hailwood Court, Hailwood Avenue, Governors Hill,
IM2 7EA
☼ 12-11 (midnight Fri & Sat) ☎ (01624) 616364
Okells Bitter; guest beers Ⓗ
A modern pub serving the Governors Hill housing
estate, situated two miles from central Douglas.
The 'Cat' has a public bar with large-screen Sky
Sports, pool and darts, and hosts a karaoke night on
the last Friday of the month. The large lounge and
conservatory leads to a spacious seating area
outside with a patio and play area. Food is served
lunchtimes and evenings (except Sun eve). A
seasonal or guest beer is usually offered alongside
the Okells Bitter. ✿✿◖&🖾(12,22)P⌐

INDEPENDENT BREWERIES

Bushy's Braddan
Okells Douglas
Old Laxey Old Laxey

ISLANDS

☻ 12-midnight (11 Sun) ☎ (01624) 897231

Moorhouse's Black Cat; Okells Bitter; guest beers ⊞
The pub was rebuilt after a fire in 1888 – it gets its
name because ginger beer was originally brewed
on site, not because of the distinctive colour of the
building. Situated on the TT course, the main bar
walls feature many pictures of the famous event.
The bar has a real log fire and a dartboard, and
there is a pool room and dining room for families.
A takeaway meal service is offered. B&B
accommodation is reasonably priced, with some
rooms en-suite.
🏨🍴☻⊙⏰⦿⚲🅿(5,6,6C)♣P🚭

Sulby Glen Hotel ✔

Main Road, IM7 2HR
☻ 12-midnight (1am Fri & Sat); 12-11 Sun
☎ (01624) 897240 ⊕ sulbyglen.net

Bushy's Bitter; Okells Bitter; guest beers ⊞
Situated on the famous TT course on a stretch
called the Sulby Straight, this is a hugely popular
destination for bike fans during the races. There's
always a friendly welcome from staff at this large
rural pub that has two lounges, a separate dining

area and a welcoming real fire in winter months.
Look for the motorcycle engine on the bar that
serves as a beer font. The home-cooked food has
an excellent reputation and the pub hosts a
popular beer festival. 🏨Q☻⚲⊙⏰⦿⚲🅿♣P🚭

Union Mills

Railway Inn

Main Road, IM4 4NE (on main A1 Douglas-Peel road)
☻ 12-midnight (1am Fri & Sat) ☎ (01624) 853006

Okells Mild, Bitter, seasonal beers; guest beers ⊞
A traditional drinkers' village local, renowned over
the years for its idiosyncratic landlords and/or
landladies. The three-roomed free house, twice
voted local CAMRA Pub of the Year, occupies a
popular spectator spot on the famous TT course. It
is headquarters to the world famous Purple
Helmets motorcycle display team – their Mad
Sunday Ride Through is legendary in the back
lounge, which features fascinating memorabilia
salvaged during renovations in 1998.
🏨⦿⚲🅿♣P🚭

Shore Hotel, Old Laxey (Photo: Tom Stainer)

The Breweries

How to use the Breweries section

Breweries are listed in alphabetical order. The independents (regional, smaller craft brewers and brew-pubs) are listed first, followed by the nationals and the globals. Within each brewery entry, beers are listed in increasing order of strength. Beers that are available for less than three months are described as 'occasional' or 'seasonal' brews. If a brewery also produces bottle-conditioned beers, this will be mentioned in the main description: these are beers that have not been pasteurised and contain live yeast, allowing them to continue to ferment and mature in the bottle as a draught real ale does in its cask.

SYMBOLS

▤ A brew-pub: a pub that brews beer on the premises.

◆ CAMRA tasting notes, supplied by a trained CAMRA tasting panel. Beer descriptions that do not carry this symbol are based on more limited tastings or have been obtained from other sources.

Tasting notes are not provided for brew-pub beers that are available in fewer than five outlets, nor for other breweries' beers that are available for less than three months of the year.

⛉ A CAMRA Beer of the Year in 2010.

▤ One of the 2011 CAMRA Beers of the Year: a finalist in the Champion Beer of Britain competition held during the Great British Beer Festival in London in August 2011, or the Champion Winter Beer of Britain competition held earlier in the year.

☺ The brewery's beers can be acceptably served through a 'tight sparkler' attached to the nozzle of the beer pump, designed to give a thick collar of foam on the beer.

⊗ The brewery's beers should NOT be served through a tight sparkler. CAMRA is opposed to the growing tendency to serve southern-brewed beers with the aid of sparklers, which aerate the beer and tend to drive hop aroma and flavour into the head, altering the balance of the beer achieved in the brewery. When neither symbol is used it means the brewery in question has not stated a preference.

ABBREVIATIONS

OG stands for Original Gravity, the measure taken before fermentation of the level of 'fermentable material' (malt sugars and added sugars) in the brew. It is only a rough indication of strength and is no longer used for duty purposes.

ABV stands for Alcohol by Volume, which is a more reliable measure of the percentage of alcohol in finished beer. Many breweries now only disclose ABVs but the Guide lists OGs where available. Often the OG and the ABV of a beer are identical, i.e. 1035 and 3.5 per cent. If the ABV is higher than the OG, i.e. OG 1035, ABV 3.8, this indicates that the beer has been 'well attenuated' with most of the malt sugars turned into alcohol. If the ABV is lower than the OG, this means residual sugars have been left in the beer for fullness of body and flavour: this is rare but can apply to some Milds or strong old ales, barley wines and winter beers.

NOTE: The Breweries section was correct at the time of going to press and every effort has been made to ensure that all cask-conditioned beers are included.

The independents

SIBA indicates a member of the Society of Independent Brewers; IFBB indicates a member of the Independent Family Brewers of Britain; EAB indicates a member of the East Anglian Brewers Co-operative. See feature on page 852.

1648 SIBA

1648 Brewing Co Ltd, Old Stables Brewery, Mill Lane, East Hoathly, East Sussex, BN8 6QB
☎ (01825) 840830
✉ brewmaster@1648brewing.co.uk
⊕ 1648brewing.co.uk
Tours by arrangement

⊠ The 1648 brewery, set up in the old stable block at the King's Head pub in 2003, derives its name from the year of the deposition of King Charles I. One pub is owned and more than 40 outlets are supplied. Seasonal beers: see website. Bottle-conditioned beers are also available.

Brew Master (OG 1040, ABV 3.9%)
A chestnut/brown-coloured bitter with a long aftertaste.

Triple Champion (OG 1041, ABV 4%)
A chestnut-coloured traditional English ale, deeply flavoured and full-bodied.

Signature (OG 1044, ABV 4.4%)
Very pale, light, crisply refreshing ale with a bitter aftertaste.

4Ts (NEW)

4Ts Brewery Ltd, Rydal Avenue, Warrington, Cheshire, WA4 6AT
☎ 07917 730184 ✉ johnwilkinson530@yahoo.co.uk

4Ts began brewing in 2010. The plant is currently located in a private garage but it is planned to relocate it to the Tavern in Warrington.

Old School Dark Mild (ABV 4%)

Bitter (ABV 4.2%)

Light (ABV 4.4%)

Dark (ABV 4.6%)

Coff-Stout-ee (ABV 6%)

8 Sail SIBA

8 Sail Brewery, Heckington Windmill, Hale Road, Heckington, Lincolnshire, NG34 9JW
☎ 07866 183479 ✉ a.pygott@btinternet.com

☺8 Sail Brewery was established in 2010 and operates on a six-barrel brew plant. The brewery nestles in the shadow of Heckington Windmill, Britain's only eight sailed windmill, from where the brewery takes its name. There are plans for the brewery shop to house a small visitor attraction – a Victorian bar displaying drinking vessels from the period up until the present day. Seasonal beers are available and bottle-conditioned beers are planned.

Ale (OG 1038, ABV 3.8%)

Merry Miller (OG 1041, ABV 4.1%)

Victorian Porter (OG 1050, ABV 5%)

Abbey Grange

See Llangollen

Abbey Ales SIBA

Abbey Ales Ltd, Abbey Brewery, Camden Row, Bath, Somerset, BA1 5LB
☎ (01225) 444437 ✉ enquiries@abbeyales.co.uk
⊕ abbeyales.co.uk
Tours by arrangement

Founded in 1997, Abbey Ales was the first brewery in Bath for over fifty years. It supplies more than 80 regular outlets within a 20-mile radius of Bath, while selected wholesalers deliver beer nationally. It has four tied houses one of which, the Star Inn in Bath, is listed on CAMRA's National Inventory of Historic Pub Interiors. Seasonal beers: see website.

Heritage (ABV 3.8%)

Bellringer (OG 1042, ABV 4.2%) ◆
A notably hoppy ale, light to medium-bodied, clean-tasting, refreshingly dry with a balancing sweetness. Citrus, pale malt aroma and dry, bitter finish.

Abbeydale SIBA

Abbeydale Brewery Ltd, Unit 8, Aizlewood Road, Sheffield, South Yorkshire, S8 0YX
☎ (0114) 281 2712
✉ info@abbeydalebrewery.co.uk
⊕ abbeydalebrewery.co.uk

⊠ Since starting in 1996, Abbeydale Brewery has grown steadily; it now produces upwards of 70 barrels a week, and the gradual expansion programme is set to continue. The regular range is complemented by ever-changing seasonals, each available for two months – see website. It also produces beers under the 'Beer Works' name.

Matins (OG 1034.9, ABV 3.6%)

Daily Bread (OG 1037, ABV 3.8%)

Brimstone (OG 1039, ABV 3.9%)
A russet-coloured bitter beer with a distinctive hop aroma.

Moonshine (OG 1041.2, ABV 4.3%)
A well-balanced pale ale with a full hop aroma. Pleasant grapefruit traces may be detected.

Absolution (OG 1050, ABV 5.3%)
A fruity pale ale, deceptively drinkable for its strength. Sweetish but not cloying.

Black Mass (OG 1065, ABV 6.7%)
A strong black stout with complex roast flavours and a lasting bitter finish.

Last Rites (OG 1097, ABV 11%) ⊓
A pale, strong barley wine.

ABC SIBA

ABC Brewery Ltd, Unit 21, Birch Road, Witton, Aston, Birmingham, B6 7DD

☎ (01942) 234976
✉ information@allgatesbrewery.com
⊕ allgatesbrewery.com
Tours by arrangement (max. of 36)

⊛AllGates commenced brewing in 2006 in a Grade II-listed building at the rear of Wigan Main Post Office. The building is an old tower brewery that has been lovingly restored, but with a modern five-barrel plant. Expansion plans are under consideration. Beers are distributed through its own estate of seven pubs, regionally and through wholesalers. Seasonal beers and monthly specials: see website.

All Black (OG 1039, ABV 3.6%) ◕
Dark brown beer with a malty, fruity aroma. Creamy and malty in taste, with blackberry fruits and a satisfying aftertaste.

California (OG 1037, ABV 3.8%)
A clean-drinking, pale gold coloured ale with a strong floral aroma. Full-bodied despite its strength and dryness.

Napoleon's Retreat (OG 1038, ABV 3.9%)
A deep golden/copper-coloured traditional session bitter.

Twitter & Busted (OG 1039, ABV 4%)
A seriously hoppy, straw-coloured ale.

Caskablanca (OG 1040, ABV 4.1%)
A generously hopped golden ale with a fruity, slightly floral aroma.

Citra (OG 1041, ABV 4.2%)
A single-hopped pale ale with citrus aromas.

Kiwi Best Bitter (OG 1041, ABV 4.2%)
Light chestnut in colour with a New Zealand twist.

All Nations

See Shires

Allsaints

Allsaints Brewery, c/o Coastal Brewery, Unit 10B, Cardrew Industrial Estate, Redruth, Cornwall, TR15 1SS
☎ 07831 388829

Formerly known as Doghouse Brewery, which closed in 2007, Allsaints recommenced production in 2008 using spare capacity at Keltek Brewery. In 2009 the brewery began using spare capacity at Coastal Brewery in Redruth. See Coastal for beer list.

Alnwick

See Hadrian & Border

Amber SIBA

Amber Ales Ltd, Unit A, Asher Lane Business Park, Pentrich, Ripley, Derbyshire, DE5 3SW
☎ (01773) 512864 ✉ info@amberales.co.uk
⊕ amberales.co.uk
Shop: Off sales from brewery tap
Tours by arrangement

Amber Ales began production in 2006 on a five-barrel plant. Amber produces five core beers and a range of experimental and seasonal ales. Its brewery tap, the Talbot Taphouse in Ripley, opened

in late 2009. Around 50 outlets are supplied direct. Bottle-conditioned beers are available and are suitable for vegetarians and vegans.

Valley Bitter (OG 1030, ABV 3.6%)

Chocolate Orange Stout (OG 1040, ABV 4%) 🏠 🍴

Original Black Stout (OG 1040, ABV 4%)

Barnes Wallis (OG 1040, ABV 4.1%)

Dambuster (OG 1051, ABV 5.5%)

Imperial IPA (OG 1058, ABV 6.5%)

Anchor Springs

Anchor Springs Brewery Co Ltd, Lineside Way, Wick, West Sussex, BN17 7EH
☎ (01903) 719842/715111
✉ debbie@jenkinslittlehampton.co.uk

Kevin Jenkins, owner of the Crown in Littlehampton, established the brewery in 2010 using the five-barrel plant previously used at the Dark Star Brewery. The beer is mostly sold in the Crown. Seasonal beers are also available.

LA Gold (OG 1039.5, ABV 3.7%)
A golden session ale. An initial sweetness leads to a citrus kick and a lingering crisp, clean finish.

IPA (OG 1042.5, ABV 4%)
A full-bodied, complex beer with a good mouthfeel and lingering hop finish. Light gold in colour, the initial sweetness gives way to malt then a dry aftertaste.

Rip Tide (OG 1045, ABV 4.1%)
Copper-coloured ale. Malted caramel nose and initial sweetness of milk chocolate leads to a complex palate and lingering bitter finish.

Undercurrent (OG 1045, ABV 4.2%)
A light, copper-coloured traditional English bitter with a modern twist. Highly hoppy aroma and initial taste leads to nutty, chocolate palate and finish.

Andwell SIBA

Andwell Brewing Co LLP, Andwell Lane, North Warnborough, Hampshire, RG29 1HA
☎ (01256) 704412 ✉ beer@andwells.com
⊕ andwells.com

⊠ Brewing commenced in 2008 on a 10-barrel plant. Beer is distributed within a 30-mile radius of the brewery and to the Isle of Wight. More than 150 outlets are supplied.

Resolute Bitter (OG 1038, ABV 3.8%) ◕
A pleasant, well-balanced session bitter. Little aroma, with an initially malty flavour with some bitterness and a sweetish finish.

Gold Muddler (OG 1039, ABV 3.9%) ◕
A light golden ale with a hoppy, citrus aroma. These characteristics are carried into the flavour with a solid bitterness, increasing maltiness and a dry, biscuity finish.

King John (OG 1042, ABV 4.2%) ◕
Malty best bitter, low in hops with a short initial bitterness and some dryness in the finish.

Ruddy Darter (OG 1047, ABV 4.6%) ◕

Angel (NEW)

Angel Ales Ltd, 62a Furlong Lane, Halesowen, West Midlands, B63 2TA
☎ 07847 300350 ✉ angelales@hotmail.co.uk
⊕ angelales.co.uk

⊙Angel Ales is the brainchild of Nick Pritchard and Andy Kirk. The brewery building is an interesting place having been a Chapel of Rest, a coffin makers workshop and a pattern makers before becoming a brewhouse. All beers are produced using organic materials. Commercial brewing began in 2011. Occasional ales are available.

Ale (OG 1042, ABV 4.2%)

Anglo Dutch

See Partners

Angus

Angus Ales, 14b Panmure Industrial Estate, Carnoustie, DD7 7NP
☎ 07708 011649 ✉ info@angus-ales.co.uk
⊕ angus-ales.co.uk
Tours by arrangement

⊗ Angus Ales was established in 2009 using a four-barrel plant. Situated in the golf town of Carnoustie, the four regular brews have golf-related names.

Gowfers' Gold (ABV 3.8%)
A refreshing golden ale.

Birdie 3 (ABV 4.1%)
A pale brown beer.

Mashie Niblick (ABV 4.2%)
A full-flavoured malty ale.

Driver Dark (ABV 4.4%)
A rich, dark stout with lots of roasted and chocolate malt.

Ann Street

See Liberation

An Teallach

An Teallach Ale Co Ltd, Camusnagaul, Dundonnell, Garve, Ross-shire, IV23 2QT
☎ (01854) 633306 ✉ ataleco1@yahoo.co.uk
Tours by arrangement

An Teallach was formed in 2001 by husband and wife team David and Wilma Orr on Wilma's family croft on the shores of Little Loch Broom, Wester Ross. The business has grown steadily each year. 60 pubs are supplied. All beers are also available bottled.

Beinn Dearg Ale (OG 1038, ABV 3.8%) ◣
A well-balanced malty, sweetish beer with a long, malty aftertaste.

Ale (OG 1042, ABV 4.2%) ◣
A classic beer in the Scottish 80/- tradition. Plenty of malt in the nicely-balanced, bittersweet taste.

Crofters Pale Ale (OG 1042, ABV 4.2%) ◣
A good quaffing, lightly-flavoured golden ale. Hops in the taste and with a slight astringency in the finish.

Suilven (OG 1043, ABV 4.3%) ◣
A refreshing golden ale with a creamy sweetish taste and a pleasant sulphurous nose.

Kildonan (OG 1044, ABV 4.4%) ◣
Plenty of fruit and a good smack of bitterness in this golden ale.

Sail Mhor (OG 1044, ABV 4.4%)

Hector (OG 1047, ABV 4.7%)

Appleford SIBA

Appleford Brewery Co Ltd, Unit 14, Highlands Farm, High Road, Brightwell-cum-Sotwell, Wallingford, Oxfordshire, OX10 0QX
☎ (01235) 848055
✉ sales@applefordbrewery.co.uk
⊕ applefordbrewery.co.uk

⊗ Appleford Brewery opened in 2006 when two farm units were converted to house an eight-barrel plant. Deliveries are made to a number of local outlets as well as nationally, via the brewery or wholesalers. Bottle-conditioned beers are available.

Brightwell Gold (OG 1041, ABV 4%)

Power Station (OG 1043, ABV 4.2%)
A copper-coloured, slightly malty bitter.

Arbor SIBA

Arbor Ales Ltd, Unit 10a, Bridge Road Industrial Estate, Bridge Road, Kingswood, Bristol, BS15 4TA
☎ (0117) 957 0899 ✉ beer@arborales.co.uk
⊕ arborales.co.uk

⊗ Arbor Ales opened in 2007 in the back of the Old Tavern pub. In 2008 it moved to Kingswood and expanded to a 5.5-barrel plant. Further expansion took place in 2009. Arbor Ales also bought its first pub, the Old Stillage, in 2009. A wide range of beers are brewed with particular pride taken in the darker ales due to the brewer's involvement with the Bristol & District Rare Ales Group (www.badrag.co.uk). Seasonal beers are available: see website. Around 160 outlets are supplied direct.

Bushcraft (OG 1039, ABV 3.9%)

Single Hop (OG 1037, ABV 4%) ◣
Very pale, well-hopped ale. While hops lead, sweet malt and fruit balance the palate while a powerful hop bitterness marks the aftertaste.

Hunny Beer (OG 1041, ABV 4.2%) ◣
Speciality bitter, pale amber in colour. Honey is discernible in the malty-fruity aroma and taste. The aftertaste is bittersweet and short.

Brigstow (OG 1042, ABV 4.3%) ◣
Fairly bitter version of the typical Bristol Best. Mid-brown with plenty of hop flavour and a hint of roasted barley.

Old Knobbley (OG 1042, ABV 4.5%)

Oyster Stout (OG 1046.5, ABV 4.6%) ◣
A smoky stout with real oysters added in the copper – a hint of the sea in the dry aftertaste. Fruity, roast and burnt flavours, liquorice notes and a creamy mouthfeel.

Beech Blonde (OG 1046, ABV 4.9%)

Archers

See Evan Evans

Arkell's SIBA IFBB

Arkell's Brewery Ltd, Kingsdown, Swindon, Wiltshire,
SN2 7RU
☎ (01793) 823026 ✉ arkells@arkells.com
⊕ arkells.com
Brewery merchandise can be purchased at
reception
Tours by arrangement

⊗ Arkells Brewery was established in 1843 and is
still run by the family. The brewery owns 105 pubs
in Berkshire, Gloucestershire, Oxfordshire and
Wiltshire. Seasonal beers: see website.

2B (OG 1032, ABV 3.2%) ◄
Light brown in colour, malty but with a smack of
hops and an astringent aftertaste. It has good body
for its strength.

3B (OG 1040, ABV 4%) ◄
A medium brown beer with a strong, sweetish
malt/caramel flavour. The hops come through
strongly in the aftertaste, which is lingering and
dry.

Moonlight Ale (OG 1046, ABV 4.5%)
A golden beer with a lingering taste and toasty
aroma.

Kingsdown Ale (OG 1051, ABV 5%) ◄
A rich, deep russet-coloured beer, a stronger
version of 3B. The malty/fruity aroma continues in
the taste, which has a hint of pears. Hops come
through in the aftertaste.

Arkwright's SIBA

Arkwright's Brewery, c/o The Real Ale Shop, 47 Lovat
Road, Preston, Lancashire, PR1 6DQ
☎ 07944 912326 ✉ info@realaleshop.net
⊕ realaleshop.net

Arkwright's began brewing at the rear of the Real
Ale Shop in 2010 using a 2.5-barrel plant.

Trouble at Mill (ABV 4%)

Run of the Mill (ABV 4.1%)

Arran SIBA

Arran Brew Ltd t/a Arran Brewery, Cladach, Brodick,
Isle of Arran, North Ayrshire, KA27 8DE
☎ (01770) 302353 ✉ info@arranbrewery.co.uk
⊕ arranbrewery.com
Shop Mon-Sat 10am-5pm; Sun 12.30-5pm
(reduced hours in winter)
Tours daily at 2pm or by appointment

⊗ The brewery opened in 2000 using a 20-barrel
plant. Production is up to 100 barrels a week with
additional bottling capability. 50 outlets are
supplied. Seasonal beers are brewed and bottle-
conditioned beer is available occasionally.

Ale (OG 1038, ABV 3.8%) 🍴 ◄
An amber ale where the predominance of the hop
produces a bitter beer with a subtle balancing
sweetness of malt and an occasional hint of roast.

Dark (OG 1042, ABV 4.3%) ◄
A well-balanced malty beer with plenty of roast
and hop in the taste and a dry, bitter finish.

Red Squirrel (OG 1038, ABV 4.5%)
A well-balanced malty, hop blend containing
suggestions of liquorice and burnt toffee with a
characteristic nutty aroma.

Blonde (OG 1048, ABV 5%) ◄
A hoppy beer with substantial fruit balance. The
taste is balanced and the finish increasingly bitter.
An aromatic strong bitter that drinks below its
weight.

Arrow

🏴 Arrow Brewery, c/o Wine Vaults, 37 High Street,
Kington, Herefordshire, HR5 3BJ
☎ (01544) 230685 ✉ deanewright@yahoo.co.uk

☺Brewer Deane Wright built his five-barrel
brewery at the rear of the Wine Vaults and started
brewing in 2005. The Wine Vaults is the only pub
outlet for Arrow Bitter.

Bitter (OG 1042, ABV 4%)

Art Brew SIBA

Art Brew, The Art Brew Barn, Northend Farm, off
Venn Lane, North Chideock, Dorset, DT6 6JY
☎ 07881 783626 ✉ artbrewdorset@googlemail.com
⊕ artbrew.co.uk

⊗ Brewing started in 2008 on a five-barrel plant
with its own water source near the Jurassic Coast.
The Royal Oak in Bath is also owned, which serves
as the brewery tap. Around 60 outlets are supplied
from Dorset towards Berkshire and London.
Seasonal beers: see website.

Art Nouveau (OG 1039, ABV 3.9%)
Golden and hoppy.

iBeer (OG 1039, ABV 4%)
Speciality vanilla beer.

Renaissance (OG 1044, ABV 4.5%)
A mid-brown bitter.

Monkey IPA (OG 1058, ABV 6.4%)
Massively hopped proper IPA.

Spanked Monkey IPA (OG 1058, ABV 6.4%)
As above but with root ginger and chilli added to
the cask.

Artisan

Artisan Brewing Co Ltd, 183a Kings Road, Cardiff,
Glamorgan, CF11 9DF
☎ 07505 401939 ✉ info@artisanbeer.co.uk
⊕ artisanbeer.co.uk
Tours by arrangement (small groups only)

⊗ Artisan was established in 2008. All beers are
unfiltered, without additives or preservatives and
suitable for vegans. Bottle-conditioned beers are
available.

Bavarian Style Wheat Beer (ABV 4.6%)

Chocolate Wheat (ABV 4.9%)

ALT Beer (ABV 5%)

Bohemian Style Pils (ABV 5%)

Helles Style Lager (ABV 5%)

Kolsch (ABV 5.1%)

The 'Real' IPA (ABV 5.6%)

Baltic Porter (Espresso) (ABV 6%)
Infused with coffee beans.

Arundel SIBA

Arundel Brewery Ltd, Unit C7, Ford Airfield Industrial Estate, Ford, Arundel, West Sussex, BN18 0HY
☎ (01903) 733111
✉ arundelbrewery@dsl.pipex.com
⊕ arundelbrewery.co.uk
Off-sales available Mon-Fri 9am-4pm at brewery

⊠ Founded in 1992, Arundel Brewery is the historic town's first brewery in more than 70 years. A range of occasional brands is available in selected months. Seasonal beers: see website.

Black Stallion (OG 1037, ABV 3.7%) ◈
A dark mild. Strong chocolate and roast aromas, which lead to a bitter taste. The aftertaste is not powerful but the initial flavours remain in the dry and clean finish.

Castle (OG 1038, ABV 3.8%) ◈
A pale tawny beer with fruit and malt noticeable in the aroma. The flavour has a good balance of malt, fruit and hops, with a dry, hoppy finish.

Sussex Gold (OG 1042, ABV 4.2%) ◈
A golden-coloured best bitter with a strong floral hop aroma. The ale is clean-tasting and bitter for its strength, with a tangy citrus flavour. The initial hop and fruit die to a dry and bitter finish.

ASB (OG 1045, ABV 4.5%)
A special bitter with a complex roast malt flavour leading to a fruity, hoppy, bittersweet finish.

Stronghold (OG 1047, ABV 4.7%) ◈
A smooth, full-flavoured premium bitter. A good balance of malt, fruit and hops comes through in this rich, chestnut-coloured beer.

Trident (OG 1050, ABV 5%)
An amber-coloured strong beer with a citrus, fruity aroma. The taste is clean and refreshing with a hoppy, fruity flavour and a pleasant dry, bitter finish.

Ascot SIBA

Ascot Ales Ltd, Unit 5, Compton Place, Surrey Avenue, Camberley, Surrey, GU15 3DX
☎ (01276) 686696 ✉ chris@ascot-ales.co.uk
⊕ ascot-ales.co.uk
Tours by arrangement

⊠ Ascot Ales began production in 2007 on a four-barrel plant. Current owners Chris & Suzanne Gill took over the brewery in late 2007. Since adding a fourth fermenter the extra capacity has given scope for more seasonal/one off brews in addition to their five regular ales. Seasonal beers: see website. Bottle-conditioned beers are also available and are suitable for vegetarians and vegans.

Alley Cat Ale (OG 1038, ABV 3.8%) ◈
A pale brown session bitter with citrus hop present throughout, but balanced by malt. Dry with a lasting bitter finish.

On the Rails (OG 1038, ABV 3.8%) ◈
Dark, fruity and roasty mild with a faint hop character throughout, bittersweet in the taste and aftertaste. Notably dry finish.

Posh Pooch (OG 1042, ABV 4.2%) ◈
A hoppy best bitter with balancing biscuity malt sweetness. The citrus fruitiness lasts throughout. Clean hoppy aftertaste.

Alligator Ale (OG 1047, ABV 4.6%) ◈
American hops provide grapefruit notes in this golden ale. Hop and bitterness dominate, but there is some balancing biscuit in the aroma and taste. A residual sweetness remains even in the sharp, dry finish.

Anastasia's Exile Stout (OG 1049, ABV 5%) ◈
Burnt coffee aromas lead to a roast malt flavour in this black beer. Notably fruity throughout. The presence of some hop feeds into the bittersweet aftertaste.

Ashley Down (NEW)

Ashley Down Brewery Ltd, 15 Wathen Road, St Andrews, Bristol, BS6 5BY
☎ (0117) 983 6567

Ashley Down began brewing in 2011 using a 3.5-barrel plant in the owner's garage.

Vanguard (ABV 3.9%)

Best (ABV 4.2%)

Pale Ale (ABV 4.3%)

Ashover SIBA

▤ Ashover Brewery, 1 Butts Road, Ashover, Chesterfield, Derbyshire, S45 0EW
☎ 07803 708526
✉ ashoverbrewery@googlemail.com
⊕ ashoverbrewery.com
Tours by arrangement

⊠ Ashover Brewery first brewed in early 2007 on a 3.5-barrel plant in the garage of the cottage next to the Old Poet's Corner pub. The brewery caters mainly for this and its sister pub, the Poet & Castle in Codnor, but other local free houses and festivals are also supplied. Seasonal beers are available.

Light Rale (OG 1038, ABV 3.7%) ◈
Light in colour and taste, with initial sweet and malt flavours, leading to a bitter finish and aftertaste.

Poets Tipple (OG 1041, ABV 4%) ◈
Complex, tawny-coloured beer that drinks above its strength. Predominantly malty in flavour, with increasing bitterness towards the end.

Hydro (OG 1043, ABV 4.2%) ◈
Easy to drink golden beer with a predominantly hoppy aroma. Hop and fruit flavours and an initial sweetness lead to a dry, clean finish and aftertaste.

Rainbows End (OG 1045, ABV 4.5%) ◈
Slightly smooth, bitter golden beer with an initial sweetness. Grapefruit and lemon hop flavours come through strongly as the beer gets increasingly dry towards the finish, ending with a bitter, dry aftertaste.

Coffin Lane Stout (OG 1050, ABV 5%) ◈
Excellent example of the style, with a chocolate and coffee flavour, balanced by a little sweetness. Finish is long and quite dry.

Butts Pale Ale (OG 1055, ABV 5.5%) ◈
Pale and strong yet easy to drink golden bitter. Combination of bitter and sweet flavours mingle with an alcoholic kick, leading to a warming yet bitter finish and aftertaste.

Aston Manor

Aston Manor Brewery Co Ltd, 173 Thimble Mill Lane, Aston, Birmingham, West Midlands, B7 5HS
☎ (0121) 328 4336 ✉ sales@astonmanor.co.uk
⊕ astonmanor.co.uk

Aston Manor is the former owner of the Highgate Brewery in Walsall (qv). Its own plant concentrates on cider. Beer is bottled at Highgate but is not bottle conditioned.

Atlantic

Atlantic Brewery, Treisaac Farm, Treisaac, Newquay, Cornwall, TR8 4DX
☎ (0870) 042 1714 ✉ stuart@atlanticbrewery.com
⊕ atlanticbrewery.com

Atlantic started brewing in 2005. All beers are organic, Soil Association certified and suitable for vegetarians and vegans. It concentrates on bottle-conditioned beers: Gold (ABV 4.6%, summer), Blue (ABV 4.8%), Red (ABV 5%), Fistral (ABV 5.2%).

Atlas

See Orkney

Atomic

Atomic Brewery, c/o 1 Lower Hillmorton Road, Rugby, Warwickshire, CV21 3ST
☎ (01788) 542170 ☎ 07986 983984
✉ sales@atomicbrewery.co.uk
⊕ atomicbrewery.com
Tours by arrangement

⊗ Atomic Brewery started production in 2006 and is run by CAMRA members Keith Abbis and Nick Pugh. One pub is owned, the Victoria Inn in Rugby, which acts as the brewery tap and features beers swapped with other micro-breweries. Atomic uses the Alexandra Ales brew plant behind the Alexandra Arms in Rugby.

Strike (OG 1039, ABV 3.7%)

Fission (OG 1040, ABV 3.9%)

Fusion (OG 1042, ABV 4.1%)

Reactor (OG 1047, ABV 4.5%)

Half-Life (OG 1051, ABV 5%)

Bomb (OG 1054, ABV 5.2%)

Power (OG 1054, ABV 5.2%)

AVS

See Loddon

Ayr SIBA

Ayr Brewing Co Ltd, 5 Racecourse Road, Ayr, KA7 2DG
☎ (01292) 263891
✉ anthony.valenti@btinternet.com
Tours by arrangement

Ayr began brewing in 2009 on a five-barrel plant and is located in the Glen Park Hotel. As well as the hotel, around 25 other outlets are supplied in central and southern Scotland and the north of England. Seasonal beers are available.

Leezie Lundie (OG 1037.5, ABV 3.8%)

Jolly Beggars (OG 1041, ABV 4.2%)

Rabbie's Porter (OG 1042.5, ABV 4.3%)

Towzie Tyke (OG 1044.5, ABV 4.6%)

B&T SIBA EAB

B&T Brewery Ltd, The Brewery, Shefford, Bedfordshire, SG17 5DZ
☎ (01462) 815080 ✉ brewery@banksandtaylor.com
⊕ banksandtaylor.com
Tours by arrangement (CAMRA branches only)

⊗ Banks & Taylor – now just B&T – was founded in 1982. It produces an extensive range of beers, including monthly special brews together with occasional beers: see website for details. There are five tied houses, all operated with guest beers as well as B&T beers.

Two Brewers Bitter (OG 1036, ABV 3.6%) ◀
Bronze-coloured bitter with citrus hop aroma and taste and a dry finish.

Shefford Bitter (OG 1038, ABV 3.8%) ◀
A pale brown beer with a light hop aroma and a hoppy taste leading to a bitter finish.

Shefford Dark Mild (OG 1038, ABV 3.8%) ◀
A dark beer with a well-balanced taste. Sweetish, roast malt aftertaste.

Golden Fox (OG 1041, ABV 4.1%)
A golden, hoppy ale, dry tasting with a fruity aroma and citrus finish.

Black Dragon Mild (OG 1043, ABV 4.3%) ◀
Black in colour with a toffee and roast malt flavour and a smoky finish.

Dunstable Giant (OG 1044, ABV 4.4%)
Dark tawny bitter with a subtle blend of malt and hops.

Dragon Slayer (OG 1045, ABV 4.5%) ◀
A golden beer with a malt and hop flavour and a bitter finish. More malty and less hoppy than is usual for a beer of this style.

Edwin Taylor's Extra Stout
(OG 1045, ABV 4.5%) ◀
A complex black beer with a bitter coffee and roast malt flavour and a dry bitter finish.

Fruit Bat (OG 1045, ABV 4.5%) ◀
A warming straw-coloured beer with a generous taste of raspberries and a bitter finish.

Shefford Pale Ale (SPA) (OG 1045, ABV 4.5%) ◀
A well-balanced beer with hop, fruit and malt flavours. Dry, bitter aftertaste.

SOS (OG 1050, ABV 5%) ◀
A rich mixture of fruit, hops and malt is present in the taste and aftertaste of this beer. Predominantly hoppy aroma. SOD is the same beer with caramel added.

Bacchus

Bacchus Brewing Co, Bacchus Hotel, 17 High Street, Sutton-on-Sea, Lincolnshire, LN12 2EY
☎ (01507) 441204 ✉ info@bacchushotel.co.uk
⊕ bacchushotel.co.uk
Tours by arrangement

Bacchus began brewing in 2010 on a one-barrel plant supplying the Bacchus Hotel.

Bittermans (OG 1043, ABV 4%)

Best Bitter (OG 1043, ABV 4.3%)

Stingo (OG 1045, ABV 4.5%)

Backyard SIBA

Backyard Brewhouse, Unit 8a, Gatehouse Trading Estate, Lichfield Road, Brownhills, Walsall, West Midlands, WS8 6JZ
☎ 07591 923370
✉ enquiries@thebackyardbrewhouse.com
⊕ thebackyardbrewhouse.com
Tours by arrangement

Backyard began brewing in 2008 on a five-barrel plant. Three core beers are produced plus seasonal and monthly specials – see website for further details. Around 40 outlets are supplied direct.

The Hoard (OG 1040, ABV 3.9%)

Blonde (OG 1041, ABV 4.1%)

D&B Porter (OG 1044, ABV 4.3%)

Heriot (OG 1043, ABV 4.4%)
Slightly sweet with hints of tangerine and fruit salad.

Penda (OG 1053, ABV 5.5%)

Badger

See Hall & Woodhouse

Ballard's SIBA

Ballard's Brewery Ltd, The Old Sawmill, Nyewood, Petersfield, GU31 5HA
☎ (01730) 821362 ✉ service@ballards-brewery.co.uk ⊕ ballards-brewery.co.uk
Shop Mon-Fri 8am-4pm
Tours by arrangement

⊠ Launched in 1980 by Mike and Carola Brown at Cumbers Farm, Trotton, Ballard's has been trading at Nyewood since 1988 and now supplies 70-80 outlets. Seasonal beers: see website. Bottle-conditioned beers are also available.

Midhurst Mild (OG 1034, ABV 3.4%)
Traditional dark mild, well-balanced, refreshing, with a biscuity flavour.

Golden Bine (OG 1038, ABV 3.8%) ◆
Amber, clean-tasting bitter. A roast malt aroma leads to a fruity, slightly sweet taste and a dry finish.

Best Bitter (OG 1042, ABV 4.2%) ◆
A copper-coloured beer with a malty aroma. A good balance of fruit and malt in the flavour gives way to a dry, hoppy aftertaste.

Wild (ABV 4.7%)
A blend of Mild and Wassail.

Nyewood Gold (OG 1050, ABV 5%) ◆
Robust golden brown strong bitter, hoppy and fruity throughout, with a balanced finish.

Wassail (OG 1060, ABV 6%) ◆
A strong, full-bodied, tawny-red, fruity beer with a predominance of malt throughout, but also an underlying hoppiness.

Bank Top SIBA

Bank Top Brewery Ltd, The Pavilion, Ashworth Lane, Bolton, Lancashire, BL1 8RA
☎ (01204) 595800 ✉ dave@banktopbrewery.com
⊕ banktopbrewery.com
Tours by arrangement

☺Bank Top was established in 1995 by John Feeney. Since 2002 the brewery has occupied a Grade II listed tennis pavilion. In 2007 the brewing capacity was doubled with the installation of a new 10-barrel plant and in 2008 David Sweeney became the sole proprietor. Bottle-conditioned beers are available.

Barley to Beer (OG 1036, ABV 3.6%)
A pale bitter with a citrus lemon and herbal finish.

Sweeney's (OG 1038, ABV 3.8%)
An amber bitter with a bold, crisp flavour and a delicate, slightly spicy aroma.

Bad to the Bone (OG 1040, ABV 4%)
A tan-coloured beer with floral qualities and delicate citrus notes.

Dark Mild (OG 1040, ABV 4%) ▣ ◆
Dark brown beer with a malt and roast aroma. Smooth mouthfeel, with malt, roast malt and hops prominent throughout.

Flat Cap (OG 1040, ABV 4%) ◆
Amber ale with a modest fruit aroma leading to a beer with citrus fruit, malt and hops. Good finish of fruit, malt and bitterness.

Gold Digger (OG 1040, ABV 4%) ◆
Golden coloured, with a citrus aroma, grapefruit and a touch of spiciness on the palate; a fresh, hoppy citrus finish.

Old Slapper (OG 1042, ABV 4%)
A blonde bitter with an initial fruitiness complemented by a pronounced hoppiness in the finish.

Pavilion Pale Ale (OG 1045, ABV 4.5%) ◆
A yellow beer with a citrus and hop aroma. Big fruity flavour with a peppery hoppiness; dry, bitter yet fruity finish.

Blonde (OG 1050, ABV 5%)
An extremely pale ale made with New Zealand hops resulting in a pleasant woody flavour and distinct berry aroma.

Port O Call (OG 1050, ABV 5%) ◆
Dark brown beer with a malty, fruity aroma. Malt, roast and dark fruits in the bittersweet taste and finish.

Leprechaun Stout (OG 1060, ABV 6%)
A pitch black stout with hints of blackcurrant and spicy fruit.

Banks's

See Marston's in New Nationals section

Barearts

Barearts Ltd t/a Barearts Brewery, 290-292 Rochdale Road, Todmorden, West Yorkshire, OL14 7PD
☎ (01706) 839305 ✉ info@barearts.com
⊕ barearts.com
Shop Wed-Fri 4-9.45pm, Sat 12-9.45pm, Sun 12-9.45pm

A four-barrel craft brewery that began production in 2005 and is named after an art gallery dedicated to nude artwork. Beer is only available from the beer shop and studio bar or by mail order. All beers are only sold in bottles or 5-litre mini casks and they are all conditioned by secondary fermentation.

Barge & Barrel

See Eastwood

Barlow SIBA

Barlow Brewery Ltd, Units 5 & 6, Shippen Rural Business Centre, Church Farm, Barlow, Derbyshire, S18 7TR
☎ (0114) 289 1767
✉ enquiries@barlowbrewery.co.uk
⊕ barlowbrewery.com
Ring for shop opening times

Barlow began brewing in 2009 using a 2.5-barrel plant located in renovated farm buildings. The Hare & Hounds in Barlow is supplied on a permanent basis as well as several other outlets in Derbyshire and South Yorkshire.

Heath Robinson (OG 1038, ABV 3.8%)
A dark bitter with a malty background and a balanced, bitter finish.

Carnival Ale (OG 1042, ABV 4%)
A light, golden pale ale with a citrus finish.

Dark Horse (OG 1043, ABV 4.2%)
A dark bitter with a coffee aroma and well-balanced finish.

Black (OG 1051, ABV 5%)
A dark ale with strong roast and malty flavours and a well-balanced, bitter finish.

Anastasia (OG 1080, ABV 8%)
Strong, dark and smooth with complex malt flavours, chocolate coffee and a hint of fruit.

Barngates SIBA

Barngates Brewery Ltd, Barngates, Ambleside, Cumbria, LA22 0NG
☎ (01539) 436575 ✉ info@barngatesbrewery.co.uk
⊕ barngatesbrewery.co.uk
Tours by arrangement

⊕Barngates Brewery started brewing in 1997 and initially provided only the Drunken Duck Inn. The brewery became a limited company in 1999 upon expansion to a five-barrel plant. Further expansion in 2008 included a brand new, purpose-built 10-barrel plant. Around 150 outlets are supplied direct throughout Cumbria, Lancashire, Yorkshire and Northumberland. Occasional beers are produced.

Cat Nap (OG 1037, ABV 3.6%) ◆
A golden beer that is unapologetically/unmistakably bitter with a dry/astringent finish.

Cracker Ale (OG 1038, ABV 3.9%) ◆
A flavoursome malty bitter, fruity but not sweet. Dry in taste rather than finish.

Pride of Westmorland (OG 1042, ABV 4.1%) ◆
A well-crafted pale brown beer with bitterness dominant throughout.

Westmorland Gold (OG 1043, ABV 4.2%) ◆

A golden ale with a good balance of malt and hops, perhaps not as intense as previously.

Tag Lag (OG 1044, ABV 4.4%) ◆
A pale amber beer, smooth and sweetly malty to begin but a lasting, bitter finish.

Red Bull Terrier (OG 1048, ABV 4.8%)
A deep red tone and a complex hop nose are complemented by tangy fruit and malt flavours with a spicy aftertaste.

Chester's Strong & Ugly (OG 1052, ABV 5.2%) ◆
Complex and well-balanced, a richly satisfying dark beer with plenty of roast and hop bitterness.

Barnsley

See Wentworth

Barrowden

▤ Barrowden Brewing Co, c/o Exeter Arms, 28 Main Street, Barrowden, Rutland, LE15 8EQ
☎ (01572) 747247
✉ enquiries@exeterarmsrutland.co.uk
⊕ exeterarmsrutland.co.uk

⊠ The brewery was established by Peter Blencowe in 1998. Martin Allsopp bought the pub and brewery in 2005, which is situated in a barn at the back of the Exeter Arms.

Pilot (OG 1028, ABV 2.6%)

Beech (OG 1040, ABV 3.8%)

Hop Gear (OG 1046, ABV 4.4%)

Blackadder (OG 1050, ABV 4.6%)

Bartrams EAB

Bartrams Brewery, Rougham Estate, Ipswich Road (A14), Rougham, Suffolk, IP30 9LZ
☎ (01449) 737655 ☎ 07768 062581
✉ marc@bartramsbrewery.co.uk
⊕ bartramsbrewery.co.uk
Shop Tue & Sat 12-6pm
Tours by arrangement

The brewery was set up in 1999. In 2005 the plant was moved to a building on Rougham Airfield, the site of Bartram's Brewery between 1894 and 1902 run by Captain Bill Bartram. His image graces the pump clips. Beers are available in a selection of local pubs and there is a large amount of trade through local farmers' markets. Marld, Beltane Braces and all porters and stouts are suitable for vegetarians and vegans, as are all bottled beers. Seasonal beers: see website.

Marld (OG 1033, ABV 3.4%)
A traditional mild. Spicy hops and malt with a hint of chocolate, slightly smoky with a light, roasted finish.

Premier (ABV 3.7%)
A traditional quaffing ale, full-flavoured but light, dry and hoppy.

Rougham Ready (OG 1038, ABV 3.8%)
A light, crisp bitter, surprisingly full bodied for its strength.

Red Queen (OG 1039, ABV 3.9%)
Typical IPA style, chocolate malt in the foreground while the resiny hop flavour lingers.

Cats Whiskers (OG 1040, ABV 4%)

A straw-coloured beer with ginger and lemons added; a unique flavour experience.

Grozet (OG 1040, ABV 4%)
Gooseberries are added to give an appealing extra dimension.

Bees Knees (OG 1042, ABV 4.2%)
An amber beer with a floral aroma; honey softness on the palate leads to a crisp, bitter finish.

Catherine Bartram's IPA (OG 1043, ABV 4.3%)
A full-bodied malty IPA style; tangy hops lead the malt throughout and dominate the dry, hoppy aftertaste.

Jester Quick One (OG 1044, ABV 4.4%)
A sweet reddish bitter using fruity American Ahtanum hops.

Beltane Braces (OG 1046, ABV 4.5%)
Smooth and dark.

Stingo (OG 1045, ABV 4.5%)
A sweetish, fruity bitter with a hoppy nose. Light honey softens the bitter finish.

Beer Elsie Bub (OG 1048, ABV 4.8%)
Originally brewed for a Pagan wedding, this strong honey ale is now brewed all year round.

Captain Bill Bartram's Best Bitter (OG 1048, ABV 4.8%)
Modified from a 100-year old recipe, using full malt and traditional Kentish hops.

Captain's Stout (OG 1049, ABV 4.8%)
Biscuity dark malt leads to a lightly smoked aroma, plenty of roasted malt character, coffee notes and a whiff of smoke.

Cherry Stout (OG 1048, ABV 4.8%)
Sensuous hints of chocolate lead to a subtle suggestion of cherries.

Suffolk 'n' Strong (OG 1050, ABV 5%)
A light, smooth and dangerously potable strong bitter, well-balanced malt and hops with an easy finish.

Comrade Bill Bartram's Egalitarian Anti-Imperialist Soviet Stout (OG 1070, ABV 6.9%)
A Russian stout by any other name, a luscious easy-drinking example of the style.

Barum SIBA

Barum Brewery Ltd, c/o Reform Inn, Pilton, Barnstaple, Devon, EX31 1PD
☎ (01271) 329994 ✉ info@barumbrewery.co.uk
⊕ barumbrewery.co.uk
Tours by arrangement

Barum was formed in 1996 by Tim Webster and is housed in a conversion attached to the Reform Inn that acts as the brewery tap and main outlet. Distribution is exclusively within Devon. Seasonal beers are brewed.

Gold (OG 1039, ABV 4%)

Original (OG 1044, ABV 4.4%)

Breakfast (OG 1048, ABV 5%)

Batemans SIBA IFBB

George Bateman & Son Ltd, Salem Bridge Brewery, Mill Lane, Wainfleet, Lincolnshire, PE24 4JE
☎ (01754) 880317 ✉ enquiries@bateman.co.uk
⊕ bateman.co.uk

Visitor Centre & Shop: ring or see website for opening times
Tours by arrangement

Bateman's Brewery is one of the few remaining independent family-owned brewers. Established in 1874 it has been brewing award-winning beers for four generations of the family. All but one of the 66 tied houses serve cask-conditioned beer. See website for seasonal and speciality beers.

Dark Mild (OG 1030, ABV 3%)
Gentle roast fruity airs preface this red-brown, caramel-infused brew. Malt and a stewed plummy sweetness initially give depth. Caramel dominates the short simple finish.

XB (OG 1037, ABV 3.7%)
A well-rounded, smooth malty beer with a blackcurrant fruity background. Hops flourish initially before giving way to a bittersweet dryness that enhances the mellow malty ending.

GHA Pale Ale (OG 1042, ABV 4.2%)

XXXB (OG 1048, ABV 4.5%)
A blend of malt, hops and fruit on the nose with a bitter bite over the top of faintly banana maltiness that stays the course.

Salem Porter (OG 1048, ABV 4.7%)
A black and complex mix of chocolate, liquorice and cough elixir.

Bath Ales SIBA

Bath Ales Ltd, Units 3-7, Caxton Business Park, Crown Way, Warmley, Bristol, BS30 8XJ
☎ (0117) 947 4797 ✉ hare@bathales.co.uk
⊕ bathales.com
Shop Mon-Fri 9am-5pm; Sat 9am-12pm
Tours by arrangement

Bath Ales started brewing in 1995 and moved in 1999 to new premises with a 15-barrel plant. The company now has a purpose-built site on the edge of east Bristol, and can brew over 350 barrels a week. Around 350 outlets are supplied direct. Ten pubs are owned, all serving cask ale. Seasonal beers are brewed. Most beers are available for purchase from the website or shop.

SPA (OG 1037, ABV 3.7%)
Nicely-balanced pale session bitter. A citrus hop aroma, fruity taste and long bitter aftertaste.

Dark Hare (OG 1040, ABV 4%)

Gem Bitter (OG 1041, ABV 4.1%)
Aroma of caramel, good body of malt and caramel in the taste ending with a short burst of fruity, caramel bitterness.

Golden Hare (OG 1045, ABV 4.4%)

Barnstormer (OG 1046, ABV 4.5%)
Malt, caramel and fruit aroma with a hint of roast and toffee. Dark brown, fruity, malty and bitter in the aftertaste – caramel present throughout.

Batham IFBB

Daniel Batham & Son Ltd, Delph Brewery, Delph Road, Brierley Hill, West Midlands, DY5 2TN
☎ (01384) 77229 ✉ info@bathams.com
⊕ bathams.com

A classic Black Country small brewery established in 1877. Tim and Matthew Batham represent the fifth generation to run the company.

The Vine, one of the Black Country's most famous pubs, is also the site of the brewery. The company has 11 tied houses and supplies around 30 other outlets. Batham's Bitter is delivered in 54-gallon hogsheads to meet demand. Seasonal beer is also brewed.

Mild (OG 1036.5, ABV 3.5%) ◆
A fruity, dark brown mild with malty sweetness and a roast malt finish.

Best Bitter (OG 1043.5, ABV 4.3%) ◆
A pale yellow, fruity, sweetish bitter, with a dry, hoppy finish. A good, light, refreshing beer.

Battledown SIBA

Battledown Brewery llp, Keynsham Works, Keynsham Street, Cheltenham, Gloucestershire, GL52 6EJ
☎ (01242) 693409 ☎ 07734 834104
✉ roland@battledownbrewery.com
⊕ battledownbrewery.com
Shop open Wed/Thu/Sat am
Tours by arrangement

⊠ Established in 2005 by Roland and Stephanie Elliott-Berry, and joined in 2006 by Ben Jennison-Phillips (ex-Whittingtons), Battledown operates an eight-barrel plant from an old engineering works and supplies more than 250 outlets. Visitors are always welcome. There is an online shop for mail order purposes. Seasonal beers are also brewed.

Standard (OG 1036, ABV 3.6%)
A golden pale ale with a refreshing aroma and sharp but smooth taste, leaving a dry, hoppy aftertaste that lingers on the palate.

Natural Selection (OG 1041, ABV 4.2%)
A deep golden beer, the malts evident but giving way to the triple hop addition that leaves a spicy and slightly citrus finish.

Premium (OG 1046, ABV 4.6%)
A rich amber ale. A malty aroma and taste with a deep satisfying, full-bodied fruit and malt texture leaving a well-rounded mellow aftertaste.

Special (OG 1050, ABV 5.2%)
A well-balanced and crisp pale ale.

Four Kings (OG 1066, ABV 7.2%)
A strong ale with a heady aroma.

Battlefield

See Tunnel

Bays SIBA

Bays Brewery Ltd, Aspen Way, Paignton, Devon, TQ4 7QR
☎ (01803) 555004 ✉ info@baysbrewery.co.uk
⊕ baysbrewery.co.uk
Shop Mon-Fri 8am-5pm
Tours by arrangement

⊠ Bays Brewery opened in early 2007 in an old steel fabrication unit in Paignton on a 20-barrel plant. Seasonal and bottle-conditioned beers are also available.

Best (OG 1037, ABV 3.7%)

Topsail (ABV 4%)

Gold (OG 1042, ABV 4.3%)

Breaker (OG 1046, ABV 4.7%)

Devon Dumpling (OG 1048, ABV 5.1%)

Bazens'

See Star

Beachy Head SIBA

Beachy Head Brewing Co Ltd, Seven Sisters Sheep Centre, Birling Manor Farm, Gilberts Drive, East Dean, East Sussex, BN20 0AA
☎ (01323) 423313 ✉ charlie@beachyhead.org.uk
⊕ beachyhead.org.uk
Tours by arrangement

⊠ The 2.5-barrel brew plant was installed at the rear of the sheep centre in late 2006. Beachy Head Brewery produces both cask and bottle-conditioned ales, supplied regularly to around 15 outlets, three of which are local pubs. The full range of ales (including seasonals) can be sampled at the Tiger Inn in East Dean village, which is the brewery tap.

Parson Darbys Hole (ABV 4%)

Southdowns Ale (ABV 4.4%)

Beachy Original (ABV 4.5%)

Legless Rambler (ABV 5%)

Beartown SIBA

Beartown Brewery Ltd, Bromley House, Spindle Street, Congleton, Cheshire, CW12 1QN
☎ (01260) 299964
✉ headbrewer@beartownbrewery.co.uk
⊕ beartownbrewery.co.uk
Shop Mon-Fri 9am-5pm
Tours by arrangement

Congleton's links with brewing can be traced back to 1272. Two of its most senior officers at the time were Ale Taster and Bear Warden, hence the name of the brewery. Both the brewery's Navigation in Stockport and the Beartown Tap have been named CAMRA regional pubs of the year. There are plans to extend the tied estate to 15 outlets over the next two years. Beartown supplies 250 outlets and owns five pubs. A new 25-barrel plant has been installed. Seasonal and bottle-conditioned beers are also available.

Ursa Minor (OG 1036, ABV 3.6%)

Bitter (OG 1037, ABV 3.7%)

Ambeardextrous (OG 1038, ABV 4%)

Bear Ass (OG 1040, ABV 4%) ◆
Dark ruby-red, malty bitter with good hop nose and fruity flavour with dry, bitter, astringent aftertaste.

Ginger Bear (OG 1040, ABV 4%)
The flavours from the malt and hops blend with the added bite from the root ginger to produce a quenching finish.

Kodiak Gold (OG 1040, ABV 4%) ◆
Hops and fruit dominate the taste of this crisp yellow bitter and these follow through to the dryish aftertaste. Biscuity malt also comes through on the aroma and taste.

Wheat Bear (OG 1050, ABV 4%)

Bearskinful (OG 1043, ABV 4.2%) ◆
Biscuity malt dominates the flavour of this amber best bitter. There are hops and a hint of sulphur on

the aroma. A balance of malt and bitterness follow through to the aftertaste.

Bearly Literate (OG 1045, ABV 4.5%)

Polar Eclipse (OG 1048, ABV 4.8%) ◄
Classic black, dry and bitter stout, with roast flavours to the fore. Good hop on the nose follow through the taste into a long dry finish.

Black Bear (OG 1050, ABV 5%) ▭ ◄
Advertised as a strong mild, this beer is rather bitter for the style. Bitter and malt flavours are balanced and there is also a good roast character along with a hint of liquorice. Aftertaste is short and reasonably dry.

Bruins Ruin (OG 1050, ABV 5%)

Beckstones

Beckstones Brewery, Upper Beckstones Mill, The Green, Millom, Cumbria, LA18 5HL
☎ (01229) 775294
✉ david@beckstonesbrewery.com
⊕ beckstonesbrewery.co.uk

⌧ Beckstones started brewing in 2003 on the site of an 18th-century mill with its own water supply. It's a five-barrel, one-man operation. The beer names often have a connection to the long-closed Millom Iron Works or local characters. The brewer also designs the distinctive pump clips. Occasional and seasonal beers are also brewed.

Barley Juice (OG 1033, ABV 3.4%) ◄
Yellow, full-flavoured, beautifully balanced, fruity, hoppy beer.

Beer O'Clock (OG 1036, ABV 3.5%) ◄
Yellow beer with a fascinating blend of flavours delivering ever-changing mouthfuls of sweet, fruity and hoppy bitterness.

**Black Gun Dog Freddy Mild
(OG 1038, ABV 3.8%)** ▭ ◄
A full-bodied, beautifully balanced ruby dark mild, replete with fruit and roast malt.

Iron Town (OG 1038, ABV 3.8%) ◄
Creamy sweet brown ale full of well-balanced fruit and hop.

Border Steeans (OG 1040, ABV 4.1%) ◄
An old-fashioned tawny bitter with a sweet start, some bitter notes and plenty of aftertaste.

Rev Rob (OG 1044, ABV 4.6%) ▭ ◄
A golden beer with a pronounced grapefruit aroma and taste. The hoppy bitterness lasts through to the aftertaste.

Beer Engine SIBA

▤ Tuttles Unique Co Ltd t/a The Beer Engine, Newton St Cyres, Devon, EX5 5AX
☎ (01392) 851282 ✉ info@thebeerengine.co.uk
⊕ thebeerengine.co.uk
Tours by arrangement

⌧ Beer Engine was developed in 1983 and is the oldest continuously-working micro-brewery in Devon, still employing the original brewer, Ian Sharp. The brewery is visible behind glass downstairs in the pub. A few outlets are supplied as well as all local beer festivals. Seasonal beers are also available.

Rail Ale (OG 1037, ABV 3.8%) ◄

A straw-coloured beer with a fruity aroma and a sweet, fruity finish.

0-4-0 Shunter (OG 1040, ABV 4%)
An amber-coloured beer with a hoppy, sweet aftertaste.

Piston Bitter (OG 1043, ABV 4.3%) ◄
A mid-brown, sweet-tasting beer with a pleasant, bittersweet aftertaste.

Sleeper Heavy (OG 1052, ABV 5.4%) ◄
A red-coloured beer with a fruity, sweet taste and a bitter finish.

Beer Works

See Abbeydale

Bees

Bees Brewery, Plot 2, Coast Road, Walcott, Norwich, NR12 0LS
☎ 07971 577526 ✉ bees-brewery@hotmail.co.uk

Bees first brewed in 2008 and was initially based at Queniborough near Leicester. It relocated to Norfolk towards the end of 2009 and the five-barrel plant is now located in a static caravan overlooking the sea. Brewer Alec Brackenbury operates the brewery on a part-time basis and mainly supplies pubs within a 10-mile radius of Walcott.

Amber (OG 1038, ABV 3.8%)

Navigator (OG 1045, ABV 4.5%)

Stripey Jack (OG 1046, ABV 4.6%)

Wobble (OG 1050, ABV 5%)

Honey (OG 1052, ABV 5.2%)

Beeston SIBA

Beeston Brewery Ltd, Fransham Road Farm, Beeston, Norfolk, PE32 2LZ
☎ (01328) 700844 ☎ 07768 742763
✉ mark_riches@tesco.net ⊕ beestonbrewery.co.uk
Tours by arrangement

The brewery was established in 2006 in an old farm building using a five-barrel plant. Brewing water comes from a dedicated borehole and raw ingredients are sourced locally whenever possible. All beers are also available bottle conditioned and in 5-litre mini casks.

The Squirrels Nuts (OG 1035, ABV 3.5%)
A mild ale.

Afternoon Delight (OG 1036, ABV 3.7%)
An easy-drinking blonde ale.

Worth the Wait (OG 1041, ABV 4.2%) ◄
Well-balanced and complex with a soft hoppy nose. An initial burst of passion fruit mingles with malt and hops in a delightful first taste. A long-lasting finish develops a bittersweet dryness.

Stirling (OG 1045, ABV 4.5%)
Rich malty red bitter with toffee notes.

The Dry Road (OG 1048, ABV 4.8%)
A robust and refreshing IPA crafted with single variety hops.

On the Huh (OG 1048, ABV 5%) ◄
Deceptively smooth bitter with a fruity raisin aroma. A bittersweet maltiness jousts with caramel

and roast. A dry hoppiness gives depth to a strong finale.

Norfolk Black (OG 1060, ABV 6%)
A warming, full-bodied strong stout.

For Brancaster Brewery:

Best (OG 1038, ABV 3.8%)

Malthouse Bitter (OG 1042, ABV 4.2%)

Belhaven

See Greene King in New Nationals section

Bellingers (NEW)

Bellingers Brewery, Station Road, Grove, Oxfordshire, OX12 0DH
☎ (01235) 772255 ✉ info@bellingersbrewery.co.uk
⊕ bellingersbrewery.co.uk
Tours by arrangement

⊗ Bellingers Brewery is a family partnership formed in 2011 to produce beers the partners want to drink. Seasonal beers: see website.

Original Bitter (OG 1040, ABV 4.1%)

Best Bitter (OG 1046, ABV 4.7%)

Belvoir SIBA

Belvoir Brewery Ltd, Crown Park, Station Road, Old Dalby, Leicestershire, LE14 3NQ
☎ (01664) 823455 ✉ colin@belvoirbrewery.co.uk
⊕ belvoirbrewery.co.uk
Tours by arrangement

⊗ Belvoir (pronounced 'beaver') Brewery was set up in 1995 by former Shipstone's and Theakston's brewer Colin Brown. Long-term expansion has seen the introduction of a 20-barrel plant that can produce 50 barrels a week. There is also a visitor centre incorporating brewery memorabilia, a bar, restaurant and shop (open seven days a week). Around 150 outlets are supplied direct. Seasonal and bottle-conditioned beers are also available.

Dark Horse (OG 1035, ABV 3.4%)

Whippling (OG 1037, ABV 3.6%)
A golden, light, crisp and refreshing beer.

Star Bitter (OG 1039, ABV 3.9%)
Reminiscent of the long-extinct Shipstone's Bitter, this mid-brown bitter lives up to its name as it is bitter in taste but not unpleasantly so.

Gordon Bennett (OG 1041, ABV 4.1%)
Light chestnut beer with a biscuity character and a pleasant hop finish.

Beaver Bitter (OG 1043, ABV 4.3%) ◄
A light brown bitter that starts malty in both aroma and taste, but soon develops a hoppy bitterness. Appreciably fruity.

Oatmeal Stout (OG 1044, ABV 4.3%)
A full-bodied creamy dark stout.

Old Dalby (OG 1050, ABV 5.1%)
A rich, smooth ruby red strong ale with a pleasant hop character.

For Hoskins Brothers, Leicester:

Hobs Best Mild (OG 1035, ABV 3.5%)

Brigadier Bitter (OG 1036, ABV 3.6%)

Hobs Bitter (OG 1040, ABV 4%)

White Dolphin (OG 1040, ABV 4%)

Tom Kelly's Stout (OG 1042, ABV 4.2%)

Ginger Tom (OG 1052, ABV 5.2%)

Beowulf SIBA

Beowulf Brewing Co, Chasewater Country Park, Pool Road, Brownhills, Staffordshire, WS8 7NL
☎ (01543) 454067 ✉ beowulfbrewing@yahoo.co.uk
⊕ beowulfbrewery.co.uk
Tours by arrangement

Beowulf Brewing Company beers appear as guest ales predominantly in the central region but also across the country. The brewery's dark beers have a particular reputation for excellence. Seasonal beers: see website. Bottle-conditioned beer is also available.

Beorma (OG 1038, ABV 3.9%) ◄
A perfectly balanced session ale with a malty hint of fruit giving way to a lingering bitterness. Background spice excites the palate.

Noble Bitter (OG 1039, ABV 4%) ◄
Golden with a sweet malty aroma. Malty start becomes very hoppy then bitter, but not an overlong finish.

Wiglaf (OG 1043, ABV 4.3%) ◄
Powerful fruity aroma from this golden ale with subtle hop and fruit tastes. Bitterness develops as a surprise from the sweet start.

Chasewater Bitter (OG 1043, ABV 4.4%) ◄
Golden bitter, hoppy throughout with citrus and hints of malt. Long mouth-watering, bitter finish.

Dark Raven (OG 1048, ABV 4.5%) ▉ ◄
So dark with apple and bonfire in the aroma, so sweet and smooth like liquid toffee apples with a sudden bitter finish.

Swordsman (OG 1045, ABV 4.5%) ◄
Pale gold, light fruity aroma, tangy hoppy flavour. Faintly hoppy finish.

Heroes Bitter (OG 1046, ABV 4.7%) ◄
Gold colour, malt aroma, hoppy taste but sweetish finish.

Mercian Shine (OG 1048, ABV 5%) ◄
Amber to pale gold with a good bitter and hoppy start. Plenty of caramel and hops with background malt leading to a good bitter finish with caramel and hops lingering in the aftertaste.

Berrow

Berrow Brewery, Coast Road, Berrow, Burnham-on-Sea, Somerset, TA8 2QU
☎ (01278) 751345
Tours by arrangement

⊗ The brewery opened in 1982 and production is now around five barrels a week. All the beers have won prizes at beer festivals. 15-20 outlets are supplied. Seasonal beers are also brewed.

Best Bitter/4Bs (OG 1038, ABV 3.9%) ◄
A pleasant, pale brown session beer, with a fruity aroma, a malty, fruity flavour and bitterness in the palate and finish.

Berrow Porter (OG 1046, ABV 4.6%)
A ruby-coloured porter with a pronounced hop character.

Topsy Turvy (OG 1055, ABV 5.9%) ◄

A gold-coloured beer with an aroma of malt and hops. Well-balanced malt and hops taste is followed by a hoppy, bitter finish with some fruit notes.

Best Mates SIBA

Best Mates Brewery Ltd, Sheep House Farm, Ardington, Wantage, Oxfordshire, OX12 8QB
☎ **(01235) 835684**
✉ **bestmatesbrewery@btconnect.com**
⊕ **bestmatesbrewery.co.uk**
Tours by arrangement

⊗ Best Mates Brewery was established in 2007 on a five-barrel plant and uses locally sourced water. Seasonal and bottle-conditioned beers are also available.

Scutchaman's Knob (OG 1036, ABV 3.6%)

Vicar's Daughter (OG 1037, ABV 3.7%)

Ardington Ale (OG 1041, ABV 4.2%)

Alfie's (OG 1044, ABV 4.4%)

Satan's Sister (OG 1045, ABV 4.5%)

Betjemen (NEW)

≣ Betjemen Brewery, Shoulder of Mutton, 38 Wallingford Street, Wantage, Oxfordshire, OX12 8AX
☎ **07870 577742** ✉ **peter@splij.com**
⊕ **themutton.co.uk**
Tours by arrangement

⊗ Established in 2011, the brewery is situated at the rear of the Shoulder of Mutton in Wantage. The brewer is award-winning Peter Fowler, late of Pitstop Brewery and now landlord of the pub.

Wantage Bells (OG 1053, ABV 5%)

Sebastopol (OG 1076, ABV 7%)

Bewdley SIBA

Bewdley Brewery Ltd, Unit 7, Bewdley Craft Centre, Lax Lane, Bewdley, Worcestershire, DY12 2DZ
☎ **(01299) 405148** ✉ **info@bewdleybrewery.co.uk**
⊕ **bewdleybrewery.co.uk**
Tours by arrangement

⊗ Bewdley began brewing in 2008 on a six-barrel plant in an old school. Brewing experience days are offered; ring for details. Beers are brewed with a railway theme for the nearby Severn Valley Railway. Seasonal beers: see website. Bottle-conditioned beers are also available.

Worcestershire Way (OG 1036, ABV 3.6%)
A light beer with citrus notes.

Old School Bitter (OG 1038, ABV 3.8%)
Session bitter with a hoppy finish.

Senior School Bitter (OG 1041, ABV 4.1%)
A premium bitter, amber-coloured with malty taste and hoppy finish.

Worcestershire Sway (OG 1049, ABV 5%)

William Mucklow's Dark Mild (OG 1060, ABV 6%)
A dark, sweetish, strong ale with a smooth, fruity flavour and slight liquorice aftertaste.

Big Lamp

Big Lamp Brewers, Grange Road, Newburn, Newcastle upon Tyne, Tyne & Wear, NE15 8NL
☎ **(0191) 267 1689**
✉ **admin@biglampbrewers.co.uk**
⊕ **biglampbrewers.co.uk**
Tours by arrangement

☺Big Lamp started in 1982 and relocated in 1997 to a 55-barrel plant in a former water pumping station. It is the oldest micro-brewery in the north-east of England. Around 35 outlets are supplied and two pubs are owned. Seasonal and occasional beers are also brewed.

Sunny Daze (OG 1036, ABV 3.6%) ◀
Golden, hoppy session bitter with a clean taste and finish.

Bitter (OG 1039, ABV 3.9%) ◀
A clean-tasting bitter, full of hops and malt. A hint of fruit with a good, hoppy finish.

One Hop (OG 1040, ABV 4%)
Dark amber beer with a smooth finish and a hint of hazelnut.

Summerhill Stout (OG 1044, ABV 4.4%) ◀
A rich, tasty stout, dark in colour with a lasting rich roast character. Malty mouthfeel with a lingering finish.

Prince Bishop Ale (OG 1048, ABV 4.8%) ◀
A refreshing, easy-drinking bitter. Golden in colour, full of fruit and hops. Strong bitterness with a spicy, dry finish.

Premium (OG 1052, ABV 5.2%) ◀
Hoppy ale with a good bitter finish.

Keelman Brown (OG 1057, ABV 5.7%)
A full-bodied ale with a hint of toffee.

Binghams SIBA (NEW)

Binghams Brewery Ltd, Unit 10, Tavistock Industrial Estate, Ruscombe Business Park, Ruscombe Lane, Ruscombe, Berkshire, RG10 9NJ
☎ **(0118) 934 4376** ✉ **chris@binghams.co.uk**
⊕ **binghams.co.uk**
Shop Mon-Thu 5-6pm; Fri 5-7pm; Sat 12-6pm; Sun 12-4pm
Tours by arrangement

⊗ Binghams started brewing in 2010 using a 10-barrel plant. Six regular beers are brewed along with seasonals.

Twyford Tipple (OG 1040, ABV 3.7%)
Tawny-coloured beer with a citrus hop finish.

Brickworks Bitter (OG 1045, ABV 4.2%)
Chestnut-coloured malty bitter.

Coffee Stout (OG 1052, ABV 5%)
Coffee mellows the dark malts.

Doodle Stout (OG 1052, ABV 5%)
Dark and complex.

Space Hoppy IPA (OG 1050, ABV 5%)
Golden, hoppy and refreshing.

Vanilla Stout (OG 1052, ABV 5%)
Infused with vanilla pods for a smooth-drinking stout.

Bird Brain

Bird Brain Brewery Ltd, 30 Hailgate, Howden, East Yorkshire, DN14 7SL
☎ **(01430) 432166** ☎ **07790 615915**
✉ **birdbrainbrewery@tiscali.co.uk**

THE BREWERIES

⊠ Bird Brain began brewing in 2009 using a two-barrel brew plant that operates two or three times a month.

Black Bird Bitter (ABV 4%)

Old Raven (ABV 4.3%)

For the Victoria Hotel, Goole:

Shiney (ABV 3.9%)

Birds SIBA

Birds Brewery, Ladybird Barn, Old Burcot Lane, Bromsgrove, Worcestershire, B60 1PH
☎ (01527) 889870
✉ brewmaster@birdsbrewery.co.uk
⊕ birdsbrewery.co.uk
Tours by arrangement

☺Birds began brewing in 2009, supplying their beers across the West Midlands. The number of beers available has been gradually increasing since then as brewer Ian Hughes experiments with different malts and hops to create a balanced range of beers. One-off brews are created for special events and bottle-conditioned, vegan versions of the range are also available.

Thunderbird (OG 1038, ABV 3.8%)
A malty beer with a hint of sweetness and a distinctive nutty finish.

Ashborough Pale (OG 1040, ABV 4%)
A light golden session beer with a crisp, dry citrus taste and hoppy aroma.

Natural Blonde (OG 1040, ABV 4%)
A pale blonde beer; floral on the nose, plenty of fruit and hops in the mouth with balanced malt. A pleasantly hoppy aftertaste with a gently crisp, bitter finish.

Black Widow (OG 1048, ABV 4.8%)
A traditional smooth and satisfying stout with a roasted malt flavour, a bitter edge and overtones of blackcurrant, raisins and liquorice.

Firebird (OG 1048, ABV 4.8%)
A dark ruby beer with a hoppy aroma, smooth malty flavour and a caramel aftertaste.

Bitter End SIBA

Bitter End Brewing Co Ltd, Unit 11, Derwent Mills, Cockermouth, Cumbria, CA13 0HT
☎ (01900) 823300
✉ sales@bitterendbrewingco.com
⊕ bitterendbrewingco.com
Tours by arrangement

☺The brewery was established by Mike Askey in 1995, behind glass at the back of the Bitter End pub, and transferred to new premises in 2009. Output from the brewery is steadily increasing with expansion into the free trade. Three regular beers are brewed along with seasonals and a range of traditional English beer styles. One-off and festival beers are also produced.

Lakeland Bitter (OG 1039, ABV 3.8%) ◆
Fruity sweet beer with some hop. Easy-drinking light mild.

Lakeland Pale Ale (OG 1042, ABV 4%)

Lakeland Best Gold (OG 1044, ABV 4.3%) ◆
Hoppy, sweet, fruity beer low in bitterness.

Blackawton

Blackawton Brewery, Barnlee Lodge, Ilsington, Devon, TQ13 9RG
☎ (01364) 661524 ☎ 07971 871546
✉ enquiries@blackawtonbrewery.co.uk
⊕ blackawtonbrewery.com

⊠ Blackawton was once Devon's oldest operating brewery, but relocated to Cornwall in 2000 and ownership changed in 2004 and again in 2010. In 2011 it returned to Devon. Around 30 outlets are supplied. Seasonal beers: see website. Bottle-conditioned beers are also available.

Original Bitter (OG 1037, ABV 3.8%)
A copper-coloured bitter; an ideal session beer with a fresh floral hop aroma.

West Country Gold (OG 1039, ABV 4.1%)
A light, golden, fresh-tasting summer beer with sweet malt flavours and delicate vanilla and fruit hints from Styrian Goldings hops.

44 Special (OG 1044, ABV 4.5%)
A premium, full-strength bitter that is rich and sweet with the aroma of ripe hops and fruit.

Moorland Ale (OG 1046, ABV 4.6%)
A dark amber-coloured premium bitter with a hoppy, bitter finish.

Exhibition Ale (OG 1047, ABV 4.7%)

Headstrong (OG 1048, ABV 5.2%)
A deceptively smooth beer with a bitter malt taste.

Blackbeck

⊟ Blackbeck Brewery, Blackbeck Inn, Egremont, Cumbria, CA22 2NY
☎ (01946) 841661
✉ drink@blackbeckbrewery.co.uk
⊕ blackbeckbrewery.co.uk

Blackbeck was established in 2009 using a five-barrel plant and was extended a year later. Beers are available in bottled form or in mini casks.

Belle (OG 1038, ABV 3.8%)
Dark and chocolatey.

Carnival Kiss (ABV 3.8%)

Trial Run (OG 1037, ABV 3.8%) ◆
A fresh and fruity yellow beer with a lasting hoppy finish.

Black Cat SIBA (NEW)

Black Cat Brewery, Eridge Road, Groombridge, Kent, TN3 9NJ
☎ 07948 387718 ✉ info@blackcat-brewery.com
⊕ blackcat-brewery.com
Tours by arrangement

⊠ Black Cat began brewing in 2011 on a 2.5-barrel brew plant. Both beers are also available bottle conditioned. Seasonal beers are planned.

Hopsmack (OG 1040, ABV 4%)
A well-hopped golden citrus beer.

Original (OG 1042, ABV 4.2%)
Full-flavoured, hoppy traditional amber bitter.

Black Country SIBA

⊟ Black Country Ales, Rear of Old Bulls Head, 1 Redhall Road, Lower Gornal, Dudley, West Midlands, DY3 2NU

☎ (01384) 480156

Office & Beer Deliveries: Unit 4, Tansey Green Road, Pensnett, Dudley, West Midlands, DY5 4TL
✉ info@blackcountryales.co.uk
⊕ blackcountryinns.co.uk
Tours by arrangement

Brewing started on the site around 1834. In 1900, oak vessels were installed that have now been refurbished and brought back into production. The brewery was closed down in 1934 but reopened in 2004, with many original features still remaining. Seasonal beers: see website. Beers are also brewed under the Thomas Guest Brewing Company name.

Bradley's Finest Golden (BFG) (OG 1040, ABV 4.2%)
A straw-coloured quaffing beer with a bold citrus hop aroma, fruity balanced sweetness and a lingering, refreshing aftertaste.

Pig on the Wall (OG 1042, ABV 4.3%)
A refreshing chestnut brown beer with a complex flavour of light hops giving way to a bittersweet blend of roasted malt. Suggestions of chocolate and coffee undertones.

Dudley Pale Ale (ABV 5%)

Fireside Bitter (OG 1047, ABV 5%)
A well-rounded premium bitter, amber in colour, clean in taste leading to a pleasant, dry finish.

Brewed under Thomas Guest Brewing Co name:

Puddlers (ABV 4.1%)
A light, creamy bitter. Initial malt and fruit notes and a mellow, dry bitterness to finish.

Cobblers (ABV 4.4%)
A pale bitter, finely balanced with a malty start leading to a long, dry finish.

Black Dog

Black Dog Brewery, The Grange, High Street, Thornton le Dale, North Yorkshire, YO18 7QW
☎ (01751) 474423 ✉ tony.bryars@btinternet.com

☺Black Dog started brewing in 1997 in the centre of Whitby, but closed in 2000. In 2006 Tony Bryars purchased the original Black Dog recipes, and re-established the brewery. The beers are currently contract brewed by Hambleton Ales (qv) in Melmerby, North Yorkshire.

Blackfriars

Blackfriars Brewery Ltd, The Courtyard, Main Cross Road, Great Yarmouth, Norfolk, NR30 3NZ
☎ (01493) 850578 ✉ pints@blackfriars-brewery.co.uk ⊕ blackfriars-brewery.co.uk
Shop: Mon-Fri 10.30am-4.30pm; Sat & Sun 12-3.30pm
Tours by arrangement

⊠ The brewery was established in 2004 using a purpose-built five-barrel plant and was extended in 2007. In 2008 the brewery relocated and now has a shop, visitor centre and fully-licensed bar. More than 50 outlets are supplied. All beers (with the exception of specials) are available in bottle-conditioned form. Specials and seasonal beers: see website.

Mild (OG 1034, ABV 3.4%) ◣
Sweet and malty in true Norfolk fashion. Red-hued with a gentle roast malt aroma. Stewed prunes and caramel lurk in the background as the finish lingers long and sweet.

Yarmouth Twos (OG 1036, ABV 3.6%)
A mix of Yarmouth Bitter and Mild.

Yarmouth Bitter (OG 1036, ABV 3.8%) ◣
Lots of blackberry and malt in the nose. a complex beer, copper coloured with a grainy mouthfeel. The initial malty fruitiness fades to a long, vinous, hoppy ending.

Mitre Gold (OG 1044, ABV 4%)

Springtide (OG 1042, ABV 4.2%)
A traditional, well-hopped bitter.

Whyte Angel (OG 1045, ABV 4.5%) ◣
Fragrant hoppy aroma leads to a strong bitter first taste. Golden hued with honey notes softening the dryness of the bitter hops. Gentle malt background throughout.

St George's Honey (OG 1046, ABV 4.6%)

Maritime (OG 1050, ABV 5%) ◣
Copper-coloured, rich, heavy and malty brew. Vinous, fruitcake characteristics supplement the richness of taste. A muted hoppy bitterness can be detected in the long finish.

Old Habit (OG 1052, ABV 5.6%) ◣
Old-fashioned mix of roast, malt and plummy fruitiness. Smooth and aromatic with coffee notes and a heavy mouthfeel. Finish softens to a malty character.

Black Hole SIBA

Black Hole Brewery Ltd, Unit 63, Ground Floor, Imex Business Park, Shobnall Road, Burton upon Trent, Staffordshire, DE14 2AU
☎ (01283) 534060 ✉ beer@blackholebrewery.co.uk
⊕ blackholebrewery.co.uk
Tours by arrangement

⊠ The brewery was established in 2007 with a purpose-built 10-barrel plant in the former Ind Coope bottling stores. Fermenting capacity has recently been increased to allow the production of four brews per week. Over 400 outlets are supplied direct and many more via wholesalers. Seasonal beers are available throughout the year and occasional beers are produced to mark special anniversaries and events.

Bitter (OG 1040, ABV 3.8%) ◣
Gentle malt and hop aroma from this amber beer. After a grassy start the bitterness develops into a satisfying hop bite. There is a dry finish with some fruitiness and malt.

Cosmic (OG 1044, ABV 4.2%)
Amber-coloured beer with a rounded bitterness and fruity character.

Titan (OG 1045, ABV 4.4%)
A rich, golden beer with a well-balanced bitterness. Subtle toffee flavours combine with fruit and spice to give this bitter an interesting finish.

Red Dwarf (OG 1046, ABV 4.5%)
A distinctive, dry bitter, ruby red in colour with an underlying toffee flavour and fruity finish.

Supernova (OG 1048, ABV 4.8%)
A premium pale ale with a floral taste.

No Escape (OG 1053, ABV 5.2%)
A smooth, dark beer with a balance of dry bitterness and spicy aroma.

Milky Way (OG 1059, ABV 6%)
A pale wheat beer; strong with a bittersweet finish.

Black Isle SIBA

Black Isle Brewing Co Ltd, Old Allengrange, Munlochy, Ross-shire, IV8 8NZ
☎ (01463) 811871 ✉ info@blackislebrewery.com
⊕ blackislebrewery.com
Shop & Visitor Centre Mon-Sat 10am-6pm
Tours by arrangement

⊠ Black Isle Brewery was set up in 1998 in the heart of the Scottish Highlands. The five-barrel plant was upgraded to a 30-barrel plant in 2010. All beers are organic and have Soil Association certification. Bottled (including bottle-conditioned) beers are suitable for vegetarians and vegans and are available by mail order to anywhere in mainland Britain. Seasonal beer: see website.

Yellowhammer IPA (OG 1038, ABV 3.9%) ◆
A refreshing, hoppy golden ale with light hop and passion fruit throughout. A short bitter finish with a light yeasty background.

Red Kite (OG 1042, ABV 4.2%) ◆
Tawny ale with light malt on the nose and some fruit on the palate. Slight sweetness in the taste and a short bitter finish.

Porter (OG 1046, ABV 4.6%) ◆
A hint of liquorice and burnt chocolate on the nose and a creamy mix of malt and fruit in the taste.

Blonde (OG 1046, ABV 5%)

Black Paw (NEW)

Black Paw Brewery, Unit 4, Westgate Road, Bishop Auckland, County Durham, DL14 7AX
☎ (01388) 602144 ☎ 07557 020664
✉ paw@blackpawbrewery.co.uk
⊕ blackpawbrewery.co.uk

Black Paw began brewing in 2011 using a 12-barrel plant. There are plans to extend the range and to bottle condition.

Bishop's Best (ABV 3.8%)

Paw's Gold (ABV 4%)

Dark Seam (ABV 5%)

Black Sheep SIBA

Black Sheep Brewery plc, Wellgarth, Masham, Ripon, North Yorkshire, HG4 4EN
☎ (01765) 689227 ⊕ blacksheepbrewery.co.uk
Visitor Centre Bistro, bar and shop 10.30am-4.30pm Sun-Wed; 10.30am-11pm Thu-Sat
Daily tours by arrangement

⊕Black Sheep was established 1992 by Paul Theakston, a member of Masham's famous brewing family, in the former Wellgarth Maltings. The traditional Yorkshire Square fermenting system is used. The company has enjoyed continued growth and now supplies a free trade of around 600 outlets, has national exposure through pubcos and wholesale channels, but owns no pubs. The brewery specialises in cask ales (75% of production) and bottled ales.

Best Bitter (OG 1038, ABV 3.8%) ◆
A hoppy and fruity beer with strong bitter overtones, leading to a long, dry, bitter finish.

Golden Sheep (OG 1039, ABV 3.9%)
A balanced blonde beer with a dry and refreshing bitterness. Light golden in colour with fresh citrus fruit flavours and a clean, crisp finish.

Ale (OG 1044, ABV 4.4%)
A premium bitter with rich fruit aromas and hints of orange and roast coffee maltiness. Bittersweet in the mouth with a dry finish with deep fruit notes.

Riggwelter (OG 1059, ABV 5.9%) ◼ ◆
A fruity bitter, with complex underlying tastes and hints of liquorice and pear drops leading to a long, dry, bitter finish.

Blackwater

Blackwater Brewery, Brewers Wholesale, Unit 2b Gainsborough Trading Estate, Rufford Road, Stourbridge, West Midlands, DY9 7ND
☎ (01384) 374050
✉ enquiries@thebrewerswholesale.co.uk
⊕ thebrewerswholesale.co.uk

Beers are contract brewed by Salopian Brewery (qv).

Blakemere

See Northern

Blencowe

See Barrowden

Blindmans SIBA

Blindmans Brewery Ltd, Talbot Farm, Leighton, Frome, Somerset, BA11 4PN
☎ (01749) 880038 ✉ info@blindmansbrewery.co.uk
⊕ blindmansbrewery.co.uk
Tours by arrangement

⊠ Blindmans Brewery was established in 2002 in a converted milking parlour and purchased by its current owners, Paul Edney and Lloyd Chamberlain, in 2004. The five-barrel brewery has its own water spring. The range of ales is regularly on tap at the Lamb Inn in Frome, which was recently renamed the Cornerhouse. Seasonal beers: see website.

Buff (OG 1036, ABV 3.6%)
Amber-coloured, smooth session beer.

Golden Spring (OG 1040, ABV 4%)
Fresh and aromatic straw-coloured beer, brewed using selected lager malt.

Eclipse (OG 1042, ABV 4.2%)

Mine Beer (OG 1042, ABV 4.2%)
Full-bodied, copper-coloured, blended malt ale.

Icarus (OG 1045, ABV 4.5%)
Fruity, rich, mid-dark ruby ale.

Siberia (OG 1047, ABV 4.7%)

Blue Anchor SIBA

▤ Blue Anchor Inn Brewery, 50 Coinagehall Street, Helston, Cornwall, TR13 8EL
☎ (01326) 565765
✉ theblueanchor@btconnect.com ⊕ spingoales.com
Tours by arrangement

⊠ Dating back to the 15th century, this is the oldest brewery in Cornwall and was originally a monks' hospice. After the dissolution of the monasteries it became a tavern brewing its own uniquely flavoured beer called Spingo at the rear of the premises. Brewing has continued to this day. Eight outlets are supplied direct. All draught beers are available in bottle-conditioned form and seasonal beers are brewed. Bragget is a recreation of a medieval beer style brewed without hops.

Spingo Jubilee/IPA (OG 1045, ABV 4.6%) ◥
Bittersweet hops and fruit dominate this golden beer, enhanced by a unique nutty, earthy character. Powerful whiff of esters and alcohol on the nose, and a long, dry fruity finish.

Ben's Stout (ABV 4.8%)
A lightly-hopped classic stout with a bittersweet taste and a roasted barley and coffee aroma.

Spingo Middle (OG 1050, ABV 5.1%) ◥
Aromatic malt and esters on the nose lead into a heavy sweet malt taste balanced by bitter hops and a unique resinous woody character. The finish fades slowly with bitterness.

Spingo Bragget (OG 1061, ABV 6.1%)

Spingo Special (OG 1066, ABV 6.7%)
Darker than Middle with a pronounced earthy character on the nose balanced by rich fruit. Fruit and peppery hops dominate the mouth, followed by a long finish with malt, fruit and hops.

Blue Ball (NEW)

Blue Ball Brewery Ltd, Units 11-12 EBL Centre, Picow Farm Road, Runcorn, Cheshire, WA7 4UA
☎ (01928) 238442 ✉ info@beerrepublic.com
⊕ blueballbrewery.com
Shop Mon-Fri 9am-5.30pm; Sat 9am-5pm

Blue Ball originally started brewing as Bridgewater Brewery in 2010 behind a homebrew shop in Frodsham. The business relocated and expanded later the same year using a five-barrel plant. Brewing takes place alongside a home brewery fabrication business and homebrew shop. A bar and restaurant, Kash, opened in Chester in 2011.

Black Hawk (OG 1054, ABV 5.2%)

Blonde Bombshell (OG 1050, ABV 5.2%)

Zeppelin (OG 1053, ABV 5.5%)

Blue Bee (NEW)

Blue Bee Brewery Ltd, Unit 29-30, Hoyland Road Industrial Estate, Sheffield, S3 8AB
☎ 07791 662484 ✉ bluebeebrewery@hotmail.co.uk
⊕ bluebeebrewery.co.uk
Tours by arrangement

Blue Bee Brewery was set up in 2010 by award-winning brewer Richard Hough. The core range is complemented by an eclectic mix of seasonal beers – see website. The beers are available to the free trade across Yorkshire, the Midlands and north west England.

Bees Knees Bitter (ABV 4%)
A russet-brown bitter with lots of hop character.

Nectar Pale (ABV 4%)
A pale, well-balanced ale with a quenching bitter finish.

Lustin' For Stout (ABV 4.8%)
A rich, complex stout. Full-bodied and black in colour with roast malt flavours continuing to a satisfying bitter finish.

Tangled Up IPA (ABV 6%)
A hoppy, floral aroma with citrus flavours and a hoppy, bitter finish.

Emergency! (ABV 9.99%)
A powerful barley wine, pale in colour with hop flavours, rich fruit on the palate and a vinous alcoholic kick.

Blue Bell

Blue Bell Brewery, Cranesgate South, Whaplode St Catherines, Lincolnshire, PE12 6SN
☎ (01406) 701000 ☎ 07813 819746
✉ beer@bluebellbrewery.co.uk
⊕ bluebellbrewery.co.uk
Tours by arrangement

☺The Blue Bell Brewery was founded in 1998 in a former potato shed located behind the Blue Bell pub, Whaplode St Catherine. The brewery operates as a separate business from the Blue Bell pub but the pub does act as the brewery tap. Around 30 outlets are supplied. Bottle-conditioned beers are available.

Frightened Pheasant (OG 1037, ABV 3.7%)

Old Honesty (OG 1040, ABV 4.1%)

Old Resurgence (OG 1043, ABV 4.3%)

For Blue Bell Inn, Whaplode St Catherine:

Ingle Dingle (OG 1054, ABV 5.1%)

Blue Buzzard (NEW)

Blue Buzzard Brewery, 17 Joseph Street, Darwen, Lancashire, BB3 3HT
☎ 07578 278013 ✉ brewery@bluebuzzards.com

Blue Buzzard is a small craft brewery run by an enthusiastic home brewer, licensed in 2010. Local festivals and the occasional pub and bar are supplied.

Dark Matter (ABV 3.8%)

Nebula (ABV 4.3%)

Eclipse (ABV 4.5%)

White Dwarf (ABV 4.8%)

Blue Cow

☐ Blue Cow Inn & Brewery, High Street, South Witham, Lincolnshire, NG33 5QB
☎ (01572) 768432 ✉ enquiries@bluecowinn.co.uk
⊕ bluecowinn.co.uk
Tours by arrangement

☺Owned by Simon Crathorn since 2005, Blue Cow is a traditional 13th-century pub with a brewery. The beer is only available in the pub.

Best Bitter (OG 1042, ABV 4%)
An amber, hoppy beer with a creamy head.

Blue Monkey SIBA

Blue Monkey Brewing Ltd, 10 Pentrich Road, Giltbrook Industrial Park, Giltbrook, Nottinghamshire, NG16 2UZ

A reddish amber beer, full-bodied with a malty aroma. Crisp and spicy with an underlying citrus flavour and a dry, malty, bitter fruit finish.

Grumpy Bastard (OG 1048, ABV 5%)

Brandy Cask

⬛ Brandy Cask Pub & Brewery, 25 Bridge Street, Pershore, Worcestershire, WR10 1AJ
☎ (01386) 552602
Tours by arrangement

☺Brewing started in 1995 in a refurbished bottle store in the garden of the pub. Brewery and pub now operate under one umbrella, with brewing carried out by the owner/landlord.

Whistling Joe (ABV 3.6%) ◣
A sweet, fruity, copper-coloured beer that has plenty of contrast in the aroma. A malty balance lingers but the aftertaste is not dry.

Brandy Snapper (ABV 4%) ◣
Golden brew with low alpha hops. Plenty of fruit and hop aroma leads to a rich taste in the mouth and a lingering aftertaste.

John Baker's Original (ABV 4.8%) ◣
A superb blend of flavours with roasted malt to the fore. The rich hoppy aroma is complemented by a complex aftertaste.

Branscombe Vale SIBA

Branscombe Vale Brewery Ltd, Branscombe, Devon, EX12 3DP
☎ (01297) 680511
✉ branscombebrewery@yahoo.co.uk
⬤ branscombebrewery.com

☒ The brewery was set up in 1992 by former dairy workers Paul Dimond and Graham Luxton in cowsheds owned by the National Trust. Paul and Graham converted the sheds and dug their own well. The NT has twice built extensions for the brewery for more space and new fermenters. In 2008 a new 25-barrel plant was added to the brewhouse. Around 80 outlets are supplied. Seasonal and bottle-conditioned beers are also available.

Dem Bones (OG 1036, ABV 3.5%)

Mild (OG 1036., ABV 3.7%)

Branoc (OG 1038, ABV 3.8%) ◣
Pale brown brew with a malt and fruit aroma and a hint of caramel. Malt and bitter taste with a dry, hoppy finish.

Draymans Best Bitter (OG 1042, ABV 4.2%)
A mid-brown beer with hop and caramel notes and a lingering finish.

BVB Best Bitter (OG 1045, ABV 4.6%) ◣
Reddy/brown-coloured beer with a fruity aroma and taste, and bitter/astringent finish.

Summa That (OG 1049, ABV 5%)
Light golden beer with a clean and refreshing taste and a long hoppy finish.

Brass Monkey SIBA

Brass Monkey Brewery Co Ltd, Unit 25, Asquith Bottom Mill, Sowerby Bridge, West Yorkshire, HX6 3BS

☎ (01422) 316040
✉ richard@thebrassmonkeybrewery.co.uk
⬤ thebrassmonkeybrewery.co.uk
Tours by arrangement

☺Brass Monkey was established in 2008 on a seven-barrel brew plant. Capacity was doubled in 2009 with the addition of two fermenters. Around 150 outlets are supplied. Seasonal beers: see website.

Son of Silverback (ABV 3.6%) ◣
Straw-coloured grainy bitter with a light hoppiness in the aroma. Fruity and hoppy in the mouth with bitterness developing in the aftertaste.

Bitter (ABV 3.8%) ◣
Pale brown, grainy bitter with a pronounced hoppy aroma and flavour. It has a long-lasting satisfying bitter finish.

Golden Monkey (ABV 4.1%) ◣
Smooth, tawny-coloured best bitter. It has a full, hoppy flavour and citrus/spicy aroma, finishing with a bitter finish.

Mandrill (ABV 4.2%) ◣
This grainy golden ale has a floral hop nose. Hops fill the mouth balanced by tangy fruit. The finish is deep and long.

Silverback (ABV 5%) ◣
Grainy yellow pale ale. A hoppy aroma is followed by a mellow fruity flavour. There is a lingering bitter aftertaste.

Braydon SIBA

Braydon Ales Ltd, The Brewhouse, Preston West Farm, Preston, Chippenham, Wiltshire, SN15 4DX
☎ (01249) 892900 ✉ info@braydonales.co.uk
⬤ braydonales.co.uk
Tours by arrangement

☒ Braydon began brewing in 2009 on a five-barrel plant. All beers have names from the old Wiltshire dialect. Seasonal beers are also available.

Gibbles (OG 1040, ABV 3.8%)
A copper-coloured, full-bodied bitter.

Yertiz (OG 1042, ABV 4.1%)
Triple-hopped, well-balanced and full-flavoured.

Galleybagger (OG 1043, ABV 4.3%)
A well-hopped, full-bodied golden bitter.

Potwalloper (OG 1043, ABV 4.4%)
A ruby-coloured ale with rich malty undertones.

Brecon (NEW)

Brecon Brewing, 8a Brecon Enterprise Park, Brecon, Powys, LD3 8BT
☎ (01874) 620800 ✉ beer@breconbrewing.co.uk
⬤ breconbrewing.co.uk

Brecon began brewing in 2011. Seasonal and special beers are planned.

Pale Beacon (ABV 3.9%)

Gold Beacon (ABV 4.2%)

Bright Beacon (ABV 4.5%)

Wandering Beacon (ABV 5%)

Breconshire SIBA

Breconshire Brewery Ltd, Ffrwdgrech Industrial Estate, Brecon, Powys, LD3 8LA

☎ (01874) 623731
✉ sales@breconshirebrewery.com
⊕ breconshirebrewery.com
Shop Mon-Fri 8.30am-4.30pm
Tours by arrangement

⊠ Breconshire Brewery was founded in 2002 as part of C H Marlow, a wholesaler and distributor of ales, beers, wines and spirits in the south Wales area for more than 30 years. The 10-barrel plant uses British malts blended with a range of British whole hops. The beers are distributed throughout Wales and the west of England to around 200 outlets. Seasonal beers: see website. Bottle-conditioned beers are also available.

Brecon County Ale (OG 1037, ABV 3.7%) ◗
A traditional amber-coloured bitter. A clean hoppy flavour, background malt and fruit, with a good thirst-quenching bitterness.

Welsh Pale Ale (OG 1037, ABV 3.7%)
Pale golden, mildy hopped session ale. Brewed to an old Welsh style of pale ale.

Golden Valley (OG 1042, ABV 4.2%) ◗
Golden in colour with a welcoming aroma of hops, malt and fruit. A balanced mix of these flavours and moderate, building bitterness lead to a satisfying, rounded finish.

Cribyn (OG 1045, ABV 4.5%) ⏚
A pale, straw-coloured aromatic best bitter. Brewed with Northdown, Challenger and Bramling Cross hops.

Red Dragon (OG 1047, ABV 4.7%)
A red-hued premium ale brewed with a complex grist and a blend of hops for extra bite.

Ramblers Ruin (OG 1050, ABV 5%) ⏚ ◗
Dark amber, full-bodied with rich biscuity malt and fruit flavours; background hops and bitterness round off the beer.

Brentwood SIBA

Brentwood Brewing Co Ltd, Frieze Hall Farm, Coxtie Green Road, South Weald, Essex, CM14 5RE
☎ (01277) 375577
✉ info@brentwoodbrewing.co.uk
⊕ brentwoodbrewing.co.uk
Shop 10am-4pm daily and online
Tours by arrangement (for groups of 10+)

⊠ Since its launch in 2006 Brentwood has steadily increased its capacity and distribution. A major expansion and relocation in 2008 included a new 20-barrel plant. 70 outlets are supplied direct.

IPA (OG 1039, ABV 3.7%)
A lightly hopped, pale session beer.

Marvellous Maple Mild (OG 1038, ABV 3.7%)
Dark brown mild with a hint of maple syrup.

Spooky Moon (OG 1040, ABV 3.8%) ◗
Well-balanced session bitter. The sweet marmalade aroma hints at the citrus bitterness to be found in the finish.

Best (OG 1042, ABV 4.2%)
A traditional, straw-coloured best bitter with a well-rounded flavour and aroma.

Gold (OG 1043, ABV 4.3%)
A heavily hopped golden beer with a fruity taste and bitter finish.

Hope & Glory (OG 1046, ABV 4.5%)
A dark, full-bodied bitter.

Lumberjack (OG 1052, ABV 5.2%)
A strong bitter with a rounded, hoppy finish.

Chockwork Orange (OG 1067, ABV 6.5%)
A dark strong ale with a hint of orange in the background.

Brew Company

Brew Company Ltd, Unit C, G4 Business Centre, Carlisle Street East, Sheffield, South Yorkshire, S4 7QN
☎ (0114) 270 9991 ✉ thebrewcompany@gmail.com
⊕ thebrewcompany.co.uk
Tours by arrangement

⊠ Brewer Pete Roberts set up this eight-barrel plant in part of a former factory in Sheffield's industrial east end in 2008. House beers are brewed for the nearby Harlequin pub, the Riverside and the Devonshire Cat. Seasonal beers: see website.

Slaker Pale Ale (OG 1038.8, ABV 3.8%)
Pale, crisp and fruity.

Brewers Gold (OG 1038.8, ABV 4%)

Elixir Bitter (OG 1038.8, ABV 4.0%)
Amber-coloured traditional English bitter with a dry roasted flavour.

Abyss Best Bitter (OG 1040.7, ABV 4.2%)
Dark walnut in colour and full of malty bitter flavours.

Hop Ripper IPA (OG 1041.7, ABV 4.3%)
A pale IPA, bitter and hoppy.

Hop Monster (OG 1043.6, ABV 4.5%)

Eclipse Porter (OG 1045.5, ABV 4.7%)
A traditional, heavy-bodied, dark, malty porter with a thick mouthfeel, a dry palate and a delicate toasted coffee grain finish.

Frontier IPA (OG 1045.5, ABV 4.7%)
Straw-coloured, crisp and dry with a bitter aftertaste.

St Petrus (OG 1048.4, ABV 5%)
For Devonshire Cat, Sheffield:
Devonshire Cat Pale Ale (ABV 3.8%)
For Harlequin, Sheffield:
Harlequin Blonde (ABV 4%)
Harlequin Best Bitter (ABV 4.2%)
For Riverside, Sheffield:
Riverside Pale Ale (ABV 4.2%)

BrewDog SIBA

BrewDog Ltd, Unit 1, Kessock Workshops, Kessock Road, Fraserburgh, AB43 8UE
☎ (01346) 519009 ✉ info@brewdog.com
⊕ brewdog.com
Tours by arrangement

BrewDog was established in 2007 by James Watt and Martin Dickie. Most of the production goes into bottles but a limited amount of cask ale is available.

Trashy Blonde (OG 1042, ABV 4.1%)
77 Lager (OG 1046, ABV 4.9%)
Punk IPA (OG 1052, ABV 6%)
Dogma (OG 1072, ABV 7.8%)

Shelford Crier (OG 1038, ABV 3.8%)
An amber-coloured session beer.

Harvest Moon Mild (OG 1040, ABV 3.9%)
Smooth fruit notes combine with coffee and
chocolate flavours, lightly hopped. A well-balanced
beer, slightly sweet with plenty of character.

Barton Bitter (OG 1040, ABV 4%) ◆
Pale brown with red and amber highlights,
balanced malt and hops and a fruity backdrop on
both nose and palate. A bittersweet flavour dries as
fruit and sweetness diminish.

CB1 Best Bitter (OG 1041, ABV 4.2%)
Amber-coloured traditional best bitter with a good
blend of malt and hops with a rounded, hoppy
finish.

Red Watch Blueberry Ale (OG 1040, ABV 4.2%)
A red-coloured beer brewed with fresh blueberries.
A refreshing, fruity ale.

Reel Ale (OG 1041, ABV 4.2%)
Straw-coloured beer with an inital malt sweetness
giving way to a long and lasting hoppy finish.

Budding Moon (OG 1043, ABV 4.5%)
A smooth, refreshing golden wheat beer, with a
citrus hop bouquet and a rich, malty fruit flavour.

Nightwatch Porter (OG 1043, ABV 4.5%)
Five types of malts, four varieties of hops plus
locally-produced honey from the Cambridge
Beekeepers Association are blended together to
create a unique and rounded flavour.

Minion of the Moon (OG 1044, ABV 4.6%)
A premium, light-coloured, full-flavoured fruity
beer. Rich malt, fruit and hops dominate the taste.
The fullness of flavour is sustained throughout
leading to a bittersweet finish.

Black Hole Stout (OG 1048, ABV 5%)
Full-bodied stout with a complex malt and caramel
profile and a dry-roasted, bitter flavour that is rich,
smooth and long-lasting.

Chocolate Orange Stout (OG 1068, ABV 6.7%)
Full-bodied, rounded soft stout. Loaded with
chocolate and coffee flavours with a good hop
balance that has a hint of orange on the nose.

Cambrinus SIBA

Cambrinus Craft Brewery, Home Farm, Knowsley
Park, Knowsley, Merseyside, L34 4AQ
☎ (0151) 546 2226 ✉ john@cambrinus.myzen.co.uk
⊠ Established in 1997, Cambrinus is housed in part
of a former farm building on a private estate. It
produces around 250 hectolitres a year on a five-
barrel plant. Around 45 outlets are supplied on a
regular basis in and around Lancashire, Cheshire
and Cumbria. Seasonal beers are also available.

Herald (OG 1036, ABV 3.7%)
Light summer drinking bitter, pale and refreshing.

Yardstick (OG 1040, ABV 4%)
Mild, malty and lightly hopped.

Deliverance (OG 1040, ABV 4.2%)
Pale premium bitter.

Endurance (OG 1045, ABV 4.3%)
IPA-style, smooth and hoppy, fermented in oak.

Camden Town

Camden Town Brewery, 55-58 Wilkin Street Mews,
Kentish Town, London, NW5 3NN
☎ (020) 7485 1671

Second Brewery: The Horseshoe, 28 Heath Street,
Hampstead, London, NW3 6TE ☎ (020) 7431 7206
✉ brewingbeer@camdentownbrewery.com
⊕ camdentownbrewery.com
Tours by arrangement

Formerly known as McLaughlin Brewhouse. In
2007 the name changed to Camden Town Brewery
and in 2010 a 20-hectolitre brewery was
established near Camden. The original plant at the
Horseshoe is now used for small batch sizes and
single runs. Seasonal beers are also available.

Bitter (OG 1038, ABV 3.8%) ◆
The aroma is predominantly malty in this pale
brown beer. The flavour has a touch of hops and
peach fruit with a bittersweet finish.

Pale Ale (OG 1045, ABV 4.5%)
A golden ale with grapefruit on the nose with a
sweet fudge character and a bitterness that lingers
into the aftertaste.

Camerons

Camerons Brewery Ltd, Lion Brewery, Stranton,
Hartlepool, Co Durham, TS24 7QS
☎ (01429) 852000
✉ martindutoy@cameronsbrewery.com
⊕ cameronsbrewery.com
Shop Mon-Sat 12-4pm
Tours by arrangement

☺Founded in 1865, Camerons was bought in 2002
by Castle Eden brewery, which moved production
to Hartlepool. In 2003 a 10-barrel micro-brewery,
the Lions Den, opened to produce and bottle small
brews of guest ales and to undertake contract
brewing and bottling. 75 pubs are owned, with five
selling real ale. Seasonal beers have been dropped
in favour of monthly guest beer production.

Best Bitter (OG 1036, ABV 3.6%) ◆
A light bitter, but well-balanced, with hops and
malt.

Strongarm (OG 1041, ABV 4%) ◆
A well-rounded, ruby-red ale with a distinctive,
tight creamy head; initially fruity, but with a good
balance of malt, hops and moderate bitterness.

Trophy Special (ABV 4%)
An amber ale, slightly sweet and malty, fruity and
hoppy from the addition of Styrian Golding hops in
the cask.

Cannon Royall SIBA

⊟ Cannon Royall Brewery Ltd, Fruiterer's Arms,
Uphampton Lane, Uphampton, Worcestershire,
WR9 0JW
☎ (01905) 621161 ✉ info@cannonroyall.co.uk
⊕ cannonroyall.co.uk
Tours by arrangement (CAMRA only)

Cannon Royall's first brew was in 1993 in a
converted cider house behind the Fruiterer's Arms.
It has increased capacity from five barrels to more
than 16 a week. The brewery supplies a number of
outlets in Worcestershire and the West Midlands.

Seasonal beers are regularly produced. Bottle-conditioned beers are also available.

Fruiterer's Mild (OG 1037, ABV 3.7%) ◆
This black-hued brew has rich malty aromas that lead to a fruity mix of bitter hops and sweetness, and a short balanced aftertaste.

King's Shilling (OG 1038, ABV 3.8%) ◆
A golden bitter that packs a citrus hoppy punch throughout.

Arrowhead Bitter (OG 1039, ABV 3.9%) ◆
A powerful punch of hops attacks the nose before the feast of bitterness. The memory of this golden brew fades too soon.

Arrowhead Extra (OG 1045, ABV 4.3%)

IPA (OG 1048, ABV 4.6%)
An aromatic hop aroma precedes a clean, citrus bitterness in this pale coloured beer.

Canterbury Ales SIBA (NEW)

Canterbury Ales, Unit 7, Stour Valley Business Park, Ashford Road, Canterbury, Kent, CT4 7HF
☎ (01227) 732541 ✉ canterbrew@gmail.com
⊕ canterbury-ales.co.uk

⊠ Brewing commenced in late 2010. Over 25 outlets are supplied direct. Seasonal beers are planned.

The Wife of Bath's Ale (OG 1038.5, ABV 3.9%) ◆
A golden beer with strong bitterness and grapefruit hop character, leading to a long, dry finish.

The Reeve's Ale (OG 1040, ABV 4.1%)

The Miller's Ale (OG 1043.6, ABV 4.5%)

Canterbury Brewers (NEW)

⬢ **Canterbury Brewers, The Foundry, Whitehorse Lane, Canterbury, Kent, CT1 2RU**
☎ (01227) 455899 ✉ t.r.sharkey@gmail.com
⊕ thefoundrycanterbury.co.uk

The Foundry is a craft brewery, restaurant and bar occupying an industrial two storey building, originally a Victorian foundry.

Gold (OG 1040, ABV 4%)

Wheat (OG 1043, ABV 4.4%)

Torpedo (OG 1044, ABV 4.5%)

Captain Cook SIBA

⬢ **Captain Cook Brewery Ltd, White Swan, 1 West End, Stokesley, North Yorkshire, TS9 5BL**
☎ (01642) 710263
✉ ashma.whiteswan@virginmedia.com
⊕ captaincookbrewery.co.uk
Tours by arrangement

⊕The Captain Cook Brewery is located within the 18th-century White Swan pub. The brewery, which started in 2009, has increased size from a four-barrel to a 6.5-barrel plant brewing up to 26 barrels a week in order to supply local and national outlets. Seasonal beers are available.

Resolution (OG 1037, ABV 3.7%)
A pale golden beer brewed with New Zealand hops.

Nee Batts (OG 1039, ABV 3.9%)
A pale golden session beer with strong citrus notes.

Sunset (OG 1040, ABV 4%)
An extremely smooth light ale with a good balance of malt and hops.

Slipway (OG 1042, ABV 4.2%)
A light-coloured hoppy ale with bitterness coming through from Challenger hops. A full-flavoured ale with a smooth malt aftertaste.

Endeavour (OG 1043, ABV 4.3%)
Mid brown ale with a bitter finish.

Black Porter (OG 1044, ABV 4.4%)
Chocolate notes and dominant roast flavours lead to a dry, bitter finish.

Discovery (OG 1044, ABV 4.4%)
A malty ale with a bitter finish.

Castle Rock SIBA

Tynemill Ltd t/a Castle Rock Brewery, Queens Bridge Road, Nottingham, NG2 1NB
☎ (0115) 985 1615
✉ admin@castlerockbrewery.co.uk
⊕ castlerockbrewery.co.uk
Shop Mon-Thu 10.30am-6pm, Fri 10.30am-4pm; Sat 10.30am-2pm
Tours by arrangement

⊕Castle Rock was established in 1998. Since then capacity has steadily increased with the largest expansion taking place in 2010 when additional brewing equipment was installed in the neighbouring building giving a total capacity of 300 barrels a week. The Visitor Centre opened in 2011. Beers are distributed through its own estate of 21 pubs and further afield through wholesalers. A different beer is brewed monthly to support the Nottinghamshire Wildlife Trust and a unique Nottinghamian Celebration beer is brewed quarterly. Seasonal beers: see website. Bottle-conditioned beers are also available.

Sheriff's Tipple (OG 1035, ABV 3.4%)
A light, tawny session bitter with distinctive hop character.

Black Gold (OG 1037, ABV 3.8%) ◆
A dark ruby mild. Full-bodied and fairly bitter.

Harvest Pale (OG 1037, ABV 3.8%) 🍷 ▦ ◆
Pale yellow beer, full of hop aroma and flavour. Refreshing with a mellowing aftertaste. Champion Beer of Britain 2010.

Preservation Fine Ale (OG 1044, ABV 4.4%) ▦ ◆
A traditional copper-coloured English best bitter with malt predominant. Fairly bitter with a residual sweetness.

Elsie Mo (OG 1045, ABV 4.7%) ▦ ◆
A strong golden ale with floral hops evident in the aroma. Citrus hops are mellowed by a slight sweetness.

Screech Owl (OG 1052, ABV 5.5%) ◆
A classic golden IPA with an intensely hoppy aroma and bitter taste with a little balancing sweetness.

Castle SIBA

Castle Brewery, Unit 9a-7, Restormel Industrial Estate, Liddicoat Road, Lostwithiel, Cornwall, PL22 0HG
☎ (01726) 871133 ☎ 07800 635831
✉ castlebrewery@aol.com

Castle started brewing in early 2008 on a two-barrel plant. Only bottle-conditioned ales are

Pheasant Plucker (OG 1038, ABV 3.7%)

Cuthberts (OG 1038, ABV 3.8%) ◆
A refreshing, hoppy beer, with hints of malt, fruit and caramel taste. Lingering bitter aftertaste.

Goat's Milk (OG 1038, ABV 3.8%) 🍺

Gravediggers Ale (OG 1038, ABV 3.8%) 🍷 ◆
A premium mild. Black and red in colour, with a complex mix of chocolate and roast flavours, it is almost a light porter.

Hop Gun (OG 1041, ABV 4.1%)

What the Fox's Hat (OG 1044, ABV 4.2%) ◆
A beer with a malty aroma, and a hoppy and malty taste with some caramel flavour.

Without a Bix (OG 1042, ABV 4.2%)

Pooh Beer (OG 1044, ABV 4.3%)
Brewed with honey.

Vicar's Ruin (OG 1044, ABV 4.4%) ◆
A straw-coloured best bitter with an initially hoppy, bitter flavour, softening to a delicate malt finish.

Pews Porter (OG 1045, ABV 4.6%) 🍷

Stout Coffin (OG 1046, ABV 4.6%)

Fallen Angel (OG 1050, ABV 5%)

For Cape of Good Hope, Warwick:

Two Llocks (ABV 4%)

City of Cambridge EAB

City of Cambridge Brewery Co Ltd, Ely Road, Chittering, Cambridge, CB5 9PH
☎ (01223) 864864 ✉ sales@cambridge-brewery.co.uk ⊕ cambridge-brewery.co.uk

⊠ City of Cambridge opened in 1997 and moved to its present site in 2002. The brewery site is in the process of being redeveloped, with the intention of keeping the brewery on the site. At present all brewing is being done under contract by Elgoods Brewery (qv). In addition to prizes for its cask beers, the brewery holds a conservation award for the introduction of native reed beds at its site to treat brewery water. Seasonal beers are also available.

City of Stirling

See Traditional Scottish Ales

Clanconnel

Clanconnel Brewing Co Ltd, PO Box 316, Craigavon, Co Armagh, BT65 9AZ
☎ 07711 626770 ✉ info@clanconnelbrewing.com ⊕ clanconnelbrewing.com
Tours by arrangement

Clanconnel started producing bottled beer in late 2008: McGrath's Irish Black (ABV 4.3%), McGrath's Irish Red (ABV 4.3%), Weaver's Gold (ABV 4.5%).

Clark's SIBA

HB Clark & Co (Successors) Ltd, Westgate Brewery, Wakefield, West Yorkshire, WF2 9SW
☎ (01924) 373328 ✉ brewery@hbclark.co.uk ⊕ hbclark.co.uk
Tours by arrangement

☺Founded in 1906 Clark's ceased brewing during the 1960s/70s but resumed cask ale production in 1982 and now delivers to around 220 outlets. Four pubs are owned, all serving cask ale. Seasonal beers are also produced.

Classic Blonde (OG 1039, ABV 3.9%)
A light-coloured ale with a citrus and hoppy flavour, a distinctive grapefruit aroma and a dry finish.

No Angel (OG 1040, ABV 4%)
A bitter with a dry hop finish, well-balanced and full of flavour. Pale brown in colour with hints of fruit and hops.

Westgate Gold (OG 1042, ABV 4.2%)
A light-coloured, fruity beer with a full body and rich aroma.

Rams Revenge (OG 1046, ABV 4.6%) ◆
A rich, ruby-coloured premium ale, well-balanced with malt and hops, with a deep fruity taste and a dry hoppy aftertaste, with a pleasant hoppy aroma.

Clearwater SIBA

Clearwater Brewery Ltd, 2 Devon Units, Hatchmoor Industrial Estate, Great Torrington, Devon, EX38 7HP
☎ (01805) 625242
✉ sales@clearwaterbrewery.co.uk
⊕ clearwaterbrewery.co.uk
Tours by arrangement

Clearwater began brewing in 1999 but a change of ownership in 2009 saw a re-branding in 2010. 50 outlets are supplied direct with beer also being available via Waverley TBS. Bottle-conditioned beers are available.

Real Smiler (OG 1036, ABV 3.7%)
A nose of crisp, fresh-cut apples and melon accompanies a honeyed tone. A light biscuit taste with the most delicate of tannins.

Devon Dympsy (OG 1041, ABV 4%) ◆
Mid-brown, full-bodied best bitter with a burnt, rich malt aroma and taste, leading to a bitter, well-rounded finish.

Proper Ansome (OG 1043, ABV 4.2%)
Fresh, immediate hoppy aromas and caramel colour, Eddying honeyed sweetness and lightly earthy scent revealing a herbal edge.

Cleveland

Cleveland Brewery, Unit 2d, Lowson Street, Stillington, TS21 1AF
☎ (01740) 630304 or (01642) 575045
⊕ clevelandbrewery.co.uk
Tours by arrangement

Established in 2010 using a four-barrel plant. The brewery is currently increasing its range to include a wider selection of interesting beers and beer styles. Clever Head (ABV 8%) is brewed to order.

Bay (ABV 3.6%)
A chestnut brown ale with a smooth finish.

Clever Blonde (ABV 3.6%)

Ironmaster (ABV 4%)
A hoppy light brown session ale.

Gold (ABV 4.2%)
A light-coloured hoppy beer with a zesty citrus finish.

Black Stuff (ABV 4.5%)

A dark ale with a velvety chocolate smoothness.

Cliff Quay

⬛ Cliff Quay Brewery, Cliff Road, Ipswich, Suffolk, IP3 0BS
☎ (01728) 684097
✉ cliffquaybrewery@btconnect.com
⬡ cliffquay.co.uk
Tours by arrangement

Cliff Quay was established in 2008 by former Wychwood brewer Jeremy Moss and John Bjornson on part of the historic Tolly Cobbold riverside site. Regular seasonal beers are brewed every two months: see website.

Bitter (OG 1035, ABV 3.4%) ◆
Pleasantly drinkable, well-balanced malty sweet bitter with a hint of caramel, followed by a sweet/malty aftertaste. A good flavour for such a low gravity beer.

Black Jack Porter (OG 1042, ABV 4.2%) ◆
Unusual dark porter with a strong aniseed aroma and rich liquorice and aniseed flavours, reminiscent of old-fashioned sweets. The aftertaste is long and increasingly sweet.

Tolly Roger (OG 1043, ABV 4.2%) ◆
Well-balanced, highly drinkable, mid-gold beer with a bittersweet hoppiness, some biscuity flavours and hints of summer fruit.

Tumblehome (OG 1047, ABV 4.7%)

Sea Dog (ABV 5.3%)
A strong, hoppy beer bursting with the flavours of lemon and grapefruit with a full maltiness in contrast.

Clockwork

⬛ The Clockwork Beer Co, Maclay Inns PLC, 1153-1155 Cathcart Road, Glasgow, G42 9HB
☎ (0141) 649 0184 ✉ clockwork@maclay.co.uk
⬡ maclay.com
Tours by arrangement

⊗ The brewpub, the oldest in Glasgow, was established in 1997. The beers are kept in cellar tanks where fermentation gases from the conditioning vessel blanket the beers on tap (but not under pressure). A wide range of ales, lagers and specials are produced. Most beers are naturally gassed while the Original Lager and Seriously Ginger are pressurised. Having taken ownership of the Maclay's cookbook when Maclay Inns took over two years ago, some old recipes including Wallace IPA (ABV 4.5%), Oat Malt Stout (ABV 4.4%), Honey Weizen (ABV 4.6%) and Maclay's 90/- (ABV 6%) have been brewed with more to come.

Amber IPA (ABV 3.8%)

Red Alt (ABV 4.4%)

Lager (ABV 4.8%)

Seriously Ginger (ABV 5%)

Clun (NEW)

⬛ Clun Brewery, White Horse Inn, The Square, Clun, Shropshire, SY7 8JA
☎ (01588) 640305 ✉ pub@whi-clun.co.uk
⬡ whi-clun.co.uk
Tours by arrangement

☺Clun was previously a 9 gallon nano-brewery but this was replaced with a 2.5-barrel plant in late 2010 for commercial production. Seasonal beers are also brewed.

Pale (OG 1040, ABV 4%)

Coach House SIBA

Coach House Brewing Co Ltd, Wharf Street, Howley, Warrington, Cheshire, WA1 2DQ
☎ (01925) 232800 ✉ djbcoachhouse@hotmail.com
⬡ coach-house-brewing.co.uk

☺Coach House was founded in 1991 following the closure of Greenall Whitley Brewery, which had a presence in Warrington since 1762. With a fermentation capacity of 240 barrels, the brewery produces 11 permanent beers, seasonal and occasional brews and a range of fruit and spiced beers.

Coachman's Best Bitter (OG 1037, ABV 3.7%) ◆
A well-hopped, malty bitter, moderately fruity with a hint of sweetness and a peppery nose.

Gunpowder Mild (OG 1037, ABV 3.8%) ◆
Biscuity dark mild with a blackcurrant sweetness. Bitterness and fruit dominate with some hints of caramel and a slightly stronger roast flavour.

Honeypot Bitter (OG 1037, ABV 3.8%)

Farrier's Best Bitter (OG 1038, ABV 3.9%)

Cheshire Gold (OG 1042, ABV 4.1%)

Dick Turpin (OG 1042, ABV 4.2%) ◆
Malty, hoppy pale brown beer with some initial sweetish flavours leading to a short, bitter aftertaste. Sold under other names as a pub house beer.

Flintlock Pale Ale (OG 1044, ABV 4.4%)

Innkeeper's Special Reserve (OG 1045, ABV 4.5%) ◆
A darkish, full-flavoured bitter. Quite fruity, with a strong, bitter aftertaste.

Postlethwaite (OG 1045, ABV 4.6%) ◆
Thin bitter with a short, dry aftertaste. Biscuity malt dominates.

Gingernut Premium (OG 1050, ABV 5%)

Posthorn Premium (OG 1050, ABV 5%) ◆
Dry golden bitter with a blackcurrant fruitiness and good hop flavours leading to a strong, dry finish. Well-balanced but slightly thin for its gravity.

Coastal SIBA

Coastal Brewery, Unit 10B, Cardrew Industrial Estate, Redruth, Cornwall, TR15 1SS
☎ (01209) 212613 ☎ 07875 405407
✉ coastalbrewery@btconnect.com
⬡ coastalbrewery.co.uk

Coastal was set up in late 2006 on a five-barrel plant by Alan Hinde, former brewer and owner of the Borough Arms in Crewe, Cheshire. It moved to larger premises in 2009. Seasonal beers and two monthly specials are produced as well as bottle-conditioned beers.

Hop Monster (OG 1038, ABV 3.7%)

Pale Sunlight (OG 1038, ABV 3.8%)

Handliner (OG 1040, ABV 4%)

Merry Maidens Mild (OG 1040, ABV 4%) 🍺

THE BREWERIES

Tours by arrangement

⊠ The brewery was set up in 2001 with a four-barrel plant in the cellar of the hotel. It was sold to Edale Brewery in 2004 and has been owned by the Walker family since 2006. Around 25 outlets are supplied direct. Seasonal and bottle-conditioned beers are also available.

Middlewood Mild (OG 1039, ABV 3.8%) ◆
A dark traditional mild with flavours of chocolate and liquorice, and toffee in the aftertaste.

**Hillsborough Pale Ale/HPA
(OG 1038, ABV 3.9%)** ◆
A straw-coloured bitter with a citrus nose, flowery head and petal undertones.

Traditional Bitter (OG 1039, ABV 4%) ◆
A traditional style, amber-coloured malty bitter.

Primrose Pale Ale (OG 1042, ABV 4.2%) ◆
Fairly bitter yellow ale with medium hoppiness and hints of grapefruit in the aftertaste.

Loxley Gold (OG 1043, ABV 4.5%) ◆
Golden coloured premium pale ale, hoppy with a clean, dry finish.

Stannington Stout (OG 1050, ABV 5%) ◆
Jet black, rich tasting, bitter yet smooth.

Samuel Berry's IPA (OG 1049, ABV 5.1%) ◆
Fairly dark IPA style fruity bitter, with some sweetness in the aftertaste.

Cuerden (NEW)

Cuerden Brewing, Smithy Farm, Blackshaw Head, West Yorkshire, HX7 7JB
☎ 07938 000530 ✉ cuerdenbrewing@gmail.com

☺Cuerden was established in 2010 using spare capacity at Bridestones Brewery. Specially designed beers for individual groups and outlets are also brewed.

Munich (ABV 3.7%)
A very pale, hoppy beer with biscuit in the background.

Mild (ABV 3.9%)

Gold (ABV 4%)

Pale (ABV 4.2%)

For the Fountaine Inn, Linton

Fountaine Pale (ABV 4.2%)

Cuillin

🍺 Cuillin Brewery Ltd, Sligachan Hotel, Sligachan, Carbost, Isle of Skye, IV47 8SW
☎ (01478) 650204 ☎ 07795 250808
✉ steve@cuillinbrewery.co.uk
⊕ cuillinbrewery.co.uk
Tours by arrangement

☺The five-barrel brewery opened in 2004 and is situated in central Skye, close to the famous Cuillin mountain. The water provides a distinctive colour and taste to the ales. Specials and seasonal ales are brewed throughout the year. The brewery is closed in winter.

Skye Ale (OG 1041, ABV 4.1%)

Black Face (OG 1043, ABV 4.3%)
A good balance of blackcurrant fruit and malts highlight this dark ruby red strong mild. Liquorice and roast also evident in the creamy mouthfeel.

Glamaig (OG 1045, ABV 4.5%)

Pinnacle (OG 1047, ABV 4.7%) ◆
The hoppy and fruity nose leads to more hop and plenty of pale malt flavour in this very drinkable golden amber bitter.

Cumberland

Cumberland Breweries Ltd, The Forge, Great Corby, Carlisle, Cumbria, CA4 8LR
☎ (01228) 560899 ☎ 07747 841671
✉ enquiries@cumberlandbreweries.co.uk
⊕ cumberlandbreweries.co.uk
Tours by arrangement

Cumberland was established in 2009 using a bespoke 10-barrel plant.

Corby Ale (ABV 3.8%) ◆
Fruity amber session beer with sweetness leading to gentle bitterness in the aftertaste.

Corby Blonde (ABV 4.2%)

Cumbrian Legendary SIBA

Cumbrian Legendary Ales Ltd, Old Hall Brewery, Esthwaite Water, Hawkshead, Cumbria, LA22 0QF
☎ (01539) 436436
✉ info@cumbrianlegendaryales.com
⊕ cumbrianlegendaryales.com
Tours by arrangement

☺The Old Hall Brewery was established in 2006 in a renovated barn on the shores of Esthwaite Water. It was taken over in 2009 by Loweswater Brewery with Hayley Barton as head brewer. The success of Loweswater Gold has meant the brewery is thriving and extra fermenting and conditioning tanks have been installed. All brewing and commercial activities for Loweswater Brewery have transferred to this site.

Melbreak Bitter (OG 1038, ABV 3.7%) ◆
A fruity, hoppy beer with a hint of bitterness and a malty finish.

Dickie Doodle (OG 1040, ABV 3.9%) ◆
Amber session ale, sweetness, fruit and hoppiness in fine balance.

Langdale (OG 1040, ABV 4%) ◆
Golden ale with fresh grapefruit aromas, hoppy fruity flavours and crisp long hop finish making for a well-balanced beer.

Grasmoor Dark Ale (OG 1044.5, ABV 4.3%) ◆
Dark fruity beer with complex character and roast nutty tones leading to a short, refreshing finish.

Loweswater Gold (OG 1041, ABV 4.3%) 🍾 ◆
A dominant fruity body develops into a light bitter finish. A beer that belies its strength.

Daleside SIBA

Daleside Brewery Ltd, Camwal Road, Starbeck, Harrogate, North Yorkshire, HG1 4PT
☎ (01423) 880022
✉ enquiries@dalesidebrewery.com
⊕ dalesidebrewery.com
Shop Mon-Fri 9am-4pm (Off sales only)

☺Opened in 1991 in Harrogate with a 20-barrel plant, the brewery delivers direct to a range of outlets including pubs, restaurants and farm shops from Newcastle to Chesterfield as well as nationally via wholesalers. Seasonal beers: see website.

Bitter (OG 1039, ABV 3.7%) ♦
Pale brown in colour, this well-balanced, hoppy beer is complemented by fruity bitterness and a hint of sweetness, leading to a long, bitter finish.

Blonde (OG 1040, ABV 3.9%) ♦
A pale golden beer with a predominantly hoppy aroma and taste, leading to a refreshing hoppy, bitter but short finish.

Pride of England (ABV 4%)
A pale golden beer with a hoppy aroma, malty tones and a subtle dry finish.

Old Legover (OG 1043, ABV 4.1%)
Well-balanced mid-brown refreshing beer that leads to an equally well-balanced fruity bitter aftertaste.

Export (ABV 5%)
Golden beer with an aromatic nose. Subtle taste of hops lead to a soft, malty finish.

Monkey Wrench (ABV 5.3%)
Powerful, strong mid-brown ale. Aromas of fruit, hops, malt and roast malt give way to well-balanced fruit hoppiness and some sweetness.

Morocco Ale (ABV 5.5%)

Dancing Duck SIBA (NEW)

Dancing Duck Brewery, 1 John Cooper Buildings, Payne Street, Derby, DE22 3AZ
☎ 07581 122122
✉ rachel@dancingduckbrewery.com
⊕ dancingduckbrewery.com

Dancing Duck was established in 2010 in a former motor engineering unit became a 10-barrel plant. The name of the brewery is inspired by the East Midland colloquial greeting 'Duck'. An increasing number of local outlets are supplied. In 2011 the brewery became partners in the operation of the Exeter Arms in Derby where the beers can always be found.

Ay Up/Ey Up (OG 1041, ABV 3.9%)
Subtle malt and floral notes are matched with citrus hop, rounded off with a slightly dry finish.

22 (OG 1044.1, ABV 4.3%)
A well-balanced best bitter with malty flavour and dark fruit notes offset by a strong hop and clean finish.

Gold (OG 1046.5, ABV 4.7%)
A modern IPA with powerful hoppy bitterness and aroma balanced with strong malt notes.

Dark Horse SIBA

Dark Horse Brewery, Coonlands Laithe, Hetton, Nr Skipton, North Yorkshire, BD23 6LY
☎ (01756) 730555

☺Formerly the Wharfedale Brewery, Dark Horse opened in late 2008 with new owners. The brewery is based in an old hay barn within the Yorkshire Dales National Park. 15 outlets are supplied direct. Bottle-conditioned beer is also available.

Best Bitter (OG 1038, ABV 3.8%) ♦
This well-balanced pale brown bitter has biscuity malt and fruit on the nose, which continue into the

taste. Bitterness increases in the finish, with a spicy hint.

Hetton Pale Ale (OG 1041, ABV 4.2%) ♦
A well-balanced and full-bodied golden pale ale with hoppy bitterness on the palate overlaying a malty base and a strong citrus fruit character.

Dark Star SIBA

Dark Star Brewing Co Ltd, 22 Star Road, Partridge Green, Horsham, West Sussex, RH13 8RA
☎ (01403) 713085 ✉ info@darkstarbrewing.co.uk
⊕ darkstarbrewing.co.uk
Shop Mon-Fri 9am-5pm; Sat 9am-1pm
Tours by arrangement

⊠ Dark Star started in the cellar of the Evening Star in Brighton, moved to a 15-barrel brewery near Haywards Heath in 2001 and in 2010 moved to its current premises using a 45-barrel plant. The range of beers is divided between permanent, seasonal and monthly specials: see website for the complete range. Copies of classic European, American or old English beer styles are regularly brewed. Bottle-conditioned beer is also available.

Hophead (OG 1040, ABV 3.8%) 🍷 🍴 ♦
A golden-coloured bitter with a fruity/hoppy aroma and citrus/bitter taste and aftertaste. Flavours remain strong to the end.

Over the Moon (OG 1040, ABV 3.8%)

Partridge Best Bitter (OG 1041, ABV 4%)
A malt flavour with a hint of smokiness is complemented by East Kent Goldings hops.

Espresso (OG 1043, ABV 4.2%) 🍷
A black beer brewed with freshly ground coffee.

American Pale Ale (OG 1047, ABV 4.7%)
Brewed with American hops and yeast.

Festival (OG 1051, ABV 5%)
A chestnut, bronze-coloured bitter with a smooth mouthfeel and fruit aroma.

Original (OG 1051, ABV 5%) 🍷 ♦
Dark, full-bodied ale with a roast malt aroma and a dry, bitter, stout-like finish.

DarkTribe

🍺 DarkTribe Brewery, Dog & Gun, High Street, East Butterwick, Lincolnshire, DN17 3AJ
☎ (01724) 782324 ✉ dixie@darktribe.co.uk
⊕ darktribe.co.uk
Tours by arrangement

☺A small brewery was built during the summer of 1996 in a workshop at the bottom of his garden by Dave 'Dixie' Dean. In 2005 Dixie bought the Dog & Gun pub and moved the 2.5-barrel brewing equipment there. The beers generally follow a marine theme, recalling Dixie's days as an engineer in the Merchant Navy and his enthusiasm for sailing. Local outlets are supplied. Seasonal beers are also produced.

Dixie's Mild (OG 1034, ABV 3.6%)

Honey Mild (OG 1032, ABV 3.6%)

Admiral Sidney Smith (OG 1034, ABV 3.8%)

Full Ahead (OG 1034, ABV 3.8%) ♦
A malty smoothness is backed by a slightly fruity hop that gives a good bitterness to this amber-brown bitter.

Durham SIBA

Durham Brewery Ltd, Unit 6a, Bowburn North Industrial Estate, Bowburn, Co Durham, DH6 5PF
☎ (0191) 377 1991 ✉ steve@durham-brewery.co.uk
⊕ durhambrewery.co.uk
Shop Mon-Fri 8am-4pm; Sat 10am-2pm
Tours by arrangement

Established in 1994, Durham now has a portfolio of around 20 beers. These are not all available as regular beers – please see website for full list. Bottles and five litre mini-casks can be purchased via the online shop and an own label/special message service is available. Seasonal beers are brewed. Bottle-conditioned beers are also available and suitable for vegans. A new visitor centre will develop tours and tastings.

Magus (ABV 3.8%) ◆
Pale malt gives this brew its straw colour but the hops define its character, with a fruity aroma, a clean bitter mouthfeel, and a lingering dry, citrus-like finish.

Earl Soham SIBA

Earl Soham Brewery, The Street, Earl Soham, Suffolk, IP13 7RT
☎ (01728) 684097 ✉ info@earlsohambrewery.co.uk
⊕ earlsohambrewery.co.uk
Shop Mon-Thu 8.30am-5pm; Fri 8.30am-6pm; Sat 9am-4.30pm; closed Sun
Tours by arrangement

Earl Soham was set up behind the Victoria pub in 1984 and continued there until 2001 when the brewery moved 200 metres down the road. The Victoria and the Station in Framlingham both sell the beers on a regular basis, as does the Brewery Tap in Ipswich. When there is spare stock, beer is supplied to local free houses and as many beer festivals as possible. 30 outlets are supplied and three pubs are owned. Seasonal beer is also brewed. Most of the beers are bottle conditioned for the shop next door and other selected outlets.

Gannet Mild (OG 1034, ABV 3.3%) ◆
A beautifully balanced mild, sweet and fruity flavour with a lingering, coffee aftertaste.

Victoria Bitter (OG 1037, ABV 3.6%) ◆
A light, fruity, amber session beer with a clean taste and a long, lingering hoppy aftertaste.

Sir Roger's Porter (OG 1042, ABV 4.2%) ◆
Roast/coffee aroma and berry fruit introduce a full-bodied porter with roast/coffee flavours. Dry roast finish.

Albert Ale (OG 1045, ABV 4.4%)
Hops dominate every aspect of this beer, but especially the finish. A fruity, astringent beer.

Brandeston Gold (OG 1045, ABV 4.5%) ◆
Beer brewed with local ingredients. Lovely sharp, clean flavour, malty/hoppy and heavily laden with citrus fruit. Malty finish.

East Coast SIBA

East Coast Brewing Co, 3 Clay House Yard, Rear of Mitford Street, Filey, North Yorkshire, YO14 9DX
☎ (01723) 514865
✉ eastcoastbrewing@hotmail.co.uk
⊕ eastcoastbrewingcompany.co.uk
Tours by arrangement

⊠ The brewery is housed in a converted stable and coach house. Six regular beers are produced plus at least one special per month. 20 outlets are supplied direct.

Bonhomme Richard (ABV 3.6%)

Mary Rose (ABV 3.8%)

Commodore (ABV 4.1%)

John Paul Jones (ABV 4.3%)

Alfred Moodies Mild (ABV 6%)

Empress of India (ABV 6%)

Eastwood

Eastwood the Brewer, Barge & Barrel, 10-12 Park Road, Elland, West Yorkshire, HX5 9HP
☎ 07949 148476 ✉ taggartkeith@yahoo.co.uk
Tours by arrangement

☺The brewery was founded by John Eastwood at the Barge & Barrel pub. 50-70 outlets are supplied direct. Seasonal beers are also available.

Stirling (ABV 3.8%)
An amber-coloured session beer with a pleasant, long-lasting, fruity finish.

Best Bitter (ABV 4%) ◆
Creamy, yellow, hoppy bitter with hints of citrus fruits. Pleasantly strong bitter aftertaste.

Gold Award (ABV 4.4%) ◆
Complex copper-coloured beer with malt, roast and caramel flavours. It has a hoppy and bitter aftertaste.

Black Prince (ABV 5%)
A distinctive strong black porter with a blend of pale and chocolate malts and roasted barley.

Eccleshall

See Slater's

Edge

See Franklin's

Edinburgh

See Greene King in New Nationals section

Elgood's SIBA IFBB

Elgood & Sons Ltd, North Brink Brewery, Wisbech, Cambridgeshire, PE13 1LN
☎ (01945) 583160 ✉ info@elgoods-brewery.co.uk
⊕ elgoods-brewery.co..uk
Shop Tue-Thu 11.30am-4.30pm (May-Sep)
Tours by arrangement

⊠ The North Brink Brewery was established in 1795 and was one of the first classic Georgian breweries to be built outside London. In 1878 it came under the control of the Elgood family and is still run today as one of the few remaining independent family breweries, with the fifth generation of the family now helping to run the company. The beers go to 42 Elgood's pubs within a 50-mile radius of Wisbech and free trade outlets throughout East Anglia, while wholesalers distribute nationally. Elgood's has a visitor centre,

INDEVNT BREWERIES · E

offering a tour of the brewery and the gardens. Seasonal beers: see website.

Black Dog (OG 1036.8, ABV 3.6%) ◆
Dry, complex dark mild. Caramel binds a good cross-section of malt, roast and dark berry fruit flavours and there is a hint of sweetness.

Cambridge Bitter (OG 1037.8, ABV 3.8%) ◆
Full-bodied copper bitter with well defined malt and plummy fruit throughout and a long, smouldering dry finish.

Golden Newt (OG 1041.5, ABV 4.1%) ◆
Golden ale with floral hops and sulphur aroma. Floral hops and a fruity presence on a bittersweet background lead to a short, muted hoppy and fruity finish.

Pageant Ale (OG 1043.8, ABV 4.3%)
A premium ale with an aroma of hops and malt giving a well-balanced bittersweet flavour and a satisfying finish.

Greyhound Strong Bitter (OG 1052.8, ABV 5.2%) ◆
A tawny/brown beer with a malty aroma. Malt and raisin fruit on the palate balanced by pleasing dryness. Dry finish with faint malt and hops.

For City of Cambridge Brewery:

Boathouse Bitter (ABV 3.7%) ◆
Copper-brown and full-bodied session bitter, starting with impressive citrus and floral hop; grassy fruit notes are present with finally a gentle bitterness.

Hobson's Choice (ABV 4.1%) ◆
This golden ale has a predominantly spicy hop aroma. Bittersweet on the palate with plenty of hops leading through to a dry, hoppy finish.

Atom Splitter (ABV 4.5%) ◆
Robust copper-coloured strong bitter with a hop aroma and taste, and a distinct sulphury edge.

Parkers Porter (ABV 5%) ◆
Impressive reddish brew with a defined roast character throughout, and a short, fruity, bittersweet palate.

Elland SIBA

Elland Brewery Ltd, Units 3-5, Heathfield Industrial Estate, Heathfield Street, Elland, West Yorkshire, HX5 9AE
☎ (01422) 377677 ✉ brewery@ellandbrewery.co.uk
⊕ ellandbrewery.co.uk
Tours by arrangement

⊙The brewery was originally formed as Eastwood & Sanders in 2002 by the amalgamation of the Barge & Barrel Brewery and West Yorkshire Brewery. The company was renamed Elland in 2006 to reinforce its links with the town. The brewery has a capacity to brew 50 barrels a week and supplies more than 150 outlets. In addition to the six regular beers there are at least four seasonal specials and a Head Brewer's Reserve available every month. Bottle-conditioned beers are also available.

Bargee (OG 1038, ABV 3.8%) ◆
Amber, creamy session bitter. Fruity, hoppy aroma and taste complemented by a bitter edge in the finish.

Best Bitter (OG 1041, ABV 4%) ◆

Creamy, yellow, hoppy ale with hints of citrus fruits. Pleasantly strong bitter aftertaste.

Beyond the Pale (OG 1042, ABV 4.2%) ◆
Gold-coloured, robust, creamy beer with ripe aromas of hops and fruit. Bitterness predominates in the mouth and leads to a dry, fruity and hoppy aftertaste.

Eden (OG 1042, ABV 4.2%) ◆
A yellow, fruity, hoppy, creamy bitter. Citrus fruit with assertively bitter taste to finish.

Nettlethrasher (OG 1044, ABV 4.4%) ◆
Grainy amber-coloured beer. A rounded nose with some fragrant hops notes followed by a mellow nutty and fruity taste and a dry finish.

1872 Porter (OG 1065, ABV 6.5%) ◆
Creamy, full-flavoured porter. Rich liquorice flavours with a hint of chocolate from roast malt. A soft but satisfying aftertaste of bittersweet roast and malt.

Elmtree SIBA

Elmtree Beers, Snetterton Brewery, Unit 10, Oakwood Industrial Estate, Harling Road, Snetterton, Norfolk, NR16 2JU
☎ (01953) 887065 ✉ sales@elmtreebeers.co.uk
⊕ elmtreebeers.co.uk
Shop Mon-Wed & Sat 11am-4pm

⊗ Elmtree was established in 2007 using a five-barrel plant and moved in 2008 to new premises. 120 outlets are supplied direct. Bottle-conditioned beers are available and are suitable for vegetarians and vegans.

Burston's Cuckoo (OG 1038, ABV 3.8%)
An aroma of floral hops with a hint of citrus rounding off into a long, dry finish.

Bitter (OG 1041, ABV 4.2%)
A well-balanced, copper-coloured crisp beer. The early malt notes give way to a complex hop finish.

Dark Horse (OG 1048, ABV 5%) ◆
A roast, slightly salty aroma and matching initial taste introduce this coal black stout. The roast notes are aided by a fruity, prune-like background. Increasingly malty finish.

Golden Pale Ale (OG 1048, ABV 5%)
A pale ale in the traditional style that is initially malty and delicately bittered. The long, dry biscuit finish is enhanced by subtle citrus aromas.

Nightlight Mild (OG 1057, ABV 5.7%) ◆
A heavy mix of liquorice, roast and malt infuses aroma and taste. The heavy character is lightened by a sweet, spicy, slowly-developing aftertaste.

Elveden EAB

Elveden Ales, The Courtyard, Elveden Estate, Elveden, Thetford, Norfolk, IP24 3TA
☎ (01842) 878922

Elveden is a five-barrel brewery based on the estate of Lord Iveagh, a member of the ennobled branch of the Guinness family. The brewery is run by Frances Moore, daughter of Brendan Moore at Iceni Brewery (qv) and produces three ales: Elveden Stout (ABV 5%) and Elveden Ale (ABV 5.2%), which are mainly bottled in stoneware bottles. The third is Charter Ale (ABV 10%) to mark the celebrations for the award of a Royal Charter for Harwich in 1604. The beer is available in cask

721

new brewery was built in 2008. Seasonal beers: see website.

Ale of Wight (OG 1037, ABV 3.7%)
An aromatic, fresh and zesty pale beer.

Scrumdiggity Bitter (ABV 4%)

Fuggle-Dee-Dum (OG 1047, ABV 4.8%) ◆
Copper-coloured strong ale with plenty of malt and hops.

Goff's SIBA

Goff's Brewery Ltd, 9 Isbourne Way, Winchcombe, Cheltenham, Gloucestershire, GL54 5NS
☎ (01242) 603383 ✉ brewery@goffsbrewery.com
⊕ goffsbrewery.com

⊠ Goff's is a family concern that has been brewing cask-conditioned ales since 1994. The ales are available regionally in more than 200 outlets and nationally through wholesalers. The addition of the seasonal Ales of the Round Table provides a range of 12 beers of which four or five are always available: see website for details.

Jouster (OG 1040, ABV 4%) ◆
A drinkable, tawny-coloured ale, with a light hoppiness in the aroma. It has a good balance of malt and bitterness in the mouth, underscored by fruitiness, with a clean, hoppy aftertaste.

Tournament (OG 1038, ABV 4%) ◆
Dark golden in colour, with a pleasant hop aroma. A clean, light and refreshing session bitter with a good hop aftertaste.

White Knight (OG 1046, ABV 4.7%) ◆
A well-hopped bitter with a light colour and full-bodied taste. Bitterness predominates in the mouth and leads to a dry, hoppy aftertaste.

Golcar

Golcar Brewery Ltd, 60a Swallow Lane, Golcar, Huddersfield, West Yorkshire, HD7 4NB
☎ (01484) 644241 ☎ 07970 267555
✉ golcarbrewrey@btconnect.com
Tours by arrangement

☺Golcar started brewing in 2001 and production has increased from 2.5 barrels to five barrels a week. The brewery owns one pub, the Rose & Crown at Golcar, and supplies other outlets in the local area.

Dark Mild (OG 1034, ABV 3.4%) 🍴 ◆
Dark mild with a light roasted malt and liquorice taste. Smooth and satisfying.

Town End Bitter (OG 1039, ABV 3.9%) ◆
Amber bitter with a hoppy, citrus taste, with fruity overtones and a bitter finish.

Alba Rose (OG 1038, ABV 4%)
A light bitter with citrus undertones.

Pennine Gold (OG 1038, ABV 4%)
A hoppy and fruity session beer.

Guthlac's Porter (OG 1047, ABV 5%)
A robust all grain and malty working man's porter.

Golden Valley

Golden Valley Ales, Old Forge Industrial Estate, Peterchurch, Herefordshire, HR2 0SD
☎ (01981) 252998 ☎ 05603 123209 / 07733 891314 ✉ beer@goldenvalleyales.co.uk

Tours by arrangement

☺Golden Valley was set up in 2009 at the Bull Ring Pub, Kingstone with equipment from the Dunn Plowman Brewery. After a year of rapid growth the brewery moved to an industrial unit in 2010 with a 35-barrel capacity and delivers direct to over 50 outlets. Seasonal beers are also available. Bottle-conditioned beers are planned.

Hay Bluff (OG 1037, ABV 3.7%)
A pale session bitter.

.410 (OG 1041, ABV 4.1%)
A traditional ale with a rounded finish.

Brewers Choice (OG 1045, ABV 4.5%)
A premium, full-flavoured ale, full of character with fruity aromas.

Kenyons Original Oatmeal Stout (OG 1047, ABV 4.7%)
A smooth stout with hints of chocolate and espresso coffee.

Golden Triangle (NEW)

Golden Triangle Brewery, c/o 42 Mile End Road, Norwich, NR4 7QX
☎ 07976 281132
✉ kevin@goldentrianglebrewery.co.uk
⊕ goldentrianglebrewery.co.uk

Golden Triangle began brewing in 2011 using spare capacity at Ufford Brewery. The brewery soon expanded, purchasing Ufford's old 10-barrel plant when the latter relocated and installing it in new premises. Further plans are planned.

City Gold (ABV 3.8%)

Goodall's

⚏ Goodall's Brewery, The Lodge, 88 Crewe Road, Alsager, Staffordshire, ST7 2JA
☎ (01270) 873669
✉ goodalls.brewery@hotmail.co.uk
Tours by arrangement

⊠ Goodall's began brewing in 2010 at the Lodge in Alsager using a 2.5-barrel plant.

Datum (OG 1039, ABV 4%)

Fur Stoat (ABV 4.5%)

Freight (ABV 4.8%)

Snoweater (OG 1049, ABV 4.9%)

Goose Eye SIBA

Goose Eye Brewery Ltd, Ingrow Bridge, South Street, Keighley, West Yorkshire, BD21 5AX
☎ (01535) 605807
✉ gooseeyebrewery@btconnect.com
⊕ goose-eye-brewery.co.uk

☺Goose Eye is a family-run brewery supplying 60-70 regular outlets, mainly in Yorkshire and Lancashire. The beers are available through national wholesalers and pub chains. It produces monthly occasional and seasonal beers with entertaining names.

Barm Pot Bitter (OG 1038, ABV 3.8%) ◆
The bitter hop and citrus flavours that dominate this amber session bitter are balanced by a malty base. The finish is increasingly dry and bitter.

Bitter (OG 1039, ABV 3.9%)

A tawny brown bitter with a pleasant balance of hops and bitterness.

Bronte Bitter (OG 1040, ABV 4%) ◆
A brown, malty best bitter. Bitterness increases to give a lingering, dry finish.

Chinook Blonde (OG 1042, ABV 4.2%) ◆
An increasingly tart, bitter finish follows an assertive grapefruit hoppiness in both the aroma and taste of this satisfying blonde brew.

Golden Goose (OG 1045, ABV 4.5%)
A straw-coloured beer light on the palate with a smooth and refreshing hoppy finish.

Over and Stout (OG 1052, ABV 5.2%) ◆
A full-bodied stout with a complex palate in which roast and malt flavours mingle with hops, dark fruit and liquorice. Look also for tart fruit on the nose and a growing bitter finish.

Pommies Revenge (OG 1052, ABV 5.2%)
An extra strong, single malt bitter.

Grafters SIBA

🍺 Grafters Brewery, Half Moon, 23 High Street, Willingham by Stow, Lincolnshire, DN21 5JZ
☎ (01427) 788340 ✉ phil@graftersbrewery.com
⊕ graftersbrewery.com
Tours by arrangement

☺Brewing started on a 2.5-barrel plant in 2007 in a converted garage adjacent to the owner's freehouse, the Half Moon. Seasonal and occasional beers are also produced.

Moonlight (OG 1038, ABV 3.6%)

Traditional Bitter (OG 1040, ABV 3.8%)

Over the Moon (OG 1041.5, ABV 4%)

Brewers Troop (OG 1043, ABV 4.2%)

Darker Side of the Moon (OG 1045, ABV 4.2%)

Golden (OG 1046, ABV 4.3%)

Wobble Gob (OG 1050, ABV 4.9%)

Grafton SIBA

Grafton Brewing Co Ltd, Unit 5, Peppers Warehouse, Blyth Road, Worksop, Nottinghamshire, S81 0TP
☎ 07837 962688

Head Office: 8 Oak Close, Worksop, Nottinghamshire, S80 1GH ✉ allbeers@oakclose.orangehome.co.uk
Tours by arrangement

☺Grafton began brewing in 2007 in a converted stable block at the Packet Inn in Retford. The recipes for the re-named beers were purchased from Broadstone Brewery when that closed in 2006. Due to expansion it moved to its current location in 2010. Around 200 outlets are supplied. Seasonal beers are also available.

Two Water Grog (OG 1040, ABV 4%)

Lady Julia (OG 1042, ABV 4.3%)

Lady Catherine (OG 1044, ABV 4.5%)

Royal Blonde (ABV 4.5%)

Blondie (OG 1046, ABV 4.8%)

Lady Mary (OG 1050, ABV 5%)

Prowler (OG 1050, ABV 5%)

Grain SIBA EAB

Grain Brewery, South Farm, Tunbeck Road, Alburgh, Harleston, Norfolk, IP20 0BS
☎ (01986) 788884 ✉ info@grainbrewery.co.uk
⊕ grainbrewery.co.uk
Shop Mon-Fri 10am-4pm; Sat 11am-3pm
Tours by arrangement

⊗ Grain Brewery was launched in 2006 by Geoff Wright and Phil Halls. The five-barrel brewery is located in a converted dairy on a farm in the Waveney Valley. 80 outlets are supplied. In 2010 Grain purchased their first pub, the Plough in Norwich. Seasonal beers: see website. Bottle-conditioned beers are also available.

Tap Room Bitter (OG 1034, ABV 3.4%)

Oak (OG 1038, ABV 3.8%) ◆
A superbly balanced mix of malt and hops with bitter overtones. A lingering hint of molasses develops in the long, uplifting finish. Tawny hued with gentle malt airs.

Blonde Ash Wheat Beer (OG 1040, ABV 4%) ◆
A wheat beer with a lemon, clove, and banana nose. This flows through to a sweet fruity beginning, ably supported by a hoppy bitterness. Caramel appears in a strong finish.

Best Bitter (OG 1042, ABV 4.2%) ◆
A rich malty aroma introduces a well-balanced, full-bodied bitter. A complex mix of flavours dominated by malt and dried fruit ably supported by hops, toffee and bitterness.

Harvest Moon (OG 1045, ABV 4.5%) ◆
An aroma of coffee and vanilla introduces this complex but well-balanced amber hued brew. Malt and hops vie with a bitter citrus fruitiness for dominance. Mandarins make a late appearance.

Blackwood Stout (OG 1050, ABV 5%)

Porter (OG 1052, ABV 5.2%) ◆
A creamy, vanilla-enhanced brew. Well-rounded maltiness flows through both bouquet and taste and gives depth to the creamy, coffee-like roast character. A big, warming finish.

India Pale Ale (OG 1062, ABV 6.5%) ◆
Copper coloured with a brooding vinous character. Malt joins forces with dried fruit and hops to begin a sustained attack on the palate. A long-lasting finish, growing in bitterness.

Grainstore SIBA

Davis'es Brewing Co Ltd, The Grainstore Brewery, Station Approach, Oakham, Rutland, LE15 6RE
☎ (01572) 770065 ✉ info@grainstorebrewery.com
⊕ grainstorebrewery.com
Tours by arrangement

Grainstore, the smallest county's largest brewery, has been in production since 1995. The company's curious name comes from the fact that it was founded by Tony Davis and Mike Davies. After 30 years in the industry Tony decided to set up his own business after finding a derelict Victorian railway grainstore building. 80 outlets are supplied. Seasonal and bottle-conditioned beers are also available.

Rutland Bitter (OG 1032, ABV 3.4%)
Light in colour and taste but a well-balanced session beer.

Rutland Panther (OG 1034, ABV 3.4%) ◆

This superb reddish-black mild punches above its weight with malt and roast flavours combining to deliver a brew that can match the average stout for intensity of flavour.

Cooking (OG 1036, ABV 3.6%) ◣
Tawny-coloured beer with malt and hops on the nose and a pleasant grainy mouthfeel. Hops and fruit flavours combine to give a bitterness that continues into a long finish.

Triple B (OG 1042, ABV 4.2%) ◣
Initially hops dominate over malt in both the aroma and taste, but fruit is there, too. All three linger in varying degrees in the sweetish aftertaste of this brown brew.

Silly Billy (OG 1043, ABV 4.3%)

Gold (OG 1045, ABV 4.5%)

Ten Fifty (OG 1050, ABV 5%) ◣
Full-bodied, mid-brown strong bitter with a hint of malt on the nose. Malt, hops and fruitiness coalesce in a well-balanced taste; bittersweet finish.

Rutland Beast (OG 1053, ABV 5.3%)
A strong beer, dark brown in colour. Well-balanced flavours blend together to produce a full-bodied drink.

Nip (OG 1073, ABV 7.3%)
A true barley wine. A good balance of sweetness and bitterness meld together so that neither predominates over the other. Smooth and warming.

For Phipps Northampton Brewery Co:

Red Star (OG 1038, ABV 3.8%)

India Pale Ale (OG 1042, ABV 4.2%)

Ratliffe's Celebrated Stout (OG 1043, ABV 4.3%)

For Steamin' Billy Brewing Co (qv):

Bitter (OG 1043, ABV 4.3%) ◣
Brown-coloured best bitter. Initial malt and hops aromas are superseded by fruit and hop taste and aftertaste, accompanied by a refreshing bitterness.

Skydiver (OG 1050, ABV 5%) ◣
Full-bodied, strong, mahogany-coloured beer in which an initial malty aroma is followed by a characteristic malty sweetness that is balanced by a hoppy bitterness.

Great Gable

Great Gable Brewing Co Ltd, Unit 2G, Bridge End Industrial Estate, Egremont, Cumbria, CA22 2RD
☎ (01946) 823846 ✉ thegreatgable@btconnect.com
⊕ greatgablebrewing.com
Tours by arrangement

Great Gable began brewing in 2002 using a five-barrel plant at the Wasdale Head Inn in Gosforth. It moved to its current location in 2010, which also saw the acquisition of its first pub, the Horse & Groom at Gosforth. Seasonal and bottle-conditioned beers are available.

Great Gable (OG 1035, ABV 3.7%) ◣
Refreshing, hoppy, fruity bitter with a pleasant, bitter aftertaste.

Wastwater Gold (OG 1041, ABV 3.9%)

Burnmoor Pale Ale (OG 1040, ABV 4.2%) ◣

A dry, hoppy bitter, refreshing and clean-tasting. Straw-coloured with a fruity taste and grapefruit overtones. Long, bitter finish.

Yewbarrow (OG 1054, ABV 5.5%) ◣
Strong, mild dark ale with robust roast flavours, rich and malty. Satisfying with hints of spice and fruit. Smooth chocolate and coffee aromas.

Great Heck SIBA

Great Heck Brewing Co Ltd, Harwinn House, Main Street, Great Heck, North Yorkshire, DN14 0BQ
☎ (01977) 661430 ☎ 07723 381002
✉ denzil@greatheckbrewery.co.uk
⊕ greatheckbrewery.co.uk

☺Great Heck began production in 2008 on a four-barrel plant in a converted slaughterhouse. Capacity was increased to 12 barrels per week in 2009. Over 100 outlets are supplied. Seasonal beers are also available.

Dave (OG 1039, ABV 3.8%)

Heck's Angel (OG 1038, ABV 3.9%)
A very dry pale ale with American hops.

Yorkshire Navigator (OG 1038, ABV 3.9%)

Yorkshire Pale Ale (OG 1043, ABV 4.3%)
A premium pale ale with a complex malt character and zesty finish.

Slaughterhouse Porter (OG 1046, ABV 4.5%)
Very black, full-bodied porter with a smooth malt character.

Staggering Genius (OG 1049, ABV 5%)
A pale Yorkshire wheat beer.

Super-Dave (OG 1050, ABV 5%)

For Bull & Fairhouse, Wakefield:

Golden Bull (OG 1036, ABV 3.8%)
A very hoppy pale ale.

Great Newsome SIBA

Great Newsome Brewery Ltd, Great Newsome Farm, South Frodingham, Winestead, East Yorkshire, HU12 0NR
☎ (01964) 612201 ☎ 07808 367386
✉ enquiries@greatnewsomebrewery.co.uk
⊕ greatnewsomebrewery.co.uk

☺Nestled in the Holderness countryside, Great Newsome began production in 2007 on a 10-barrel plant, brewing in renovated farm buildings. Beer is distributed throughout Yorkshire as well as North Lincolnshire. Seasonal beers: see website.

Sleck Dust (OG 1037, ABV 3.8%)
Straw-coloured, refreshingly bitter session beer with floral aroma and subtle dry finish.

Pricky Back Otchan (OG 1042, ABV 4.2%)
Hoppy golden bitter with fresh citrus aroma.

Frothingham Best (OG 1042, ABV 4.3%)
Dark amber best bitter with subtle dry finish.

Holderness Dark (OG 1042, ABV 4.3%)
Dark, strong mild. Malty notes with a hint of sweetness.

Jem's Stout (OG 1044, ABV 4.3%)
Dark, smooth beer with smoky, roasted malt flavours and aroma.

Great Oakley SIBA

Great Oakley Brewery, Bridge Farm, 11 Brooke Road, Great Oakley, Northamptonshire, NN18 8HG
☎ (01536) 744888 ☎ 07850 327658
✉ sales@greatoakleybrewery.co.uk
⊕ greatoakleybrewery.co.uk
Tours by arrangement

⊠ The brewery started production in 2005 and is housed in converted stables on a former working farm. It is run by husband and wife team Phil and Hazel Greenway. More than 60 outlets are supplied, including the Malt Shovel Tavern in Northampton, which is the brewery tap. Seasonal beers: see website. Bottle-conditioned beers are also available.

Welland Valley Mild (OG 1037, ABV 3.6%)
A dark, traditional mild. Full of flavour.

Eleanor Cross (OG 1039, ABV 3.8%)
An amber gold easy-drinking ale.

Wagtail (OG 1040, ABV 3.9%)
Light coloured with a unique bitterness derived from New Zealand hops.

Wot's Occurring (OG 1040, ABV 3.9%) ⚐
Amber gold session bitter with a subtle hop finish.

Marching In (OG 1041, ABV 4.1%)
A golden, clean-tasting beer.

Harpers (OG 1045, ABV 4.3%)
Traditional mid-brown bitter with a malty taste.

Gobble (OG 1047, ABV 4.5%) ⚐
A golden beer with a pleasant hop aftertaste.

Delapre Dark (OG 1047, ABV 4.6%)
A dark, full-bodied ale made from five different malts.

Abbey Stout (OG 1050, ABV 5%)
A dark, rich stout.

Tailshaker (OG 1051, ABV 5%)
A full-bodied golden ale with a great depth of character.

Great Orme SIBA

Great Orme Brewery Ltd, Nant y Cywarch, Glan Conwy, Conwy, LL28 5PP
☎ (01492) 580548 ✉ info@greatormebrewery.co.uk
⊕ greatormebrewery.co.uk

☺Great Orme is a five-barrel micro-brewery situated on a hillside in the Conwy Valley between Llandudno and Betws-y-Coed, with views of the Conwy Estuary and the Great Orme. Established in 2005, it is housed in a number of converted farm buildings. Around 50 outlets are supplied.

Cambria (ABV 3.8%)
A modern IPA with a full hop flavour and dry finish.

Welsh Black (OG 1042, ABV 4%) ◥
Smooth-tasting dark beer with roast coffee notes in aroma and taste. Sweetish in flavour and having some characteristics of a mild ale with hoppiness also present in the aftertaste.

Orme (OG 1043, ABV 4.2%) ◥
Malty best bitter with a dry finish. Faint hop and fruit notes in aroma and taste, but malt dominates throughout.

Celtica (OG 1045, ABV 4.5%) ▪ ◥

Yellow in colour with a zesty taste full of citrus fruit flavours. Some initial sweetness followed by peppery hops and a bitter finish.

Merlyn (OG 1051, ABV 5%)
A strong ale with balanced hop bitterness and sweet malt.

Great Western SIBA

Great Western Brewing Co Ltd, Stream Bakery, Bristol Road, Hambrook, Bristol, BS16 1RF
☎ (0117) 957 2842
✉ contact@greatwesternbrewingcompany.co.uk
⊕ greatwesternbrewingcompany.co.uk
Shop Mon-Fri 10am-5pm; Sat 10am-2pm
Tours by arrangement

⊠ Great Western is a 12-barrel brewery set up in 2008 by Kevin Stone in a former bakery. The property has been renovated resulting in a bespoke showpiece brewery retaining many of the building's original features. 200 outlets are supplied and one pub is owned. Seasonal beers are also available.

HPA (OG 1040, ABV 4%)

Maiden Voyage (OG 1040, ABV 4%) ◥
An amber bitter with a strong aroma of malt and fruit. The taste is initially sweet and fruity (damson notes) but the slightly astringent finish is dry and biscuity.

Bees Knees (OG 1041, ABV 4.2%) ◥
A powerful aroma of honey with hints of malt and meadow flowers leads to a taste of honey and malt developing in bitterness through a slightly astringent but finely balanced aftertaste.

Classic Gold (OG 1044, ABV 4.6%) ◥
Golden ale with subtle aroma of malt and pale fruits – pears, melons and golden plums. The taste is fruity with balancing hop character rapidly fading into a slightly astringent finish.

Green Dragon

🏠 Green Dragon Brewery, Green Dragon, 29 Broad Street, Bungay, Suffolk, NR35 1EF
☎ (01986) 892681
Tours by arrangement

⊠ The Green Dragon pub was purchased in 1991 and the buildings at the rear converted to a brewery. In 1994 the plant was expanded and moved into a converted barn. The doubling of capacity allowed the production of a larger range of ales, including seasonal and occasional brews. The beers are available at the pub and beer festivals.

Chaucer Ale (OG 1037, ABV 3.8%)

Gold (OG 1045, ABV 4.4%)

Bridge Street Bitter (OG 1045, ABV 4.5%)

Strong Mild (OG 1054, ABV 5.4%)

Greene King

See under New Nationals section

Greenfield SIBA

Greenfield Real Ale Brewery, Unit 8 Waterside Mills, Greenfield, Saddleworth, Greater Manchester, OL3 7NH
☎ (01457) 879789 ✉ office@greenfieldrealale.co.uk
⊕ greenfieldrealale.co.uk
Shop 9am-5pm daily
Tours by arrangement

☺ Greenfield was launched in 2002 using a five-barrel plant. The brewery is in an old spinning mill next to the River Chew on the edge of the Peak District National Park. Spring water from the National Park is used for brewing. Floor area doubled in 2008 to provide additional space for cask storage and bottling facilities. More than 200 outlets are supplied in the north-west and further afield via distributors. Seasonal beers: see website. Bottle-conditioned ales are also available.

Black Five (OG 1040, ABV 4%) ◆
A dark brown beer in which malt, roast, toffee, fruit and chocolate can all be found in aroma and taste. Smooth, malty aftertaste.

Monkey Business (OG 1041, ABV 4%) ◆
Yellow in colour with a fruit and hop aroma. Hops and grapefruit in the mouth, with a dry, astringent finish.

Delph Donkey (OG 1041, ABV 4.1%)

Dobcross Bitter (OG 1041, ABV 4.2%)

Summer Ice (OG 1041, ABV 4.2%)

Green Jack SIBA

Green Jack Brewing Co Ltd, Argyle Place, Love Road, Lowestoft, Suffolk, NR32 2NZ
☎ (01502) 562863 ✉ info@green-jack.co.uk
⊕ green-jack.com
Tours by arrangement

Green Jack started brewing in 2003 and in 2009 moved to a 35-barrel brew house built in an old Lowestoft smoke house. 150 outlets are supplied and three pubs are owned. Seasonal beers: see website. Bottle-conditioned beers are also available. Beers are also brewed for Hektors Brewery Ltd.

Excelsior (OG 1037, ABV 3.7%)

Orange Wheat Beer (OG 1041, ABV 4.2%) ◆
Strong citrus aroma with hints of elderflower, leading to a distinctly tangerine, tart-tasting, unusually clear wheat beer. Refreshing.

Trawlerboys Best Bitter (OG 1045, ABV 4.6%)

Lurcher Stout (OG 1046, ABV 4.8%) ◆
Rich, roasty dark ale with mature blackcurrant in the aroma and fruity, hoppy bitterness in the taste quickly giving way to a long, sweetish aftertaste.

Mahseer IPA (OG 1048, ABV 5%)

Gone Fishing ESB (OG 1052, ABV 5.5%)

Ripper Tripel (OG 1074, ABV 8.5%)

Baltic Trade Export Stout (OG 1092, ABV 10.5%)

Green Mill SIBA

☐ **Green Mill Brewery, Cask & Feather, 1 Oldham Road, Rochdale, OL16 1UA**
☎ 07967 656887 ✉ greenmillbrewery@msn.com
⊕ greenmillbrewery.co.uk

Green Mill started brewing in 2007 on a 2.5-barrel plant. The brewery moved in 2010 to the rear of the Cask & Feather with plans for further expansion. A number of seasonal and occasional ales are brewed. Around 30 outlets are supplied either directly or through wholesalers.

Gold (OG 1034, ABV 3.4%)

A Bitter T'ale (OG 1039, ABV 4%)

Chief (OG 1041, ABV 4.2%)

Northern Lights (OG 1045, ABV 4.5%)

Greenodd

☐ **Greenodd Brewery, Ship Inn, Main Street, Greenodd, Cumbria, LA12 7QZ**
☎ 07782 655294
Tours by arrangement

Greenodd was established in 2010 in a building behind the Ship Inn using a two-barrel plant. There is a viewing window from the street behind the pub.

Kiln (OG 1038, ABV 3.8%)

Blonde (OG 1040, ABV 4%)

Best Bitter (OG 1040, ABV 4.1%)

GPA (Greenodd Pale Ale) (OG 1044, ABV 4.4%)

Green Room

Green Room Ales Ltd, c/o St Stephen Road, Sticker, St Austell, Cornwall, PL26 7HA
☎ 07843 010950 ✉ letstalk@greenroomales.co.uk
⊕ greenroomales.co.uk

Stephen Burton started brewing in 2009 on a 2.5-barrel plant at the listed address. Due to increased demand he started using spare capacity at Keltek Brewery (qv), along with its bottling facilities. Production was relocated from early 2010, with the original plant subsequently moved to Keltek to increase flexibility. Cask beers are produced but much of the output is bottled, although at present only some of the special brews are bottle-conditioned.

Icon (ABV 4%)

IPA (ABV 4%)

Kudos (ABV 5%)

Rogue (ABV 7.6%)

Green Tye EAB

Green Tye Brewery, Green Tye, Much Hadham, Hertfordshire, SG10 6JP
☎ (01279) 841041 ☎ 07770 766376
✉ info@gtbrewery.co.uk
Tours by arrangement for small groups

⊠ Established in 1999 near Much Hadham, on the edge of the Ash Valley. Green Tye supplies the local free trade, neighbouring counties and further afield via beer agencies and swaps with other micro-breweries. Seasonal and bottle-conditioned beers are also available.

Union Jack (OG 1036, ABV 3.6%)
A copper-coloured bitter, fruity with a citrus taste and a hoppy, citrus aroma, with a balanced, bitter finish.

Hadham Gold (OG 1040, ABV 4%)

Hamm

Hammer
Road, Po
☎ (0190:
brewery.

⊠ Hamm
five-barr
barrel pl:
Bottle-co

Shooting

HPA (OG
A light, g
flavour.

Red Hun
A ruby re

Woodcot
A tangy

Madgwi
A golden

Hanby

See Shro

Ha'pe

Ha'penny
8, Aldbor
Essex, IG:
☎ (020)
⊠ info@
⊕ hapen
Tours by

⊠ Ha'pe
CAMRA r
had a fo
Aldborou

Sixteen-!
A fruity
througho
lingers ir
toffee.

London
Spring-H
London

Gog Mag
A dark g
with flor
sweet ar

Mrs Love
Porter (/
A light-d
aroma. R
flavour v
dryness.

Happy

Happy Va
Cheshire,
☎ 07758
⊠ dave@
⊕ happy

⊠ Happy
and Nicc

A pale straw-coloured bitter with a light and fruity body and a dominant fruity aroma.

Gribble

▤ Gribble Brewery Ltd, Gribble Inn, Oving, West Sussex, PO20 2BP
☎ (01243) 786893 ⊠ info@gribbleinn.co.uk
⊕ gribbleinn.co.uk

⊠ The Gribble Brewery was established in 1980. Until 2005 it was run as a managed house operation by Hall & Woodhouse (qv) but is now an independent micro-brewery owned by the publicans of the inn on the same site. Around 20 outlets are supplied direct. Seasonal beer is also available.

CHI P A (ABV 3.8%)

Ale (ABV 4.1%)

Fuzzy Duck (ABV 4.3%)

Reg's Tipple (ABV 5%)
Reg's Tipple was named after a customer from the early days of the brewery. It has a smooth nutty flavour with a pleasant afterbite.

Plucking Pheasant (ABV 5.2%)

Pig's Ear (ABV 5.8%)

Griffin

▤ Griffin Brewery, Church Road, Shustoke, Warwickshire, B46 2LB
☎ (01675) 481205
Tours by arrangement

☺Brewing started in 2008 in the old coffin shop premises adjacent to the pub (formerly occupied by Church End Brewery). The brewery is a venture between Griffin licensee Mick Pugh and his son Oliver. A number of seasonal ales and specials are brewed throughout the year. At present the brewery only supplies the Griffin Inn and beer festivals.

Ramblers Ruin (OG 1041, ABV 4.1%)
A light refreshing session beer with a citrus aftertaste.

Gorgeous George (OG 1044, ABV 4.4%)
A golden ale; full-flavoured with a hoppy aftertaste.

BMW (Black Magic Woman) (OG 1051, ABV 5.1%)
A strong dark bitter with a blackcurrant aftertaste.

Bitter (OG 1052, ABV 5.2%)
Malty flavour with a strong hop balance and a slightly sweet finish.

Pale Ale (OG 1059, ABV 5.9%)
A light-coloured beer with citrus and grapefruit flavours.

Gwaun Valley

Gwaun Valley Brewery, Kilkiffeth Farm, Pontfaen, Fishguard, SA65 9TP
☎ (01348) 881304
⊠ enquiries@gwaunvalleybrewery.co.uk
⊕ gwaunvalleybrewery.co.uk
Shop & Visitor Centre 10am-6pm daily
Tours by arrangement

⊠ Gwaun Valley began brewing in 2009 on a four-barrel plant in a converted granary.

Bitter Ale (ABV 4%)
A rich, smooth bitter with a lasting hoppy flavour.

Light Ale (ABV 4%)
An easy-drinking ale with fruity undertones and a clean aftertaste.

Dark Ale (ABV 4.2%)
A smooth, mild dark ale with a hint of chocolate.

St Davids Special (ABV 4.2%)

Gwynant

▤ Bragdy Gwynant, Tynllidiart Arms, Capel Bangor, Aberystwyth, Ceredigion, SY23 3LR
☎ (01970) 880248 ⊕ tynllidiartarms.com
Tours by arrangement

⊠ Brewing started in 2004 in a 4' 6" x 4' former men's toilet at the front of the pub, with a brew length of nine gallons. Beer is only sold in the pub. The brewery has now been recognised as the smallest commercial brewery in the world by the Guinness Book of Records. Brewing recommenced in late 2009 after a period of suspension. Bottled beers are planned.

Cwrw Gwynant (ABV 4.5%)

Hadrian Border SIBA

Alnwick Ales Ltd t/a Hadrian Border Brewery, Unit 5, The Preserving Works, Newburn Industrial Estate, Shelley Road, Newburn, Newcastle upon Tyne, Tyne & Wear, NE15 9RT
☎ (0191) 264 9000 ⊠ hadrianborder@yahoo.co.uk
⊕ hadrian-border-brewery.co.uk
Tours by arrangement

Hadrian Border was based at the former Four Rivers 20-barrel site in Newcastle but relocated to Newburn in 2011 with a new 30-barrel brewery. The company's brands are available from Glasgow to Yorkshire, and nationally via wholesalers.

Gladiator (OG 1036, ABV 3.8%) 🍷 🍂
Tawny-coloured bitter with plenty of malt in the aroma and palate leading to a strong, bitter finish.

Tyneside Blonde (OG 1037, ABV 3.9%) 🍂
Refreshing blonde ale with zesty notes and a clean, fruity finish.

Farne Island Pale Ale (OG 1038, ABV 4%) 🍂
A copper-coloured bitter with a refreshing malt/hop balance.

Flotsam (OG 1038, ABV 4%)
Bronze coloured with a citrus bitterness and a distinctive floral aroma.

Legion Ale (OG 1040, ABV 4.2%) 🍂
Well-balanced, amber-coloured beer, full bodied with good malt flavours. Well hopped with a long bitter finish.

Newcastle Pioneer (OG 1041, ABV 4.2%) 🍂
Light amber ale, well hopped with only Pioneer hops to give a light spicy/fruity finish.

Secret Kingdom (OG 1042, ABV 4.3%)
Dark, rich and full-bodied, slightly roasted with a malty palate ending with a pleasant bitterness.

Reiver's IPA (OG 1042, ABV 4.4%)
Golden bitter with a clean citrus palate and aroma with subtle malt flavours breaking through at the end.

Centurion Best Bitter (OG 1043, ABV 4.5%) 🍂

THE BREWERIES

Hoppy, crisp, straw-coloured bitter with floral notes and a dry finish.

Squirrels' Hoard (OG 1040, ABV 4%)

Nemesis (OG 1041, ABV 4.1%)

Pinches IPA (OG 1043, ABV 4.3%)

Val (Addiction) (OG 1048, ABV 4.8%)

Hart of Stebbing EAB

Hart of Stebbing Brewery, White Hart, High Street, Stebbing, Essex, CM6 3SQ
☎ (01371) 856383
✉ nick@hartofstebbingbrewery.co.uk
⊕ hartofstebbingbrewery.co.uk

The brewery was established in 2007 by Bob Dovey and Nick Eldred, who is also the owner of the White Hart pub where the brewery is based. At present only the White Hart and local beer festivals are supplied. Occasional specials are also brewed.

Hart IPA (OG 1035, ABV 3.5%)

Harveys IFBB

Harvey & Son (Lewes) Ltd, Bridge Wharf Brewery, 6 Cliffe High Street, Lewes, East Sussex, BN7 2AH
☎ (01273) 480209 ✉ maj@harveys.org.uk
⊕ harveys.org.uk
Shop Mon-Sat 9.30am-5.30pm
Tours by arrangement (currently two year waiting list)

Established in 1790, this independent family brewery operates from the banks of the River Ouse in Lewes. A major development in 1985 doubled the brewhouse capacity and subsequent additional fermenting capacity has seen production rise to more than 45,000 barrels a year. Harveys supplies real ale to all its 48 pubs and 450 free trade outlets in Sussex and Kent. Seasonal beers: see website. Bottle-conditioned beer is also available.

Sussex XX Mild Ale (OG 1030, ABV 3%) ◆
A dark copper-brown colour. Roast malt dominates the aroma and palate leading to a sweet, caramel finish.

Hadlow Bitter (OG 1033, ABV 3.5%)
Formerly Sussex Pale Ale

Sussex Best Bitter (OG 1040, ABV 4%) ◆
Full-bodied brown bitter. A hoppy aroma leads to a good malt and hop balance, and a dry aftertaste.

Armada Ale (OG 1045, ABV 4.5%) ◆
Hoppy amber best bitter. Well-balanced fruit and hops dominate throughout with a fruity palate.

Harviestoun SIBA

Harviestoun Brewery Ltd, Alva Industrial Estate, Alva, Clackmannanshire, FK12 5DQ
☎ (01259) 769100 ✉ info@harviestoun.com
⊕ harviestoun.com
Tours by arrangement

Harviestoun started in a barn in the village of Dollar in 1985 with a five-barrel brew plant, but now operate on a state-of-the-art 60-barrel brewery in Alva. The brewery supplies local outlets direct and nationwide via wholesalers. It was bought by Caledonian Brewing Co in 2006 but is now independent following the takeover of Caledonian by Scottish & Newcastle in 2008.

Further expansion is planned. Seasonal beers: see website.

Bitter & Twisted (OG 1038, ABV 3.8%) ◆
Refreshingly hoppy beer with fruit throughout. A bittersweet taste with a long, bitter finish. A golden session beer.

Haggis Hunter (OG 1044, ABV 4.3%)
A fruity, hoppy, balanced beer.

Schiehallion (OG 1048, ABV 4.8%) ◆
A Scottish cask lager, brewed using a lager yeast and Hersbrucker hops. A hoppy aroma, with fruit and malt, leads to a malty, bitter taste with floral hoppiness and a bitter finish.

Harwich Town EAB

Harwich Town Brewing Co, Station Approach, Harwich, Essex, CO12 3NA
☎ (01255) 551155 ✉ info@harwichtown.co.uk
⊕ harwichtown.co.uk
Shop – see website
Tours by arrangement

Brewing started in 2007 on a five-barrel plant next to Harwich Town railway station. The brewer is a CAMRA member and former customs officer. Beers are named after local landmarks, characters or events. 50 outlets are supplied. An annual festival special is brewed for Harwich & Dovercourt Bay Winter Ale Festival in December. Seasonal and bottle-conditioned beers are also available.

Ha'Penny Mild (ABV 3.6%)

Leading Lights (ABV 3.8%)

Misleading Lights (ABV 4%)

Bathside Battery Bitter (OG 1042, ABV 4.2%)

Redoubt Stout (ABV 4.2%)

Parkeston Porter (ABV 4.5%)

Lighthouse Bitter (ABV 4.8%)

Phoenix APA (OG 1052, ABV 5.1%)

Imperial Redoubt Stout (OG 1084, ABV 8%)

Hastings SIBA (NEW)

Hastings Brewery Ltd, Unit 12, Conqueror Industrial Estate, Moorhurst Road, St Leonards, East Sussex, TN38 9NB
☎ 07708 259342 ✉ info@hastingsbrewery.co.uk
⊕ hastingsbrewery.co.uk

The brewery was founded in 2010 by Brett Ross, alongside father and son Andy and Pete Mason. It exclusively produced vegan-friendly beers. The initial brewery had a one-barrel brew length, which was replaced in 2011 by a 5.25-barrel system.

Blonde (OG 1038, ABV 3.7%)

Best (OG 1044, ABV 4.1%)

Havant SIBA

Havant Brewery, c/o 29 Gladys Avenue, Cowplain, Waterlooville, Hampshire, PO8 8HT
☎ (02392) 252118
✉ mike@thehavantbrewery.co.uk
⊕ thehavantbrewery.co.uk

Havant began brewing in 2009 on a one-barrel plant with two fermenters. Expansion is planned with production increasing to 16 barrels per week. Seasonal beers: see website.

Started (OG 1042, ABV 4%)

Finished (OG 1051, ABV 5%)

Hawkshead SIBA

Hawkshead Brewery Ltd, Mill Yard, Staveley, Cumbria, LA8 9LR
☎ (01539) 822644
✉ info@hawksheadbrewery.co.uk
⊕ hawksheadbrewery.co.uk
Shop 12-5pm daily

☺Hawkshead brewery complex is a showcase for real ale. The brewery expanded in 2006, having outgrown its original site (opened in 2002) in a barn at Hawkshead. Further expansion in 2010 added a second bar to the Beer Hall, which is the visitor centre and brewery tap. A kitchen serves 'beer tapas' to complement the beer. Windows throughout look into the cellar, specialist beer shop, brew house and the new fermentation room, which is in the main bar. Pubs are supplied throughout the north west. Bottle-conditioned beers are available. Bottle-conditioned Pure Brewed Organic Stout is suitable for vegans.

Windermere Pale (OG 1036, ABV 3.5%) ◆
Crisp and fruity yellow beer with hints of melon and grapefruit and a strong bitter aftertaste.

Bitter (OG 1037, ABV 3.7%) ▮ ◆
Well-balanced, thirst-quenching beer with fruit and hops aroma, leading to a lasting bitter finish.

Red (OG 1042, ABV 4.2%) ◆
An impressive colour for this richly flavoured beer; lots of fruitiness and good hop flavour with a lingering aftertaste.

Lakeland Gold (OG 1043, ABV 4.4%) ◆
Fresh, well-balanced fruity, hoppy beer with a clean bitter aftertaste.

Pure Brewed Organic Stout (OG 1044, ABV 4.5%) ◆
Well-crafted and smooth, consistently deep and powerful in its stoutiness.

Lakeland Lager (OG 1045, ABV 4.8%)
A cask-conditioned lager.

Brodie's Prime (OG 1048, ABV 4.9%) ◆
Complex, dark brown beer with plenty of malt, fruit and roast taste. Satisfying full body with clean finish.

Triple X Brodie's Prime (OG 1075, ABV 8.5%)

Haworth Steam (NEW)

Haworth Steam Brewing Co, Main Street, Haworth, West Yorkshire, BD22 0HB
☎ (01535) 646212 ☎ 07798 636705
✉ haworthsteambrew@gmail.com
⊕ haworthsteambrewery.co.uk

Brewing began in 2011 using a five-barrel plant.

True Tyke (ABV 3.8%)

WD Austerity (ABV 3.8%)

Ironclad 957 (ABV 4.3%)

Fallwood XXXX (ABV 5.2%)

Haywood Bad Ram

Haywood Bad Ram Brewery, Callow Top Holiday Park, Sandybrook, Ashbourne, Derbyshire, DE6 2AQ
☎ (01335) 344020 ☎ 07974 948427
✉ acphaywood@aol.com ⊕ callowtop.co.uk
Shop 9am-5pm (seasonal)
Tours by arrangement

⊠ The brewery was based in a converted barn but a new 2,500 sq ft brewery and bottling plant became operational in 2010. One pub is owned (on site) and several other outlets are supplied. The brewery is not operational during the winter. Bottle-conditioned beers are available.

Dr Samuel Johnson (ABV 4.5%)

Bad Ram (ABV 5%)

Lone Soldier (ABV 5%)

Woggle Dance (ABV 5%)

Callow Top IPA (OG 1050, ABV 5.2%)

Heart of Wales

▤ Neuadd Arms Brewing Co t/a Heart of Wales Brewery, Stables Yard, Zion Street, Llanwrtyd Wells, Powys, LD5 4RD
☎ (01591) 610236
✉ Lindsay@heartofwalesbrewery.co.uk
⊕ heartofwalesbrewery.co.uk
Shop 10am-6pm daily
Tours by arrangement

⊠ The brewery was set up with a six-barrel plant in 2006 in old stables at the rear of the Neuadd Arms Hotel. Beers are brewed using water from the brewery's own borehole. Seasonal brews celebrate local events such as the World Bogsnorkelling Championships. Seasonal and bottle-conditioned beers are available. All bottle-conditioned beers are suitable for vegetarians and vegans. Cambrian Heart was commissioned by and is brewed for the Cambrian Mountains Initiative, inspired by the Prince of Wales, which aims to promote and support rural producers and communities in the region.

Irfon Valley Bitter (ABV 3.6%)

Aur Cymru (ABV 3.8%)

Bitter (ABV 4.1%)

Welsh Black (ABV 4.4%) ▮

Cambrian Heart Ale (ABV 4.5%)

Noble Eden Ale (ABV 4.6%)

Inn-stable (ABV 6.8%)

Hebridean

Hebridean Brewing Co, 18a Bells Road, Stornoway, Isle of Lewis, HS1 2RA
☎ (01851) 700123 ✉ info@hebridean-brewery.co.uk ⊕ hebridean-brewery.co.uk
Shop open in summer months only
Tours by arrangement

☺The company was set up in 2001 on a steam powered plant with a 14-barrel brew length. A shop is attached to the brewery. Seasonal beers are produced for Mods, Gaelic festivals that are the Scottish equivalent of the Welsh Eisteddfod.

Celtic Black Ale (OG 1036, ABV 3.9%)

THE BREWERIES

Manor in 2000. In 2007 Highgate was bought by Global Star, a pub group. The brewery closed during 2010 and reopened later the same year as the Highgate & Walsall Brewery Company. The brewery supply Molson Coors with Dark Mild as well as having a contract to brew Smiles beers. Seasonal beers are available.

Davenports Fat Catz (OG 1040, ABV 4%)

Davenports IPA (OG 1040.8, ABV 4%)

Davenports Original (OG 1040, ABV 4%)

Davenports England Glory (OG 1044, ABV 4.4%)

Davenports Fox's Nob (OG 1044, ABV 4.4%)

Davenports Highland Whisky Ale (OG 1044, ABV 4.4%)

Davenports Irish Whiskey Ale (OG 1044, ABV 4.4%)

For Coors:

M&B Mild (OG 1034.8, ABV 3.2%)

For Smiles:

Blonde (OG 1038.8, ABV 3.8%)

Best (OG 1041, ABV 4.1%)

Bristol IPA (OG 1044, ABV 4.4%)

Heritage (OG 1052, ABV 5.2%)

High House Farm SIBA

High House Farm Brewery, Matfen, Newcastle upon Tyne, Tyne & Wear, NE20 0RG
☎ (01661) 886192/886769 (Sales line)
✉ info@highhousefarmbrewery.co.uk
⊕ highhousefarmbrewery.co.uk
Shop Sun-Tue 10.30am-5pm, Thu-Sat 10.30am-9pm, closed Wed
Tours by arrangement

⊠ The brewery was founded in 2003 on a working farm with visitor centre, brewery shop and exhibition and function room. Over 350 outlets are supplied. Seasonal beers: see website.

Auld Hemp (OG 1038, ABV 3.8%) ◆
Tawny coloured ale with hop, malt and fruit flavours and a good bitter finish.

Nel's Best (OG 1041, ABV 4.2%) ◆
Golden hoppy ale full of flavour with a clean, bitter finish.

Matfen Magic (OG 1046.5, ABV 4.8%) ◆
Well-hopped brown ale with a fruity aroma. Malt and chocolate overtones with a rich, bitter finish.

Highland SIBA

Highland Brewing Co Ltd, Swannay Brewery, by Evie, Swannay, Orkney, KW17 2NP
☎ (01856) 721700
✉ info@highlandbrewingcompany.co.uk
⊕ highlandbrewingcompany.co.uk
Tours by arrangement

⊕ Brewing began in 2006 and bigger plant was installed a year later. A visitor centre, café and 20-barrel plant are planned. Around 300 outlets are supplied. Seasonal beers are also available.

Orkney Best (OG 1038, ABV 3.6%) ◆
A refreshing, light-bodied, low gravity golden beer bursting with hop, peach and sweet malt flavours. The long, hoppy finish leaves a dry bitterness.

Island Hopping (OG 1039, ABV 3.9%) ◆
Fruity hoppiness with some caramel. Dry aftertaste.

Dark Munro (OG 1040, ABV 4%) ◆
The nose presents an intense roast hit which is followed by summer fruits in the mouth. The strong roast malt continues into the aftertaste.

Scapa Special (OG 1042, ABV 4.2%)
A good copy of a typical Lancashire bitter, full of bitterness and background hops, leaving your mouth tingling in the lingering aftertaste.

Orkney IPA (OG 1048, ABV 4.8%) ◆
A traditional bitter, with light hop and fruit flavour throughout.

St Magnus Ale (OG 1049, ABV 5.2%) ◆
A complex, tawny bitter with a stunning balance of malt and hop and some soft roast. Full-bodied.

Orkney Blast (OG 1058, ABV 6%) ◆
Plenty of alcohol in this warming strong bitter/barley wine. A mushroom and woody aroma blossoms into a well-balanced smack of malt and hop in the taste.

Highlands & Islands

See Orkney

Highwood (Chelmsford) (NEW)

Cann Do Beers Ltd t/a The Highwood Brewery, Pool's Lane, Highwood, Essex, CM1 3QL
☎ (01245) 249300 ✉ canndobeers@btconnect.com

Brewing began in 2011 using a five-barrel plant. Further beers are planned.

Essex IPA (ABV 3.6%)

Highwood

See Tom Wood (under W)

Hilden SIBA

Hilden Brewing Co, Hilden House, Hilden, Lisburn, Co Antrim, BT27 4TY
☎ (02892) 660800
✉ irishbeers@hildenbrewery.co.uk
⊕ hildenbrewery.co.uk
Shop Tue-Sun 12-2.30pm (3pm Sun) – Taproom Restaurant
Tours by arrangement (Tue-Sat 11.30am & 6.30pm)

⊕ Set up in 1981, Hilden is Ireland's oldest independent brewery. Now in the second generation of the family-owned business, the beers are widely distributed across the UK. Occasional brews plus seasonals are also produced.

Linenhall Special (ABV 3.7%)
A light, hoppy session bitter.

Ale (OG 1038, ABV 4%) ◆
An amber-coloured beer with an aroma of malt, hops and fruit. The balanced taste is slightly slanted towards hops, and hops are also prominent in the full, malty finish.

Scullion's Plain Stout (ABV 4.2%)
Irish stout with a good head and lingering dark malts.

Silver (OG 1042, ABV 4.2%)

A pale ale, light and refreshing on the palate but with a satisfying mellow hop character.

Molly Malone (OG 1045, ABV 4.6%)
Dark ruby-red porter with complex flavours of hop bitterness and chocolate malt.

Scullion's Irish (OG 1045, ABV 4.6%)
A bright amber ale, initially smooth with a slight taste of honey that is balanced by a long, dry aftertaste.

Cathedral Quarter (ABV 5.3%)
A classic red Irish ale with a full-bodied flavour.

Halt (OG 1058, ABV 6.1%)
A premium traditional Irish red ale with a malty, mild hop flavour.

For College Green Brewery:

Molly's Chocolate Stout (OG 1042, ABV 4.2%)
A dark chocolate-coloured beer with a full-bodied character.

Headless Dog (OG 1042, ABV 4.3%)
A well-hopped bright amber ale.

Hill Island SIBA

Michael Griffin t/a Hill Island Brewery, Unit 7, Fowlers Yard, Back Silver Street, Durham, DH1 3RA
☎ 07740 932584 ✉ mike@hillisland.freeserve.co.uk
⏚ myspace.com/hillisland

☺Hill Island is a literal translation of Dunholme from which Durham is derived. The brewery began trading in 2002 and stands by the banks of the Wear in the heart of Durham City. Many of the beers produced have names reflecting local history and heritage. Brews can also be made exclusively for individual pubs. Around 40 outlets are supplied. The brewery is open to visitors one weekend most months for a mini beer festival, during which six different house ales are served. Bottled ales and draught beer can be bought most Saturdays from the brewery's stall in Durham open market. Seasonal beers are also available.

Peninsula Pint (OG 1036.5, ABV 3.7%)
Blonde and hoppy with a zesty aroma.

Bitter (OG 1038, ABV 3.9%)
Red-gold in colour with pronounced caramel notes, balanced with grassy hop aromas.

Dun Cow Bitter (OG 1041, ABV 4.2%)
Golden ale with hints of caramel and citrus hop flavours.

Cathedral Ale (OG 1042, ABV 4.3%)
Ruby red with hints of roast malts and crisp bitterness.

Griffin's Irish Stout (OG 1045, ABV 4.5%)
Black and bitter. Traditional Irish-style stout.

Hillside

See Deeside

Hobden's

See Wessex

Hobsons SIBA

Hobsons Brewery & Co Ltd, Newhouse Farm, Tenbury Road, Cleobury Mortimer, Shropshire, DY14 8RD
☎ (01299) 270837 ✉ beer@hobsons-brewery.co.uk
⏚ hobsons-brewery.co.uk
Shop Mon-Fri 9am-5pm
Tours by arrangement

☺ Established in 1993 in a former sawmill, Hobsons relocated to a farm site with more space in 1995. A second brewery, bottling plant and a warehouse have been added along with significant expansion to the first brewery. It now uses environmentally sustainable technologies where possible. Beers are supplied within a radius of 50 miles and two pubs are owned. Hobsons also brews and bottles for the local tourist attraction, the Severn Valley Railway (Manor Ale, ABV 4.2%). Seasonal and bottle-conditioned beers are also available.

Mild (OG 1034, ABV 3.2%) 🏷 🍴
A classic mild. Complex layers of taste come from roasted malts that predominate and give lots of flavour.

Twisted Spire (OG 1036, ABV 3.6%)
A blond beer with a sweet, floral aroma. The initial sweetness gives way to a burst of hop flavour which lingers through to a crisp, dry finish.

Best Bitter (OG 1038.5, ABV 3.8%) 🍴
A pale brown to amber, medium-bodied beer with strong hop character throughout. It is consequently bitter, but with malt discernible in the taste.

Town Crier (OG 1044, ABV 4.5%) 🍴
An elegant straw-coloured bitter. The hint of sweetness is complemented by subtle hop flavours, leading to a dry finish.

Hoggleys SIBA

Hoggleys Brewery, Unit 12, Litchborough Industrial Estate, Northampton Road, Litchborough, Northamptonshire, NN12 8JB
☎ (01327) 831308 ✉ hoggleys@hotmail.com
⏚ hoggleys.co.uk
Tours by arrangement

⊗ Hoggleys was established in 2002 as a part-time brewery. It expanded to an eight-barrel plant in 2006, became full-time and moved to larger premises. Seasonal and bottle-conditioned beers are also available. Solstice Stout and Mill Lane Mild are suitable for vegans as are all bottle-conditioned beers.

3/6 (OG 1036, ABV 3.6%)

Kislingbury Bitter (OG 1040, ABV 4%)

Mill Lane Mild (OG 1040, ABV 4%)

Northamptonshire Bitter (OG 1040, ABV 4%)

Reservoir Hogs (OG 1042, ABV 4.3%)

Pump Fiction (OG 1045, ABV 4.5%)

Solstice Stout (OG 1050, ABV 5%)

Hogs Back SIBA

Hogs Back Brewery Ltd, Manor Farm, The Street, Tongham, Surrey, GU10 1DE
☎ (01252) 783000 ✉ info@hogsback.co.uk
⏚ hogsback.co.uk
Shop & Visitors' Centre – see website
Tours by arrangement

☺ This traditionally-styled brewery, established in 1992, boasts an extensive range of award-winning ales, brewed from the finest malted barley and whole English hops. The shop sells all the brewery's beers and related merchandise plus over 400 beers and ciders from around the world. Fully guided tours with tastings are available. Over half a million bottles are produced annually for home and export. Seasonal beers: see website.

HBB/Hogs Back Bitter (OG 1039, ABV 3.7%) ◆
An aromatic session beer. Biscuity aroma with some hops and lemon notes. Well-balanced, plenty of hop impact in the mouth with a long-lasting dry, hoppy, bitter aftertaste.

**TEA/Traditional English Ale
(OG 1044, ABV 4.2%)** ◆
A tawny-coloured best bitter with both malt and hops present in the nose. These carry through into a well-rounded flavour with malt slightly dominant and more fruity sweetness than bitterness.

Hop Garden Gold (OG 1048, ABV 4.6%) ◆
Pale golden best bitter. Full-bodied and well-balanced with an aroma of malt, hops and fruit. Hoppy bitterness grows in an increasingly dry aftertaste with a hint of sweetness.

**A Over T/Aromas Over Tongham
(OG 1094, ABV 9%)** ◆
A full-bodied, tawny-coloured barley wine. The malty aroma with hints of vanilla lead to a well-balanced taste where the hops cut through the underlying sweetness and dominate in the finish.

Hogswood SIBA

Hogswood Brewing Co, Higher Goshen, Mithian, St Agnes, Cornwall, TR5 0QE
☎ (01872) 554224 ✉ vaughan@hogswood.com
⊕ hogswood.com

⊠ Hogswood was established in 2009. Five outlets are supplied direct. Seasonal beer is also available.

Stoked (ABV 3.6%)
A light session beer.

Goshen Ale (ABV 4%)
A rich bronze session bitter with a distinctive hoppy aroma combined with a malt taste. A hoppy, bitter finish.

Broken Piston (ABV 4.2%)
Rich malt dominates this copper beer from start to finish. Sweet caramel is balanced by bitterness.

Black Boar (OG 1047, ABV 4.6%)
A dark beer with a powerful malt flavour, hints of dark fruit and sweet roots.

Holden's SIBA IFBB

Holden's Brewery Ltd, Hopden Brewery, George Street, Woodsetton, Dudley, West Midlands, DY1 4LW
☎ (01902) 880051 ✉ holdens.brewery@virgin.net
⊕ holdensbrewery.co.uk
Shop Mon-Fri 9am-5pm; Sat 9-11am
Tours by arrangement

☺ A family brewery spanning four generations, Holden's began life as a brew-pub in the 1920s. The company continues to expand with 20 tied pubs and supplies around 70 other outlets. Plans are in place for the construction of a new brewhouse to cope with demand. Seasonal beers: see website.

Black Country Mild (OG 1037, ABV 3.7%) ◆

A good, red/brown mild; a refreshing, light blend of roast malt, hops and fruit, dominated by malt throughout.

Black Country Bitter (OG 1039, ABV 3.9%) ⌂ ◆
A medium-bodied, golden ale; a light, well-balanced bitter with a subtle, dry, hoppy finish.

XB (OG 1042, ABV 4.1%) ◆
A sweeter, slightly fuller version of the Bitter. Sold in a number of outlets under different names.

Golden Glow (OG 1045, ABV 4.4%)
A pale golden beer with a subtle hop aroma plus gentle sweetness and a light hoppiness.

Special (OG 1052, ABV 5.1%) ◆
A sweet, malty, full-bodied amber ale with hops to balance in the taste and in the good, bittersweet finish.

Holland

Holland Brewery, 5 Browns Flats, Brewery Street, Kimberley, Nottinghamshire, NG16 2JU
☎ (0115) 938 2685
✉ hollandbrew@btopenworld.com

Len Holland, a keen home-brewer for 30 years, went commercial in 2000, in the shadow of now closed Hardys & Hansons. Seasonal beers are also available.

Chocolate Clog (OG 1038, ABV 3.8%)

Golden Blond (OG 1040, ABV 4%)

Lipsmacker (OG 1040, ABV 4%)

Cloghopper (OG 1042, ABV 4.2%)

Double Dutch (OG 1045, ABV 4.5%)

Mad Jack Stout (OG 1045, ABV 4.5%)

Holsworthy (NEW)

Holsworthy Ales, Unit 5, Circuit Business Park, Clawton, Holsworthy, Devon, EX22 6RR
☎ (01566) 783678 ☎ 07879 401073
✉ dave@holsworthyales.co.uk
⊕ holsworthyales.co.uk

Holsworthy began brewing in 2011 using a six-barrel plant. Further beers are planned.

Tamar Sauce (ABV 4.1%)

Holt IFBB

Joseph Holt Ltd, The Brewery, Empire Street, Cheetham, Manchester, M3 1JD
☎ (0161) 834 3285 ⊕ joseph-holt.com
Shop Mon-Fri 9am-4pm

The brewery was established in 1849 by Joseph Holt and his wife Catherine. It is still a family-run business in the hands of the great, great-grandson of the founder. Joseph Holt supplies approximately 100 outlets as well as its own estate of 129 tied pubs. A dedicated 30-barrel brew plant is used for seasonal beers: see website. Fewer and fewer Holts pubs are dispensing cask Mild since the introduction of Keg Black.

Mild (OG 1033, ABV 3.2%) ◆
A dark brown/red beer with a fruity, malty nose. Roast, malt, fruit and hops in the taste, with strong bitterness for a mild, and a dry malt and hops finish.

IPA (ABV 3.8%)

A fresh-tasting, traditional golden IPA with a good floral hop aroma.

Bitter (OG 1040, ABV 4%) ◆
Copper-coloured beer with malt and hops in the aroma. Malt, hops and fruit in the taste with a bitter and hoppy finish.

Hook Norton SIBA IFBB

Hook Norton Brewery Co Ltd, The Brewery, Brewery Lane, Scotland End, Hook Norton, Oxfordshire, OX15 5NY
☎ (01608) 737210 ✉ info@hook-norton-brewery.co.uk ⊕ hooky.co.uk
Visitor Centre & Shop Mon-Fri 9am-5pm; Sat & summer bank hols 9.30am-4.30pm
Tours by arrangement (01608 730384)

⊗ Hook Norton was founded in 1849 by John Harris, a farmer and maltster. The current premises were built in 1900 and Hook Norton is one of the finest examples of a Victorian tower brewery. A 25hp steam engine, which was used for most of its motive power, now only operates occasionally. Hook Norton owns 47 pubs and supplies approximately 300 free trade accounts. Seasonal beers: see website. Bottle-conditioned beers are also available.

Hooky Dark (OG 1033, ABV 3.2%) ◆
A chestnut brown, easy-drinking mild. A complex malt and hop aroma give way to a well-balanced taste, leading to a long, hoppy finish that is unusual for a mild.

Hooky Bitter (OG 1036, ABV 3.6%) ◆
A classic golden session bitter. Hoppy and fruity aroma followed by a malt and hops taste and a continuing hoppy finish.

Hooky Gold (OG 1042, ABV 4.1%)
A golden, crisp beer with a citrus aroma and a fruity, rounded body.

Old Hooky (OG 1048, ABV 4.6%) ◆
A strong bitter, tawny in colour. A well-rounded fruity taste with a balanced bitter finish.

Hop Back SIBA

Hop Back Brewery plc, Units 22-24, Batten Road Industrial Estate, Downton, Salisbury, Wiltshire, SP5 3HU
☎ (01725) 510986 ✉ info@hopback.co.uk
⊕ hopback.co.uk

⊗ Started by John Gilbert in 1987 at the Wyndham Arms in Salisbury, the brewery has expanded steadily ever since. It went public via a Business Expansion Scheme in 1993 and has enjoyed rapid continued growth. Summer Lightning has won many awards. The brewery has 11 tied houses and also sells to some 500 other outlets. Seasonal beers are produced on a monthly basis. Entire Stout is suitable for vegans. Bottle-conditioned beers are also produced.

GFB/Gilbert's First Brew (OG 1035, ABV 3.5%) ◆
A golden beer, with a light, clean quality that makes it an ideal session ale. A hoppy aroma and taste lead to a good, dry finish.

Odyssey (OG 1040, ABV 4%)
A darker bitter with toasted malty overtones from the use of three dark malts in the recipe.

Crop Circle (OG 1041, ABV 4.2%) ◆

A refreshingly sharp and hoppy summer beer. Gold coloured with a slight citrus taste. The crisp, dry aftertaste lingers. A dry hopped version is called Spring Zing.

Taiphoon (OG 1041, ABV 4.2%)
A light gold speciality beer flavoured with lemongrass.

Entire Stout (OG 1043, ABV 4.5%) 🍷 🍴 ◆
A rich, dark stout with a strong roasted malt flavour and a long, sweet and malty aftertaste.

Summer Lightning (OG 1048, ABV 5%) ◆
A pleasurable pale bitter with a good, fresh, hoppy aroma and a malty, hoppy flavour. Finely balanced, it has an intense bitterness leading to a long, dry finish.

Hop Me Up

See Sleaford

Hopdaemon SIBA

Hopdaemon Brewery Co Ltd, Unit 1, Parsonage Farm, Seed Road, Newnham, Kent, ME9 0NA
☎ (01795) 892078 ✉ info@hopdaemon.com
⊕ hopdaemon.com
Tours by arrangement

⊗ Tonie Prins originally started brewing in Tyler Hill near Canterbury in 2000 and moved to the present site in 2005. The brewery supplies more than 100 outlets and is working at full capacity. Bottled beers are mostly contract bottled to keep up with demand and are no longer bottle conditioned.

Golden Braid (OG 1039, ABV 3.7%) 🍴 ◆
A refreshing golden session bitter with a good blend of bittering and aroma hops underpinned by pale malt.

Incubus (OG 1041, ABV 4%) ◆
A well-balanced, copper-hued best bitter. Pale malt and a hint of crystal malt are blended with bitter and slightly floral hops to give a lingering hoppy finish.

Skrimshander IPA (OG 1045, ABV 4.5%)
An aromatic copper-coloured pale ale with a fruity finish.

Green Daemon (OG 1048, ABV 5%)
A golden beer with tropical fruit aromas and a crisp, clean finish. Brewed in the style of a Bavarian Helles.

Dominator (OG 1050, ABV 5.1%)

Leviathan (OG 1057, ABV 6%)
A strong ruby ale with spicy hop aromas and a rich, malty finish.

Hope Valley (NEW)

Hope Valley Brewing Company Ltd, Castleton Youth Hostel, Castle Street, Castleton, Derbyshire, S33 8WG

Beers were first seen in 2009. The location is a brewing school and it does not produce beer commercially. However beers sometimes appear at beer festivals. The two-barrel plant was formerly used by Edale.

Dovedale (OG 1044, ABV 4.4%)
A copper bitter with a crisp finish.

Hairy Helmet (OG 1047, ABV 4.7%)
Pale bitter, well hopped but with a sweet finish.
Ginger Helmet is the same beer with ginger.

Bespoke (OG 1050, ABV 5%)
Full-bodied, well-rounded premium bitter.

Scary Hairy (ABV 5.9%)

Leeds SIBA IFBB

Leeds Brewery Co Ltd, 3 Sydenham Road, Leeds, West Yorkshire, LS11 9RU
☎ (0113) 244 5866 ✉ sales@leedsbrewery.co.uk
⊕ leedsbrewery.co.uk
Tours by arrangement

☺Leeds Brewery began production in 2007 using a 20-barrel plant. It is the largest independent brewer in the city and uses a unique strain of yeast originally used by another, now defunct, West Yorkshire brewery. Four pubs are owned and around 300 outlets are supplied direct. Seasonal beers: see website. See also Brewery Tap.

Pale (OG 1037.5, ABV 3.8%) ◣
Well-balanced light ale, citrus in both aroma and flavour. Gold in colour with a refreshing bitter, hoppy finish.

Yorkshire Gold (ABV 4.2%)
A golden ale with a well-balanced, bitter finish.

Best (OG 1041, ABV 4.3%) ◣
A full flavoured, moderately hoppy beer, balanced with malt, leading to a slightly hoppy, lingering bitter aftertaste.

Midnight Bell (OG 1047.5, ABV 4.8%) 🍷 🍴 ◣
A malty, rich, fruity aroma carries through in the taste along with touches of chocolate and vanilla. Sweetness and roast malt flavours linger. Deep red, almost black in colour.

Leek

Staffordshire Brewing Ltd t/a Leek Brewery, Unit 2a, Churnet Court, Cheddleton, Staffordshire, ST13 7EF
☎ (01538) 361919 ☎ 07971 808370
✉ leekbrewery@hotmail.com
⊕ beersandcheese.co.uk
Shop Mon-Fri 9am-5pm
Tours by arrangement

⊗ Brewing started in 2002 with a 4.5-barrel plant located behind the owner's house, before moving to Cheddleton in 2004. The brewery upgraded to a six-barrel plant in 2007 and to a 20-barrel plant in 2010. In recent years the brewery has concentrated on producing bottle-conditioned beers but the new upgrade means that cask-conditioned beers will be regularly available again. A range of beer cheeses is made in the dairy, next door to the brewery.

Staffordshire Gold (OG 1035, ABV 3.8%) ◣
Light, straw-coloured with a pleasing hoppy aroma and a hint of malt. Bitter finish from the hops, making it easily drunk and thirst-quenching.

Danebridge IPA (OG 1038, ABV 4.1%) ◣
Full fruit and hop aroma. Flowery hop start with a bitter taste. Finish of hops and flowers.

Staffordshire Bitter (OG 1040, ABV 4.2%) ◣
Amber with a fruity aroma. Malty and hoppy start with the hoppy finish diminishing quickly.

Black Grouse (OG 1042, ABV 4.5%)

Hen Cloud (OG 1042, ABV 4.5%)

St Edwards (OG 1043, ABV 4.7%)

Rudyard Ruby (OG 1044, ABV 4.8%)

Double Sunset (OG 1050, ABV 5.2%)

Rocheberg Blonde (OG 1052, ABV 5.6%)

Lees IFBB

J W Lees & Co (Brewers) Ltd, Greengate Brewery, Middleton Junction, Manchester, M24 2AX
☎ (0161) 643 2487 ✉ mail@jwlees.co.uk
⊕ jwlees.co.uk
Tours by arrangement

☺ Lees is a family-owned brewery founded in 1828 by John Lees and run by the sixth generation of the family. Brewing takes place in the 1876 brewhouse designed and built by John Willie Lees, the grandson of the founder. The current head brewer is a family member. The brewhouse has been completely modernised in recent years to give greater flexibility. The company has a tied estate of around 180 pubs, mostly in North Manchester, with 30 in North Wales; almost all serve cask beer. Seasonal beers are brewed four times a year.

Brewer's Dark (OG 1032, ABV 3.5%) ◣
Formerly GB Mild, this is a dark brown beer with a malt and caramel aroma. Creamy mouthfeel, with malt, caramel and fruit flavours and a malty finish. Becoming rare.

Bitter (OG 1037, ABV 4%) ◣
Copper-coloured beer with malt and fruit in aroma, taste and finish.

Scorcher (OG 1039, ABV 4%)

Coronation Street (OG 1042, ABV 4.2%)
First brewed in 2009, the name is licensed to Lees by ITV.

John Willie's (OG 1041, ABV 4.5%)
A well-balanced, full-bodied premium bitter.

Moonraker (OG 1073, ABV 7.5%) ◣
A reddish-brown beer with a strong, malty, fruity aroma. The flavour is rich and sweet, with roast malt, and the finish is fruity yet dry. Available only in a handful of outlets.

Leila Cottage SIBA

🍺 Leila Cottage Brewery, Countryman, Chapel Road, Ingoldmells, Skegness, Lincolnshire, PE25 1ND
☎ (01754) 872268
✉ countryman_inn@btconnect.com
⊕ countryman-ingoldmells.co.uk
Tours by arrangement

⊗ Leila Cottage started brewing in 2007 using a 0.5-barrel plant, which was upgraded in 2009 to a 2.5-barrel one. The brewery is situated at the Countryman pub – Leila Cottage was the original name of the building before it became a licensed club and more recently a pub. The brewery now owns its own bottling line meaning that all beers are also available bottle conditioned including seasonals.

Ace Ale (OG 1040, ABV 3.8%)

Leith Hill

▤ Leith Hill Brewery, c/o Plough Inn, Coldharbour Lane, Coldharbour, Surrey, RH5 6HD
☎ (01306) 711793 ✉ theploughinn@btinternet.com
🌐 ploughinn.com
Tours by arrangement

⊗ Leith Hill was established in 1996 using home-made equipment to produce nine-gallon brews in a room at the front of the pub. The brewery moved to converted storerooms at the rear of the Plough Inn in 2001 and increased capacity to 2.5-barrels in 2005. All beers brewed are sold only on the premises.

Beautiful South (OG 1036, ABV 3.6%)
A session beer with some hop and malt character.

Crooked Furrow (OG 1040, ABV 4%) ◆
A malty beer, with some balancing hop bitterness. Pale brown in colour with an earthy malty aroma and a long, dry and bittersweet aftertaste. Some fruit is also present throughout.

Tallywhacker (OG 1048, ABV 4.8%) ◆
Dark, sweet and fruity old ale with good roast malt character.

Leyden SIBA

▤ Leyden Brewing Ltd, Lord Raglan, Walmersley Old Road, Nangreaves, Greater Manchester, BL9 6SP
☎ (0161) 764 6680 🌐 lordraglannangreaves.co.uk
Tours by arrangement

☺ The brewery was built by Brian Farnworth and started production in 1999. Additional fermenting vessels have been installed, allowing a maximum production of 12 barrels a week. One pub is owned and 30 outlets are supplied. In addition to the permanent beers, a number of seasonal and occasional beers are brewed.

Balaclava (OG 1040, ABV 3.8%)

Black Pudding (OG 1040, ABV 3.8%)
A dark brown, creamy mild with a malty flavour, followed by a balanced finish.

Nanny Flyer (OG 1040, ABV 3.8%)
A drinkable session bitter with an initial dryness, and a hint of citrus, followed by a strong, malty finish.

Light Brigade (OG 1043, ABV 4.2%) ◆
Copper in colour with a citrus aroma. The flavour is a balance of malt, hops and fruit, with a bitter finish.

Rammy Rocket (OG 1042, ABV 4.2%)

Forever Bury (OG 1047, ABV 4.5%)

Raglan Sleeve (OG 1047, ABV 4.6%) ◆
Dark red/brown beer with a hoppy aroma and a dry, roasty, hoppy taste and finish.

Crowning Glory (OG 1068, ABV 6.8%)

Liberation

Liberation Brewery, Tregear House, Longueville Road, St Saviour, Jersey, JE2 7WF
☎ (01534) 764089 ✉ paulhurley@victor-hugo-ltd.com 🌐 liberationgroup.com
Tours by arrangement

☺ Following the closure of the original brewery in Ann Street in 2004, the brewery is now located in an old soft drinks factory using a 40-barrel plant.

Formerly known as the Jersey Brewery it was renamed in 2010 to the Liberation Brewery following its sale to the Liberation Group. Its flagship beer, Liberation Ale, is now regularly seen on the UK mainland. 66 pubs are owned with around two-thirds of these serving cask ale. Seasonal beers are brewed on the five-barrel plant formerly at the Tipsy Toad Brewery.

Liberation Ale (OG 1039, ABV 4%)
Golden beer with a hint of citrus on the nose.

Lichfield

Lichfield Brewery Co Ltd, Lichfield, Staffordshire
✉ robsondavidb@hotmail.com

Does not brew; beers mainly contracted by Tower Brewery (qv).

Linfit

▤ Linfit Brewery, Sair Inn, 139 Lane Top, Linthwaite, Huddersfield, West Yorkshire, HD7 5SG
☎ (01484) 842370

A 19th-century brew-pub that started brewing again in 1982. The beer is only available at the Sair Inn. English Guineas is suitable for vegetarians and vegans. Due to a serious fire in 2011 the brewery temporarily ceased operations.

Bitter (OG 1035, ABV 3.7%) ◆
A refreshing session beer. A dry-hopped aroma leads to a clean-tasting, hoppy bitterness, then a long, bitter finish with a hint of malt.

Gold Medal (OG 1040, ABV 4.2%)
Very pale and hoppy. Use of the dwarf variety of English hops, First Gold, gives an aromatic and fruity character.

Special (OG 1041, ABV 4.3%) ◆
Dry-hopping provides the aroma for this rich and mellow bitter, which has a very soft profile and character: it fills the mouth with texture rather than taste. Clean, rounded finish.

Swift (OG 1041, ABV 4.3%)

Autumn Gold (OG 1045, ABV 4.7%) ◆
Straw-coloured best bitter with hop and fruit aromas, then the bittersweetness of autumn fruit in the taste and the finish.

English Guineas (OG 1045, ABV 4.7%)

Old Eli (OG 1050, ABV 5.3%)
A well-balanced premium bitter with a dry-hop aroma and a fruity, bitter finish.

Leadboiler (OG 1063, ABV 6.6%)

Lion's Tale SIBA

▤ Lion's Tale Brewery, Red Lion, High Street, Cheswardine, Shropshire, TF9 2RS
☎ (01630) 661234 ✉ cheslion96@yahoo.co.uk

The building that houses the brewery was purpose-built in 2005 and houses a 2.5-barrel plant. Jon Morris and his wife have owned the Red Lion pub since 1996. Seasonal beers are also available.

Blooming Blonde (OG 1041, ABV 4.1%)

Lionbru (OG 1041, ABV 4.1%)

Chesbrewnette (OG 1045, ABV 4.5%)

Bamboozle (OG 1049.5, ABV 4.8%) ◆
Full-bodied and well balanced. Distinctive bittersweet flavour with hop and caramel to accompany.

Forbury Lion (OG 1056, ABV 5.5%)
A malty IPA with a strong complex hop finish.

For AVS Wholesale:

Gravesend Shrimpers (OG 1042.8, ABV 4.1%)

Long Lane (NEW)

Long Lane Brewery, Matchless Home Brewing, 32 Belvoir Road, Coalville, Leicestershire, LE67 3PN
☎ (01530) 813800

This small 100-litre brewery was established in 2010 and is based in the Matchless Homebrew shop. Beers are mostly bottle-conditioned but cask beers can be produced to order.

Loose Cannon SIBA

Loose Cannon Brewery, Unit 6, Suffolk Way, Abingdon, Oxfordshire, OX14 5JX
☎ (01235) 531141 ✉ will@lcbeers.co.uk
⊕ lcbeers.co.uk
Shop Mon-Sat 9am-5pm

Loose Cannon began production in 2010 using a 15-barrel brew plant. Owner and head brewer Will Laithwaite previously worked at Rebellion Brewery.

Abingdon Bridge (OG 1041, ABV 4.1%)
Full-flavoured and smooth with well-rounded bitterness and a light citrus and floral finish.

Lord Conrad's

Lord Conrad's Brewery, Unit 21, Dry Drayton Industrial Estate, Scotland Road, Dry Drayton, Cambridgeshire, CB23 8AT
☎ 07736 739700 ✉ lordconrads@gmail.com
⊕ lordconradsbrewery.co.uk

⊗ Lord Conrad's began commercial brewing in 2011 using a 2.5-barrel plant. Beer festivals and local outlets are supplied. Seasonal and bottle-conditioned beers are also available.

3 Villages (ABV 3.8%)

Conkerwood (ABV 4.5%)

Pheasant's Rise (ABV 5%)

Lovibonds

Lovibonds Brewery Ltd, Rear of 19-21 Market Place, Henley-on-Thames, Oxfordshire, RG9 2AA
☎ (01491) 576596 ✉ info@lovibonds.com
⊕ lovibonds.com
Shop Fri 3-8pm; Sat 11am-5pm; Sun 11am-4pm
Tours by arrangement

Lovibonds Brewery was founded by Jeff Rosenmeier in 2005 and is named after Joseph William Lovibond, who invented the Tintometer to measure beer colour. Brewing takes place on the Old Luxters Brewery plant (qv), 5 miles from Henley-on-Thames. Only test brewing takes place in Henley. Beers are only available bottled or in mini kegs.

Loweswater

See Cumbrian Legendary Ales

Luckie

Luckie Ales, c/o 14 Kingsmill Drive, Kennoway, Fife, KY8 5LX
☎ (01333) 352801 ✉ info@luckie-ales.com
⊕ luckie-ales.com

Luckie Ales was established in 2009. Beer is brewed at an unnamed Scottish brewery.

Midnycht Myld (OG 1037, ABV 3.4%)

Amber Ale (OG 1040, ABV 3.7%)

80/- (OG 1056, ABV 5%)

19th Century IPA (ABV 6.5%)

Edinburgh Export Stout (ABV 7.5%)

Edinburgh 68/- (ABV 8.5%)

Ludlow SIBA

Ludlow Brewing Co Ltd, The Railway Shed, Station Drive, Ludlow, Shropshire, SY8 2PQ
☎ (01584) 873291
✉ gary@theludlowbrewingcompany.co.uk
⊕ theludlowbrewingcompany.co.uk
Shop Mon-Fri 10am-5pm; Sat 10am-2pm
Tours by arrangement

⊗ The brewery opened in 2006 in a renovated malthouse. During 2010 a move to larger premises, a former railway sidings shed on the same site, took place. In addition a new 20-barrel plant was installed. The premises also functions as the brewery tap and a visitor centre. Bottle-conditioned beer is also available.

Best (ABV 3.7%)

Gold (ABV 4.2%)

Black Knight (ABV 4.5%)

Boiling Well (ABV 4.7%)

Stairway (ABV 5%)

Lymestone SIBA

Lymestone Brewery Ltd, The Old Brewery, Mount Road, Stone, Staffordshire, ST15 8LL
☎ (01785) 817796 ☎ 07891 782652
✉ brad@lymestonebrewery.co.uk
⊕ lymestonebrewery.co.uk
Shop Mon-Fri 8am-5pm, Sat & Sun by arrangement
Tours by arrangement

☺Lymestone commenced brewing in 2008 on a 10-barrel brew plant and has since doubled fermenting capacity. 300 outlets are supplied direct with beer also being available via wholesalers.

Stone Cutter (OG 1038, ABV 3.7%) ◆
Sulphurous aroma gives way to a caramel sweet start and pleasing hop and fruit balance. The mouth-watering hoppy promise is fulfilled in to the finish.

Stone Faced (OG 1042, ABV 4%)
Subtle citrus and toffee flavours balanced by a hoppy aroma and bitter finish.

Foundation Stone (OG 1047, ABV 4.5%) ◆

An IPA-style beer with pale and crystal malts. Faint biscuit and chewy, juicy fruits burst on to the palate then the spicy Boadicea and Pilot hops pepper the taste buds to leave a dry bitter finish.

Ein Stein (OG 1052, ABV 5%)
A continental-style blonde ale. Biscuit malts give way to a fresh hop aftertaste.

Stone The Crows (OG 1056, ABV 5.4%) ◆
A rich dark beer from chocolate malts. Fruit, roasts and hops abound to leave a deep lingering bitterness from the Styrian Goldings and Millennium hop mix.

Lytham SIBA

Lytham Brewery Ltd, Unit 8, Campbells Court, Lord Street, Lytham St Annes, Lancashire, FY8 5HU
☎ (01253) 737707 ✉ info@lythambrewery.co.uk
⊕ lythambrewery.co.uk
Tours by arrangement

Lytham started brewing in 2008 at the Hastings Club in Lytham but moved to larger premises soon after due to demand. The brewery originally used a 2.5-barrel plant which was upgraded to a 10-barrel plant in 2010. The brewery burnt down in May 2011 and has moved to its present address. The 2.5-barrel plant was salvaged and brewing has recommenced with eight new fermenters and six new conditioning tanks.

Amber (OG 1037, ABV 3.6%)
A traditional malty beer using English hops.

Blonde (OG 1038, ABV 3.8%)
A pale golden beer with a subtle hop aroma and a smooth, dry finish.

Gold (OG 1042, ABV 4.2%)
A golden beer with a fruity aroma and lasting bitter finish.

Royal (OG 1044, ABV 4.4%)
A full-bodied English ale with a crisp fruity aroma and a smooth, dry finish.

Dark (OG 1047, ABV 5%)
Dark chocolate malt with a hint of vanilla and a smooth, dry finish.

IPA (OG 1054, ABV 5.6%)
A pale bitter with a fresh, sweet, hoppy flavour leading to a long, dry finish.

McGivern

McGivern Ales, c/o The Bridge End Inn, 5 Bridge Street, Ruabon, LL14 6DA
☎ (01978) 810881 ☎ 07891 676614
✉ mcgivernmatt@hotmail.com
⊕ mcgivernales.co.uk

☺The brewery was established in early 2008 and is based at the brewer's home in Wrexham but will move in 2011 to the Bridge End Inn in Ruabon. Bottle-conditioned beers are available occasionally.

Amber Ale (OG 1040, ABV 4%)

Cascade Pale Ale (ABV 4%)

Crest Pale (OG 1041, ABV 4%)

Stout (OG 1042, ABV 4.2%)

Porter (ABV 4.5%)

McGuinness

See Offa's Dyke

McLaughlin

See Camden

McMullen SIBA IFBB

McMullen & Sons Ltd, 26 Old Cross, Hertford, Hertfordshire, SG14 1RD
☎ (01992) 584911 ✉ contact@mcmullens.co.uk
⊕ mcmullens.co.uk

⊠ McMullen is Hertfordshire's oldest independent brewery, celebrating 185 years of brewing in 2012. A new brewhouse opened in 2006, giving the company greater flexibility to produce its regular cask beers and up to eight seasonal beers a year. Cask beer is served in all 140 pubs.

AK (OG 1035, ABV 3.7%) ◆
A pleasant mix of malt and hops leads to a distinctive, dry aftertaste that isn't always as pronounced as it used to be.

Cask Ale (OG 1039, ABV 3.8%)
A light and refreshing beer marked by the use of Styrian Goldings and English Fuggle hops.

Country Bitter (OG 1042, ABV 4.3%) ⊓ ▮ ◆
A full-bodied beer with a well-balanced mix of malt, hops and fruit throughout.

IPA (OG 1047, ABV 4.8%)
A strong bitter with deep rich flavours created with specially kilned amber malts.

Maclay

See Greene King in New Nationals section

Madcap

Madcap Brewery Ltd, Unit 3, Broadmeadow Industrial Estate, Ecclefechan, Dumfriesshire, DG11 3LG
☎ (01461) 203495 ☎ 07801 699161

Registered Office: Greenknowe Avenue, Annan, Dumfriesshire, DG12 6ER
✉ john@madcapbrewery.com
⊕ madcapbrewery.com
Tours by arrangement

Madcap Brewery started production in 2009 using a one-barrel plant in a small outbuilding at the rear of the family home. In 2010 the brewery moved to its present address with a new five-barrel plant. Seasonal and bottle-conditioned beers are also available. All bottle-conditioned beers are also available cask-conditioned upon request: see website for details.

Fechan Ale (ABV 5%)

Magic Rock (NEW)

Magic Rock Brewing Co Ltd, The Bed Factory, Quarmby Mills, Tanyard Road, Oakes, Huddersfield, West Yorkshire, HD3 4YP
☎ (01484) 649823 ✉ sales@magicrockbrewing.com
⊕ magicrockbrewing.com
Tours by arrangement

☺Magic Rock began brewing in 2011 in the Old Bed Factory attached to the Rockshop Wholesale Company in Huddersfield. The brewery developed from the online myBrewerytap.com business. Bottle-conditioned beers are available.

Curious (ABV 3.9%)

Rapture (ABV 4.5%)

Highwire (ABV 5.5%)

Magpie SIBA

Magpie Brewery, Unit 4, Ashling Court, Ashling Street, Nottingham, NG2 3JA
☎ 07738 762897 ✉ info@magpiebrewery.com
⊕ magpiebrewery.com

☺ Magpie is a six-barrel brewery launched in 2006. It is located a few feet from the perimeter of the Meadow Lane Stadium, home of Notts County FC (the Magpies) from which the brewery name naturally derived. Seasonal and occasional beers: see website.

Fledgling (OG 1035.9, ABV 3.8%) ◆
A hoppy and bitter golden ale.

Best (OG 1040.7, ABV 4.2%) ◆
A malty traditional pale brown best bitter, with balancing hops giving a bitter finish.

Thieving Rogue (OG 1042, ABV 4.5%) ◆
A hoppy golden ale with a long-lasting, bitter finish.

Monty's Firkin (OG 1043, ABV 4.6%) ◆
A well-balanced premium amber best bitter. Originally brewed for the Queen Adelaide in Nottingham, and named after the pub dog.

Midnight Porter (OG 1049.4, ABV 5%)

Home IPA (OG 1047.5, ABV 5.2%)

JPA (Jackson Pale Ale) (OG 1048.6, ABV 5.2%)

Maldon

See Farmer's Ales

Mallard SIBA

Mallard Brewery, Unit A, Maythorne, Nottinghamshire, NG25 0RS
☎ (01636) 812365 ☎ 07811 193930
✉ stevenhussey@tiscali.co.uk
Tours by arrangement

☺ Phil Mallard built and installed a two-barrel plant in a shed at his home and started brewing in 1995. The brewery was taken over in 2010 and moved to its current address. There are plans to expand the plant, increase the range of beers and introduce bottle-conditioned ales.

Duck 'n' Dive (OG 1039, ABV 3.7%) ◆
A bitter, pale golden beer, with a dry finish. Brewed with First Gold hops.

Quacker Jack (OG 1040, ABV 4%)

Feather Light (OG 1040, ABV 4.1%) ◆
A straw-coloured lager style beer with a hoppy taste and aroma.

Duckling (OG 1041, ABV 4.2%) ◆
A dry-hopped, golden ale. Very bitter; hops dominate in the aroma and aftertaste.

Webbed Wheat (OG 1043, ABV 4.3%)

A wheat beer with a fruity, hoppy nose and taste.

Spittin' Feathers (OG 1044, ABV 4.4%) ◆
A mellow, malty, reddish-brown bitter with a slightly sweet and fruity taste.

Drake (OG 1045, ABV 4.5%)
A full-bodied premium bitter, with malt and hops on the palate, and a fruity finish.

Duck 'n' Disorderly (OG 1050, ABV 5%)

Friar Duck (OG 1050, ABV 5%)
A pale, full malt beer, hoppy with a hint of blackcurrant flavour.

Mallinsons

Mallinsons Brewing Co, Plover Road Garage, Plover Road, Huddersfield, West Yorkshire, HD3 3HS
☎ (01484) 654301 ✉ info@drinkmallinsons.co.uk
⊕ drinkmallinsons.co.uk

☺The brewery was set up in early 2008 on a six-barrel plant in a former garage by CAMRA member Tara Mallinson. A range of one-off specials is brewed along with bottle-conditioned beers.

Emley Moor Mild (ABV 3.4%)
Black with a ruby hint. A full-bodied mild with a nutty taste and slightly bitter finish.

Stadium Bitter (ABV 3.8%)
Straw-coloured with a clean, bitter taste and dry, fruity finish.

Station Best Bitter (ABV 4.2%)
An amber-coloured best bitter with a balance of malt and fruity hops.

Castle Hill Premium (ABV 4.6%)
A golden-coloured premium bitter, hoppy with citrus tones.

Malt B

≣ Malt B Brewing Co, Crown Inn, Beesby Road, Maltby le Marsh, Lincolnshire, LN13 0JJ
☎ (01507) 450100 ✉ nigelwalpole007@o2.co.uk
⊕ thecrowninnmaltby.co.uk
Tours by arrangement

Malt B started brewing in early 2008. Until the 1970s the building that houses the brewery was an outside toilet, hence some beer names incorporate toilet humour. Seasonal beers are also available.

P.E.A. (Proper English Ale) (OG 1037, ABV 3.6%)

Old Reliable (OG 1042, ABV 4.2%)

Regal Flush (OG 1042, ABV 4.3%)

Smarty's Night Porter (OG 1045, ABV 4.5%)

Malvern Hills SIBA

Malvern Hills Brewery Ltd, 15 West Malvern Road, Malvern, Worcestershire, WR14 4ND
☎ (01684) 560165 ✉ beer@tiscali.co.uk
⊕ malvernhillsbrewery.co.uk
Tours by arrangement

Founded in 1998 in an old quarrying dynamite store and now an established presence in the Three Counties, Birmingham and the Black Country. Limited use of wholesalers can spread the ales further afield. The core beers are supplemented by a rolling programme of monthly specials. 2011 saw the first steps taken into bottling with plans for significant future growth in this area.

Santler (OG 1036, ABV 3.6%)

Feelgood (OG 1038, ABV 3.8%)

Swedish Nightingale (OG 1040, ABV 4%)

Priessnitz Plzen (OG 1043, ABV 4.3%)
A mix of soft fruit and citrus give this straw-coloured brew its quaffability, making it ideal for quenching summer thirsts.

Black Pear (OG 1044, ABV 4.4%)
A sharp citrus hoppiness is the main constituent of this golden brew that has a long, dry aftertaste.

Mansfield

See Marston's in New Nationals section

Marble SIBA

Marble Beers Ltd, 73 Rochdale Road, Manchester, M4 4HY
☎ (0161) 819 2694
✉ thebrewers_marblebeers@msn.com
Tours by arrangement

☺ Marble opened at the Marble Arch Inn in 1997 and produces organic and vegan beers as well as some non-organic ales. It is registered with the Soil Association and the Vegetarian Society. Marble currently owns four pubs and supplies around 10 outlets. In 2009 a second, 12-barrel plant was installed at Unit 41, Williamson Street, Manchester. All brewing now takes place at this site. A number of bottle-conditioned beers are available as well as regular seasonals.

Pint (OG 1038.5, ABV 3.9%)
A pale, dry and extremely hoppy beer.

Dobber (OG 1057, ABV 4%)

Manchester Bitter (OG 1042, ABV 4.2%)
Yellow beer with a fruity and hoppy aroma. Hops, fruit and bitterness on the palate and in the finish.

JP Best (OG 1043, ABV 4.3%)
Pale tawny in colour. Hoppy with a good malt balance, assertively bitter.

Ginger (OG 1046, ABV 4.5%)
Intense and complex. Full-bodied and fiery with a sharp, snappy bite.

Stouter Stout (OG 1048, ABV 4.7%)
Black in colour, with roast malt dominating the aroma. Roast malt and hops in the mouth, with a little fruit. Pleasant, dry, bitter aftertaste.

Lagonda IPA (OG 1047.5, ABV 5%)
Golden yellow beer with a spicy, fruity nose. Fruit, hops and malt in the mouth, with a dry fruitiness continuing into the bitter aftertaste.

Chocolate Marble (OG 1054.5, ABV 5.5%)
A strong, stout-like ale.

Marlpool

Marlpool Brewing Co Ltd, 5 Breach Road, Marlpool, Heanor, Derbyshire, DE75 7NJ
☎ (01773) 711285 5118
✉ enquiries@marlpoolbrewing.co.uk
⊕ marlpoolbrewing.co.uk
Shop – see website for opening hours
Tours by arrangement

Marlpool was set up in 2010 using a 2.5-barrel plant situated in an old slaughterhouse. It operates on a part-time basis and supplies local pubs within a 10-mile radius of the brewery. Although next to the Queens Head pub it is completely independent.

Otters Pocket (OG 1040, ABV 4%)
An easy-drinking, smooth amber ale.

Stratty Ratty (OG 1044, ABV 4.4%)
A pale ale, lightly hopped with a bitter, dry finish.

Marston Moor

Marston Moor Brewery Ltd, PO Box 9, York, North Yorkshire, YO26 7XW
☎ (01423) 359641
✉ info@marstonmoorbrewery.co.uk
⊕ rudgatebrewery.co.uk

☺ Established in 1983 in Kirk Hammerton, the brewery had a re-investment programme in 2005, moving brewing operations to nearby Tockwith, where it shares the site with Rudgate Brewery (qv). Two special beers are available each month. Around 250 outlets are supplied.

Cromwell's Pale (OG 1036, ABV 3.8%)
A golden beer with hops and fruit in strong evidence on the nose. Bitterness as well as fruit and hops dominate the taste and long aftertaste.

Matchlock Mild (OG 1038, ABV 4%)
Traditional, full-flavoured dark mild.

Mongrel (OG 1038, ABV 4%)
A balanced bitter with plenty of fruit character.

Fairfax Special (OG 1039, ABV 4.2%)
A full-bodied premium bitter, pale in colour with a well-balanced slightly citrus aroma.

Merriemaker (OG 1042, ABV 4.5%)
A premium straw-coloured ale with a typical Yorkshire taste.

Brewers Droop (OG 1045.5, ABV 5%)
A powerful golden ale with a sweet taste.

Marston's

See Marston's in New Nationals section

Matthews

See Dawkins

Mauldons SIBA EAB

Mauldons Ltd, Black Adder Brewery, 13 Church Field Road, Sudbury, Suffolk, CO10 2YA
☎ (01787) 311055 ✉ sims@mauldons.co.uk
⊕ mauldons.co.uk
Shop Mon-Fri 9.30am-4pm
Tours by arrangement

☒ The Mauldon family started brewing in Sudbury in 1795. The brewery with 26 pubs was bought by Greene King in the 1960s. The current business, established in 1982, was bought by Steve and Alison Sims – both former employees of Adnams – in 2000. They relocated to a new brewery in 2005, with a 30-barrel plant that has doubled production. The brewery tap was bought in 2008 and a second pub in 2010. Around 150 outlets are supplied. There is a rolling programme of seasonal beers: see website.

Micawber's Mild (OG 1035, ABV 3.5%)

Fruit and roast flavours dominate the nose, with vine fruit and caramel on the tongue and a short, dry, coffeeish aftertaste. Full-bodied and satisfying.

Moletrap Bitter (OG 1038, ABV 3.8%) ◆
Delicate hop aroma leading to a refreshing bitter hoppiness, finishing with a citrus aftertaste with hints of orange peel and grapefruit. An excellent session beer, which belies its strength.

Silver Adder (OG 1042, ABV 4.2%)
A light-coloured bitter with five hop and malt combinations giving a refreshing, crisp finish.

Suffolk Pride (OG 1048, ABV 4.8%) ◆
A full-bodied, copper-coloured beer with a good balance of malt, hops and fruit in the taste.

Black Adder (OG 1053, ABV 5.3%) 🏆 ◆
Superbly balanced dark, sweet ale, but with rich vine fruit throughout. The brewery's flagship beer.

Mayfields SIBA

Mayfields Brewery, No. 8 Croft Business Park, Leominster, Herefordshire, HR6 0QF
☎ (01568) 611197 ✉ info@mayfieldsbrewery.co.uk
⊕ mayfieldsbrewery.co.uk
Shop Wed-Fri 10am-4pm (other times by appt)

Established in 2005 Mayfields is a small family brewery located in the heart of one of England's major hop growing regions. 2008 saw a change of location and ownership. Since then the range of core beers have been changed and updated. Around 50 outlets are supplied. Seasonal beers are brewed on a monthly basis: see website. The brewery also distributes draught and bottled traditional local cider.

Copper Fox (OG 1037, ABV 3.8%)
A copper-coloured ale with a fresh malt body and lots of hop character.

Priory Pale Ale (OG 1039, ABV 4%)
A light golden ale with a refreshing malt body and plenty of hops in the aroma leading to a gentle bitter finish.

Ducking Stool (OG 1043, ABV 4.2%)
A refreshing golden amber-coloured ale with plenty of hop character throughout.

Aunty Myrtle's (OG 1044, ABV 4.5%)
A dark copper-coloured ale with gentle malt flavours and strong hop finish.

Mayflower

🕱 Mayflower Brewery, Tower Hill Brewery, Wellcross Farm, Tower Hill Road, Up Holland, Lancashire, WN8 0DS
☎ 07984 404567 ✉ info@mayflowerbeer.co.uk
⊕ mayflowerbeer.co.uk
Tours by arrangement

☺ Established in 2001 Mayflower is a 2.5-barrel, family-run micro-brewery located in a renovated barn in rural West Lancashire. A number of real ale pubs throughout the north-west are supplied. Beers are brewed on a rotating cycle. Seasonal/occasional beers are also available.

Black Diamond (OG 1038, ABV 3.6%)

Tower Hill (OG 1039, ABV 3.8%)

Douglas Valley Ale (OG 1041, ABV 4%)

Maypole

Maypole Brewery Ltd, North Laithes Farm, Wellow Road, Eakring, Newark, Nottinghamshire, NG22 0AN
☎ 07971 277598/07971 277592
✉ maypolebrewery@aol.com
⊕ maypolebrewery.co.uk

⊕ The brewery opened in 1995 in a converted 18th-century farm building. After changing hands in 2001 it was bought by the former head brewer, Rob Neil, in 2005. Seasonal beers can be ordered at any time for beer festivals: see website for details and list.

Little Weed (OG 1038, ABV 3.8%)

Mayfly Bitter (OG 1038, ABV 3.8%)

Celebration (OG 1040, ABV 4%)

Gate Hopper (OG 1040, ABV 4%)

Mayfair (OG 1040, ABV 4.1%)

Maybee (OG 1041, ABV 4.3%)

Major Oak (OG 1042, ABV 4.4%)

Flanagan's Extra Stout (OG 1044, ABV 4.5%)

Wellow Gold (OG 1044, ABV 4.6%)

Kiwi IPA (OG 1046, ABV 4.8%)

Mayhem (OG 1048, ABV 5%)

Platinum Blonde (OG 1048, ABV 5%)

For Olde Red Lion, Wellow:

Olde Lions Ale (ABV 3.9%)

Meantime SIBA

Meantime Brewing Co Ltd, Units 4 & 5, Lawrence Trading Estate, Blackwall Lane, London, SE10 0AR
☎ (020) 8293 1111 ✉ info@meantimebrewing.com
⊕ meantimebrewing.com
Shop Mon-Fri 8am-5pm
Tours by arrangement

⊗ Founded in 2000, Meantime brews a wide range of continental style beer and traditional English bottle-conditioned ales. Two pubs are owned. In 2010 the brewery relocated to larger premises in Greenwich. Bottle-conditioned beers are produced, all suitable for vegetarians and vegans. A six-barrel brewery is also owned at the Old Brewery, the Old Royal Naval College in Greenwich and is used to brew limited edition beers.

London Pale Ale (OG 1042, ABV 4.3%) ◆
Amber-coloured best bitter with a citrus hop aroma. The malty sweetness is balanced by strong bitter hops on the palate that fade in the slightly dry finish.

Kellerbier (ABV 4.6%)
Only available at the Old Brewery.

Meesons

See Old Bog

Melbourn

Melbourn Bros Brewery, All Saints Brewery, All Saints Street, Stamford, Lincolnshire, PE9 2PA
☎ (01780) 752186

Tours by arrangement (minimum 10 people, £6 per head including tastings)

A famous Stamford brewery that opened in 1825 and closed in 1974. It re-opened in 1994 and is owned by Samuel Smith of Tadcaster (qv). Melbourn brews three handcrafted, organic fruit beers (Cherry, Strawberry and Raspberry) using the antique steam-driven brewing equipment. The beers are all suitable for vegans and are organic. The beers are only available bottled (not bottle-conditioned).

Merlin SIBA (NEW)

Merlin Brewing Co Ltd, 3 Springbank Farm, Congleton Road, Arclid, Cheshire, CW11 2UD
☎ (01477) 500893
✉ brewing@merlinbrewing.co.uk
⊕ merlinbrewing.co.uk
Tours by arrangement

⊗ In 2010 David and Sue Peart started brewing in rural Cheshire using an eight-barrel plant. Beers are principally supplied to outlets within a 30-mile radius. All beers are also available bottle conditioned.

Merlin's Gold (OG 1038, ABV 3.8%)
A light golden ale with a floral, rounded, citrus flavour.

Spellbound (OG 1040, ABV 4%)
A premium English ale, full-flavoured and bitter with a dry finish. Light chestnut in colour.

The Wizard (OG 1042, ABV 4.2%)
Light amber in colour and bursting with hop aroma and flavour.

Merry Miner (NEW)

Merry Miner Brewery Ltd, Grendon House Farm, Warton Lane, Grendon, Warwickshire, CV9 3DT
☎ 07811 932721 ✉ merryminerbrewer@aol.co.uk
Tours by arrangement

⊗ Merry Miner began brewing in 2010 using a 2.5-barrel plant previously used by Discovery Ales. The owner was a miner and played for the Merry Miner football team, hence the name. Seasonal beers are also available.

Warwickshire's Finest (OG 1036, ABV 3.8%)

Davey's Lamp (OG 1038, ABV 4%)

Cap Lamp (OG 1039, ABV 4.2%)

Pit Pony (OG 1041, ABV 4.5%)

Methane (OG 1045, ABV 5%)

Mersea Island

Mersea Island Brewery, Rewsalls Lane, East Mersea, Essex, CO5 8SX
☎ (01206) 385900 ✉ beers@merseawine.com
⊕ merseawine.com
Shop Wed-Sun 10.30am-4pm, closed Mon & Tue

The brewery was established at Mersea Island Vineyard in 2005, producing cask and bottle-conditioned beers. The brewery supplies several local pubs on a guest beer basis as well as most local beer festivals. The brewery holds its own festival of Essex-produced ales over the four-day Easter weekend.

Yo Boy! (OG 1038, ABV 3.8%) ◆

Pale session beer. Peach and orange on the aroma and taste, leading to a pleasantly bitter finish.

Lion Bitter (OG 1038, ABV 3.9%)
A pale amber bitter with nutty and caramel flavours.

Gold (OG 1043, ABV 4.5%)
A lager/Pilsner style.

Skippers Bitter (OG 1047, ABV 4.8%) ◆
Strong bitter, whose full character is dominated by pear drops and juicy malt. A raspberry tartness follows.

Oyster (OG 1048, ABV 5%)

Mighty Oak

Mighty Oak Brewing Co Ltd, 14b West Station Yard, Spital Road, Maldon, Essex, CM9 6TW
☎ (01621) 843713
✉ sales@mightyoakbrewing.co.uk
⊕ mightyoakbrewing.co.uk
Tours by arrangement

⊗ Mighty Oak was formed in 1996 and moved in 2001 to Maldon, where capacity was increased. Around 250 outlets are supplied. Twelve monthly ales are brewed based on a theme.

IPA (OG 1035.6, ABV 3.5%) ◆
Light-bodied, pale session bitter. Hop notes are initially suppressed by a delicate sweetness but the aftertaste is more assertive.

Oscar Wilde (OG 1039.5, ABV 3.7%) ▣ ◆
Roasty dark mild with suggestions of forest fruits and dark chocolate. A sweet taste yields to a more bitter finish.

Captain Bob (OG 1039, ABV 3.8%)

Maldon Gold (OG 1039.5, ABV 3.8%) ◆
Pale golden ale with a sharp citrus note moderated by honey and biscuity malt.

Burntwood Bitter (OG 1041, ABV 4%) ◆
Full-bodied bitter with an unusual blend of caramel, roast grain and grapefruit.

Goods Shed Buffer Ale (OG 1042, ABV 4.2%)

Simply The Best (OG 1044.1, ABV 4.4%) ◆
Well-balanced, mid-strength bitter with a sweet start and a dry, bitter finish.

English Oak (OG 1047.9, ABV 4.8%) ◆
Strong tawny, fruity bitter with caramel, butterscotch and vanilla. A gentle hop character is present throughout.

Mighty Hop SIBA (NEW)

Mighty Hop Brewery Ltd, Silverdale, Woodmead Road, Lyme Regis, Dorset, DT7 3AD
☎ (01297) 445358
✉ enquiries@mightyhopbrewery.co.uk
⊕ mightyhopbrewery.co.uk

Mighty Hop began brewing in 2010 using a one-barrel plant and only produces bottle-conditioned ales for the licensed trade.

Milestone SIBA

Milestone Brewing Co Ltd, Great North Road, Cromwell, Newark, Nottinghamshire, NG23 6JE

THE BREWERIES

☎ (01636) 822255 ✉ info@milestonebrewery.co.uk
⊕ milestonebrewery.co.uk
Shop Mon-Fri 8am-5pm; Sat 9am-3pm
Tours by arrangement

☺ The brewery has been in production since 2005 on a 12-barrel plant. Around 150 outlets are supplied. Seasonal and bottle-conditioned beers are also available.

Lions Pride (OG 1038, ABV 3.8%)

Shine On (OG 1039, ABV 4%)

Loxley Ale (OG 1042, ABV 4.2%)

Black Pearl (OG 1043, ABV 4.3%)

Crusader (OG 1044, ABV 4.4%)

Rich Ruby (OG 1044, ABV 4.5%)

Olde English (OG 1049, ABV 4.9%)

Game Keeper (OG 1052, ABV 5.2%)

Raspberry Wheat Beer (OG 1055, ABV 5.6%)

Milk Street SIBA

⊟ Milk Street Brewery Ltd (MSB Ltd), The Griffin, 25 Milk Street, Frome, Somerset, BA11 3DL
☎ (01373) 467766 ✉ rjlyall@hotmail.com
⊕ milkstreetbrewery.co.uk
Tours by arrangement

Milk Street was established in 1999 in a former porn cinema situated behind a pub. The cinema is long gone and now houses the brewery, which expanded in 2005 and is now capable of producing 30 barrels per week. It mainly produces for its own estate of three outlets with direct delivery to pubs in a 30-mile radius. Wholesalers are used to distribute the beers further afield.

Gulp (ABV 3.5%)
A session beer with a pleasant lemon and citrus aroma and a full mouthfeel with good hop balance. The finish has a clean bitterness with spicy and blackcurrant notes.

Funky Monkey (OG 1040, ABV 4%)
Copper-coloured summer ale with fruity flavours and aromas. A dry finish with developing bitterness and an undertone of citrus fruit.

Mermaid (OG 1041, ABV 4.1%)
Amber-coloured ale with a rich hop character on the nose, plenty of citrus fruit on the palate and a lasting bitter and hoppy finish.

Amarillo (OG 1043, ABV 4.3%)
Brewed with American hops to give the beer floral and spicy notes. Initially soft on the palate, the flavour develops to that of burnt oranges and a pleasant herbal taste.

Zig-Zag Stout (OG 1046, ABV 4.5%) 🍺
A dark ruby stout with characteristic roastiness and dryness with bitter chocolate and citrus fruit in the background.

Beer (OG 1049, ABV 5%)
A blonde beer with musky hoppiness and citrus fruit on the nose, while more fruit surges through on the palate before the bittersweet finish.

Mill Green SIBA

⊟ Mill Green Brewery, White Horse, Edwardstone, Sudbury, Suffolk, CO10 5PX

☎ (01787) 211118
✉ enquiries@millgreenbrewery.co.uk
⊕ millgreenbrewery.co.uk

⊠ Mill Green started brewing in 2008 as an eco brewery in a new complex behind the White Horse pub. Brewing liquor is heated by solar panels, wood boiler and wind turbine. 20 outlets are supplied. Seasonal and bottle-conditioned beers are also available.

Mawkin Mild (OG 1028, ABV 2.9%) ✦
A superb complex mild, with a strong aroma and flavour for such a low gravity beer. Bitter coffee notes in the taste and aftertaste.

White Horse Bitter (OG 1036, ABV 3.6%)
A traditional session bitter with a spicy, bitter, lasting finish.

Green Goose (OG 1040, ABV 4%)
A dark bitter, rich in flavour with a hedgerow fruit aroma.

Loveleys Fair (OG 1040, ABV 4%)
A modern-style pale ale, golden in colour and heavily hopped with a tangy, citrus bite.

Good Ship Arbella (OG 1054, ABV 5.4%)
An American pale ale style, strong on hop.

Millis

Millis Brewing Co Ltd, St Margaret's Farm, St Margaret's Road, South Darenth, Dartford, Kent, DA4 9LB
☎ (01322) 866233 ⊕ millisbrewing.com
Shop Mon-Fri 12-5pm; Sat 10am-2pm

☺ John and Miriam Millis started with a half-barrel plant at their home in Gravesend. Demand outstripped the facility and Millis moved in 2003 to its current location – a former farm cold store – with a 10-barrel plant. They now supply around 40 outlets within a 50-mile radius. Wetherspoon's pubs are supplied within a 30-mile radius with Kentish Gold (ABV 4.8%). Seasonal and bottle-conditioned beers are also available.

Kentish Dark (OG 1035, ABV 3.5%)
Well-balanced, easy-drinking dark mild.

Gravesend Guzzler (OG 1037, ABV 3.7%)
Pale, easy-drinking, fruity session beer.

Kentish Best (OG 1040, ABV 4%)
A copper-coloured best bitter; tangy, fruity and dry.

Dartford Wobbler (OG 1043, ABV 4.3%)
A tawny-coloured, full-bodied best bitter with complex malt and hop flavours and a long, clean, slightly roasted finish.

Kentish Red Ale (OG 1043, ABV 4.3%)
A traditional red ale with complex malt, hops and fruit notes.

Millstone SIBA

Millstone Brewery Ltd, Unit 4, Vale Mill, Micklehurst Road, Mossley, nr Oldham, OL5 9JL
☎ (01457) 835835 ✉ info@millstonebrewery.co.uk
⊕ millstonebrewery.co.uk

Established in 2003 by Nick Boughton and Jon Hunt, the brewery is located in an 18th-century textile mill. The eight-barrel plant produces a range of pale, hoppy beers including five regular and seasonal/occasional beers (including the 'pub name' series). Over 50 outlets are supplied.

Vale Mill (OG 1039, ABV 3.9%)
A pale gold session bitter with a floral and spicy aroma building upon a crisp and refreshing taste.

Three Shires Bitter (OG 1040, ABV 4%) ◆
Yellow beer with hop and fruit aroma. Fresh citrus fruit, hops and bitterness in the taste and aftertaste.

Tiger Rut (OG 1040, ABV 4%)
A pale, hoppy ale with a distinctive citrus/grapefruit aroma.

Grain Storm (OG 1042, ABV 4.2%) ◆
Yellow/gold beer with a grainy mouthfeel and fresh fruit and hop aroma. Citrus peel and hops in the mouth, with a bitter finish.

True Grit (OG 1049, ABV 5%)
A well-hopped strong ale with a mellow bitterness and a citrus/grapefruit aroma.

Milton SIBA EAB

Milton Brewery Cambridge Ltd, 111 Cambridge Road, Milton, Cambridgeshire, CB24 6AT
☎ (01223) 226198
✉ enquiries@miltonbrewery.co.uk
⊕ miltonbrewery.co.uk
Tours by arrangement

⊗ The brewery has grown steadily since it was founded in 1999 and now operates pubs in Cambridge, London, Peterborough and Norwich through a sister company, Individual Pubs Ltd. Beers are available nationally via wholesalers. Regular seasonal beers are brewed. Nero is suitable for vegetarians and vegans.

Minotaur (OG 1035, ABV 3.3%) ◆
Red/brown mild with a defined malt and roast nose, then a sweetish malt and fruit balance with roast adding depth. The malt and sweetness remain in the aftertaste with little bitterness.

Jupiter (OG 1037, ABV 3.5%) ◆
A copper-coloured bitter with malt and hops in balance on nose and palate. Some caramel sweetness, but butterscotch lingers on in the aftertaste.

Neptune (OG 1039, ABV 3.8%) ◆
Delicious hop aromas introduce this well-balanced, nutty and refreshing copper-coloured ale. Good hoppy finish.

Pegasus (OG 1043, ABV 4.1%) 🎁 🍴 ◆
This copper-coloured beer balances malty aroma and flavour with some kiwi fruit and faint toffee. Pleasing dry aftertaste.

Sparta (OG 1043, ABV 4.3%) ◆
A golden ale that is dominated by floral hops throughout with some citrus fruit on the palate. Refreshingly dry with a moderately bitter finish.

Electra (OG 1045, ABV 4.5%)

Nero (OG 1050, ABV 5%) 🍴 ◆
A creamy black stout. Prunes and raisins on the nose lead in to flavours of sweet chocolate, malt and roast with layers of fruit. The aftertaste develops to chocolatey dryness.

Cyclops (OG 1055, ABV 5.3%)
Deep copper-coloured ale, with a rich hoppy aroma and full body; fruit and malt notes develop in the finish.

Mitchell Krause

Mitchell Krause Brewing Ltd, PO Box 86, Workington, Cumbria, CA14 9BD
☎ 07825 580694 ✉ graeme@mkbrewing.co.uk
⊕ mkbrewing.co.uk

Mitchell Krause was set up in 2009 and produces three bottled beers, two of which are brewed at the Bitter End Brewery in Cockermouth (Bavarian Hefe Weiss is bottle-conditioned). The other beer is contract brewed at Hepworth Brewery.

Mithril

Mithril Ales, Mithril, Aldbrough St John, Richmond, North Yorkshire, DL11 7TL
☎ (01325) 374817 ☎ 07889 167128
✉ mithril58@btinternet.com ⊕ mithrilales.co.uk

☺Mithril started brewing in 2010 in an old stables opposite the brewer's house on a 2.5-barrel plant. Owner/brewer Pete Fenwick is a well-known craft brewer who brews twice a week to supply the local area of Darlington and Richmond. Weekly specials are available.

Dere Street (OG 1039, ABV 3.8%)
Amber-coloured bitter with a fruity, malty sweetness and a smooth, hoppy finish.

Route A66 (OG 1041, ABV 4%)
A crisp, refreshing, satisfying golden beer. A dry bitterness with a lingering citrus and spicy hop taste and aroma.

Flower Power (OG 1042, ABV 4.2%)
A pale ale with a massive citrus, fruity hop flavour. Hints of grapefruit and floral on the tongue from the late addition of elderflowers.

Moles

Moles Brewery (Cascade Drinks Ltd), 5 Merlin Way, Bowerhill, Melksham, Wiltshire, SN12 6TJ
☎ (01225) 704734/708842 ✉ sales@moles-cascade.co.uk ⊕ molesbrewery.com
Shop Mon-Fri 9am-5pm; Sat 9am-12pm
Tours by arrangement

⊗ Moles was established in 1982 by Roger Catte, a former Ushers brewer, using his nickname to name the brewery. 10 pubs are owned, all serving cask beer. Over 200 outlets are supplied direct. Seasonal beers: see website.

Tap Bitter (OG 1035, ABV 3.5%)
A session bitter with a smooth, malty flavour and clean bitter finish.

Double MM Mild (OG 1036, ABV 3.6%)
A light-bodied dark mild with fruit and toasted toffee flavours and a smooth bitterness.

Best Bitter (OG 1040, ABV 4%)
A well-balanced, amber-coloured bitter, clean, dry and malty with some bitterness, and delicate floral hop flavour.

Elmo's Fire (OG 1044, ABV 4.4%)
A medium-bodied pale ale. Refreshingly bitter with a fruity, spicy aroma.

Landlords Choice (OG 1045, ABV 4.5%)
A dark, strong, smooth porter, with a rich fruity palate and malty finish.

Rucking Mole (OG 1045, ABV 4.5%)
A chestnut-coloured premium ale, fruity and malty with a smooth bitter finish.

THE BREWERIES

Mole Catcher (OG 1050, ABV 5%) 🍷
A copper-coloured ale with a delightfully spicy hop aroma and taste, and a long bitter finish.

Monty's SIBA

Monty's Brewery Ltd, Unit 1, Castle Works, Hendomen, Montgomery, Powys, SY15 6HA
☎ (01686) 668933 ✉ info@montysbrewery.co.uk
🌐 montysbrewery.co.uk
Tours by arrangement

Monty's began brewing in 2009 and was the first brewery in Montgomeryshire since the Eagle brewery in Newtown closed in 1990. Pump clips are available in English and Welsh. One pub is owned, the Sportsman in Newtown. Seasonal beers: see website. Bottle-conditioned beers are also available.

Mojo (OG 1039, ABV 3.8%)
A golden, slightly toasty brew, with a hint of marmalade.

Manjana (OG 1039.5, ABV 3.9%)
A well-balanced chestnut bitter.

Midnight (OG 1040, ABV 4%)
A dark, smooth, creamy stout.

Moonrise (OG 1040, ABV 4%)
A copper-coloured, gently malty, well-balanced traditional brew.

Sunshine (OG 1041, ABV 4.2%)
A golden, hoppy, floral/citrus ale with a pleasantly dry finish.

Mischief (OG 1050, ABV 5%)
A strong golden ale with a good balance of malt and hop bitterness.

Moodley's

Moodley's Ltd, Bowen's Farm, Poundsbridge Lane, Penshurst, Kent, TN11 8AJ
☎ (01892) 821366 ☎ 07788 889877
✉ yudhistra@moodleys.co.uk 🌐 moodleys.co.uk
Tours by arrangement

Moodleys was established in 2008, moving to its current site in 2010. At present only bottle-conditioned beers are produced, all approved by the Vegetarian Society. Seasonal beers are also available. Cask-conditioned ale is planned. The beers are available at local pubs, farm shops and online.

Moonstone

🔲 Moonstone Brewery (Gem Taverns Ltd), Ministry of Ale, 9 Trafalgar Street, Burnley, Lancashire, BB11 1TQ
☎ (01282) 830909 ✉ meet@ministryofale.co.uk
🌐 moonstonebrewery.co.uk
Tours by arrangement

😊 A small, 2.5-barrel brewery, based in the Ministry of Ale pub. Brewing started in 2001 and beer is generally only available in the pub. Seasonal beers are also brewed.

Black Star (OG 1037, ABV 3.4%)

Blue John (ABV 3.6%)

Tigers Eye (OG 1037, ABV 3.8%)

White Sapphire (OG 1037, ABV 3.9%)

Trafalgar Stout (OG 1050, ABV 4.9%)

Moor SIBA

Moor Beer Co Ltd, c/o Chapel Court, Pitney, Somerset, TA10 9AE
☎ 07887 556521 ✉ justin@moorbeer.co.uk
🌐 moorbeer.co.uk
Tours by arrangement

Moor Beer was founded in 1996 and rescued from oblivion by award-winning brewer Justin Hawke in 2006. The brewery's capacity was quadrupled in 2010 to meet demand. Special, seasonal and bottle-conditioned beers are also available.

Revival (OG 1038, ABV 3.8%) 🍷
An immensely hoppy and refreshing pale ale.

Northern Star (ABV 4.1%)

Southern Star (ABV 4.1%)

Merlin's Magic (OG 1045, ABV 4.3%) 🍷
Dark amber-coloured, complex, full-bodied beer, with fruity notes.

Illusion (ABV 4.5%)
A black IPA with powerful hop flavours.

Peat Porter (OG 1047, ABV 4.5%) 🍷
Dark brown/black beer with an initially fruity taste leading to roast malt with a little bitterness. A slightly sweet malty finish.

Ported Peat Porter (OG 1049, ABV 4.7%)
Peat Porter with added Reserve Port.

Somerland Gold (OG 1052, ABV 5%)
Hoppy blonde ale with hints of honey and a long, hoppy finish.

Hoppiness (ABV 6.5%)
Rich malt and fruit flavours of a barley wine with the hoppy crispness of a pale ale.

Old Freddy Walker (OG 1075, ABV 7.3%) 🍷
Rich, dark, strong ale with a fruity complex taste, leaving a fruitcake finish.

JJJ IPA (OG 1085, ABV 9%) 🍷
Copper-coloured, new world IPA. Immensely hoppy and malty.

Moorhouse's SIBA

Moorhouse's Brewery (Burnley) Ltd, The Brewery, Moorhouse Street, Accrington Road, Burnley, Lancashire, BB11 5ZN
☎ (01282) 422864 ✉ info@moorhouses.co.uk
🌐 moorhouses.co.uk
Shop Mon-Fri 10am-4.30pm
Tours by arrangement

Established in 1865 as a drinks manufacturer, the brewery started producing cask-conditioned ale in 1978 and has achieved recognition by winning more international and CAMRA awards than any other brewery of its size. A new brewhouse and visitors centre were completed in 2010. The company owns six pubs, all serving cask-conditioned beer. Seasonal beers: see website.

Black Cat (OG 1036, ABV 3.4%) 🍷
A dark mild-style beer with delicate chocolate and coffee roast flavours and a crisp, bitter finish.

Premier Bitter (OG 1036, ABV 3.7%) 🍷
A clean and satisfying bitter aftertaste rounds off this well-balanced hoppy, amber session bitter.

Pride of Pendle (OG 1040, ABV 4.1%) ◥
Well-balanced amber best bitter with a fresh initial hoppiness and a mellow, malt-driven body.

Blond Witch (OG 1045, ABV 4.5%) ◥
Light ale, fruity with lasting finish.

Pendle Witches Brew (OG 1050, ABV 5.1%) ◥
Well-balanced, full-bodied, malty beer with a long, complex finish.

Moorview SIBA

Moorview Brewery, Upper Austby Farm, Nesfield, North Yorkshire, LS29 0EQ
☎ 07833 337289

Office: 1a Silverdale Close, Guiseley, Leeds, West Yorkshire, LS20 8BQ ☎ (01943) 878154
✉ eric.cusack@btopenworld.com
⊕ moorviewbrewery.co.uk

☺Moorview began brewing in 2008 using the old brew plant from the Turkey Inn at Goose Eye. Water is supplied from their own bore hole. Around 15 outlets are supplied direct.

First Born Bitter (ABV 3.4%)

Full Mashings (ABV 3.6%)

Golden Butts (ABV 3.7%)

Amber Gambler (ABV 3.8%)

Silicone Blonde (ABV 4.4%)

Cocker-Doodle-Brew (ABV 5.2%)

Mordue SIBA

Mordue Brewery, Units D1 & D2, Narvic Way, Tyne Tunnel Estate, North Shields, Tyne & Wear, NE29 7XJ
☎ (0191) 296 1879
✉ enquiries@morduebrewery.com
⊕ morduebrewery.com
Shop: see website for opening times
Tours by arrangement

☺ In 1995 the Fawson brothers revived the Mordue Brewery name (the original closed in 1879). High demand required moves to larger premises and replacing the original five-barrel plant with a 20-barrel one. The beers are distributed nationally and 200 outlets are supplied direct. Seasonal beers: see website.

Five Bridge Bitter (OG 1038, ABV 3.8%) ◥
Crisp, golden beer with a good hint of hops, the bitterness carries on in the finish. A good session bitter.

Geordie Pride (OG 1042, ABV 4.2%) ◥
Well-balanced and hoppy copper-coloured brew with a long, bitter finish.

Workie Ticket (OG 1045, ABV 4.5%) ▯ ◥
Complex tasty bitter with plenty of malt and hops, long satisfying bitter finish.

Radgie Gadgie (OG 1048, ABV 4.8%) ▯ ◥
Strong, easy-drinking bitter with plenty of fruit and hops.

IPA (OG 1051, ABV 5.1%) ◥
Easy-drinking golden ale with plenty of hops, the bitterness carries on in the finish.

Morrissey Fox

Morrissey Fox Breweries Ltd, Tickton Hall, Tickton, Beverley, East Yorkshire, HU17 9RX

☺Morrissey Fox Breweries was developed in 2008 and filmed by Channel 4. The brewery was initially based at Ye Olde Punchbowl in Marton cum Grafton, North Yorkshire but the company left the pub in 2009. Beers are contract brewed elsewhere reportedly including Cropton Brewery and Celt Experience.

Bitter (OG 1040, ABV 3.9%)

Blonde (OG 1043, ABV 4.2%)

Morton

Morton Brewery, Unit 10, Essington Light Industrial Estate, Essington, Wolverhampton, WV11 2BH
☎ 07988 069647

Office: 96 Brewood Road, Coven, Staffordshire, WV9 5EF ✉ mortonbrewery@aol.com
⊕ mortonbrewery.co.uk
Tours by arrangement

Morton was established in 2007 on a three-barrel plant by Gary and Angela Morton, both CAMRA members. The brewery moved to Essington in 2008 to increase production. Essington Ale was introduced to celebrate the move and became so popular with the locals that a full range of Essington beers is brewed regularly. 30 outlets are supplied direct plus various beer festivals. Seasonal and special beers: see website. Bottle-conditioned beers are also available.

Penkside Pale (OG 1035, ABV 3.6%)

Essington Bitter (OG 1037, ABV 3.8%)

Merry Mount (OG 1037, ABV 3.8%)

Essington Blonde (OG 1039, ABV 4%)

Forever In Darkness (OG 1040, ABV 4%)

Essington Ale (OG 1041, ABV 4.2%)

Jelly Roll (OG 1041, ABV 4.2%)

Essington Gold (OG 1043, ABV 4.4%)

Gregory's Gold (OG 1043, ABV 4.4%)

Essington Supreme (OG 1046, ABV 4.6%)

Scottish Maiden (OG 1045, ABV 4.6%)

Essington IPA (OG 1047, ABV 4.8%)

Moulin

⬛ Moulin Hotel & Brewery, 2 Baledmund Road, Moulin, Pitlochry, Perthshire, PH16 5EL
☎ (01796) 472196 ✉ enquiries@moulinhotel.co.uk
⊕ moulinhotel.co.uk
Shop 12-3pm daily
Tours by arrangement

☺ The brewery opened in 1995 to celebrate the Moulin Hotel's 300th anniversary. Two pubs are owned and four outlets are supplied. Bottle-conditioned beer is available.

Light (OG 1036, ABV 3.7%) ◥
Thirst-quenching, straw-coloured session beer, with a light, hoppy, fruity balance, ending with a gentle, hoppy sweetness.

Braveheart (OG 1039, ABV 4%) ◥
An amber bitter, with a delicate balance of malt and fruit and a Scottish-style sweetness.

Ale of Atholl (OG 1043.5, ABV 4.5%) ◥

Ruby red in colour with toffee, Ribena and roast barley in aroma. Gentle hop notes, fruity and soft mouthed.

Port Stout (OG 1046, ABV 4.8%) 🍺 ◆
A black beer with roast malt in the aroma that remains in the taste but gives way to hoppy bitterness in the aftertaste.

Stormstay (OG 1048, ABV 5%)
A ruby-coloured complex ale with a toffee and floral hop aroma and a surprisingly clean and citrus finish after the malt toffee and biscuit flavours.

Oakham SIBA EAB

Oakham Ales, 2 Maxwell Road, Woodston, Peterborough, Cambridgeshire, PE2 7JB
☎ (01733) 370500 ✉ info@oakhamales.com
⊕ oakhamales.com
Shop Mon-Fri 9am-5pm
Tours by arrangement

⊗ The brewery started in 1993 in Oakham, Rutland and moved to Peterborough in 1998. The brewery's head office and main production site is a 75-barrel plant. An additional six-barrel plant is located at its brew pub central to the city, which allows special and one-off brews including beers made especially for its elite customers as members of the 'Oakademy of Excellence', which was launched in late 2008. Around 350 outlets are supplied and three pubs are owned. Seasonal beers: see website.

Jeffrey Hudson Bitter/JHB (OG 1038, ABV 3.8%) ◆
Lemon, grapefruit and spicy hop notes abound on aroma and palate of this straw-coloured golden ale. Good bittersweet finish.

Inferno (OG 1039, ABV 4%) 🍺 ◆
Impressive golden ale with explosive fruity hop fumes. The palate comprises a powerful resiny and spicy hop character with complex fruit flavours and a satisfying bitterness. Strong, dry, hoppy finale.

Citra (OG 1041, ABV 4.2%)
A light, refreshing beer with pungent grapefruit, lychee and gooseberry aromas leading to a dry, bitter finish.

White Dwarf (OG 1042, ABV 4.3%) ◆
A speciality beer with fruit and hops on the aroma and in the taste. Dry and faintly astringent on the palate, leading to a strong, dry and moderately astringent finish.

Bishops Farewell (OG 1046, ABV 4.6%) ◆
Citrus and grassy hops on the nose of this golden ale. A spirited spicy hop tang is coupled with strong bitterness and leads into an intense, dry, hoppy aftertaste.

Oakleaf SIBA

Oakleaf Brewing Co Ltd, Unit 7, Clarence Wharf Industrial Estate, Mumby Road, Gosport, Hampshire, PO12 1AJ
☎ (023) 9251 3222 ✉ info@oakleafbrewing.co.uk
⊕ oakleafbrewing.co.uk
Shop Mon-Fri 9am-5pm; Sat 10am-1pm
Tours by arrangement

⊗ Ed Anderson set up Oakleaf with his father-in-law, Dave Pickersgill, in 2000. The brewery stands on the side of Portsmouth Harbour. Some 350 outlets are supplied direct with national deliveries

via wholesalers. Seasonal beers: see website/facebook. Bottle-conditioned beers are also available.

Some Are Drinking (ABV 3.9%)
An easy-drinking light summer ale, pale and refreshing with a zesty hop finish.

Quercus Folium (OG 1040, ABV 4%)
A traditional mid-brown bitter with an inital malty flavour leading to a long hoppy finish.

Nuptu'ale (OG 1042, ABV 4.2%) ◆
A full-bodied pale ale, strongly hopped with an uncompromising bitterness. An intense hoppy, spicy, floral aroma leads to a complex hoppy taste. Well-balanced with malts and citrus flavours and a hint of sweetness making for a refreshing bitter.

Pompey Royal (OG 1046, ABV 4.5%)
A traditional mid-brown malty ale with a delicate hop balance.

Hole Hearted (OG 1048, ABV 4.7%) ◆
An amber-coloured strong bitter with strong floral hop and citrus notes in the aroma. These continue to dominate the flavour and lead to a long, bittersweet finish.

Blake's Gosport Bitter (OG 1053, ABV 5.2%) ◆
Packed with berry fruits and roastiness, this is a complex strong bitter. Malt, roast and caramel are prevalent as both bitterness and sweetness build at the same time to an uncompromising vinous finish. Warming, spicy, well-balanced and delicious.

For Suthwyk Ales:

Old Dick (OG 1038, ABV 3.8%) ◆
Formerly known as Bloomfield Bitter, this is a pleasant, clean-tasting pale brown bitter. Easy-drinking and well-balanced. Beer is brewed by Oakleaf for Suthwyk using ingredients grown on the farm.

Liberation (OG 1042, ABV 4.2%)

Skew Sunshine Ale (OG 1046, ABV 4.6%) ◆
An amber-coloured beer. Initial hoppiness leads to a fruity taste and finish. A slightly cloying mouthfeel.

Palmerston's Folly (OG 1047, ABV 4.8%)

Oakwell SIBA

Oakwell Brewery, PO Box 87, Pontefract Road, Barnsley, South Yorkshire, S71 1EZ
☎ (01226) 296161
Tours by arrangement

⊙ Brewing started in 1997. Oakwell supplies around 30 outlets.

Old Tom Mild (OG 1033.5, ABV 3.4%) ◆
A malty mild with sweet fruit and caramel flavours. A smooth, clean finish.

Barnsley Bitter (OG 1036, ABV 3.8%) ◆
A fruity and malty bitter with a hoppy, clean, bitter and mellow finish.

Oban

Oban Ales Ltd, Kilmelford Craft Brewery, Kilmelford, PA34 4XA
☎ (01852) 200731 ✉ sales@obanales.co.uk
⊕ obanales.co.uk
Tours by arrangement

☺Oban Ales was established in 2010 using the former Black Mountain Brewery plant. Brewing is currently suspended.

Rocky Pass (OG 1039, ABV 4%)

Oban Bay

▤ Oban Bay Brewery, Cuan Mor, 60 George Street, Oban, Argyll, PA34 5DS
☎ (01631) 565078

Brewing began in 2009. 20 outlets are supplied. Bottle-conditioned beers are available.

Kilt Lifter (ABV 3.9%)

Skinny Blonde (ABV 4.1%)

Skelpt Lug (ABV 4.2%)

Fair Puggled (ABV 4.5%)

Odcombe

▤ Odcombe Brewery, Masons Arms, 41 Lower Odcombe, Odcombe, Somerset, BA22 8TX
☎ (01935) 862591
✉ paula@masonsarmsodcombe.co.uk
⊕ masonsarmsodcombe.co.uk
Tours by arrangement

Odcombe Brewery opened in 2000 and closed a few years later. It re-opened in 2005 with assistance from Shepherd Neame. Brewing takes place once a week and beers are only available at the pub. Seasonal beers are also available.

No 1 (OG 1040, ABV 4%)

Spring (OG 1041, ABV 4.1%)

Roly Poly (OG 1042, ABV 4.2%)

Offa's Dyke

▤ Offa's Dyke Brewery, Barley Mow Inn, Chapel Lane, Trefonen, Oswestry, Shropshire, SY10 9DX
☎ (01691) 656889 ⊕ offasdykebrewery.com
Shop Mon-Fri 5-11pm; Sat & Sun 12-12
Tours by arrangement

⊗ Offa's Dyke was established in 2007. The brewery and adjoining pub straddle the old England/Wales border, Offa's Dyke. The owner grows barley locally and is experimenting with small-scale hop cultivation. An Oswestry brewery tap opened in 2010, Olde Vaults. Bottle-conditioned beers are available.

Barley Gold (OG 1038, ABV 3.6%)

Offa's Pride (OG 1040, ABV 3.8%)

D.O. (ABV 4%)

Thirst Brew (OG 1042, ABV 4%)

Honey Blonde (OG 1045, ABV 4.2%)

Grim Reaper (OG 1050, ABV 5%)

Offbeat SIBA (NEW)

Offbeat Brewery Ltd, Unit 6, Thomas Street, Crewe, Cheshire, CW1 2BD
☎ 07502 096438 ✉ beer@offbeatbrewery.com
⊕ offbeatbrewery.com
Tours by arrangement

☺Offbeat began brewing at the Borough Arms in Crewe before quickly expanding to a six-barrel

plant at the current address. Specials and bottle-conditioned beers are also available.

Outlandish Pale (ABV 3.9%)
A session ale with a big, hoppy hit.

Odd Ball Red (ABV 4.8%)
A ruby red ale with a spicy flavour and finish.

Out Of Step IPA (ABV 5.8%)
A generously hopped IPA with abundant citrus flavours leading to a dry, bitter finish.

Okells SIBA

Okell & Son Ltd, Kewaigue, Douglas, Isle of Man, IM2 1QG
☎ (01624) 699400 ✉ mac@okells.co.uk
⊕ okells.co.uk
Tours by arrangement

☺ Founded in 1874 by Dr Okell and formerly trading as Isle of Man Breweries, this is the main brewery on the island, having taken over and closed the rival Castletown Brewery in 1986. The brewery moved in 1994 to a new, purpose-built plant at Kewaigue to replace the Falcon Brewery in Douglas. All the beers are produced under the Manx Brewers' Act 1874 (permitted ingredients: water, malt, sugar and hops only – amended in 1998 to allow the brewing of wheat and fruit beers). Approximately three quarters of the company's 48 Isle of Man pubs and three of the four in England and Wales sell cask beer and some 70 free trade outlets are also supplied. Seasonal beers: see website.

Mild (OG 1034, ABV 3.4%) ◄
Sweet dark brown mild, easy-drinking.

Bitter (OG 1035, ABV 3.7%) ◄
Well-balanced malt and hops with some fruitiness leading to a short, bitter finish.

Dr Okell's IPA (OG 1044, ABV 4.5%)
A light-coloured beer with a full-bodied taste. The sweetness is offset by strong hopping that gives the beer an overall roundness with spicy lemon notes and a fine dry finish.

Red (OG 1047, ABV 4.7%)
A ruby red ale with a spicy citrus hop aroma. An initial sweetness leads to a smooth, easy-diniking beer.

Alt (OG 1050, ABV 5%) ▩ ◄
Well-rounded, hoppy, rich and dark with plenty of finish.

Old Bear SIBA

Old Bear Brewery, Unit 1, Aireworth Mills, Aireworth Road, Keighley, West Yorkshire, BD21 4DH
☎ (01535) 601222 ✉ sales@oldbearbrewery.co.uk
⊕ oldbearbrewery.co.uk
Shop Mon-Fri 9am-4pm, Sat 10am-1pm
Tours by arrangement

☺ Old Bear is a family business founded in 1993 at the Old White Bear in Crosshills. The brewery moved to Keighley in 2004 to a purpose-built unit to cater for increased production. The original 10-barrel plant was retained and refurbished and there is now a one-barrel plant for special ales. Beers are supplied within a 60-mile radius of Keighley and are available nationally via wholesalers. All cask beers are also available bottle conditioned.

O5 Gold (ABV 5%)

OG (ABV 5.4%) 🍺

O8 (OG 1077.5, ABV 7.5%) 🍺
A pale and strong ale, deceptively smooth.

Otter SIBA

Otter Brewery Ltd, Mathayes, Luppitt, Honiton, Devon, EX14 4SA
☎ (01404) 891285 ✉ info@otterbrewery.com
⊕ otterbrewery.com
Tours by arrangement

Otter Brewery was set up in 1990 by the McCaig family and has grown into one of the West Country's major producers of beers. The brewery is located in the Blackdown Hills, between Taunton and Honiton. 2009 saw the completion of Otter's 'eco cellar', partly underground and built with clay blocks and a grass roof. The beers are made from the brewery's own springs and are delivered to more than 500 pubs across the south-west including the family's first pub, the Holt, in Honiton. Seasonal beers: see website.

Bitter (OG 1036, ABV 3.6%) ◆
Well-balanced amber session bitter with a fruity nose and bitter taste and aftertaste.

Amber (OG 1040, ABV 4%) 🍴 ◆
Amber-coloured as the name suggests, with a fruity nose and fruit and hop taste. Well-balanced with a lingering bitter finish.

Bright (OG 1039, ABV 4.3%) ◆
Pale yellow/golden ale with a strong fruit aroma, sweet fruity taste and a bittersweet finish.

Ale (OG 1043, ABV 4.5%) ◆
A full-bodied best bitter. A malty aroma predominates with a fruity taste and finish.

Head (OG 1054, ABV 5.8%)
Fruity aroma and taste with a pleasant bitter finish. Dark brown and full-bodied.

Ouseburn Valley (NEW)

Ouseburn Valley Brewery, 11 Dilston Terrace, Gosforth, Newcastle upon Tyne, NE3 1XX
☎ (0191) 285 0937
✉ nige@ouseburnvalleybrewery.co.uk
⊕ ouseburnvalleybrewery.co.uk

⊠ Ouseburn Valley is currently operating from the owner's garage with plans to increase capacity and move to the cellar of the Brandling Villa in Newcastle.

Armstrong Bitter (OG 1042, ABV 4.1%)

Elderflower Gold (OG 1042, ABV 4.1%)

Brandling Porter (OG 1044, ABV 4.4%)

IPA (OG 1045, ABV 4.7%)

Grainger Special (OG 1046, ABV 4.8%)

Outlaw

See Roosters

Outstanding

Outstanding Brewing Co Ltd, Britannia Mill, Cobden Street, Bury, Lancashire, BL9 6AW

☎ (0161) 764 7723 ✉ info@outstandingbeers.co.uk
⊕ outstandingbeers.com

The brewery was set up as a collaboration between Paul Sandiford, Glen Woodcock, David Porter and Alex Lord. The 15-barrel plant went into production in 2008. Selective free trade accounts are supplied nationally.

Red (OG 1042, ABV 4.4%)
A mid range copper-coloured ale with a distinctive hop finish.

Blond (OG 1044, ABV 4.5%)
Pale and lightly bittered with citrus flavours and a floral nose.

Ginger (OG 1044, ABV 4.5%)
Light brown beer with a noticeable hint of ginger.

SOS (OG 1044, ABV 4.5%)
Light brown bitter, dry and intensely bitter.

White (OG 1048, ABV 5%)
A cloudy wheat beer with earthy, spicy, lemony flavours.

Standing Out (OG 1053, ABV 5.5%)
A pale golden ale, dry and bitter with lots of hop aroma.

Stout (OG 1057, ABV 5.5%)
Thick, jet black and bitter with liquorice overtones.

Owenshaw Mill (NEW)

Owenshaw Mill Brewery Ltd, Old Cawsey, Sowerby Bridge, West Yorkshire, HX6 2AJ
☎ (01422) 839010
✉ info@owenshawmillbrewery.co.uk
⊕ owenshawmillbrewery.co.uk

☺Owenshaw Mill began production in 2011 using an eight-barrel plant.

Katy's Blonde (OG 1037, ABV 3.6%)
A pale, fruity session beer.

Oxfordshire Ales SIBA

Bicester Beers & Minerals Ltd, 12 Pear Tree Farm Industrial Units, Bicester Road, Marsh Gibbon, Bicester, Oxfordshire, OX27 0GB
☎ (01869) 278765 ✉ john@oxfordshireales.co.uk
⊕ oxfordshireales.co.uk
Tours by arrangement

⊠ The company first brewed in 2005. The five-barrel plant was previously at Picks Brewery but has now been upgraded to a 10-barrel plant with the purchase of a larger copper. It supplies 50-60 outlets as well as several wholesalers. Seasonal beers are produced.

Triple B (OG 1037, ABV 3.7%) ◆
This pale amber beer has a huge caramel aroma. The caramel diminishes in the initial taste, which changes to a fruit/bitter balance. This in turn leads to a long, refreshing, bitter aftertaste.

Pride of Oxfordshire (OG 1042, ABV 4.1%) ◆
An amber beer, the aroma is butterscotch/caramel, which carries on into the initial taste. The taste then becomes bitter with sweetish/malty overtones. There is a long, dry, bitter finish.

Marshmellow (OG 1047, ABV 4.7%) ◆
The slightly fruity aroma in this golden-amber beer leads to a hoppy but thin taste, with slight caramel notes. The aftertaste is short and bitter.

Palmers SIBA IFBB

JC & RH Palmer Ltd, The Old Brewery, West Bay Road, Bridport, Dorset, DT6 4JA
☎ (01308) 422396
✉ enquiries@palmersbrewery.com
⊕ palmersbrewery.com
Shop Mon-Sat 9am-6pm
Tours by arrangement Easter-Sep (Please ring 01308 427500)

⊗ Palmers is Britain's only thatched brewery and dates from 1794. It is situated in Bridport, the heart of the Jurassic Coast in south-west Dorset. The company continues to make substantial investment in its 53 tenanted pubs, all serving cask ale. Around 400 outlets are supplied.

Copper Ale (OG 1036, ABV 3.7%) ◆
Beautifully balanced, copper-coloured light bitter with a hoppy aroma.

Best Bitter (OG 1040, ABV 4.2%) ◆
Hop aroma and bitterness stay in the background in this predominately malty best bitter, with some fruit on the aroma.

Dorset Gold (OG 1046, ABV 4.5%) ◆
More complex than many golden ales thanks to a pleasant banana and mango fruitiness on the aroma that carries on into the taste and aftertaste.

200 (OG 1052, ABV 5%) ◆
This is a big beer with a touch of caramel sweetness adding to a complex hoppy, fruit taste that lasts from the aroma well into the aftertaste.

Tally Ho! (OG 1057, ABV 5.5%) ◆
A complex dark old ale. Roast malts and treacle toffee on the palate lead in to a long, lingering finish with more than a hint of coffee.

Panther EAB (NEW)

Panther Brewery, Unit 1, Collers Way, Reepham, Norfolk, NR10 4SW
☎ 07766 558215 ✉ martin@pantherbrewery.co.uk
⊕ pantherbrewery.co.uk
Shop Mon-Fri 9am-6pm; Sat 10am-3pm
Tours by arrangement

Panther began brewing in 2010 on an industrial estate near the old railway station, formerly the home of Reepham Brewery. The entrance incorporates a small shop selling its bottle-conditioned ales and other merchandise.

Golden Panther (OG 1039, ABV 3.7%)

Pink Panther (OG 1042, ABV 4%)

Red Panther (OG 1043, ABV 4.1%) ◆
A nutty, full-flavoured brew. Plenty of roasted malt in both aroma and taste. Hops, and a residual sweetness, provide balance.

Black Panther (OG 1053, ABV 4.5%)

Paradise

Paradise Coach House Ltd (Paradise Brewery), Bird in Hand, Trelissick Road, Hayle, Cornwall, TR27 4HY
☎ (01736) 753974
✉ birdinhand@paradisepark.org.uk
Tours by arrangement

⊙Brewing first started in 1981 under the name Paradise Brewery, named after its location, the Paradise Bird Park. The name was changed to Wheal Ale in 1995. Brewing ceased in 2004 but re-started in 2009 under the original Paradise name.

Bitter (OG 1036, ABV 3.6%) ◆
Gentle malt and fruit on the nose, followed by a dominantly bitter flavour balanced by sweet malt and fruity hop. The finish is bitter.

Artist Ale (OG 1055, ABV 5.2%) ◆
Full-bodied tawny ale with a faint aroma of malt. Heavy sweet malt and bubblegum esters in the mouth with a balance of hops. Dryness and bitterness in the finish.

Parish

Parish Brewery, 6 Main Street, Burrough on the Hill, Leicestershire, LE14 2JQ
☎ (01664) 454801 ☎ 07715 369410
✉ trudygrants@yahoo.co.uk
Tours by arrangement

⊗ Parish began in 1983 and operates on a 20-barrel plant located in a 400-year-old building and former stables next to Grant's Freehouse, which is the main outlet for the full range of beers. In addition to the regular range, Poacher's Ale (ABV 6%), a blended ale comprising one part Baz's Bonce Blower and two parts PSB, is also available. Other local outlets are also supplied and special one-off brews are produced for beer festivals held across Leicestershire, Rutland and Cambridgeshire. Baz's Bonce Blower is also available bottle conditioned.

PSB (OG 1039, ABV 3.9%)
Hoppy session beer with malty aftertaste.

Trudy's Tipple (OG 1039, ABV 3.9%)
Refreshing full bodied golden ale with light crisp tones, with naturally grown elderflower leaving citrus after taste.

Farm Gold (OG 1041, ABV 4.2%)
Light-coloured beer with distinctive hoppy taste and powerful aroma.

Burrough Bitter (OG 1047, ABV 4.8%)
Darker version of PSB with medium to strong bitterness and more pronounced malty aftertaste.

Poacher's Ale (OG 1060, ABV 6%)
Deep ruby red full-bodied malty blended beer. Not to be underestimated in strength.

Baz's Bonce Blower (OG 1100, ABV 12%)
Strong, dark beer with a rich, malty character.

Partners SIBA

Partners Brewery Ltd, Unit 12, Saville Bridge Mill, Mill Street East, Dewsbury, West Yorkshire, WF12 9AF
☎ (01924) 457772 ✉ sales@partnersbrewery.co.uk
Tours by arrangement

⊗ Formerly known as Anglo Dutch, Paul Klos (Dutch) set up the brewery with Mike Field (Anglo) in a former dye mill near Dewsbury Minster in 2000. In 2011 the brewery was bought by Paul Horne and Richard Sharp and renamed the Partners Brewery. The new owners intend to continue brewing the current range as well as developing a new range of regular ales and seasonal brews.

Apistus (OG 1040, ABV 4%)
A pale honey beer.

Dusk Till Dawn (OG 1040, ABV 4%)

THE BREWERIES

Yellow in colour, with a hoppy, fruity nose. Soft maltiness and a strong hop/citrus flavour lead to a dry, bitter finish.

Alchemists Ale (OG 1043, ABV 4.3%) 🍺
Yellow beer with generous hop and fruit on the nose and palate. Good bitter hop finish.

Pied Bull (NEW)

▤ Pied Bull Brewery, Pied Bull Hotel, 57 Northgate Street, Chester, CH1 1HQ
☎ (01244) 325829 ✉ contact@piedbull.co.uk
⊕ piedbull.co.uk

Pied Bull began brewing in 2011 using a one-barrel plant. Beer is mainly for in-house consumption but local beer festivals are supplied and occasional brewery swaps occur. Seasonal and special ales are also available.

Bull Races (ABV 4%)

Pied Eyed (ABV 4%)

Bull's Hit (ABV 4.3%)

The Bee and the Bull (ABV 4.4%)

Black Bull (ABV 5.2%)

Pilgrim SIBA

Pilgrim Brewery, 11 West Street, Reigate, Surrey, RH2 9BL
☎ (01737) 222651
✉ pilgrimbrewery@googlemail.com ⊕ pilgrim.co.uk

⊗ Pilgrim was set up in 1982 in Woldingham, Surrey, and moved to Reigate in 1985. The original owner, Dave Roberts, is still in charge. Beers are sold mostly in the Surrey area to around 30 outlets. Seasonal beers: see website.

Surrey Bitter (OG 1037, ABV 3.7%) 🍺
Pineapple, grapefruit and spicy aromas in this well-balanced quaffing beer. Initial biscuity maltiness with a hint of vanilla give way to a hoppy bitterness that becomes more pronounced in a refreshing bittersweet finish.

Weald Ale (OG 1038, ABV 3.7%)

Moild (OG 1038, ABV 3.8%)

Progress (OG 1041.5, ABV 4%) 🍺
A well-rounded tawny-coloured bitter. Predominantly sweet and malty with an underlying fruitiness and a hint of toffee. The flavour is well-balanced overall with a subdued bitterness.

Porter (OG 1042, ABV 4.1%) 🍺
Black beer with a good balance of dark malts plus berry fruit flavours. Roast character present throughout to give a bitter finish.

Pin-Up (NEW)

Pin-Up Beers Ltd, c/o 5 Hanover Terrace, Brighton, East Sussex, BN2 9SN
☎ (01273) 906956 ✉ info@pinupbeers.com
⊕ pinupbeers.com

Pin-up began brewing in 2011. Beers are contract brewed at an unnamed Essex brewer while suitable premises are found.

Natural Blonde (ABV 3.8%)

Red Head (ABV 4.2%)

Pitfield SIBA

Pitfield Brewery, Ashlyns Farm, Epping Road, North Weald, Epping, Essex, CM16 6RZ
☎ (01787) 282360 ☎ 07999 517231
✉ sales@pitfieldbeershop.co.uk
⊕ pitfieldbeershop.co.uk
Shop daily 10am-4pm
Tours by arrangement

⊗ After 24 years in London, Pitfield Brewery left the capital in 2006 and moved to new premises in Essex. It has since moved again to an organic farm with 25 acres of organic barley for the brewery's use. The beers are sold at farmers' and organic markets in the south-east of England. Pitfield also produces organic fruit wines, cider and perry. The beers are on sale in the brewery shop (at North Weald) but the brewery itself is located further afield on the farm. Seasonal beers are also available. All beers are organically produced to Soil Association standards and are vegan-friendly. Two further beers are produced using non-organic ingredients under the Epping Brewery name.

Dark Mild (OG 1036, ABV 3.4%)

Bitter (OG 1036, ABV 3.7%)

Lager (OG 1036, ABV 3.7%)

Pure Gold (OG 1039, ABV 3.9%)
A golden ale, initially malty with a complex bitter finish.

Shoreditch Stout (OG 1038, ABV 4%) 🍺
Chocolate and a raisin fruitiness on the nose lead to a fruity roast flavour and a sweetish finish with a little bitterness.

Eco Warrior (OG 1043, ABV 4.5%) 🍺
Golden ale with a vivid, citrus hop aroma. The hop character is balanced with a delicate sweetness in the taste, followed by an increasingly bitter finish.

Red Ale (OG 1046, ABV 4.8%) 🍺
Complex beer with a full, malty body and strong hop character.

1850 London Porter (OG 1048, ABV 5%) 🍺
Big-tasting dark ale dominated by coffee and forest fruits. The finish is dry but not acrid.

N1 Wheat Beer (OG 1048, ABV 5%)

1837 India Pale Ale (OG 1065, ABV 7%)

1792 Imperial Stout (OG 1085, ABV 9.3%)

For Epping Brewery:

Dark (OG 1034, ABV 3.4%)

Forest Bitter (OG 1036, ABV 3.7%)

Plain Ales SIBA

Plain Ales Brewery, Unit 17 b & c, Deverill Road Trading Estate, Sutton Veny, Wiltshire, BA12 0LG
☎ (01985) 841481 ✉ james@plainales.co.uk
⊕ plainales.co.uk
Tours by arrangement

⊗ Plain Ales started production in 2008 on a 2.5-barrel plant in a garange and expanded to a 10-barrel plant at the current location in 2009.

Sheepdip (ABV 3.8%)

Innocence (ABV 4%)
A straw-coloured, fragrant bitter.

Inntrigue (ABV 4.2%)

Inncognito (ABV 4.8%)

Inndulgence (ABV 5.2%)
A dark ruby porter with coffee, chocolate and a hint of smoke.

Plassey SIBA

Plassey Brewery, Eyton, Wrexham, LL13 0SP
☎ (01978) 781111 ☎ 07050 327127
✉ plassey@globalnet.co.uk ⊕ plasseybrewery.co.uk
Shop open office hours
Tours by arrangement

The brewery was founded in 1985 on the 250-acre Plassey Estate, which also incorporates a touring caravan park, craft centres, a golf course, three licensed outlets for Plassey's ales, and a brewery shop. Some 30 free trade outlets are also supplied. Seasonal beer: Ruddy Rudolph (ABV 4.5%, Xmas).

Original Border Mild (ABV 3.6%) ◆
A traditional dark mild, true to the style, based on an old Border Breweries (Wrexham) recipe. Full-bodied and smooth with good roast notes and some initial sweetness but also quite hoppy with a bitter finish.

Welsh Border Exhibition Ale (OG 1036, ABV 3.8%)

Bitter (OG 1041, ABV 4%) ◆
Full-bodied and distinctive best bitter. Good balance of hops and fruit flavours with a lasting dry, bitter aftertaste.

Offa's Dyke Ale (OG 1043, ABV 4.3%) ◆
Sweetish and fruity refreshing best bitter with caramel undertones. Some bitterness in the finish.

Owain Glyndwr's Ale (OG 1043, ABV 4.3%)

Fusilier (OG 1046, ABV 4.5%)

Cwrw Tudno (OG 1048, ABV 5%) ◆
A mellow, sweetish premium beer with classic Plassey flavours of fruit and hops.

Dragon's Breath (OG 1060, ABV 6%)
A fruity, strong bitter, smooth and quite sweet, though not cloying, with an intense, fruity aroma.

Plockton

Plockton Brewery, 5 Bank Street, Plockton, Ross-shire, IV52 8TP
☎ (01599) 544276
✉ andy@theplocktonbrewery.com
⊕ theplocktonbrewery.com
Tours by arrangement

⊗ The brewery started trading in 2007 and expanded to a 2.5-barrel plant in 2009. Bottle-conditioned beers are available and are suitable for vegetarians.

Plockton Bay (OG 1044, ABV 4.6%) ◆
A well-balanced, tawny coloured best bitter with plenty of hops and malt that give a bittersweet, fruity flavour.

Poachers SIBA

Poachers Brewery, 439 Newark Road, North Hykeham, Lincolnshire, LN6 9SP
☎ (01522) 807404 ☎ 07954 131972
⊕ poachersbrewery.co.uk
Tours by arrangement

Brewing started in 2001 on a five-barrel plant. In 2006 it was downsized to a 2.5-barrel plant and

relocated by brewer George Batterbee at the rear of his house. Regular outlets are supplied throughout Lincolnshire and surrounding counties; outlets further afield are supplied via wholesalers. Seasonal and bottle-conditioned beers are also available.

Trembling Rabbit Mild (OG 1034, ABV 3.4%)
Rich, dark mild with a smooth malty flavour and a slightly bitter finish.

Shy Talk Bitter (OG 1037, ABV 3.7%)
Clean-tasting session beer, pale gold in colour; slightly bitter finish, dry hopped.

Poachers Pride (OG 1040, ABV 4%)
Amber bitter brewed using Cascade hops that produce a citrus flavour and aroma that lingers.

Bog Trotter (OG 1042, ABV 4.2%)
A malty, earthy-tasting best bitter.

Lincoln Best (OG 1042, ABV 4.2%)

Billy Boy (OG 1044, ABV 4.4%)
A mid-brown beer hopped with Fuggles and Mount Hood.

Black Crow Stout (OG 1045, ABV 4.5%)
Dry stout with burnt toffee and caramel flavour.

Hykeham Gold (OG 1045, ABV 4.5%)
A cask-conditioned lager.

Monkey Hanger (OG 1045, ABV 4.5%)
A ruby red bitter with a smooth fruity flavour balanced by bitter hops.

Jock's Trap (OG 1050, ABV 5%)
A strong, pale brown bitter; hoppy and well-balanced with a slightly dry fruit finish.

Trout Tickler (OG 1055, ABV 5.5%)
Ruby bitter with intense flavour and character, sweet undertones with a hint of chocolate.

Porter

See Outstanding

Port Mahon

See Little Ale Cart

Potbelly SIBA

Potbelly Brewery Ltd, Sydney Street Entrance, Kettering, Northamptonshire, NN16 0JA
☎ (01536) 410818 ☎ 07834 867825
✉ toni@potbelly-brewery.co.uk
⊕ potbelly-brewery.co.uk
Tours by arrangement

Potbelly started brewing in 2005 on a 10-barrel plant and supplies some 200 outlets. The brewery has won more than 30 awards for its beers in only six years of brewing. Seasonal beers: see website. Bottle-conditioned beers are also available.

Best (OG 1036.9, ABV 3.8%)
A traditional chestnut-coloured bitter.

Aisling (OG 1038.5, ABV 4.4%)
A smooth pale bitter with a good balance of hops and malt.

Beijing Black (OG 1045, ABV 4.4%)
A strong dark mild.

Pigs Do Fly (OG 1041, ABV 4.4%)

THE BREWERIES

A light and golden ale.

Bellowhead (OG 1045, ABV 4.5%)
A light-coloured bitter with a citrus hoppy finish. Brewed with the help of Bellowhead, a local band.

Crazy Daze (OG 1050, ABV 5.5%)
A light golden bitter with hidden strength.

Potton SIBA

Potton Brewery Co Ltd, 10 Shannon Place, Potton, Bedfordshire, SG19 2SP
☎ (01767) 261042 ✉ info@potton-brewery.co.uk
⊕ potton-brewery.co.uk

Set up by the late Clive Towner and Bob Hearson in 1998, it was Potton's first brewery since 1922. The brewery expanded from 20 barrels a week to 50 in 2004 and further expansion is now taking place. Around 150 outlets are supplied. Seasonal and bottle-conditioned beers are also available.

Shannon IPA (OG 1035, ABV 3.6%) 🍾
A well-balanced session bitter with good bitterness and fruity late-hop character.

Potton Porter (OG 1040, ABV 4%)
A ruby sweet traditional porter with a burnt aftertaste and a hint of liquorice.

Gold (OG 1040, ABV 4.1%)
Golden-coloured, refreshing beer with a spicy/citrus late-hop character.

Shambles Bitter (OG 1043, ABV 4.3%)
A robust pale and heavily hopped beer with a subtle dry hop character imparted by Styrian Goldings.

Village Bike (OG 1042, ABV 4.3%) ◆
Classic English premium bitter, amber in colour, heavily late-hopped.

Pride of Potton (OG 1057, ABV 6%) ◆
Impressive, robust amber ale with a malty aroma, malt and ripe fruit in the mouth, and a fading sweetness.

Prescott SIBA

Prescott Brewery LLP, Unit 1, The Bramery Business Park, Alstone Lane, Cheltenham, Gloucestershire, GL51 8HE
☎ 07526 934866 ✉ info@prescottales.co.uk
⊕ prescottales.co.uk
Tours by arrangement

Prescott started brewing in 2009 on a 10-barrel plant.

Hill Climb (ABV 3.8%)

Track Record (ABV 4.4%)

Grand Prix (ABV 5.2%)

Preseli

Preseli Brewery, Unit 15, The Salterns, Tenby, Pembrokeshire, SA70 8EQ
☎ 07824 512103 ✉ preseli-brewery@hotmail.com
⊕ preseli-brewery.co.uk

⊠ Preseli began brewing in 2009 on a six-barrel plant. Seasonal beers are also available.

Even Keel (OG 1038, ABV 3.8%)

Old Mariners (OG 1040, ABV 4%)

Baggywrinkle (OG 1045, ABV 4.5%)

Powder Monkey (OG 1045, ABV 4.5%)

Prestonpans

Prestonpans Ales, 227-229 High Street, Prestonpans, East Lothian, EH32 9BE
☎ (01875) 819922 ☎ 07974 740248
✉ pans.ales@virginmedia.com
⊕ prestoungrange.org
Tours by arrangement

Prestonpans Ales opened as Fowler's in 2004 during the refurbishment of the Prestoungrange Gothenburg, the adjacent pub. After a period of inactivity, Roddy Beveridge, a member of Scottish Craft Brewers, continued the range of beers left by the previous brewer with some twists. The Prestoungrange Gothenburg offers all the beers, which are also distributed to pubs in Edinburgh and the Lothians and throughout Britain. Seasonal beers are brewed.

Prestonpans IPA (OG 1041, ABV 4.1%)
Light, crisp, refreshing malt with complex hop bitterness and a dry hop aroma.

Prestonpans 80/- (OG 1042, ABV 4.2%)
Complex malt with marked caramel notes and solid bitterness with a green hoppy finish.

Gothenburg Porter (OG 1043, ABV 4.4%)
Pronounced roast barley character and a long, dark chocolate and espresso coffee finish.

Princetown

See Dartmoor

Prior's Well

Prior's Well Brewery, The Old Kennels, Clumber Park, Hardwick Village, Nottinghamshire, S80 3PB
☎ 07971 277598 ✉ priorswell@aol.com
⊕ priorswell.co.uk

⊠ A sister brewery to Maypole, established in early 2010 on the Clumber Park Estate and housed in the former estate kennels, built in 1891 for the then duchess, which were abandoned in the mid-1960s and have now been sympathetically restored by the National Trust, which owns the property. The five-barrel plant was previously used at Tydd Steam and before that Oldershaws Brewery. Natural Clumber water from the estate is used in the brewing process. Bottle-conditioned beers are planned. Seasonal beers are also available.

Gardener's Tap (OG 1037, ABV 3.8%)

Silver Chalice (OG 1040, ABV 4.1%)

Father Hawkins (OG 1044, ABV 4.5%)

Priors Gold (OG 1045, ABV 4.7%)

Prospect SIBA

Prospect Brewery Ltd, Unit 11, Bradley Hall Trading Estate, Bradley Lane, Standish, Wigan, Lancashire, WN6 0XQ
☎ (01257) 421329 ✉ sales@prospectbrewery.com
⊕ prospectbrewery.com
Tours by arrangement

⊕Brewing commenced in 2007 on a five-barrel plant from Bank Top Brewery. The brewery was originally situated at the top of Prospect Hill – hence the name – but moved to new premises in 2010 using a 12-barrel plant. Most of the beers are named along prospecting/mining themes. More than 150 outlets are supplied direct. Seasonal beers are also available. A brewery bar is now open to the public (Thu 4-7pm; Fri 4-7.30pm).

Silver Tally (OG 1037, ABV 3.7%)
A clean, pale golden bitter with citrus aromas and a full hop flavour with a dry bitter finish.

Nutty Slack (OG 1039, ABV 3.9%) ◆
Dark brown mild ale with malt and fruit in the aroma. Creamy and chocolatey on the palate, with both malt and fruit in evidence. Malty and moderately bitter finish.

Hop Vine Bitter (OG 1040, ABV 4%)
A pale golden beer with citrus hops and a satisfying sweet balance.

One Twenty (OG 1040, ABV 4%)
A yellow/gold beer wiht zesty citrus notes; clean tasting and refreshing.

Panned Out (OG 1040, ABV 4%)
A tawny beer with full-bodied rounded bitterness and spicy notes.

Pioneer (OG 1040, ABV 4%)
A light bodied amber beer with aromas of dry pale malt and earthy hops.

Blinding Light (OG 1042, ABV 4.2%)
A pale refreshing beer with citrus and spicy notes.

Gold Rush (OG 1045, ABV 4.5%)
A deep golden ale with hoppy and bitter flavours, light fruity notes and a grassy, floral finish.

Big John (OG 1047, ABV 4.8%)
A dark stout bursting with smoky liquorice flavour with a satisfying bitter aftertaste.

Purity SIBA

Purity Brewing Co Ltd, The Brewery, Upper Spernall Farm, Great Alne, Warwickshire, B49 6JF
☎ (01789) 488007 ✉ sales@puritybrewing.com
⊕ puritybrewing.com
Shop Mon-Fri 8am-5pm; Sat 10am-1pm
Tours by arrangement

☺ Brewing began in 2005 in a purpose-designed plant housed in converted barns in the heart of Warwickshire. The brewery incorporates an environmentally-friendly effluent treatment system. It supplies the free trade within a 70-mile radius and delivers to more than 500 outlets.

Pure Gold (OG 1039.5, ABV 3.8%) 🍷
An easy-drinking beer with a dry, bitter finish.

Mad Goose (OG 1042.5, ABV 4.2%)
Light copper in colour with a zesty hop character and citrus overtones.

Pure Ubu (OG 1044.8, ABV 4.5%)
An amber-coloured beer, well-balanced and full-flavoured.

Purple Moose SIBA

Bragdy Mws Piws Cyf/Purple Moose Brewery Ltd, Madoc Street, Porthmadog, Gwynedd, LL49 9DB
☎ (01766) 515571 ✉ beer@purplemoose.co.uk
⊕ purplemoose.co.uk
Shop Mon-Fri 9am-5pm
Tours by arrangement

A 10-barrel plant opened in 2005 by Lawrence Washington in a former saw mill and farmers' warehouse in the coastal town of Porthmadog. The names of the beers reflect local history and geography. The brewery now supplies around 250 outlets. Seasonal and monthly special beers: see website.

Cwrw Eryri/Snowdonia Ale (OG 1035.3, ABV 3.6%) 🍷 🍴 ◆
Golden, refreshing bitter with citrus fruit hoppiness in aroma and taste. The full mouthfeel leads to a long-lasting, dry, bitter finish.

Cwrw Madog/Madog's Ale (OG 1037, ABV 3.7%) ◆
Full-bodied session bitter. Malty nose and an initial nutty flavour but bitterness dominates. Well balanced and refreshing with a dry roastiness on the taste and a good dry finish.

Talyllyn Pioneer (ABV 3.9%)
Brewed to celebrate 60 years of preservation on the Talyllyn Railway.

Cwrw Glaslyn/Glaslyn Ale (OG 1040.5, ABV 4.2%) 🍴 ◆
Refreshing light and malty amber-coloured ale. Plenty of hop in the aroma and taste. Good smooth mouthfeel leading to a slightly chewy finish.

Ochr Tywyll y Mws/Dark Side of the Moose (OG 1045, ABV 4.6%)
A delicious dark ale with a deep malt flavour and a fruity bitterness.

Quantock SIBA

Quantock Brewery, Unit E, Monument View, Summerfield Avenue, Chelston Business Park, Wellington, Somerset, TA21 9ND
☎ (01823) 662669 ✉ rob@quantockbrewery.co.uk
⊕ quantockbrewery.co.uk

Quantock began brewing in 2008 on an eight-barrel plant. Bottle-conditioned beers are available.

Ale (ABV 3.8%)

Sunraker (ABV 4.2%)

Wills Neck (ABV 4.3%)

Stout (ABV 4.5%)

White Hind (ABV 4.5%)

Royal Stag IPA (ABV 6%)

UXB (ABV 9%)

Quartz SIBA

Quartz Brewing Ltd, Archers, Alrewas Road, Kings Bromley, Staffordshire, DE13 7HW
☎ (01543) 473965 ✉ scott@quartzbrewing.co.uk
⊕ quartzbrewing.co.uk
Shop Mon, Wed & Fri 9.30am-4.30pm; Sat 10am-2pm
Tours by arrangement

☺ Quartz was established in 2005 by Scott and Julia Barnett. There are four regular beers produced in cask, bottle and mini-cask, supplemented with seasonal specials. Around 50 outlets are supplied direct.

Blonde (OG 1038, ABV 3.8%) ◆
Little aroma, gentle hop and background malt. Sweet with unsophisticated sweetshop tastes.

Crystal (OG 1040, ABV 4.2%) ◆
Sweet aroma with some fruit and yeasty Marmite hints. Hoppiness begins but dwindles to a bittersweet finish.

Extra Blonde (OG 1042, ABV 4.4%) ◆
Sweet malty aroma with a touch of fruit. Sweet start, smooth with a hint of hops in the sugary finish.

Heart (OG 1045, ABV 4.6%) ◆
Pale brown with some aroma of fruit and malt. Gentle tastes of fruit and hops eventually clear to leave a bitter finish.

Quay

See Dorset

Quercus

Quercus Brewery & Beer House, Unit 2M, South Hams Business Park, Churchstow, Kingsbridge, Devon, TQ7 3QH
☎ (01548) 854888 ✉ info@quercusbrewery.com
⊕ quercusbrewery.com
Shop Wed-Thu 12-5pm, Fri 10am-5pm, Sat 10am-3pm (Winter Fri & Sat 10am-5pm)

⊠ Quercus began trading in 2007 and is a small, family-run brewery using an eight-barrel brew plant. A specialist beer shop is also owned and the lease on the King's Arms Hotel in Kingsbridge has recently been acquired, a local outlet for Quercus beers. Seasonal beers: see website.

Origin (OG 1039, ABV 3.9%)
A smooth, easy-drinking amber ale with the sweetness of the malt balanced by the refreshing aroma and taste of Fuggles hops.

Prospect (OG 1039, ABV 4%)
Subtle bitterness and sweet malt flavour with a rich aroma and colour.

Shingle Bay (OG 1041, ABV 4.2%)
A light, golden, easy-drinking ale with fruity citrus aroma and taste giving a subtle, crisp bite to refresh the palate.

QB (Quercus Bitter) (OG 1044, ABV 4.5%)
A full-bodied best bitter with a hint of oak-smoked aroma and taste.

Ramsbury SIBA

Ramsbury Estates Ltd, Priory Farm, Axford, Marlborough, Wiltshire, SN8 2NN
☎ (01672) 520647/541407
✉ dgolding@ramsburyestates.com
⊕ ramsburybrewery.com
Tours by arrangement

⊠ Ramsbury started brewing in 2004 and is situated high on the Marlborough Downs in Wiltshire. The brewery uses home grown barley from the Ramsbury Estate. At present a 10-barrel plant is used but there are plans to increase capacity.

Bitter (OG 1036, ABV 3.6%)
Amber-coloured beer with a smooth, delicate aroma and flavour.

Sunsplash (ABV 4%)

Kennet Valley (OG 1040, ABV 4.1%)
A light amber, hoppy bitter with a long, dry finish.

Flint Knapper (OG 1041, ABV 4.2%)
Rich amber in colour with a malty taste.

Gold (OG 1043, ABV 4.5%)
A rich golden-coloured beer with a light hoppy aroma and taste.

Chalk Stream (ABV 5%)

Rum Truffle (ABV 5.6%)

Ramsgate SIBA

Ramsgate Brewery Ltd, Unit 1, Hornet Close, Pyson's Road Industrial Estate, Broadstairs, Kent, CT10 2YD
☎ (01843) 868453 ✉ beer@ramsgatebrewery.co.uk
⊕ ramsgatebrewery.co.uk
Shop Mon-Fri 10am-5pm; Sat 10am-1pm
Tours by arrangement

⊠ Ramsgate was established in 2002 at the back of a Ramsgate pub. In 2006 the brewery moved to its current location, allowing for increased capacity and bottling. Bottle-conditioned beers are available. Seasonal and monthly specials: see website.

Gadds' No. 7 (OG 1037, ABV 3.8%)

Gadds' Seasider (OG 1042, ABV 4.3%)

Gadds' No. 5 (OG 1043, ABV 4.4%)

Gadds' No. 3 (OG 1047, ABV 5%)

Gadds' Dogbolter (OG 1054, ABV 5.6%)

Randalls SIBA

RW Randall Ltd, La Piette Brewery, St Georges Esplanade, St Peter Port, Guernsey, GY1 2BH
☎ (01481) 720134 ✉ tours@rwrandall.co.uk
⊕ randallsbrewery.co.uk
Tours by arrangement

Randalls has been brewing since 1868 and was bought in 2006 by a group of private investors. It moved a few years ago to new premises with a 36-barrel brewhouse. 18 pubs are owned and a further 50 outlets are supplied.

Patois (OG 1045, ABV 4.5%)

Raw SIBA

Raw Brewing Co Ltd, Units 3 & 4, Silver House, Adelphi Way, Staveley, Derbyshire, S43 3LJ
☎ (01246) 475445 ✉ contact@rawbrew.com
⊕ rawbrew.com
Tours by arrangement

⊠ Raw began brewing in 2010 using a five-barrel plant from Prospect Brewery of Wigan. Three core beers are available with plans to extend the range and produce seasonal specials.

Blonde Pale (OG 1039, ABV 3.9%)

JR Best (OG 1042, ABV 4.2%)

Dark Peak (OG 1045, ABV 4.5%)

Anubis (OG 1051, ABV 5.2%)

Grey Ghost (OG 1056, ABV 5.9%)

RCH SIBA

RCH Brewery, West Hewish, Weston-Super-Mare, Somerset, BS24 6RR

☎ (01934) 834447 ✉ rchbrew@aol.com
⊕ rchbrewery.com

⊠ The brewery was originally installed in the early 1980s behind the Royal Clarence Hotel at Burnham-on-Sea. Since 1993 brewing has taken place in a former cider mill at West Hewish. A 30-barrel plant was installed in 2000. RCH supplies 150 outlets and the award-winning beers are available nationwide through its own wholesaling company, which also distributes beers from other small independent breweries. Seasonal and bottle-conditioned beers are also available.

Hewish IPA (OG 1036, ABV 3.6%) ◆
Light, hoppy bitter with some malt and fruit, though slightly less fruit in the finish. Floral citrus hop aroma; pale brown/amber colour.

PG Steam (OG 1039, ABV 3.9%) 🍷 🍺 ◆
Powerful hop and malt flavour with just a hint of fruit. Very bitter aftertaste with the merest suggestion of roast.

Pitchfork (OG 1043, ABV 4.3%) ◆
Yellow best bitter with a citrus hop aroma with pale malt. Hops predominate in a taste whose underlying sweetness becomes slightly astringent before ending with bitter hops.

Old Slug Porter (OG 1046, ABV 4.5%) 🍷 ◆
Smoky, roast malt and hops with lots of body and dark fruit. Complex, dark-brown slightly sour porter. Sweetness fades leaving a smoky, bitter-sour aftertaste.

East Street Cream (OG 1050, ABV 5%) ◆
Robust tawny-coloured strong bitter. Sweet-and-sour fruit flavours fill the mouth, some balancing hop leading to a slightly astringent finish.

Double Header (OG 1053, ABV 5.3%) ◆
Light brown, full-bodied strong bitter. Nicely balanced flavours of malt, hops and tropical fruits are followed by a long, bittersweet finish. Refreshing and easy-drinking for its strength.

Firebox (OG 1060, ABV 6%) ◆
Full-bodied pale-brown strong bitter; faint aroma of malt and hops with banana notes. Sweet malt and fruit in the mouth soon turn to a bitter astringency; bittersweet aftertaste.

Reality

Reality Brewery, 127 High Road, Chilwell, Nottingham, NG9 4AT
☎ 07801 539523

Reality began brewing in 2010 using a 2.5-barrel plant in the unused space of an IT business. Its relation to this and real ale formed the name. The brewery relocated to nearby premises in 2011 and fermentation capacity was increased. Beers are usually themed around the brewery name.

Virtuale Reality (OG 1038, ABV 3.8%)

Bitter Reality (OG 1044, ABV 4.4%)

Rebellion SIBA

Rebellion Beer Co, Marlow Brewery, Bencombe Farm, Marlow Bottom, Buckinghamshire, SL7 3LT
☎ (01628) 476594 ✉ info@rebellionbeer.co.uk
⊕ rebellionbeer.co.uk
Shop Mon-Fri 8am-6pm; Sat 9am-6pm
Tours by arrangement

⊠ Established in 1993, Rebellion filled the void left when Wethereds ceased brewing in 1987 in Marlow. Steady growth led to larger premises being sought and a relocation in 1999. Rebellion's nearby Three Horseshoes pub is the brewery tap. Rebellion Mild is only available in this pub and a few other locals. Around 500 other outlets are supplied. Seasonal beers: see website. Bottle-conditioned beer is also available.

IPA (OG 1039, ABV 3.7%) ◆
Copper-coloured bitter, sweet and malty, with resinous and red apple flavours. Caramel and fruit decline to leave a dry, bitter and malty finish.

Smuggler (OG 1042, ABV 4.1%) ◆
A red-brown beer, well-bodied and bitter with an uncompromisingly dry, bitter finish.

Mutiny (OG 1046, ABV 4.5%) ◆
Tawny in colour, this full-bodied best bitter is predominantly fruity and moderately bitter with crystal malt continuing to a dry finish.

Rectory SIBA

Rectory Ales Ltd, Streat Hill Farm, Streat Hill, Streat, Hassocks, East Sussex, BN6 8RP
☎ (01273) 890570 ✉ rectoryales@hotmail.com
Tours by arrangement (Easter-Sep)

⊠ Rectory was founded in 1995 by the Rector of Plumpton, the Rev Godfrey Broster, to generate funds for the maintenance of his three parish churches. 107 parishioners are shareholders. The brewing capacity is now 20 barrels a week. All outlets are supplied from the brewery. A different seasonal beer is produced each month – please ring for details.

All Saints Tipple (OG 1041, ABV 4.1%)
A traditional style bitter. Mid-brown in colour.

Redemption SIBA

Redemption Brewing Co Ltd, Unit 2, Compass West Industrial Estate, 33 West Road, Tottenham, London, N17 0XL
☎ (020) 8885 5227 ☎ 07919 416046
✉ andy.moffat@redemptionbrewing.co.uk
⊕ redemptionbrewing.co.uk
Tours by arrangement for local organisations and CAMRA groups

⊠ Redemption began brewing in 2010 on a 12-barrel plant. Most of the beer is supplied to pubs in north and central London.

Pale Ale (OG 1037.5, ABV 3.8%) ◆
A well-balanced, amber bitter with hops and citrus orange throughout. The sweet maltiness fades in the aftertaste leaving a slightly dry bitter finish. Orange and peach on the nose.

Hopspur (OG 1044.5, ABV 4.5%)
An amber ale with chewy biscuit malt flavours, slightly sweet with some roast malt throughout. Hops provide citrus and pine flavours and an easy, bitter finish.

Urban Dusk (OG 1044, ABV 4.6%) ◆
Full-bodied brown best bitter; chocolate and some toffee in the aroma. Citrus, creamy fudge and dark roast chocolate on the palate, drying to leave a slightly dry bitter finish.

THE BREWERIES

Horsham (qv) and occasionally elsewhere. All beers listed are available cask and bottle-conditioned. Six strong (ABV 6-9%) bottle-conditioned Christmas beers are produced annually, principally for export to the U.S.

Bitter (OG 1040, ABV 4%)

Organic Beer/ROB (OG 1043, ABV 4.3%)

Blue (OG 1049, ABV 5%)

Ivanhoe (OG 1050, ABV 5.2%)

IPA (OG 1055, ABV 5.5%)

Foreign Export Stout (OG 1078, ABV 8%)

For Coniston Brewing:

Bluebird (ABV 4.2%)

XB (ABV 4.4%)

Old Man (ABV 4.8%)

Ridleys

See Greene King in New Nationals section

Ringmore

Ringmore Craft Brewery Ltd, Higher Ringmore Road, Shaldon, Devon, TQ14 0HG
☎ (01626) 873114
✉ geoff@ringmorecraftbrewery.co.uk

☺Ringmore was established in 2007 on a one-barrel plant and is the first brewery in Shaldon since 1920. It expanded to a 2.5-barrel plant in 2009 to keep up with demand. Bottle-conditioned beers are also available, including seasonals.

Oarsome Ale (OG 1046, ABV 4.6%)

Ringwood

See Marston's in New Nationals section

Riverhead

⬛ Riverhead Brewery Ltd, 2 Peel Street, Marsden, Huddersfield, West Yorkshire, HD7 6BR
☎ (01484) 841270 (Pub) ☎ (01924) 261333 (Brewery) ✉ brewery@ossett-brewery.co.uk
⊕ ossett-brewery.co.uk
Tours by arrangement (through Ossett Brewing Co)

☺ Riverhead is a brew-pub that opened in 1995 after conversion from an old grocery shop. Ossett Brewing Co purchased the site in 2006 but runs it as a separate brewery. It has since opened The Dining Room on the first floor, which uses Riverhead beers in its dishes. All original recipes have been retained with new beers also being added. The core range of beers are named after local reservoirs, with the height of the reservoir relating to the strength of the beer. There are many rotating beers produced as well as seasonals.

Sparth Mild (ABV 3.6%)

Butterley Bitter (OG 1038, ABV 3.8%) ◗
A dry, amber-coloured, hoppy session beer.

March Haigh (OG 1046, ABV 4.6%)
A golden-brown premium bitter. Malty and full-bodied with moderate bitterness.

Redbrook Premium (ABV 5.5%)

Riverside

Riverside Brewery, Bee's Farm, Wainfleet, Lincolnshire, PE24 4LX
☎ (01754) 881288 ☎ 07779 280996

☺ Riverside started brewing in 2003, almost across the road from Bateman's, using a five-barrel plant. In 2008 the brewery moved to new premises. Eight barrels a week are produced, with some 15-20 outlets supplied. Seasonal beers are also available.

Dixon's Major (OG 1038, ABV 3.9%)

Dixon's Hoppy Daze (OG 1041, ABV 4.2%)

Dixon's Old Diabolical (OG 1043, ABV 4.4%)

John Roberts

See Three Tuns

Robinson's IFBB

Frederic Robinson Ltd, Unicorn Brewery, Lower Hillgate, Stockport, Cheshire, SK1 1JJ
☎ (0161) 612 4061 ✉ brewery@frederic-robinson.co.uk ⊕ frederic-robinson.com
Tours by arrangement

☺ Robinson's has been brewing since 1838 and the business is still owned and run by the family (fifth and sixth generations). It has an estate of just under 400 pubs. Contract beers are also brewed. Seasonal beers: see website.

Hatters (OG 1032, ABV 3.3%) ◗
A light mild with a malty, fruity aroma. Biscuity malt with some hop and fruit in the taste and finish. (A darkened version is available in a handful of outlets and badged Dark Hatters.)

Old Stockport (OG 1034, ABV 3.5%) ◗
A beer with a refreshing taste of malt, hops and citrus fruit, a fruity aroma, and a short, dry finish.

Dizzy Blonde (OG 1037, ABV 3.8%)
A straw-coloured summer ale with a distinctive hop aroma. A light, refreshing beer with a clean, zesty, hop-dominated palate complemented by a crisp, dry finish.

Dark Hatters (OG 1032, ABV 4%)

Hartleys XB (OG 1040, ABV 4%) ◗
An overly sweet and malty bitter with a bitter citrus peel fruitiness and a hint of liquorice in the finish.

Cumbria Way (OG 1040, ABV 4.1%)
A pronounced malt aroma with rich fruit notes. Rounded malt and hops in the mouth, long dry finish with citrus fruit notes. Brewed for the Hartley's estate in Cumbria.

Unicorn (OG 1041, ABV 4.2%) ◗
Amber beer with a fruity aroma. Malt, hops and fruit in the taste with a bitter, malty finish.

Double Hop (OG 1050, ABV 5%) ◗
Pale brown beer with malt and fruit on the nose. Full hoppy taste with malt and fruit, leading to a hoppy, bitter finish.

Old Tom (OG 1079, ABV 8.5%) 🍷 🍴 ◗
A full-bodied, dark beer with malt, fruit and chocolate on the aroma. A complex range of flavours includes dark chocolate, full maltiness,

port and fruits and lead to a long, bittersweet aftertaste.

Rockingham SIBA

Rockingham Ales, c/o 25 Wansford Road, Elton, Cambridgeshire, PE8 6RZ
☎ (01832) 280722 ✉ brian@rockinghamales.co.uk
⊕ rockinghamales.co.uk

⊠ A part-time brewery established in 1997 that operates from a converted farm building near Blatherwycke, Northamptonshire (business address as above). The two-barrel plant produces a prolific range of beers and supplies several local outlets. The regular beers are brewed on a rota basis, with special beers brewed to order. Seasonal beers are also available.

Forest Gold (OG 1039, ABV 3.9%)
A hoppy blonde ale with citrus flavours. Well-balanced and clean finishing.

Hop Devil (OG 1040, ABV 3.9%)
Six hop varieties give this golden ale a bitter start and spicy finish.

A1 Amber Ale (OG 1041, ABV 4%)
A hoppy session beer with fruit and blackcurrant undertones.

Saxon Cross (OG 1041, ABV 4.1%)
A golden-red ale with nut and coffee aromas. Citrus hop flavours predominate.

Fruits of the Forest (OG 1043, ABV 4.2%)
A multi-layered beer in which summer fruits and several spices compete with a big hop presence.

Dark Forest (OG 1050, ABV 5%)
A dark and complex beer, similar to a Belgian Dubbel, with malty/smoky flavours that give way to a fruity bitter finish.

Rodham's

Rodham's Brewery, 74 Albion Street, Otley, West Yorkshire, LS21 1BZ
☎ (01943) 464530

Michael Rodham began brewing in 2005 on a one-barrel plant in the cellar of his house. Capacity has gradually increased and is now 2.5 barrels. All beers produced are malt-only, using whole hops. Occasional seasonal and bottle-conditioned beers are available.

Relish (OG 1035, ABV 3.7%)
A pale ale with creamy malt and citrus fruit flavours with a lasting hoppy bitterness.

Rubicon (OG 1039, ABV 4.1%)
Amber-coloured with a nutty, malt and light fruit taste. A dry, peppery and bitter aftertaste.

Wheat Beer (OG 1039, ABV 4.1%)
Naturally cloudy, sharp and refreshing.

Royale (OG 1042, ABV 4.4%)
A golden beer with a citrus, hoppy taste, underlying malt with a bitter finish.

Old Albion (OG 1048, ABV 5%)
A dark garnet-coloured porter with a complex taste of roast malt and tart fruit with a balancing bitterness.

IPA (OG 1053, ABV 5.7%)
Rich malt combines with tart citrus hops giving a long, bitter finish.

Rooster's SIBA

Rooster's Brewing Co Ltd, Unit 3-4, Grimbald Park, Wetherby Road, Knaresborough, North Yorkshire, HG5 8LJ
☎ (01423) 865959 ✉ tom@roosters.co.uk
⊕ roosters.co.uk
Tours by arrangement

☺ Rooster's was opened in 1993 by Sean and Alison Franklin. From 1996 one-off and seasonal specials have been brewed under the Outlaw Brewery Co name. The brewery moved to larger premises in 2001. The brewery has been bought by Ian Fozzard of Market Town Taverns. Sean and Alison will run the brewery until they retire, when Ian's son will take over. Seasonal and bottle-conditioned beers are also available.

Leghorn (OG 1043, ABV 4.3%)

Yankee (OG 1043, ABV 4.3%) ◣
A straw-coloured beer with a delicate, fruity aroma leading to a well-balanced taste of malt and hops with a slight evidence of sweetness, followed by a refreshing, fruity/bitter finish.

YPA (Yorkshire Pale Ale) (OG 1043, ABV 4.3%)
A pale-coloured beer with pronounced raspberry and flower aromas.

Under Outlaw Brewery name:

Wrangler (ABV 3.7%)

Wild Mule (ABV 3.9%)

Roseland

⬛ Roseland Brewery, c/o Roseland Inn, Philleigh, nr St Mawes, Truro, Cornwall, TR2 5NB
☎ (01872) 580254 ☎ 07977 472484

Roseland was established in 2009 by Phil Heslip at his pub, the Roseland Inn. The beers are mainly named after local birds and are generally only available in the Roseland Inn or its sister pub, the Victory Inn at St Mawes though beers can be found at local beer festivals.

Cornish Shag (OG 1037, ABV 3.8%)
A copper-coloured session bitter.

Full Marks (OG 1039, ABV 4%)
A dark amber bitter, well-balanced with a dry, hoppy finish.

Choughed to Bits (OG 1042, ABV 4.2%)
A mid-brown hoppy bitter.

Gullable (OG 1044, ABV 4.5%)
A golden ale with citrus overtones.

High as a Kite (OG 1047, ABV 4.8%)
A dark, hoppy bitter.

Rossendale

⬛ Rossendale Brewery Ltd, Griffin Inn, 84 Hud Rake, Haslingden, Lancashire, BB4 5AF
☎ (01706) 214021 ⊕ rossendalebrewery.co.uk

☺Formerly known as Pennine Ales, the brewery acquired the brew plant previously used by Porter Brewing Co in 2007 and is based in the cellar of the Griffin Inn in Haslingden. It produces seven regular cask ales.

Floral Dance (OG 1035, ABV 3.6%)
A pale and fruity session beer.

Hameldon Bitter (OG 1040, ABV 3.8%)

THE BREWERIES

A dark traditional bitter with a dry and assertive character that develops in the finish.

Glen Top (OG 1045, ABV 4%)

Ale (OG 1045, ABV 4.2%)
A malty aroma leads to a complex, malt dominated flavour, supported by a dry, increasingly bitter finish.

Halo Pail (OG 1045, ABV 4.5%)

Pitch Porter (OG 1050, ABV 5%)
A full-bodied, rich beer with a slightly sweet, malty start, counter balanced with sharp bitterness and a roast barley dominance.

Sunshine (OG 1055, ABV 5.3%)
A hoppy and bitter golden beer with a citrus character. The lingering finish is dry and spicy.

Rother Valley SIBA

Rother Valley Brewing Co, Gate Court Farm, Station Road, Northiam, East Sussex, TN31 6QT
☎ (01797) 252922 ☎ 07798 877551
Tours by arrangement

⊠ Rother Valley was established in Northiam in 1993 overlooking the Rother Levels. Hops grown on the farm and from Sandhurst are used. Brewing is split between cask and an ever-increasing range of filtered bottled beers. Around 100 outlets are supplied. A monthly seasonal ale is available.

Honeyfuzz (OG 1038, ABV 3.8%)
A pale bitter flavoured with Sussex honey, subtle but not sweet with a citrus twang on the finish.

Smild (OG 1038, ABV 3.8%)
A full-bodied, dark, creamy mild with hints of chocolate.

Level Best (OG 1040, ABV 4%) 🗍 ◆
Full-bodied tawny session bitter with a malt and fruit aroma, malty taste and a dry, hoppy finish.

Copper Ale (OG 1041, ABV 4.1%)
A copper-coloured ale with a good balance of malt and hops.

Hoppers Ale (OG 1044, ABV 4.4%)
A copper-coloured ale. The initial burst of hop is followed by a pleasant caramel taste.

Boadicea (OG 1045, ABV 4.5%)
A straw-coloured beer with a delicate, fruity flavour.

Blues (OG 1050, ABV 5%)
A dark brew full of complex tastes such as chocolate, raisins and a roast finish. Deceptively smooth.

Rotters

Rotters Brewery, Tower Hotel, Talgarth, Powys, LD3 0BW
☎ (01874) 711253 ⊠ rottersbrewery@gmail.com
⊕ rottersbrewery.co.uk
Tours by arrangement

☺Rotters Brewery opened in 2010. Seasonal beer: Whipping Tree (ABV 3.6%, summer). Rotters Stout is suitable for vegans.

Stout (OG 1046, ABV 4.5%)
A creamy stout with a roasted barley character.

Grounds For Divorce (OG 1048, ABV 4.7%)
A premium ruby ale.

Rowditch

🗏 Rowditch Inn Brewery, Rowditch Inn, 246 Uttoxeter New Road, Derby, DE22 3LL
☎ (01332) 343123

Rowditch began brewing in 2010 using a three-barrel plant on the premises of the Rowditch pub.

BSB (Bog Standard Beer) (OG 1040, ABV 3.8%)

RSB (Rowditch Special Beer) (OG 1050, ABV 5%)

Rowton

Rowton Brewery Ltd, Stone House, Rowton, Telford, Shropshire, TF6 6QX
☎ 07746 290995

Rowton was established in 2008 on a four-barrel plant in an old cow shed on the owner's farm. Water is from a borehole on site. Meteorite is named after a meteorite that landed on the farm in the 19th century and is now in a London museum. Seasonal beers are also available.

Bitter (ABV 3.9%)

Comet (ABV 4.3%)

Meteorite (ABV 4.7%)

Royal Tunbridge Wells SIBA

Royal Tunbridge Wells Brewing Co Ltd, Spa Brewery, 18H Chapman Way, Royal Tunbridge Wells, Kent, TN2 3EF
☎ (01892) 618140
⊠ info@royaltunbridgewellsbrewing.co.uk
⊕ royaltunbridgewellsbrewing.co.uk
Tours by arrangement

Brewing began in 2010 using a 10-barrel plant. Around 250 outlets are supplied direct. Seasonal and bottle-conditioned beers are also available.

Dipper (OG 1038, ABV 3.7%)
A full-flavoured beer with a crisp hop bitterness.

Sovereign (OG 1039, ABV 3.8%)
A delicate sweet nose and full hop bitterness.

Royal (OG 1042, ABV 4.1%) ◆
This typically Kentish best bitter has a strong bitter hop character tempered by malt, with hints of fruit in the mouth and a long finish.

Rudgate SIBA

Rudgate Brewery Ltd, 2 Centre Park, Marston Moor Business Park, Tockwith, York, North Yorkshire, YO26 7QF
☎ (01423) 358382 ⊠ sales@rudgatebrewery.co.uk
⊕ rudgatebrewery.co.uk

☺ Rudgate Brewery was founded in 1992 and is located in an old armoury building on a disused World War II airfield. It has a 15-barrel plant and six open fermenting vessels, producing more than 70 barrels a week. Around 350 outlets are supplied direct. Seasonal beers are also available.

Jorvik Blonde (OG 1036, ABV 3.8%)
Flaxen blonde ale with a balanced hoppy bitterness and a crisp, fruity finish.

Viking (OG 1036, ABV 3.8%) ◆
An initially warming and malty, full-bodied beer, with hops and fruit lingering into the aftertaste.

Battleaxe (OG 1040, ABV 4.2%) ◆
A well-hopped bitter with slightly sweet initial taste and light bitterness. Complex fruit character gives a memorable aftertaste.

Ruby Mild (OG 1041, ABV 4.4%) ▦ ◆
Nutty, rich ruby ale, stronger than usual for a mild.

Special (OG 1042, ABV 4.5%)
Moderately bitter leading to a citrus, hoppy finish.

Well Blathered (OG 1046, ABV 5%)
A premium bitter, golden-coloured with distinctive lemon on the nose.

Rugby

See Wood Farm

Saddleworth

🍺 Church Inn & Saddleworth Brewery, Church Lane, Uppermill, Oldham, Greater Manchester, OL3 6LW
☎ (01457) 820902/872415
Tours by arrangement

☺ Saddleworth started brewing in 1997 in a brewhouse that had been closed for around 120 years. Brewery and inn are set in a historic location at the top of a valley overlooking Saddleworth Moor and next to St Chads Church, which dates from 1215. Seasonal beers are also available.

Mild (OG 1038, ABV 3.6%)

More (OG 1038, ABV 3.8%)

St George's Bitter (OG 1038, ABV 3.8%)

Blue Tree Bitter (OG 1040, ABV 4%)

Honey Smacker (OG 1042, ABV 4.1%)

Hop Smacker (OG 1042, ABV 4.1%)

Indya Pale Ale (OG 1042, ABV 4.1%)

Shaftbender (OG 1060, ABV 5.4%)

Sadler's SIBA

Sadler's Ales Brewery, 7 Stourbridge Road, Lye, Stourbridge, West Midlands, DY9 7DG
☎ (01384) 895230 ✉ beer@sadlersales.co.uk
⊕ sadlersales.co.uk
Tours by arrangement

☺Thomas Alexander Sadler founded the original brewery in 1900 adjacent to the Windsor Castle Inn, Oldbury. Fourth generation brewers John and Chris Sadler re-opened the brewery in its new location in 2004. The brewery tap house was built and opened in 2006 next to the brewery. Around 250 outlets are supplied. An extensive range of bottle-conditioned beers is available as well as beer-based cheeses and condiments.

JPA (OG 1038, ABV 3.8%)

Red House Mild (OG 1040, ABV 4%)

Mellow Yellow (OG 1041, ABV 4.1%)
A pale ale brewed with plenty of hop and honey.

Worcester Sorcerer (OG 1043, ABV 4.3%)
Brewed with English hops and barley with hints of mint and lemon, creating a floral aroma and crisp bitterness.

Thin Ice (OG 1045, ABV 4.5%)
A pale ale. Bitter but with an orange and lemon finish.

Stumbling Badger (OG 1049, ABV 4.9%)
A well-balanced strong ale, packed with flavour and aroma with hints of fruit and a hoppy finish.

Mud City Stout (OG 1066, ABV 6.6%)
Rich, full-bodied strong stout brewed with raw cocoa, fresh vanilla pods, oats, wheat and dark malts.

Saffron SIBA

Saffron Brewery, The Cartshed, Parsonage Farm, Henham, Essex, CM22 6AN
☎ (01279) 850923 ☎ 07747 696901
✉ tb@saffronbrewery.co.uk ⊕ saffronbrewery.co.uk
Tours by arrangement

⊗ Founded in 2005, Saffron is situated near the historic East Anglian town of Saffron Walden, famous for its malting industry in the 18th century. The brewery was upgraded to a 15-barrel plant in early 2008 and re-located to a converted barn at Parsonage Farm by Henham church, with a purpose-built reed bed for environmentally friendly disposal of waste products. 40 outlets are supplied direct. Seasonal and bottle-conditioned beers are also available.

Muntjac (OG 1037, ABV 3.7%)

Pledgdon Ale (OG 1037, ABV 3.7%)

Essex Pale Ale (OG 1039, ABV 3.9%)

Ramblers Tipple (OG 1040, ABV 3.9%)
A rich, copper-coloured bitter with toffee and caramel flavours.

Brewhouse Bell (OG 1041, ABV 4%)
Golden amber in colour with citrus and hop flavours balancing well for a clean, fresh finish.

Saffron Blonde (OG 1044, ABV 4.3%)
A light golden ale with a delicate balance of citrus and smooth, malty flavours and a crisp finish.

Squires Gamble (OG 1044, ABV 4.3%)
Traditional style copper ale; soft, mellow, full-flavoured and hoppy with citrus and biscuit hints.

Tiddly Vicar (OG 1051, ABV 5%)
Dark copper nutty beer with a light, spicy finish.

St Austell SIBA IFBB

St Austell Brewery Co Ltd, 63 Trevarthian Road, St Austell, Cornwall, PL25 4BY
☎ (01726) 74444 ✉ info@staustellbrewery.co.uk
⊕ staustellbrewery.co.uk
Shop Mon-Fri 9am-5pm; Sat 10am-4pm
Tours by arrangement

St Austell Brewery celebrated 150 years of brewing in 2001. Founded by Walter Hicks in 1851, the company is still family owned, with a powerful commitment to cask beer, available in all 169 licensed houses, as well as in the free trade throughout Cornwall, Devon and Somerset. A visitor centre offers guided tours and souvenirs from the brewery. Seasonal and bottle-conditioned beers are also available: see website.

Dartmoor Best Bitter (OG 1035, ABV 3.5%)

Trelawny (OG 1039, ABV 3.8%)

Black Prince (OG 1041, ABV 4%) ▦ ◆
Creamy dark mild with aroma of lightly roasted malt and caramel. Malt and sweetness dominate the flavour balanced by traces of bitterness and fruity hops, fading away.

Tribute (OG 1043, ABV 4.2%) 🍺 ◆
Gold-amber ale with complex flowery aroma with a trace of tangy ester. Citrus maltiness dominates the flavour balanced by bitter hops reminiscent of elderflower. Ends refreshingly bitter with a hint of astringency.

Proper Job (OG 1046, ABV 4.5%) 🍺 ◆
Floral, aromatic hops greet the nose and persist in the mouth but are mellowed by a sweet, well-rounded and full-bodied palate that disappears in a bittersweet aftertaste.

Hicks Special Draught/HSD (OG 1052, ABV 5%) ◆
An aromatic, fruity, hoppy bitter that is initially sweet with an aftertaste of pronounced bitterness, but whose flavour is fully rounded.

St George's SIBA

St George's Brewery Ltd, The Old Bakery, Bush Lane, Callow End, Worcestershire, WR2 4TF
☎ (01905) 831316 ✉ info@stgeorgesbrewery.co.uk
⊕ stgeorgesbrewery.co.uk
Tours by arrangement

⊗ The brewery was established in 1998 in old village bakery premises. It was acquired in 2006 by Duncan Ironmonger. Andrew Sankey has been the brewer and brewery manager for a number of years. The brewery supplies local freehouses and wholesalers for a wider distribution. At least two monthly specials are usually available.

Valour (OG 1038, ABV 3.8%)
A refreshing beer with a hoppy character and citrus undertones.

Friar Tuck (OG 1040, ABV 4%)
A smooth golden bitter with a citrus character.

Honour (OG 1040, ABV 4%)
Amber-coloured with a spicy taste to start and a lasting bitter finish.

Worcester Sauce (OG 1043, ABV 4%)
A well-balanced amber beer; hoppy with a fruity aftertaste.

Charger (OG 1046, ABV 4.6%)
A light golden beer with a citrus blast and a hint of grapefruit.

Dragons Blood (OG 1048, ABV 4.8%)
A ruby red beer with a hint of chocolate and an earthy, slightly spicy aroma.

St Jude's

St Jude's Brewery Ltd, 2 Cardigan Street, Ipswich, Suffolk, IP1 3PF
☎ (01473) 413334 ☎ 07870 358834
✉ gt6xxx@yahoo.co.uk ⊕ stjudesbrewery.co.uk
Shop by prior appt Mon-Sat 10am-5pm
Tours by arrangement

⊗ St Jude's was established in 2006 on a seven-barrel plant. It bottles on site and supplies to many outlets in the UK. Seasonal and bottle-conditioned beers are also available.

Brandon's Mild (OG 1034, ABV 3.4%)

Royal Tudor Honey Ale (OG 1040, ABV 4%)

St Francis (OG 1049, ABV 4%) ◆
Pale golden. Surprisingly malty aroma but the taste is all fruit and hops. Suitable for vegetarians and vegans.

Gypeswic Bitter (OG 1044, ABV 4.4%) ◆
Fruity beer with a toffeish palate, elderflower and a clean aftertaste with lingering hop flavour.

Ipswich Bright (OG 1042, ABV 4.4%) ◆
A refreshing, golden bitter beer with a long, hoppy aftertaste.

Coachman's Whip (OG 1052, ABV 5.2%)
A well-balanced ale with a bitter, rich flavour.

Devereaux's Dark Porter (OG 1055, ABV 5.5%)

John Orford's Strong Brown Ale (OG 1055, ABV 5.5%) ◆
Strong caramel and malt aroma and taste.

Wolsey's Winter Warmer (OG 1062, ABV 6.2%)

St Mary's Stout (OG 1068, ABV 6.5%) ◆
Intense fruit aroma leading to incredibly rich flavour, with raisins and red berries in the taste and aftertaste.

St Peter's SIBA EAB

St Peter's Brewery Co Ltd, St Peter's Hall, St Peter South Elmham, Suffolk, NR35 1NQ
☎ (01986) 782322 ✉ beers@stpetersbrewery.co.uk
⊕ stpetersbrewery.co.uk
Shop Mon-Fri 9am-5pm; Sat, Sun & Bank Hols 11am-4pm
Tours by arrangement

⊗ St Peter's Brewery is based in a moated medieval hall near Bungay, Suffolk. Established in 1996 it concentrates in the main on bottled beer (85% of capacity) but has a rapidly increasing cask market. Two pubs are owned. 40% of production is exported to 32 countries worldwide. Seasonal beers are also available.

Best Bitter (OG 1038, ABV 3.7%) ◆
A complex but well-balanced hoppy brew. A gentle hop nose introduces a singular hoppiness with supporting malt notes and underlying bitterness. Other flavours fade to leave a long, dry, hoppy finish.

Mild (OG 1037, ABV 3.7%)
Sweetness balanced by bitter chocolate malt to produce a rare but much sought after traditional mild.

Organic Best (OG 1041, ABV 4.1%) ◆
A very dry and bitter beer with a growing astringency. Pale brown in colour, it has a gentle hop aroma which makes the definitive bitterness surprising. One for the committed.

Ruby Red (ABV 4.3%)
A tawny red ale with subtle malt undertones and a distinctive spicy hop aroma.

Organic Ale (OG 1045, ABV 4.5%) ◆
A rich toffee apple aroma and a smooth grainy feel. Malt and caramel initially match the dry hoppy bitterness. As the flavours mature, liquorice dryness develops. Full-bodied.

Golden Ale (OG 1047, ABV 4.7%) ◆
Amber-coloured, full-bodied, robust ale. A strong hop bouquet leads to a mix of malt and hops combined with a dry, fruity hoppiness. The malt quickly subsides, leaving creamy bitterness.

Grapefruit Beer (OG 1047, ABV 4.7%) 🍾 ◆
With a very strong aroma and taste of grapefruit, this refreshing beer is exactly what it says on the tin. A superb example of a fruit beer.

IPA (OG 1055, ABV 5.5%)
A full-bodied, highly hopped pale ale with a zesty character.

Salamander SIBA

Salamander Brewing Co Ltd, 22 Harry Street, Bradford, West Yorkshire, BD4 9PH
☎ (01274) 652323
✉ salamanderbrewing@fsmail.net
⊕ salamanderbrewing.co.uk
Tours by arrangement

⊗ Salamander first brewed in 2000 in a former pork pie factory. Expansion in 2004 took the brewery to 40-barrel capacity. There are direct deliveries to more widespread areas such as Cumbria, East Yorkshire and Lancashire in addition to the established trade of about 100 outlets throughout Lancashire, Manchester, North Yorkshire and Derbyshire.

Axolotl (OG 1038, ABV 3.9%)

Mudpuppy (OG 1042, ABV 4.2%) ◆
A well-balanced, copper-coloured best bitter with a fruity, hoppy nose and a bitter finish.

Golden Salamander (OG 1045, ABV 4.5%) 🍺 ◆
Citrus hops characterise the aroma and taste of this golden premium bitter, which has malt undertones throughout. The aftertaste is dry, hoppy and bitter.

Salopian SIBA

Salopian Brewery, 67 Mytton Oak Road, Shrewsbury, Shropshire, SY3 8UQ
☎ (01743) 248414
✉ enquiries@salopianbrewery.co.uk
⊕ salopianbrewery.co.uk
Shop Mon-Fri 9am-4pm
Tours by arrangement

⊗ The brewery was established in 1995 in an old dairy on the outskirts of Shrewsbury and, having grown steadily, now produces 80 barrels a week. 2010 saw the installation of a new brewhouse. Salopian also brews under the Blackwater Brewery name.

Shropshire Gold (OG 1037, ABV 3.8%) 🍺 🍺
A light, copper-coloured ale with an unusual blend of body and dryness.

Oracle (OG 1040, ABV 4%)
A crisp golden ale with a striking hop profile. Dry and refreshing with a long-balanced aromatic finish.

Darwins Origin (OG 1042, ABV 4.3%)
A light copper ale with a striking hop profile.

Hop Twister (OG 1044, ABV 4.5%)
A premium bitter with a citrus flavour and complex hop finish. Refreshing and crisp.

Golden Thread (OG 1048, ABV 5%)
A bright gold ale. Strong and quite bitter but well-balanced.

Saltaire SIBA

Saltaire Brewery Ltd, Unit 6, County Works, Dockfield Road, Shipley, West Yorkshire, BD17 7AR
☎ (01274) 594959 ✉ info@saltairebrewery.co.uk
⊕ saltairebrewery.co.uk
Tours by arrangement

☺ Launched in 2006, Saltaire Brewery is an award-winning brewery based in a former Victorian power station. A mezzanine bar gives visitors views of the brewing plant and the chance to taste the beers. More than 300 pubs are supplied across West Yorkshire and the north of England.

Blonde (OG 1042, ABV 4%) ◆
A thirst-quenching quaffing ale, this straw-coloured beer has a slightly sweet, fruity, hoppy finish.

Raspberry Blonde (OG 1042, ABV 4%)
Blonde infused with a hint of raspberries.

Cascade Pale Ale (OG 1050, ABV 4.8%) ◆
A well-balanced golden ale with floral hop aromas and pronounced bitterness, culminating in a long dry finish and dry aftertaste.

Triple Chocoholic (OG 1050, ABV 4.8%) ◆
A smooth, dark brown, roast, chocolate-flavoured stout with a dry, bitter finish and a rich chocolate aroma.

Sambrook's SIBA

Sambrook's Brewery Ltd, Units 1 & 2, Yelverton Road, Battersea, London, SW11 3QG
☎ (020) 7228 0598
✉ sales@sambrooksbrewery.co.uk
⊕ sambrooksbrewery.co.uk
Shop Mon-Fri 10am-6pm; Sat 10am-1pm
Tours by arrangement

⊗ Sambrooks was established in 2008 by Duncan Sambrook and David Welsh using a 20-barrel plant. Seasonal and bottle-conditioned beers are available.

Wandle Ale (OG 1038, ABV 3.8%) ◆
A touch of dryness balances the rounded sweetish malt flavour of this fruity, quaffable pale brown bitter. Some peach and citrus notes and hops are noticeable when fresh.

Junction Ale (OG 1044, ABV 4.5%) ◆
Soft fruit and figs on the nose of this well-balanced best bitter. The fruit on the palate is a little more citrussy plus creamy toffee. Sweetish dry aftertaste.

Sandstone SIBA

Sandstone Brewery LLP, Unit 5, Wrexham Enterprise Park, Preston Road, off Ash Road North, Wrexham Industrial Estate, Wrexham, LL13 9JT
☎ 07851 001118 ✉ info@sandstonebrewery.co.uk
⊕ sandstonebrewery.co.uk
Tours by arrangement

Sandstone Brewery was established in 2008 by three CAMRA members on a four-barrel brew plant. More than 60 regular outlets are supplied direct. The beers, apart from the signature beer Sandstone Edge, are named after fictitious village characters. Seasonal beers are also available.

Edge (OG 1039, ABV 3.8%) ◆
A satisfying session ale, this pale, dry, bitter beer has a full mouthfeel and a lingering hoppy finish that belies its modest strength.

Sleeping Policeman (OG 1043, ABV 4.2%) ◆
Clean-tasting best bitter, chestnut in colour with a fruity aroma continuing into the taste. Peppery hops increasingly evident in the aftertaste and dry, bitter finish.

Poacher's Pale (OG 1046, ABV 4.4%)

Sherborne

🍺 Sherborne Brewery Ltd, 257 Westbury, Sherborne, Dorset, DT9 3EH
☎ (01935) 812094 ⊕ sherbornebrewery.co.uk

☺ Sherborne Brewery started in late 2005 on a 2.5-barrel plant. It moved in 2006 to new premises at the rear of the brewery's pub, Docherty's Bar. Beer is supplied to the pub and to 15-20 other local outlets as a guest beer.

257 (OG 1039, ABV 3.9%) ◀
Light-coloured best bitter with fruit-hop aromas and flavour with burnt astringent undertones.

Cheap Street (OG 1044, ABV 4.4%) ◀
Faint hop fruit aromas lead to strong astringent flavours and a lingering dry burnt aftertaste; reminiscent of a German Rauch (smoked) beer but with a thinner body.

Sherfield Village SIBA (NEW)

Sherfield Village Brewery, Goddards Farm, Goddards Lane, Sherfield on Loddon, Hampshire, RG27 0EL
☎ 07906 060429
✉ pete@sherfieldvillagebrewery.co.uk
⊕ sherfieldvillagebrewery.co.uk

Sherfield began brewing in 2011 using a five-barrel plant. Seasonal and occasional beers are also brewed; the 'Solo' range is produced using New World hops.

Threesome (ABV 3%)

Pewter Suitor (ABV 4.4%)

Foursight (ABV 4.5%)

Pioneer Stout (ABV 5%)

Ship Inn

🍺 Ship Inn Brewery, Ship Inn, Newton Square, Low Newton by the Sea, Northumberland, NE66 3EL
☎ (01665) 576262 ⊕ shipinnnewton.co.uk

The Ship Inn commenced brewing in 2008 on a 2.5-barrel plant. The brewery now produces 7.5 barrels per week and all regular beers are brewed in constant rotation, brewing three times per week. The beers are only available at the Ship Inn. Seasonal and bottle-conditioned beers are also available. A special beer (4.2% ABV) is brewed for every 100 brews.

Red Herring (ABV 3.8%)

Sandcastles at Dawn (ABV 3.8%)

Sea Coal (ABV 4%)

Sea Wheat (ABV 4%)

Ship Hop Ale (ABV 4%)

White Horses (ABV 4%)

Autumn Rye (ABV 4.1%)

Rye P.A. (ABV 4.1%)

Sea Dog (ABV 4.2%)

Dolly Daydream (ABV 4.3%)

Indian Summer (ABV 4.4%)

Shires

🍺 Shires Brewery, All Nations Brewhouse, 20 Coalport Road, Madeley, Shropshire, TF7 5DP

☎ (01952) 580570 (Brewery) ☎ (01746) 769606 (Office) ✉ info@shiresbrewery.co.uk
⊕ shiresbrewery.co.uk

☺Shires Brewery (formerly Worfield) was launched in 2009 and is based at the historic All Nations Brewhouse in Madeley near Telford, which has a brewing tradition stretching back to 1831. Mike Handley supervises the 10-barrel plant. The brewery supply the All Nations tap house next door as well as other outlets. Seasonal beers: see website.

Coalport Mild (OG 1034, ABV 3.5%)
Traditional dark mild, full of nutty flavour from dark malts and full-bodied for its strength.

Best Bitter (OG 1039, ABV 3.8%)
Pale in colour with fruity undertones and a hint of citrus. A tasty session beer. Sold in the All Nations as Dabley Ale.

OBJ (Oh Be Joyful!) (OG 1043, ABV 4.2%) ◀
A light and sweet bitter; delicate flavour belies the strength.

Shropshire Pride (OG 1045, ABV 4.5%)
A mid-coloured bitter, very full-bodied and malty with a pleasant bittersweet balance.

Severn Gorgeous (OG 1048, ABV 4.8%)
A light-bodied ale with full hop bitterness accompanying pine and citrus aromas.

Dabley Gold (OG 1050, ABV 5%)
The big brother of Dabley Ale, produced from the same recipe but brewed to a higher gravity giving a sweeter, fuller flavour.

Shoes SIBA

🍺 Shoes Brewery, Three Horseshoes Inn, Norton Canon, Hereford, HR4 7BH
☎ (01544) 318375
Tours by arrangement

Landlord Frank Goodwin was a keen home brewer who decided in 1994 to brew on a commercial basis for his pub. The beers are brewed from malt extract and are normally only available at the Three Horseshoes. Each September Canon Bitter is brewed with 'green' hops fresh from the harvest. All beers are also available bottle conditioned.

Norton Ale (OG 1038, ABV 3.6%)

Canon Bitter (OG 1040, ABV 4.1%)

Peploe's Tipple (OG 1060, ABV 6%)

Farriers Ale (OG 1114, ABV 15%)

Shotover SIBA

Shotover Brewing Co Ltd, Coopers Yard, Manor Farm Road, Horspath, Oxfordshire, OX33 1SD
☎ (01865) 876770 ☎ 07801 570444
✉ ed@shotoverbrewing.com
⊕ shotoverbrewing.com
Shop: please ring or email first
Tours by arrangement

⊠ Shotover is a family-run craft brewery four miles from Oxford city centre. It began brewing in 2009. 10 outlets are supplied direct. Bottle-conditioned beers are available and are suitable for vegetarians and vegans. Vegetarian cask ale can be supplied on request.

Prospect (OG 1040, ABV 3.7%)
A pale copper, hoppy session bitter.

Scholar (OG 1046, ABV 4.5%)
A mid-copper classic English bitter.

Shugborough SIBA

Shugborough Brewery, Shugborough Estate, Milford, Staffordshire, ST17 0XB
☎ (01782) 823447 ⊕ shugborough.org.uk
Tours daily Mar-Oct

Brewing in the original brewhouse at Shugborough, home of the Earls of Lichfield, restarted in 1990 but a lack of expertise led to the brewery being a static museum piece until Titanic Brewery of Stoke-on-Trent (qv) began helping in 1996. Brewing takes place every weekend during the visitor season with museum guides in period costume.

Miladys Fancy (OG 1048, ABV 4.6%)

Lordships Own (OG 1054, ABV 5%)

Silhill SIBA (NEW)

Silhill Brewery Ltd, PO Box 15739, Solihull, West Midlands, B93 3FW
☎ 0845 519 5101 ✉ info@silhillbrewery.co.uk
⊕ silhillbrewery.co.uk

☺Silhill began brewing in 2010. 50 outlets are supplied direct.

**3.7 Per Cent Premium Session Ale
(OG 1037, ABV 3.7%)**
A full-flavoured light amber session ale.

4.0 Per Cent Pale Ale (OG 1040, ABV 4%)
A pale ale with a light, full-hopped taste.

Silverstone

Silverstone Brewing Co Ltd, Kingshill Farm, Syresham, nr Silverstone, Northamptonshire, NN13 5TH
☎ (01280) 850629
✉ services@silverstonebrewingcompany.com
⊕ silverstonebrewingcompany.com
Tours by arrangement

☒ The brewery, which is located near the celebrated motor racing circuit, opened in 2008. In keeping with its motor racing theme the brewery is the proud sponsor of Formula V10. 60 outlets are supplied direct.

Pitstop Bitter (OG 1038, ABV 3.8%)

Pole Position (ABV 4.1%)

Sinclair

See Orkney

Six Bells SIBA

🍺 **Six Bells Brewery, Church Street, Bishop's Castle, Shropshire, SY9 5AA**
☎ (01588) 638930 ⊕ sixbellsbrewery.co.uk
Tours by arrangement

Neville Richards – 'Big Nev' – started brewing in 1997 with a five-barrel plant and two fermenters. Alterations in 1999 included two more fermenters, a new grain store and mashing equipment. He supplies a number of customers both within the county and over the border in Wales. A new 12-

barrel plant opened in 2007. In addition to the core beer range, 12 monthly specials are produced.

Big Nev's (OG 1037, ABV 3.8%)
A pale, fairly hoppy bitter.

Ow Do! (ABV 4%)

Cloud Nine (OG 1043, ABV 4.2%)
Pale amber-colour with a slight citrus finish.

Skinner's SIBA

Skinner's Brewing Co Ltd, Riverside, Newham Road, Truro, Cornwall, TR1 2SU
☎ (01872) 271885 ✉ info@skinnersbrewery.com
⊕ skinnersbrewery.com
Shop & Visitor Centre open daily 9am-5pm
Tours by arrangement (ring 01872 245689)

☒ Skinner's brewery was founded in 1997. To increase production the brewery moved to bigger premises in 2003, opening a brewery shop and visitor centre. The brewery is now a 25-barrel plant with production capacity of 375 barrels a week. Since opening, the brewery has won numerous awards. Merchandise and beer are available to purchase online. Seasonal beers: see website.

Ginger Tosser (OG 1038, ABV 3.8%)
Hoppy golden ale fused with Cornish honey. The rounded finish has a hint of ginger.

Spriggan Ale (OG 1038, ABV 3.8%) ◆
A light golden, hoppy bitter. Well-balanced with a smooth bitter finish.

Betty Stogs (OG 1040, ABV 4%) ▱ ◆
Refreshing copper ale with balance of citrus hops and apple fruit, sweet malt and bitterness. Faint aroma of malt and hops. Bitter finish is slow to develop but long to fade.

Heligan Honey (OG 1040, ABV 4%) ▰ ◆
Pale brown beer with added Cornish honey detectable in the aroma. The creamy taste is dominated by sweetness and butterscotch balanced by bitterness and a little hops. Lingering bittersweet aftertaste.

Keel Over (OG 1041, ABV 4.2%)
A classic Cornish bitter, amber in colour, beautifully balanced with a smooth finish.

Cornish Knocker Ale (OG 1044, ABV 4.5%) ◆
Refreshing, amber ale with hops all the way through. Spice and fruit in the mouth balanced by bitter and faint malt undertones, with a clean and lasting bitter finish.

Figgy's Brew (OG 1044, ABV 4.5%) ◆
With subdued fruit and malt on the nose, a pale brown beer that is gently malty and sweet in the mouth, leading to bitterness that becomes dry in the finish.

Hunny Bunny (OG 1045, ABV 4.5%)
A premium strength golden ale with subtle hints of Cornish honey. Clean-tasting with a hoppy aroma.

Cornish Blonde (OG 1048, ABV 5%)
A combination of wheat malt and English and American hops makes this light-coloured wheat beer deceptively easy to drink.

Slater's SIBA

Eccleshall Brewing Co Ltd, Slater's Brewery, St Albans Road, Common Road Industrial Estate, Stafford, ST16 3DR

☎ (01785) 257976 ✉ sales@slatersales.co.uk
⊕ slatersales.co.uk
Shop Mon-Fri 9am-5pm, Sat 10am-12pm
Tours by arrangement

☺ The brewery was opened in 1995 and in 2006 moved to new, larger premises, resulting in a tripling of capacity. It has won numerous awards from CAMRA and SIBA and supplies more than 1,100 outlets. One pub is owned, the George at Eccleshall, which serves as the brewery tap.

Why Knot (OG 1036, ABV 3.6%)
A golden bitter with balanced malt and hops leading to a long, pleasant astringency.

Original (OG 1040, ABV 4%) ◆
Amber bitter. Malty aroma with caramel notes, hoppy taste develops into a dry hoppy finish with a touch of sweetness.

Top Totty (OG 1040, ABV 4%) ◆
Great yellow colour with a fruit and hop nose. Hop and fruit balanced taste leads to citrus hints with mouth-watering edges. Dry finish with tangs of lemon.

Queen Bee (OG 1042, ABV 4.2%) ◆
Golden with a sweet and spicy aroma and hop background. Honey sweet taste followed by a gentle bitter finish on the tongue.

Premium (OG 1044, ABV 4.4%) ◆
Pale brown bitter with malt and caramel aroma. Malt and caramel taste supported by hops and some fruit provide a warming descent and satisfyingly bitter mouthfeel.

Slaughterhouse SIBA

Slaughterhouse Brewery Ltd, Bridge Street, Warwick, CV34 5PD
☎ (01926) 490986
✉ enquiries@slaughterhousebrewery.com
⊕ slaughterhousebrewery.com
Tours by arrangement

Production began in 2003 on a four-barrel plant in a former slaughterhouse. Due to its success, beer production now consists mainly of Saddleback, supplemented by monthly special and seasonal beers. Around 30 outlets are supplied. The brewery premises are licensed for off-sales direct to the public.

Saddleback Best Bitter (OG 1038, ABV 3.8%)
Amber-coloured session bitter with a distinctive Challenger hop flavour.

Pale Ale (OG 1041, ABV 4.1%)
A classic English pale ale with a dry quenching balance of malt and hops and a long finish with light fruit notes.

Wild Boar (OG 1052, ABV 5.2%)
A robust dark beer produced using both dark crystal and chocolate malts.

Sleaford SIBA (NEW)

Hop Me Up Ltd – Sleaford Brewery, 21 Pride Court, Enterprise Park, Sleaford, Lincolnshire, NG34 8GL
☎ 07854 829718 ✉ hopmeup@hotmail.co.uk
⊕ hopmeup.co.uk
Tours by arrangement

⊗ Sleaford began brewing in 2011 using a six-barrel brew plant. More than 20 outlets are supplied direct. All beers are also available bottle conditioned.

Cats Eyes IPA (ABV 3.7%)

Pale Ale (ABV 3.9%)

Pleasant Pheasant (ABV 4.3%)

Midnight Runner (ABV 5.2%)

Small Paul's

Small Paul's Brewery, 27 Briar Close, Gillingham, Dorset, SP8 4SS
☎ (01747) 823574 ✉ smallbrewer@aol.com
Tours by arrangement

⊗ Launched in 2006, this half-barrel brewery is located in the owner's garage. There are usually two brews a month but consideration is being given to increasing capacity following success at beer festivals. A small number of local pubs and clubs are supplied direct and beers can be designed and brewed to order. Seasonal beers are also available.

Gylla's Gold (OG 1039, ABV 3.8%) ◆
Drinkable session ale. Mild fruit/hop aromas lead to bitter hop flavours and a lingering dry hop aftertaste.

Challenger II (OG 1045, ABV 4.3%)
A copper-coloured malty bitter.

Wyvern (OG 1044, ABV 4.4%) ◆
Red-brown, well-balanced best bitter with malt and caramel flavours and a short, bittersweet finish.

Gillingham Pale (OG 1045, ABV 4.5%) ◆
Fruity, caramel aromas lead to complex bittersweet flavours and a short, dry finish.

Samuel Smith

Samuel Smith Old Brewery (Tadcaster), High Street, Tadcaster, North Yorkshire, LS24 9SB
☎ (01937) 832225 ⊕ samuelsmithsbrewery.co.uk

☺ A fiercely independent, family-owned company. Tradition, quality and value are important, resulting in brewing without any artificial additives. All real ale is supplied in wooden casks, though nitrokeg has replaced cask beer in some pubs in recent years. An unfiltered draught wheat beer is a recent addition. Around 200 pubs are owned. A bottle-conditioned beer was introduced in 2008 (Yorkshire Stingo, ABV 8%) but is only available in specialist off-licences.

Old Brewery Bitter/OBB (OG 1040, ABV 4%) ◆
Malt dominates the aroma, with an initial burst of malt, hops and fruit in the taste, which is sustained in the aftertaste.

Snowdonia

⌨ Snowdonia Brewery, Snowdonia Parc Brewpub & Campsite, Waunfawr, Caernarfon, Gwynedd, LL55 4AQ
☎ (01286) 650409 ✉ info@snowdonia-park.co.uk
⊕ snowdonia-park.co.uk

Snowdonia started brewing in 1998 in a two-barrel brewhouse. The brewing is now carried out by the owner, Carmen Pierce. The beer is brewed solely for the Snowdonia Park pub and campsite.

Snowdonia Gold (OG 1040, ABV 4%)

Carmen Sutra (OG 1043, ABV 4.4%)

Welsh Highland Bitter (OG 1048, ABV 5.2%)

Son of Sid

▤ Son of Sid Brewery, The Chequers, 71 Main Road, Little Gransden, Bedfordshire, SG19 3DW
☎ (01767) 677348
✉ chequersgransden@btinternet.com

Son of Sid was established in 2007 on a 2.5-barrel plant in a separate room of the pub. The brewery can be viewed from the lounge bar. It is named after the father of the current landlord, who ran the pub for 42 years. His son has carried the business on for the past 19 years as a family-run enterprise. Beer is sold in the pub and at local beer festivals.

Muckcart Mild (OG 1035, ABV 3.5%) ◆
Black mild with a resounding roast malt presence and a caramel background in aroma and taste. There is some sweetness but the balance is predominantly dry and bitter, with increasing bitterness in the aftertaste.

Golden Shower (OG 1039, ABV 3.9%)
Full-bodied golden beer with a light hop character and a defined maltiness.

South Hams SIBA

South Hams Brewery Ltd, Stokeley Barton, Stokenham, Kingsbridge, Devon, TQ7 2SE
☎ (01548) 581151
✉ info@southhamsbrewery.co.uk
⊕ southhamsbrewery.co.uk
Tours by arrangement

⊗ The brewery moved to its present site, a milking parlour, in 2003, with a 10-barrel plant and plenty of room to expand. It supplies more than 60 outlets in Plymouth and south Devon. Wholesalers are used to distribute to other areas. Three pubs are owned. Seasonal beers: see website. Bottle-conditioned beers are also available.

Devon Pride (OG 1039, ABV 3.8%)

Re'session Ale (ABV 4%)

XSB (OG 1043, ABV 4.2%) ◆
Amber nectar with a fruity nose and a bitter finish.

Wild Blonde (ABV 4.4%)

Eddystone (OG 1050, ABV 4.8%) ⬚

Southport SIBA

Southport Brewery, Unit 3, Enterprise Business Park, Russell Road, Southport, Merseyside, PR9 7RF
☎ 07748 387652 ✉ southportbrewery@fsmail.net
⊕ southportbrewery.co.uk

☺ The Southport brewery opened in 2004 as a 2.5-barrel plant but moved to a five-barrel plant due to demand. Around 30 pubs are supplied in the North-west. It also supplies the free trade via Boggart Brewery (qv). Seasonal beers: see website.

Cyclone (OG 1039.5, ABV 3.8%)
A bronze-coloured bitter with a fruity blackcurrant aftertaste.

Sandgrounder Bitter (OG 1039.5, ABV 3.8%)
Pale, hoppy session bitter with a floral character.

Carousel (OG 1041.5, ABV 4%)
A refreshing, floral, hoppy best bitter.

Golden Sands (OG 1041.5, ABV 4%)
A golden-coloured, triple hopped bitter with citrus flavour.

Natterjack (OG 1043.5, ABV 4.3%)
A premium bitter with fruit notes and a hint of coffee.

For Southport Football Club:

Grandstand Gold (OG 1039.5, ABV 3.8%)
A gold-coloured bitter, available for all home matches.

Spectrum SIBA EAB

Spectrum Brewery, Unit 11, Wellington Road, Tharston, Norwich, NR15 2PE
☎ 07949 254383 ✉ info@spectrumbrewery.co.uk
⊕ spectrumbrewery.co.uk
Tours by arrangement

⊗ Proprietor and founder Andy Mitchell established Spectrum in 2002. The brewery moved premises in 2007 as well as increasing brew length and gaining organic certification for all beers. Seasonal and bottle-conditioned beers are also available. Dark beers produced are suitable for vegans.

Light Fantastic (OG 1035.5, ABV 3.7%) ◆
Golden hued with a refreshing citrus character on nose and taste. Grapefruit notes add depth to the hoppy bitterness in the beginning. Initial malt background fades to a sharp, slightly astringent finish.

Dark Fantastic (OG 1041, ABV 3.8%) ◆
A rich vine fruit and roast aroma introduces this dark mild. Heavy chocolate notes permeate the malty sweetness, contrasting with the underlying bitterness. A long, rich, tapering ending.

Bezants (OG 1037.5, ABV 4%) ◆
Dry golden ale with a direct bitterness and a light hop flavour.

43 (OG 1040.5, ABV 4.3%) ◆
Sulphurous notes in the nose do not transfer to the taste. Although bitterness is the outstanding flavour there is more than a trace of both malt and soft fruits. A quick, crisp ending.

Black Buffle (OG 1047, ABV 4.5%) ◆
The deep roast backbone is softened by a blackcurrant fruitiness. Malt is in evidence but is soon masked by a growing bitterness. A satisfying spectrum of aroma and taste.

Wizzard (OG 1047.5, ABV 4.9%) ◆
Rich and fruity in nose and taste. A full-bodied, complex brew with raisin and cherry matching the heavy malt overtones. Well-balanced refreshing and creamy with an increasingly bitter finish.

Old Stoatwobbler (OG 1064.5, ABV 6%) ◆
Rich and creamy old ale with a dark chocolate digestive flavour. Roast and vine fruits with a touch of caramel mask a background hoppy bitterness. A long sustained finish.

Trip Hazard (OG 1061.5, ABV 6.5%) ◆
A sweet, fruity brew with bubblegum notes throughout. Smooth bodied and easy drinking. A bitter hop undertow lightens the sweet resinous maltiness towards the end.

Abraham Thompson was set up in 2004 to return Barrow-brewed beers to local pubs. This was achieved in 2005 after an absence of more than 30 years following the demise of Case's Brewery in 1972. With a half-barrel plant, this nano-brewery has concentrated almost exclusively on dark beers, reflecting the tastes of the brewer. As a result of the small output, finding the beers outside the Low Furness area is difficult. The only frequent stockist is the Black Dog Inn between Dalton and Ireleth.

Lickerish Stout (ABV 3.8%)
A black, full-bodied stout with heavy roast flavours and good bitterness.

Oatmeal Stout (ABV 4.5%)

Porter (ABV 4.8%)
A deep, dark porter with good body and a smooth chocolate finish.

Letargion (ABV 9%)
Black, bitter and heavily roast but still very drinkable. A meal in a glass.

John Thompson

🍺 John Thompson Inn & Brewery, Ingleby, Melbourne, Derbyshire, DE73 7HW
☎ (01332) 862469 ⊕ johnthompsoninn.com
Tours by arrangement

John Thompson set up the brewery in 1977. The pub and brewery are now run by his son, Nick. Seasonal beers are also available.

JTS XXX (OG 1041, ABV 4.1%)

Thornbridge SIBA

Thornbridge Brewery, Riverside Business Park, Buxton Road, Bakewell, Derbyshire, DE45 1GS
☎ (01629) 641000
✉ alex@thornbridgebrewery.co.uk
⊕ thornbridgebrewery.co.uk
Shop Mon-Fri 9am-4pm
Tours by arrangement

⊛ The first Thornbridge craft beers were produced in 2005 using a 10-barrel brewery, housed in the grounds of Thornbridge Hall. The beers have gained considerable success with over 190 CAMRA and SIBA awards being won. A 30-barrel brewery opened in Bakewell in 2009. The original site continues to develop new, seasonal and speciality beers. 200 outlets are supplied direct. Five pubs are owned. Unfiltered and bottle-conditioned beers are available.

Wild Swan (OG 1035, ABV 3.5%) ◆
Extremely pale yet flavoursome and refreshing beer. Plenty of lemony citrus hop flavour, becoming increasingly dry and bitter in the finish and aftertaste.

Lord Marples (OG 1041, ABV 4%) ◆
Smooth, traditional, easy-drinking bitter. Caramel, malt and coffee flavours fall away to leave a long, bitter finish.

Ashford (OG 1043, ABV 4.2%)
A brown ale with a floral hoppiness, a smooth, malty kick and a delicate coffee finish.

Hopton (OG 1043, ABV 4.3%)
A burnt gold English pale ale. Medium-bodied with some biscuit character and citrus present in the mouth. The finish shows a clean bitterness with a touch of lingering grassiness.

Blackthorn (OG 1044, ABV 4.4%)

Jawick (OG 1047, ABV 4.8%)

Kipling (OG 1050, ABV 5.2%) ◆
Golden pale bitter with aromas of grapefruit and passion fruit. Intense fruit flavours continue throughout, leading to a long bitter aftertaste.

Jaipur IPA (OG 1055, ABV 5.9%) 🍺 🍴 ◆
Flavoursome IPA packed with citrus hoppiness that's nicely counterbalanced by malt and underlying sweetness and robust fruit flavours.

Halcyon (OG 1071, ABV 7.7%)

Saint Petersburg (Imperial Russian Stout) (OG 1072.4, ABV 7.7%) 🍴 ◆
Good example of an imperial stout. Smooth and easy to drink with raisins, bitter chocolate and hops throughout, leading to a lingering coffee and chocolate aftertaste.

Thorne SIBA

Thorne Brewery (Yorkshire) Ltd, Unit A2, Thorne Enterprise Park, King Edward Road, Thorne, South Yorkshire, DN8 4HU
☎ (01405) 741685 ✉ info@thornebrewery.com
⊕ thornebrewery.com
Tours by arrangement

⊛ Thorne Brewery Community Interest Company was set up in 2008 to bring brewing back to Thorne. In early 2009 a 10-barrel brew plant was purchased and the first beers were available shortly after. Profits are re-invested in the local community to help improve the area.

Best Bitter (OG 1039, ABV 3.9%)
Malt dominates the taste with caramel, chocolate and fruitcake flavours. The hops complement this with a full-bodied bitterness and notes of orange peel, pepper and herbal aromas.

Pale Ale (OG 1041, ABV 4.2%)
English hops give a fruity flavour and a resinous, grassy aroma. Well-balanced bitterness gives a clean finish.

Three B's SIBA

🍺 Three B's Brewery, Black Bull, Brokenstone Road, Tockholes, Lancashire, BB3 0LL
☎ (01254) 207686 ✉ robert@threebsbrewery.co.uk
⊕ threebsbrewery.co.uk
Tours by arrangement

Three B's was established by Robert Bell in 1998 in Blackburn using a two-barrel plant. Expansion saw a move to Feniscowles with a 10-barrel plant and in 2011 the brewery relocated again to a building behind the Black Bull in Tockholes. Seasonal beers: see website. Bottle-conditioned beers are also available.

Bee Thrifty (OG 1036, ABV 3.4%)
A light and refreshing amber-coloured beer.

Stoker's Slake (OG 1038, ABV 3.6%) ◆
Lightly roasted coffee flavours are in the aroma and the initial taste. A well-rounded, dark brown mild with dried fruit flavours in the long finish.

Honey Bee (OG 1039, ABV 3.7%)
A golden honey beer with honey apparent in both aroma and taste.

Bobbin's Bitter (OG 1038, ABV 3.8%)

A golden bitter with warm aromas of nutty grain and a full, fruity flavour with a light, dry finish.

Oatmeal Stout (OG 1040, ABV 3.8%)
A black roast beer with roast barley flavour and aroma and a complex hop taste.

Bee Blonde (OG 1041, ABV 4%)
A distinctive, pale bitter with a light, dry, balance of grain and hops and a delicate finish with citrus fruits.

Tackler's Tipple (OG 1044, ABV 4.3%)
A dark best bitter with full hop flavour, biscuit tones on the tongue and a deep, dry finish.

Doff Cocker (OG 1045, ABV 4.5%) ◆
Yellow with a hoppy aroma and initial taste giving way to subtle malt notes and orchard fruit flavours. Crisp, dry finish.

Pinch Noggin (OG 1046, ABV 4.6%)
A dark, strong best bitter with full hop flavour and a long aftertaste.

Knocker Up (OG 1047, ABV 4.8%) ◆
A smooth, rich, creamy porter. The roast flavour is foremost without dominating and is balanced by fruit and hop notes.

Shuttle Ale (OG 1050, ABV 5.2%)
A rustic-coloured traditional strong pale ale.

Three Castles SIBA

Three Castles Brewery Ltd, Unit 12, Salisbury Road Business Park, Pewsey, Wiltshire, SN9 5PZ
☎ (01672) 564433 ☎ 07725 148671
✉ sales@threecastlesbrewery.co.uk
⊕ threecastlesbrewery.co.uk
Shop Mon-Fri 9am-4pm; Sat 9am-1pm
Tours by arrangement

⊗ Three Castles is an independent, family-run brewery, established in 2006. Its location in the Vale of Pewsey has inspired the names for its range of ales. Seasonal beers: see website. Bottle-conditioned beers are also available and are suitable for vegetarians.

Barbury Castle (OG 1039, ABV 3.9%)
A balanced, easy-drinking pale ale with a hoppy, spicy palate.

Uffington Castle (OG 1042, ABV 4.2%)
Dark brown ale with a malty, nutty palate and a pleasant bitterness. The hop comes through well with a big spicy aroma.

Vale Ale (OG 1043, ABV 4.3%)
Golden-coloured with a fruity palate and strong floral aroma.

Tanked Up (OG 1050, ABV 5%)
Strong ale with a vibrant aroma.

Three Peaks

Three Peaks Brewery, 7 Craven Terrace, Settle, North Yorkshire, BD24 9DB
☎ (01729) 822939

⊗ Formed in 2006, Three Peaks is run by husband and wife team Colin and Susan Ashwell. The brewery is located in the cellar of their home. Two beers are brewed at present on their 1.25-barrel plant but more are planned.

Pen-y-Ghent Bitter (OG 1040, ABV 3.8%) ◆

Malt and fruit flavours dominate this mid-brown session bitter, with some bitterness coming through afterwards.

Ingleborough Gold (OG 1041, ABV 4%)

Three Tuns SIBA

Three Tuns Brewery, 16 Market Square, Bishop's Castle, Shropshire, SY9 5BN
☎ (01588) 638392 ✉ tunsbrewery@aol.com
⊕ threetunsbrewery.co.uk
Shop Mon-Fri 9am-5pm
Tours by arrangement

Brewing started on the site sometime in the 16th century. The brewery was licensed in 1642 and is the oldest licensed brewery in the country. Recent refurbishment has resulted in a significant increase in capacity and styles of beers. Seasonal beers: see website.

1642 Bitter (OG 1042, ABV 3.8%)
A golden ale with a light, nutty maltiness and spicy bitterness.

XXX (OG 1046, ABV 4.3%) ◆
A pale, sweetish bitter with a light hop aftertaste that has a honey finish.

Cleric's Cure (OG 1059, ABV 5%)
A light tan-coloured ale with a malty sweetness. Strong and spicy with a floral bitterness.

Thwaites IFBB

Daniel Thwaites plc, Star Brewery, PO Box 50, Blackburn, Lancashire, BB1 5BU
☎ (01254) 686868
✉ marketing@danielthwaites.com
⊕ danielthwaites.com
Tours by arrangement

☺ Established in 1807, Thwaites is still controlled by the Yerburgh family, descendants of the founder, Daniel Thwaites. The company owns around 360 pubs. Real ale is available in more than 60% of these but Nutty Black is hard to find. A monthly Signature range beer is produced and landlords joining the company's 1807 Cask Club can sell a guest beer from an outside brewer as provided by Thwaites. Two bottle-conditioned beers are also available.

Nutty Black (OG 1036, ABV 3.3%) ◆
A tasty traditional dark mild presenting a malty flavour with caramel notes and a slightly bitter finish.

Original (OG 1036, ABV 3.6%) ◆
Hop driven, yet well-balanced amber session bitter. Hops continue through to the long finish.

Indus IPA (OG 1039, ABV 3.9%)
A well-hopped amber ale.

Wainwright (OG 1042, ABV 4.1%)
A straw-coloured bitter with soft fruit flavours and a hint of malty sweetness.

Lancaster Bomber (OG 1044, ABV 4.4%) ◆
Well-balanced, copper-coloured best bitter with firm malt flavours, a fruity background and a long, dry finish.

Tigertops

Tigertops Brewery, 22 Oakes Street, Flanshaw, Wakefield, West Yorkshire, WF2 9LN

intact, despite having lain idle for more than 100 years. The brewery has been run by Peter's daughter, Catherine Maxwell Stuart, since his death in 1990. The Maxwell Stuarts are members of the Stuart clan, and the main Bear Gates will remain shut until a Stuart returns to the throne. All the beers are oak-fermented and 60 per cent of production is exported. Seasonal and occasional beers are also available.

Traquair House Ale (OG 1069, ABV 7%)

Tring SIBA

Tring Brewery Co Ltd, Dunsley Farm, London Road, Tring, Hertfordshire, HP23 6HA
☎ (01442) 890721 ✉ info@tringbrewery.co.uk
⊕ tringbrewery.co.uk
Shop Mon-Tue 11am-5pm, Wed-Fri 9am-6pm, Sat 9am-5pm, closed Sun
Tours by arrangement

⊗ Founded in 1992, Tring Brewery brews 90 barrels a week. Most of the beers take their names from local myths and legends. In addition to the regular and seasonal ales it brews a selection of monthly specials. The brewery relocated to larger premises in 2010. Seasonal beers: see website.

Side Pocket For A Toad (OG 1035, ABV 3.6%)
Citrus notes from American Cascade hops balanced with a floral aroma and a crisp, dry finish in a straw-coloured ale.

Brock Bitter (OG 1036, ABV 3.7%)
A light brown session ale with hints of sweetness and caramel, gentle bitterness and a floral aroma from Styrian hops.

Mansion Mild (OG 1036, ABV 3.7%)
Smooth and creamy dark ruby mild with a fruity palate and gentle late hop.

Blonde (OG 1039, ABV 4%)
A refreshing blonde beer with a fruity palate, balanced with a lingering hop aroma.

Ridgeway (OG 1039, ABV 4%)
Balanced malt and hop flavours with a dry, flowery hop aftertaste.

Jack O'Legs (OG 1041, ABV 4.2%)
A combination of four types of malt and two types of aroma hops provide a copper-coloured premium ale with full fruit and a distinctive hoppy bitterness.

Colley's Dog (OG 1051, ABV 5.2%)
Dark but not over-rich, strong yet drinkable, this premium ale has a long dry finish with overtones of malt and walnuts.

Trinity EAB

Trinity Ales, Church Road, Gisleham, Suffolk, NR33 8DS
☎ (01502) 743121 ✉ graham@trinityales.co.uk
⊕ trinityales.co.uk

⊗ Trinity Ales was launched in 2009 using a four-barrel plant. Pure spring water is used from an ancient well along with Suffolk hops and barley from local farms. Outlets are supplied within a 30-mile radius of the brewery. Bottle-conditioned beers are also available.

Wishing Well (OG 1039, ABV 3.8%)

High Light (OG 1040, ABV 4%)

Snow Plough (OG 1040, ABV 4%)

Black Street Smithy (OG 1050, ABV 4.5%)

Church Key (OG 1050, ABV 4.5%)

Gisleham Gold (OG 1045, ABV 4.5%)

Triple fff SIBA

Triple fff Brewing Co, Magpie Works, Station Approach, Four Marks, Alton, Hampshire, GU34 5HN
☎ (01420) 561422 ✉ sales@triplefff.com
⊕ triplefff.com
Shop Mon-Fri 9am-5pm, Sat 10am-12pm
Tours by arrangement

⊗ The brewery was founded in 1997 with a five-barrel plant. Since then demand has rocketed with the brewery growing in size to a 50-barrel plant. The brewery has two of its own outlets, the Railway Arms in Alton and the White Lion in Aldershot, as well as supplying over 300 other outlets. Three core beers are available all year round, supplemented by some old favourites and occasional new brews: see website for details.

Alton's Pride (OG 1039, ABV 3.8%) 🍺 🍴 🌾
An excellent, clean-tasting brown session beer. Full-bodied for its strength with a glorious aroma of floral hops. An initially malty flavour fades as citrus notes and hoppiness take over, leading to a lasting hoppy/bitter finish.

Moondance (OG 1045, ABV 4.2%) 🌾
A golden ale, well-hopped, with an aromatic citrus hop nose, balanced by bitterness and a noticeable sweetness in the mouth. Bitterness increases in the finish as the fruit declines, leading to a bittersweet finish.

Trossach's Craft

See Traditional Scottish Ales

Truman's

Truman's Beer, Top Floor, 8 Elder Street, London, E1 6BT
☎ (020) 7247 1147 ✉ trumans@trumansbeer.co.uk
⊕ trumansbeer.co.uk

Founded in 1666, Truman's was brewed for over 300 years until its closure in 1989. In 2010 it was re-established and the owners plan to build a new brewery in East London. The one beer is currently brewed by Nethergate (qv).

Tryst SIBA

Tryst Brewery, Lorne Road, Larbert, Stirlingshire, FK5 4AT
☎ (01324) 554000 ✉ john@trystbrewery.co.uk
⊕ trystbrewery.co.uk
Shop Mon-Fri office hours; Sat am
Tours by arrangement

⊗ John McGarva, a member of Scottish Craft Brewers, started brewing in 2003 in an industrial unit near Larbert station. Monthly specials are brewed and all beers are also available bottle conditioned.

Brockville Dark (OG 1039, ABV 3.8%)
A full-tasting session ale with hints of liquorice and roasted grains.

Brockville Pale (OG 1039, ABV 3.9%)
A pale golden session ale, smooth on the palate.

Bla'than (OG 1041, ABV 4%)
A strong floral nose and refreshing taste enhanced with elderflower and pale malts.

Drovers 80/- (OG 1041, ABV 4%)
A traditional, well-malted 80/- with an element of sweetness. A gentle nose complements a smooth finish.

RAJ IPA (OG 1055, ABV 5.5%) ▨
Exclusively English hopped with balanced flavours, with a hoppy aroma and palate.

Tunnel SIBA

Tunnel Brewery Ltd, Old Stable Block, Red House Farm, Nuneaton Road, Church End, Warwickshire, CV10 0QU
☎ (024) 7639 4386 ☎ 07765 223110
✉ info@tunnelbrewery.co.uk
⊕ tunnelbrewery.co.uk
Shop Mon-Fri 10am-4pm; Sat 10am-12pm
Tours by arrangement

☺ Bob Yates and Mike Walsh started brewing in 2005, taking the name from a rail tunnel that passes under the village. Originally brewing at the Lord Nelson Inn, the brewery relocated in 2011. Seasonal beers: see website. Tunnel also brews for Battlefield Brewery, which will take over production once the brewery is built at Bosworth Battlefield Visitor Centre in Leicestershire. Bottle-conditioned beers are also available and are suitable for vegans (for both Tunnel and Battlefield). One pub is owned, the Horseshoes in Nuneaton.

Linda Lear Beer (OG 1038, ABV 3.7%)
A dark amber, fruity beer with a grassy hop finish.

Late Ott (OG 1040, ABV 4%)
A golden ale with a very dry, hoppy finish.

Legend (OG 1044, ABV 4%)
A malty ale with a good hop balance.

Trade Winds (OG 1045, ABV 4.6%)
An aromatic, copper-coloured beer with an aroma of Cascade hops and a clean, crisp hint of citrus, followed by fruity malts and a dry finish full of scented hops.

Parish Ale (OG 1047, ABV 4.7%)
A reddish-amber, malty ale with a slight chocolate aroma enhanced by citrus notes. It becomes increasingly fruity as the English hops kick in. Smooth, gentle hop bitterness in the finish.

Shadow Weaver (OG 1047, ABV 4.7%)
A sweet stout with a hint of chocolate.

Jean 'Cloudy' Van Damme (OG 1048, ABV 5%)
A Belgian-style wheat beer with a hint of spice.

Munich Style Lager (OG 1052, ABV 5%)

Stranger In The Mist (OG 1048, ABV 5%)
A German-style wheat beer.

Nelson's Column (OG 1051, ABV 5.2%)
A ruby red, strong old English ale.

Boston Beer Party (OG 1056, ABV 5.6%)
A full-flavoured, copper-coloured IPA.

For Battlefield Brewery:

Let Battle Commence (OG 1038, ABV 3.8%)
A sweet vanilla, amber session beer.

Richard III (OG 1042, ABV 4.2%)
A light, refreshing pale ale.

Henry Tudor (OG 1052, ABV 5%)
A fruity red ale with a malty finish.

Twickenham SIBA

Twickenham Fine Ales Ltd, Ryecroft Works, Edwin Road, Twickenham, Middlesex, TW2 6SP
☎ (020) 8241 1825 ✉ info@twickenham-fine-ales.co.uk ⊕ twickenham-fine-ales.co.uk
Tours by arrangement

The 10-barrel brewery was set up in 2004 and was the first brewery in Twickenham since the 1920s. The brewery supplies pubs and clubs within 25 miles of the brewery, including central London. It expanded into new premises in 2009 and is planning to increase brewing capacity and introduce bottled ales. Seasonal beers: see website.

Sundancer (OG 1035, ABV 3.7%) ◥
A light, zesty, golden ale with citrus notes dominating from beginning to end. The finish is bitter but balanced by biscuity sweetness that stops the aftertaste being too intense.

Original (OG 1041, ABV 4.2%) ◥
A malty, honey sweetness is balanced by hops and fruit throughout this pale brown best bitter with a creamy mouthfeel . Dryish, slightly bitter aftertaste.

Naked Ladies (OG 1043, ABV 4.4%) ◥
Dark golden ale with a perfumed nose and a touch of spicy hop, which is in the initial flavour but fruit dominates. There is a lasting bitterness with some dryness.

Two Bridges SIBA

Two Bridges Brewery, 37 Ardler Road, Caversham, Reading, Berkshire, RG4 5AE
☎ 07714 899770
✉ kevin.durkan@twobridgesbrewery.co.uk
⊕ twobridgesbrewery.co.uk

Two Bridges Brewery was founded in 2009 by husband and wife Kevin and Kerri Durkan, with help from Kerri's mum. The Two Bridges are those over the Thames from Caversham to Reading. The 2.5-barrel plant has outgrown the owner's garage and a move is planned to a larger location in Caversham. Local outlets are supplied direct and those further afield through the SIBA list. Polypins are available for off-sales. Seasonal beers are also brewed.

Stormy Weather (ABV 4%)

Woodcutter (ABV 4%)

Golden Cygnet (OG 1045, ABV 4.8%)

Two Roses SIBA (NEW)

Two Roses Brewery, Unit 9, Darton Business Park, Barnsley Road, Darton, South Yorkshire, S75 5QX
☎ 07780 701254
✉ enquiries@tworosesbrewery.co.uk
⊕ tworosesbrewery.co.uk
Tours by arrangement

Two Roses commenced brewing in 2011 on an eight-barrel plant and is situated in industrial units on the site of an old carpet factory on the outskirts of Barnsley. All beers are also available bottle conditioned.

☺The brewery was set up at an equestrian centre in 1993. In 2011 a new brewery was built a mile from the original site, which has increased the capacity.

Best Bitter (OG 1038.5, ABV 3.8%) ◀
Pale brown beer with an assertive bitterness and a lingering dry finish. Despite initial sweetness, peppery hops dominate throughout.

Mad Hatter (OG 1038.5, ABV 3.9%)
A red-brown beer with fruity and malty flavours throughout. Brewed with American Amarillo hops to give spicy and floral notes.

Cheshire Cat (ABV 4%) ◀
Pale, dry bitter with a spritzy lemon zest and a grapy aroma. Hoppy aroma leads through to the initial taste before fruitiness takes over. Smooth creamy mouthfeel and a short, dry finish.

Eastgate Ale (OG 1043.5, ABV 4.2%) ◀
Well-balanced and refreshing clean amber beer. Citrus fruit flavours predominate in the taste and there is a short, dry aftertaste.

Old Dog Bitter (OG 1045, ABV 4.5%) ◀
Robust, well-balanced amber beer with a slightly fruity aroma. Rich malt and fruit flavours are balanced by bitterness. Some sweetness and a hint of sulphur on nose and taste.

Ambush Ale (OG 1047.5, ABV 4.8%) ◀
Full-bodied malty, premium bitter with initial sweetness balanced by bitterness and leading to a long-lasting dry finish. Blackberries and bitterness predominate alongside the hops.

Oasthouse Gold (OG 1050, ABV 5%) ◀
Straw-coloured, crisp, full-bodied and fruity golden ale with a good dry finish.

Welbeck Abbey (NEW)

Welbeck Abbey, Lower Motor Yard, Welbeck, Nottinghamshire, S80 3LR
☎ (0114) 249 4804

A joint venture between Kelham Island Brewery and Welbeck Estates, which started brewing in 2011. The brewery is housed in a listed barn in the centre of the Welbeck Estate. The 10-barrel plant was originally used at Kelham Island.

Wellington

See Crown

Wells & Young's

See New Nationals section

Welton's SIBA

Welton's North Downs Brewery Ltd, 1 Mulberry Trading Estate, Foundry Lane, Horsham, West Sussex, RH13 5PX
☎ (01403) 242901/251873 ✉ sales@weltons.co.uk
⊕ weltonsbeer.com
Tours by arrangement

Ray Welton moved his brewery to a factory unit in Horsham in 2003, which has given him space to expand. Over 100 different beers were brewed during the past year. Around 400 outlets are supplied. Bottle-conditioned beers are also available.

Pride 'n' Joy (ABV 2.8%) ◀
A light brown bitter with a slight malty and hoppy aroma. Fruity with a pleasant hoppiness and some sweetness in the flavour, leading to a short malty finish.

Horsham Bitter (ABV 3.8%)
Amber-coloured, bitter but with a huge aroma.

Old Cocky (OG 1043, ABV 4.3%)

Horsham Old (OG 1046, ABV 4.6%) ◀
Roast and toffee flavours predominate with some bitterness in this traditional old ale. Bittersweet with plenty of caramel and roast in a rather short finish.

Export Stout (ABV 4.7%)
Hints of burnt toast, balanced by good levels of hops with a long finish.

Old Harry (OG 1051, ABV 5.2%)

Wensleydale SIBA

Wensleydale Brewery Ltd, Manor Road, Bellerby, North Yorkshire, DL8 5QH
☎ (01969) 622463 ☎ 07900 264235
✉ enquiries@wensleydalebrewery.co.uk
⊕ wensleydalebrewery.co.uk
Shop Mon-Fri 9am-5pm
Tours by arrangement

Wensleydale Brewery (formerly Lidstone's) was set up in 2003 on a two-barrel plant in Yorkshire Dales National Park. A year later the brewery relocated to larger premises six miles away and is now operating on a 4.5-barrel plant. Most beers are available in bottles – some bottle conditioned. Around 100 outlets are supplied. Seasonal beers are also available.

Lidstone's Rowley Mild (OG 1037, ABV 3.2%) ◀
Chocolate and toffee aromas lead into what, for its strength, is an impressively rich and flavoursome taste. The finish is pleasantly bittersweet.

Bitter (OG 1038, ABV 3.7%) ◀
Intensely aromatic, straw-coloured ale offering a superb balance of malt and hops on the tongue.

Falconer Session Bitter (OG 1040, ABV 3.9%)
A fruity, malt-based session ale, copper-coloured with a long, bitter, dry finish.

Semerwater Summer Ale (OG 1041, ABV 4.1%)
A pale ale with citrus aromas. A clean, hoppy nose is balanced by a light, malty sweetness.

Coverdale Gamekeeper (OG 1042, ABV 4.3%)
A well-balanced, copper-coloured best bitter with spicy hop flavours and a juicy malt flavour.

Black Dub Oat Stout (OG 1044, ABV 4.4%)
Black and silky, enriched with roast barley, chocolate malt and malted oats. Named after a deep, dark pool (or Dub) in the River Cover to the rear of Middleham Castle.

Sheep Rustler Nut Brown Ale (OG 1041, ABV 4.4%)
A dark, reddish brown beer with a sweetish roast malt taste leading to a long-lasting, roasted, slightly bitter finish.

Gold (OG 1043, ABV 4.5%)
Aromatic and spicy hop flavours combine with light malt to make this a highly quaffable, light golden best bitter.

Coverdale Poacher IPA (OG 1049, ABV 5%) ◀

Citrus flavours dominate both aroma and taste in this pale, smooth, refreshing beer; the aftertaste is quite dry.

Wentwell (NEW)

Wentwell Brewery, 15 Wingfield Drive, Derby, DE21 4PW
☎ 07900 475755 ✉ contact@wentwellbrewery.com
⊕ wentwellbrewery.com

Wentwell began commercial brewing in early 2011 using a one-barrel plant, upgrading to a three-barrel plant soon after. All beers are also available bottle conditioned. Further beers are planned.

Derbyshire Gold (ABV 3.9%)
A light, hoppy, zesty beer.

Barrel Organ Blues (ABV 4.5%)
A golden-brown malty beer with a hint of chocolate.

Wentworth SIBA

Wentworth Brewery Ltd, Power House, Gun Park, Wentworth, South Yorkshire, S62 7TF
☎ (01226) 747070
✉ info@wentworthbrewery.co.uk
⊕ wentworthbrewery.co.uk
Tours by arrangement

The brewery was founded in 1999 in the power house in the grounds of Wentworth Woodhouse. A new custom-built 30-barrel brewery was commissioned in 2006. Wentworth produces around 20 core bottled beers under both the Wentworth brand and the Barnsley Beer Company. Two monthly specials are also produced in addition to the seasonal range.

Imperial Ale (OG 1038, ABV 3.8%)
A tawny, bitter beer with a floral nose. There is a slight hint of sweetness on the aftertaste.

WPA (OG 1039.5, ABV 4%) ◆
An extremely well hopped IPA-style beer that leads to some astringency. A very bitter beer.

Best Bitter (OG 1040, ABV 4.1%) ◆
A hoppy, bitter beer with hints of citrus fruits. A bitter note dominates the aftertaste.

Bumble Beer (OG 1043, ABV 4.3%)
A pale golden beer, made with local honey, which gives it a unique and distinctive flavour throughout the year.

Short n Stout (OG 1044, ABV 4.5%)
A smooth mellow stout with rich coffee overtones.

Black Zac (OG 1046, ABV 4.6%)
A mellow, dark ruby-red ale with chocolate and pale malts leading to a bitter taste, with a coffee finish.

Oatmeal Stout (OG 1050, ABV 4.8%) ◆
Black, smooth, with roast and chocolate malt and toffee overtones.

Rampant Gryphon (OG 1062, ABV 6.2%) ◆
A strong, well-balanced golden ale with hints of fruit and sweetness but which retains a hoppy character.

Wessex

CF Hobden t/a Wessex Brewery, Rye Hill Farm, Longbridge Deverill, Warminster, Wiltshire, BA12 7DE
☎ (01985) 844532
✉ wessexbrewery@tinyworld.co.uk
Tours by arrangement

✖ The brewery went into production in 2001 and moved to its current location in 2004. 15 local outlets are supplied. Beers are also available through selected wholesalers. Seasonal beers are also produced.

Potter's Ale (OG 1038, ABV 3.8%)
A classic bitter.

Longleat Pride (OG 1040, ABV 4%)
A pale, hoppy bitter.

Crockerton Classic (OG 1041, ABV 4.1%)
A full-bodied, tawny, full-flavoured bitter; fruity and malty.

Merrie Mink (OG 1041, ABV 4.2%)
A full-flavoured best with a strong hop aroma.

Deverill's Advocate (OG 1046, ABV 4.5%)
A well-balanced golden premium ale.

Warminster Warrior (OG 1045, ABV 4.5%)
Full-flavoured premium bitter.

The Beast of Zeals (ABV 6.66%)

Russian Stoat (OG 1080, ABV 9%)
Dark, strong and obvious.

For Isle of Avalon Brewery:

Isle Ale (OG 1038, ABV 3.8%)

Jake's Mild (OG 1039, ABV 4%)

Sunset (OG 1043, ABV 4.3%)

Sunrise (OG 1050, ABV 5%)

Arthur's Ale (OG 1071, ABV 7%)

West SIBA

⊟ **West Brewery, Bar & Restaurant, Binnie Place, Glasgow Green, Glasgow, G40 1AW**
☎ (0141) 550 0135 ✉ info@westbeer.com
⊕ westbeer.com
Tours by arrangement

No real ale. West opened in 2006 and produces a full range of European-style beers. The brewery's copper-clad system, visible from the 300-seat bar and restaurant, is a fully-automated German one with an annual capacity of 1.5 million litres. Brewing is in strict accordance with the Reinheitsgebot, the German purity law, importing all malt, hops and yeast from Germany. Five regular beers are produced along with a range of seasonals. Beers: Hefeweizen (ABV 4.9%), St Mungo (ABV 4.9%), Helles Light (ABV 3.9%), Dunkel (ABV 4.9%), Munich Red (ABV 4.9%).

West Berkshire SIBA

West Berkshire Brewery Co Ltd, Old Bakery, Yattendon, Thatcham, Berkshire, RG18 0UE
☎ (01635) 202968 ✉ info@wbbrew.co.uk
⊕ wbbrew.com
Shop Mon-Fri 10am-4pm; Sat 10am-1pm
Tours by arrangement

✖ The brewery, established in 1995 at the Potkiln pub in Frilsham, moved its main site to Yattendon and in 2006 extended the brewhouse and installed a new plant; the original five-barrel plant at the Potkiln pub in Frilsham has now closed. In 2011 a new brewery was built 600 yards down the road,

THE BREWERIES

and chocolate undertones and a lovely blackcurrant aroma.

Birds & Bees (OG 1040, ABV 4.3%)
Fruity golden ale with refreshing hop and elderflower aromas.

Cock O' The Walk (OG 1046, ABV 4.3%)

Good Times (OG 1045, ABV 4.5%)
Refreshing, fruity, malty and aromatic.

Red (OG 1045, ABV 4.5%)
A rich ruby-red beer with toffee flavours and citrus hop aromas.

Ceilidh (OG 1048, ABV 4.7%)
A premium lager.

Joker IPA (OG 1047, ABV 5%)
Very hoppy, bright amber bitter with strong hop aromas.

Seven Giraffes (OG 1047, ABV 5.1%)
Classic IPA with late infusion of elderflower, cone hops and lemon.

Midnight Sun (OG 1056, ABV 5.6%)
A rich, black, smooth porter.

Willy's

▤ **Willy's Wine Bar Ltd, 17 High Cliff Road, Cleethorpes, Lincolnshire, DN35 8RQ**
☎ **(01472) 602145**
Tours by arrangement

The brewery opened in 1989 to provide beer for its two pubs in Grimsby and Cleethorpes. It has a five-barrel plant with maximum capacity of 15 barrels a week. The brewery can be viewed at any time from pub or street.

Original (OG 1039, ABV 3.9%) ◥
A light brown 'sea air' beer with a fruity, tangy hop on the nose and taste, giving a strong bitterness tempered by the underlying malt.

Last Resort (OG 1044, ABV 4.3%)

Coxswains Special (OG 1050, ABV 4.9%)

Willy Good (NEW)

Willy Good Ale, The Old Forge, Hartley's Farm, Winsley, Wiltshire, BA15 2JB
☎ **07711 364202** ✉ **willygoodale@live.co.uk**

Willy Good Ale was established in 2010. It quickly reached maximum production levels and upgraded to a six-barrel plant in 2011. Bottle-conditioned beers are available.

Willy Hop! (ABV 4%)

High Five (ABV 5%)

Wheat a Minute (ABV 5.7%)

Wincle SIBA

Wincle Beer Co Ltd, Towles Farm Barn, Dane Bridge, Wincle, Cheshire, SK11 0QE
☎ **(01260) 227777** ✉ **sales@winclebeer.co.uk**
⊕ **winclebeer.co.uk**
Shop 10am-4pm daily
Tours by arrangement

☺Wincle began brewing in 2008 on a five-barrel plant in an old milking parlour. The brewery relocated in 2011. 120 outlets are supplied direct

within a 25-mile radius. Bottle-conditioned beers are also available.

Wincle Waller (OG 1038, ABV 3.8%)

Sir Phillip (OG 1041, ABV 4.2%)

Wibbly Wallaby (OG 1043, ABV 4.4%)

Undertaker (OG 1044, ABV 4.5%)

Mr Mullin's IPA (OG 1047, ABV 4.8%)

Windsor Castle

See Sadler's

Windsor & Eton SIBA

Windsor & Eton Brewery, Unit 1, Vansittart Estate, Duke Street, Windsor, Berkshire, SL4 1SE
☎ **(01753) 854075** ✉ **sampleroom@webrew.co.uk**
⊕ **webrew.co.uk**
Shop 9am-5pm Mon-Thu; 9am-7pm Fri (check website for further opening times)
Tours by arrangement

⊠ Windsor & Eton Brewery was established in 2010 on an 18-barrel plant bringing brewing back to Windsor 79 years after the closure of both Noakes and Burge & Co. 130 outlets are supplied direct.

Knight of the Garter (OG 1037, ABV 3.8%)
An easy-drinking golden ale with an Amarillo hop flavour.

Guardsman (OG 1041, ABV 4.2%)
A tangy session best bitter with a fresh, hoppy finish.

Conqueror (OG 1049, ABV 5%)
A complex black IPA with an intense hop flavour.

Winster Valley

▤ **Winster Valley Brewery, Brown Horse Inn, Winster, Cumbria, LA23 3NR**
☎ **(01539) 443443**
✉ **craig@winstervalleybrewery.co.uk**
⊕ **winstervalleybrewery.co.uk**
Tours by arrangement

☺Winster Valley was established in 2009 using a 2.5-barrel plant at the Brown Horse Inn in Winster.

Best Bitter (ABV 3.7%)
A full-bodied beer with a roasted malt flavour with a hint of caramel.

Old School (ABV 3.9%)
A pale ale, full-tasting with floral aromas.

Winter's

Winter's Brewery, 8 Keelan Close, Norwich, NR6 6QZ
☎ **(01603) 787820**

⊠ David Winter, who had previous award-winning success as brewer for both Woodforde's and Chalk Hill breweries, decided to set up on his own in 2001. He purchased the brewing plant from the now defunct Scott's Brewery in Lowestoft. The local free trade is supplied.

Mild (OG 1036.5, ABV 3.6%) ◥
Classic dark mild, red-brown with a nutty roast character. A good balance of malt caramel and roast abetted by both sweetness and a light, hoppy

bitterness. Lingering finish develops a plummy feel.

Bitter (OG 1039.5, ABV 3.8%) ◆
A well-balanced amber bitter. Hops and malt are balanced by a crisp citrus fruitiness. A pleasant hoppy nose with a hint of grapefruit. Long, sustained, dry, grapefruit finish.

Golden (OG 1040, ABV 4.1%) ◆
Just a hint of hops in the aroma. The initial taste combines a dry bitterness with a fruity apple buttress. The finish slowly subsides into a long, dry bitterness.

Revenge (OG 1047, ABV 4.7%) ◆
Blackcurrant notes give depth to the inherent maltiness of this pale brown beer. A bittersweet background becomes more pronounced as the fruitiness gently wanes.

Storm Force (OG 1053, ABV 5.3%) ◆
A well-defined, sweetish brew. Hops and vine fruit give depth to the malty backbone of this pale brown strong beer. All flavours hold up well as the finish develops a warming softness.

Tempest (OG 1062, ABV 6.2%)

Wirksworth SIBA

Wirksworth Brewery, 25 St John Street, Wirksworth, Derbyshire, DE4 4DR
☎ (01629) 824011
✉ wirksworthbrewery@hotmail.co.uk
⊕ wirksworthbrewery.co.uk
Off sales: Fri & Sat 10am-5pm

☺Jeff Green started brewing in 2007 with a 2.5-barrel plant in a converted stone workshop. Wirksworth supplies Derbyshire pubs with its core beers and supplements these with at least one seasonal offering. Every September there is a brew house open weekend giving visitors the opportunity to gain an insight into the brewing process and taste the real ales.

Cruckbeam (OG 1040, ABV 3.9%)

Sunbeam (OG 1040, ABV 4%)

First Brew (OG 1042, ABV 4.2%)

T'owd Man (OG 1050, ABV 4.9%)

Wissey Valley

Wissey Valley Brewery, 1 High Street, Downham Market, Norfolk, PE38 9DA
☎ (01366) 386658
✉ thehopandhog@btconnect.com
⊕ norfolkfoodanddrink.co.uk
Shop Wed-Sun 9am-5pm
Tours by arrangement

⊠ After several moves since starting up in 2002 (as Captain Grumpy's), the brewery is now located at the rear of the local produce store, team room and restaurant, the Hop & Hog.

**Captain Grumpy's Best Bitter
(OG 1039, ABV 3.9%)**

Khaki Sergeant Strong Stout (OG 1059, ABV 6%)

Wizard SIBA

Wizard Ales, Unit 4, Lundy View, Mullacott Cross Industrial Estate, Ilfracombe, Devon, EX34 8PY

☎ (01271) 865350 ✉ mike@wizardales.co.uk
⊕ wizardales.co.uk
Tours by arrangement

⊠ Brewing started in 2003 on a 1.25-barrel plant, since upgraded to five barrels. The brewery moved from Warwickshire to Devon in 2007. Around 20 local outlets are supplied. Bottle-conditioned beers are also available.

Apprentice (OG 1038, ABV 3.6%)

Lundy Gold (OG 1042, ABV 4.1%)

Old Combe (OG 1043, ABV 4.2%)

Druid's Fluid (OG 1048, ABV 5%)

Wold Top SIBA

Wold Top Brewery, Hunmanby Grange, Wold Newton, Driffield, East Yorkshire, YO25 3HS
☎ (01723) 892222
✉ enquiries@woldtopbrewery.co.uk
⊕ woldtopbrewery.co.uk

☺Wold Top commenced brewing in 2003 and is an integral part of Hunmanby Grange, a family farm. It uses home and Wold-grown malting barley and chalk-filtered water from the farm's borehole. The brewery installed a bottling line in 2008 and contract bottles for other breweries. Over 600 outlets are supplied. Seasonal beers: see website.

Bitter (OG 1037, ABV 3.7%)
A crisp, clean, aromatic session bitter. Full-flavoured with a long, hoppy finish.

Falling Stone Bitter (OG 1041, ABV 4.2%)
A full-bodied, smooth best bitter. Named after the first recorded meteorite in England, which fell in Wold Newton.

Mars Magic (OG 1044, ABV 4.6%)
An aromatic premium ale with a red glow and smooth, malty flavour.

Wold Gold (OG 1046, ABV 4.8%)
A blonde summer beer with a soft, fruity flavour with a hint of spice.

Wolf SIBA

WBC (Norfolk) Ltd t/a The Wolf Brewery, Rookery Farm, Silver Street, Besthorpe, Attleborough, Norfolk, NR17 2LD
☎ (01953) 457775 ✉ info@wolfbrewery.com
⊕ wolfbrewery.com
Shop Mon-Fri 9am-5pm
Tours by arrangement

⊠ The brewery was founded in 1996 on a 20-barrel plant, which was upgraded to a 30-barrel one in 2006. Over 300 outlets are supplied. Seasonal beers: see website.

Golden Jackal (OG 1039, ABV 3.7%) ◆
A hoppy, citrus nose carries through to the initial taste. The citrus notes remain right to the end as the initial hoppiness is replaced by a dry bitterness.

Lavender Honey (OG 1037, ABV 3.7%)
Honey from the Norfolk Lavender Company is added during the brewing process to give this beer a delicate flavour.

Wolf In Sheep's Clothing (OG 1039, ABV 3.7%) ◆
A malty aroma with fruity undertones introduce this reddish-hued mild. Malt, with a bitter background that remains throughout, is the dominant flavour of this clean-tasting beer.

THE BREWERIES

Initial sweetness is quickly balanced by subtle fruitiness and moderate hop bitterness. A full-flavoured beer with a bittersweet aftertaste.

Golden Bitter (OG 1039, ABV 4%)
A light, refreshing beer with fruity aftertones finished with a well-balanced bitter taste.

Undercliff Experience (OG 1040, ABV 4.1%)
An amber ale with a bittersweet malt and hop taste with a dry, lemon edge that dominates the bitter finish.

Blonde Ale (OG 1045, ABV 4.5%)
A golden beer with a malty aroma, laced with floral, citrus hops. The taste is hoppy and bitter to start, with smooth malt support and light lemon notes. Dry, hoppy aftertaste.

Holy Joe (OG 1050, ABV 4.9%) ◣
Strongly bittered golden ale with pronounced spice and citrus character, and underlying light hint of malt.

Wight Winter (ABV 5%)
A ruby ale with malty milk chocolate in the nose at first then plenty of orange fruit. Bitter, malty and roasted to taste with perfumed bitter orange notes always present.

YSD/Special Draught (OG 1056, ABV 5.5%) ◣
Easy-drinking strong, amber ale with pronounced tart bitterness and a refreshing bite in the aftertaste.

Wight Old Ale (ABV 6%)
Roasted crystal malts give a full-bodied taste with citrus fruits and port in the aftertaste.

Yule Be Sorry (ABV 7.6%) ⌂
A rich, full-bodied beer.

Yeovil SIBA

Yeovil Ales Ltd, Unit 5, Bofors Park, Artillery Road, Lufton Trading Estate, Yeovil, Somerset, BA22 8YH
☎ (01935) 414888 ✉ rob@yeovilales.com
⊕ yeovilales.com
Sales counter Fri pm only until 5.30pm
Tours by arrangement

⊗ Yeovil Ales was established in 2006 using an 18-barrel plant. Production has steadily increased and up to 350 outlets are supplied across six counties in the south west. Seasonal beers: see website.

Glory (OG 1039, ABV 3.8%)
A well-balanced bitter with citrus hop notes.

Star Gazer (OG 1042, ABV 4%)
Dark copper bitter with late-hopped floral bouquet.

Summerset (OG 1043, ABV 4.1%)
Blonde ale with fruity hop finish.

Ruby (OG 1047, ABV 4.5%)
Red bitter with rich malt depth.

P.O.S.H. (OG 1054, ABV 5.4%)
A strong IPA with a fruity body and hoppy finish.

Yetman's

Yetman's Brewery, Bayfield Farm Barns, Bayfield Brecks Farm, Bayfield, Norfolk, BR25 7DZ
☎ 07774 809016 ✉ peter@yetmans.net
⊕ yetmans.net

⊗ A 2.5-barrel plant built by Moss Brew was installed in restored medieval barns in 2005. The

brewery supplies local free trade outlets. Bottle-conditioned beers are available.

Red (OG 1036, ABV 3.8%)

Orange (OG 1040, ABV 4.2%) ◣
Well-balanced and smooth-drinking. A light fruity aroma leads into a stirring mix of malt and hops supported by a bittersweet background. A big finish combines malt and a vinous fruitiness.

Green (OG 1044, ABV 4.8%)

York SIBA

York Brewery Ltd, 12 Toft Green, York, North Yorkshire, YO1 6JT
☎ (01904) 621162 ✉ info@york-brewery.co.uk
⊕ york-brewery.co.uk
Shop Mon-Sat 12-6pm
Tours by arrangement (ring for daily tour times)

York started production in 1996, the first brewery in the city for 40 years. It has a visitor centre with bar and gift shop, and was designed as a show brewery, with a gallery above the 20-barrel plant and viewing panels to fermentation and conditioning rooms. The brewery owns several pubs and in 2006 additional space was acquired to increase production capacity. More than 400 outlets are supplied. The brewery was bought by Mitchell's Hotels & Inns in 2008. Seasonal beers – see website.

Guzzler (OG 1036, ABV 3.6%) ⌂ ▣ ◣
Refreshing golden ale with dominant hop and fruit flavours developing throughout.

Constantine (ABV 3.9%)

Yorkshire Terrier (OG 1041, ABV 4.2%) ◣
Refreshing and distinctive amber/gold brew where fruit and hops dominate the aroma and taste. Hoppy bitterness remains assertive in the aftertaste.

Centurion's Ghost Ale (OG 1051, ABV 5.4%) ◣
Dark ruby in colour, full-tasting with mellow roast malt character balanced by light bitterness and autumn fruit flavours that linger into the aftertaste.

Yorkshire Heart SIBA (NEW)

Yorkshire Heart Brewery, Frank Lane, Nun Monkton, York, YO26 8EL
☎ (01423) 330716 ✉ chris.yhv@mypostoffice.co.uk
⊕ yorkshireheartwinesandbeers.co.uk

Yorkshire Heart began brewing in 2011 and is situated on the site of the Yorkshire Heart Vineyard and Winery, not far from York. Further beers are planned. Bottle-conditioned beers are also available.

Yorkshire Hearty (OG 1037, ABV 3.7%)

JRT Best Bitter (OG 1042, ABV 4.2%)

Yorkshire Dales

Yorkshire Dales Brewing Co Ltd, Seata Barn, Elm Hill, Askrigg, North Yorkshire, DL8 3HG
☎ (01969) 622027 ☎ 07818 035592
✉ rob@yorkshiredalesbrewery.com
⊕ yorkshiredalesbrewery.com

⊛ Situated in the heart of the Yorkshire Dales, brewing started in 2005. Installation of a five-barrel plant and additional fermenters at the converted milking parlour increased capacity to 20 barrels a week. Over 150 pubs are supplied throughout the North of England. Four monthly special are always available, including a dark mild. Bottle-conditioned beers are also available.

Butter Tubs (OG 1037, ABV 3.7%)
A pale golden beer with a dry bitterness complemented by strong citrus flavours and aroma.

Leyburn Shawl (OG 1038, ABV 3.8%)
A crisp, dry, pale ale with an underlying sharpness.

Buckden Pike (OG 1040, ABV 3.9%)
A refreshing blonde beer with a crisp, fruity finish.

Nappa Scar (OG 1041, ABV 4%)
A golden ale brewed with a trio of American hops for citrus and peach flavours throughout.

Muker Silver (OG 1041, ABV 4.1%)
A blonde lager-style ale, very crisp with a sharp, hoppy finish.

Askrigg Ale (OG 1043, ABV 4.3%)
A pale golden ale with intense aroma that generates a crisp, dry flavour with a long, bitter finish.

Garsdale Smokebox (OG 1057, ABV 5.6%)
A complex ale created by smoked and dark malts. Deep, rich chocolate and coffee flavours are complemented by the smokiness.

Young's

See Wells & Young's in New Nationals section

Zerodegrees

Blackheath: Zerodegrees Microbrewery, 29-31 Montpelier Vale, Blackheath, London, SE3 0TJ ☎ (020) 8852 5619

Bristol: Zerodegrees Microbrewery, 53 Colston Street, Bristol, BS1 5BA ☎ (0117) 925 2706

Cardiff: 27 Westgate Street, Cardiff, CF10 1DD ☎ (029) 2022 9494

Reading: 9 Bridge Street, Reading, Berkshire, RG1 2LR ☎ (0118) 959 7959
✉ info@zerodegrees.co.uk ⊕ zerodegrees.co.uk
Tours by arrangement

Brewing started in 2000 in Greenwich, London and incorporates a state-of-the-art, computer-controlled German plant, producing unfiltered and unfined ales and lagers, served from tanks using air pressure (not CO2). Four pubs are owned. All beers are suitable for vegetarians and vegans. All branches of Zerodegrees follow the same concept of beers with natural ingredients. There are regular seasonal specials including fruit beers.

Wheat Ale (OG 1045, ABV 4.2%) ◆
Authentic Munich-style wheat beer with Hallertau hops and Munich wheat malt. Strong aroma of wheat malt, a flavour of cloves and lemons lasts in a sweetish aftertaste.

Pale Ale (OG 1046, ABV 4.6%) ◆
Malt and fruit on the nose of the American-style pale ale lead to an increasingly bitter taste and finish.

Black Lager (OG 1048, ABV 4.8%) ◆
A Czech-style stout based on wheat malt and Continental hops. Strong roast and burnt malt flavours with hints of prunes and fresh coriander.

Pilsner (OG 1048, ABV 4.8%) ◆
Spicy, zesty Continental lager with sweetish lemony taste and bitter, slightly astringent aftertaste. The peppery malt aroma has hints of camomile and rosemary.

REPUBLIC OF IRELAND BREWERIES

Bay

Bay Brewery, The Oslo, Upper Salthill Road, Salthill, Co Galway 00353 91 448390 ⊕ winefoodbeer.com/Brewery.aspx

Based at The Oslo Bar and Restaurant in Salthill, just outside Galway City, Bay Brewery produces a red ale and a Vienna lager. Sold in keg at the owners' other pubs in Galway and Dublin, both are served direct from the conditioning tanks in The Oslo.

Ale (ABV 4.2%)

Lager (ABV 4.2%)

Beoir Chorca Dhuibhne/West Kerry

Beoir Chorca Dhuibhne/West Kerry Brewery, Tig Bhric, nr Ballyferriter, Co Kerry 00353 66 915 6325 ✉ info@tigbhric.com ⊕ tigbhric.com/grudlann.html

Beer is brewed on a 400-litre plant in a remote area where Irish is the main language. The beers are available on draught in two pubs: Tig Bhric (adjacent to the brewery) and Tig Ui Chathain in nearby Ballyferriter village. Bottle-conditioned versions are also produced.

Beal Ban (ABV 4.1%)

Carraig Dubh (ABV 4.1%)

Cul Dhorca (ABV 4.1%)

Brew-Eyed (NEW)

Brew-Eyed Beers, Unit 5, Enterprise Centre, Banagher, Co Offaly 00353 86 125 0283 ✉ info@brewed.com ⊕ breweyed.com

Established in 2011 in Banagher in County Offaly. The first beer was a lager but the regular range will include both cask and bottle-conditioned ales.

Burren (NEW)

Burren Brewery, Roadside Tavern, Kincora Road, Lisdoonvarna, Co Clare 00353 65 707 4084 ✉ roadsidetavern@gmail.com

Brewpub run by the owners of the Burren Smokehouse, specialising in local food, drink and music. The in-house brewery produces three keg beers for day-to-day sale, but cask editions are also available at the pub several times a year during festivals.

Carlow

Carlow Brewing Co, Muine Bheag Business Park, Royal Oak Road, Carlow, Co Carlow 00353 59 972 0509 ✉ info@carlowbrewing.com ⊕ carlowbrewing.com

One of the bigger Irish independents with a good range of cask beers.

O'Hara's Irish Stout (ABV 4.3%)

THE BREWERIES

O'Hara's Red Ale (ABV 4.3%)

Curim Gold Wheat Beer (ABV 4.7%)

O'Hara's Pale Ale (ABV 5.2%)

Leann Follain Stout (ABV 6%)

Dingle (NEW)

Dingle Brewing Co, Spa Road, Dingle, Co Kerry
✉ hello@thedinglebrewingco.com
⊕ thedinglebrewingco.com

Launched in the summer of 2011 with a lager commemorating Antarctic explorer Tom Crean, former proprietor of the South Pole Inn in Annascaul on the Dingle Peninsula. Occasional cask beers are available.

Dungarvan

Dungarvan Brewing Co, Westgate Business Park, Dungarvan, Co Waterford 00353 58 24000
✉ info@dungarvanbrewingcompany.com
⊕ dungarvanbrewingcompany.com

Established 2010 and producing three beers in bottle-conditioned format, increasingly available cask-conditioned.

Black Rock (ABV 4.3%)

Copper Coast (ABV 4.3%)

Helvick Gold (ABV 4.9%)

Eight Degrees (NEW)

Eight Degrees Brewing Co, Unit 3, Coolnanave, Dublin Road, Mitchelstown, Co Cork 00353 86 159 4855
✉ scott@eightdegrees.ie ⊕ eightdegrees.ie

A recent start-up by two County Cork-based Antipodean entrepreneurs. All beers are bottle-conditioned; Howling Gale (ABV 5%), Sunburnt Irish Red (ABV 5%), Knockmealdown Porter (ABV 5%).

Franciscan Well

Franciscan Well Brewery, 14 North Mall, Cork City, Co Cork 00353 59 913 4356
✉ info@franciscanwellbrewery.com
⊕ franciscanwellbrewery.com

Small brewery that brings choice to a city dominated by Beamish and Murphy, both owned by Heineken, which has closed Beamish. Franciscan Well brews Blarney Blond, Rebel Red, Shandon Stout, Purgatory Pale Ale and Friar Weisse, all keg beers but are occasionally produced in cask form for special events. The brewery hosts beer festivals that feature beers from other Irish cask brewers.

Galway Hooker

Galway Hooker Brewery, Roscommon Business Park, Racecourse Road, Roscommon, Co Roscommon 00353 87 77 62823 ✉ aidan@galwayhooker.ie
⊕ galwayhooker.ie

Galway Hooker produces filtered keg beer for the Irish market but produces occasional casks for festivals in both Britain and Ireland.

Irish Pale Ale (ABV 4.4%)

Messrs Maguire

Messrs Maguire Brewing Co, 1-2 Burgh Quay, Dublin 2 00353 16 705 7777 ✉ info@messrsmaguire.ie
⊕ messrsmaguire.ie

Pub, brewery and restaurant in the historic O'Connell Bridge area of the city. It brews a range of keg beers, including porter, red ale and wheat beer. Revitalised in 2010 with a new brewster, a refurbished basement bar serving real ale, a new menu and a new range of seasonals.

Pale Ale (ABV 4.3%)

Brown Ale (ABV 5.5%)

Metalman (NEW)

Metalman Brewing Co Ltd, c/o 82 Flodh Mor, Ferrybank, Waterford City, Co Waterford
✉ info@metalmanbrewing.com
⊕ metalmanbrewing.com

Though the company is based in Waterford, early beers have been brewed by owners Grainne and Tim at White Gypsy while the brewhouse is under construction. Occasional casks are produced for festivals and pubs with real ale taps.

Pale Ale (ABV 4.3%)

Windjammer (ABV 4.8%)

Porterhouse

Porterhouse Brewing Co, Unit 6D, Rosemount, Park Road, Ballycoolin, Blanchardstown, Dublin 15 00353 1 822 7417 ⊕ theporterhouse.ie

The oldest surviving craft brewery in the Republic of Ireland. It has three pubs in Dublin: 16-18 Parliament Street, Temple Bar, Dublin 2; Porterhouse North, Cross Guns Bridge, Glasnevin, Dublin 9; Porterhouse Central, 45-47 Nassau Street, City Centre South, Dublin 2 plus Porterhouse Bray, Strand Road, Co Wicklow. There are also branches in Covent Garden, London and Pearl Street, New York City. Only one permanent cask ale is produced, but a number of other stouts and ales are produced occasionally in cask form for sale in the Temple Bar flagship and as guest ales in other pubs.

TSB (ABV 3.7%)

Trouble

Trouble Brewing, Allenwood, Co Kildare 00353 87 908 6658 ✉ info@troublebrewing.ie
⊕ troublebrewing.ie

Small craft brewery producing two cask ales plus occasional specials and seasonals.

Or (ABV 4.3%)
A golden ale.

Dark Arts Porter (ABV 4.4%)

White Gypsy

White Gypsy, Railway Road, Templemore, Co Tipperary 00353 86 17 24520 ✉ info@whitegypsy.ie
⊕ whitegypsy.ie

Produces a wide range of cask and keg ales and lagers, plus a range of bottle-conditioned strong beers. The brewery features Ireland's only commercial hop garden and produces the only beer made from 100% Irish ingredients. It is also experimenting with barrel aging, producing a number of blends of its vintage stout.

Raven
ABV varies. Oak-aged stout.

Emerald IPA (ABV 5%)
Made from all-Irish ingredients.

Bock (ABV 7%)

Scottish Ale (ABV 7%)

Imperial Porter (ABV 7.5%)

India Pale Ale (ABV 7.5%)

R.I.P.

The following breweries have closed, gone out of business or suspended operations since the 2011 Guide was published:

Atlas Mill, Brighouse, West Yorkshire
Avon, Bristol, Gloucestershire & Bristol
Baskerville, Yelland, Devon
Birmingham, Birmingham: Nechells, West Midlands
Bridgnorth, Bridgnorth, Shropshire
Bryson's, Morecambe, Lancashire
Buckle Street, Honeybourne, Worcestershire
Carter's, Machen, Glamorgan
Dartmouth, Newton Abbot, Devon
Discovery, Little Packington, Warwickshire
Far North, Reay, Highlands & Western Isles
Forgotten Corner, Maker Heights, Cornwall
Goldfinch, Dorchester, Dorset
Headless, Derby, Derbyshire
Hidden, Dinton, Wiltshire
Norfolk Cottage, Norwich, Norfolk
Pitstop, Grove, Oxfordshire
Rainbow, Allesley Village, West Midlands
Red Rose, Great Harwood, Lancashire
Shropshire/Wem, Whitchurch, Shropshire
Taunton, West Bagbrough, Somerset
Toad, Doncaster, South Yorkshire
Tudor, Abergavenny, Gwent
WC, Mickle Trafford, Cheshire
White, Bexhill-on-Sea, East Sussex
Willoughby, Whitbourne, Worcestershire

FUTURE

The following new breweries have been notified to the Guide and will start to produce beer during 2011/2012. In a few cases, they were in production during the summer of 2011 but were too late for a full listing in the Guide:

Albion, Warrington, Cheshire
Aylesbury, Aylesbury, Buckinghamshire
Barnsley, Barnsley, South Yorkshire
Black Iris, Derby, Derbyshire
Brewshed, Bury St Edmunds, Suffolk
Bronte, Brighouse, West Yorkshire
Cellar Rat, Stockport, Cheshire
Cromarty, Cromarty, Highlands & Western Isles
Daft Monk, Leiston, Suffolk
Fakir, Great Yarmouth, Norfolk
Faringdon, Faringdon, Oxfordshire
Flightpath, Stockport, Cheshire
Geeves, Barnsley, South Yorkshire
Hunsbury Craft, Northampton, Northamptonshire
James & Kirkman, Pontefract, West Yorkshire
Just A Minute, Spennymoor, County Durham
Kinneil, Bo'ness, Edinburgh & The Lothians
Laverstoke Park, Overton, Hampshire
Llynas, Llwyndyrys, North West Wales
Loch Lomond, Alexandria, Loch Lomond, Stirling & The Trossachs
Longdog, Basingstoke, Hampshire
May Hill, Longhope, Gloucestershire & Bristol
Milltown, Huddersfield, West Yorkshire
Moncada, London: W10, Greater London
Problem Child, Parbold, Lancashire
Redchurch, London, Greater London
Rosebud, Brightlingsea, Essex
Rough Draft, Leeming Bar, North Yorkshire
St Ives, St Ives, Cornwall
Scarborough, Scarborough, North Yorkshire
Shottle Farm, Shottle, Derbyshire
Tom Smith, Kettering, Northamptonshire
Tickenham Farm, Tickenham, Somerset
Treboom, York, North Yorkshire
Trent Navigation, Nottingham, Nottinghamshire
Trowel, Chesham, Buckinghamshire
Urban, Birmingham: Hockley, West Midlands
Vens, Rawreth, Essex
Weighbridge, Swindon, Wiltshire
XT, Long Crendon, Buckinghamshire

hops. The brewery was badly damaged in the Cumbrian floods of 2009 and was out of operation for three months. Marston's commitment to the plant was shown by the rapid repairs at a cost of several million pounds. Regular specials reflect the Cumbrian heritage of Jennings and include Sticklepike (ABV 3.8%), Crag Rat (ABV 4.3%), Golden Host (ABV 4.3%) and Tom Fool (4%).

Dark Mild (OG 1031, ABV 3.1%) ◆
A well-balanced, dark brown mild with a malty aroma, strong roast taste, not over-sweet, with some hops and a slightly bitter finish.

Bitter (OG 1035, ABV 3.5%) ◆
A malty beer with a good mouthfeel that combines with roast flavour and a hoppy finish.

Cumberland Ale (OG 1039, ABV 4%) ◆
A light, creamy, hoppy beer with a dry aftertaste.

Cocker Hoop (OG 1044, ABV 4.6%)
A rich, creamy, copper-coloured beer with raisiny maltiness balanced with a resiny hoppiness, with a developing bitterness towards the end.

Sneck Lifter (OG 1051, ABV 5.1%) ◆
A strong, dark brown ale with a complex balance of fruit, malt and roast flavours through to the finish.

Only Pedigree is fermented in the unions but yeast from the system is used to ferment the other beers.

EPA (OG 1036, ABV 3.6%)

Burton Bitter (OG 1037, ABV 3.8%) ◆
Overwhelming sulphurous aroma supports a scattering of hops and fruit with an easy-drinking sweetness. The taste develops from the sweet middle to a satisfyingly hoppy finish.

Pedigree (OG 1043, ABV 4.5%) ◆
Pale brown with a gentle aroma of sweet malt and a dash of hops. Light in taste with no dominant flavours but a sweet aftertaste.

Old Empire (OG 1057, ABV 5.7%) ◆
Sulphur dominates the aroma over malt. Malty and sweet to start but developing bitterness with fruit and a touch of sweetness. A balanced aftertaste of hops and fruit leads to a lingering bitterness.

For AB InBev:

Draught Bass (OG 1043, ABV 4.4%) ◆
Pale brown with a fruity aroma and a hint of hops. Hoppy but sweet taste with malt, then a lingering hoppy bitterness.

Marston's

Marston, Thompson & Evershed, Marston's Brewery, Shobnall Road, Burton upon Trent, Staffordshire, DE14 2BW
☎ (01283) 531131 ✉ enquiries@marstons.co.uk
⊕ marstons.co.uk
Shop Mon-Fri 10am-5pm; Sat 9.30am-12pm (excluding Bank Holidays)
Tours can be booked on (01283) 507391

☺Marston's has been brewing cask beer in Burton since 1834 and the current site is the home of the only working 'Burton Union' fermenters, housed in rooms known collectively as the 'Cathedral of Brewing'. Burton Unions were developed in the 19th century to cleanse the new pale ales of yeast.

Ringwood

Ringwood Brewery Ltd, Christchurch Road, Ringwood, Hampshire, BH24 3AP
☎ (01425) 471177
✉ enquiries@ringwoodbrewery.co.uk
⊕ ringwoodbrewery.co.uk
Shop Mon-Sat 9.30am-5pm
Tours Sat & Sun afternoon

Ringwood was bought in 2007 by Marston's for £19 million. The group plans to increase production to 50,000 barrels a year. Some 750 outlets are supplied and seven pubs are owned. Seasonal beers are available.

Best Bitter (OG 1038, ABV 3.8%) ◆

Brewery organisations

There are three organisations mentioned in the Breweries section to which breweries can belong.

The Independent Families Brewers of Britain (IFBB) represents around 35 regional companies still owned by families. As many regional breweries closed in the 1990s, the IFBB represents the interests of the survivors, staging events such as the annual Cask Ale Week to emphasise the important role played by the independent sector.

The Society of Independent Brewers (SIBA) represents the growing number of small craft or micro brewers: some smaller regionals are also members. SIBA is an effective lobbying organisation and played a leading role in persuading the government to introduce Progressive Beer Duty. It has also campaigned to get large pub companies to take beers from smaller breweries and has had considerable success with Enterprise Inns, the biggest pubco.

The East Anglian Brewers' Co-operative (EAB) was the brainchild of Brendan Moore at Iceni Brewery. Finding it impossible to get their beers into pub companies and faced by the giant power of Greene King in the region, the co-op makes bulk deliveries to the genuine free trade and also sells beer at farmers' markets and specialist beer shops. EAB also buys malt and hops in bulk for its members, thus reducing costs.

A malty session bitter with strong toffee notes in the aroma, leading to a short, bittersweet finish. Malt tends to dominate throughout.

Boondoggle (OG 1043, ABV 4.2%)

Fortyniner (OG 1049, ABV 4.9%) ◆
Despite a change of ownership, this remains a beer with a fruity, biscuity aroma leading to a sweet but well-balanced taste with malt, fruit and hop flavours all present. The finish is bittersweet with some fruit.

Old Thumper (OG 1055, ABV 5.6%) ◆
A powerful, sweet, copper-coloured beer. A fruity aroma preludes a strong, sweet, malty taste with soft fruit and caramel, which is not cloying and leads to a surprisingly bittersweet aftertaste.

Wychwood

Wychwood Brewery Ltd, Eagle Maltings, The Crofts, Witney, Oxfordshire, OX28 4DP
☎ (01993) 890800 ✉ info@wychwood.co.uk
⊕ wychwood.co.uk
Shop Sat 2-6pm
Tours on Saturdays: booking essential

Wychwood Brewery is located on the fringes of the ancient medieval forest, the Wychwood. The brewery was founded in 1983 on a site dating back to the 1880s, which was once the original maltings for the town's brewery, Clinch's. Monthly seasonal beers are produced.

Hobgoblin (OG 1045, ABV 4.5%)
The beer was reduced in strength early in 2008 by the previous owner, Refresh UK.

WELLS & YOUNG'S
Wells & Young's IFBB

Wells & Young's Brewing Co, Bedford Brewery, Havelock Street, Bedford, MK40 4LU
☎ (01234) 272766
✉ postmaster@wellsandyoungs.co.uk
⊕ wellsandyoungs.co.uk
Merchandise available online
Tours by arrangement

Wells & Young's was created following the merger of the brewing and brands divisions of Charles Wells of Bedford and Young & Co of Wandsworth in 2006, creating Britain's largest private brewery.

Brewing has been synonymous with Bedford since 1876 when the founder, Charles Wells, established a brewery on the banks of the Great Ouse River. Since then the company has thrived, to become a major force in the brewing industry. Wells and Young's run separate pub estates. In 2007, Wells & Young's acquired the Courage brands from Scottish & Newcastle (now Heineken UK). Seasonal beers include Young's Waggle Dance. Bottle-conditioned beers are also available.

Eagle IPA (OG 1035, ABV 3.6%) ◆
A refreshing, amber session bitter with pronounced citrus hop aroma and palate, faint malt in the mouth, and a lasting dry, bitter finish.

Young's Bitter (OG 1036, ABV 3.7%) ◆
This light drinking amber bitter has citrus initially on the palate with sweet malt and a hint of hops that linger into a slightly dry and bitter finish.

Courage Best Bitter (OG 1038, ABV 4%)
Malt and hops on the nose, with a full palate of malt, fruit and hops, and a dry and bitter finish.

Wells Bombardier (OG 1042, ABV 4.1%)

Young's Special (OG 1044, ABV 4.5%) ◆
Pale brown in colour, this rounded best bitter has citrus throughout plus some slight creamy toffee, which balances the bitterness that grows in the aftertaste.

Courage Directors Bitter (OG 1045.5, ABV 4.8%)
A chestnut-coloured beer with a rich, malty aroma, fruit and hops in the mouth and a long, malty, fruity and hoppy finish.

Young's London Gold (ABV 4.8%) ◆
A dark gold beer with a smooth mouthfeel. Citrus and malt in the low aroma, coming through more strongly on the palate and aftertaste with a little peach. Dry finish.

Young's Winter Warmer (OG 1055, ABV 5%) ◆
Rich malt and raisins are the main flavours in this ruby-brown beer that is complemented by roast and a little burnt bitter dryness. Blackberry, citrus and toffee overtones.

SIBA Direct Delivery Scheme

In 2003 the Society of Independent Brewers (SIBA) launched a Direct Delivery Scheme (DDS) that enables its members to deliver beer to individual pubs rather than to the warehouses of pub companies. Before the scheme came into operation, small craft brewers could only sell beer to the national pubcos if they delivered beer to their depots. In one case, a brewer in Sheffield was told by Punch Taverns that the pubco would only take his beer if he delivered it to a warehouse in Liverpool and then returned to pick up the empty casks. In the time between delivery and pick-up, some of the beer would have been delivered by Punch to...Sheffield.

Now SIBA has struck agreements with Admiral Taverns, Edinburgh Woollen Mills, Enterprise Inns, New Century Inns, Orchard Pubs, and Punch, as well as off-licence chains Asda and Thresher to deliver direct to their pubs or shops. The scheme has been such a success that DDS is now a separate but wholly-owned subsidiary of SIBA.

See **www.siba.co.uk/dds_site**

THE BREWERIES

Global giants

Eight out of ten pints of beer brewed in Britain come from the international groups listed below. They concentrate their production and marketing budgets on promoting processed beers – lagers and 'smooth-flow' keg ales – but they are slowly starting to grasp the reality of a changing beer scene in which the only small growth comes from the cask beer sector. Heineken UK, Britain's biggest brewer,who took over the Scottish & Newcastle pub and brewing operations, announced in June 2011 a scheme called Cask Orders that offers its free trade customers a portfolio of 42 regional and seasonal ales sourced from 20 smaller brewers. Cask Orders initially was for the 2011 summer season but if successful it could become a permanent feature of Heineken's operation: let us hope one swallow makes a successful summer. June 2011 saw the end of brewing at the historic Tetley plant in Leeds, a cause for sorrow well beyond Yorkshire. The Tetley cask brands are now brewed for Carlsberg by Marston's and they are being given some much-needed promotion by their owner, with the promise of seasonal beers to follow. The most dramatic sign of the globals interest in the cask sector came in February 2011 when Molson Coors bought the successful Sharp's brewery in Cornwall, best known for its Doom Bar bitter, while it invested £1 million in a new craft beer plant, the William Worthington's Brewery, in Burton-on-Trent. The penny has yet to drop at AB InBev, the world's biggest brewer, who still believes the future lies with American Budweiser and Stella Artois and has put up for sale such legendary cask beers as Draught Bass, Boddingtons and Flowers. Heineken and the Belgian directors of AB InBev speak roughly the same language and perhaps the Dutch could have a quiet word in Flemish ears.

AB INBEV
AB InBev

AB InBev UK Ltd, Porter Tun House, 500 Capability Green, Luton, Bedfordshire, LU1 3LS
☎ (01582) 391166
✉ name.surname@interbrew.co.uk ⊕ inbev.com

The biggest merger in brewing history in 2008 created AB InBev, when InBev of Belgium and Brazil bought American giant Anheuser-Busch, best-known for the world's biggest (but not best) beer brand, Budweiser. The giant is a major player in the European market with such lager brands as Stella Artois and Jupiler. It has a slight interest in ale brewing with the cask- and bottle-conditioned wheat beer, Hoegaarden, and the Abbey beer Leffe. It has a ruthless track record of closing plants and disposing of brands: it has already announced the closure of the historic Stag Brewery in Mortlake, London, formerly Watney's, where the British version of Budweiser is brewed. It's not known where the brand will be produced following the closure of the Mortlake plant but it's unlikely that many readers of the Good Beer Guide will care. In 2000 Interbrew, as it was then known, bought both Bass's and Whitbread's brewing operations, giving it a 32 per cent market share. The British government told Interbrew to dispose of parts of the Bass brewing group, which were bought by Coors, now Molson Coors (qv). Draught Bass has declined to around 37,000 barrels a year: it once sold close to one million barrels a year, but was sidelined by the Bass empire. It is now brewed under licence by Marston's (see New Nationals section). Only 30 per cent of draught Boddingtons is now in cask form and this is brewed under licence by Hydes of Manchester (qv Independents section). AB InBev has put Draught Bass, Boddingtons and Flowers cask beers up for sale for £15 million.

Brewed for AB InBev by Brain's of Cardiff:

Flowers IPA (ABV 3.6%)

Flowers Original (ABV 4.5%)

AB InBev Magor

AB InBev Magor Brewery, Magor, Gwent, NP26 3DA
No real ale.

AB InBev Samlesbury

AB InBev Samlesbury, Cuerdale Lane, Samlesbury, Preston, Lancashire, PR5 0XD
No real ale.

CARLSBERG
Carlsberg UK

Carlsberg Brewing Ltd, PO Box 142, The Brewery, Leeds, West Yorkshire, LS1 1QG
☎ (0113) 259 4594 ⊕ carlsberg.co.uk/carlsberg.com

Tetley, the historic Leeds brewery, closed in June 2011. The two Tetley Milds are produced by Marston's at its Burton-on-Trent site and cask Tetley Bitter moved to Banks's Brewery in Wolverhampton. Carlsberg UK is a wholly-owned subsidiary of Carlsberg Breweries of Copenhagen, Denmark, Carlsberg is an international lager giant. In Britain its lagers are brewed at a dedicated plant in Northampton.

Brewed for Carlsberg by JW Lees:

Draught Burton Ale (OG 1047, ABV 4.8%) ◣
A beer with hops, fruit and malt present throughout, and a lingering complex aftertaste, but lacking some hoppiness compared to its Burton original.

Brewed for Carlsberg by Marston's:

Tetley Dark Mild (OG 1031, ABV 3.2%)

Tetley Mild (OG 1034, ABV 3.3%) ◣
A mid-brown beer with a light malt and caramel aroma. A well-balanced taste of malt and caramel follows, with good bitterness and a satisfying finish.

Tetley Bitter (OG 1035, ABV 3.7%) ◣
A smooth, creamy bitter with a hoppy nose. Hops are joined by a good dose of balancing malt until both give way to the long, bitter finish.

Carlsberg Northampton

Carlsberg UK, Carlsberg Brewing Ltd, Bridge Street, Northampton, NN1 1PZ
☎ (01604) 668866

No real ale.

MOLSON COORS
Molson Coors SIBA

Molson Coors Brewers Ltd, 137 High Street, Burton upon Trent, Staffordshire, DE14 1JZ
☎ (01283) 511000 ⊕ molsoncoorsbrewers.com

Molson Coors is the result of a merger between Molson of Canada and Coors of Colorado, U.S. Coors established itself in Europe in 2002 by buying part of the former Bass brewing empire, when Interbrew (now AB InBev) was instructed by the British government to divest itself of some of its interests in Bass. Coors owns several cask ale brands. It brews 110,000 barrels of cask beer a year (under licensing arrangements with other brewers) and also provides a further 50,000 barrels of cask beer from other breweries. In February 2011 Molson Coors bought Sharp's brewery in Cornwall in a bid to increase its stake in the cask beer sector.

M&B Mild (OG 1034, ABV 3.2%)

Stones Bitter (OG 1037, ABV 3.7%)
Brewed under contract by Everards.

Worthington's White Shield (ABV 5.6%)
Bottle-conditioned: Sweet aroma, woody tastes with angelica, nettles and sharp apples. Ever-changing tastes but a long hoppy finish. Due to the success of the beer since it returned to Burton, production has moved to the main Coors brewery where more than 100,000 barrels a year are produced. The beer has been a major success in Sainsbury's stores and increased production has allowed the beer to go on sale in Asda, Morrisons and Waitrose outlets.

Brewed for Molson Coors by Brains of Cardiff:

Hancock's HB (OG 1038, ABV 3.6%) ◆
A pale brown, slightly malty beer whose initial sweetness is balanced by bitterness but lacks a noticeable finish. A consistent if inoffensive Welsh beer.

Worthington's Bitter (OG 1038, ABV 3.6%)
A pale brown bitter of thin and unremarkable character.

M&B Brew XI (OG 1039.5, ABV 3.8%)
A sweet, malty beer with a hoppy, bitter aftertaste.

Molson Coors Alton

Molson Coors Brewers Ltd (Alton), Manor Park Brewery, Alton, Hampshire, GU34 2PS
No real ale.

Sharp's

Sharp's Brewery, Pityme Business Centre, Rock, Cornwall, PL27 6NU
☎ (01208) 862121
✉ enquiries@sharpsbrewery.co.uk
⊕ sharpsbrewery.co.uk
Shop Mon-Fri 9am-5pm
Tours by arrangement

Sharp's was bought for £20 million by Molson Coors in February 2011. The brewery was founded in 1994. Within 15 years it had grown from producing 1,500 barrels a year to 60,000. The company owns no pubs and delivers beer to more than 1,200 outlets across the south of England via temperature-controlled depots in Bristol and London. Molson Coors has stressed that it will maintain production in Cornwall . Seasonal beer: see website. Bottle-conditioned beer is also available.

Cornish Coaster (OG 1035.2, ABV 3.6%) ◆
A smooth, easy-drinking beer, golden in colour, with a fresh hop aroma, and dry malt and hops in the mouth. The finish starts malty but becomes dry and hoppy.

Cornish Jack (OG 1037, ABV 3.8%)
Light, candied fruit dominates the aroma, underpinned with fresh hops. The flavour is a delicate balance of light sweetness, fruity notes and fresh, spicy hops. Subtle bitterness and dry fruit notes linger in the finish.

Doom Bar (OG 1038, ABV 4%) ◆
Flowery, spicy hop and berries on the nose lead to malt and fruit in the mouth with fresh bitterness running through the long, sweet finish.

Own (OG 1042, ABV 4.4%) ◆
Full-bodied, deep golden brown beer, rich in nutty malt and hops on the tongue. Bitterness develops, persisting in the finish, together with some hoppy dryness and malt.

Special (OG 1048.5, ABV 5%) ◆
Deep golden brown with a fresh hop aroma. Dry malt and hops in the mouth; the finish is malty but becomes dry and hoppy.

Molson Coors Tadcaster

Molson Coors Brewers Ltd (Tadcaster), Tower Brewery, Wetherby Road, Tadcaster, North Yorkshire, LS24 9SD
No real ale.

William Worthington's Brewery

National Brewery Centre, Horninglow Street, Burton upon Trent, Staffordshire, DE14 1YQ
☎ (01283) 532880 ⊕ nationalbrewerycentre.co.uk

Molson Coors invested £1 million on this brewing plant in 2011, set within the brewery centre; the brewery is named after one of the famous Burton brewers from the 18th and 19th centuries who developed the pale ale style that transformed brewing in Britain. The brewery is open for visitors as part of the brewery centre tours. There's a shop and also a restaurant and bar where beers from the brewery can be sampled. There are regular monthly and seasonal beers, including Spring, Summer, Autumn and Winter Shields. The new brewery has replaced the on-site White Shield Brewery, but this can still be visited and beers from the Worthington plant are pumped to the old site where fermentation takes place.

Allowance Ale (OG 1033, ABV 3.5%)

Worthington's Red Shield (OG 1038, ABV 4.2%)

Brewery Tap (OG 1042, ABV 4.5%)

Worthington E (OG 1044, ABV 4.8%)
Cask version of one of the infamous keg beers of the 1970s.

Worthington's White Shield (OG 1049, ABV 5.6%)

Beers index

These beers refer to those in bold type in the breweries section (beers in regular production) and so therefore do not include seasonal, special or occasional beers that may be mentioned elsewhere in the text.

Dragon Slayer B&T *674*
Dragon Bowland *688*
Dragon's Blood
  Sawbridgeworth *806*
Dragon's Breath Plassey *793*
Dragonhead Orkney *787*
Dragons Blood St George's *804*
Dragon's Wheat North Wales *780*
Drake Mallard *768*
Draught Bass Marston's *852*
Draught Burton Ale Lees
  (Carlsberg UK) *854*
Draymans Best Bitter
  Branscombe Vale *690*
Dreadnought Chalk Hill *702*
  Nottingham *781*
Dream Weaver Leadmill *761*
Dreckly Forge *728*
Drift Wood Red Rock *798*
Driver Dark Angus *671*
Drop of Nelson's Blood Farmer's
  Ales *725*
Drovers 80/- Tryst *827*
Druid's Fluid Wizard *841*
Drummer Woodlands *843*
Drunken Duck George Wright *844*
Dry Hop Franklin's *728*
The Dry Road Beeston *679*
Dry Stout O'Hanlon's *781*
Dubonni Saxon City *806*
Duchess Leadmill *761*
Duck 'n' Disorderly Mallard *768*
Duck 'n' Dive Mallard *768*
Duck Soup Warwickshire *832*
Ducking Stool Mayfields *770*
Duckling Mallard *768*
Dudbridge Donkey
  Nailsworth *776*
Dudley Pale Ale Black
  Country *683*
Duerr's Blossom Honey Beer
  Dunham Massey *719*
Dun Cow Bitter Hill Island *747*
Dun Hogs Head Ale Islay *754*
Dunham Dark Dunham
  Massey *719*
Dunham Light Dunham
  Massey *719*
Dunham Milk Stout Dunham
  Massey *719*
Dunham Porter Dunham
  Massey *719*
Dunham Stout Dunham
  Massey *719*
Dunscar Bridge Dunscar
  Bridge *719*
Dunstable Giant B&T *674*
Durdle Door Dorset *717*
Dursley Steam Bitter Severn
  Vale *806*
Dusk Ruby Bitter Cross Bay *711*
Dusk Till Dawn Partners *789*
Dusty Penny Flipside *727*
Dynamo Wantsum *831*

E

Eagle IPA Wells & Young's *853*
Eagley Brook Dunscar Bridge *719*
Earl's Ale Tollgate *824*
Earl's RDA Island *754*
East Anglian Pale Ale Cox &
  Holbrook *710*
  Humpty Dumpty *751*
East Coast Mild Waveney *833*

East India Pale Ale
  Whitstable *838*
East Mill Tower *824*
East Street Cream RCH *797*
Eastgate Ale Weetwood *834*
Easy Rider Kelham Island *757*
Eazy Peazy Neath *777*
Ebony Moon Tonbridge *824*
Eccles Cake Ale Garthela *732*
Eclipse Porter Brew Company *691*
Eclipse Blindmans *684*
  Blue Buzzard *685*
Eco Warrior Pitfield *792*
Eddystone South Hams *811*
Eden Elland *721*
Edgar's Golden Ale Vale *830*
Edge Kinver *759*
  Sandstone *805*
Edinburgh 68/- Luckie *766*
Edinburgh Export Stout
  Luckie *766*
Edinburgh Gold Stewart *814*
Edinburgh No.3 Premium Scotch
  Ale Stewart *814*
Edinburgh Pale Ale Belhaven *851*
Edmund Tyrell Artis Castor *702*
Edwin Taylor's Extra Stout
  B&T *674*
Ein Stein Liverpool One *765*
  Lymestone *767*
Elderado Bowman *688*
Elderflower Gold Ouseburn
  Valley *788*
Elderquad Downton *718*
Eleanor Cross Great Oakley *737*
Electra Milton *773*
Elemental Porter Tempest *819*
Elixir Bitter Brew Company *691*
Elmo's Fire Moles *773*
Elsie Mo Castle Rock *701*
Elveden Forest Gold Iceni *752*
Emanation Pale Ale Tempest *819*
Emerald IPA White Gypsy *849*
Emerald Festival *726*
Emergency! Blue Bee *685*
Emley Moor Mild Mallinsons *768*
Empress of India East Coast *720*
Endeavour Ale Cropton *711*
Endeavour Captain Cook *701*
Endurance Cambrinus *700*
Engel's Amber Ale Opa Hay's *786*
Engel's Best Bitter Opa Hay's *786*
Engel's Pale Ale Opa Hay's *786*
English Ale West Country *836*
English Best Brodie's *694*
English Guineas Linfit *763*
English Oak Mighty Oak *771*
English Pale Ale Buxton *699*
Enigma Spire *812*
Entire Stout Hop Back *749*
Entire Olde Swan *785*
EPA Marston's *852*
Erosion Coastal *706*
The Erradale Old Inn *785*
Errmmm... Strands *815*
ESB Fuller's *730*
Espresso Dark Star *713*
Essex Beast Nethergate *778*
Essex Border Nethergate *778*
Essex Boys Best Bitter Crouch
  Vale *711*
Essex IPA Highwood
  (Chelmsford) *746*
Essex Pale Ale Saffron *803*
Essington Ale Morton *775*

Essington Bitter Morton *775*
Essington Blonde Morton *775*
Essington Gold Morton *775*
Essington IPA Morton *775*
Essington Supreme Morton *775*
Estivator Old Bear *784*
Even Keel Preseli *794*
Everyday Ale Bryncelyn *695*
Evolution Ale Darwin *714*
Evolution Blue Monkey *686*
Excelsior Green Jack *738*
  Ossett *787*
Exciseman's 80/- Broughton *694*
Exeter Old Bitter Exe Valley *723*
Exhibition Ale Blackawton *682*
Exhibition Bristol Beer
  Factory *693*
EXP Franklin's *729*
Explorer Adnams *668*
Export Ale Rhymney *799*
Export Stout Welton's *834*
Export Daleside *713*
Extinction Ale Darwin *714*
Extra Blonde Quartz *796*
Extra Pale Ale Nottingham *781*
Extra Special Bitter
  Hopshackle *750*
Extreme Concertina *707*

F

Fagin's Itchen Valley *755*
Fair Puggled Oban Bay *783*
Fairfax Special Marston Moor *769*
Fairtrade Ginger Pale Ale Little
  Valley *764*
Falconer Session Bitter
  Wensleydale *834*
Fallen Angel Church End *704*
Falling Stone Bitter Wold Top *841*
Fallwood XXXX Haworth
  Steam *743*
Falstaff Warwickshire *832*
Farm Gold Parish *789*
Farmer Ray Ale Corvedale *708*
Farmer's IPA Farmer's Ales *725*
Farmers Ale North Wales *780*
Farmers Bitter Bradfield *688*
Farmers Blonde Bradfield *688*
Farmers Brown Cow
  Bradfield *688*
Farmers Joy Verulam *830*
Farmers Pale Ale Bradfield *688*
Farmers Sixer Bradfield *688*
Farmers Stout Bradfield *688*
Farmhouse Ale Spitting
  Feathers *812*
Farne Island Pale Ale Hadrian
  Border *739*
Farrier's Best Bitter Coach
  House *705*
Farriers 1606 Farriers Arms *725*
Farriers Ale Shoes *808*
Father Hawkins Prior's Well *794*
Father Mike's Dark Rich Ruby
  Brunswick *695*
Feather Light Mallard *768*
Feathers Fuzzy Duck *731*
Fechan Ale Madcap *767*
Feckless Redwillow *799*
Feelgood Malvern Hills *769*
Felstar Felstar *726*
Fen Tiger Iceni *752*
Fenny Popper Concrete Cow *707*
Ferryman Exeter *723*

Chalk Hill 702
Cleveland 704
Copthorne 708
Cuerden 712
Dancing Duck 713
Dorking 717
Exmoor 723
Festival 726
FILO 727
Grainstore 736
Green Dragon 737
Green Mill 738
Hunter's 751
Ilkley 753
Kingstone 759
Ludlow 766
Lytham 767
Mersea Island 771
Neath 777
North Curry 779
Potton 794
Ramsbury 796
Sawbridgeworth 806
Tap House 818
Tatton 818
Wayland's Sixpenny 833
Wensleydale 834
Williams 839
Goldbade Wheat Beer
O'Hanlon's 781
Golden Ale Coles 706
Isca 754
North Yorkshire 780
St Peter's 804
Yates 845
Golden Arrow Cottage 710
Golden Bear Warwickshire 832
Golden Best Timothy Taylor 818
Golden Bine Ballard's 675
Golden Bitter Yates' 846
Golden Blond Holland 748
Golden Boar Farmer's Ales 725
Golden Bolt Box Steam 688
Golden Braid Hopdaemon 749
Golden Bud Speciale
Brampton 689
Golden Bud Brampton 689
Golden Bull Great Heck 736
Golden Butts Moorview 775
Golden Chalice Glastonbury 733
Golden Crown Star 813
Golden Cygnet Two Bridges 827
Golden Delicious Burton
Bridge 697
Golden Drop Ufford 828
Golden Fleece Dent 715
Golden Fox B&T 674
Golden Ginseng North
Yorkshire 780
Golden Globe Shaws 807
Golden Glow Holden's 748
Golden Goose Goose Eye 735
Loch Leven 765
Golden Guild Hart of Preston 741
Golden Hare Bath Ales 677
Golden Hinde Coastal 706
Golden Hop Shardlow 807
Golden Jackal Wolf 841
Golden Kiwi Tydd Steam 828
Golden Lance Keltek 757
Golden Monkey Brass
Monkey 690
Golden Newt Elgood's 721
Golden Oat Bitter Derwent 716
Golden Pale Ale Elmtree 721

Golden Panther Panther 789
Golden Pheasant Old
Chimneys 784
Golden Pig Country Life 710
Golden Pippin Copper
Dragon 708
Golden Plover Allendale 669
Buntingford 696
Golden Salamander
Salamander 805
Golden Sands Coastal 706
Southport 811
Golden Scotch Ale Belhaven 851
Golden Seahawk Premium Beer
Cotleigh 709
Golden Sheep Black Sheep 684
Golden Shower Son of Sid 811
Golden Sovereign Flipside 727
Golden Spire Northcote 779
Golden Spring Blindmans 684
Golden Thread Salopian 805
Golden Valley Breconshire 691
Golden Warrior Empire 722
Golden Archers (Evan Evans) 722
Grafters 735
Winter's 841
Goldfield Hambleton 740
Goldihops Kelburn 757
Goldilocks Old Bear 784
Goldings Leatherbritches 761
Goldrush Cottage 710
Gone Fishing ESB Green Jack 738
Gone For A Burton Tower 824
**The Good, the Bad and the
Drunk** Falstaff 724
Good Knight Felstar 726
Good Old Boy West Berkshire 836
Good Ship Arbella Mill Green 772
Good Times Williams 840
Goodcock's Winner Cox &
Holbrook 710
Goodens Gold Flowerpots 727
Goods Shed Buffer Ale Mighty
Oak 771
Gordon Bennett Belvoir 680
Gorge Best Cheddar Ales 702
Gorgeous George Griffin 739
Gorlovka Imperial Stout
Acorn 668
Gorslas Ale Kite 760
Goshen Ale Hogswood 748
Gothenburg Porter
Prestonpans 794
Gothic Enville 722
Gowfers' Gold Angus 671
GPA (Greenodd Pale Ale)
Greenodd 738
Grain Storm Millstone 773
Grainger Special Ouseburn
Valley 788
Grand Prix Prescott 794
Grand Slam Wood Farm 843
Grandstand Gold Southport 811
Grange No 1 Llangollen 765
Granny Wouldn't Like It Wolf 842
Grans's Lamb Nant 776
Grantham Gold Newby Wyke 778
Grantham Stout Oldershaw 785
Grapefruit Beer St Peter's 804
Grasmoor Dark Ale Cumbrian
Legendary 712
Grasshopper Kentish Bitter
Westerham 836
Gravediggers Ale Church End 704
Gravesend Guzzler Millis 772

Gravesend Shrimpers
Loddon 766
Gravitas Vale 830
Great Bear Old Bear 784
Great Bustard Stonehenge 814
Great Cockup Porter Hesket
Newmarket 745
Great Gable Great Gable 736
Great Northern Fernandes 726
Great Raft Bitter Old
Chimneys 784
Green Barrel Dawkins 714
Green Bullet Neath 777
Green Daemon Hopdaemon 749
Green Dragon Whittlebury 838
Green Goose Mill Green 772
Green Yetman's 846
Gregory's Gold Morton 775
Grenville's Renown Jollyboat 756
Grey Ghost Raw 796
Greyhound Strong Bitter
Elgood's 721
Griffin's Irish Stout Hill Island 747
Grim Reaper Offa's Dyke 783
Gringo's Gold Botley 687
Gritstone Bollington 687
Grizzly Beer Fox 728
Grog Y VoG Vale of
Glamorgan 830
Grounded Devon Earth 716
Grounds For Divorce Rotters 802
Grozet Bartrams 677
Grumpling Premium Ale
Vale 830
Grumpy Bastard Brandon 690
Grunter Idle 752
Guardsman Windsor & Eton 840
Guerrilla Blue Monkey 686
Guilsborough Gold Nobby's 778
Gull Rock Tintagel 822
Gullable Roseland 801
Gulp Milk Street 772
Gulping Fellow Fellows 726
Gun Dog Bitter Wall's 831
Gun Dog Teignworthy 818
Gun Flint Brandon 689
Gunhill Adnams 668
Gunner's Daughter Old
Cannon 784
Gunpowder Mild Coach
House 705
Guthlac's Porter Golcar 734
Guzzler York 846
Gylden Ringer Croglin 711
Gylla's Gold Small Paul's 810
Gypeswic Bitter St Jude's 804

H

H&H Bitter Greene King 850
H&H Olde Trip Greene King 850
Ha'penny Ale Halfpenny 740
Ha'Penny Mild Harwich
Town 742
Hadham Gold Green Tye 738
Hadley's Gold Red Rat 798
Hadley's Red Rat 798
Hadlow Bitter Harveys 742
Haggis Hunter Harviestoun 742
Hairy Helmet Leatherbritches 762
Halcyon Daze Burton Old
Cottage 697
Halcyon Thornbridge 820
Half Bore Hunter's 751
Half Centurion Kinver 759

Pubs transport guide
Leave the car behind and travel to the pub by bus, train or tram

Using public transport is an excellent way to get to the pub, but many people use it irregularly, and systems can be slightly different from place to place. This guide is designed to help you.

Information

You should find route and timetable information at bus stop or platform timetable cases, which usually give contact telephone numbers and details of text messaging services. You can also get information from information centres run nationally, regionally or locally. Remember that many operators will not tell you about other operators' services.

Information by phone

The national **Traveline** system (0871 200 22 33) gives information on all bus and local rail services throughout England, Scotland and Wales. Calls are put through to a local call centre and if necessary your call will be switched through to a more relevant centre. Mobile phone users will be given a series of menu options to locate the relevant centre. In London use Traveline or the **Transport for London** information line, 020 7222 1234. For **National Rail Enquiries** telephone 08457 48 49 50.

On the net

Try Transport Direct, **www.transportdirect.info**, or Traveline, **www.traveline.org.uk**. For London try **www.tfl.gov.uk**. National Rail Enquiries are at **www.nationalrail.co.uk/times_fares**. Scotland has its own planner at **www.travelinescotland. com**, with a link from Traveline. Just a tip – it can help to know the post code of the pub(s) you want to visit!

Coach

The two main UK coach sites are:
National Express, 08717 818181,
www.nationalexpress.com
Scottish Citylink, 08705 505050,
www.citylink.co.uk

Using the bus

If there are a number of bus stops in an area, make sure the service you want is listed on the bus stop plate or timetable case. If no services are listed then all buses should stop there, apart perhaps from some 'express' buses. Give a clear signal to the driver to stop the bus.

Some routes operate on a 'hail and ride' principle where the bus will stop anywhere it is safe to do so. Ask the enquiry service or operator, or, if you use a stop on the outward journey, ask the driver. If you don't know where to get off, ask the driver to let you know. It's often worth asking the driver where your return stop is, as sometimes it's not too obvious.

Some buses run 'on demand' so you'll have to telephone in advance. The information centre should know, and give you the contact number.

Paying your fare

Have some small change ready to pay the driver as some companies operate a 'fast fare' system and don't give change. In central London and on many tram systems you need to buy a ticket in advance from a nearby machine.

The most economical and convenient way to travel around in London, on buses, trams, underground and most trains, is with an oyster card which can be obtained from oyster ticket shops, Underground and some rail stations. There is a refundable £3 deposit for one.

Special fares

Where available, return tickets are often cheaper than two singles. Many operators, and some local authorities, offer 'network' tickets for a number of journeys. If buying an operator's multi-journey ticket check that you can use it on other operators' services – important if more than one company operates the route.

On trains, standard and 'saver' return tickets allow you to break your journey, so if you are visiting a number of pubs by train, book to the furthest station. This may not apply to other types of rail ticket – ask in advance.

Concessionary fares

There are concessionary fares schemes for seniors and people with certain disabilities. The English national concessionary fares scheme provides free travel for pass-holders on buses anywhere in England between 9.30am and 11pm, and at any time at weekends or on bank

holidays. It does not provide free bus travel outside England, nor is it generally valid on trains, trams or ferries. However, there are local exceptions where the scheme is enhanced, either for local residents or for everyone. It is worth checking locally.

The Scottish, Welsh and Northern Irish schemes are slightly different. Eligible people should enquire locally. As in England, there are local enhancements.

National Express offer half fare discounts for people over 60 or with certain disabilities on most of their services throughout the United Kingdom. If you think you are eligible, ask before you book. If you have a concessionary fares card, this will generally give proof of entitlement. Scottish passes are valid on long distance coaches within Scotland, such as those operated by Scottish CityLink. This entitlement is only for Scottish residents.

National Rail sell a range of rail cards, including ones for people over 60, with certain disabilities, or between the ages of 16 and 25. These give a discount of 34% on most tickets, and there can be other advantages. Either ask at your nearest staffed station, telephone National Rail Enquiries, or look on the National Rail web site

Complaints, problems & lost property

If you have any complaints, problems or lose anything when using public transport, please contact the operator running the service as soon as possible. Keep your ticket. The information is important. If you feel your complaint is not dealt with satisfactorily, contact the relevant Transport Authority who may be able to help. Service reliability is improving rapidly but occasionally things do go wrong and the bus doesn't turn up. If, because of this, you need get a taxi, ask for a receipt and send it in with your complaint. You may get reimbursed.

Outside Mainland UK, but within the area of this Guide, information services are:

NORTHERN IRELAND

Translink, 02890 666630,
www.translink.co.uk
or **www.traveline.org.uk**

ISLE OF MAN

Isle of Man Transport, 01624 662525,
www.iombusandrail.info

JERSEY

Telephone 01534 877772,
www.thisisjersey.com

GUERNSEY

Island Coachways 01481 720210,
www.buses.gg

NOTE: All information was correct at the time of writing, however CAMRA cannot be held responsible for any changes made since that date.

West F
Dewsk

Wa
℣ Gla
Red C
Gwael
Lorele
Railwa

℣ Gw
Coach
Clytha

℣ Mi
Ancie

℣ No
Tap &
Pictur

℣ We
Ship &
Frien
Pemb

Ship

Sc
℣ Al
Eliza

℣ A
Salt

℣ D
Cave

Readers' recommendations

Suggestions for pubs to be included or excluded

All pubs are regularly surveyed by local branches of the Campaign for Real Ale to ensure they meet the standards required by the *Good Beer Guide*. If you would like to comment on a pub already featured, or on any you think should be featured, please fill in the form below (or a copy of it), and send it to the address indicated. Alternatively, email **gbgeditor@camra.org.uk**. Your views will be passed on to the branch concerned. Please mark your envelope/email with the county where the pub is, which will help us to direct your comments efficiently.

Pub name:

Address:

Reason for recommendation/criticism:

Pub name:

Address:

Reason for recommendation/criticism:

Pub name:

Address:

Reason for recommendation/criticism:

Your name and address:

Please send to: [Name of county] Section, Good Beer Guide,
230 Hatfield Road, St Albans, Hertfordshire AL1 4LW

Pub name:

Address:

Reason for recommendation/criticism:

Pub name:

Address:

Reason for recommendation/criticism:

Pub name:

Address:

Reason for recommendation/criticism:

Pub name:

Address:

Reason for recommendation/criticism:

Your name and address:

Please send to: [Name of county] Section, Good Beer Guide,
230 Hatfield Road, St Albans, Hertfordshire AL1 4LW

Have your say

Feedback on the Good Beer Guide

We are always trying to improve the *Good Beer Guide* for our readers and we welcome your feedback. If you have any suggestions for how the *Good Beer Guide*, Good Beer Guide Mobile Edition or sat-nav POI could be improved, please let us know. Simply fill out the form below (or a copy of it) and send it to the address indicated, or make your comments on our website at: **www.camra.org.uk/gbgfeedback**. Thank you.

Colour sections:

Pubs section:

Brewery section:

Good Beer Guide e-book:

Good Beer Guide Mobile:

Good Beer Guide sat-nav POI:

What other suggestions do you have?

Please send to: Good Beer Guide – Have your say,
230 Hatfield Road, St Albans, Hertfordshire, AL1 4LW

Preserving Britain's Pub heritage

CAMRA's National Inventory of Historic Pub Interiors

Pubs with a star (★ or ☆) in this Guide are among those identified by CAMRA as Britain's Real Heritage Pubs. Here, in addition to enjoying great real ale, you can do so in genuinely historic surroundings. It's a real irony that, although the pub is such a great traditional institution in our country, there are now very few that have not been radically altered in recent decades. A major CAMRA achievement over recent years has been to identify those that remain and campaign for their preservation.

The very best of our heritage pubs are now identified in the National Inventory of Historic Pub Interiors. This comes in two parts. Part One (★) lists pubs that are wholly or very largely intact since before the Second World War plus a few select examples built up to 1970. Part Two (☆) contains those which, although altered, have particular rooms or features of national historic significance.

Britain's real heritage pubs are an immensely varied bunch, ranging from small, unspoilt rural classics like the Birch Hall Inn at Beck Hole in North Yorkshire to the great palatial pubs built at the end of the Victorian era, represented most magnificently by the Philharmonic in Liverpool. To find Britain's real heritage pubs look up CAMRA's Heritage Pubs website highlighted at the end of this page. You will find interior photographs of the pubs and full descriptions that will tell you what to look out for.

In addition to these national treasures, there are other pubs which, perhaps not so complete or with such important features, still have genuine heritage to be savoured and saved. Examples in the *Good Beer Guide* include the Colpitts in Durham, a typical multi-room Victorian urban pub; the Holly Bush, Hampstead, London NW3, also with much Victorian work; the Volunteer Arms,

Tiled fireplace in the Forester, Ealing, London

Musselburgh, Edinburgh & The Lothians, with its fine display of spirit casks mounted behind the bar; and the Shakespeare's Head, Leicester, a now-rare survival from the early 1960s.

CAMRA has recently published *Yorkshire's Real Heritage Pubs* which, along with *Scotland's True Heritage Pubs, Real Heritage Pubs of Wales* and guides to London, East Anglia and the North East, can be purchased from CAMRA. In addition, you can find details on the CAMRA Pub Heritage website, where Scotland, London, East Anglia, North East and Northern Ireland real heritage-pubs guides are available for printing.

CAMRA members can get additional information about the regional inventories of historic pub interiors in preparation for the surveying of other areas of the country by logging in to the members' area of the CAMRA Pub Heritage website.

For further details of CAMRA's real heritage pubs, visit **www.heritagepubs.co.uk**. To buy heritage pubs guides, visit **www.camra.org.uk/books**.

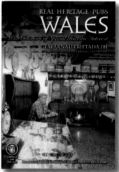

For further details of CAMRA's real heritage pubs, visit **www.heritagepubs.co.uk**.
To buy heritage pubs guides, visit **www.camra.org.uk/books**.

Books for beer lovers

100 Belgian Beers to Try Before You Die!

Tim Webb & Joris Pattyn

100 Belgian Beers to Try Before You Die! showcases 100 of the best Belgian beers as chosen by internationally-known beer writers Tim Webb and Joris Pattyn. Lavishly illustrated throughout with images of the beers, breweries, Belgian beer bars and some of the characters involved in Belgian brewing, the book encourages both connoisseurs and newcomers to Belgian beer to sample them for themselves, both in Belgium and at home.

£8.50 ISBN 987-1-85249-248-9   CAMRA members' price £7.50

300 Beers to Try Before You Die!

Roger Protz

300 beers from around the world, handpicked by award-winning journalist, author and broadcaster Roger Protz to try before you die! A comprehensive portfolio of top beers from the smallest microbreweries in the United States to family-run British breweries and the world's largest brands. This book is indispensible for both beer novices and aficionados.

£12.99 ISBN 978-1-85249-273-1   CAMRA members' price £10.99

A Beer a Day

Jeff Evans

Written by leading beer writer Jeff Evans, *A Beer a Day* is a beer lover's almanac, crammed with beers from around the world to enjoy on every day and in every season, and celebrating beer's connections with history, sport, music film and television. Whether it's Christmas Eve, Midsummer's Day, Bonfire Night, or just a wet Wednesday in the middle of October, *A Beer a Day* has just the beer for you to savour and enjoy.

£9.00 ISBN 978-1-85249-235-9   CAMRA members' price £8.00

Brew Your Own British Real Ale

Graham Wheeler

The perennial favourite of home-brewers, *Brew Your Own British Real Ale* is a CAMRA classic. This new edition is re-written, enhanced and updated with new recipes for contemporary and award-winning beers, as well as recipes for old favourites no longer brewed commercially. Written by home-brewing authority Graham Wheeler, *Brew Your Own British Real Ale* includes detailed brewing instructions for both novice and more advanced home-brewers, as well as comprehensive recipes for recreating some of Britain's best-loved beers at home.

£14.99 ISBN 978-1-85249-258-8   CAMRA members' price £12.99

Cider

Photography by Mark Bolton

Proper cider and perry – made with apples and pears and nothing but, is a wonderful drink – but there's so much more to it than that. *Cider* is a lavishly illustrated celebration of real cider, and its close cousin perry, for anyone who wants to learn more about Britain's oldest drink. With features on the UK's most interesting and characterful cider and perry makers, how to make your own cider, foreign ciders, and the best places to drink cider – including unique dedicated cider houses, award-winning pubs and year-round CAMRA festivals all over the country – *Cider* is the essential book for any cider or perry lover.

£14.99 ISBN 978-1-85249-259-5   Sale price £10.00 CAMRA members' price £8.00

Good Bottled Beer Guide
Jeff Evans

A pocket-sized guide for discerning drinkers looking to buy bottled real ales and enjoy a fresh glass of their favourite beers at home. The 7th edition of the *Good Bottled Beer Guide* is completely revised, updated and redesigned to showcase the very best bottled British real ales now being produced, and detail where they can be bought. Everything you need to know about bottled beers; tasting notes, ingredients, brewery details, and a glossary to help the reader understand more about them.

£12.99 ISBN 978-1-85249-262-5 CAMRA members' price £10.99

Good Beer Guide Belgium
Tim Webb

The completely revised and updated 6th edition of the guide so impressive that it is acknowledged as the standard work for Belgian beer lovers, even in Belgium itself. The *Good Beer Guide Belgium* includes comprehensive advice on getting there, being there, what to eat, where to stay and how to bring beers back home. Its outline of breweries, beers and bars makes this book indispensible for both leisure and business travellers a well as for armchair drinkers looking to enjoy a selection of Belgian brews from their local beer store.

£14.99 ISBN 978-1-85249-261-8 CAMRA members' price £12.99

Edinburgh Pub Walks
Bob Steel

A practical, pocket-sized travellers' guide to the pubs in and around Scotland's capital city. Featuring 25 town, park and costal walks, Edinburgh Pub Walks enables you to explore the many faces of the city, while never straying too far from a decent pint. Featuring walks in the heart of Edinburgh, as well as routes through its historic suburbs and nearby towns along the Firth of Forth, all accessible by public transport.

£9.99 ISBN 978-1-85249-274-8 Members' price £7.99

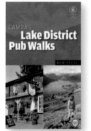

Lake District Pub Walks
Bob Steel

A pocket-sized, traveller's guide to some of the best walking and best pubs in the Lake District. The walks are grouped geographically around tourist hubs with plenty of accommodation, making the book ideal for a visitor to the Lakes. The book is fully illustrated, with clear Ordnance Survey mapping and written directions to help readers navigate the routes. Features explore some of the region's fascinating historical and literary heritage as well as its thriving brewing scene.

£9.99 ISBN 978-1-85249-271-7 CAMRA members' price £7.99

London's Best Beer Pubs & Bars
Des de Moor

London's Best Beer, Pubs & Bars is the essential guide to beer drinking in London. This practical book is packed with detailed maps and easy-to-use listings to help you find the best places to enjoy perfect pints in the capital. Laid out by area, find the best pubs serving the best British and international beers wherever you are. Features tell you more about London's rich history of brewing and the city's vibrant modern brewing scene, where well-known brands rub shoulders with tiny micro-breweries.

£12.99 ISBN 978-1-85249-285-4 CAMRA members' price £10.99

Order these and other CAMRA books online at **www.camra.org.uk/books**, ask your local bookstore, or contact: CAMRA, 230 Hatfield Road, St Albans, AL1 4LW. Telephone 01727 867201

An offer for CAMRA members
Good Beer Guide annual subscription

Being a CAMRA member brings many benefits, not least a big discount on the Good Beer Guide. Now you can take advantage of an even bigger discount on the Guide by taking out an annual subscription.

Simply fill in the form below and the Direct Debit form on p907 (photocopies will do if you don't want to spoil your book), and send them to CAMRA at 230 Hatfield Road, St Albans, Hertfordshire AL1 4LW.

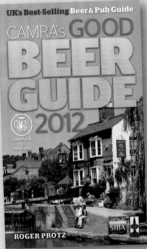

You will then receive the **Good Beer Guide** automatically every year. It will be posted to you before the official publication date and before any other postal sales are processed.

You won't have to bother with filling in cheques every year and you will receive the book at a lower price than other CAMRA members (for instance, the **2012** Guide was sold to annual subscribers **for just £10** including postage & packing).

So sign up now and be sure of receiving your copy early every year.

Note: This offer is open only to CAMRA members and is only available through using a Direct Debit instruction to a UK bank. This offer applies to the **Good Beer Guide 2013** onwards.

CAMRA's **GOOD BEER GUIDE**

Name

_____

CAMRA Membership No.

_____

Address and Postcode

_____

_____

_____

_____

I wish to purchase the *Good Beer Guide* annually by Direct Debit and I have completed the Direct Debit instructions to my bank which are enclosed.

Signature _____   Date _____

Find Good Beer Guide pubs on the move – any time, anywhere!

CAMRA is pleased to offer two hi-tech services for beer lovers – **Good Beer Guide Mobile** and the **Good Beer Guide POI** sat-nav file. Together, these offer the perfect solution to pub-finding on the move

Good Beer Guide Mobile

Good Beer Guide Mobile provides detailed information on local *Good Beer Guide* pubs, breweries and beers wherever you are or wherever you're going! Simple to use, Good Beer Guide Mobile offers the following features:

- Search results with full pub and brewery descriptions and detailed visitor information.
- CAMRA tasting notes for hundreds of regular beers.
- Interactive maps help you find your way.
- Search from a postcode, place name or auto locate using GPS.
- Available on a wide range of mobile phones

For iPhone/iPod Touch visit the **App Store** and for Android phones visit the **Android Market**. For other phones visit **http://m.camra.org.uk**

(NOTE: Your standard network charges apply when using this service)

FREE 7 DAY TRIAL WITH NO OBLIGATION
(Excludes iPhone/iPod Touch/Android)

PACKED WITH USEFUL FEATURES FOR JUST £5
(£4.99 for iPhone/iPod Touch/Android)

Available on the **App Store**

Available from the **Android™ Market**

Find Good Beer Guide pubs using satellite navigation!

The Good Beer Guide POI (Points of Interest) file allows users of TomTom, Garmin and Navman sat-nav systems to see the locations of all the 4,500-plus current *Good Beer Guide* pubs and plan routes to them. So, now, wherever you are, there is no excuse for not finding your nearest *Good Beer Guide* pub!

The file is simple to install and use and full instructions are provided. Priced at just £5.00, it is the perfect tool for any serious pub explorer. No more wasting time thumbing through road atlases or getting lost down country lanes. Navigate your way easily, every time, and make the most of Britain's best pubs.

- To download the file vist: **www.camra.org.uk/gbgpoi**

Good Beer Guide e-book

The future of pub guides has arrived...

In September 2012, to coincinde with the publication of this new 2012 edition of the *Good Beer Guide*, CAMRA Books will be launching the *Good Beer Guide* 2012 e-book in the widely compatible ePUB and Kindle formats. This further addition to CAMRA's digital *Good Beer Guide* products presents exciting new possibilities for users of the Guide. The e-book provides all the benefits of searchable, adaptable and portable digital content while also making it readable in real size and fully interactive, taking advantage of GPS, mobile and Internet connectivity (where the e-reader allows) to bring exciting new features to the Guide.

Please check the CAMRA website **www. camra.org.uk/gbg** for further information and for details of where to buy the *Good Beer Guide* e-book.

- Portable, electronic version of the printed *Good Beer Guide*
- Fully interactive, searchable content in ePUB and Kindle formats
- Includes full colour features and images from the printed book as well as complete pubs and breweries listings*
- Active e-mail and web links within entries*
- Postcode links to Google maps to help you navigate*

*Where e-reader allows.

ePUB

amazonkindle

detached and retained this section

CAMPAIGN FOR REAL ALE

Instruction to your Bank or Building Society to pay by Direct Debit

DIRECT Debit

Please fill in the form and send to: Campaign for Real Ale Ltd. 230 Hatfield Road, St. Albans, Herts. AL1 4LW

Name and full postal address of your Bank or Building Society

To The Manager	Bank or Building Society

Address

Postcode

Originator's Identification Number

9	2	6	1	2	9

FOR CAMRA OFFICIAL USE ONLY
This is not part of the instruction to your Bank or Building Society

Membership Number

Name

Postcode

Name (s) of Account Holder (s)

Bank or Building Society account number

Branch Sort Code

Reference Number

Instruction to your Bank or Building Society

Please pay CAMRA Direct Debits from the account detailed on this Instruction subject to the safeguards assured by the Direct Debit Guarantee. I understand that this instruction may remain with CAMRA and, if so, will be passed electronically to my Bank/Building Society

Signature(s)

Date

Banks and Building Societies may not accept Direct Debit Instructions for some types of account

It takes all sorts to Campaign for Real Ale

CAMRA, the Campaign for Real Ale, is an independent not-for-profit, volunteer-led consumer group. We promote good-quality real ale and pubs, as well as lobbying government to champion drinkers' rights and protect local pubs as centres of community life.

CAMRA has over 125,000 members from all ages and backgrounds, brought together by a common belief in the issues that CAMRA deals with and their love of good quality British beer. From just £20 a year – that's less than a pint a month – you can join CAMRA and enjoy the following benefits:

- A monthly colour newspaper and quarterly magazine informing you about beer and pub news and detailing events and beer festivals around the country.
- Free or reduced entry to over 150 national, regional and local beer festivals.
- Money off many of our publications including the *Good Beer Guide* and the *Good Bottled Beer Guide*.
- A 20% discount on hotel bookings with Ramada Jarvis, a 10% discount on all holidays booked with Cottages4you and an 8% discount on all holidays booked with Thomas Cook online.
- £20-worth of JD Wetherspoon real ale vouchers (40 x 50 pence off a pint).

Do you feel passionately about your pint? Then why not join CAMRA

Just fill in the application form (or a photocopy of it) and the Direct Debit form on the previous page to receive 15 months membership for the price of 12!*

If you wish to join but do not want to pay by Direct Debit, please fill in the application form below and send a cheque, payable to CAMRA, to: CAMRA, 230 Hatfield Road, St Albans, Hertfordshire, AL1 4LW. Please note than non Direct Debit payments will incur a £2 surcharge. Figures are given below.

Please tick appropriate box	Direct Debit		Non Direct Debit	
Single membership (UK & EU)	£20	☐	£22	☐
Concessionary membership (under 26 or 60 and over)	£14	☐	£16	☐
Joint membership	£25	☐	£27	☐
Concessionary joint membership	£17	☐	£19	☐

Life membership information is available on request.

Title _____ Surname _____

Forename(s) _____

Address _____

_____ Postcode _____

Date of Birth _____ Email address _____

Signature _____

Partner's details (for Joint Membership)

Title _____ Surname _____

Forename(s) _____

Date of Birth _____ Email address _____

CAMRA will occasionally send you e-mails related to your membership. We will also allow your local branch access to your email. If you would like to opt-out of contact from your local branch please tick here ☐ (at no point will your details be released to a third party).

Find out more at **www.camra.org.uk/joinus** or telephone **01727 867201**

*15 months membership for the price of 12 is only available the first time a member pays by Direct Debit.

NOTE: Membership benefits are subject to change.   REF: GBG2012